Oracle Application Server 10*g* Web Development

Christopher Ostrowski
Bradley D. Brown

McGraw-Hill/Osborne

New York Chicago San Francisco
Lisbon London Madrid Mexico City Milan
New Delhi San Juan Seoul Singapore Sydney Toronto

The McGraw·Hill Companies

McGraw-Hill/Osborne
2100 Powell Street, 10th Floor
Emeryville, California 94608
U.S.A.

To arrange bulk purchase discounts for sales promotions, premiums, or fund-raisers, please contact **McGraw-Hill/**Osborne at the above address. For information on translations or book distributors outside the U.S.A., please see the International Contact Information page immediately following the index of this book.

Oracle Application Server 10g Web Development

4567890 CUS CUS 019876

ISBN 0-07-225511-0

Acquisitions Editor
Lisa McClain

Project Editor
Julie M. Smith

Acquisitions Coordinator
Athena Honore

Technical Editor
Brian Conneen

Copy Editor
Lauren Kennedy

Proofreader
Susie Elkind

Indexer
Valerie Perry

Composition
Lucie Ericksen, Dick Schwartz

Illustrators
Melinda Lytle, Kathleen Edwards

Series Design
Jani Beckwith, Peter F. Hancik

Cover Series Design
Damore Johanne Design, Inc.

This book was composed with Corel VENTURA™ Publisher.

This book is dedicated to the
five great women in my life:
My mother, Carole, never wavered in her love for me,
sacrificed so much so that I might have a chance
at a better life and who instilled in me the basic
values that I carry with me as a man today;
My aunt, Gladys, who is incapable of suppressing her love
and who squeezes me harder when she sees me than
any body check I've ever received playing hockey;
My grandmother, Jennie, who, despite a lifetime of sickness
and physical pain, remains the most positive, upbeat,
happy and unconditionally loving person I know;
My wife, Karen, who has loved and accepted me and who has
always inspired me to reach beyond what I thought I was
capable of (including writing this book);
and finally my daughter, Kelsey, who has taught me more about
my place in the world in the last three years than I learned
in the 34 years I was on the planet before her combined
and who has opened up within me a well of love
and devotion I did not believe I possessed
I love you all.....

Chris

This book is dedicated to my partners Joe and Rich and to the employees who have worked so hard to make TUSC a success. It is an absolutely honor and privilege to wake up each day knowing that each and everyone at TUSC is striving to make a difference in the world. We have forever changed IT and will continue to do so!

Brad

Contents at a Glance

PART I
Overview

PART II
Oracle Tools

PART III
Oracle Portal

PART IV
Java

7

Contents

PART IV

Java

Foreword

racle Application Server 10G is an integrated suite of middleware technology designed to help you build Enterprise Applications, Web Sites and Web Services, Enterprise Portals, Business Processes, Business Intelligence, and other systems. To help understand how to get started with the product and to best exploit its technological capabilities, you need to have the advise of experts who have worked for years with Oracle Application Server and Middleware Technologies to implement both simple and complex solutions for real world customers. Bradley Brown and Chris Ostrowski are among the foremost experts on Oracle's technology in the world. Their book brings their real world expertise in using Oracle Application Server to you. They not only provide insight on how to get started with it but they have incorporated many very valuable best practices and examples for advanced users.

This book covers a wide range of topics, including: Oracle Application Server 10g Architecture, Oracle Forms 10g, Oracle Reports 10g, Oracle Discoverer 10g, OracleAS Portal, Oracle JDeveloper 10g, and other Java-based technologies like XML and Web Services.

This is the best and most comprehensive book that I have seen on Oracle Application Server 10G and it should be invaluable help to you as you use the product.

Thomas Kurian
Senior Vice President
Oracle Server Technologies Division

Acknowledgments

Both Brad and Chris would like to thank everyone at TUSC:
Janet Bacon, Rusty Barnett, Roger Behm, Dave Bevins, Greg Bogode, James, Broniarczyk, Eric Broughton, Deb Bryda, Mike Butler, Larry Caldwell, Bill Callahan, Patrick Callahan, Alain Campos, Brian Carignan, Mark Carlstedt, Tony Catalano, Paul Chmelik, Rob Christensen, Holly Clawson, Liz Coffee, Teri Collins, Judy Corley, Matthew Cox, Tony DaGiau, Janet Dahmen, Terry Daley, Susan Difabio, Michelle Dodge, Barb Dully, Bernie Eder, Brett Feldmann, Dave Fornalsky, Sergio Frank, George Frederick, Robert Freeman, Kathy Gates, Kevin Gilpin, Gary Goebel, Helmut Goebel, Jason Grandy, Eric Guyer, Rex Halbeisen, Don Hammer, Scott Heaton, Amy Horvat, Joseph Hurth, Mohammad Jamal, Mary Kardaris, Charles Kaufman, Teri Kemple, Mike Killough, Gary King, Mike King, Angela Kmiec, Melissa Knight, Matt Kundrat, Felix Lacap, Lynn LaFleur-Dragonfly, Larry Linnemeyer, Scott Lockhart, Toni Lopez, Steven Lowe, Tammy Mackart, Matt Malcheski, Ray Mansfield, J.R. Mariottini, Mike Martin, Dan Martino, Ed Marwitz, Sharon Maynard, Kim McGinley, Reymer Mendez, Dave Muehlius, James Nash, Dan Norris, Brian O'Neil, Jay Oliphant, David Parker, John Parker, Gregory Partenach, Marsha Ramos, Heidi Ratini, Bob Reczek, Sheila Reiter, Mark Reidel, Jamie Rocks, Johnny Sadkauskas, Alwyn Santos, Sabina Schoenke, Chad Scott, Burk Sheva, Jolene Shrake, John Smiley, Tony Solosky, Ed Stayman, Jack Stein, Jenny Tao, Kimberly Tate, Bob Taylor, Chris Thoman, Graham Thornton, Jeff Tieri, Dave Trch, Joel Tuisl, Tom Usher, Dave Ventura, Barry Wiebe, Ted Williams, Lisa Wright and Bob Yingst

–Brad

There are so many people involved in writing a book like this and so many of the people I have worked with during this process have been incredibly gracious and selfless I'm afraid that my words will not fully express how profoundly grateful I am for having had the opportunity to work with all of you, but here goes:

Karen Ostrowski—my wife Karen has made incredible sacrifices to give me the opportunity to write this book. There is no way I would have been able to complete it without her support and encouragement. I can't imagine a life without you. I love you with all of my heart.

Brad Brown—thank you so much for giving me the opportunity to do this and for creating a company where everyone is encouraged to grow not only as employees, but also as human beings. Your unselfish words of encouragement kept me going through many a dark hour. I am so grateful for having the opportunity to work along side you and I admire you for living the "Traits of the Uncommon Leader" every day. Brad also provided technical edits for all of the chapters, which he was able to fit in his schedule while running a company, volunteering for various worthy causes, performing in triathlons and being one of the most devoted fathers to his children that I know. I will always look at your life with incredulity wondering how you do it.

Julie Smith/Lisa McClain/Athena Honore - Julie, Lisa and Athena make up the Osborne/ McGraw-Hill team that I dealt with every day during the writing of this book. Their professionalism, encouragement and patience (through my various missed deadlines) was indispensable for a first-time author. Come out to Denver and we'll go out for a beer—I'm buyin'!

Mark Bullen: Mark wrote Chapter 7 (the only chapter to be returned from the technical editors with absolutely no modifications whatsoever) and part of Chapter 16. Mark unselfishly gave up his time to help me out in his areas of specialty and because of this, I was able to overlook the fact that he is a Red Wings fan. Thanks, Mark! (Go Avs!)

Brian Conneen: Technical Editor extraordinaire!, Lisa Goldstein, the publisher liaison for the App Server group, and Peter Farkas, Brian's manager who is helping ensure he has time to get the reviews done

Everyone at TUSC, but especially:

Robin Fingerson: Robin wrote Chapter 3 and was always available with a joke when times got hard. If you see Robin, ask about her dogs, but whatever you do, don't talk to her about politics!

Shaun O'Brien and Brad Gibson jumped in and each wrote a chapter (Shaun wrote Chapter 13, Brad wrote Chapter 14) at the last minute when deadlines were looming large. The book would not have been completed without their incredibly unselfish offer to write those two chapters. Guys, I owe you one, BIG TIME!

Kevin Loney told it to me straight about the effort and commitment needed to write a book, unselfishly gave of his time to answer any questions I had about the process and sent me unsolicited emails asking about my progress. Thanks, Kevin!

Gillian Kofal wrote part of Chapter 16 and, along with everyone else at TUSC, unselfishly gave of her time even during a very busy time in her life. Thanks, Gillie!

Mark Pelzel, Chelsea Graylin and William Lewkow, for forming the best management team I have EVER worked for in any company (and being a consultant, I've had a chance to work with a LOT of companies).

A very special acknowledgement goes out to someone who went so far and above the call of friendship that I am truly in awe of him as a friend. Gregg Petri not only wrote Chapter 12, but he provided detailed feedback on every single chapter of the book. All of this while raising three small children and with nothing but humor and compassion in his voice at all times. Gregg did all of this with absolutely no prodding on my part whatsoever. Along with Brad and my wife Karen, this book would not have been possible without your tireless and selfless efforts. I am so grateful for having a best friend like you. A special thanks also goes out to Gregg's family: Aimee, Chase, Madgian and Taryn.

My friends and family: My Dad, Robert Ostrowski, my "other" Dad, Andrew Fedak, Diana, Richard, Michael and Thomas McKinley, Betty Thompson, Greg, Cindy, Chris, Brittany and Ryan Free, Joyce Free, Stephen, Pat, Drew, Stevie and Jack Fedak, Denise Fedak, Darron DeRosa, Fred, Stephanie and Carrie Wilcoxson, Bob and Denise May, Ken, Tracy, Jessica and Chris Hei, Deb, Richard, Melanie, Emily and Natalie Clarke, William Heath, Bill Haas, Paul Haines, Eric Linneman, Quentin, Claudine, Cassadee and Quincy Jaksch, Carl Strauss, Jason Stueve, Rick Hata, Mike and Kady Kofal, The "Vroom School Crew" of Bayonne, NJ: Jeff Finkelstein, John Guterman, Marc Geffen and David Ripps (in memoriam), Stacey, Brandon, Kendall and Riley Tinianov, Sheila Heitzig, Allison Leech, Wayne McGurk

–Chris

Introduction

Programming used to be easy.

Well, maybe "easy" isn't the right word, but it sure was a lot easier a few years ago. When I graduated college, my first job was writing COBOL code for an appliance company in New Jersey. I didn't have to worry about things like network protocols, presentation layers, web security, transaction processing or database schemas. There weren't any real-time transactions—the clerks processed all transactions locally on their registers (PCs) and at night, a "polling" program, running on an HP 3000, would grab all of the transactions from the PCs and process them, updating inventory, customer and billing tables in an HP Image database and creating "pick lists" and delivery schedules for the appliances to be placed on trucks to be delivered the next day.

It is almost inconceivable that a system like this could be implemented today. Customers and managers demand real-time, up-to-the-second information. A writer in Wired magazine went so far as to suggest that large public institutions dispense with yearly and quarterly earnings reports and put their real-time financial data on-line so that investors had a chance to view it before making decisions. While that's unlikely to happen anytime soon (if at all), it is an indication of the current mentality: if the information is out there, users want to see it now, and it should be up-to-the-second accurate.

The Web was supposed to make everything simpler and it sure has accomplished this, hasn't it (note sarcasm)? Because of the dynamic nature of modern Web development, developers are presented with the classic double-edged sword—loose enforcement of standards allows creative programmers to extend and enhance the Web experience for end-users but those extensions come at a cost - a non-standard environment where browser incompatibilities, scalability anomalies and hard-to-track-down security holes are all introduced.

Oracle, in particular, has weathered this storm of changing paradigms spectacularly well. How? By making the effort to create an environment that both embraces new technologies and supports legacy applications. By making this effort, Oracle has ensured that organizations can continue to maintain their competitive advantages by making use of newer technologies *on their timetable*. Organizations, while encouraged to upgrade their applications to maintain an acceptable service level with Oracle Support, have never been forced to abandon a development platform like Forms or Reports even through the paradigm shift we have experienced over the last couple of years from client-server to Web-based applications (OK, OK - those of you running DOS-based Forms 2.5 were probably forced to abandon that platform, but that's rare exception).

The result of this effort is the Oracle Application Server 10g. It is a stunning piece of software that allows developers and organizations to exploit the latest Java technologies (like JSPs, JAAS, etc.), build portals from an integrated, Web-based environment (OracleAS Portal), use a set of Oracle-specific security features (Oracle Internet Directory, Single Sign-On) and maintain support for those legacy applications that need to be moved to the Web quickly and easily (Oracle Forms, Oracle Reports, Oracle Discoverer). It is secure, scalable and stable and offers a set of features unmatched by any other application server available today.

This book will introduce you to the various development environments supported by Oracle Application Server 10g. Towards the end of each section, there is a chapter on integrating those technologies with the server, except for OracleAS Portal which is already integrated with Oracle Application Server 10g. This book does not discuss the administration tasks associated with Oracle Application Server 10g. For that, see "Oracle Application Server 10g Administration Handbook" by John Garmany and Donald Burleson, Oracle Press, ISBN: 0072229586

Components needed

To run all of the examples in this book you will need Oracle Application Server 10g, Business Intelligene and Forms installation option

If you are running an Intel-based machine (Windows or Linux) you will need a PC with at least a 1.5GHz processor, 2GB of RAM and 15GB of disk space.

If you are running a Unix-based machine, the guidelines above should meet all of your needs, but check with your installation guide for specifics.

The above requirements are just for the application server; if you plan on running the components listed below on the same machine, add some more CPU power, RAM and disk space. These components include Oracle Developer Suite 10g - which includes the following components discussed in this book: Oracle Forms Developer 10g, Oracle Reports Developer 10g, Oracle JDeveloper 10g, Oracle Discoverer Administration Edition

If you are running on an Intel-based machine (Windows or Linux) you will need a PC with at least a 1.5GHz processor, 512MB of RAM and 15GB of disk space.

If you are running on a Unix-based machine, the guidelines above should meet all of your needs, but check with your installation guide for specifics.

The above requirements are just for the development suite; if you plan on running the application server on the same machine, add some more CPU power, RAM and disk space.

If your application server is on one machine and you're going to do the examples in the book on another, some chapters will require you to move files between machines. To move a file to a Unix machine, you will need ftp access. To move a file to a Windows machine, you will need a shared directory. If you don't have these privileges, contact your system administrator.

Audience

This book is intended for those developers who wish to develop Web-based applications that use Oracle development technologies. No one development tool is perfect for every circumstance, so this book discusses all of the major development tools available today. Since the book was designed to discuss the many different development options available to developers today, it is a "wide" book - that is, it discusses many different technologies and gives you the basics of getting started with each tool. For a "deeper" discussion of the topics in these chapters, see Appendix A.

How this book is organized

Oracle Application Server 10g Web Development is broken into four parts, including an overview (Part I), Oracle developmental tools (Part II), Oracle Portal (Part III), and the most common-used Java technologies and methods for deploying those application (Part IV).

Chapter 1: Overview Of Technologies

This chapter provides an overview of what Oracle Application Server is capable of. It lists the technologies available to you, the developer, how Oracle implements various Web-based standards and introduces the security features Oracle has built into the application server.

Chapter 2: Application Server Architecture

Chapter 2 discusses the architecture of Oracle Application Server 10g and focuses on Oracle's Containers for Java (OC4J). OC4J provides a full set of Java services to the application server that surpasses the features found in any other application server on the market today.

Chapter 3: Oracle Forms

Oracle Forms is one of Oracle's most mature development environments. It is tightly integrated with the Oracle database and provides developers with an intuitive graphical development environment. This chapter discusses the basics of developing Forms and Chapters 6 and 11 discuss integrating Forms with the Application Server and Portal environments, respectively.

Chapter 4: Oracle Reports

Along with Oracle Forms, Oracle Reports is one of Oracle's most mature development environments. It is tightly integrated with the Oracle database and provides developers with an intuitive graphical development environment to design sophisticated reports easily. This chapter discusses the basics of developing Reports and Chapters 6 and 11 discuss integrating Reports with the Application Server and Portal environments, respectively.

Chapter 5: Oracle Discoverer

Oracle Discoverer is a tool for allowing end-users to construct ad-hoc reports without seriously affecting the impact on your database. Chapter 5 discusses how this works, how to create Discoverer workbooks and worksheets and how to view them via the web.

Chapter 6: Incorporating Forms, Reports & Discoverer into AS

Once your Forms, Reports and Discoverer objects are created, how do you move them to the web easily and securely? Chapter 6 discusses moving the forms, reports and Discoverer objects, re-compilation on the target server, how do secure the objects and how to access them.

Chapter 7: The PLSQL Web Toolkit and PSPs

The PL/SQL toolkit allows you to write code as database procedures, functions and packages that Oracle Application Server can call directly. This feature eliminates the need to use a development tool to access Oracle data over the web. This chapter discusses the fundamentals of the web toolkit and discusses PL/SQL Server Pages (PSPs) - the PL/SQL programmer's answer to Java Server Pages (JSPs).

Chapter 8: Portal Architecture

OracleAS Portal allows you to develop portlets (Portal components like forms and reports) and content pages (for unstructured data like Microsoft Word documents) easily. The Portal environment, while straightforward, is probably unlike any development environment you've seen before. This chapter explores the OracleAS Portal environment and walks you through the creation of a simple OracleAS Portal component.

Chapter 9: Portal Development Part 1

There are many different types of components you can create in OracleAS Portal. This chapter discusses the most common components you are likely to come across: OracleAS Portal Forms, OracleAS Portal Reports, OracleAS Portal Charts, OracleAS Portal Dynamic Pages, OracleAS Portal Lists Of Values and OracleAS Portal XML Components.

Chapter 10: Portal Development Part 2

This chapter continues the discussion of OracleAS Portal components by discussing OracleAS Portal Calendars, OracleAS Portal Hierarchies, OracleAS Portal Menus, OracleAS Portal URLs, OracleAS Portal Links and OracleAS Portal Data Components. This chapter also discusses content, content management and OracleAS Portal Page Design.

Chapter 11: Incorporating Forms, Reports & Discoverer into Portal

This chapter talks about ways to take Oracle Forms, Oracle reports and Oracle Discoverer workbooks and worksheets and integrate them with OracleAS Portal Pages. By doing this, we can integrate these components with OracleAS Portal's security features and visual templates, allowing you to maintain a consistent look across your portal.

Chapter 12: Java in the Oracle Database

There are so many options for integrating application that use Java technologies that developers often overlook one of the simplest ways: storing your Java code directly in the Oracle database. This chapter shows how to store and call Java code in the Oracle database.

Chapter 13: JDeveloper

Oracle JDeveloper 10g has won numerous development awards and it's easy to see why. It is one of the most complete IDEs available on the market today. While entire books are devoted to it, this chapter introduces the basics of Oracle JDeveloper 10g and will have you writing Java applications in a very short period of time.

Chapter 14: JSPs

Java Server Pages are a really cool technology that allows you to greatly enhance the functionality of your web pages easily. This chapter introduces you to JSPs, talks about scopes, syntax and configuration and talks about extending JSP functionality by way of tag libraries.

Chapter 15: Deploying EARs, WARs, JARs and JSPs to AS

After you've done all of this work on your Java-based application, how do you move it to the application server? This chapter talks about the three basic ways of performing this task with the pros and cons of each method discussed.

Chapter 16: XML

For many developers, XML is a scary subject. They know it's becoming ubiquitous, but few understand how it related to Web-based applications using Oracle data sources. This chapter outlines the XML basics along with Oracle's implementation of XML-related technologies.

Chapter 17: Web Services

Have you tried to learn Web Services, but were overwhelmed by the amount of "pre-requisite" knowledge you needed to have before you could start putting all of the pieces together? This chapter clearly outlines the basics of web services, how they can make you a better developer and how they fit into the Oracle Application Server 10g technology stack.

Getting the most out of this book

With the advent of Beatlemania in the 60's, a new type of magazine started hitting the newsstands - one devoted to the once-taboo music of Rock and Roll. John Lennon once (in)famously said that reading about rock and roll was like reading about sex. He used a much cruder term than "sex", but this is a family book, so we'll leave it at that. I would like you to take the spirit of Lennon's words when approaching this book. There is a lot to learn by simply reading the pages, but to truly experience all it has to offer, I encourage you to "listen to the music" by sitting down and working through the examples. It is only this way that you'll have a full appreciation for the techniques described in this book.

In order to do this, you'll need access to some serious hardware. The examples in this book were written and tested on a server that consisted of an Intel-based machine with a 2.4 GHz Pentium 4 processor and 2GB of RAM running Windows 2000 Service Pack 4. Every attempt was made to use the latest and greatest versions of the various pieces of software made available by Oracle. Not every patch was applied (an entire book could be written on that subject alone), but I tried to use my best judgment in determining whether a particular patch was essential or not. I accessed that machine by way of my laptop, which is a 2.0GHz Pentium 4 with 1GB of RAM over an 802.11b wireless network. I was the only one on the server, so performance metrics are meaningless, but even when doing CPU and disk intensive activities in the background (like deploying an application or installing the ADF runtime files, both of which are described in Chapter 15), I was able to perform other actions (like editing Portal pages) with no discernable slowdown.

Experiment, play around, but most importantly, have fun!

Chris Ostrowski
Brad Brown
October 2004
orawebdev@tusc.com

PART I

Overview

CHAPTER 1

Overview of Technologies

eveloping applications for the Web is a complex process. The number of programming languages, Application Programming Interfaces (APIs), frameworks, and development platforms is much higher than it has been in years past and it continues to grow at a lightning pace. IT departments wanting to maintain their competitive advantage are asked to evaluate and embrace new technologies faster than ever before. This leads to shorter development times for projects and shorter times for developers to absorb new technologies. These factors, coupled with the fact that developers are increasingly called upon to have a working knowledge of and provide input on things such as database design, networking, development methodologies, code-generating tools, Java frameworks, and source code management, has led to a crisis in the development world where developers don't have enough hours in the day to learn all of the aspects of the tasks they need to know to be productive members of their IT departments. Luckily for Oracle developers, Oracle has provided a series of products that allows you to create and test applications quickly, interface with the Oracle database seamlessly, and deploy those applications to the Web securely and with minimal effort. Oracle's development and Application Server products have the added advantage of maturity: they are stable, proven technologies used in a wide range of production environments throughout the world.

At the core of your development efforts is the Oracle Application Server, sometimes incorrectly referred to as a web server (web servers are a subcomponent of the Application Server). The Application Server takes requests from a client application, most likely a web browser such as Internet Explorer or Netscape Navigator, processes the requests, and returns the results. It then, depending on the type of request it receives, can call other programs or speak to databases to satisfy the client's request. The Application Servers uses Transmission Control Protocol/Internet Protocol (TCP/IP), the protocol defining the rules for establishing connections between computers and HyperText Transfer Protocol (HTTP) to control the communication between a web browser and a web server.

Oracle Application Server 10*g* is a product designed to meet all of the challenges your organization faces when putting your applications on the Web. While the details of installing and administrating the Application Server are beyond the scope of this book, all Oracle developers can benefit from an understanding of the basic framework of web development and Oracle's solutions for each of these framework pieces. In the language used in Oracle's documentation, the implementation of these solutions is called *services*, and services are integrated into the Application Server 10*g* product stack.

For more information regarding installation and administration of Oracle Application Server 10*g*, see the Oracle Application Server 10*g* Administration Handbook by John Garmany and Donald K. Burleson (Oracle Press, 2004).

The amount of tools and services provided by Application Server 10*g* can seem overwhelming. You are certainly not required to implement every service provided by Application Server 10*g*; services that are installed and configured but not used waste resources, so choose your installation options carefully. Organizations can pick and choose those services they wish to exploit. Even if a particular service is not selected during installation, it is possible to go back and add that functionality to Application Server 10*g* at a later date without affecting your current production setup. This provides tremendous flexibility as developers can change direction without abandoning work performed up to that point.

A good example of this would be the Oracle Forms Server that is part of Application Server 10*g*. This service allows you to take existing Oracle Forms and serve them up over the Web. Perhaps your organization has begun by using Oracle Portal to quickly develop some forms and reports that are published over the Web to your employees. This initial project has proven to be so popular that the decision has been made to move Oracle Forms, Oracle Reports, and Oracle Discoverer worksheets (which have richer feature sets than their equivalent components in Portal) to the Web and to integrate some of those components with Portal. An administrator can reconfigure Application Server 10*g* to add the necessary functionality without affecting any of the work performed up to this point.

By doing this, your organization can move to a web-based model without losing the time and effort already invested in Forms, Reports, or Discoverer development. As your needs grow, it is possible to augment your development efforts with PL/SQL server pages (PSPs) or a tool such as JDeveloper to implement technologies like JavaServer Pages (JSPs), Enterprise JavaBeans (EJBs), Struts, or Java applets. As the site traffic grows, you can increase performance by implementing the Oracle Web Cache service to cache the most heavily used pages. Power users can create their own ad-hoc reports using Discoverer. You can expand your Portal to integrate content, web-based components (such as forms, reports, or XML-based portlets) and content from external sites with a minimal investment in development and design time. The feature set of Application Server 10*g* can tackle virtually any development challenge organizations face today.

The architecture of Application Server 10*g* allows you to scale by adding more Application Servers (called *mid-tiers* in Oracle's documentation) and more Web Cache servers. You can even allow others to incorporate your content through the use of XML and Enterprise JavaBeans. All of this is managed through a single web interface, the Oracle Enterprise Manager Application Server Control.

One could argue that as a developer, it is not necessary to understand the architecture of Application Server 10*g*. While we have met many developers with this philosophy, we strongly urge you to make the effort to understand the fundamentals of how the Application Server does its basic functions. The administrative details of Application Server 10*g* will probably be handled by a systems administrator or a DBA, but, as we'll see in later chapters, there are many steps that fall upon the developer's shoulders as you test and implement your development efforts. A basic knowledge of Application Server 10*g*'s structure is important and will make your job easier moving forward.

What Is Oracle Application Server 10*g*?

Oracle Application Server 10*g* is an application server designed to support all major web development languages and frameworks. It is a collection of services designed together to integrate seamlessly with Oracle databases and deliver content dynamically over the Web. Some of its features include:

- **Oracle HTTP Server** Application Server 10*g* includes an HTTP server based on the Apache HTTP Server, version 1.3.28. The Apache server is the most popular web server in use today. It is highly customizable and its architecture fully supports enhancements via modules.

- **Oracle Portal** Portal is a complete, web-based development environment that allows you to develop and implement production-quality applications quickly and easily.

- **Oracle Wireless** Wireless provides complete support for enabling your applications on a multitude of wireless devices.
- **Oracle Identity Management** Identity Management has security features that can be applied across all types of applications served up by Application Server 10*g*.
- **PL/SQL integration** Procedural Language extension to Structured Query Language (PL/SQL) integration gives you the ability to call PL/SQL stored procedures directly from your HTML-based applications via the PL/SQL Web Toolkit and the mod_plsql module included with Apache.
- **Oracle Forms, Oracle Reports, and Oracle Discoverer Servers** These servers give you the ability to serve Forms, Reports and Discoverer workbooks and worksheets over the Web and integrate those components with Portal.

On top of all of these features, Application Server 10*g* also supports the full Java 2 Enterprise Edition technology stack, including:

- **Enterprise JavaBeans (EJBs)** EJBs enable applications to use entity, session, and message-driven beans. They come with an EJB container that provides services for you. Services include transaction, persistence, and lifecycle management.
- **Servlets** Servlets can generate dynamic responses to web requests.
- **JavaServer Pages (JSP)** Enable you to mix Java and HTML to author web applications easily. JSP also enable you to generate dynamic responses to Web requests. Servlets and JSP run within a "web container," which also provides services similar to those provided by the EJB container.
- **Java Authentication and Authorization Service (JAAS)** JAAS enables you to authenticate users (ensures that users are who they claim to be) and authorizes users (checks that users have access to an object before executing or returning the object).
- **Java Message Service (JMS)** JMS enables you to send and receive data and events asynchronously.
- **Java Transaction API (JTA)** JTA enables your applications to participate in distributed transactions and access transaction services from other components.
- **J2EE Connector Architecture** The J2EE Connector Architecture enables you to connect and perform operations on enterprise information systems.

Out of the box, Application Server 10g also includes various programs and web pages for the administration of this complex environment. The Enterprise Manager Application Server Control provides numerous pages for monitoring the various services in Application Server 10*g* and gives administrators the ability to edit configuration files and review log files via a web browser. This is invaluable for remote administration of application server instances when it is difficult to provide direct access to a server and simplifies the administrator's job by not having to make them remember the file names and directory paths of the many log and configuration files used by Application Server 10*g*. Certain configuration editor pages even have syntax checking functionality built into them, allowing administrators to verify their changes before attempting to implement modifications to components on the Server. Most of the tasks that can be performed on these pages are administrative and are of little interest to the developer, but, as we'll see in later chapters, there are pages devoted to the creation and maintenance of containers, which give developers the ability to deploy their applications quickly and easily through a graphical interface.

The power of Application Server 10*g* lies in its seamless integration with various Internet and programmatic standards and the Oracle database. It has evolved into a product that enables you and your organization to benefit from the true power of the Internet by providing a reliable, scalable, and secure deployment platform. Figure 1-1 provides a visual representation of the Application Server 10*g* product.

The boxes at the top of each section represent the different categories of services. The ovals represent Oracle's implementation of those services. This chapter discusses, at a high level, the

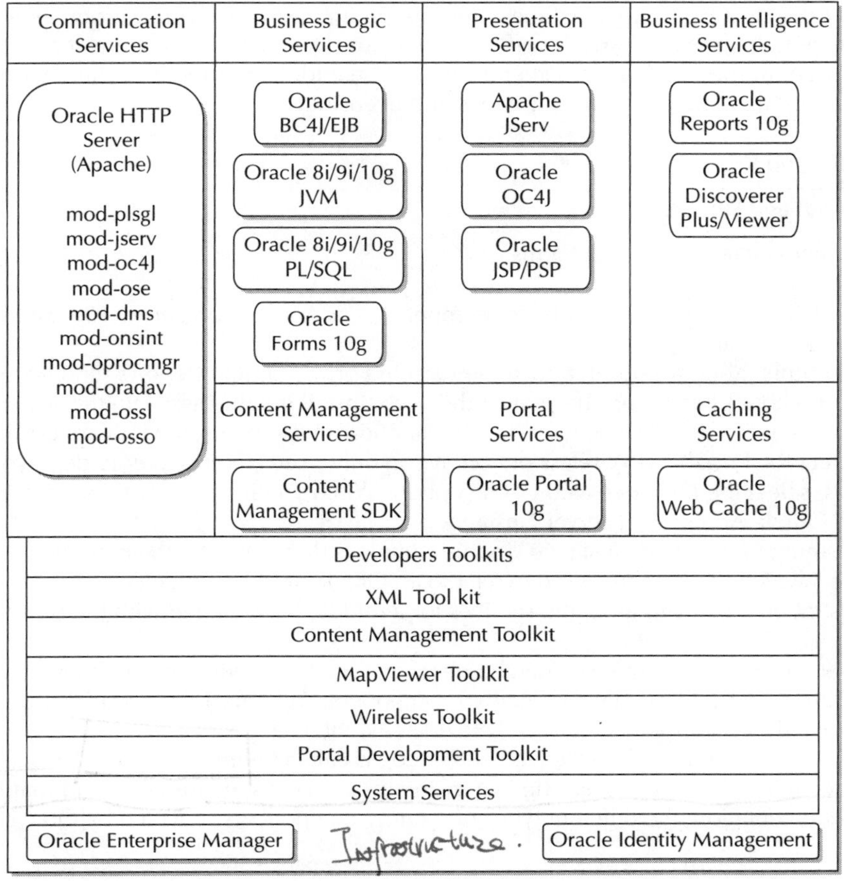

FIGURE 1-1. *Oracle Application Server 10g Architecture*

various services that Application Server 10*g* provides and why you, as a developer, are interested in them. Chapter 2 discusses Oracle's implementation of these services in detail. The architecture of Application Server 10*g* may seem overly complex, but this is necessary as it reflects Oracle's commitment to the numerous open standards and frameworks that constitute modern web development. The architecture also gives Application Server 10*g* a level of scalability and reliability not seen in most application servers.

There are two major pieces of Application Server 10*g*: the middle tier, which provides components for deploying and running applications over the Web, and the infrastructure, which maintains security and clustering information. In a one-to-many relationship, a single infrastructure can maintain security and clustering information for one or many middle tiers. When you install Application Server 10*g*, you must decide if you'll need an infrastructure because that piece needs to be installed first. We cover the different types of middle-tier installations, and if they are dependent on an infrastructure, next.

What is an infrastructure and a middle tier composed of? Each piece is composed of a series of programs, which provide various services to the Apache server. As an analogy, think of the services that run on a Windows machine—they are programs that provide various services to the operating system. In the same way, the programs that constitute the infrastructure and middle tiers provide services to the Application Server instance. The middle tier has three different versions that you can install, depending on your needs and licensing:

- J2EE and Web Cache
- Portal and Wireless
- Business Intelligence and Forms

Table 1-1 lists the different middle-tier components of Application Server 10*g* configured with each type of installation.

Based on this table, if you plan to serve Oracle Forms, Oracle Reports, and/or Oracle Discoverer workbooks and worksheets over the Web, install the Business Intelligence and Forms option. If you want to use Portal and/or develop applications to be used with wireless (handheld) devices, select the Portal and Wireless option. If you only need a web server to deploy J2EE applications, select the J2EE and Web Cache option. When you install the middle tier, you are creating an Oracle Application Server "instance."

The meaning of the word "instance" in this context is different from the more general use of "instance," which is commonly used to refer to an Oracle database instance. Figure 1-2 shows the administration page with all of the services for a middle tier installed with the Business Intelligence and Forms option.

As of version 8.1.7 of the Oracle database server, Oracle includes an HTTP server as part of its installation. It provides only the first two components in Table 1-1: an HTTP server and Oracle Application Server Containers for J2EE (OC4J) containers.

The second major piece of Application Server 10*g* is called the *infrastructure.* The infrastructure is an instance of Application Server 10*g* that maintains security and clustering information. In Oracle's documentation, the different types of security components provided by Oracle are

Component	J2EE and Web Cache	Portal and Wireless	Business Intelligence and Forms
Oracle HTTP Server	X	X	X
Oracle Application Server Containers for J2EE (OC4J)	X	X	X
Oracle Application Server Web Cache	X	X	X
Oracle Enterprise Manager web site	X	X	X
Oracle Application Server TopLink	X	X	X
Oracle Application Server Portal		X	X
Oracle Application Server Wireless		X	X
Oracle Application Server Personalization			X
Oracle Application Server Discoverer			X
Oracle Application Server Reports Services			X
Oracle Application Server Forms Services			X

TABLE 1-1. *Middle-Tier Components by Installation Type*

called "Identity Management." The Identity Management components provide directory, security, and user management functionality. The Identity Management components are

- Oracle Internet Directory
- Oracle Application Server Single Sign-On
- Oracle Delegated Administration Services
- Oracle Directory Integration and Provisioning
- Oracle Application Server Certificate Authority

Each of the Identity Management components are discussed in Chapter 2. For both the Business Intelligence and Forms option and the Portal and Wireless option, an infrastructure is required. The infrastructure, by default, uses an Oracle 9*i* Database to store Identity Management information, but an Oracle9*i* or Oracle Database 10*g* can be manually specified. The Identity Management information is referenced through a Lightweight Directory Access Protocol (LDAP) server provided by Oracle called Oracle Internet Directory (OID). You can instruct the installer to use an existing Oracle9*i* Database or Oracle Database10*g* instance or have the installer create a new database instance for you. Figure 1-3 shows the administration page with all of the services for an infrastructure.

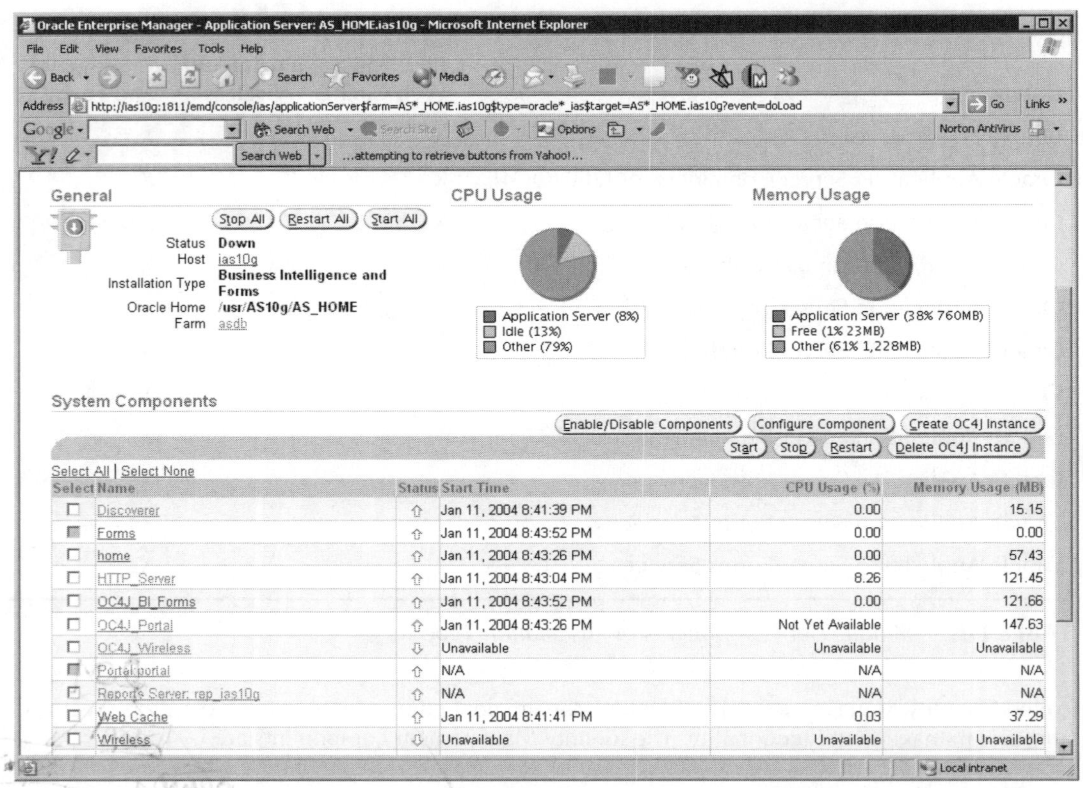

FIGURE 1-2. *A Middle-tier administration screen*

Technically, the Forms and Reports servers can be configured to *not* use an infrastructure in Application Server 10*g*, but it is far more common to use one.

"Topology" describes the layout of Application Server 10*g* instances installed in your organization. Application Server 10*g* can be installed in so many different ways that there is an entire chapter on it, entitled "Recommended Topologies," in the installation guide. The most common topology is to install the infrastructure on one machine and the middle tier on another, although you can install both the infrastructure and middle tier on the same machine, provided you have enough disk and memory resources (as each instance needs to be installed in its own ORACLE_HOME), or numerous middle tiers on numerous servers. Figure 1-4 lists some common topologies. In an effort to provide organizations with a high amount of flexibility, the infrastructure and middle tiers do not have to be running on the same hardware or operating system platform. They do, however, have to be running the same version of the Oracle Application Server 10*g* software.

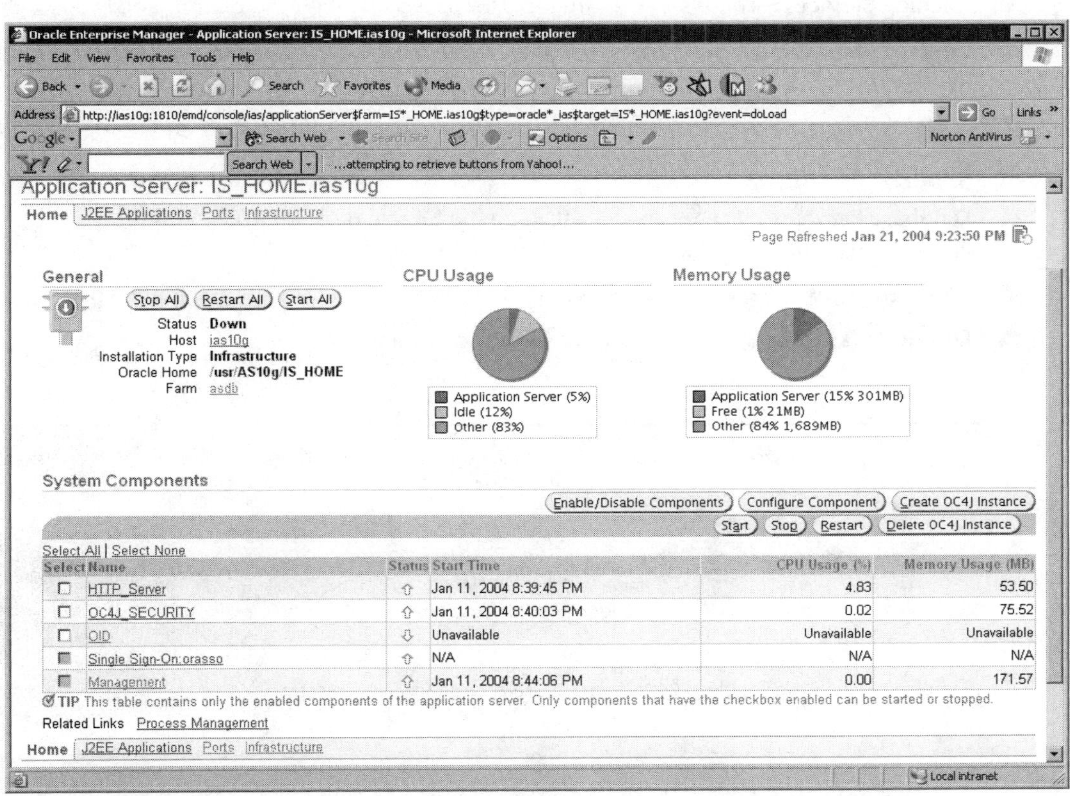

FIGURE 1-3. *Administration screen for the infrastructure*

Since all instances **must** be running the same version of the software, this means that any patch applied to an Oracle Application Server 10*g* instance must be applied to **all** instances, even if they're running on the same machine.

The different categories of the Application Server architecture (see Figure 1-1) discussed in this chapter are grouped according to the type of function they provide:

- **Communication Services** These services handle requests to and from the Web.
- **Business Logic Services** These services are the development tools and languages for building applications.
- **Presentation Services** These service are the development tools and languages for building dynamic web pages.

- **Caching Services** These services are tools for improving web site performance.
- **Content Management Services** These services are tools for managing documents in the database.
- **Portal Services** These services provide publishing features for content and portlets.
- **Business Intelligence Services** These services provide reports and ad-hoc queries.
- **Database Services** These services make up the Oracle database for storing application data.
- **Persistence Layer Services** These services provide an object-relational framework.
- **Developer's Toolkits** APIs to aid in the creation of applications.

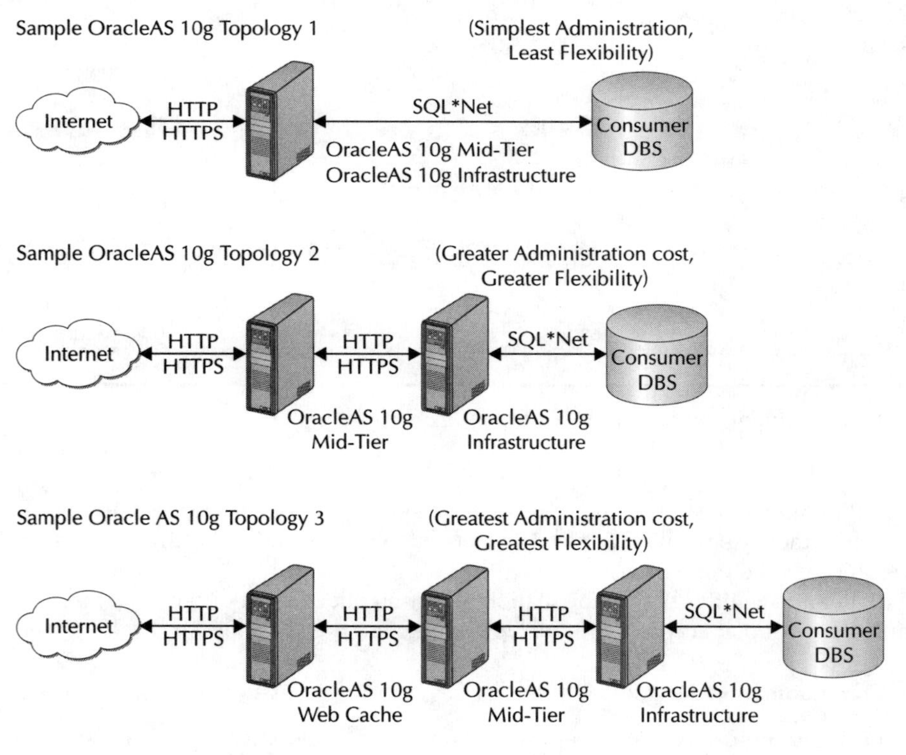

FIGURE 1-4. *Common topologies*

Communication Services

Communication services provide connectivity between clients (most likely a PC or a Macintosh running a web browser) and a server over the Internet or, more accurately, a TCP/IP connection. The most common way of interaction is through a web browser, which uses a protocol called HTTP. HTTP can handle multimedia communication services such as audio, video, and data. Tools like Oracle Portal take advantage of these features to seamlessly store and retrieve almost any type of data from an Oracle database. For the purposes of Oracle web development, the communication services are the web server.

Starting with Oracle9*i* Application Server Release 1, Oracle has used Apache as its web server, referred to in the Oracle documentation as the HTTP Server. Apache has a large base of knowledge available for its administration, as it is the most popular web server used today. A quick search of a popular technical book site turned up no less than 35 books related to Apache administration and configuration. By standardizing on the Apache web server, Oracle has provided a great amount of flexibility to administrators and organizations that wish to move their Oracle-based applications to the Web.

The designers of Apache were smart enough to know that there was no way they could anticipate every conceivable way people might want to use their web server, so they designed it with an open-ended interface that incorporates a modular architecture through which additional functionality can be added. These enhancements are commonly referred to as "mods" (modules) as they all begin with the prefix "mod_." Modules may be linked statically to the web server or may be loaded dynamically at run time using Dynamic Shared Object (DSO) support on Unix or Dynamically Linked Libraries (DLLs) on Windows. The API for these modular components is based on the C programming language. Table 1-2 lists the mods that come with the Apache server provided with Application Server 10*g*.

Module	Functionality Provided to the Apache Server	Provided by Oracle?	Supported by Oracle?
mod_access	The directives provided by mod_access are used in <Directory>, <Files>, and <Location> sections as well as .htaccess files to control access to particular parts of the server.	No	Yes
mod_actions	The Action directive lets you run CGI scripts whenever a file of a certain type is requested. The Script directive lets you run Common Gateway Interface (CGI) scripts whenever a particular method is used in a request.	No	Yes
mod_alias	The directives contained in this module allow for manipulation and control of Uniform Resource Locators (URLs) as requests arrive at the server. The Alias and ScriptAlias directives are used to map between URLs and filesystem paths.	No	Yes

TABLE 1-2. *Apache Modules Provided in Oracle Application Server 10g*

Module	Functionality Provided to the Apache Server	Provided by Oracle?	Supported by Oracle?
mod_asis	This module provides the handler send-as-is, which causes Apache to send the document without adding most of the usual HTTP headers.	No	Yes
mod_auth	This module allows the use of HTTP Basic Authentication to restrict access by looking up users in plain text password and group files.	No	Yes
mod_auth_anon	This module does access control in a manner similar to anonymous File Transfer Protocol (FTP) sites; i.e., have a "magic" user id "anonymous" and the e-mail address as a password.	No	Yes
mod_auth_db	This module provides an alternative to DBM files for those systems that support DB (Berkeley database files) and not DBM (indexed Berkeley database files).	No	No
mod_auth_dbm	This module provides for HTTP Basic Authentication, where the usernames and passwords are stored in DBM-type database files.	No	No
mod_auth_digest	This is an updated version of mod_digest using MD5 authentication (experimental).	No	No
mod_autoindex	This module provides for automatic directory indexing.	No	Yes
mod_cern_meta	This module emulates the CERN HTTPD Meta file semantics. Meta files are HTTP headers that can be output in addition to the normal range of headers for each file accessed.	No	No
mod_cern_headers	This module allows reverse proxies that terminate Secure Sockets Layer (SSL) connections in front of Oracle HTTP Server to transfer information regarding SSL connection to Oracle HTTP Server.	No	Yes
mod_cgi	Any file that has the mime type application/x-httpd-cgi or handler cgi-script is treated as a CGI script, and run by the server, with its output being returned to the client.	No	Yes
mod_define	This module provides support for Distributed Authoring and Versioning.	No	Yes (Unix only)
mod_digest	This module implements an older version of the MD5 Digest authentication; use mod_auth_digest.	No	Yes
mod_dir	The DirectoryIndex directive sets the name of a file written by the user, typically called index.html, used as the index of a directory.	No	Yes

TABLE 1-2. *Apache Modules Provided in Oracle Application Server 10g* (continued)

Module	Functionality Provided to the Apache Server	Provided by Oracle?	Supported by Oracle?
mod_dms	This module enables you to monitor the performance of site components with Oracle's Dynamic Monitoring Service (DMS).	Yes	Yes
mod_env	This module allows for control of the environment that will be provided to CGI scripts and SSI pages.	No	Yes
mod_example	The files in the src/modules/example directory under the Apache distribution directory tree are provided as an example to those that wish to write modules that use the Apache API.	No	No
mod_expires	This module provides for the generation of Expires HTTP headers (an instruction to the client about the document's validity and persistence) according to user-specified criteria.	No	Yes
mod_fastcgi	This module routes requests to fastcgi modules.	No	Yes
mod_headers	This module provides for the customization of HTTP response headers.	No	Yes
mod_imap	This module processes .map files, thereby replacing the functionality of the imagemap CGI program.	No	No
mod_include	This module provides a handler, which will process files before they are sent to the client.	No	Yes
mod_info	This module provides a comprehensive overview of the server configuration, including all installed modules and directives in the configuration files.	No	Yes
mod_isapi	This module implements the Internet Server extension API. It allows Internet server extensions (e.g., ISAPI DLL modules) to be served by Apache for Windows.	No	No
mod_jserv	This module converts HTTP requests to servlet requests, returning HTTP responses to the client. It is disabled by default in the Oracle HTTP Server distribution; use mod_oc4j instead.	No	Yes
mod_log_agent	This module provides for logging of user agents. It's deprecated; use mod_log_config instead.	No	No
mod_log_config	This module provides for logging of the requests made to the server, using the Common Log Format or a user-specified format.	No	Yes
mod_log_referer	This module provides for logging of the documents that reference documents on the server. It's deprecated; use mod_log_config instead.	No	Yes

TABLE 1-2. *Apache Modules Provided in Oracle Application Server 10g* (continued)

Module	Functionality Provided to the Apache Server	Provided by Oracle?	Supported by Oracle?
mod_mime	This module is used to determine various bits of "meta information" about documents. The directives AddCharset, AddEncoding, AddHandler, AddLanguage, and AddType are all used to map file extensions onto the meta-information for that file.	No	Yes
mod_mime_magic	This module provides for determining the MIME type of a file by looking at a few bytes of its contents. It is intended as a "second line of defense" for cases that mod_mime can't resolve.	No	Yes
mod_mmap_static	This module maps a list of statically configured files into memory. It is an experimental module and should be used with care.	No	No
mod_negotiation	This module provides for content selection that's defined as the selection of a document that best matches the client's capabilities.	No	Yes
mod_oc4j	This module routes requests to the OC4J instances.	Yes	Yes
mod_onsint	This module provides integration support with Oracle Notification Service (ONS) and Oracle Process Manager and Notification Server (OPMN).	Yes	Yes
mod_oprocmgr	This module provides process management and load balancing services to JServ processes. It is provided for legacy users of JServ. JServ is disabled by default in the Oracle HTTP Server configuration. Oracle recommends using OC4J and `mod_oc4j` (which are enabled by default).	Yes	Yes
mod_oradav	This module provides enhancements to mod_dav to allow Oracle DB as a backing store.	Yes	Yes
mod_ossl	This module enables strong cryptography for Oracle HTTP Server. It is very similar to `mod_ssl; mod_ossl` is based on the Oracle implementation of SSL, which supports SSL, version 3.	Yes	Yes
mod_osso	This module supports single sign-on across sites and applications.	Yes	Yes
mod_perl	This module runs perl programs.	No	Yes
mod_plsql	This module routes requests to pl/sql programs in databases; it enables requests to database stored procedures to be made from the browser.	Yes	Yes
mod_proxy	This module implements proxying capability for FTP, CONNECT (for SSL), HTTP/0.9, HTTP/1.0, and (as of Apache 1.3.23) HTTP/1.1.	No	Yes

TABLE 1-2. *Apache Modules Provided in Oracle Application Server 10g* (continued)

Module	Functionality Provided to the Apache Server	Provided by Oracle?	Supported by Oracle?
mod_rewrite	This module uses a rule-based rewriting engine (based on a regular-expression parser) to rewrite requested URLs on the fly.	No	Yes
mod_setenvif	This module allows you to set environment variables according to whether different aspects of the request match regular expressions you specify.	No	Yes
mod_so	On selected operating systems, this module can be used to load modules into Apache at run time via the Dynamic Shared Object (DSO) mechanism, rather than requiring a recompilation; mod_so is experimental.	No	Yes
mod_speling	This module attempts to correct misspellings of URLs that users might have entered by ignoring capitalization and allowing up to one misspelling.	No	Yes
mod_status	This module allows server administrators to find out how well their servers are performing. A HTML page is presented that gives the current server statistics in an easily readable form.	No	Yes
mod_unique_id	This module provides a magic token for each request, which is guaranteed to be unique across "all" requests under very specific conditions. The unique identifier is even unique across multiple machines in a properly configured cluster of machines.	No	Yes
mod_userdir	This module provides for user-specific directories. The UserDir directive sets the real directory in a user's home directory to use when a request for a document for a user is received.	No	Yes
mod_usertrack	This module uses cookies to provide for a clickstream log of user activity on a site. Oracle Application Server 10*g* contains a service called Clickstream Intelligence that enhances this functionality.	No	Yes
mod_vhost_alias	This module creates dynamically configured virtual hosts by allowing the IP address and/or the Host: header of the HTTP request to be used as part of the pathname to determine what files to serve.	No	Yes

TABLE 1-2. *Apache Modules Provided in Oracle Application Server 10g* (continued)

A page provided by Oracle in the Enterprise Manager web site called the Module Metrics page lists various Apache modules and how often they have been accessed since the startup of the HTTP Server (see Figure 1-5).

The mods provided by Oracle will be discussed at various times in this book. For more information about Apache, go to http://www.apache.org.

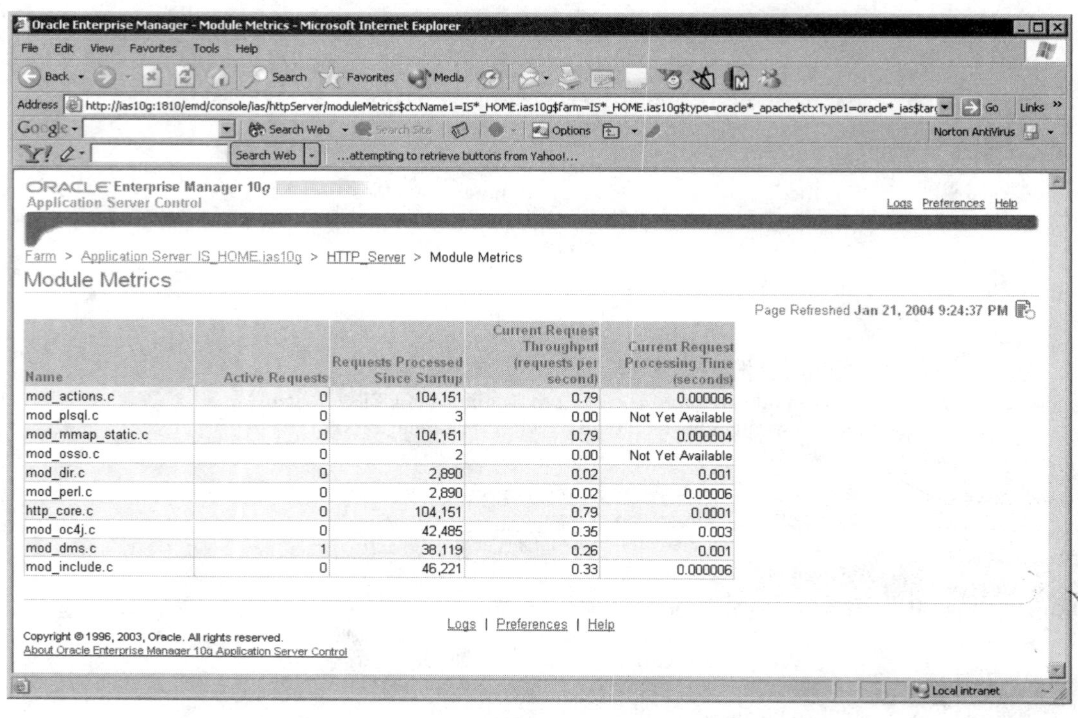

Name	Active Requests	Requests Processed Since Startup	Current Request Throughput (requests per second)	Current Request Processing Time (seconds)
mod_actions.c	0	104,151	0.79	0.000006
mod_plsql.c	0	3	0.00	Not Yet Available
mod_mmap_static.c	0	104,151	0.79	0.000004
mod_osso.c	0	2	0.00	Not Yet Available
mod_dir.c	0	2,890	0.02	0.001
mod_perl.c	0	2,890	0.02	0.00006
http_core.c	0	104,151	0.79	0.0001
mod_oc4j.c	0	42,485	0.35	0.003
mod_dms.c	1	38,119	0.26	0.001
mod_include.c	0	46,221	0.33	0.000006

FIGURE 1-5. *The Module Metrics page for the HTTP Server*

Content Management Services

All organizations have different types of data that they use on a regular basis in the course of their activities. Some of this data is in spreadsheets, some in Oracle databases, some in non-Oracle databases, some is in picture and sound files—the list goes on and on. "Content Management" refers to the process of capturing, storing, sorting, codifying, integrating, updating, and protecting any and all of an organization's information. Oracle Application Server 10*g* provides content management services that allow organizations to store, manage, and retrieve all different types of data in a central place; namely, an Oracle database.

Storing disparate data is not the only objective, however. For any content management service to be truly useful, it must also take into account such factors as connecting to other people's information, approval and publication processes, indexing, search and retrieval capabilities, security, collaboration, accessibility, reuse, and digital rights management. In Oracle9*i* Application Server Release 1, Oracle introduced the Oracle Internet File System (iFS), which stored files in an Oracle 8*i* Database or Oracle 9*i* Database. iFS, in effect, made all content available in a file hierarchy that could be accessed through a web browser, Windows networking, or FTP, independent of platform (except for Windows networking, of course). Application Server 10*g* has added many new features to its content management capabilities and renamed it the Oracle Content Management Software Development Kit (SDK). The Content Manager SDK has support for all major content management services listed above. Oracle Ultra Search can be used to search across corporate web servers, databases, mail servers, file servers, and Oracle 10*g* Portal instances. Ultra Search is based on Oracle 10*g* Text technology and is an out-of-the box solution that requires no SQL coding. It uses a crawler to index documents (the documents stay in their own repositories), and the crawled information is used to build an index that stays within your firewall in an Oracle database.

Business Logic Services

As we will see over the course of this book, the various technologies we can use for our web-based applications all have benefits and limitations. Not every technology is appropriate for every circumstance and no one tool is the "right" one to go with. Some of the technologies are good for displaying (or "presenting") data, and are generally classified under the category "Presentation Services." Other technologies are better for holding application logic, and are generally classified under "Business Logic Services." That's not to say these technologies are mutually exclusive—you could put your business logic into a technology designed for presenting data (like a JSP application) if you wanted to—but the Presentation and Business Logic Services were designed with the idea of separating the code that drives the business from the code that controls how the end user interacts with data, and the intent of making applications easier to maintain and enhance, particularly in a collaborative environment where numerous programmers with different skill sets will be working on a single project.

Traditionally, the technology used for web-based Business Logic Services were Enterprise JavaBeans. Enterprise JavaBeans technology is the server-side component architecture for the Java 2 Platform, Enterprise Edition (J2EE) platform. EJB technology enables development of distributed, transactional, secure, and portable applications based on Java technology. The EJB specification is one of the several Java APIs in the J2EE platform. The specification details how an Application Server provides server-side objects with:

- Web Services
- Persistence
- Transactions
- Concurrency control
- Events using JMS (Java messaging service)
- Naming and directory services
- Security
- Deployment of components in an application server

Might want to disclude this from the list, or lower it. CORBA support isn't exactly the shining star of te J2EE platform. Maybe add Web Services or something else.

If you search for a definition of "persistence" on the Internet, you'll find so many different variations that you'll probably be more confused after searching than you were before. The one that most closely matches my idea of persistence comes from the unlikely source http://www.posc.org: "That quality of an instance of data related to its existence beyond and outside of the life of its creating process or the lives of other processes that use it. In this context, persistence is normally used in describing the life of objects relative to sessions; that is, whether or not they live beyond sessions." See the discussion of TopLink later in this chapter under the section " Persistence Layer Services" for more information on Oracle's strategic direction regarding persistence implementation for OC4J.

Additionally, the EJB specification defines the roles played by the EJB container and the EJBs, as well as how to deploy the EJBs in a container.

Central to the understanding of EJBs in the concept of patterns; Sun Microsystems defines a pattern as "a recurring solution to a problem in a context. A context is the environment, surroundings, situation, or interrelated conditions within which something exists. A problem is an unsettled question, something that needs to be investigated and solved. A problem can be specified by a set of causes and effects. Typically, the problem is constrained by the context in which it occurs. Finally, the solution refers to the answer to the problem in a context that helps resolve the issues." A solution to a problem is not considered a pattern unless there is some way to show that the solution can be applied to recurring types of problems in the solution's definition. Patterns are described by five main characteristics: context, problem, solution, forces, and consequences.

EJBs, however, are notoriously difficult to program and maintain. In response to this, Oracle created a business logic service framework called Oracle Business Components for Java (BC4J), which seeks to remove much of the complexity of EJBs while it continues to provide all of the EJBs' functionality. With BC4J, developers can author and test object-oriented business logic in components that automatically integrate with relational databases, reuse business logic through multiple views of data, and access and update those views from servlets or JSPs.

You may be asking yourself why it is even necessary to store business logic in the middle tier: Don't most Oracle-based applications store their business logic in database packages, procedures, functions, and triggers? There are several reasons for implementing business logic via BC4J:

- You do not want to mix object-oriented and relational paradigms in your application.
- You will be accessing the database only through clients using Business Components for Java.Your programming staff is skilled in Java and not in PL/SQL.
- You will be accessing both Oracle and non-Oracle databases.

Some companies may not want to be "locked into Oracle"—that is, they want to have database vendor freedom. This is generally a bad practice (for example, you won't maximize the performance of your Oracle application), but if you have a generic product (i.e., Peoplesoft, SAP, etc.), this may make sense.

Designing, authoring, debugging, documenting, delivering, and maintaining a J2EE design pattern framework takes a significant amount of time and effort. BC4J implements patterns for developers, giving them a significant advantage in getting their J2EE applications built, deployed, and enhanced more quickly.

It is not a requirement, of course, to store your business logic in the middle tier. Traditionally, Oracle developers have stored their business logic inside the Oracle database in the form of packages, procedures, functions, triggers, and constraints. To assist in the development of web-based applications, Oracle provides an Apache module called mod_plsql that allows you to make requests to stored procedures in the database directly from the browser. As of Oracle 8.1.7, a group of packages called the PL/SQL Web Toolkit has been included as part of the built-in packages in the database. By using the toolkit, you can generate web pages; query, retrieve, and display data from an Oracle database; dynamically calculate the contents of web pages; and much more. The details of using the PL/SQL Web Toolkit are discussed in Chapter 7.

Oracle also provides an installation script that can be run against databases prior to 8.1.7 to install the PL/SQL Web Toolkit packages.

Another place business logic can be stored is within an Oracle Form. Oracle Application Server 10*g*, when installed with the Business Intelligence and Forms option, can serve Oracle Forms over the Web to a client's web browser where the form is displayed as a Java applet containing the user interface for the forms run-time engine. When you submit a URL to launch an Oracle Forms-based application, the web listener accepts the request and downloads the Oracle Forms applet to your browser. The Oracle Forms applet then establishes a persistent connection to an Oracle Forms run-time engine. All processing takes place between the Oracle Forms applet and the Oracle Forms Services run-time engine, which seamlessly handles any queries or commits to the database. The Oracle Forms Server can be configured to use Application Server 10*g*'s single sign-on (SSO) and OID capabilities to secure access. Oracle Forms can also be integrated into Oracle Portal to use its publishing capabilities. SSO and OID are discussed in Chapter 2, and Oracle Forms, their implementation in a web environment, their integration with Portal, and the configuration of the Forms Server are discussed in Chapters 3, 6, and 11. Figure 1-6 shows an Oracle Form served up to a web browser.

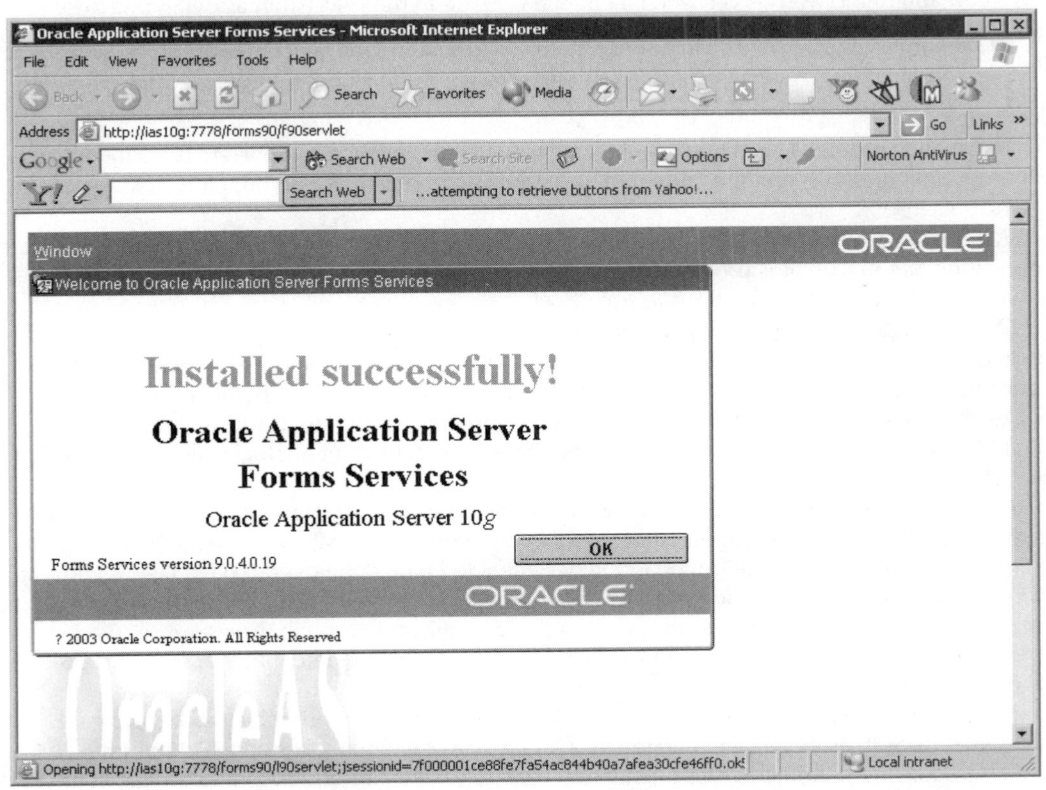

FIGURE 1-6. *An Oracle Form viewed through a web browser*

Presentation Services

As we have seen, technologies such as BC4J and Oracle Forms are good for writing, testing, and maintaining your business logic. There are other technologies, however, that are better suited for displaying your applications. "Presentation Services" deliver dynamic content to client browsers, supporting servlets, business intelligence, PL/SQL Server Pages, JavaServer Pages, Perl/CGI scripts, and PHP. You can use Presentation Services to build your presentation layer for your web applications. While Oracle puts these services into a separate group, you can think of them grouped with the Business Logic Services in that your application logic can reside within these components. We recommend, however, that you break your business logic into executable components, which can then be called or invoked by these services.

Apache JServ (mod_jserv) is a module for the Apache web server that implements Sun Microsystems's Java Servlet API for running server-side Java code. Java servlets must be executed from within a Java Virtual Machine (JVM), and hence any servlet execution environment must include a JVM. The complexity of adding a JVM to the Apache server would degrade the Apache architecture, so the solution adopted for Apache JServ was to separate the JVM from the Apache server. This separation provides several benefits:

- It allows the use of any compatible JVM from any vendor. No modifications need be made to the web server when a change is made to the JVM (such as by an upgrade).
- It improves stability by separating the processes, allowing process-level protections by the operating system. If the JVM should crash or be mis-configured, the web server will still operate normally.
- It allows for advanced functionality, including automatic startup, separate JVMs for different configurations, and the capability to support load balancing on high traffic sites.

While the Apache module for handling servlet requests (mod_jserv) is still available in Oracle Application Server 10*g*, it is provided for backwards compatibility only. Oracle recommends converting your legacy applications to use OC4J.

OC4J is the core J2EE run-time component of Application Server 10*g* implemented as a module (mod_oc4j) in the Apache web server. OC4J is J2EE 1.3 compatible and runs on Java 2 Platform, Standard Edition (J2SE) distributions, making it easy to use and highly productive for developers, while at the same time offering outstanding performance and scalability for production environments. OC4J provides complete support for the technologies listed in Table 1-3.

OC4Js are discussed in Chapters 12, 13, and 15.

JSPs is a server-side technology that is an extension to the Java Servlet technology. JSPs have a dynamic scripting capability that works in tandem with HTML code, separating the user interface from content generation, enabling designers to change the overall page layout without altering the underlying dynamic content. Developers can benefit by using JSP technology without having to learn the Java language; they extend the JSP language through the use of simple tag handlers and easily maintain pages through the use of the JSP Standard Tag Library (JSTL). JSPs are discussed in Chapters 14 and 15.

PSPs is a technology provided by Oracle. It works on the same principles as JSPs, except that it uses PL/SQL as its scripting language. This can be beneficial for shops with minimal Java expertise. PSPs are compiled components executed as Oracle Stored Procedures. The Oracle PSP service includes the PSP Compiler and the PL/SQL Web Toolkit. Existing web pages can be made dynamic by embedding PL/SQL tags to perform database operations and display the results.

Java Technology	Version of Specification Supported in Oracle Application Server 10*g*
JSPs	1.2
Servlets	2.3
EJBs	2.0
JMS	1.0.2b
Java Database Connectivity (JDBC)	2.0
Simple Object Access Protocol (SOAP)	1.1
Web Services Description Language (WSDL)	1.1
Universal Description, Discovery, and Integration (UDDI)	2.0

TABLE 1-3. *Java Technologies Supported by OC4J*

Because PSPs are executed as stored procedures, it is important to note that the processing of PSPs occurs on the Oracle Database server. All of the other technologies discussed in this book execute on the Oracle Application Server. Chapter 7 discusses PSPs.

Business Intelligence Services

Business Intelligence Services can help you gain insight into internal business operations, customers, and suppliers. The basic Business Intelligence requirements usually include data quality, data analysis, and information access. The ultimate goal of Business Intelligence Services is to provide up-to-the-second business insight, most commonly provided with reporting tools. Oracle provides two enterprise-quality reporting tools: Oracle Reports and Oracle Discoverer. The choice of which tool to implement (or the decision to implement both) will be based on the needs and skill level of the employees in your organization. Both of these tools, in conjunction with Oracle Application Server 10*g*, provide the capability to easily make reports available over the Web.

Similar to the Forms Server discussed earlier, the Reports Server allows you to publish Oracle Reports on an internal company intranet, an external company extranet, or over the Web. In addition, the Reports Server can interface with a mail server to automatically deliver reports to the mailbox of selected users or groups. The Reports Server consists of the server component, run-time engines, and the servlet runner. When a client submits a request for a report, the Oracle HTTP Server web listener routes that request to the Oracle Reports Services server component. The server then routes the request to the Oracle Reports Services run-time engine, which runs the report. The report output is then sent back to the client through the Oracle HTTP Server web listener. Reports can be formatted as HTML, XML, PDFs (Adobe Acrobat), or as plain text for the user. Developers can also easily customize them for import into Microsoft Excel or any other commonly supported Multipurpose Internet Mail Extensions (MIME) document type. The Oracle Reports Server can be configured to use Application Server 10*g*'s SSO and OID capabilities to secure access. Reports can also be integrated easily with Oracle Portal so that they can take advantage of Portal's publishing, security, and visual template features. Chapters 4, 6 and 11 discuss Oracle Reports and the Reports Server. Figure 1-7 shows an Oracle Report served up over the Web.

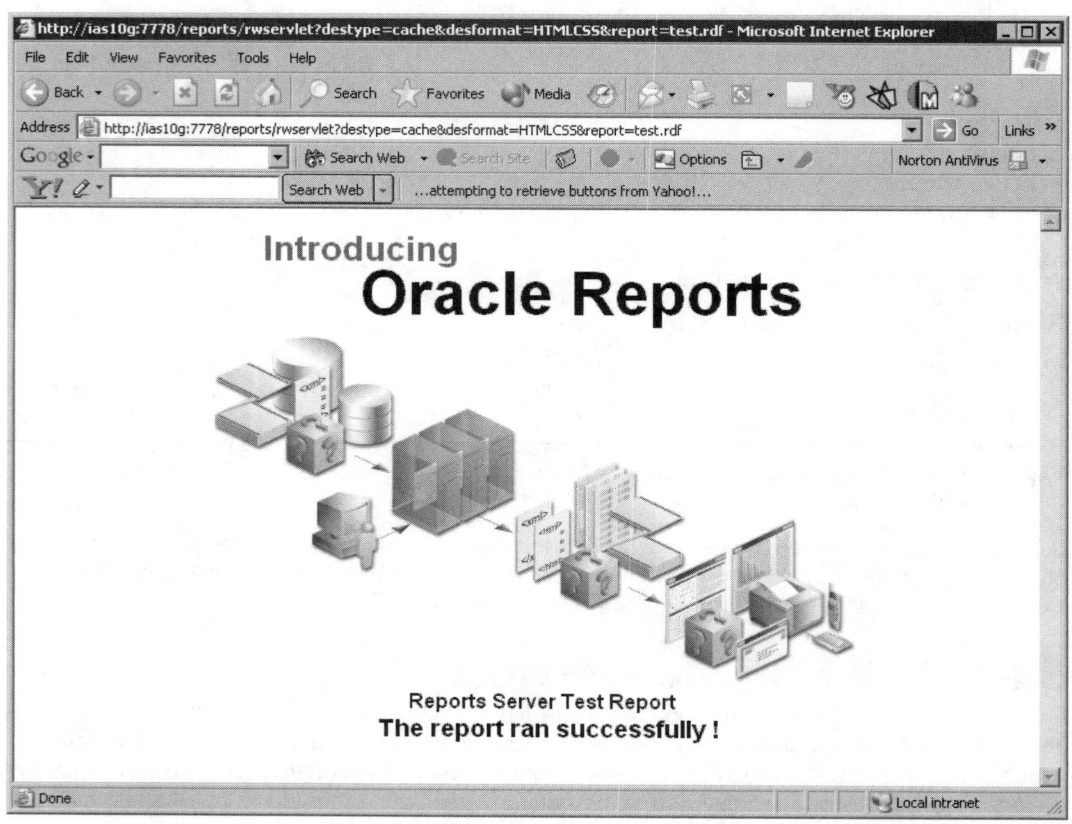

FIGURE 1-7. *An Oracle Report viewed through a web browser*

Oracle Discoverer is a reporting tool that gives ad-hoc query capabilities to your end users. Targeted at power users, Discoverer enables you to access information from the database and create dynamic reports that accept parameters and have drill-down or data pivoting capabilities, all without the need to learn SQL. Invoking the Discoverer workbook or worksheet over the Web can be made as simple as clicking a URL that invokes the Discoverer web component called Discoverer Viewer. This link can be constructed to invoke a particular workbook query automatically, giving the user the results in a web browser with the ability to interact with the query results to drill up or down, enter values into optional parameters, or to follow links to other workbooks or applications. Figure 1-8 shows an Oracle Discoverer workbook displayed in Discoverer Plus.

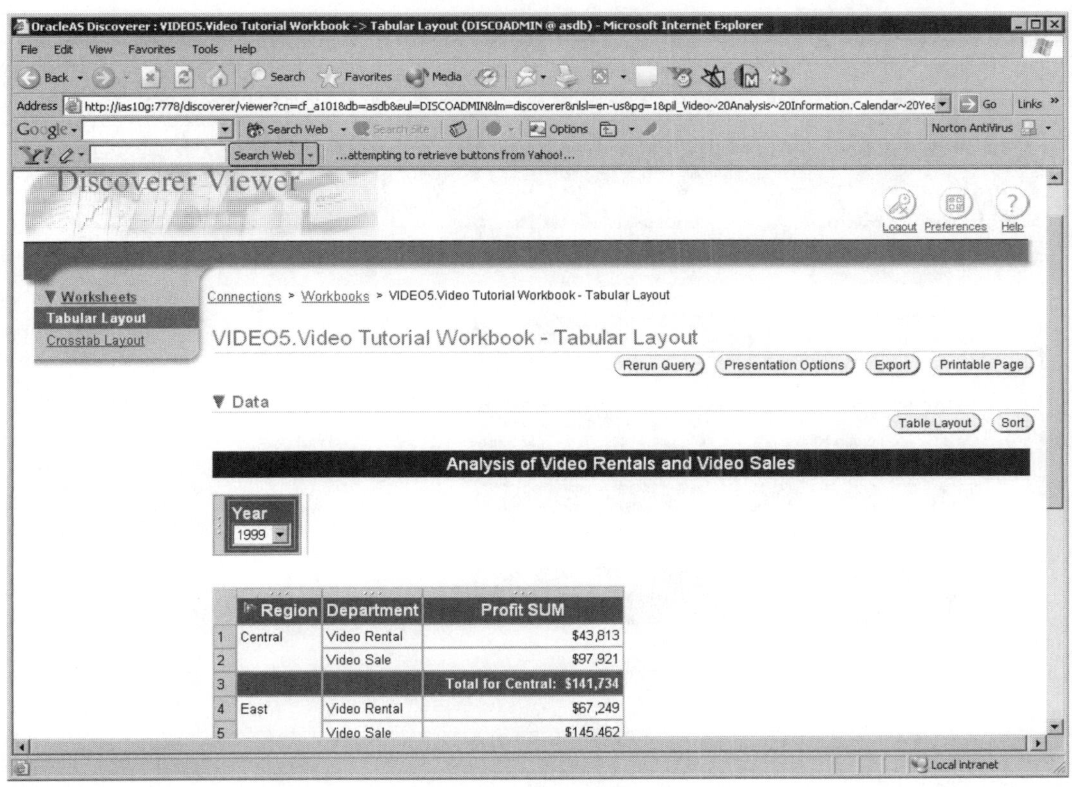

FIGURE 1-8. *An Oracle Discoverer worksheet viewed through a web browser*

There is no environment in Application Server 10*g* to develop Oracle Forms and Reports. The Forms Server and Reports Server components exist solely to take Forms and Reports and serve them up on the Web. Oracle Discoverer Server has the capability to serve Discoverer Workbooks and Worksheets over the Web, but it also has the capability to develop Workbooks and Worksheets using a web browser as its interface. This piece of the Discoverer Server, called Discoverer Plus, can be used as a replacement to the Oracle Discoverer Desktop. By using the Discoverer Plus web interface, you will no longer have to install the Discoverer Desktop software on every client that needs to create and manage workbooks and worksheets. The Discoverer Administrator program, which is used to administer End-User Layers (EULs) and Discoverer privileges, is still required. Figure 1-9 shows an Oracle Discoverer worksheet displayed over the Web in the Discoverer Plus environment.

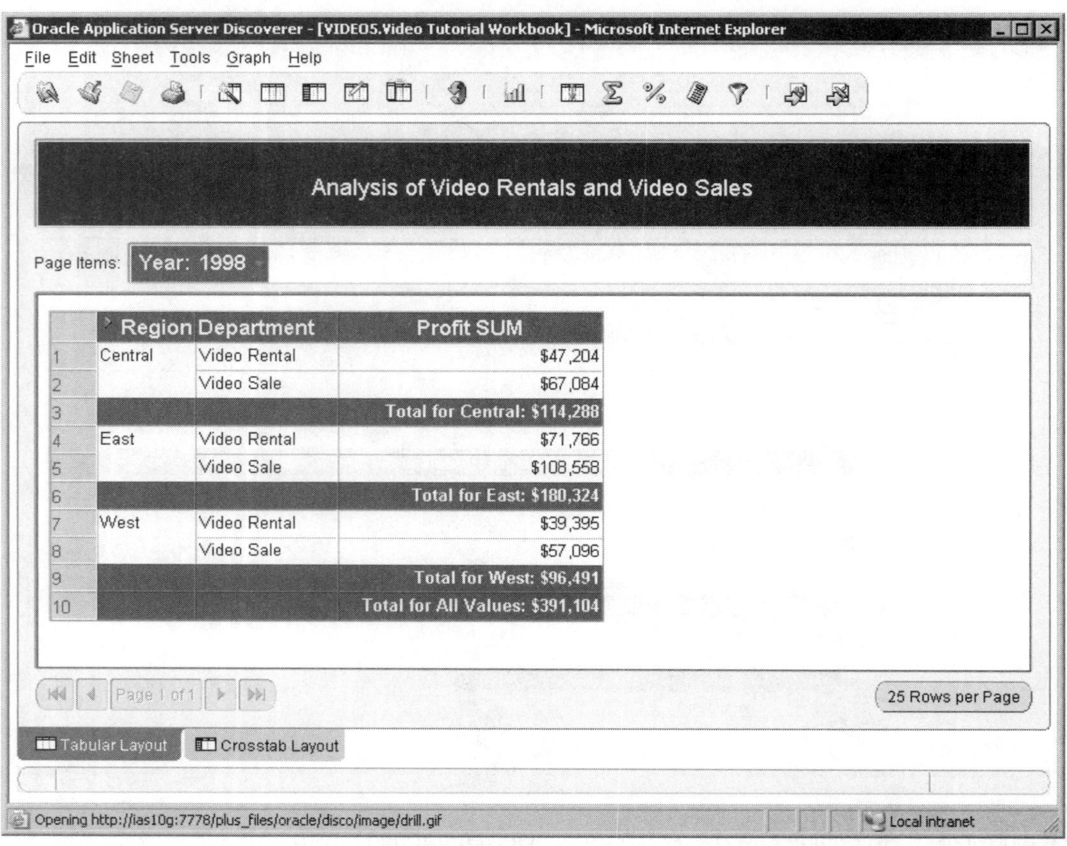

FIGURE 1-9. *The Discoverer Plus development environment*

Portal Services

An enterprise portal is defined as an application that enables organizations to unlock internally and externally stored information and provide users a single gateway to personalized information needed to make informed business decisions. By providing end users with relevant data from across multiple data sources and presenting that information in a context that is meaningful to the user, portals offer the promise of providing a competitive advantage through new business processes, increasing productivity by putting more power into the hands of business users, and increasing effectiveness through knowledge sharing and reduced search time.

Oracle Portal can handle and display virtually any type of data, giving you the ability to create portals that give users access to web applications, business documents, business intelligence reports, charts, and links to other forms of data that can exist both inside and outside your corporate intranet. Portal pages contain regions, which can hold items of content, such as spreadsheet or word processor files or portlets that provide access to web resources such as applications or other web pages. After portlets are written and tested, then can be published to a page, where they will be viewable by those users who have access to the page. Depending on the level of expertise of your end users and the amount of flexibility you're willing to give them, the Portal page can be set up so that the end users can modify their pages by adding, removing, or modifying content, similar to a site like http://my.yahoo.com. Portal is unique in the sense that its development environment is itself a Portal application. Once your developers and administrators become comfortable with the Portal environment, it will be easy for them to understand the mechanics of Portal development. Combined with the wizard-based approach to developing Portal applications, your developers can be productive in a very short period of time. Portal is discussed in Chapters 8 through 11. Figure 1-10 shows a Portal development screen.

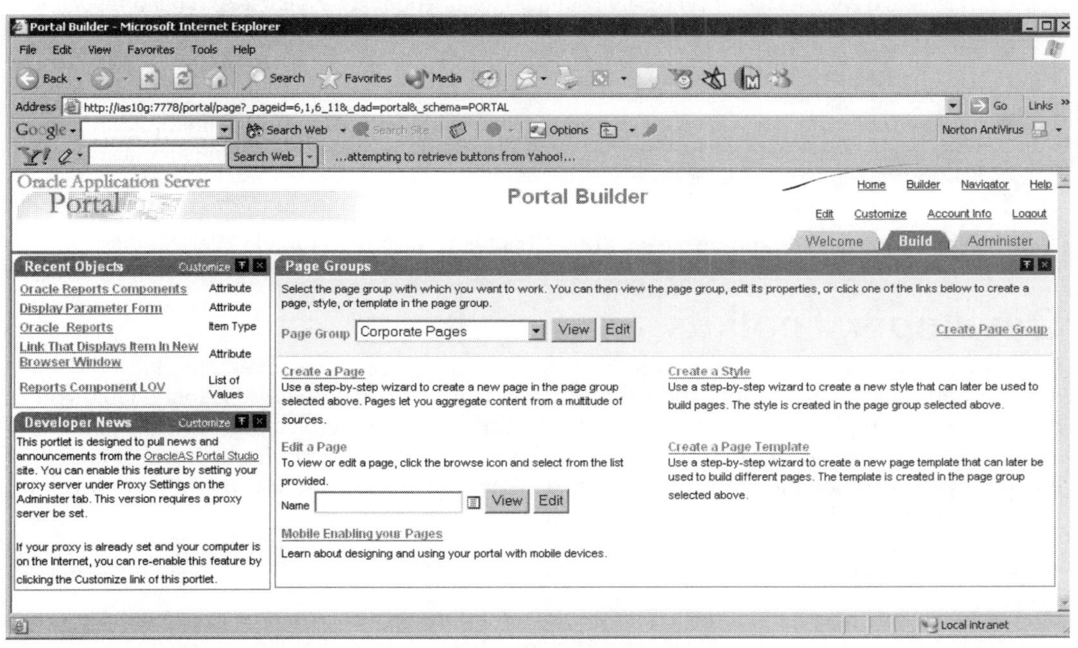

FIGURE 1-10. *A screen of the Portal development environment*

Web Services

Web Services are web-based applications that dynamically interact with other web applications using open standards that include eXtensible Markup Language (XML), Simple Object Access Protocol (SOAP) and Universal Description, Discovery, and Integration (UDDI). Such applications typically run behind the scenes, with one program "talking to" another (server to server). Using the UDDI discovery system, the goal of Web Services is to register the service on the Internet, allow an application to search for and find the service, and then to seamlessly exchange data with it. Web Services are either a request and response or a one-way style, and they can use either synchronous or asynchronous communication. The fundamental unit of exchange between Web Services clients and Web Services, of either style or type of communication, is a message.

Web Services enable software components to interact with each other around the world. Given Web Services use open, XML-based protocols that are lightweight and simple, their acceptance and use has gained a tremendous amount of support in recent years. A Web Service does the following things:

- *It exposes and describes itself.* A Web Service defines its functionality and attributes so that other applications can understand it. By providing a Web Services Description Language (WSDL) file, a Web Service makes its functionality available to other applications.
- *It allows other services to locate it on the Web.* A Web Service can be registered in a UDDI Registry so that applications can locate it.
- *It can be invoked.* Once a Web Service has been located and examined, the remote application can invoke the service using an Internet standard protocol (such as HTTP or SMTP).

Chapter 16 introduces and discusses XML. Chapter 17 discusses Oracle Web Services.

Developer Toolkits

To support application development and deployment, Oracle provides several toolkits containing libraries and tools. Oracle Application Server Developer Kits 10*g* provide APIs that enable you to develop Oracle Application Server Portal, Oracle Application Server Wireless, XML, and LDAP applications. Developer kits are used in development environments, not in staging or production environments. The code in a developer kit is deployed in production. It is possible to develop your own developer kits.

XML Toolkit

Oracle XML Developer's Kit 10*g* (XDK) is a set of components, tools, and utilities available in Java, C, and C++, and in Oracle Database 10*g* and Oracle Application Server 10*g* that ease the task of building and deploying XML-enabled applications. The production Oracle XDK is fully supported and comes with a commercial redistribution license. Oracle XDK consists of the following components:

- **XML parsers** XML parsers create and parse XML using Document Object Model (DOM), Simple API for XML (SAX), and Java API for XML Processing (JAXP) interfaces.

You're able to directly access XMLType in the Oracle Database 10*g* with unified C DOM interfaces. DOM support includes the 3.0 specification.

- **eXtensible Stylesheet Language Transformation (XSLT) processors** XSLT processors transform or render XML. They now include XSLT 2.0 Java support.
- **XSLT VM** XSLT VM and Compiler provides high performance C XSLT transformation engine using compiled stylesheets.
- **XML schema processors** XML schema processors support XML schema validation. It now includes validator interfaces for stream-based processing.
- **XML JavaBeans** XML JavaBeans parse, transform, diff, retrieve, and compress XML documents via Java components.
- **XML Class Generator** Now supporting JAXP, XML Class Generator automatically generates classes from Document Type Definitions (DTDs) and XML schemas to send XML from web forms or applications.
- **XML SQL Utility** XML SQL Utility generates XML documents, DTDs, and XML schemas from SQL queries in Java and inserts XML documents into Oracle databases.
- **XSQL Servlet** XSQL Servlet combines XML, SQL, and XSLT in the server to deliver dynamic web content and build sophisticated database-backed web sites and services.
- **XML Pipeline Processor** XML Pipeline Processor invokes Java processes through XML control files.
- **TransX Utility** TransX Utility makes it easier to load globallized seed data and messages into Oracle databases.

Chapter 16 introduces and discusses XML.

Content Management Toolkit

Oracle Content Management SDK provides a set of Java APIs for folders, versioning, check-in/check-out, security, searching, extensible metadata, and other standard operations for the development of content-oriented applications. You can access your content with your choice of tools through the following protocols:

- **File Transfer Protocol (FTP)** FTP allows the transfer of one or more files from one machine to another across the Internet.
- **Server Message Block (SMB)** SMB is a protocol for sharing files, printers, serial ports, and communications abstractions such as named pipes and mail slots between computers.
- **Web Distributed Authoring and Versioning (WebDAV)** WebDAV is a mechanism to support collaborative development of web pages.
- **Network File System (NFS)** NFS is a protocol suite developed and licensed by Sun Microsystems that allows different makes of computers running different operating systems to share files and disk storage.

- **Apple Filing Protocol (AFP)** AFP is Apple's network protocol providing file server/client access in an AppleShare network.
- **Internet Messaging Access Protocol 4 (IMAP4)** IMAP4 is a network standard that allows users to manage e-mail messages and folders from multiple locations and systems. Users can choose to store their messages on their own local computers (or clients), or on a server.
- **Simple Mail Transfer Protocol (SMTP)** SMTP is a protocol used to send e-mail on the Internet. It is a set of rules regarding the interaction between a program sending e-mail and a program receiving e-mail.

Developers can also create custom/proprietary protocol servers. Oracle Content Management SDK is fully integrated with Oracle Text, Oracle Workflow, Oracle *inter*Media, Oracle Advanced Queueing, and other Oracle API products. It is also integrated with Oracle platform infrastructure products such as Oracle Internet Directory. It was formerly known as Oracle Internet File System.

Oracle Application Server MapViewer Toolkit

Geographic and location data are managed in a native type within Oracle Database 10*g*. Oracle provides the following technologies to make use of geographic information:

- **Oracle Locator** Oracle Locator provides core location functionality to support a variety of Location Based Services (LBS) and third-party Geographic Information Systems (GIS) solutions.
- **Oracle Spatial** Oracle Spatial is a database option for Oracle9*i* and Oracle Database 10*g* Enterprise Edition that provides advanced spatial features to support high-end GIS and LBS solutions.
- **Oracle MapViewer** Oracle MapViewer is an Oracle Application Server Java component and JDeveloper extension used for map rendering and viewing geospatial data managed by Oracle Spatial or Locator.

Wireless Toolkit

Oracle Application Server Wireless is a comprehensive and flexible wireless and voice platform. Enterprises can deploy wireless browser-based applications, voice applications, notifications, Java 2 Micro Edition (J2ME), and two-way messaging applications. It helps enterprises and service providers efficiently build, manage, and maintain wireless and voice applications. Some of the main features of Application Server Wireless include:

- **Multichannel server** A multichannel server enables applications to be accessed through multiple delivery methods such as Short Message Service (SMS), voice access, Wireless Application Protocol (WAP), Pocket PCs, etc. Developers can focus on creating mobile applications for any channel in one, future-proof open standards language.
- **J2ME support** J2ME provides a lightweight run-time environment for mobile devices enabling client-side development based on industry standards instead of proprietary device interfaces.

- **J2ME Developer's Kit** The J2ME Developer's Kit offers the capability to extend Web Services to J2ME devices.
- **J2ME Provisioning System** The J2ME Provisioning System is a web-based application manager that allows users to upload J2ME applications to the database repository for efficient management and secure storage.
- **Notifications and multimedia messaging** Notifications and multimedia messaging enhance intelligent messaging with new functionality for actionable alerts, message adaptation, and failover delivery control.
- **Web clipping** Web clipping allows clipping and scraping of existing web content to create wireless applications that reuse existing PC browser-based applications.
- **Location services** Location services give access to the full LBS functionality, such as user positioning, geocoding, mapping, driving directions, and business directory lookup.

To develop mobile applications, Oracle has created the Wireless Developer's Kit, a download that provides developers with documentation, samples, code templates, and wizards for common mobile user interface constructs. The Wireless Development Kit can be used on any PC or laptop, connected or disconnected, to build and test wireless and voice applications. Developers can use any IDE to develop their mobile applications, including Oracle JDeveloper. The JDeveloper Wireless Extension includes built-in simulators allowing developers to preview the mobile application, code templates, wizards, code insight, and automatic deployment to Oracle Application Servers.

Wireless applications can be deployed in the following ways:

- **Hosted services** Oracle provides a hosting service that maintains logins and allows access to a secure repository. This is the fastest way to implement your wireless development.
- **In-house deployment** Corporations deploy and maintain their own firewall-based security infrastructure.
- **In-house with hosted Web Services** Corporations install the Oracle9*i* Application Server Wireless infrastructure within their own premises while using the desired features as a Web Service.

Security is provided through a number of different protocols depending on the type of wireless application:

- **Browser-based applications** 802.11: HTTPS, WAP 1.2, WAP 2.0.
- **Short Message Service (SMS)** General Packet Radio Service (GPRS) security; applications can use symmetric shared encryption keys.
- **E-mail** Security is usually guaranteed in the domain if the e-mail server and application server are located at the mobile operator. If the servers reside at the enterprise, a secure channel—SSL, Transport Layer Security (TLS)—needs to be used.

- **Voice** HTTPS can secure the channel between the voice gateway and the application server.

Oracle Application Server Wireless supports the following messaging capabilities:

- **Push messaging** Push messaging sends messages to mobile users using the notifications engine or a custom application.
- **Mobile-initiated pull messaging** Mobile users send a message to invoke a server-side application, which replies by sending a message to the mobile user.
- **Server-initiated pull messaging** The server sends a message to which the mobile user can respond.

Out-of-the-box, the following channels and protocols are supported in Oracle Application Server Wireless:

- **SMS, Enhanced Messaging Systems (EMS), SmartMessages** Short Message Peer to Peer or SMPP (Logica, CMG, Comverse), UCP (CMG), CIMD (Nokia), Nokia Global System for Mobiles (GSM) phone modems with data cable, Mobileway V-SMSC, Vodafone VVSP
- **MMS** SMTP (Ericsson, LogicaCMG), External Application Interface or EAIF (Nokia), MM7 (Ericsson, LogicaCMG)
- **E-mail** IMAP, POP3, SMTP
- **Fax** Captaris RightFax
- **Voice notifications** VoiceGenie Voice Gateway
- **Pagers** Wireless Communications Transfer Protocol (WCTP)
- **Instant Messaging (IM)** Jabber (also as Gateway to AOL, MSN, Yahoo!, ICQ, etc.)

Portal Development Kit

The wizard-based approach to developing Portal components allows developers to create and deploy web-based components and applications extremely quickly. There are, however, serious limitations to any type of wizard-based development environment. The ability to customize and extend the functionality of components generated through a wizard-based development environment is arduous at best, and impossible in many cases.

The Portal Development Kit (PDK) provides developers with tools and articles that provide advanced techniques for extending the functionality of Portal components beyond what is available through the component wizards in Portal. The PDK is a framework that enables development of portlets for seamless integration with Oracle Application Server Portal. Using the PDK, developers can create portlets either as PL/SQL stored procedures (database providers) or in any other web language, including Java, Web Services, XML, Application Server Pages (ASP), Perl, etc. (web providers). The PDK includes the following:

- **PDK Services for Java (JPDK)** JPDK provides APIs for creating Java-based and Web Services-based portlets.
- **Java Portlet Container** Java Portlet Container provides a run-time environment for portlets coded to the JPDK Portlet API.
- **OmniPortlet** OmniPortlet provides wizards that enable Portal page designers to publish SQL, XML, Web Service, spreadsheet, and existing web page data directly to a Portal page.
- **Web Clipping Portlet** The Web Clipping Portlet enables page designers to collect existing web content into centralized Portal pages as a means of content consolidation. Page designers can clip page content from an existing web site and deliver it as a portlet to a Portal page.
- **PL/SQL Development Kit** The PL/SQL Development Kit provides APIs for developing database providers.
- **Utilities** Utilities simplify the development and testing of portlets.
- **Java Portlet Wizard** The Java Portlet Wizard is a JDeveloper Add-in that provides a wizard-based utility for creating JPDK-based portlets.
- **PL/SQL Generator** The PL/SQL Generator is a hosted utility that simplifies creation of PL/SQL-based portlets.
- **Test suite** The test suite includes the Provider Test and Test Harness utilities for testing web providers without having an installation of the Oracle Application Server Portal.
- **Samples** This includes various code samples highlighting development solutions.
- **Articles** This includes development white papers explaining development issues in depth.

Go to http://portalstudio.oracle.com for more information about downloading and installing the PDK.

Persistence Layer Services

When developing Java applications that interface with Oracle, the integration between Java's object-oriented features such as object references, business rules, complex relationships and inheritance, and Oracle's relational database features such as stored procedures, tables, rows, columns, and foreign keys (referred to as object-relational[O-R] mapping) requires an effort that is commonly underestimated by both developers and project managers. The problem of bridging object-oriented and relational technologies is referred to as object-relational impedance mismatch and the fundamental differences in modeling, design, and skill sets can prolong development work. This can lead to deployed applications that are, at best, difficult to maintain and, at worst, unreliable and impossible to enhance. In addition to these issues, developers also need the ability to translate object-oriented data into relational data, referred to as O-R mapping. A product that easily enables the integration of relational database and Java technologies, while allowing database designers and Java developers to maintain database and application design principles, would be invaluable. Oracle recognized the developer's need for these features and has created a product that not only addresses all of the complex issues mentioned above, but also adds features such as:

- A query framework that allows developers to define queries using various technologies
- A transaction framework that provides object-level transaction support
- Performance enhancements that includes a fully-configurable cache that ensures object-identity

Oracle Application Server TopLink integrates the object and relational worlds. It allows applications and application developers to manage Java objects using relational databases. TopLink is robust enough to work with any Java-supporting database and any application server that supports Java and J2EE containers. Some of the major features of Oracle Application Server TopLink include:

- **The Oracle Application Server Mapping Workbench** The Oracle Application Server Mapping Workbench is a visual tool that creates and maps metadata describing the relationship between Java classes and relational tables.
- **Advanced mapping support** Advanced mapping support includes support for the following mappings:
    - Direct-to-field
    - One-to-one
    - Variable one-to-one
    - One-to-many
    - Many-to-many
    - Aggregate Object
    - Aggregate-collection
    - Transformation
    - Object type
    - Type conversion
    - Serialized object
    - Direct collection
    - Nested tables
    - VArrays and OREFS
    - Multitable
    - Inheritance

- **Object caching** Object caching stores data returned as objects from the database for future use, minimizing database and network access. The following cache types are supported:
  - **Soft** Objects are maintained through garbage collection sweeps until memory is at a premium.
  - **Hard** Objects are not garbage collected.
  - **Weak** Objects exist in the cache as long as they are being used.
  - **Full** Objects are cached but not removed.
- **Query Flexibility** Developers can define queries using:
  - An object-oriented expression framework
  - Query By Example (QBE)
  - Enterprise Java Beans Query Language (EJB QL)
  - SQL
  - Stored procedures
- **Object-level transaction support** Transactions are supported through the "Unit of Work," a Java-based transaction. During a Unit of Work, the application modifies business objects; when the Unit of Work is committed, Oracle Application Server TopLink updates the database, based on what has changed, thereby executing the minimally required SQL.

Oracle Application Server TopLink consists of three main components:

- **Development tools** Development tools consist of the Oracle Application Server Mapping Workbench (which creates and manages the mapping metadata that describes the relationship between Java classes and relational tables) and the Oracle Application Server Sessions Editor (which describes how TopLink communicates with the datasource at run time by creating the session.xml file).
- **Run-time tools** Development tools consist of the web client, an interface to interact with any Oracle Application Server TopLink server session, and the Performance Profiler, providing performance tuning and run-time diagnostics.
- **Class libraries** Class libraries consist of the TopLink API, which is called at run time to retrieve and store Java objects.

Caching Services

Web caching is the process of keeping frequently used pages in memory so that the HTTP server can display them quickly instead of repeatedly processing requests for those URLs. By implementing caching, clients experience faster page retrievals and the load on the web server is greatly reduced. It is one of the most effective ways to scale your application without the need for r-coding or purchasing new hardware.

Oracle Application Server 10*g* contains a component called the Web Cache. It is a content-aware service that improves the performance, scalability, and availability of web sites. Application Server Web Cache 10*g* uses caching and compression technologies to optimize application performance and more efficiently utilize low-cost, existing hardware resources. Built-in workload management features ensure application reliability and help maintain quality of service under heavy loads. And new in this release, end-user performance monitoring features provide unparalleled insight into end-user service levels. The real power of Application Server Web Cache is its capability to cache both static and dynamically-generated pages.

The Web Cache can be configured to run on its own server or on the middle-tier server (see Figure 1-11). In either configuration, the Web Cache is placed in front of the web server to cache pages and provide content to those browsers that request it. If the Web Cache, acting as a virtual server or virtual request router, can satisfy the request, it will provide content to the client. If the requested content is not cached by the Web Cache or has been marked invalid for any reason, the content is retrieved from the web server and cached in the Web Cache. Application Server Web Cache allows you to define invalidation rules, which can be used to control the amount and types of cached content in your server. Some of the key benefits of Application Server Web Cache can be measured by dramatic improvements in the following areas:

- **Resource usage** Higher throughput and scalability
- **User experience** Faster response times without sacrificing personalization
- **Availability** Intelligent workload management
- **Productivity** No need to roll your own cache means faster time-to-market
- **Bottom line** Reduced infrastructure load translates into cost savings
- **Intelligence** Better visibility into end-user service levels

Some of the key features of Application Server Web Cache include:

- Efficient use of low-cost hardware
- Fine-grained cache control
- Workload management and reliability
- End-user experience management
- Advanced networking
- Single-vendor manageability and integration
- Flexible deployments

The new features of Application Server Web Cache include enhancements in the following categories:

- **End-user performance management** This is the most significant new Web Cache feature. Administrators can configure Application Server Web Cache to measure end-user response times for individual URLs, sets of URLs, or even entire web-based applications, regardless of whether the URLs are cached. The Analyze functionality lets you view detailed reports in context by group, URL, domain, visitor, or application as well as in a daily, weekly, or monthly context. Further drill-downs provide administrators with response time and load distribution information to help balance web server resources.

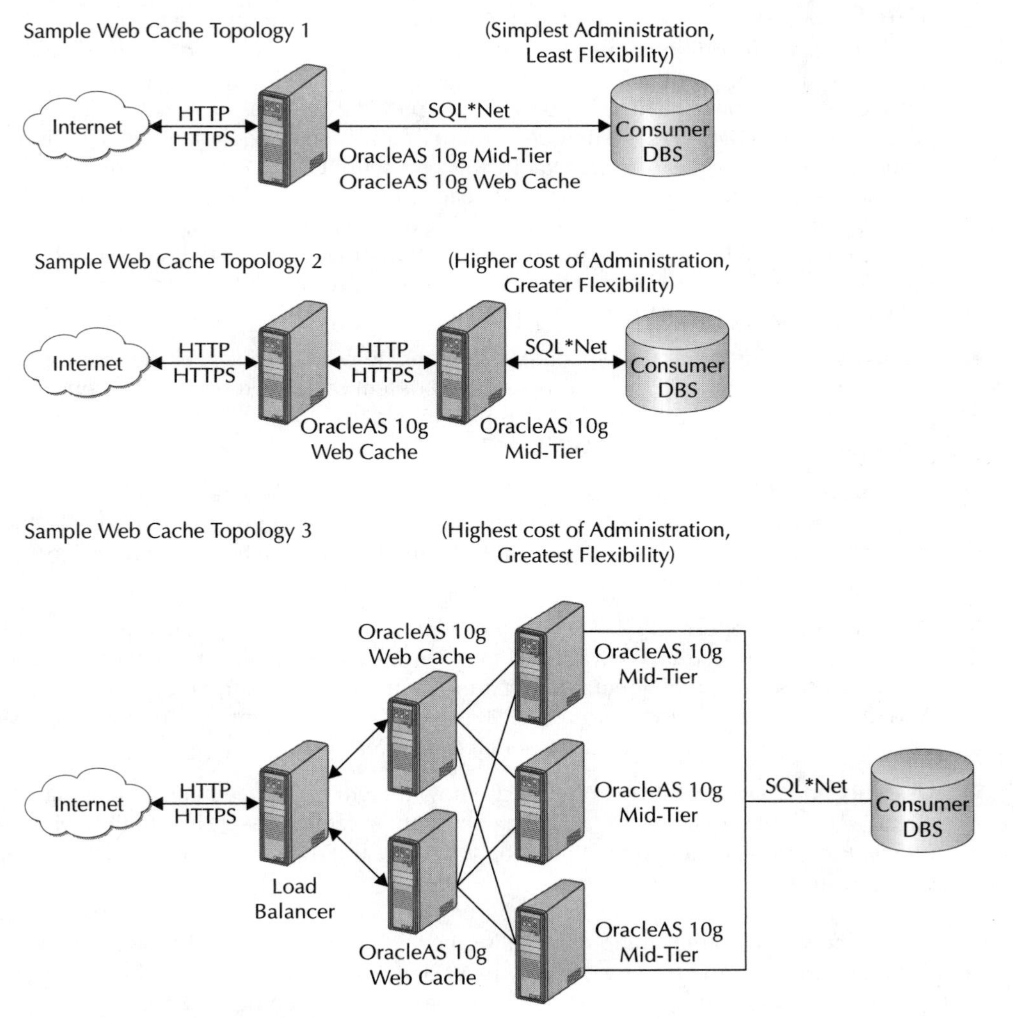

FIGURE 1-11. *Possible Web Cache topologies*

- **Security** Web Cache now supports applications that require client-side SSL certificates for PKI-based authentication. Oracle Application Server now supports nCipher's BHAPI-compliant hardware for deployment on servers running Web Cache and/or Oracle HTTP Server.
- **Caching** Previously, administrators could either cache one version of a page for all browsers, or they could cache one version for each browser type and version. Now, administrators can customize the caching rules to define groups of browsers that will share a cached version of a page.
- **Invalidation** The 9.0.4 release of Web Cache introduces an inline invalidation mechanism as an additional means of managing content freshness. Inline invalidation provides a useful way for origin servers to "piggyback" invalidation messages on transactional responses sent to Web Cache. In previous releases of Web Cache, the URL-based cache key was the unique identifier for a cached document. Invalidation requests needed to specify either exact URLs or a set of URLs and headers matching a regular expression in order to invalidate cached objects. Because it can be difficult for applications to map URLs to the underlying data used to generate those URLs, Web Cache invalidation has been extended in 9.0.4 to support search keys. Cached objects can now be associated with multiple application-specified search keys, with the URL-based key being the primary key.
- **Compression** The Web Cache compression engine now supports self-describing compression policies and more compressible content by compressing documents containing session-encoded URLs, Edge Side Includes (ESI) tags, or the <!–WEBCACHETAG–> and <!–WEBCACHEEND–> tags.
- **Load balancing and request routing** Support for session binding in a cache cluster allows Web Cache to bind a user session to a particular origin web server. This feature is used to consecutively route requests for a unique session to the same origin server, allowing stateful load balancing.
- **HTTP protocol support** Web Cache now supports chunked transfer encoding. HTTP 1.0 (with connection keep-alive) was used in prior releases of Web Cache, which caused problems for servers that generated dynamic content with unknown content length. Application Servers's support for HTTP 1.1 allows for persistent connection to the Web Cache, even when content length is undetermined.
- **Usability and manageability** Web Cache now includes improved access logging, event logging, and diagnostics, reporting on popular cache misses, integration with Oracle Process Manager and Notification (OPMN), and dynamic configuration for select parameters.

Figure 1-12 shows the administration screen for the Web Cache server. The Web Cache is an administration function, and is therefore only mentioned briefly in this book. The Database Cache, introduced in Oracle9*i* Application Server Release 1, has been discontinued.

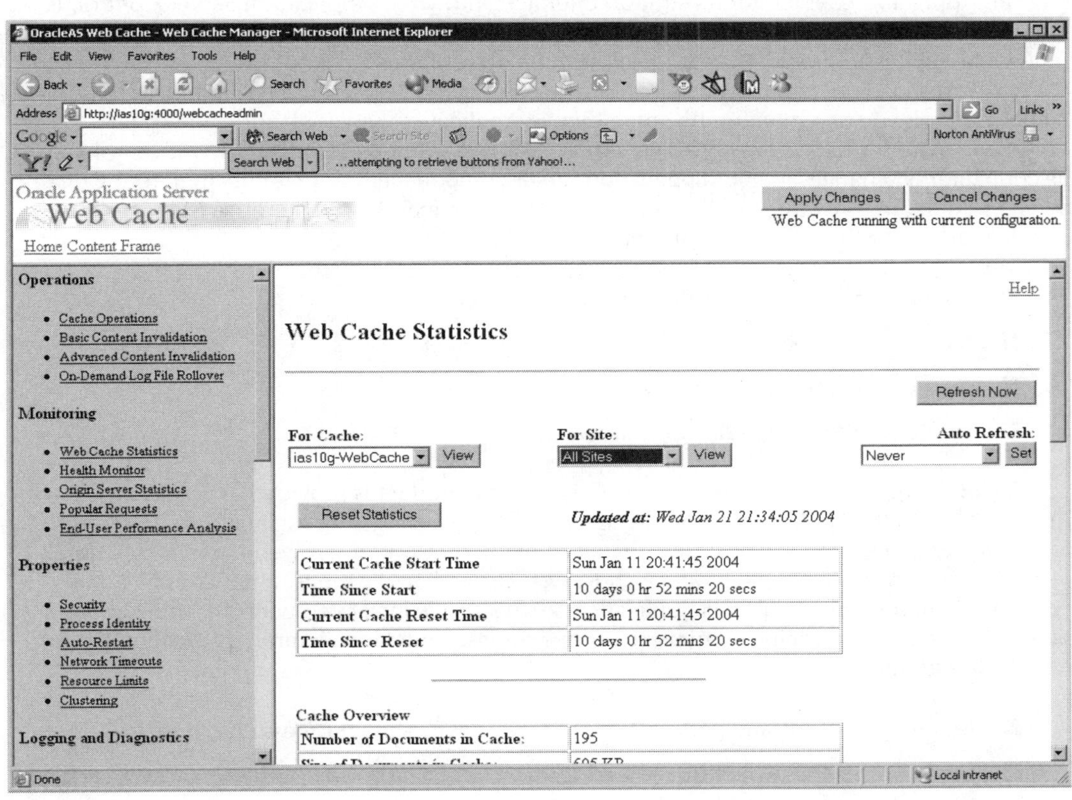

FIGURE 1-12. *The Web Cache administration screen*

System Services

Oracle provides numerous system services to help make your interaction with Oracle Application Server 10*g* easier. Most of the system services made available through the Enterprise Manager Application Server Control web pages are of interest mainly to administrators, but developers will benefit from an understanding of the Application Server Control pages when the deployment of applications is discussed in Chapter 15.

Enterprise Manager 10*g* Grid Control

Oracle Application Server 10*g* is supported by a web-based management system, Oracle Enterprise Manager 10*g*. Enterprise Manager provides both a simple, out-of-box application server administration interface and a comprehensive system for managing and monitoring large-scale Oracle systems.

The Application Server administration interface, known as Application Server Control, is automatically installed with Application Server 10*g*. It is designed to help you manage your individual application server instances, application server farms (an Application Server grouped with its corresponding infrastructure), and Oracle Application Server clusters. From the Application Server Control, you can monitor the entire Oracle Application Server platform—from J2EE to Portal and Wireless to Business Intelligence components—and perform administrative tasks, such as configuration changes to your application server components and real-time monitoring of all services configured in your Application Server 10*g* instances. With Enterprise Manager 10*g* Application Server Control, administrators can:

- Manage and configure application server components
- Monitor server performance and application server logs
- Create and configure J2EE services
- Deploy and monitor J2EE applications

The complete Enterprise Manager 10*g* Grid Control product is provided as an optional installation with the application server. The two can be used together as an integrated system for complete application server system management. Grid Control is a web-based system for central management of Oracle products, host systems, and applications. It provides a central console for monitoring distributed application servers and is integrated with the Application Server Control for performing administration operations. With Grid Control, application server administrators can:

- Monitor the status and performance of servers across the business enterprise
- Maintain service-level requirements for web applications
- Maintain system and software configurations
- Manage the entire system stack employed by the application server system

Figures 1-2 and 1-3 are screens for administering the middle tier and infrastructure instances, respectively, via the Enterprise Manager Application Server Control web site.

Development Tools

Does your web application have to be written in Java? Many developers believe that to be true, but as we will see, there are many options available to us as Oracle developers. Oracle provides numerous tools that allow us to leverage existing (or legacy) code into applications that can be deployed over the Web with minimal effort. In general, there are two types of web applications:

- **HTML-based** Application code (residing on the server or in an Oracle database) producing a series of HTML pages. There is no limitation as to what language is used to generate these pages.

- **Applet-based** Java code downloaded to the client's browser and executed there. Applets give the developer full control of the interface, but at a price—the time needed to download the applet may be prohibitive for all but the most trivial of applications.

Except for Discoverer Plus and Portal, there is no development environment provided with Oracle Application Server 10*g*.You will have to make a descision as to what technology to use when beginning your development. There is no "one" tool that is perfect for solving all of your development needs and virtually all organizations use a combination of different tools and technolgies. The most valuable developers in modern IT shops are those that are fluent in numerous technologies.

Choosing the right development tool is not an easy task and it is not a decision to enter into lightly. Human nature being what it is, people tend to gravitate to things they know and feel comfortable with. Some hard questions need to be answered before deciding on a technology, or a combination of technologies:

How Will Your Application Be Accessed?

It is not enough to deploy an application over the Web and not worry about how users will access it, although this was the original promise of browser-based applications. There are three basic ways of delivering your application, and each one of these will affect the development decisions you will need to make:

- **Intranet** In this environment, users access the application over a network inside a company or organization, which uses software like that used on the Internet, but the intranet is for internal use only and is not accessible to the public. This option gives you the most flexibility in your development decisions as there is a good likelihood that all users of your application will have fast network connections and that your organization has standardized on a single browser.
- **Extranet** In this environment, users access the application over a private network that uses the Internet protocols and the public telecommunication system to share a business's information, data, or operations with external suppliers, vendors, or customers. An extranet can be viewed as the external part of a company's intranet. Here, your development options begin to decrease, as there will be questions regarding browser types and firewall issues, which may block certain types of communications between the clients and server.
- **Internet** In this environment, users can access the application from anywhere in the world. This option has the least amount of flexibility regarding your development decisions as the application will have to be "generic" enough to support all types of browsers and all types of access (dial-up, broadband, etc.). It will be almost impossible to deliver any applet-based application via this method.

How Complex Is the User Interface?

Applets give the developer the greatest control over the look and feel of the user interface. As mentioned before, this comes at a great price: namely, the time required to download the applet to the browser. In an intranet or extranet setting, this may be acceptable, but it will be virtually impossible to serve applets over the Internet. If the decision is to go with an HTML-based application, whether users can be productive with a standard interface or if sophisticated HTML tools (such as Dreamweaver) will need to be utilized to create something more complex must be determined.

What Types of Users Will Be Using Your Application?

In general, users can be broken into three categories:

- **Casual users** For these users, speed is the most important factor. Casual users will probably demand that an application start with minimal load time and provide data access immediately. These users will usually be satisfied with HTML-based applications.
- **"Heads-down" users** These users work with an application for an extended period of time, and a startup period of a minute will probably be acceptible in a tradeoff to the productivity gains realized throughout the day. These users may benefit from an Applet-based application.
- **Power users** These users demand applications they can customize: either the interface of the application or the types queries and data used in the application. For these users, flexibility and interaction are the most important features, which will probably require an Applet-based application.

Oracle Forms

Oracle Forms is one of Oracle's oldest and most mature development products. It has been traditionally used to create client/server applications. It is similar in design and philosophy to Microsoft's Visual Basic development environment. Countless Forms-based applications are still in production environments around the world today.

As development efforts started moving towards web and browser-based deployments, the demand to create an environment that still supported Forms-based development (preserving legacy code and knowledge) and introduced web deployment (eliminating the high cost of maintaining clients with mutilple operating systems, nonstandard configurations, etc.) began to grow. Oracle began developing technologies that allowed existing Forms to be served over the Web. These initial efforts were called "cartridges" and were designed to "plug into" the web server, enhancing its functionality.

Oracle Application Server 10*g* includes a service called the Forms Server that is installed with the Business Intelligence and Forms option. It handles serving Oracle Forms over the Web, gathering metrics to assist in administration and tuning, and integration with Oracle's Identity Mangement features. There are numerous configuration parameters to modify virtually every aspect of the Forms environment on the Web. These parameters are discussed in detail in Chapter 6.

Starting with Oracle Forms 9*i* (the current version is Oracle Forms 10*g*), Oracle no longer provided the Forms run time to deploy Forms in a traditional client-server environment. The only way to test an Oracle Form you have developed is to run it as a web form through a forms server provided with the Oracle Forms 10*g* development environment. It was the final indication that

Oracle believed (and still firmly believes) that web-based applications is where organizations will be putting their development resources in the future. Chapter 3 discusses the Oracle Forms development environment. Chapters 6 and 11 discuss integrating Forms with Oracle Application Server 10*g* and Oracle Portal, respectively.

Oracle Reports

Much of what has been said about Oracle Forms also applies to Oracle Reports. It is a mature and stable product that allows developers to create reports quickly and easily. It also suffers from the high administration costs of deployment as Reports run-time libraries need to be installed and maintined on every machine that needs to run an Oracle Report. In response to this, Oracle developed cartridges for the Oracle Application Server (before Oracle standardized on Apache as its web server), which eventually became the Reports Server engine that is included with Oracle Application Server 10*g* today. The Reports Server can be configured to integrate with Oracle's Identity Management features for security. Like Oracle Forms 9*i*, every version of Oracle Reports since 9*i* (the current version is Oracle Reports 10*g*) no longer provides the Reports run-time environment to run Oracle Reports in a traditional client/server environment. The only way to test a Report you have developed is to run it as a web report through a reports server provided with the Oracle Reports 10*g* development environment.

Multiple Reports servers can be defined for each middle tier in Oracle Application Server 10*g*. This gives another layer of scalability for your environment. If you wish to integrate Reports with Oracle Portal, calendars can be created in Portal to limit the access times for certain reports, Report servers, and printers. You can also use the Portal security model to limit access to any of these components. Chapter 4 discusses the Oracle Reports development environment. Chapters 6 and 11 discuss integrating Reports into Oracle Application Server 10*g* and Oracle Portal, respectively.

Oracle Discoverer

As mentioned earlier in this chapter, Oracle Discoverer server contains a component to view and interact with Discoverer worksheets over the Web (Discoverer Viewer) and a component to create and modify Worksheets (Discoverer Plus). The ad-hoc capabilities of Discoverer can allow your developent staff to off-load report design and generation to power users. By putting the full capabilities of the Discoverer desktop on to the Web, Oracle makes the implementation of Discoverer a simple experience for most organizations.

Discoverer also integrates seamlessly with Oracle Portal via an internal portlet provider provided by Oracle called the Discoverer portlet. This portlet allows you to define the workbook and worksheet you wish to display, any parameters to be passed to the worksheet, and a refresh options setting that allows you to specify AUs: Okay to make active here? the length of time a particular report will be cached (in Portal's Cache, not the Web Cache). The Discoverer worksheet becomes a portlet and can have any of Portal's security and display properties applied to it. Chapter 5 discusses viewing and creating Discoverer workbooks and worksheets via the Web, and Chapters 6 and 11 discuss how to integrate Discoverer with Oracle Application Server 10*g* and Oracle Portal.

Java Tools

An Integrated Development Enivornment (IDE) is a development environment in which the tools have been integrated to collaborate with each other (e.g., the output of one tool can be used as the input to another tool). Attempting to build Java applications without an IDE using the free Java compiler provided in the Java Software Development Kit from Sun Microsystems is possible, but it is a less than optimal environment. Oracle's Java IDE, JDeveloper, has so many essential tools, only the hardiest of Java programmers would ever attempt to build production-quality Java applications without it. JDeveloper will be covered in Chapter 13, but a quick list of its prominent features include:

- Three profiling modes that enables you to create a statistical analysis of the performance of your application with respect to its functionality both at compile time and run time, its use of memory in the Java heap, and the occurrence and duration of various events.
- A public Extension SDK that enables its development environment to be extended and customized.
- Native support for SQL, PL/SQL, and XML. This support includes syntax highlighting and code insight, as well as PL/SQL development, PL/SQL debugging, and SQL tuning. Additionally, JDeveloper provides direct access to the database, allowing you to view, create, modify, and delete tables, views, triggers, indexes, sequences, and more.
- Robust debugging support for both Java and PL/SQL. Debugging in these two environments is seamlessly integrated when using an Oracle9*i* database, providing the capability to step from Java code directly into PL/SQL code within the same debugging session.
- Class diagrams. The goal of class modeling is to visualize classes or components, and the relationships between them, that comprise all or part of a system design. Classes and components modeled on a class diagram are synchronized to ensure that changes made to modeled elements are reflected in their implementation files, and that changes to the implementation files are visualized on the diagram.
- Activity diagrams. Processes performed in a business or system can be visualized using modeled activities, flows, and states on activity diagrams. An activity can represent a single process, or it can represent a subactivity model (that is, the activity can be broken down into a set of subactivities which themselves form an activity model).
- All aspects of EJB development from conception to implementation. EJB support includes: modeling and wizard-based development of EJB session, entity, and message-driven beans, the ability to add, edit, and delete EJBs and EJB properties using the EJB Module Editor, reverse-engineering of database tables and foreign key relationships as Container-Managed Persistence (CMP) entity beans and Container Managed Relationships (CMRs), the ability to test EJBs locally in the IDE, and the ability to check EJBs for deployment errors and inconsistencies using the EJB Verifier.

- J2EE deployment, which allows developers to package and assemble J2EE modules into standard archives such as EJBs, JARs, WARs, and EARs. These archives can be deployed with a single-click to Oracle Application Server Containers for J2EE (OC4J).
- A built-in J2EE Applications Framework. Oracle Business Components for Java (BC4J) is a standards-based, server-side framework for creating scalable, high-performance J2EE applications. The framework provides design-time facilities and run-time services to simplify the task of building, debugging, customizing, and reusing business components.
- An application Development Framework (ADF). This is the most exciting new feature of JDeveloper for developers. The ADF is Oracle's solution to the ever-increasing complexity of the J2EE platform. Based on the Model-View-Controller (MVC) architecture, Oracle ADF lets application developers focus on the business domain rather than on the underlying technologies. By using visual, declarative, and guided-coding techniques, the framework allows application developers who are not J2EE experts to quickly become productive. The framework is based on industry standards allowing applications built with ADF to be deployed on any J2EE server and connect to any SQL database.
- Integration of the TopLink Mapping Workbench. Oracle JDeveloper 10*g* seamlessly integrates with the Mapping Workbench (see Figure 1-13), giving developers the ability to:
    - Automatically map descriptors
    - Generate database schemas from object models
    - Generate object models from database schemas
    - Generate both CMP and Bean-Managed Persistence (BMP) entity beans
    - Import an object model from any IDE or UML modeling tool
    - Connect and interact with any relational database with a JDBC-compliant driver

HTML DB

HTML DB occupies a unique space in the world of Oracle web development. It is a web development tool, but it is not part of the Oracle Application Server 10*g* product stack. The Oracle HTML DB engine is stored in the database, and its accessible via the HTTP server that comes standard with the Oracle 10*g* database. It is intended primarily for simple web-based applications that do not require the sophisticated features provided with Application Server 10*g*. HTML DB is composed of three main pieces:

- **Application Builder** Application Builder helps you assemble an HTML user interface on top of database objects. The Oracle HTML DB engine takes care of presenting your application using templates and UI elements.

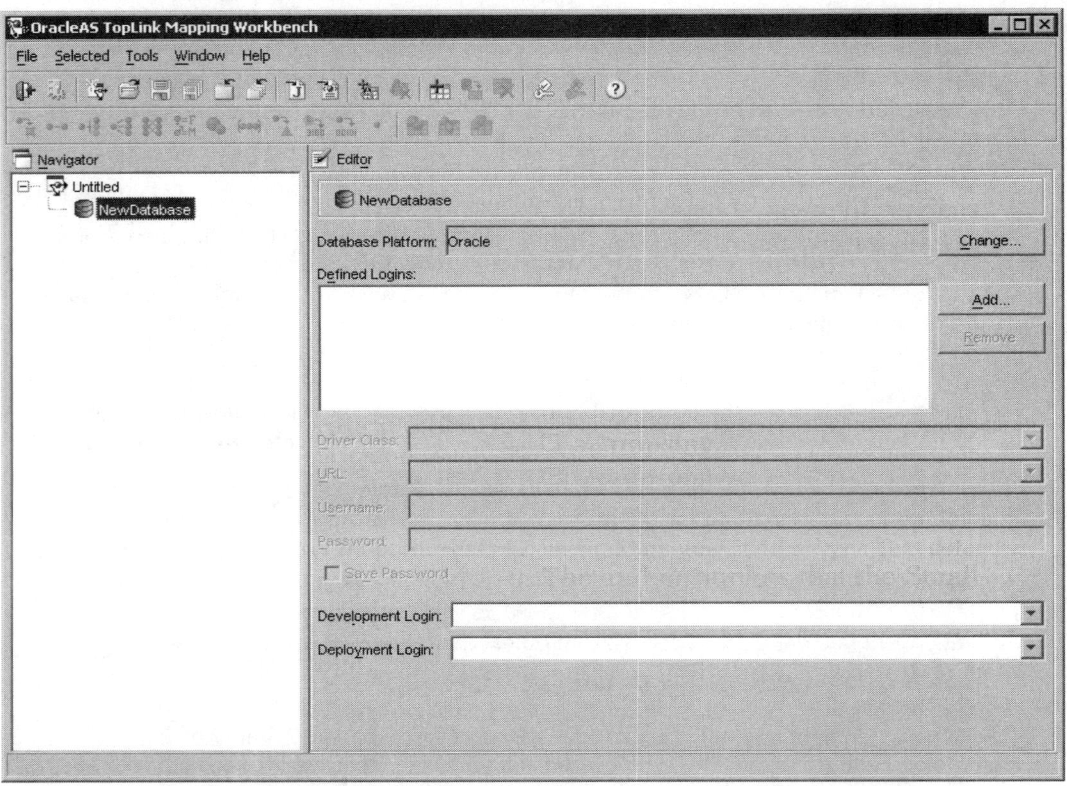

FIGURE 1-13. *The TopLink Mapping Workbench*

- **SQL Workshop** SQL Workshop enables you to interact with the database through a web browser. With it, you can view or create database objects, run SQL commands, and query by example.
- **Data Workshop** Data Workshop helps you import plain text and spreadsheet data into database tables and export data from database tables.

All HTML DB applications are displayed in your browser from data queried from the database, called *application definitions.* This metadata provides information about your application to the HTML DB engine, and therefore no code is generated (or needed). The Oracle HTML DB rendering engine reads the application definition and displays the application accordingly. Figure 1-14 shows an example of an HTML DB page.

FIGURE 1-14. *An HTML DB page*

Database Tools

The PL/SQL Web Toolkit, a set of packages, procedures, and functions that directly interface with the mod_plsql module included with Apache is discussed in Chapter 7, but there are many enhancements to the PL/SQL language and Oracle's support of SQL in Application Server 10*g* that are mentioned here. Some of the major SQL enhancements include:

- Operators, functions, and constraints for new, native floating point datatypes
- The introduction of regular expression support
- Performance and size limit of large objects (LOBs) has been enhanced

Some of the major PL/SQL enhancements include:

- A rewritten, optimizing PL/SQL code generator for the PL/SQL Virtual Machine (PVM)
- Support for binary_float and binary_double datatypes
- Built-ins to support regular expression manipulation: regexp_like, regexp_instr, regexp_substr, and regexp_replace
- Multiset operations on nested table instances, supporting operations like equals, union, intersect, except, member
- Support for a user-defined quote character
- INDICES OF and VALUES OF syntax for FORALL

Summary

Web applications are applications based on open, public web standards that use a web browser as the client. They fall into one of two categories: HTML-based or applet-based. How you decide to code your application depends on numerous factors, as there is no one "right" way to code an application. Various technologies exist that excel at different aspects of web application development. In all but the smallest IT departments, you will be called upon to use a combination of these technologies.

Oracle offers all the software you need to build production-quality web applications. At the core of your Oracle-based web development is Oracle Application Server 10*g*, an Application Server designed to support all major web development languages, APIs, and frameworks, and to provide unparalelled flexibility, security, scalability, and reliability. Application Server 10*g* supports the full J2EE technology stack as well as Oracle-specific technologies such as Forms, Reports, and Discoverer. Oracle is committed to open standards, allowing developers to use the capabilities of Application Server 10*g* to solve virtually any development challenge.

CHAPTER 2

Oracle Application Server 10*g* Architecture

In Chapter 1, we looked at some of the components that make up Oracle Application Server 10*g* and how those components support the various development standards and frameworks available to developers today. On the development side, we've seen that Oracle Application Server 10*g*:

- Supports the full J2EE stack, including elements such as JavaServer Pages (JSPs), Enterprise JavaBeans (EJBs), and servlets
- Provides support for existing Oracle Forms, Oracle Reports, and Oracle Discoverer worksheets
- Provides a complete development, deployment, and administrative portal environment
- Supports various wireless devices and their corresponding protocols
- Provides full support for Web Services

If this was the extent of the Oracle Application Server 10*g* product stack, it would be an incredibly powerful product. Oracle, however, has added numerous features in addition to those already mentioned that further enhance its usefulness and functionality. While developers and administrators are not required to use any of these features, the work taken to master and implement these technologies will provide productivity benefits that will, in most cases, far outweigh ignoring them.

This chapter deals with features specific to Oracle Application Server 10*g* that provide developers with an environment that is secure, stable, scalable, and reliable. These technologies augment existing methods, saving developers and administrators the overhead of mastering these new technologies from scratch. In most cases, developers and administrators can take their existing knowledge of application development and deployment and enhance it with the topics discussed in this chapter to speed application development time, create more secure applications, decrease application deployment and user provisioning time, and increase the availability of deployed applications. The topics addressed in this chapter include:

- Oracle Application Server Containers for J2EE (OC4J)
- Oracle Application Server 10*g* security architecture
- Oracle Process Manager and Notification Server (OPMN)

Oracle Application Server Containers for J2EE (OC4J)

Java development and deployment is discussed in detail in Part IV of this book, but it is helpful to talk about OC4J now and discuss some of its important features. OC4J provides developers with a consistent framework that allows the deployment of Java applications to the Web easily. A developer must understand, however, the directory naming convention and meanings of various deployment files before attempting to deploy applications to an OC4J instance contained within Application Server 10*g*. Oracle's Java development tool, Oracle JDeveloper 10*g*, has enhancements that allow Java applications developed there to be deployed to an Application Server 10*g* OC4J instance with minimal effort. JDeveloper 10*g* and the deployment of applications developed there will be discussed in detail in Chapter 13.

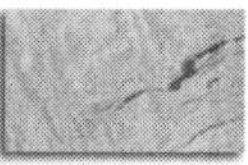

NOTE
It is important to note that while OC4J is an integral part of Oracle Application Server 10g, it is also available as a separate download from the Oracle Technology Network (http://otn.oracle.com).

Most Java applications are built using a variety of Java technologies, some of which were discussed in Chapter 1. When an application made up of these different Java technologies is deployed, the Java 2 Platform, Enterprise Edition (J2EE) specification mandates that the files that constitute your application be placed in specifically named directories and include deployment files that describe your application's directory structure. These deployment files are used as the application is deployed under an OC4J container in the middle tier of your application server farm. Oracle takes the information contained in these deployment files and automatically constructs various web pages that allow deployed applications to be monitored via the Enterprise Manager Application Server Control web site. Figure 2-1 shows an example of an Enterprise Manager web site page for an application named "portal," deployed under the OC4J container named OC4J_Portal.

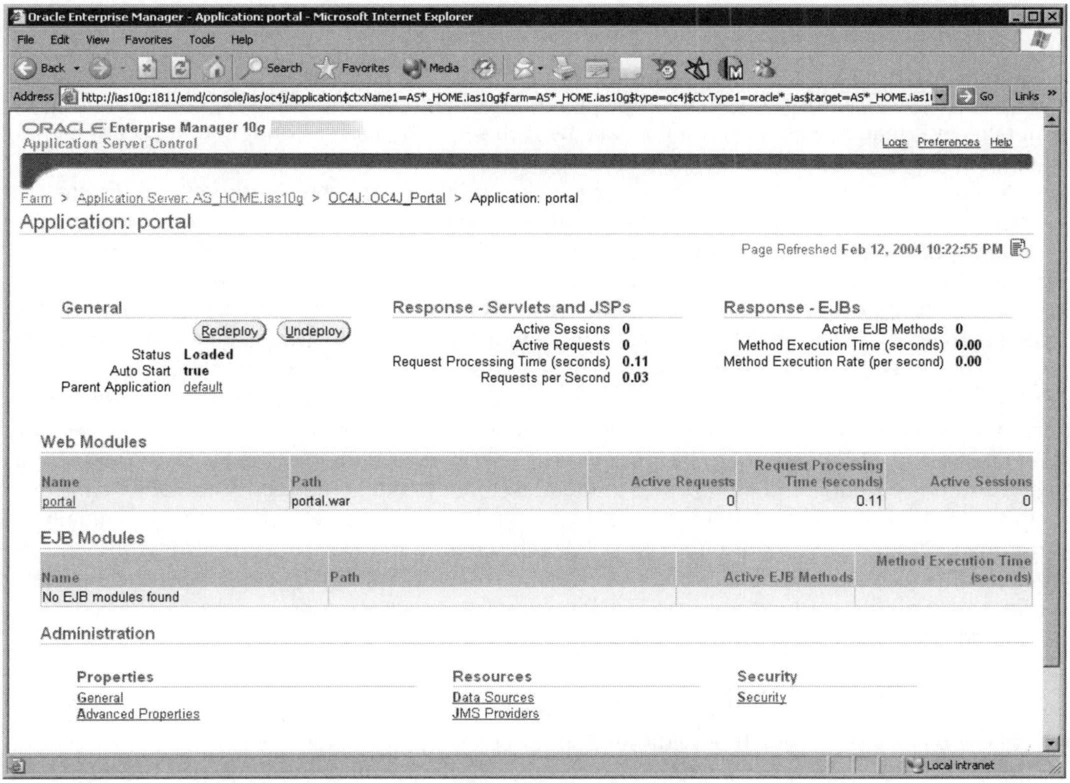

Oracle Enterprise Manager - Application: portal - Microsoft Internet Explorer

ORACLE Enterprise Manager 10g
Application Server Control

Farm > Application Server: AS_HOME.ias10g > OC4J: OC4J_Portal > Application: portal

Application: portal

Page Refreshed Feb 12, 2004 10:22:55 PM

General

Status Loaded
Auto Start true
Parent Application default

Response - Servlets and JSPs

Active Sessions 0
Active Requests 0
Request Processing Time (seconds) 0.11
Requests per Second 0.03

Response - EJBs

Active EJB Methods 0
Method Execution Time (seconds) 0.00
Method Execution Rate (per second) 0.00

Web Modules

Name	Path	Active Requests	Request Processing Time (seconds)	Active Sessions
portal	portal.war	0	0.11	0

EJB Modules

Name	Path	Active EJB Methods	Method Execution Time (seconds)
No EJB modules found			

Administration

Properties: General, Advanced Properties
Resources: Data Sources, JMS Providers
Security: Security

FIGURE 2-1. *An Enterprise Manager web site page for application "portal"*

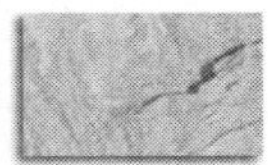

NOTE
In this example, the page displayed in Figure 2-1 gives metrics for all aspects of the Oracle Portal environment, including development, administration, and the generation and delivery of Oracle Portal pages. If you have a heavily or moderately used Portal environment, viewing the metrics on this page can give a good indication of the types of metrics that can be used to tune any of your OC4J instances.

Some terminology needs to be explored before the structure and content of the files that make up an OC4J server and the application to be deployed can be discussed. Some of the terminology discussed here may be thoroughly understood by experienced Java developers, but it is important to remove any ambiguities before proceeding.

A *servlet* is a small Java program that runs on a web server, as opposed to an *applet,* which is a Java program that runs in a client browser. When a client HTTP request calls a servlet, the web server passes the HTTP request to a "container" (discussed shortly). The container translates the HTTP request into a Java method invocation and then passes the request to the servlet. Servlets take client HTTP requests from a browser, generate dynamic content (with data queried from an Oracle database as an example), and provide an HTTP response back to the browser. Unlike a Java client program, a servlet has no static main() method. Therefore, a servlet must execute under the control of an external container.

The Apache server, however, does not have a Java Virtual Machine (JVM) built into it. Sun Microsystems maintains the specification of the Java language and the Apache Foundation maintains the Apache web server. If the Apache web server had a JVM built into it, coordinating changes in the Java specification with Apache would be almost impossible as Sun and the Apache Foundation have different (and sometimes conflicting) motivating factors. In response to the attempt to create a Java environment that Apache could use, the concept of a container was born.

Strictly speaking, a container is a component that contains other components, but for our purposes, we can think of a container as a program that provides a Java environment and associated services to support that Java environment to the Apache web server. Because the container is not part of the Apache server, it can be updated to reflect Sun's enhancements of the Java language, independent of any changes (such as upgrades, bug fixes, or security patches) made to the Apache web server. Traditionally, the container is associated with and communicates with the Apache web server by way of an Apache module called mod_jserv. When a client HTTP request calls a servlet, the web server passes the HTTP request to the container. The container translates the HTTP request into a Java method invocation and then passes the request to the servlet. The servlet container calls the methods of the servlet and provides services to the servlet while it is executing. A servlet container is usually written in Java and is either part of a web server (if the web server is also written in Java) or otherwise associated with and used by a web server. The servlet container provides the servlet easy access to properties of the HTTP request, such as its headers and parameters.

In general, there are two types of containers:

- *Web containers*, which provide support for servlets and JSPs
- *EJB containers*, which provide support for Enterprise Java Beans (EJBs)

The Apache server provided with Oracle Application Server 10g has the mod_jserv module disabled by default as Oracle has created its own module, mod_oc4j (Oracle Containers For J2EE), which encompasses all of the functionality of the mod_jserv module and adds many features to it. mod_oc4j can be considered both a web container (as it provides all the services needed by servlets and JSPs) and an EJB container (as it provides support for EJBs). OC4J includes a fully standards-compliant servlet container. In addition, Oracle provides Oracle Business Components for Java (BC4J), an XML-powered framework that enhances the EJB architecture and helps developers quickly build, test, and deploy multitier database applications from business components. BC4J greatly assists in the development of EJBs by implementing many of the common patterns used by developers of Oracle-based web applications. Oracle encourages all developers of applications deployed through Application Server 10*g* to use BC4J and OC4J.

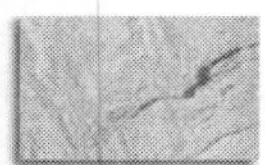

TIP
Not only is mod_oc4j much faster than mod_jserv, but it also has an EJB container and much greater functionality

Most of the administration tasks of creating and editing the files associated with an OC4J instance, as well as the tasks associated with deploying applications to an OC4J instance, can be handled through the Oracle Enterprise Manager Application Server Control web site, although it is not a requirement to do so. Through this web site, you can create OC4Js, deploy applications, and monitor the container's performance as well as set characteristics that can be used to cascade down to other applications deployed within an OC4J instance. Figure 2-2 shows the main page of an OC4J instance.

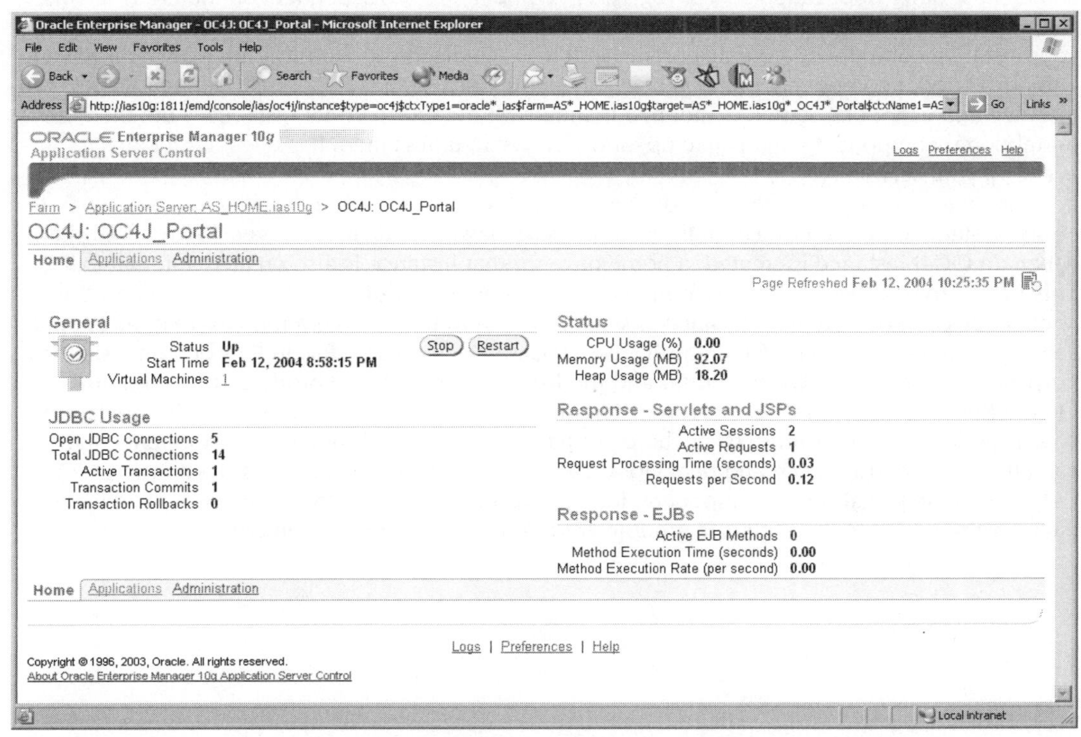

FIGURE 2-2. *The main page of an OC4J container*

Chapter 15 will explore the various tasks that need to be performed when deploying Java applications to an Application Server 10*g* OC4J instance. This chapter discusses the basic tasks involved in OC4J creation and administration. As part of the Application Server 10*g* installation, a number of OC4J instances are created automatically. To see what has been installed and configured already, point your browser to:

```
http://<Middle-tier>:<Enterprise Manager Port>
```

The development machine used for all examples contained in this book is named xpas10*g*, and the Enterprise Manager Application Server Control web site is listening on the default port of 1810; the Uniform Resource Locator (URL) to access the site is

```
http://xpas10g:1810
```

After you log in, the farm page is presented (a farm is an infrastructure and all of its associated middle tiers). Select the middle-tier instance. A page similar to the one in Figure 2-3 should be displayed.

The components displayed may look different depending on the type of installation you have chosen, but at the very least, a couple of components that begin with "OC4J_" should be visible. These components are OC4J instances and are created, by default, to support Oracle processes. Some of the other Application Server 10*g* system components are dependent on the OC4J servers. For example, if the "Portal and Wireless" or "Business Intelligence" options were chosen during your install, a component named "portal:portal" will be displayed with its check box grayed out. The portal:portal component check box is grayed out because it is dependent on the OC4J_Portal instance and cannot be started or stopped manually. If the OC4J_Portal instance is up, then the portal:portal component will also be up, and vice versa, unless there has been an unexpected event on your server.

If the two components are dependent on each other, you may wonder why they are separate on the system components page of the Enterprise Manager Application Server Control web site. When an OC4J instance is created, a home page for that instance is also created automatically. This page provides various real-time information metrics about the OC4J instance and the applications deployed to that instance as well as access to the configuration files that make up any applications deployed there. In most cases, this is sufficient for a developer's or administrator's purposes. In the case of Oracle Portal and the Business Intelligence products (Oracle Forms, Oracle Reports, and Oracle Discoverer), Oracle has created other metrics and administration pages specific to those products, as there are parameters for each of these components that can affect their performance and behavior outside of the parameters associated with the OC4J instance. In the portal:portal component, for example, an administrator or developer can view the performance of the providers (a grouping of Portal objects, most commonly portlets) that

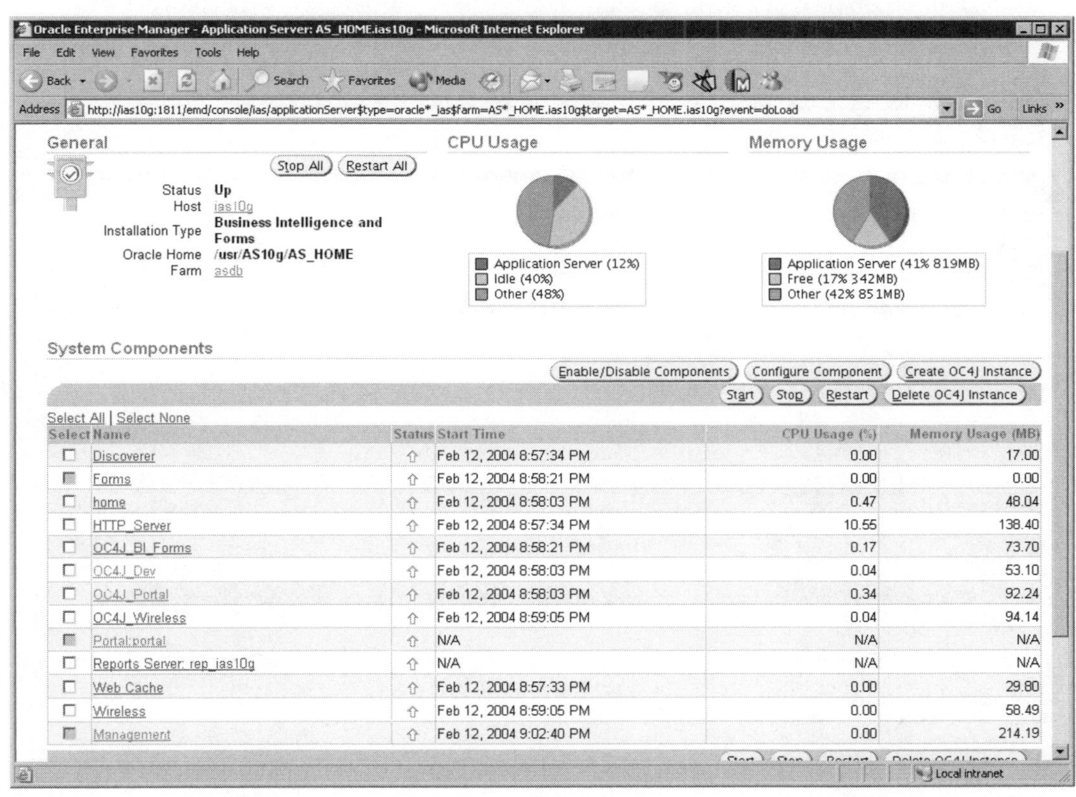

FIGURE 2-3. *Components installed in the middle tier*

have been created in your Portal environment and even drill down to individual components in the provider (such as Portal forms or Portal Reports) to view their metrics (see Figure 2-4). In the Forms system component (which is dependent on the OC4J_BI_Forms instance), you can view metrics for the users currently connecting to Application Server 10*g* via an Oracle Forms application (see Figure 2-5) and change the configuration files that drive the Forms server. Chapter 6 will look at the Forms, Reports, and Discoverer servers running under Oracle Applications Server 10*g*, along with their configuration and monitoring.

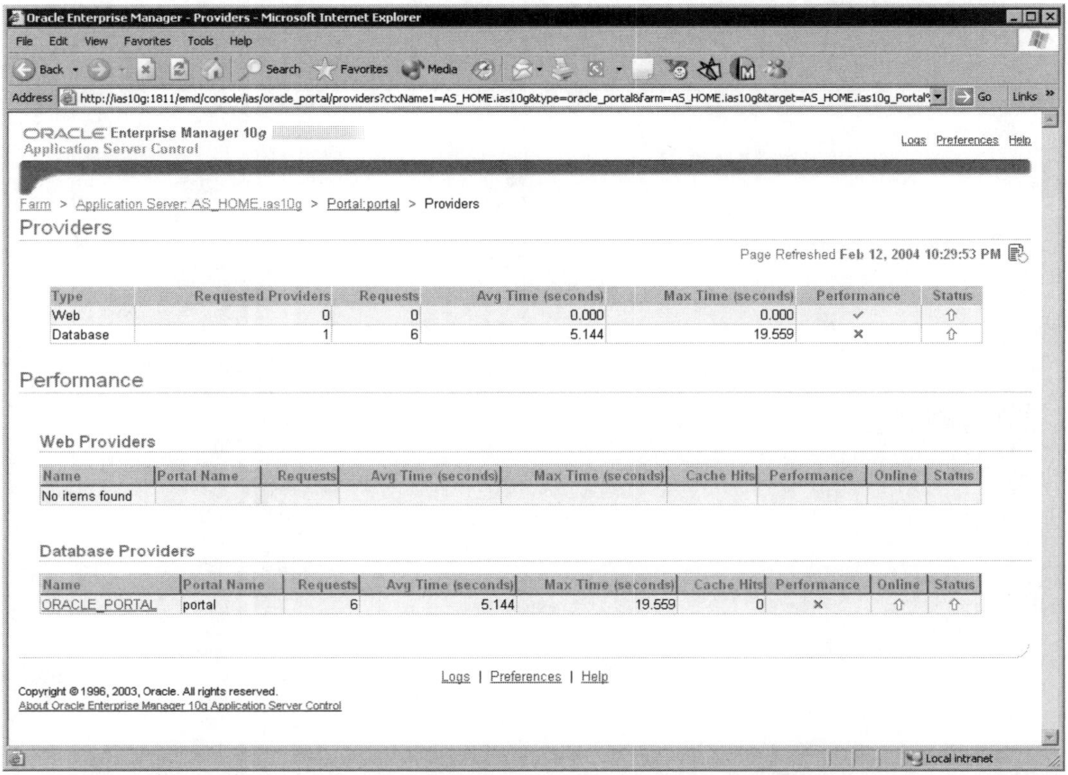

FIGURE 2-4. *Metrics of a Portal component*

TIP
The parameter em_mode must be set to 1 in the Oracle Forms configuration file (formsweb.cfg) to see the metrics in Figure 2-5.

Although you could deploy your application to one of these existing OC4J instances, it is a much better idea to go ahead and create your own OC4J instance.

NOTE
The existing OC4J instances have settings that are unique to the applications deployed there. The OC4J_Portal instance, for example, has settings that influence the behavior of the Portal application. Deploying an application there and changing any of the settings for the OC4J_Portal instance could, at the very least, cause the Portal application to behave erratically and, at the very worst, stop the Portal application from functioning altogether.

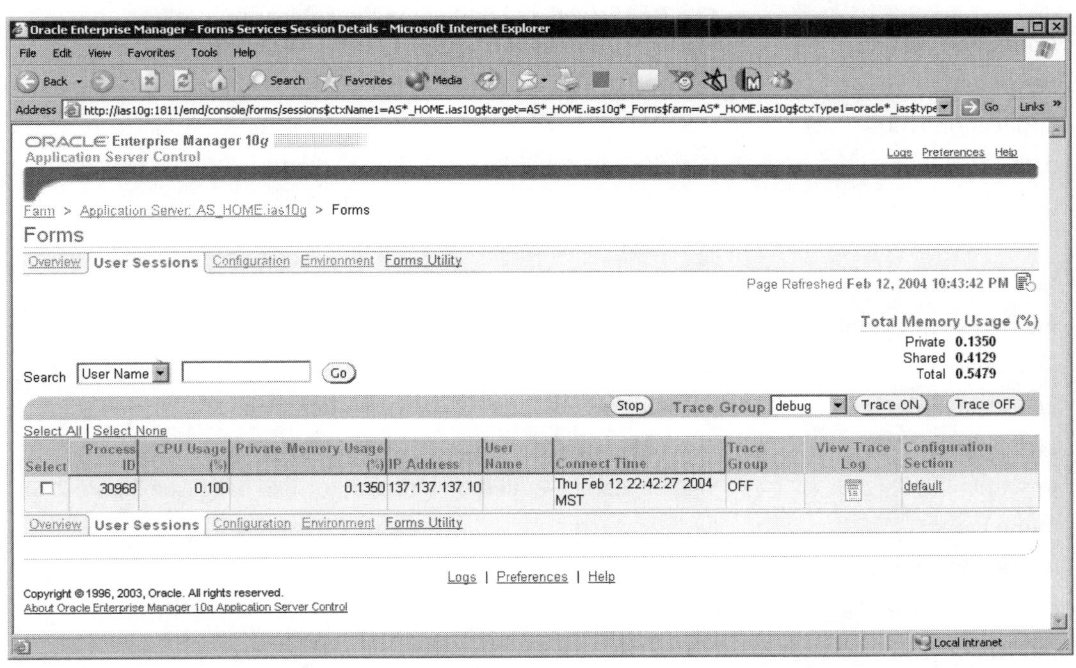

FIGURE 2-5. *Metrics for users connecting to Oracle Application Server 10g via a Forms application*

All of the administrative actions associated with an OC4J instance (creating a new instance, deploying an application, etc.) could be performed from the command line. As we will see, however, there are a number of configuration files that must be in place and the Enterprise Manager Application Server Control web site will handle a lot of the work of creating these files and populating them with values for us if we choose to use it to create our OC4J instance. The configuration files fall into two categories:

- **OC4J server configuration files** Those files that affect the behavior of the OC4J instance
- **Application deployment files** Those files that describe the structure of the application we wish to deploy

This chapter will take a look at the OC4J server configuration files. Although it's mentioned briefly in this chapter, the content and directory structure associated with application deployment files will be explored in depth in Chapter 15.

The major advantage of using the Enterprise Manager Application Server Control web site, aside from its graphical user interface (GUI) interface, is its capability to do a lot of the work for us by setting up the location and structure of many of the files needed to configure OC4J instances. If the Enterprise Manager Application Server Control web site is used to create an OC4J instance, the files are created and populated automatically, as shown in Table 2-1.

Configuration File	Can Be Viewed and Edited via the Enterprise Manager Application Server Control Web Site
server.xml	Yes; file can be edited on a text editor-like page (see Figure 2-6)
application.xml	No
data-sources.xml	Yes; file can be updated via a web interface
default-web-site.xml	Yes; file can be edited on a text editor-like page (see Figure 2-6)
global-web-application.xml	Yes; file can be edited on a text editor-like page (see Figure 2-6)
http-web-site.xml	No
internal-settings.xml	No
java2.policy	No
jazn-data.xml	Yes; file can be updated via a web interface
jazn.xml	Yes; file can be updated via a web interface
jms.xml	Yes; file can be edited on a text editor-like page (see Figure 2-6)
mime.types	No
oc4j-connectors.xml	No
oc4j.properties	No
principals.xml	No
rmi.xml	Yes; file can be edited on a text editor-like page (see Figure 2-6)

TABLE 2-1. *OC4J Server Configuration Files*

While it is certainly possible to use command-line tools to create OC4J instances and deploy applications, the approach taken in this book is to use the Enterprise Manager Application Server Control web site to perform these tasks. Oracle **strongly** recommends using the Enterprise Manager Application Control web site as errors introduced into these files can corrupt your repository.

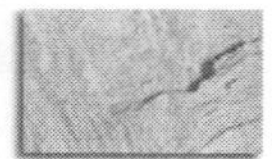

NOTE
*If you would like to see the process of configuring the various XML files manually and using the command-line interface to deploy applications, see Oracle9iAS Building J2EE Applications by Nirva Morisseau-Leroy, et al (Osborne Oracle Press, 2002). Although that book is aimed at the version of OC4J included with Oracle9i Application Server Release 2 (9.0.3), the process is, with very minor exceptions, the same. Remember, however, that Oracle **strongly** recommends using the Enterprise Manager Application Server Control web site to update these files.*

The OC4J server configuration files are located in <ORACLE_HOME>/j2ee/<OC4J instance name>/config. They are listed below in alphabetical order except for server.xml, which, among other things, serves to reference other configuration files.

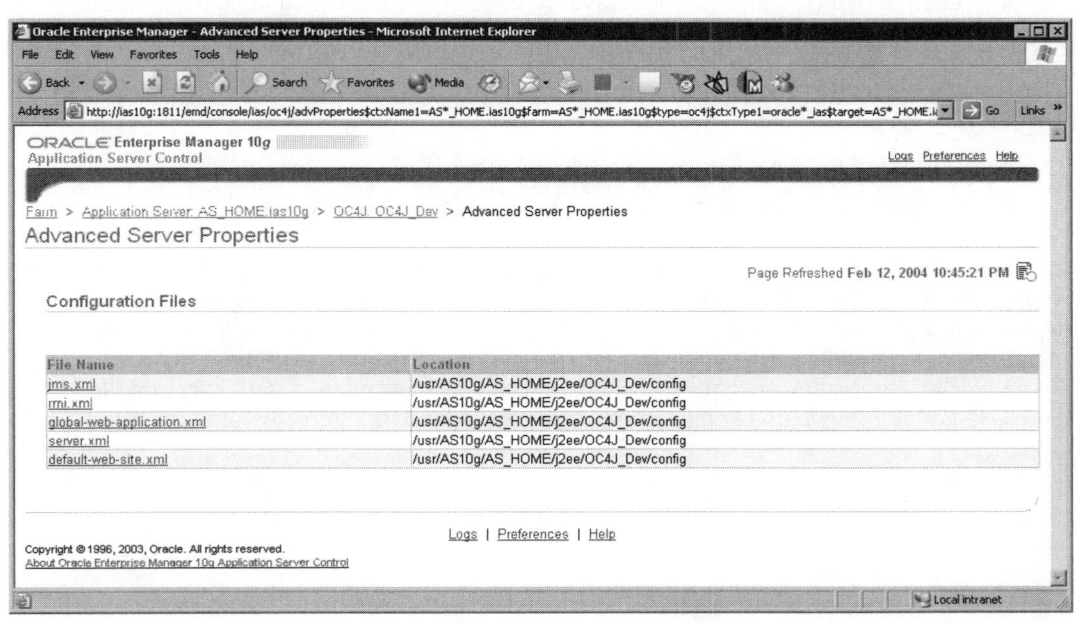

FIGURE 2-6. *Page listing configuration files that can be edited via the Oracle Enterprise Manager Application Server Control web site*

server.xml

This file maintains configuration information about the OC4J server. It is considered to be the "root" configuration file as it contains references to other configuration files. The configuration parameters specified in a server.xml file include:

- Library path, located in the application deployment descriptor
- Global application, global web application, and default web site served
- Maximum number of HTTP connections the server allows
- Logging settings
- Java compiler settings
- Cluster ID
- Transaction time-out
- SMTP host
- Location of the data-sources.xml configuration

- Location of the configuration for Java Message Service (JMS), an interface providing point-to-point queuing and publish/subscribe behavior, frequently used by EJBs that need to start another process asynchronously; and Remote Method Invocation (RMI), a technology that allows Java programs to access the objects of another Java program running on a different computer
- Location of the default and additional web sites
- Pointers to all applications for the container to deploy and execute

The server.xml provides a good example of the benefits of using the Enterprise Manager Application Server Control web site to deploy applications: every time a new application is deployed to an OC4J instance, an entry must be created in this file. By using the Enterprise Manager Application Server Control web site, the process of updating this file is handled automatically, eliminating possible syntax errors. Here is an example of the server.xml file for the OC4J_Portal instance (the line numbers have been added for discussion after the listing):

```
<?xml version="1.0" standalone='yes'?>
<!DOCTYPE application-server PUBLIC "Orion Application Server Config"
"http://xmlns.oracle.com/ias/dtds/application-server-9_04.dtd">
<application-server
application-directory="../applications"
deployment-directory="../application-deployments"
connector-directory="../connectors"
>
<rmi-config path="./rmi.xml" />
<!- Interoperability config link ->
<sep-config path="./internal-settings.xml" />
<!- JMS-server config link, uncomment to activate the JMS service ->
<jms-config path="./jms.xml" />
<javacache-config path="../../../javacache/admin/javacache.xml" />
<log>
<file path="../log/server.log" />
<!- Uncomment this if you want to use ODL logging capabilities
<odl path="../log/server/" max-file-size="1000" max-directory-
 size="10000"/>
->
</log>
<global-application name="default" path="application.xml" />
<application name="jocdemo" path="../applications/jocdemo.ear" auto-start="true" />
<application name="ojspdemos" path="../applications/ojspdemos.ear" auto-start="true" />
<application name="reportsDemo" path="../applications/reportsDemo.ear" auto-start="true" />
<application name="sqljdemos" path="../applications/sqljdemos.ear" auto-start="true" />
<application name="jazndemos" path="../applications/jazndemos.ear" auto-start="true" />
<application name="BC4JJSPDemo" path="../applications/BC4JJSPDemo.ear" auto-start="true" />
<global-web-app-config path="global-web-application.xml" />
<!- <web-site path="./secure-web-site.xml" /> ->
<web-site default="true" path="./default-web-site.xml" />
<!-  Uncomment to add http-web-site, and make sure there's no
port confliction among multiple OC4J instances.
<web-site path="./http-web-site.xml" />
->
<!-
Demos available for download at:
http://otn.oracle.com/tech/java/oc4j/demos/904
```

```
37 Refer to the iAS Admin or OC4J User's Guide for details on dcmctl and
38 Oracle Enterprise Manager (EM) tools for J2EE application deployment.
39 ->
40 <!- Compiler, activate this to specify an alternative compiler such
41 as jikes for EJB/JSP compiling. ->
42 <!- <compiler executable="jikes" classpath="/myjdkdir/jre/lib/rt.jar"
43 ->
44 </application-server>
```

All lines beginning with <!– and terminating with –> are comment lines.

- Lines 1-2 provide the header and document type definition for the XML parser.
- Lines 3-7 provide the container with the locations of the various application deployment files relative to directory location of the OC4J server (by default <ORACLE_HOME>/j2ee/<OC4J name>/config).
- Line 8 provides the location of the RMI (discussed shortly) configuration file.
- Lines 9-10 provide the location of internal-settings.xml, which specifies server extension provider properties.
- Lines 11-12 provide the location of the JMS (discussed shortly) configuration file.
- Line 13 provides the location of the javacache.xml file, which is mainly used to specify the Java Object Cache port number.
- Lines 14-19 provide the location and parameters of log files associated with this OC4J instance.
- Line 20 specifies the default name of the default application associated with this OC4J instance. If an application deployed under this instance does not specify a value for a parameter, the application will take the parameter value from what is specified for the default application for the OC4J instance.
- Lines 21-26 list applications deployed to this OC4J instance.
- Line 27 specifies the location of the global-web-application.xml file (discussed below).
- Line 28 is a commented line. If we wanted multiple web sites associated with this OC4J instance, they could be specified like this commented line.
- Line 29 tells the OC4J server that the web site specified in Line 20 is the default for this OC4J instance.
- Lines 30-33 are similar to Line 28; we could comment out these lines for an additional web site (see entry for http-web-site.xml below).
- Lines 34-39 are comments provided by Oracle.
- Lines 40-43 allow the specification of an EJB/JSP compiler other than the default provided by Oracle.
- Line 44 is the closing XML tag for the server.xml file.

application.xml

There two categories of application.xml files:

- **Global** An application.xml file associated with the OC4J container
- **Local** Individual application.xml files associated with each application deployed to that container

This chapter, given we are looking at the creation and administration of OC4J instances, will deal with the global application file. The local application file will be discussed in Chapter 15.

The global application.xml file contains common settings for all applications in a particular OC4J instance. It also defines the location of the security definition file (jazn-data.xml) and the data source definition file (data-sources.xml). Here is an example of a global application.xml file:

```
<?xml version="1.0" standalone='yes'?>
<!DOCTYPE orion-application PUBLIC "-//Evermind//DTD J2EE Application
runtime 1.2//EN" "http://xmlns.oracle.com/ias/dtds/orion-application-
9_04.dtd">
<!- The global application config that is the parent of all the other
applications in this server. ->
<orion-application autocreate-tables="true" default-data-
source="jdbc/OracleDS">
<web-module id="defaultWebApp" path="../../home/default-web-app"/>
<web-module id="dms0" path="../../home/applications/dms0.war"/>
<web-module id="dms" path="../../home/applications/dms.war"/>
<commit-coordinator>
<commit-class class="com.evermind.server.OracleTwoPhaseCommitDriver"/>
<property name="datasource" value="jdbc/OracleDS"/>
<!- Username and password are the optional properties
replace with your commit_co-ordinator_super_user
<property name="username"
value="system" />
<property name="password"
value="->pwForSystem" />
->
</commit-coordinator>
<persistence path="../persistence"/>
<!- Path to the libraries that are installed on this server.
These will be accessible for the servlets, EJBs etc ->
<library path="../applib"/>
<library path="../../../BC4J/lib"/>
<library path="../../../jlib/ojmisc.jar"/>
<library path="../../../ord/jlib/ordim.jar"/>
<library path="../../../ord/jlib/ordhttp.jar"/>
<library path="../../../jlib/uix2.jar"/>
<library path="../../../jlib/share.jar"/>
<library path="../../../jlib/regexp.jar"/>
<library path="../../../jlib/jdev-cm.jar"/>
<library path="../../../lib/dsv2.jar"/>
```

```
33 <library path="../../../rdbms/jlib/xsu12.jar"/>
34 <!- Path to the taglib directory that is shared
35 among different applications. ->
36 <library path="../../../j2ee/home/jsp/lib/taglib"/>
37 <library path="../../../uix/taglib"/>
38 <library path="../../../lib/oraclexsql.jar"/>
39 <library path="../../../lib/xsqlserializers.jar"/>
40 <!- Comment the following element to use principals.xml ->
41 <principals path="./principals.xml"/>
42 <log>
43 <file path="../log/global-application.log"/>
44 <!- Uncomment this if you want to use ODL logging capabilities
45 <odl path="../log/global-application/" max-file-size="1000" ma
46 x-directory-size="10000"/>
47 ->
48 </log>
49 <jazn provider="XML" location="./jazn-data.xml"/>
50 <data-sources path="data-sources.xml"/>
51 <connectors path="./oc4j-connectors.xml"/>
52 <namespace-access>
53 <read-access>
54 <namespace-resource root="">
55 <security-role-mapping>
56 <group name="administrators"/>
57 </security-role-mapping>
58 </namespace-resource>
59 </read-access>
60 <write-access>
61 <namespace-resource root="">
62 <security-role-mapping>
63 <group name="administrators"/>
64 </security-role-mapping>
65 </namespace-resource>
66 </write-access>
67 </namespace-access>
68 </orion-application>
```

- Lines 1-2 provide the header and document type definition for the XML parser.
- Lines 3-4 are comments provided by Oracle.
- Lines 5-68 provide information that will be used as default settings for all applications deployed in this instance. The tag is called *orion-application* as the OC4J technology has been licensed by Oracle from IronFlare, makers of the Orion application server.
- Line 6 specifies the location of any files associated with the default web application.
- Lines 7-8 specify the location of the Dynamic Monitoring Service (DMS); do not modify these lines.
- Lines 9-19 specify a Java Database Connectivity (JDBC) data source, a default username and password for that data source, and a Java class to handle transactions. See the data-sources.xml file section below.

- Lines 20-39 specify the various libraries to be used in the applications deployed in this OC4J instance.
- Lines 40-41 specify the location of the principals.xml file. See the principals.xml file section below.
- Lines 42-48 specify logging information for all applications deployed to this OC4J server.
- Line 49 specifies the location of the jazn-data.xml file. See the jazn-data.xml file section below.
- Line 50 specifies the location of the data-sources.xml file. See the data-sources.xml file section below.
- Line 51 specifies the location of the oc4j-connectors.xml file. See the oc4j-connectors.xml file section below.
- Lines 52-67 specify the namespace (naming context) security policy for RMI clients, resources with specific security settings, and the run-time mapping (to groups and users) of a role.
- Line 68 is the closing XML tag for the application.xml file.

data-sources.xml

This file provides configuration information for data sources used by applications deployed in this OC4J instance. In addition, it contains information on how to retrieve JDBC connections. In the data-sources.xml file, you can specify the following:

- JDBC driver
- JDBC URL
- Java Naming and Directory Interface (JNDI) paths to which to bind the data source. JNDI is a set of Application Programming Interfaces (APIs) that assists with the interfacing to multiple naming and directory services.
- User/password for the data source
- Database schema to use
- Inactivity time-out
- Thread policy
- Garbage collection granularity
- Maximum number of connections allowed to the database

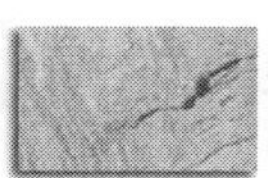

TIP
Creating JDBC connections with data sources is described in detail in Chapter 13.

Here is an example of a data-sources.xml file:

```
1  <?xml version="1.0" standalone='yes'?>
2  <!DOCTYPE data-sources PUBLIC "Orion data-sources"
   "http://xmlns.oracle.com/ias/dtds/data-sources-9_04.dtd">
3  <data-sources>
4  <!-
5  An example/default DataSource that uses
6  Oracle JDBC-driver to create the connections.
7  This tag creates all the needed kinds
8  of data-sources, transactional, pooled and EJB-aware sources.
9  The source generally used in application code is the "EJB"
10 one - it provides transactional safety and connection
11 pooling. Oracle thin driver could be used as well,
12 like below.
13 url="jdbc:oracle:thin:@host:port:sid"
14 ->
15 <data-source
16 class="com.evermind.sql.DriverManagerDataSource"
17 name="OracleDS"
18 location="jdbc/OracleCoreDS"
19 xa-location="jdbc/xa/OracleXADS"
20 ejb-location="jdbc/OracleDS"
21 connection-driver="oracle.jdbc.driver.OracleDriver"
22 username="scott"
23 password="->pwForScott"
24 url="jdbc:oracle:thin:@localhost:1521:oracle"
25 inactivity-timeout="30"
26 />
27 </data-sources>
```

- Lines 1-2 provide the header and document type definition for the XML parser.
- Line 3 is the beginning of the data sources specification.
- Lines 4-14 are comments provided by Oracle.
- Lines 15-16 specify the class containing JDBC driver manager.
- Line 17 specifies the name of the data source (referenced in Line 11 of the global application.xml file).
- Lines 18-20 are the location, xa-location, and ejb-location attributes. These are JNDI names that this data source is bound to within the JNDI namespace. While all three must be specified, Oracle recommends that only the ejb-location JNDI name in the JNDI lookup for retrieving this data source be used.
- Line 21 specifies the class containing the actual JDBC driver.
- Lines 22-24 specify the default connection information for the JDBC driver.
- Line 25 specifies the parameters associated with this JDBC driver specification.
- Line 26 is the closing XML tag for this data source.
- Line 27 is the closing XML tag for the data-sources.xml file.

default-web-site.xml

Multiple web sites, under the control of a single server.xml file, can be defined. Each of these web sites can have its own configuration files and act independently of the other web sites. If only one web site is used, the configuration parameters for that web site will come from this file. If multiple web sites are used, a file called web-site.xml can be used to specify different parameters. Each web site that is recognized by the server has a web site XML file to configure it. In Oracle Application Server, there is just one web site. OC4J standalone is a separate download available from Oracle that provides just the OC4J containers included with Oracle Application Server 10*g*. In the OC4J standalone, there is typically one web site; however, you might use a second web site for "shared" applications. For example, you might do this where some communication is through HTTP and some through HTTPS. It is also possible for there to be no web sites, if the OC4J instance is not used for web modules. The default-web-site.xml file provides configuration information for a default web site and contains the following:

- Host name or IP address, virtual host settings for this site, listener ports, and security using Secure Sockets Layer (SSL)
- Default web application for this site
- Additional web applications for this site
- Access-log format
- Settings for user web applications (for /~user/ sites)
- SSL configuration
- Restrict access to the site from one or more hosts

```
<?xml version="1.0" standalone='yes'?>
<!DOCTYPE web-site PUBLIC "OracleAS XML Web-site"
"http://xmlns.oracle.com/ias/dtds/web-site-9_04.dtd">
<!- change the host name below to your own host name. Localhost will
->
<!- also add cluster-island attribute as below
<web-site host="localhost" port="0"  protocol="ajp13"
display-name="OracleAS Java Web Site" cluster-island="1" >
->
<web-site port="0"  protocol="ajp13"
display-name="OracleAS Java Web Site">
<!- Uncomment the following line when using clustering ->
<!- <frontend host="your_host_name" port="80" /> ->
<!- The default web-app for this site, bound to the root ->
<default-web-app application="default" name="defaultWebApp"
root="/j2ee"
/>
<web-app application="default" name="dms" root="/dmsoc4j" />
<!- Access Log, where requests are logged to ->
```

```
17 <access-log path="../log/default-web-access.log" />
18 <!- Uncomment this if you want to use ODL logging capabilities
19 <odl-access-log path="../log/default-web-access" max-file-size="1000"
   ma
20 x-directory-size="10000"/>
21 ->
22 </web-site>
```

- Lines 1-2 provide the header and document type definition for the XML parser.
- Lines 3-8 are comments provided by Oracle.
- Lines 9-10 specify parameters to be used by the default web site associated with this OC4J instance. ajp13 in Line 9 stands for Apache JServ Protocol (version 1.3).
- Lines 11-12 are comments showing how to configure OC4J clustering.
- Lines 13-15 are information about the default web application deployed to the default web site associated with this OC4J instance.
- Line 16 is information about the DMS application referenced in Line 8 of application.xml.
- Lines 17-22 provide logging information regarding this web site.
- Line 23 is the closing XML tag for the default-web-site.xml file.

global-web-application.xml

This file contains OC4J-specific global web application configuration information that contains common settings for all web modules in this OC4J instance.

http-web-site.xml

This is the default web site descriptor in an OC4J standalone environment. As this book concerns itself with Oracle Application Server 10*g*, it is not discussed.

jazn.xml and jazn-data.xml

These files provide security information for the Oracle Application Server Java Authentication and Authorization Service (JAAS) Provider. JAAS is a set of Java packages that enable services to authenticate and enforce access controls upon users. These files define the user and group configuration for employing JAZNUserManager, the default user manager with the primary purpose of leveraging the JAAS Provider as the security infrastructure for OC4J. The jazn.xml file tells OC4J which data source to use, although by default, OC4J uses the jazn-data.xml file. The following are specified in the jazn-data.xml file:

- Username and password for the client-admin console
- Name and description of users/groups, and real name and password for users

jms.xml

This file contains the configuration for the OC4J Java Message Service (JMS) implementation. JMS is an interface to provide point-to-point queuing and topic (publish/subscribe) behavior. JMS is frequently used by EJBs that need to start another process asynchronously. In the jms.xml file, specify the following:

- Host name or IP address, and port number to which the JMS server binds
- Settings for queues and topics to be bound in the JNDI tree
- Log settings

oc4j-connectors.xml

This file contains global OC4J-specific configuration for connectors. Sun Microsystems defines a connector as "a standard extension mechanism for containers to provide connectivity to enterprise information systems". A connector is specific to an enterprise information system and consists of a resource adapter and application development tools for enterprise information system connectivity. The resource adapter is plugged into a container through its support for system-level contracts defined in the connector architecture.

principals.xml

By default, the JAAS Provider types (discussed in the jazn-data.xml section above) are used to enable services to authenticate and enforce access controls upon users. In the orion-application.xml file (discussed in Chapter 15), you can specify the <principals> element to tell OC4J to use the UserManager described in a principals file, normally principals.xml. A <principals> element in the orion-application.xml file has one attribute, <path>, which specifies a path for the principals file, normally principals.xml. For example, <principals path="myprincipals.xml" />.

The principals.xml file contains a <principals> element; this contains two sub-elements, <groups> and <users>. The <groups> element contains one or more <group> elements, and the <users> element contains one or more <user> elements. Groups in principals.xml correspond to roles in the JAAS Provider. The principals.xml file does not support any equivalent of the JAAS Provider's concept of realms. Permissions granted to groups may be checked explicitly, and OC4J does check for the special permissions listed above. However, group permissions are not integrated with the usual permission checking performed by a Security Manager. The XMLUserManager class is supported for backward compatibility in that Oracle recommends you use one of the JAAS Provider types. Figure 2-7 shows how to specify the User Manager for a deployed application. Figure 2-8 shows the Security page for an application where users, groups, and roles can be entered, modified, and deleted via the web interface.

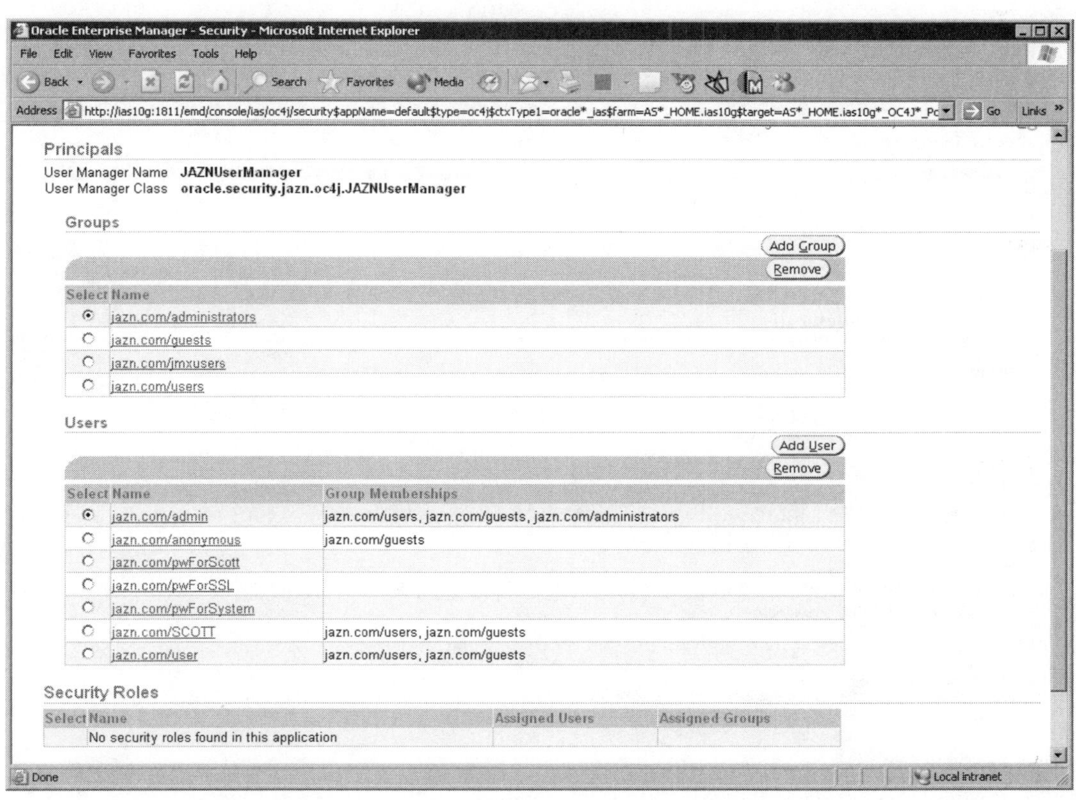

FIGURE 2-7. *The User Manager section of the Properties page of a deployed application in the Enterprise Manager Application Server Control web site*

rmi.xml

This file provides configuration information for the RMI system. RMI enables communication between different Java programs running in different JVMs, or in our case, different OC4J instances. This can be incredibly useful for creating distributed applications. Say, for instance, you have created an application that uses critical business logic encapsulated in an EJB. A second application needs the same business logic. If you have coded your EJB with enough flexibility to satisfy the request of the second application, you can use RMI to remotely call (invoke) the EJB and get access to its logic. OC4J supports RMI over HTTP, a technique known as *RMI tunneling*.

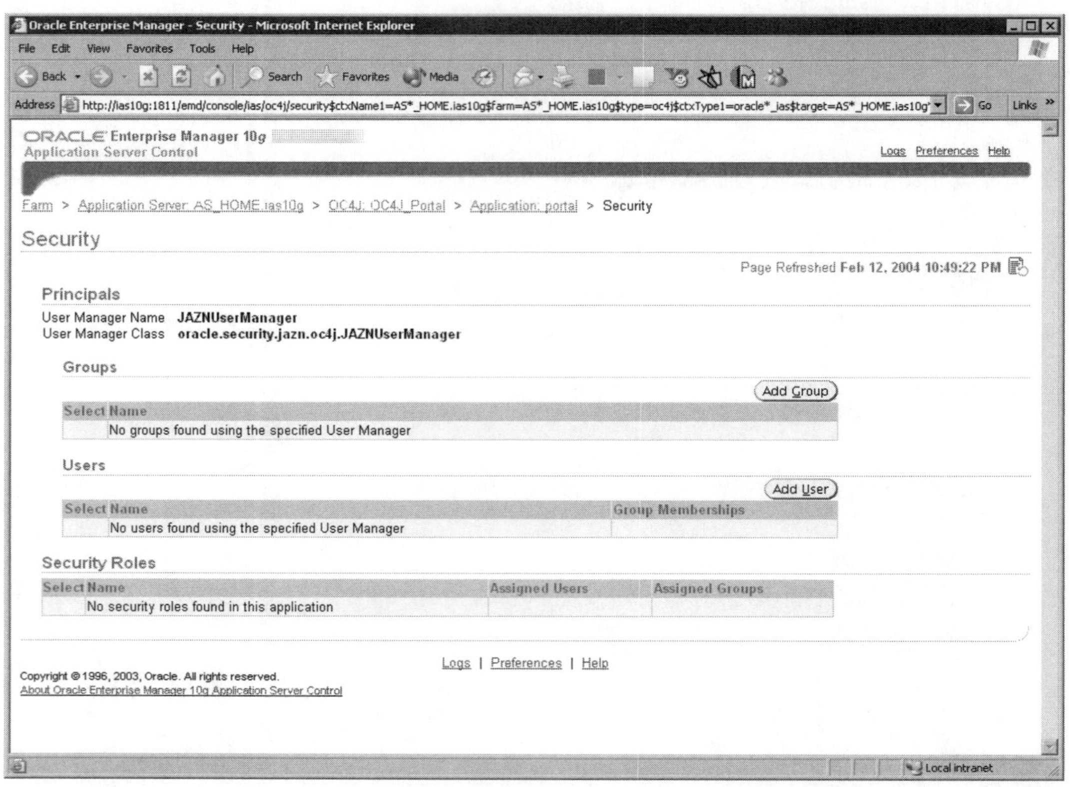

FIGURE 2-8. *The Security page for a deployed application*

By using the technique of encapsulating RMI calls within an HTTP POST request, Java programs can make outgoing RMI calls without being stopped by a local firewall. The following are specified in the rmi.xml file:

- Host name or IP address, and port number to which the RMI server binds
- Remote servers to which to communicate
- Clustering settings
- Log settings

Here is an example of an rmi.xml file:

```
1  <?xml version="1.0" standalone='yes'?>
2  <!DOCTYPE rmi-server PUBLIC "Orion RMI-server"
   "http://xmlns.oracle.com/ias/dtds/rmi-server-9_04.dtd">
3  <rmi-server port="23791" >
4  <!- A remote server connection example ->
5  <!- <server host="the.remote.server.com" username="adminUser"
   password="123abc" /> ->
6  <!- path to the log-file where RMI-events/errors are stored ->
7  <log>
8  <file path="../log/rmi.log" />
9  <!- Uncomment this if you want to use ODL logging capabilities
10  <odl path="../log/rmi/" max-file-size="1000" max-directory-size=
11 "10000"/>
12 ->
14 </log>
15 </rmi-server>
```

- Lines 1-2 provide the header and document type definition for the XML parser.
- Line 3 specifies the port RMI will communicate on.
- Lines 4-6 are comments provided by Oracle providing an example of how to configure an RMI server. The host specified in Line 5 is where the remote method exists.
- Lines 7-13 specify logging information for the RMI process.
- Lines 14 is the closing XML tag for the rmi.xml file.

Creating an OC4J Instance

To create an OC4J instance, click the Create Instance button on the top right of Figure 2-9. When you create an OC4J instance, an OC4J home page for configuring and managing your OC4J instance is created, along with the necessary files to configure the new instance. Each OC4J instance has its own OC4J home page. You can drill down to any of the running OC4J instances by selecting the name of the instance in the System Components table. The Application Server Control displays the OC4J home page for that instance (see Figure 2-9).

As you can see, the Home tab shows basic metrics regarding the OC4J instance. Other than the Start (not pictured because the OC4J instance is currently running), Stop, and Restart buttons, there is not much you can do to the OC4J. The Applications tab (see Figure 2-10) gives us a lot more opportunity to actively work with our OC4J instance.

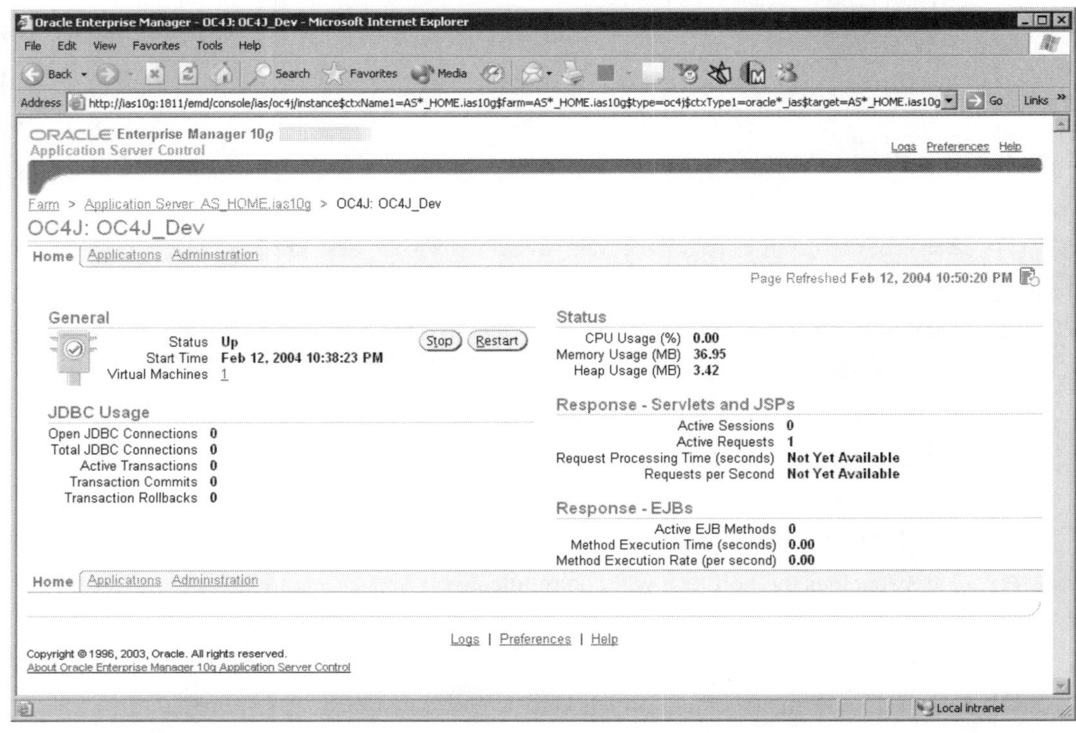

FIGURE 2-9. *The home page for an OC4J instance*

In this tab, we can view and get information about applications deployed to this OC4J instance. Also of note are the Deploy EAR file and Deploy WAR file buttons in the top right of the page. Clicking these buttons will start wizards that will do much of the work of configuring the various deployment files we will need to successfully deploy our application.

Java Archive Files (EAR, WAR, and JAR files)

What, exactly, are EAR and WAR files? **E**nterprise **Ar**chive (EAR) and **W**eb **Ar**chive (WAR) files are special types of **J**ava **Ar**chive (JAR) files that incorporate the different types of Java components (or programs) that comprise your application. It is not uncommon to have an application use a number of different Java technologies: for example, EJBs to store business logic and JSPs to handle the look and feel of an application and compiled class files that make up a servlet. Each of these components must be stored in a structured set of directories, with various directories containing .xml files describing the contents of subdirectories. Once these directories, XML files, and various Java files are in the correct locations, they can be grouped together into a single file using the `jar` command-line utility. In Chapter 15, we will look at the creation of an application with various Java components and how the jar utility is used to create an EAR or a WAR file.

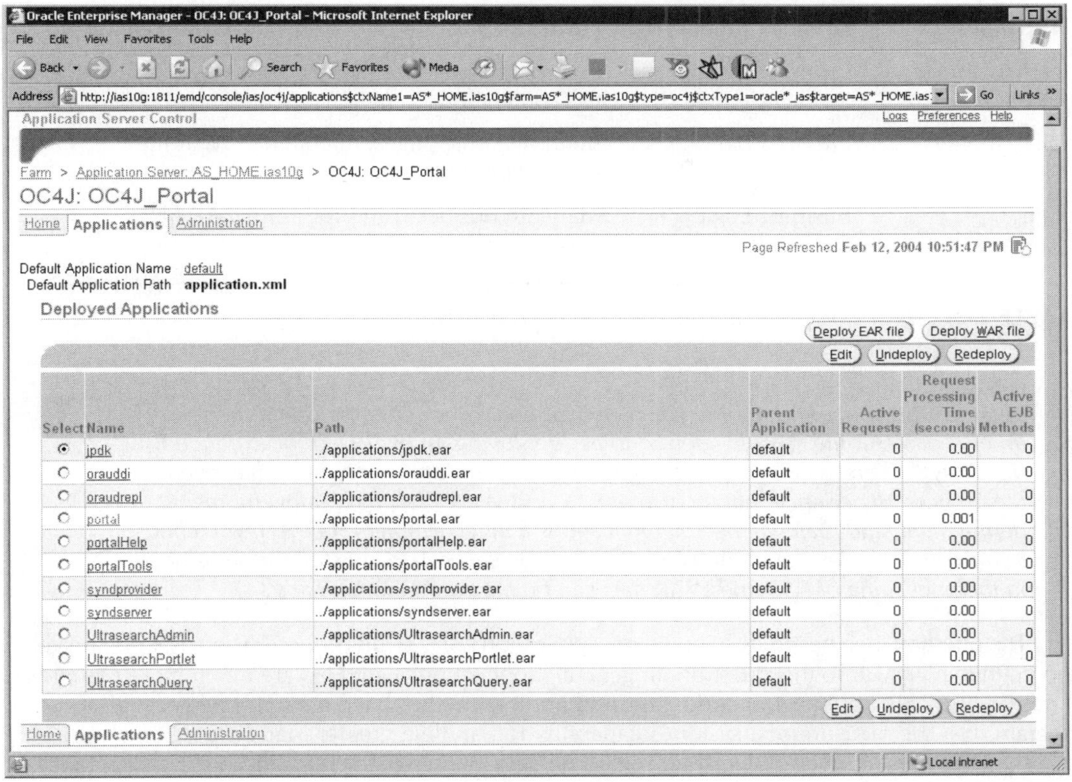

Oracle Enterprise Manager - OC4J: OC4J_Portal - Microsoft Internet Explorer

File Edit View Favorites Tools Help

Address http://ias10g:1811/emd/console/ias/oc4j/applications$ctxName1=AS*_HOME.ias10g$farm=AS*_HOME.ias10g$type=oc4j$ctxType1=oracle*_ias$target=AS*_HOME.ias

Application Server Control — Logs Preferences Help

Farm > Application Server: AS_HOME.ias10g > OC4J: OC4J_Portal

OC4J: OC4J_Portal

Home | Applications | Administration

Page Refreshed Feb 12, 2004 10:51:47 PM

Default Application Name default
Default Application Path **application.xml**

Deployed Applications

Deploy EAR file | Deploy WAR file
Edit | Undeploy | Redeploy

Select	Name	Path	Parent Application	Active Requests	Request Processing Time (seconds)	Active EJB Methods
⦿	jpdk	../applications/jpdk.ear	default	0	0.00	0
○	orauddi	../applications/orauddi.ear	default	0	0.00	0
○	oraudrepl	../applications/oraudrepl.ear	default	0	0.00	0
○	portal	../applications/portal.ear	default	0	0.001	0
○	portalHelp	../applications/portalHelp.ear	default	0	0.00	0
○	portalTools	../applications/portalTools.ear	default	0	0.00	0
○	syndprovider	../applications/syndprovider.ear	default	0	0.00	0
○	syndserver	../applications/syndserver.ear	default	0	0.00	0
○	UltrasearchAdmin	../applications/UltrasearchAdmin.ear	default	0	0.00	0
○	UltrasearchPortlet	../applications/UltrasearchPortlet.ear	default	0	0.00	0
○	UltrasearchQuery	../applications/UltrasearchQuery.ear	default	0	0.00	0

Edit | Undeploy | Redeploy

Home | Applications | Administration

Local intranet

FIGURE 2-10. *The Applications tab of an OC4J home page*

The difference between an EAR file and a WAR file depends on the types of Java components that make up your application, and thus define your application type. An application that does not contain EJBs is considered a web application and is usually deployed as a WAR file. An application that contains EJBs is considered an EJB (or Enterprise) application, and is deployed as an EAR file (see Table 2-2). Note that we said that web applications are *usually* deployed as WAR files—you could deploy a web application as an EAR file by leaving the directories for EJB modules empty. This is commonly referred to as "wrapping" a WAR file into an EAR file. If the application contains EJBs, however, it must be deployed as an EAR file. EAR files are further complicated by the fact that they contain WAR files—the web-tier components of the application.

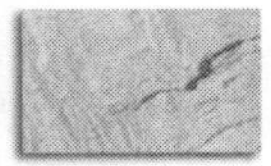

NOTE
The method of "wrapping" a WAR file into an EAR file is what Oracle does when you click the "Deploy WAR file" button on the home page for the OC4J container.

Technology	Service Category	Purpose	Where Deployed
HTML, images, PDFs, etc.	Communication Services	Present the user interface of the application	WAR file
JSPs, servlets	Presentation Services	Build dynamic pages, maintain state, control page flow	WAR file
EJBs	Business Logic Services	Maintain business rules for application	EAR file

TABLE 2-2. *Java Components and Their Deployment Locations*

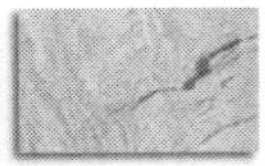

NOTE
Technically, you could deploy your applications without first grouping them into an EAR or WAR file. This is referred to as "deploying an exploded (or expanded) directory." There is certainly nothing wrong with this approach, but it has been the authors' experience that the use of EAR and WAR files makes development, deployment, and maintenance of applications a much simpler process. If you choose to do your Java development using Oracle JDeveloper 10g, most of the steps needed in the packaging of EAR and WAR files can be handled automatically.

The question then becomes, "Should my application contain EJBs or not?" There is, unfortunately, no definitive answer to this question. In general, applications with EJBs are much more complex and require a greater effort to code, test, and implement, but have a much higher level of scalability—the measure of a system's capability to handle a greater load by applying more hardware to it. A number of questions regarding development resources, in-house knowledge, desired flexibility, and maintainability of the application will have to be addressed before beginning any design and development work.

Building applications using EJBs is closer to the spirit of the J2EE specification, which encourages distributing an application's various technologies among discrete tiers outlined in the services discussed in Chapter 1 and in Table 2-2. By using EJBs, the presentation layer remains thin (less code) while the business logic layer is robust (more code). In a web application, the presentation layer contains the business logic (violating the basic J2EE premise that encourages the separation of business and presentation logic) and the business logic layer is not used at all.

The simpler of the two types of files is the WAR file. A WAR file contains all web-tier components for a J2EE application (see Table 2-2), including servlet .class. EAR files have the added functionality of giving the developer the option of either deploying the entire EAR file or just deploying selected components of the EAR file. Figure 2-11 depicts an application directory structure.

The directory names enclosed in <> are arbitrarily named. The directories and filename in *italics* must be named exactly to the specification. If your application does not contain any EJBs, you can create a WAR file by running the JAR utility from the <web module> directory. You can create an EAR file by running the JAR utility from the <appname> directory. It is important to note that the application.xml file in the META-INF directory is the local application.xml file, which serves a different purpose than the global application.xml file discussed earlier in this chapter. The content and structure of the italicized files in Figure 2-11 will be explored in detail in Chapter 15.

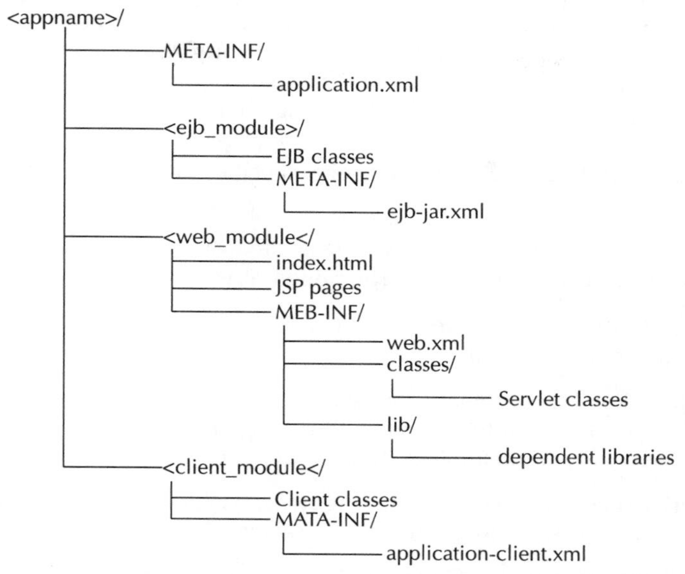

FIGURE 2-11. *A development directory structure*

Security Architecture

In the previous section, Java Authentication and Authorization Service (JAAS), a set of Java packages that enable services to authenticate and enforce access controls upon users, was discussed briefly. This is far from the only security method available to you when developing applications to be deployed in Oracle Application Server 10*g*. Oracle has provided a robust framework that gives you the ability to develop applications that are highly secure. There are a number of different technologies, all with differing capabilities and complexity. Oracle has grouped these different technologies under the term "Identity Management."

Oracle Identity Management is an integrated set of services for managing users and their privileges. It provides a complete security life cycle for both end users and network entities, including devices, processes, applications, web services, or anything else that needs to interact in a networked environment. By grouping the various security components under an easily managed infrastructure, Oracle makes it easy for security administrators to create an environment that enhances application security while speeding up application deployments. This saves both time and money as it eliminates the error-prone process of attempting to maintain various credentials on different machines, while improving accuracy and security. Although it was released as part of Oracle Application Server 10*g*, all Oracle products (Oracle Database, Application Server, Collaboration Suite, and E-Business Suite) have been designed to use Oracle Identity Management out of the box. It provides a highly scalable environment, native support for Oracle products, and a single point of administration, greatly reducing the overhead needed to deploy and maintain applications within an organization. It also supports integration with third-party identity management solutions so that the need for "integration points," those places in the organization where security information must be synchronized between disparate systems, can be eliminated. Oracle Identity Management will support the following standards in the future:

- **SAML** Security Assertions Meta Language; specifies interoperation between security services.
- **SPML** Service Provisioning Meta Language; an XML standard that defines the protocol **between service components and provisioned services agents.**
- **DSML** Directory Services Markup Language; allows developers to express LDAP functions and retrieve data in XML.
- **XKMS** XML Key Management Specification; a specification that significantly extends the public key infrastructure (PKI) model by using XML to provide new levels of ease and interoperability when implementing secure applications.
- **WS-Security standards** Web-Services security; enables applications to construct secure Simple Object Access Protocol (SOAP) message exchanges.
- **Liberty Alliance standards** Open standards for federated network identity management and identity-based services. For more information, go to http://www.projectliberty.org/.

The "g" in Oracle Application Server 10*g* and Oracle Database 10*g* stands for "grid" and it reflects Oracle's commitment to the emerging technology of grid computing. *Grid computing* is defined in general terms as "an effort to develop an environment in which individual users can access computers, databases, and experimental facilities simply and transparently, without having to consider where those facilities are located." For our purposes, Oracle defines grid computing as "a software architecture designed to effectively pool together large amounts of low cost modular storage and servers to create a virtual computing resource across which work can be transparently distributed to use capacity very efficiently, at low cost, and with very high availability." Without some sort of centralized way of maintaining users and privileges across an architecture like this (one that will, most likely, contain heterogeneous hardware, networking, and operating systems), the effort to create and maintain users (called "provisioning" in Oracle's documentation) would become time and resource prohibitive in all but the most simplest of environments. Oracle Identity Management is a manageable, secure, and centralized infrastructure that can be utilized on all Oracle components in an Oracle Grid.

Some of the key features of Identity Management include:

- **Integration with Microsoft Windows** Oracle provides three features to integrate information about users with an existing Windows environment. They include:
  - **Windows Directory Connector** This connector provides the ability to map and synchronize users defined in the Windows environment with those defined in Oracle's Identity Management environment.

- **Windows Authentication** This plug-in allows security administrators to maintain passwords in a single location. Microsoft's Active Directory passes authentication information onto the Oracle Identity Management system. The plug-in also has bidirectional features, allowing Windows passwords to be updated from the Oracle Identity Management environment.
- **Native Authentication** This technology allows users to use their Windows logins as their authentication to access applications served up by Application Server 10*g*. Oracle Single Sign-On receives Kerberos tokens as its authentication method.

- **Multilevel authentication** This allows the security administrator to assign different authentication levels to different applications.
- **Deployment options** The Application Server 10*g* security components can use all of the networking technologies commonly implemented within organizations to support their needs, including the use of proxy servers, load balancers, and firewalls segmented into multiple DMZs.

The major components that constitute Oracle Identity Management are

- **Oracle Internet Directory (OID)** An application deployed on an Oracle 9*i* (or higher) database, OID is a Lightweight Directory Access Protocol (LDAP) V3 directory service that is considered to be the de facto Internet standard for directory services. OID has the benefits of scalability and high availability, as it uses an Oracle database to store its information. It provides various layers of access control including entry level, attribute level, and prescriptive access control. In Application Server 10*g*, Oracle has enhanced password policy enforcement in OID, which includes the ability to prevent users from using previous passwords as their current passwords, forcing users to change their passwords upon initial login and IP-based account lockout.
- **Oracle Directory Synchronization** This service allows OID to synchronize data with other repositories. It is not limited to other LDAP servers, however; it can synchronize data from text files, relational databases, network operating system (NOS) directories (such as Novell's NetWare, Banyan's VINES, or IBM's LAN Server) and includes a preconfigured solution to synchronize with Microsoft Active Directory.
- **Oracle Delegated Administration Services (DAS)** A component of OID that provides administration of directory information by users and application administrators. The Self Service Console, a web-based application that allows security administrators to create and modify users and privileges is built into the DAS framework. Figure 2-12 shows the Self-Service Console.
- **Oracle Application Server Single Sign-On** This service provides a single sign-on (SSO) for users to sign in once and be authenticated to multiple web applications, including Oracle Portal, Oracle E-Business Suite, and other non-Oracle applications. It can be configured to run standalone or with your existing infrastructure. It uses all modern Internet standards including HTTP/HTTPS, cookies, and X.509 certificate for

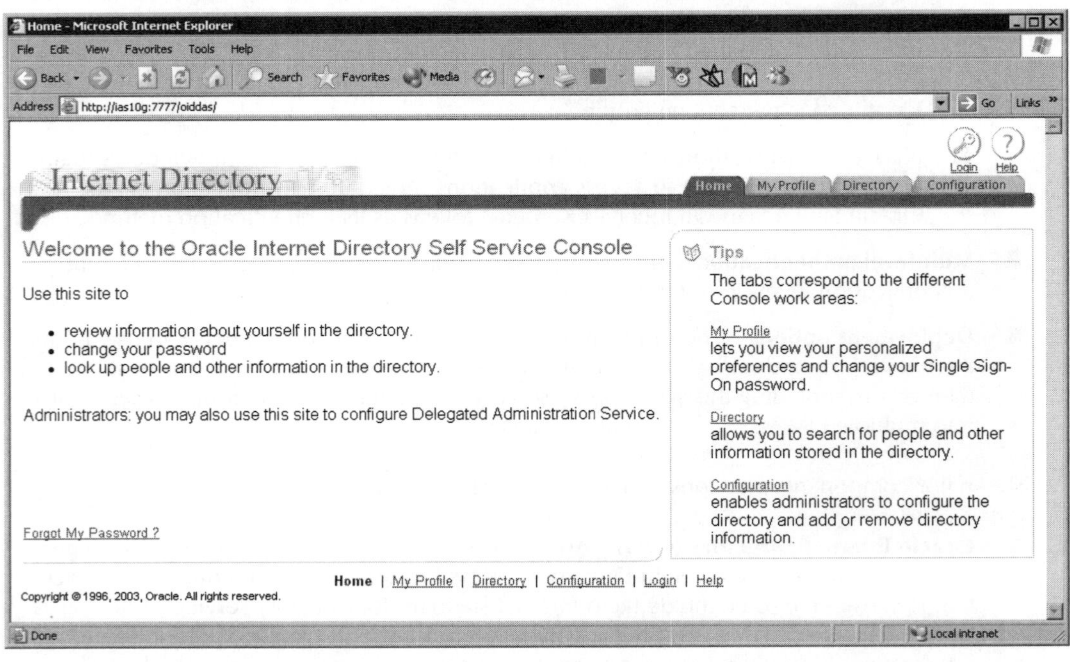

FIGURE 2-12. *The Self-Service Console*

user tokens. SSO has been enhanced in Application Server 10*g* to include multilevel authentication and Windows native authentication, both discussed earlier.

- **Oracle Application Server Certificate Authority** This service generates and publishes X.509 v3 PKI certificates. X.509 is an international standard, which defines the prevailing technology for digital certificates and other security measures. X.509 defines two types of digital certificates: a public key certificate, which asserts identity, and an attribute certificate, which asserts privilege. Through the Application Server Certificate Authority, a security administrator can easily request certificates through a web interface.

Oracle Process Manager and Notification Server (OPMN)

The Oracle Process Manager and Notification Server (OPMN) is used, primarily, to control and monitor single or multiple Oracle Application Server components and instances via a command line interface. It has many features that allow a site to obtain high availability of the components that constitute Application Server 10*g*. Of particular note is the capability of OPMN to detect a process that has died and restart it again. This gives developers the ability to deploy their applications in an environment where administrators can concern themselves with performance monitoring and security and hand the details of process death detection and restart to an automatic, centralized process. OPMN has many other capabilities that are primarily of interest to the Application Server 10*g* administrator and will not be discussed in detail here, except to note that the control program for OPMN, opmnctl, is now the recommended way to start and stop all system components. This section will focus on the aspects of OPMN that relate to the system components most Oracle web developers interact with: OC4J servers, Oracle Reports Services, and Oracle Discoverer.

NOTE
In previous versions of the application server, the Distributed Configuration Management (dcmctl) shell script, along with programs specific to system components (such as oidctl for the Oracle Internet Directory and webcachectl for the Web Cache), were used to start and stop system components. While those tools are still available, the only tool supported by Oracle to start and stop system components under Application Server 10g is opmnctl. When you start and stop components via the Enterprise Manager Application Server Control web site, the opmnctl executable is called to perform the necessary tasks. For more information regarding administration of Application Server 10g, see the Oracle Application Server 10g Administration Handbook by John Garmany and Donald K. Burleson (Osborne Oracle Press Series, 2004).

OPMN is made up of three components:

- **Oracle Notification Server** This process communicates with the system components that make up Application Server 10*g*. Server components "subscribe" to the notification server and, based on system events, have information "published" to them.
- **Oracle Process Manager** This process is used to start, stop, restart, and detect the unexpected death of Application Server 10*g* system components. opmn.xml is used to specify the components that Oracle Process Manager manages.
- **Process Manager modules** These modules handle component-specific functionality. The Process Manager modules test system components to see if a component is alive and responding and holds information that is specific to that Application Server 10*g* component.

In previous versions (9.0.2 and 9.0.3), you were limited to using OPMN to control the Oracle HTTP Server and OC4J instances. In version 9.0.4 (the one included with Application Server 10*g*), you can also use OPMN to control the following components:

- Distributed Configuration Management (DCM) daemon (server)
- Oracle Application Server Log Loader
- Oracle Internet Directory
- Oracle Application Server Port Tunnel
- Oracle Application Server Web Cache
- Oracle Application Server Discoverer
- Oracle Application Server Wireless
- Oracle Application Server Reports Services
- Oracle Application Server ProcessConnect

Other components, such as Oracle Forms, Oracle Single Sign-On, and Oracle Portal, are implicitly managed by OPMN as they are implemented as applications running under OC4J containers. The only other processes required for Application Server 10*g* that do not fall under the control of OPMN are

- **The metadata repository** The Oracle database used by the infrastructure; this must be started using the `startup` command after connecting to the idle instance in Structured Query Language (SQL)*Plus as sysdba.
- **The listener for the metadata repository** Use the `lsnrctl` command to start the listener.
- **The Enterprise Manager Application Server Control web site** Use the `emctl start iasconsole` command to start the Application Server Control.

The opmnctl program requires the OPMN server be running before any commands can be passed to it. To start the OPMN server manually, use the `opmnctl start` command. To start the OPMN server and all of the processes specified in the opmn.xml file, use the `opmnctl startall` command. To stop the OPMN server and all of the processes specified in the opmn.xml file, use the `opmnctl stopall` command. The OPMN process does not read the opmn.xml file dynamically, so if you make any changes to it, you must tell the OPMN process to reread it. This can be accomplished with the `opmnctl reload` command. `opmnctl` can also be used to perform any of the operations mentioned above on individual components specified in the opmn.xml file or, by specifying the scope, all components within a specific instance, cluster, or farm. `opmnctl` commands can also be run in synchronous or asynchronous mode, which aids in the writing of scripts to startup or shutdown components.

`opmnctl validate` is used to validate the syntax in the opmn.xml file and `opmnctl status` is used to get the status of those components specified in the opmn.xml file. All of the opmnctl commands have an information page associated with them, similar to man pages in Unix. To see a command's information page, use the `opmnctl usage <command>` command.

NOTE
The opmn.xml file is too large to include here in its entirety. In the following sections, parts of the opmn.xml will be listed with commentary to illustrate its behavior.

With Oracle Application Server 10g, most of the OPMN settings can be configured either through the Oracle Enterprise Manager web site or through OPMN's command-line utility opmnctl. Oracle *strongly* discourages editing the opmn.xml file by hand.

One of the main benefits of using OPMN to administer system components is its capability to start components in order. Many system components are dependant on other components running before they can be started. By default, OPMN is installed with all of the necessary start order dependencies for the components installed based on your installation type. This feature allows you to start all components with a single command: `opmnctl startall`. The open nature of OPMN and its corresponding opmn.xml file allows you to add your own components and their associated dependencies when starting up your application server.

Nor are you limited to just restarting a system component upon its expected or unexpected termination. Event scripts, similar to triggers in the database, can be configured to run and perform various tasks based on a components change of state. The event script types include prestart, prestop, and post-crash. Here is a section of the opmn.xml file that includes a prestart section that will run a shell script called restartoad.sh before starting the Oracle Discoverer server:

```
<category id="EventScript">
   <data id="prestart" value="/usr/AS10g/AS_HOME/discoverer
/util/restartoad.sh"/>
</category>
```

Configuring OPMN for OC4J

After we created a new OC4J instance called OC4J_Dev, the following lines were created for us by Oracle in the opmn.xml file:

```
1  <process-type id="OC4J_Dev" module-id="OC4J">
2  <module-data>
3  <category id="start-parameters">
4  <data id="java-options" value="-server -
   Djava.security.policy=/usr/AS10g/AS_HOME/j2ee/OC4J_Dev
   /config/java2.policy -Djava.awt.headless=true"/>
5  <data id="oc4j-options" value="-properties"/>
6  </category>
7  <category id="stop-parameters">
8  <data id="java-options" value="-
   Djava.security.policy=/usr/AS10g/AS_HOME/j2ee/
   OC4J_Dev/config/java2.policy -Djava.awt.headless=true"/>
9  </category>
10 </module-data>
11 <start timeout="900" retry="2"/>
12 <stop timeout="120"/>
13 <restart timeout="720" retry="2"/>
14 <port id="ajp" range="3301-3400"/>
15 <port id="rmi" range="3201-3300"/>
16 <port id="jms" range="3701-3800"/>
17 <process-set id="default_island" numprocs="1"/>
18 </process-type>
```

- Line 1 begins the section that specifies the OPMN settings for a process; in this case, it's the OC4J_Dev instance.
- Line 2 begins the module data section where the data OPMN will use to manage this component will be specified.
- Lines 3-6 specify parameters passed to the Java environment upon startup of this container.
- Lines 7-9 specify parameters passed to the Java environment upon shutdown of this container.
- Lines 11-13 specify timeout parameters for this container.
- Lines 14-16 specify port ranges for Apache JServ Protocol (AJP), RMI, and JMS services for this container.
- Line 17 specifies the number of JVMs that will be used by the JMS server.

Configuring OPMN for Reports

Given the Reports server is made up of two components, the Reports server and the OC4J_BI_Forms instance, there are two sections of the opmn.xml file that need to be configured. This section lists the entry for the OC4J_BI_Forms instance:

```
1  <process-type id="OC4J_BI_Forms" module-id="OC4J">
2  <environment>
3  <variable id="DISPLAY" value="localhost:0"/>
4  <variable id="LD_LIBRARY_PATH"
   value="/usr/AS10g/AS_HOME/lib:/usr/AS10g/AS_HOME
   /lib:/usr/AS10g/AS_HOME/network/lib::/usr
   /AS10g/AS_HOME/jdk/jre/lib/i386:/usr/AS10g/AS_HOME
   /jdk/jre/lib/i386/server:/usr/AS10g/AS_HOME/jdk
   /jre/lib/i386/native_threads"/>
5  </environment>
6  <module-data>
7  <category id="start-parameters">
8  <data id="java-options" value="-server -
   Djava.security.policy=/usr/AS10g/AS_HOME/j2ee/OC4J_BI_Forms
   /config/java2.policy -Djava.awt.headless=true -Xmx512M -
   Xbootclasspath^/p:/usr/AS10g/AS_HOME/vbroker4/lib/vbjboot.jar "/>
9  <data id="oc4j-options" value="-properties -userThreads "/>
10 </category>
11 <category id="stop-parameters">
12 <data id="java-options" value="-
   Djava.security.policy=/usr/AS10g/AS_HOME/j2ee/OC4J_BI_Forms
   /config/java2.policy -Djava.awt.headless=true"/>
13 </category>
14 <category id="urlping-parameters">
15 <data id="/reports/rwservlet/pingserver?start=auto" value="200"/>
16 </category>
17 </module-data>
18 <dependencies>
19 <database infrastructure-key="portal"/>
20 <managed-process process-type="HTTP_Server" process-set="HTTP_Server" ias-
component="HTTP_Server" autostart="true"/>
21 </dependencies>
22 <start timeout="900" retry="2"/>
23 <stop timeout="120"/>
24 <restart timeout="720" retry="2"/>
25 <port id="ajp" range="3301-3400"/>
26 <port id="rmi" range="3201-3300"/>
27 <port id="jms" range="3701-3800"/>
28 <process-set id="default_island" numprocs="1"/>
29 </process-type>
```

- Line 1 begins the section that specifies the OPMN settings for a process; in this case, it's the OC4J_BI_Forms instance.

- Lines 2-5 specify environment variables that will be used by this OC4J instance.
- Lines 6-10 specify Java parameters that will be used to start up this OC4J instance.
- Lines 11-13 specify Java parameters that will be used to shut down this OC4J instance.
- Lines 14-17 specify parameters for ping operations as part of OC4J process ping operations. AJP13 protocol is used to directly connect to the OC4J process and the HTTP return code is validated against the configured code.
- Line 15 specifies the URL in the OC4J process that will be pinged; value is the expected HTTP return code.
- Lines 18-21 specify dependencies for this OC4J container.
- Line 20 specifies the component that must be running before attempting to start this component. In this case, the HTTP server must be up and running before an attempt is made to start the OC4J_BI_Forms instance.
- Lines 22-24 specify timeout parameters for this container.
- Lines 25-27 specify port ranges for AJP, RMI, and JMS services for this container.
- Line 28 specifies the number of JVMs that will be used by the JMS server.

This code listing shows the opmn.xml entry for a specific Reports server:

```
1  <ias-component id="rep_DevServer1" status="enabled" id-
matching="false">
2  <process-type id="rep_DevServer1" module-id="ReportsModule">
3  <process-set id="rep_DevServer1" restart-on-death="true" numprocs="1">
4  <environment>
5  <variable id ='PATH' value="<Path to uname command>" append="true"/>
6  </environment>
7  <module-data>
8  <category id="general-parameters">
9  <data id="batch" value="yes"/>
10 </category>
11 <category id="restart-parameters">
12 <data id="reverseping-timeout"value="300"/>
13 </category>
14 </module-data>
15 <start timeout="300" retry="3"/>
16 <stop timeout="300"/>
17 <restart timeout="300"/>
18 <ping timeout="30" interval="30"/>
19 </process-set>
20 </process-type>
21 </ias-component>
```

- Lines 1-3 define the Reports server.
- Lines 4-6 specify environment variables for the Reports server.

- Line 5 specifies where the uname command is.
- Lines 7-14 specify a category that collects all the data that is common to the various process management tasks.
- Lines 8-10 specify parameters used to construct the command line for starting and stopping of the Oracle Application Server Reports Services server.
- Lines 11-13 specify parameters used in death detection.
- Lines 15-18 specify timeout parameters for this container.

Configuring OPMN for Discoverer

The Oracle Discoverer server requires the following entries in the opmn.xml file for the OPMN process to manage it:

```
<ias-component id="Discoverer">
<environment>
<variable id="VBROKER_HOME" value="/usr/AS10g/AS_HOME/vbroker4"/>
<variable id="OSAGENT_PORT" value="16001"/>
<variable id="DISCO_DIR" value="/usr/AS10g/AS_HOME/"/>
<variable id="DISCO_JRE" value="/usr/AS10g/AS_HOME/jdk/jre"/>
<variable id="DISCO_PREFERENCE"
value="ias10gOracleDiscovererPreferences9"/>
<variable id="LD_LIBRARY_PATH"
value="/usr/lib:/usr/AS10g/AS_HOME/discoverer
/lib:/usr/AS10g/AS_HOME/vbroker4/lib:/usr/AS10g/AS_HOME/lib"
append="true"/>
<variable id="OAD_VERBOSE_LOGGING" value=""/>
<variable id="DC9_REG" value="/usr/AS10g/AS_HOME/discoverer/"/>
<variable id="PATH"
value="/usr/AS10g/AS_HOME/jdk/jre/bin:/usr/AS10g
/AS_HOME/vbroker4/bin:/bin" append="true"/>
</environment>
<process-type id="OSAgent" module-id="Disco_OSAgent" working-
dir="/usr/AS10g/AS_HOME/discoverer/util">?report
<ping interval="300"/>
<process-set id="OSAgent" numprocs="1">
<module-data>
<category id="EventScript">
<data id="prestart"
value="/usr/AS10g/AS_HOME/discoverer/util/restartoad.sh"/>
</category>
</module-data>
</process-set>
</process-type>
<process-type id="OAD" module-id="Disco_OAD" working-
dir="/usr/AS10g/AS_HOME/discoverer/util">
<dependencies>
```

```
25 <managed-process ias-component="Discoverer" process-type="OSAgent"
    process-set="OSAgent" autostart="true"/>
26 </dependencies>
27 <ping interval="0"/>
28 <process-set id="OAD" numprocs="1">
29 <module-data>
30 <category id="bounce-parameters">
31 <data id="bounce-process" value="false"/>/OC4J_Dev
32 <data id="bounce-time" value="23:55"/>
33 </category>
34 <category id="sessionserver-parameters">
35 <data id="shutdown-event-name"
    value="/usr/AS10g/AS_HOME/opmn/bin/opmn"/>
36 <data id="reverse-ping-interval" value="600"/>
37 </category>
38 </module-data>
39 </process-set>
40 </process-type>
41 <process-type id="PreferenceServer" module-id="Disco_PreferenceServer"
   working-dir="/usr/AS10g/AS_HOME/discoverer" status="enabled">
42 <process-set id="PreferenceServer" numprocs="1"/>
43 </process-type>
44 </ias-component>
```

- Lines 1-12 specify the Discoverer component and the environment variables needed by the Discoverer server.
- Line 13: id="OSAgent" must match the ID.
- Line 14 specifies a time of five minutes for the ping interval of the OSAgent process (defined in Line 13).
- Lines 17-19 define a script to be executed before the Discoverer server process is initiated.
- Line 23: id="OAD" must match the targets.xml entry; module-id="Disco_OAD" defines the type of process and associates this configuration with a process module; working-dir="/usr/AS10g/AS_HOME/discoverer/util" specifies where the log file associated with the OAD process will exist.

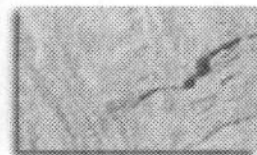

NOTE
OAD stands for Object Activation Daemon (OAD). It is a background process that runs and manages Discoverer session components.

- Lines 24-26 specify dependencies that must be running before this system component can begin.
- Line 27 specifies the ping interval for the OAD process (defined in Line 23).
- Line 28 specifies the number of OAD instances started for this process set. There should be at most one OAD instance running in one Oracle Application Server instance.

- Lines 30-33 specifiy the bounce parameters for OAD. OAD can be scheduled for restart every day for a specific time period. It must run for 24 hours prior to scheduled setup.
- Lines 34-37 are the category to specify the parameters for the session servers started by OAD. The session server is an Oracle Application Server Discoverer process that is launched during a user session. The Discoverer session server performs such operations as connecting to a database or opening a workbook. It provides the link between the Application Server Discoverer servlet or applet to the database.
- Line 41: id="PreferenceServer" is required and cannot be changed. The name must match the entry in the targets.xml file or elements and attributes will not work; module-id= "Disco_PreferenceServer" defines the type of process and associates the configuration with a process module; working-dir="/usr/AS10g/AS_HOME/discoverer" specifies the location of the log file associated with the dis51pr process.
- Line 42 specifies the number of preference server instances started for the process set. There should be at most one instance running in one Application Server instance.

Summary

Security, development environment, and process management are essential aspects of any web-based application deployment. Long gone are the days when these concerns can be easily dismissed as "someone else's problem." It is everyone's responsibility within the development, implementation, and administration teams to contribute to the security and stability of an organization's production environment. In response to these complex demands, Oracle has created technologies that assist developers in creating and deploying applications, making sure those applications are secure and giving administrators ways of ensuring the highest possible availability for those applications after they have been deployed. Oracle's technologies for these demands include:

- **OC4J** Oracle's Application Server Containers for J2EE, providing developers with a robust, secure, and scalable Java environment.
- **Oracle Identity Management** Providing developers with an easy way of maintaining various levels of security for their applications in a secure, centralized location.
- **Oracle Process Manager** Providing administrators with the ability to maintain applications deployed to OC4J instances easily and restart those processes automatically in the event of an unexpected termination.

If Oracle included the Apache web server and the Oracle Forms, Oracle Reports, and Oracle Discoverer servers as the only elements of the Oracle Application Server 10*g* product stack, it would still be an incredibly powerful product. The supplemental tools provided by Oracle discussed in this chapter enhance the existing components to make Application Server 10*g* a true world-class product, suitable for virtually any type of production, web-based application.

PART II

Oracle Tools

CHAPTER 3

Oracle Forms 10*g*

Things have come a long way from the early incarnations of the Oracle Forms toolkit. Early versions were not only crude, text-only forms, but they were also platform-specific as well. Later versions have added a graphical user interface (GUI) development environment and support for web deployment and Java, resulting in a robust, flexible development environment.

History

Oracle has made an attempt to synchronize the versions of each of their tools. With the release of Oracle 10*g*, a new version of the Forms development toolkit has also been released. The changes between the previous version (Forms 9*i*) and Oracle Forms 10*g* are surprisingly few. Internally, the current release of the Oracle Forms tools is version 9.0.4. If you are familiar with the toolset for 9*i*, using the latest version won't require many changes.

Major changes in functionality marked the migration from Oracle Forms version 6 to Oracle Forms 9*i*. With Oracle Forms 9*i*, Oracle finally moved away from the client-server model and fully embraced web deployment for all forms. The crude support for Web Forms in Forms 6*i* gave way to a fully web-enabled toolkit. Dropping the client-server deployment option for Forms was a big change for most developers.

New Functionality in 10*g*

Oracle Forms 10*g* has added support for Java Development Kit (JDK) 1.4, giving developers access to the latest Java functionality. In addition, Oracle Forms 10*g* has added more robust support for WebUtil, which allows the form in the browser to interact with the local machine to read and write files, providing parity with the desktop capabilities of client/server Forms, among other things.

Deciding to use Oracle Forms 10*g*

Oracle Forms 10*g* is a comprehensive toolset used for developing interactive GUI screens with robust data validation and data manipulation capabilities. Oracle Forms 10*g* easily manages inserting, updating, and deleting underlying data in the database with automated Data Manipulation Language (DML) functionality. Oracle Forms 10*g* can manage complex data structures behind the scenes without requiring independent SQL commands for each transaction.

There are, of course, other options to using the Oracle Forms 10*g* toolkit to develop user applications. Java, Hypertext Markup Language (HTML) forms, JavaServer Pages (JSPs), Application Server Pages (ASPs), and other dynamic web application tools can also be used to create the GUI and data management functionality of online forms. However, these options may involve considerably more coding to match the data validation and DML capabilities of Oracle Forms 10*g*. If your shop's core competency is Forms, you'll be comfortable here, but remember that Forms uses a fat client and requires JInitiator. Those two aspects will prevent you from using Forms in an Internet environment.

Development Server Components

Oracle Forms 10*g* is part of the Oracle 10*g* Developer Suite, which includes the following tools:

- Oracle Forms Developer
- Oracle Reports Developer

- Oracle JDeveloper
- Business Components for Java
- SQL*Plus
- Oracle Reports Developer
- Oracle Designer
- Oracle Software Configuration Manager
- Oracle Discoverer Administration Edition
- Oracle Discoverer Desktop Edition

Oracle Forms 10*g* is part of the Rapid Application Development (RAD) environment from Oracle.

Building Forms

This chapter is designed to give a short introduction to the Oracle Forms 10*g* toolset and the basic components of a forms application. Chapter 6 will discuss deploying Oracle Forms in a web environment and Chapter 11 will discuss incorporating Oracle Forms into Oracle Application Server Portal. This chapter will cover the following topics:

- Basic Forms concepts
- Form elements
- The Object Navigator
- Wizards
- Built-ins
- Triggers
- Object Groups and Libraries

Basic Forms Concepts

A form simply allows you to work visually with the data in the database. It is a representation of the data in the database tables, a collection of objects that yields a graphic interface to the data.

Every form, no matter how simple, contains the following pieces:

- At least one block
- At least one item
- At least one canvas
- At least one window

Most Oracle Forms 10*g* have multiples of each of these objects, but the basics are the same, no matter how simple or complex the form.

In addition to the basic objects in a form, the toolkit supports a wide variety of widgets and interface items to build the user experience: buttons, toolbars, check boxes, radio buttons, even Java-bean controls. PL/SQL code behind these objects (and in the database) controls validation and behavior in the form.

All of these items are created using the Form Builder.

Data Blocks

Blocks are the form elements that connect the displayed items on the screen to the database. The block itself is never seen when a form is running; only the items that it contains are displayed on the canvas (Figure 3-1).

Blocks can be based on single database tables, multiple tables (via a view), and even the returned values from a PL/SQL package. Blocks can also be created that are not connected to (not bound) to the database at all. These are commonly called Control Blocks or non-base table blocks (NBTs). Control Blocks can be used to hold working variables, reference values, or any other data that is used or displayed within the Form.

When a block is associated with tables in the database, Oracle Forms 10*g* handles the standard DML functions automatically. Select, Insert, Update, and Delete are supported for these blocks without having to write additional code. When the block is based on a view, limited ability to perform DML is supported (based on the rules for updatable views).

When the block is based on PL/SQL code, or when you want to perform nonstandard functions when the user attempts to update or delete items in the form, then PL/SQL code can be written to perform the desired action and override the standard DML functions. For example, if a user

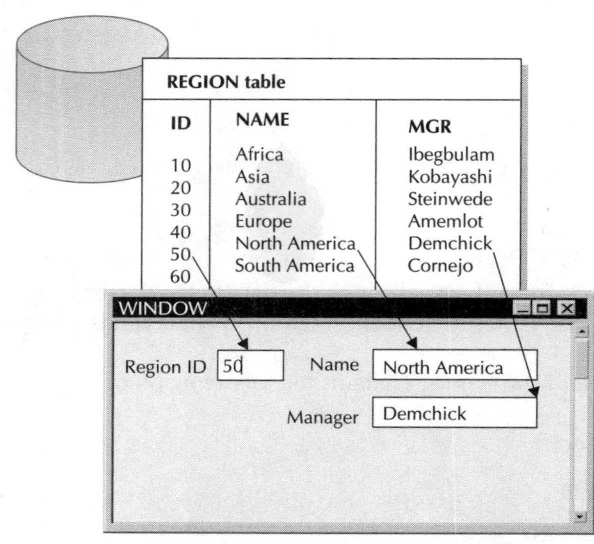

FIGURE 3-1. *A graphical description of database tables and Oracle Forms 10g canvases*

deletes a record on screen, but the system requires that items never be deleted (they must be marked inactive instead), then the delete function can be "replaced" by PL/SQL code to set the appropriate flags invisibly to the user. For the standard behavior, however, no code is required. Oracle Forms 10*g* handles the interaction automatically.

TIP
A form can have an unlimited number of blocks, but a logical limit is ten. If you have more than ten blocks, you should consider breaking the form up into smaller modules.

Items and Data Items

Items are the form elements that connect the form to a column in the database table (or, as noted in the preceding section, "Data Blocks," a returned value from PL/SQL). Items can only be created within blocks. They are the pieces of a block that are seen when the form is running. The items may be bound to the database, in which case they represent a column in the table or view being bound, or a value returned by a PL/SQL package. Or, the item may be a calculated value or reference value from a Control Block.

Cursor Navigation

Cursor navigation at run time is controlled by the orientation of the data blocks and items set at design time in the Object Navigator. By default, the cursor goes to the first item on the first block of the form, and then moves through each block and item in the form. By rearranging the data blocks and items, the navigation sequence at run time can be controlled.

There are other ways to control navigation: programmatically or by hard-coding the sequence of items. It is always preferable to use the physical ordering of item and blocks to control navigation.

Finally, you can specify what behavior should occur when you reach the last item in a record. The cursor can return to the first item in the same record, can move to the next record, or can move to the next block in the form.

Single-Record and MultiRecord Blocks

Blocks can be displayed on the canvas either as a single-record-per-screen (form layout), or with multiple records displayed (tabular format). Which layout you use depends on the kind of data displayed and the functionality of the forms. For example, maintaining a list of codes is more easily done when the data is displayed in multiple rows, spreadsheet-fashion. Working with customer data, on the other hand, may require showing more details, and a forms-type layout is more readable.

Master-Detail Relationships

Oracle Forms 10*g* easily manages the concept of parent-child relationships between blocks. A parent-child (or Master-Detail) relationship between tables in the database, such as a customer having many locations, or an order having many lines, is usually represented by foreign-key relationships between the tables. However, a master detail relationship does not require that this database relationship exist.

Within Oracle Forms 10*g*, the relationship between the master and detail blocks ensures that the detail block displays only those records that are associated with the current master record, and coordinates querying, data entry, and deletion between the blocks. The detail block must be created after the master block is created (the easiest way to do this is to use the wizard, which will allow you to set up the relationship automatically). An important component of the relationship is how the blocks remain coordinated. Forms can either automatically query the detail information every time the master record is viewed, or querying the detail blocks can be deferred until they are needed and then they're either automatically queried on first use, or manually queried via code.

By far the most common master-detail relationship is one parent and one child. For example, an order header and order lines. One parent and many children is common for informational forms, such as customer information which has various subtables of information such as addresses, shipping and billing information, and contacts.

It is uncommon to have one child record belong to more than one parent record. This situation requires that you manipulate the auto-generated triggers for master-detail relationships.

Canvases, Windows, and Views

Canvases, windows, and views are the components of Forms that the user sees when the form is run; each is a different "layer" in the display of the form on screen (Figure 3-2). The canvas is the object on which the GUI is drawn, the "background" of the form. All the other visible objects in the form are drawn on the canvas. The window is the frame through which the canvas is seen. The View is the object that controls how much of the canvas can be seen at any given time.

The canvas can be any size (within reason), while the window controls the ultimate size of the interface. It controls how much of the canvas can be seen at any one time. If the canvas is larger than the window, then only what can fit into the window will be visible.

In Figure 3-2, the canvas is twice as wide as the window, so only about half of the canvas can be seen at one time. The window itself is fairly large, but the view port in it is just large enough to view the items on the canvas and cover the remaining items. The canvas could be scrolled to display the remaining half and the items on it within the confines of the view port.

In many cases, the window, canvas, and view are the same size.

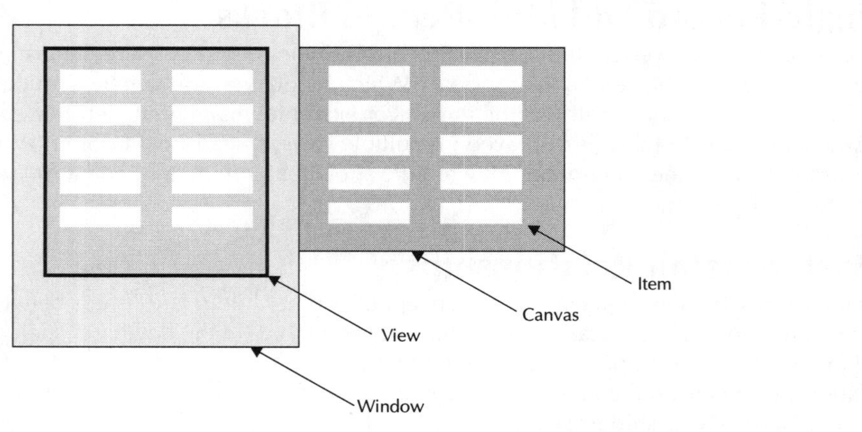

FIGURE 3-2. *A graphical representation of windows, views, canvases, and items*

Windows

When a Forms application is displayed, it is enclosed in a master window, called the Multiple Document Interface (MDI) window. This is the outer "container" window for the application; other windows will open within the MDI.

There are two types of windows within Forms: a document window and a dialog window. The document window is the "standard" window of an application, while a dialog window is a "pop-up" window that is independent of the application and can be moved outside of the MDI window.

Dialog windows have an additional property that controls their behavior. The modal property determines if the dialog window has a synchronous or an asynchronous display. A modal window must be explicitly dismissed before the user can return to another window. A nonmodal window allows the user to switch back and forth between open windows. Error messaging and confirmation dialog windows are usually modal windows: processing stops until the user acknowledges the message.

An application may have a single window into which all canvases are displayed, or it may have multiple windows. Some forms display each canvas in the same window, while others display each canvas in its own window and have multiple popup displays of different sizes. There is no practical limit to the number of windows in a form. In practice, however, there are rarely more than five to ten.

Canvases

Canvases are the Form components that are used to display items on the screen. By arranging items on one or more canvases, they can be presented logically to the user. There are several types of canvases that can be displayed within the windows of the Form. These include Content, Stacked, Tabbed, and Toolbar canvases.

Content Canvas

A Content canvas is the "background" of the window. It is a type of canvas that completely fills the window that it is in. If the canvas is larger than the window, it is cropped; if the canvas is smaller than the window, Forms will fill in the extra space with the specified background color. Since a content canvas completely fills the window, only one content canvas can be seen at any time. If the form navigates to an item on a different canvas, then that new content canvas replaces the currently displayed canvas.

If the canvas is larger than the window/view in which it is displayed, scrollbars can be added to the window to display all the items. Good design principles, however, suggest that you do not scroll more than two window-widths in any direction, and do not allow scrolling both horizontally and vertically in one form.

Stacked Canvas

A stacked canvas can be layered on top of a content canvas, and is used to hide part of the content canvas or display alternate data. For example, a form designed to display customer information may display the common customer information at the top of the canvas and allow either financial data, order data, or contact information to be displayed on the bottom half of the window. Each set of data is arranged on a stacked canvas that is displayed in the same position. When the user wants to see order data, the stacked canvas with order data is "brought to the top."

In most cases, the size of a stacked canvas is smaller than the window it is displayed in, because the stacked canvases are used to cover up only part of the content canvas in the window. If it is not smaller than the existing canvas, then the stacked canvas will completely obscure the content canvas, which defeats the purpose of having an alternate view.

Stacked canvases can be displayed and hidden programmatically. They are also displayed automatically when the user navigates to an item on the canvas. A stacked canvas will remain in view until it is explicitly dismissed or replaced by another canvas.

A common error that can occur is that stacked canvases can disappear at inopportune times. This is usually related to the automatic re-ordering that Forms uses to display the active item. In this case, something that has to be displayed in order to show the active item has overlapped the stacked canvas and caused it to be pushed farther down in the stack of displayed canvases.

Tabbed Canvas

Tabbed canvases are a specialized type of stacked canvas that has multiple pages of information identified by folder-like tabs across the top or side of the display. Each tab page can contain different data, which is easily accessed by clicking the identifying tab.

Tabbed canvases are two-part objects: the Tab Canvas itself is the container, which contains multiple Tab Pages. Remember that Forms insists that the "active item" is displayed at all times. This can cause confusion when working with Tabbed canvasses. Because Forms considers the Tab Canvas itself as the display canvas, not the individual pages, it is possible to have a Tab Page displayed that does not contain the current item. As long as the Tab Canvas is displayed, Forms is satisfied.

Toolbar Canvas

Finally, Forms has a special type of canvas for custom button bars. Forms has a default "smartbar" toolbar that is included in each Form to provide the standard functionality for cut and paste, save, etc., and can be seen in Figure 3-3. If you need a custom toolbar, this type of canvas can be used as a replacement.

Like windows, there is no practical limit to the number of canvases in a form. However, a logical limit is 10-15 canvases. If the form is complex enough to require more canvases to display data, the Form should probably be broken up into multiple smaller forms.

Behavior

When a form is displayed in the browser window, the "active" item—that is, the item with focus—must be displayed. Using the order of blocks and items, Forms determines which item should be the "starting" place in the form. Forms will do whatever is necessary to display that item within the open view port on screen. If the item is not in the current view, then the Form will manipulate the layers of display to ensure that the item can be seen. When the user (or internal code) navigates to another item, that item will then be brought into the view port if it is not already visible.

Using Form Builder - Object Navigator

The Object Navigator is part of the Forms toolkit. It is displayed automatically when Forms Developer starts and shows all the objects that you create in Forms designer (Figure 3-4).

The Object Navigator organizes the modules and objects within the workspace. It consists of a toolbar and hierarchical object management section. Objects are grouped into nodes based on

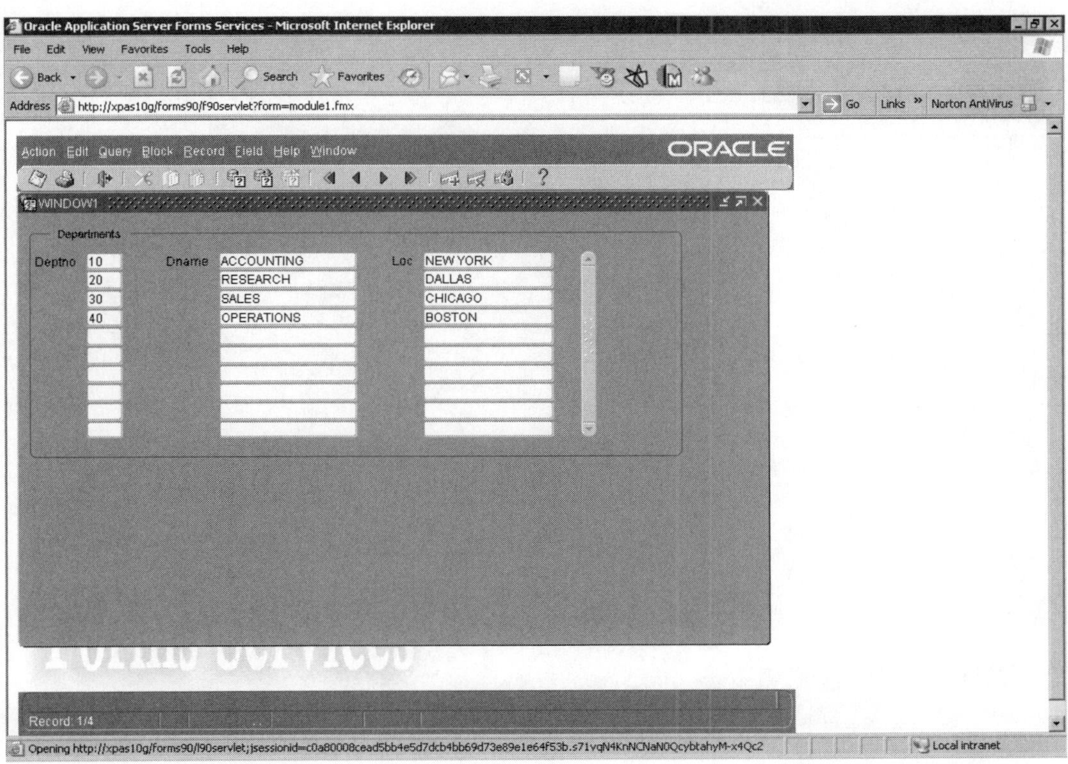

FIGURE 3-3. *Displaying a simple form in a web browser*

type (menus, forms, blocks, items, etc.). You can view all the objects in a form by expanding and collapsing the nodes in the form. You can view items in three ways:

- **Ownership View** Grouped by type (see Figure 3-4).
- **Visual View** Objects are shown organized by containers so that canvases are contained in windows, and items are shown in canvases, etc.
- **PL/SQL Only** Only objects with associated PL/SQL code are displayed in either view.

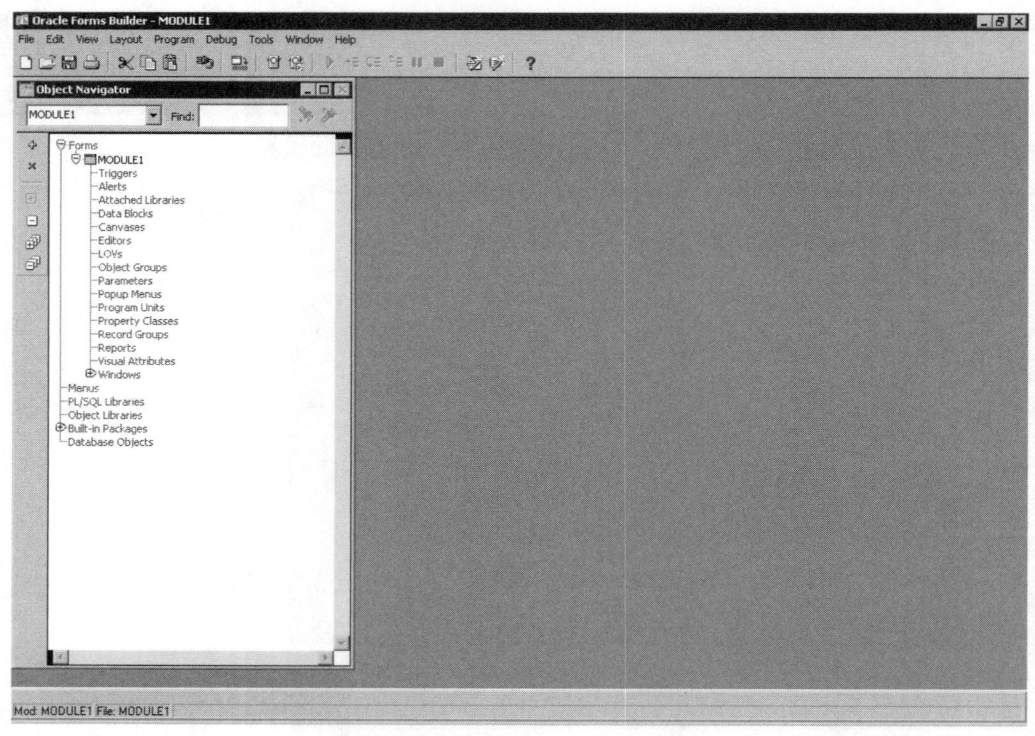

FIGURE 3-4. *The Forms Builder module*

Wizards

While forms can be built manually, Forms provides a number of wizards to assist with development:

- Data Block Wizard
- Layout Wizard
- LOV Wizard

Wizards can speed the development of Forms by providing default behavior and layouts, and all of them are reentrant. In many cases, making changes to the objects by using the wizard is much easier than manually updating each property. Note, however, that rerunning the wizards can overwrite the changes you have made with the defaults from Forms.

Exercise: Building a Simple Form

There are four basic steps to creating a simple form that allows Select, Update, Insert, and Delete on a single table:

- Create a new form module in the Object Navigator
- Create a block based on a database table
- Arrange the items in the block on a canvas
- Run the form

Instead of discussing in detail how to create and run a form, let's create a simple form and then discuss the results. This should make it easier to understand how the basic elements function. Just follow along with the steps:

1. Create a new Form module (highlight the node under forms and click the green plus sign). When you open Forms Builder, you may be offered the option to open an existing form or create a new one, and by default, a new, empty module is created (Figure 3-4).
2. The Data Block Wizard automates the task of creating blocks and items. It is the fastest way to create a default block and layout, and is the basis for most forms (Figure 3-5). Give focus to the Data Blocks node and press the green + button (create). Select Use Data Block Wizard to continue.

You can also create data blocks manually by choosing Build New Data Block Manually. This is used to create Control blocks. While it is possible to build a table-based block manually, it is not recommended and can be quite tedious! It is nearly always easier to start with the wizard-generated block and made adjustments as necessary.

1. If the Welcome screen is displayed, click OK. Select Table or View as the type of data block and press the Next button (Figure 3-6).
2. Click Browse and log in to the database if you are prompted to (Figure 3-7).
3. Select the S_DEPT table from the list and click OK (Figure 3-8). This list of values can display those items that belong to your user, or those that belong to another user.
4. The Available columns will display all the columns in the table. Use the arrow buttons to move the columns into the database items region. Only the columns in the database items region will be incorporated into the form. Press Next (Figure 3-9).

FIGURE 3-5. *The New Data Block dialog box*

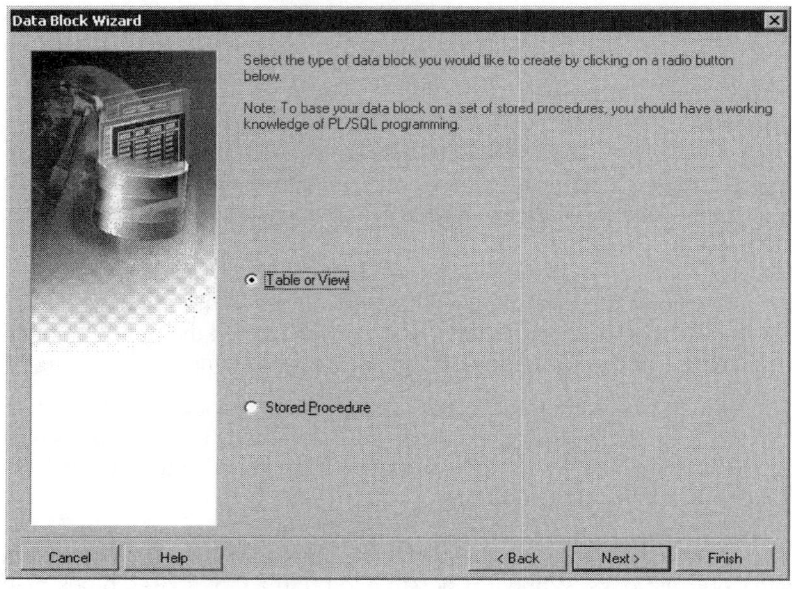

FIGURE 3-6. *The first step of the Data Block Wizard*

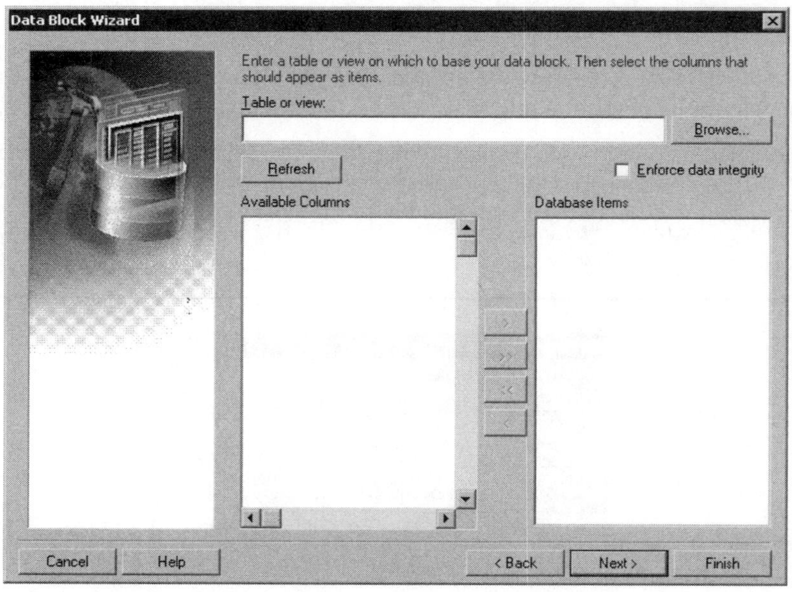

FIGURE 3-7. *The second step of the Data Block Wizard*

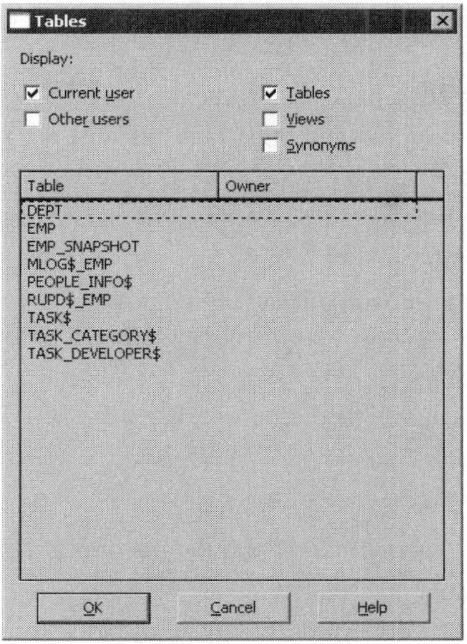

FIGURE 3-8. *The Tables dialog box*

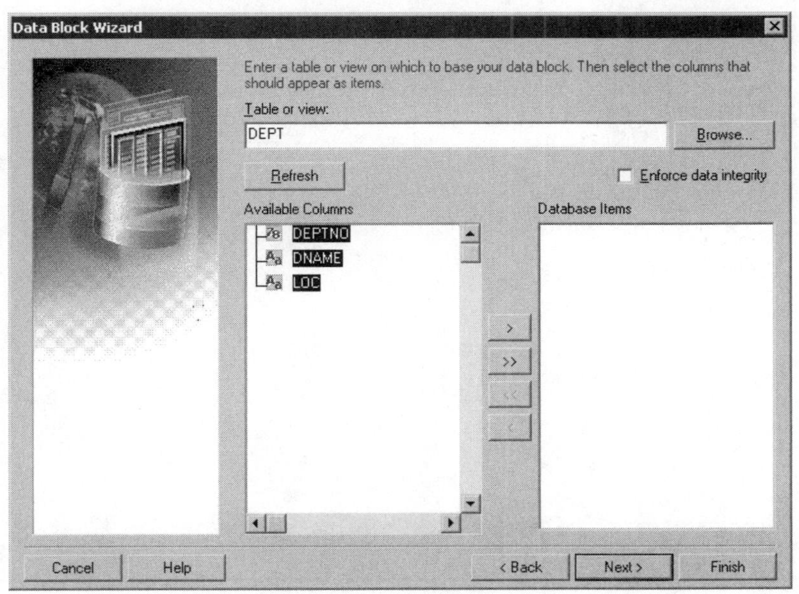

FIGURE 3-9. *The Data Block Wizard with the selected table displayed*

5. Enter a name for the data block (Figure 3-10). This name will default to the name of the table or view you are basing the block on. Normally, you will not want to override this name.
6. When the Congratulations dialog box is displayed, select Create the Data Block, then call the Layout Wizard option and press Finish (Figure 3-11).
7. The Layout Wizard will assist in creating a default canvas and window, and arranging the selected items on it (Figure 3-12). Accept the default settings of New Canvas and Content and press Next.
8. The Available Items region will display the columns that you chose from the previous wizard. Use the arrow buttons to move the columns into the Displayed Items region. Press Next (Figure 3-13).
9. Change the Prompt value for the columns (Figure 3-14). This page allows you to control the physical display of the items. Do not change anything yet. Press Next.
10. Select Tabular and press Next (Figure 3-15).
11. Set the Frame Title to "Departments" and the Records Displayed to 10. Check Display Scrollbar. Press Next.
12. Press the Finish button. Your Forms toolkit should look something like this (Figure 3-16).

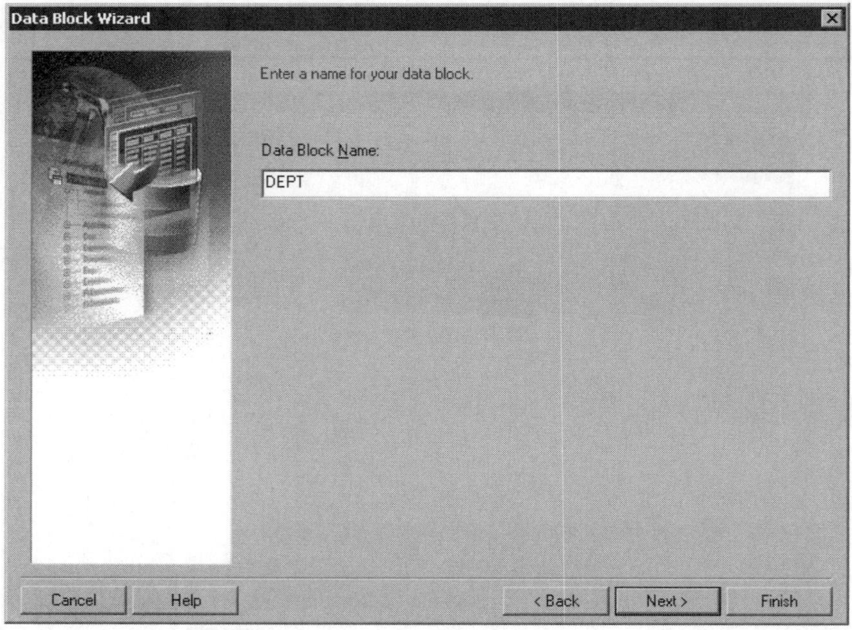

FIGURE 3-10. *Entering a name for the data block*

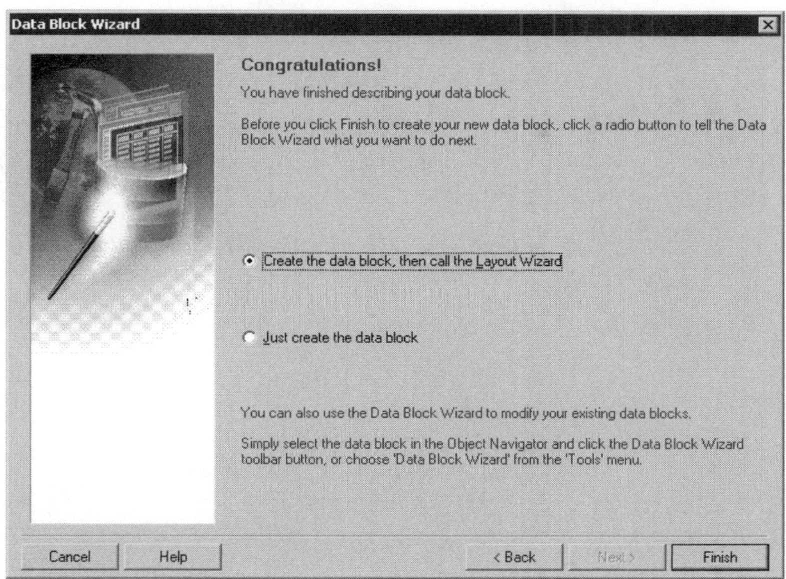

FIGURE 3-11. *The final step of the Data Block Wizard*

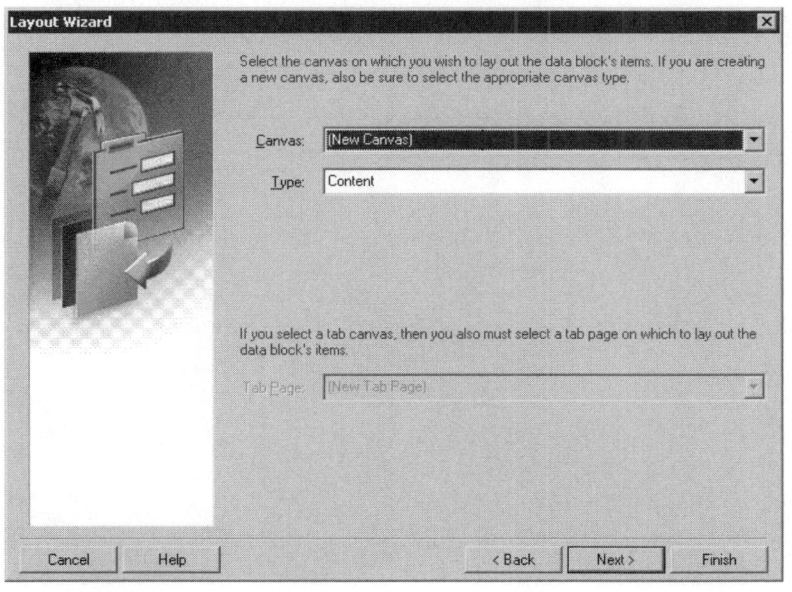

FIGURE 3-12. *The first page of the Layout Wizard*

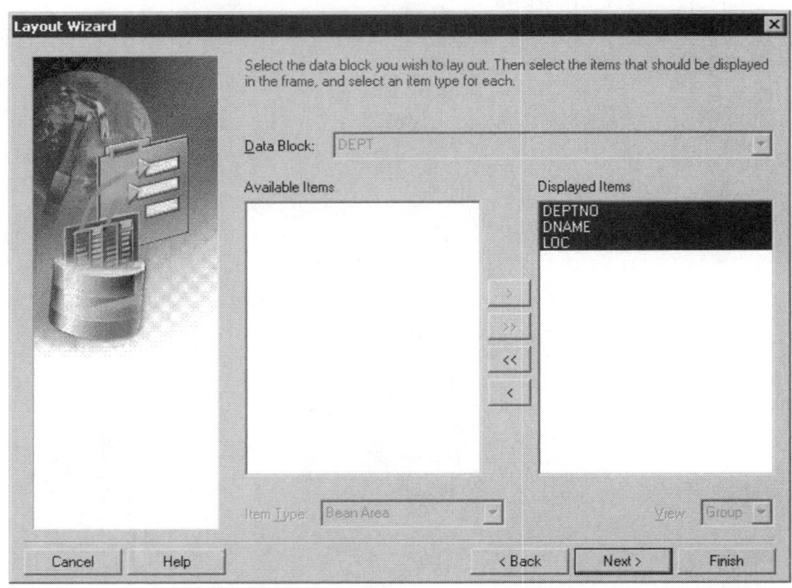

FIGURE 3-13. *The Layout Wizard with items selected*

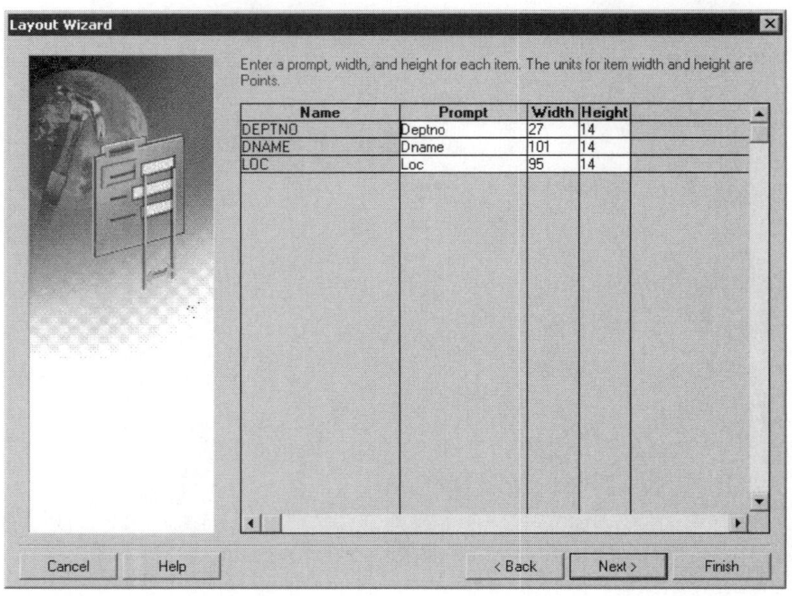

FIGURE 3-14. *Setting item attributes in the Layout Wizard*

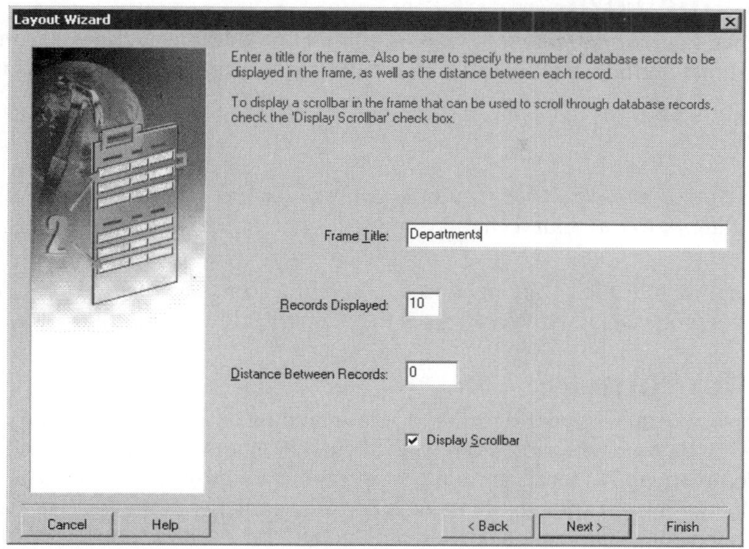

FIGURE 3-15. *Setting attributes for the frame in the Layout Wizard*

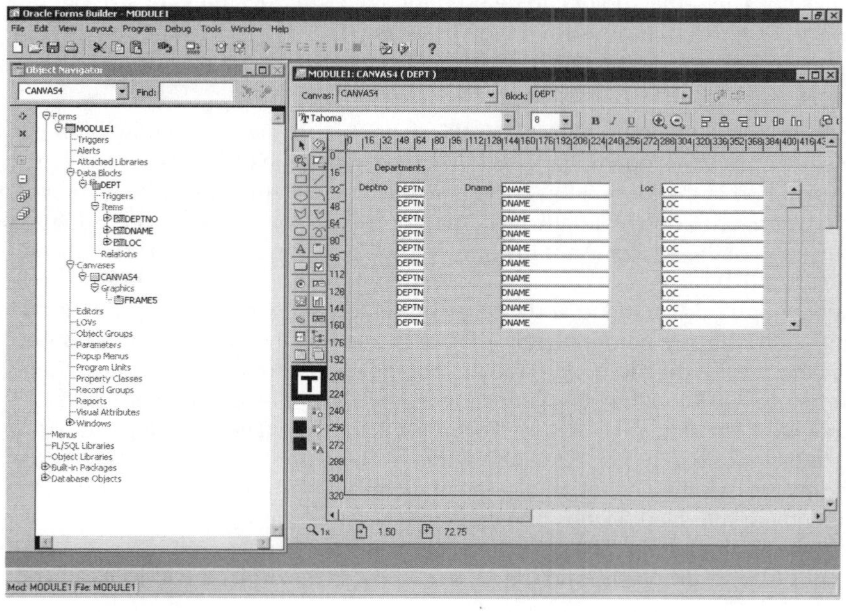

FIGURE 3-16. *Forms Builder after successfully generating the form*

Compiling the Form

Make sure to save your work. Note that there is a limitation in the way the web run time reads directory names that include spaces; make sure that you save the form into a directory that can be read.

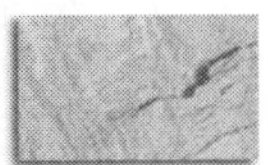

NOTE
If you store files in a directory with spaces, you will receive an error when you attempt to run your form.

The Forms compiler is the component used to compile Form source code (.fmb) into executable code (.fmx) that can be run on the Web. This is the "deployable" version of the form.

Running the Form

Previous versions of Forms supported a client-server implementation, which required that a run-time engine be installed or accessible from each client machine. Forms 10*g* no longer supports client-server deployment. All forms are run on the Web via a browser.

One of the major misconceptions about Web Forms in earlier versions was that the form was built and compiled in the Forms Designer, and then run through some sort of "converter" to generate the Java code that runs the form in the browser. This is not the case.

However, running a form for the first time does require some Java support, in the form of a thin Java applet that handles the display of the Oracle form in the browser. The applet is downloaded and cached on the client machine. The Forms Applet provides the user interface for the form and is responsible for rendering the display. It does not contain any specific application logic (that is, in the form itself). The same applet can be used for any form, regardless of size or complexity. Preferences control how the forms run in the browser.

Using OC4J

Testing the forms locally requires that an OC4J instance is running. In Windows, this can be started from the menu Forms Developer | Start OC4J Instance. Once the OC4J instance is running, simply press the Run button in the form. If this is the first time you have run forms from within Forms Builder, you will have to download the Java Applet code. Follow the instructions to perform the default installation of the Applet. After the applet loads, we can test our form displayed in the browser (Figure 3-17).

Note that the pull-down menu and toolbar presented in your form are fully functional. They are default options that are automatically attached to every new form. The form is functional "right out of the box." You can query, update, and delete records; scroll through them; and even insert records—although you will need to be sure to create a unique identifier!

The large window that you see is the Forms MDI window. This is a standard window management technique in which all other windows of the application are contained with the parent window. This is the default management technique for Forms applications. However, a Single Document Interface (SDI) is also available.

In the browser, the Forms MDI window appears within the Java Applet space. By default, this applet space is 650 x 500 pixels, and the MDI window is maximized within it. The default size of

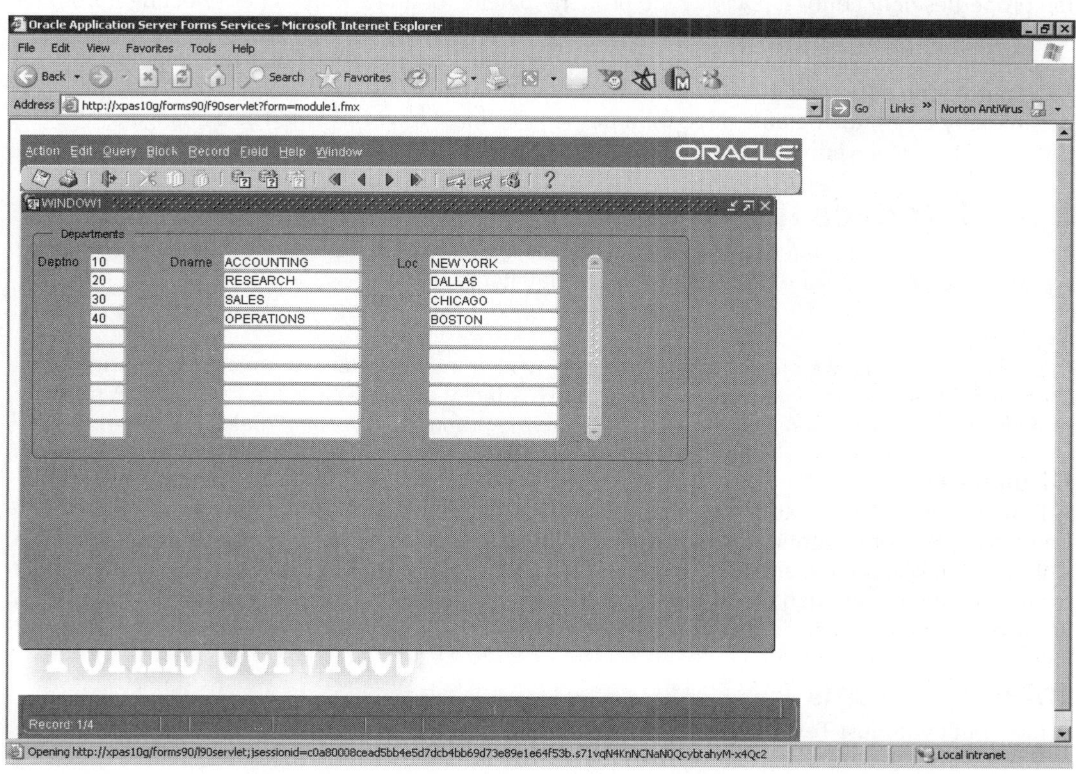

FIGURE 3-17. *The generated form displayed in a web browser*

the Applet frame can be changed by editing the height and width properties in the following file: $ORACLE_HOME/forms90/formsweb.cfg. This should be set to the normal expected size of the browser window. In most cases, 800 x 600 is the lowest common denominator size and forms should be designed to fit within that window. However, the value can be set higher if each of the users can support the configuration. Do not design at higher resolutions unless you can ensure that all users can view the forms.

Property Palettes

Every item in a form has properties that control its behavior and appearance. Using the Wizard sets these properties to default values, which can then be changed to customize the item. The appearance and behavior of form objects (and even the form itself) can be altered by changing the properties defined for it. Display the property palette for an item by either selecting it from the Tools menu, double-clicking on the object in the Object Navigator (except for canvases, when double-clicking simply displays the canvas), or right-clicking the object and selecting Property Palette from the popup menu.

In many cases, the default value for a property is fine. However, when you change a property, it is displayed with a small green square next to the name.

Basic Interface Items

Items that the user can interact with on the canvas are called interface items. The most common types of interface items are Text Items and Display Items.

Text Items

In the basic form that we created above, the only type of interface item we created was a simple Text Item. These interface items allow the user to interact with the data in the form field. A majority of items in a form are often text items, as these are the primary "data entry" fields for a form.

Display Items

A Display Item is (as its name suggests) an interface item for display only. They are similar to Text Items, but the user cannot update the data displayed in them. The same effect can be attained by setting enterable, update allowed, and insert allowed properties of a text item to prohibit the user from changing it, although this is not the preferred way of handling displayed data. Display items are not navigable.

Interface Items

A form built with just Text Items and Display Items is functional, but they are not easy for the user to work with. Older applications often required that users memorize or look up complex codes for things, and required developers to write code to handle verification of the data a user would type in. Was that a "Y" or "yes" that you need to type in for Preferred Customer? What are the codes for shipping?

Constraints in the database can be used to catch these data entry issues, and hints could be provided, but there is a much better approach. Using Check Boxes, Radio Groups, and List Boxes can control the data entry for specific fields.

All of these interface items are used to give the user a choice of multiple values that map back to a single value in the database. No matter how many Radio Buttons you can choose from, or how many items are in a list, only one value is stored in the database. One of the other advantages of using these interface items is that the displayed value is not necessarily the value that is stored in the database. A Check Box may be labeled "Require Phone Number?" but the value stored is either a Y or N.

These alternate interface items can be created by simply drawing the appropriate object type in the Layout Editor (from the object buttons on the left), or by selecting the item and changing its item type property in the property palette.

Check Boxes

Check Boxes are used when there are two choices for a field: on or off. A Check Box should have a clear binary choice between opposite values – YES/NO, ON/OFF, PREFFERED/NOT PREFERRED. The checked and unchecked values should be intuitive. You would probably not use a Check Box for MALE/FEMALE (unless you were tracking Dennis Rodman).

Most Check Boxes are backed up by a not null constraint and a check constraint in the database. Check Boxes have several properties that control their behavior:

- **Value when checked** The value that will be inserted into the database when the Check Box is checked.
- **Value when unchecked** The value that will be inserted into the database when the Check Box is not checked.
- **Check Box Mapping of Other Values** This property controls how records queried from the database will be handled if the value in the database is not one of the two values allowed by the Check Box. The erroneous value may be shown as checked or unchecked, or it may be NOT ALLOWED, which will ignore the record and not display it in the form (which is often confusing to users, since the data can be seen in other tools).

For example, if the Check Box is set up to allow the values Y and N, but somehow an M is present in the data, forms can either pretend the M is a Y or N, or discard the record entirely. Note that displaying the "bad value" as one of the allowed values does not automatically change the value to the allowed value. It remains an M in the database unless it is explicitly changed.

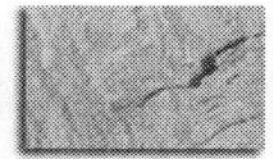

TIP
Do not use a series of Check Boxes that behaves like a radio group (i.e., writing code to allow the user to check only one of the many checkboxes and uncheck the rest). Use a radio group instead.

Radio Group

For those of us old enough to remember old car radios, the similarity of this widget to the little push-buttons to change the stations is obvious. Only one item can be selected at a time.

A Radio Group is used when there are two to six values to choose from, and the user must select one value. Like the Check Box, Radio Groups are usually backed up by not null constraints and either a check constraint or foreign key relationship in the database.

The Radio Group is the container, which is bound to the database item, and contains radio buttons. The group itself has no physical representation on the canvas; only the buttons are shown. The buttons have associated values that are inserted into the database.

The Radio Group has a Mapping of Other Values property (like Check Boxes and List Boxes). Leaving the property NULL disregards the invalid value. Otherwise, the value can be displayed as one of the valid radio choices.

List Boxes

List Boxes, or drop-down boxes, display a list of valid values to the user. One value can be selected. Each List Box must have an associated list of values (which can be hard-coded into the list box item, or dynamically attached from a Record Group).

The following properties control List Boxes:

- **Elements in list** The display value and database value pairs for the list.
- **Mapping of Other Values** Controls how records queried in the database will be handled if the value in the list column does not match the value of an item currently in the list.

Leaving this property NULL means disregarding the record and not displaying it on screen. Setting the value of one of the items in the list will display the record as though it had that value. Again, it does not change the bad value to an accepted one, it only displays it.

List Boxes come in several flavors, which behave slightly differently.

- **Pop list** The standard List Box, which initially displays a single value that can be expanded to view the rest of the list. This is the most common type of list box.
- **T-List** This List Box is less common, but can be used when there are only a few items to display. It takes of a lot of screen real estate, and because of the multiline display users often attempt to select multiple items. Even though multiple lines are displayed, the user can still only choose one value. ·
- **Combo Box** Combo Boxes are rarer yet. Initially, they behave just like a Pop list. However, a Combo Box allows the user to type in a value that is not in the list and have that value saved to the database. However, if the list is hardcoded (in the Element in List property), the new value will not display in the list the next time it is used. In order to have a Combo Box display user-entered data immediately, it must dynamically build the list-of-values (LOVs).

Buttons

After text items, Buttons are the most common interface item in forms. Buttons are a specific widget designed to mimic an actual push button, and perform an action when they are pressed. Buttons are not bound to database items.

Buttons have the following properties:

- **Label** The wording that appears on the button. Buttons can also be iconic.
- **Default button** The button indicating it's the default button for the block. It will be displayed with default highlighting. It is important to remember that the default button for a screen should never be a "destructive" button. Users have a tendency to press Return blindly and the action performed by the button should not be one that makes permanent changes to data or begins processing. For example, do not make the default button OK on a confirmation dialog window, since this may mean that the user will inadvertently perform that complete delete because he did not read the dialog message.
- **Mouse navigation** This property indicates if the cursor should move focus to the button when it is pressed, or whether the cursor should remain where it is, and no navigation should occur.

Record Groups

Record Groups are internal Forms structures that behave like tables in memory. They have no visual representation, and by themselves, have no values. However, they are used to drive other interface items such as LOVs and List Boxes.

Record Groups can be based on a list of static values (although this is not common) or on queries. The query can be as simple or complex as necessary to return the values you need. Record Groups can reference forms objects, system objects, or other variables.

List of Values

A list-of-values (LOVs) displays a pop-up listing of available values for a form field. It is based on a record group. The LOV Wizard can easily create a list of values (and the associated Record Group).

The Record Group behind an LOV can have as many columns as you want to display, for informational purposes. Each column in the LOV can be "linked" to a displayed field so that when the LOV item is selected, it can populate a number of fields on screen. Each column in the LOV can return to only one field in the form.

When one of the values of the LOV is returned to the form, you have the option to "attach" the LOV to one of the fields so the users can invoke the list to select a value. An LOV is assigned to a text item in the form by setting the following properties:

- **List of values** Which LOV to associate with this item.
- **List X Position/List Y Position** Specific location to display the LOV.
- **Validate from List** Indicates that the LOV should be used to determine that the data entered into the field is valid. When data is typed into the field, the LOV is consulted to determine if the value entered is included in the LOV. For this property to work, the first column of the LOV must be the column that is bound to the form item.

Layout Editor

Each of the interface items listed above has a property palette, which includes information about location, size, color, and font. Each item can be customized by changing the value in the property palette, but it is much easier using the Layout Editor (Figure 3-18).

The Layout Editor is a graphical tool for working with the visual elements of a form. The Layout Editor, Property Palette, and Object Navigator are linked together—if you make a change in one, the others are automatically synchronized.

Layout Editor Buttons

Using the buttons and Layout Menu, you can design the look and feel of the form easily. See Figure 3-19 for the layout buttons in the Layout Editor.

To find out what a specific button does, simply point to it with the cursor—a Tooltip will display describing the button's function. The toolbar on the left-hand side of the Layout Editor includes these buttons:

A. Use these buttons to select, rotate, zoom, or reshape items

B. Use these buttons to create boilerplate graphics objects such as boxes or lines. Boilerplate items are read-only and the user cannot interact with them.

C. Use these buttons to create boilerplate text. Remember that item prompts are now properties that are associated with the item itself. Do not use boilerplate for item prompts.

D. Use this button to create a new frame object that can be used for auto-layout.

E. Use these buttons to create interface items such as buttons, check boxes, radio buttons, text items, images, charts, JavaBean areas, display items, list items, and hierarchical tree items. Note that you can create these items in the layout editor

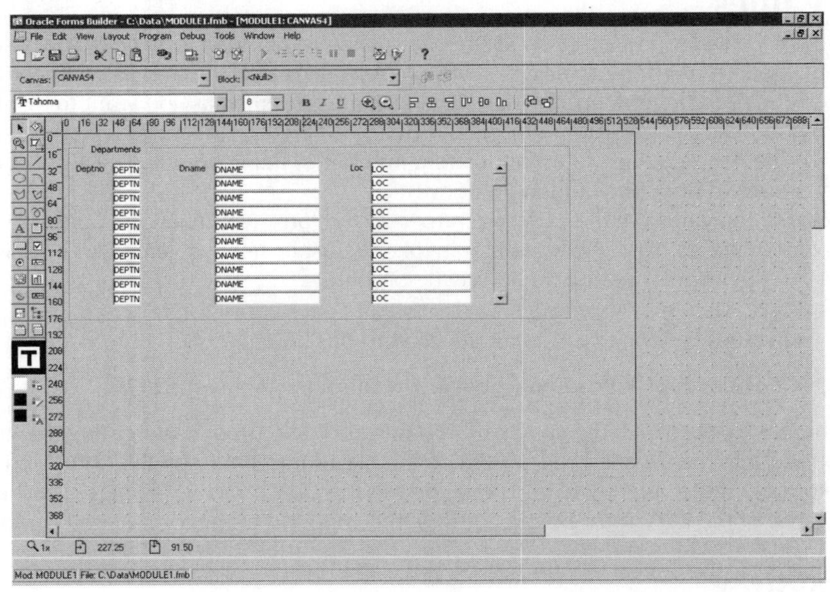

FIGURE 3-18. *The Layout Editor*

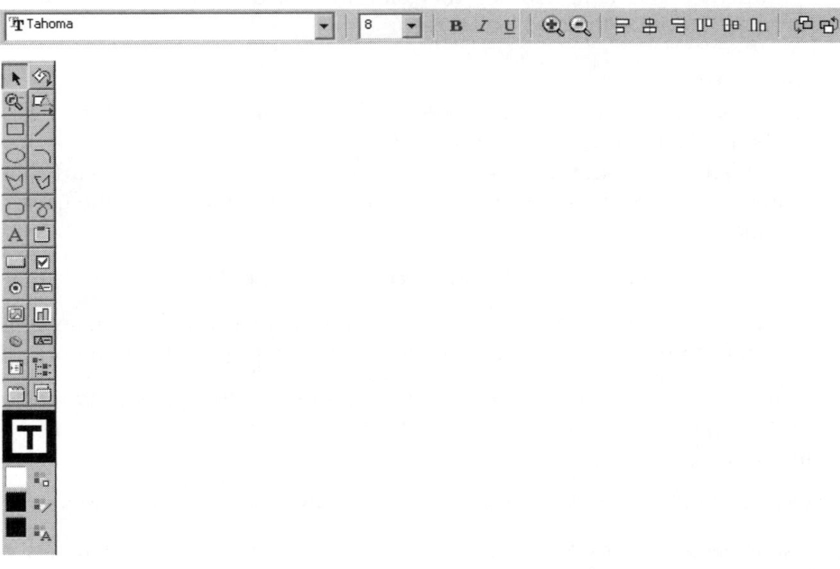

FIGURE 3-19. *Buttons in the Layout Editor*

and they will be created in the data block that has current focus, or the first block in the form if none of them have focus.

F. Use this button to create a tab canvas.

G. Use this button to create a stacked canvas on top of this one.

H. Use these buttons to control the background/fill color, line color, and text color.

Across the top of the Layout Editor are additional layout buttons:

1. Use these drop-down menus to set the font and size for items.
2. Use these buttons to set the font attributes (bold, italic, underline) for items, prompts, and boilerplate.
3. Use these buttons to zoom in and out.
4. Use these buttons to align multiple objects, horizontally and vertically. You can also align objects using the menu selection Layout | Align Components. Note that aligning left will align the object with the one that is farthest left; aligning top will align the objects with the object that is highest, etc.
5. Use these buttons to change the layout order of the items by moving items to the front or moving them behind other objects.

Adding Functionality

So far, forms are collections of objects displayed on a canvas. Users can invoke the built-in functionality for DML actions (Select, Insert, Update, Delete). Our forms might look nice, but they don't do much yet.

Functionality is added to the Form using interface items and adding PL/SQL code "behind the scenes" to make the form work. Oracle Forms 10*g* is event driven; that is, code is run in response to specific actions by the user or generated by the form. Events are predefined actions that occur within a form.

Events

Users generate events by moving the mouse, clicking a mouse button, tabbing from one item to another, changing the data in an item, or other interaction with the GUI. The form itself generates events for nearly every action that it takes. Opening a form, opening or closing a window, moving from one item to another or one block to another, coordinating master-detail relationships are all examples of forms-generated events.

Every predefined event in the form can be "trapped" by a corresponding trigger. Triggers allow us to add functionality to the form to augment or replace the default behavior. Each predefined event has a specific trigger associated with it. For example, when a button is pressed, it is captured by a when-button-pressed trigger. There are user-defined triggers, but they are of minimal use and are more a hold-over from an early version of Forms (which had a limited number of recognized events) than current functionality.

There are four types of events in a form:

- Interface Events are generated by the user's interaction with the form.

- Keyboard Events are generated by the user pressing a function key or key combination that performs an action.
- Internal Processing events occur as a result of run-time processing and are often generated by other events.
- User-defined events.

Triggers

Triggers intercept the default behavior of the form and replace it, or add custom logic to the form. Triggers "fire"—are executed—in response to the events in the form. In most places, multiple events occur in response to actions in the form, so multiple triggers may fire in the sequence of events.

The level at which a trigger is defined determines its scope. A trigger defined at the item level applies only to that item. A trigger defined at the block level applies to every appropriate item in that block. At the form level, a trigger fires for every item in the form. For example, if a when-button-pressed trigger is placed on an individual button, it will fire only when that button is pressed. If the same trigger is placed at the block level, it will fire for all the buttons in the block. And if it is placed at the form level, it will fire for each button on the form.

Some triggers can be defined at only one level; others can be defined at multiple levels.

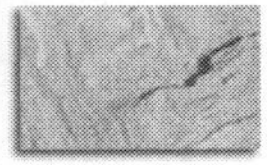

NOTE
Only one trigger of each type can exist at each level (item, block, form); to perform additional actions in response to an event, simply add code to the existing trigger.

By default, Forms executes the trigger code at the lowest level (item) first. If there is no trigger for the event at the item level, forms will look at the block level, then the forms level. Only one trigger of each type will fire by default. However, you can change the way triggers interact by setting the Execution Hierarchy property for the trigger. The Execution Hierarchy property for the trigger can have the following values:

- **Override** The default; fires the lowest level trigger fires.
- **Before** The current trigger will fire before firing the same trigger at the next higher scope. If an item trigger and a block trigger exist, Forms will first fire the item trigger and then fire the block trigger.
- **After** Fires the current trigger after it fires the trigger at the next higher scope.

It is very rare to change the default of OVERRIDE for triggers. This is the expected behavior of forms. However, using a high-level trigger to perform common functionality for multiple blocks or items and setting the properties in the triggers to allow them both to fire can be efficient. If you do change this property, document it well. Developers often overlook this property because it is "never changed," and it can make troubleshooting very difficult.

Writing Triggers

Triggers are written using standard PL/SQL structure and syntax, and contain anonymous PL/SQL blocks. If you have no variable declarations, the BEGIN and END statements are optional; Forms will automatically add them to the block. If there are variable declaration, then the standard format of

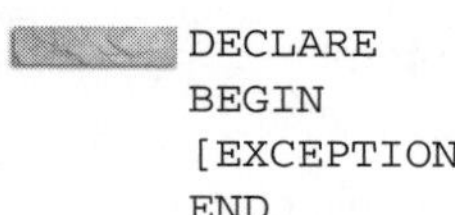

```
DECLARE
BEGIN
[EXCEPTION]
END
```

is required.

Triggers can reference forms objects, Forms built-ins, and all PL/SQL syntax and DML Statements are always allowed in triggers. Triggers can refer to Forms objects by name or ID, system variables, database packages, procedures, and functions.

Types of Triggers

Trigger can be generally divided into the following categories:

- **Block-processing triggers** Fire in response to events related to record management in a block.
- **Interface Event triggers** Fire in response to events that occur in the form interface as a result of user interaction.
- **Navigational triggers** Fire as Forms navigates internally through different levels of the object hierarchy, either in response to user interaction or to internal navigation.
- **Transactional triggers** Fire in response to events that occur as a form interacts with the database. Some transactional triggers replace default behavior and allow forms to run against non-Oracle data sources.
- **Validation triggers** Fire when Forms validates data in an item or record. Validation is performed during navigation that occurs in response to user input or programmatic control, or by default processing such as commit.
- **Query-time triggers** Fire just before and after the execution of a query. They are used to change the behavior of queries or augment the values returned from a query.
- **Message Handling triggers** (on-error and on-message) Fire when errors or messages are presented by the Form.
- **Master-detail triggers** Fire when navigating between parent and child data blocks to keep all related information coordinated. These triggers are generated automatically when a master-detail relationship is created. Unless you are developing your own custom block-coordination, you should not edit these triggers.
- **Key triggers** Fire in response to pressing a function key or combination of keys to perform an action in the form.

The next couple of sections will discuss some of the more commonly used triggers. Forms Developer has many more triggers. The Help system has a complete listing of triggers and their characteristics.

Block Processing Triggers

The following Block Processing triggers are available to the Oracle Forms 10*g* developer:

- **When-Clear-Block** Performs an action whenever Form Builder flushes the current block; that is, removes all records from the block.
- **When-Create-Record** Performs an action whenever Form Builder attempts to create a new record in a block. For example, it's used to set complex, calculated, or data-driven default values that must be specified at run time, rather than design time.
- **When-Remove-Record** Performs an action whenever a record is cleared or deleted. For example, it used to adjust a running total that is being calculated for all of the records displayed in a block.
- **When-Button-Pressed** Initiates an action when an operator selects a button, either with the mouse or through keyboard selection.

Interface Event Triggers

The following Interface Event triggers are available to the Oracle Forms 10*g* developer:

- **When-Button-Pressed** Initiates an action when the user presses a button, either with the mouse or through a keyboard selection.
- **When-Checkbox-Changed** Initiates an action when the user toggles the state of the check box, either with the mouse or with a keyboard action.
- **When-List-Changed** Initiates an action when the user selects a value from the list item.
- **When-Radio-Changed** Initiates an action when the user selects a radio button in a radio group.

The preceding triggers are often used to perform validation that the user has selected a valid value, or prevent changing an item if other values have not been set properly.

- **When-Timer-Expired** Performs an action when an internal forms timer expires.
- **When-Image-Activated** Initiates an action when the user uses the mouse to single- or double-click on an image item.
- **When-Image-Pressed** Initiate an action when the user single- or double-clicks on an image item.
- **When-Window-Activated** Initiates an action when the user or application activates a window.
- **When-Window-Closed** Initiates an action when the user closes a window, or the application does so programmatically.
- **When-Window-Deactivated** initiate an action when the window becomes deactivated as a result of another window becoming the active window
- **When-Window-Resized** Initiates an action whenever the window is resized, either by the user or programmatically.

Navigation Triggers

The following Navigation triggers are available to the Oracle Forms 10*g* developer:

- **Pre-Form** Performs an action just before Form Developer navigates to the form from "outside" the form, such as at form startup.
- **Pre-Block** Performs an action before Form Developer navigates to the block level from the form level.
- **Pre-Record** Performs an action before Form Developer navigates to a record from the block level.
- **Pre-Text-Item** Performs an action before navigating to a text item in the form.
- **Post-Text-Item** Manipulates an item when Form Developer leaves the text item.
- **Post-Record** Manipulates a record when Form Developer leaves it.
- **Post-Block** Manipulates the current record in the block when Form Developer navigates out of a block and to another block.
- **Post-Form** Performs an action before Form Developer navigates "outside" the form, such as when exiting.

When-New-Instance Triggers

The following When-New-Instance triggers are available to the Oracle Forms 10*g* developer:

- **When-New-Form-Instance** Performs an action at form startup.
- **When-New-Block-Instance** Performs an action immediately after the input focus moves to an item in a block other than the block that previously had focus.
- **When-New-Record-Instance** Performs an action immediately after the input focus moves to an item in a different record. If the new record is in a different block, this fires after the when-new-block-instance trigger, but before the when-new-item-instance trigger.
- **When-New-Item-Instance** Performs an action immediately after the input focus moves to a different item. If the new item is in a different record or block, then the when-new-record-instance and when-new-block-instance triggers also fire.

Transactional Triggers

On-triggers are normally used against a non-Oracle database; or when basing blocks on PL/SQL procedures, when the default behavior of delete, insert, update, and select must be handled explicitly by code. When a block is based on a PL/BLOCK, Forms Developer will generate these triggers for you:

- **On-Delete** Replaces the default processing for handling deleted records during transaction posting.
- **On-Insert** Replaces the default processing for insertion of records into the database.
- **On-Update** Replaces the default processing for handling updated records.

- **On-Select** Replaces the default processing for opening a cursor and executing the query to identify the records in the block that are identified by the block properties.
- **Pre-Commit** Performs an action immediately before the Post and Commit transactions are processed in the database.
- **Pre-Delete** Manipulates a record prior to its being deleted from the database during the default Post and Commit transactions; for example, to prevent deletion of the record if certain conditions are met.
- **Pre-Update** Validates or modifies a record prior to its being updated in the database.
- **Pre-Insert** Manipulates a record prior to its being updated in the database.
- **Pre-Select** Performs an action during the execute query and count query processing when the block is queried. The actual statement performed by the block can be retrieved in the pre-select trigger.
- **Pre-Logon** Performs an action just before Forms Developer initiates the logon procedure. Usually used against a non-Oracle database.

Validation Triggers

The following When-New-Instance triggers are available to the Oracle Forms 10*g* developer:

- **When-Validate-Item** Augments the standard validation of an item performed by Forms Developer.
- **When-Validate-Record** Augments the standard validation of a completed record.

Query Triggers

The following Query triggers are available to the Oracle Forms 10*g* developer:

- **Pre-Query** Validates the current query criteria, or provides additional query criteria programmatically, just before sending the SELECT statement to the database. It can be used to modify the query criteria by adding default values.
- **Post-Query** Performs an action (usually a query to retrieve additional data) after fetching a record from the database.
    - Fires once for each record retrieved by the block.
    - Often used to populate control items or items in other blocks.

Key Triggers

Key triggers are a bit different than those triggers listed above. A predefined set of logical functions are assigned to every form. These are mapped to function keys, which are operating system specific. Every keyboard has a physical set of keys that are mapped to logical functions, but the keyboard is dependent on the type of computer and OS.

Forms cannot generally be coded to look for the press of a physical key—say F1. Instead, Forms looks for the press of a key that results in that specific logical function—the key that executes a query, or displays a list box, for example. You can programmatically mimic the pressing of the function key using the do-key built-in.

Key triggers change the default behavior of a function key. A function key can be disabled by writing a NULL trigger. Note that key triggers must contain explicit instructions if you want them to perform their default functionality in addition to custom logic.

Each key-trigger fires when the key combination for the corresponding function is pressed. Each key-trigger also has a corresponding built-in.

Built-Ins

Built-ins are simply functions or procedures that allow PL/SQL code to interact seamlessly with Forms objects in PL/SQL. They extend PL/SQL with form-specific functionality.

Key Trigger	Function	Built-In
Key-clrblk	Clearing the block	CLEAR_BLOCK;
Key-clrfrm	Clearing the form	CLEAR_FORM;
Key-clrrec	Clearing the record	CLEAR_RECORD;
Key-crerec	Creating a new record	CREATE_RECORD;
Key-delrec	Deleting the current record	DELETE_RECORD;
Key-up	Moving the cursor up a record	UP;
Key-down	Moving the cursor down	DOWN;
Key-next-item	Navigating to the next item	NEXT_ITEM;
Key-prev-item	Navigating to the previous item	PREVIOUS_ITEM;
Key-nxtblk	Navigating to the next block	NEXT_BLOCK;
Key-prvblk	Navigating to the previous block	PREVIOUS_BLOCK;
Key-nxtrec	Navigating to the next record	NEXT_RECORD;
Key-nxtset	Navigating to the next fetched set of records	NEXT_SET;
Key-scrdwn	Scrolling down a screen	SCROLL_DOWN;
Key-scrup	Scrolling up a screen	SCROLL_UP;
Key-commit	Committing a record	COMMIT_FORM
Key-exit	Exiting the form	EXIT_FORM
Key-entqry	Entering a query	ENTER_QUERY
Key-exeqry	Executing a query	EXECUTE_QUERY
Key-others	When any other key is pressed	

TABLE 3-1. *Key triggers and their functions*

Invoking Multiple Forms

Most applications consist of a number of separate forms, which each handle a specific task. These multiple forms interact seamlessly to provide the user with a single, unified GUI. In order to do this, forms must be able to invoke and run other forms. There are several built-ins that control how the application invokes multiple forms:

- **New_Form** Closes the currently active form (after performing all validation and committing changed data) and opens a new form.
- **Call_Form** Suspends the currently active form and opens another one. The calling form remains "open," but it is in the background and cannot be interacted with. As soon as the current form exits, the calling form is resumed at the point where it was suspended. Note that committing in the newly opened form will commit all pending transactions in both (all) forms.

NOTE
This can take up a lot of memory, since the "call stack" remains open.

- **Open_Form** Opens a completely new form, while leaving the calling form open and active as well. The user can switch between the forms. By default, the new form is opened in the same session, but it could be opened in a separate session in order to have asynchronous transactions.

Testing Built-Ins

Any built-in that could result in an application error should be explicitly tested using forms_failure, form_fatal, or form_success (these are also built-ins). It is not necessary to test all built-ins for success, but any built-in that performs navigation should be tested if there is a chance that the failure would disrupt the form. For example,

```
go_block('s_dept');
if not FORM_SUCCESS then
     message('Failed to navigate to the Departments Block');
end if;
```

Restricted Built-Ins

Built-ins are classified as either restricted or unrestricted. In general, a restricted built-in performs navigation as it executes, an unrestricted built-in does not. In addition, some built-ins can execute when the form is querying, and some may not. These characteristics define which triggers may include the built-in.

System Variables

System Variables keep track of run-time information and allow access to information about the application and the status of the forms. Some common system variables include:

- Block_status
- Current_datetime

- Current_form
- Cursor_block
- Cursor_item
- Cursor_record
- Cursor_value
- Effective_date
- Form_status
- Last_query
- Last_Record
- Message_level
- Mode
- Mouse_button_pressed
- Mouse_button_shift_state
- Mouse_canvas
- Mouse_item
- Mouse_record
- Mouse_x_pos
- Mouse_y_pos
- Record_status
- Suppress_working
- Trigger_block
- Trigger_item
- Trigger_record

Reusable Components

One of the primary goals of developing forms is to avoid duplicating work, and allow for easy maintenance. It is tedious and error-prone to maintain each item separately. Using Visual Attribute Groups (VAGs) and Property Classes to create "templates" of properties for items speeds application design, provides a common look and feel to the application, and makes it easier to implement design changes.

Visual Attribute Groups

Visual Attribute Groups (VAGs) control the appearance of an object by defining properties for fonts, colors, and patterns. VAGs are user-defined sets of properties. They are "shortcuts" to apply font, color, and pattern properties to an item without updating each property individually.

Changing a property in the VAG automatically propagates that change to each item that references the VAG.

VAGs can be assigned to Prompts, Frame title information, and all other interface items. When dealing with font and color properties, it is important that you do not leave any of the properties in the section set to the default value of <unspecified>. Doing so can lead to unpredictable results at run time.

VAGs are created under the Visual Attributes node in the Object Navigator. A VAG does not have a physical representation. Instead, it is used by other objects using the Visual Attribute Group property of that object.

Multiple-record blocks often have the current row highlighted, so the user can more easily see what data she is working with. This is accomplished by creating a new VAG with the font and color properties for the highlighted row. The VAG is then assigned to the Current Record Visual Attribute Group property for the block, or assigned to each individual item.

Property Classes

VAGs only allow the properties for colors, fonts, and patterns to be applied. To allow the same user-defined template for nonvisual attributes, Property Classes must be used.

Property Classes do for other properties what VAGs do for visual attribute properties. A Property Class can control size, location, behavior, and other properties. With Property Classes, you can assemble multiple properties and their values into groups, and then assign these groups to various form objects. Properties can be added and removed from the Property Class property sheet and have a value assigned to them.

Objects that have properties assigned to them in this way are called subclassed items. Subclassing an object creates a link between the "master object" and the item you are linking it to. All the properties of the Property Class are assigned to the object.

As with VAGs, if the properties of the Property Class are changed, the new values are propagated to all the subclassed items. If one part of the VAG or Property Class is overridden manually, the remaining inherited properties will remain synchronized.

Object Groups

Object Groups are simply a way of bundling together various elements in a form so they can be used by many forms in the application. Having VAGs and Property Classes set up in each form still means that you would have to change each form to implement a system-wide change. Putting these items in an Object Group means that they can be shared. The Object Group is simply a container that is then associated with each form that you want to share the object with. Adding or removing any object from the object group automatically updates any form that includes the object group.

Items are added to Object Groups in the Object Navigator by dragging and dropping the object you want to include. The Object Group is then referenced in each form.

Object Libraries

However, Object groups are used to collect items for easy transport into an Object Library, which expands the concept of reuse even further. Object Libraries are used by the development team only and are not part of the application itself, but they provide a common library of reusable items.

There are several benefits to using Object Libraries during application development:

- Object Libraries are automatically reopened when you start up Forms Builder.

- Object Libraries can be updated and the changes immediately are available to the development team
- You can associate multiple Object Libraries with an application. For example, you may have a generic library that contains corporate-wide standards, and a smaller library for project-specific items.
- You can use an Object Library to create, maintain, and distribute standard reusable objects, rapidly create application using predefined objects that can be dropped into a form, and enforce standards for the look and feel and behavior in an application.

Any Forms object can be stored in an Object Library, except for a form itself. The Object Library can be used to create reusable blocks, triggers, and other major components of the application. Additionally, Object Libraries support the creation of "SmartClasses," a special type of object that makes building forms as easy as drag-and-drop.

Simply create a library (in the Object Library Node of the Navigator) and drag and drop the items into it. Save the library and it becomes available to Forms Builder. To use an object from the Object Library, drag it from the Object Library into the destination form. You have the option to subclass the object, which creates a link to the "master" object in the Object Group; or to copy the item, which creates an independent copy of the object in the destination form and "disconnects" it from the master.

The VAGs, Property Classes, and other objects are instantly available. Like the properties of a VAG or Property Class, items within the object library propagate to the linked forms automatically.

SmartClasses

A SmartClass is a special type of object that is created within an object library. It is a "rubber stamp" to create objects with the same properties, or to apply the properties to an existing object. An object based on a SmartClass is subclassed; it inherits its functionality and appearance from the SmartClass. You can SmartClass nearly every type of object in a form: windows, canvases, blocks, buttons, etc.

SmartClasses can be used two ways:

- You can create new objects in the form based on the SmartClass by dragging the SmartClass object from the object library into the form.
- You can apply the SmartClass properties to an existing object by choosing the SmartClass from the pop-up menu.

SmartClasses support a "building-block" approach to application development. They can be used to easily distribute design standards by creating SmartClass objects for each type of item in your application and distributing these SmartClasses within an object library to the development team.

Shared PL/SQL Code

One of the most important ways to speed development and reuse Oracle Forms 10*g* components is to share the code that is written in triggers. You can do this by using Program Units, PL/SQL Libraries, and by referencing PL/SQL code in the database.

Program Units provide a means of writing PL/SQL code that can be called from multiple triggers. Program Units contain PL/SQL code that is local to the form and may contain packages, procedures, and functions. Program Units within the form can reference forms objects, system objects, and global objects. However, putting the Program Units into PL/SQL Libraries allows you to share the code across multiple forms. PL/SQL Libraries are collections of packages, procedures, and functions that are deployed as separate modules in your application. Like their local counterparts, PL/SQL Libraries can reference forms objects, systems objects, and global objects. However, because they are outside of the form scope, they must use special built-ins to reference the objects within a form indirectly. These special built-ins are listed below.

- **Name_in** References the object by the name you specify. For example:
  - name_in('s_emp.photo');
- **Copy** Copies the specified value into the object with the name you specify. For example:
  - copy('myvalue', 's_emp.photo');

Think of indirect referencing as dealing with the value of the object that has the name you specify.

A PL/SQL Library is deployed as an executable file just like your forms are. When the form runs, it tries to reference the code in the library (.plx or .pll) files that are located in a specific location. When you attach a library to a form, you have the option of hard-coding the path into the attachment or removing it:

- If you do not remove the path, Forms will look in the specified directory only for the file you have attached. If you move the file, the form will no longer be able to attach the library.
- If you remove the path, Forms will look in the path specified by your forms90_path and oracle_path in the registry/environment variables. In a production environment, you nearly always remove the library path.

At run time, Forms Developer prefers the compiled version (.plx) of a PL/SQL Library. However, if the compiled version cannot be found, then the source version (.pll) will be used. If you have problems with changes in your code not "seeming to take effect," it may be because there is a compiled older version of your code in the directory direct path path. As long as you do not change the signature of any of the program units in the library, a new version of a PL/SQL library can be created and deployed without having to recompile any of the forms that use it.

Finally, Forms can reference any code in the database. However, PL/SQL code in the database cannot reference forms items because the PL/SQL engine in the database does not understand the Forms built-ins.

Summary

Oracle Forms 10*g* is a powerful development environment that integrates with Oracle database seamlessly. It is one of the most mature Oracle development tools and, as such, has a rich feature set, large installed base of Oracle Forms developers, and an extensive amount of material available regarding Oracle Forms programming techniques on sources such as Oracle Technology Network (http://otn.oracle.com) and Oracle MetaLink (http://metalink.oracle.com) to assist the Oracle developer in overcoming virtually any development challenge. Starting with Oracle Forms 9*i* and continuing with Oracle Forms 10*g*, Oracle has made the commitment to web-based deployment, streamlining the process for deploying Oracle Forms to the Web via Oracle Application Server 10*g*. The process and details for deploying Oracle Forms on the Web are covered in Chapter 6.

CHAPTER 4

Oracle Reports 10g

s the development and deployment requirements of Oracle-based applications have grown increasingly complex, Oracle has responded to the challenge by providing development tools that not only seamlessly integrate with the Oracle database, but also provide development teams with all of the tools necessary to meet the challenges of the intricate development and deployment requirements imposed upon them. One of the most mature and stable development tools of the Oracle Internet Development Suite (iDS) is Oracle Reports 10*g*. This tool allows the creation of highly complex reports satisfying virtually every reporting need within an organization.

The goal of Oracle Reports 10*g* is to provide the developer with an environment to publish "*any* data in *any* format, *anywhere*." This design goal is necessary as modern developers face significant integration issues where homogeneous hardware and software environments are a thing of the past. Oracle Reports 10*g*, like all of Oracle's other development tools, fully embraces open standards and gives organizations the flexibility to integrate different types of data and deliver it in all major formats used in modern web deployment. The data sources that can be used include:

- SQL
- PL/SQL
- XML
  - File-based
  - Online (via HTTP, HTTPS, or FTP)
- Java Database Connectivity (JDBC)
- Text files
- Oracle Online Analytical Processing (OLAP)

Oracle also provides an open Java Application Programming Interface (API) for adding additional data sources.

Publishing Reports

"Publishing" refers to the way a report is delivered to end users. When it comes to reports, both paper and web-based reports are used in almost every organization. It is, therefore, a requirement that any reporting tool be flexible enough to publish reports in a variety of different formats. Optimally, the reporting tool would allow these reports to be published in these different formats without requiring any significant changes to the code or structure of the report. As we'll discuss in this chapter, Oracle Reports 10*g* allows developers to publish reports in the following formats with virtually no modification to the report itself:

- Paper layout:
  - **RTF (Rich Text Format)** Allows report to be opened in Microsoft Word, StarOffice, or OpenOffice

- **PDF (Portable Document Format)** Allows report to be opened and viewed in Adobe Acrobat
- **HTML/HTMLCSS** For printing from a web page

- Web layout:
  - JSP (JavaServer Pages)
  - HTML/HTMLCSS?CSS stands for Cascading Style Sheets
  - XML (eXtensible Markup Language)

Delivering the finished report to those who need access to it is not a task to be taken lightly. While the simplest method (that of making the report available on a web server and having users access it through a web browser) is relatively simple to implement, other delivery methods can be more demanding. Luckily, Oracle Reports 10*g* provides numerous methods of delivering the finished report. These methods include:

- File
- Printer
- Cache (to be displayed directly in a browser)
- E-mail (via SMTP, or Simple Mail Transfer Protocol)
- Oracle Portal 10*g*
- FTP (File Transfer Protocol)
- WebDAV (Web Distributed Authoring and Versioning)

Oracle Reports and Oracle Portal

If you have any familiarity with Oracle Portal, you know that it contains wizards to create both forms and reports. While blessed with a very small learning curve, the capabilities and features sets of the forms and reports components in Oracle Portal pale in comparison to the equivalent Oracle Forms 10*g* and Oracle Reports 10*g* products. We discuss Oracle Portal and the integration of Oracle Reports in Chapters 8 through 11.

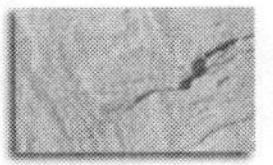

NOTE
This is not to imply that the forms and reports components of Oracle Portal 10g are not worthy of investigation—they are incredibly powerful wizard-based components that allow the developer to create forms and reports to be deployed exclusively on the Web with sophisticated features such as advanced security and visual templates in a very short period of time. The Oracle Forms 10g and Oracle Reports 10g products have richer feature sets, however, allowing the developer to control virtually every aspect of the deployed application. The forms and reports components of Oracle Portal will be discussed in detail in Chapter 9. Integrating forms and reports developed with Oracle Forms 10g and Oracle Reports 10g into Oracle Portal is discussed in Chapter 11.

Oracle provides a migration tool that allows you to import reports developed in Oracle Portal 10*g* into Oracle Reports 10*g*. This way, an Oracle Portal report that needs to be enhanced beyond what is available in Oracle Portal can be modified in Oracle Reports 10*g*. It is then possible to re-integrate the report back into Oracle Portal.

Oracle Reports 10*g* Development Environment

All of these features would be irrelevant if the process for developing reports was arduous for developers. Oracle Reports 10*g* provides a WYSIWYG editor (WYSIWYG stands for what you see is what you get) and tools to preview your work for both paper and web-based layouts and a JavaServer Pages (JSP) engine. The developer has the choice of using layout and data wizards to generate much of the code necessary for a finished report, or to bypass these wizards entirely, giving the developer total control of all report aspects. Even if the wizards are used, the developer still has the ability to enhance the code generated by the wizards. The wizards are what is termed "reentrant," meaning that even after manual modifications to the reports have been made by the developer, the wizards can be run again with fields in the wizards populated with the changes (and vice versa).

There are many advanced features of Oracle Reports 10*g*. Some of these include:

- A Java import program to generate wrapper PL/SQL packages for Java classes. (This is new to Reports, but PL2Java has been around for some time.)
- Oracle JDeveloper 10*g* integration for development and debugging of Reports JSPs.
- Oracle Software Configuration Management (SCM) integration for source control.

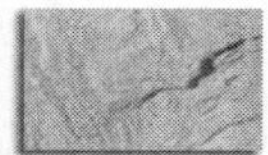

TIP

These advanced features are beyond the scope of this book. For more information, see the online Reports documentation at http://docs.oracle.com or http://tahiti.oracle.com.

Reports Builder

Reports Builder is the program that allows developers to create and test all of the objects that constitute an Oracle Report. These report objects include:

- Data model objects
- Layout objects
- Parameter Form objects
- PL/SQL objects
- References to external PL/SQL libraries
- Code shown in the Web Source view (for JSP-based web reports)

Data Model Objects

These objects provide the data that will be displayed on the report. They include:

- **Queries** Queries are used to query database(s) and provide the base data for your reports. They can be built using report or data wizards or can be constructed manually.

As mentioned before, multiple data sources are available including Oracle (SQL and PL/SQL), XML, JDBC, etc.

- **Groups** Groups are used to organize columns in a report. They can be used to either separate a query's data into sets producing break levels in a report, or filter a query's data, conditionally removing records from result sets. This is a very powerful feature of Oracle Reports as it allows queries run against the database to be as simple as possible and shifts complex reporting requirements (summaries, grouping, etc.) to the reports engine, distributing the load more evenly among your hardware components.
- **Groups** When you define a query for your report, Reports Builder automatically creates a corresponding column in the data model. The real power of columns is in their flexibility. Developers can:
  - Create new columns manually for summary and formula columns
  - Reassign columns to a different group
  - Define a column as a graphic column, allowing graphics to be read out of the database (or from a file on the server) and displayed directly on reports
  - Define Formula columns (user-created columns that get data from a PL/SQL function or expression, a SQL statement, or a combination), Summary columns (columns that perform a computation on another column's data), and Placeholder columns (columns for which the datatype and value are set by the developer in PL/SQL)
- **Links** Links are used to link data on a report made up of a master-detail query. The query that provides the detail data is executed once for each record in the parent group matching the criteria.

Layout Objects

These objects are used to control the look of your report:

- **Frames** Used to protect objects on your report from being overwritten or moved by other objects. Frames are commonly used to protect column headings and all objects in a group to ensure they maintain their relative positions during printing.
- **Repeating frames** Used on the fields that are created for a group's columns to protect them from being overwritten or moved by other objects. Repeating frames fire once for each record of the group. Repeating frames can enclose any layout object, including other repeating frames.
- **Fields** Used as placeholders for parameters, columns, etc. The most common usage for fields is to display data queried from the database, but they are also useful for displaying information that does not come directly from the database or is derived from data queried from the database. Examples of this include values specified on a parameter form, page number of the report, date report was executed, user executing the report, etc. Formulas (PL/SQL functions) are commonly used to populate fields.
- **Boilerplate** Used to print text or draw graphics that appear every time a report is executed. In the paper layout of the report editor, there are numerous tools in the tool

palette to help developers draw the necessary boilerplate objects to be used in their reports. The report editor is discussed later in this chapter. Boilerplate objects can also be links to a file or even to a URL where the image is located.

- **Anchors** Used to align objects. Anchors fasten an edge of one object to an edge of another object, ensuring that they maintain their relative positions. When data is queried, it is possible that the size of some layout objects may be altered by the data being returned. Anchors maintain the relative positions of objects. Implicit anchors are generated that determine which objects, if any, can overwrite an object. By default, objects are anchored to the upper-left corner of their enclosing object. Developers can also create explicit anchors, which will automatically override any implicit anchoring for an object.

Parameter Form Objects

Reports Builder includes a tool called the Parameter Form Builder that allows the developer to define which parameters the end user can enter before running a report. You are not limited, however, to the standard parameter display generated by the Parameter Form Builder tool. Additionally, the developer can create boilerplate text with HTML tags for adding hyperlinks or any other HTML tagged text to your Paper Parameter Form, insert parameter fields with JavaScript (for defining input or select events), or create a Parameter Form header or footer for placing a logo or link in the header or footer of the HTML Parameter Form.

PL/SQL Objects

The PL/SQL objects supported by Oracle Reports 10*g* can be broken down into two categories:

- **Program units** Reports Builder includes the PL/SQL editor. This editor allows developers to create PL/SQL objects (packages, functions, or procedures) *stored and executed in the report*. These PL/SQL objects are sometimes referred to as local program units. PL/SQL objects created with this editor have no corresponding PL/SQL object created in the database. By embedding the PL/SQL code in the report, the execution of the PL/SQL program handled by the Reports Server and the load is more evenly distributed (assuming, of course, that the reports server is on a machine other than the database). Local program units can be used by other reports by placing them into a library. These libraries can then be attached to other reports, giving the report access to all packages, functions, and procedures contained within the library. Reports Builder also includes the Stored PL/SQL editor, which allows the creation and modification of PL/SQL program units stored in the database, sometimes referred to as stored program units.
- **Triggers** Report triggers execute PL/SQL functions at specific times during the execution and formatting of your report. There are five report triggers available (developers cannot create report triggers), the names of which should be self-explanatory:
    - **Before Report trigger** Fires before the data is fetched and the report is executed but after the queries are parsed.
    - **After Report trigger** Fires after report output is sent to a specified destination. (There is a Java API included with Reports for writing your own destination.)

- **Between Pages trigger** Fires before each page of the report is formatted, except the very first page.
- **Before Parameter Form trigger** Fires before the Runtime Parameter Form is displayed.
- **After Parameter Form trigger** Fires after the Runtime Parameter Form is displayed.

Reports Builder Components

Reports Builder provides a number of wizards and graphical editing tools to assist developers in creating reports. This chapter will start off by using the wizards to create a simple master-detail report, and then explore the advanced features of Oracle Reports 10*g* by enhancing the report manually. Chapter 6 will explore how to incorporate Oracle Reports into your web environment and Chapter 11 will discuss how to incorporate Reports into OracleAS Portal.

NOTE
*The example report created in this chapter is created off of the demo schemas that are included with the infrastructure database installed as a part of Oracle Application Server 10*g.

Reports Builder consists of various programs and wizards that provide the developer with all the necessary tools to build reports that are robust, scalable, and secure. Navigating around these integrated tools all happens within the Reports Builder desktop. Oracle Reports 10*g* provides great flexibility by not only giving the developer numerous ways of accomplishing almost any task, but by also providing numerous ways of invoking the various tools and wizards within Reports Builder. One of the obstacles many beginning Reports developers struggle with is determining where a task, such as creating a report trigger or altering the layout of a report, is performed. Oracle Reports 10*g* is a mature product with many advanced features, and mastering these features will take a reasonable amount of time. The development tools and wizards have been assembled in a logical manner, thankfully, so while the Reports Builder windows may seem like a dizzying array of graphical objects, the learning curve is surprisingly short. In this chapter, we'll cover building a simple report using the Report Wizard, and then explore the advanced features of Oracle Reports 10*g* by manually adding enhancements to it.

Wizards

Reports Builder is made up of numerous wizards to assist in the construction of your report. The report objects created and the code they generate is available for modification and enhancement to the developer at all times. One of the most powerful features of the wizards is the capability to run them over and over. After the initial code and layout has been generated, the wizards will automatically pick up on any modifications you have made to your report manually if you choose to run them again.

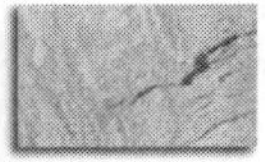

TIP
It is not necessary to use any of the wizards provided with Oracle Reports 10g. For developers uncomfortable with such tools, it is entirely possible to create every aspect of a report by hand.

The Report Wizard

Unless it has specifically been turned off, a dialog box asking how you would like to begin using Reports Builder is displayed upon starting the program. Selecting the first option, "Designing: Use the Report Wizard," begins the Report Wizard that walks the developer through a series of questions regarding the following characteristics of a report:

- **Layout** Reports can have a web layout (for reports designed to be displayed on the Web), a paper layout (for reports designed to be printed), or the wizard can generate both types of layouts.
- **Style** The most common types of reports are
  - **Tabular** The report is organized in a multicolumn, multirow format, with each column corresponding to a column selected from the database. The output is similar to that of a spreadsheet.
  - **Group Left/Above** These reports suppress the repetition of values in a report by "breaking," or dividing, the rows of table based on a common value in one of the columns. Group Left reports prints the common value to the left of the associated rows; Group Above prints the common value above the associated rows and is a good choice for master-detail reports where the master record does not contain a lot of information.
  - **Matrix reports** These reports need grouping calculations performed on both its rows and columns simultaneously. Matrix reports are beyond the scope of this book.
- **Data source** The data source defines where the data is queried. See the list of data sources listed earlier in this chapter.
- **Query** Query defines the query.
- **Fields displayed on the report** Not all fields specified in the query have to be printed on the report. It is possible, for example, to write a trigger at the group level to display a particular value based on the value of a column retrieved from the database, without displaying the retrieved column.
- **Summary columns** Summary columns define where functions such as count, average, or sum are applied to any of the columns in a report.
- **Templates** Templates define visual temples for your finished report.

In most cases, the Report Wizard is the first step the developer performs to build a report.

The Data Wizard

The Data Wizard is a subset of the Reports Wizard incorporating the Data Source, Query, Fields Displayed on the Report, and Summary columns pages. The Data Wizard can be used to modify queries already defined for the report without having to revisit all of the questions posed by the Report Wizard.

The Graph Wizard

The Graph Wizard is used to create graphs that become part of your report. The graphs that are produced become JSP tags. Graph attributes include title, subtitle, footnote, and axis title. References to user parameters, system parameters, and columns in the text can be used to display their value at run time. The Graph Wizard includes templates to create all of the standard graphs commonly found on reports: bar, line, area, pie, and combination graphs.

Major Reports Components

There are many components of Oracle Reports Builder 10*g* that are intended to provide the developer with a rich graphical environment. These components are designed so that the developer has complete control over virtually every aspect of the report, yet needs to write a minimum of code to achieve the objectives of the report. Navigating your way through the many components of Oracle Reports 10*g* can be difficult even for experienced developers. The following paragraphs detail the major components of Oracle Reports 10*g*, their functions, and what they look like.

NOTE

Like any rich development environment, Oracle Reports 10g provides the developer with numerous ways of solving problems. It cannot be stressed enough that there is no single "right" way to solve a particular problem. As such, the example tutorial in this chapter is but one way to create a basic report. As a developer, your goal should be to get yourself to the point where you can solve a variety of different problems using different tools and techniques quickly and efficiently. The more flexibility and creativity you can demonstrate, the more invaluable you'll become to your company. An analogy we often use is to compare software development with the construction of a house. If you were to take on the task of building a house, you had better become proficient at using a variety of tools. Would you try to build a house using just a hammer? (You wouldn't need a hammer to build Larry Ellison's house as there are no nails anywhere, but that's another story.) As the saying goes, "People who only have a hammer see every problem as a nail." Don't be the developer who only has a hammer in your toolbox.

Object Navigator

The Object Navigator (see Figure 4-1) is designed to give a hierarchical view of all of the elements that make up your report. As you expand the categories (by clicking the "plus" signs to the left of each heading), you'll see that there are a multitude of different objects that can make up your report. It may seem overwhelming if you count up how many different objects can be used to make up a report (even a simple one), but by walking through basic report elements, it will be demonstrated how easy it is to build a simple report quickly and find the necessary report objects in the Object Navigator when it comes time to modify them.

Property Inspector

Almost every element that makes up your report has properties that describe how it looks and behaves. If we were to describe a car, it has various properties that describe it, such as its make, model, year, color, engine size, etc. If we were to list the attributes of a laptop computer, it would have some properties similar to a car: make, model, color, but other properties unique to a laptop: memory, hard disk size, etc. (Yes, yes, we know that some cars have MP3 players with hard disks in them, but ignore that for now.) Likewise, the objects that make up an Oracle Report have numerous attributes, some of which are shared among different reports objects.

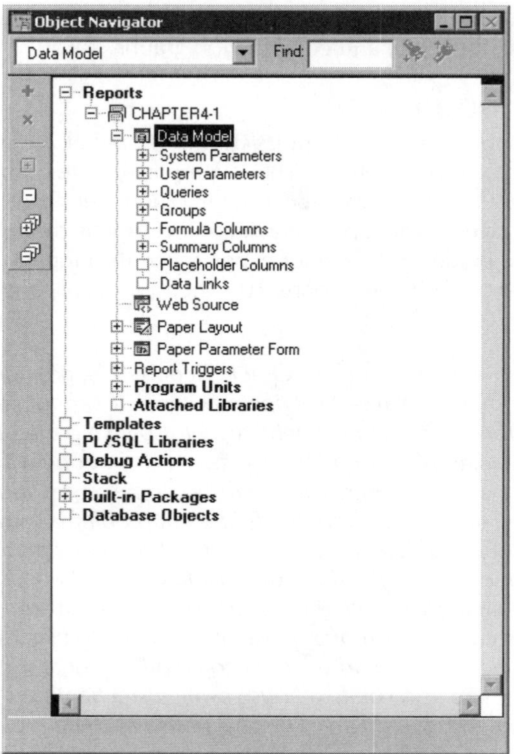

FIGURE 4-1. *The Object Navigator*

The Property Inspector (see Figure 4-2) shows all of the properties of a particular report object or group of objects. As we'll discuss shortly, the Property Inspector gives you the ability to compare and set properties for multiple report objects simultaneously. This is invaluable for maintaining a consistent look and feel in your report.

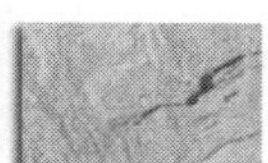

NOTE

*Figure 4-2 was purposely taken from a Unix version of Oracle Reports 10g (running on Red Hat Linux Advanced Server 2.1) to show the subtle differences in the display between the Microsoft Windows and Unix versions of Oracle Reports 10*g*. While some of the Reports Builder screens and windows display differently, all the functionality of Oracle Reports 10*g* is the same between platforms.*

Report Editor

The Report Editor is one of the more complex screens in Oracle Reports 10*g*. When the Report Editor is invoked, the developer has the option of viewing five different aspects of the report corresponding to the five buttons in the top left of the Report Editor window (see Figure 4-3).

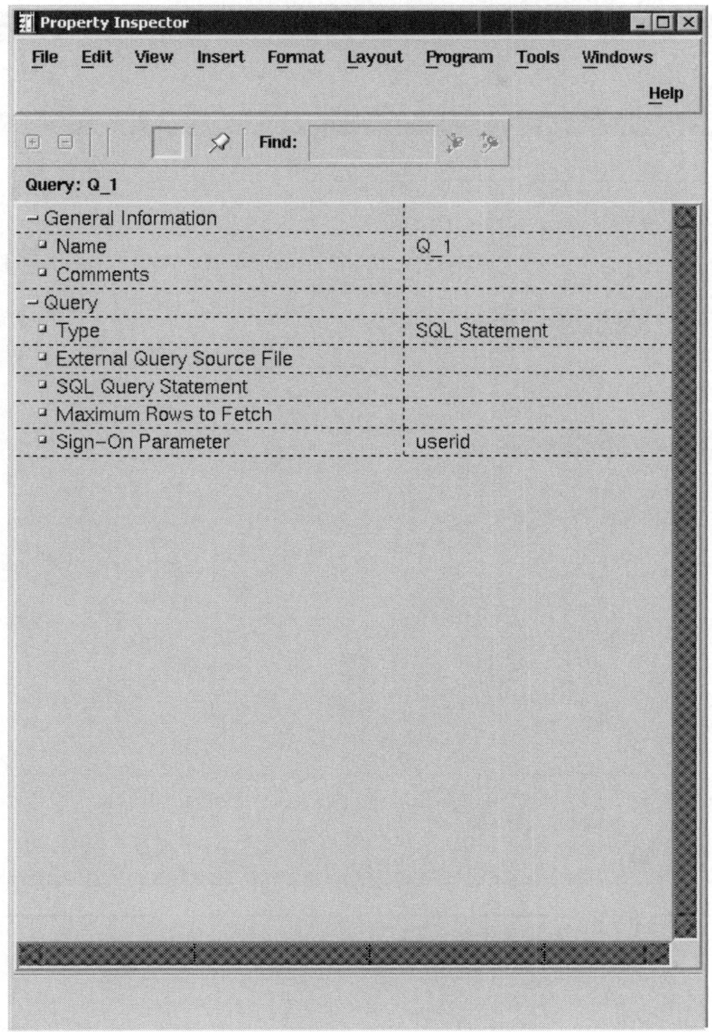

FIGURE 4-2. *The Property Inspector*

The first (left-most) button corresponds to the Data Model view (which is displayed in Figure 4-3). This window shows a graphical representation of the query (or queries) that drives the report. It allows the developer to construct or modify a query and to visualize the relationships between tables. For a simple query involving one or two tables, this screen may not seem to be of much use, but can greatly assist the developer when creating complex reports involving

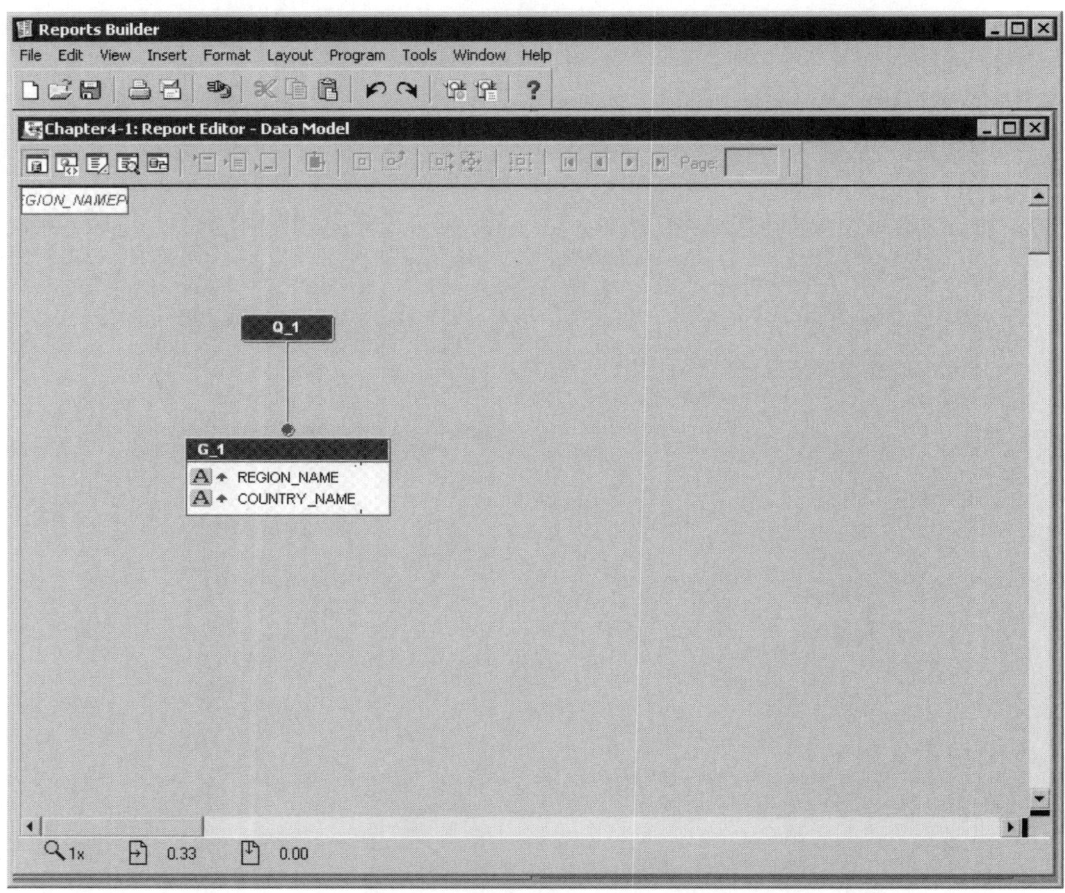

FIGURE 4-3. *The Report Editor window*

numerous tables. Like almost all of the wizards and reports components, the data model can be reentered after changes have been made. An example of this would be the use of the Reports Wizard to modify an existing query. Reentering the data model will reflect any changes made there (and vice versa).

The second left-most button corresponds to the Web Source view (see Figure 4-4). If the Reports Wizard was chosen to construct the report, an option is presented to generate a Paper Layout, a Web Layout, or both. Choosing a Web Layout or both will automatically generate JSP

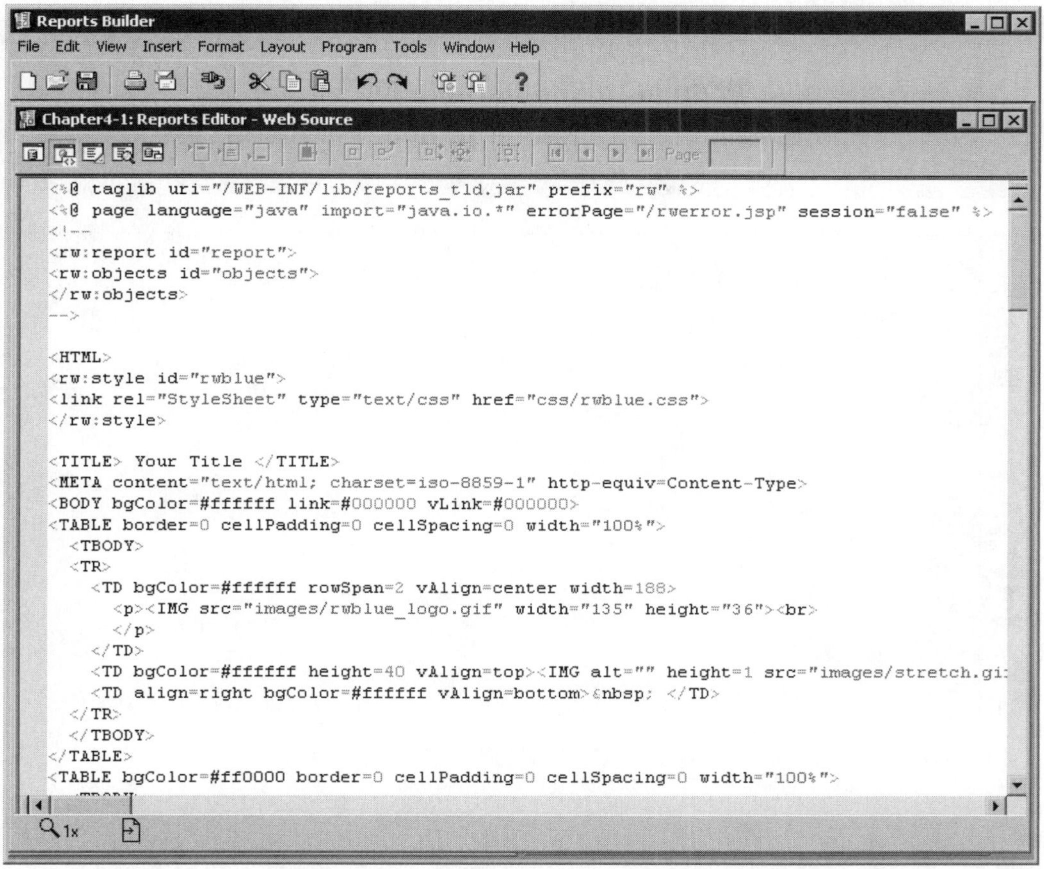

```
<%@ taglib uri="/WEB-INF/lib/reports_tld.jar" prefix="rw" %>
<%@ page language="java" import="java.io.*" errorPage="/rwerror.jsp" session="false" %>
<!--
<rw:report id="report">
<rw:objects id="objects">
</rw:objects>
-->

<HTML>
<rw:style id="rwblue">
<link rel="StyleSheet" type="text/css" href="css/rwblue.css">
</rw:style>

<TITLE> Your Title </TITLE>
<META content="text/html; charset=iso-8859-1" http-equiv=Content-Type>
<BODY bgColor=#ffffff link=#000000 vLink=#000000>
<TABLE border=0 cellPadding=0 cellSpacing=0 width="100%">
  <TBODY>
  <TR>
    <TD bgColor=#ffffff rowSpan=2 vAlign=center width=188>
      <p><IMG src="images/rwblue_logo.gif" width="135" height="36"><br>
      </p>
    </TD>
    <TD bgColor=#ffffff height=40 vAlign=top><IMG alt="" height=1 src="images/stretch.gi
    <TD align=right bgColor=#ffffff vAlign=bottom>  </TD>
  </TR>
  </TBODY>
</TABLE>
<TABLE bgColor=#ff0000 border=0 cellPadding=0 cellSpacing=0 width="100%">
```

FIGURE 4-4. *The Web Source view of the Report Editor window*

code. The JSP code can be moved to your Reports Server to deploy Oracle Reports on the Web quickly and easily.

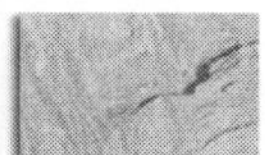

TIP
*The process of generating JSPs from within Oracle Reports 10*g *and moving them to the Web is discussed in Chapter 6.*

The third button corresponds to the Paper Layout view for the report (see Figure 4-5). On this page, the developer can arrange the elements of the report graphically, insert graphs driven by the data on the report, and insert header and footer text and graphics. The fourth button runs the

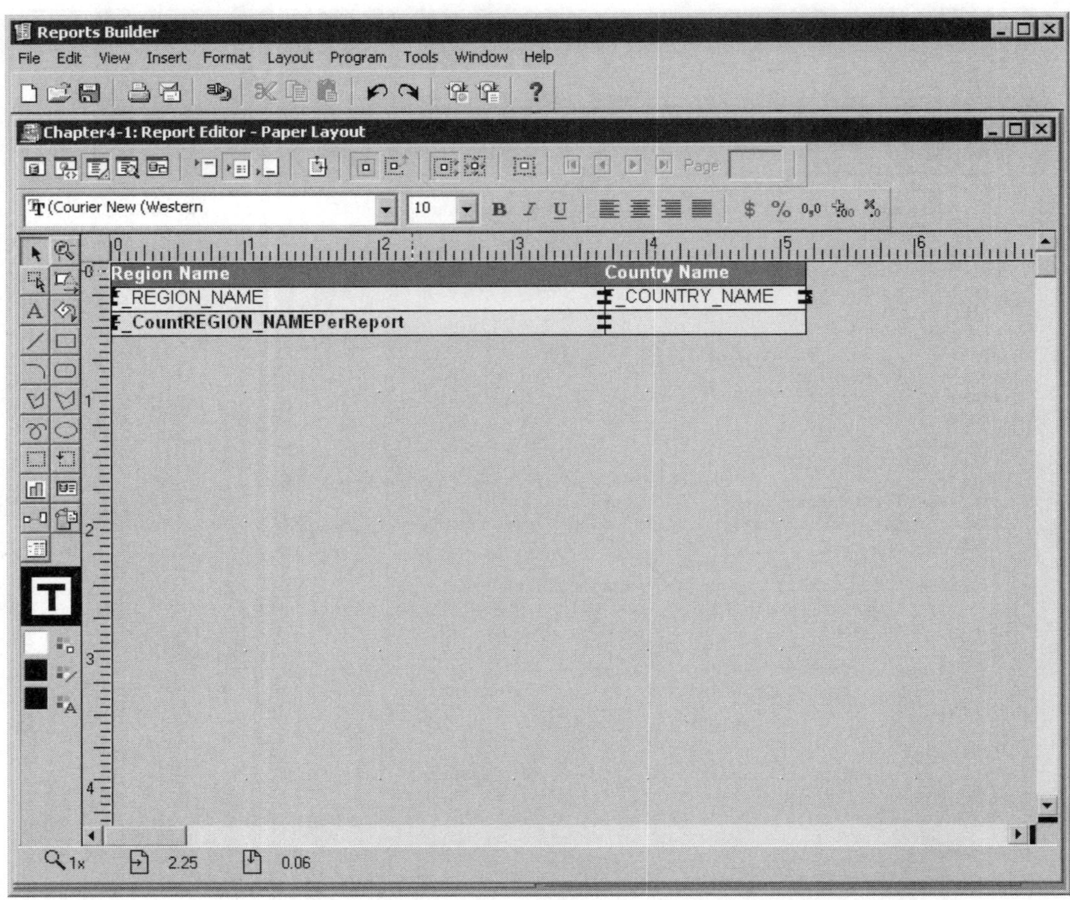

FIGURE 4-5. *The Paper Layout view of the Report Editor window*

report and displays the paper layout. The fifth button displays the Paper Parameter Form, where it is possible to design the form the end user will use to enter values that will drive the report (see Figure 4-6).

PL/SQL Editors

Two PL/SQL editors are provided with Oracle Reports 10*g* (see Figure 4-7). The Stored PL/SQL editor allows the developer to create PL/SQL program units that are stored in the database. The

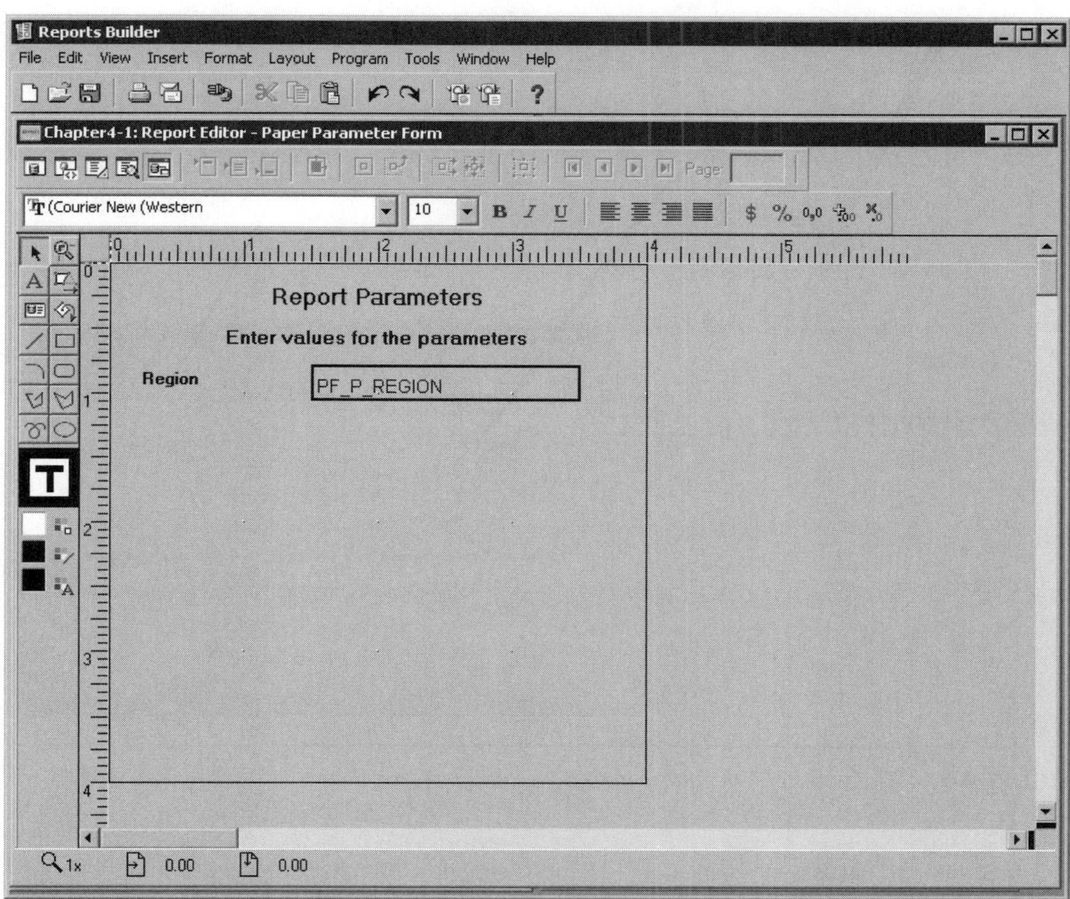

FIGURE 4-6. *The Paper Parameter Form view of the Report Editor window*

PL/SQL editor allows the developer to create PL/SQL program units stored in the report. In this manner, the developer has access to all of the benefits of a PL/SQL environment without the overhead of making calls over a network.

Triggers

The Database Trigger editor (see Figure 4-8) allows the creation of database triggers.

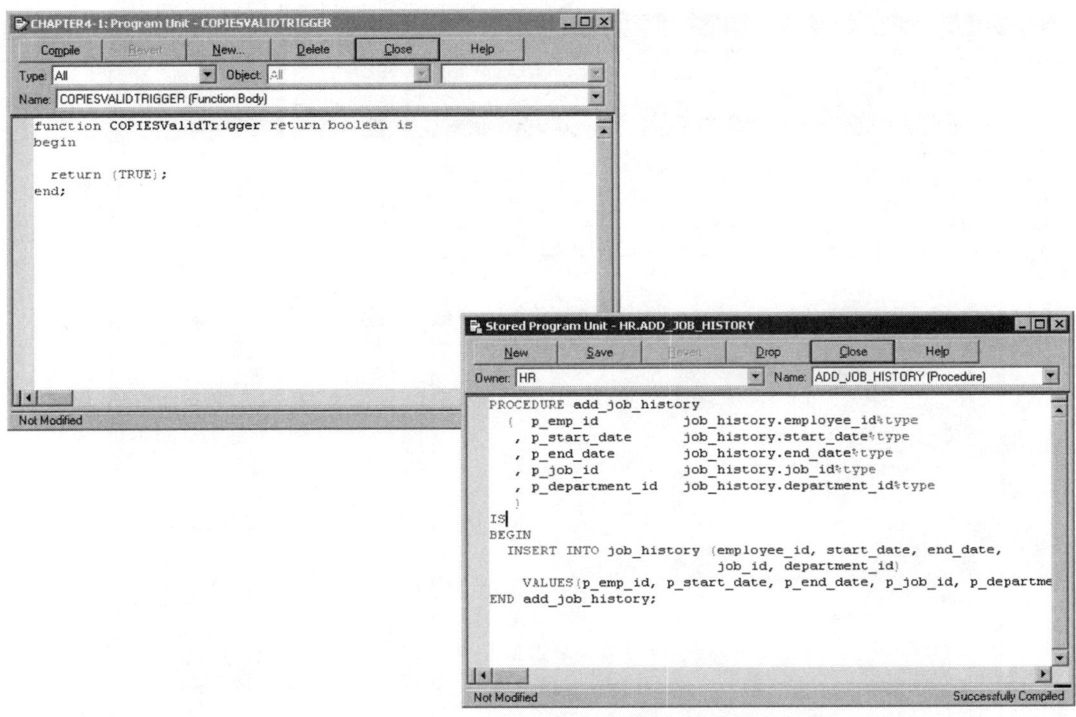

FIGURE 4-7. *The two PL/SQL editors in Oracle Reports 10g*

In addition to database triggers, Oracle Reports supports formatting triggers at both the group and field level. As we discussed earlier, there are also five report triggers defined by Oracle Reports 10*g* at the report level. Some of their most common uses include:

- **Before Parameter Form** Commonly used to get or initialize settings for the report before any interaction with the end user
- **After Parameter Form** Particularly useful for constructing a SQL statement to drive your report from values on your parameter form that do not correspond to values in the database; for example:
  - The database may contain values such as 10, 20, and 30 for regions in your company. While you could provide a drop-down list with 10, 20, 30 etc. in it, users will find greater meaning in values such as 'Asia', 'Europe', 'North America', etc. The After Parameter Form trigger can be used to translate a value in the drop-down list of a parameter form (i.e., 'Asia') to a value in the database (i.e., 10).
  - To provide a complex series of sorting or ordering criteria to your end users.

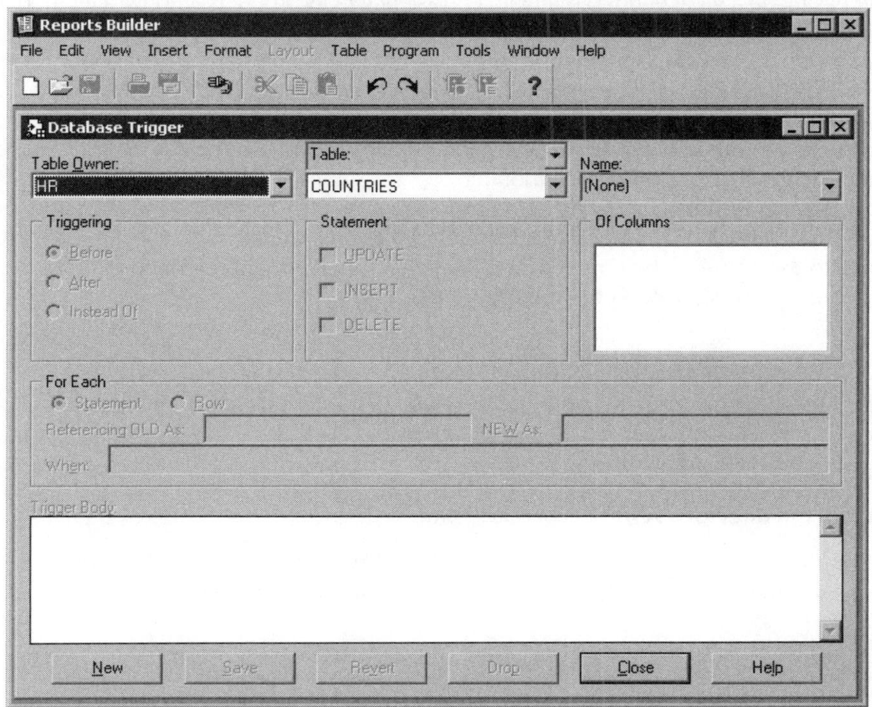

FIGURE 4-8. *The Database Trigger editor*

- **Before Report** Can be used to alter the report based on what parameters the end users select.
- **Between Pages** Executed between pages of a report; of limited practical use.
- **After Report** Useful for post-report processing such as sending an e-mail notification to selected users that a report has been generated.

Starting Reports Builder

Reports Builder is part of the Oracle Internet Developer Suite 10*g*. It is available for the Solaris, HP-UX, Linux, and Windows platforms.

NOTE
Oracle provides a certification matrix on the Oracle Technology Network (http://otn.oracle.com) that lists what products are officially supported on what platforms. This matrix is invaluable as it lists the service packs and operating system patches required for all Oracle products. Given this changes frequently, it is the authors' recommendation to visit this web site before attempting to install any Oracle products.

Oracle has made a great effort to maintain consistency in its products among different platforms. While the installation and look-and-feel of the products may appear identical between the Windows and Unix platforms, the method to invoke the executables and the necessary settings to run the executables differs greatly. This book gives examples for both Windows and Unix platforms (Red Hat Linux Advanced Server 2.1 was used, but there should be no significant differences between commands issued on a Linux machine and other Unix platforms, and where differences do occur, they are annotated).

To start Reports Builder on Windows, follow this path: Start -> Programs -> Oracle Developer Suite - <ORACLE_HOME> -> Reports Developer -> Reports Builder where <ORACLE_HOME> corresponds to the name of the Oracle home that was specified when Oracle Internet Developer Suite was installed. To start Reports Builder on Unix:

1. Open a command window.
2. Make sure your ORACLE_HOME environment variable points to the directory where Oracle Developer Suite 10*g* is installed. (This is critical if you have different Oracle products installed on your machine.)
3. cd to the directory $ORACLE_HOME/bin.
4. Run the rwbuilder.sh script (In Figure 4-9, ORACLE_HOME is /usr/iDS10*g*). After the splash screen, you should see a screen similar to the one in Figure 4-10.

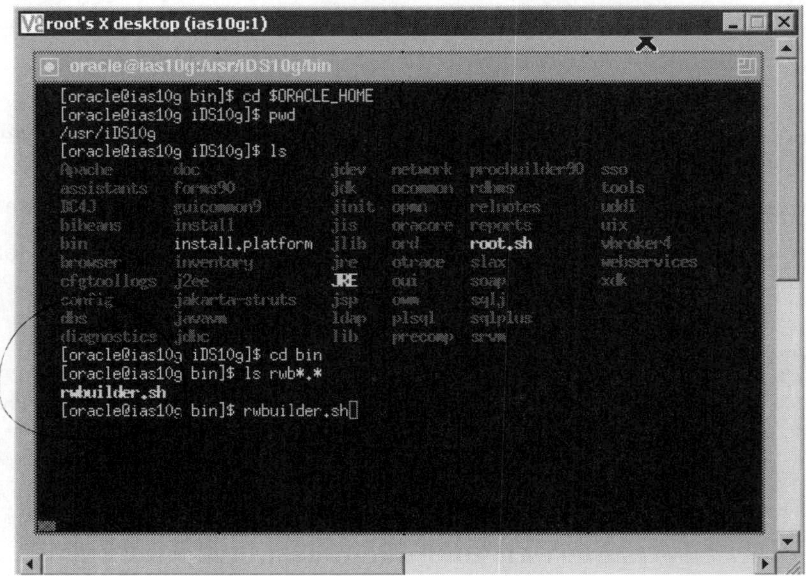

FIGURE 4-9. *Starting Report Builder in Unix*

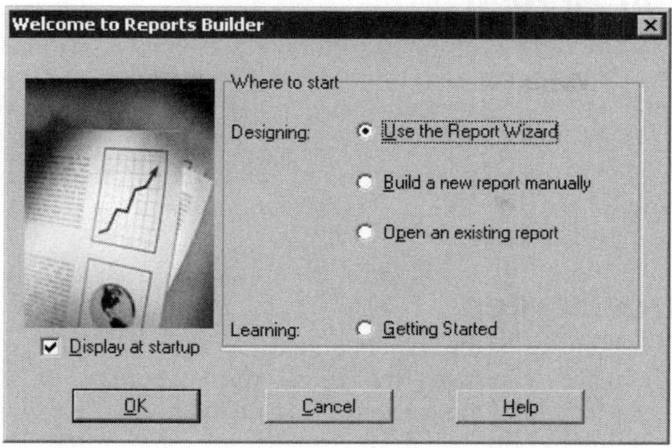

FIGURE 4-10. *The First Reports Builder page*

While it is certainly possible to build reports from scratch, in most cases, it is more productive to use the wizards to construct the report and manually enhance it later. For the example reports in this chapter, the hr schema that is included in the demo schemas included with the 9*i* infrastructure database will be used.

NOTE
If the demo schemas have not been added to your infrastructure database, you can add them manually by running the Database Configuration Assistant and selecting them in Step 4.

Building a Report with the Report Wizard

The Report Wizard creates all of the basic elements of an Oracle Report including the layout of the report, the query that will drive the report, the columns from the query to be displayed on the report, any calculations on those fields, the formatting of the displayed fields, and a template (if desired) to use when displaying the report. It is possible to build a report from scratch without using the reports wizard (by selecting the "Build a new report manually" radio button in Figure 4-10), but in most cases, it is more productive to use the reports wizard to define your report, and then add enhancements to it manually later. On the "Welcome to Report Builder" screen, select the "Use the Report Wizard" radio button and click OK.

The Layout Screen

The Report Wizard begins with a welcome screen. The next page of the reports wizard asks what type of layout will be used for the report. Layouts can be defined as a specification of how a report will be displayed. An Oracle report can have both a web layout and a paper layout, so that the report appears one way when displayed on the web and differently when printed. For now, select the "Create both Web and Paper layout" radio button and click "Next >."

The Report Style Screen

The next page of the Report Wizard allows developers to specify a report style. A report style defines how the report will group the rows returned by the query (or queries) that will drive the report. The most common choices are Tabular, Group Left, and Group Above. One of the most powerful features of the Report Wizard is the capability to go back and change any of the settings after the report is generated (you can also do this manually in the Object Navigator, which we discuss shortly). For now, select the "Tabular" radio button, name the report "Example1," and click "Next >."

The Data Source Screen

The next page of the wizard asks for the specification of a data source. Depending on what is selected on this screen, the following wizard page will display options for that particular type of query. This is another example of the powerful features built into Oracle Reports 10*g*, as the developer has the ability to pull data from virtually any data source. The data sources included are

- **Express Server Query** Lets you create a query that selects data from an Express Server. This feature is provided for backward compatibility only as Oracle Express Server, an OLAP database intended for data warehousing, has been discontinued by Oracle. Most of Oracle Express's sophisticated data warehousing technologies have been incorporated into the Oracle Database Server product.
- **JDBC Query** Lets you access any JDBC-enabled data source. The key word in that sentence is "any." As long as a valid JDBC driver is installed on the system and used to execute the report, Oracle Reports can pull data from it. This is an extremely powerful feature allowing reports to be built incorporating data from multiple databases in a single report without having to develop and test ETL (Extract, Transform, Load) programs or purchase expensive gateways. JDBC drivers exist for traditional data sources (SQL databases) such as Microsoft SQL Server, IBM DB2, and MySQL, but also exist for nontraditional data sources such as Microsoft Excel spreadsheets or ACT! (contact management) databases.

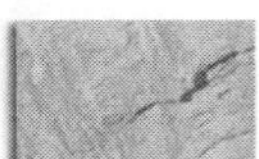

NOTE
JDBC drivers come in various levels, with a level 1 JDBC driver having the fewest number of features and a level 4 JDBC driver having the most. The cost of the higher-level drivers is greater, but is required for all but the most elemental forms of data access. For more information about JDBC drivers, go to http://java.sun.com/products/jdbc/driverdesc.html.

- **OLAP Query** Lets you create a query that selects from multidimensional Oracle Online Analytical Processing (OLAP) data stored in an Oracle database. For these types of queries, it is common to use a matrix layout on the previous page (report style) of the reports wizard.
- **SQL Query** The most common selection; highlighted automatically when entering this page of the wizard. Selecting this option will display a page that allows the

construction of a query to drive the report graphically. The Query Builder allows developers to select tables and columns to be included in the report while maintaining and displaying all referential integrity constraints. After building the query graphically, the developer has the option of modifying the query (such as adding where clauses, as an example).

- **Text Query** Allows developers to construct a report that queries data from a text file. Out of the box, Oracle Reports 10*g* supports three formats: Apache log file, text files with comma-delimited fields, and text files with space-delimited fields. Additional formats can be included via Pluggable Data Sources (PDS). See Chapter 42 of the Building Reports manual (Oracle Part # B10602-01),"Building a Report with a Text Pluggable Data Source," for more information on PDS.
- **XML Query** Lets you access an XML data file. A Document Type Definition (DTD) file, defining the elements and data structure contained in an XML document, is needed.

The Data Query Screen

Select "SQL Query" and click "Next >." The next page of the Report Wizard is where the definition of the query that will drive the report is specified. The developer has the option of typing out the query manually in the Data Source definition field, running the Query Builder to build the query graphically, or importing the query from a text file. To continue building the example report for this chapter, click the "Query Builder..." button to start the Query Builder. If this is the first time Query Builder has been selected in the current session, a dialog box requesting logon information is displayed. If a connection has already been established in the current Reports Builder session, Query Builder will automatically use that connection information. If a connect has already been established and a different connection is desired, click the "Connect..." button before clicking the "Query Builder..." button (different connection information can also be specified by selecting "File," then "Connect" in the Reports Builder menu). Connect to the HR schema in the database that gets installed with the infrastructure.

TIP
Alternatively, if you have access to another database with the HR demo schema and do not wish to connect directly to the Oracle Application Server 10g infrastructure database, feel free to do that.

NOTE
If you have Oracle E-Business Suite installed at your location, do not try to connect to the HR schema in that instance and attempt to create the report in the chapter against it. The HR schema in Oracle E-Business Suite is very different from the demo HR schema included with version 9i of the Oracle database.

On the Query Builder page, a dialog box with the tables and views owned by the schema, you are logged in, as shown in Figure 4-11. You can select tables, views, or snapshots from other schemas by selecting <LOCAL> in the drop-down box in the dialog and then selecting another schema. Only tables, views, and snapshots you have been granted select privileges on will be available. As the HR user, double-click on Regions, then double-click on Countries, then click "Close." A screen similar to Figure 4-12 is displayed.

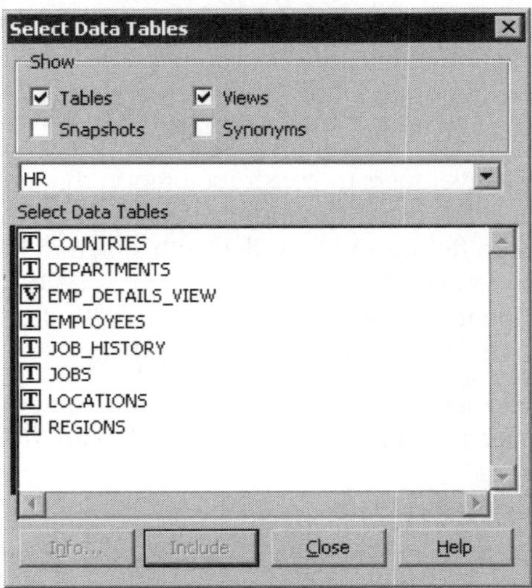

FIGURE 4-11. *Objects owned by the HR schema*

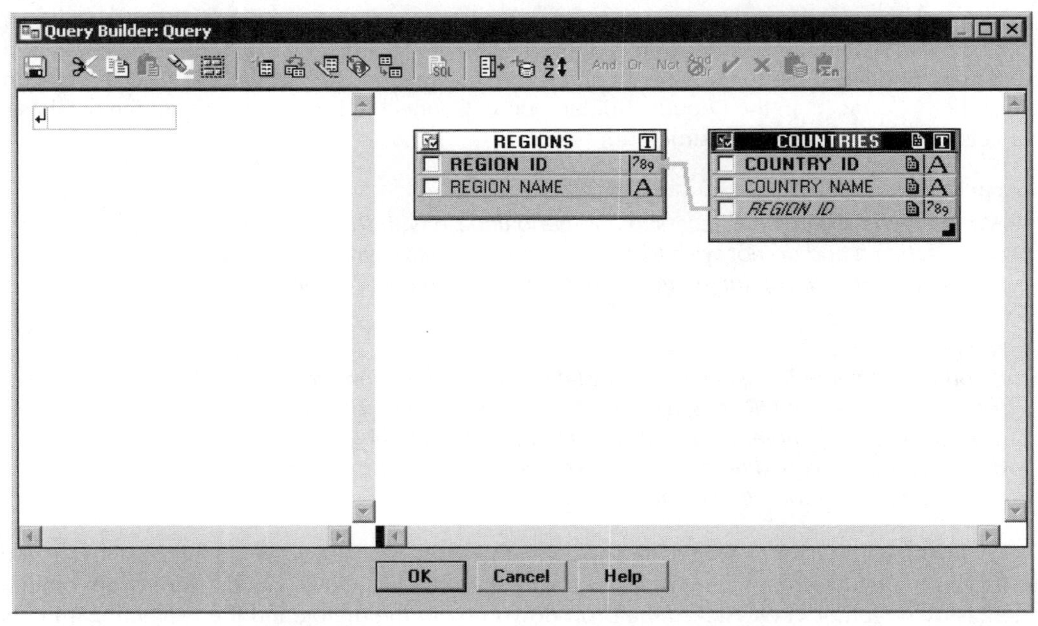

FIGURE 4-12. *The Query Builder screen*

The arrow connecting the two tables is a reflection of a foreign key relationship between the countries and regions tables. In this example, there is a one-to-many relationship between the two that can be stated like this: A single region is made up of one or many countries. Now that the tables making up the query have been selected, it's time to select the fields (columns) from those tables that will make up our query. Select the check boxes next to region_name and country_name and click "OK." Just because a column is selected on this screen, it does not necessarily mean it will be displayed on the report. The check boxes here only serve to specify which columns will be included in the query. Why would a column ever be selected to be part of the query, but not be displayed on a report? It is possible to alter the formatting of a group based on a value in the database, while not actually displaying the value. For example, a manager may want a report that prints products sold by the company that have the highest margins in a different color without actually printing the margin percentage. The margin percentage might be selected (or derived) from the database and used in a conditional formatting trigger to print the row corresponding to the product in a different color.

The data source definition now contains the following SQL that will be used to drive the report:

```
SELECT ALL REGIONS.REGION_NAME, COUNTRIES.COUNTRY_NAME
FROM REGIONS, COUNTRIES
WHERE (COUNTRIES.REGION_ID = REGIONS.REGION_ID)
```

The Data Columns and Data Calculations Screens

Click "Next >." The Fields page of the Report Wizard provides the capability to specify which fields will be displayed on the report. Click the double greater-than signs (>>) to move all of the columns to the right-hand pane. Click "Next >." The next page in the wizard allows calculations of the fields in the report to be specified. To see the total number of rows, make sure REGION_NAME is selected in the left-hand pane and click the "COUNT >" button in between the two frames. Click "Next >."

The Labels Page

The Labels page allows the developer to change the headings on the report. Oracle will make a guess based on the name of the column you are selecting out of the database. You can also change the width of the columns that will hold the data queried from the database. To see the effect of this, change the label that says "Count:" to "Region count:" and make its width 25. Click "Next >."

The Template Page

The final page of the wizard allows the developer to specify a template to be used when displaying the report. There are predefined templates, but they are of limited use as they include a graphic that says "Your Company, Inc.," which is hardly appropriate for a production report. The developer is not limited to these templates, as they can be created or modified. Choose "Blue" in the predefined template list and click "Finish." The report is then executed and the results are displayed on the screen (see Figure 4-13).

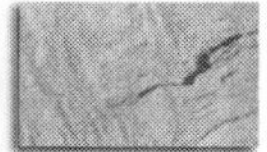

NOTE

Name this report Chapter4-1 and save it as a Reports Binary (.rdf) file. An .rdf file is specific to an operating system. In other words, it is not possible to take an .rdf developed on, say, a Microsoft Windows machine and run it on a Linux machine. In Chapter 6, we'll cover the steps to take a report developed on one machine to be run on another machine with a different operating system, as well as discuss saving the report as a JSP.*

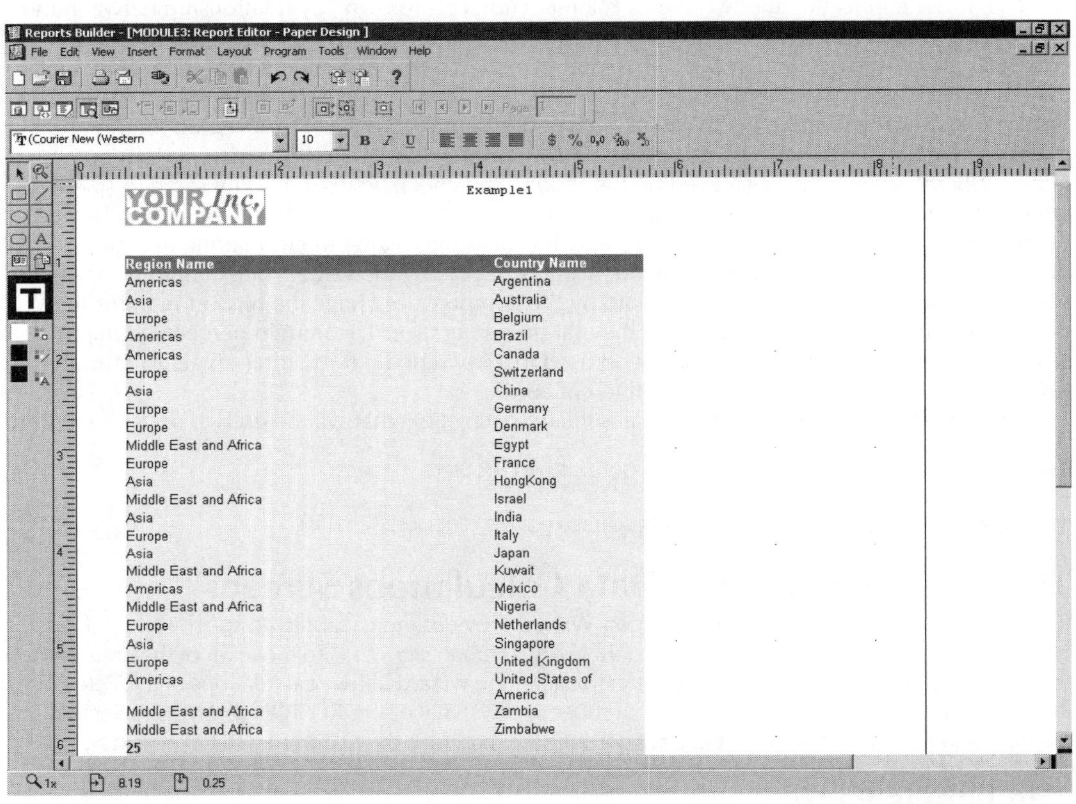

FIGURE 4-13. *An Oracle Report displayed in the Report Editor*

Enhancing the Report

Congratulations! You have just created your first Oracle Report. As you can see, for basic reports, there is virtually no coding necessary. Most reports, however, have requirements that go beyond what the wizards can provide. Figure 4-13 is part of the Reports Builder called the Report Editor. In the top right of the screen are two rows of icons familiar to all users of Windows-based programs: the Minimize button (which looks like an underscore (_), the Restore Down button, which looks like one box in front of another, and the Close button, which is an X. Click the Restore Down button on the lower row of icons. Drag the Report Editor window over to the right. Your screen should look something like the one in Figure 4-14.

Working with the Object Navigator

On the left-hand side of the screen is a window called the Object Navigator. It can be displayed at any time by either selecting Tools -> Object Navigator from the Reports Builder menu or by pressing F5. As a developer, you will get to know the Object Navigator well. The Object Navigator has an entry for every report object and provides a graphical, hierarchical view of all the objects

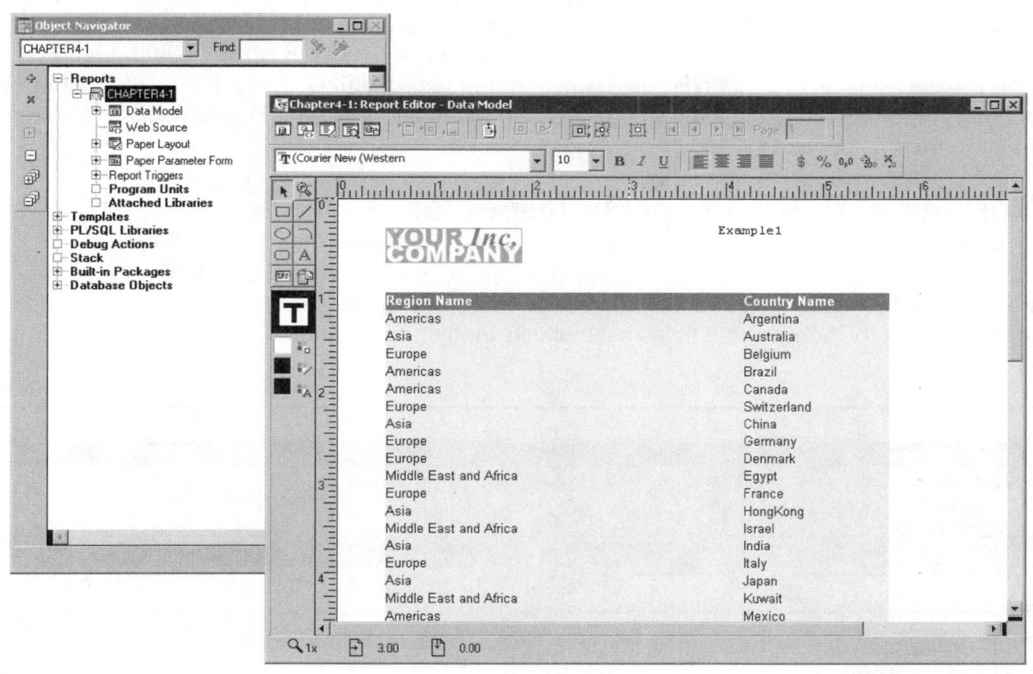

FIGURE 4-14. *The Reports Builder showing the Object Navigator*

that constitute your report. It organizes report objects into logical groups so that they can be retrieved and modified easily. Changes made in the object navigator will be automatically reflected in the graphical layouts of your report and vice versa. Under the example report entry (Chapter4-1), there are seven groupings: Data Model, Web Source, Paper Layout, Paper Parameter Form, Report Triggers, Program Units, and Attached Libraries. There are other groupings not under the Report grouping (Templates, PL/SQL Libraries, etc.) that will be discussed shortly.

Clicking the small plus sign to the left of "Data Model" expands the group to display more hierarchical report elements. All of the elements in the data model reflect the result of what was selected in the Reports Wizard when building the report.

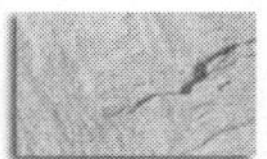

NOTE

When it comes time for the developer to go back and modify or enhance the report, there are three ways of accomplishing the task: 1) the Reports Wizard can be run again and the answers to the various questions, modified; 2) the developer can use the graphical editors to modify the report; or 3) the developer can use the object navigator to modify the attributes of elements on the report, add new elements, or remove existing elements. For this example, the modification of elements using the Object Navigator and Property Inspector will be demonstrated.

Click on the small plus sign next to "Queries." This element expands to include a sub-element named "Q_1." (The name "Q_1" and all of the other report elements in this example were chosen arbitrarily by the Reports Wizard.) There is no plus sign next to "Q_1," which implies that this is the lowest level that can be drilled down to. But what, exactly, is "Q_1"? To find out more about this report element, click the small SQL icon to the left of "Q_1." Your screen should look similar to the one in Figure 4-15.

Working with the Property Inspector

The Property Inspector lists all of the properties (attributes) of query "Q_1." The help system included with Oracle Reports 10*g* is context-sensitive, so any of the fields in the Property Inspector can be highlighted and F1 can be used to display the help screen associated with that particular property. Some of the fields have blanks in their right-hand column. This does not

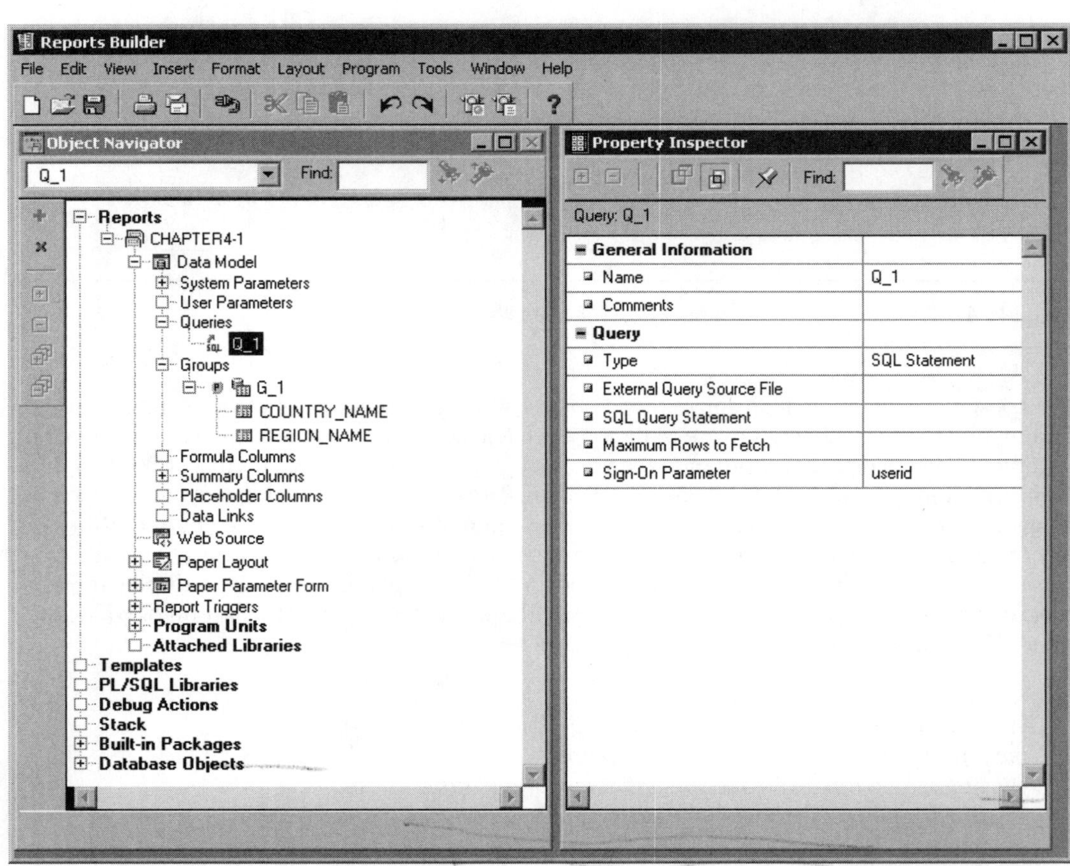

FIGURE 4-15. *Reports Builder with the Property Inspector page displayed*

necessarily mean that there is not a value associated with the property. To see an example of this, click the row that says "SQL Query Statement" in the Property Inspector. A button appears in the right-hand column. Clicking that button will take you to the SQL Query Statement window that allows the developer to modify the query that drives this report. If you notice, the query is taken from the Reports Wizard demonstrated earlier in this chapter that was used to construct our report. If we wanted to modify the query (or if we were building the report from scratch), we could do so here, run the Reports Wizard to modify it using a wizard-based interface, or use the Data Model page of the Report Editor (discussed shortly) to do so graphically. Oracle Reports 10*g* gives developers the flexibility to use the tool they are most comfortable with.

Like the Object Navigator, you will become very familiar with the Property Inspector. Almost every element on your report has properties that affect how it looks and behaves. The Property Inspector gives you the ability to view and modify these properties. The fields displayed on the Property Inspector change depending on what is selected in the Object Navigator. To see an example of this, click the plus sign next to "Groups" in the Object Navigator, then click the icon directly to the left of the element "G_1." The Property Inspector changes to reflect the fact that groups have different properties than queries.

One of the most difficult concepts for many beginning Reports developers to grasp is the concept of scope when discussing an object's attributes. Some elements have parents (for lack of a better word) that can have properties assigned to them; others don't. To see an example of this, click the "Q_1" element in the Object Navigator. You will notice that the properties for "Q_1" are displayed in the Property Inspector. If you click on "Queries," which is one level up in the hierarchy, there is nothing displayed in the Property Inspector. Therefore, element "Q_1" does not have any parents with properties. The same cannot be said for groups. If you click the plus sign next to "Groups" in the Object Navigator, then the plus sign next to "G_1," you'll see two elements under "G_1" named COUNTRY_NAME and REGION_NAME. In this case, both the child elements (the two columns) and the parent element (group "G_1") have attributes. The Property Inspector can be used to select multiple objects simultaneously and see if any of the common attributes between them are different.

To see this functionality, click the "G_1" element in the Object Navigator once so it is highlighted. While holding the control button down on your keyboard, single-click the "COUNTRY_NAME" and "REGION_NAME" elements in the Object Navigator. All three elements should now be highlighted. The Property Inspector changes to reflect the fact that multiple elements are now highlighted in the Object Navigator by stating "Multiple Selection: G_1, COUNTRY_NAME, REGION_NAME" underneath its toolbar. In the toolbar, the icon that looks like either a "U" or a rounded "n" becomes selectable (clicking the icon will toggle between these two selections). This icon represents the type of union that is occurring between the multiple fields highlighted in the Object Navigator. If the icon looks like a "U" (the set symbol for union), the Property Inspector shows all attributes for all objects selected. If the icon looks like an "n" (the set symbol for intersection), the Property Inspector will only display attributes that are common to the multiple elements you have selected (see Figure 4-16). If the attribute is undefined for the multiple selections, the Property Inspector will display a blank. If the attribute is not blank, but the same value for all objects selected, it will display the value. If the attribute is not blank, but is different for any of the objects selected, five asterisks are displayed. If any value is modified while in this mode, the change is propagated to all objects selected.

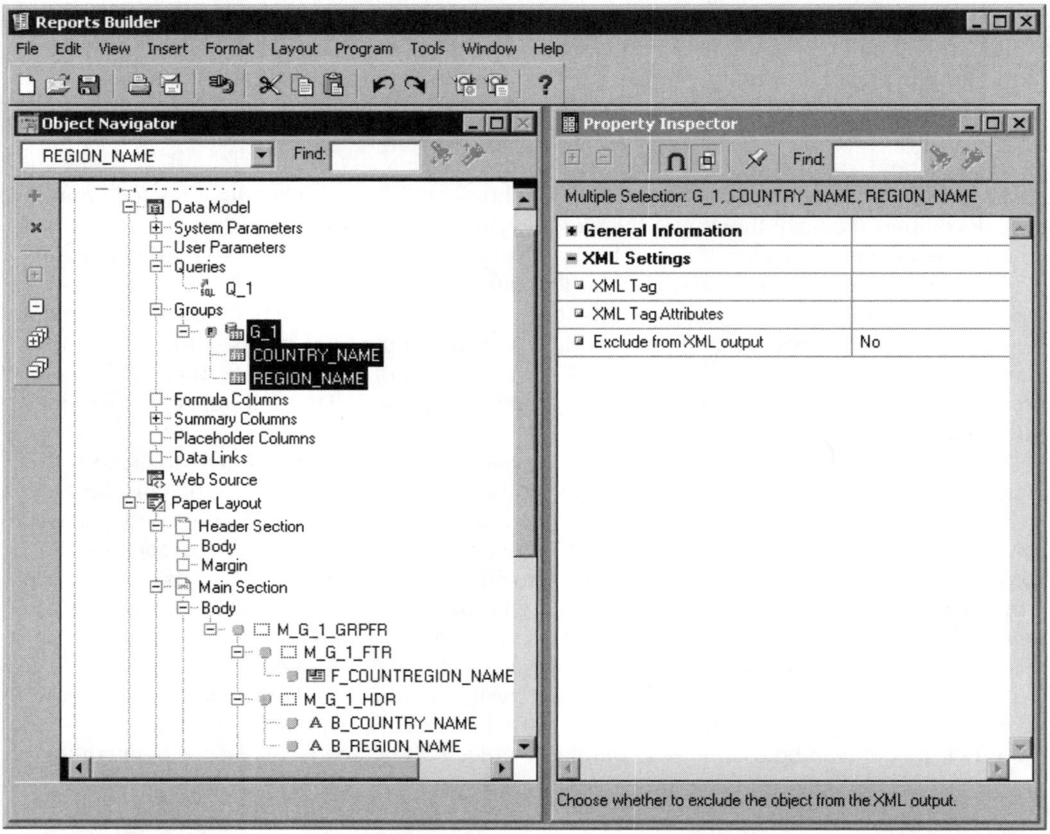

FIGURE 4-16. *Multiple selections in the Object Navigator*

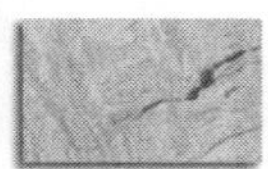

NOTE

In this example, using the Property Inspector to view the differences in attributes between three elements may seem trivial, but as you build more and more complex reports containing dozens (or even hundreds) of elements, this feature become invaluable.

Under the data model heading, we've looked at Queries, which are pretty self-explanatory, and groups, which are used to separate a query's data into sets and filter a query's data. If you click on "G_1" in the Object Navigator, the properties for the group are displayed. In the middle of the Property Inspector are two properties: Filter Type and PL/SQL filter. Here, the developer has the ability to filter data at the group level (later you'll see how to filter data at the query level). If "First" or "Last" are selected, the developer must enter a number in the "Number of Records" field just below the "Filter Type" property. This value will return the first or last *n* records when the report is executed. By selecting PL/SQL as the filter type, the developer can write a PL/SQL block to limit the rows returned by the query.

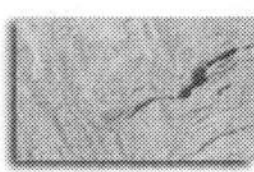

NOTE

Note that while this may sound similar to the conditional formatting discussed earlier, the PL/SQL blocks defined here can only be used to limit rows based on complex criteria or format rows returned by the query. It does not affect the actual display of the field on the report.

Filter Types are very convenient for returning the first or last *n* number of rows from a query, but they aren't much use for conditional statements. You could write a PL/SQL block to filter out rows, but in most cases that is overkill as there are simpler methods to limiting the types of rows returned on a report. Two of the most common include altering the SQL statement to include a WHERE clause and providing a parameter form for the user, so that at run time end users can determine what data they would like to see on the report.

Limiting Rows Returned by a Query

Altering the query to include a WHERE clause restricting rows is very simple to do, but it carries with it the obvious limitation of inflexibility. Once the query is defined, it remains that way until a developer modifies it and generates a new report. In many circumstances, this is impractical. However, reports with fixed WHERE: clauses in them, commonly referred to as canned reports, are very useful in many organizations. Some examples of canned reports include daily (or monthly, quarterly, yearly, etc.) inventory reports, sales reports, HR reports, etc. For reports where the criteria for querying data changes frequently, canned reports are not a good fit.

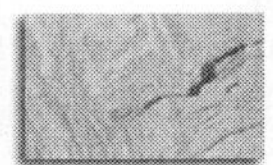

NOTE

*Later in this chapter we will discuss creating reports with parameter forms that give end users the ability to select values before running their reports. For true ad-hoc reporting capabilities, however, Oracle provides a sophisticated tool called Oracle Discoverer 10*g *that allows users to create their own reports based on their specific needs. Oracle Discoverer 10*g *also has a full featured web development environment (unlike Oracle Forms 10*g *and Oracle Reports 10*g*) called Discoverer Plus, that gives knowledgeable end users the ability to create their own Discoverer Reports via a web interface. Oracle Discoverer 10*g *integrates seamlessly with Oracle Application Server 10*g *and Oracle Application Server Portal. Oracle Discoverer 10*g *is discussed in detail in Chapters 5, 6, and 11.*

To modify an existing query, select the query in the Object Navigator. In the Property Inspector, click the row that says "SQL Query Statement." A button on the right side of the row appears. Clicking that button takes you to the SQL Query Statement editor. From here, you can click the Query Builder button to graphically build your query, use the Import SQL Query button to read the query from a file on disk, or simply edit the query in the edit window. Figure 4-13 displayed the results of the query with no WHERE change clauses. If we want our report just to reflect the countries in Asia, we can alter the query to look like this:

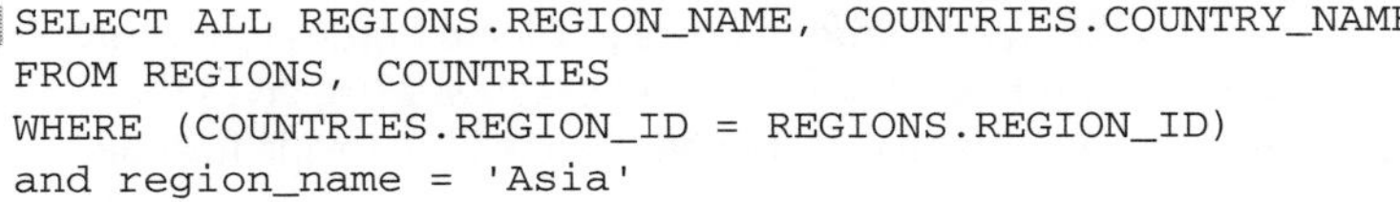

```
SELECT ALL REGIONS.REGION_NAME, COUNTRIES.COUNTRY_NAME
FROM REGIONS, COUNTRIES
WHERE (COUNTRIES.REGION_ID = REGIONS.REGION_ID)
and region_name = 'Asia'
```

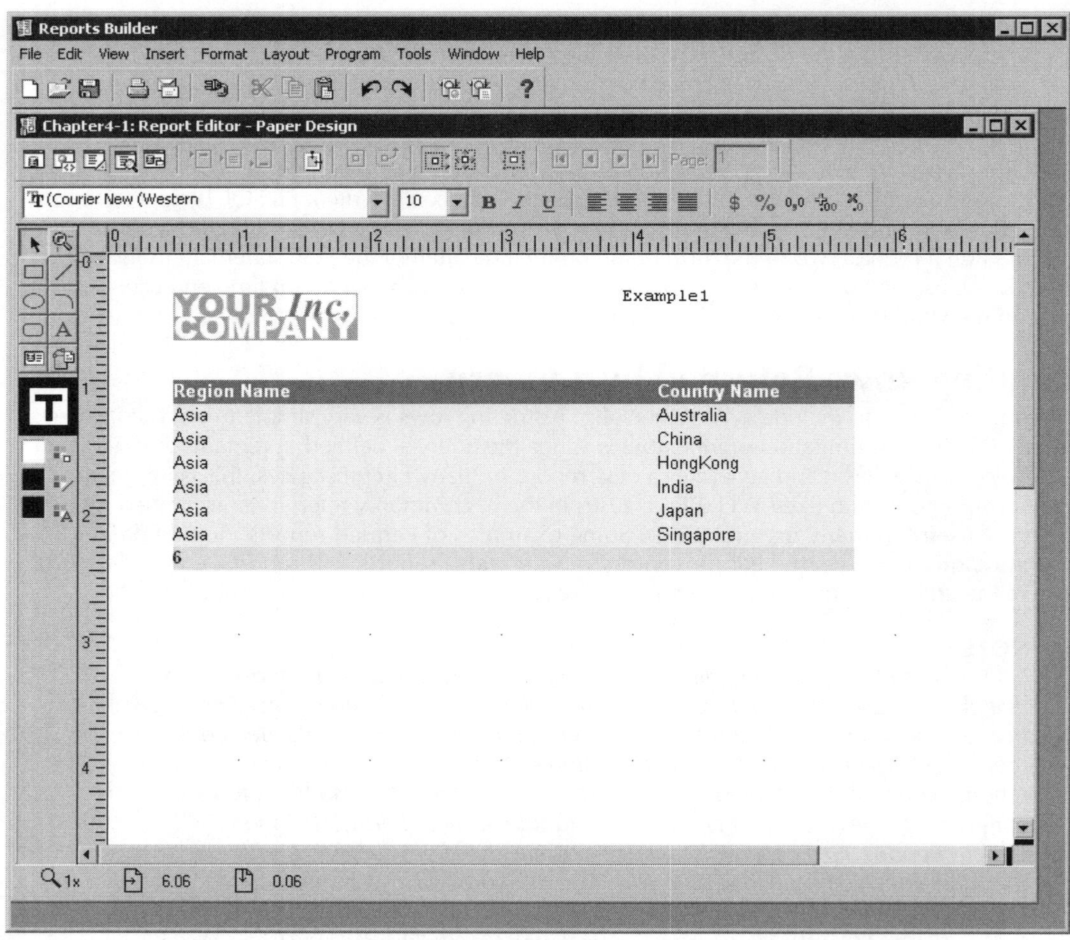

FIGURE 4-17. *The example report with just countries in Asia*

After clicking OK, run the report by clicking the Run Paper Layout icon from the toolbar. You will see a report similar to the one in Figure 4-17.

Adding User Parameters to a Report

The process outlined in the previous section is fine for a canned report, but the report would be much more flexible if we gave the end users the ability to select what data they would like to see on the report. This greatly cuts down on the need for developers to create hordes of custom reports, each tailored slightly to an individual end user's needs. Oracle Reports 10*g* gives the developer the ability to create user parameters that can be used to filter the data to provide flexibility.

Static Parameter Values

In the Object Navigator, under the Data Model heading for our report, there is an element called "User Parameters." Double-clicking "User Parameters" creates a new user parameter called "P_1." In the Property Inspector, change the name of the user parameter to "P_REGION."

NOTE
While it doesn't affect the functionality or performance of the report, it's a good idea to give the objects that make up your report meaningful names. For a small report like this, it may seem trivial, but will prove invaluable when you attempt to create larger reports with dozens of report objects. The Report Wizard used to generate this report will choose names like P_1 for parameters, Q_1 for queries, and R_1 for regions.

The datatype of P_REGION defaults to number. Since we want to give the end user the ability to select a Region, change the datatype to character. The property right below that specifies the parameter's width. Will we ever have a region greater than 20 characters? Earlier we looked at "Groups" in the Object Navigator and saw that REGION_NAME was included in the default group, "G_1," that was created for us. If you click on "REGION_NAME" under "G_1" in the Object Navigator, the properties of the field that will hold data retrieved from the database are displayed. In the middle of the Property Inspector, you can see that width of the database column is 25 characters, so it is entirely possible to have values greater than 20 characters. Change the width of the P_REGION user parameter to 25. We can leave the parameter field blank, but that leaves a large margin for user error. If the end user was, for example, looking for countries in the "Asia" region, entering "asia," "Asia " (with a space at the end), or "ASIA" would not return the data the end user is looking for. It is much more beneficial to provide the end user with a list from which they can select the values they are interested in. Single-click the "List of Values" row—your screen should look like the one in Figure 4-18.

Clicking the button in the right column of the List of Values row brings us to the "Parameter List Of Values" dialog box. From Figure 4-13, we know of the following regions in our database: Americas, Asia, Europe, and Middle East and Africa. We can add those values to our parameter list by entering the values (watching for case-sensitivity) and clicking the "Add >>" button (see Figure 4-19).

Next we need to incorporate our new report object into the query. Click the "Q_1" report element under "Queries" in the Object Navigator. Click "SQL Query Statement" in the Property Inspector and then the button to launch the SQL Query Statement dialog box. The user parameter we've created, P_REGION, can be referenced like a bind variable. Add the following line to your SQL statement:

```
SELECT ALL REGIONS.REGION_NAME, COUNTRIES.COUNTRY_NAME
FROM REGIONS, COUNTRIES
WHERE (COUNTRIES.REGION_ID = REGIONS.REGION_ID)
and region_name = :p_region
```

Creating the Parameter Form

Now that a parameter is in place, the next step is to create a parameter form. If you look in the Object Navigator towards the bottom under our Chapter4-1 heading, you will see an element named "Paper Parameter Form." This would seem like the logical place to start, but clicking the "Paper Parameter Form," or any of the elements underneath it, does not give us the ability to define anything. Instead, we need to use a wizard that creates the parameter form for us. Under

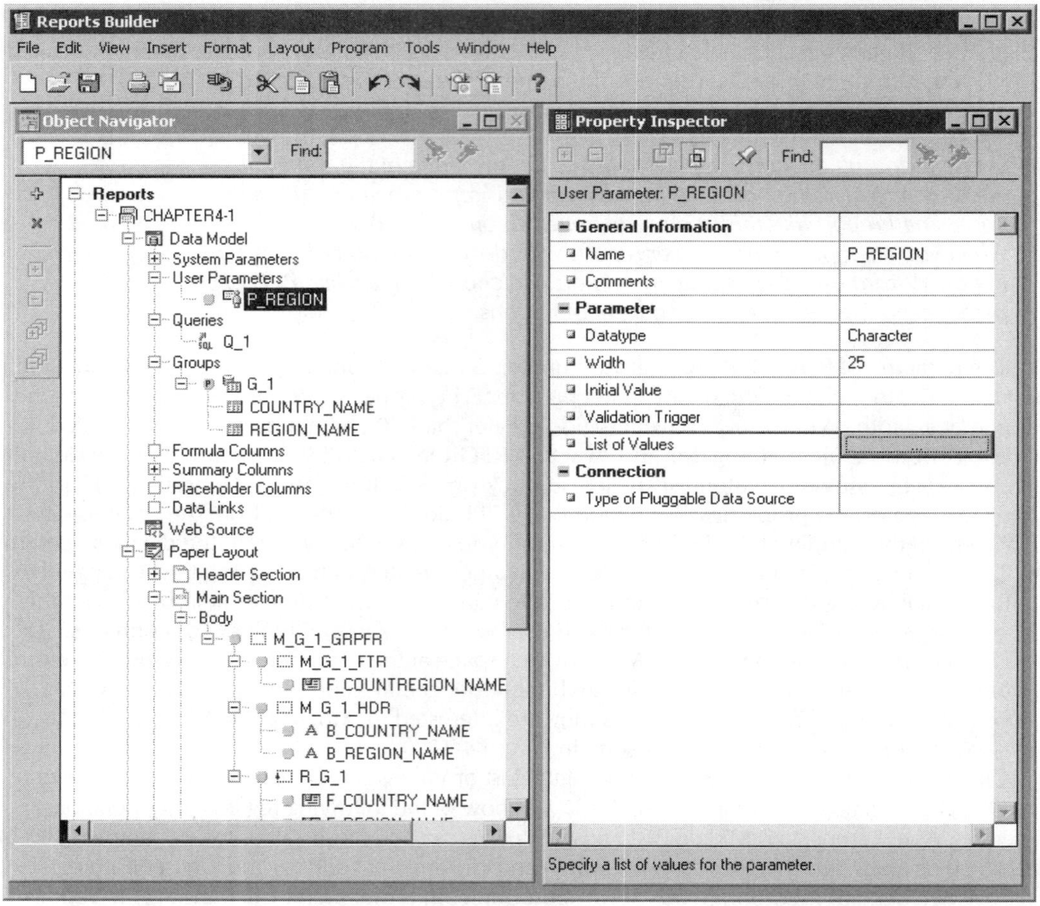

FIGURE 4-18. *The Property Inspector showing the P_REGION report object*

"Tools," in the Reports Builder menu, is an item called "Parameter Form Builder." Select this menu item to create the parameter form.

NOTE

It's important to note that the Parameter Form Builder is different from the Paper Parameter Form view of the Report Editor in Figure 4-6. The Parameter Form Builder gives the developer the ability to specify what is displayed on the Parameter Form for the report. The Parameter Form view of the Report Editor gives the developer the ability to determine how the parameters are displayed to the end user.

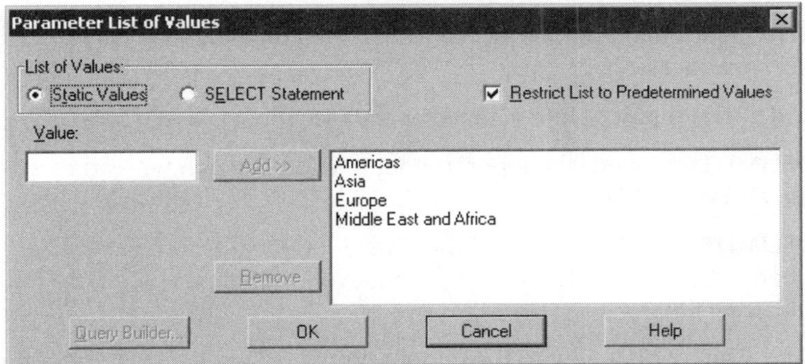

FIGURE 4-19. *Adding static values to a report's parameter list*

All system and user parameters defined for this report are available for you to put on your parameter form. System parameters are defined for all reports. They include:

- **DESTYPE** Stands for destination type; can be set to the following values:
  - **Screen** Provided for backwards compatibility; developers can still set the DESTYPE system parameter to SCREEN to format a report to display screen fonts or printer (preview) fonts in the Reports Builder user interface.
  - **File** Sends the output to the file on the server; used in conjunction with the DESNAME parameter.
  - **Printer** Sends the output to the printer on the server; used in conjunction with the DESNAME parameter.
  - **Mail** Sends the output to mail users; used in conjunction with the DESNAME parameter.
  - **Sysout** Sends the output to the client machine's default output device.
  - **Cache** Sends the output to the Oracle Reports cache.
  - **Localfile** Sends the output to a file on the client machine.
- **DESFORMAT** Stands for destination format; can be set to the following values:
  - **HTML** Sends the report output to a file that is in HTML format.
  - **HTMLCSS** Sends the report output to a file that includes style sheet extensions.
  - **PDF** Sends the report output to a file that is in PDF format and can be read by a PDF viewer (such as Adobe Acrobat).

    - **POSTSCRIPT** Sends the report output to a file that is in PostScript format.
    - **RTF** Sends the report output to a file that can be read by standard word processors (such as Microsoft Word).
    - **XML** The report output is saved as an XML file.
    - **DELIMITED** Sends the report output to a file that can be read by standard spreadsheet utilities.
    - **DELIMITED DATA** Provides the same functionality as DELIMITED, and is used when you have problems running large volume reports with DESFORMAT= DELIMITED
    - **dflt** The report is sent to the current printer driver. If a printer has not been selected, then PostScript is used by default.
- **DESNAME** Used to specify a cache destination, file name, printer name, Oracle Application Server Portal, or e-mail ID. For printer names, you can optionally specify a port.
- **MODE** Specifies whether to run the report in character mode or bitmap. Valid values are bitmap, character, or default. Character mode is only available on Windows; the Reports Builder ASCII driver will be used to produce editable ASCII output.
- **ORIENTATION** Valid values are default, landscape, and portrait. default uses the default printer setting for orientation.
- **PRINTJOB** Toggles between showing and hiding the print job dialog box before a report is run.
- **COPIES** The number of copies to generate when the report is run; only valid when DESTYPE is PRINTER.

To select which parameters will appear on the parameter form, single-click the parameter name (P_REGION) in the left-hand column of the dialog box. Change the label to something meaningful and click "OK" (see Figure 4-20).

Run the report by clicking the "Run Paper Layout" icon in the Reports Builder toolbar. You are presented with a drop-down box with the static values that were entered in Figure 4-19. Selecting one of them and clicking the "Run Report" icon in the toolbar of the Runtime Parameter Form window will produce a report similar to the one in Figure 4-21.

Dynamic Parameter Values

The parameter form associated with this report makes it much more functional and useful than a canned report, but there is always an inherent danger with hard-coding values used to drive a report. Suppose that a decision is made to make "Middle East and Africa" into two distinct regions? If the values in the database change, the developer will be forced to recode the report to reflect those changes. A better solution would be to query the database to get the current values and populate the parameter form dynamically. To do this, select "P_REGION" in the Object Navigator under User Parameters. In the Property Inspector, click the button in the right-hand column next

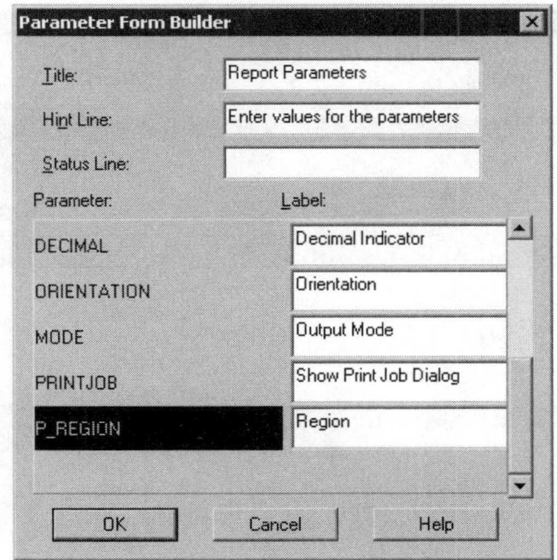

FIGURE 4-20. *The Parameter Form Builder dialog box*

to "List of Values." In the "Parameter List of Values" dialog box, click the "SELECT Statement" radio button. The SQL Query Statement editor can be used to create a SQL statement that will populate our drop-down box on the report's parameter form. The developer has the option of entering the query manually or using the Query Builder to build a SQL query graphically. In the edit window, enter:

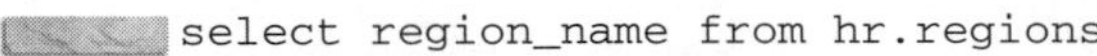

```
select region_name from hr.regions
```

Run the report to view the values in the drop-down box of the parameter form. It has now been built dynamically by reading the database and constructing the values found there.

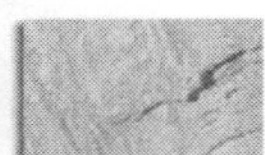

NOTE
Note that it is not necessary to use the distinct keyword when querying data to populate a parameter form field. Oracle Reports 10g is smart enough to remove duplicate values automatically. Nor is it necessary to end the SQL statement with a semicolon.

The parameter values are correct, but it's a good idea to order the list so that users can find the value they're looking for quickly. In the "Parameter List of Values" dialog box, add the following code to return values in alphabetical order:

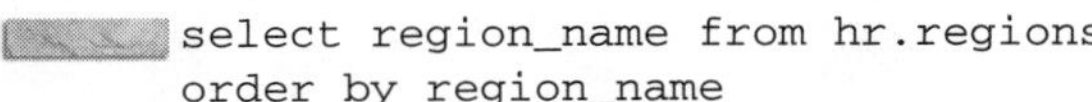

```
select region_name from hr.regions
order by region_name
```

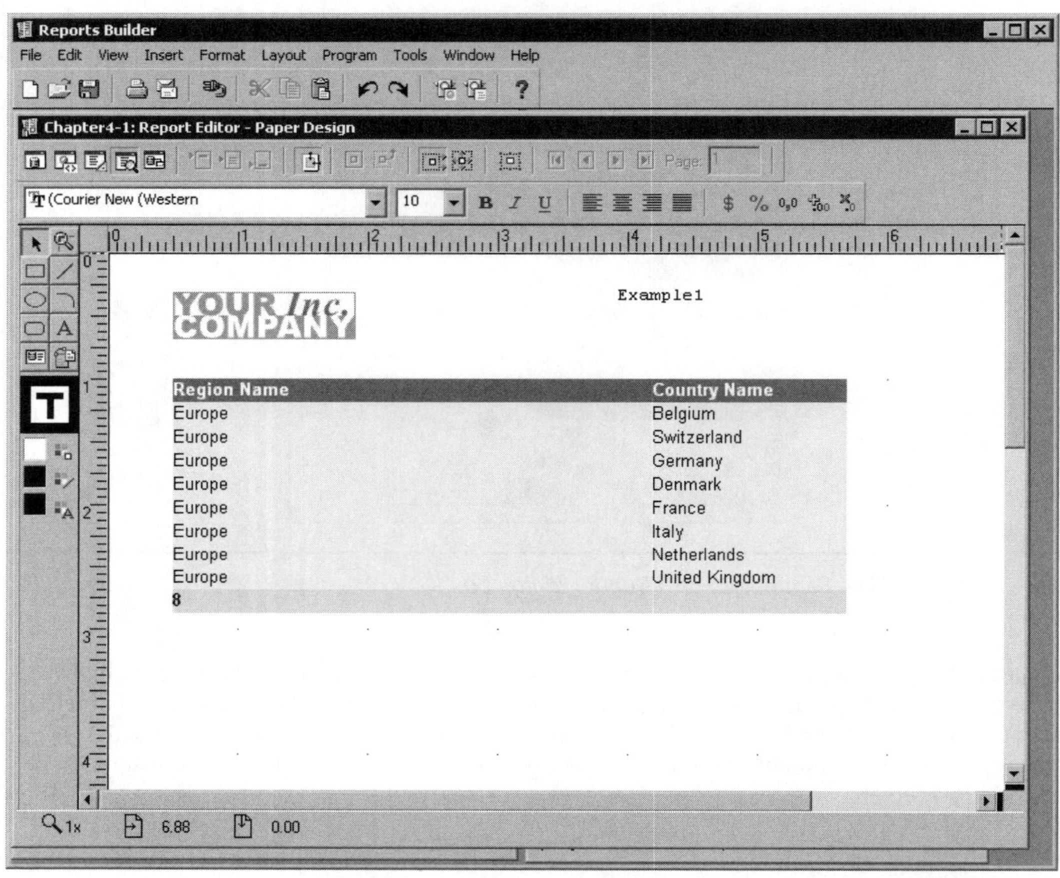

FIGURE 4-21. *Report output with filter applied to REGION_NAME*

Adding Additional Parameter Values to a Dynamically-Built List

The parameter form will allow the selection of different regions, but what if the end user wishes to see all regions? Two changes will have to be made:

- The query that populates the drop-down box in the parameter form will need to display 'All.' This is a relatively simple code modification. In addition to the regions queried from the select statement above, we can add the word 'All' by unioning the query:

  ```
  select 'All' from dual
  union
  SELECT ALL REGIONS.REGION_NAME
  FROM REGIONS
  ```

  This will place the word 'All' at the top of the drop-down box.

- The query that drives the report will need to be modified so that when the user selects 'All,' no records are excluded. For this, we need to revisit the Report Triggers discussed earlier. Constructing a SQL statement that can handle these different sorting criteria can be challenging. By using the After Parameter Form trigger, you can construct a variable that can be incorporated into your SQL statement. The After Parameter Form trigger may contain code like this (line numbers have been added manually):

```
1  function AfterPForm return Boolean is
2  v_region_where          varchar2(100);
3   begin
4     if :P_REGION = 'All' then
5        v_region_where := 'and 1 = 1'
6     else
7        v_region_where := 'and region_name = ''' || :P_REGION || '''';
8     end if;
9     :P_REGION_WHERE := v_region_where;
10    return (true);
11  end;
```

- Line 1 is the function for the After Parameter Form trigger. There are five functions associated with the different report triggers.
- Line 2 defines the variable that will hold our WHERE clause.
- Line 4 tests to see if the end user selected 'All' in the parameter form for the reports
- Line 5 shows if 'All' is selected, a WHERE clause is created to select all records,
- Line 7 shows if a specific region was selected, the v_region_where field is constructed to hold a WHERE clause to select a single region; the three single quotes before || : P_REGION put a single quote in the v_region_where field (the first two single quotes) and then close the string (the third single quote); in the four single quotes after :P_REGION |, the first single quote starts a new text field, the middle two quotes insert a single quote into the v_region_where variable, and the fourth single quote closes the string. If :P_REGION were equal to Europe, then the v_region_where variable would equal:

```
and region_name = 'Europe'
```

- Line 9 shows the scope of variable v_region_where limits its use to the After Parameter Form function. When the function completes, the memory allotted to the variable is released, so in order to preserve the value, we must assign it to a variable defined at the form level (P_REGION_WHERE).

If you try to compile the trigger at this point, you will receive an error, as P_REGION_WHERE has not been defined in the form yet. With the After Parameter Form PL/SQL window still open, single-click "User Parameters" in the Object Navigator. With "User Parameters" highlighted, click the green plus sign towards the top left of the Object Navigator to create a new parameter. With the new parameter (P_1) highlighted, go to the Property Inspector and change its name to P_REGION_WHERE, its datatype to character, and its width to 40. Go back to the After Parameter Form PL/SQL window and click "Compile."

Now that the WHERE clause is constructed properly, how can the query that drives the report access it? The driving query looked like this:

```
SELECT ALL REGIONS.REGION_NAME, COUNTRIES.COUNTRY_NAME
FROM REGIONS, COUNTRIES
WHERE (COUNTRIES.REGION_ID = REGIONS.REGION_ID)
and region_name = :p_region
```

If the end user selects 'All,' this query won't work as it will return 0 records. We want the query to reflect the WHERE clause constructed in the After Parameter Form trigger. To do that, the query can be modified like this:

```
SELECT ALL REGIONS.REGION_NAME, COUNTRIES.COUNTRY_NAME
FROM REGIONS, COUNTRIES
WHERE (COUNTRIES.REGION_ID = REGIONS.REGION_ID)
&p_region_where
```

Conditional Formatting at the Group or Field Level (Manual Coding)

In Figure 4-17, it was demonstrated how to modify a query so that only certain rows are returned. In the preceding section, "Adding Additional Parameter Values to a Dynamically-Built List," we demonstrated how to use parameters to give your report greater flexibility. While these features of Oracle Reports 10*g* are very powerful, they are not the only ways to customize your report. Developers have the option of formatting rows at the group or field level.

Suppose, for example, a new requirement for the report we have been developing gets assigned to you. This new requirement states that all rows in the 'Asia' region are to be highlighted in red on the report. Certainly, there is no SQL statement that can accomplish that for you. Reports, thankfully, provides the capability to fire triggers at the group level that allow the developer to insert conditional PL/SQL statements that can format data.

Selecting the group that encloses a set of fields can be difficult in the Report Editor Paper Layout view. In Figure 4-22, there is a repeating group (which is where we want to add the formatting code) surrounding the row that includes the F_REGION_NAME and F_COUNTRY_NAME fields. If you click either of the fields, they become the ones selected. How can you select the group that encloses these fields? The answer lies in the Object Navigator.

As we mentioned earlier, the Object Navigator is a hierarchical representation of all of the elements that constitute your report. The key word there is "hierarchical." By selecting any of the field objects in your report, the graphical representation in the Object Navigator will show what group (parent) that field belongs to. Single-click the F_REGION_NAME field in the Report Layout window and press F5 to display the Object Navigator. As you can see in Figure 4-23, the Object Navigator highlights the corresponding field (F_REGION_NAME) in the hierarchy. From this, we can determine that the F_REGION_NAME field is part of the R_G_1 repeating group. To place a formatting trigger to affect all rows in this repeating group, double-click the small grey circle to the left of R_G_1.

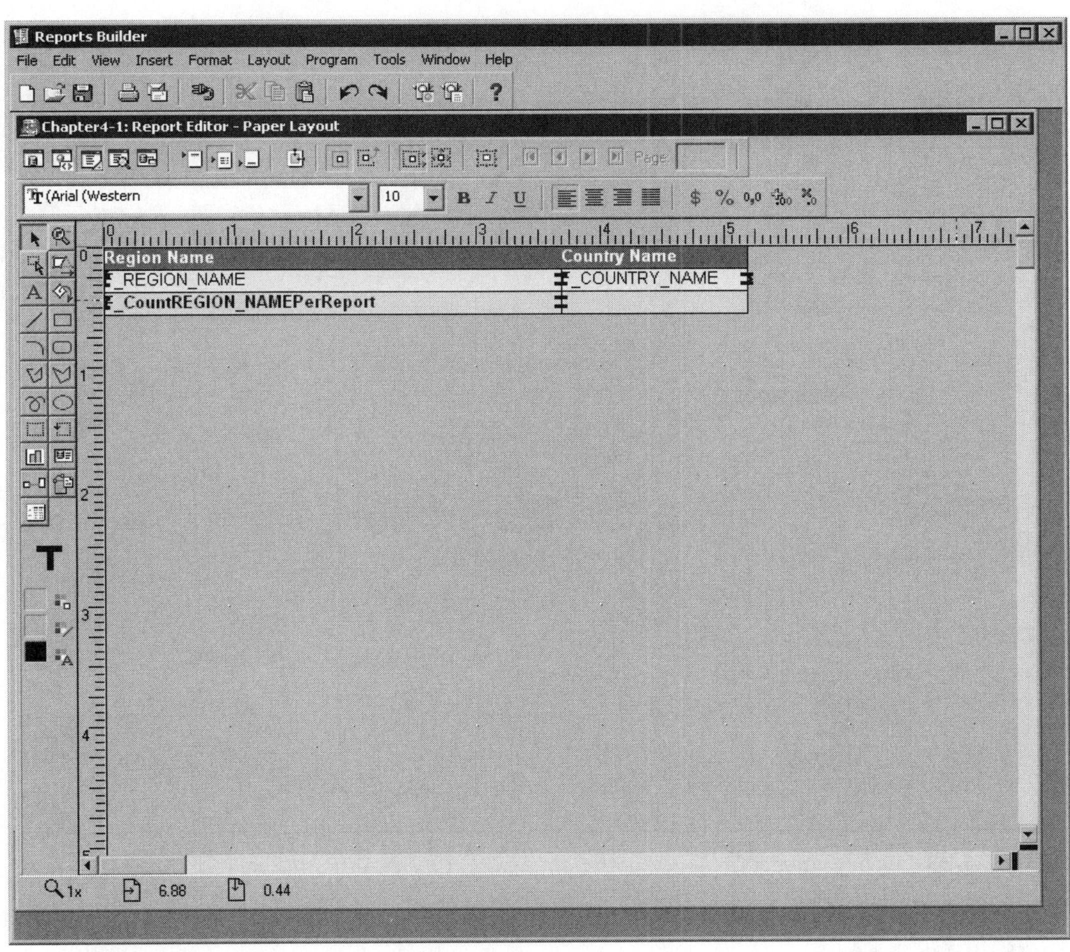

FIGURE 4-22. *The Paper Layout view in the Report Editor*

The following code will format every row with 'Asia' as the region_name in red:

```
function R_G_1FormatTrigger return boolean is
begin
  if :region_name = 'Asia' then
      srw.set_background_fill_color('red');
  end if;
  return (TRUE);
end;
```

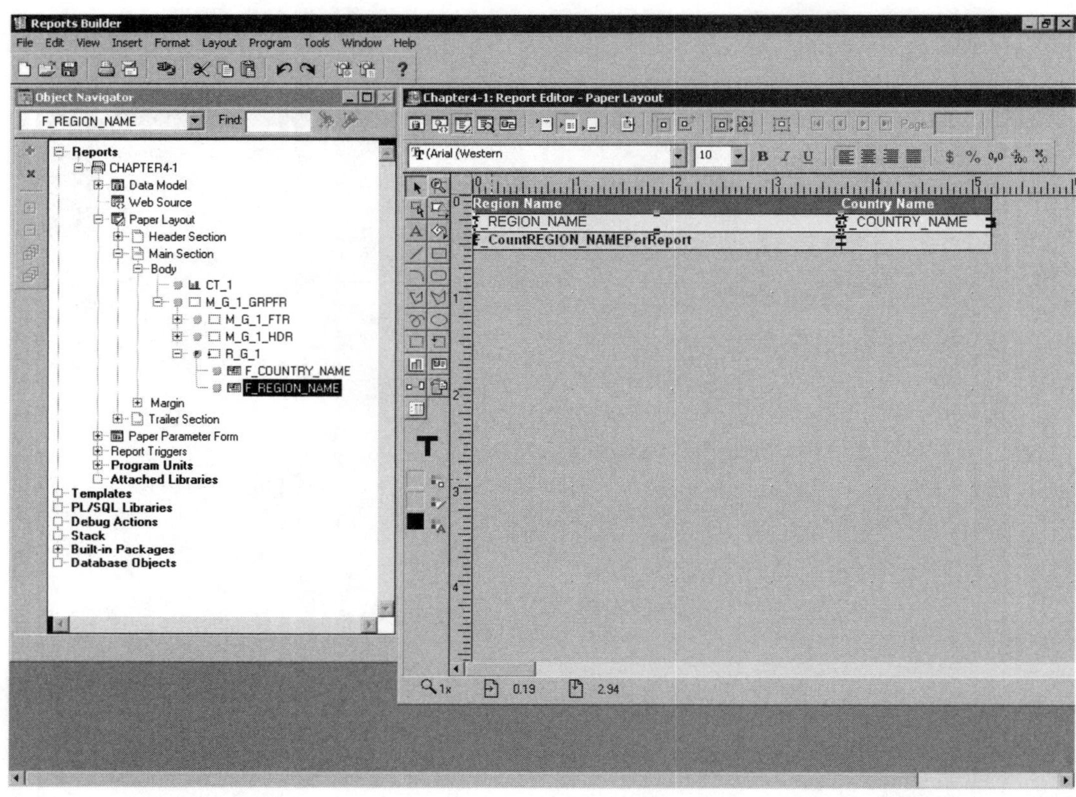

FIGURE 4-23. *The Object Navigator with field F_REGION_NAME highlighted*

The fourth line in the code above makes use of a Reports built-in package called Reports Builder is shipped with numerous built-in packages which are collections of PL/SQL functions, procedures, and exceptions that can be referenced in any of your libraries or reports. The PL/SQL objects provided by the SRW package enable you to perform such actions as change the formatting of fields, run reports from within other reports, create customized messages to display in the event of report error, and execute SQL statements. You can reference the contents of the SRW package from any of your libraries or reports without having to attach it. To view all of the functions and procedures in the SRW package, click the "Built-In Packages" object in the Object Navigator, then select the SRW package (Figure 4-24).

This is the one case, unfortunately, where the context-sensitive help won't help much. You may expect that highlighting one of the package objects and hitting F1 would bring you to the help screen for that package, but it does not. To view help on using the built-in packages, type either "srw package examples" or "Built-in packages examples." Run the report to see how the R_G_1 group trigger can change the way data is formatted on your report.

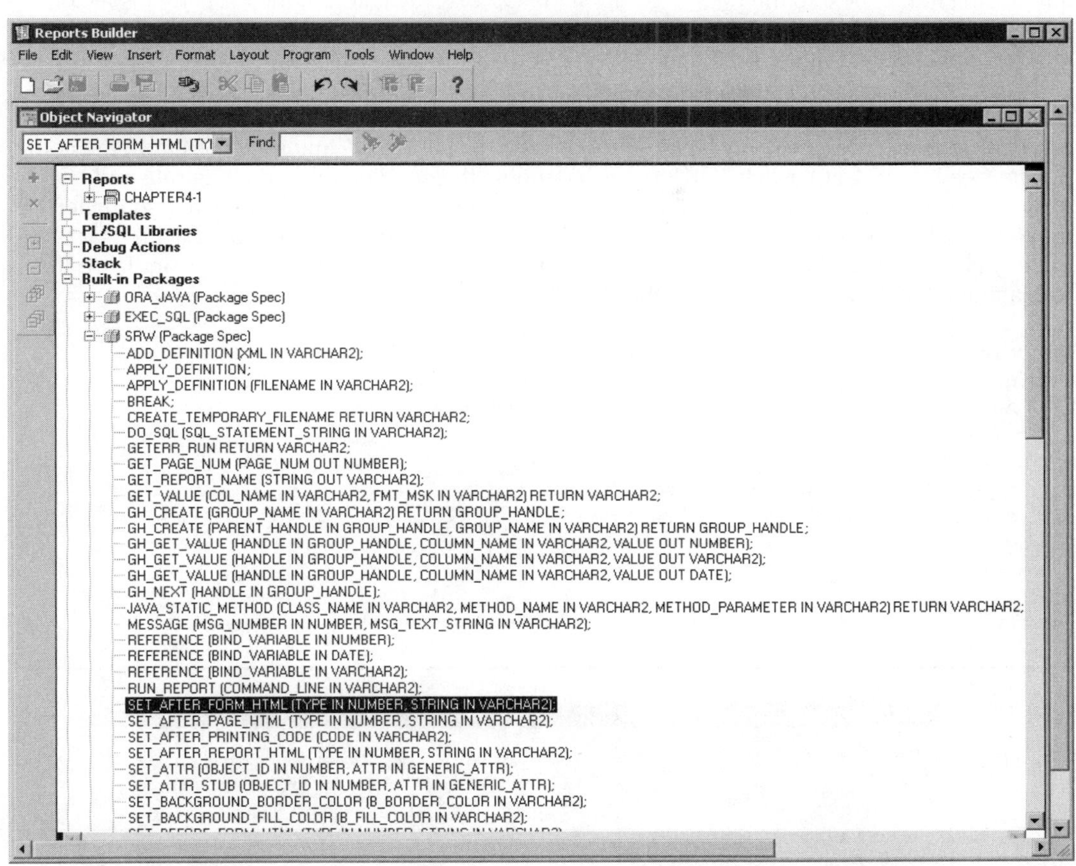

FIGURE 4-24. *A listing of the PL/SQL objects in the srw built-in package*

Note also that the third line in the code listing above references region_name and not F_REGION_NAME. You cannot reference layout objects—in order to write conditional PL/SQL formatting blocks, you must reference the source field of the layout objects. We can also define conditional formatting at the field level if we just want to change the appearance of a specific field within a row.

Conditional Formatting at the Group or Field Level (Using the Conditional Formatting Wizard)

There is also a wizard available to the developer to assist in the creation of formatting code at either the group or field level. Double-click the rectangle with an arrow pointing down (symbolizing a repeating frame) next to the R_G_1 group in the Object Navigator. In the Property Inspector, click the button to the right of the "Conditional Formatting" property. The Conditional formatting window appears (see Figure 4-25).

Click "New" to create a new formatting condition. Select REGION_NAME in the first drop-down box, "equals" in the second drop-down box, and type "Asia" (without the quotes) in the third box, noting case sensitivity. Click the icon next to "Fill Color" and select red from the color palette (see Figure 4-26). Click "OK" to finish defining the conditional formatting rule and "OK" again to close the Conditional formatting window. If you click the small gray circle to the left of the R_G_1 object in the Object Navigator (which now has a small "P" in it to reflect the fact that there is PL/SQL code attached to this report object), you will see code that is very similar to the formatting PL/SQL we wrote about in the previous section:

```
function R_G_1FormatTrigger return boolean is
begin
  - Automatically Generated from Report Builder.
  if (:REGION_NAME = 'Asia')
  then
    srw.set_foreground_fill_color('red');
    srw.set_fill_pattern('solid');
  end if;
  return (TRUE);
end;
```

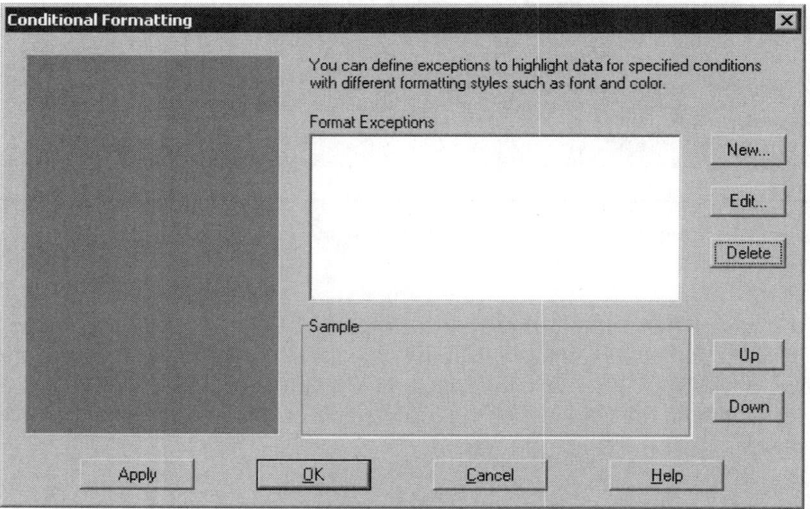

FIGURE 4-25. *The Conditional Formatting window*

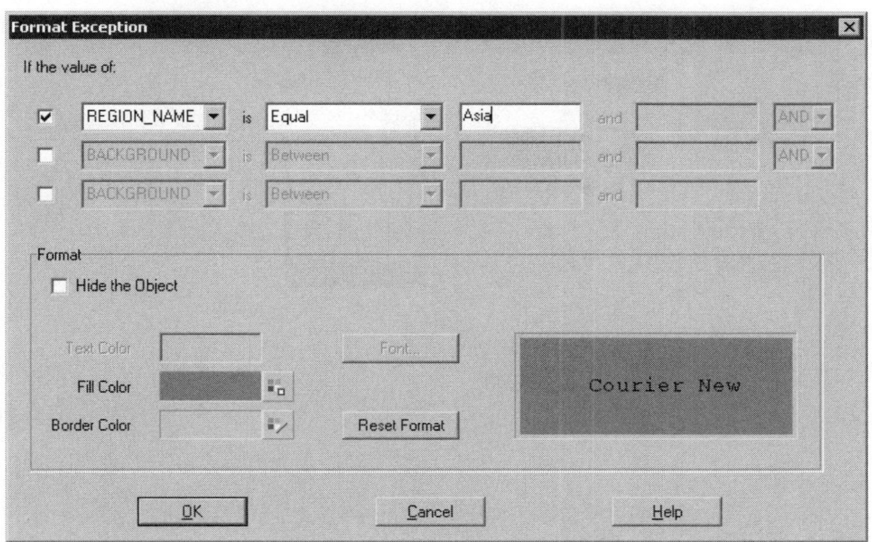

FIGURE 4-26. *The Format Exception dialog box*

Adding a Graph to the Report

Adding a graph to a report is a relatively painless process as Oracle Reports 10*g* provides the Graph Wizard to create and insert graphs easily. Finding the Graph Wizard can be difficult as it is not on the Reports Builder menu, nor is there a button for it anywhere. To run the graph wizard, display the Report Editor by either pressing F7 or right-clicking on any of the report elements in the Object Navigator and selecting "Report Editor." Select the "Paper Layout" icon in the top left of the Report Editor. Right-click on any blank area in the Paper Layout window and select "Graph Wizard."

The Graph Wizard is a Java application that allows developers to quickly create graphs and embed them in reports. As you can see from Figure 4-27, the Graph Wizard can display data in a multitude of formats. All of the major graphing types are included out of the box and are displayed on the left-hand side of the Graph Wizard. For even greater functionality, each of the graph types has a subtype, allowing developers to further customize the graphs to be displayed. For the example report in this chapter, we will create a bar graph at the bottom of the report that graphs the number of countries corresponding to each region. On the first page of the Graph Wizard, select "Bar" in the "Graph type:" window on the left and "Bar" in the "Graph subtype:" window on the right and click "Next >."

The next screen of the graph wizard asks if the graph should be displayed at the beginning or end of the report. Select "at the end of the report" and click "Next >." The X-axis in the following

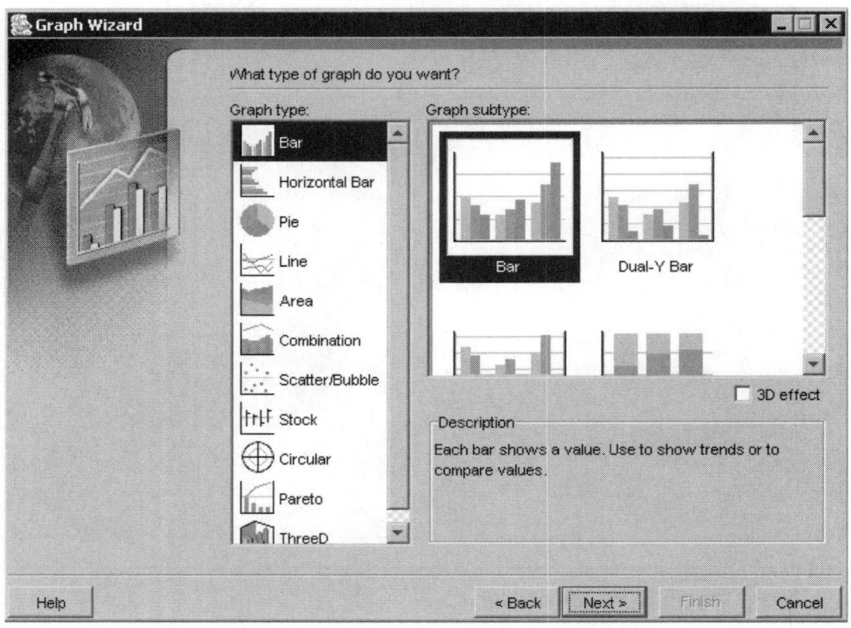

FIGURE 4-27. *A listing of the different graph types supported by Oracle Reports 10g*

screen is what the graph wizard will use to display horizontally in your report. If we had selected "Horizontal Bar" as the Graph type, the column selected on this screen would be displayed vertically. Select REGION_NAME and click the greater-than button (>) to move the REGION_NAME column to the right window. Click "Next >."

The next screen of the Graph Wizard asks for the column that will provide the numerical data for our graph. The only numeric column available for us to select is CountREGION_NAMEPerReport. Select that column to move it to the right-hand window and click "Next >." The next screen of the Graph Wizard allows the developer to change the layout of items on the graph. The bars box is only applicable for Pie-bar and Ring-bar graphs. It specifies the data items for the bars that show details about a slice of the pie. The Groups box is used to specify data items for the groups of the graph. Leave both of these boxes unchanged and click "Next >." In the titles page, you can specify Titles, Sub-Titles, and Footnotes for your graph. You can enter boilerplate text or insert values from your report by selecting the drop-down boxes. For this report example, click the check box next to "Show Title" and type "Report #1" (without the quotes) in the text box just below "Show Title." Click "Next >."

The Legend page allows you to change the colors that are displayed in the graph. Leave the values as they are and click "Next >." The X-axis page allows you to modify the characteristics of what is printed along the X-axis of your report. Leave the values unchanged and click "Next >." The Y-axis page provides the same functionality for the Y-axis of your report. Again, leave the values unchanged and click "Next >." The next page allows you to define how data is plotted on your graph. Leave the values unchanged and click "Next >." The final page gives developers the option of creating a link in the graph that would allow an end user to click on the graph and be taken to a web site. Leave this field blank and click "Finish." The graph is now created as an object in your report.

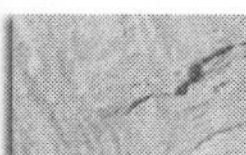

NOTE
If you noticed carefully, right after you specified what columns would make up your X- and Y- axis, the "Finish" button became available in the lower right-hand part of the Graph Wizard window. You can click "Finish" at any point from that moment on to take default values for the rest of the wizard pages.

Click the "Run Paper Layout" in the menu bar of Reports Builder. You should see a graph at the bottom of the report similar to Figure 4-28.

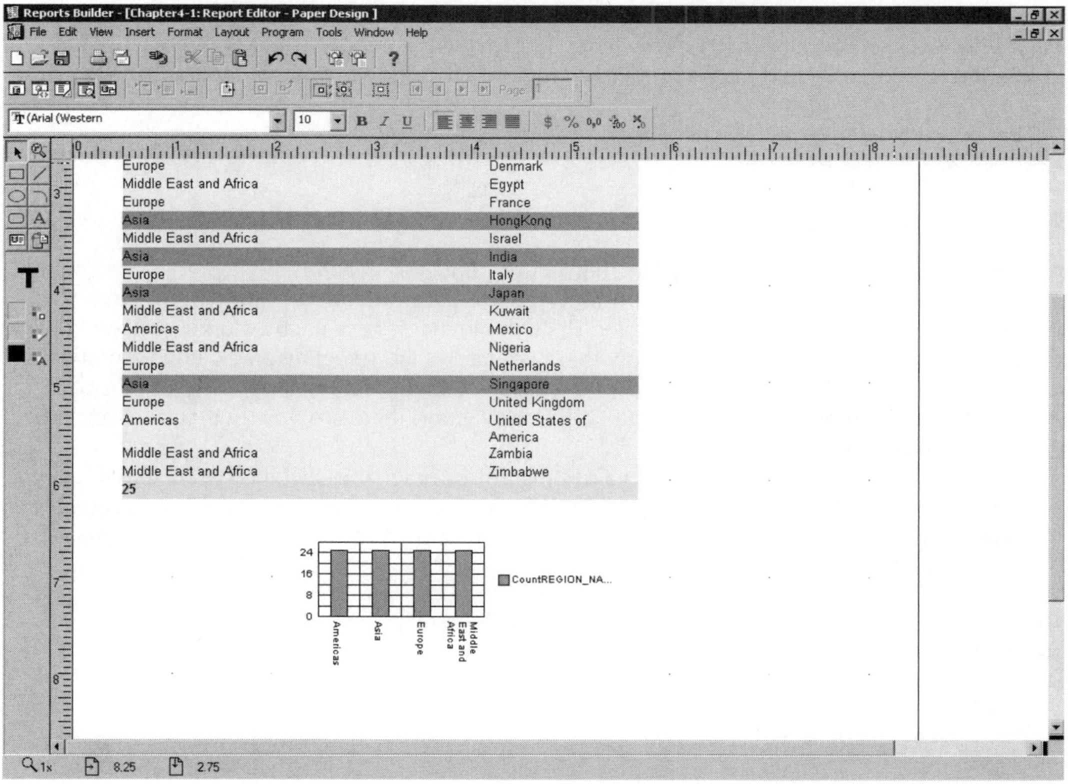

FIGURE 4-28. *The report with the first version of the graph*

The results returned are obviously not correct. What happened? All of the bars in our graph show 25, which is the total number of records for our report. Right-click on the graph and select "Graph Wizard." This runs the Graph Wizard again, but we are now in reentrant mode. The wizard has a set of tabs along the top of it that allows us to jump to any point and make modifications to our graph. Looking at the graph in Figure 4-28, it appears that the X-axis has the correct values, but the Y-axis does not. Click the "Data" tab of the Graph Wizard to display the page where the columns that make up the Y-axis of our graph are specified.

As we were walking through the steps of the wizard, the only column available to us when we came to this page was the CountREGION_NAMEPerReport column. This column, if you remember, was a summary column that totaled the number of records for the report (Reports gives you a hint by putting the "PerReport" at the end of its name when naming the variable). This variable will not provide the data needed for the graph. The query we created to drive the report does not have a column that corresponds to the data we wish to display on the graph. The solution is to create another query for the report.

Many reports will require only one query, but developers are not limited to one query per report. Multiple queries can be defined and will execute automatically after processing the parameter form (if it exists). To create another query, select the Data Model view in the Report Editor. Right-click on a blank spot in the editor and select the "Data Wizard." The new query is named Q_2. Click "Next >," select "SQL Query," and click "Next >" again. In the data source definition, we need to construct a query that will provide the two axes that will make up our graph: the region name and the count of each region. The following query accomplishes this:

```
SELECT region_NAME, count(region_name) reg_count
FROM REGIONS, COUNTRIES
WHERE (Regions.REGION_ID = Countries.REGION_ID)
group by region_name;
```

I have aliased the count of regions as "reg_count," but I did not alias the region_name column. There are now two queries in the report that query a column called region_name. Reports automatically creates a layout object called F_<column_name> for each column queried from the database. Will there be a conflict now that two queries are selecting an exactly named field? It turns out that Reports is smart enough to avoid potential conflict by appending a "1" (or "2" or "3," etc.) to the reports variable. In the Object Navigator, there are now two queries and two groups (see Figure 4-29).

This query will, however, return all values regardless of what is specified in the parameter form for the report (and, therefore, display values for all regions in the graph). If this is acceptable, the query can be left as it is. If you want the graph to reflect what is selected in the parameter form, we need to add the following line:

```
SELECT region_NAME, count(region_name) reg_count
FROM REGIONS, COUNTRIES
WHERE (Regions.REGION_ID = Countries.REGION_ID)
&p_region_where
group by region_name;
```

We now need to modify our graph to pull data from the second query (Q_2). Return to the Graph Wizard by pressing F7 to return to the Report Editor. Click the "Paper Layout" icon in the top left of the page, right-click on the graph on the bottom of the report, and select the "Graph Wizard." There is now a new tab on the top of the wizard called "Group." This tab allows us to select what group of data will be used to drive our graph. In Figure 4-29, Reports created a new

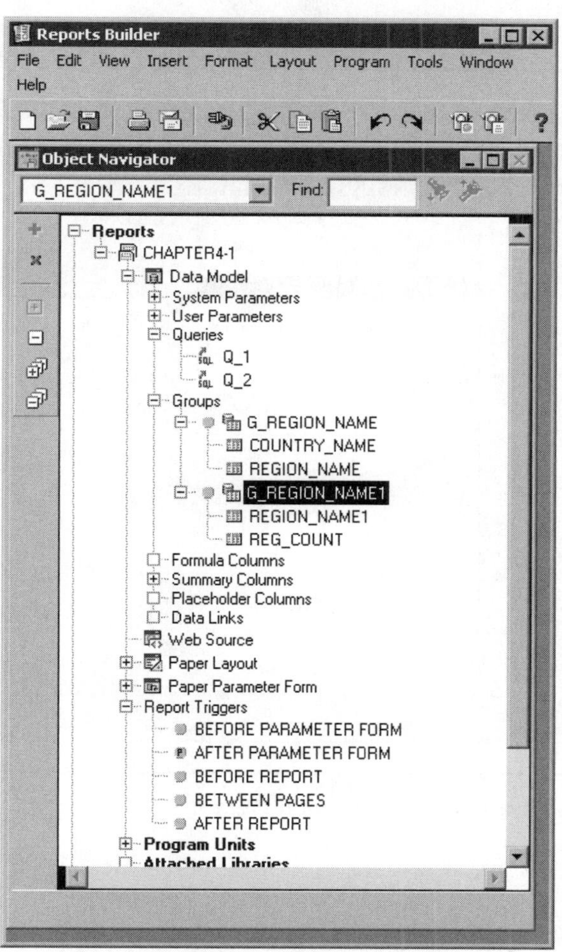

FIGURE 4-29. *The Object Navigator showing two queries and two groups*

group called G_REGION_NAME1 that corresponds to our new query, Q_2. Select G_REGION_NAME1 in the left window of the wizard and, holding down the control key on your keyboard, select both columns in the right window (see Figure 4-30).

In the Category tab, select region_name1 and in the Data tab, select reg_count. Click "Finish" to return to the Report Editor inside Reports Builder. Click the "Run Paper Layout" icon in the Reports Builder menu. Select "All" on the parameter form. The bottom of your report should look like the one in Figure 4-31.

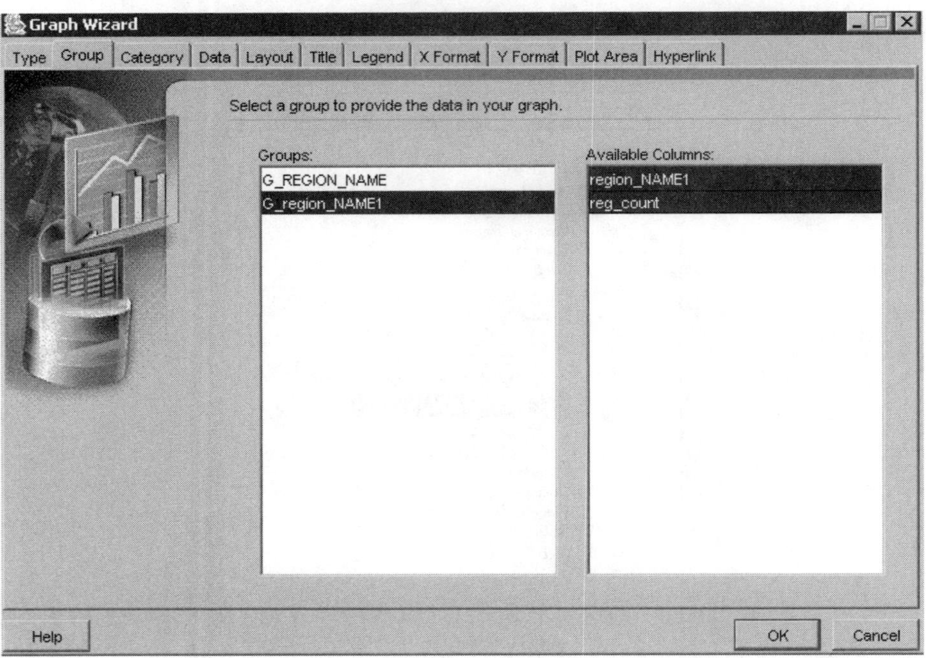

FIGURE 4-30. *Selecting columns in the Graph Wizard*

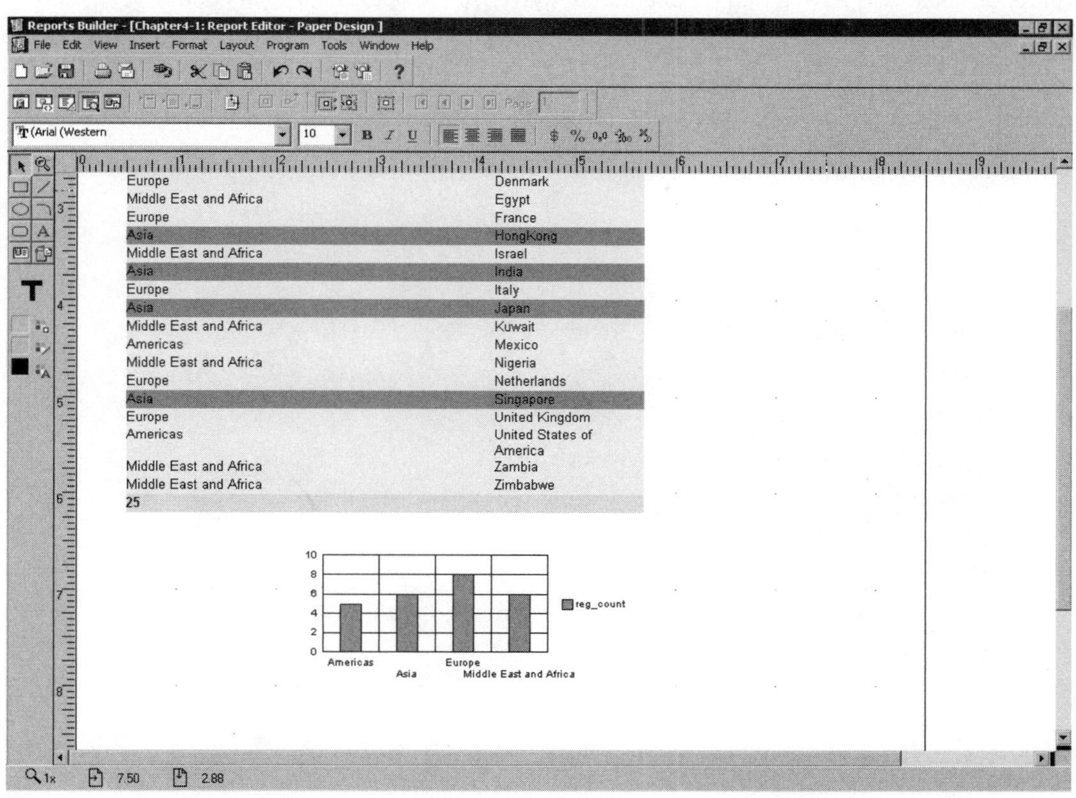

FIGURE 4-31. *The report with the second version of the graph*

Summary

Oracle Reports 10*g* is a robust, scalable reports development environment that gives developers an abundant set of graphical tools to create reports quickly. Through the use of the Report Wizard, developers can construct reports in a very short period of time with a minimal amount of coding.

All reports elements have a rich set of attributes, giving developers near-total control of all reports aspects. Sophisticated wizards for the creation of queries, parameter forms, and graphics allow the developer to enhance reports quickly and easily. PL/SQL program units can be stored and exectued from within the form. Oracle Reports 10*g* contains a robust feature set, stability and maturity, full integration with Oracle databases, the capability to pull data from heterogeneous data sources, and seamless integration with Oracle Portal.

CHAPTER 5

OracleAS Discoverer 10*g*

racleAS Discoverer 10*g* is an end-user ad hoc query, reporting, analysis, and web-publishing tool. It opens up the analytic capabilities of the Oracle databases within your organization to all levels of end users without the need for any training in SQL or extended resource usage from your IT department. OracleAS Discoverer 10*g* is the tool to enable users to gain insight into their business and operations and make informed business decisions using up-to-the-second data. All of these features would be of little value if the tool itself had a large learning curve (hindering the productivity of the end users) or required huge database resources (hindering the ability of the database to provide information to those who need it). Luckily, OracleAS Discoverer 10*g* has been designed with these factors in mind.

Fewer developers and end users work with OracleAS Discoverer 10*g* than with other Oracle tools such as Oracle Forms and Oracle Reports, and that's a shame because it's an incredibly powerful product. As you'll see in this chapter, OracleAS Discoverer 10*g* gives end users the ability to define and run complex reports with advanced features such as graphing, data pivoting, drill-downs, parameters, and correlated subqueries (just to name a few), all without requiring the end users to have advanced knowledge of SQL and all of its nuances. On top of all of these features, OracleAS Discoverer 10*g* contains a full web-based development environment (unlike Oracle Forms and Oracle Reports) that gives Discoverer developers the ability to create and run Oracle Discoverer Workbooks and Worksheets on the web via their web browser. This eliminates many of the licensing and maintenance costs of maintaining the client machines previously needed for the Oracle Discoverer Desktop. Since OracleAS Discoverer Plus (the web-based Discoverer development tool) and OracleAS Discoverer Viewer (the tool for viewing Discoverer reports over the web) are true collaborative environments, the creation and sharing of Oracle Discoverer Reports between users within a department or organization is a very simple process. OracleAS Discoverer 10*g* can be integrated with Oracle Application Server 10*g*'s Identity Management features, including Single-Sign On.

The Discoverer End-User Layer

All of this amazing functionality comes at a cost, albeit a small one. Before end users can begin to exploit the features of OracleAS Discoverer 10*g* just outlined and manipulate the data in your databases via Discoverer Workbooks, Worksheets, and reports, a set of tables and views, called an End-User Layer, needs to be built into the database. What is an End-User Layer? From Oracle's documentation:

"The End User Layer (EUL) is the metadata (i.e., data about the actual data in a database) that is simple and easy for Discoverer end users to understand. You use Discoverer Administrator to create, customize, and maintain this view for your users so they can easily access data in Discoverer. You must have access to at least one EUL in order to use Discoverer. Access is granted using the Privileges dialog."

When using OracleAS Discoverer Viewer (the web-based tool to view Discoverer Workbooks and Worksheets over the Web, discussed in Chapter 6), the first thing you are prompted for is the Discoverer connection you would like to begin working with. The OracleAS Discoverer connection is made up of a username, a password, a connect string, and an End-User Layer (Discoverer connections also include a responsibility and security group, but these fields are of use only to Oracle's E-Business Suite, formerly knows as Oracle Financials). The End-User Layer is required before you begin working with Oracle Discoverer.

Oracle Discoverer Administrator

Building the EUL is the only part in the process that cannot be performed over the Web. The tool used to build the EULs, called Oracle Discoverer Administrator, is part of the Oracle10*g* Internet Development Suite. This tool can also modify and delete EULs. To start the Oracle Discoverer Administrator on Windows, follow this sequence:

Start | Oracle Developer Suite – <ORACLE_HOME> | Discoverer Administrator | Oracle Discoverer Administrator

To start the Oracle Discoverer Administrator on Unix, enter these commands:

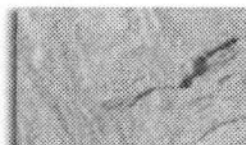

```
export ORACLE_HOME = <directory where developer suite is installed>
cd $ORACLE_HOME/bin
. ./dis51adm.sh
```

The username you specify here may or may not have an EUL built already. If it does, you will connect to it and be given the option of modifying it. If it does not, you will be presented with the option of building one (Figure 5-1). The user must exist in the database before attempting to connect.

Click Create an EUL. The first page of the Create EUL Wizard (Figure 5-2) allows you to specify who will own the EUL tables and views, whether they are available to all users in the database, and if the EUL is intended for Oracle Applications (also known as E-Business Suite).

TIP
If you logged in as a user with CREATE USER privileges, the radio button next to Create A New User will be available. You can create a new user to own the EUL tables and views at this point, if you wish.

If the Grant Access To PUBLIC check box is selected, the new EUL will be accessible to all users in the current database. Clear this check box to specify that the EUL owner is the only database user that is able to access data through this EUL. Clicking Finish here will begin the process of creating the tables and views that make up the EUL.

The Discoverer EUL tables and views now exist, but they are not populated with any data. We now have to begin the process of specifying what database objects will be accessed through OracleAS Discoverer 10*g*. After that task is completed, Discoverer will populate the newly created tables and views with metadata. After you click Close, Oracle Discoverer Administrator reconnects as the user specified and a Load Wizard page is displayed.

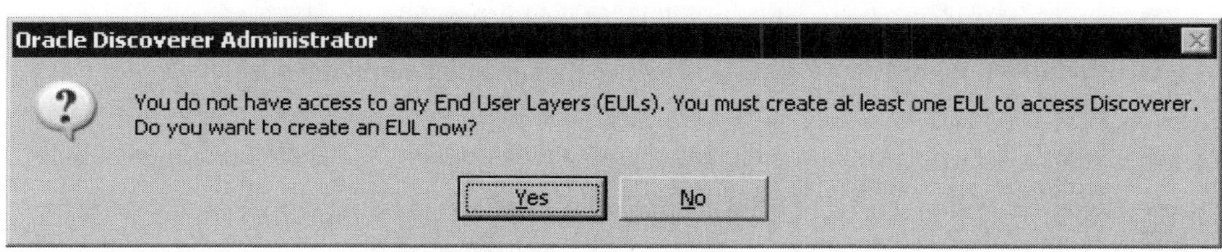

FIGURE 5-1. *The dialog to create an EUL*

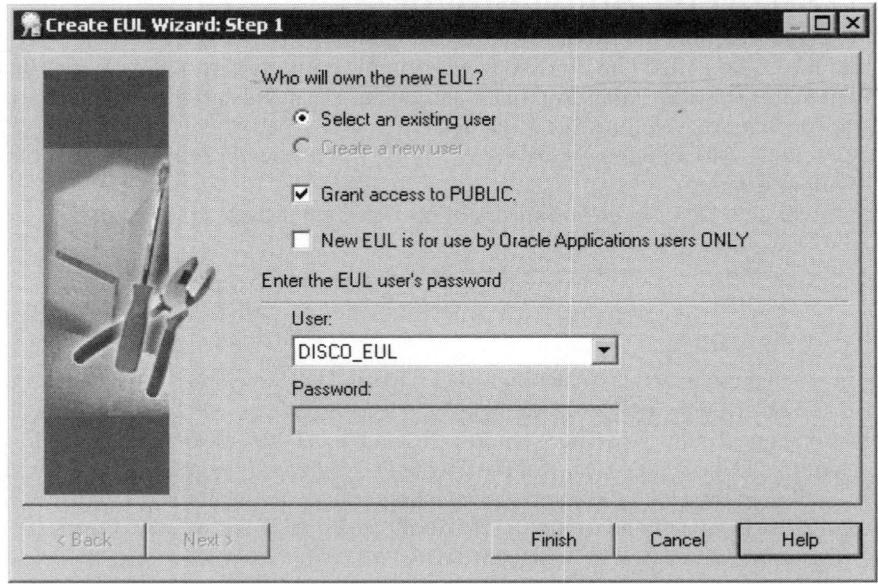

FIGURE 5-2. *The first page of the Create EUL Wizard*

You are prompted to either create a new business area or open an existing one. What, exactly, is a business area? From Oracle's documentation:

"Business areas are conceptual groupings of tables and/or views designed to match Discoverer end users specific data requirements."

You can put any schema object you like into a business area, but business areas are intended to group tables and views that end users would normally reference together. As you will see later, we can define relationships within the business area that give Discoverer end users greater functionality, and obviously, those relations cannot be created between schema objects not included in the business area. There is a one-to-many relationship between EULs and business areas: namely, that an EUL consists of more business areas and that a business area can belong to only one EUL. Creating the business area involves these things:

- Specifying what schema objects will be in the business area
- Whether joins are created between master/detail tables when the business area is populated
- Whether data hierarchies are created and whether default aggregate on numeric items are computed in the business area
- Naming the business area

The business area can be modified later, so the choices made here are not permanent. The second page of the Load Wizard (Figure 5-3) specifies what schemas will be used. If any links are defined in your database, they will be available to you in the drop-down box on the top of the dialog box.

NOTE
It's important to note that even though all schemas in the database are listed here, only those tables and views you have been granted privileges on will be available for you in the next page of the wizard, where individual tables and views are selected.

Clicking Next takes you to the third step in the wizard (Figure 5-4). Here is where you will select the individual tables and views that will make up your business area. Views have an "eye" icon next to them.

Click Next to display the fourth page of the Load Wizard (Figure 5-5). Here's where things really start to get interesting. This page is where you can define some of the advanced features of OracleAS Discoverer 10*g*. This page has five check boxes along the left side of the wizard:

- **Yes, create joins from** Use this check box to create joins on items in the business area.
- **Primary/foreign key constraints** Use this option to create joins on primary and foreign keys when primary and foreign key constraints are defined in the database. It saves you having to create the joins manually, and Discoverer will always create joins that are correct (i.e., the master and detail relationships are specified the right way round).

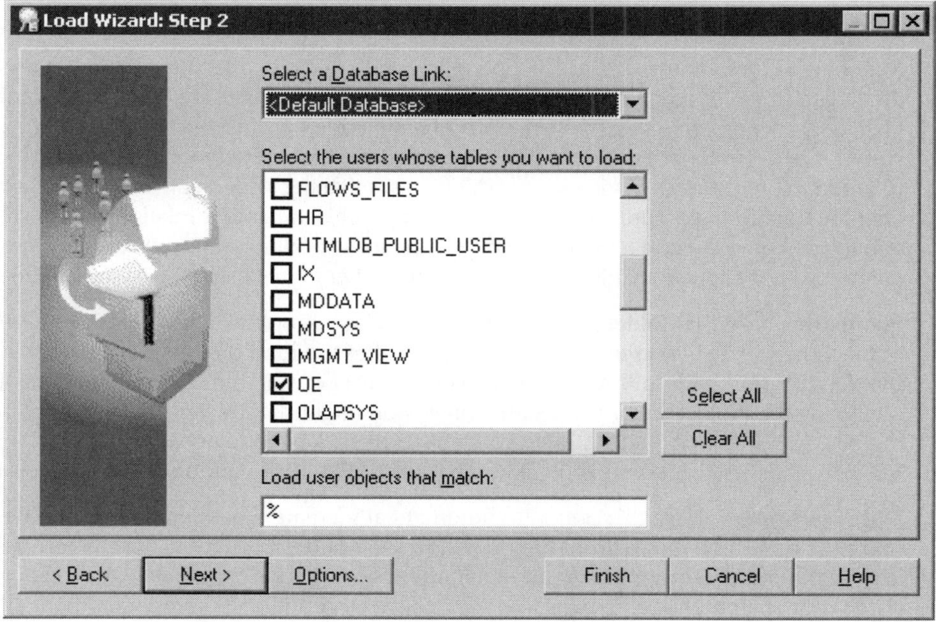

FIGURE 5-3. *The second step of the Load Wizard*

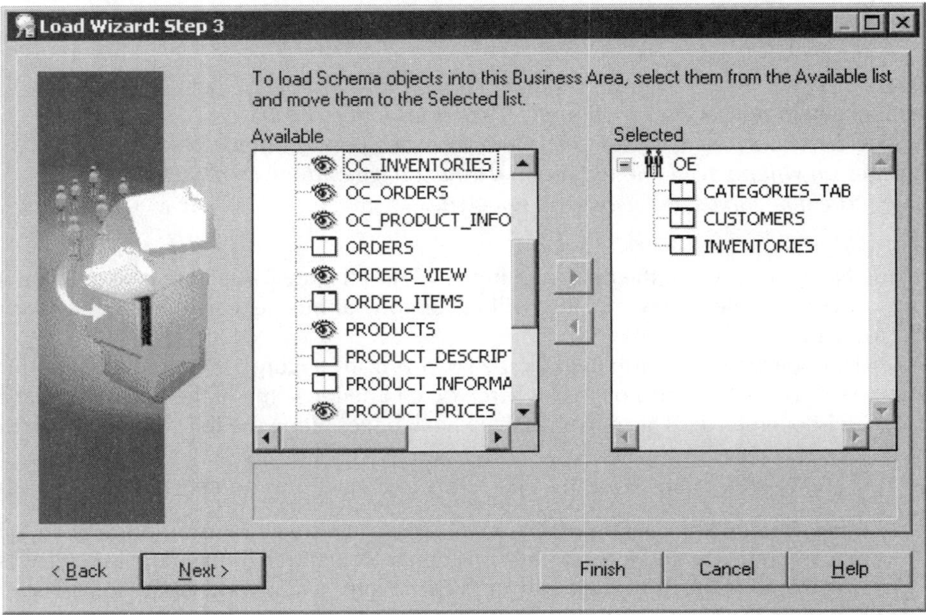

FIGURE 5-4. *The third step of the Load Wizard*

- **Matching column names** Use this option to create joins on matching column names in the database tables when no primary and foreign key constraints are defined. Discoverer checks every column name of every object being loaded against every other column name. As the number of columns that are loaded increases, the amount of processing required also increases. A side effect of doing this is that the joins created must be checked after the load to make sure they are valid. The master-detail folder relationship must be verified as being the correct way round, and the join condition must be verified as being valid (e.g., not created accidentally by two different columns using the same name).
- **Summaries based on folders that are created** Use this option to use automated summary management (ASM) to create summary folders after the load process, based on folders that Discoverer creates. ASM attempts to create a set of suitable summary folders after analyzing the table structure. Selecting this option might slightly increase the duration of the business area load, but it should give end users improved query performance. Note: Do not choose this option if you are going to run ASM, or if your database space is low.
- **Date hierarchies** Use this option to automatically create date hierarchies for date items. Choose a hierarchy from the drop-down list of default date hierarchy formats. The date hierarchy is applied to all date columns in the business area. Creating a date hierarchy enables end users to drill up/down through date items. Automatically

generating date hierarchies inserts additional (e.g., calculated) items into the folder. An extra item is created for every date item in each node in the date hierarchy.

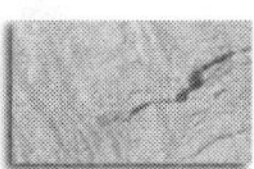

NOTE
Hierarchies are used to provide Discoverer end users the ability to either drill up to a more general level of detail or drill down to a finer level of detail (hierarchies are discussed later in this chapter).

- **Default aggregate on data points** Use this option to specify a default aggregate for numeric items. Choose an aggregate from the drop-down list. The default aggregate is SUM. This will create an aggregate for every numeric column in the tables you specified on the previous page. Most times, this is inefficient. It is much more likely that you will create individual aggregates based on your needs.
- **List of values (LOVs) for items of type** Use this option to generate LOVs based on the types you select. This option automatically creates LOVs for each axis item of each type specified, except character items longer than 40 characters. The values are derived from the values in the database column. LOVs make interacting with reports much more intuitive for end users. Selecting this option will create an LOV for every column specified. Most times, this is inefficient. It is much more likely that you will create individual LOVs to meet your needs.

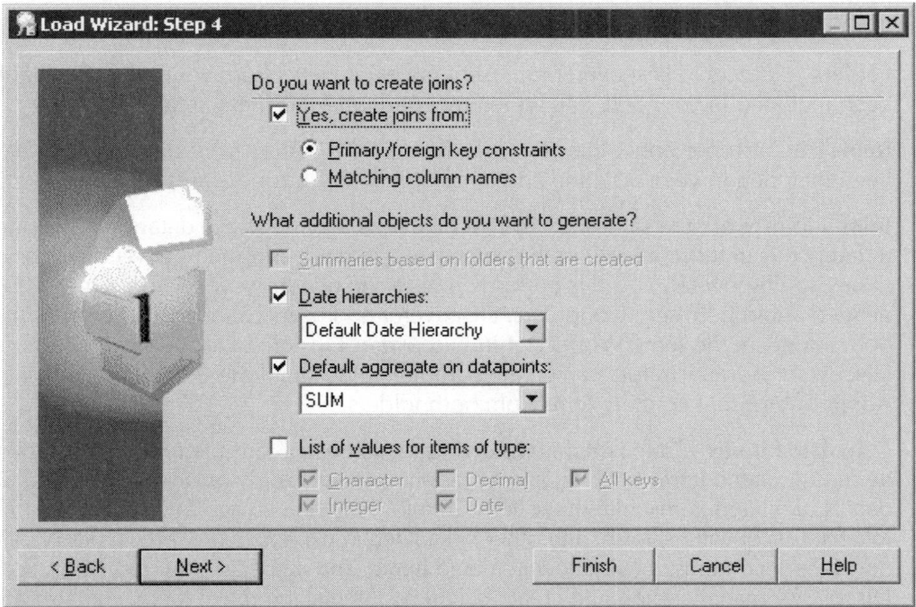

FIGURE 5-5. *The fourth page of the Load Wizard*

The final page of the Load Wizard is where the business area is named, and table and view names can be altered when added to the business area. When you click Finish, the business area is populated with data.

Oracle Discoverer Administrator Workarea

From this moment onward, when your run Oracle Discoverer Administrator and log in as the user you created, you will be asked to either create a new business area or open an existing business area. To demonstrate, log out of Discoverer Administrator and log back in again. Select Open An Existing Business Area, specify the business area you just created, and click Finish. You will see the Discoverer Administrator Workarea.

In the bottom right of the screen is a small window called the Administration Tasklist. This window provides a quick way of running the various wizards built into Oracle Discoverer Administrator to enhance your EUL and provide greater functionality and capabilities to your Discoverer end users. The Administration Tasklist acts both as a reminder of the basic steps involved in preparing a business area and as an interactive method of launching the listed tasks. You do not have to use the Administration Tasklist, but it may be helpful to track your progress.

The Load Wizard is great for creating your EUL and setting global properties that apply to all elements in your business area(s). The Discoverer Administrator Workarea is used to create specific attributes in your business area (joins, calculated items, conditions, etc.). The four tabs at the top of the Workarea enable you to access the pages of the Workarea. Each tab enables you to work with a different element of the business area design. The Workarea is your primary view of the business area, where you modify folders and items to create the business view of data for the end user.

Discoverer Terminology Now is a good time to take a small detour and discuss the terms Discoverer uses.

- **Folders** Folders in Discoverer represent tables or views from your database that have been included in your EUL and added to a particular business area.
- **Items** Items represent columns in the tables or views from your database that have been included in your EUL and added to a particular business area.
- **Joins** Joins work the same way in Discoverer as they do in the database. The only difference is in terminology: in the database, a join is performed between two or more *tables*; in Discoverer, a join is performed between two or more *folders*. Once you have defined a join between two folders, Discoverer end users can include items from both folders in the same Worksheet in Discoverer Plus (and Discoverer Desktop) and Discoverer Administrators can create complex folders and hierarchies in Discoverer Administrator that contain items from both folders.
- **Calculated items** Calculated items are items that use a formula to derive data for the item. Calculated items enable Discoverer end users to apply business calculations to the data. Calculated items (like other items in a folder) can be used in conditions, summary folders, lists of values, joins, and other calculated items. There are three types of calculated items: derived items, aggregate calculated items, and aggregate derived items. As the Discoverer manager, you can create calculated items and make them available for inclusion in Workbooks. Creating calculated items provides the following benefits:

- Discoverer end users can include a complicated calculation in their Worksheets simply by selecting a calculated item.
- You can add new items to a folder that do not exist as columns in the underlying database tables.
- You create calculated items using expressions that can contain existing items, operators, literals, and functions.
- **Conditions** Conditions filter Worksheet data, enabling Discoverer end users to analyze only the data they are interested in. You also use conditions to restrict access to sensitive data. By imposing mandatory conditions, you assure that only nonsensitive data is made available to Discoverer users. You can make sure that Discoverer end users see only the data that you want them to see. As a Discoverer Administrator, you can anticipate commonly used conditions and make them available to Discoverer end users so they can apply them in Worksheets. This enables Discoverer end users to work efficiently (Discoverer Plus users can also create their own conditions). Conditions are categorized as follows:
- **Simple conditions** These contain a single condition statement.
- **Advanced conditions** These contain two or more condition statements.
- **Nested conditions** These contain condition statements that are defined within other condition statements.
- **Advanced nested conditions** These contain two or more condition statements and also include condition statements defined within the advanced condition. As an alternative to creating advanced conditions, you might want to create two or more single conditions and apply them at the same time. This enables Discoverer users to be more selective about which parts of the condition they use.

  Conditions work in Discoverer by matching condition statements against Worksheet data so that data matching your condition statements is displayed in Workbooks. There are two types of conditions:
- Mandatory conditions are always applied to a Worksheet that contains one or more items from the folder that contains the condition. Discoverer Plus users are not notified of mandatory conditions and cannot turn them off.
- Optional conditions can be turned on or off as required by Discoverer Plus users. They can also view a condition's formula, but they are not allowed to edit the formula.

  Table 5-1 shows further differences between mandatory and optional conditions.
- **Hierarchies** Hierarchies were discussed briefly earlier, but to quickly review: hierarchies are created between items in a business area to provide Discoverer end users with the ability to drill up to a more general level of detail or drill down to a finer level of detail. There are two kinds of hierarchies:
- **Item hierarchies** Relationships between items other than dates.

Mandatory Condition	Optional Condition
Always applied to the results of a folder.	Applied to the results of a folder only if selected in Discoverer Plus.
Used by the Discoverer manager to permanently restrict the rows returned by a folder.	Provided by the Discoverer manager as a shortcut to help users build conditions more easily.
Invisible in Discoverer Plus.	Visible (but not editable) in Discoverer Plus.
When created in a complex folder, can reference items in the source folders.	When created in a complex folder, can reference only items in the complex folder.
Affects the result set (in the database) of the folder definition in the EUL.	Does not affect the result set (in the database) of the folder definition in the EUL (because an optional condition is used only when applied in Discoverer Plus).
When added, changed, or deleted, causes any summaries based on the folder to become invalid, because their result set no longer matches that of the folder. These summaries are set to "Refresh required" and must be refreshed to be made available again.	When added, changed, or deleted, has no affect on summaries based on the folder.

TABLE 5-1. *Differences Between Mandatory and Optional Conditions in Discoverer*

- **Date hierarchies** Relationships between date items. Oracle Discoverer Administrator contains a date hierarchy template and the ability for Discoverer Administrators to define custom date hierarchies.
- **Item classes** Item classes are groups of items that share some similar properties. An item class enables you to define item properties once and then assign the item class to other items that share similar properties. Discoverer uses item classes to implement the following features: lists of values, alternative sorts, and drill-to-detail links. As the Discoverer manager, it is your responsibility to create suitable item classes to support these Discoverer features. You can create a different item class for each feature, or you can specify that Discoverer uses the same item class for more than one feature. Note that an item class to support an alternative sort must also support a list of values.
- **Summary folders** Summary folders are a representation of queried data (created in Discoverer Administrator) that has been saved for reuse. The data is stored in the database in one of the following forms (depending on the version of Oracle):
- **Materialized views** Discoverer uses materialized views to store summarized data in Oracle 8.1.7 (or later) Enterprise Edition databases.
- **Tables** Discoverer uses tables to store summarized data in Oracle Standard Edition databases.

  Summary folders improve the response time of a query because the query accesses preaggregated and prejoined data rather than querying against the detail database tables.

Discoverer Connections

Oracle Discoverer requires its own connection information, as it is possible, depending on privileges granted in the database, for a user to connect to different End-User Layers (EULs). A Discoverer connection can be created in one of two ways:

- By having an administrator create a Discoverer connection via the Oracle Enterprise Manager web site
- By configuring Discoverer Server so that users are allowed to create their own connections (this feature can be disabled)

Creating a Discoverer Connection in the Enterprise Manager Web Site

This is the preferred way to set up connections and the way most administrators will configure their systems. In the Enterprise Manager Web Application Server Control web site for your middle tier, select the Discoverer component. Select Public Connections. Click Create Connections. You'll be presented with a page similar to Figure 5-6.

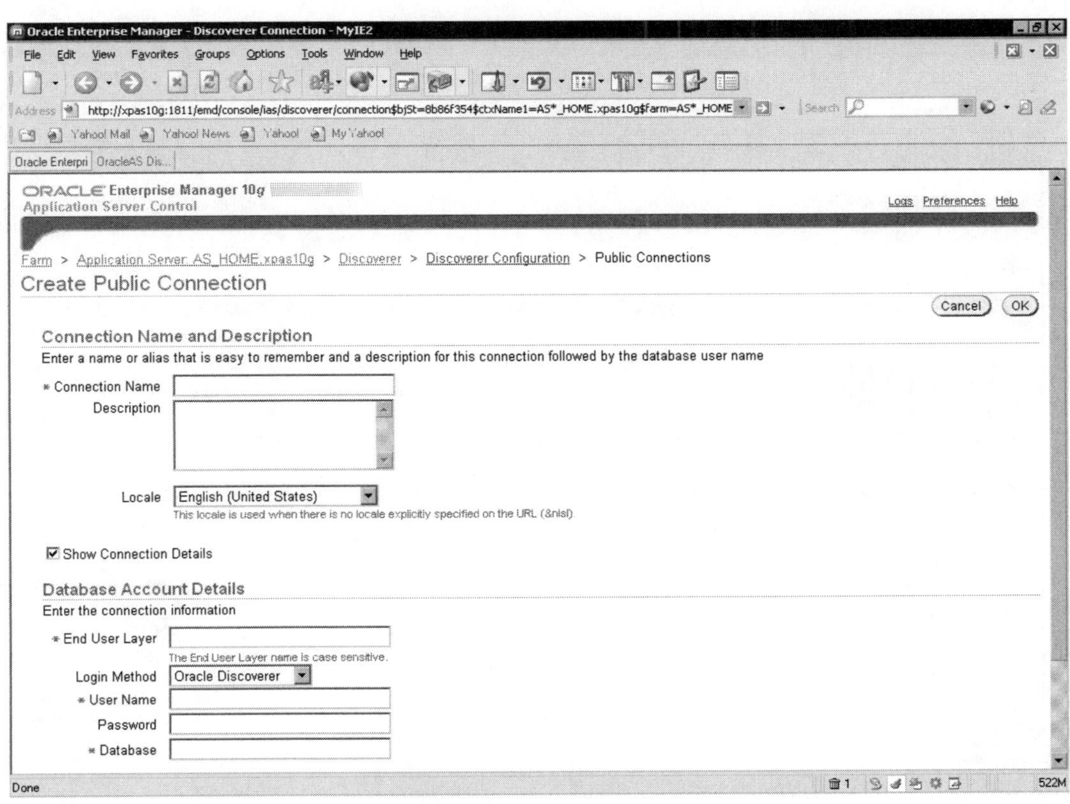

FIGURE 5-6. *The Create Public Connection screen for Discoverer*

On this page, you'll name your connection, select the End-User Layer you wish to connect to, and enter the username/password/connection string information. Asterisks denote required fields, and you'll notice that there is no asterisk next to the Password field under User Account Details—this allows the administrator to create connections that prompt a user for a password before connecting to the database.

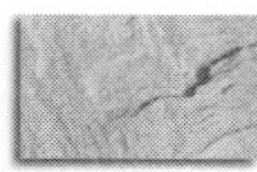

Tip
The hint on this page states that the End-User Layer is case-sensitive, but this can be misleading. I used the following code to create a user named "disco" that was going to hold my End-User Layer tables and views:

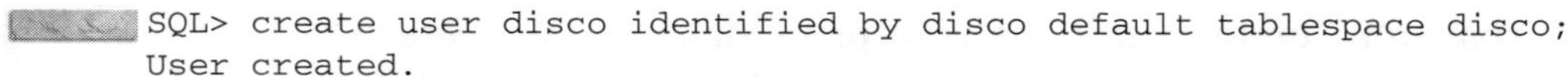

```
SQL> create user disco identified by disco default tablespace disco;
User created.
```

Although it looks as if the username is in lowercase, it's stored in the data dictionary as uppercase. Attempting to access it in Discoverer Viewer with an End-User Layer entered with lowercase letters (or anything, for that matter, not in all CAPS) will result in a page similar to Figure 5-7.

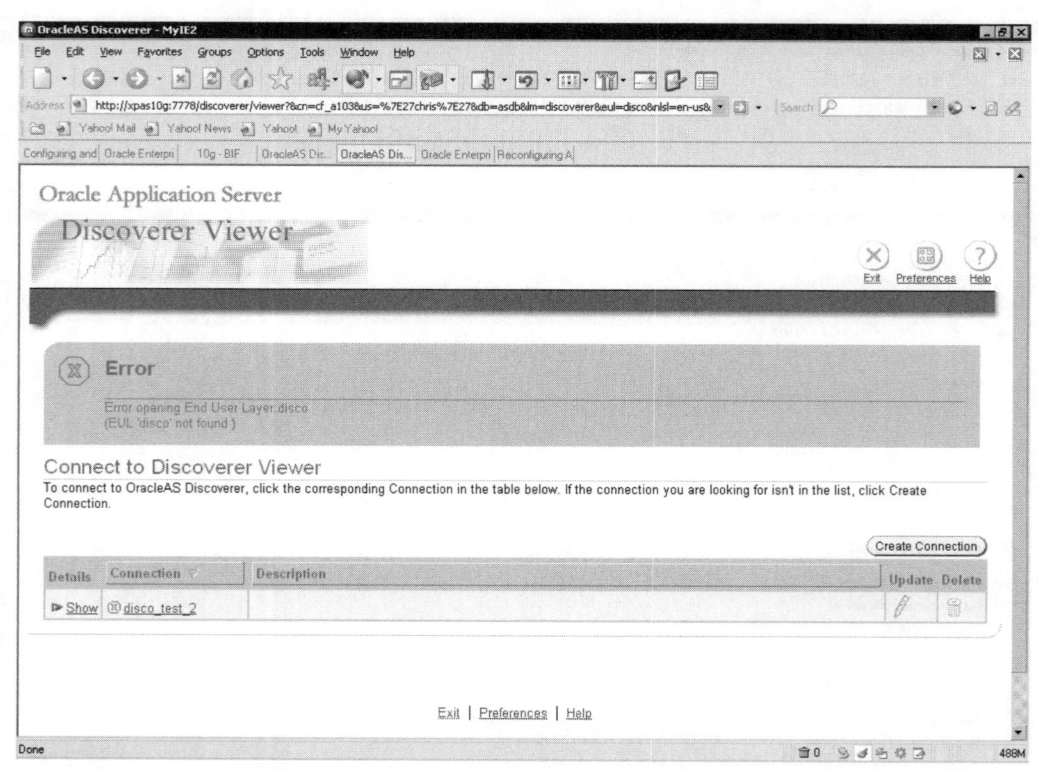

FIGURE 5-7. *An error when trying to access an EUL in lowercase*

Allowing Users to Create Their Own Discoverer Connections

If we return to the Discoverer configuration page on the Enterprise Manager Web site, you'll notice that in the middle of the page, there is a check box next to a line that says "Allow users to define and use their own private connections in Discoverer Plus and Discoverer Viewer." By default, this check box is selected, allowing end users to create their own Discoverer connections. This is generally a bad idea, as it is possible for an end user to connect to a "wrong" database. It also further introduces security risks by letting end users know username/password/connection string information, allowing knowledgeable users direct connections to your database with (potentially) malicious tools like SQL*Plus. It's a good idea to disable this feature by deselecting this option, but if you determine that this functionality is worth the risks, leave the default. Users will see a Create Connection button on the top right part of the screen (as in Figure 5-10). If this feature is disabled, the button will not appear. Any connections created using this method are valid for as long as the browser is open.

Building a Discoverer Report

The following pages walk through an example of creating a Discoverer report from scratch. As an extremely simple example, let's say I want to build a Discoverer Report of my CD collection. Although it's overkill for an example this simple, let's work off the following tables:

```
create table artists (
artist_id        number              primary key,
artist_lname     varchar2(30)        not null,
artist_fname     varchar2(20));

create table genres (
genre_id         number             primary key,
genre             varchar2(20)       not null);

create table sub_genres (
sub_genre_id     number             primary key,
sub_genre        varchar2(20)       not null);

create table cds (
cd_id            number             primary key,
artist_id        number
constraint artist_id_fk references artists (artist_id),
genre_id         number
constraint genre_id_fk references genres (genre_id),
sub_genre_id     number
constraint sub_genre_id_fk references sub_genres (sub_genre_id),
title            varchar2(30)        not null,
rating           number);
```

To populate the tables, I ran the following insert statements:

```
insert into artists values (1,'Morrison','Van');
insert into artists values (2,'Counting Crows', null);
```

```
insert into artists values (3,'Beatles, The', null);
insert into artists values (4,'Coltrane', 'John');
insert into artists values (5,'Dylan', 'Bob');

insert into genres values (1,'Classic Rock');
insert into genres values (2,'Modern Rock');
insert into genres values (3,'Jazz');
insert into genres values (4,'Pop');

insert into sub_genres values (1,'60s');
insert into sub_genres values (2,'70s');
insert into sub_genres values (3,'80s');
insert into sub_genres values (4,'90s');
insert into sub_genres values (5,'Folk - Acoustic');
insert into sub_genres values (6,'Folk - Electric');
insert into sub_genres values (7,'R and B');
insert into sub_genres values (8,'Psychedelic');
insert into sub_genres values (9,'Be-Bop');
insert into sub_genres values (10,'Experimental');
insert into sub_genres values (11,'Country Rock');

insert into cds values (1,1,1,2,'Moondance',10);
insert into cds values (2,1,1,1,'Astral Weeks',10);
insert into cds values (3,1,4,7,'The Healing Game',7);
insert into cds values (4,2,2,4,'August and Everything After',9);
insert into cds values (5,2,2,4,'Recovering The Satellites',9);
insert into cds values (6,3,1,1,'Rubber Soul',9);
insert into cds values (7,3,1,1,'Revolver',10);
insert into cds values (8,3,1,8,'Sgt Pepper',8);
insert into cds values (9,3,1,1,'Abbey Road',10);
insert into cds values (10,3,1,2,'Let It Be',6);
insert into cds values (11,4,3,9,'Blue Train',10);
insert into cds values (12,4,3,9,'Dakar',8);
insert into cds values (13,4,3,10,'A Love Supreme',10);
insert into cds values (14,5,1,5,'Another Side Of',8);
insert into cds values (15,5,1,6,'Highway 61 Revisited',10);
insert into cds values (16,5,1,11,'New Morning',8);
```

Next, we'll walk through the steps of creating an EUL. Start up Discoverer Administrator Desktop and connect to the user who owns these tables. If no EUL exists for this user, you will be prompted to create an EUL. In step 1 of the Create EUL Wizard, select Select An Existing User, Grant Access To PUBLIC, and the user who owns the preceding tables in the User field, and then click Finish. This will build the EUL tables and views in the user's schema. Click No when asked if you want to install the tutorial data. Click Close to exit the Create EUL Wizard.

The Load Wizard then begins automatically. Select Create A New Business Area. Make sure On-Line Dictionary is selected and click Next. In step 2 of the wizard, select the user who owns the tables you have created. Click Next.

In step 3 of the Load Wizard, all of the tables and views owned by the cd user are displayed. All the items that start with "EUL5_" are the Discoverer End-User Layer tables and views. Select the four tables we created previously and click the arrow pointing to the right in the middle of the dialog box (Figure 5-8). Click Next.

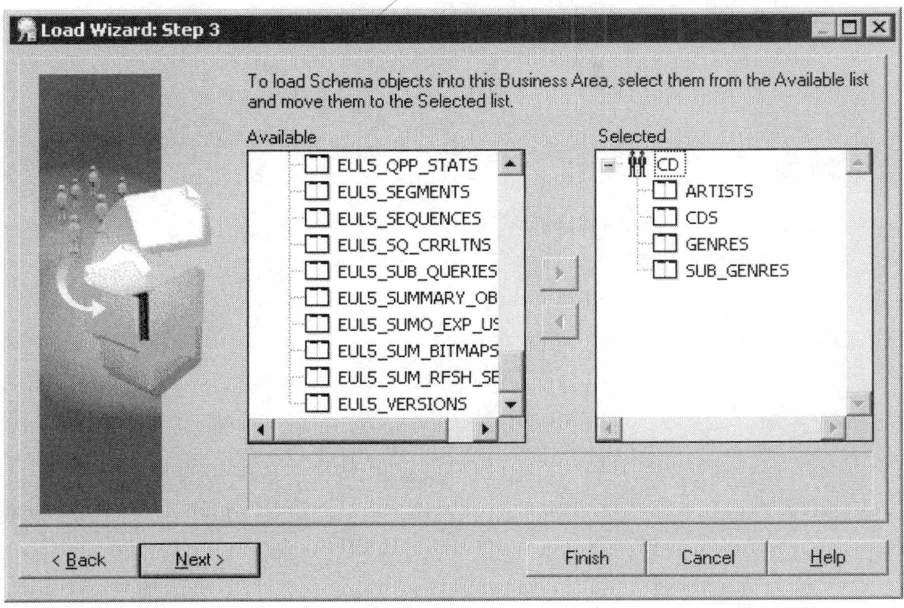

FIGURE 5-8. *Selecting the cd tables*

Step 4 of the Load Wizard presents us with some interesting decisions. At the top of Figure 5-9, we are prompted to create joins. If you select this, Discoverer will keep some extra information in the End-User Layer regarding tables that are joined on a regular basis. Since we created primary and foreign keys when creating our tables, select the Primary/Foreign Key Constraints radio button. Because there are no dates in our tables, there is no need to generate any date hierarchies, so uncheck that box.

The next box asks if we want to generate a default aggregate on datapoints; the aggregate specified defaults to SUM. An aggregate is a calculation performed on a particular column. If you select the drop-down box, you'll see that Discoverer specified the following aggregates: AVG, Count, Detail, MAX, MIN, and SUM. Aggregates allow Discoverer to maintain calculated data in the End-User Layer, which, in turn, helps complex reports run faster. Selecting this check box will generate the selected aggregate for all numeric data selected in step 3 of the Load Wizard. Table 5-2 shows the numeric items in our tables.

Here is where it will take some understanding of your data to make the best decisions when building your business areas. All of the numeric fields shown in Table 5-2, except rating in the cds table, are used as primary or foreign keys. Would we ever want to see the average of a primary key? Would we ever want to see the sum of a foreign key? Probably not; it's rare that aggregates are ever applied to primary and foreign keys. That eliminates seven of the eight numeric fields, so selecting Default Aggregate On Datapoints, which will generate aggregates for all numeric fields selected, does not make sense in this scenario. What about the rating column in the cds table? What type (if any) of aggregate might we want to perform on that field? We'll revisit this later. For now, uncheck Default Aggregate on Datapoints.

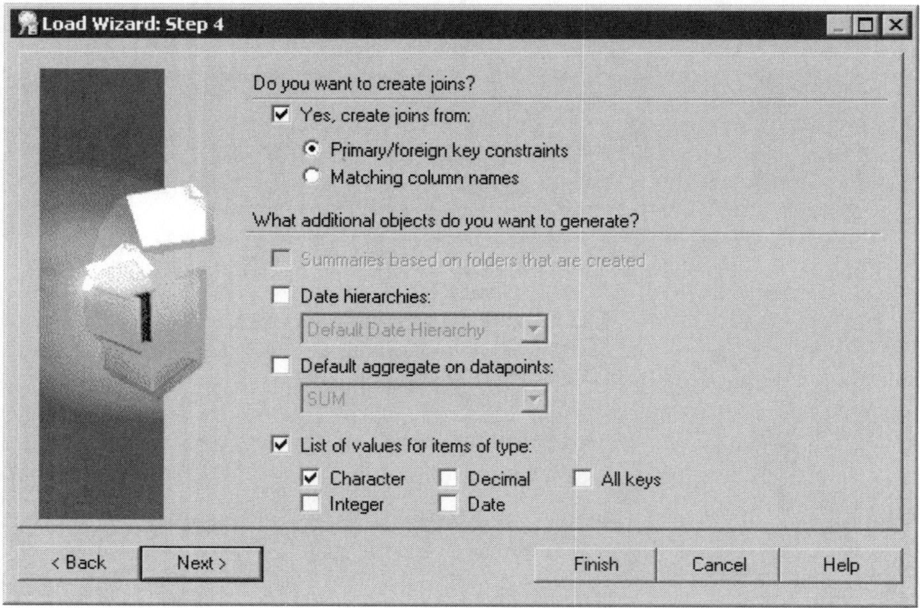

FIGURE 5-9. *Step 4 of the Load Wizard*

The last check box on step 4 of the Load Wizard asks if we want to generate lists of values (LOVs) in our Workbook. LOVs are extremely helpful for end users when selecting data, particularly in ad hoc queries. This requires, however, knowledge of the data that will constitute your report. For example, would a state field be a good candidate for an LOV? If you run a small business with

Table	Numeric Item
artists	artist_id
genres	genre_id
sub_genres	sub_genre_id
cds	cd_id
cds	artist_id
cds	genre_id
cds	sub_genre_id
cds	rating

TABLE 5-2. *Numeric Items in the cd Schema*

clients in five states, then an LOV on state is a very good idea. What if you do business in all 50 states? What if you do business internationally? As more and more entries get added to your LOV, it becomes less and less beneficial. If your company sells or stocks thousands of products, an LOV on a field like product_id is a bad idea. The check box on this screen, if selected, will generate LOVs for *every* field that matches the secondary criteria (character, integer, decimal, etc.). Usually, you will want to create individual LOVs for specific fields, but in this example, since our tables are so small, leave List Of Values For Items Of Type and Character selected. Click Next. In the last step of the wizard, give the business area a name and description and uncheck everything below the description field. Click Finish.

Connecting to Discoverer Plus

Discoverer Plus is a rich, web-based environment for creating Oracle Discoverer Workbooks and Worksheets. Running Discoverer Plus is as simple as pointing your browser to the Discoverer Plus Environment built into Oracle Application Server 10*g*:

```
http://<server>:<port>/discoverer/plus
```

The server I have been using for the examples in this book is called xpas10g. The infrastructure is running on port 7777, and the middle tier is running on 7778. To connect to Discoverer running on my machine,

```
http://xpas10g:7778/discoverer/plus
```

Everything mentioned in this section can be accomplished using Oracle Discoverer Desktop 10*g*. It is certainly not a requirement that you use Oracle Discoverer Plus to create your Discoverer Workbooks and Worksheets, but since this is a book on Oracle Web Development, Discoverer Plus is used for the development of Discoverer Workbooks and Worksheets. In order to connect to Discoverer Plus, two things need to be checked first:

- The Discoverer Web component must be "up."
- The Discoverer Plus subcomponent must be enabled.

If all of the pieces are in place, you will be presented with a screen like Figure 5-10.

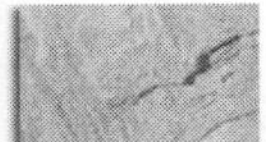

NOTE
If this is the first time you are connecting to Discoverer Plus, you will be prompted to download a browser plug-in called JInitiator. Oracle JInitiator enables users to run OracleAS Discoverer applications using Netscape Navigator or Internet Explorer. It provides the ability to specify the use of a specific Java Virtual Machine (JVM) on the client, rather than using the browser's default JVM. Oracle JInitiator runs as a plug-in for Netscape Navigator and as an ActiveX component for Internet Explorer. Oracle JInitiator does not replace or modify the default JVM provided by the browser. Rather, it provides an alternative JVM in the form of a plug-in.

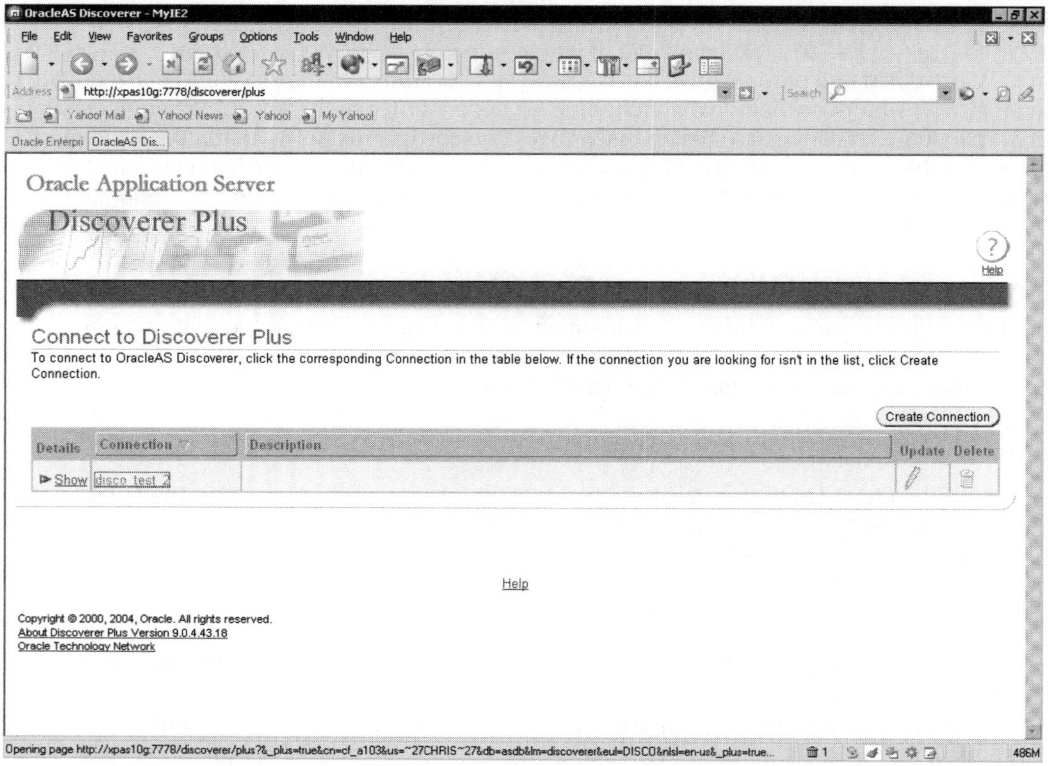

FIGURE 5-10. *The Select Discoverer Connection page*

Discoverer Plus begins with a wizard that prompts the developer to either open an existing Workbook or create a new one. Selecting Create A New Workbook displays the screen in Figure 5-11.

NOTE

We've been discussing Workbooks and Worksheets a lot up to this point without taking the time to define them. Workbooks are Discoverer files that contain Worksheets displaying data retrieved from the database. Workbooks typically contain data that is related in some way but organized to show different perspectives. Worksheets contain the data that you want to analyze, together with a number of Discoverer components to help you analyze the data. Worksheets are created in a Workbook. There is a one-to-many relationship between Workbooks and Worksheets; namely, a Workbook is made up of one or more Worksheets, and a Worksheet can belong to one and only one Workbook.

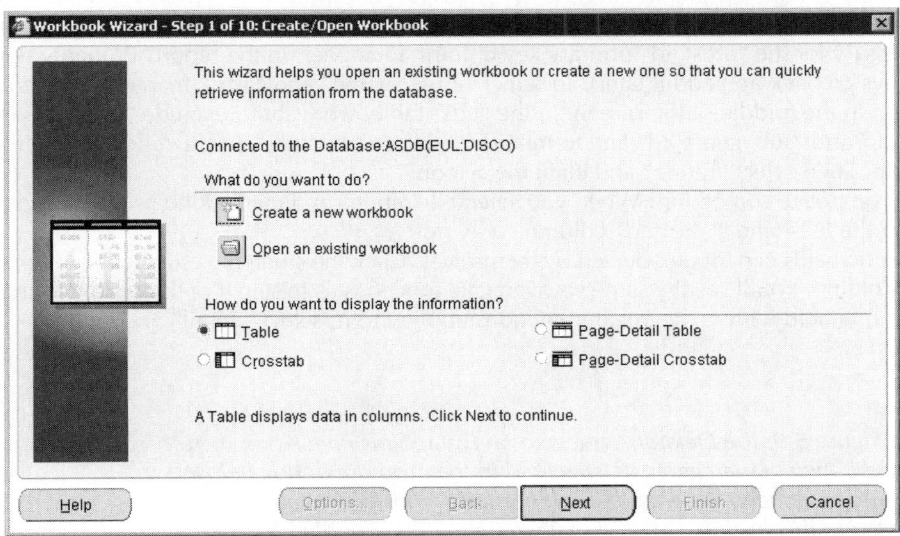

FIGURE 5-11. *Step 1 of the Create Workbook Wizard*

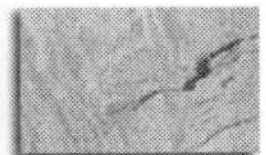

NOTE
The name Workbook Wizard is a little misleading. What we are really doing here is creating the first Worksheet within this Workbook.

There are four options for displaying your data in a Discoverer Worksheet:

- **Table** Use this option to display data in columns. This style is similar to a spreadsheet layout.
- **Crosstab** Use this option to display data in rows and columns that can be pivoted along the top and side axes.
- **Page-Detail Table** Use this option to display data in columns grouped by the items in the Page Axis area.
- **Page-Detail Crosstab** Use this to option display data in rows and columns grouped by the items in the Page Axis area.

Creating a Table-Based Report

The simplest type of Discoverer report is one based on a table. Later in this chapter, we'll discuss Crosstabs, the other common type of Discoverer report. In the Workbook Wizard, select Table and click Next.

The second page of the Workbook Wizard allows us to specify what items (columns) will appear on our report. What types of columns should appear on our CD report? The "ARTISTS" folder (table) is made up of the "ARTIST_ID," "ARTIST_LNAME," and "ARTIST_FNAME" items (columns). Certainly, we would want the artist's first and last names to appear on the report, but is it necessary for the "artist_id" primary key column to appear on the report? Probably not (we can always go back and add it later), so select "artist_lname" and "artist_fname" and then click the > icon in the middle of the screen. In the "cds" table, we want to exclude "cd_id," "artist_id," "genre_id," and "sub_genre_id" and to include "title" and "rating." Select "title" and then click the > icon. Then select "rating" and click the > icon.

Did you notice something? When you selected "rating" and clicked the > icon, it did not appear in the left-hand "Selected" column. Why not?

Numeric fields cannot be selected by themselves. Click the small plus sign to the left of the "rating" column. You'll see the same six aggregate functions as in step 4 of the Load Wizard. To see the rating field with no aggregate functions applied to it, select "detail" and then the > icon (Figure 5-12).

NOTE
If, in Figure 5-9, the Default Aggregate on Datapoints check box were selected, the default aggregate specified in the drop-down box below it would have been generated for all numeric fields in the tables selected in this business area. If that were the case, double-clicking the "rating" item would have moved the default aggregate generated for that item into the right-hand column.

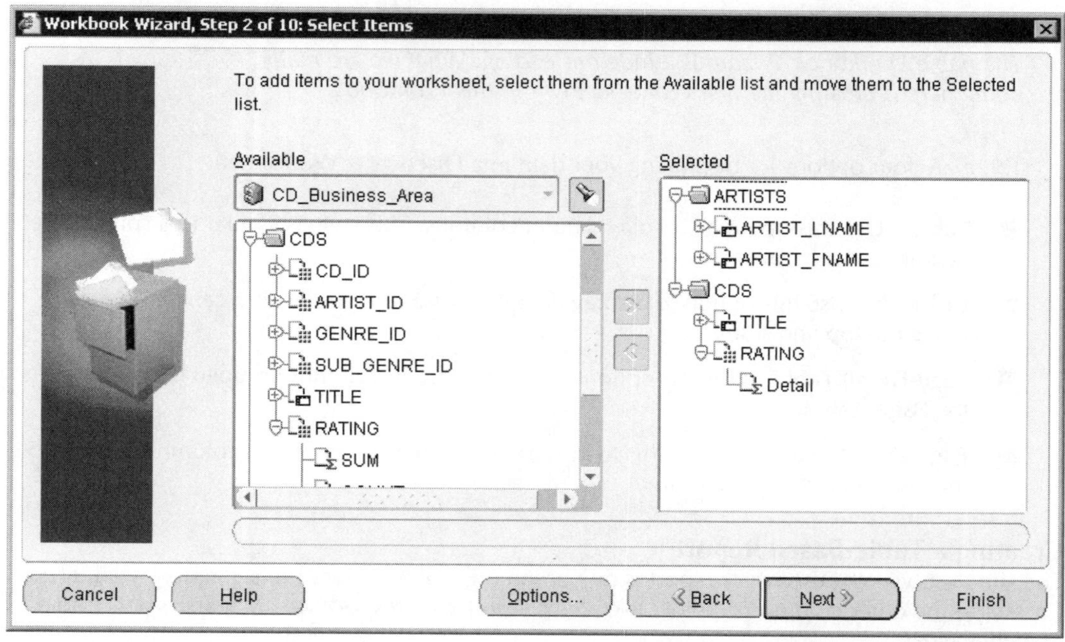

FIGURE 5-12. *Selecting the detail of the "rating" column in the Workbook Wizard*

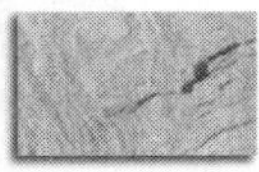

NOTE

The six aggregate functions in Figure 5-12 are the same six as the functions we could have specified (but didn't) in Figure 5-9. If we didn't specify them in the Load Wizard, why do they show up here? Just because we didn't specify any aggregate columns in the Load Wizard, that doesn't mean those functions are unavailable to us. It's a question of how and when the column is aggregated. If we chose to build an aggregate column in the Load Wizard (or manually, after the EUL and Workarea[s] were built), a column would be built in one of the EUL tables that would maintain values for the aggregated column. Querying that column would return a value almost instantly. By not creating an aggregate column but instead applying the function here in the Workbook Wizard, we specify that the report will force the database to calculate the value(s) at run time and work that much harder to return its value(s).

Finish this page up by selecting the genre item (column) from the genres folder (table) and the sub_genre item from the sub_genres folder. At this point, we can skip the last eight steps of the wizard by clicking Finish in the lower right of the window. Later, we'll enhance our report by modifying it in the Edit Worksheet window, which will duplicate the functionality of the wizard pages we're skipping now. When you click Finish, the report is generated in the database and is run (Figure 5-13).

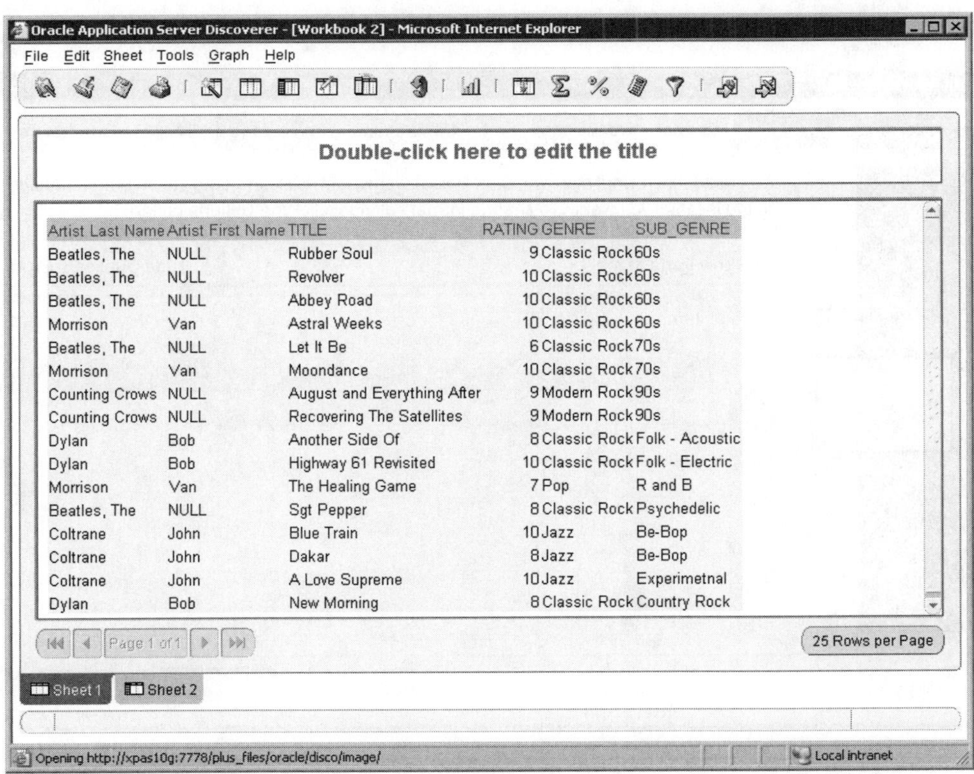

Artist Last Name	Artist First Name	TITLE	RATING	GENRE	SUB_GENRE
Beatles, The	NULL	Rubber Soul	9	Classic Rock	60s
Beatles, The	NULL	Revolver	10	Classic Rock	60s
Beatles, The	NULL	Abbey Road	10	Classic Rock	60s
Morrison	Van	Astral Weeks	10	Classic Rock	60s
Beatles, The	NULL	Let It Be	6	Classic Rock	70s
Morrison	Van	Moondance	10	Classic Rock	70s
Counting Crows	NULL	August and Everything After	9	Modern Rock	90s
Counting Crows	NULL	Recovering The Satellites	9	Modern Rock	90s
Dylan	Bob	Another Side Of	8	Classic Rock	Folk - Acoustic
Dylan	Bob	Highway 61 Revisited	10	Classic Rock	Folk - Electric
Morrison	Van	The Healing Game	7	Pop	R and B
Beatles, The	NULL	Sgt Pepper	8	Classic Rock	Psychedelic
Coltrane	John	Blue Train	10	Jazz	Be-Bop
Coltrane	John	Dakar	8	Jazz	Be-Bop
Coltrane	John	A Love Supreme	10	Jazz	Experimetnal
Dylan	Bob	New Morning	8	Classic Rock	Country Rock

FIGURE 5-13. *The CD report*

The report is correct, but not in the state we would need it to be in production. We can enhance the report by selecting Sheet | Edit Worksheet in the menu. The Edit Worksheet window appears. The tabs along the top correspond to steps 2–10 in the Create Worksheet Wizard. The leftmost tab (Select Items) should look familiar—it's the last step we performed before clicking Finish and generating the report in the Create Workbook Wizard. In this tab, developers can add or remove items from the report.

The next tab, Table Layout, serves two specific functions. First, it allows the reordering of columns in the report. Simply drag a column to the left or right and it is automatically repositioned on the report (in Figure 5-14, "rating" was dragged to the right side of the report). The second feature of this tab is the specification of page items. Page items are a way to filter data on a report and to give end users a method of seeing different types of data without having to recode the report for different types of conditions. To enable Page Items, click the Show Page Items check box. A small box called Page Items appears (Figure 5-14).

To see how this feature works, select "ARTIST_LNAME" and drag it into the Page Items box, as shown in Figure 5-15. Select OK to run the report again. You now have a report with a drop-down box automatically populated with the values in that column. Selecting different values will automatically generate a new report based on that value.

Selecting All will produce the same report as in Figure 5-13. We can continue enhancing the report to make it more presentable. Bring up the Edit Worksheet window again by selecting Sheet | Edit Worksheet. Click the Format tab (Figure 5-16).

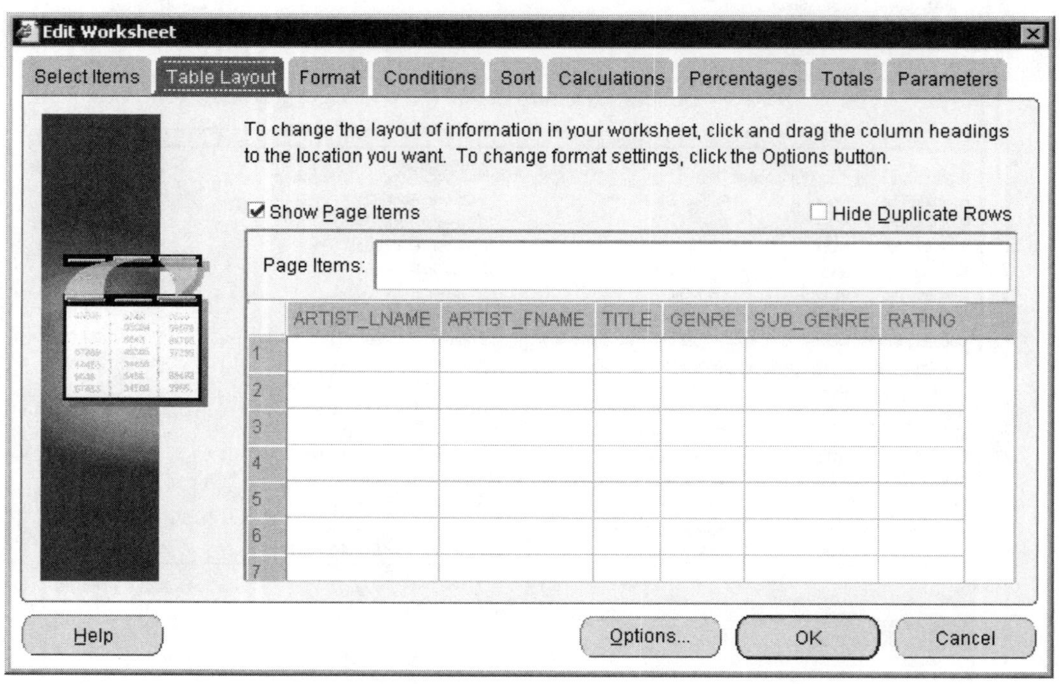

FIGURE 5-14. *The Edit Worksheet window with Page Items selected*

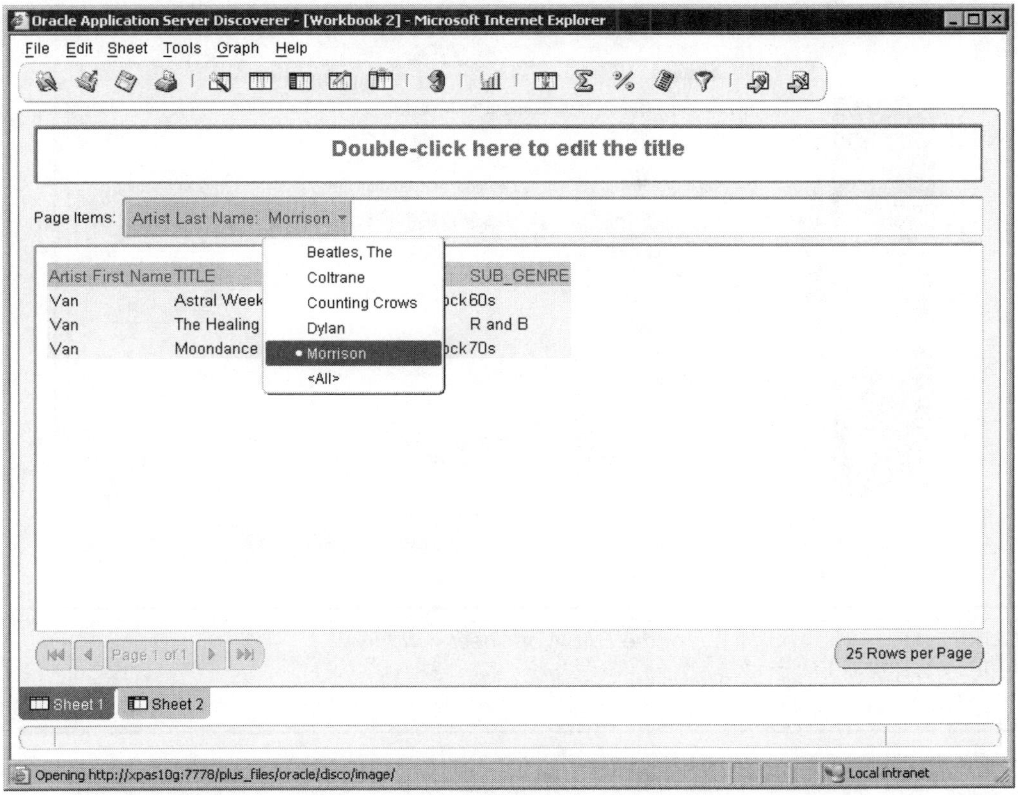

FIGURE 5-15. *The CD report with the Page Items drop-down box*

The headings in our report are not very intuitive. Click ARTIST_FNAME and then select Edit Heading. Change each of the headings to something more intuitive. From this page of the wizard, you can also change the background color of the report, the font used, and its size and numerical formats.

The fourth tab in the Edit Worksheet window allows developers to define conditions for the report. Just because a condition is defined, that does not mean it must be used in the report. This is especially useful for creating numerous or complex queries and allowing Discoverer end users (usually power users) to apply different criteria to the data depending on their needs without having to recode, test, and maintain multiple reports. Click New to define a new condition.

NOTE
The ability to disable and enable conditions exists only in Discoverer Plus. It does not exist in Discoverer Viewer.

Figure 5-17 shows the New Condition window. Here, you can create a condition based on any of the columns in any of the tables that make up your report, even those not displayed.

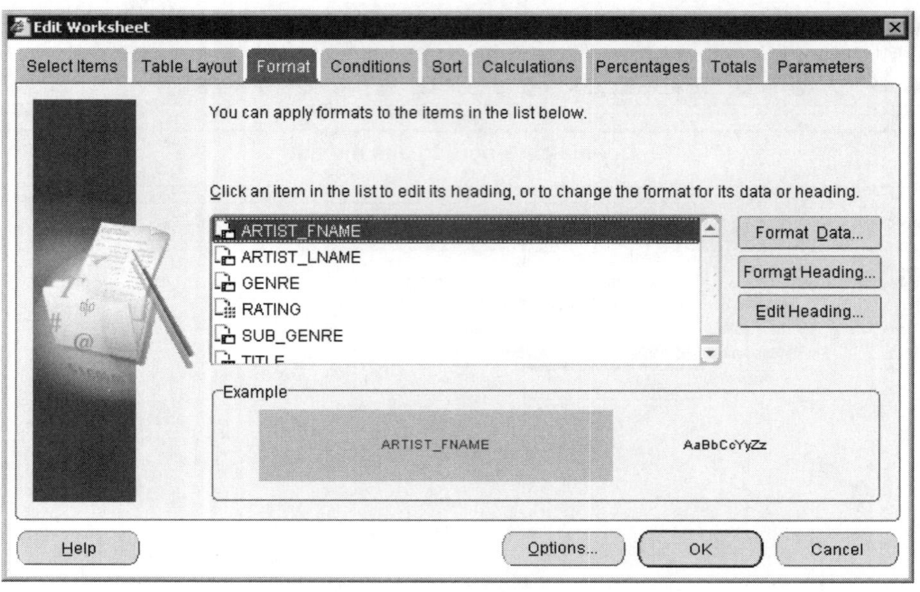

FIGURE 5-16. *The Format tab of the Edit Worksheet window*

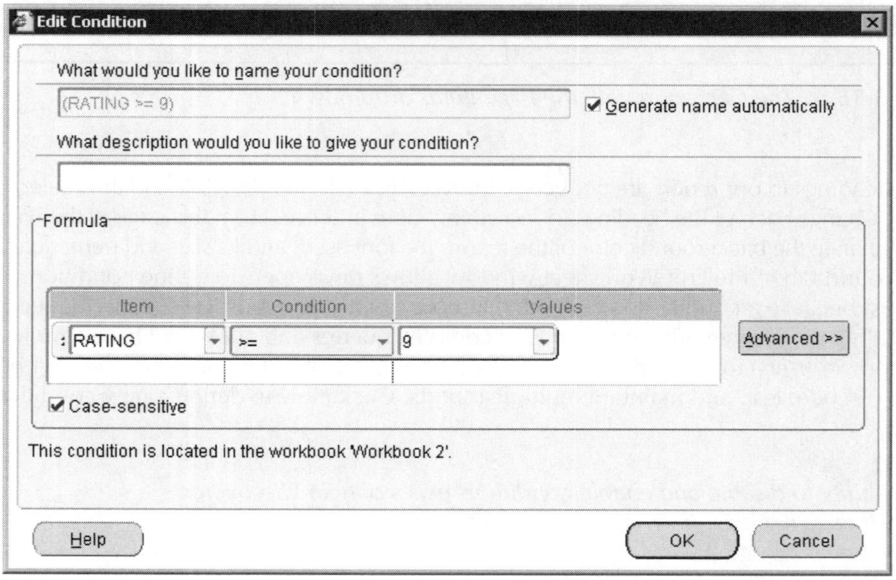

FIGURE 5-17. *A condition where the rating must be greater than or equal to 9*

Clicking the drop-down box next to the "Item" column will display all of the columns you can define a condition for. Included in that list is the Create Calculation selection, which allows developers to perform mathematical calculations (on numeric fields) or concatenation (on non-numeric fields) before defining the condition criteria. Clicking the Advanced button allows the definition of multiple criteria separated by the following four clauses: "and," "or," "not and," and "not or." For a simple test, let's create a condition so that only CDs with a rating of 9 or higher will be displayed.

Back in the Edit Worksheet window, the condition is displayed with a check box next to it. If it is left checked, the criteria will be applied when the report is run. To run the report without the criteria, simply uncheck the box next to the criteria (Figure 5-18).

The next tab, Sort, is pretty self-explanatory. This tab allows developers to define the sorting criteria for the report. You can sort on any of the columns in the report, defining whether the specified columns are to be sorted low-to-high or high-to-low, whether they are "grouped" (repeating columns do not display the rows values over and over again), and whether the column is displayed or hidden on the report.

The sixth tab in the Edit Worksheet window, Calculations, allows developers to define calculations for items on the report. The important thing to note here is that these calculations are at the row level; that is, this is not the place to define sums or averages for your entire report (later on we'll look at the Totals tab in the Edit Worksheet window). Calculations defined here are applicable only to the data in a particular row. For example, you may think you could define a calculation that averages the rating for a particular artist by defining a calculation. The results, however, would not be particularly useful (Figure 5-19).

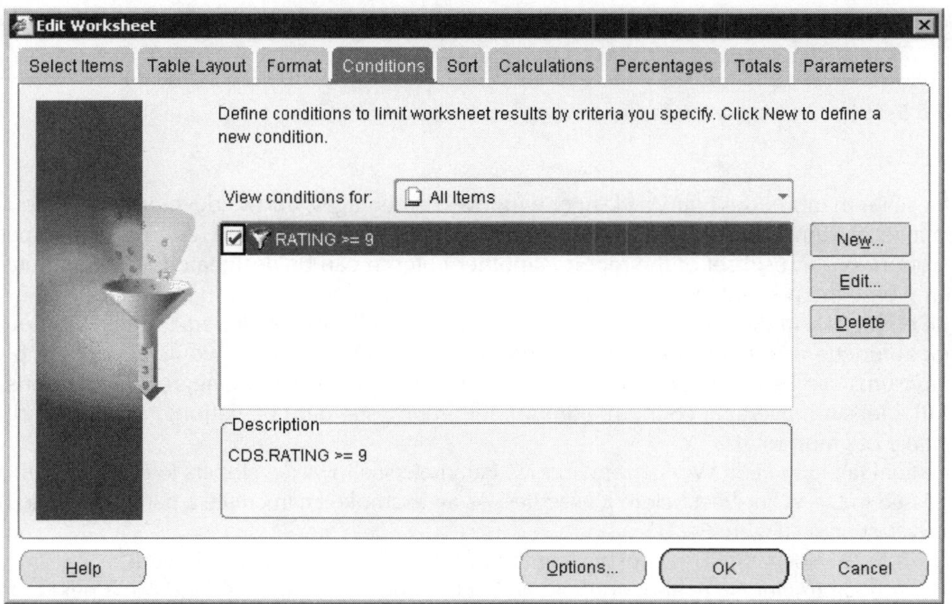

FIGURE 5-18. *Enabling/disabling a condition*

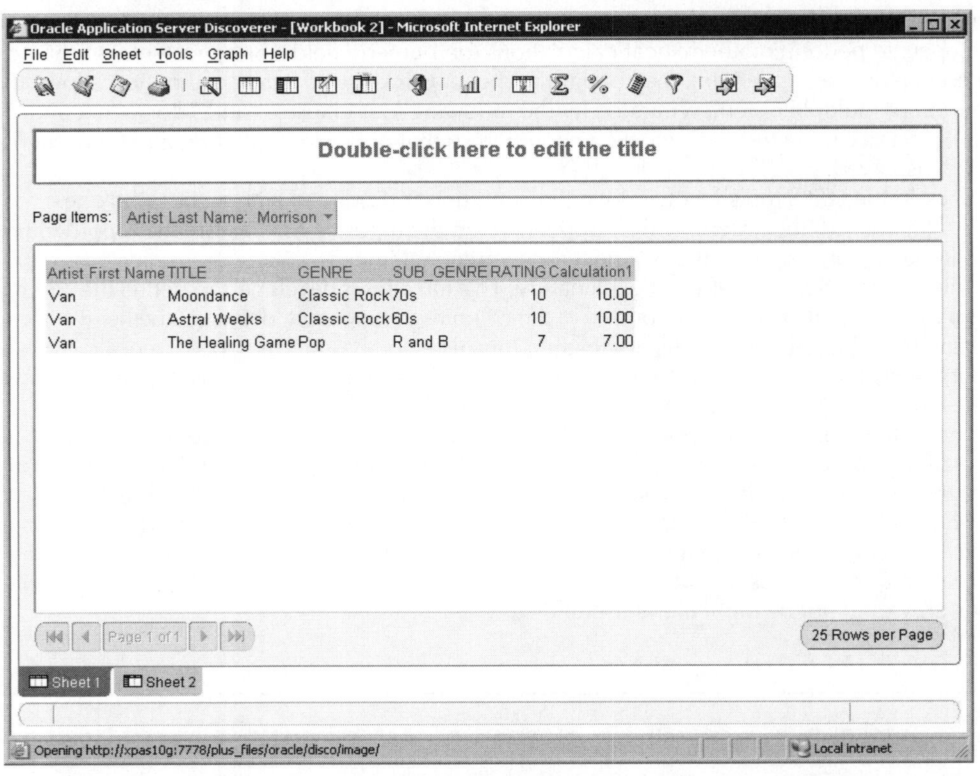

FIGURE 5-19. *The report with the "wrong" calculation*

The seventh tab in the Edit Worksheet window, Percentages, allows developers to calculate percentages of items in their report. The percentage can be for the whole report, for each page in the report, or for a subset of the report—another column can be designated as the subtotal column where the percentage is calculated each time the subtotal column changes.

The eighth tab in the Edit Worksheet window, Totals, allows developers to define various numerical functions to their reports (see Figure 5-20). The word "totals" would seem to imply that only sums can be calculated, but that is not the case. The following aggregate functions are available: sum, average, count, maximum, minimum, standard deviation, variance, and percentage of grand total.

The final tab in the Edit Worksheet window, Parameters, allows developers to define parameters to be passed to the Worksheet before it executes. As an example, I can create a parameter based on the artist's last name (Figure 5-21).

Figure 5-22 shows the results of adding the parameter in Discoverer Viewer.

After the parameter is created, you can go back to the Conditions tab and see a new entry (Figure 5-23).

Edit Total
Which data point would you like to create a total on?
RATING
What kind of total do you want?
f(x) Average
Adds all the values and divides by the number of values.
Where would you like your total to be shown?
Grand total at bottom
Subtotal at each change in:
All Group Sorted Items
Don't display total for a single row
Which page items do you want to include?
Calculate totals only for current page items.
Calculate totals for all page items.
Example
The example above shows a Sum total calculated from sample data.
What label do you want to be shown?
Average
Format Heading...
Generate label automatically
Format Data...
Help
OK
Cancel

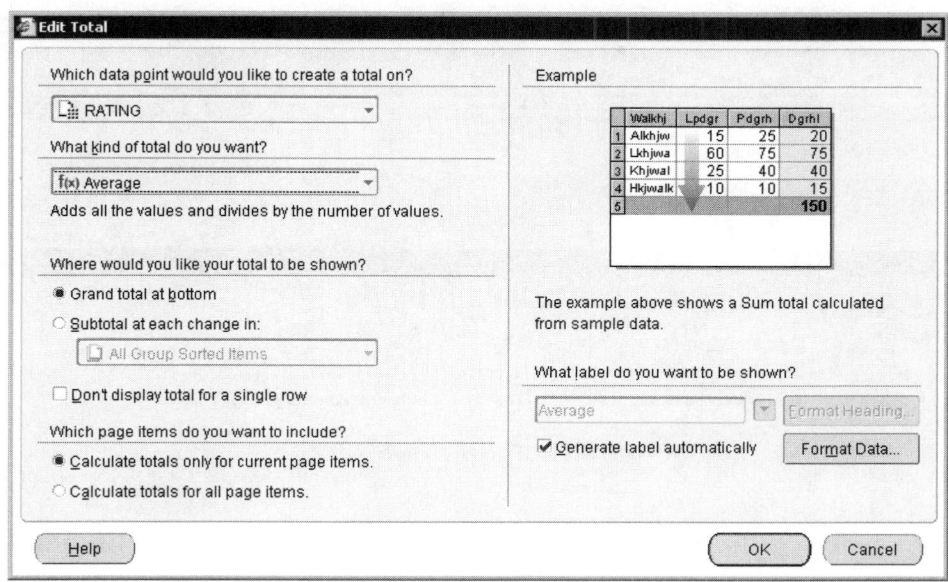

FIGURE 5-20. *The Edit Total page*

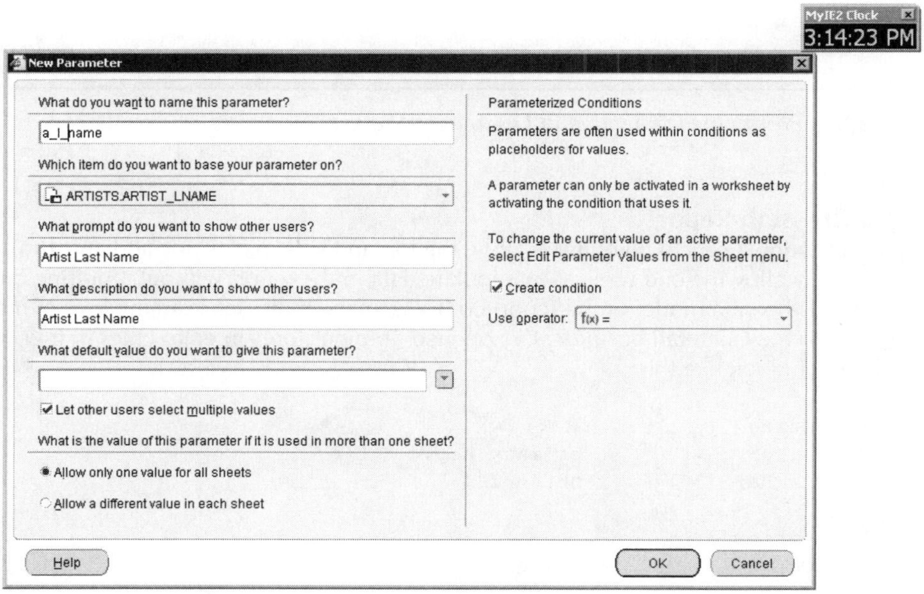

MyIE2 Clock
3:14:23 PM
New Parameter
What do you want to name this parameter?
a_l_name
Which item do you want to base your parameter on?
ARTISTS.ARTIST_LNAME
What prompt do you want to show other users?
Artist Last Name
What description do you want to show other users?
Artist Last Name
What default value do you want to give this parameter?
Let other users select multiple values
What is the value of this parameter if it is used in more than one sheet?
Allow only one value for all sheets
Allow a different value in each sheet
Parameterized Conditions
Parameters are often used within conditions as placeholders for values.
A parameter can only be activated in a worksheet by activating the condition that uses it.
To change the current value of an active parameter, select Edit Parameter Values from the Sheet menu.
Create condition
Use operator:
f(x) =
Help
OK
Cancel

FIGURE 5-21. *The Create Parameter page*

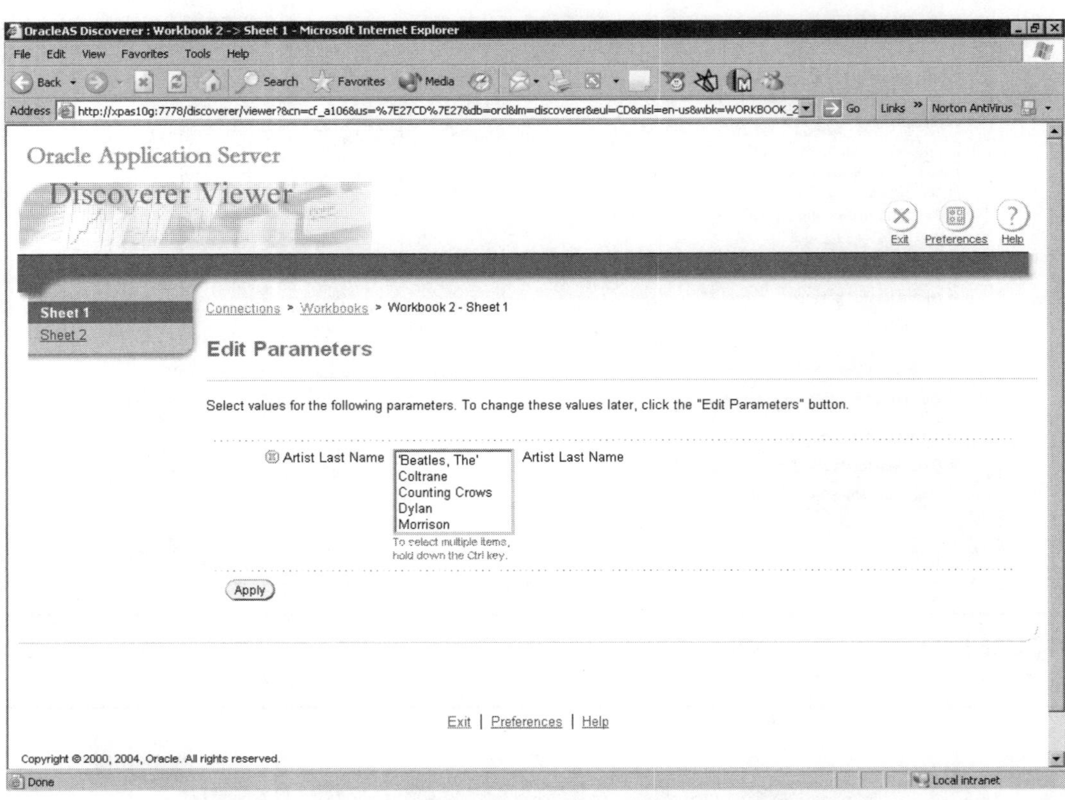

FIGURE 5-22. *Prompting for a value in Discoverer Viewer*

Creating a Crosstab Report

Crosstab reports allow users to pivot items along the top and side axes. They add an extra layer of functionality by allowing end users to manipulate data in the report without requiring complex changes in either the data model or the report code. As an example, let's say my love of music has taken me into the CD retail business. I've opened up nine stores in eight cities in four states. My database might look like this:

```
create table states (
state_id     number              primary key,
state_name   varchar2(30)        not null);

create table cities (
city_id      number              primary key,
state_id     number
```

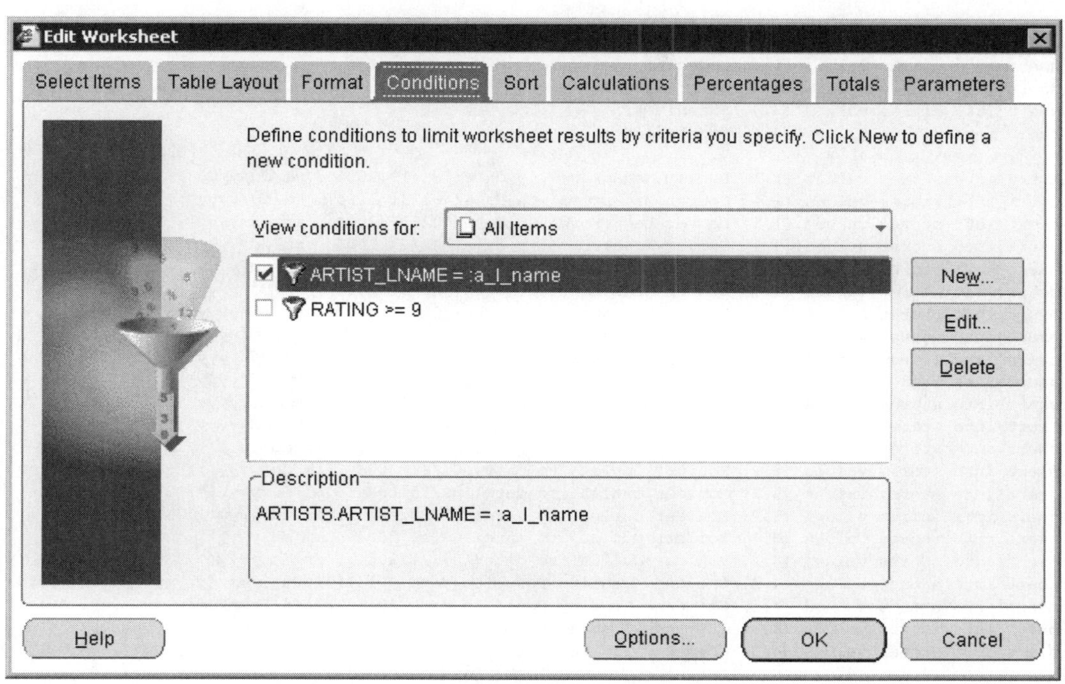

FIGURE 5-23. *Viewing the new condition after parameter creation*

```
constraint state_id_fk references states (state_id),
city_name   varchar2(20)      not null);

create table stores (
store_id    number,
city_id     number
constraint city_id_fk references cities (city_id),
store_name  varchar2(30),
sales_date  date,
total_sales number);
```

The data for the first quarter of 2004 for my stores might look something like this:

```
insert into states values (1,'Colorado');
insert into states values (2,'Wyoming');
insert into states values (3,'Utah');
insert into states values (4,'Arizona');

insert into cities values (1,1,'Denver');
```

```
insert into cities values (2,1,'Boulder');
insert into cities values (3,2,'Cheyenne');
insert into cities values (4,2,'Gilette');
insert into cities values (5,3,'Ogden');
insert into cities values (6,3,'Salt Lake City');
insert into cities values (7,4,'Phoenix');
insert into cities values (8,4,'Scottsdale');

insert into stores values (1,1,'Denver Megastore',to_date('01/15/2004','mm/dd/yyyy'),1234.56);
insert into stores values (1,1,'Denver Megastore',to_date('01/31/2004','mm/dd/yyyy'),3562.33);
insert into stores values (1,1,'Denver Megastore',to_date('02/15/2004','mm/dd/yyyy'),2345.67);
insert into stores values (1,1,'Denver Megastore',to_date('02/28/2004','mm/dd/yyyy'),3455.87);
insert into stores values (1,1,'Denver Megastore',to_date('03/15/2004','mm/dd/yyyy'),3456.78);
insert into stores values (1,1,'Denver Megastore',to_date('03/31/2004','mm/dd/yyyy'),9368.95);
insert into stores values (2,1,'Denver Ministore',to_date('01/15/2004','mm/dd/yyyy'),234.56);
insert into stores values (2,1,'Denver Ministore',to_date('01/31/2004','mm/dd/yyyy'),458.14);
insert into stores values (2,1,'Denver Ministore',to_date('02/15/2004','mm/dd/yyyy'),345.67);
insert into stores values (2,1,'Denver Ministore',to_date('02/28/2004','mm/dd/yyyy'),418.39);
insert into stores values (2,1,'Denver Ministore',to_date('03/15/2004','mm/dd/yyyy'),456.78);
insert into stores values (2,1,'Denver Ministore',to_date('03/31/2004','mm/dd/yyyy'),457.14);
insert into stores values (3,2,'Boulder Outlet',to_date('01/15/2004','mm/dd/yyyy'),1234.56);
insert into stores values (3,2,'Boulder Outlet',to_date('01/31/2004','mm/dd/yyyy'),4544.89);
insert into stores values (3,2,'Boulder Outlet',to_date('02/15/2004','mm/dd/yyyy'),1234.56);
insert into stores values (3,2,'Boulder Outlet',to_date('02/28/2004','mm/dd/yyyy'),3454.54);
insert into stores values (3,2,'Boulder Outlet',to_date('03/15/2004','mm/dd/yyyy'),1234.56);
insert into stores values (3,2,'Boulder Outlet',to_date('03/31/2004','mm/dd/yyyy'),3209.09);
insert into stores values (4,3,'Cheyenne Trading Post',to_date('01/15/2004','mm/dd/yyyy'),1234.56);
insert into stores values (4,3,'Cheyenne Trading Post',to_date('01/31/2004','mm/dd/yyyy'),453.46);
insert into stores values (4,3,'Cheyenne Trading Post',to_date('02/15/2004','mm/dd/yyyy'),123.56);
insert into stores values (4,3,'Cheyenne Trading Post',to_date('02/28/2004','mm/dd/yyyy'),876.38);
insert into stores values (4,3,'Cheyenne Trading Post',to_date('03/15/2004','mm/dd/yyyy'),12.56);
insert into stores values (4,3,'Cheyenne Trading Post',to_date('03/31/2004','mm/dd/yyyy'),90.89);
insert into stores values (5,4,'Gilette Swap n Trade',to_date('01/15/2004','mm/dd/yyyy'),1234.56);
insert into stores values (5,4,'Gilette Swap n Trade',to_date('01/31/2004','mm/dd/yyyy'),402.98);
insert into stores values (5,4,'Gilette Swap n Trade',to_date('02/15/2004','mm/dd/yyyy'),2222.22);
insert into stores values (5,4,'Gilette Swap n Trade',to_date('02/28/2004','mm/dd/yyyy'),346.74);
insert into stores values (5,4,'Gilette Swap n Trade',to_date('03/15/2004','mm/dd/yyyy'),3333.33);
insert into stores values (5,4,'Gilette Swap n Trade',to_date('03/31/2004','mm/dd/yyyy'),930.76);
insert into stores values (6,5,'Ogden Outlet',to_date('01/15/2004','mm/dd/yyyy'),333.33);
insert into stores values (6,5,'Ogden Outlet',to_date('01/31/2004','mm/dd/yyyy'),934.06);
insert into stores values (6,5,'Ogden Outlet',to_date('02/15/2004','mm/dd/yyyy'),444.44);
insert into stores values (6,5,'Ogden Outlet',to_date('02/28/2004','mm/dd/yyyy'),4890.76);
insert into stores values (6,5,'Ogden Outlet',to_date('03/15/2004','mm/dd/yyyy'),555.55);
insert into stores values (6,5,'Ogden Outlet',to_date('03/31/2004','mm/dd/yyyy'),9856.55);
insert into stores values (7,6,'Salt Lake Megastore',to_date('01/15/2004','mm/dd/yyyy'),56.78);
insert into stores values (7,6,'Salt Lake Megastore',to_date('01/31/2004','mm/dd/yyyy'),2293.65);
insert into stores values (7,6,'Salt Lake Megastore',to_date('02/15/2004','mm/dd/yyyy'),78.90);
insert into stores values (7,6,'Salt Lake Megastore',to_date('02/28/2004','mm/dd/yyyy'),4698.76);
insert into stores values (7,6,'Salt Lake Megastore',to_date('03/15/2004','mm/dd/yyyy'),67.89);
insert into stores values (7,6,'Salt Lake Megastore',to_date('03/31/2004','mm/dd/yyyy'),908.39);
insert into stores values (8,7,'Phoenix Hot Tracks',to_date('01/15/2004','mm/dd/yyyy'),135.79);
insert into stores values (8,7,'Phoenix Hot Tracks',to_date('01/31/2004','mm/dd/yyyy'),345.08);
insert into stores values (8,7,'Phoenix Hot Tracks',to_date('02/15/2004','mm/dd/yyyy'),246.80);
insert into stores values (8,7,'Phoenix Hot Tracks',to_date('02/28/2004','mm/dd/yyyy'),9803.47);
insert into stores values (8,7,'Phoenix Hot Tracks',to_date('03/15/2004','mm/dd/yyyy'),987.65);
insert into stores values (8,7,'Phoenix Hot Tracks',to_date('03/131/2004','mm/dd/yyyy'),5398.74);
insert into stores values (9,8,'Scottsdale Ministore',to_date('01/15/2004','mm/dd/yyyy'),11.22);
insert into stores values (9,8,'Scottsdale Ministore',to_date('01/31/2004','mm/dd/yyyy'),3679.47);
insert into stores values (9,8,'Scottsdale Ministore',to_date('02/15/2004','mm/dd/yyyy'),22.33);
insert into stores values (9,8,'Scottsdale Ministore',to_date('02/28/2004','mm/dd/yyyy'),865.23);
insert into stores values (9,8,'Scottsdale Ministore',to_date('03/15/2004','mm/dd/yyyy'),33.44);
insert into stores values (9,8,'Scottsdale Ministore',to_date('03/31/2004','mm/dd/yyyy'),857.91);
```

The End-User Layer created earlier does not have these tables in it, so we'll have to go back and modify the EUL. In the Discoverer Administrator Desktop, select Create A New Business Area in step 1 of the Load Wizard. Select the user who owns the tables defined in the preceding code fragment in the second step and select the "Cities," "States," and "Stores" tables in step 3. In step 4 (shown in Figure 5-24), select

- Yes, Create Joins From and Primary/Foreign Key Constraints
- Date Hierarchies and Default Date Hierarchy
- Default Aggregate On Datapoints and SUM
- List Of Values For Items Of Type and Character

Give the business area a name and description and deselect all check boxes. Click Finish. Now, let's go back into Discoverer Plus and create a crosstab report to view this data. In step 1 of the Workbook Wizard, select the Crosstab radio button. Click Next. On the second page of the wizard, select "CITY_NAME" from the cities table, "STATE_NAME" from the states table, and "STORE_NAME," "TOTAL_SALES:Detail" (remember to click the small plus sign next to TOTAL_SALES and then select "Detail"), and "SALES_DATE:Year" from the stores table (Figure 5-25).

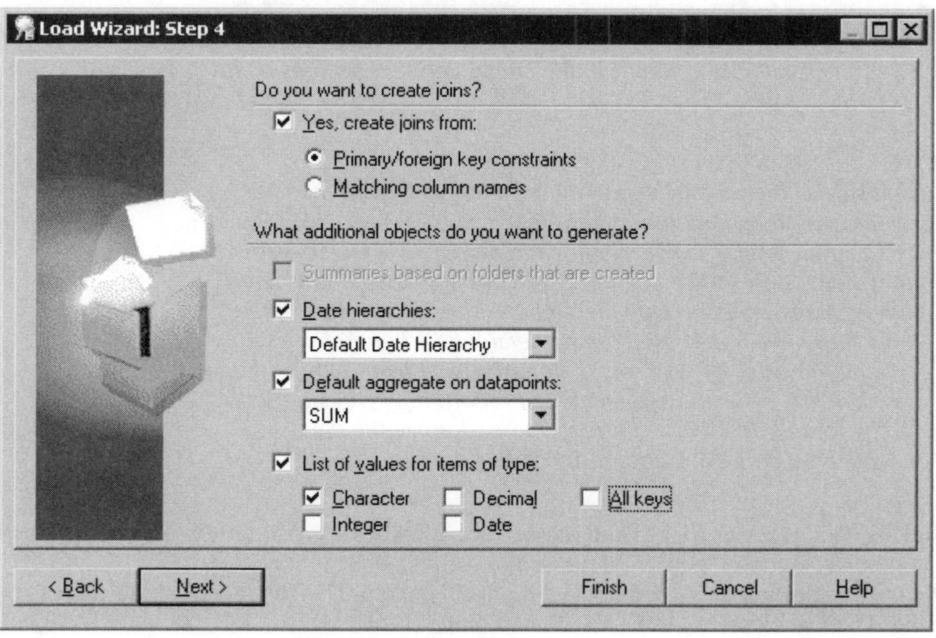

FIGURE 5-24. *Load Wizard step 4 for the new business area*

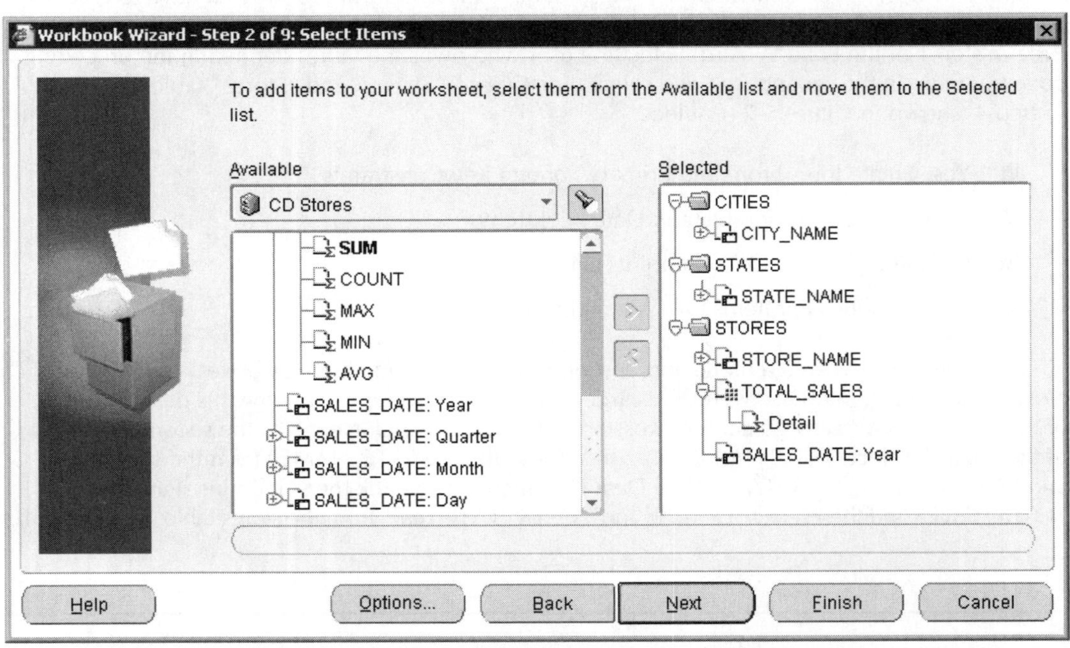

FIGURE 5-25. *Available columns in the cities, states, and stores tables*

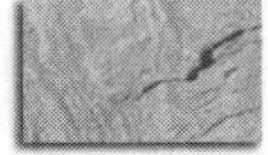

NOTE
The left side of the second step of the Workbook Wizard includes four items (columns) not in our table: SALES_DATE:Year, SALES_DATE:Quarter, SALES_DATE:Month, and SALES_DATE:Day. Where did they come from? Back in Figure 5-24, we told the Load Wizard to automatically generate date hierarchies. This is the result—there are now four new items based on the default date hierarchy: one organizing the dates by year, one by quarter, one by month, and one by day. We'll see (when we execute our report) how we can use this hierarchy to drill down into our report to customize the data displayed, all without any additional coding.

Clicking Next takes us to the third page of the Workbook Wizard. Before we can do anything, the dialog box shown in Figure 5-26 pops up.

Click OK to display the Crosstab Layout page (Figure 5-27). The layout of this page can be confusing. The five elements at the top (Data Point:TOTAL_SALES, CITY_NAME, STATE_NAME, STORE_NAME, and SALES_DATE:Year) are what will be displayed at the top of the report (the horizontal x-axis). There has to be at least one column on the vertical y-axis, or the report won't return any rows.

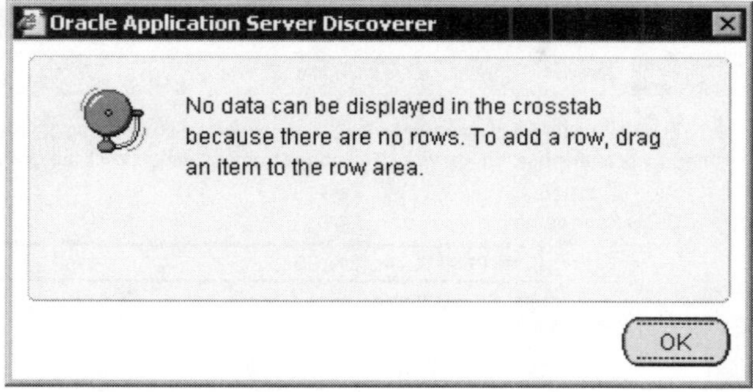

FIGURE 5-26. *Crosstab dialog*

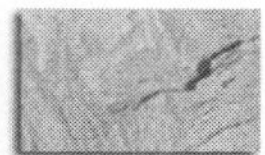

TIP
When you first begin creating crosstab reports, it may be hard to visualize the intersection of data, so you may struggle deciding what columns should be on which axis, but Oracle Discoverer 10g is flexible enough for you to experiment with different configurations. After a while, it will seem like second nature.

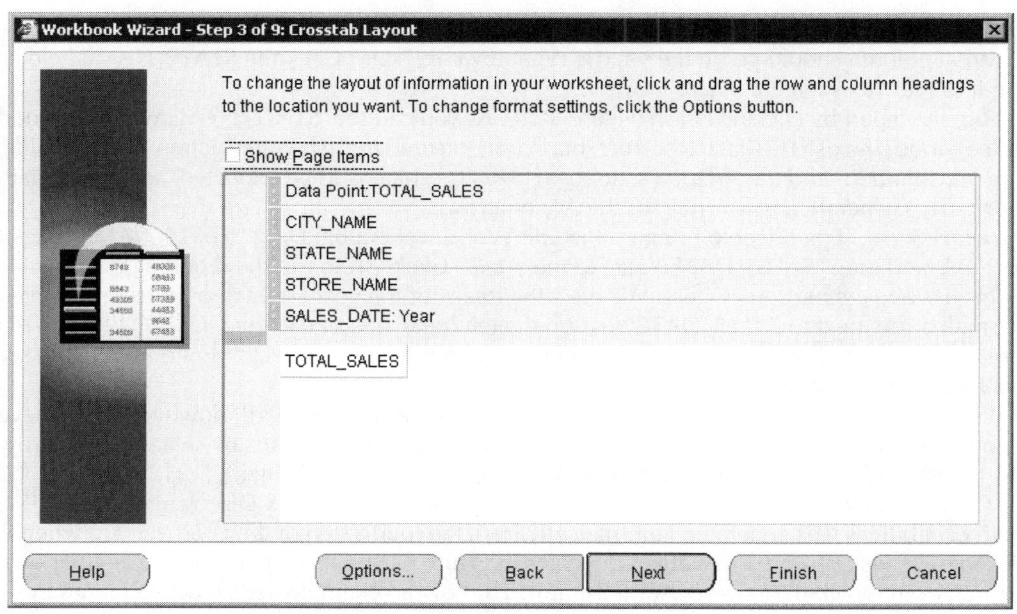

FIGURE 5-27. *The Crosstab layout page*

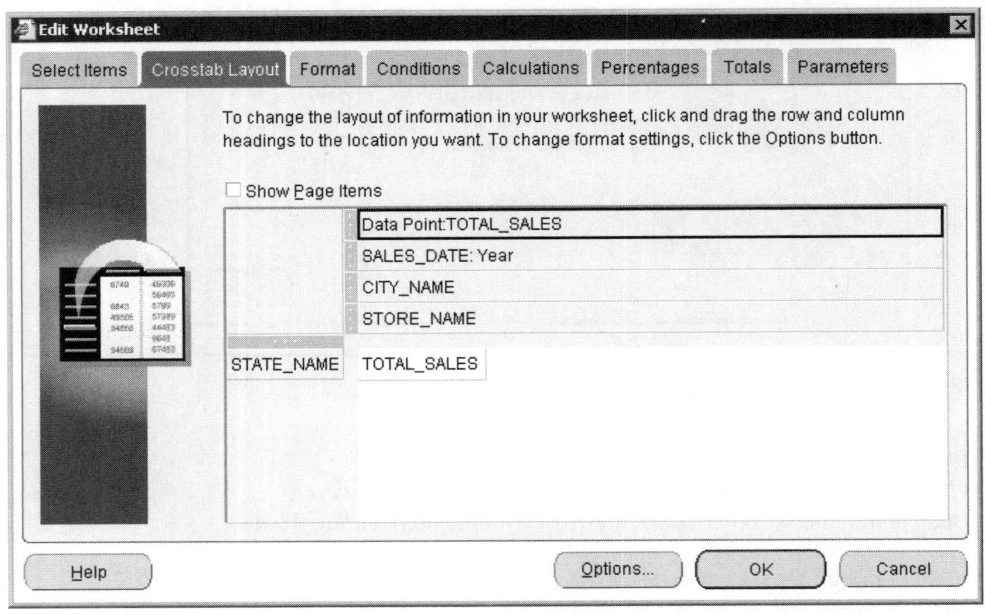

FIGURE 5-28. *The STATE_NAME field dragged into the y-axis*

What column should go on the y-axis? What if we try state? Click the STATE_NAME field and drag it to the y-axis (Figure 5-28).

Run the report by clicking Finish (Figure 5-29). As you can see, STATE_NAME was not a good choice for our y-axis. The data is correct, but hardly meaningful. The intersection of the Boulder store (in Colorado) and the Arizona state row is NULL, which is to be expected, as the Boulder store cannot generate any revenue for the Arizona row.

Select Sheet | Edit Sheet to bring up the Edit Worksheet dialog. Drag "STATE_NAME" back to the x-axis and drag "SALES_DATE:Year" to the y-axis. Click OK to run the report again.

Now we're getting somewhere. We have the totals for the year for each of our stores. Note the small arrow next to SALES_DATE:Year on the left-hand side of the page. Clicking that displays a small menu that allows you to drill down further into the report. Select "Month in Year" to see data by month (Figure 5-30).

Clicking any of the arrows next to the three months allows you to drill down to the day level, or you can display the report drilled down to the day level for all months by selecting the arrow next to "SALES_DATE:Month" and drilling down to "Day in Month" (Figure 5-31).

The hierarchy that was used in this report to demonstrate OracleAS Discoverer 10g's drill-down capabilities was generated automatically from the fourth step of the Load Wizard when we clicked the check box next to Date Hierarchies in Figure 5-24. Developers can create their own hierarchies in Oracle Discoverer Administrator. To show an example, let's create a hierarchy between the cities and states tables. Start up Oracle Discoverer Administrator on your desktop, log in as the user who owns the EUL, select Open An Existing Business Area, and select the

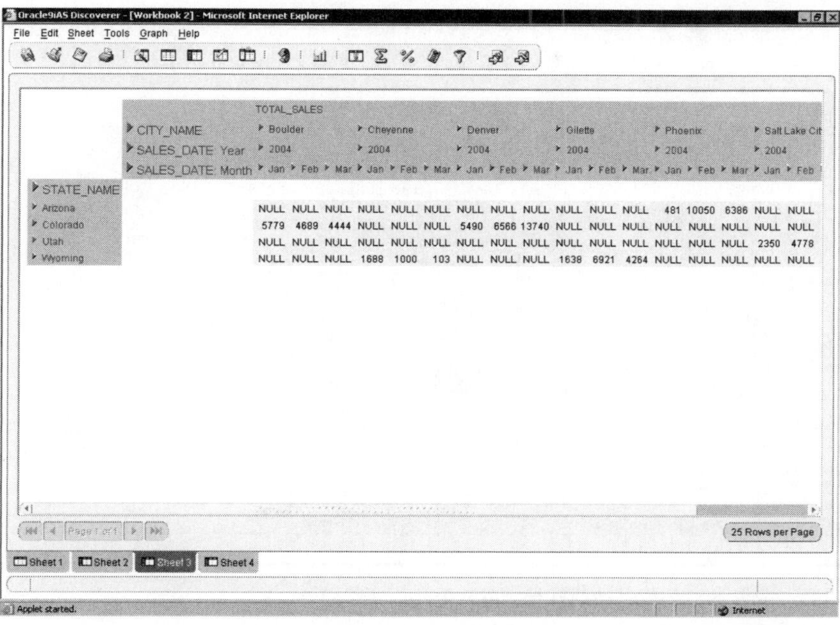

FIGURE 5-29. *The report with STATE as the y-axis*

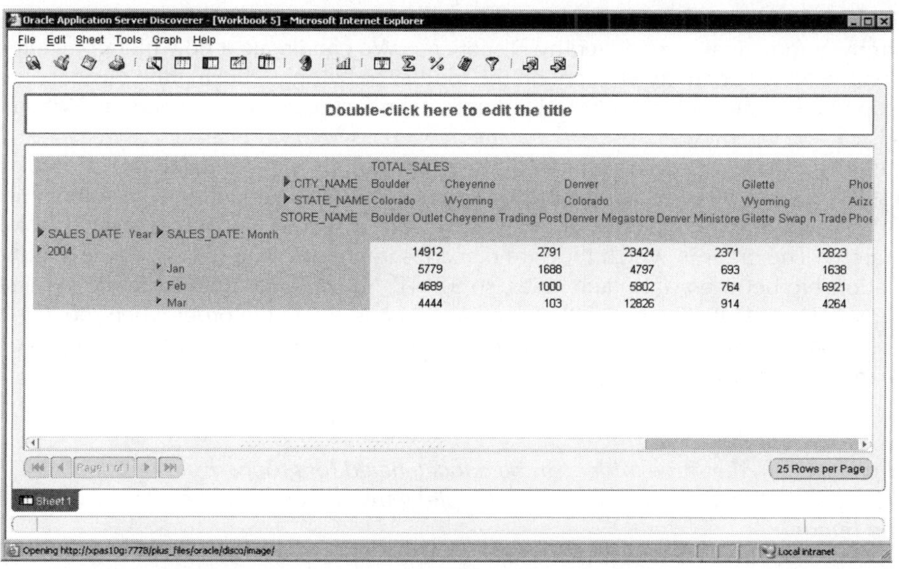

FIGURE 5-30. *Report drilled down to monthly level*

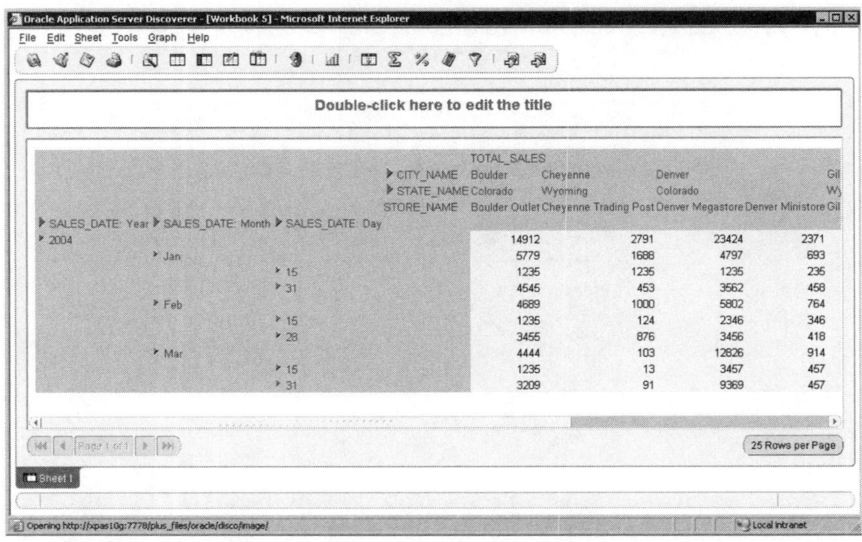

FIGURE 5-31. *Report drilled down to daily level*

business area that holds the STATES, CITIES, and STORES tables. Click the Hierarchies tab and click the plus signs to expand the hierarchy elements. Your screen should look something like Figure 5-32.

The SALES_DATE item in the STORES folder has been expanded to show the structure of the hierarchy automatically generated by Discoverer. We can create a new hierarchy either by clicking on the New Hierarchy element on the toolbar or by right-clicking the business area in the desktop window and selecting New Hierarchy. The first page of the Hierarchy Wizard is displayed.

Hierarchies can be based on either items (nondate columns in the database) or date columns. Since this example involves creating a hierarchy between states and cities, select Item Hierarchy and click Next. On the second page of the wizard, you will specify which items will make up your hierarchy. The order in which they are placed is important. In this case, there is a one-to-many relationship between states and cities, so STATE_NAME is selected to be moved first, followed by CITY_NAME (Figure 5-33). If you make a mistake in the order when moving items into your hierarchy, you can rearrange items by using the Promote and Demote buttons on the right side in step 2 of the Hierarchy Wizard.

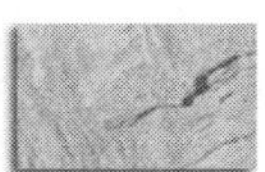

TIP
Multiple items in the same folder can be concatenated (or grouped) as hierarchy elements by selecting the multiple items and clicking the Group button.

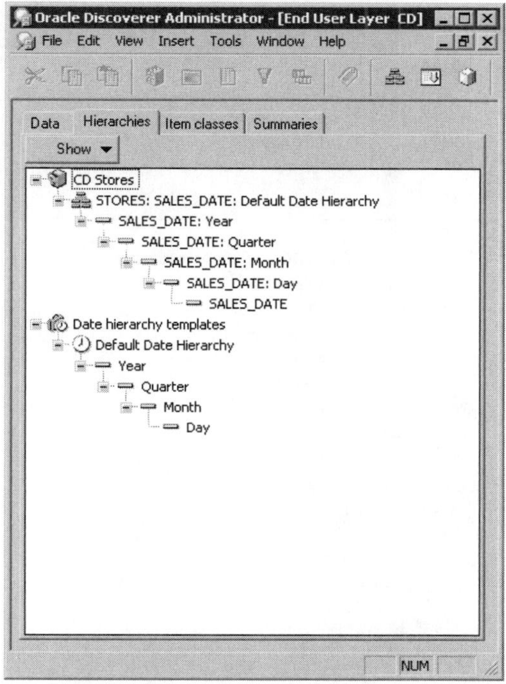

FIGURE 5-32. *The Hierarchies tab in the Oracle Administrator desktop*

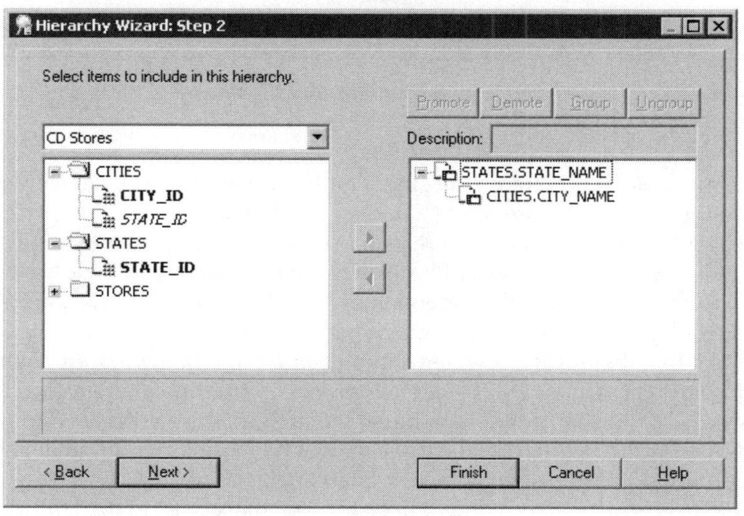

FIGURE 5-33. *Step 2 of the Hierarchy Wizard*

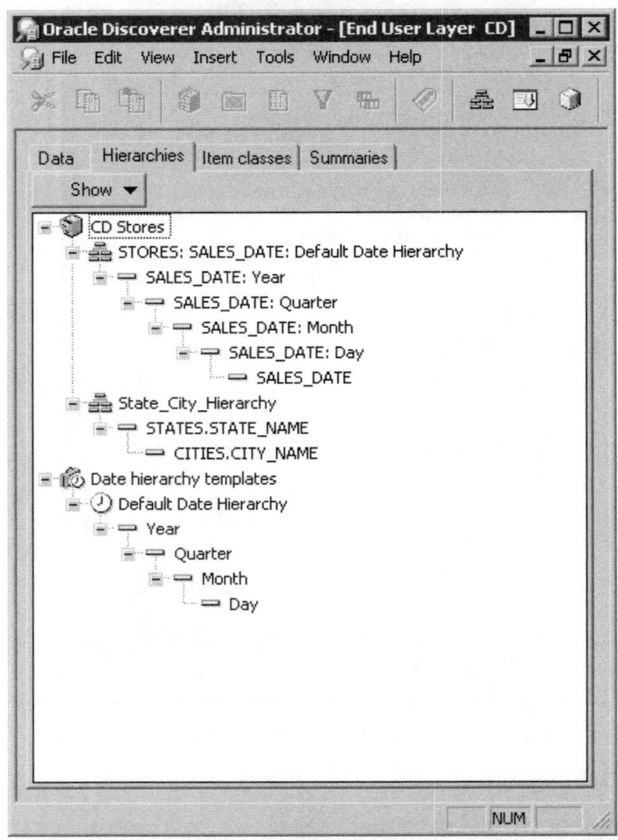

FIGURE 5-34. *Discoverer desktop with new hierarchy displayed*

Click Next and name your hierarchy in step 3 of the wizard. Clicking Finish will display the new hierarchy in the desktop (Figure 5-34).

To see the effect of the next hierarchy, create a new Worksheet in your existing Workbook by selecting Sheet | New Sheet in Discoverer Plus. Select the Crosstab table, click Next, and select the same items you did before, with the exception of STORE_NAME (CITY_NAME, STATE_NAME, TOTAL_SALES:Detail, and SALES_DATE:Year). When we performed this step previously, we pointed out the fact that there were new items in the left-hand window based on our date hierarchy (SALES_DATE:Year, SALES_DATE:Quarter, etc.). This time, there are no new items reflecting our State_City_Hierarchy. For item-based hierarchies, there is no need to specify them in this step of the wizard. The drill-down capability will be there for us automatically when running the report. Click Next to specify the Crosstab layout.

Grab the STATE_NAME field and drag it from the top (the x-axis) to the left side (the y-axis). Grab CITY_NAME and drag it to the y-axis. Click Finish to run your report (Figure 5-35).

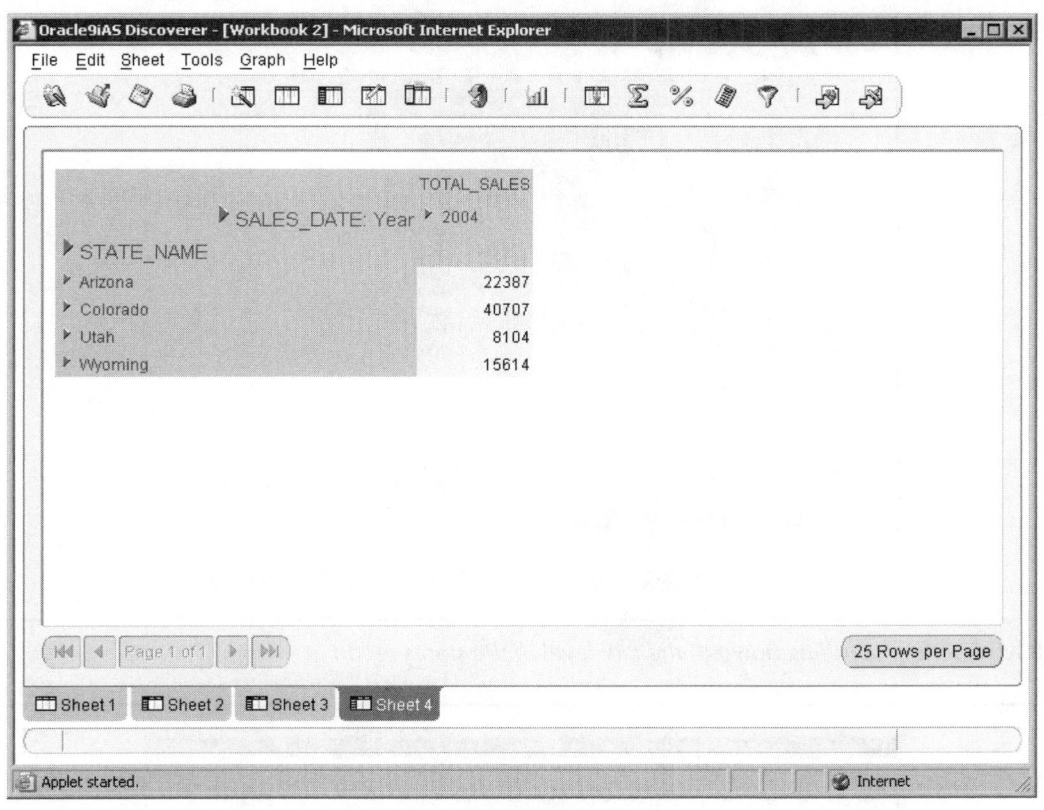

FIGURE 5-35. *The store report with the state_city_hierarchy*

Clicking the small arrowheads next to any of the states allows you to drill down to the city level (Figure 5-36).

You still have the ability to drill down on the date field created earlier (Figure 5-37).

Figure 5-38 shows the report in Discoverer Viewer.

Creating Graphs

As you have seen, OracleAS Discoverer 10*g* gives users incredible flexibility when viewing data from the database. It provides the ability to drill down; use parameters and conditions to filter data; and define calculations, percentages, and totals to enhance the data that is returned in Discoverer Worksheets. We can also define items in the business areas of our EUL that keep numerical functions (such as SUM, AVG, etc.) in the database, allowing developers to create reports that utilize aggregate columns on large sets of data without sacrificing performance.

OracleAS Discoverer 10*g* also provides graphing capabilities that give users an additional way of viewing their data. The graphing component is build into Discoverer Plus, and once a graph is defined for a Worksheet, it becomes part of the Worksheet, viewable in Discoverer Viewer and exportable to formats like HTML.

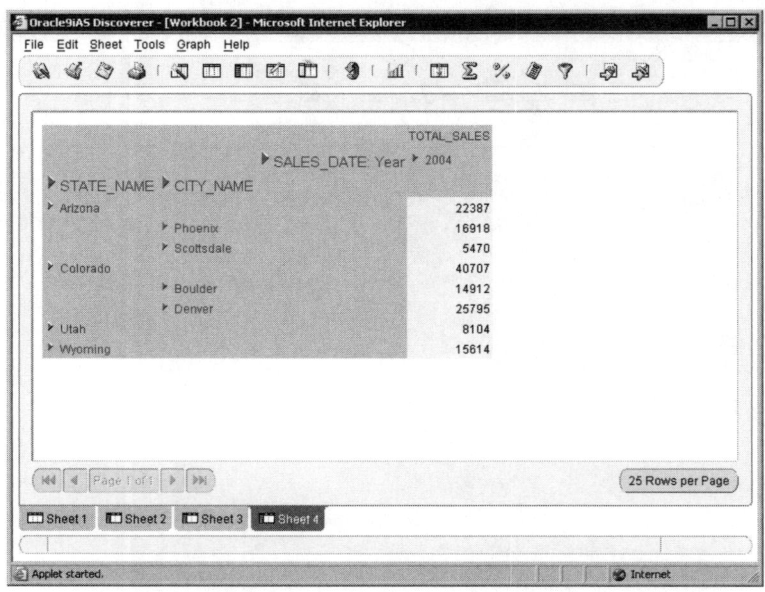

FIGURE 5-36. *Drilling down to the city level in the stores report*

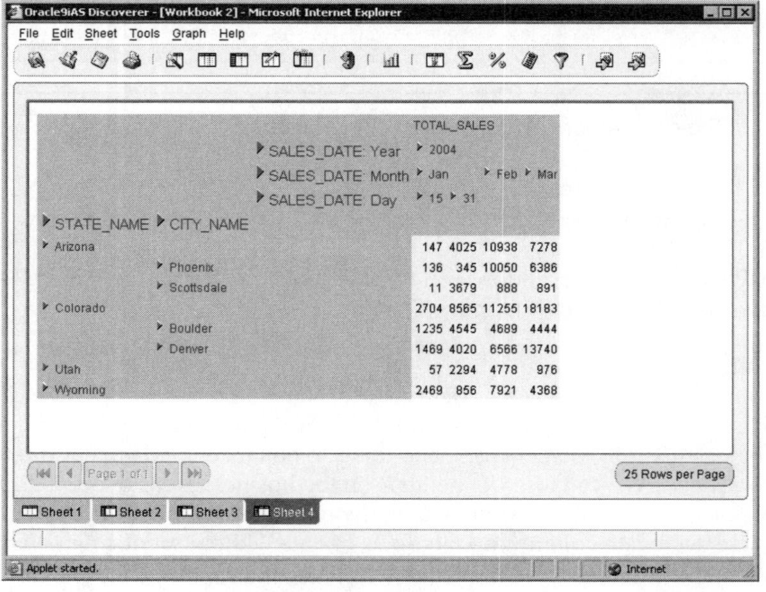

FIGURE 5-37. *Drilling down on both city and date*

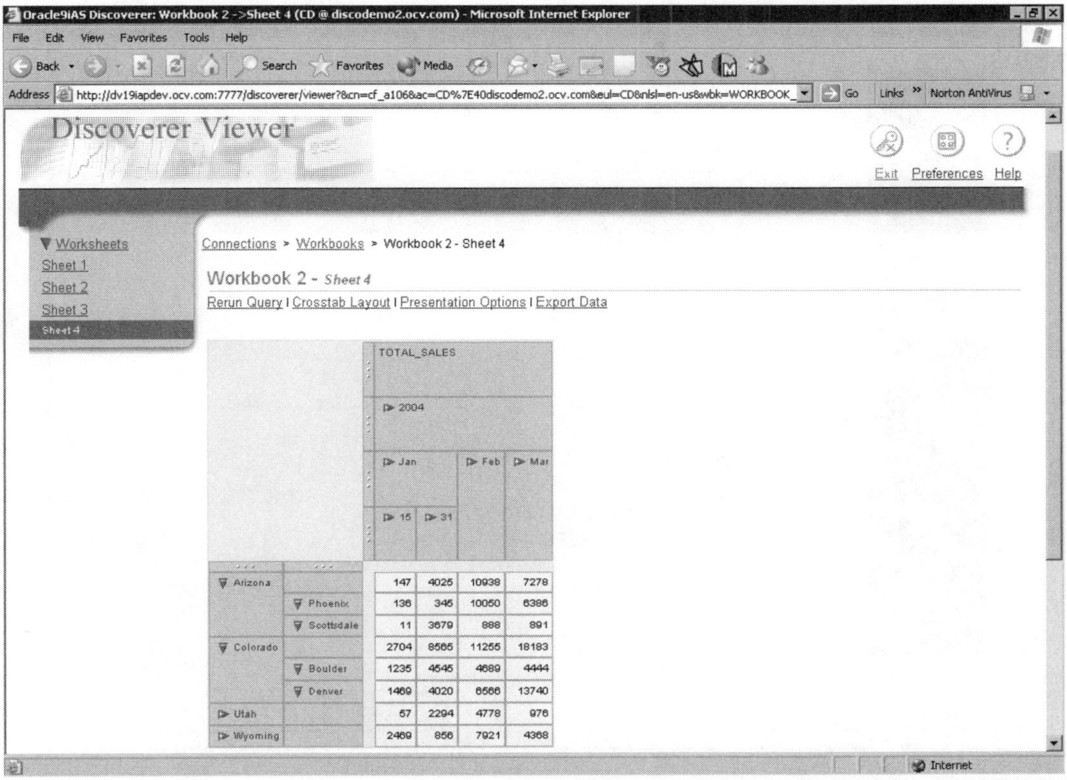

		TOTAL_SALES			
		2004			
		Jan		Feb	Mar
		15	31		
Arizona		147	4025	10938	7278
	Phoenix	136	345	10050	6386
	Scottsdale	11	3679	888	891
Colorado		2704	8565	11255	18183
	Boulder	1235	4545	4689	4444
	Denver	1469	4020	6566	13740
Utah		57	2294	4778	976
Wyoming		2469	856	7921	4368

FIGURE 5-38. *The stores report in Discoverer Viewer*

To create a graph for a Worksheet, select Graph | New Graph in Discoverer Plus. The first page of the Graph Wizard lists the different types of graphs available to you. Some of the graph types have subtypes, giving you further graphing options. For now, select the Bar type and the Bar subtype. Click Next.

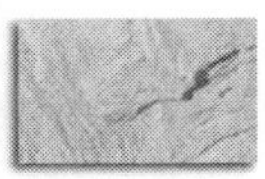

NOTE
The wizard has different steps depending on the type and subtype of graph you select, so the pages may not be the same as the pages described in this example if a different type of graph is selected.

Page 2 of the Graph Wizard (Figure 5-39) gives developers the ability to give the graph a title, select what is to be displayed in the graph, and decide whether to graph data by rows or columns. Don't make any changes to this page and click Next.

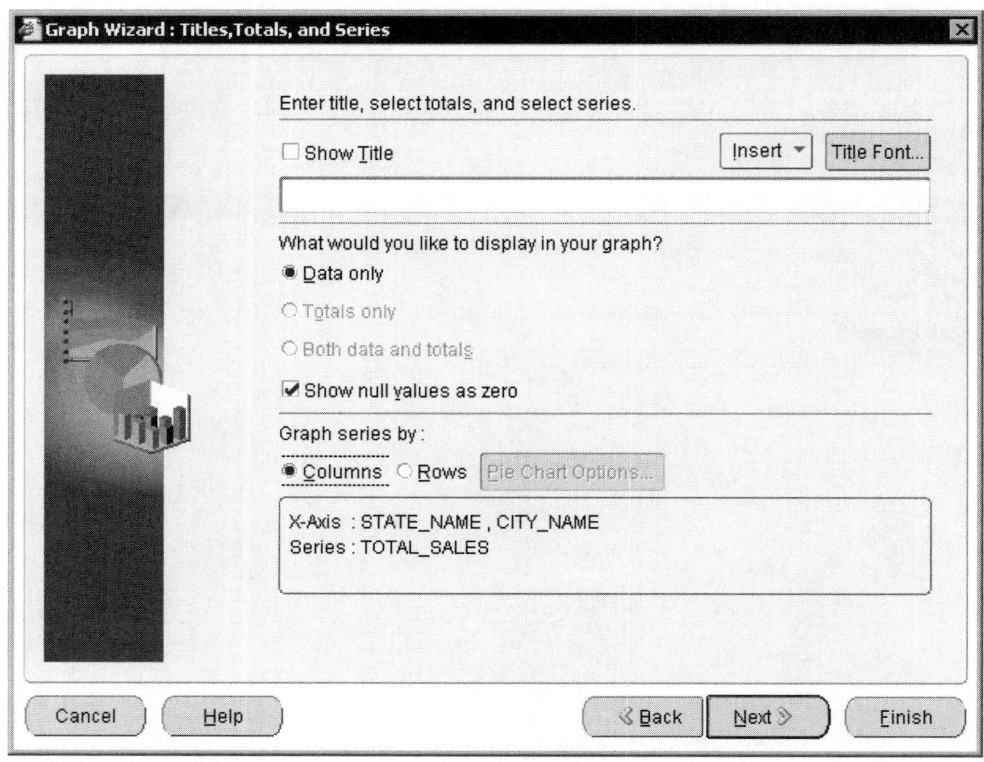

FIGURE 5-39. *The second page of the Graph Wizard*

TIP

Right from the first page of the Graph Wizard, the Finish button is available to you on the bottom right of the window. This is very similar to the Workbook/Worksheet Wizards, where we had the ability to skip over steps and take the default values for our graph. Just as with the Workbook/Worksheet Wizards, we can edit the graph upon completion and make changes to it.

The third page of the Graph Wizard allows developers to modify how the x-axis is displayed. Do not change anything on this page; just click Next. The fourth page allows developers to modify how the y-axis is displayed. Do not change anything on this page; just click Next. The fifth page allows developers to define characteristics of the plot area of the graph. Do not change anything on this page; just click Next. The sixth page allows developers to define characteristics of the legend area of the graph. Do not change anything on this page; just click Finish to display the graph.

The graph created is "dynamic"; that is, it will change depending on what is selected in the report section. For example, "collapsing" Arizona and Utah in the report will remove the associated city graph objects (Figure 5-40).

Figure 5-41 shows the graph as it will appear to your end users in Discoverer Viewer.

Exporting Data

One of the most powerful features of OracleAS Discoverer is its ability to export data directly into other tools for further analysis. An incredibly cool feature is OracleAS Discoverer's ability to automatically generate macros that preserve many of the drill-down capabilities described in the preceding sections in an Excel spreadsheet. To see an example of this, save the Discoverer Worksheet by selecting File | Save from the menu. Open up another web browser and enter the URL for Discoverer Viewer:

```
http://<server>:<port>/discoverer/viewer
```

Select the Discoverer connection and then select the Workbook you just saved. Click the Export Data link, then select Microsoft Excel Workbook (*.xls), and click Export Data. Excel (if installed on your machine) will start automatically (Figure 5-42).

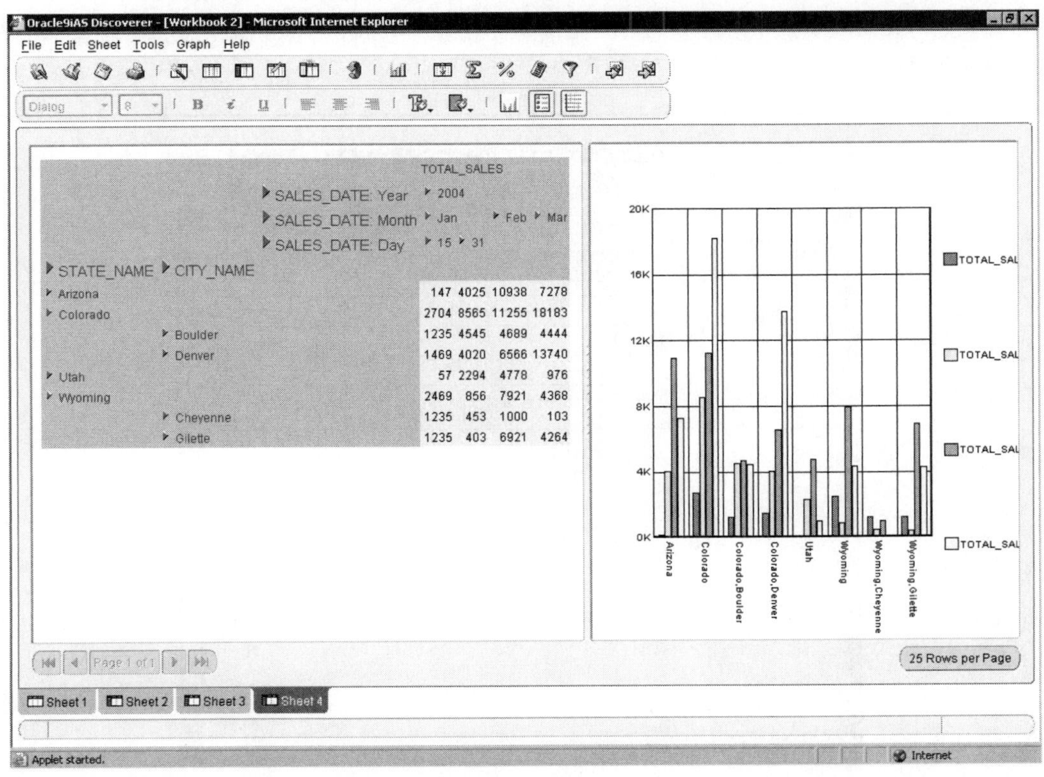

FIGURE 5-40. *Stores graph with Arizona and Utah "collapsed"*

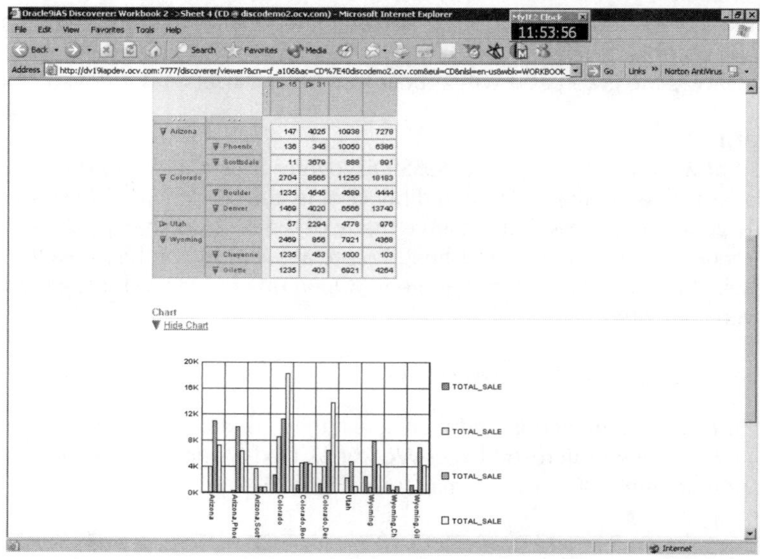

FIGURE 5-41. *The graph in Discoverer Viewer*

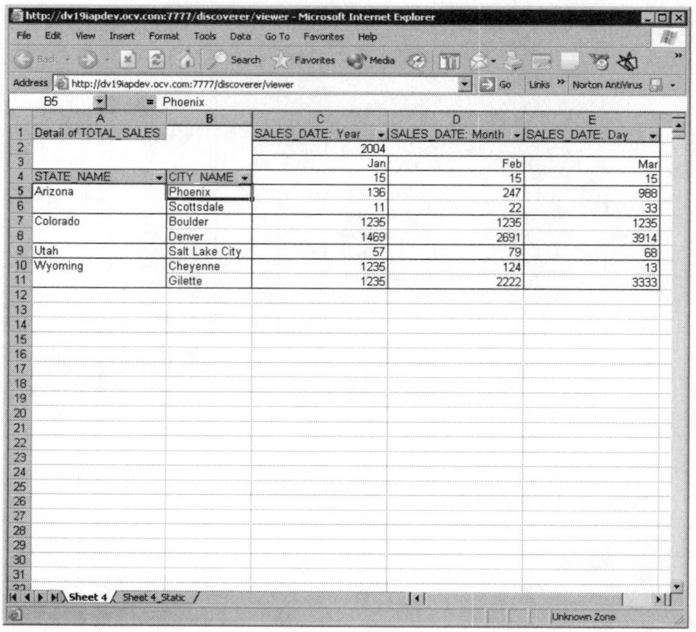

FIGURE 5-42. *Exported data in Excel*

One of the really slick features of the exporting capabilities of OracleAS Discoverer 10*g* is its ability to preserve drop-down information within the spreadsheet. In Figure 5-43, you'll notice that there are drop-down boxes for the fields that are part of hierarchies. While these drop-down boxes do not have the full functionality of drill-down in Discoverer Plus/Viewer, they still provide a limited form of ad hoc queries to those end users more comfortable working with Excel spreadsheets.

Options in Discoverer Viewer and Discoverer Plus

Both Discoverer Viewer and Discoverer Plus provide options pages that allow developers and end users to modify the behavior and characteristics of how reports are run and displayed in these environments. Discoverer Plus has options that control things like these (discussed in detail in the following section):

- If queries in Worksheets are run automatically
- How NULL values are displayed
- The default values for data, headings, and totals
- Whether automatic querying, fan traps, and multiple join path detection are enabled or disabled
- What default EUL is used
- Query Governor settings

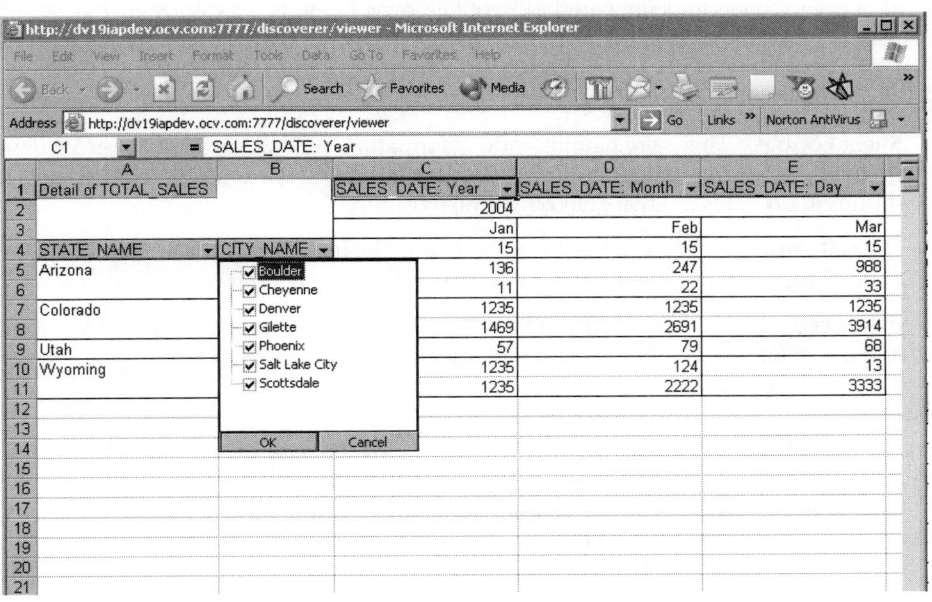

FIGURE 5-43. *Excel spreadsheet with drop-down boxes*

Discoverer Viewer has options that control preferences:

- **Query Governor settings** These options set limits on how many resources (disk I/O, CPU time, etc) can be used by a query.
- **Worksheets** These options set how NULLs are displayed, the number of rows per page.
- **Summary Data** These options determine when to use summary data.
- **Fan-Trap Detection** This setting detects and prevents certain queries that could return ambiguous results.
- **End-User Layer** You can select a default EUL for Discoverer to use each time you create a new connection to your database.
- **Locale Selection** You can select the locale that you want Oracle9*i*AS Discoverer to use when displaying text and presentation options (Figure 5-44).

Discoverer Plus Options

To see the options available to developers in Discoverer Plus, select Tools | Options from the menu in Discoverer Plus. The Options window is displayed with six tabs along the top:

- **General** This tab allows developers to define when the query associated with a Workbook is run, options for scheduled Workbooks, and if the graphics on Wizard pages should be displayed.
- **Query Governor** One of the most powerful features of Discoverer, the Query Governor allows developers to define thresholds for Discoverer reports. This is invaluable, as end users can manipulate reports in such a way as to use up large amounts of database resources (CPU time, I/O, etc.). The Query Governor can be used to limit the execution of reports beyond various time thresholds and retrieved numbers of rows thresholds.
- **Sheet Format** This page defines various formatting options on Discoverer Worksheets, including how null values are displayed, how many rows are displayed per page, and if drill-down items are displayed in inline or outline format.
- **Default Formats** Allows developers to define defaults formats (font, font size, alignment, text color, background color, etc.) for data, heading, and total fields.
- **Advanced** Allows developers to enable or disable automatic querying of Worksheets and the detection of fan traps and multiple join paths.

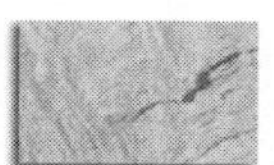

NOTE
From Oracle's Documentation: "Fan traps occur when the data items in two folders are not directly related but do have a relationship based on the data items in a third folder. Multiple join paths occur when two tables can be linked in more than one way."

- **EUL** Allows developers to specify a default EUL to use each time a connection is established to a database.

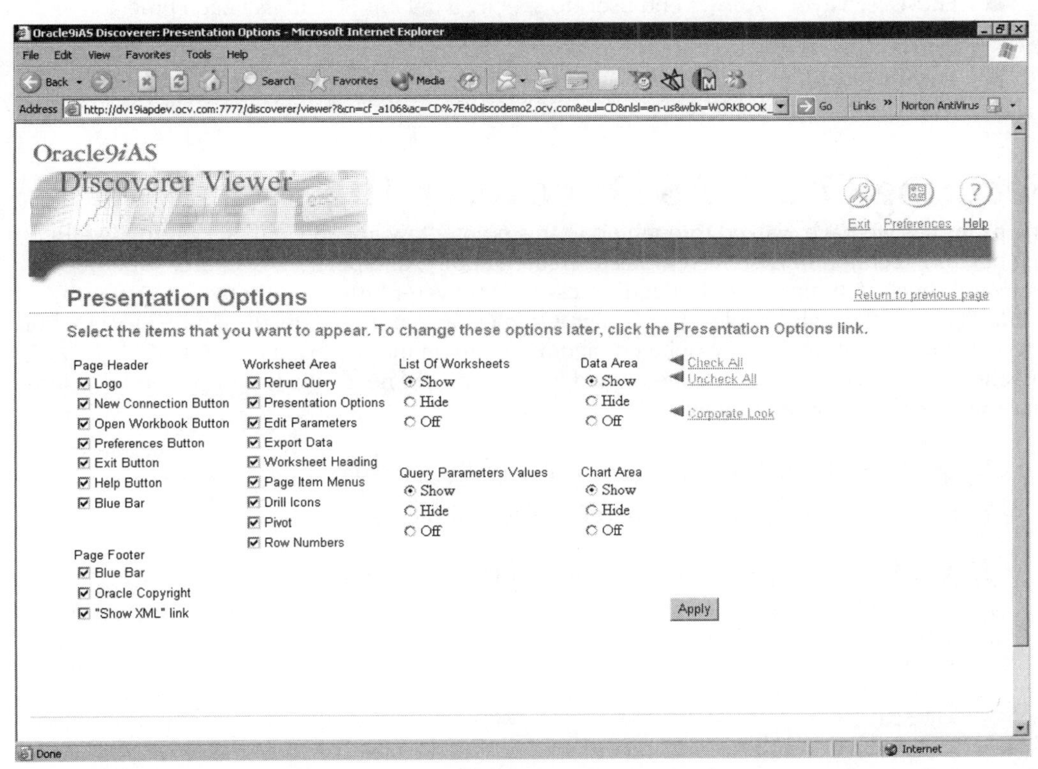

FIGURE 5-44. *The Presentation Options page in Discoverer Viewer*

Discoverer Viewer Options

To see the options available to end users in Discoverer Viewer, select the Preferences icon on the top right of any Discoverer Viewer page. An HTML page is displayed with six sections:

- **Query Governor** One of the most powerful features of Discoverer, the Query Governor allows end users to define thresholds for Discoverer reports. This is invaluable, as end users can manipulate reports in such a way as to use up large amounts of database resources (CPU time, I/O, etc.). The Query Governor can be used to limit the execution of reports beyond various time thresholds and retrieved numbers of rows thresholds.
- **Worksheets** This page defines various formatting options on Discoverer Worksheets, including how null values are displayed and how many rows are displayed per page.
- **Summary Data** Defines when summary data should be used.
- **Fan-Trap Detection** Defines whether Discoverer will detect queries that could return ambiguous results.

- **End-User Layer** Allows end users to specify a default EUL to use each time a connection is established to a database.
- **Locale Selection** Allows end users to select the locale that OracleAS Discoverer will use when displaying text.

Securing OracleAS Discoverer 10*g*

The examples we have walked through up to this point allow anyone with access to the URL that begins execution of Discoverer Plus to create, modify, and delete Discoverer Workbooks and Worksheets. Limiting unauthorized access to Discoverer Plus and Discoverer Viewer by validating users through Oracle's Single Sign-On mechanism is a relatively simple process, but it requires modification of an Apache configuration file on the server. In the $ORACLE_HOME/Apache/Apache/conf directory, a file named mod_osso.conf needs the following modifications (back up the file before modifying it):

1. Open the file mod_osso.conf file located on the middle tier.
2. Find the following line: # # Insert Protected Resources: ....
3. Add the following lines immediately after the line mentioned in step 2:

```
<Location /discoverer/plus>
require valid-user
AuthType Basic
</Location>
<Location /discoverer/viewer>
Header unset Pragma
OssoSendCacheHeaders off
require valid-user
AuthType Basic
</Location>
```

Summary

OracleAS Discoverer 10*g* gives end users incredible flexibility when viewing complex reports over the Web. By having the complex aspects of SQL encapsulated in the Discoverer End-User Layer, you enable end users to manipulate reports without having to master the intricate details of SQL syntax. By giving end users the power to manipulate reports, multiple benefits are realized, including these:

- Empowering end users to make decisions quicker and with greater confidence
- Decreased burden on programming, QA, and implementation staff
- Increased understanding of data through the use of graphs
- The ability to export data into tools like Excel for further analysis and reporting

OracleAS provides a production-quality web-based development environment, Discoverer Plus, which decreases Total Cost of Ownership (TCO) by reducing licensing fees and maintenance fees involved in maintaining client PC configurations. Discoverer Plus provides wizards for virtually every aspect of Discoverer report development, allowing developers to change aspects of their reports on the fly before saving the finished product to the database. As Discoverer Workbooks and Worksheets are stored within the database, viewing them over the Web requires no conversion work whatsoever, something that is not true for Oracle Forms and Oracle Reports.

Discoverer Viewer is a powerful web-based application that allows end users to view Discoverer Workbooks and Worksheets over the Web. All advanced Discoverer features used in Discoverer Plus, such as drill-downs and LOVs, are available to end users in Discoverer Viewer. Discoverer Viewer includes a powerful export feature that allows end users to export Discoverer data into various formats for further analysis or reporting.

The features, along with OracleAS Discoverer 10*g*'s integration with Oracle Identity Management and Oracle Web Cache, make Discoverer a true world-class solution for virtually any organization's reporting needs.

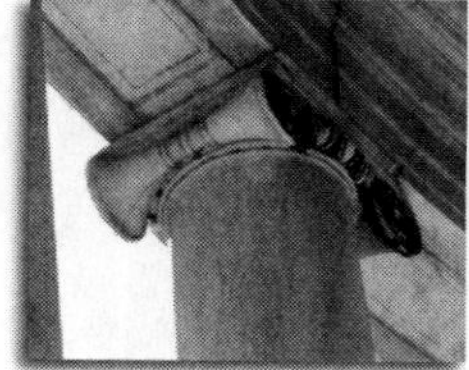

CHAPTER 6

Deploying Oracle Tools to the Web

A book with "Oracle Web Development" in the title would be of use mainly as a paperweight if it didn't discuss the issues and methods surrounding deploying and running applications over the Web. Up until this point, we have looked at development tools that were not specifically created for the development of web-enabled applications (Parts III and IV, which discuss Oracle Portal and Java respectively, will discuss development environments that have their basis in web deployment). This potential limitation is mitigated by the advanced features of Oracle Application Server 10*g* that provide developers and administrators the ability to serve these components over the Web in an environment that is secure, stable, and scalable. This chapter will discuss techniques for deploying these components in such a way as to minimize the impact of moving to a deployment architecture that is fundamentally different from the client/server architecture you may be accustomed to. As we will see, Oracle has made a great effort to make the transition of these legacy applications to the Web simple, while giving developers and administrators all of the benefits of web-based applications.

NOTE
It is important to note that when discussing "web applications" in this chapter, we are referring to intranet-based or extranet-based web applications. Due to performance, download times, footprint, and JInitiator requirements, it is not practical to deploy these applications in an Internet environment.

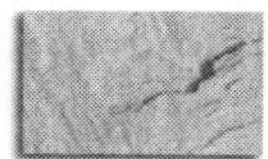

NOTE
In this chapter, Form(s) with a capital "F" refers to the form(s) developed with the Oracle Forms Builder tool that comes as part of the Oracle Development Suite as opposed to an HTML form, and Report(s) with a capital "R" refers to reports developed with Oracle Reports.

If Oracle provides environments such as Oracle Portal and tools such as JDeveloper that have their basis in web deployments, why even bother with tools such as Oracle Forms, Oracle Reports, and Oracle Discoverer? There are many reasons for this (discussed in the appropriate chapters), but some of the prevalent reasons include:

- *Legacy applications and legacy knowledge.* The move to the Web greatly decreases administration costs, particularly for large installations where many users are spread over a large distance. Keeping the client machines (which probably have different versions of operating systems, different service packs, etc.) consistent enough to allow all of them to run Oracle's tools (Forms runtime, Discoverer Desktop, etc.) can be daunting at best and impossible at worst. Moving applications to the Web allows system administrators to simplify their deployment environments, but does your organization have the resources to rewrite all of your applications in a web-based tool such as Oracle Portal or Java? Most organizations will not take on the task of rewriting all of the applications that drive their business for the Web. In many organizations, the knowledge regarding the business rules and practices of the organization has been accumulated by developers that do not have the skills in Oracle Portal or Java to translate those business rules into web-based applications quickly without a significant investment in training.

- *Tool feature set incompatibilities and complexity.* Oracle Portal has wizards that allow the development of forms and reports, but these Portal components do not have all of the functionality of the respective Oracle Forms and Oracle Reports products. Oracle JDeveloper 10*g* allows complete control of all aspects of your application, but has a much higher learning curve.
- *Impedance mismatch.* This term refers to the inherent difficulties between working with an object-oriented language such as Java and the relational aspects of a relational database such as Oracle. Oracle provides an extremely robust tool called TopLink that simplifies and eliminates many of the barriers of communication between Java and Oracle, but it is one more tool that your developers will need to be trained on.

In Chapter 1, we discussed the different types of Oracle Application Server 10*g* installations. You will recall that there were three different types of installations:

- **J2EE and Web Cache** Provides a HyperText Transfer Protocol (HTTP) server and Oracle Application Server Containers for J2EE (OC4J) containers for the deployment of Java applications.
- **Portal and Wireless** Provides all of the components in the J2EE and Web Cache installation plus support for wireless devices and the Oracle Portal environment.
- **Business Intelligence and Forms** Includes support for serving Oracle Forms, Oracle Reports, and Oracle Discoverer workbooks and worksheets over the Web. This chapter focuses on the Business Intelligence and Forms features of Oracle Application Server 10*g*.

In Chapters 3, 4 and 5, we discussed the major Oracle development tools, Oracle Forms, Oracle Reports, and Oracle Discoverer (we discuss the fourth major Oracle development tool, Oracle JDeveloper 10*g*, in Chapter 14). There are many issues when moving these components to the Web, not the least of which is the fundamental architecture change from client/server to web deployment. This chapter addresses the major issues and provides a road map for a seamless transition of Oracle Forms, Reports, and Discoverer workbooks and worksheets to the Web.

Displaying Oracle Forms on the Web

In Chapter 3, we discussed Oracle Forms and their development. Oracle Forms is an extremely robust environment that incorporates all of the modern components that users have come to expect from applications. In a sign that Oracle acknowledges that the client/server architecture model is obsolete, Oracle Forms, from version 9*i* onward, does not even have the capability of generating Forms to be deployed in a client/server environment. The sole focus is now on web-based applications. You can still test your Forms locally on your development machine, but testing them requires the developer to run a small web server locally.

The Forms engine (the program that will display your Forms on the Web) included with Oracle Application Server 10*g* is 9.0.4. This version corresponds to the Forms Developer version included with Oracle Developer Suite 10*g*. Table 6-1 shows the versions associated with each release of the application server.

Application Server Version	Forms Engine Version	Corresponding Development Suite
Oracle Application Server 10*g*	9.0.4	Oracle Developer Suite 10*g*
Oracle 9*i* Application Server Release 2	9.0.2	Oracle9 Developer Suite Release 2 v9.0.2
Oracle 9I Application Server Release 1	6*i*	N/A - Forms Developer 6 standalone

TABLE 6-1. *Forms Engine Version Included with the Application Server*

The Forms engine has not changed drastically between these versions, so it is possible to take an Oracle Form developed under one version of Forms and deploy it on an Application Server with a different version of the Forms engine without modifying it (provided that the development machine and the application server are running the same version of the operating system).

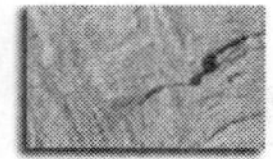

TIP
If the Form is developed on one platform (say, Windows) and deployed on another (say, Unix/ Linux), the form MUST be recompiled.

This can be a risky proposition, however, as features are modified, enhanced, or dropped between versions of Forms. It is also possible (although rare) that a slight difference in operating systems (a developer using a machine with Windows 2000 Service Pack 3 and a server with Windows XP Service Pack 2, for example) will cause unexpected behavior when a Form is moved to the Web and deployed. The safest method is to recompile the Form on the target platform before attempting to access it via the Web. If you choose to recompile your Forms, there are two methods you can follow: recompilation and migration.

Using the Forms Compiler

Recompilation is the easier of the two. It involves running an executable included with every installation of Oracle Application Server 10*g* to recompile your Forms. On Windows, this executable is called ifcmp90; on Unix, it is called f90genm.sh. If no parameters are passed, the Forms Compiler program will come up in display mode, prompting you for the various parameters (this is true on Unix provided you have an X Server running). The parameters can also be entered on the command line, which is very useful if you have numerous forms to recompile and want to put them into a batch file or script (see Figure 6-1).

The parameters the Forms Compiler accepts are shown in Table 6-2.

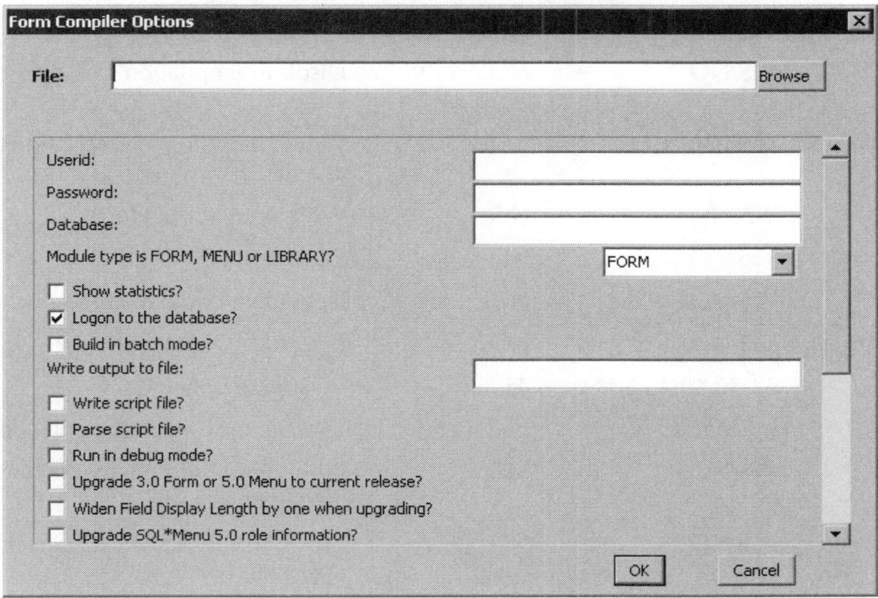

FIGURE 6-1. *The Forms Compiler Options window*

Parameter	Values	Default Value	Comment
module_type	FORM / MENU / LIBRARY	FORM	Specifies the type of form component to compile.
statistics	YES/NO	NO	Show statistics associated with recompilation?
logon	YES/NO	YES	Log on to database before compilation? Note: Because this parameter defaults to YES, you must provide a user/password@connect_string combination if you don't specify logon=no (see examples below).

TABLE 6-2. *Parameters Accepted by the Forms Compiler*

Parameter	Values	Default Value	Comment
batch	YES/NO	NO	Display compilation messages on screen?
output_file	<filename>	none	Write output from compilation process to a file.
script	YES/NO	NO	Write out a script file?
parse	YES/NO	NO	Parse script file?
upgrade	YES/NO	NO	Upgrade module to current version?
upgrade_roles	YES/NO	NO	Upgrade SQL*Menu roles?
version	23,30,40,45,50,60	45	Version to upgrade.
crt_file	<filename>	none	CRT file for version 2.x upgrade.
build	YES/NO	YES	Build runform/runmenu file when upgrading?
add_triggers	YES/NO	NO	Add KEY-UP/DOWN triggers during upgrade?
nofail	YES/NO	NO	Add NOFAIL keyword to trigger steps?
debug	YES/NO	NO	Build with debug information?
compile_all	YES/NO	NO	Compile all PL/SQL code?
strip_source	YES/NO	NO	Strip PL/SQL source code from library?
window_state	NORMAL / MAXIMIZE / MINIMIZE	NORMAL	Root window state.
help	YES/NO	NO	Show help information?
options_screen	YES/NO	NO	Display options window? (for bitmap only)
widen_fields	YES/NO	NO	Add one character to display width?
print_version	YES/NO	NO	Print version used to save module?
forms_doc	YES/NO	NO	Print forms documentation report?

TABLE 6-2. *Parameters Accepted by the Forms Compiler* (continued)

If you have numerous Forms that need to be recompiled, a batch file like this will recompile all forms in whatever directory this batch file is run from (replace username/password@connect_string with the appropriate connection information):

```
Echo compiling Forms....
for %%f IN (*.fmb) do ifcmp90 userid=username/password@connect_string
module=%%f batch=yes module_type=form compile_all=yes window_state=minimize
upgrade=yes
ECHO FINISHED COMPILING
```

On Unix, the equivalent shell script would look like this:

```
for form in 'ls *.fmb'
do
   echo Compiling Form $form ....
   f90genm userid= username/password@connect_string batch=yes module=$form
module_type=form compile_all=yes window_state=minimize upgrade=yes
done
```

Check the <form name>.err files to see if all Forms were recompiled correctly. Note that the Forms Compiler takes files with the extension .fmb as its input. .fmx files are compiled Forms specific to the operating system they were compiled on. The Forms Compiler takes the binary version of the Form (.fmb) and compiles it into an .fmx specific to the operating system on which they are to be deployed. This is why a Form developed on a client machine that has a different operating system where it is to be deployed *must* be recompiled before attempting to access it.

If you specify script=YES, then no .fmx is generated. A different type of Forms file is generated—an .fmt file. .fmt files are text versions of the .fmb. To convert a .fmt back to a .fmt, specify parse= YES in the Reports Compiler parameter list.

If you use ftp to move your .fmb files to the deployment server, make sure you transfer your files in binary mode. You will not be able to compile them if they are transferred in ASCII mode (which many ftp clients default to).

Even if the client where the Form was developed and the server where the form is to be deployed are the same, it never hurts to recompile on the server. We've seen developers struggle with unexpected behavior in their web-deployed forms for days, only to recompile their Forms and see the issues go away. Because the Forms Compiler can be called from a command line, it is possible to compile the Forms automatically as part of a "build" if you are using a version control system like ClearCase, PVCS, CVS, or StarTeam.

Using the Forms Migration Assistant

If you anticipate problems due to usage of obsolete item types, properties, or built-ins, it may be more efficient to use the Forms Migration Assistant. Like the Forms Compiler, the Forms Migration Assistant can upgrade all Forms modules (Forms, Menus, Object Libraries, and PL/SQL Libraries), but it also has the following capabilities:

- Performs PL/SQL substitutions defined in the /forms90/search_replace.properties file
- Updates PL/SQL code where possible
- Converts RUN_PRODUCT calls for running reports into RUN_REPORT_OBJECT calls (the rp2rro.pll library must exist in the FORMS90_PATH prior to migration)
- Alerts you to obsolete item types, properties, and built-ins

- Alerts you to the presence of V2-style triggers or triggers defined at incorrect levels
- Generates Forms module executable files (command-line interface only)

Similar to the Forms Compiler, the Forms Migration Assistant has a different executable name on Windows and Unix:

Windows	ifplsqlconv90 module=<filename>.<file_extension> userid=<connect_string> log=<filename>
UNIX	f90plsqlconv.sh module=<filename>.<file_extension> userid=<connect_string> log=filename

You can see that the Forms Migration Assistant has much fewer parameters available than the Forms Compiler (to see the parameters, type the appropriate executable name without specifying any parameters).

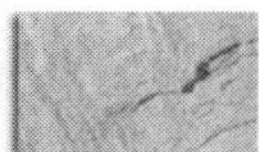

NOTE
It is very important to note that the Forms Migration Assistant cannot create a separate output file from the module being upgraded. It is advisable to copy the files to be migrated to a separate directory prior to running the Forms Migration Assistant.

The behavior of the Forms Migration Assistant can be configured by modifying the $ORACLE_HOME/forms90/converter.properties file. For example, if you want to perform module generation (possible only with the command-line interface), you can set the following properties in the converter.properties file:

```
default.generateruntime=true
default.connectdb=true (if a database connection is required)
```

Here's an example of the converter.properties file that comes with Oracle Developer Suite 10*g*:

```
#Converter Settings
#Wed May 05 12:37:52 MDT 2004
default.usequeuetables=false
default.desname=
default.logfiledir=
ui.options.size=494.0 276.0
ui.main.size=699.0 351.0
default.reports_servername=
default.destype=cache
default.servletname=rwservlet
ui.options.pos=390.0 107.0
ui.progress.size=454.0 331.0
default.use_orarrp=false
default.lastfiledirectory=C\:\\Data\\Forms
```

```
default.orarrp_virtual_directory=
default.welcomepage=true
ui.main.pos=92.0 63.0
default.browser=iexplorer
default.logfilename=converter.log
default.reportshost=/
default.orarrp_physical_directory=
ui.helpHome=C\:\\IDS_HOME
ui.progress.pos=245.0 44.0
default.desformat=html
default.backupwarning=true
default.servletdir=/reports/
```

You can supply the user ID if required either in the converter.properties file or as part of the command line.

There are two ways to run the Forms Migration Assistant: either through the command line (making it useful for batch upgrading Forms) or through the Wizard (for those users more comfortable with a graphical interface, or GUI). On Windows, the Forms Migration Assistant is located in:

Start -> Programs -> Oracle Developer Suite - <Oracle_HOME> -> Forms Developer -> Oracle Forms Migration Assistant (GUI Mode)

On Unix, you can run the Forms Migration Assistant in graphical mode by specifying mode= wizard at the end of the command:

```
f90plsqlconv.sh mode=wizard
```

The graphical version of the Forms Migration Assistant, as shown in Figure 6-2, has all of the functionality of the command-line version except that it cannot generate Forms executables (.fmxs). After you have used the Migration Assistant Wizard to convert a module, you can then use the Forms Compiler to generate the executable file.

The first page of the Migration Assistant Wizard (after the Welcome page) enables you to choose the modules to upgrade. You can choose one or more modules (.fmb, .mmb, .olb, or .pll files) from one or more directories. It's important to note that the upgraded modules will be written to the same location; there is no option to create a different output file. Keep a backup copy of your Forms modules in a different directory so that you will not overwrite them. The second page of the Migration Assistant Wizard (see Figure 6-3) enables you to specify whether you want a separate log file for each module, or whether you want to combine all messages into one log file. You can choose the name and location for the combined file using the browse button to help you select the location. If you choose to create a separate file for each module, you can use the browse button to choose the location, but the file will have a name of the format <modulename>_<moduletype>.log.

If the Forms to be upgraded use RUN_PRODUCT to call Reports, you must specify options for calling Reports from Forms. Three of these options, Reports Server Name, Reports Servlet Virtual Directory, and Reports Servlet, are shown on the main page. The Advanced Options button will display a page (see Figure 6-4) where the developer or administrator can specify additional options (including options for creating a Report Object in the form). You can also

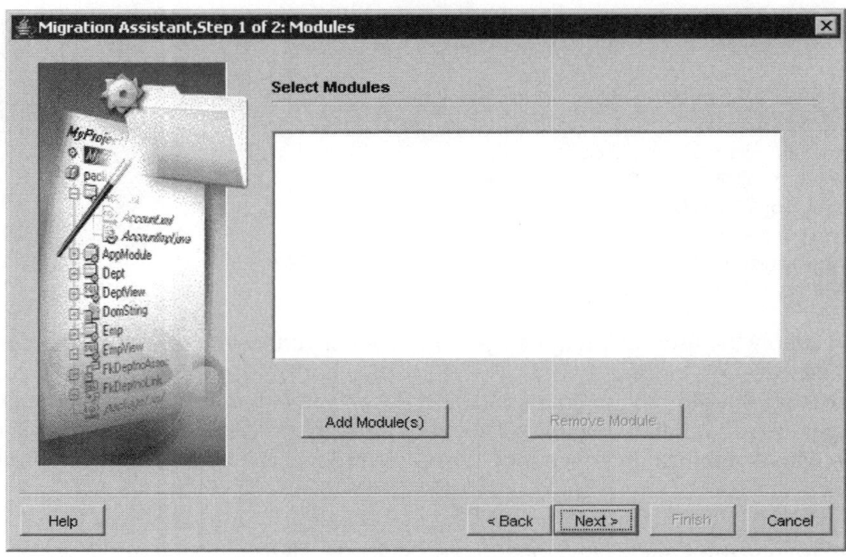

FIGURE 6-2. *The Forms Migration Assistant*

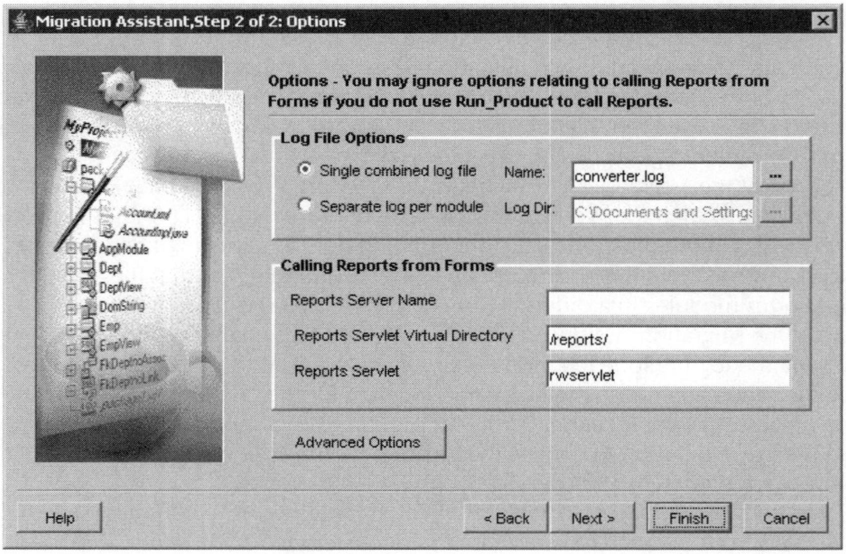

FIGURE 6-3. *The second page of the Forms Migration Assistant*

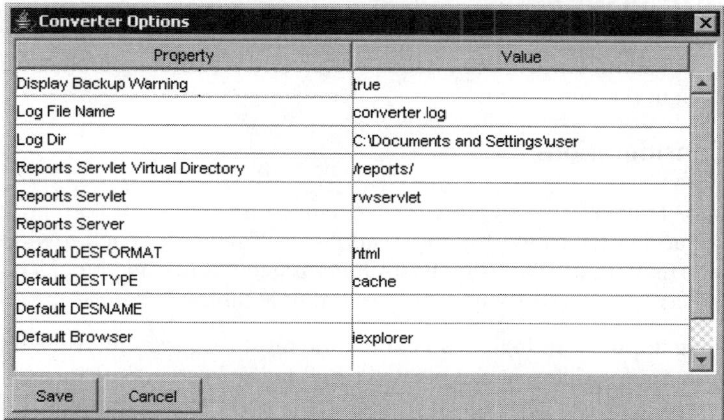

FIGURE 6-4. *The Converter Options page of the Forms Migration Assistant*

modify the converter.properties files graphically from this page. Before the upgrade begins, the Migration Assistant saves the options that you have selected to the converter.properties file.

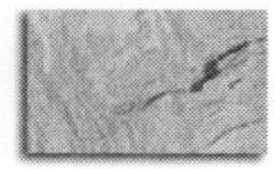

TIP
RUN_REPORT_OBJECT should be used in place of RUN_PRODUCT

Essential to the upgrade process is the verification of the process via detailed inspection of the log files generated. The log files give you the following information:

- Modules that were upgraded
- PL/SQL substitutions that were performed
- Other actions taken by the Migration Assistant, such as changing RUN_PRODUCT to RUN_REPORT_OBJECT
- Obsolete usage that should be corrected

If you used the command-line Forms Migration Assistant and chose to generate the executable, or if you used the Forms Compiler to generate the executable directly, then you should examine the module's .err file to ensure that the module compiled successfully. If not, you can open the module in Forms Builder to correct the reported problems. Even if the module generated correctly, it may not function correctly when it is run. For example, a form may be using built-ins that are not obsolete, but which now run on the application server rather than on the client. This could produce run-time errors or undesirable results. You should test all functionality of the application to ensure that it performs as it did when it was run in client-server mode.

Post-Upgrade Issues

After the Forms have been converted, they can be deployed and viewed on the Web via a web browser, but there are some fundamental issues that should be addressed before attempting to use them in a production environment:

Performance Considerations

- **Post-Query Triggers** Post-Query triggers can cause serious performance issues, as they require an additional round-trip to the application server for each row retrieved from the database. An alternative to using Post-Query triggers is to code blocks based on stored procedures or views to display data from multiple tables.
- **Partitioning application logic** Spreading the most resource-intensive parts of your application among different servers will result in the best architecture for performance. For example, a stored procedure on the data server can be called by the Form to distribute the resource requirements evenly. Web-deployed Forms can also take advantage of an additional tier of application partitioning by exploiting technologies such as JavaBeans or Pluggable Java Components to perform certain tasks on the client.
- **Promoting object similarities** Message "diff-ing" is a technique used by Forms to increase performance of web-deployed Forms by only sending messages to the client that reflect changes in the previous messages. Using this technique, the network traffic between the server and client is greatly reduced. Using similar objects allows the Forms engine to exploit the benefits of Message "diff-ing." Here are some steps you can take as a developer to encourage consistency between objects:
  - Accept default values for properties, and change only those attributes needed for the object
  - Use SmartClasses (defined in Object Libraries) to describe groups of objects
  - Lock the look-and-feel into a small number of visual attributes

Features that Work Differently on the Web

The Forms Migration Assistant will get your Forms ready for web deployment, but it is important for developers and users to understand that not all Forms' functionality is preserved when deploying Forms on the Web. There are some subtle, yet significant, behavioral differences that must be addressed through either recoding of the Forms or education of end users. Some of the significant differences include:

- **Redesigning menus** Web-deployed Forms only support pull-down menus, so any block, full-screen, or Lotus-style in your applications will need to be recoded.
- **Font mapping** In a traditional client/server web deployment, fonts were aliased in the uifont.ali file and the default font was defined by the FORMS60_DEFAULTFONT environment variable. Web-deployed Forms use the registry.dat (located in the $ORACLE_HOME/forms90/java/oracle/forms/registry directory) to specify these values. The code listing below shows the section of the registry.dat that deals with default fonts

and font mapping. Because the Java Runtime Environment (JRE) is used to display Forms via the Web, we are limited to the fonts provided in the JRE, which is a much smaller subset than, say, the fonts provided with Microsoft Windows. Any Form developed using fonts not in the JRE will be converted when displayed on the Web. This can lead to Forms that look completely different when deployed on the Web. At run time, Forms Services maps application fonts to their Java equivalents. Java then renders the font in a predefined font for the deployment platform. How fonts are displayed at run time can be affected by modifying the default font mappings. There are two types of font mapping that developers can perform:

- **Defining the default font.** The default font definition applies to text where the font characteristics (name, size, style, and weight) are unspecified, or where the specified font has no Java equivalent.
- **Mapping application fonts to Java equivalents.** You can map equivalent Java fonts for text with a specified font name that does not exist in Java. The JRE then renders the font in a predefined font for the deployment platform.

```
#
# Defaults for the Font details, all names are Java Font names.  Each of
# these parameters represents the default property to use when none is
# specified.
#
# defaultFontname represents the default Java fontName.
# defaultSize     represents the default fontSize.  Note that the size is
#                 multiplied by 100 (e.g. a 10pt font has a size of 1000).
# defaultStyle    represents the default fontStyle, PLAIN or ITALIC.
# defaultWeight   represents the default fontWeight, PLAIN or BOLD.
#
default.fontMap.defaultFontname=Dialog
default.fontMap.defaultSize=900
default.fontMap.defaultStyle=PLAIN
default.fontMap.defaultWeight=PLAIN
#
# Default Font Face mapping.
#
# appFontname  represents a comma delimited list of Application Font Names.
# javaFontname represents a comma delimited list of Java Font Names.
#
# The number of entries in the appFontname list should match the number in
# the javaFontname list.  The elements of the list are comma separated and
# *all* characters are taken literally, leading and trailing spaces are
# stripped from Face names.
#
# Note that this file uses the Java 1.1 Font names in order to be able to
# handle the NLS Plane (BUG #431051)
#
default.fontMap.appFontnames=Courier
New,Courier,courier,System,Terminal,Fixed,Fixedsys,Times,Times New Roman,MS
Sans Serif,Arial
default.fontMap.javaFontnames=MonoSpaced,MonoSpaced,MonoSpaced,Dialog,MonoSp
aced,Dialog,Dialog,Serif,Serif,Dialog,SansSerif
```

- **Using images in web-deployed Forms.** Images that are loaded into a form with the `READ_IMAGE_FILE` built-in can be loaded from either the directory referenced by the FORMS90_PATH environment variable or from a URL. Images to be displayed in a Forms image item that is populated with READ_IMAGE_FILE can be deployed to the application server machine in a directory that is included in the FORMS90_PATH environment variable. If the images and icons that you use in your application have different extensions (.gif and .jpg), you should use this method to deploy image files. Using a URL to load the image requires recoding the READ_IMAGE_FILE command:
  - **Eliminate the file extension.** The URL that is dynamically constructed at run time to load the image item appends to the file name the default extension specified in iconpath of the Forms registry file.
  - **Change the file type to URL.** You can deploy such images to be loaded from the middle tier by locating them in the codebase directory of the middle-tier machine (assuming that imageBase is set to codebase), or to another virtual directory defined for the web server. If you do this, you must also specify the location in the iconpath parameter. You must also specify iconextension. The specification of iconextension affects all image files loaded with a URL, such as icons, so all must have the same extension when images are deployed by this method.
  - **Optionally, deploy such images so that they are downloaded to the client.** This reduces the network traffic to the application server as the application runs. If you choose this option, you must place the images in a Java Archive (JAR) file and place it in the codebase directory. You must also include the JAR file in the appropriate archive parameter.
- **Icons** Client-server forms use platform-specific icon files, such as .ico files on Windows platforms. Forms Builder still uses these platform-specific files, although beginning with version 9.0.4, .gif or .jpg files can also be used to display icons at design time. At run time, it is common to see button icons not displaying on buttons that developers have created in applications that were formerly client-server deployed. This is because icon files for web applications must be .gif or .jpg format. All icons must use the same format, because you must specify the file extension in the iconextension parameter. You must perform additional configuration to deploy the icon files. If you deploy them to the middle tier, you set iconpath to the virtual directory where the icon files are located, such as the codebase directory (assuming that imageBase is set to codebase). However, the best option for deploying icons is to place them in a JAR file to download to the client machine, which reduces network traffic to the application server as the application runs. Place the JAR file in the `codebase` directory. You must also include the JAR file in the appropriate archive parameter, and set iconpath to blank `(default.icons.iconpath= )`.
- **Key mappings** Key mappings for Oracle Forms on the Web are contained in the fmrweb.res resource file. It is a text file that can be modified with any text editor. You no longer use Oracle Terminal to define key mappings. The file defines key mappings by combining five columns: Java function number (JFN), Java modifiers number (JMN), User-readable key sequence (double-quoted) (URKS), Forms function number (FFN),

User-readable function description (double-quoted) (URFD). Each key mapping is of the format:

```
JFN : JMN : URKS : FFN : URFD
```

- The key mappings defined by default in fmrweb.res differ from those in client-server applications. If you want to provide key mappings similar to those of client-server applications, you can use the fmrpcweb.res file that is also provided by performing the following steps:
  - Make a backup copy of fmrweb.res, naming it fmrweb.res.old
  - Make a copy of fmrpcweb.res and name the copy fmrweb.res
- **Calling reports from Forms.** When you call reports from an Oracle Forms version 9.0.*x* application, you must call Reports Services using either the `RUN_REPORT_OBJECT` or the `WEB.SHOW_DOCUMENT` built-in. You cannot use `RUN_PRODUCT.` There are several things to consider when integrating Reports with Forms.
- **The search path must be set properly to find the report.** If you are calling reports from a Forms application, the Reports Server must know where the Report files are located. If the Reports Server cannot find the report at run time, an "FRM-41214: Unable to run report" error is displayed. To set a search path for Reports, do the following before starting the Reports Server:
  - For Windows platforms:
    Set REPORTS_PATH in the Windows registry (HKEY_LOCAL_MACHINE > SOFTWARE > ORACLE > HOMEx).
  - On Unix:
    Set REPORTS_PATH by revising the shell script that defines the initial default values: $ORACLE_HOME/bin/reports.sh. This script is called when starting any Reports Server.
- **The Reports Server must be started prior to calling the report from Forms.** The Reports Server being used to run the report from Forms must be running prior to calling the report. If it is not running, users receive an error at run time: FRM-41213 Unable to connect to the Reports Server. There are three ways to start the Reports Server:
- **Start the in-process server from a URL.** The in-process server runs in the same process as the servlet, and is started the first time a report is requested without providing a value for the server parameter in the request.
- **Install and start the Reports Server as a service (on Windows).**
- **Start the Reports Server from the command line:**
  - For Windows platforms:
    rwserver server=<reports server name>
  - On UNIX:
    rwserver.sh server=<reports server name> batch=yes &

- **How you call the Report determines whether you can use the in-process server.** If the Forms application uses the RUN_REPORT_OBJECT built-in to call the Report, you cannot use the in-process Reports Server. You will have to explicitly start the Reports Server, either as a service on NT or from the command line. However, if the Forms application calls a Report by passing a URL to the web.show_document built-in, then you can use the in-process Reports Server.
- **The Reports Server that you use should not have an underscore in the name.** The default Reports Server for Oracle Application Server has a name of the format rep_<server>. However, if you use a Report object in a Form that has an underscore in the name, the name becomes truncated, and Forms is unable to connect to it. To work around this problem, start a Reports Server with a different name that does not contain an underscore.
- **Reports access control must be disabled.** If the Reports Server is configured for access control, you may be able to run a Report from Forms, but you will not be able to display the results. You will probably receive an error: FRM-41217 Unable to get report job status. To work around this problem, you can disable access control for a particular Reports Server. Open the <server>.conf file and comment out the entire security section. Insert "!–" after the opening "<", and insert "–" before the closing ">" of the entire security section. Alternatively, you can delete the security section completely.
- **Single sign-on mode for the Reports Servlet must match that being used for the Forms Servlet.** To call a report from Forms, both the Forms Servlet and the Reports Servlet must have the same Single Sign-On (SSO) mode. By default, SSO is turned on for Reports but off for Forms. With the default settings, the Report will run, but will not display results. You will probably receive the same error as when access control is implemented for the Reports Server: FRM-41217 Unable to get report job status. You can turn off SSO for Reports by setting SINGLESIGNON=NO in the rwservlet.properties file. If you comment out or delete the setting, SSO will revert to the default, which is on, so it must be explicitly set to NO. In Oracle Application Server 10g, SSO for Forms is enabled or disabled with the ssoMode parameter in the formsweb.cfg file (discussed shortly).

NOTE
In the rwservlet.properties file, the values listed for the attributes that are commented out represent the default values for those attributes. This explains why, even though SINGELSIGNON is commented out, its default value is YES. This is true for all attributes in the file.

Running an Oracle Form on the Web

Now that you've converted your Forms to the appropriate version, it's time to display them on the Web. We'll start by taking a look at the easiest method, but, as we'll quickly see, it is not the optimal way to do it in a production environment.

Before attempting to display Forms on the Web, the Forms Server component of Oracle Application Server must be up and running. The Forms Server is a subcomponent of the OC4J_BI_Forms component, meaning that it cannot be stopped or started by itself. It is provided as a separate component on the Enterprise Manager Web Page so that administrators can configure the Forms component and monitor the performance of the Forms Server. There are two ways to check to see if the Forms Server is up and running:

- **Through the Enterprise Manager Application Server Web Page.** This page gives a graphical description of the components that make up the Application Server. The forms component will have a check mark in the status column if it is up and running. It cannot be started individually (you'll notice that its check box is grayed out), so the only way to start it is to start the OC4J_BI_Forms component. If, for some reason, the OC4J_BI_Forms component is up, but the Forms component is not, there may be a configuration problem on your system.
- **By using the Distributed Configuration Management Program.** dcmctl is a command line program provided by Oracle to get the status of Oracle Application Server 10*g* components and, if necessary, start or stop them. It is located in the $ORACLE_HOME/dcm/bin directory. To check the status of your components, type:

  ```
  dcmctl getstate -v
  ```

  Your output will look like this:

  ```
  C:\AS_HOME\dcm\bin>dcmctl getstate -v
  Current State for Instance:AS_HOME.xpas10g
      Component               Type           Up Status      In Sync Status
  ==========================================================================
  1   HTTP_Server             HTTP_Server    Up             True
  2   OC4J_BI_Forms           OC4J           Up             True
  3   OC4J_Portal             OC4J           Up             True
  4   OC4J_Wireless           OC4J           Up             True
  5   home                    OC4J           Up             True
  ```

  To start any components that are down, type:

```
dcmctl start -v
```

By default, the Forms Server starts by looking at the $ORACLE_HOME/forms90 directory on your middle tier middle tier for Forms to display on the Web. You can augment the directories that the Forms Server will search through by setting the FORMS90_PATH environment variable. The simplest way to display a Form through a web browser is by using the following format for your URL:

```
http://<servername>:<port number>/forms90/f90servlet?form=<form name>
```

The server used for the screen shots in this chapter is called xpas10g, so to display the test.fmx form that is included as part of the Oracle Application Server 10*g* installation (which is placed in the $ORACLE_HOME/forms90 directory), your URL would look like this:

```
http://xpas10g:7778/forms90/f90servlet?form=test.fmx
```

Everything included in the URL after the question mark is a parameter (or set of parameters) that is passed to the f90servlet executable. All parameters are in the format *parameter=value* and are separated by ampersands (&). form=<form name> is one of many parameters that can be passed to the f90servlet executable. Table 6-3 lists the parameters that can be specified in the URL when invoking the f90servlet executable (for a detailed description, see Oracle Application Server Forms Services Deployment Guide 10*g* (9.0.4), Part No. B10470-01).

Parameter	**Required?**	**Description**
escapeparams	Optional	Set this parameter to false if you want runform to treat special characters in run-form parameters as it did in releases prior to 9.0.4.
heartBeat	Optional	Use this parameter to set the frequency at which a client sends a packet to the server to indicate that it is still running. Define this number value in minutes or in fractions of minutes; for example, 0.5 for 30 seconds. The default is two minutes. If the heartbeat is less than FORMS90_TIMEOUT, the user's session will be kept alive, even if she is not actively using the form.
form	Required	Specifies the name of the top level Forms module (fmx file) to run.
userid	Optional	Login string. For example: scott/tiger@ORADB.
otherparams	Optional	This setting specifies command line parameters to pass to the Forms run-time process in addition to form and userid. Default is: otherparams=buffer_records=%buffer% debug_messages=%debug_messages% array=%array% obr=%obr% query_only=%query_only% quiet=%quiet% render=%render% record=%record% tracegroup=%tracegroup% log=%log% term=%term% Note: Special syntax rules apply to this parameter when it is specified in a URL: a + may be used to separate multiple name=value pairs. For production environments, in order to provide better control over which run-form parameters end users can specify in a URL, use the restrictedURLparams parameter.
debug	Optional	Allows running in debug mode. Default value is No.
buffer	Optional	Supports running and debugging a form from the Builder. Subargument for otherparams Default value is No.
debug_messages	Optional	Supports running and debugging a form from the Builder. Subargument for otherparams Default value is No.
allow_debug	Optional	When set to true, all admin functions from the forms90/f90servlet/admin screen are activated. forms90/f90servlet/xlate runs Forms Trace Xlate on a specified trace file. This parameter must be set to true before trace logs can be viewed from the Forms EM User Sessions screen. The default value is false; the test.fmx application is executed if an administrative function is attempted.
array	Optional	Supports running and debugging a form from the Builder. Default value is No.
query_only	Optional	Supports running and debugging a form from the Builder. Default value is No.
quiet	Optional	Supports running and debugging a form from the Builder. Default value is Yes.

TABLE 6-3. *Parameters That Can Be Passed to the f90servlet Executable*

Parameter	Required?	Description
render	Optional	Supports running and debugging a form from the Builder. Default value is No.
host	Optional	Supports running and debugging a form from the Builder. Default value is Null.
port	Optional	Supports running and debugging a form from the Builder. Default value is Null.
record	Optional	Supports running and debugging a form from the Builder. Default value is Null.
tracegroup	Optional	Supports running and debugging a form from the Builder. Default value is Null.
log	Optional	Supports running and debugging a form from the Builder. Default value is Null.
term	Optional	Supports running and debugging a form from the Builder. Default value is Null.
serverURL	Required	/forms90/l90servlet (see Chapter 1, Forms Listener Servlet)
codebase	Required	Virtual directory you defined to point to the physical directory <ORACLE_HOME>/forms90/java, where, by default, the applet JAR files are downloaded from. The default value is /forms90/java.
imageBase	Optional	Indicates where icon files are stored. Choose between: codeBase, which indicates that the icon search path is relative to the directory that contains the Java classes (use this value if you store your icons in a JAR file (recommended)) and documentBase, which is the default. In deployments that make use of the Forms Server CGI, you must specify the icon path in a custom application file.
logo	Optional	Specifies the .gif or GIF (no period) file that should appear at the Forms menu bar. Set to NO for no logo. Leave empty to use the default Oracle logo.
restrictedURLparams	Optional	Specified by an administrator to restrict a user from using certain parameters in the URL. If the number of parameters is more than one, then they should be separated by a comma. The restrictedURLparams itself cannot be the value of this parameter; i.e., restrictedURLparams. Default value is HTMLbodyAttrs,HTMLbeforeForm, pageTitle,HTMLafterForm,log,allow_debug,allowNewConnections.
formsMessageListener	Optional	Forms applet parameter.
recordFileName	Optional	Forms applet parameter.
width	Required	Specifies the width of the form applet, in pixels. Default is 650.
height	Required	Specifies the height of the form applet, in pixels. Default is 500.
separateFrame	Optional	Determines whether the applet appears within a separate window. Legal values: True or False.

TABLE 6-3. *Parameters That Can Be Passed to the f90servlet Executable* (continued)

As an example, if you wanted to display the Form with a narrower width than Figure 6-5, you could specify the following (the width parameter defaults to 650; see Figure 6-6).

```
http://xpas10g:7778/forms90/f90servlet?form=test.fmx&width=500
```

Note how the Form is "chopped off" on its right-hand side.

The text.fmx form that is provided by Oracle does not connect to any database; therefore, no connection information is needed for the Form to run successfully. In the real world, your Form will always connect to a database. There are three options for authenticating users: you can prompt users for connection information, provide them with connection information that connects end users to their data source automatically, or turn on SSO (described above) to authenticate users via Oracle's SSO mechanism. If you choose the first method, you simply specify the form name in the URL and the user is prompted for his login information automatically (see Figure 6-7).

Alternatively, you can provide the connection information directly in the URL:

```
http://xpas10g:7778/forms90/f90servlet?form=test.fmx&width=500&userid=chris/
viewonly@christest
```

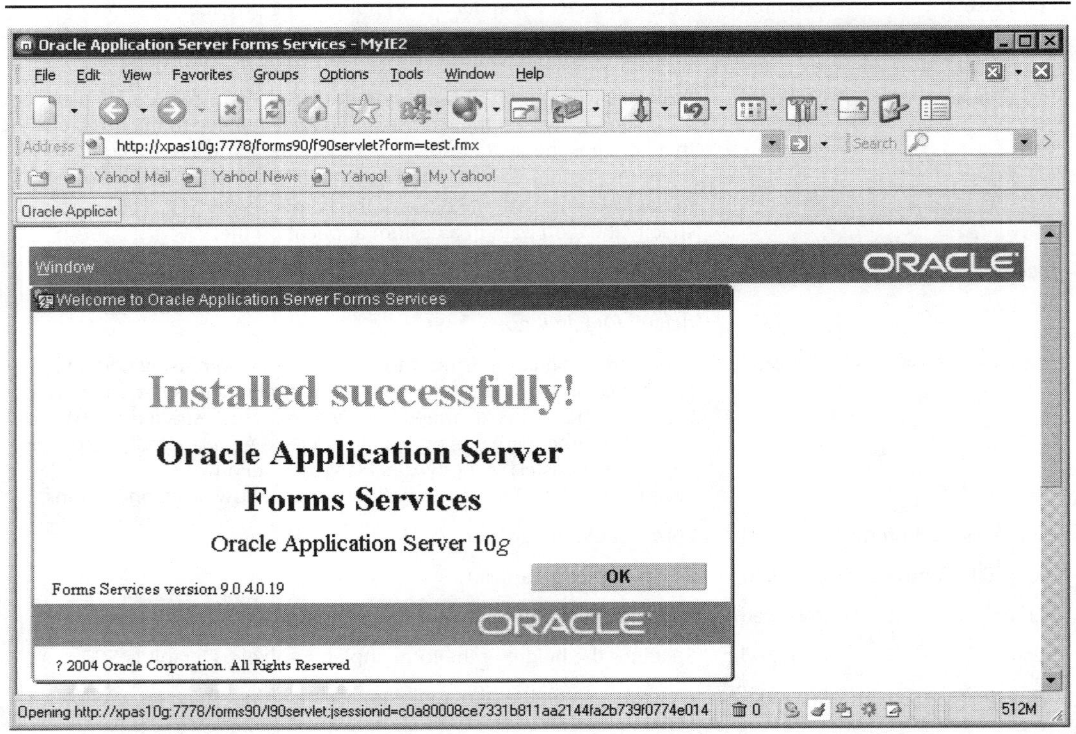

FIGURE 6-5. *Displaying the test form*

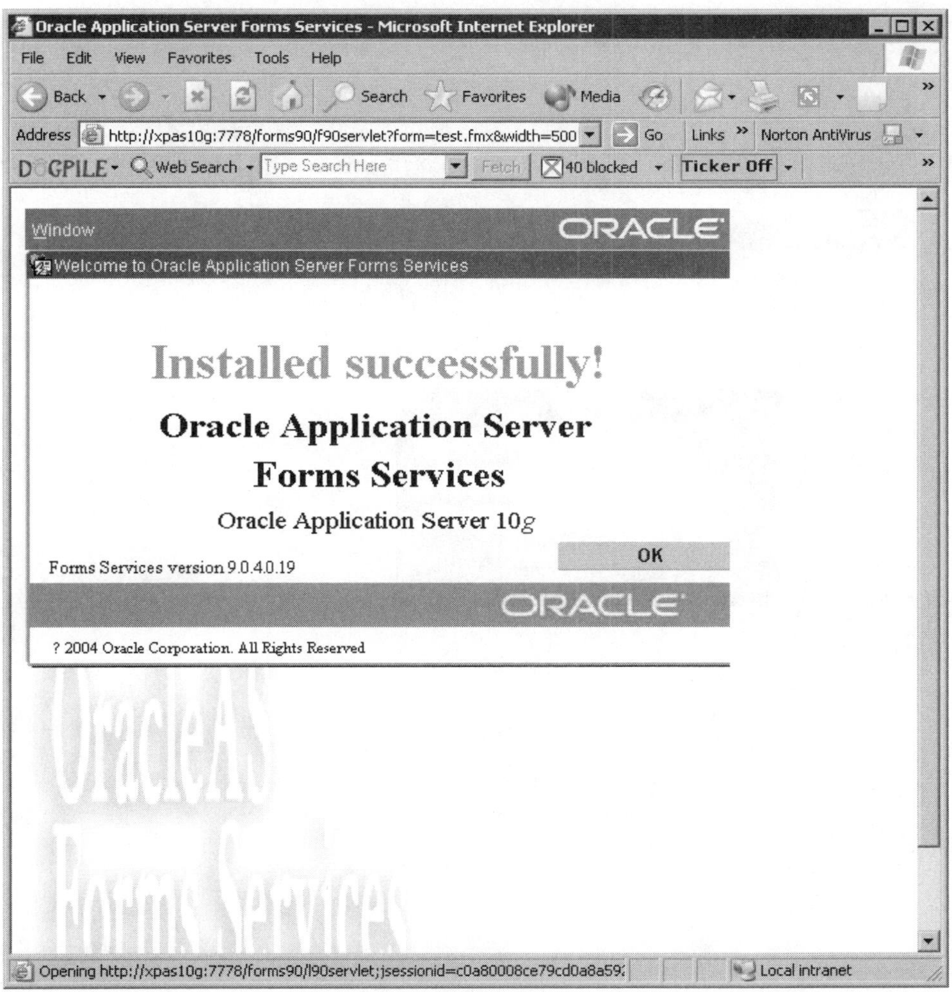

FIGURE 6-6. *The test form displayed with a shorter width*

The obvious problem with this is that you are not only exposing a lot of information about your Form, but also a lot of information about databases on your system. The database connection specified in the URL is a valid database connection that a knowledgeable user could use to get access to your database. Even if the user only has read (select) privileges on tables in your database, it is still a gaping security hole to provide users with a URL like the preceding example.

Another problem comes into play as more and more parameters are added to your URL. Many browsers have limits as to how many characters can be specified and, even if you provide the long URLs to your end users in the form of links, they can be difficult to maintain. Fortunately, Oracle has provided a simple solution: the Forms Servlet Configuration file.

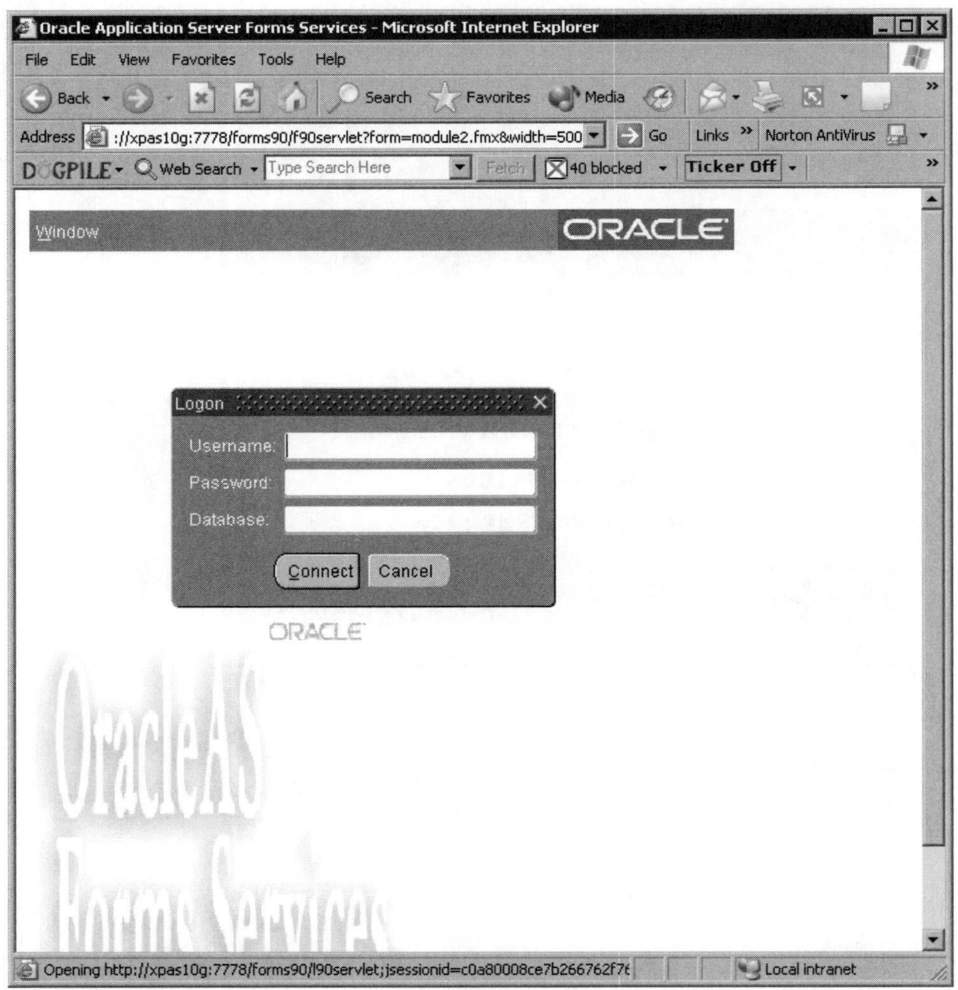

FIGURE 6-7. *Forms prompting for a user login*

formsweb.cfg

In the $ORACLE_HOME/forms90/server directory, there is a file called formsweb.cfg. This file, known as the Forms Servlet Configuration file, is used to create what are referred to as *named configurations*. These named configurations encapsulate the parameters that can be passed to the f90servlet executable and hide the details (form name, database login, etc.) from the end user. The URL simply references the named configuration and all Form implementation details are effectively hidden. Here's an example of the BOTTOM of a formsweb.cfg file (we'll discuss the top part in a moment):

```
# Example Named Configuration Section
# Example 1: configuration to run forms in a separate browser window with
# "generic" look and feel (include "config=sepwin" in the URL)
# You may define your own specific, named configurations (sets of parameters)
# by adding special sections as illustrated in the following examples.
# Note that you need only specify the parameters you want to change.  The
# default values (defined above) will be used for all other parameters.
# Use of a specific configuration can be requested by including the text
# "config=<your_config_name>" in the query string of the URL used to run
# a form.  For example, to use the sepwin configuration, your could issue
# a URL like "http://myhost.mydomain.com/servlet/f90servlet?config=sepwin."
[sepwin]
separateFrame=True
lookandfeel=Generic

# Example Named Configuration Section
# Example 2: configuration affecting users of MicroSoft Internet Explorer
5.x.
# Forms applet will run under the browser's native JVM rather than using
Oracle JInitiator.
[ienative]
IE=native

# Example Named Configuration Section
# Example 3: configuration forcing use of the Java Plugin in all cases (even if
# the client browser is on Windows)
[jpi]
baseHTMLJInitiator=basejpi.htm
baseHTMLie=basejpi.htm

# Example Named Configuration Section
# Example 4: configuration running the Forms ListenerServlet in debug mode
# (debug messages will be written to the servlet engine's log file).
[debug]
serverURL=/forms90/l90servlet/debug
```

Each named configuration starts with [named configuration]. All parameters specified after that are part of that named configuration. The named configuration ends when either another named configuration is specified or the end of the file is reached. In the above code listing, four named configurations are specified: sepwin, ienative, jpi, and debug. None of the above examples uses the form parameter, so let's create a typical-looking named configuration. At the end of the formsweb.cfg file, the following lines were added:

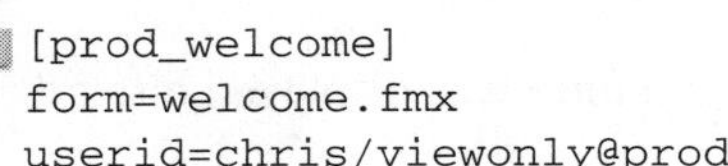

```
[prod_welcome]
form=welcome.fmx
userid=chris/viewonly@prod
```

```
width=900
height=900
lookAndFeel=Oracle
background=images/welcome.gif
splashScreen=images/welcome_splash.gif
logo=images/mycompanylogo.gif
```

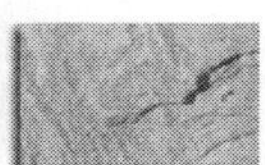

TIP

Even if your Forms Server is running on a Windows machine, use forward-slashes (/) when separating directories in your configuration files.

To run the Form and hide all of its implementation details, use the config= parameter in the URL to reference the named configuration:

```
http://xpas10g:7778/forms90/f90servlet?config=prod_welcome
```

It is important to note that the [default] configuration (the section at the beginning of the formsweb.cfg—discussed shortly) is always read by the Forms Server. The parameters you specify in your named configurations "overwrite" whatever is specified there, so if you change a value in the [default] section, it will affect all Forms called by way of a named configuration, unless the parameter is specified in the named configuration. In this way, you can create default behavior for all Forms (by changing values in the [default] section) and give individual Forms specific behavior by specifying values in the named parameter section.

If, for whatever reason, you do not wish to use the location or filename of the default Forms Servlet Configuration file, you can change it by modifying the web.xml file in the $ORACLE_HOME/j2ee/OC4J_BI_Forms/applications/forms90app/forms90web/WEB-INF directory. The following lines need to be uncommented and the new filename and directory specified:

```
<!-
  <init-param>
     <param-name>configFileName</param-name>
     <param-value><your configuration file name goes here></param-value>
  </init-param>
->
```

The OC4J_BI_Forms container will need to be stopped and started before changes will take effect.

So far, we have looked at creating named configurations with parameters that can be specified in the URL calling the f90servlet executable, but there are other parameters that can only be specified in the formsweb.cfg, as shown in Table 6-4.

Here's an odd Forms behavior: If you haven't modified your formsweb.cfg file, try putting in a named configuration not specified in the formsweb.cfg:

```
http://xpas10g:7778/forms90/f90servlet?config=bogusbogusbogus
```

You would expect an error to be displayed (I know we did), but a form was displayed instead (see Figure 6-8).

Parameter	Required?	Description
baseHTML	Required	The default base HTML file.
baseHTMLJInitiator	Required	The physical path to HTML file that contains JInitiator tags.
connectionDisallowedURL	Required	This is the URL shown in the HTML page that is not allowed to start a new session.
baseHTMLjpi	Optional	The physical path to HTML file that contains Java Plug-in tags. Used as the baseHTML file if the client browser is not on Windows and the client browser is either Netscape or Internet Explorer (IE) without the IE native settings.
baseHTMLie	Optional	The physical path to the HTML file that contains Internet Explorer 5 tags; e.g., the CABBASE tag. The default path is <ORACLE_HOME>/forms90/server/baseie.htm. This is required when using the IE native JVM.
HTML delimiter	Required	The delimiter for variable names. Defaults to %.
workingDirectory	Required	Defaults to <ORACLE_HOME>/forms90 if not set.
envFile	Required	This is set to default.env in the formsweb.cfg file.
defaultcharset	Optional	Specifies the character set to be used in servlet requests and responses. Defaults to iso-8859-1 (also known as Latin-1). Ignored if the servlet request specifies a character set (e.g., in the content-type header of a POST). The values of this parameter may be specified either as an IANA character set name (e.g., SHIFT_JIS) or as an Oracle character set name (e.g., JA16SJIS). It should match the character set specified in the NLS_LANG environment variable, and it should also be a character set that the browser is capable of displaying. Also, if the browser allows multibyte characters to be entered directly into a URL; e.g., using the IME, as opposed to URL escape sequences; and if you wish to allow end users to do this, then the value of this parameter should match the character set that the browser uses to convert the entered characters into byte sequences. Note: If your configuration file contains configuration sections with names that contain characters other than 7-bit ASCII characters, then the following rules apply. If a config parameter is specified in a URL or in the body of a POST request with no specified character set, and the value contains non-7-bit ASCII characters, then the value is interpreted using a character set whose name is derived from the value of the defaultcharset parameter. However, only the language-dependent default section and the language-independent default section of the configuration file is searched for the defaultcharset parameter. No configuration section is searched because the name is not yet known.

TABLE 6-4. *formsweb.cfg System Parameters that Cannot Be Specified in the URL*

Parameter	Required?	Description
IE	Recommended if there are users with IE 5.0 or above browsers	Specifies how to execute the Forms applet under Microsoft IE 5.0 or above. If the client is using an IE 5.0 or above browser, either the native JVM or JInitiator can be used. A setting of "JInitiator" uses the basejini.htm file and JInitiator. A setting of "Native" uses the browser's native JVM.
log	Optional	Supports running and debugging a form from the Builder. Default value is Null.
pageTitle	Optional	HTML page title, attributes for the BODY tag, and HTML to add before and after the form.
HTMLbodyAttrs	Optional	Attributes for the <BODY> tag of the HTML page.
HTMLbeforeForm	Optional	HTML content to add to the page above the area where the Forms application will be displayed.
HTMLafterForm	Optional	HTML content to add to the page below the area where the Forms application will be displayed.

TABLE 6-4. *formsweb.cfg System Parameters that Cannot Be Specified in the URL* (continued)

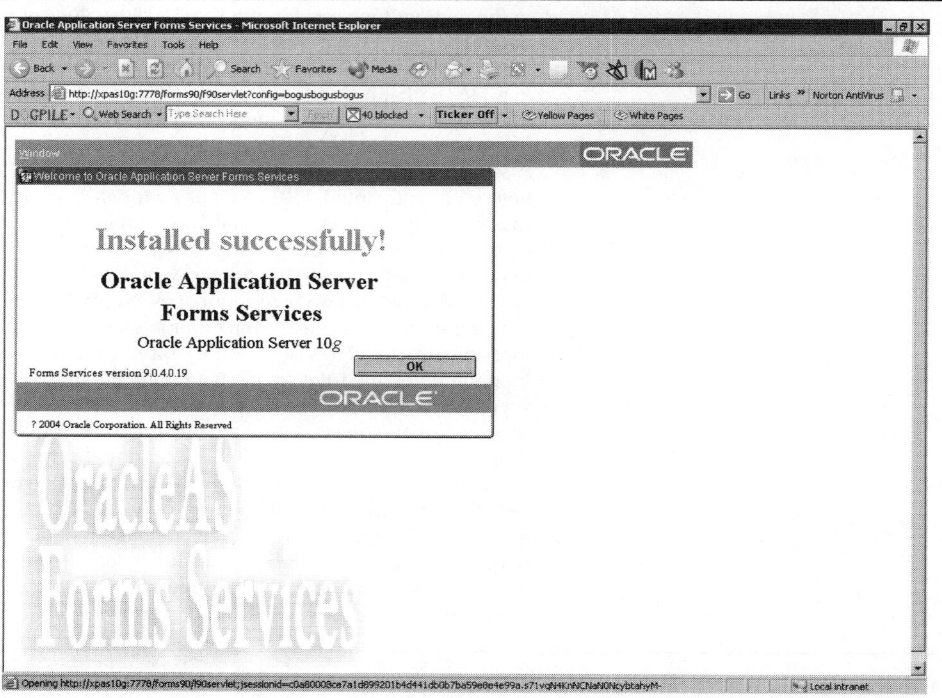

FIGURE 6-8. *Form displayed with bogus named configuration specified*

To understand what is going on, we need to revisit our formsweb.cfg file and examine the beginning part of it. The first couple of lines (after the comment lines that begin with a "#") look like this:

```
[default]
# System parameter: default base HTML file
baseHTML=base.htm
# System parameter: base HTML file for use with JInitiator client
baseHTMLjinitiator=basejini.htm
# System parameter: base HTML file for use with Sun's Java Plug-In
baseHTMLjpi=basejpi.htm
# System parameter: base HTML file for use with Microsoft Internet Explorer
# (when using the native JVM)
baseHTMLie=baseie.htm
# System parameter: delimiter for parameters in the base HTML files
HTMLdelimiter=%
# System parameter: working directory for Forms runtime processes
# WorkingDirectory defaults to <oracle_home>/forms90 if unset.
workingDirectory=
# System parameter: file setting environment variables for the Forms runtime processes
envFile=default.env
# System parameter: JVM option for Microsoft Internet Explorer.
# This parameter specifies how to execute the Forms applet under
# Microsoft Internet Explorer 5.x or above.  Put IE=native if you want
# the Forms applet to run in the browser's native JVM.
IE=JInitiator

# Forms runtime argument: whether to escape certain special characters
# in values extracted from the URL for other runtime arguments
escapeparams=true
# Forms runtime argument: which form module to run
form=test.fmx
# Forms runtime argument: database connection details
userid=
```

You'll notice that it begins with a named configuration section called [default]. The [default] section is always read, so if no parameters, or a bogus-named configuration, is specified in the URL, the Forms Server will take information from the [default] section of the formsweb.cfg. This is why even though we specified config=bogusbogusbogus in Figure 6-8, a Form (test.fmx) was still displayed.

Displaying Oracle Reports on the Web

Oracle Forms requires the most work before moving to a web-deployment. Moving Oracle Reports and Oracle Discoverer worksheets to the Web are relatively simple in comparison. As with Oracle Forms, Oracle provides a compiler for Oracle Reports included with every installation of Oracle Application Server 10*g*. On Windows, it can be found in Start -> Programs -> Oracle <Oracle_HOME> -> Reports Services -> Reports Converter (see Figure 6-9). On Unix, you can run the rwconverter.sh script.

There are two main types of Reports files you can generate from Oracle Reports Developer: Reports Binary files (.rdf) and Report Binary Run-only files (.rep). RDFs for Reports are equivalent

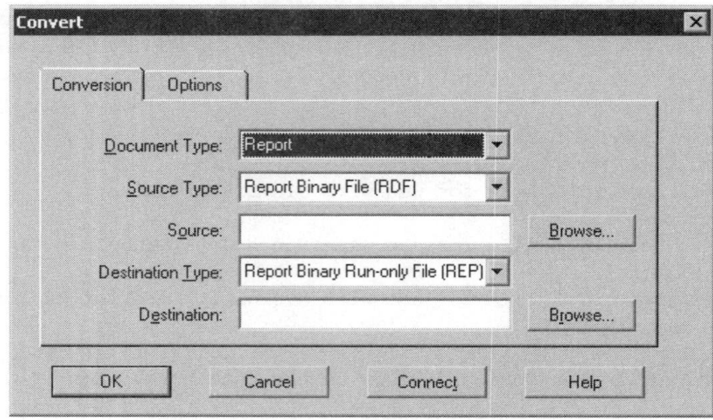

FIGURE 6-9. *The Reports converter executable*

to FMBs for Forms and REPs are equivalent to FMXs for Forms in the sense that .REPs and FMXs are platform specific (i.e., an .rep of FMX developed on, say, a Windows machine cannot be moved to a Linux machine and executed there) while RDFs and FMBs are not. There is a crucial difference, however, between the Forms and Reports Servers included with Oracle Application Server 10*g*: the Forms Server requires FMXs; the Reports Server can run RDFs with no problems. What this implies for the developer is that a Form developed on one platform MUST be recompiled before deploying on a different platform; Reports, however, can be developed on one platform and deployed on another without recompilation. As is the case of Forms, the Oracle Application Server 10*g* Reports Server can serve Reports via the Web developed with Reports 6*i* onward without modification.

TIP
Just like Forms, it's a good idea to recompile your Reports on your production server just to make sure there are no anomalies.

Reports and Fonts

Perhaps the biggest issue to consider when moving reports to the Web involves the fonts used in the Reports. The Reports Server will use the character set on the server displaying the Reports, which may have a different character set than what is on your development machine(s). During Report formatting, fonts associated with the layout objects are first checked against the font alias file, uifont.ali. If an entry in the font alias file is found, the mapped font is used instead of the original one. The mapped font is then looked up in the list of fonts available on the system or printer. If a particular font is not found, Oracle Reports will look for the nearest matching font under the same character set that can be used instead.

On Windows, the font lookup mechanism is simple due to the availability of printer drivers, which have the capability of uploading fonts from the system as needed. Oracle Reports considers both the printer and the system fonts when looking for the available fonts. On Unix, the fonts available for generating output are either one of the following: the fonts available on the printer, specifically the fonts defined in the PPD or TFM files if no printer is specified, or the fonts available in the ScreenPrinter file, screenprinter.ppd.

The following steps describe how Oracle Reports generates a list of the available fonts for generating output (e.g., for the screen, printer, or file):

- Oracle Reports looks in the printer configuration file uiprint.txt for all the printers that are listed for the application. If no printers are defined or available, Oracle Reports uses ScreenPrinter.
- Oracle Reports gets their type, version, and printer definition file.
- Oracle Reports checks for the existence of these printers in the system.
- If the printers are present, the printer definition files are loaded and the information in these files is read along with the information related to the fonts available for the printer. If these printers are not found, then Oracle Reports uses ScreenPrinter.
- The AFM files (Adobe Font Metric—used to provide information on Adobe fonts), which are named the same as the font names given in the PPD files, are searched.
- If found, Oracle Reports then reads the AFM files for all the valid keywords, checks for their correctness and, in case of any discrepancy, default values are used for those keywords.
- If the AFM file is not found, Oracle Reports marks the font as unusable.

Substituting Fonts

If a particular font is needed but not found in the PPD file or if an AFM file is not found, Oracle Reports will look for the nearest matching font according to its matching rules. If it cannot find any matching font for this character set, Oracle Reports searches for a font that has a character set for the environment in which the application is running. After finding a set of fonts with a similar character set, Oracle Reports picks the closest match to the requested font based on the font weight, style, etc. If more than one font has the same parameters, Oracle Reports picks the first one and uses it instead of the original font.

Font Matching Rules

When attempting to match a font, Oracle Reports will try to find the closest match according to the following criteria for fonts with the same character set:

fontface > fontsize > fontstyle > fontweight > fontwidth

If Oracle Reports can't match the font face, it will try to match the font size; if it can't match the size, it will try to match the font style; and so on. If a font matches the font size but nothing else and another font matches the style, weight, and width but not the font size, then Oracle Reports will pick the font with the same font size. It should be noted that irrespective of any font in the output file, the final printed output will depend solely on the fonts installed in the printer.

Because a report may have to run in many different environments, Oracle Reports always tries to approximate a font for the original font when the original is unavailable. This algorithm is not entirely foolproof. When you create a report, you must be aware of the fonts defined and you should always consider whether those same fonts will be available on the platform where users will run the report. If the font that you have defined is not available in the run-time environment, Oracle Reports substitutes another font that is available on the machine. This process can lead to unexpected and undesirable results, such as strange characters in the report output and incorrect formatting of objects. If you are encountering these kinds of problems, you should use font aliasing to control the font substitutions made by Oracle Reports. Oracle Reports follows the preceding described mechanisms for all output file generation except PDF, which has the PDF font sub setting/embedding capabilities.

Printing

For printing, Oracle Reports generates output based upon the printer driver, in the case of Windows, or the printer, in the case of Unix. On Windows, the output generation is handled by the printer driver. The fonts in this case can either be from the system or from the printer. For fonts that are not available on the printer, the printer will get the fonts from the system through Windows Application Programming Interfaces (APIs).

Font Configuration Files

The following list describes all of the files associated with font configuration for Oracle Reports.

- uiprint.txt (Unix only)

  The printer configuration file contains a list of printers installed for the application along with the type of printer, its version, and the printer definition file. The list of available fonts for run time is taken from the printer definition file. If no printer is present, Oracle Reports chooses a PostScript printer as the default and default.ppd file as the printer definition file.

- screenprinter.ppd (Unix only)

  screenprinter.ppd is used when a printer is not available on Unix. screenprinter.ppd is in ORACLE_HOME/guicommon9/tk90/admin/PPD.

- uifont.ali

  This file contains mapping information for fonts which can be substituted for other fonts at run time. Oracle Reports has added three new sections to the uifont.ali file:

  - **[PDF]** Used for font aliasing and multibyte language support
  - **[PDF:Subset]** Used for TrueType font subsetting and multibyte language support
  - **[PDF:Embed]** Used for Type1 font embedding

- PPD and AFM files (UNIX only)

PostScript Printer Definition (PPD) files and AFM files are supplied by Adobe and by printer vendors. These files contain information about the printer. Along with other parameters, these files are read for the information about the available fonts for the printer, which Oracle Reports will use. For all the fonts listed in the PPD file, Oracle Reports searches for the corresponding

AFM file according to the font name and loads all of the fonts for which there is an available AFM. From the fonts perspective, you should modify these files when you add new fonts for the printer and want these changes reflected in Oracle Reports. The AFM files contain information such as the font attributes (style, weight, width, encoding scheme), whether the font is fixed pitch or proportional, and how large each character is. After looking for the font names from the PPD files, Oracle Reports searches for the AFM files with the same name as the font.AFM files are NOT font files; they are metrics files, which give Oracle Reports information on how to properly format the character for the printer. If you have an AFM file, but the font is not available on the printer, then Oracle Reports cannot generate the font. Because the AFM files are NOT fonts themselves, if you wish to have more PostScript printer fonts available, you need to:

- Purchase the fonts and have them installed on the printer
- Obtain revised AFM and PPD files from the font/printer vendor
- Obtain matching X Server display fonts (if necessary)

Running an Oracle Report on the Web

Oracle Reports uses a Reports Server to serve up reports to your browser over the Web. You can have multiple Reports Servers running simultaneously, each with different characteristics depending on the nature of reporting in your company. During the installation of Oracle Application Server 10*g*, a Reports Server is created for you automatically. It is given the name rep_<servername> and can have its status checked in the Enterprise Manager Application Server Control web site for the middle tier. Unlike the Forms Server we discussed earlier, the Reports Server has no dependencies and can be started or stopped independently.

As with Oracle Forms, there is an easy way to display your Reports on the Web, but it is for illustrative purposes only—you would not use this method in a production environment. The rwservlet executable is used to serve Oracle Reports over the Web. Its URL format is:

```
http://<host>:<port>/reports/rwservlet?<parameters>
```

A typical Reports URL might look like this:

```
http://xpas10g:7778/reports/rwservlet?destype=cache&desformat=PDF&report=tes
t.rdf&userid=chris/viewonly@test&repserver=rep_xpas10g
```

This is not a good way to do it because of the same issue we discussed earlier with Forms: namely, that too much Reports implementation and database information is exposed in the URL for all to see. For Forms, Oracle provides the Forms Servlet Configuration File (formsweb.cfg) to hide Forms implementation details. For Reports, Oracle provides a similar file but its naming and format are different.

cgicmd.dat

The cgicmd.dat file is referred to in Oracle documentation as the Key Map file. It is located in the $ORACLE_HOME/reports/conf directory, and it performs a similar role for Reports that the formsweb.cfg file provides for Forms. Its format is slightly different:

<key>:<parameters>

The preceding request to run the Report:

```
http://xpas10g:7778/reports/rwservlet?destype=cache&desformat=PDF&report=tes
t.rdf&userid=chris/viewonly@test&server=rep_xpas10g
```

can have its details hidden like this in the cgicmd.dat file:

```
test_report: destype=cache desformat=PDF report=test.rdf userid=chris/
viewonly@test server=rep_xpas10g
```

Note that parameters are separated by blank spaces and NOT ampersands as with the URL. To reference this key, simply specify it at the end of your URL:

```
http://xpas10g:7778/reports/rwservlet?test_report
```

The rwservlet executable can accept numerous parameters, the most common of which are described as follows (for a complete list, refer to Oracle Application Server Reports Services Publishing Reports to the Web 10g (9.0.4), Part Number B10314-01):

- **ARRAYSIZE** Use ARRAYSIZE to specify the size (in kilobytes) for use with Oracle9*i* array processing. Generally, the larger the array size, the faster the report will run.
- **BLANKPAGES** Use BLANKPAGES to specify whether to suppress blank pages when you print a report. Use this keyword when there are blank pages in your report output that you do not want to print.
- **BUFFERS** Use to specify the size of the virtual memory cache in kilobytes. You should tune this setting to ensure that you have enough space to run your reports, but not so much that you are using too much of your system's resources.
- **COPIES** Use to specify the number of copies of the report output to print.
- **DATEFORMATMASK** Use to specify how date values display in your delimited report output.
- **DESFORMAT** Use DESFORMAT to specify the format for the job output and to specify the printer driver to be used when DESTYPE is FILE and DESNAME=filename. The values are listed in Table 6-5.
- **DESNAME** Use DESNAME to specify the name of the cache, file, printer, Oracle Application Server Portal, or e-mail ID (or distribution list) to which the report output will be sent.
- **DESTYPE** Use DESTYPE to specify the type of device that will receive the report output. If you have created your own pluggable destination via the Oracle Reports Destination API, this is how the destination you created gets called. The values for DESTYPE are listed in Table 6-6.
- **HELP** Use HELP to display a help topic that lists the keywords you can use with the rwservlet command.

Value	Description
DELIMITED	The report output is sent to a file that can be read by standard spreadsheet utilities, such as Microsoft Excel. If you do not specify a delimiter (via the DELIMITER keyword), the default delimiter is a TAB. See Usage Notes.
DELIMITEDDATA	Provides the same functionality as DELIMITED, and is used when you have problems running large volume reports with DESFORMAT= DELIMITED. See Usage Notes.
HTML	This report output is sent to a file that is in HTML format.
HTMLCSS	This report output is sent to a file that includes style sheet extensions.
PDF	This report output is sent to a file that is in PDF format and can be read by a PDF viewer, such as Adobe Acrobat. PDF output is based upon the currently configured printer for your system. The drivers for the currently selected printer are used to produce the output; you must have a printer configured for the machine on which you are running the report.
POSTSCRIPT	This report output is sent to a file that is in PostScript format.
PRINTER DEFINITION	If DESTYPE=FILE and DESNAME=<filename> then PRINTER DEFINITION is used to specify how to format the report. If MODE= BITMAP, specify the name of the printer. If MODE=CHARACTER, specify the character-mode printer definition file (.prt file), such as hpl, hplwide, dec, decwide, decland, dec180, dflt or wide. Ask your system administrator for a list of valid printer definitions.
RTF	The report output is sent to a file that can be read by word processors (such as Microsoft Word). When you open the file in Microsoft Word, you must choose View -> Page Layout to view all the graphics and objects in your report.
XML	This report output is saved as an XML file. This report can be opened and read in an XML-supporting browser, or your choice of XML viewing application.

TABLE 6-5. *Values for the DESFORMAT parameter*

- **KILLJOBID** Use KILLJOBID to kill a Reports Server job with the specified job ID *n*.
- **MODULE | REPORT** Use MODULE or REPORT to specify the name of the report to run.
- **ORIENTATION** ORIENTATION controls the direction in which the pages of the report will print {DEFAULT|LANDSCAPE|PORTRAIT}.

Value	Description
CACHE	Sends the output directly to the Reports Server cache.
LOCALFILE	Sends the output to a file on the client machine, synchronously or asynchronously.
FILE	Sends the output to the file on the server named in DESNAME.
PRINTER	Sends the output to the printer on the server named in DESNAME. You must have a printer that the Oracle Application Server Reports Services can recognize as installed and running.
MAIL	Sends the output to the mail users specified in DESNAME. You can send mail to any mail system that works with SMTP. Note: The configuration file rwbuilder.conf must include the pluginParam mailServer with the outgoing mail server name. This applies in both Windows and Solaris environments.
ORACLEPORTAL	Sends the output to Oracle Application Server Portal. Relevant keywords include EXPIREDAYS, ITEMTITLE, OUTPUTPAGE, PAGEGROUP, REPLACEITEM, SCHEDULE, STATUSPAGE.
FTP	Sends the output to the specified FTP server.
WEBDAV	Sends the output to the specified WebDAV URL so that the report can be published directly.
name_of_pluggable_destination	If you have created your own pluggable destination via the Oracle Reports Destination API, this is what you use to call the destination you created.

TABLE 6-6. *Values for the DESTYPE parameter*

- **PAGESTREAM** PAGESTREAM enables or disables page streaming (pagination) for the report when formatted as HTML or HTMLCSS output, using the navigation controls set by either of the following:
  - The Page Navigation Control Type and Page Navigation Control Value properties in the Report Property Palette
  - PL/SQL in a Before Report trigger (SRW.SET_PAGE_NAVIGATION_HTML)
- **SERVER** Use SERVER to specify the name of the Reports Server you want to use to run this report.
- **SSOCONN** Use SSOCONN to specify one or more connect strings to use to connect to one or more data sources in a single sign-on (SSO) environment.

- **USERID** Use USERID only if you're not using SSO. Use USERID to specify your Oracle user name and password, with an optional database name for accessing a remote database. If the password is omitted, then a database logon form opens automatically before the user is allowed to run the report.

Reports Server Configuration Files

There are several files that make up the configuration of the Reports Server. The two most prominent ones are the rwservlet.properties and rep_<server name>.conf files, both of which are located in the $ORACLE_HOME/reports/conf directory.

rwservlet.properties Any parameter specified here applies to all Reports Servers running on that machine. There are many parameters that can be specified in this file (see Chapter 3, "Configuring OracleAS Reports Services" in "Oracle Application Server Reports Services Publishing Reports to the Web 10g (9.0.4)", Part Number B10314-01). In the list below are those parameters most commonly specified:

- SERVER_IN_PROCESS=YES

The in-process server is an instance that gets started through the Reports Servlet "rwservlet," when the report is requested for the first time. By default (starting with Oracle9iAS R2 onward), when the Business Intelligence and Forms option is selected during installation, an in-process Reports Server is configured automatically and is named rep_<hostname>.This process is not listed in the process list of the OS. Hence, this service cannot be stopped/disabled as it can be done with a normal process. By specifying this to yes, you do not have to specify the server=<servername> parameter in either the URL calling the report or the cgicmd.dat file. The server specified in the SERVER parameter (discussed in the following text) will be used when the report is executed.

- #SINGLESIGNON=YES

Even though it is commented out by default in the rwservlet.properties file, the default value for the SINGLESIGNON parameter is still yes. This allows administrators to take advantage of Oracle's SSO capabilities from within Oracle Reports. Why is this desirable?

Consider an organization where there are hundreds of reports run over the Web every day. Most likely, this organization has multiple databases. If one username and password is used to access a specific report, you run into the danger of having the username/password combination fall into the wrong hands. At best, in this scenario, there are now people with access to data on the reports that should not have it. At worst, a knowledgeable user can now gain access to your database with a (potentially) malicious tool such as SQL*PLUS. It also becomes impossible to trace the source of the leak, as anyone who has been given that username/password combination is a potential suspect.

A better solution would be a way to define database resources and grant them to users as they need them. This way a user is solely responsible for his/her password and, when a breach of security is detected, the individual's login can be quarantined without affecting all other users on the system.

This also makes it easier to track down the unauthorized user, as Oracle has monitoring tools that can pinpoint when and where a particular user accesses the system.

Oracle's SSO capabilities allow the creation of users who can access Oracle Application Server 10*g* components such Oracle Reports and Oracle Portal. These users are not to be confused with database users—no database user is created when these users are created—they are stored in Oracle's Lightweight Directory Access Protocol (LDAP) implementation, Oracle Internet Directory.

This is where it gets a little confusing: Where is the LDAP data stored from Oracle Internet Directory? Why, in an Oracle database (the infrastructure instance), of course! The Oracle Internet Directory service stores encrypted LDAP data in tables in the database.

For each of these LDAP users, it is possible to create resources (database username/password/connection string combinations). This way, the end user only needs to log in once (and, therefore, only has to remember one password) and the person responsible for security in your organization can grant or revoke access to a report by defining or deleting resources. To create a single sign-on user, enter the URL of the Delegated Administration Service on your infrastructure machine:

```
http:<server name>:<port name>/oiddas
```

You will be presented with a screen like the one in Figure 6-10.

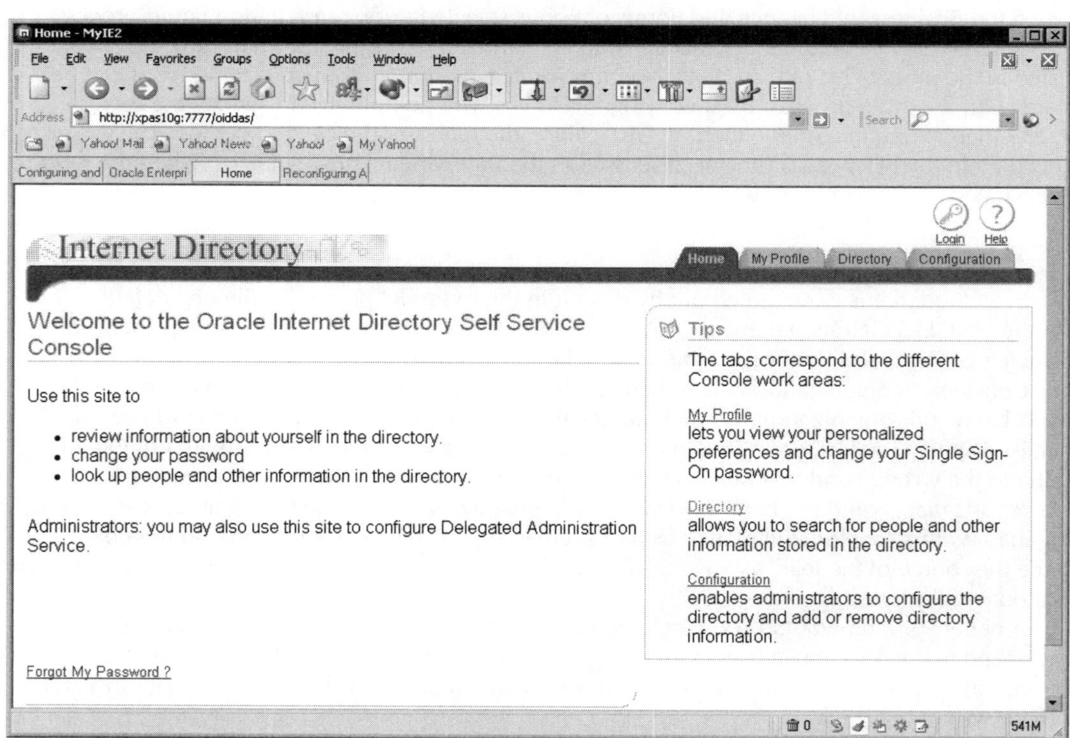

FIGURE 6-10. *The login screen for Oracle Internet Directory*

Log in using the orcladmin username and the password you enter when creating the infrastructure instance (not the database instance) when installing Oracle Application Server 10*g*. Click the "Directory" tab, then the Create button in the middle of the screen. Fill in the required fields at the top of the screen (see Figure 6-11), then click Resource Access Information on the top right of the screen to be taken to the bottom of the page (see Figure 6-12).

Click the "Create" button and enter a name for your database resource. Click "Next" and enter a username/password/connect string combination.

It can be confusing determining where the connect string specified when creating a database resource for a user is resolved. First of all, it is **not** resolved on the user's local machine, even though the Report is displayed there. The connect string is resolved where the report is executed, not displayed. Secondly, it is **not** resolved on the infrastructure server (or, in the case of a server with both infrastructure and middle tier on the same machine, it is **not** resolved in the ORACLE_HOME for the infrastructure). This confuses many administrators—didn't we just log in to the infrastructure to define the user and the resource for that user? Yes, but again, this is not where the Report is actually executed—the infrastructure is simply where we define and store the connection information for the resource. Finally, it **is** resolved on the middle tier (or, in the case of a server with both infrastructure and middle tier on the same machine, in the ORACLE_HOME for the

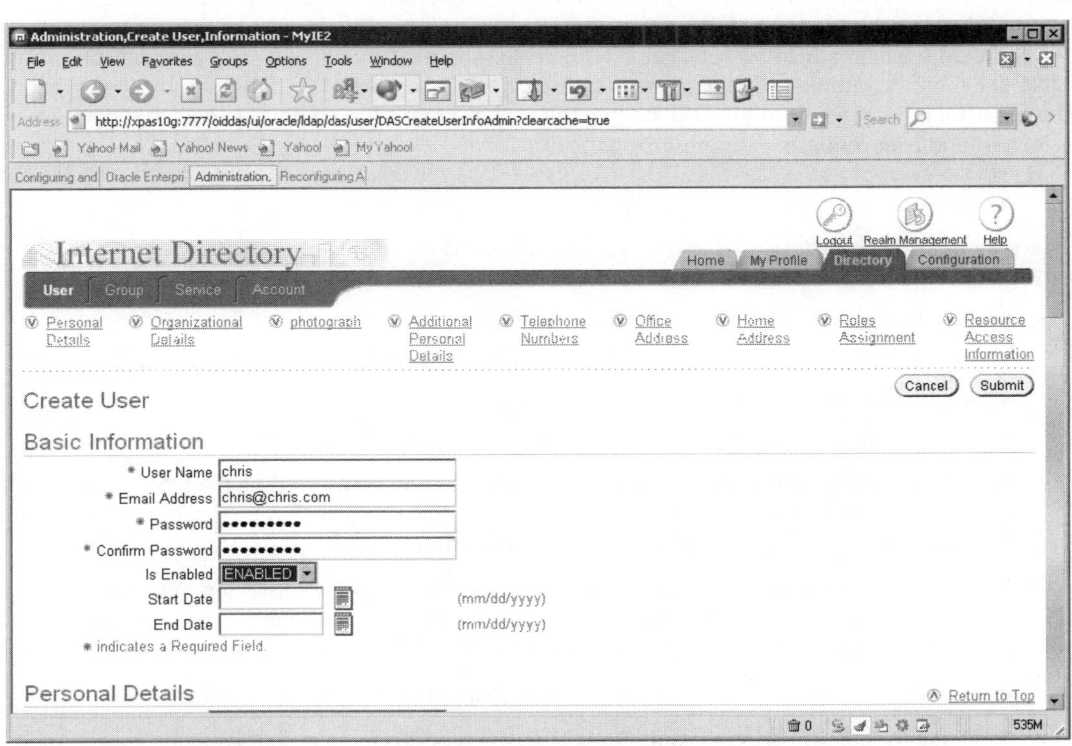

FIGURE 6-11. *The Create User screen*

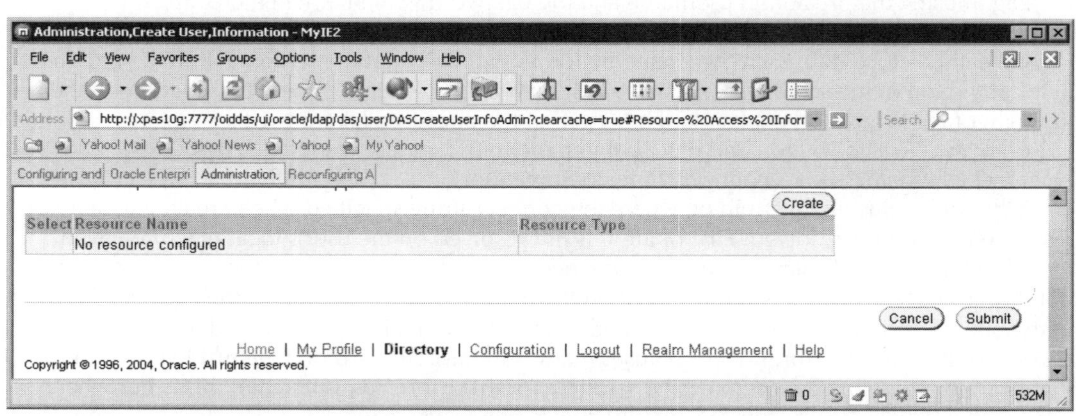

FIGURE 6-12. *The create resource section of the Create User screen*

middle tier). This means that the tnsnames.ora file on the middle tier is what will be used to attempt a connection to the database.

How do we take advantage of Oracle's single sign-on functionality? By first making sure the SINGLESIGNON parameter in the rwservlet.properties files is set to YES, and then by specifying the SSOCONN parameter in the URL calling the report. Here's the chain of events that happens when an end user requests a report through SSO:

1. The user specifies a URL in their browser similar to this one:

   ```
   http://xpas10g:7778/reports/rwservlet?destype=cache&desformat=
   PDF&report=test.rdf&ssoconn=ssotest
   ```

   or if there is an entry like this in the cgicmd.dat:

   ```
   ssotestkey: destype=cache desformat=PDF report=test.rdf ssoconn=ssotest
   ```

   a URL like this:

   ```
   http://xpas10g:7778/reports/rwservlet?ssotestkey
   ```

2. The Reports Server determines that SSO has been enabled by reading the SINGLESIGNON parameter from the rwservlet.properties file and passes control to the infrastructure server. The user is then prompted for a login and password.

3. If authentication is successful, control is passed back to the middle tier. Why the middle tier? The Reports Server checks for the existence of a resource for that user matching the name specified in the SSOCONN parameter in the URL (in this example, ssotest).

4. The Reports Server then attempts to establish a connection to that database.

5. If the connection is successful, the SQL in the report is executed, the results are returned to the Reports Server, and the report output is displayed in the end user's web browser.

Metalink note 222332.1, "A Detailed Explanation of Oracle 9*i* Reports Security," is an excellent primer for understanding the issues related to securing Oracle Reports on the Web. Even though it was written for Oracle 9*i* Reports, the concepts are applicable to Oracle Reports 10*g*.

- SERVER=rep_oski

This is the server that is used when the SERVER_IN_PROCESS parameter is set to YES and no server is specified in either the URL or the cgicmd.dat Key Map file.

rep_<server name>.conf The rep_<server name>.conf file is an XML file that maintains information about Reports Servers on your system. Unlike the rwservlet.properties file, changes to this file will only affect the individual Reports Server. It can be very difficult to read (being an XML file), but the section below outlines the major sections of the file:

```
<engine id="rwEng" class="oracle.reports.engine.EngineImpl" initEngine="1"
maxEngine="1" minEngine="0" engLife="50" maxIdle="30"
callbackTimeOut="60000">
```

This line specifies the basic characteristics of your Reports Server:

- **initEngine** Specifies the number of Reports Server engines started when this Reports Server is started.
- **maxEngine** and **minEngine** Specify the maximum and minimum engines used by this Reports Server.
- **engLife** Specifies the number of jobs this Reports Server will process before shutting itself down and restarting itself (this is to attempt to avoid memory leaks).
- **maxIdle** The number of minutes of allowable idle time before the engine is shut down, provided the current number of engines is higher than minEngine.
- **callbackTimeOut** The number of milliseconds of allowable waiting time between when the server calls an engine and the engine calls the server back.

An optional parameter, although not listed in the example above, is the classPath attribute. This attribute of the engine element is used in any environment that uses the Java Importer. The value of this attribute represents the Java classpath used by the reports engine. All Java classes that are used in a report need to be found along this path. Any custom java class that is added to the REPORTS_CLASSPATH environment variable for use during design needs to be added to this attribute for deployment. The main difference between the REPORTS_CLASSPATH environment variable and the classpath attribute is that REPORTS_CLASSPATH contains all Java objects that are part of the reports services environment (data sources, destinations, other plug-ins, etc.), while the classpath attribute contains all the java objects that are used by Reports during execution (barcode beans, etc.).

```
<connection maxConnect="20" idleTimeOut="15">
```

MAXCONNECT must be equal to the SUM of your anticipated MAX CLIENT and MAX SERVER processes. For every client request on the Reports Server, the minimum number of connections required is two (2): one for the server and one for the client. If you anticipate or tune your Reports Server to handle a maximum of 20 engines, you must allow MAXCONNECT to be set to at least 40. idleTimeOut represents the maximum time of inactivity between a Reports client (e.g., RWCLIENT, RUN_REPORT_OBJECT, RWSERVLET) and the Reports Server. If a report contains SQL or PL/SQL, which takes a long time to execute on the RDBMS side, a REP-56109 timeout message may occur as a result of the idleTimeOut setting.

Running Oracle Discoverer on the Web

Oracle Discoverer is unique in the sense that Oracle Application Server 10*g* not only provides an environment to view Oracle Discoverer workbooks and worksheets via the Web (discussed here), but also provides an environment to develop Oracle Discoverer workbooks and worksheets (discussed in Chapter 5). This makes it extremely attractive for organizations looking to reduce their total cost of ownership (TCO): there is much less work configuring developer's machines and less licensing costs (as it is no longer necessary to install Discoverer Desktop on all developer and power-user's machines).

Another significant benefit to this architecture is the reduction in time spent moving Discoverer objects to the Web. Because Discoverer Plus and Discoverer Viewer are fully integrated with Oracle Application Server 10*g*, there is a significant reduction in time and effort needed to configure your environment when displaying Oracle Discoverer workbooks and worksheets. And given Oracle Discoverer workbooks and worksheets are stored within the database, there is no need for any type of conversion or recoding. Of the three development tools discussed in this chapter, Oracle Discoverer is the easiest to integrate with the Web.

Discoverer Connections

Some of this material was covered earlier, but is repeated here for those readers who are only interested in running Discoverer workbooks and worksheets on the Web and have skipped Chapter 5. If you have read through Chapter 5 and are comfortable creating and maintaining Discoverer connections, you can safely skip this section.

Oracle Discoverer requires its own connection information, as it is possible for a user to connect to different End-User Layers (EULs).

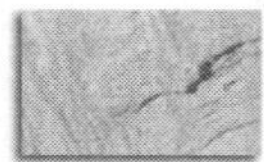

NOTE
An End-User Layer is a set of tables and views that maintains metadata (data about data) about the data in your database. The EUL allows users to create sophisticated Discoverer Reports without knowing the advanced features of SQL and insulates them from the complexity usually associated with databases. It provides an intuitive, business-focused view of the database using terms that Discoverer end users are familiar with and can easily understand. This enables Discoverer end users to focus on business issues instead of data access issues. The EUL contains the metadata that defines one or more business areas. A business area is a conceptual grouping of tables and/or views that apply to a user's specific data requirements. Business areas can be set up to reflect the needs of the user or group of users accessing the EUL.

A Discoverer connection can be created in one of two ways:

- By having an administrator create a Discoverer connection via the Oracle Enterprise Manager web site.
- By allowing users to create their own connections in Discoverer Viewer (this feature can be disabled).

Creating a Discoverer Connection in the Enterprise Manager Web Site

This is the preferred way to set up connections and the way most administrators will configure their systems. In the Enterprise Manager Web Application Server Control web site for your middle tier, select the Discoverer component (see Figure 6-13). Select Public Connections. Click the Create Connections button. You'll be presented with a page similar to Figure 6-14.

On this page, you'll name your connection, select the End-User Layer you wish to connect to, and enter the username/password/connection string information. Asterisks denote required fields and you'll notice that there is no asterisk next to the Password field under Database

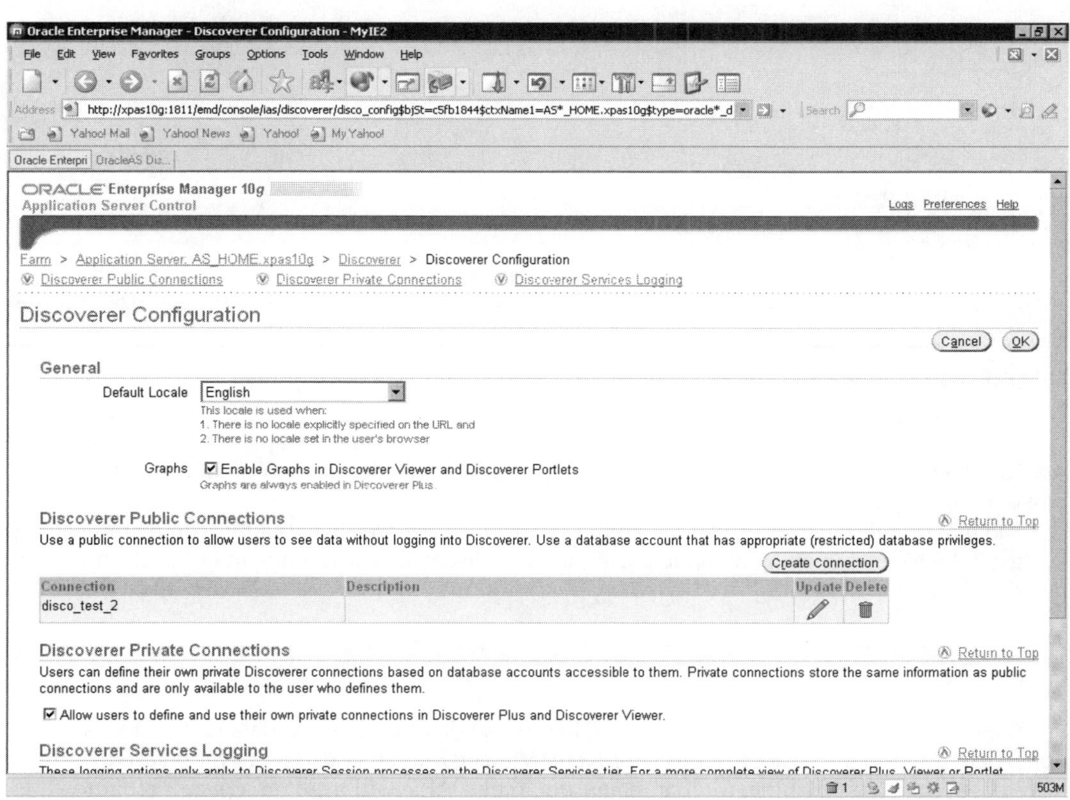

FIGURE 6-13. *The Discoverer properties page in the Enterprise Manager Application Server web page*

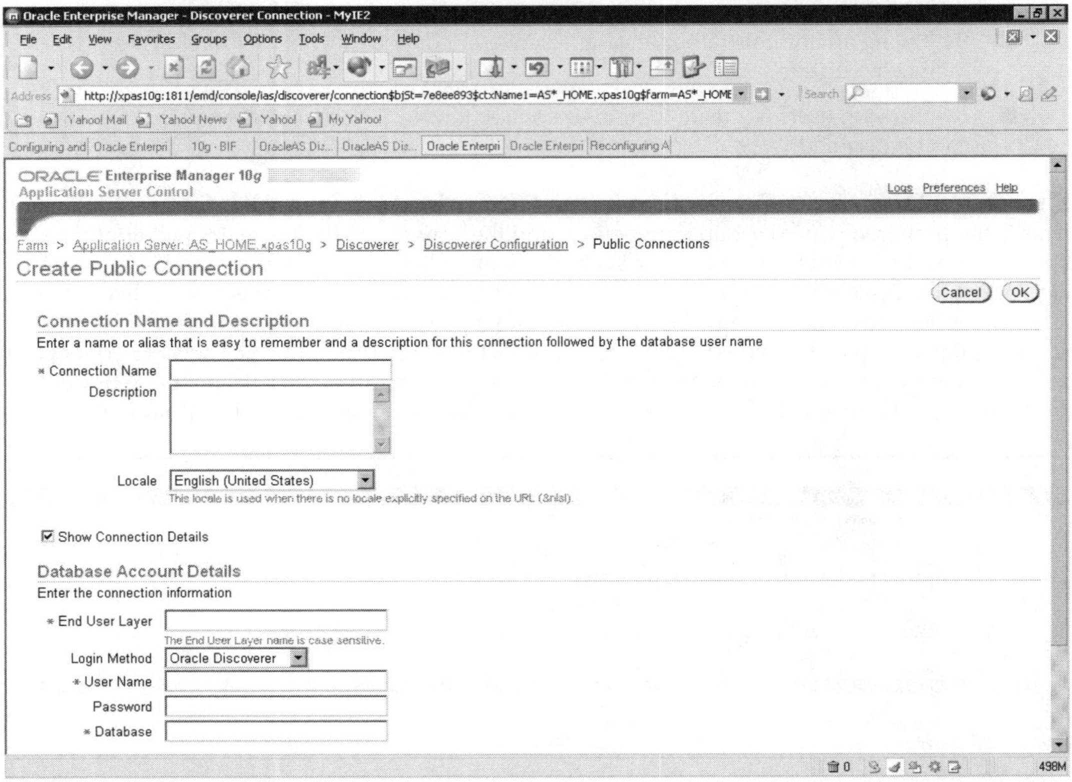

FIGURE 6-14. *The Create Public Connection Screen for Discoverer*

Account Details; this allows the administrator to create connections that prompt a user for a password before connecting to the database.

The hint on this page states that the End-User Layer is case sensitive, but this can be misleading. We used the following code to create a user named "disco" that was going to hold my End-User layer tables and views:

```
SQL> create user disco identified by disco default tablespace disco;
User created.
```

Although it looks like the username is in lowercase, it's stored in the data dictionary as uppercase. Attempting to access it in Discoverer Viewer with an End-User Layer entered with lowercase letters (or anything, for that matter not in all CAPS) will result in a page similar to Figure 6-15.

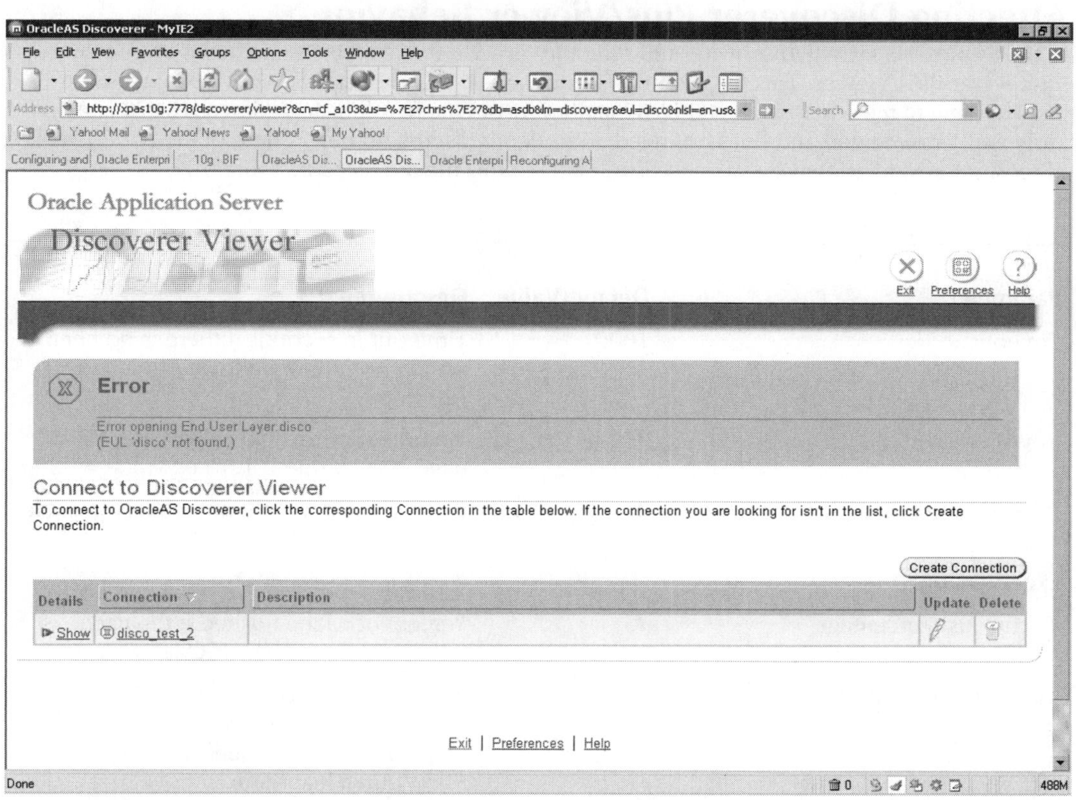

FIGURE 6-15. *An error when trying to access an EUL in lowercase*

Allowing Users to Create their Own Discoverer Connections

If we return to Figure 6-13, you'll notice that in the middle of the page, there is a check box next to a line that says "Allow users to define and use their own private connections in Discoverer Plus and Discoverer Viewer." By default, this check box is selected, allowing end users to create their own Discoverer connections. This is generally a bad idea as it is possible for an end user to connect to a "wrong" database. It also further introduces security risks by having end users know username/password/connection string information. It's a good idea to disable this feature by deselecting this option, but if you determine that this functionality is worth the risks, leave the default. Users will see a "Create Connection" button on the top-right part of the screen (as in Figure 6-15). If this feature is disabled, the button will not appear. Any connections created using this method are valid for as long as the browser is open.

Affecting Discoverer Plus/Viewer Behavior

In the $ORACLE_HOME/discoverer/util directory is a file that affects the behavior of Oracle Discoverer Plus/Viewer. This file, pref.txt, is known as the Discoverer Server Preferences File. Unlike many of the other parameter files included with Oracle Application Server 10*g*, pref.txt is fairly well commented and does not need an in-depth discussion here. Some of the parameters of most interest to administrators and developers in this file are listed in Table 6-7.

Parameter	Default Value	Description
Timeout	1800	Time out in seconds if there is no client activity. Minimum allowed time is 180 seconds.
RowsPerHTML	25	# Number of rows to display per HTML page. Min. value = 1. Max. value = 999.
PrintHeadersOnce	0	# turns off Print Column headers in each page (0 = Off , 1 = On)
ExcelVersion	"Excel95"	# ex Excel95,Excel97
CacheFlushPercentage	25	Percent of cache flushed if the cache is full. Valid values: 0 - 100%.
MaxVirtualDiskMem	1024000000	# Maximum amount of disk memory allowed for the data cache. Should be greater than or equal to MaxVirtualHeapMem.
MaxVirtualHeapMem	5120000	Maximum amount of heap memory allowed for the data cache.
QueryBehavior	0	Action to take after opening a workbook (0 = Run Query Automatically, 1 = Don't Run Query, 2 = Ask for Confirmation)
AxisLabelBehavior	1	Controls the behavior of when axis labels are displayed; valid values are: 1 -> "Always show axis labels" 2 -> "Never show axis labels" 3 -> "Show or hide axis labels as set in Discoverer Desktop."
NullValue	"NULL"	
ExcelExportWithMacros	1	If this is made 0, the exported Excel file won't have any macros and hence no formatting.

TABLE 6-7. *Discoverer Parameters*

Parameter	Default Value	Description
ItemClassDelay	15	Time out in seconds for LOV retrieval.
PredictionThresholdSeconds	60	Warn the user if the predicted query time exceeds the following value (seconds). Min. value = 1. Max. value = N.A. (see description at the beginning of file for range of valid values).
PredictionThresholdSecondsEnabled	1	Query prediction threshold disabled (0) or enabled (1).
QueryTimeLimit	1800	Limit on query time in seconds. Min. value = 1. Max. value = N.A. (see description at the beginning of file for range of valid values).
QueryTimeLimitEnabled	1	Query time limit disabled (0) or enabled (1).
RowFetchLimit	10000	Max rows fetched. Min. value = 1. Max. value = N.A. (see description at the beginning of file for range of valid values).
RowFetchLimitEnabled	1	Row fetch Limit disabled (0) or enabled (1).
MaxRowsPerFetch	250	Maximum permissible value for Incremental fetch. Min. value = 1. Max. value = 10,000.
RowsPerFetch	250	Incremental Fetch. Min. value = 1. Max. value = 10,000.
DefaultEUL	"VIDEO5"	Default EUL to connect to.

TABLE 6-7. *Discoverer Parameters* (continued)

Invoking Discoverer Plus

Displaying an Oracle Discoverer Worksheet on the Web is as simple as invoking Discoverer Plus from your web browser. The URL will be in the format similar to:

```
http://<server name>:<port number>/discoverer/viewer
```

For the examples in this chapter, we have been referencing a server named xpas10g:

```
http://xpas10g:7778/discoverer/viewer
```

The first screen you will see is similar to Figure 6-16. This screen allows you to select which predefined Discoverer connection the end user wants to use to view

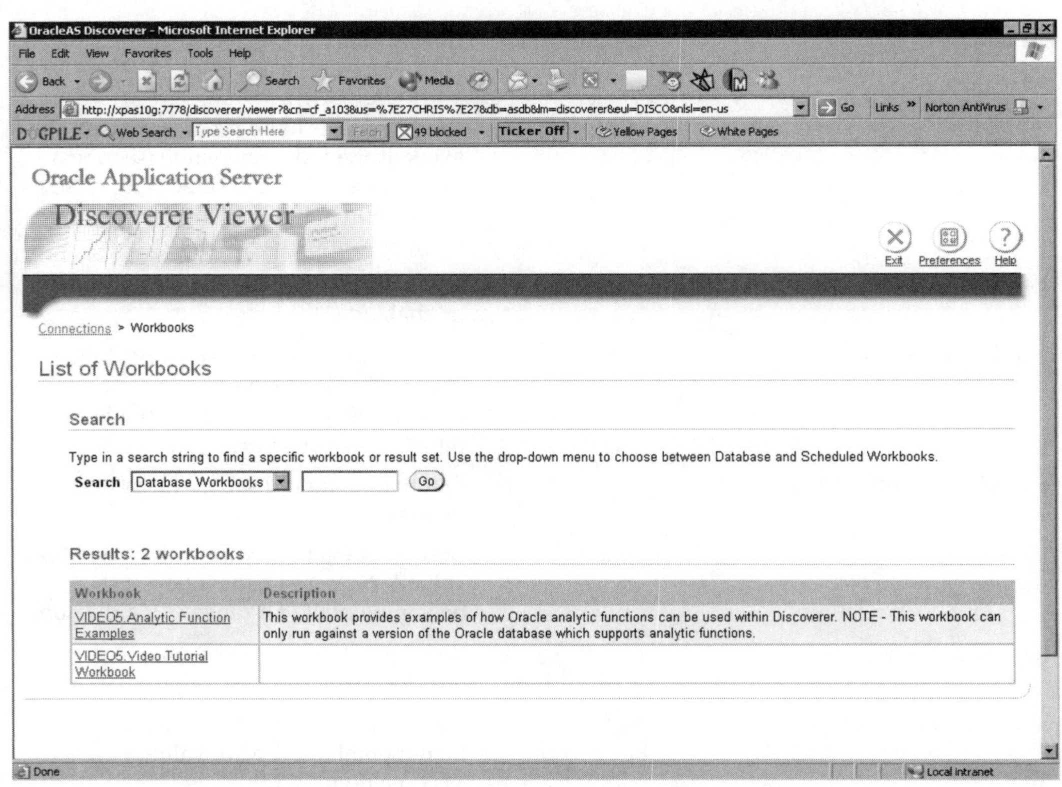

FIGURE 6-16. *Discoverer workbooks available*

Discoverer data. Upon selecting a connection, you are presented with the workbooks available for that user.

You now have the full functionality of the Discoverer product to view and run Discoverer Reports that was described in Chapter 5.

Summary

Oracle Application Server 10*g* gives organizations incredible flexibility when making decisions to move applications to the Web. Oracle has made a great effort to ease the transition to web-based deployments by providing robust support for legacy applications developed with tools not originally designed for web-based deployments such as Oracle Forms, Oracle Reports, and Oracle Discoverer. This chapter has explored the methods available to move Oracle Forms, Oracle Reports, and Oracle Discoverer workbooks and worksheets to the Web along with migration tools that make the process of this transition as seamless and painless as possible. In Chapter 11, we will discuss integrating these legacy components into Portal and how we can exploit the benefits of Oracle Portal pages, templates, and security.

CHAPTER 7

The PL/SQL Web Toolkit and PSPs

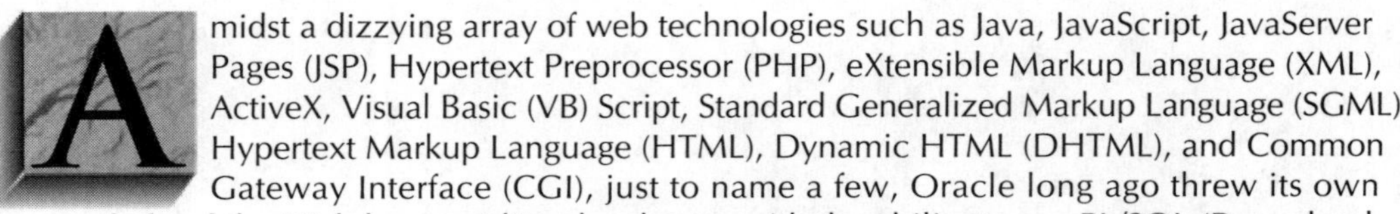

Amidst a dizzying array of web technologies such as Java, JavaScript, JavaServer Pages (JSP), Hypertext Preprocessor (PHP), eXtensible Markup Language (XML), ActiveX, Visual Basic (VB) Script, Standard Generalized Markup Language (SGML), Hypertext Markup Language (HTML), Dynamic HTML (DHTML), and Common Gateway Interface (CGI), just to name a few, Oracle long ago threw its own support behind the Web by providing developers with the ability to use PL/SQL (Procedural Language extension to Structured Query Language) as a medium for dynamic web content generation. With the advent of WebDB, the Oracle Application Server and the PL/SQL cartridge, Oracle has provided developers who are already well versed in PL/SQL and HTML with the ability to create dynamic web applications based on data driven content without the need to learn an entirely new language.

Today, the platform for this capability is the Apache-based Oracle Application Server 10*g* (formerly known as Oracle9*i* Application Server) and the mod_plsql Apache module, but the basic concept for accomplishing the task works the same.

How PL/SQL Works as a Web Technology

Oracle offers two PL/SQL technologies for web content generation: the PL/SQL Web Toolkit and PL/SQL Server Pages (PSPs). As we'll discuss in this chapter, these two technologies are tightly integrated. In fact, PSPs require the PL/SQL Web Toolkit and are essentially another way to make use of the PL/SQL Web Toolkit.

Regardless of the technology used, web content reaches a web browser in the same manner. In order for PL/SQL to do its work, several components need to be in place and configured properly. First and foremost, a client machine with an installed web browser that can reach the network where the web application server resides is necessary. This is the easiest task given it is hard to find a computer in operation today that doesn't have a web browser installed. A web application server is required, in this case Oracle Application Server 10*g*, to serve the HTML to the client's web browser. The Application Server 10*g* install also includes an Apache module called mod_plsql (also referred to as the PL/SQL gateway) that allows Apache to communicate directly with the Oracle database's PL/SQL engine. A database access descriptor (DAD) that maps a virtual path to a database connection also needs to be configured. Finally, an Oracle database with the PL/SQL Web Toolkit installed (installed by default on versions 8.1.7 and later) is required, which provides the mechanism of generating HTML from PL/SQL.

Figure 7-1 shows a typical PL/SQL web application architecture. The key to having all of these components work correctly is in the Uniform Resource Locator (URL) requested by the web browser. The URL for a PL/SQL web application equates to a PL/SQL procedure on the target database server. When a client requests a URL for a PL/SQL web application (or when an HTML link from a static page provides it), Apache determines that a PL/SQL subprogram is being called and routes the request through the mod_plsql module. The mod_plsql module examines the URL, determines the correct DAD to use (there can be multiple DADs configured on a single application server), and opens a connection to the database, if the connection is not already established. Once the connection is open, mod_plsql passes any parameters specified and control to the target database's PL/SQL engine, which executes the procedure specified in the URL. The HTML results

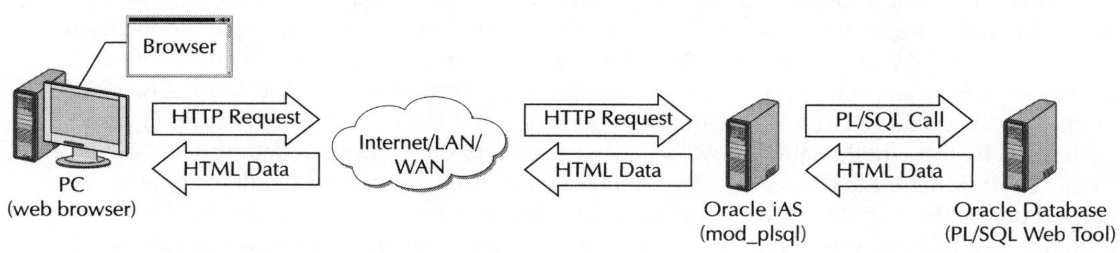

FIGURE 7-1. *A typical PL/SQL web application architecture*

are then returned back through mod_plsql and then on to the client's web browser. An example URL looks like this:

```
http://hostname/pls/DADname/progname
```

or

```
http://hostname/pls/DADname/<package>.<procedure>
```

The "hostname" part of the URL is the hostname of the web application server, the "pls" in the URL tells Apache to hand the URL off to mod_plsql to handle the call. "DADname" is the name of the Database Access Descriptor (DAD), which provides the database connection information, and "progname" is the name of the PL/SQL procedure being called.

If the installation and configuration of Application Server 10*g* is too daunting for the purposes of getting your feet wet or access to an installation of Application Server is not available, there is an alternative. If a development instance of the Oracle database is available, then all of the components needed to run the examples in this chapter are available. By default, all versions of the Oracle database since 8.1.7 include the Apache web server, the mod_plsql module, and the PL/SQL Web Toolkit. The only tasks required are the creation of a schema in the database for your PL/SQL web application subprograms, and the configuration of a DAD using the Apache server.

Why PL/SQL?

Now that the fundamentals of how the PL/SQL Web Toolkit functions have been discussed, the logical question to ask as a developer is, "Why would I want to use PL/SQL for web development?" While it's not appropriate for every development circumstance, there are many good reasons for using PL/SQL and the PL/SQL Web Toolkit to develop your web-based applications. Two major considerations are the scope of the web application and the talent pool within your organization available for its development, deployment, and maintenance.

While PL/SQL is good at pushing HTML out and very good at manipulating data stored in an Oracle database, scalability can sometimes be an issue. When developing an application using the PL/SQL Web Toolkit, the application server becomes, essentially, a "pass-through" server—that is, a server that does nothing more than pass requests back and forth between the client and the database. The HTML that is generated using the PL/SQL Web Toolkit is work performed by the Oracle database, which also must carry out its normal data processing duties. In this environment, the Oracle database server is now doing work that would ordinarily be carried out by the middle-tier web application server. This may not be a problem in a small- to medium-sized application scope, but in a large enterprise web application, a database server experiencing a heavy load servicing data requests must now also make PL/SQL function calls to generate HTML, a nontrivial task.

The PL/SQL engine in the Oracle 10*g* database has been upgraded and now incorporates many new performance-enhancing features. Both Oracle Portal and HTML DB use PL/SQL extensively and have references of extreme scalability. In a Real Application Cluster (RAC) environment, additional performance gains are realized through Oracle's capability for each node in a cluster to execute PL/SQL simultaneously.

Using the PL/SQL Web Toolkit also takes server clustering at the middle tier out of the equation of system performance considerations as well. In larger enterprise environments, a traditional architecture incorporating J2EE technologies—including JSPs, Oracle Application Server Containers for J2EE (OC4J), and Enterprise JavaBeans (EJBs)—may be a better option, as the burden of generating the front end of the application is shifted to the application server. In recent years, a significant effort was undertaken to improve the performance and scalability of J2EE applications. However, a similar effort has not been undertaken for PL/SQL web application development. It is the developer's responsibility to carefully consider the current and likely future scope of an application to make sure the PL/SQL Web Toolkit makes sense.

Along with considerations of application use and scope, factors focusing on the skill set of developers needed to develop and maintain the application need to be addressed. The PL/SQL Web Toolkit is a good fit for organizations that already have PL/SQL expertise, but lack the equivalent expertise in Java. Use of the PL/SQL Web Toolkit is appropriate if the scope of the application is relatively small and will be primarily used internally. In this scenario, requisitioning outside Java talent or training existing employees in Java, both of which can be financially prohibitive, can be avoided.

In the spectrum of computer languages, HTML is easy to learn, so with a minimal amount of study and training, PL/SQL developers can be easily tapped to develop web applications using the PL/SQL Web Toolkit. PL/SQL server pages (PSPs), discussed later in this chapter, can be used to partition the task of writing HTML to people within the organization that specialize in web front-end design and development, leaving the PL/SQL developers to the task of writing code.

PL/SQL Web Toolkit: The Basics

The best way to introduce the PL/SQL Web Toolkit is to start with the ubiquitous "Hello World" example:

```
CREATE OR REPLACE PROCEDURE hello
IS
BEGIN
   htp.htmlopen;
   htp.headopen;
   htp.title('Hello World Program');
   htp.headclose;
   htp.bodyopen(null, 'text="#000000" bgcolor="#FFFFFF"');
   htp.bold('Hello World!');
   htp.br;
   htp.br;
   htp.print('System date and time is: ' || to_char(sysdate, 'MM/DD/YYYY
HH24:MI:SS'));
   htp.br;
   htp.print('Oracle user is: ' || user);
   htp.bodyclose;
   htp.htmlclose;
END hello;
```

Implementation issues need to be addressed before discussing the mechanics of the code. In order for the code to function, the PL/SQL procedure needs to be loaded into a target Oracle database. For this example, a user called webdev has been created in the Oracle database instance where the web toolkit resides. A DAD called TEST that contains the Transparent Network Substrate (TNS) connection information (username, password, and connect string) that points to the database has also been configured. Figure 7-2 shows an example DAD configuration page.

To get to the DAD configuration page, browse to the hostname of your application server (i.e., http://<hostname>/). If the Apache server is functioning correctly, a menu page such as the one in Figure 7-3 will be displayed.

If an error saying that the host did not respond is displayed, verify that the Apache Web Service is running on the application server.

From the Apache menu, follow these steps:

1. Click the "MOD_PLSQL Configuration Menu" link; this will display the gateway configuration menu.
2. Select "Gateway Database Access Descriptor Settings"; this will display a page with a link to add a new DAD.
3. Choose the "Add Default" option.

There is a lot of information to specify on the DAD configuration page. For this example, the most important information resides at the top of the page. A name for the DAD must be specified along with the username, password, and connect string that mod_plsql will use to access the database where your web application resides. If your web application will need access to multiple users or multiple databases, then multiple DADs will need to be configured. Clear out the other

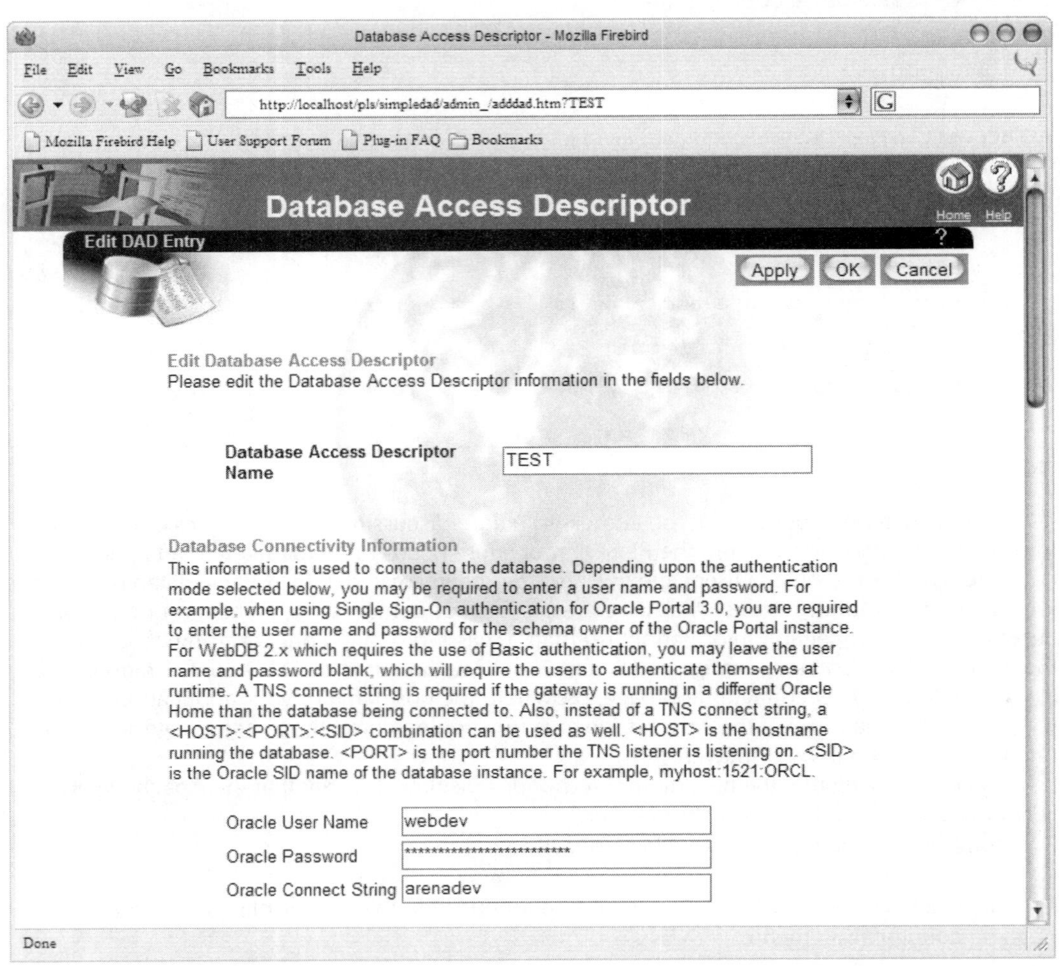

FIGURE 7-2. *Database Access Descriptor Configuration*

settings or leave them at their defaults as they will not be needed. Be sure to click the OK button at the top of the page when you are finished.

Once the DAD is configured and the PL/SQL procedure is loaded into the database, start your browser and call the appropriate URL. The "Hello World" page shown in Figure 7-4 should be displayed.

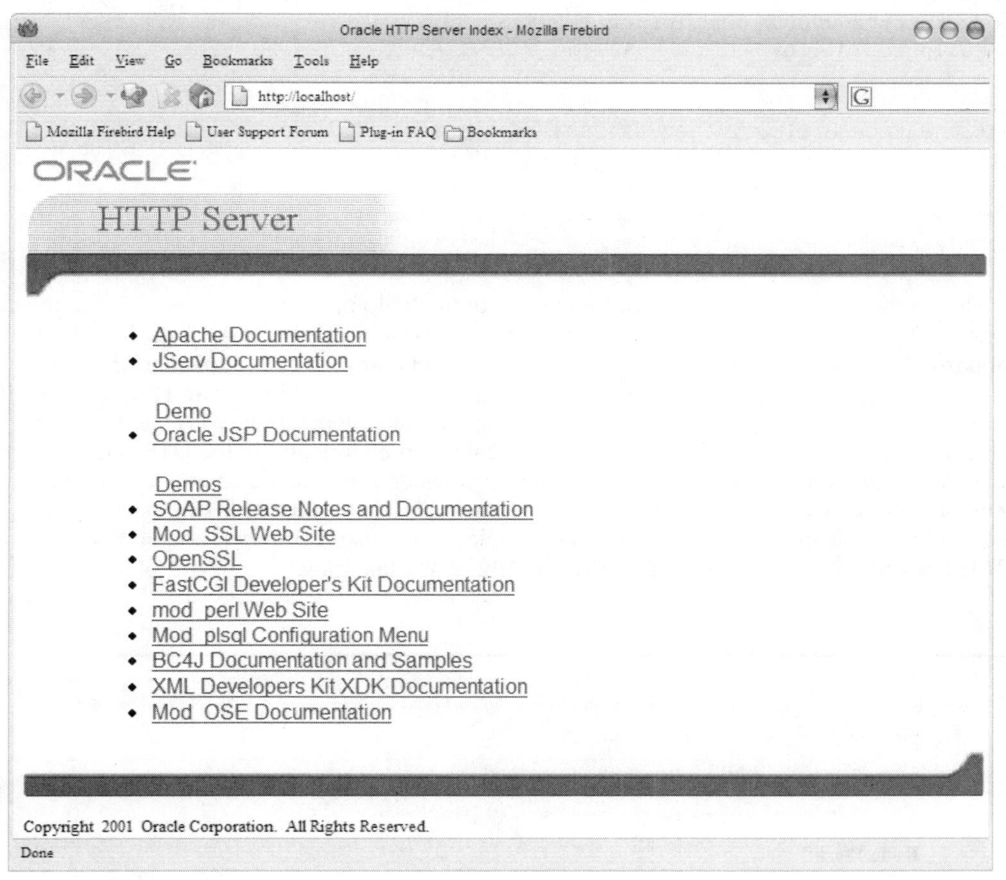

FIGURE 7-3. *Apache web server home page*

Notice that the URL follows the expected pattern:

```
http://<hostname>/pls/<DADname>/<PL/SQL procedure name>
```

If you look at the page source in your browser, you'll notice that it's just "plain vanilla" HTML:

```
<html>
<head>
<title>Hello World Program</title>
```

```
</head>
<body text="#000000" bgcolor="#FFFFFF">
<b>Hello World!</b>
<br>
<br>
System date and time is: 02/03/2004 16:21:36
<br>
Oracle user is: WEBDEV
</body>
</html>
```

How does it work? The first detail to note about the hello program in Listing 7-5, are the calls to the HTP package. The HTP package contains a procedure to generate each tag in the HTML standard. The package name HTP is an acronym for Hypertext Procedures and there is a corresponding package called HTF, for Hypertext Functions. For all intents and purposes, HTP and HTF serve the same purpose, which is the programmatic generation of HTML. For every procedure in the HTP package, there is an identically named function in the HTF package. The parameter requirements and internal functionality between the procedures and functions are identical with the exception that the HTP procedures directly output the HTML back to mod_plsql on the application server for immediate display in the user's browser, and HTF returns the HTML back to a PL/SQL program as a VARCHAR2 character string.

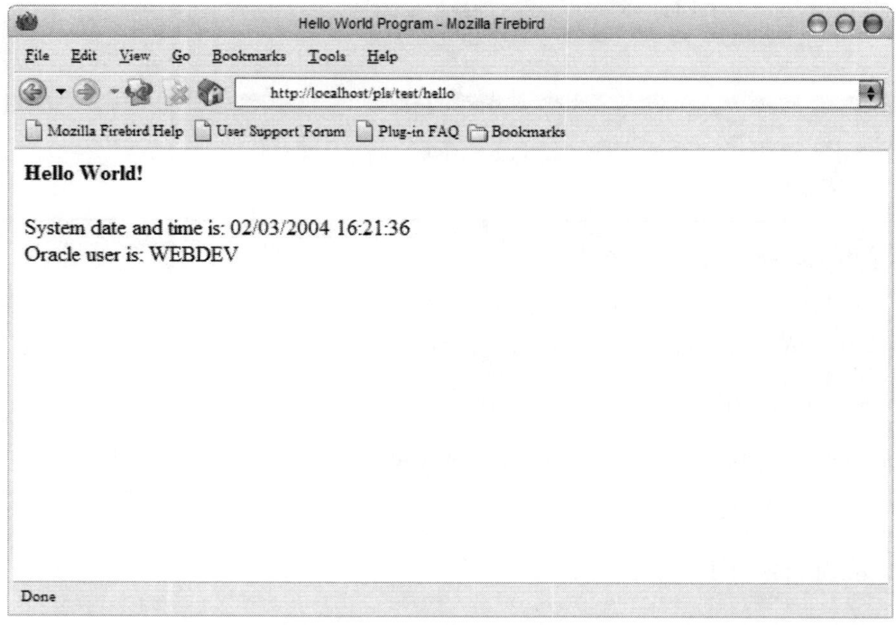

FIGURE 7-4. *The resultant web page generated by the hello PL/SQL module*

To illustrate this duality, let's look at the call structures for HTP.TITLE and HTF.TITLE from the PL/SQL Web Toolkit Reference:

```
htp.title (ctitle in varchar2);

htf.title (ctitle in varchar2) return varchar2;
```

Usage:

```
htp.title('Hello World Program');—sends HTML directly to browser

html_txt := htf.title('Hello World Program');—puts HTML in variable
```

In the former case, the output <TITLE>Hello World Program</TITLE> is sent directly to the browser for display, and in the latter, it's put into the html_txt variable, which would be defined as a VARCHAR2 datatype. The HTF package is most useful if some direct manipulation of the HTML is desired before sending it to the application server or you want to nest output from an HTF function into a parameter passed to an HTP procedure. The Hello program output needs no such tweaking, so HTP is used throughout.

If you are already familiar with HTML and its structure, you can probably already guess what our program is doing. The flow of the PL/SQL program exactly follows the flow of the HTML page we're generating. In fact, we can place the code and page source next to each other and easily see how the output comes from the code, as shown in Table 7-1.

PL/SQL Block

```
begin
  htp.htmlopen;
  htp.headopen;
  htp.title('Hello World Program');
  htp.headclose;
  htp.bodyopen(null, 'text="#000000"
bgcolor="#FFFFFF"');
  htp.bold('Hello World!');
  htp.br;
  htp.br;
  htp.print('System date and time is: ' || to_
char(sysdate, 'MM/DD/YYYY HH24:MI:SS'));
  htp.br;
  htp.print('Oracle user is: ' || user);
  htp.bodyclose;
  htp.htmlclose;
end hello;
```

HTML Output

```
<html>
<head>
<title>Hello World Program</title>
</head>
<body text="#000000" bgcolor="#FFFFFF">

<b>Hello World!</b>
<br>
<br>
System date and time is: 02/03/2004 16:21:36

<br>
Oracle user is: WEBDEV
</body>
</html>
```

TABLE 7-1. *PL/SQL Code and Resulting Generated HTML*

The HTP.HTMLOPEN and HTP.HEADOPEN procedures generate <HTML> and <HEAD> tags, respectively. These are examples of paired tags, which by HTML standards means that there is both an opening and closing tag to fully specify the particular markup. In other words, we also need something that will generate </HTML> and </HEAD> tags, right? If you look at the fourth HTP call in the code snippet above, you'll see a call to HTP.HEADCLOSE, and at the end of our PL/SQL block, you'll see a call to HTP.HTMLCLOSE. These, of course, generate the needed </HEAD> and </HTML> tags in the correct places.

It's important to remember if a procedure or function, such as HTP.HTMLOPEN, has a closing tag analog, you'll need to include it in your code at the appropriate point. Some browsers can be picky about missing closing tags while others are quite forgiving, which can lead to mixed results depending on which browser a user happens to use when interacting with your web application. In general, it's desirable to produce a web application that will work properly when accessed using any web browser. This can be impractical, given differing features and scripting support, but at a minimum, the application should work when using one of the most popular browsers. Using an editor that has the capability to set up code clip libraries allows the developer to create a clip library to generate code for the tag pairs, eliminating the need to remember closing tags.

Many procedures take parameters, such as HTP.TITLE. In this case, not only does the procedure call generate both of the necessary HTML tags (i.e., <TITLE> and </TITLE>), but it also embeds the user supplied text between the tags. Procedures such as HTP.BODYOPEN take parameters that are used to populate the attributes of the tag it generates. The call structure for HTP.BODYOPEN shows this:

```
htp.bodyOpen(cbackground in varchar2 DEFAULT NULL,
             cattributes in varchar2 DEFAULT NULL);
```

cbackground is a URL for an image file to be used as a background for the web page, and cattributes is a freeform string of any other attributes that the <BODY> tag will accept. Because the Hello program does not use a background image, the call to HTP.BODYOPEN leaves this first parameter null. Because the parameters are defaulted to null, the BODYOPEN command could have been specified using named notation rather than supplying a NULL for the first parameter:

```
htp.bodyopen(cattributes => 'text="#000000" bgcolor="#FFFFFF"');
```

Two procedures, HTP.PRINT and HTP.PRN, do not generate HTML tags but instead echo the text supplied to them back as the output. These two procedures can be used to provide free-form text in the HTML output (such as the date/time and user name messages in the "Hello World" example) or, as discussed later in this chapter, can be used to generate an entire HTML page. The only difference between HTP.PRINT and HTP.PRN is that HTP.PRINT adds a linefeed (\n) to the end of the string you pass it. This only affects the way the HTML source looks when it is viewed in a browser, not how the HTML output is rendered because HTML ignores linefeeds in the source—use <BR> to get a "linefeed" into HTML output.

Using HTF Functions

As stated earlier in this chapter, the HTF package is virtually a functional clone of the HTP package, with the exception that all of its subprograms are functions that return VARCHAR2 strings containing the generated HTML to the caller instead of pushing it directly to the browser.

A common usage of HTF functions is to nest them inside HTP calls. In the following example, htp.center and htf.header are combined to display text in a centered, level 1 heading:

```
htp.center(htf.header(1, 'Sales vs. Orders'));
```

The following HTML would be produced:

```
<CENTER><H1>Sales vs. Orders</H1></CENTER>
```

The HTF package also gives the developer a means of dynamically altering HTML generated code before it is sent to the client's browser. As an example: a request is made by an end user to color code salary listings. Salaries of 25,000 and less appear in green; salaries between 25,000 and 75,000 appear in black; salaries between 75,000 and 100,000 appear in yellow; and salaries of 100,000 and more appear in red. Code Listing 2 can be used to accomplish this:

```
CREATE OR REPLACE PROCEDURE html_emp_list
IS
     cursor emp_cur
     is
          select e.emp_last_name || ', ' || e.emp_first_name emp_name,
                 d.dept_name,
                 e.salary
            from webapp.emps e,
                 webapp.depts d
           where e.dept_id = d.dept_id
           order by 1;
     v_sal_color           varchar2(8) := '#000000';
BEGIN
     htp.htmlopen;
     htp.headopen;
     htp.title('Employee Salary Listing');
     htp.headclose;
     htp.bodyopen(null, 'text="#000000" bgcolor="#FFFFFF"');
     htp.center(htf.header(1, 'Employee Salary Listing'));
     htp.br;
     htp.br;
     htp.tableopen(cborder => 'BORDER="1"',
                   calign => 'center',
                   cattributes => 'CELLPADDING="5"');
     htp.tablerowopen;
     htp.tableheader('Name');
     htp.tableheader('Dept');
     htp.tableheader('Salary');
     htp.tablerowclose;
     for emp_rec in emp_cur
     loop
          htp.tablerowopen;
          htp.tabledata(emp_rec.emp_name);
          htp.tabledata(emp_rec.dept_name);
          v_sal_color :=
```

```
            case
                when emp_rec.salary <= 25000 then '#00FF00'
                when emp_rec.salary between 75001 and 99999 then '#FFFF00'
                when emp_rec.salary >= 100000 then '#FF0000'
                else '#000000'
            end;
        htp.tabledata(cvalue => htf.fontopen(v_sal_color) || to_char(emp_
rec.salary, '9,999,999,999') || htf.fontclose,
                      calign => 'right');
        htp.tablerowclose;
    end loop;
    htp.tableclose;
    htp.bodyclose;
    htp.htmlclose;
END html_emp_list;
```

After creating demo tables for the employees and departments, pointing a browser to http://localhost/pls/test/html_emp_list will produce the output in Figure 7-5.

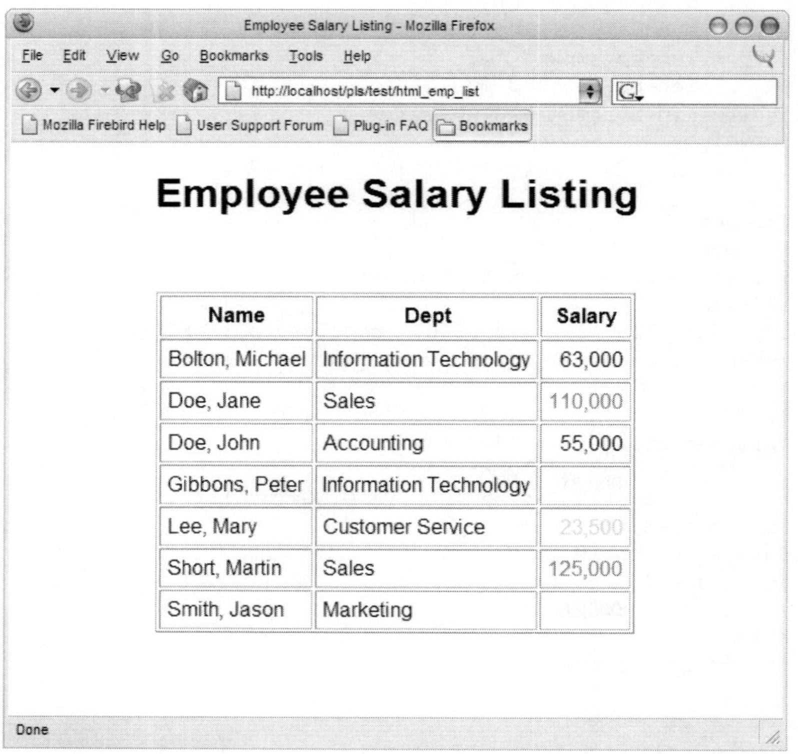

FIGURE 7-5. *html_emp_list output*

This is an example of a dynamic, data-driven application, albeit a very simple one. It contains data from the database, and uses the data itself (i.e., the salary) to alter the presentation. The flexibility offered by the HTF package is very powerful.

Using HTP.PRINT and HTP.PRN vs. the Specialized Tag Generation API

Given the HTP.PRINT and HTP.PRN procedures push whatever is fed to them directly to the browser, the hello program could be written as follows:

```
CREATE OR REPLACE PROCEDURE hello2
IS
BEGIN
   htp.print('<HTML>' ||
             '<HEAD>' ||
             '<TITLE>Hello World Program</TITLE>' ||
             '</HEAD>' ||
             '<BODY text="#000000" bgcolor="#FFFFFF">' ||
             '<B>Hello World!</B>' ||
             '<BR>' ||
             '<BR>' ||
             'System date and time is: ' || to_char(sysdate, 'MM/DD/YYYY HH24:MI:SS') ||
             '<BR>' ||
             'Oracle user is: ' || user ||
             '</BODY>' ||
             '</HTML>');
END hello2;
```

In Listing 3, htp.p can be substituted for htp.print. Syntactically, there is no difference between the two, but this small stylistic difference often turns into a passionate debate among developers, particularly those sensitive to standards and code consistency. Typically, HTML developers like htp.p and Oracle developers prefer htp.toolkit_name. PSPs (discussed later) solve this battle.

Installing this new procedure into the database with SQL*Plus as hello2, Figure 7-6 verifies that the same output is produced.

While there is no difference in the output between hello and hello2, our hello program has gone from being more like the structured PL/SQL most Oracle developers are well versed in to HTML user interface regurgitation. The hello2 program is, in essence, just doing a PRINT command, which most experienced PL/SQL developers are likely to consider poor programming practice. No experienced PL/SQL developer would want to maintain a piece of code like the hello2 version of the hello program.

The advantage to the PRINT method, however, is that the hello2 version of the program will execute faster than the hello version. Each PL/SQL call made in the hello version adds to the overhead of the program. Additionally, generating HTML tags incurs a very high cost. The PL/SQL engine has to maintain code pointers and create call stacks for each call with very little real work being done other than text manipulation and output. The hello version of the program contains 13 calls to HTP procedures; hello2 only has one. The hello program is a simple example, but as the complexity of a page increases and as looping is introduced, this difference in performance is even more pronounced.

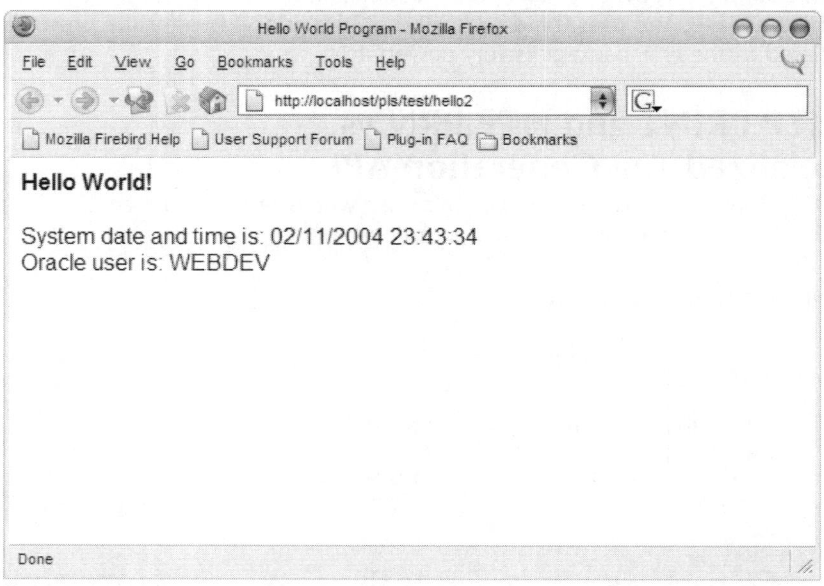

FIGURE 7-6. *Output of hello program written with HTP.PRINT calls*

How do we balance performance against maintainable code? As you will see later, this is the question PL/SQL server pages (PSPs) strive to answer. PSP functionality converts HTML-based server scripts with embedded PL/SQL into PL/SQL procedures that rely heavily on HTP.PRN statements, which helps with performance and also alleviates the PL/SQL developer from having to maintain ugly HTP.PRN code. All maintenance of the page can be done on the original PSP script without ever having to touch the PL/SQL subprogram on the server directly.

Another important note: The PL/SQL Web Toolkit is an inefficient way to produce purely static web pages (i.e., pages that don't contain data from the database), because of the overhead costs incurred. Any web server can serve a static page from a local directory much faster than Oracle can produce it using PL/SQL. The realization of reduced overhead and elimination of network traffic between the web application server and the database server more than justifies keeping static pages on the web server.

Additional Web Toolkit Packages

In addition to the HTP and HTF packages, Oracle has supplied some additional packages in the PL/SQL Web Toolkit to provide additional functionality for PL/SQL web applications. These packages, which all begin with the prefix OWA_, enable developers to work with browser cookies, set mime headers, and interact with image maps, to name just a few features. What follows is only a partial listing of the most common packages. (See the PL/SQL Packages and Types Reference (Oracle Part number B10802-1) for complete documentation on the available OWA_ packages.)

Managing Cookies with OWA_COOKIE

HTTP is a stateless protocol. This means that at the network transport protocol layer, the web server is unable to keep track of user session state information. Unlike some transport protocols, there are no facilities built into HTTP to distinguish you from other users browsing the site. In essence, your connection to the web server is seen as just another HTTP request that the web server needs to generate an HTTP response for. Browser cookies are one way to keep track of user and session information. Simply put, a cookie is a name value pair. For example, cookies can be used:

- So that the web site can identify that user during the session and on subsequent returns to the web site. This methodology can be used by site counters to record how many times a particular user has visited the site.
- To provide automatic authentication of the user to the web site, so users don't have to type in usernames and passwords each time they access their account information.
- To store user preferences (page layouts, color schemes, etc.) for the site.
- To implement a shopping cart on an e-commerce site.

The OWA_COOKIE package contains subprograms that allow the web developer to send cookies to and retrieve cookies from the user's web browser. The OWA_COOKIE package includes the following datatypes and subprograms:

- **owa_cookie.cookie datatyp**e The standard governing cookies allows a single cookie to have multiple values. It is defined in the package as follows:

```
type cookie is RECORD (
name varchar2(4096),
vals vc_arr,
num_vals integer);
```

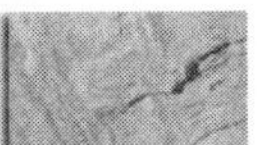

NOTE
vc_arr is defined in the OWA.COOKIE package as a binary integer indexed table of varchar2(4096) elements. There are also several vc_arr datatypes defined in the OWA packages but the sizes of the elements vary. If you need to define a PL/SQL table to hold cookies, make sure you use owa_cookie.vc_arr in your definition. Also, the documentation for the PL/SQL Web Toolkit tends to list the length of the VARCHAR2 strings as 4,000 characters; they are actually a full 4KB, or 4,096 bytes, in size.

- **owa_cookie.get function** The get function will retrieve a named cookie (returned as the cookie record datatype shown above) from the user's browser. If no cookie was sent by the user's browser, an empty cookie is returned to the caller.

NOTE
Cookie names are case sensitive, so calling the get function looking for Userid will not return a result if the cookie sent by the browser was named userid.

- **owa_cookie.get_all procedure** This procedure is similar to the get function above, except that it will retrieve all cookies sent by the web browser. The procedure has three OUT parameters, two defined as vc_arr for the cookie names and values and one integer that holds the count of elements in the two arrays.
- **owa_cookie.remove procedure** You use this procedure to force the expiration of a certain cookie. It accepts three VARCHAR2 parameters: the name and value of the cookie to remove, and the path if there was one when the cookie was set. Note though, that even as recent as Oracle 9*i* Release 2, the path parameter is not actually implemented in the Web Toolkit procedure's code, so you can ignore it. It's defaulted to NULL in the procedure prototype, so you can leave it out of the parameter list entirely.
- **owa_cookie.send procedure** This procedure sends a cookie to the browser to be stored for later retrieval. The prototype for the procedure is as follows:

```
procedure send(name     in varchar2,
   value   in varchar2,
               expires in date     DEFAULT NULL,
               path    in varchar2 DEFAULT NULL,
               domain  in varchar2 DEFAULT NULL,
               secure  in varchar2 DEFAULT NULL);
```

You only need to specify the name and value parameters to create a simple cookie. Providing just the name and value creates a session persistent cookie. Note that the cookie is not expired if you just browse to another site; the browser must be closed down and restarted before the cookie is expired. To create a cookie that doesn't expire from the browser until sometime in the future, supply a date in the future as the value for the expires parameter. The path and domain parameters serve to further document the cookie information and are optional. If you supply anything other than NULL for the secure parameter, the cookie is marked as secure.

IMPORTANT NOTE
The owa_cookie.send and owa_cookie.remove procedures must be called in the context of an HTTP header. In other words, you must have an open HTTP header and the calls cannot be made once an HTP call has been made for the page, because doing that will close the header. We've found the easiest way to do this is to use something similar to the following code:

```
owa_util.mime_header('text/html', false);
      owa_cookie.send('MyCookie', '1', to_date('20050101 09:15', 'YYYYMMDD
HH24:MI'));
      owa_util.http_header_close;
```

This code fragment, as long as it comes before any HTP calls for the page, will set a cookie on the user's browser. It first opens the HTTP response header by setting the mime type to text/html (the default for a web page). Notice that the false Boolean parameter is needed in the owa_util.mime_header call to keep the HTTP header open; otherwise, by default owa_util.mime_header will close it. It then puts a "Set-Cookie: MyCookie=1 expires=Saturday, 01-Jan-2005 09:15:00 GMT;" line in the header and finally closes the HTTP header. This cookie will stay in the browser's cookie list until 9:15am on January 1st, 2005.

Setting the Mime Type of a Page with OWA_UTIL

Mime types are used by content providers to inform a browser what type of content is being sent to it, so the browser can decode the data or instantiate the proper helper application. If you are generating pages that contain only HTML, the mime type of the page does not have to be specified, as all modern browsers will assume a 'text/html' mime type. What if application requirement specifies something other than text display on a page, such as an image or a Word document? If you don't tell the browser what is being sent, it will default to text. The result will be a nonsensical stream of American Standard Code for Information Interchange (ASCII) characters displayed in the browser window instead of the desired output. The solution to this is to set the mime type in the header of the page. The PL/SQL Web Toolkit procedure owa_util.mime_header accommodates this:

```
   procedure mime_header(ccontent_type in varchar2 DEFAULT 'text/html',
                         bclose_header in boolean  DEFAULT TRUE,
                ccharset      in varchar2 DEFAULT 'MaGiC_KeY')
```

Most of the time, only content_type needs to be specified. The other two parameters can be set if the HTTP header needs to be kept open or a different character set needs to be specified for the browser. For example:

```
owa_util.mime_header('text/plain', false, 'ISO-8859-4');
```

will generate a mime-type header as follows:

```
Content-type: text/plain; charset=ISO-8859-4
```

When the browser receives the data that makes up the page, it will know that it is getting plain text and to use the ISO-8859 character set to render it.

As with the owa_cookie send and remove subprograms, mime_header needs to be called in the context of the HTTP header, so it must come before any HTP calls.

As an example, let's enhance the employee salary list web page. A new requirement has been given to you, the developer, specifying that small photos will be loaded into the database for each employee and the end users want to be able to click a name in the list and see the photo belonging to that employee. First, a new procedure for our web application that will read an image from a binary large object (BLOB) in the database and stream the data back to the web browser is needed. Listing 4 provides a simple example:

```
create or replace procedure show_emp_photo(p_emp_id
webapp.emp_photos.emp_id%TYPE)
```

```
is
     v_blob                  blob;
     v_chunksize             number := 4096;
     v_offset             number := 1;
     v_rawdata             raw(4096);
begin
     select emp_image into v_blob
       from webapp.emp_photos
      where emp_id = p_emp_id;
      owa_util.mime_header('image/jpeg');
     begin
        loop
           dbms_lob.read(v_blob, v_chunksize, v_offset, v_rawdata);
           htp.prn(utl_raw.cast_to_varchar2(v_rawdata));
           v_offset := v_offset + v_chunksize;
           v_chunksize := 4096;
        end loop;
     exception
        when no_data_found then
           null;
     end;
exception
   when no_data_found then
      null;
end show_emp_photo;
```

Listing 4

The show_emp_photo procedure retrieves a BLOB from the database using the employee ID passed to it. In this example, the images are stored as JPEGs, so the code sets the mime type to 'image/jpeg' (owa_util.mime_header('image/jpeg');). The procedure retrieves the image data using dbms_lob.read and then calls the htp.prn procedure to send the binary image data to the web browser.

With a fairly simple change to our original html_emp_list procedure, we can complete this enhancement. The first modification is to turn the employee's name into a hyperlink that, when clicked, will display that employee's photo.

htp.tabledata(emp_rec.emp_name);

changes to:

```
htp.tabledata(htf.anchor(curl => '#',
     ctext => emp_rec.emp_name,
     cattributes => 'ONCLICK="open(''//' ||
     vc_hostname || vc_app_path || 'show_emp_photo?p_emp_id='
     || to_char(emp_rec.emp_id)
     ||''',''EmpPic'',''resizable=no,height=105,width=105'');"'));
```

Setting the URL to '#', normally used for jumping to named anchors on a page, allows you to have a link that doesn't go anywhere. It is used in this example to demonstrate the ability to specify an ONCLICK method for the hypertext link that contains a JavaScript call that opens a new window and displays the employee photo. Note the call to show_emp_photo. The ?

denotes a parameter list. The parameter p_emp_id is matched against the input parameter p_emp_id in our show_emp_photo code in Listing 4. The other two parameters passed to the JavaScript open() command give the new window a referential name and set some of its properties.

Two additional lines are added in the procedure declaration:

```
vc_app_path     varchar2(255) := owa_util.get_owa_service_path;
vc_hostname     varchar2(255) := owa_util.get_cgi_env('HTTP_HOST');
```

These are used to construct the URL in the modified tabledata statement. It is always a good idea to avoid hard coding in applications when possible. In a larger application, these can be included in a parameter package (so that the code isn't repeated) and then the package variables can be referenced when needed in the application. Using this technique, it is not necessary to traipse through the code to change hard-coded references to the application server URL if the configuration of the application server ever needed to be changed. The calls to owa_util.get_owa_service_path and owa_util.get_cgi_env will automatically compensate if the application server is changed.

After making the changes and revisiting the URL for the employee list, Figure 7-7 reflects that each employee's name is now a hypertext link and when one is clicked, a new browser window containing the picture is opened.

The owa_util.mime_header procedure can be used to send various other types of data to a client's browser; XML data and/or Macromedia Flash content and audio/video streams are just a few of the other possibilities. Also, most browsers allow users to add additional mime types and configure helper applications to handle the data for the new type.

It is the developer's responsibility to check that the mime type being set with owa_util.mime_header is compatible with all the browsers you intend to support. For instance, what if we had used "image/jpg" in our application? While Mozilla-based browsers have no problem with this mime type, Internet Explorer does not necessarily recognize it properly and might ask for permission to save the file rather than displaying it in a new window.

Optimistic Locking Using OWA_OPT_LOCK

If your web application will only insert new records into or query existing records from the Oracle database, then row locking will not be a serious concern. If, however, your application needs to update existing data, another side effect of HTTP's stateless nature will need to be addressed. Just as is the case with any other data entry application, there can be long periods of time between querying data, updating it, and committing it back to the database. When you're using tools such as Oracle Forms, update conflicts are resolved automatically using Oracle database row locks. In the context of a web application, however, a user's connection to the application server is stateless. Therefore, the connection from the application server to the database is stateless as well and no such resolution can be done automatically by the database. The OWA_OPT_LOCK package allows you to manage these conflicts manually in the context of a web application.

Consider the following example. You have an online banking account with Bank Y. You just moved recently and sent them a change of address notice. Let's say also that you made a mistake that you didn't catch on the notice before you sent it. You listed your street address as 15 Cherry Lane and it's actually 17 Cherry Lane. Upon logging into your account and checking your online profile, you see that a clerk at the bank has not yet corrected your address info (i.e., it's still shown as the old address), so you decide to update it online. Unknown to you, the clerk has already

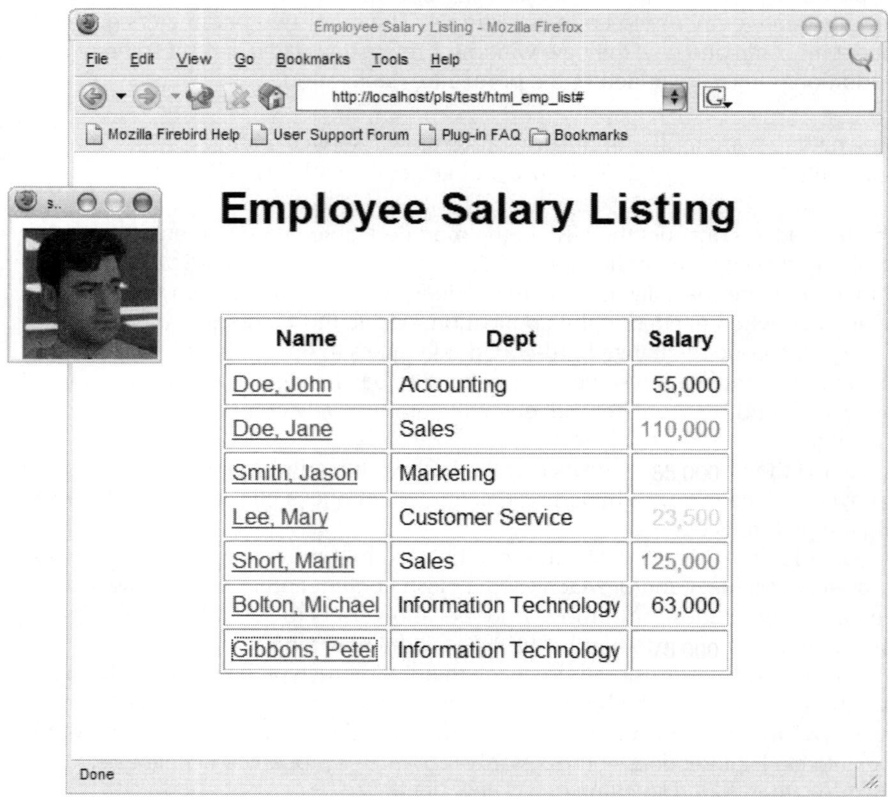

FIGURE 7-7. *Revised employee list page with photo image enhancement*

pulled up your record and was in the process of updating it, but is on coffee break. You update the address with the new address info as 17 Cherry Lane (the correct address), save your profile, and log off. However, the next day you log in to make sure your address info is still correct and see that your address has changed from 17 Cherry Lane to the incorrect 15 Cherry Lane.

What happened? The web application that both the clerk and the customer used didn't account for the possibility that data in the database might change between the time it was displayed and the time an update was committed. After you logged off, the data entry clerk at the bank came back from coffee break, finished the entry, and committed it to the database. In the process, the clerk unknowingly overwrote your corrected address with the incorrect one.

OWA_OPT_LOCK helps web application developers avoid this pitfall by doing the following:

- Provide a means of recording the state of a record at the time it was queried from the database table.

- Provide a means of comparing the current state of the record against the original state of the record. This is done just prior to performing the update.
- Provide a means of acting on the result of the comparison of the record states. If the record states differ, then the record was modified and the application needs to be able to reject the change.

It's important to note that while optimistic locking techniques will allow an application to detect intervening updates to data, it cannot prevent them, given there is no actual database lock being imposed. In other words, in the case of Bank Y, optimistic locking wouldn't prevent the customer from pulling up address information and updating it while the clerk had the same information in another browser window. However, optimistic locking would have been able to detect that the data had been changed when the clerk tried to commit the address change transaction because the current state of the data would not match the original state of the data recorded just after it was queried.

The OWA_OPT_LOCK package provides two different methods of ensuring data integrity:

- **The hidden fields method** OWA_OPT_LOCK includes a procedure to generate hidden form fields in your HTML form that it uses to store the "Post-Query" values of the record to be updated. Another procedure is available to validate those fields against the current data in the record just prior to update to make sure the record in the database hasn't changed.
- **The checksum method** OWA_OPT_LOCK also includes a procedure that will calculate a 32-bit checksum on either a string passed to it or the actual row in a table.

The hidden fields method is a very common technique used when a web application involves data entry. It uses the following subprograms in OWA_OPT_LOCK:

```
owa_opt_lock.store_values(p_owner in varchar2
                          p_tname in varchar2
                          p_rowid in rowid);
owa_opt_lock.verify_values(p_old_values in vcArray) return boolean;
```

The store_values procedure does a few things automatically that would otherwise need to be performed manually. Using the owner, table name, and rowid parameters passed to it, the store_values procedure reads the current state of the record that will potentially be updated from the database and creates hidden form fields to store this state. This procedure call needs to be included at the bottom of your HTML form (before the </FORM> tag or HTP.FORMCLOSE call) where it can add the hidden fields into the HTML form code.

Once the form is submitted and the update procedure is invoked, the owa_opt_lock.verify_values function can be called to make sure the record hasn't been changed. The procedure is called by the form's submit command and will receive a PL/SQL table of the hidden form fields data. Pass the PL/SQL table of hidden field data into the p_old_values parameter and it will check the old values against the current record state. If the record has changed, the function will return a FALSE Boolean and a message stating that the data has changed can be shown, requesting that the end user take appropriate action. If the function returns a TRUE, then your web application can continue and commit the change.

Checksums can also be used to verify that a record has not changed. Instead of storing field values, this method calculates a 32-bit checksum (a unique numeric representation of a given set of data) of the column values in the record to be updated.

```
owa_opt_lock.checksum(p_buff in varchar2) return number;
owa_opt_lock.checksum(p_owner in varchar2
                      p_tname in varchar2
                      p_rowid in rowid) return number;
```

The owa_opt_lock.checksum function is overloaded, so the developer has the choice of either supplying a VARCHAR2 string to base the checksum on or having the function perform all the work of checking the current record state by supplying the owner, table name, and rowid, just as in the hidden field method.

The basic idea is essentially the same: when the HTML form is displayed to the user, a checksum is calculated to capture the current state of the data. Just before the application makes the update, the owa_opt_lock.checksum function is invoked again to get a checksum for the latest state of the record. If the checksums don't match, then the data has been changed and your application can reject the update.

One important thing to note when using the first version of owa_opt_lock.checksum (the one that accepts the VARCHAR2 string): it is the developer's responsibility to make sure the strings submitted to the function are consistent. The follow code snippet shows a common mistake:

Initial record state capture:

```
chksum1 := owa_opt_lock.checksum(col1 || ':' || col2 || ':' || col3 || ':' || col4);
```

Pre-update state capture:

```
chksum2 := owa_opt_lock.checksum(col1 || col2 || col3 || col4);
```

Check:

```
if chksum1 = chksum2 then
   b_ok_to_upd := true;
else
   b_ok_to_upd := false;
end if;
```

The Boolean variable b_ok_to_upd will always be false because the missing colon (:) characters in the second checksum call will throw off the calculation even if the record hasn't changed. Because a checksum value is dependent on the position of data as well as content, it will return a false value if anything is out of position (i.e., values are concatenated in the wrong order). It has been our experience that the second version is the better one to use as it will get the data values and calculate the checksum without the possibility of an error being introduced between the two checksum calculations.

Passing Parameters to a PL/SQL Web Application

A web application would be of limited use if data could not be passed between pages or between the browser and the application. Fortunately, the HTML standard provides developers with some tools for this very purpose:

- **GET Method** This method uses a Common Gateway Interface (CGI) environment variable on the application server called QUERY_STRING to pass information from one page to another. All hypertext links (anchor tags) use this method to pass a URL to the web server to serve up a new page. HTML forms can also use this method, although the POST Method (discussed next) is preferred and more common. It is the simplest method to use, but the data appears on the browser URL (a significant security issue) and there are limitations on the length of the URL passed.
- **POST Method** The POST Method passes data directly to the called page (or PL/SQL subprogram in our case) without the data showing up on a URL and without the length limitation that the GET method imposes.
- **Cookies** Cookies are often used to identify users during an online session. They store persistent identifiers such as login information and user preferences. A more detailed discussion of cookies can be found in the "Managing Cookies with OWA_COOKIE" section earlier in the chapter.

GET Method

The employee salary listing program (html_emp_list) shown earlier in this chapter is an example of making use of the GET method. The generic form of a URL encoded using the GET method is as follows:

```
http://hostname/virtual_path/modulename?parameter1=value1&parameter2=
value2&parameter3=value3.../
```

Recall the tabledata call that was modified to make the employee name into a hypertext link:

```
htp.tabledata(htf.anchor(curl => '#',
                         ctext => emp_rec.emp_name,
                    cattributes =>
   'ONCLICK="open(''//' || vc_hostname || vc_app_path ||
   'show_emp_photo?p_emp_id=' || to_char(emp_rec.emp_id)
   ||''',''EmpPic'',''resizable=no,height=105,width=105'');"'));
```

The important part of the statement, in terms of this discussion, is the URL encoded into the JavaScript open() command. Replacing vc_hostname and vc_app_path with the hostname and virtual path used in the rest of the examples produces:

```
http://localhost/pls/test/show_emp_photo?p_emp_id=<emp_id>
```

The question mark (?) tells the web server to use the GET method to pass this data. The Apache mod_plsql module will pick up on this and pass the <emp_id> value into the p_emp_id parameter in the show_emp_photo procedure.

Make sure that each of the parameter names you supply in your URL matches the desired input parameter in the PL/SQL subprogram or your values won't get passed in properly. These are **not** case sensitive (as they are in most web languages).

```
create or replace procedure show_emp_photo(p_emp_id
webapp.emp_photos.emp_id%TYPE)
```

The GET method is very simple and transparent to the user. Unfortunately, this simplicity and transparency causes problems in a number of areas, the most serious of which is the fact that the URL is submitted to the web server and as the client's browser navigates to the new page, the URL is displayed in its entirety in the web browser. In our employee salary list application (assuming the window displaying the photo had shown the address field that we told it not to do in the open() JavaScript call), the entire URL would have been displayed, including the data we passed in the address bar.

As an example, suppose a login package, like the one in Listing 5, has been created:

```
create or replace package bad_login
is
   procedure login;
   procedure start_page(p_userid    varchar2,
                        p_password  varchar2);
end bad_login;
/
create or replace package body bad_login
is
   procedure login
   is
      vc_app_path     varchar2(255) := owa_util.get_owa_service_path;
      vc_hostname     varchar2(255) := owa_util.get_cgi_env('HTTP_HOST');
   begin
      htp.htmlopen;
      htp.formopen(curl => 'http://' || vc_hostname || vc_app_path ||
'bad_login.start_page',
                   cmethod => 'GET');
      htp.print('Enter UserID: ');
      htp.formtext(cname => 'p_userid');
      htp.br;
      htp.print('Enter Password: ');
      htp.formpassword(cname => 'p_password');
      htp.br;
      htp.formsubmit;
      htp.formclose;
      htp.htmlclose;
   end login;
   procedure start_page(p_userid    varchar2,
                        p_password  varchar2)
```

```
   is
   begin
      htp.htmlopen;
      htp.bold('User: ' || p_userid || ' is now logged in.');
      htp.htmlclose;
   end start_page;
end bad_login;
```

This section of code is a package rather than procedures and functions that have been used in the code example up until this point in the chapter. Using package subprograms is no different than using standalone procedures and functions. It is referenced in the URL the same way procedures and functions are referenced in PL/SQL (i.e., using dot notation). For a sizable web application with many pages, we recommend using a package or a set of packages over many standalone procedures. Packages provide a way of keeping all interface code together and promote data encapsulation, improving maintenance, and security. Because they are loaded into memory on the server as a unit, the application will only take the overhead hit of loading the package into memory once when it is first accessed, as long as the connection from the application server to the Oracle server remains open, which improves overall application performance. Packages also reduce memory fragmentation, which improves memory management performance. It's also worth noting that when you recompile a package body, it does not invalidate all of the referencing program units.

It's important to note that PSPs don't support packaging.

The login form shown in Figure 7-8 is displayed when the client's browser is pointed to the correct URL.

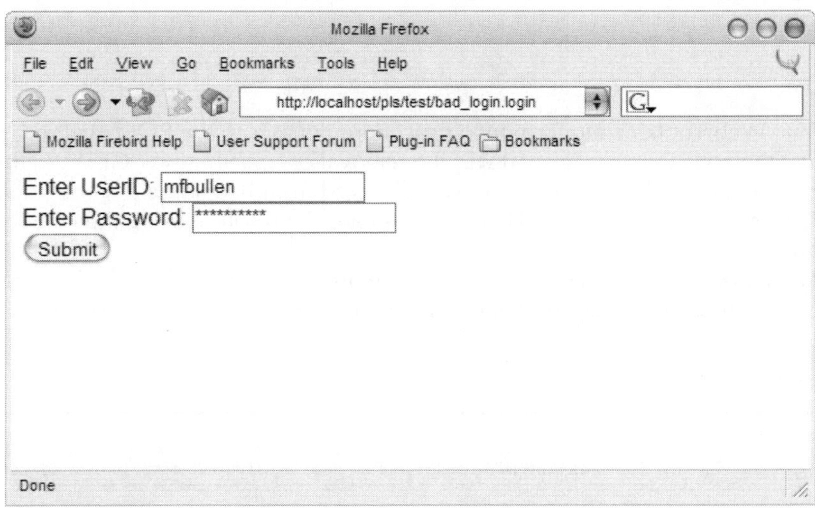

FIGURE 7-8. *A simple login form*

When the submit button is clicked, however, the password in the address field is displayed, as shown in Figure 7-9.

This is unacceptable for all production applications. The effort to hide the password using a password type text input field in the HTML form is totally negated by the appearance of the password in the address field of the browser. To make matters worse, because the information is added to the URL, the user can easily bookmark it and bypass the login page from that moment forward. The GET method is not the right choice for preventing users from seeing information passed between forms.

Another GET method issue is that parameter values cannot contain spaces or other characters that are illegal in a URL without having them escaped, which involves passing the entire URL through a function like utl_url.escape (see the PL/SQL Packages and Types Reference documentation to convert the illegal characters to legal representations). HTML allows you to include such characters using a %<two digit ASCII hex> notation. So a space character, which is ASCII hex 20, could be represented legally in a URL as %20.

As the number and/or size of parameters you want to pass on increases, you will run into a limitation on the size of the URL itself. Many web servers do not check this and may crash if your URL becomes too lengthy (1,000 characters is a common limit). At the very least, there is a danger of one or more of your parameters getting truncated if the URL is too long.

POST Method

The POST method uses the C standard input (STDIN) device to pass parameters and data to a called module. In this manner, it circumvents all of the aforementioned problems with the GET method because the STDIN device hides the parameters from the user and there is no size limit to the data sent using it. Moreover, the Apache mod_plsql module handles parameter passing with either the GET or POST method seamlessly, so there is no additional work for your PL/SQL code to do to use the POST method.

We can quickly fix our login screen issue from the previous section by changing one piece of code:

```
htp.formopen(curl => 'http://' || vc_hostname || vc_app_path || 'bad_login.start_page');
```

The PL/SQL Web Toolkit's htp.formopen procedure defaults to the POST method, so the only modification to the code that was needed was the removal of "cmethod => 'GET'". In this example, the package name (and any references to it) was changed from bad_login to good_login. We now have a much more secure login page. Figure 7-10 shows the result of using the POST method to pass information.

The parameters were passed as evidenced by the username being displayed on the start page, but nothing shows in the address field on the browser other than the module name for the start page.

FIGURE 7-9. *GET Method side effect*

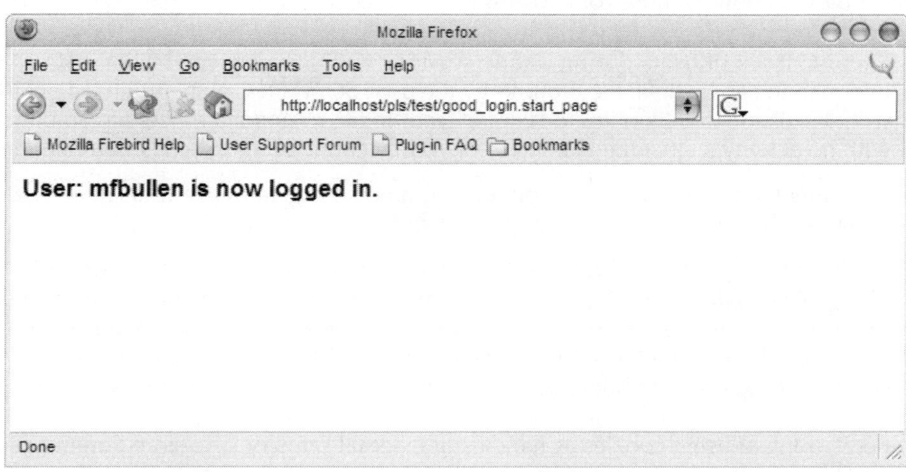

FIGURE 7-10. *Start page that results when called using the POST method*

Using Cookies to Improve Web Applications

The previous two sections deal mainly with passing fairly small amounts of internal application data between web pages. Cookies can be harnessed to even greater uses. When a web site is visited that keeps track of some kind of information that uniquely identifies you, the user is typically taken a registration page. The site asks you to create a username, enter a password and your e-mail address, and provide some other personal information about yourself. When the page is submitted, the web application creates an account record in a database, probably creates some default preference information for you based on some answers you provided in the registration page (especially if it contains a mini-survey about your wants, needs, etc.), and creates a unique identifier for you. The unique ID is typically then sent back to your browser to be stored as a persistent cookie (i.e., with an expiration date, usually far in the future), which is nothing more than a small, encrypted file stored on your hard drive. There could be megabytes of data stored in the site database about you, which is incredibly powerful (but may not be such a good thing if you're paranoid about sites keeping tracking data about you, but that's a topic for another book). The only piece that connects end users to all of this information is the tiny cookie containing your basic identifying information on your hard drive.

Have you ever been back to a site you haven't visited in a long time? You've forgotten your account information, yet the site somehow knows who you are and can e-mail your username and a new temporary password so that you can log into and change your password to a new one. You can thank a browser cookie containing your unique ID that was set way back when you registered for the site for this functionality. Assuming you haven't manually deleted the cookies from within your browser, the information will still be there and has enabled the site to look up account information, including the username and e-mail address, without any intervention from the end user.

Some additional powerful uses of cookies are

- Keeping track of users during online sessions with the web site so that user specific information can be linked to requests by the user. Some sites, such as online banking sites, will also use session cookies to "expire" your login session after a certain amount of time with no activity so that the likelihood of your account being hijacked is greatly reduced.
- Implementating a shopping cart on an e-commerce site, allowing users to order items and keep them separated from other users ordering items simultaneously.
- Implementating user configurable interfaces or "skins" for a web site. A simple ID stored as a cookie could be used to give the user the option of seeing interface A, B, or a default that's suited to the user's personal taste. A portal site is an example of this: the user is allowed to specify the layout and content for her portal page. Maybe she wants sports, stock quotes, and news but not local weather (she has an office with a window).

In general, think of using cookies as handles or external primary keys stored on the client side that reference larger sets of data stored in the site's database.

PL/SQL Server Pages (PSPs)

It is often necessary to have two different teams working on a web application. One team, perhaps HTML and web front-end design experts, concerns itself with the details of the application's user interface while the other team, the software developers, concern itself with the business logic that makes the application work. Modern application frameworks such as Java 2 Platform, Enterprise Edition (J2EE) and .NET separate presentation and business logic into distinct tools. This allows large development teams to develop discrete portions of the application while not being directly dependent upon the work of other development team members. See Chapter 1 for a discussion of the different types of technologies (called services) that are outlined in the J2EE specification and how they are implemented by Oracle Application Server 10*g*.

This is the purview of server page scripting—an HTML file with executable script code embedded and mingled with HTML tags. The idea is to have one focus of development that both teams can work on without the pitfall of user-interface designers getting mired in code and developers getting mired in user-interface details. A server page source file can be opened in a web page authoring tool such as Macromedia Dreamweaver or Microsoft Front Page, and the HTML can then be edited by the web designers just like any standard HTML page, leaving the embedded code intact. Likewise, software developers can open the PSP in any developer text editor and make changes to the code, leaving the HTML as is.

In addition to visual editing tools such as Dreamweaver and FrontPage, Oracle JDeveloper 10*g* now has an extremely powerful visual HTML editor. JDeveloper is discussed in detail in Chapter 13.

PL/SQL Server Pages, or PSPs as they are commonly known, are roughly analogous to JavaServer Pages (JSPs). PSPs, in fact, use the same script tag syntax that JSPs, Microsoft's Active Server Pages (ASP), and other server page technologies use. Like JSPs, PSPs are not actually executed, but are compiled into executable modules. JSPs are compiled into Java servlets that call Java class APIs to output HTML; PSPs are compiled into PL/SQL procedures that call the PL/SQL Web Toolkit API to output HTML. The major difference is that JSPs are compiled and executed on the application server and PSPs are compiled and loaded into the Oracle database and executed by the database's PL/SQL engine.

As a method of introducing PSPs, let's turn to the "Hello World" program developed earlier in this chapter into a PSP. Listing 6 shows the equivalent PSP file.

```
<!- Hello3.PSP          ->
<%@ page language="PL/SQL" contentType="text/html"%>
<%@ plsql procedure="hello3"%>
<HTML>
<HEAD>
<TITLE>Hello World Program</TITLE>
</HEAD>
<BODY text="#000000" bgcolor="#FFFFFF">
<B>Hello World!</B>
<BR>
<BR>
System date and time is: <%=to_char(sysdate, 'MM/DD/YYYY HH24:MI:SS')%>
<BR>
Oracle user is: <%=user%>
</BODY>
</HTML>
Listing 6
```

The HTML in the preceding listing is easy to recognize; what's new are the script elements. PSP script elements start with "<%" and end with "%>." Without getting into the scripting elements, the ease with which both web designers and developers work with a server page technology such as PSP should be evident. HTML designers can work with the file in a web page authoring tool, can change HTML interface elements at will, and can ignore the script elements because the base document is HTML. PL/SQL developers can open the same file and change the script elements at will, ignoring the HTML interface tags.

Figure 7-11 shows the result of the hello3.PSP program, which is the same as the code earlier in this chapter centering on the HTP package.

Early in the chapter, we mentioned that PSPs offer a good balance between performance and maintainability. We also mentioned, in the beginning of this section, that the PSP is not, in itself, what is being executed. A PSP must be compiled into a PL/SQL procedure and loaded into the database before it can be served up by the application server. Listing 7 shows the PL/SQL procedure that is result of this compile and load of hello3.PSP into the database.

```
CREATE OR REPLACE  PROCEDURE "WEBDEV"."HELLO3"
AS
BEGIN
NULL;
owa_util.mime_header('text/html');
htp.prn('<!- Hello3.PSP          ->');
htp.prn('');
htp.prn('
<HTML>
<HEAD>
<TITLE>Hello World Program</TITLE>
</HEAD>
<BODY text="#000000" bgcolor="#FFFFFF">
```

```
<B>Hello World!</B>
<BR>
<BR>
System date and time is: ');
htp.prn(to_char(sysdate, 'MM/DD/YYYY HH24:MI:SS'));
htp.prn('
<BR>
Oracle user is: ');
htp.prn(user);
htp.prn('
</BODY>
</HTML>
');
 END;
```

The resultant code is not easily maintainable (and this is after Listing 7 was manually cleaned up). The print statements are broken oddly across multiple lines and indentation is nonexistent. In fact, it looks a lot like our hello2 program from Listing 3. "Pretty," executable code, however, is not the object of PSPs. The use of the HTP.PRN calls will generally perform better than the specialized tag procedures in HTP and HTF.

As a PL/SQL developer who decides to use PSPs, there's no benefit in trying to make this code look presentable. A Java developer writing JSPs would not write a JSP initially and make modifications to the resultant Java Servlet from then on. In the same manner, you should write off the procedure generated by the compile and load of a PSP and focus your development efforts on the original PSP file—then recompile it and reload, thereby replacing the previous version of the procedure.

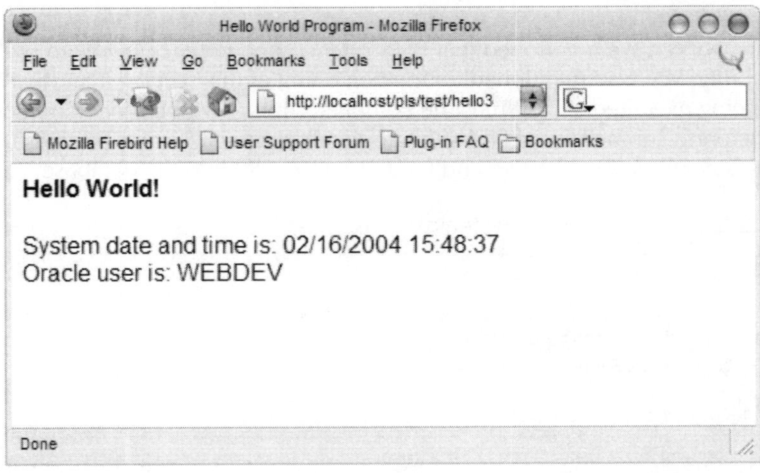

FIGURE 7-11. *Output from the PSP version of the Hello Program*

Loading PSPs into the Database

Once you have a PSP file written and ready to be compiled and loaded, use the following command:

```
loadPSP [-replace] -user <logon> [<page1> <page2> ...]
```

This is an operating system command found in the %ORACLE_HOME%/bin directory, not one that can be issued at a SQL*Plus prompt.

The PSP loader will read each PSP submitted, compile it, and then load each resulting procedure into the database. If you are loading an updated PSP, the –replace flag must be specified so that loadPSP will replace the old procedure with the new version. The –user flag is used to specify a standard Oracle connection string (i.e., user/pass@DB). You must include the file extension of the PSP files and the extension must be .PSP.

The following command is used to load hello3.PSP into a test database:

```
loadPSP -replace -user webdev/webdev@arenadev hello3.PSP
```

The loadPSP executable will examine the file for errors and will abort if it finds any. If the file is error-free, then it will compile it into a PL/SQL procedure and load it into the schema specified in the connect string. If you do not specify the generated procedure name in the PSP script, the default name of the procedure is the same as the name of the source file, without the .PSP extension. It is important to note that PSPs will only be generated as standalone procedures; loadPSP cannot create packages. If you wish to have your PSP code packaged together, you will have to do so manually. Unlike other PL/SQL code that provides business logic, it has been the author's experience that packaging procedures generated from PSPs will cause a maintenance nightmare if they are updated with any frequency. It is much more efficient to load your PSPs into their own schema and apply appropriate grants to access the database schema containing the data as needed.

PSP Elements

The real power of PSPs come from their script elements. All PSP script elements start with <% and end with %> and are used to embed compiler instructions or code into the underlying HTML document. A special element called the scriptlet allows the developer to embed whole blocks of free-form PL/SQL code into the page.

There are four types of PSP elements as shown in Table 7-2.

Directives

Directive elements are similar to compiler directives in other languages. They impart information about the page to the compiler, which in the case of PSPs, is loadPSP. Most of them do not translate into actual executable code in the resultant PL/SQL procedure, with the exception of the mime-type specification, which generates a call to owa_util.mime_header. Directives should be at the top of your PSP (as in Listing 6).

There are four different directives:

- **Page directive** The page directive specifies the scripting language the page uses, the content type (i.e., mime-type and character set), and an error page to navigate to in case there is a problem with the page.

PSP Element	Element Type
<%@ ... %>	Directive: Used to provide information to loadPSP about the PSP, such as the mime type, page language, character set, PL/SQL procedure name, and parameters.
<%! ... %>	Declaration: Used to declare PL/SQL variables that have a page global scope.
<%= ... %>	Expression: PL/SQL expression is evaluated and the result is placed at the location of the expression tag.
<% ... %>	Scriptlet: PL/SQL executable code.

TABLE 7-2. *PSP Element Types*

Syntax:

```
<%@ page [language="PL/SQL"] [contentType="content type string"] [errorPage="file.PSP"] %>
```

The contentType and errorPage attribute names are case sensitive.

- **Procedure directive** The procedure directive is particular to PSPs and tells the compiler what to name the PL/SQL procedure it creates. If this directive isn't specified, then loadPSP will use the file name of the PSP (without the .PSP extension). The procedure name specified in this directive does not need to match the filename.

  Syntax:

  ```
  <%@ plsql procedure="procedure_name" %>
  ```

- **Parameter directive** Also specific to PSPs, this directive allows you to specify input parameters for the resultant PL/SQL procedure. These parameters are passed to your procedure by another page that is calling it (i.e., using the GET or POST method).

  There is no capability to specify data direction (i.e., IN or OUT). All parameters in PSPs are IN only.

  Syntax:

  ```
  <%@ plsql parameter="parameter_name" [type="PL/SQL_datatype"]
  [default="value"] %>
  ```

  When specifying PL/SQL literals, you must enclose the literal in both double quotes and single quotes.

  For example:

  ```
  <%@ plsql parameter="p_username" type="varchar2" default = "'guest'" %>
  ```

- **Include directive** The include directive allows you to statically incorporate an external file into your PSP. The include file can contain any combination of plain text, HTML, and PSP elements but it cannot have a PSP extension (INC is typical), and the directory path specified in the directive must match the directory path used when it is specified to loadPSP. Include files are especially useful when you have a fairly static interface element or scriptlet that is used in many PSPs and you want to avoid copying the code into each PSP. Keep in mind, though, that this is a compile-time include only. Once the procedure is created, changing the include file will not affect the code in the procedure in the database. To apply an include file change to existing procedures, it is necessary to reload all affected PSPs. If a more dynamic behavior is desired, put the code into a procedure or package subprogram and call it in the PSP with a scriptlet.

Syntax:

```
<%@ include file="path name" %>
```

Declarations

The declaration element allows you to specify PL/SQL types and variables. This element can span multiple lines, with individual declarations separated by semicolon just like they would be in a normal PL/SQL block. These declarations have scope for the entire PSP page and are equivalent to the declarations in the outermost BEGIN/END block in a PL/SQL procedure.

Syntax:

```
<%! PL/SQL declaration;
[ PL/SQL declaration; ] ... %>
```

Example:

```
<%! username varchar2(15);
    password varchar2(15); %>
```

Because a declaration element is in scope for the entire page, the author recommends placing them at the top of the PSP page, just under the directives (if any) and before any HTML or PL/SQL code.

Expressions

The expression element allows you to insert any PL/SQL expression that evaluates to either a VARCHAR2 string or a value that can be typecast to a VARCHAR2, such as a numeric datatype. Hello3.PSP in Listing 6 makes use of expressions to show the user name and the current date and time. Unlike some of the other elements, only one expression can be specified and because it's not a complete PL/SQL statement on its own, you don't need to include a semicolon.

Syntax:

```
<%= PL/SQL expression %>
```

Example:

```
<%@ page language="PL/SQL" contentType="text/html" %>
<%@ plsql procedure="next_meet" %>
<%@ plsql parameter="p_next_meet_dt" type="date" %>
<HTML>
<BODY>
The next meeting date is: <%= to_char(p_next_meet_dt, 'DD-MON-YYYY') %>
```

```
</BODY>
</HTML>
```

Scriptlets

Scriptlets are the most powerful of the PSP script elements and provide the bulk of your interface logic.

Syntax:

```
<% PL/SQL statement;
[PL/SQL statement;] %>
```

These PL/SQL statements will make up the body (between the outer BEGIN/END keywords) of the generated procedure. Scriptlets are extremely flexible as they can contain an entire PL/SQL block or be conditional fragments of PL/SQL code wrapped around HTML text.

Consider the example of a complete PL/SQL block enclosed in a scriptlet as shown in Listing 8.

```
<%@ page language="PL/SQL" contentType="text/html" %>
<%@ plsql procedure="table_dump" %>
<%@ plsql parameter="p_table_name" type="varchar2" %>
<!- table_dump.PSP ->
<HTML>
<HEAD>
<TITLE>Table Dump</TITLE>
</HEAD>
<BODY bgcolor="#FFFFFF">
<H2>Table Dump of <%= p_table_name %></H2>
<BR>
<%
   declare
      b_ok_flag  boolean;
   begin
      b_ok_flag := owa_util.tableprint(p_table_name, 'border');
   end;
%>
<BR>
</BODY>
</HTML>
```

The output appears in Figure 7-12. The owa_util.tableprint procedure is very useful for querying the contents of a database table quickly and displaying it in an HTML page. With a small amount of effort, another small PSP containing an HTML form that allows the user to enter the table name in a form field then calls table_dump passing the table name to it could be developed.

Note that in the PL/SQL block scriptlet, a Boolean (b_ok_flag) variable is needed to receive a TRUE/FALSE value return from owa_util.tableprint. A declaration element at the top of the PSP can be used, but it's only needed in the scope of the local block. In general, it is good programming practice to declare a variable in its smallest scope, as opposed to its largest. It breaks with generally accepted PL/SQL programming guidelines, but the trade-off is that it makes the scriptlets more readable. When writing PSPs, you become less of a PL/SQL developer and

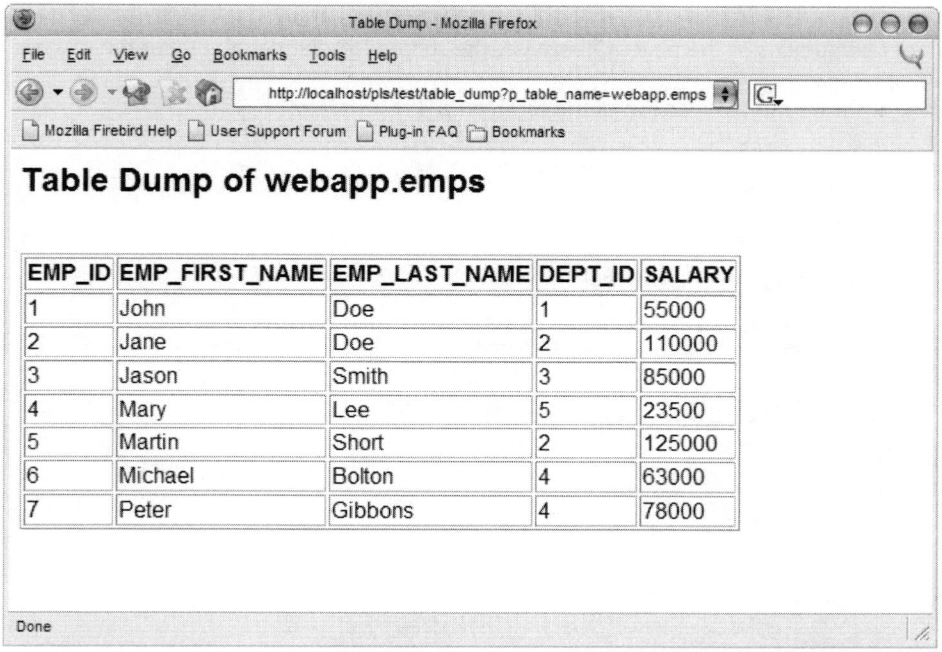
Table Dump - Mozilla Firefox
File Edit View Go Bookmarks Tools Help
http://localhost/pls/test/table_dump?p_table_name=webapp.emps
Mozilla Firebird Help
User Support Forum
Plug-in FAQ
Bookmarks
Table Dump of webapp.emps
EMP_ID EMP_FIRST_NAME EMP_LAST_NAME DEPT_ID SALARY
1 John Doe 1 55000
2 Jane Doe 2 110000
3 Jason Smith 3 85000
4 Mary Lee 5 23500
5 Martin Short 2 125000
6 Michael Bolton 4 63000
7 Peter Gibbons 4 78000
Done

FIGURE 7-12. *Output of the emps table data from table_dump.PSP*

more of a web application developer. Having said that, it is certainly not our intention to advocate the abolishment of all PL/SQL standards, but it would be beneficial for developers to approach the development of PSPs with a slightly different mindset, one that is necessary because of the interface logic embedded within PSP code.The developer also has the freedom to split PL/SQL logic and use it to conditionally cause things to print or not print, whichever the case might be.

```
…
<% if b_spec_disclaim then %>
   <BR>
   This is the special disclaimer text …
   <BR>
<% else %>
   <BR>
   This is the standard disclaimer text …
   <BR>
<% end if %>
…
```

Just as in other scripting languages, it's important not to put a lot of business logic in the PSPs. Business logic belongs in the program units.

This code snippet contains three separate scriplets that work together as one IF-THEN-ELSE-END IF statement. It checks the value of the Boolean variable, then, if it's set to TRUE, the first disclaimer text appears in the page. Otherwise, the second disclaimer text (after the <% else %> scriptlet) appears.

Listing 9 shows the PSP version of the html_emp_list program.

```
<%@ page language="PL/SQL" contentType="text/html" %>
<%@ plsql procedure="PSP_emp_list" %>
<!- PSP_emp_list.PSP ->
<HTML>
<HEAD>
<TITLE>Employee Salary Listing</TITLE>
</HEAD>
<BODY text="#000000" bgcolor="#FFFFFF">
<CENTER><H1>Employee Salary Listing</H1></CENTER>
<BR>
<BR>
<TABLE BORDER="1" ALIGN="CENTER" CELLPADDING="5">
<TR>
<TH>Name</TH>
<TH>Dept</TH>
<TH>Salary</TH>
</TR>
<%
   declare
      cursor emp_cur
      is
      select e.emp_id,
             e.emp_last_name || ', ' || e.emp_first_name emp_name,
             d.dept_name,
             e.salary
        from webapp.emps e,
             webapp.depts d
       where e.dept_id = d.dept_id
       order by 1;
       vc_virt_path    varchar2(255) := owa_util.get_cgi_env('HTTP_HOST')
|| owa_util.get_owa_service_path;
    begin
       for emp_rec in emp_cur
       loop
%>
         <TR>
         <TD><A HREF="#" ONCLICK="open('//<%= vc_virt_path
%>show_emp_photo?p_emp_id=<%= emp_rec.emp_id
%>','EmpPic','resizable=no,height=105,width=105');">
             <%= emp_rec.emp_name %></A></TD>
         <TD><%= emp_rec.dept_name %></TD>
         <TD ALIGN="RIGHT"><FONT COLOR="<%= case
                                 when emp_rec.salary <= 25000 then '#00FF00'
                                 when emp_rec.salary between 75001 and 99999
then '#FFFF00'
                                 when emp_rec.salary >= 100000 then '#FF0000'
                                 else '#000000'
                                 end %>">
                             <%= to_char(emp_rec.salary, '9,999,999,999') %>
                             </FONT>
         </TD>
         </TR>
<%
```

```
      end loop;
   end;
%>
</TABLE>
</BODY>
</HTML>
```

The cursor and virtual path variable (which combines the hostname and virtual path information into one variable this time) are declared local to the PL/SQL block containing the for loop, given that's the only place they are needed. The example also contains logic to perform a direct substitution of the case evaluation into the <FONT> tag's color attribute. It is possible to have kept the vc_sal_color variable and defined it in the declaration section of the local block, then evaluated the case result into it just like in the original version of the program. However, since it was only needed once, the code was constructed in such a way as to not preserve it.

You can also call any PL/SQL procedure or package subprogram using a scriptlet.

```
<% web_utils.navbar; %>
```

This could be a standardized HTML navbar included in each PSP page at the top to make navigation of your site easier. The navbar procedure could be written to generate HTML, button images, and JavaScript (to make the rollover buttons work) using the specialized HTP or HTP.PRINT/PRN calls. Whatever the navbar procedure prints using the HTP package will show up at the scriptlet position on the page.

This is a very powerful technique that allows you to build HTML interface libraries into your web application. When you need a user interface widget, it can be called via a scriptlet. If a widget needs to be changed, the procedure in the library package can be modified (in one place!) and all pages in the application are automatically updated.

Commenting PSPs

Because PSPs are a hybrid of HTML and PL/SQL code, either HTML comments, PL/SQL comments, or both can be used to comment your PSP. Developers must take care when using comments: only HTML comments can be used in the HTML part of the PSP (i.e., outside PSP elements).

For example:

```
<% begin
      <!- My HTML comment ->
      for emp_rec in emp_cur…
…
%>
```

will result in an error because an HTML comment has (illegally) been placed inside a piece of PL/SQL code.

Likewise:

```
<HTML>
<BODY>
- My PL/SQL comment
```

```
/* My other PL/SQL comment */
...
</BODY>
</HTML>
```

will also fail. PL/SQL comments must appear in scriptlets and HTML comments can only appear outside PSP scriptlets.

Building Applications Using the PL/SQL Web Toolkit

Now that we've covered all of the basics, a discussion on the bigger picture of application development using the PL/SQL Web Toolkit is in order. Some of the questions that should be visited before beginning development are

- Should I develop using only the programmatic function calls of the toolkit?
- Should I use PSPs?
- What about code partitioning between presentation and business logic layers?
- What about application security and architecture?

If your application will be sizable, you will quickly find that a homogeneous solution consisting exclusively of only hand-coded PL/SQL procedures using HTP/HTF calls or only PL/SQL server pages, is far too limiting. A successful implementation of a large application will likely be a mixture of both techniques. For user interface generation and basic page display logic that will build pages, it will most likely be determined that PSPs enable development teams to easily partition work between developers and user interface designers. PSPs are also easier and quicker to develop as opposed to the tedious coding of HTP/HTF calls. Additionally, both groups will enjoy the productivity benefit of simpler maintenance. For very focused user interface elements, the development team will benefit from first building a PL/SQL package (or packages) that serve as an interface widget library and then referencing them in your PSPs. This method will not only promote code reusability, but also will make the interface easy to update across the board.

In web application development, the goal is to separate the application presentation (interface) from the business logic. For example, code that contains logic that processes a user's shopping cart items and creates orders inside a PSP in not desireable. PSPs should contain only presentation logic and the PL/SQL code that does all the heavy lifting in the database should only be referenced or called by the page.

The security of your web application is another essential area of focus. Looking at the examples in this chapter, you might have noticed that two different schemas were involved. The WEBDEV schema was used by the database access descriptor to log in to the database—it held the interface procedures and packages, such as html_emp_list. The WEBAPP schema contained data tables and (if there was any) the heavy-duty data manipulation logic such as the shopping cart order generation logic mentioned in the previous paragraph.

By partitioning things this way, the attempt has been made to "firewall" the data. The WEBDEV user is the only user granted rights necessary for the web application to work. If the WEBDEV user connection becomes compromised through the application server and an attacker somehow gains access, no data is at risk because the most damage an attacker can do (by compromising the WEBDEV user) is to destroy the interface packages and bring the application down.

An important application architecture consideration is the organization of the code. If business logic is separated properly from user interface logic, making significant changes to the user interface will be easier. In fact, if a disciplined design approach is adhered to, the user interface can be entirely replaced without affecting any of the underlying business logic.

Summary

The chapter has introduced most, if not all, of the necessary weapons in the PL/SQL Web Toolkit arsenal needed to start developing web applications using PL/SQL. Additional documentation on PL/SQL web development can found in the following documentation sources available on Oracle's Technology Network at http://otn.oracle.com/tech/pl_sql/index.html:

Oracle Application Server 10*g*, PL/SQL Web Toolkit Reference, 10g (9.0.4), Part no. B12098-01

Oracle Database, Application Developer's Guide—Fundamentals, 10*g* Release 1 (10.1), Part no. B10795-01

PART III

Oracle Portal

CHAPTER 8

Oracle Application Server Portal— Architecture

racle defines Oracle Application Server Portal as "a rich, declarative environment for creating a portal web interface, publishing and managing information, accessing dynamic data, and customizing the portal experience, with an extensible framework for J2EE-based application access." While that one-sentence summarization is quite a mouthful, it does not do Oracle Application Server Portal justice. Oracle Application Server Portal is an incredibly powerful environment that allows developers to create and test sophisticated applications, all while writing and maintaining a very small amount of code. Like any truly powerful development environment, Oracle Application Server Portal can be used in a multitude of ways. For example, beginning developers can use Oracle Application Server Portal's wizards to generate applications consisting of forms, reports, and graphs and deploy those Oracle Application Server components quickly, easily, and with a minimum of coding. Advanced developers can enhance the generated components through the use of the Oracle Application Server Portal Application Programming Interface (API) or even bypass the wizards altogether and use Java and/or PL/SQL to create Oracle Application Server Portal portlets. The portal you create can pull data from a single database, multiple databases (including non-Oracle databases), and even from other sites on the Web. Oracle Application Server Portal can be used to create portlets that interact with other sites on the Web and use their content in your portal.

Oracle Application Server Portal leverages the open standards, enabling developers to build Java 2 Platform, Enterprise Edition/eXtensible Markup Language (J2EE/XML) components that can be exposed within the framework as pure HTML. With the introduction of Web Services for Remote Portals (WSRP) and Java Specification Request (JSR) 168, Oracle Application Server Portal support will include the capability to build interoperable applications that can be deployed across multiple vendor platforms. Furthermore, since Oracle Application Server Portal is a component of the Oracle Application Server, it can integrate with other components such as Oracle Application Server Discoverer and Oracle Application Server Reports to expose rich Business Intelligence Reports. As part of the Oracle Application Server, Oracle Application Server Portal can also be deployed in a number of different architectures to support scalability and high-availability scenarios.

What is a Portlet?

Oracle's definition is that they're "reusable building blocks for easily publishing information and applications." You can think of a portlet as a small application that performs a specific function. Portlets are then placed and arranged on a page so that the end user can interact with them. Portlets can be forms, reports, graphs, links to other web sites, ad hoc query tools—the list goes on and on (we'll explore the different types of portlets in Chapter 9). All portlets come from a data source registered within Oracle Application Server Portal, called a portlet provider. You can publish pages, navigation pages, and other Oracle Application Server Portal components as portlets, or use Oracle Application Server Portal's wizards to easily create reports, forms, charts, and other types of dynamic components. You can also build components with your own tools and integrate them through Oracle Application Server Portal's APIs, available in the Portal Developer Kit (PDK).

One of the most difficult, yet ultimately beneficial, concepts for many beginning Oracle Application Server Portal developers to grasp is the fact that the Oracle Application Server Portal development environment is itself an Oracle Application Server Portal application. All forms, pages, and wizards that developers use to generate Oracle Application Server Portal components are Oracle Application Server Portal elements themselves, stored in the Oracle Application Server Portal repository. This is beneficial to developers because they can work with a well-designed portal environment and understand the basics of Oracle Application Server Portal development, architecture, and navigation before attempting to build and deploy their first portal.

This chapter is designed to show the architecture of Oracle Application Server Portal and to provide a roadmap so that developers and administrators can find their way around Oracle Application Server Portal quickly. Subsequent chapters in this section will explore such topics as Oracle Application Server Portal development, administration, and incorporating Forms, Reports, and Discoverer into Oracle Application Server Portal. Even though Oracle Application Server Portal is a true declarative development environment that requires little, if any, coding for a complete application, it is still beneficial to define and explore the structure of Oracle Application Server Portal and how applications and portals are constructed. Given Oracle Application Server Portal is a true web-based development environment, you are probably anxious to jump in and start creating Oracle Application Server Portal portlets and applications immediately; some of the material in this chapter may appear dry in that context, but mastering the basics of Oracle Application Server Portal navigation will save you much time as your development efforts move forward.

Logging in to Oracle Application Server Portal for the First Time

When Oracle Application Server 10*g* is installed with either the Portal and Wireless or Business Intelligence and Forms options, Oracle Application Server Portal is installed also. Before we can access the Oracle Application Server Portal environment, the necessary components must be up and running. Use the dcmctl tool (in the $ORACLE_HOME/dcm/bin directory) to see if the Oracle Application Server Portal Oracle Application Server Containers for J2EE (OC4J) container is running:

```
C:\AS_HOME\dcm\bin>dcmctl getstate -v
Current State for Instance:AS_HOME.xpas10g
   Component                  Type          Up Status      In Sync Status
=====================================================================
1  HTTP_Server                HTTP_Server   Up             True
2  OC4J_BI_Forms              OC4J          Up             True
3  OC4J_Portal                OC4J          Up             True
4  OC4J_Wireless              OC4J          Up             True
5  home                       OC4J          Up             True
```

If you are running on a server that has both the infrastructure and middle tier on the same machine, make sure you run this command from the ORACLE_HOME location of the middle tier. If the OC4J_Portal component is not running for any reason, you can start it by executing the following command:

```
dcmctl start -co OC4J_Portal -v
```

Oracle Application Server Portal also depends on the security functions built into Oracle Application Server 10*g*. To check to make sure that the security piece is up and running, cd to the ORACLE_HOME of your infrastructure, then to the dcm\bin directory. Execute the following command:

```
C:\IS_HOME\dcm\bin>dcmctl start -v
```

```
Current State for Instance:IS_HOME.xpas10g
   Component                Type          Up Status     In Sync Status
=========================================================================
1  HTTP_Server              HTTP_Server   Up            True
2  OC4J_SECURITY            OC4J          Up            True
3  home                     OC4J          Down          True(Disabled)
```

If the OC4J_SECURITY component is not running for any reason, start it with the following command:

```
dcmctl start -co OC4J_SECURITY -v
```

To access Oracle Application Server Portal for the first time, enter the URL in your web browser from the following template:

http://<server>:<port>/pls/portal

The machine I used for the examples in this chapter is called xpas10*g* and the middle tier was installed on port 7778, so to access Oracle Application Server Portal on this server:

```
http://xpas10g:7778/pls/portal
```

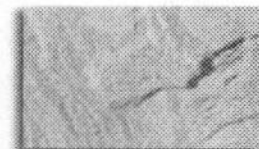

TIP

During installation, Oracle will attempt to use port 7777 for your Oracle Application Server 10g instance. If, for whatever reason, port 7777 is not available, Oracle will try 7778, then 7779, and so on. If your middle tier and infrastructure installations are on separate machines, then both will use 7777 (unless some other application is using that port). If you chose to install both the infrastructure and middle tier on the same machine, then, most likely, the infrastructure will use 7777 and the middle tier will use 7778. Oracle Application Server Portal lives in the middle tier, so use the middle tier port number to access it. It is important to note that while Oracle Application Server's Portal Page Engine (PPE) lives in the middle tier, it is dependant on both the middle-tier and the infrastructure for both meta-data and identity management.

If all of the necessary components are up and running, you should see a page similar to Figure 8-1.

As with virtually every Oracle Application Server Portal page you will work with, a lot of information is displayed. This page serves as both a welcome to the Oracle Application Server Portal environment and as an example of a typical Oracle Application Server Portal page. As you work with Oracle Application Server Portal, you will become comfortable with the basic layout of an Oracle Application Server Portal page (although, as a developer, you have great flexibility to make your Oracle Application Server Portal pages look like whatever they want) and this welcome page contains all of the basic Oracle Application Server Portal page elements.

Along the top of the page (above the first horizontal line) there is a page region called the banner. Although your portal pages do not have to contain a banner, it is included in all Oracle Application Server Portal templates when it comes time to build and deploy your Oracle Application

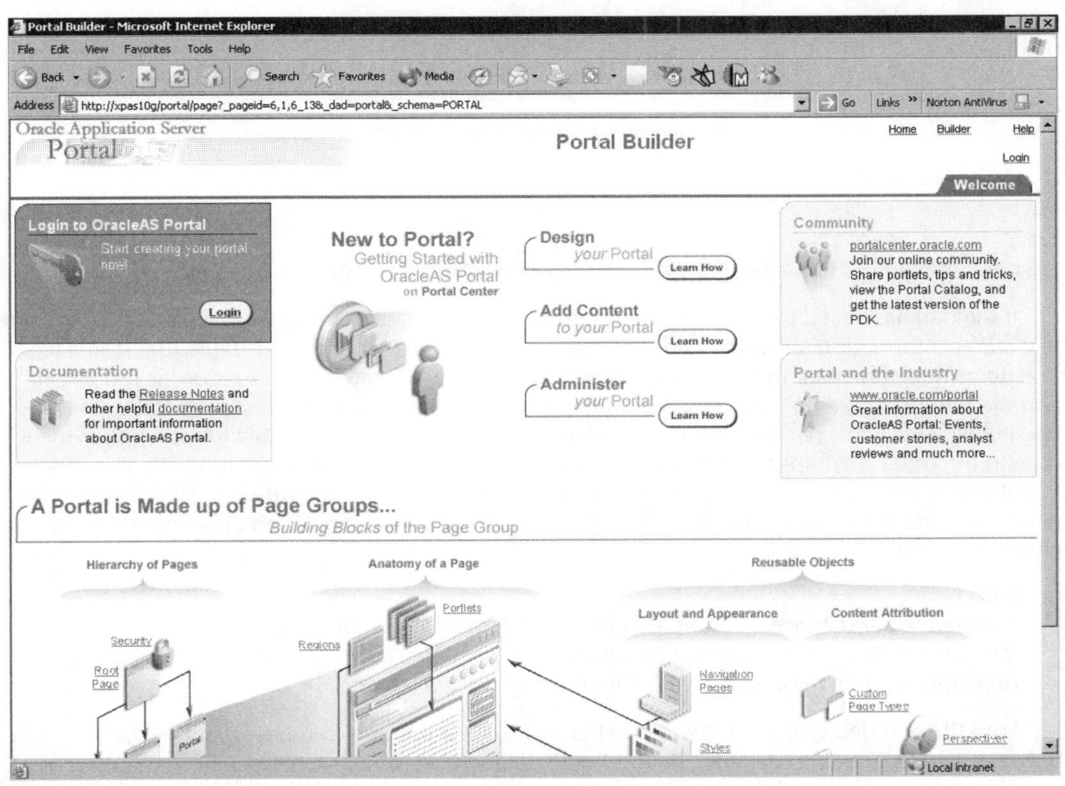

FIGURE 8-1. *The initial Oracle Application Server Portal page*

Server Portal pages. There is an image on the left, a title (Portal Builder), and links on the right. Below the links on the right is a tab that says Welcome. Tabs are like banners—they are not required, but are included as standard page elements in Oracle Application Server Portal. Below the Welcome tab is the main part of the page.

A key concept to understand when working with Oracle Application Server Portal and the various Oracle Application Server Portal elements is the one-to-many relationship. Oracle used this concept many times when constructing the Oracle Application Server Portal environment. A one-to-many relationship describes one where there is one parent record and one or more child records. Child records cannot exist without a parent record, but a parent record may exist without any child records. As an example, say one of us walks into our local bookstore and purchases some books. The invoice might look like this:

```
Order # 12345
Customer: 67890     Ostrowski, Chris
                  215 Union Blvd
               Lakewood, CO 80228
```

```
Quantity     Title
1           Oracle Application Server 10g Web Development, Ostrowski/Brown,
Oracle Press
1           Oracle9i Performance Tuning Tips & Techniques, Niemiec, Oracle
Press
1           Oracle PL/SQL Tips and Techniques, Trezzo, Oracle Press

Total:       179.97
Tax:         10.80
Total:       190.77
Payment Method: Mastercard xxxx-xxxx-xxxx-1234 Exp: 01/05
```

If the database used to store this information is normalized, there would be a database record that stores information about the order (Order id = 12345) and a line-items table that stores the line items that constitute this order (the three books). In this case, the order record is the parent and the line items are the children. The parent (the order) consists of one or more children (the line items). Line items cannot exist independent of an order. It is also possible to split the payment due on the order. Perhaps Chris has a gift certificate for $100. The payment to satisfy this order might constitute the $100 gift certificate and $90.77 charged to his credit card. Anticipating this possibility, the database is also designed with a one-to-many relationship between the orders and payments tables.

NOTE
Normalized and Normalization are fancy words for structuring your database so that there is as little redundancy as possible. The objective is to increase capacity by eliminating wasted storage.

For DBA-minded types out there, another example of the one-to-many relationship is the one between tablespaces and datafiles in an Oracle database. A tablespace (the parent) consists of one or more datafiles (children). A datafile cannot exist independent of a tablespace.

In Oracle Application Server Portal, developers will visit this one-to-many relationship many times, and here is the first example of it. Every Oracle Application Server Portal page, including the Welcome page in Figure 8-1, is made up of regions. A region is nothing more than a section of a page. Many aspects of content display are defined at the region level, such as the width of the region or whether to display borders around the portlets in a portlet region. Regions can also include one or more tabs. A region can be defined to hold portlets, items, subpage links, and tabs, or it can exist as undefined (undefined regions become defined when an Oracle Application Server Portal object first gets placed on them). You cannot add portlets to an item region, nor can you add items to a portlet region. You cannot add anything to a subpage links region; these regions automatically populate with links to subpages of the current page. You cannot add anything to a tab region; although you can configure the tab to include, for example, rollover images. There is a one-to-many relationship between pages and regions. In regions defined as portlet regions, there is also a many-to-many relationship between regions and portlets. These relationships are shown in Figure 8-2.

NOTE
Another way to think about regions is to picture each Oracle Application Server Portal page divided into a section of web real estate. Each region exposes an Oracle Application Server Portal object such as portlet or an item and can be seen as a container. Every Oracle Application Server Portal page is comprised of one or more regions.

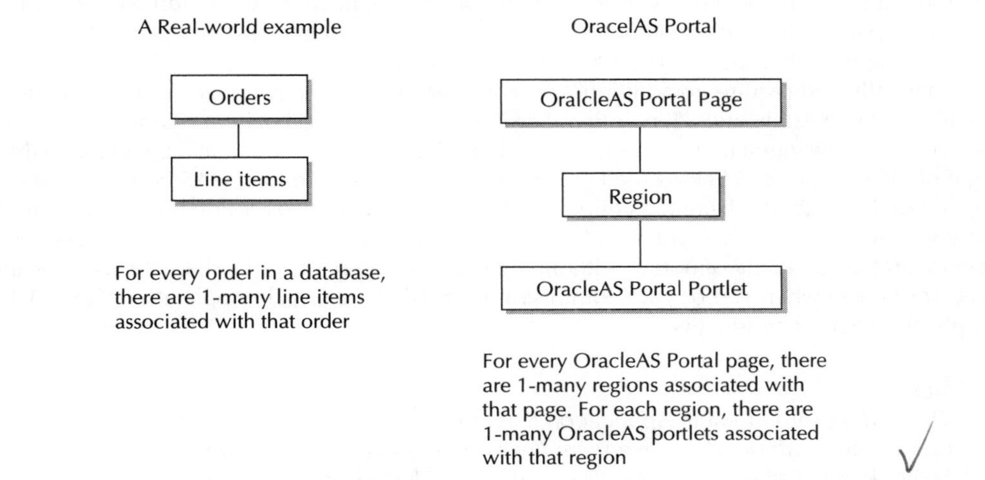
A Real-world example
Orders
Line items
For every order in a database, there are 1-many line items associated with that order
OracleAS Portal
OralcleAS Portal Page
Region
OracleAS Portal Portlet
For every OracleAS Portal page, there are 1-many regions associated with that page. For each region, there are 1-many OracleAS portlets associated with that region

FIGURE 8-2. *One-to-many relationship between pages, regions, and portlets*

The many-to-many relationship is slightly different than the one-to-many relationship discussed earlier. In this example, one region may have many portlets placed on it, but a portlet may be placed on one or many different regions on different pages. Item regions have the same many-to-many relationship: an item region may contain many items and a single item may be placed on more than one region.

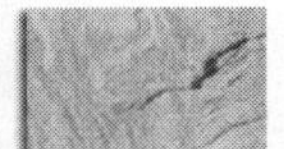

NOTE
What, exactly, are items? To fully understand items, we must take a step back and look at the definition of a portal. In the most general sense, a portal is a highly trafficked web site with a wide range of content, services, and vendor links. It acts as a middleman by selecting the content sources and assembling them in a simple-to-navigate, customizable interface for presentation to the end user. Based on this definition, there are many pieces that constitute a typical portal that don't fit into traditional programming constructs like forms or reports. A good example might be a company's internal portal site that delivers private company information to its employees. Some of these portal elements may be things like Microsoft Word documents or Adobe Portable Document Format (PDF) files that outline company policies. The designers of Oracle Application Server Portal were smart enough to know that some (if not most) information included in a typical portal would be nonstructured data like the aforementioned Word documents or PDF files. Item regions hold these nonstructured items and are discussed in detail in Chapter 10.

One of the many benefits of developing in Oracle Application Server Portal is the ability to display pages with certain elements shown and others hidden based on the privileges of the user signing in to your portal. These changes are handled by Oracle Application Server Portal automatically and require no additional programming from the developer. As an example, let's log in to Oracle Application Server Portal as if we were going to begin our Oracle Application Server Portal development work. You can log in by either clicking the small Login link on the top right of the page, or by clicking the Login link under the Login to OracleAS Portal portlet on the top left of the page. By default, a couple of Oracle Application Server Portal logins are created for you automatically when you install Oracle Application Server Portal. In the login screen, login with the username of portal (without the quotes). The password will be the same as the password given when you or your administrator installed the Oracle Application Server 10*g* Application Server middle tier.

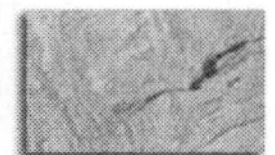

NOTE
The portal user in Oracle Application Server Portal is similar to the sys user in the database. It has every privilege within Oracle Application Server Portal and should be used very sparingly. Just like the sys user in the database, you should never create Oracle Application Server Portal objects as the portal user. The portal user should be used for system administration purposes only.

After a successful login, you should see a page similar to Figure 8-3.

The page looks similar to Figure 8-1 and, in fact, the URL is exactly the same. But if you look closely, you'll notice that there are many new elements on the page. On the top right of the page there are many more links. Previously, only Home, Builder, Help, and Logon were displayed. Now, Navigator, Edit, Customize, and Account Info are displayed and the Login link has been replaced with the Logout link. We also have three tabs along the top right: Welcome, Build, and Administer. Finally, the login portlet on the top left of the page has been replaced with a Quick Tips portlet. This is an example of how your Oracle Application Server Portal pages can be designed to behave differently depending on who is looking at them, with no additional programming whatsoever. When we first viewed the Welcome page, we had not authenticated ourselves to Oracle Application Server Portal (authenticated is a fancy word for logging in). After we logged in, we became part of an Oracle Application Server group called the Authenticated Users group. As a member of that group, we saw a different version of the page. Our user login portal also gave us privileges to see other aspects of the page.

A Quick Tour of Oracle Application Server Portal Pages

There are so many pages and tabs available to developers after they log in to Oracle Application Server Portal, it is easy to become quickly overwhelmed. This section will walk through the basic Oracle Application Server Portal pages and give a brief explanation of each so that later on, we can easily navigate among them as we visit them in detail.

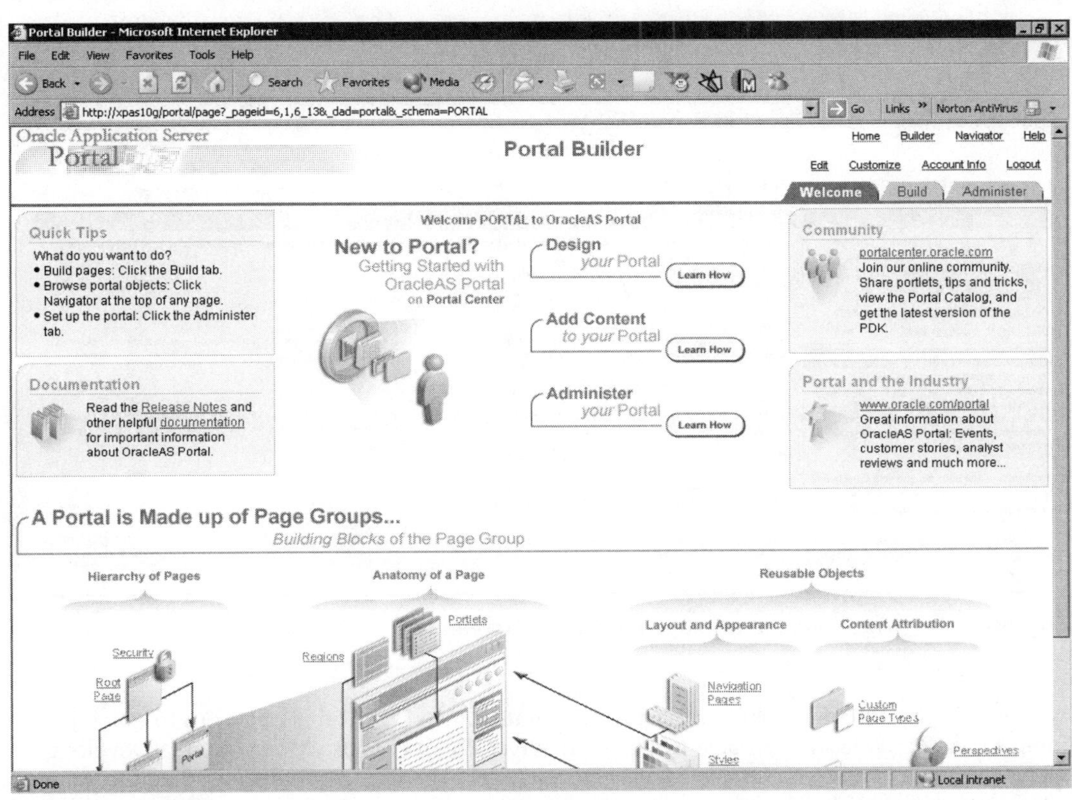

FIGURE 8-3. *The Oracle Application Server Portal welcome page after a successful login*

Like most Oracle development tools, Oracle Application Server Portal provides developers with many ways of performing the basic tasks of Oracle Application Server Portal development and administration. None of these methods are the right way of doing things—they are simply different techniques for accomplishing your development goals that give developers the ability to choose which methods are suitable for them. Some of the methods require more steps than others, so after exploring the different methods, we will (generally) use those techniques requiring the fewest number of steps.

As the portal user, you have all privileges in Oracle Application Server Portal. As we have already discussed, Oracle Application Server Portal pages display different elements based on privileges granted to the user logging in, so many of these pages will look subtlety different if you should log on as a different user. Clicking the Build tab in the top right will display a page similar to the one in Figure 8-4.

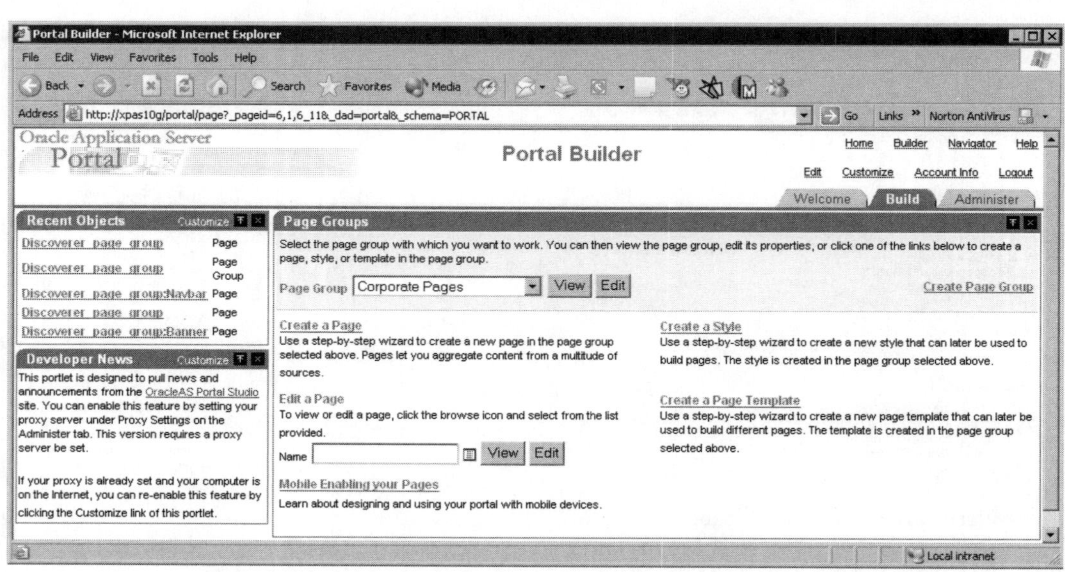

FIGURE 8-4. *The Build tab displayed in Oracle Application Server Portal*

On this page, there are three portlets—a Recent Objects portlet that allows us to quickly jump to one of the last five Oracle Application Server Portal objects we've edited, a Developer News portlet with a link to Oracle's Portal Development site (http://portalcenter.oracle.com), and a portlet that allows developers to work with Page Groups—along with the banner page element discussed earlier. Page Groups are at the top of the hierarchy in Figure 8-2. Pages are children of Page Groups and cannot, therefore, exist without them. Every Page Group has a default root page and any attribute defined for a Page Group automatically cascades down to its Pages (although many attributes can be overridden at the Page level).

The two portlets on the left-hand side of the page—Recent Objects and Developer News—give an example of Oracle Application Server Portal's security mechanism. Both have a Customize link in their title bars. These Customize links allow end users to change certain characteristics of the portlet. Depending on the privileges granted to a particular user, the Customize links will appear or be hidden. Any changes made to the portlet will be made for that user only. For example, if the portal user chooses to customize the Recent Objects portlet to limit the list to only the three most recent objects (Figure 8-5), another user logging in will still see the five most recent objects in that portlet.

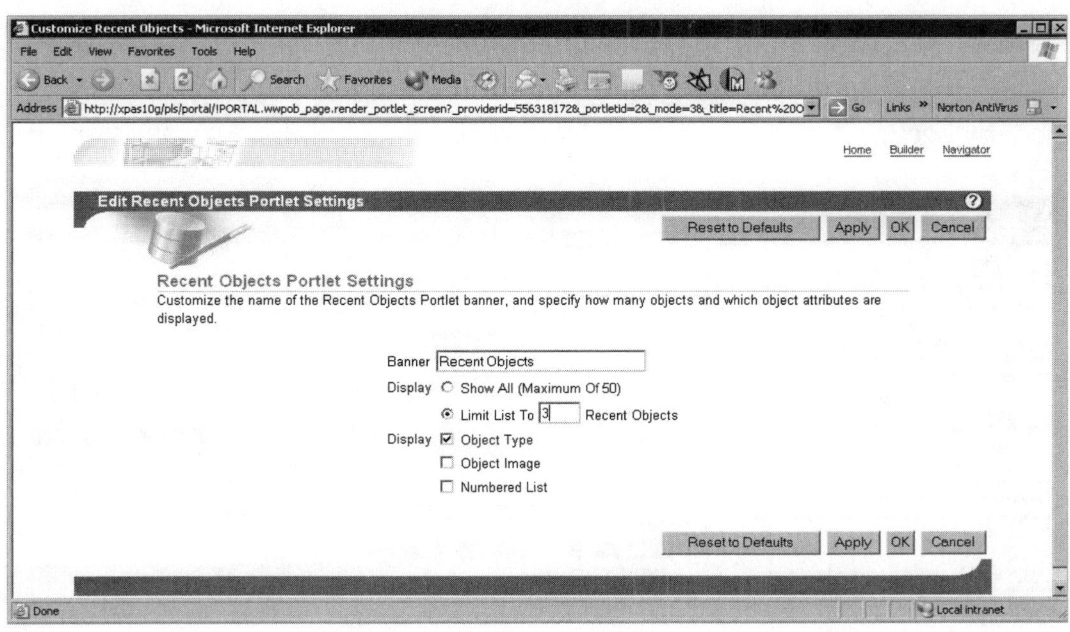

FIGURE 8-5. *The Customize Recent Objects portlet screen*

The third tab in Figure 8-4, Administer, is where Oracle Application Server Portal administrators will spend most of their time. It has three subtabs along the left-hand side: Portal, Portlets, and Database. The Portal subtab (see Figure 8-6) has portlets that allow administrators to change the basic functionality of the Oracle Application Server Portal as a whole. The Portlets subtab (see Figure 8-7) has portlets that allow administrators to display the Portlet Repository and to define remote providers. The portlets on these two subtabs will be discussed in Chapter 10.

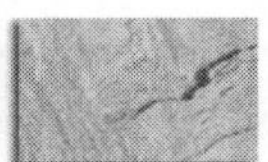

NOTE
A provider can be thought of as a way of grouping portlets together. Any attribute assigned to the provider will cascade down to the portlets in that provider (unless it's overridden by the portlet). In addition, providers are also members of provider groups, which can also define attributes. This is yet another example of the one-to-many relationships that you will find throughout the Oracle Application Server Portal product. The provider is the parent, and the Oracle Application Server Portal components (forms, reports, graphs, etc.) that can eventually become portlets are the children.

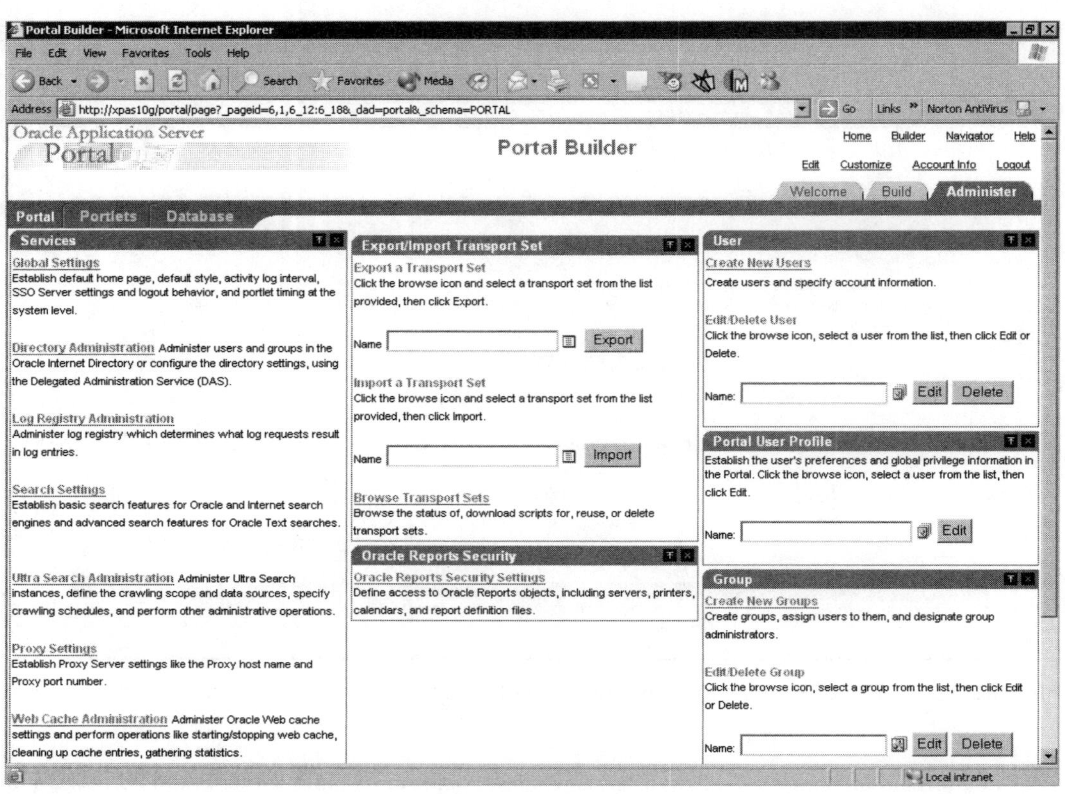

FIGURE 8-6. *The Portal subtab in the Administer tab*

The last subtab, Database (see Figure 8-8), allows administrators to create and modify both database objects and rows within a table. This functionality is limited to the infrastructure database.

Here is another example of Oracle Application Server Portal's security mechanism: Out of the box, Oracle Application Server Portal defines Groups that have various privileges within Oracle Application Server Portal (the portal user, of course, has all privileges). Becoming a member of any Oracle Application Server Portal group automatically grants all privileges to that user. Three of the basic groups defined during the install of Oracle Application Server Portal are: PORTAL_ADMINISTRATORS, PORTAL_DEVELOPERS, and PORTLET_PUBLISHERS. The Oracle Application Server Portal elements on each of the tabs displayed along the top of the page will differ depending on what groups the Oracle Application Server Portal user is assigned to. As an example, if a user is only a member of the PORTAL_DEVELOPERS group, nothing will be displayed in the Database subtab of the Administer tab. In general, these default groups were set up with the following privileges and for the following reasons:

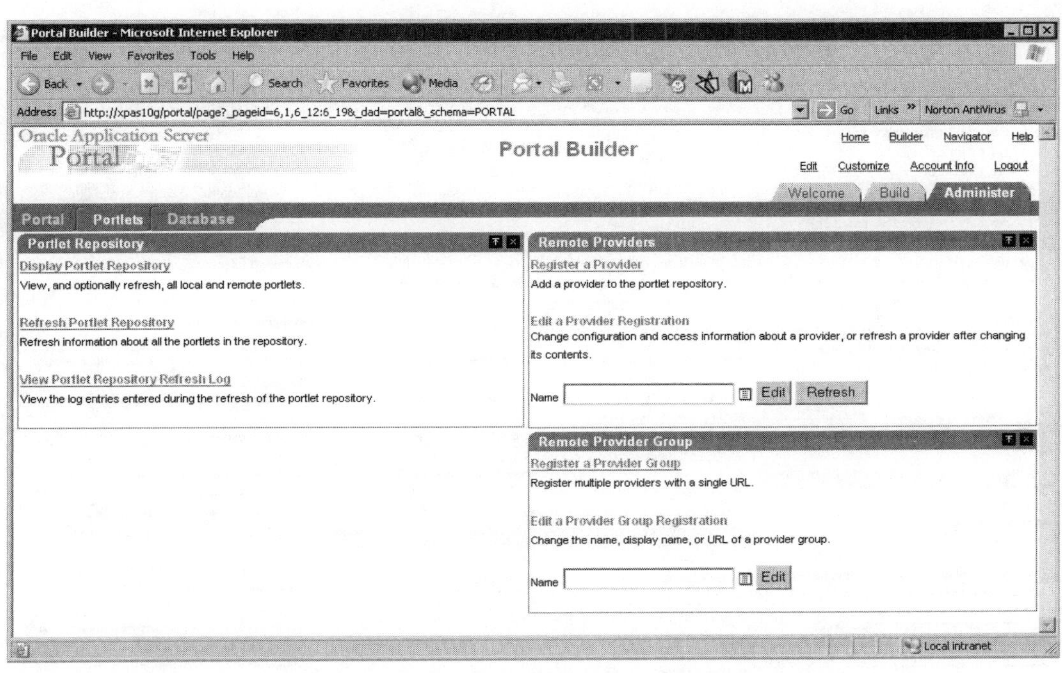

FIGURE 8-7. *The Portlets subtab in the Administer tab*

- **PORTAL_DEVELOPERS** Users in this group can create portlets, but cannot place them on a page. In general, users in this group are usually more concerned with the functionality of the various portlets that will make up an Oracle Application Server Portal site and less concerned with the look and feel of a site.
- **PORTLET_PUBLISHERS** Users in this group can take developed portlets and place them on a page, and can construct pages and page templates but cannot create new portlets. In general, users in this group are generally more concerned with the aesthetics of a portal site and less concerned with the code that makes up the various portlets to be placed on a site.
- **PORTLET_ADMINISTRATORS** Users in this group have responsibilities across all facets of the site, including creation and deletion of users and groups, design and code modifications, and overall Oracle Application Server Portal functionality. In general, users in this group have control over all aspects of the Oracle Application Server Portal site.

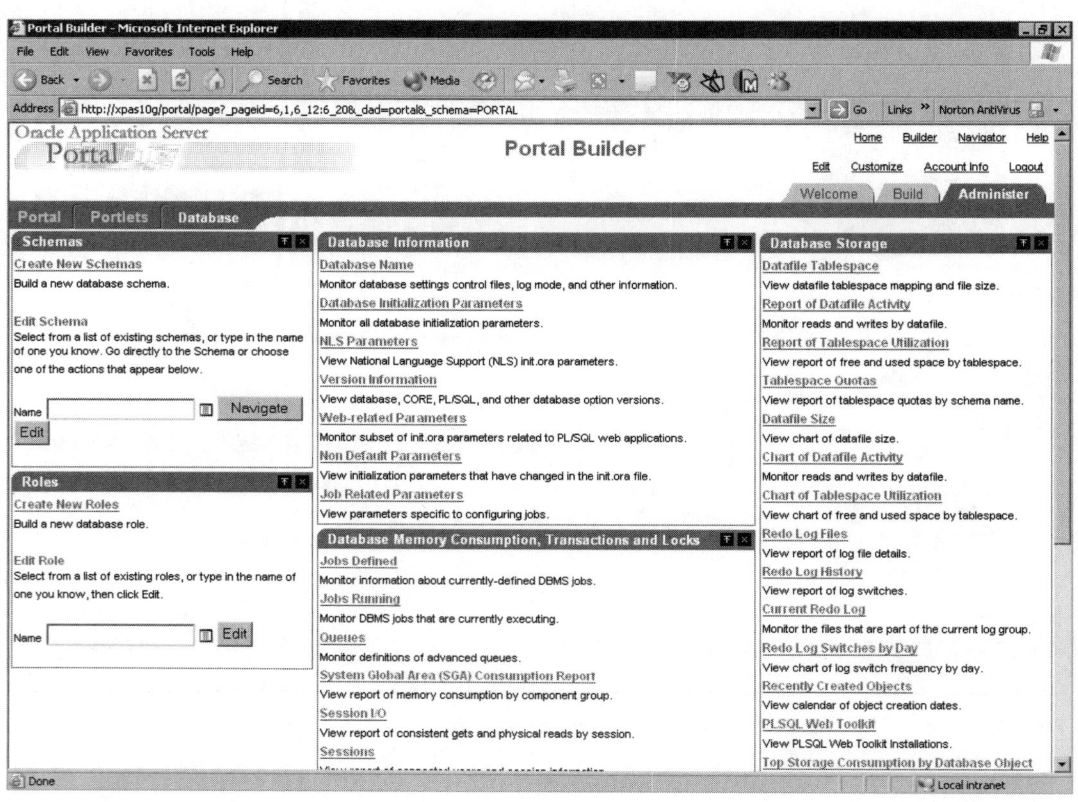

FIGURE 8-8. *The Database subtab in the Administer tab*

You are not limited to these groups as you can create other groups that have distinct privileges and assign users to these groups. At some sites, there may be a group of portlet users that are in charge of both designing portlets and placing them on pages. In this case, a new group with the privileges of both PORTAL_DEVELOPERS and PORTLET_PUBLISHERS can be created and users can be assigned to that (or, users can just be assigned to both groups). If you have a really small amount of administrators and developers at your Oracle Application Server Portal site, you may not even need groups at all, as you can assign these privileges directly to Oracle Application Server Portal users.

The Navigator

Up until this point, we have seen pages where developers can create users and groups, page groups, register providers, and change Oracle Application Server Portal settings and database objects among other things. What we haven't seen is the ability to design pages or create Oracle

Application Server portlets such as forms and reports. To do those things, we'll need to explore another major piece of Oracle Application Server Portal: the Oracle Application Server Portal Navigator.

The Oracle Application Server Portal Navigator (see Figure 8-9) is where developers will spend most of their time. Its three tabs, Page Groups, Providers, and Database Objects, allow developers to create, modify, and delete all of the Oracle Application Server Portal objects that make up a portal. Again, only certain tabs and certain options within those tabs will be available to the Oracle Application Server Portal developer based on their privileges. You can exit the Navigator at any time by clicking the Builder link in the top right of the page.

The Page Groups Tab

The Page Groups tab allows the creation of all page elements. On this tab, developers can perform the following actions:

Create a new Page Group This action, which automatically creates the "root" page of that group, is used to define a group that will incorporate pages that make up your portal or a section of your portal. As an example, an organization may have a set of Oracle Application Server Portal pages with a certain look for a corporate office, another set for external suppliers, and other sets of pages for various satellite locations. Any attributes applied at the Page Group level cascade down to all subpages (unless they're overridden at the subpage level).

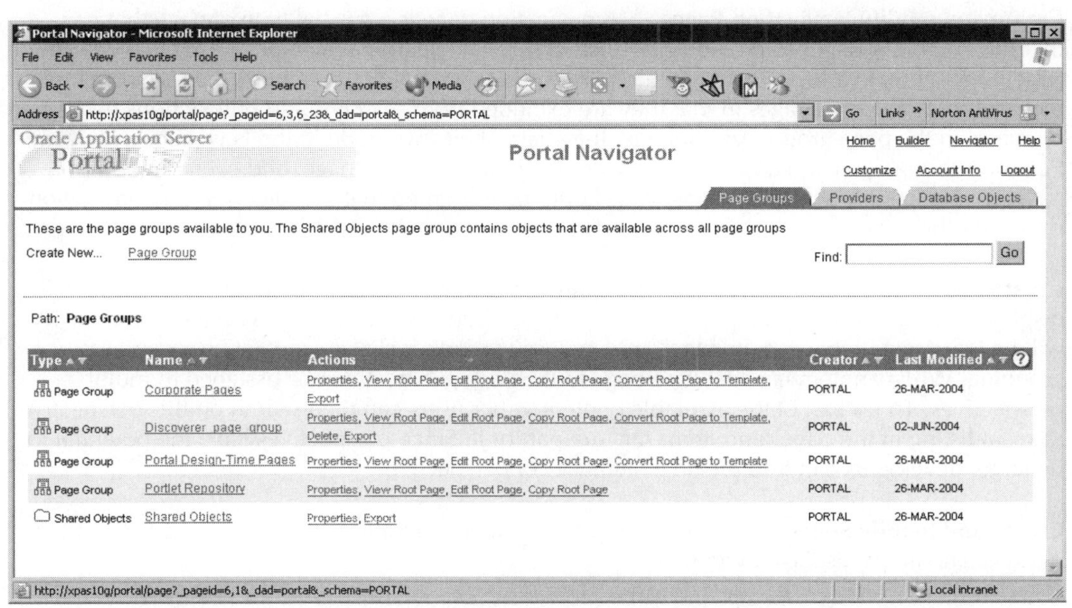

FIGURE 8-9. *The Page Groups tab of the Portal Navigator*

Edit properties of the Page Group This action allows developers to define attributes of the Page Group such as the total amount of disk space used for items placed on pages within this page group, whether privileged users can alter the pages within the Page Group, what types of pages can exist within the Page Group, how items are to be displayed and versioned, if language translations are to be made available, and which users can perform which actions against pages in the page group.

Create new subpages Every page group has a "root" page; other pages can be created as subpages to the root page. A "breadcrumb" menu, showing where the user is in the hierarchy of pages, is generated automatically.

Edit the root page or any of the subpages This is where developers (or, more accurately, those users in the PORTLET_PUBLISHERS group) will design pages and place portlets and items on them.

Create, modify and apply Templates These are used for enforcing a particular layout, style, set of privileges, and content for multiple pages

Create and modify Categories The purpose of categories is to enable users to quickly display a listing of a particular type of content. Categories answer the question, "What is this item or page?" and are used to classify content. For every item or page that you create, you can assign it to one category

Create and modify Navigation Pages A navigation page is a special type of page that can be included on other pages to provide a consistent set of navigational elements. A typical navigation page might contain a logo, the page title, a login link, and a link to the home page. Navigation pages differ from other pages in that they are excluded from searches and bulk actions performed on pages in the page group. Additionally, they have their own node in the Navigator (Navigation Pages). Although you can add any item or portlet to a navigation page, and even divide your navigation page into several regions, you should bear in mind that the idea is to add navigation pages to other pages.

Create and modify Perspectives The purpose of perspectives is to enable users to quickly display a listing of content that is pertinent to them. Perspectives often answer the question, "Who will be interested in this item or page?" and are used to further classify content by a cross-category grouping. When an item is added to a page to the page group, it can be assigned to multiple perspectives. To find all of the available content, other users can then search on this perspective to see a listing of the pages and items that are part of it. Since perspectives have the potential to be large, developers can also create a hierarchy of perspectives.

Create and modify Styles A style controls the colors and fonts used by pages and all the tabs, portlets, and items displayed within them.

Create and modify Attributes There are two types of attributes:

- **Content attributes** These are associated with item types and page types, and store information about an item or page. Administrators can create their own item types and page types and specify what information they want users to supply by choosing which attributes to include. In addition, page group administrators can create their own attributes for containing extra information. The following table lists built-in content attributes:

Attribute	Description
Author	The name of the author of the item.
Category	The name of the category to which the item or page belongs.
Description	A short text description of the item or page.
Display Name	The display name of the item or page.
Display Option	Information about how the item or portlet should be displayed: — Item Displayed Directly In Page Area — Link That Displays Item In Full Browser Window — Link That Displays Item In New Browser Window
Enable Item Check-Out	Information about whether or not the item can be checked out and checked in. This provides document control, allowing groups of users to edit items and not overwrite each other's work. Users cannot edit items that are checked out by another user.
Expiration Period	Information about how long an item should be displayed on a page.
Image	The image associated with the item or page.
Image Alignment	Information about where the item image should appear in the page.
Keywords	Keywords that describe the content or purpose of the item or page. When a user performs a search, the user's search criteria are compared to the keywords to find a match.
Perspectives	The names of the perspectives associated with the item or page.
Publish Date	The date (in the format, DD-MON-YYYY HH12:MI PM) when the item should start being displayed to users.
Rollover Image	The second image associated with the item or page. This image is displayed whenever a user moves the mouse cursor over the original image on a navigation bar or tab.

TABLE 8-1. *Content Attributes*

- **Display attributes** These are associated with regions, and display information about an item or portlet, such as the author, display name, and creation date. Page designers can choose which attributes to display in a region. Some content attributes, such as author and description, are also display attributes. The following table lists built-in display attributes:

Attribute	**Description**
Associated Functions	Links to functions associated with the item if the item is of a custom item type that includes function calls.
Author	The name of the author of the item.
Category	The name of the category to which the item or portlet belongs.
Create Date	The date when the item or portlet was added to the page.
Creator	The user name of the user who added the item or portlet to the page.
Date Updated	The date when the item or portlet was last updated.
Description	The short text description of the item or portlet.
Display Name	The display name of the item or portlet.
Display Name Link	The display name of the item or portlet as a link pointing to the item or portlet content.
Display Name And Image Link	The display name and image of the item or portlet as links pointing to the item or portlet content. If the item has both a display name and an image, these will appear next to each other. If the item does not have an associated image, only the display name will appear.
Document Size	The size of the uploaded file.
Expire Date	The date (in the format, DD-MON-YYYY HH12:MI PM) when the item is due to expire.
Gist	The Gist icon () next to items. Users can click this icon to display an overview of the item created by Oracle Text.
Help URL	The help icon () next to the portlet item. Users can click this icon to display help for the portlet.
Image	The image associated with the item. If the item does not have an associated image, nothing is displayed.
Image Link	The image associated with the item as a link pointing to the item content. If the item does not have an associated image, nothing is displayed.
Image Or Display Name Link	The image associated with the item as a link pointing to the item content. If the item does not have an associated image, the display name is displayed instead.

TABLE 8-2. *Display Attributes*

Attribute	Description
Image URL	The image icon () next to the portlet item. Users can click this icon to display a preview of the portlet.
Item Content	The content of the item.
Keywords	The keywords associated with the item or portlet.
Last Updated By	The user name of the user who last updated the item or portlet.
Mime Type Image	The image associated with the mime type of the uploaded file.
New Item Indicator	The New icon () next to a new item or portlet. Users can click this icon to display a list of all new content in the page group.
Perspectives	The names of the perspectives associated with the item or portlet.
Portlet Content	The portlet itself if the Item Displayed Directly In Page Area display option is selected.
Portlet ID	The ID of the portlet.
Portlet Name	The name of the portlet.
Property Sheet	The Property Sheet icon () next to items and portlets. Users can click this icon to view the properties of an item or portlet.
Provider ID	The ID of the provider.
Provider Name	The name of the provider.
Publish Date	The date when the item is published on the page (i.e., when the item is visible to users in View mode).
Subscribe	The Subscribe () or Unsubscribe () icon next to items. Users can click this icon to subscribe to an item and be notified, via the Notifications portlet, when it is updated.
Themes	The Themes icon () next to items. Users can click this icon to display the nouns and verbs appearing most often within an item.
Translations	A list of the languages in which the item or portlet is available.
Updated Item Indicator	The Recently Updated icon () next to a recently updated item or portlet. Users can click this icon to display a list of all recently updated content in the page group.
Versions	The Versions icon () next to items that have multiple versions. Users can click this icon to view other versions of the item.
View As HTML	The View As HTML icon () next to items. Users can click this icon to view an HTML version of an item.
View As HTML With Highlight	The View As HTML With Highlight icon () next to items. Users can click this icon to view an HTML version of an item with search terms highlighted.

TABLE 8-2. *Display Attributes* (continued)

Create and modify Page Types Page types define the contents of a page and the information that is stored about a page. The information stored about a page is determined by the attributes of the page type. There are five base page types included with Oracle Application Server Portal:

- **Standard** Displays items and portlets
- **URL** Displays the contents of a particular URL
- **Mobile** Displays item and portlets in a hierarchical tree structure for viewing on a mobile device
- **PL/SQL** Displays the results of executing PL/SQL code
- **JSP** Displays the results of executing a Java Server Page (JSP)

In addition to these base page types, developers and page designers can also create custom page types:

Create and modify item types Items are one of the basic components of a portal page. Items in Oracle application Server Portal are based on item types. Item types define the contents of an item and the information that is stored about an item. The information stored about an item is determined by the attributes of the item type. There are two types of item types:

- **Base item types**
- **Extended item types**

Base Item Types Base items can broken down further into two subtypes:

- **Content item types** These allow users to add content (for example, images, documents, or text) to a page. Base content item types are not available for users to add to pages. Oracle Application Server Portal provides extended item types (listed below) that are based on the base content items. The following are the base content item types provided by Oracle:
  - **Base File** Uploads a file and stores it in the page group.
  - **Base Image Map** Uploads an image and allows the contributor to identify areas within the image that users can click to go to different URLs.
  - **Base Image** Uploads an image and stores it in the page group.
  - **Base PL/SQL** Executes PL/SQL code and displays the results.
  - **Base Page Link** Links to another page in the page group.
  - **Base Text** Displays text (up to 32KB).
  - **Base URL** Links to another web page, web site, or document
- **Navigation item types** These allow users to add navigational elements (for example, a login/logout link, basic search box, or list of objects) to a page. The following are the base navigation item types provided by Oracle:

- **Portal Smart Link** Adds a smart link (and associated image) to the page. A smart link is a link that users can click to access areas of the Oracle Application Server Portal quickly, such as Account Information, Advanced Search, Contact Information, Help, and Home.
- **Login/Logout Link** Adds links and/or icons to the page that users can click to log in or log out of the portal.
- **Basic Search Box** Adds a basic search box (and associated image) to the page in which users can enter search criteria. Users can specify whether users of the search box can search all page groups or only the page group specified.
- **List of Objects** Adds a list of objects (pages, categories, and perspectives) that users specify to the page. Users can choose to display this list as a drop-down list or as links (with or without associated images).
- **Portal Smart Text** Adds smart text, such as the current date, current user, or current page to the page.
- **Object Map Link** Adds a map of objects available in the portal.
- **Page Path** Adds the page path to the page. Users can choose the number of levels for the path, and the character that separates the path levels.
- **Page Function** Adds a page function to the page. If there are no page functions associated with the current page, this item type is not displayed.

Extended item types These types are available to users to add to pages:

- **File and Simple File**
- **Simple Image**
- **Image and Simple Image Map**
- **PL/SQL and Simple PL/SQL**
- **Page Link and Simple Page Link**
- **Text and Simple Text**
- **URL and Simple URL**
- **Zip File**

The Providers Tab

As we mentioned earlier, a provider can be thought of as a way of grouping portlets together. On the Provider tab of the Navigator in Figure 8-10, you can see that there are three categories of providers available to you:

- **Locally Built Providers** This is where developers will define providers when they are ready to build Oracle Application Server Portal objects such as Oracle Application Server Portal forms, reports, and graphs.

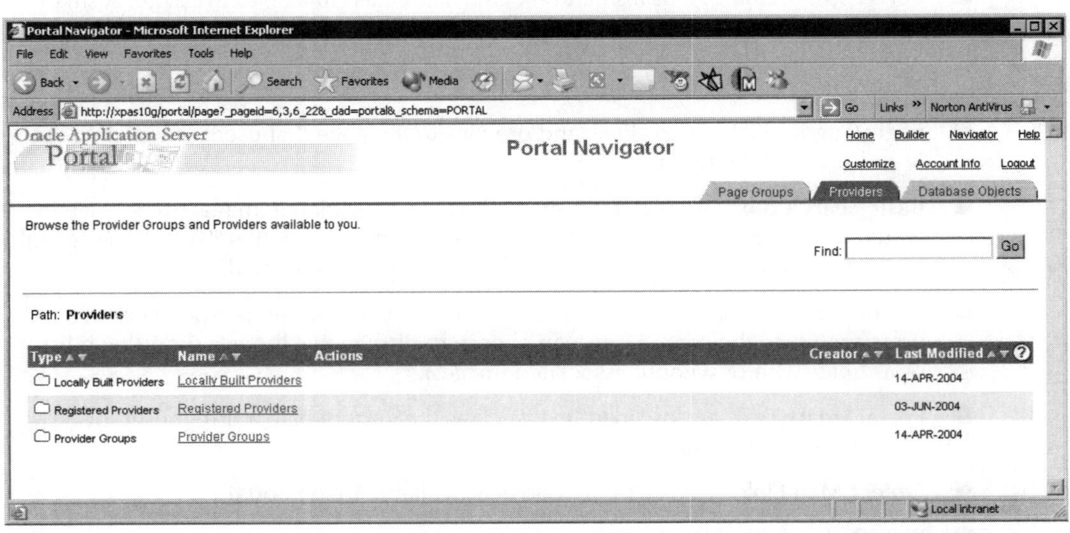

FIGURE 8-10. *The Providers tab of the Oracle Application Server Portal Navigator*

- **Registered Providers** This is where providers built outside of Oracle Application Server Portal are.
- **Provider Groups** A provider group is a mechanism for organizing and simplifying the registration of providers. Provider groups often define a group of providers that share a common feature, such as belonging to the same organization, or providing similar content or functions.

The Database Objects Tab

The Database Objects tab allows Oracle Application Server Portal users with the necessary privileges to manipulate database objects in the infrastructure database (see Figure 8-11). Some of the actions that can be performed include:

- Creating new schemas
- Creating and modifying these database objects: tables, views, procedures, functions, packages, sequences, synonyms, indexes, triggers, database links, Java objects, and scripts
- Querying rows in tables and views
- Modifying columns and column attributes
- Modifying rows in tables and views
- Viewing able constraints and column attributes

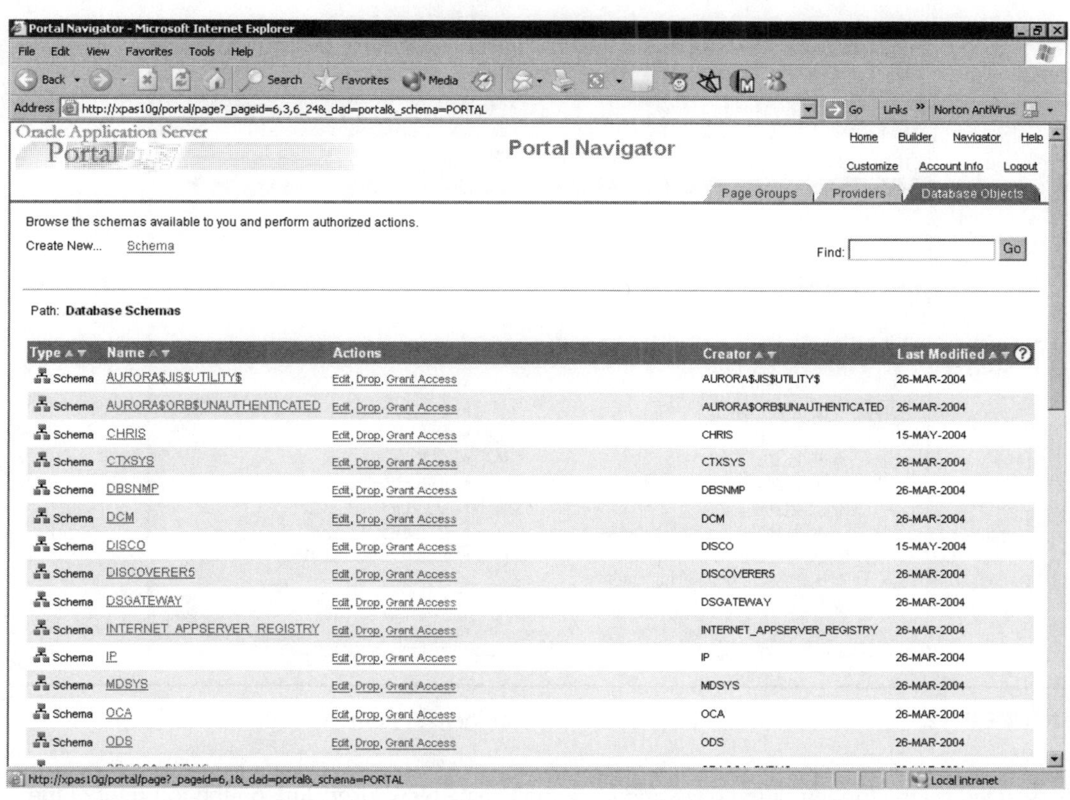

FIGURE 8-11. *The Database Objects tab of the Oracle Application Server Portal Navigator*

The Help System

Last, but certainly not least, is the Oracle Application Server Portal Help system (see Figure 8-12). Oracle has greatly improved the help system included with Oracle Application Server Portal, although it is important to note that it is not context-sensitive. Selecting the Help icon on any Oracle Application Server Portal screen will bring you to the window pictured in Figure 8-12. The Search tab on this page is invaluable, as it allows developers to search through all of the Oracle Application Server Portal documentation in one place.

Creating an Oracle Application Server Portal User

The first order of business we should take care of is the creation of a user to develop Oracle Application Server Portal objects. The creation of initial users is one of the main reasons you would ever log in to your portal as the portal user. Assuming you are still logged in as the portal user, click the Administer tab on the top right of the Welcome page. Make sure the Portal subtab

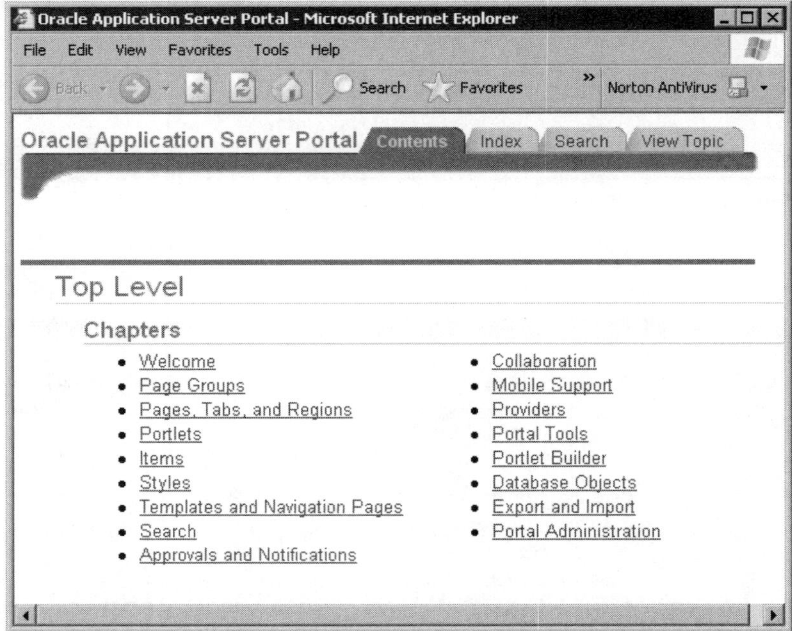

FIGURE 8-12. *The Oracle Application Server Portal help system*

is selected on the top left of the page and click the Create New Users link on the top right of the page. After selecting that link, your browser will be directed to a long URL that starts something like this:

http://<infrastructure server>:<infrastructure port>/oiddas/ui/oracle/ldap/das/user/AppCreateUserInfoAdmin …

The examples in the chapter have been taken from a server named xpas10*g* with both the infrastructure (port 7777) and the middle tier (port 7778) installed on it. On this machine, the redirected URL begins like this:

http://xpas10g:7777/oiddas/ui/oracle/ldap/das/user/AppCreateUserInfoAdmin …

It is important to note this for the following reason: when we're creating Oracle Application Server Portal users, we're creating users in Oracle's implementation of the Lightweight Directory Access Protocol (LDAP) standard, Oracle Internet Directory. Creating an Oracle Application Server Portal user does not create a user in the Infrastructure database.

LDAP stands Lightweight Directory Access Protocol, and it is a set of protocols for accessing information directories. LDAP is based on the standards contained within the X.500 standard, but is significantly simpler. And unlike X.500, LDAP supports TCP/IP, which is necessary for any type of Internet access. LDAP makes it possible for almost any application running on virtually any computer platform to obtain directory information, such as e-mail addresses and public keys. Because LDAP is an open protocol, applications need not worry about the type of server hosting the directory.

NOTE
You can also create and edit Oracle Internet Directory users at any time by going to http://<infrastructure server>:<infrastructure port>/oiddas. The root user for Oracle Internet Directory is orcladmin and the password will be the same one assigned to the infrastructure instance during installation of the infrastructure.

We will now create users to handle the various tasks associated with development and administration of our portal. After selecting the Create New Users link, you should see a page similar to the one in Figure 8-13. On this page, you will create a new user and assign privileges that will allow that user to create Oracle Application Server Portal components. Fill in the required fields for a user you will use for Oracle Application Server Portal development and click the Roles Assignment link (see Figure 8-14).

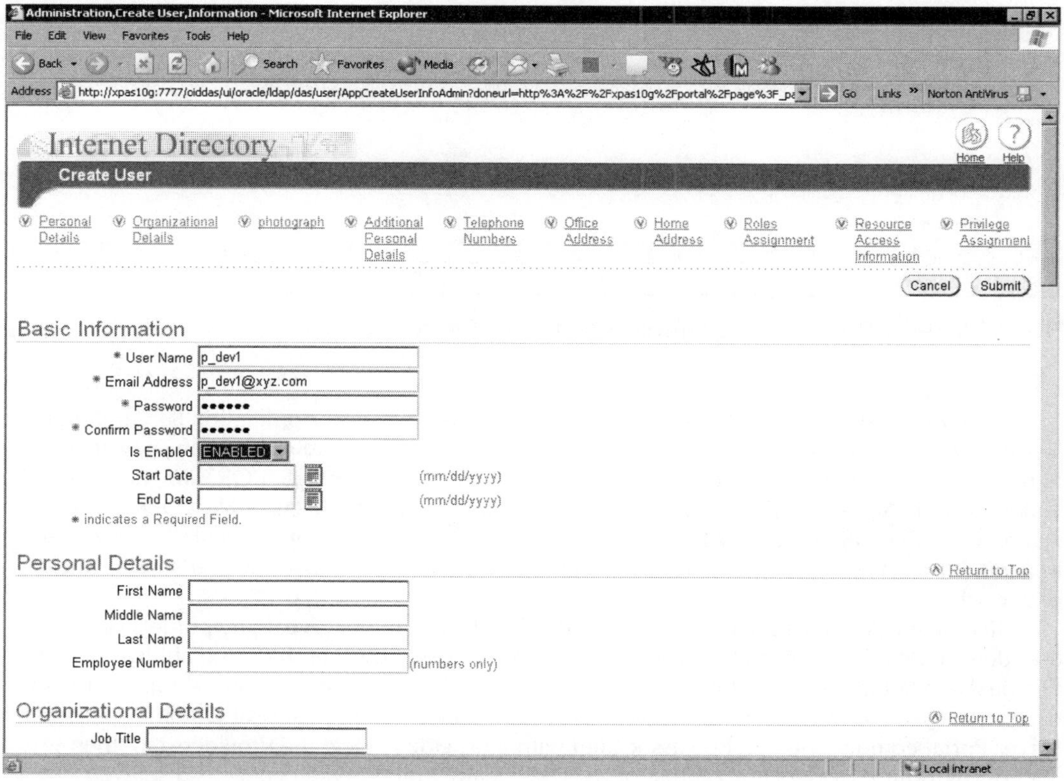

FIGURE 8-13. *The Create User page of the Oracle Internet Directory*

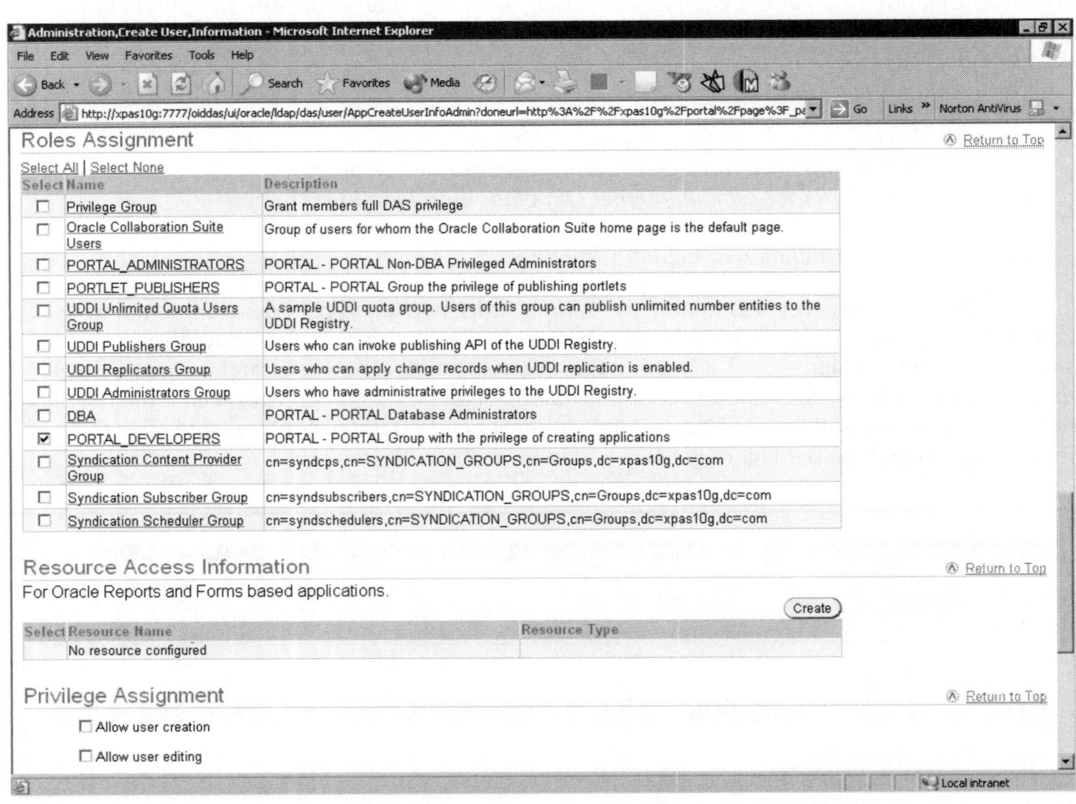

FIGURE 8-14. *The Roles Assignment section of the Create User page*

Figure 8-14 lists the default roles that are provided when Oracle Application Server Portal is installed. You are not limited to these default roles; you can create your own. For now, pay attention to the roles listed earlier in this chapter, namely PORTAL_DEVELOPERS, PORTLET_PUBLISHERS, and PORTLET_ADMINISTRATORS. Click the check box next to PORTAL_DEVELOPERS, as in Figure 8-14. Click the Return to Top link, and then click the Submit link to create the new user. In another browser, log in to Oracle Application Server Portal with this new user's name and password.

Clicking the Administration tab and then the Database will not reveal any portlets since this user does not have administration privileges. This user does, however, have the ability to create Oracle Application Server Portal components. Click on the Navigator link on the top right of the page to be taken to the Oracle Application Server Portal Navigator. Since all Oracle Application Server Portal components must be associated with a provider, select the Providers tab, then select the Locally Built Providers link on that page. The Locally Built Providers page is displayed (see Figure 8-15), but it contains no links to create a new provider. This is one of the security features that frustrate many new Oracle Application Server Portal developers. Instead of presenting a link or option that brings you to a page or screen explaining the fact that the Oracle Application Server Portal user does not have sufficient privileges to perform an action, the link or option simply is not displayed on the screen. The user we have created has been granted the privileges in the PORTAL_DEVELOPERS group, which gives us the ability to create Oracle Application Server Portal components, but not Oracle Application Server Providers. Why?

As we will see in the next chapter, the Oracle Application Server Portal wizards that are used to generate forms, reports, and graphs (among other Oracle Application Server Portal components) are really sophisticated code generators. While you have the ability to embed JavaScript code with your Oracle Application Server Portal Forms and Reports, the majority of code that will drive your portal will be PL/SQL code. This PL/SQL code needs to be stored somewhere: it is stored in the infrastructure database. When we create an Oracle Application Server Portal Provider, one of the first things we will need to specify is a database schema that this provider is associated with. This database schema is the one that will be used to hold the generated PL/SQL code that makes up the various Oracle Application Server Portal objects that we generate from the wizards. In order to create an Oracle Application Server Provider, we must have access to the database to specify which schema we want to use. In most cases, you would not want to give that privilege to an Oracle Application Server Portal developer, which is why our user does not have the ability to create a new provider.

What if we want that user to have the ability to create a provider? There are a couple of ways to do it. We can either grant a provider privilege explicitly to that user or we can make that user a

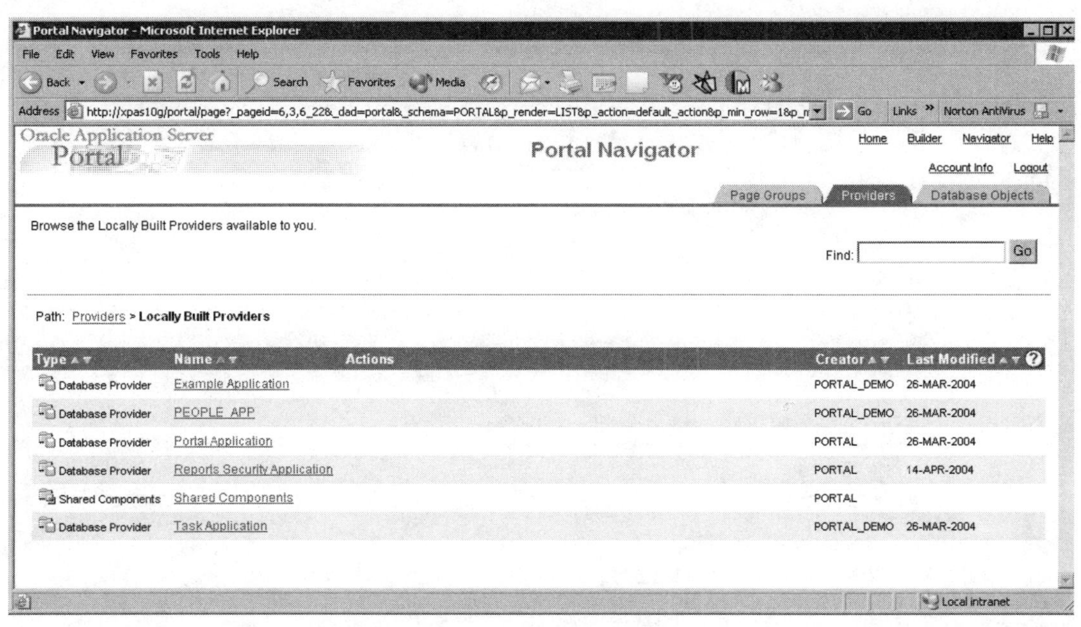

FIGURE 8-15. *The Locally Built Providers page*

member of a group with the necessary provider privilege so that the user implicitly gets the necessary privilege. Let's look at explicitly granting the privilege first.

Log into Oracle Portal Provider Portal as a user with administration privileges (you can use the portal user we've been using in this chapter). Click the Administer tab. On the right-hand side of the screen, you'll see four portlets: User, Portal User Profile, Group, and Portal Group Profile. To change the Oracle Application Server Portal privileges for a user, you might think you need to go into the User portlet, but you would be incorrect. The User portlet is only used for things like the Oracle Application Server Portal user's personal information (username, password, group memberships, etc.). To edit an Oracle Application Server Portal user's privileges, we will use the Portal User Profile portlet. Click the small icon between the Name: field and the Edit button to bring up a list of Oracle Application Server Portal users defined on your system. Select the user that was just created and click Select to close the selection window. Click the Edit button to bring up the Edit Portal User screen. Click the Privileges tab to display privileges for that user (see Figure 8-16).

It looks like this user does not have any privileges to do anything in our portal, but remember that the user inherits the privileges of any group they are assigned to. In this case, no explicit

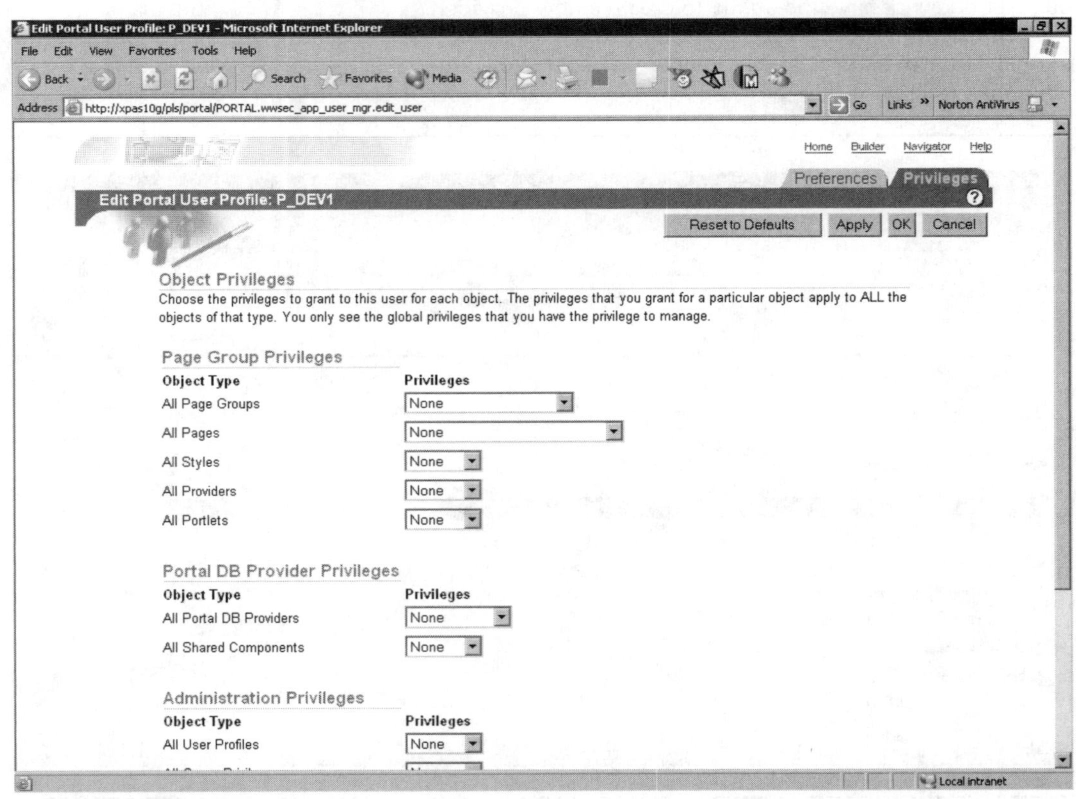

FIGURE 8-16. *The Privileges tab of the Edit Portal User Profile screen*

privileges have been assigned to this user, but he has implicitly inherited the privileges from the PORTAL_DEVELOPERS group. Click the Builder link on the top right of the screen, then click the small icon between the Name: field and the Edit button in the Portal Group Profile portlet at the bottom of the page. Select the PORTAL_DEVELOPERS group, click the Edit, and select the Privileges page. As you can see in Figure 8-17, members of the PORTAL_DEVELOPERS group have the ability to Create Oracle Application Server Providers.

So what's going on here? We know that the user we have just created is a member of the PORTAL_DEVELOPERS group and that the PORTAL_DEVELOPERS group has the ability to create providers. Why doesn't the Create Provider link show up when we log in as that user? Remember we said that providers must be associated with a database schema so that the PL/SQL packages that are generated from the various Oracle Application Server Portal wizards can be stored? The Oracle Application Server Portal user must have privileges on those schemas so that these packages can be created. We must grant an additional privilege to this Oracle Application Server Portal user so that they may create providers. On the Administration tab and on the Portal subtab, type the name of your Oracle Application Server Portal user in the name field of the Portal User Profile portlet and click Edit. On the Privileges tab, select the drop-down box next to All Schemas. You'll

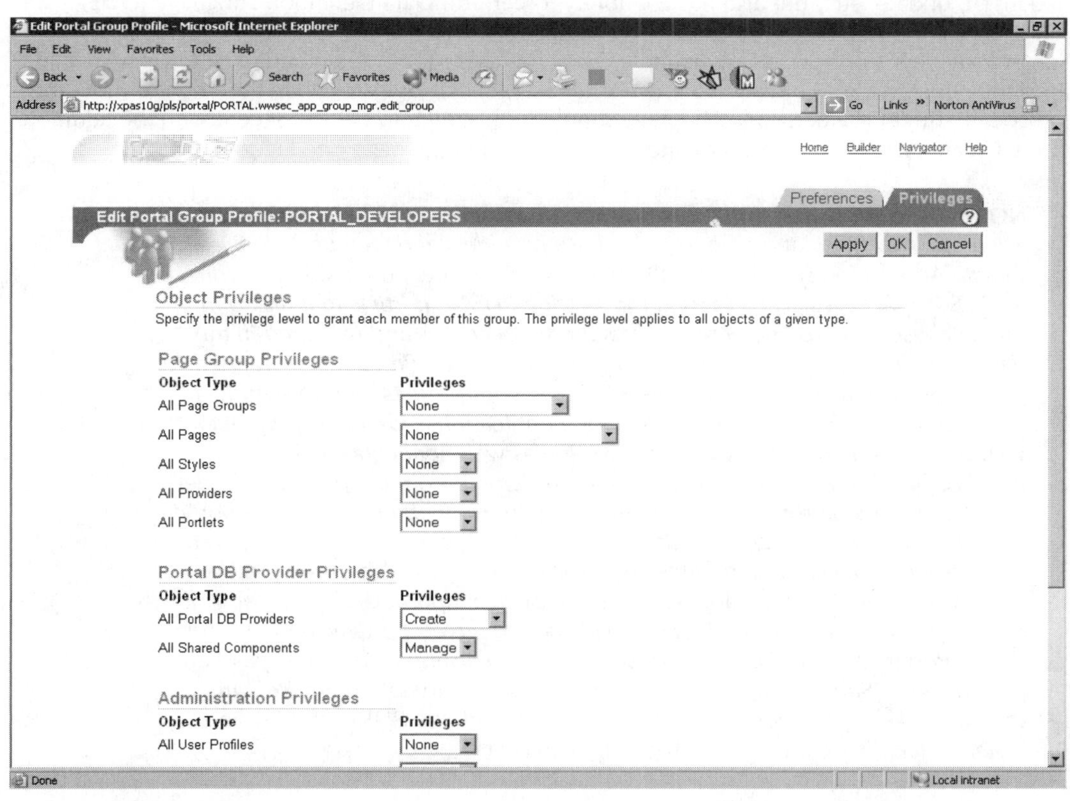

FIGURE 8-17. *The Privileges tab for the PORTAL_DEVELOPERS group*

see six options: Create, View Data, Insert Data, Modify Data, Manage, and None. The order in which they are listed is a little confusing: moving from the bottom of the list (Create) up, the privileges encompass more and more capabilities, except for the topmost selection (None), which revokes all privileges. It would seem to make more sense to put None at the bottom of the list, but it is at the top for all drop-down boxes on this page.

Create gives the Oracle Application Server Portal user the ability to create a new schema in the infrastructure database, but nothing else. View Data gives the Oracle Application Server Portal user the ability to create a schema and to query the data in that schema, but no privileges to add or insert data. Insert Data has all of the privileges of those below it, plus the ability to insert data into the schema. Granting our Oracle Application Server Portal user any of the three privileges we've mentioned will not give the user the ability to create an Oracle Application Server Portal Provider. Providers not only need the ability to view and insert data as various elements of the Oracle Application Server Portal components are created, but also need the ability to modify data in that schema as Oracle Application Server Portal components are changed and updated. We need a privilege higher than Insert Data before our Oracle Application Server Portal user will have the ability to create providers. The last two options—Modify Data, which has all of the privileges below it plus the ability to actually modify data in the schemas, and Manage, which has the ability to not only perform Data Manipulation Language (DML) statements like insert, update, etc., but also has the ability to perform Data Definition Language (DDL) statements like Create Index—give the necessary privileges for our user to create Oracle Application Server Providers. For now, as an example, grant the user Modify Data and click OK. Log back in as the new Oracle Application Server Portal user, click Navigator, then the Providers tab, then the Locally Built Providers link. The page should look similar to before, except with the addition of the Create New… Database Provider link at the top of the page (see Figure 8-18).

NOTE

There are two types of providers—database providers and web providers—in Oracle Application Server Portal. Database providers are those packages written as PL/SQL packages. They're used for creating PL/SQL portlets that reside in the database and are implemented as stored procedures and executed in the database. They can be written in PL/SQL or Java Stored Procedures wrapped in PL/SQL. You use PL/SQL portlets whenever your portlets require significant database interaction or when the development team has Oracle experience. web providers are those applications written as web applications. They are installed and hosted on a web server and are remote from the portal. A portlet exposed as a web provider can be developed in any web language. The portal communicates to the web provider using the HTTP protocol. There are several benefits when developing portlets and exposing them as web providers: You can leverage existing web application code to create portlets, manage outside of Oracle Application Server Portal, provide hosted servers for Oracle Application Server Portal users, and create portlets using any existing web language. Web providers use Simple Object Access Protocol (SOAP) to communicate with the Portal. Web providers, such as OC4J (along with the PDK) can also be installed locally on the Oracle Application Server.

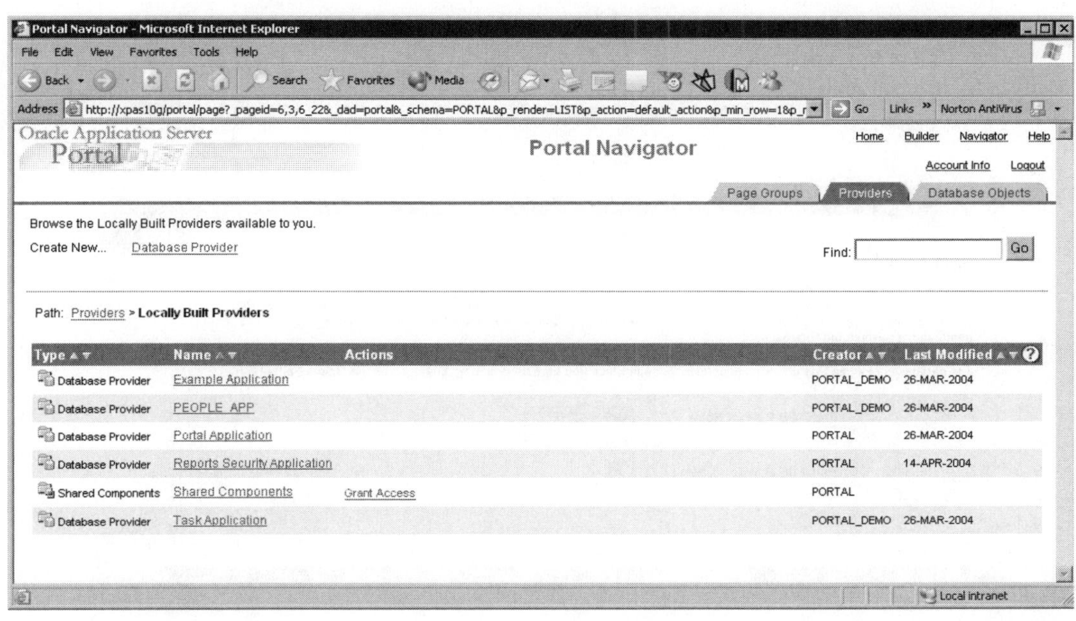

FIGURE 8-18. *The Locally Built Providers page of the Portal Navigator with the Create New Database Provider link available*

The example we just discussed illustrates how tightly security is built into Oracle Application Server Portal. It also serves to demonstrate that it is not always intuitively obvious how and where to make the changes necessary to grant access to your Oracle Application Server Portal users.

Now that we have the ability to create providers, let's go ahead and create one to see what options are available to us. As the Oracle Application Server Portal user created in this chapter, click the Navigator link in the top right of the screen, then the Providers tab, then the Database Provider link on the top left of the screen. You should see a screen similar to the one in Figure 8-19.

The first two fields are self-explanatory: the internal name of the application (which cannot contain any spaces or special characters) and the display name of the application (which can contain spaces and special characters and will be what is displayed in the Oracle Application Server Portal Navigator). The third field is more troublesome in this example. It requires us to specify which schema in the infrastructure database we will use to store our PL/SQL packages. As you can see in Figure 8-19, no schemas are available to us, preventing us from continuing. What's happening here?

When we were modifying this user earlier, we gave the Oracle Application Server Portal user the ability to Modify Data in any schema in our infrastructure database. When we use the Oracle Application Server Portal wizards to create forms, reports, graphs, etc., we will need the ability to create various database objects in the schema; granting Modify Data privileges doesn't give us the ability to actually create any new database objects, so no database schemas are available to us.

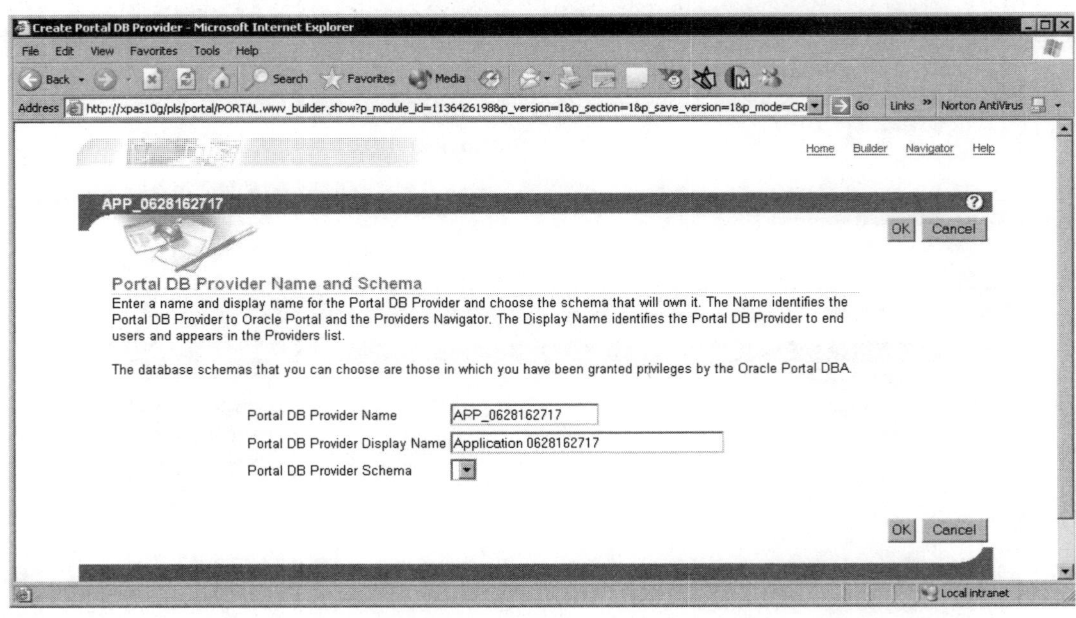

FIGURE 8-19. *The Create Portal Database Provider screen*

So the answer is simple, right? Go back and grant Execute privileges to our Oracle Application Server Portal development user. That will give the Oracle Application Server Portal developer the necessary privileges to create a provider, but that may not be such a great idea, either. By granting that privilege, an Oracle Application Server Portal developer can do anything to any of the schemas in the infrastructure database. The potential for disaster, unintentionally or on purpose, is great in this scenario. A better solution would be to define a schema to hold Oracle Application Server Portal-generated PL/SQL packages and grant privileges on that schema to the necessary Oracle Application Server Portal developer(s).

You can use Oracle Application Server Portal to create a schema in the database. Log in as a user with administration privileges and select the Navigator link. Select the Database Objects link and then the Create New… Schema link. Fill in the necessary fields and make sure the Use this Schema for Portal Users check box is selected. Click Create. Back on the Navigator page, select the Grant Access link next to the schema you just created. You should see a page similar to the one in Figure 8-20. On this page, you can grant privileges to Oracle Application Server Portal user on the selected database schema. Similar to the privileges tab discussed earlier, the privileges you can select on this page (view, insert, modify, and manage) are in order from least powerful (view) to most powerful (manage). Granting view, insert, or modify will not grant enough privileges for the Oracle Application Server Portal user to use this schema to begin creating Oracle Application Server Portal components for a provider. You must grant the Manage privilege for your Oracle Application Server Portal developer to use this schema. Click the Add button before clicking the OK button, which closes the page.

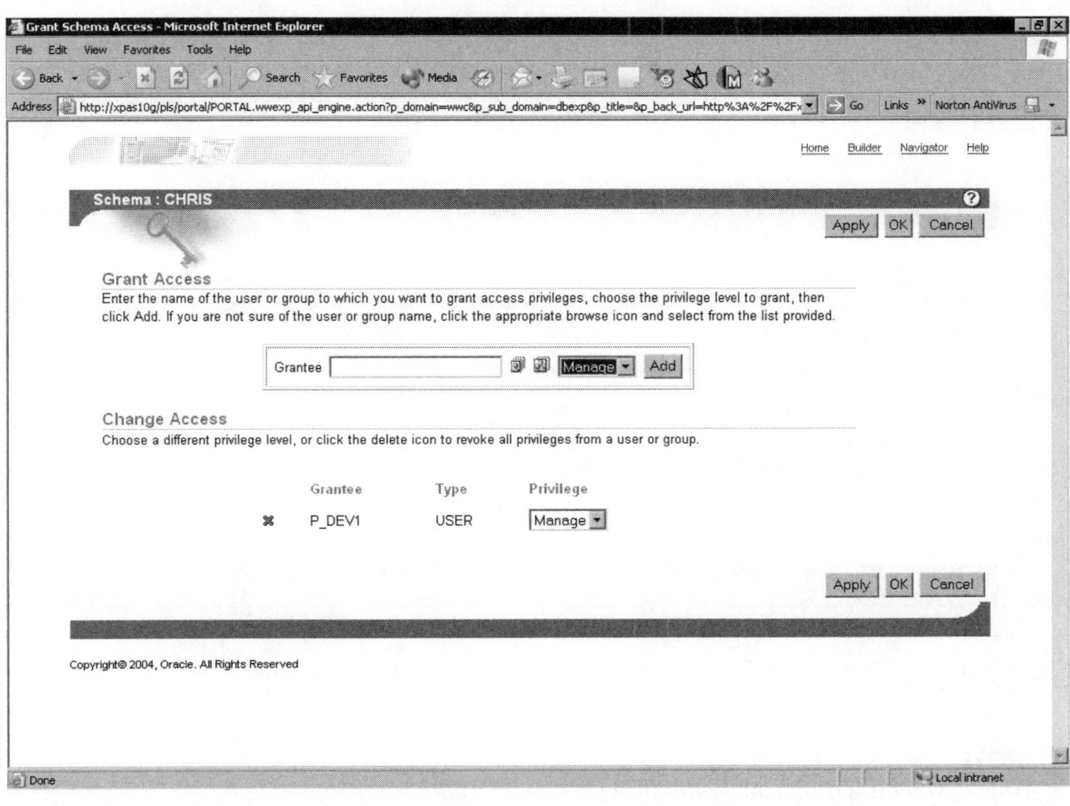

FIGURE 8-20. *The Grant Access page*

Logging back into Oracle Application Server Portal as the developer user, you can now create a new provider using the schema that has been granted the necessary privileges (see Figure 8-21).

The granting of Manage privileges on the Chris schema in the preceding example is all the Oracle Application Server Portal developer user needs to create providers (along with, of course, the Create Provider privilege implicitly granted by being a member of the PORTAL_DEVELOPERS group). There is no need to grant the individual user the Modify Data privilege for all users that we performed earlier (just before Figure 8-18). To keep security tight in your database, it's best to go back and revoke that privilege.

Creating Your First Oracle Application Server Portal Objects

Now that our Oracle Application Server Portal development user has the ability to create a provider, let's go ahead and start creating some Oracle Application Server Portal components. We'll finish the chapter by taking some components and placing them on an Oracle Application Server Portal page.

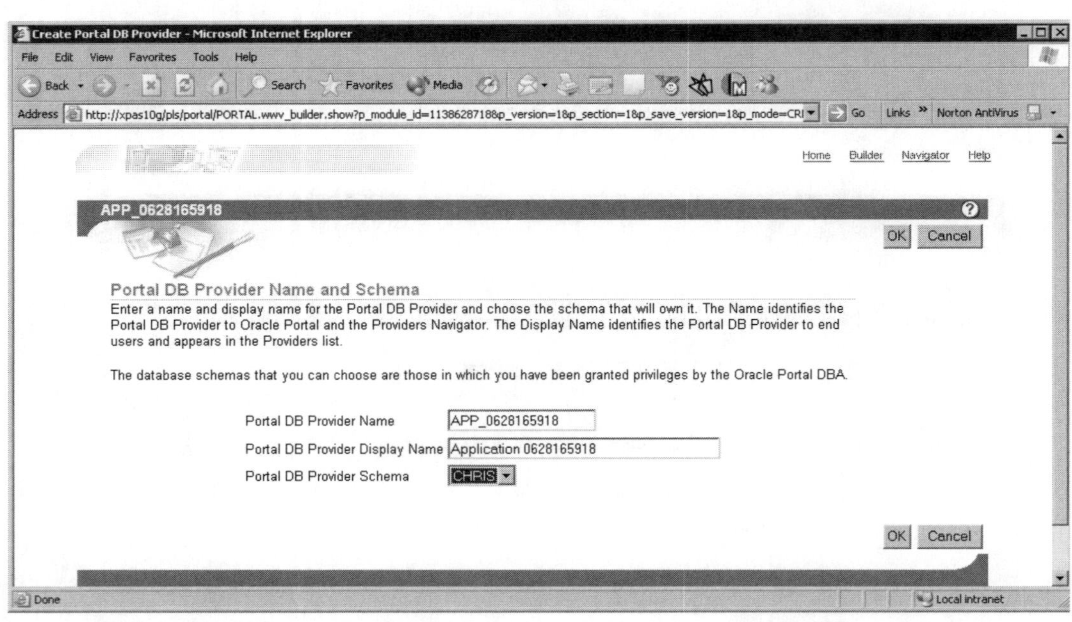

FIGURE 8-21. *The Create Provider page with the available Chris schema*

NOTE
This chapter is a rudimentary trip through Oracle Application Server Portal. In the next chapter, we will discuss the various development options available to developers in depth.

If you are not logged in already, log in as the development user created earlier in this chapter. Select the Navigator link and click the Create New… Database Provider link. Give your Provider a name (no spaces or special characters), a display name, and select a database schema to use for this application (see Figure 8-22). Click OK.

Back in the Oracle Application Server Portal Navigator screen, click the link with your provider's name. You are taken to a navigator page where you can build the following Oracle Application Server Portal objects:

- **Form** The form displays a customized form that can be used as an interface for updating tables, executing stored procedures, and generating other customized forms. You can build three types of forms:
    - A form based on a table or view enables end users to insert, update, and delete data in a database table or view.

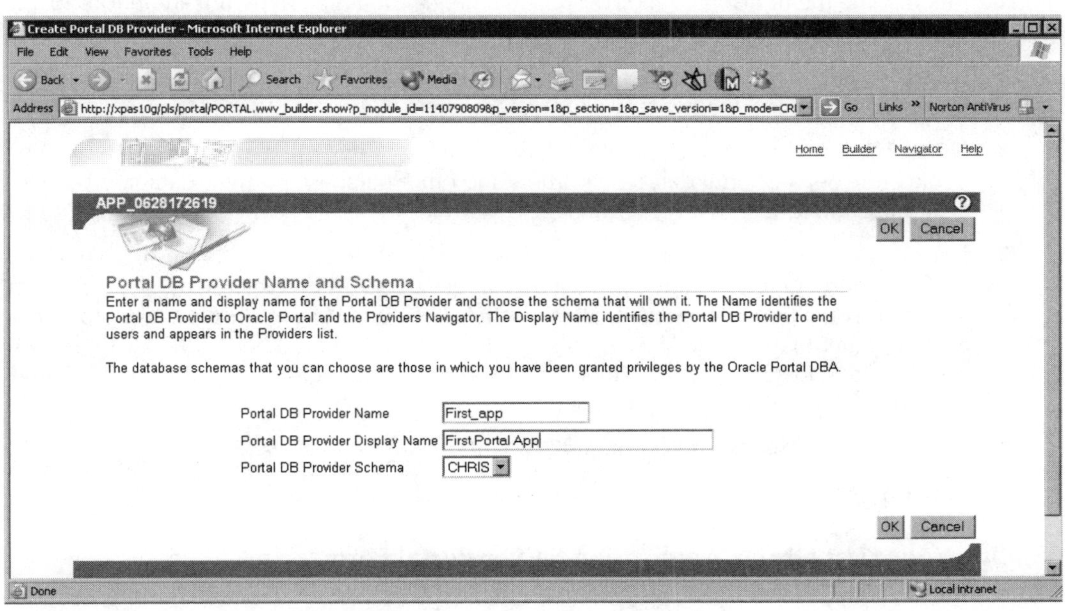

FIGURE 8-22. *The Create Portal DB Provider screen*

- A master-detail form displays a master row and multiple detail rows within a single HTML page. The form contains fields for updating values in two database tables or views.
- A form based on a procedure enables end users to insert, update, and delete data in a database stored procedure.

- **Report** The report displays data you select from the database table or view in a report. It can have a tabular, form, or custom layout.
- **Chart** The chart displays data you select from a database table or view as a bar chart. You can also create Java-based image charts.
- **Data component** The data component displays data in spreadsheet format.
- **Calendar** The calendar displays data you select from a database table or view as a calendar.
- **Dynamic page** The dynamic page displays dynamically-generated HTML content on a web page.
- **Hierarchy** The hierarchy displays data you select from a database table or view as a graphical hierarchy of items containing up to three levels.

- **Menu** The menu displays an HTML-based menu containing hyperlinked options to other menus, Oracle Application Server Portal database portlets, or URLs.
- **Frame driver** The frame driver displays a web page with two frames. End-user queries in one frame control the contents of the other frame.
- **Link** The link displays a clickable link that provides a hypertext jump between Oracle application Server Portal database portlets and other database portlets, database portlet customization forms, or any HTML page.
- **List-of-values (LOVs)** LOVs enable end users to choose entry field values in a form or database portlet customization form. You can use LOVs when creating database portlets to preselect the possible values in an entry field. The end user clicks the mouse to select a value rather than type it. You can also build LOVs based on other LOVs. LOVs are assigned to fields on a Form or Report and are the only Oracle Application Server Portal components not placed directly on a page
- **URL** The URL displays the contents of a URL.
- **XML Component** The XML component displays an XML page.

Building Your First Oracle Application Server Portal Form

An Oracle Application Server Portal Form is one of the fundamental developer pieces to query, insert, update, and delete data from an Oracle database. To begin creating your first Oracle Application Server Portal Form, click the Form link in the top left of the screen. The first page of the Form wizard (see Figure 8-23) provides the developer with options to create an Oracle Application Server Portal form based on a single table or view, a master-detail form, or a form based on a PL/SQL procedure stored in the database. For this example, select Form based on a table or view. You should then see a screen similar to the one in Figure 8-24.

There are a couple of common elements on this page that we will see time and time again as we develop our Oracle Application Server Portal components. There is a marker at the top of the page that shows us where we are in terms of the number of steps to create our Oracle Application Server Portal component; in this case, Step 1 of 8. Different components (forms, reports, graphs, etc.) have different numbers of steps and, depending on options selected on the first couple of steps of the wizards, we may skip over later steps in the wizards. Oracle will take the choices we make in these steps and generate PL/SQL code after the final step and store the result in the infrastructure database as a PL/SQL package. Afterwards, we can go back and modify any of our Oracle Application Server Portal components, and Oracle will regenerate the necessary PL/SQL code to reflect our changes.

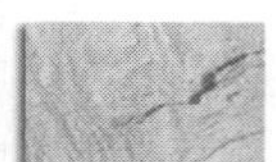

NOTE

There are two important things to note at this time: 1) If you decide to make changes to your Oracle Application Server components, Oracle Application Server Portal gives developers the option of keeping as many versions of the generated component as desired so that they can be recovered; and 2) The steps of the wizard that are documented in this section are only available in this form when you create an Oracle Application Server Portal component for the first time. If and when you go back to modify the component, the screens look a little different.

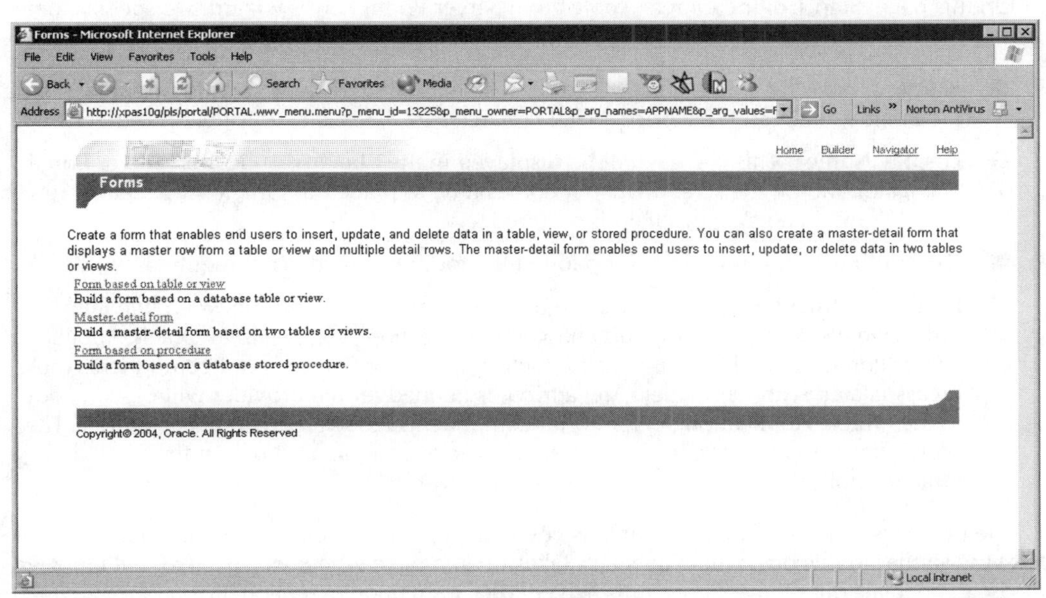

FIGURE 8-23. *The first page of the Oracle Application Server Portal Form wizard*

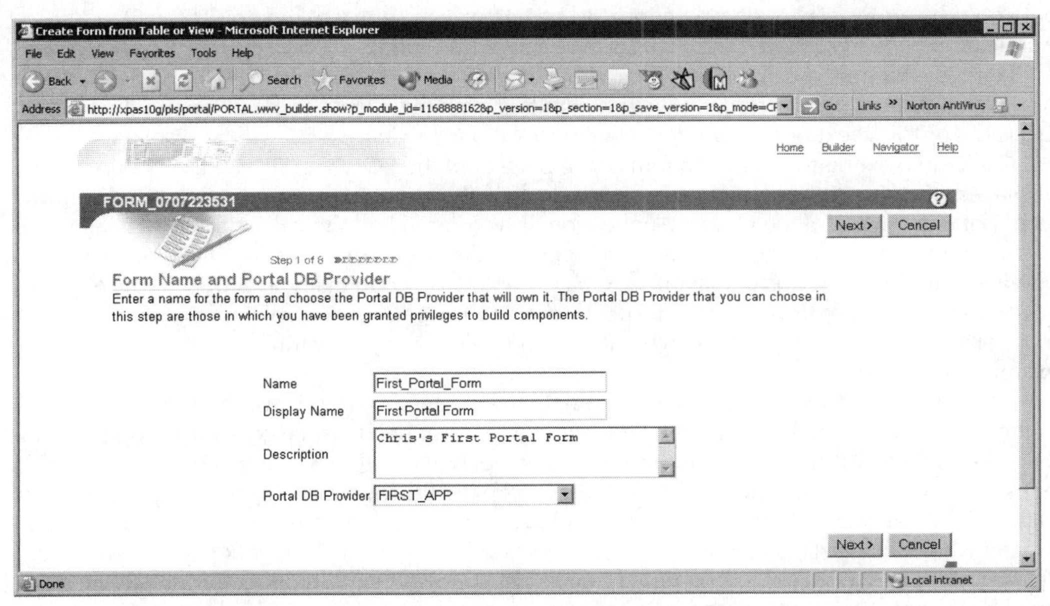

FIGURE 8-24. *The first step of the Oracle Application Server Portal Create Form wizard*

On this page, Step 1 of the Oracle Application Server Portal Forms wizard, we specify some basic elements of our form:

- **Name** This is the name that Oracle will use internally to store the form in the database. It cannot contain any spaces or illegal characters (",", ";", etc); this field is required.
- **Display Name** This is what will be displayed in the Oracle Application Server Portal Navigator and on the screen when it comes time to place our Oracle Application Server Portal Form on a page; this field is required.
- **Description** This is a text description of the form; this field is not required.
- **Portal DB Provider** Like the one-to-many relationship analogy between line items and orders we discussed earlier in this chapter in the section "Logging in to Oracle Application Server Portal for the First Time," all Oracle Application Server Portal components must be associated with a provider. Any attributes defined for the provider will cascade down to the Oracle Application Server Portal components associated with this provider. The individual components can, of course, override any of the attributes at the individual Oracle Application Server Portal component level.

The first page of most of the components you can create in Oracle Application Server Portal look very similar to this one. Clicking Next> takes up to a page where we specify what table we will use to populate our Oracle Application Server Portal form upon execution. If you look carefully, you'll see that, at the top of the screen, we are now at Step 3 of 8 (see Figure 8-25).

What happened to Step 2? We mentioned earlier that decisions made in early wizard steps affect later steps. You may be thinking that on the first page, if we had selected a Master-detail form or a Form based on a procedure, we would not have skipped over Step 2 of the wizard, but you'd be wrong. There doesn't appear to be any way to see Step 2 in any of the Oracle Application Server Forms wizards. This is probably a minor bug.

Here, developers specify the table or view that will be used to drive the data when the Oracle Application Server Portal Form is executed. For this example, click the small icon to the right of the Table or View text box. A window similar to the one in Figure 8-26 will be displayed.

Click the Next button at the bottom of the page until the PORTAL_DEMO.EMP table is displayed. Click that table to select it, and then click Next> back on the screen that is displaying Step 3 of 8. In Step 4 of the Oracle Application Server Portal Form wizard, developers select the layout of the form. Selecting Tabular will display results in a format based on the information you provide in this wizard. Custom layouts are based on HTML code that you supply in the Custom Layout steps. Because developers can specify their own HTML code, developers can create a more elaborate and sophisticated layout than you could using a structured layout. For this example, select Tabular.

Before clicking Next>, it is important to note the existence of the Finish button on this page of the wizard. Up until this point, the Finish button has not been displayed. This is due to the fact that all of the wizard steps up until this point have been mandatory. From this point on, all of the steps in the wizard are optional—that is, we can step over them and accept default values for our Oracle Application Server Portal form. One annoying thing to note: the Finish button is located exactly where the Next> button was on the earlier steps in the wizard. I mention this because, as you get more and more proficient with the wizards, you will begin stepping through them very quickly. On more than one occasion, I have inadvertently clicked the Finish button when I meant to click Next>. Not a huge deal, but it can be very time-consuming. Do not click Finish at this point for this example. Click Next>.

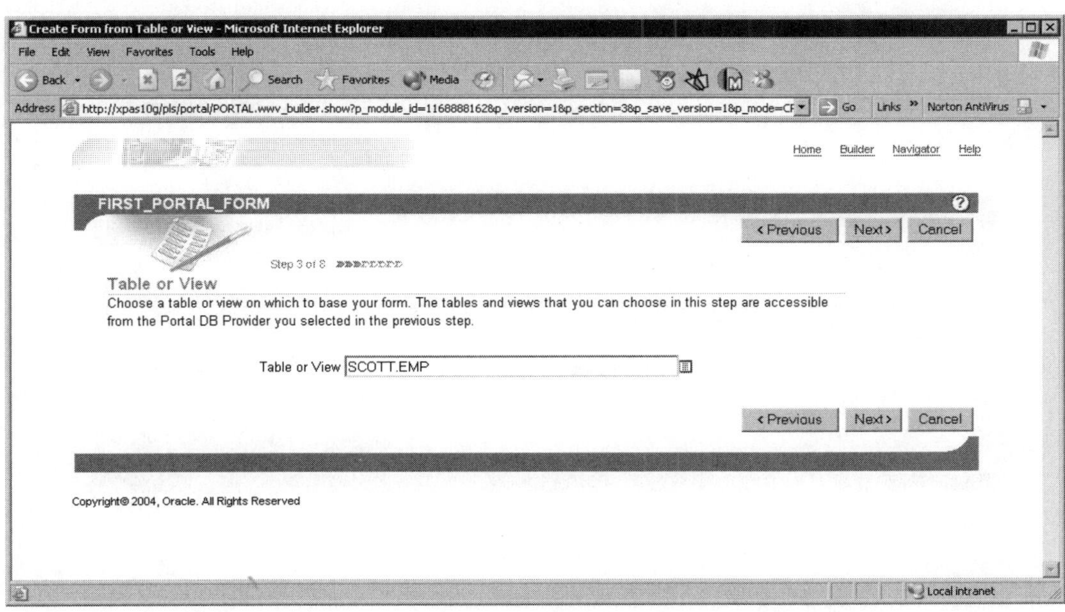

FIGURE 8-25. *Step 3 of the Oracle Application Server Portal Form wizard*

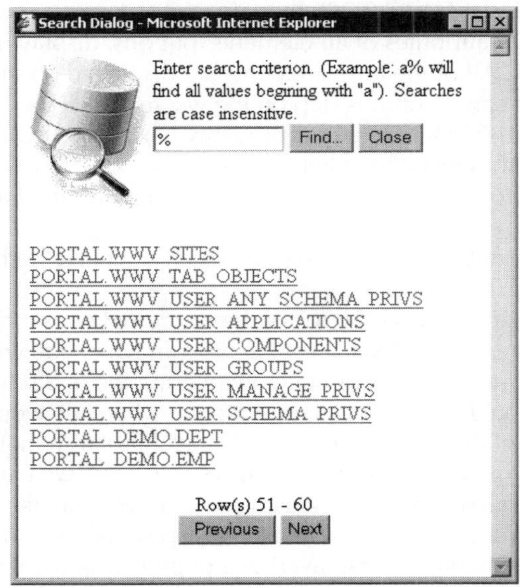

FIGURE 8-26. *The search dialog*

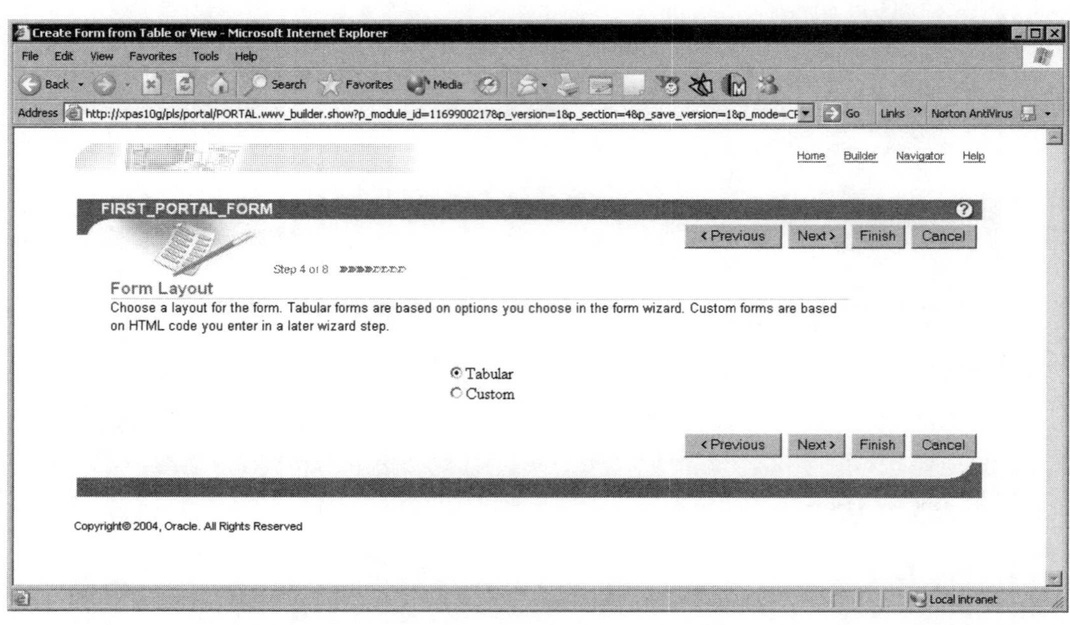

FIGURE 8-27. *Step 4 of the Oracle Application Server Portal Form wizard*

In Step 5 of the wizard (see Figure 8-28), there is a lot going on. This page in the wizard allows developers to modify attributes of all elements (buttons, display fields, check boxes, LOVs, etc.) displayed on the form. All of the form elements are displayed on the left-hand side. As a quick example of what we can do on this step on the wizard, click the EMPNO link on the left-hand side of the window. The EMPNO field is probably a primary key in our table and, therefore, not something we want end users to be able to update. After EMPNO is selected, the right-hand part of the screen changes to reflect the attributes that can be modified for this selected form element (see Figure 8-29).

In the Label field, change EMPNO to Employee # and uncheck the Updatable and Insertable boxes. Click Next>.

The next screen (see Figure 8-30) is Step 7 of the wizard. Here is a real example of how decisions made earlier in the wizard steps affect the order in which the wizard steps are presented to us (unlike the skipping over of Step 2 discussed earlier). If we had selected a Custom layout in Step 4 of the wizard, we would have been taken to Step 6, where we would have had to specify the HTML code for the layout of our form. Since we selected Tabular in that step, we bypassed Step 6. In Step 7 of the Oracle Application Server Portal Form wizard, we can specify a template (used to specify things like background and foreground colors, fonts, etc.), for the text that will appear in the header or footer of the form, text that will appear in a pop-up window if the user clicks the Help icon on the form, and text that will be displayed in a pop-up window if the user clicks the About icon on the form.

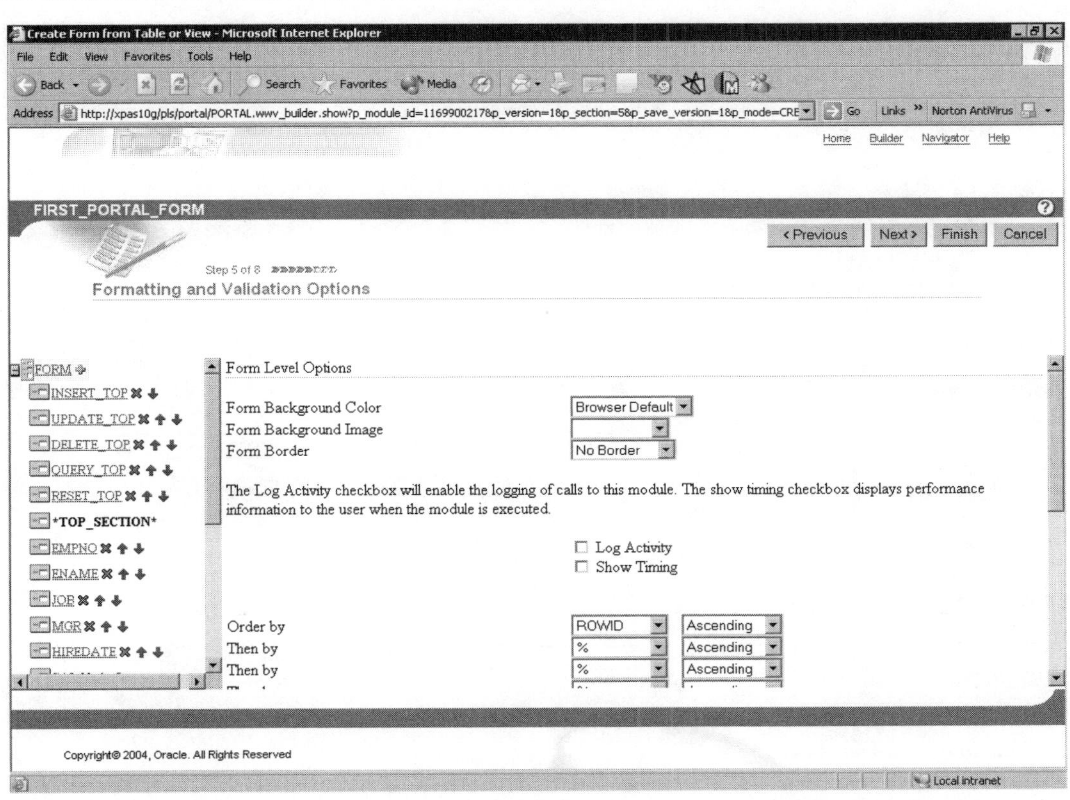

FIGURE 8-28. *Step 5 of the Oracle Application Server Portal Form wizard*

Templates take a little explaining. If you place your Oracle Application Server Portal form on a page, the template you select will never be displayed; the page attributes will determine what the Oracle Application Server Portal form looks like. If that's the case, what purpose do templates serve? When you generate an Oracle Application Server Portal component, developers have the option of turning that component into a portlet (to be placed on an Oracle Application Server Portal page) or the individual Oracle Application Server Portal component can be referenced via a URL and displayed outside of the context of an Oracle Application Server Portal page. If the latter is chosen, the template selected in this step will be used to determine how the Oracle Application Server Portal form is displayed in your browser. It is also important to note that Oracle Application Server Portal Pages can have page templates associated with them, which are different from the template that can be specified on this page.

To see an example of a template, click the Preview Template button. You'll see a window similar to the one in Figure 8-31.

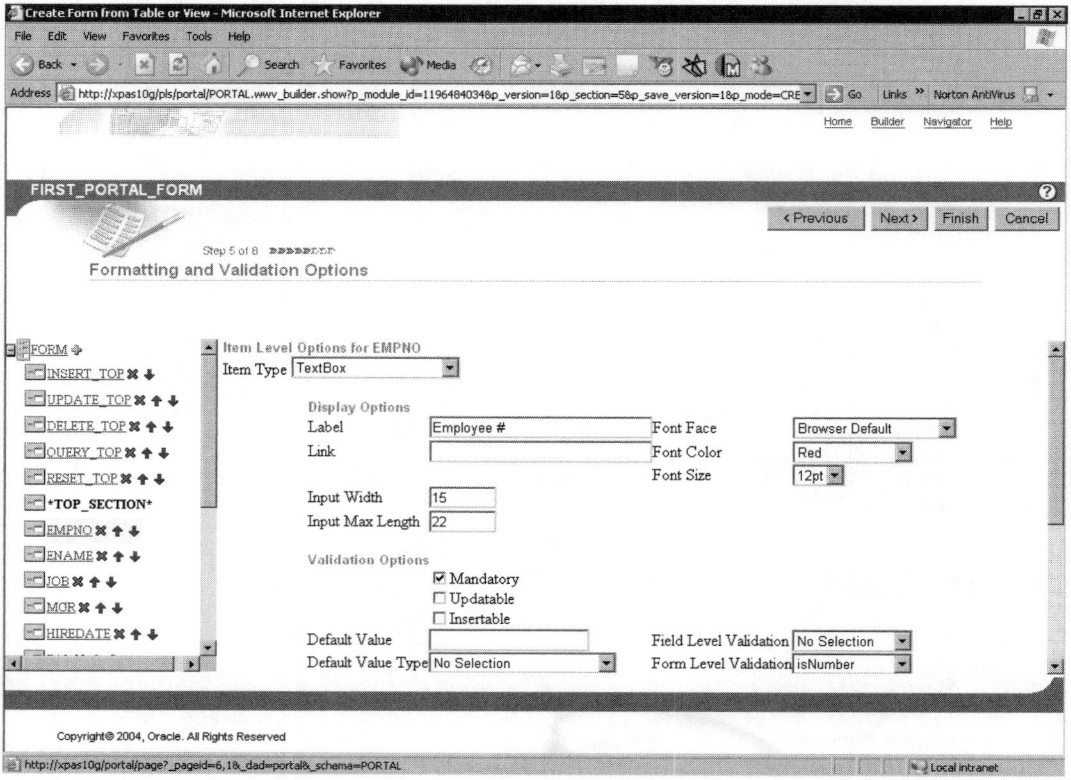

FIGURE 8-29. *Step 5 of the Oracle Application Server Portal Form wizard with the EMPNO field selected*

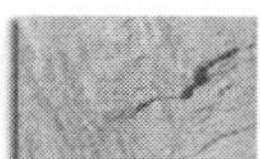

NOTE

Page templates enforce the structure or how the real estate of an Oracle Application Server Portal page should be allocated for all pages that are associated with that template. User interface, or UI, unstructured templates enable developers to build rich custom interfaces that will support JavaScript and stylesheets. Oracle Application Server Portal developers are not limited to the default templates provided by Oracle as part of the standard Oracle Application Server Portal installation. They can create their own templates that can be used here.

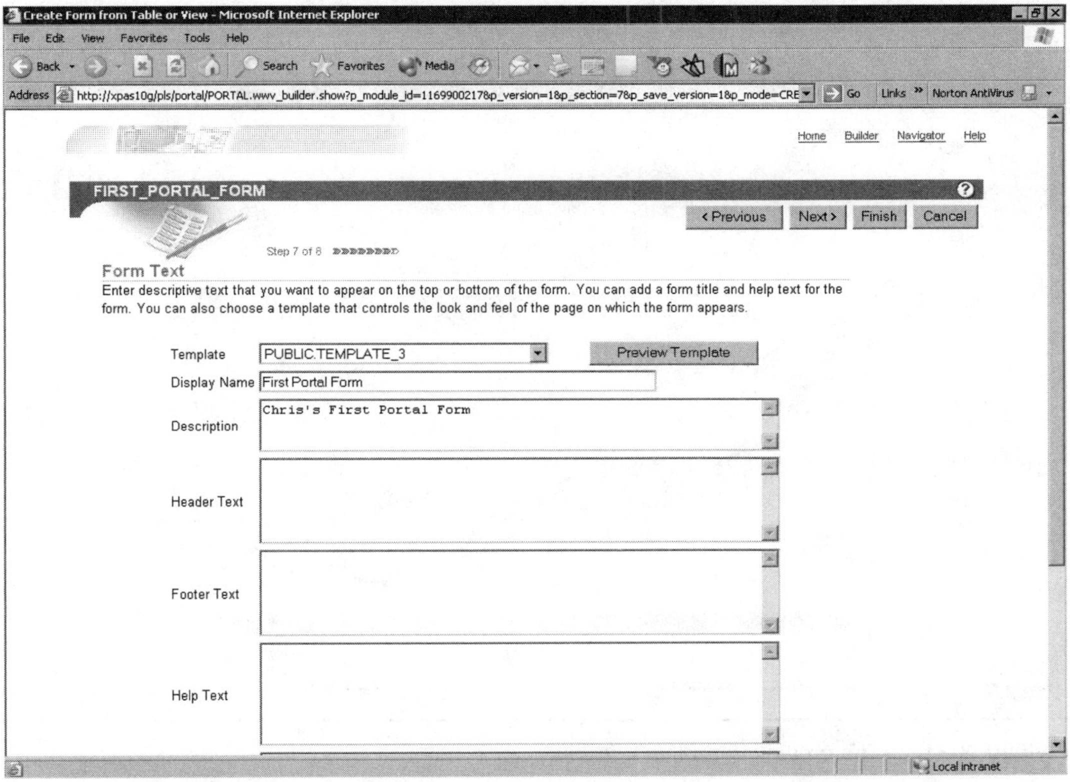

FIGURE 8-30. *Step 7 of the Oracle Application Server Portal Form wizard*

The three icons in the top right are generated automatically. Clicking the large question mark icon will display a window with whatever text you type in the Help Text text box in Step 7 of the Oracle Application Server Portal form wizard. Clicking the small question mark icon that looks like it's on the cover of a book will display a window with whatever text you type in the About Text text box. The Home icon will redirect user's browsers to a home page which can be specified programmatically. Close the preview window and click Next> on the wizard page.

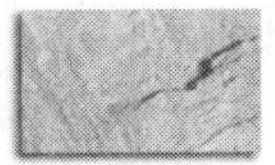

NOTE
*You can use HTML tags, like <b> to **bold** display text, in any of the text boxes in Step 7 of the Oracle Application Server Portal form wizard.*

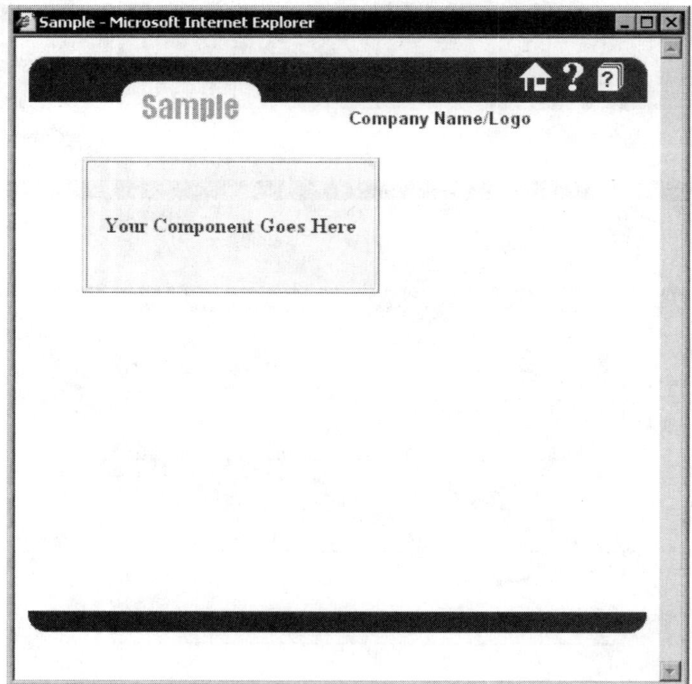

FIGURE 8-31. *The preview template window*

The next page of the Oracle Application Server Portal Form wizard is the final one: Step 8 of 8 (see Figure 8-32). On this page, we can specify triggers that fire (execute) PL/SQL code as the user progresses through the form.

Clicking Finish as this point will send the infrastructure database into a frenzy, as the wizard will begin generating the PL/SQL code to reflect the selections you have made in the steps of this wizard. After a few moments, your browser will be directed to the Manage Component screen, which should look like the screen in Figure 8-33.

This screen provides a wealth of information to the developer: the name of the form, which provider it is associated with, what archive versions are available, the current production version, when it was last altered, the link that can be used programmatically to invoke the component, the PL/SQL that was generated by the wizard when creating the component and the call interface, listing the parameters that can be passed to the component along with examples of invoking the component from a stored procedure and from a URL in a browser.

The links on the bottom of the screen are

- **Edit** Edits the existing (production) version of the component; no archiving takes place
- **Edit as New** Creates a new version of the component and archives the existing production version of the component

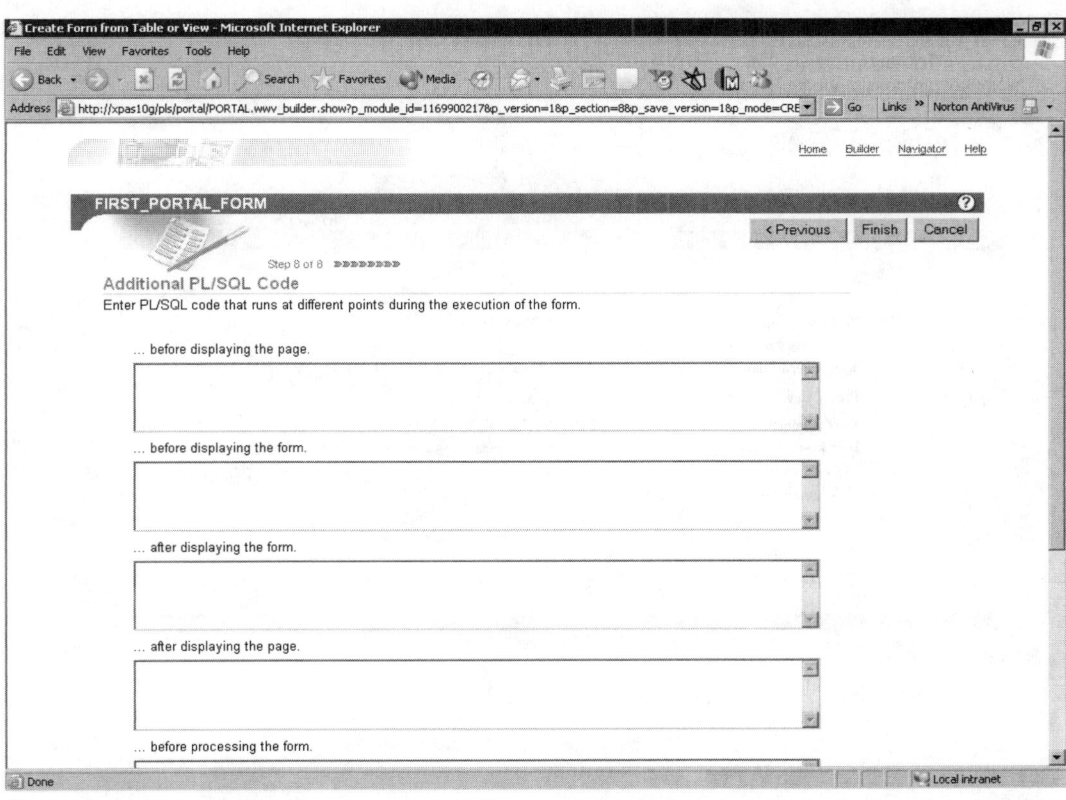

FIGURE 8-32. *Step 8 of the Oracle Application Server Portal Form wizard*

- **Run** Runs the component outside of the Portal page structure
- **Run as Portlet** Runs and displays the component as what it will look like when placed on a page (page attributes and templates can override this)
- **Customize** Allows developers to specify parameters that end users can modify when displaying portlets
- **Add to Favorites** Adds component to Favorites Portlet
- **About** Gives detailed information about the component
- **Delete** Deletes PL/SQL that constitutes component from infrastructure database

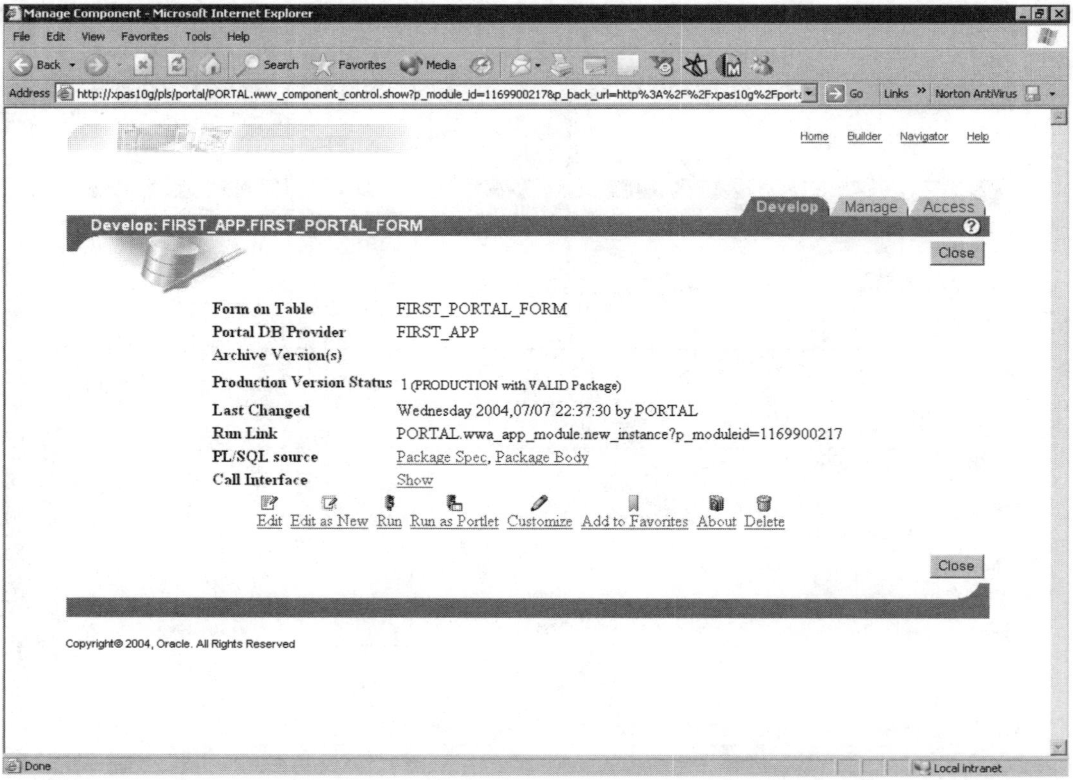

FIGURE 8-33. *The Manage Component screen*

NOTE

Where is the Favorites portlet? By default, it is not visible, but it is very easy to display it. On any Oracle Application Server Portal screen, click the Builder link in the top-right part of the screen. Click the Customize link in the top right after the Builder page is displayed. On the left-hand side of the page, you'll see a region that has Recent Objects and Developer News listed. Click the icon right above that that looks like two small boxes and a plus sign. You'll be taken to the Add Portlets page. In the search box, type favorites (without the quotes) and click the Go button. When the Favorites portlet appears in the left-hand column, single-click it and it will appear in the right-hand column. Click OK. The Customize Page with Favorites in the left-hand column will display. Click Close and the Build tab will redisplay with the Favorites portlet in the left-hand column.

Click Run as Portlet to see what the completed Oracle Application Server Portal form will look like as a portlet. Click the Query button to retrieve the first record (see Figure 8-34).

Note how the changes we made in Step 5 (see Figures 8-28 and 8-29) are reflected here: the label next to the EMPNO database column has been changed to Employee #. Notice also that after retrieving the record, that field cannot be updated, as we have deselected the Updatable check box for that column.

Figure 8-35 depicts running the form by clicking the Run link in the Manage Component screen. Note that the background, colors, and fonts reflect the template we chose for this form in Step 7 (see Figure 8-30).

If we select Edit in the Manage Component screen, we will be editing the production version (in this case, version 1) of the form. If we should edit and save the form and realize we made a mistake, we will be out of luck at that point, as we were editing the only version of the form. It's much safer (and smarter) to use the Edit as New link when modifying an Oracle Application Server Portal component. By clicking this link, a copy of the production component is made, the current production component is archived and the editing screen for that component is executed with the new component. To try this out, return to the Manage page for the Form and click the Edit as New link. A screen similar to Figure 8-36 will appear.

This looks similar to Step 5 of the Oracle Application Server Portal Form Wizard. It is, in fact, exactly similar to that step in the wizard in every way, except for the tabs at the top right of the screen. These tabs correspond to steps in the wizard that we have completed already. The current tab we're on corresponds to Step 5 of the wizard. The second tab corresponds to Step 7 (remember, we skipped Step 6 since we chose Tabular for our layout style) and the third tab corresponds to the final step: Step 8. For this example, click the ENAME column in the left-hand pane of the window, change the label for the ENAME field to Emp Name (without the quotes), and change the font color to blue (see Figure 8-37). At this point, you can either click another tab to make additional changes or click OK to generate a new version of the form. For this example, click OK.

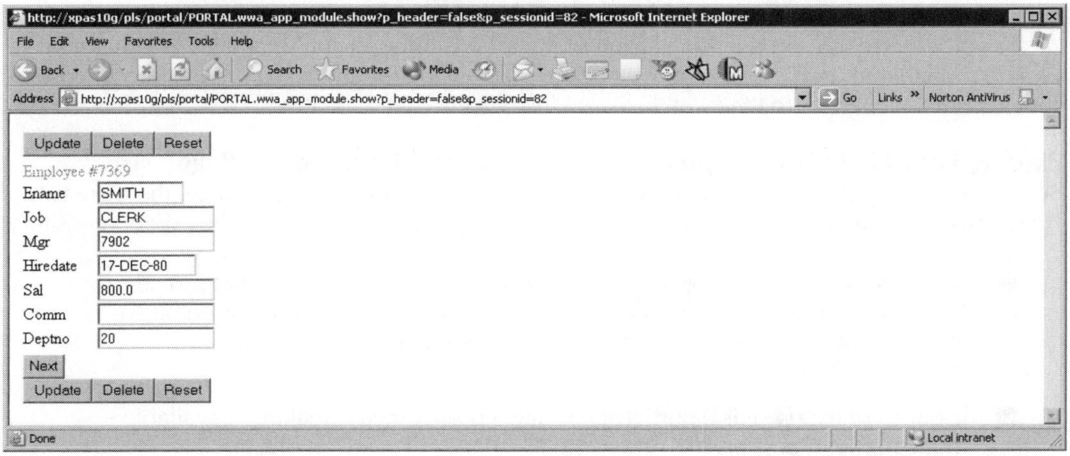

FIGURE 8-34. *The completed form displayed as a portlet*

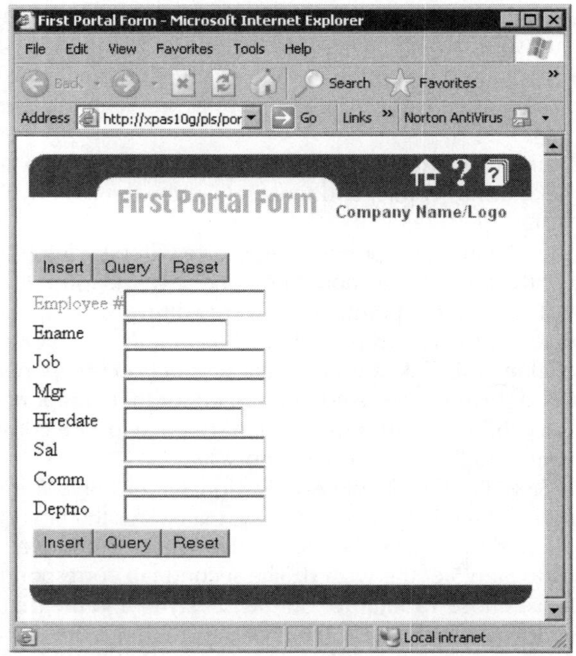

FIGURE 8-35. *The completed form run as a web form*

The Manage Component screen for this form will display. It should look something like the screen in Figure 8-38.

As you can see, our production version of the form is now version 2, and there is an archived version available to us if we need to roll back to that version for any reason. Click Run to note the effect of the changes to the form that were just made.

Placing Your First Oracle Application Server Portal Form onto a Page

Before we can place our new Oracle Application Server Portal Form onto a page, there are two conditions that need to be checked to make sure our new form shows up in the portlet repository:

- Is the provider that our form is associated with designated as a portlet provider? Database and web providers can have their provider designation turned off so that none of the components associated with it will be visible in the portlet repository.
- Is our form exposed as a portlet? Exposing a portlet means making it available to the portlet repository.

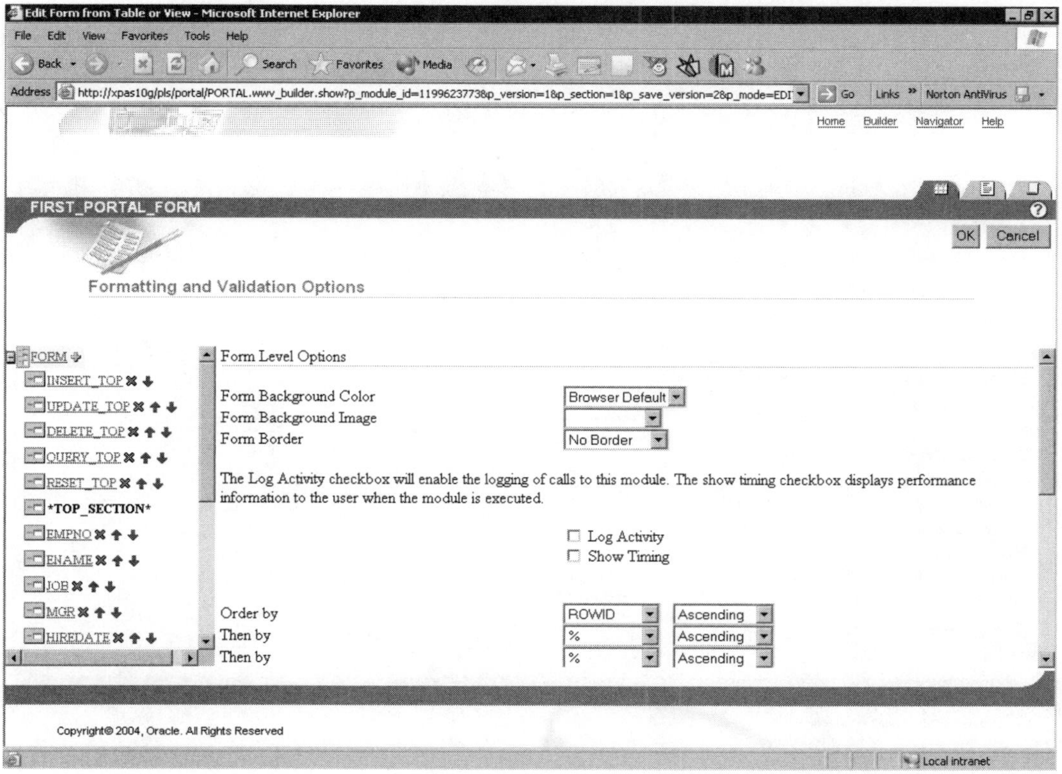

Edit Form from Table or View - Microsoft Internet Explorer

FIRST_PORTAL_FORM

Formatting and Validation Options

Form Level Options

Form Background Color Browser Default
Form Background Image
Form Border No Border

The Log Activity checkbox will enable the logging of calls to this module. The show timing checkbox displays performance information to the user when the module is executed.

Log Activity
Show Timing

Order by ROWID Ascending
Then by % Ascending
Then by % Ascending

FORM INSERT_TOP UPDATE_TOP DELETE_TOP QUERY_TOP RESET_TOP *TOP_SECTION* EMPNO ENAME JOB MGR HIREDATE

Copyright© 2004, Oracle. All Rights Reserved

FIGURE 8-36. *The Formatting and Validation Options screen*

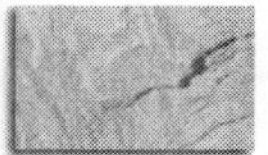

NOTE
The portlet repository is a list of portlets that can be placed on a page. If either of the above two conditions are not met, the portlet will not show up in the portlet repository.

To check the first condition, select the Grant Access link next to the database provider that owns your Oracle Application Server Portal component in the Providers tab of the Oracle Application Server Portal Navigator. Make sure the Expose as Provider check box is checked. To check the second condition, click the provider's name and select Grant Access next to the individual component you have just developed. Make sure the Publish as Portlet box is checked. Now that we are sure both conditions have been met, we can place our form onto an Oracle Application Server Portal page.

Pages belong to page groups, so we will need to create one. In the Oracle Application Server Portal Navigator, click the Page Groups tab. Click the Create New… Page Group link on the top left of the screen. Fill in the necessary fields and click Create (see Figure 8-39).

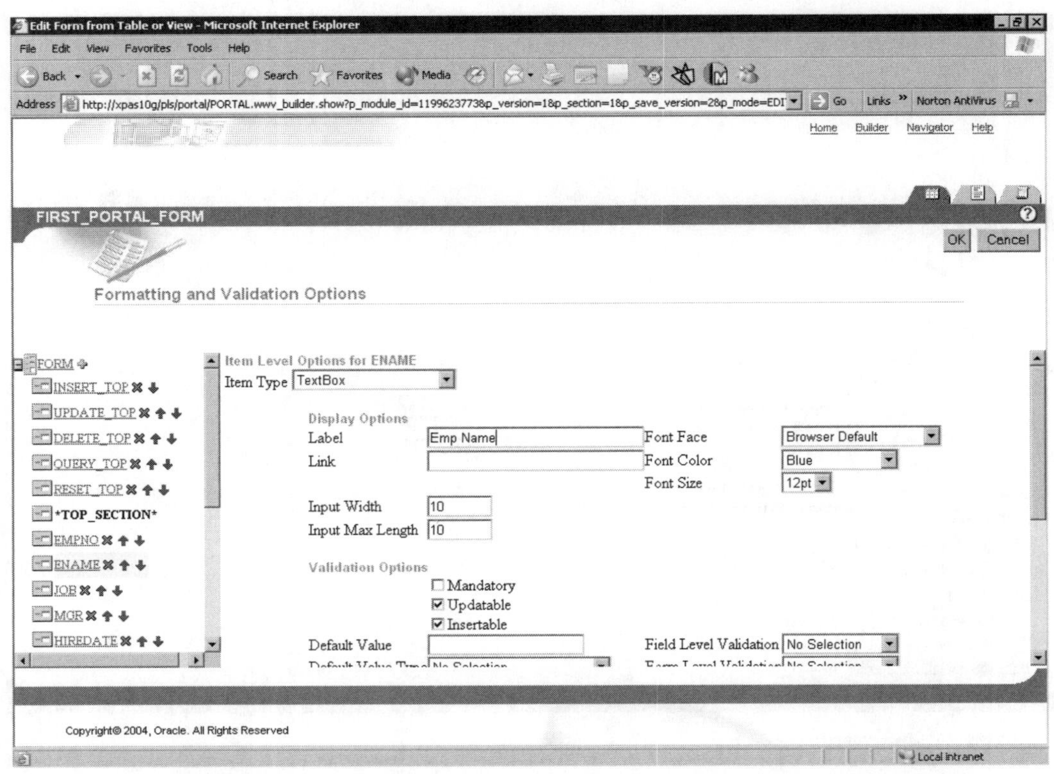

FIGURE 8-37. *Modifying the ENAME field in the portal form wizard*

After clicking that page, you will be taken to a graphical representation of the root page for that page group (see Figure 8-40). It looks like there's a lot going on on this page, but it's all laid out in a logical manner so that when developers understand the layout of the screen, it becomes easy to modify it quickly. The top three rows of the page (the ones starting with Editing Views:, Page Group:, and Path:) display information about the page and what mode the page is currently being edited in. The current mode is listed in bold (in this example, we are editing the page in Graphical mode). You can switch between Graphical, Layout, and List while editing your page. They all perform the same basic functions (adding/moving/removing portlets, etc.), but just display the information in a different manner. The one you'll pick is a matter of personal preference. The Graphical mode is the one that will be demonstrated in the Portal chapters of this book (Chapters 8-11).

The fourth row is a series of icons. This row represents the actions you can perform for a particular region. A region is a section of the page. If you remember back to the beginning of this chapter, we said that, using the one-to-many analogy, an Oracle Application Server Portal page has a one-to-many relationship with regions and a region has a one-to-many relationship with portlets. You'll notice that that row of icons is repeated lower on the page. This row represents the actions that can be performed with portlets for the second, lower region on the page.

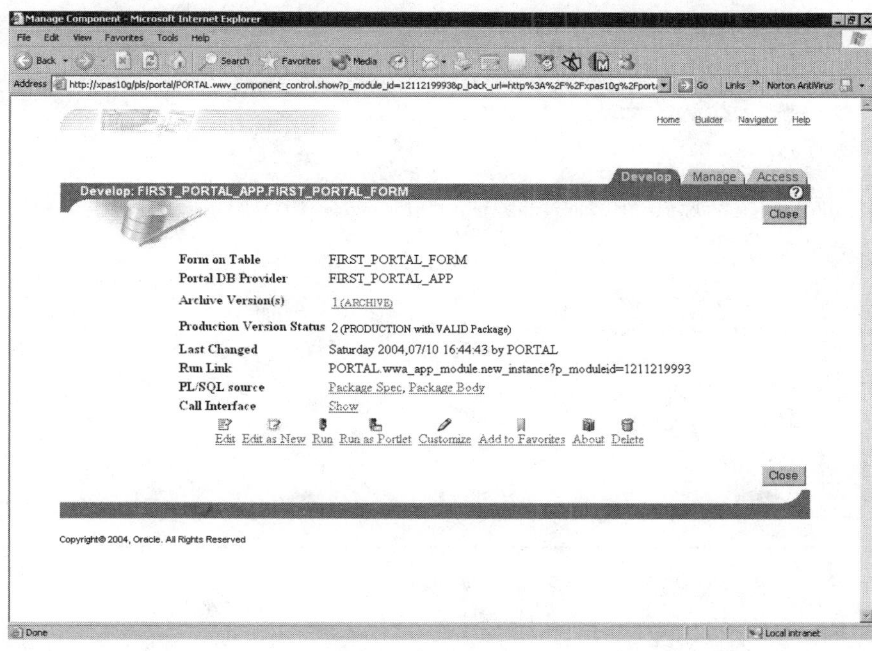

FIGURE 8-38. *The Manage Component screen for the form after our first modification*

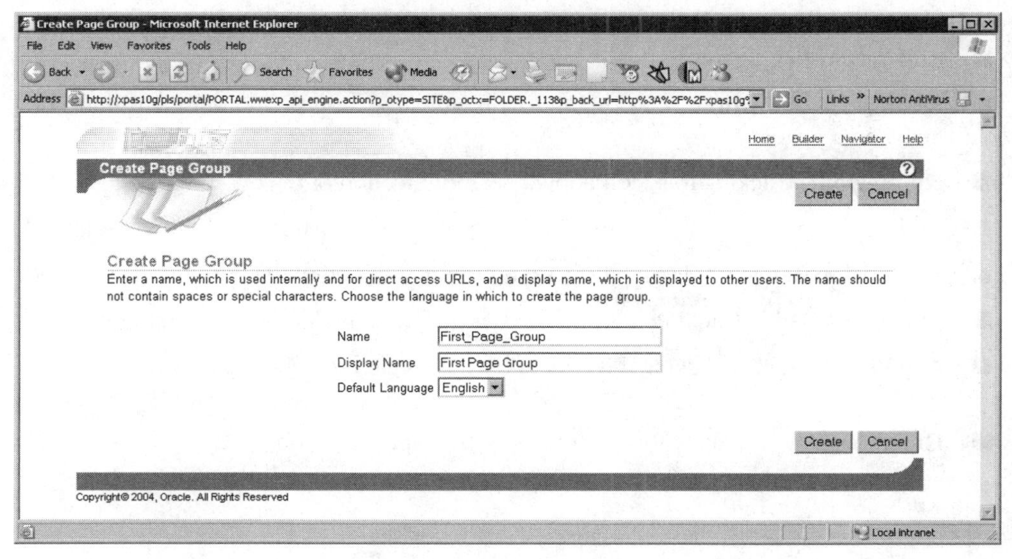

FIGURE 8-39. *The Create Page Group screen*

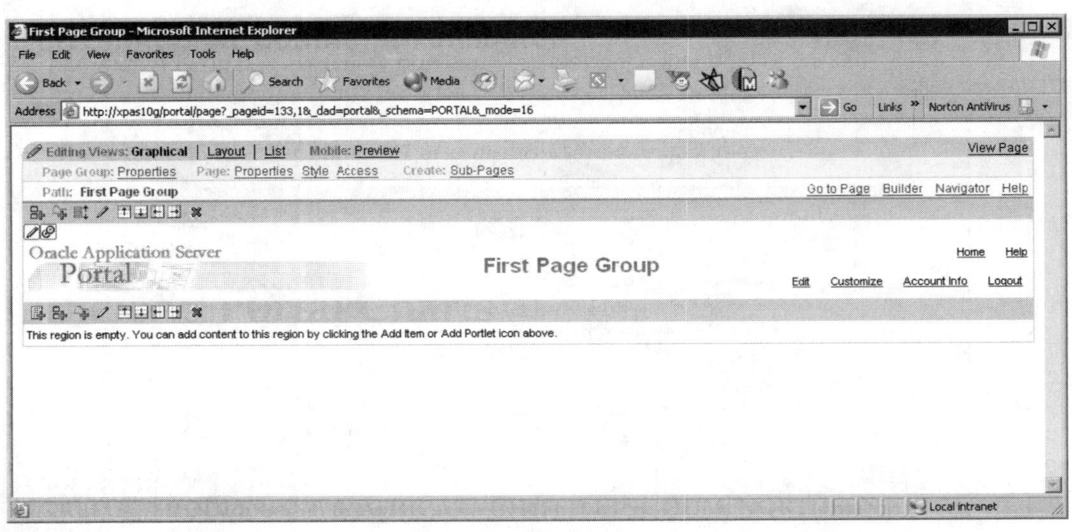

FIGURE 8-40. *The root page in Graphical mode*

If you move your mouse over the icons, a small help-text window will pop up telling you the action each of the icons performs. Moving from left to right:

- **Add Item/Portlet** Clicking this icon will allow you to add either portlets or items, depending on whether the region is defined as a portlet region or an item region.
- **Add Tab** Clicking this icon will add a tab to the region.
- **Arrange Items/Portlets** Clicking this icon will allow you to re-order the portlets or items on a page.
- **Edit Region** Clicking this icon allows the modification of region attributes.
- **Add Region Above** Clicking this icon adds a region above the current one selected.
- **Add Region Below** Clicking this icon adds a region below the current one selected.
- **Add Region Left** Clicking this icon adds a region to the left of the current one selected.
- **Add Region Right** Clicking this icon adds a region to the right of the current one selected.
- **Delete Region** Clicking this icon deletes the selected region.

NOTE

Items are things you would like to place on your portal that don't fit traditional database constructs such as forms or reports. Examples of items are spreadsheet files, images, sounds, documents, etc.

For the bottommost region, click the Add Portlet icon. The Add Portlets screen appears (see Figure 8-41). The bottom-left of the screen shows the Portlet Repository with all available portlets organized into groups. The right-side of the page shows what portlets have been placed on the region.

In previous versions of Portal, to find a component to be placed in a region, you'd have to traverse the various groupings to find the component you were looking for. With Oracle Application Server Portal, Oracle has made this process simpler by introducing the search box that allows you to search for portlets from a single location. The name we will be searching for is the internal

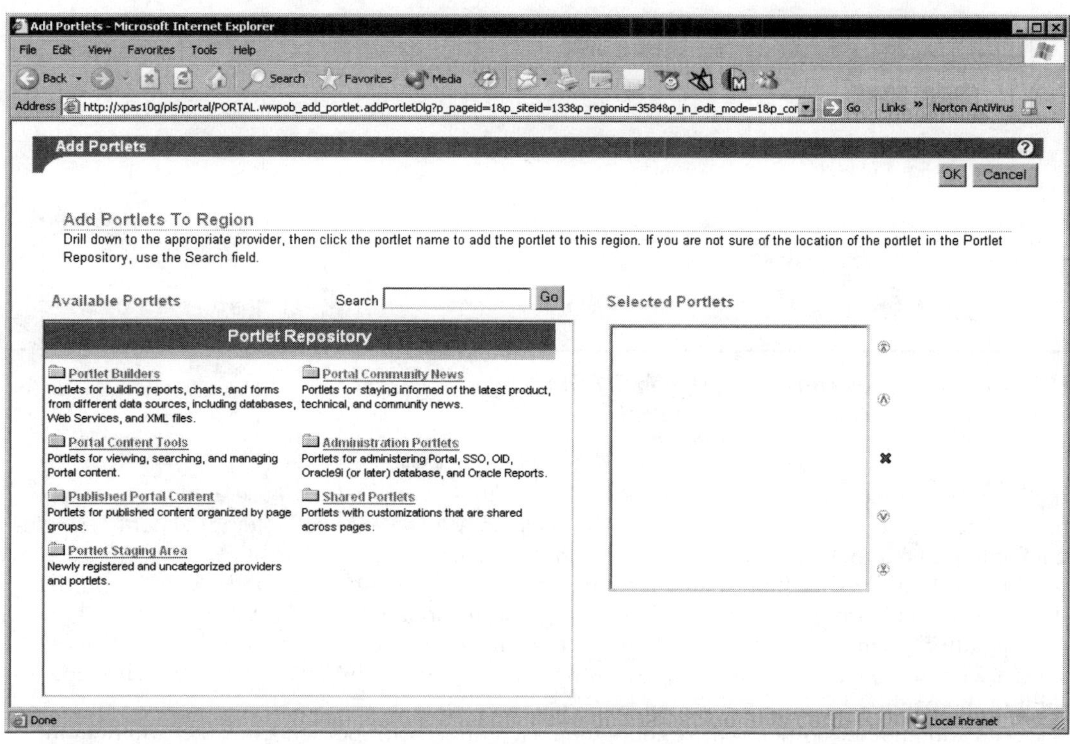

FIGURE 8-41. *The Add Portlets page displaying the Portlet Repository*

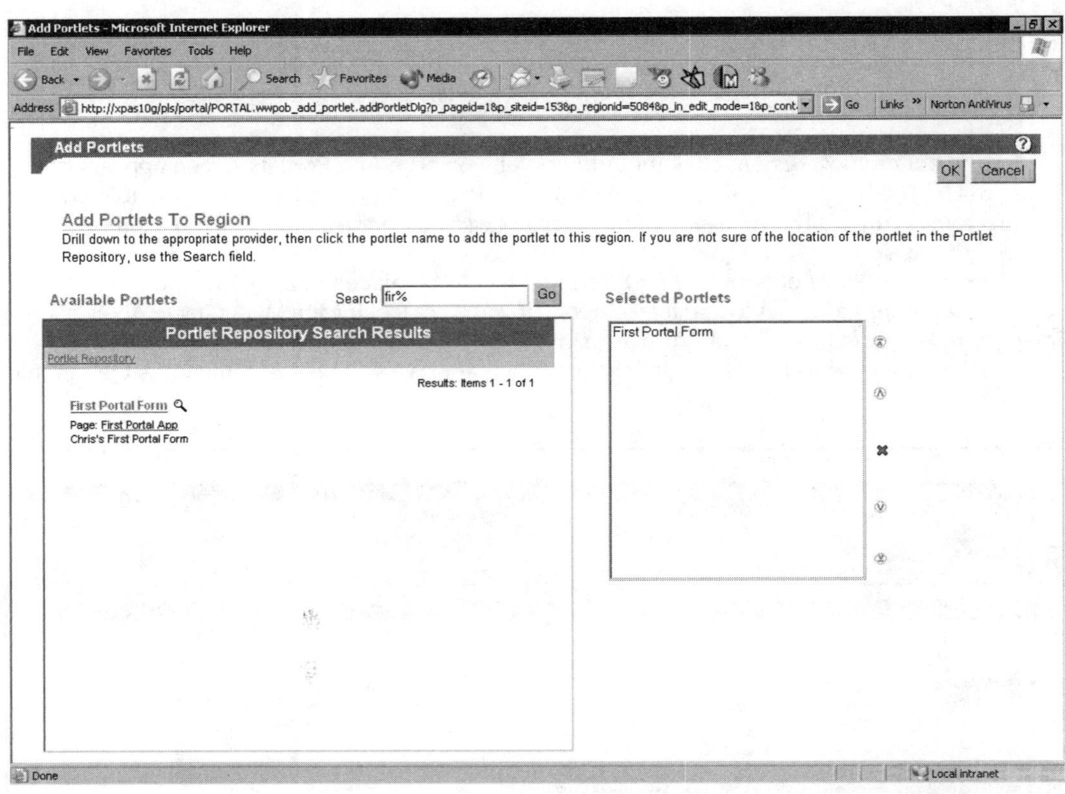

FIGURE 8-42. *Selecting the First_Portal_Form portlet*

name of the component we have developed (First_Portal_Form). We can use wildcards, so type fir% (without the quotes) in the search field and click Go. When the search returns the portlet, single-click it to move it to the right-side of the screen (see Figure 8-42).

Click OK and you will be returned to the page in graphical-editing mode with the portlet displayed (see Figure 8-43). It is a fully working portlet, so feel free to test it by hitting the Query button, then the Next and Previous buttons to scroll through the records in that table. To see what the page will look like when it's deployed, click the View Page link in the top right of the page.

Let's add another portlet to the right of the First_Portal_Form portlet. Click the Add Region Right icon (eighth icon from the left). A new region will be placed to the right of the existing

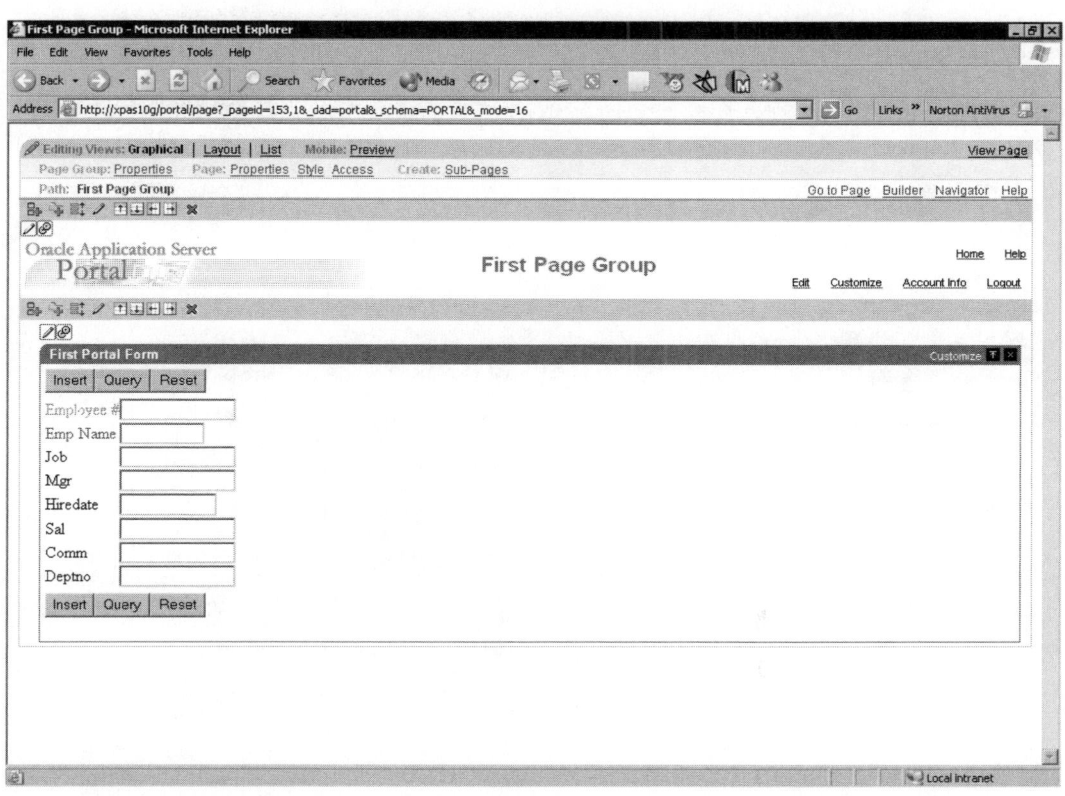

FIGURE 8-43. *Graphically editing the page with the First_Portal_Form portlet placed on it*

region. Click the Add Portlets icon for the new region (if the icon displays Add Item when you move your mouse over it, click the pencil icon and change the region type to Portlets, then go back and click the Add Portlets icon for the new region). Click the Portlet Staging Area link, then the Example Application link. Finally, click the Report from SQL Query link to move it to the right side of the page. Click OK to re-display the First_Portal_Page with two regions and two portlets (see Figure 8-44). Click View Page on the top right of the screen to see how the page will look when it's deployed.

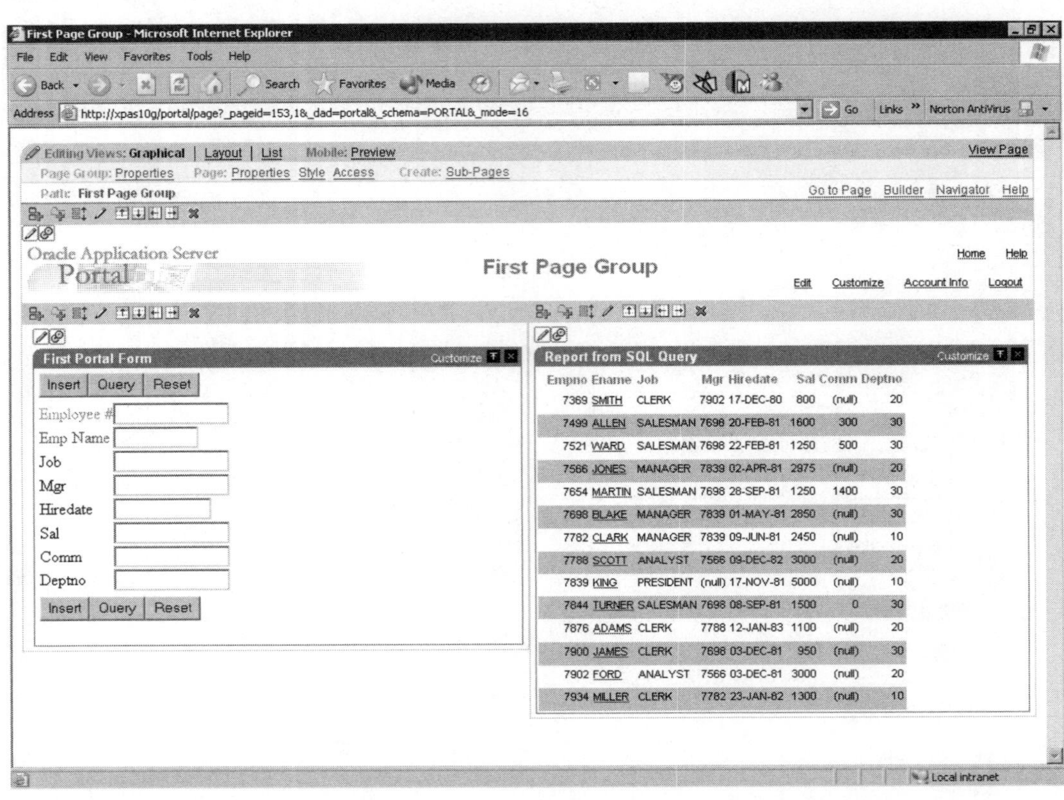

FIGURE 8-44. *The portal page with two regions and two portlets*

Summary

Oracle Application Server Portal is a feature-rich development environment that gives developers a multitude of tools and constructs that allow the creation and deployment of web-based applications quickly and easily. This chapter has introduced the basic architecture of Oracle Application Server Portal, but we've just scratched the surface of what it is truly capable of. In subsequent chapters, details of Oracle Application Server Portal development; security and advanced topics, such as the integration of external sites; and Oracle Forms, Oracle Reports, and Oracle Discoverer Workbooks and Worksheets in Oracle Portal will be discussed.

CHAPTER 9

OracleAS Portal—Development—The Basic OracleAS Portal Components

evelopers new to the OracleAS Portal environment are often amazed at how easy it is to create web applications, portlets, and OracleAS Portal pages using the OracleAS Portal wizards. By taking advantage of these wizards, developers can concentrate on developing and deploying OracleAS Portal objects to the Web quickly and easily. Without being marketed as such, OracleAS Portal provides a rapid application development (RAD) environment that allows developers and architects to take full advantage of the various RAD methodologies (as opposed to the more traditional "waterfall" methods of development) pictured in Figure 9-1.

RAD methodologies allow developers, business analysts, project managers, and end users to interact throughout the development lifecycle, increasing the likelihood that a development project will succeed. OracleAS Portal provides an environment where OracleAS Portal components can be modified and deployed on the spot, allowing end users and developers to interact instantaneously. One thing many developers fail to grasp is how much flexibility the OracleAS Portal wizards provide for them. OracleAS Portal is an incredibly rich development environment that provides developers with a plethora of tools and methods to accomplish their tasks. All of this includes a seamless integration with Oracle databases, of course.

In the preceding chapter, we walked through the creation of an OracleAS Portal component: an OracleAS Portal Form. The OracleAS Portal Form was then placed on an OracleAS Portal Page and displayed. This chapter will discuss the major components developers can create using the OracleAS Portal wizards:

- OracleAS Portal Forms
- OracleAS Portal Reports

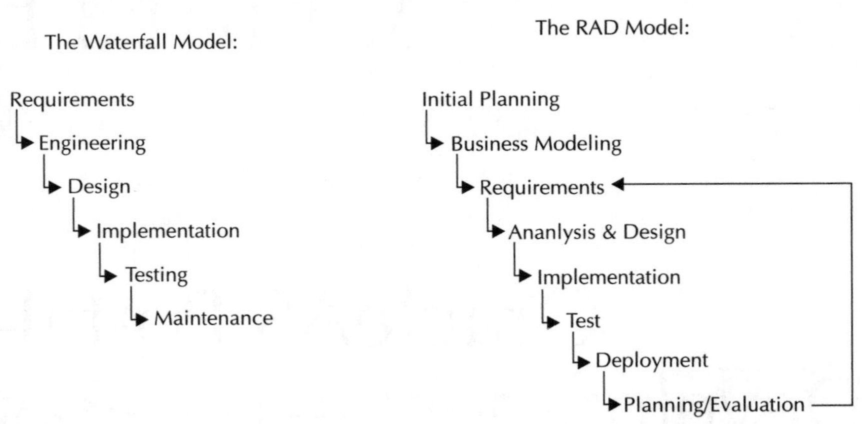

FIGURE 9-1. *A comparison of waterfall and RAD methodologies*

- OracleAS Portal Charts
- OracleAS Portal Dynamic Pages
- OracleAS Portal Lists of Values
- OracleAS Portal XML Components

In Chapter 10, the following advanced OracleAS Portal components and topics are discussed:

- OracleAS Portal Calendars
- OracleAS Portal Hierarchies
- OracleAS Portal Menus
- OracleAS Portal URLs
- OracleAS Portal Links
- OracleAS Portal Data Components
- OracleAS Portal Page Design
- OracleAS Content and Content Management

OracleAS Portal Forms

One of the basic OracleAS Portal components is that of an OracleAS Portal Form. A form allows end users to interact directly with the database and can be designed to query, insert, update, or delete data, or most likely, to enable the end user to perform a combination of these activities. The OracleAS Portal wizard used to create an OracleAS Portal Form, like all of the other wizards discussed in this chapter and the next, can be used to create a component that can be run by itself over the Web and accessed via a web browser. These components run outside of OracleAS Portal's security and page structure and can be used to create components that are not placed on OracleAS Portal pages. Running the OracleAS Portal components in this manner is commonly referred to as "full-page" or "stand-alone" mode. As this is unusual, the focus of this chapter and the next will be on the creation of OracleAS components that are designed to be used as portlets (i.e., those to be placed on an OracleAS Portal page).

As you have seen in the preceding chapter, an OracleAS Portal component cannot exist by itself—it must be associated with a provider. An OracleAS Portal provider is a way of grouping OracleAS Portal components together. If you have not created an OracleAS Portal database provider, return to Chapter 8 and follow the steps to do so now. If you already have a provider, select the Navigator link on the top right of any OracleAS Portal screen, the Providers tab, the Locally Built Providers link, and then the provider you have created. You will see a screen similar to Figure 9-2.

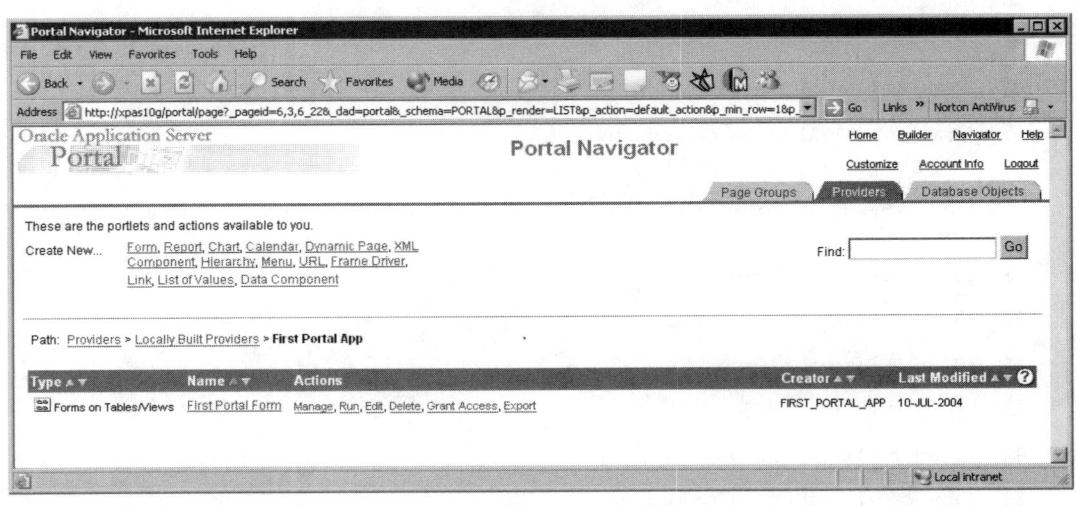

FIGURE 9-2. *The OracleAS Portal Navigator with the "First Portal App" provider selected*

NOTE
There are two types of providers in OracleAS Portal: database providers and web providers. Database providers store the PL/SQL code that constitutes the components associated with the provider in the infrastructure database that is installed as part of the Oracle Application Server 10g installation. Web providers use code stored on the server (commonly Java) to build OracleAS Portal application components. A web provider is a web-based application that communicates with the portal using the HTTP or HTTPS protocol. Since the web provider communicates using HTTP, it can be installed on any web application server that the portal can contact. A discussion of web providers is beyond the scope of this book. For more information, see: http://www.oracle.com/technology/products/ias/portal/html/primer_pdkjava_provider_framework_v2.html.

Clicking the Create New... Form link will bring you to a screen similar to Figure 9-3.

As you can see from this wizard page, we can create three basic types of OracleAS Portal Forms using the OracleAS Portal Form Wizard. If you need a form to select and modify a record from a single table or view, choose the first selection, "Form based on a table or view."

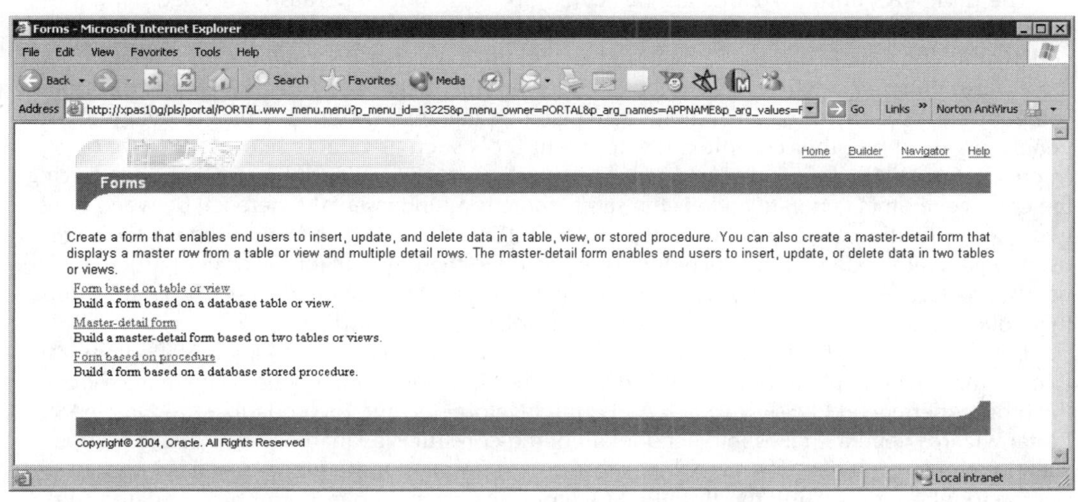

FIGURE 9-3. *The first page of the Create New Form Wizard*

NOTE

If you select a view to serve as the basis of your OracleAS Portal form, the options available to the end user, with regard to updating, deleting, and inserting records, will be determined by how the view was created. An updatable join view is a join view that involves two or more base tables or views, where UPDATE, INSERT, and DELETE operations are permitted. The data dictionary views ALL_UPDATABLE_COLUMNS, DBA_UPDATABLE_COLUMNS, and USER_UPDATABLE_COLUMNS contain information that indicates which of the view columns are updatable. In order to be inherently updatable, a view cannot contain any of the following constructs: set operators; DISTINCT operators; an aggregate or analytic function; a GROUP BY, ORDER BY, CONNECT BY, or START WITH clause; a collection expression in a SELECT list; a subquery in a SELECT list; or a join (with some exceptions).

As its name implies, selecting "Form based on a table or view" will start the OracleAS Portal Forms Wizard and will prompt you to answer questions regarding how you would like an OracleAS Portal Form that is based on a single table or view to display and behave.

The OracleAS Portal wizards are basically glorified code generators. By specifying the attributes of your OracleAS Portal components, you are instructing the wizard how to generate code within the Oracle database (the infrastructure database that is installed when installing the Infrastructure piece of Oracle Application Server 10*g*). Beginning OracleAS Portal developers sometimes mistakenly draw an analogy between the OracleAS Portal wizards and the template generators used by other complex development tools such as Oracle JDeveloper 10*g* or Microsoft C#. While the process of answering questions about your application and then having the code generators generate code is the same, there is a fundamental difference between the two: the application code generators in the Oracle JDeveloper 10*g* and Microsoft C# tools are used to generate code that the developer is expected to then modify for his or her particular needs. The OracleAS Portal wizards are designed to generate all of the necessary PL/SQL code that your OracleAS Portal pages will use when displaying your work.

Is it possible to go back and modify the PL/SQL code generated by the OracleAS Portal wizards to customize your application? Yes, it is possible, but it would definitely be a challenge for even the most experienced PL/SQL / OracleAS Portal developer. Why? The code that the OracleAS Portal wizards generate takes into account all of the constructs available to you as a developer, such as templates, styles, custom colors, etc. Support for all of these pieces results in a lot of overhead when generating the final PL/SQL code. As an example, if you have created the basic OracleAS Portal form in the preceding chapter, open another browser window and log in to OracleAS Portal. Select Navigator, then the Providers tab, then the Locally Built Providers link, and then the link of the provider you have already created. Select the Manage link next to the OracleAS Portal Form you created in the preceding chapter. With the Develop tab selected, click the Package Body link in the middle of the screen. You will see the PL/SQL code that has been generated for this form (a sample is shown in Figure 9-4). If you remember, the OracleAS Portal Form we created was very simple and had almost no special conditions placed in it, and still, over 1,000 lines of PL/SQL code are generated! So while it is possible to modify the generated PL/SQL code, OracleAS Portal was designed so that you use the wizards to make modifications to your OracleAS Portal components.

CAUTION
Additionally, it is critical to note that any changes that are made to the package outside of the OracleAS Portal Wizards (e.g., in JDeveloper) will be overwritten (i.e., lost!) as soon as the wizard is invoked again on this package.

After the generators have done their work, you can edit the OracleAS Portal component at any time to make changes. The editing procedure allows you to revisit the wizard pages (all represented on a single OracleAS Portal page as tabs along the top right of the screen) and make the necessary modifications to your OracleAS Portal components. Clicking OK on any of these screens signals the OracleAS Portal engine to generate a new version of your OracleAS Portal component.

Note how JavaScript code is created within our OracleAS Portal components. It may be a little confusing for developers to understand how this code is stored and executed in our OracleAS Portal components. As you will see, certain screens of the wizards allow you to embed JavaScript code to enhance the functionality of our OracleAS Portal components. Where is this

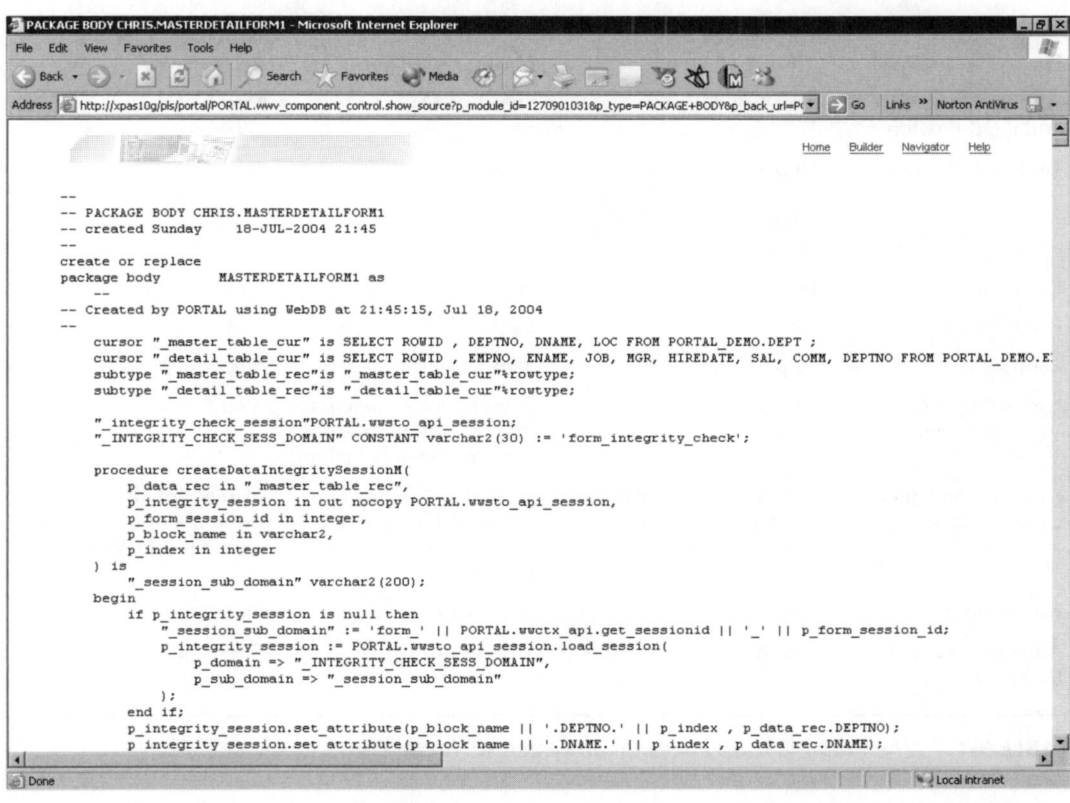

FIGURE 9-4. *The PL/SQL code generated for a simple OracleAS Portal Form*

code stored? It is actually stored as part of the PL/SQL code that is generated when the OracleAS Portal Component Wizard completes. This code is then executed by the OracleAS Portal engine when the component is run on a page. There is no need to write HTML code with JavaScript in it—the code is "embedded" in the OracleAS Portal component and is stored, as part of a PL/SQL package for that component, in the infrastructure database of your Oracle Application Server 10*g* installation.

Table 9-1 lists the OracleAS Portal wizard pages, showing how your choice of OracleAS Portal Form type will affect which pages are displayed.

As you can see, many of the wizard pages are common to all OracleAS Portal Form types. The first wizard page prompts the developer for a name, a display name, a description, and what Portal database provider the form will be associated with:

- The name field is what OracleAS Portal will use to store the information about your form internally. As such, it cannot contain spaces or any special characters.

Portal Wizard Page	Form Based on a Table or View	Master Detail Form	Form Based on a Procedure
Form Name and Portal DB Provider	Step 1 of 8	Step 1 of 11	Step 1 of 8
Table(s) or View(s)	Step 3 of 8 (if you remember from Chapter 8, there is no step 2 in the Forms wizards)	Step 3 of 11	N/A
Procedure	N/A	N/A	Step 3 of 8
Join Conditions	N/A	Step 4 of 11	N/A
Form Layout	Step 4 of 8	Step 5 of 11	Step 4 of 8
Formatting and Validation Options	Step 5 of 8	Steps 6/7 of 11 (one page for the master table, one page for the detail table)	Step 5 of 8
Form Layout Editor – Custom Layout	Step 6 of 8 (displayed if, on step 4 of 8, "Custom" layout is selected)	Steps 8 of 11, 9 of 11 (displayed if, on step 5 of 11, "Custom" layout is selected)	Step 6 of 8 (displayed if, on step 4 of 8, "Custom" layout is selected)
Form Text	Step 7 of 8	Step 10 of 11	Step 7 of 8
Additional PL/SQL Code	Step 8 of 8	Step 11 of 11	Step 8 of 8

TABLE 9-1. *The Portal Wizard Pages for an OracleAS Portal Form*

- The display name is what will be displayed when you view the OracleAS Portal objects in the Navigator.
- The comment field is a text field to enter comments about this particular OracleAS Portal component.
- The Portal DB Provider field lists the different providers that can be used. By default, the OracleAS Portal Provider selected in the previous screens will be highlighted as the default.

The next page of the wizard asks for information about the table/view, master/detail table/views, or procedure you will base your form on. If you are creating a master/detail form, the next page of the wizard will prompt you for a join condition. If you are using parent key/foreign key constraints to maintain referential integrity in your database, OracleAS Portal will automatically populate those fields for you. For this example, select the PORTAL_DEMO.DEPT table.

The next page of the wizard, the Form Layout page (Figure 9-5), is where many of the options that determine how our form will look and act can be specified.

The left side of the window includes a hierarchical representation of all of the objects that are placed on the form. Depending on which object is selected (highlighted in yellow), the options provided for that object will appear in the right-hand side of the window. In Figure 9-5, the Form

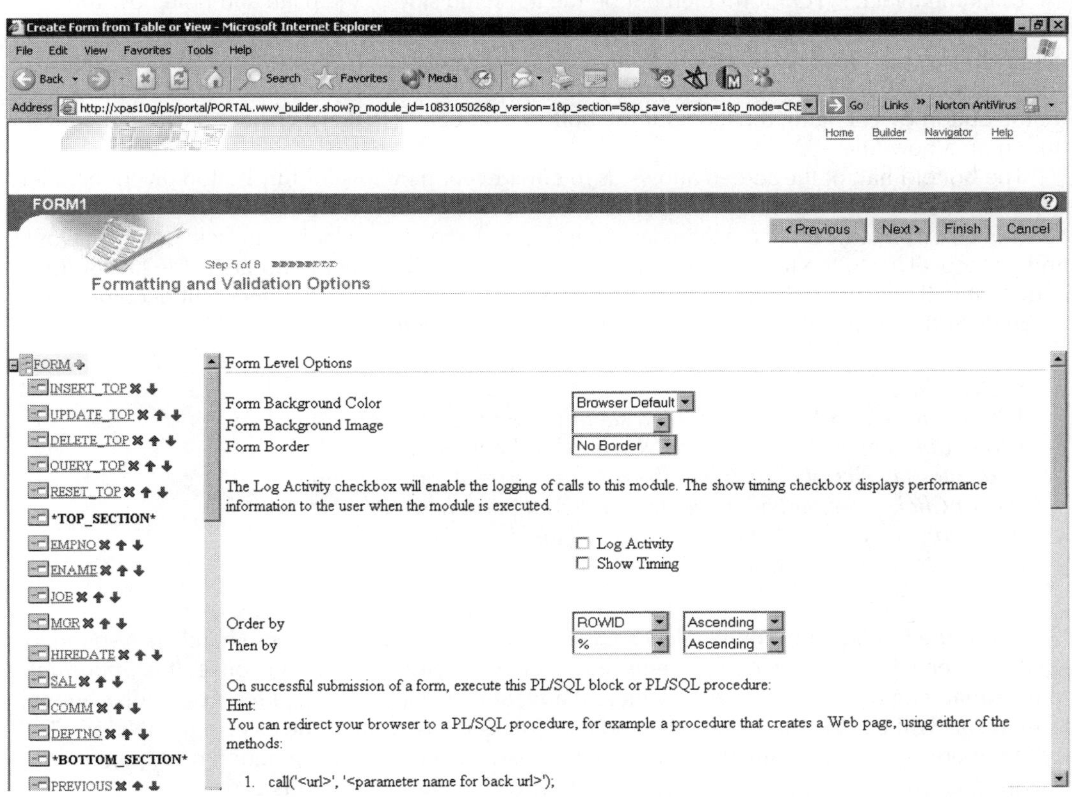

FIGURE 9-5. *The Form Layout page of the OracleAS Portal Form Wizard*

object is selected, so the right-hand pane displays options that can be set for the entire form (form background color, form background image, the order of rows to be returned to the form, etc.).

You will notice that the OracleAS Portal has automatically generated a set of buttons (one under the group "Top Section" and another set under the group "Bottom Section" in the left-hand frame). These buttons represent the standard actions that can be performed on data entered into a form: insert, update, delete, query, and reset (which clears all of the fields on the form). Next to each of these buttons is a red *x* and two blue up and down arrows (except for the first element on the page, the insert_top button). Clicking the red *x* will remove the component from the form. This makes it easy to create an OracleAS Portal Form with specific functionality. Suppose your requirements specify that an end user can insert new records and query existing records, but cannot delete or update existing records. You can create a form with the update and delete buttons removed (remember to remove them from both the top and bottom sections), which would remove that functionality from the completed form. The blue up and down arrows allow you to move form elements around. After you click one of these arrows, the OracleAS Portal page you are currently developing will redraw itself showing the reordered form components.

Click the INSERT_TOP form element on the left-hand side of the page and note how the right-hand side changes to reflect the options for the INSERT_TOP form element. The right-hand pane will also change depending on the item type selected from the drop-down box next to it. For this example, INSERT_TOP is defined as a button. We can specify what is to be displayed on the button by changing the label for the button, and below that is a check box to create the button on a new line.

The bottom half of the screen allows us to enter event handlers for this button. Event handlers will perform actions when a specific action is initiated (similar to a trigger in a database). For items of type "Button," there are three JavaScript event handlers available: onClick, onMouseDown, and onMouseUp. In the text box to the right of the JavaScript event handlers is the JavaScript code that will execute when the specific event occurs. Any code written here will become part of the PL/SQL package that the OracleAS Portal wizard will generate.

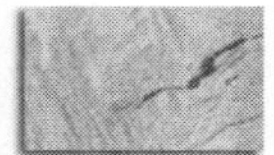

NOTE
While onClick and onMouseDown seem to be the same, there are subtle differences. The onMouseDown event handler is defined as "executes JavaScript code when the user depresses a mouse button," and onClick is defined as "executes JavaScript code when an object on a form is clicked." For buttons, both of these are the same, but for radio buttons, only onClick is defined.

Below the JavaScript event handlers are the PL/SQL event handlers. These handlers respond to specific events for the form components and execute PL/SQL code in response. It is important to note that if an onClick Javascript event and a PL/SQL event are defined for a particular button, both events will be executed when the end user clicks the button. In the case of the INSERT_TOP button, there is no code defined for the query, update, delete, reset, pagination next, pagination previous, or custom PL/SQL events. The insert PL/SQL event includes this code:

```
-- Type your PL/SQL code here...
doInsert;-- This is the default handler
-- ...and here, thanks...
```

This piece of code calls the default procedure for OracleAS Portal (named doInsert) that takes the values currently displayed on the form and attempts to insert them into the database. If, for whatever reason, you need other functionality to go along with your application when you insert records, you can add the necessary PL/SQL code here. Do not put PL/SQL code in more than one PL/SQL event for a button.

Click the DEPTNO field in the left-hand side of the screen. This field is defined as a text box. On the right-hand side, we can set values for the label; decide if the label should be treated as an HTTP link; set the height, width, and font to be used; set default values and/or format masks; determine whether predefined JavaScript validations (isAlpha, isDate, isNum, isNull, etc.) should be applied; and enable a new set of JavaScript event handlers, where we can further define functionality at the form level.

Three of the most important attributes are the three check boxes in the middle of the page: mandatory, updatable, and insertable. Mandatory will reflect whether the field is defined as NOT NULL in the database. Updatable and insertable allow you to prohibit the end user from modifying fields in a way that is not appropriate. For example, a field like DEPTNO may be used as a parent key to the employee table. Altering that value may create orphan records in the EMP table. As part of the requirements for your application, it may be advantageous to deselect the updatable attribute for that field.

The bottom section of the Formatting and Validation options has the same buttons as the top sections (insert, update, delete, query, reset) plus two additional buttons: Previous and Next. These buttons allow the end user to scroll through a set of records, one by one. The PL/SQL events tied to each of those buttons correspond to the Pagination Previous and Pagination Next PL/SQL events. Once again, each of these events has a default handler—doPrevious and doNext, respectively. These default handlers provide OracleAS Portal with the default functionality needed to scroll through a result set of database records.

You are not limited to the top and bottom buttons, along with the fields from the table(s) or view(s) you have selected for your form. Clicking the green plus sign next to the Form entry in the left-hand frame on the page will allow you to add form elements. These form elements can be used for page formatting items such as horizontal lines or images, or else for buttons to upload objects like images or sounds to your database.

If, in the fourth step of the wizard, you selected a custom layout, clicking Next> on the Formatting and Validation Options screen will bring you to the Form Layout Editor – Custom Layout page of the wizard. This page allows you to write your own HTML code to format how the fields will appear on your screen. If Tabular is chosen on the fourth page of the wizard, records will be returned in a tabular format similar to those in Figure 9-6.

The next step of the Forms Wizard provides you with the opportunity to use a template to display your form; enter the display name for your form; and enter header, footer, help, and about text for your form. If you click the Preview Template button, you will see an example of how the colors and background of the form will be displayed. On the top right, there are three icons displayed: the "house" icon will return the user to a specified URL, the question mark icon

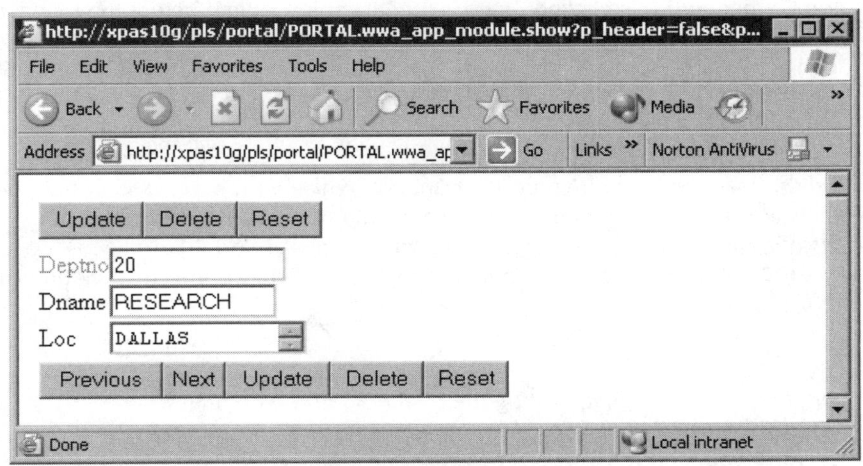

FIGURE 9-6. *Records returned in a tabular format*

will display whatever is entered in the Help Text field, and the "book" icon will display anything that is entered in the About Text field. You can use HTML tags (like <b> for bold) to format the data in the Help Text and About Text fields.

NOTE
In regard to the Form Text page, there is a similar page for almost every type of OracleAS Portal component that we can create (reports, calendars, etc.). Earlier in this chapter, it was mentioned that an OracleAS Portal component can be displayed as a portlet (something to be placed on a page) or stand-alone. The options on this page of the wizard are only applicable for OracleAS components in stand-alone mode. Anything entered here will not be used if the OracleAS Portal component is displayed as a portlet.

The final page of the wizard allows developers to add PL/SQL code that "fires" at various times during the life of a portlet and a page. The six options available are

- Before displaying the page
- Before displaying the form
- After displaying the form
- After displaying the page
- Before processing the form
- After processing the form

all of which should be self-explanatory.

At this point, when Finish is clicked, there is a noticeable lag time before the Manage screen (Figure 9-7) appears. During this time, the OracleAS Portal Form Wizard generates the necessary PL/SQL code in the Oracle Application Server 10*g* infrastructure database. After the PL/SQL code has been generated, clicking the Package Body link in the middle of the Manage page will show you what was generated.

To see what the new OracleAS Portal Form looks like, you can click either the Run or Run as Portlet link on the Manage page. If you click Run, you will see the OracleAS Portal Form run as a web form (stand-alone mode). This will give you an opportunity to test the various icons and see the effects of choosing different templates for the OracleAS Portal Form. Most developers, however, use Oracle Portal to develop components to be used as portlets. Click the Run As Portlet link to see how your form will look as a Portlet.

CAUTION
It is important to note here that running the OracleAS Portal Form as a portlet will display the portlet using default, generic settings for things like color, font type, and font size. In the next chapter, we will see how setting parameters at the page level greatly affects the look of your OracleAS Portal pages.

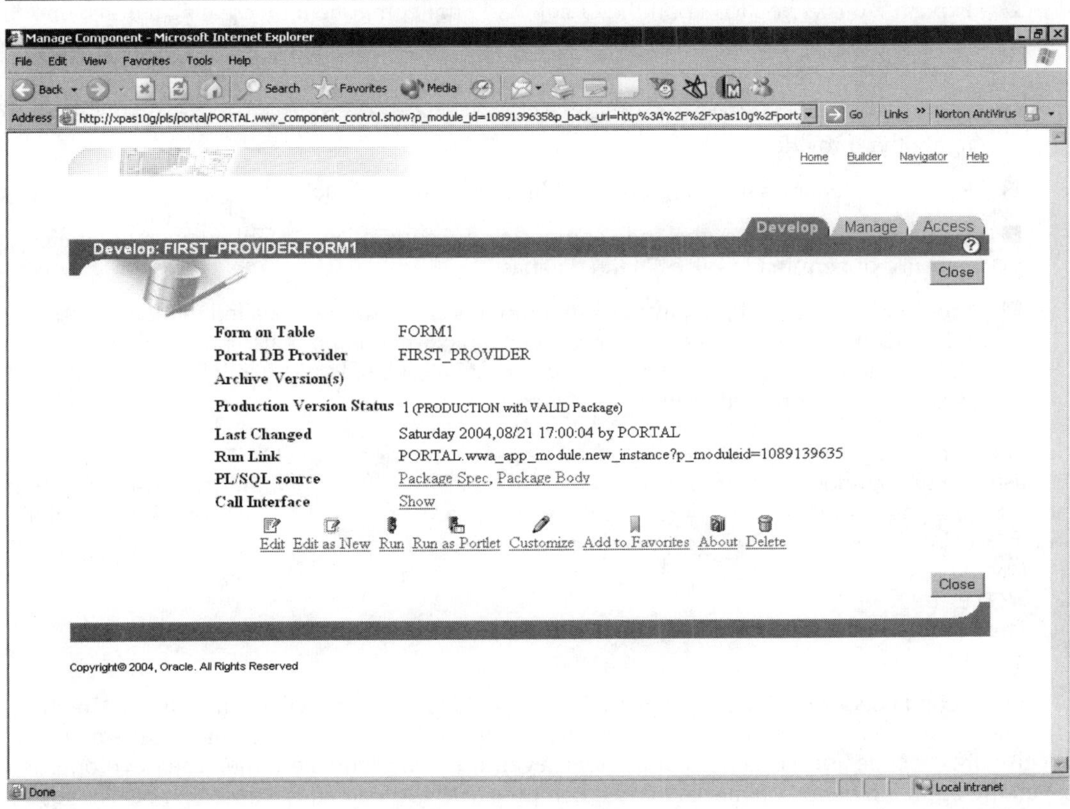

FIGURE 9-7. *The Manage screen for OracleAS Portal components*

The Edit and Edit As New links on the bottom left of the Manage page allow developers to modify their OracleAS Portal components after they have been generated. By using the Edit As New link, developers can take advantage of OracleAS Portal's versioning mechanism: clicking this link will copy your component and allow you to begin working on a new version. When you generate the new component, the Manage page will show a current (production) version and an archived version. OracleAS Portal will keep as many archived versions as you wish, if you repeatedly modify your component by using the Edit As New link. If you select the Edit link, the current version of the component is edited, which can be dangerous if you modify an OracleAS Portal component and then need to undo the changes.

The Manage tab allows you to perform various maintenance activities on your form:

- **Export** Allows you to export the OracleAS Portal component by creating a transport set (the metadata for the OracleAS component) and an export file (the definition of the OracleAS component).
- **Copy** Allows you to copy the OracleAS component; can be used to copy components to another provider.
- **Rename** Renames the component within the current provider.
- **Generate** Regenerates the code composing the component; useful if generation failed because of permission issues in the database.
- **Monitor** OracleAS Portal introduces a monitoring mechanism called the log registry; this registry can be used to monitor various OracleAS components; if this OracleAS Portal component was selected for monitoring in the Log Registry, clicking this link would list a report of all accesses.

The Access tab allows developers to set privileges for their components. The first check box, Publish As Portlet, adds the component to the portlet registry. The portlet registry is used to place portlets on a page. If Publish As Portlet is not checked, the page designer will not see the portlet in the Add Portlets section when constructing a page.

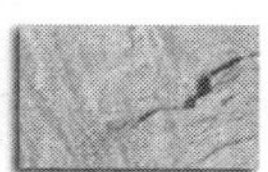

NOTE
Page design and construction are discussed in the next chapter.

The second check box, Inherit Privileges From Portal DB Provider, will change the look of this page depending on its state. If it is checked, any privileges that have been defined at the provider level will "cascade" down to the component level. If it is not checked, then the developer is given the option to define privileges for that component. If the state of the check box is changed (from unchecked to checked or from checked to unchecked), the page will automatically redraw itself and present the developer with the appropriate options. Clicking Close at this point will return you to the Navigator page, displaying your completed component (Figure 9-8).

From this page, you can use the links to the right of the component name to perform various actions:

- **Manage** Brings you to the Manage page.
- **Run** Runs the component in stand-alone mode.
- **Edit** Edits the component. (Note: This does *not* perform an Edit As New, so you will be editing the production version of the component. To use versioning, select the Manage link and then the Edit as New link.)
- **Delete** Deletes the component (if you have multiple versions, you will be prompted for which version[s] you wish to delete).
- **Grant Access** Brings you directly to the Access tab of the Manage page for the component.
- **Export** Brings you directly to the export page for the component.

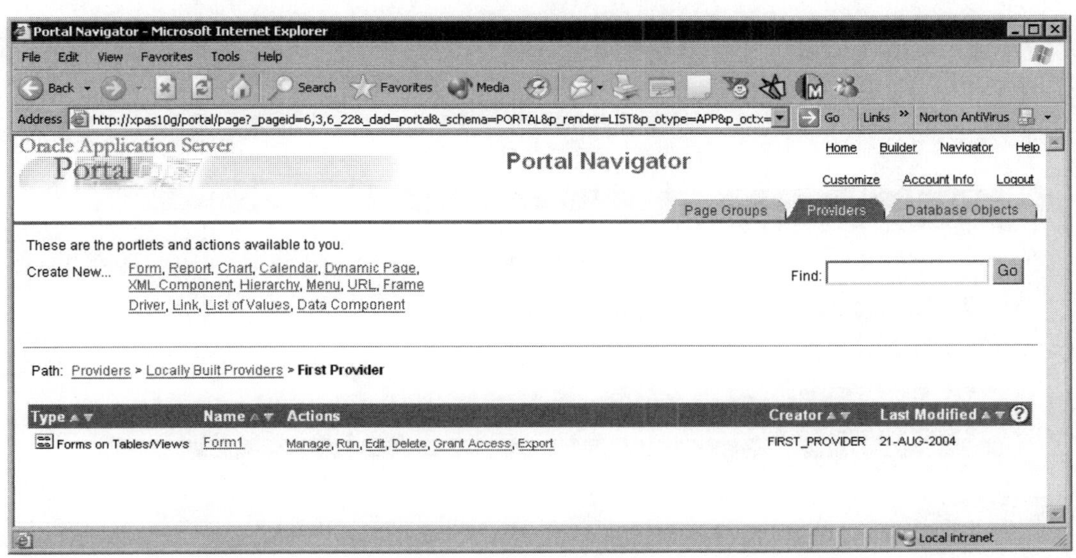

FIGURE 9-8. *The Navigator page listing the completed form*

NOTE
The Forms component of OracleAS Portal is extremely powerful, yet it does not contain all of the functionality of the Oracle Forms 10g product. See Chapter 11 for a discussion of integrating forms created in Oracle Forms 10g with OracleAS Portal.

OracleAS Portal Reports

The Reports component of OracleAS Portal gives developers the ability to create great-looking OracleAS Portal Reports. As you will see, developers can change the look of the report according to values queried (or calculated) from the database, and then they can grant power users the ability to modify the query used to drive the report and can even create links in their reports that allow users to click a report and be taken to another OracleAS Portal component.

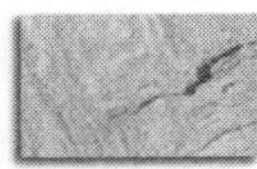

NOTE
Links in OracleAS Portal are discussed in the next chapter.

When you select the Create New... Report link in the Navigator, you are presented with a page similar to the one used to create our first OracleAS Portal Form (Figure 9-9).

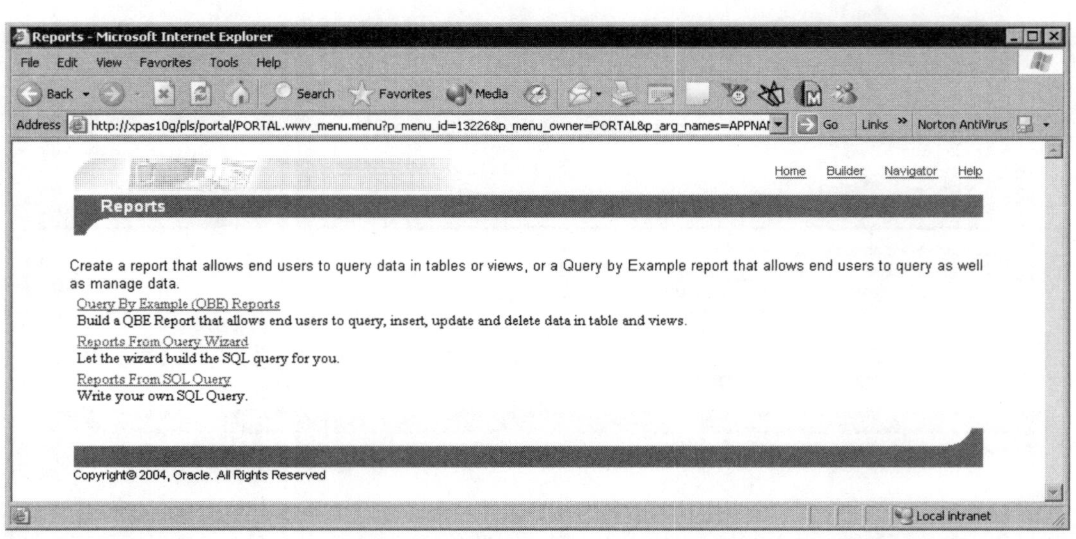

FIGURE 9-9. *The first page of the OracleAS Portal Report Wizard*

Choosing from the three different types of OracleAS Portal Reports will depend on your reporting requirements:

- **Query By Example (QBE) Reports** Choosing this type of report will not only generate the report itself but will also generate a customization screen along with the OracleAS Portal Report. Power users can be granted privileges that allow them to modify what data is returned to the portlet and to insert/update/delete records in the reports' tables.
- **Reports from Query Wizard** This type of report is similar to a QBE report except for the fact that the customization page contains many fewer options—the ability to insert/update/delete records is not available, nor is the ability to change the where clause of the query driving the report.
- **Reports from SQL Query** This option allows developers to write their own query that will drive the report.

Table 9-2 shows the different OracleAS Portal Report Wizard pages presented to the developer depending on the type of report chosen.

Click the Query By Example (QBE) link to build a QBE report for this example. The first page of the wizard should look familiar. In fact, all of the OracleAS Portal components we can build will have a screen similar to Figure 9-10.

Enter meaningful values for your OracleAS Portal Report and click Next >. The next page of the wizard prompts for a table or view that will drive this report. Clicking the small notepad

Wizard Page	QBE Report	Report from Query Wizard	Report from SQL Query
Report Name and Portal Provider	Step 1 of 10	Step 1 of 16	Step 1 of 13
Table(s) or View(s)	Step 3 of 10 (as in the wizard for OracleAS Portal Forms, there doesn't appear to be a step 2 anywhere)	Step 3 of 16	N/A
SQL Query	N/A	N/A	Step 3 of 13
Table/View Columns	Step 4 of 10 (erroneously labeled "Step 5 of 10" on actual wizard page)	Step 5 of 16	N/A
Column Conditions	N/A	Step 6 of 16	N/A
Report Layout	N/A	Step 7 of 16	Step 4 of 13
Column Formatting	Step 5 of 10	Step 8 of 16	Step 5 of 13
Formatting Conditions	Step 6 of 10	Step 9 of 16	Step 6 of 13
Display Options	Step 7 of 10	Step 12 of 16	Step 9 of 13
Report Layout Editor	N/A	N/A	Step 10 of 13
HTML Code	N/A	Step 13 of 16	N/A
Customization Form Options	Step 8 of 10	Step 14 of 16	Step 11 of 13
Report and Customization Form Text	Step 9 of 10	Step 15 of 16	Step 12 of 13
Additional PL/SQL Code	Step 10 of 10	Step 16 of 16	Step 13 of 13

TABLE 9-2. *The Portal Wizard Pages for an OracleAS Portal Report*

icon to the right of the text box will bring up a list of all tables and views you have access to in the database.

This can be confusing for developers new to OracleAS Portal. We've already mentioned that when a user is created in OracleAS Portal, an entry is made for that user in Oracle's LDAP implementation, Oracle Internet Directory (OID). No user is created in the database. If no user is created in the database, how can a developer determine what tables and views they have access to? The answer lies in the schema that is associated to the OracleAS Portal provider upon creation of the provider. Any attempt to create an OracleAS Portal Form or Report (or any OracleAS Portal object for that matter) that needs with query the database to see a list of available objects for inclusion on that OracleAS Portal component will "talk" to the database as the user specified when the OracleAS Portal database provider is defined. For DBA types out there, the list of objects that is presented to the OracleAS Portal developer will reflect those objects in the ALL_TABLES and ALL_VIEWS views. A second point of confusion relates to accessing data on separate instances. Oracle recommends that the infrastructure database not be used for storing any data that is not directly used by Oracle Application Server 10*g* to perform its functions. It is considered

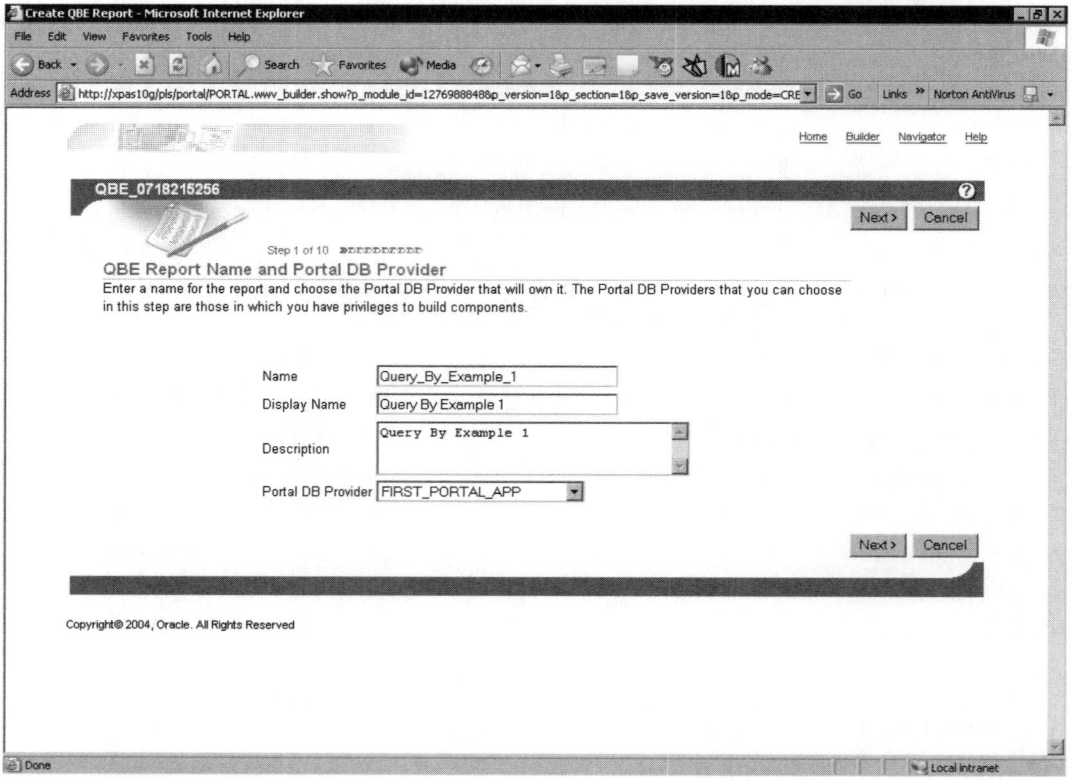

FIGURE 9-10. *The first step of the OracleAS Portal Reports Wizard*

bad practice to mingle data used by the various Oracle Application Server 10*g* components with application data found in your organization. OracleAS Portal accesses data not in the infrastructure database through the use of links, as is demonstrated in the following example.

TIP
As of OracleAs10g, the Portal Repository can be installed into a new or existing Oracle database, versions 9.2.x or 10g. This is done using the RepCA (Repository Creation Assistant CD, part of the distribution). If your portal will be accessing data from only one database instance, you can install the Portal Repository there and reference the data locally—this is far superior to using db links. If your portal will be referencing data from multiple Oracle database instances, you will have to use database links.

As it is common (and good practice) to store your company's production data outside of the infrastructure database, this example will make use of a database link. By default, the Oracle Application Server 10*g* infrastructure database is called asdb. On a separate server, I have an older Oracle 9*i*AS R2 database running named iasdb. In that database, I have a schema named user1. For this example, we will build an OracleAS Portal Report off of the test1 table owned by the user1 user in the iasdb database. What are the steps to perform this?

First, we must build a database link in the asdb instance. In order for the database link to work properly, an entry is needed in the tnsnames.ora file in the infrastructure home of my Oracle Application Server 10*g* installation. In this example, my home for the infrastructure instance on my xpas10g server is C:\IS_HOME, so the tnsnames.ora file that needs modification is in the C:\IS_HOME\NETWORK\ADMIN directory. In the next example, you will see the entry for the Oracle Application Server 10*g* infrastructure database (asdb on the xpas10g server) and the new entry for the database link about to be created (iasdb on the 192.168.0.2 server):

```
ASDB =
  (DESCRIPTION =
    (ADDRESS_LIST =
      (ADDRESS = (PROTOCOL = TCP)(HOST = xpas10g)(PORT = 1521))
    )
    (CONNECT_DATA =
      (SERVICE_NAME = asdb.world)
    )
  )

IASDB =
  (DESCRIPTION =
    (ADDRESS_LIST =
      (ADDRESS = (PROTOCOL = TCP)(HOST = 192.168.0.2)(PORT = 1521))
    )
    (CONNECT_DATA =
      (SID = iasdb)
    )
  )
```

For simplicity's sake, I created a public database link called iasdb in the asdb instance:

```
SQL> create public database link iasdb connect to user1 identified by user1 using 'iasdb';
Database link created.
SQL> desc test1@iasdb
 Name                                      Null?    Type
 ----------------- ---- ------------
 FIELD1                                             VARCHAR2(20)
 FIELD2                                             VARCHAR2(20)
SQL> select * from test1@iasdb;
FIELD1               FIELD2
---------- ----------
xxxxxxxxx            yyyyyyyyy
xxxxxxxxx            yyyyyyyyy
```

```
xxxxxxxxxx          yyyyyyyyy
xxxxxxxxxx          yyyyyyyyy
xxxxxxxxxx          yyyyyyyyy
xxxxxxxxxx          yyyyyyyyy
xxxxxxxxxx          yyyyyyyyy
xxxxxxxxxx          yyyyyyyyy
xxxxxxxxxx          yyyyyyyyy
xxxxxxxxxx          yyyyyyyyy
```

Now that we have confirmed the validity of the iasdb database link in the asdb instance, let's specify the test1 table in the third page of the OracleAS Portal Reports Wizard by clicking the small notepad icon to the right of the text box on that page, as shown in Figure 9-11.

If you search through all of the available tables and views, you will see that no objects resolved through the database link are displayed. OracleAS Portal is not "smart" enough to resolve any of the database links (public or private) for a specified user. Nor can you specify the link in the Search dialog (Figure 9-12).

You can, however, specify the full table or view name with the database link directly in the Table or View field in the third step of the OracleAS Portal Reports wizard (Figure 9-13).

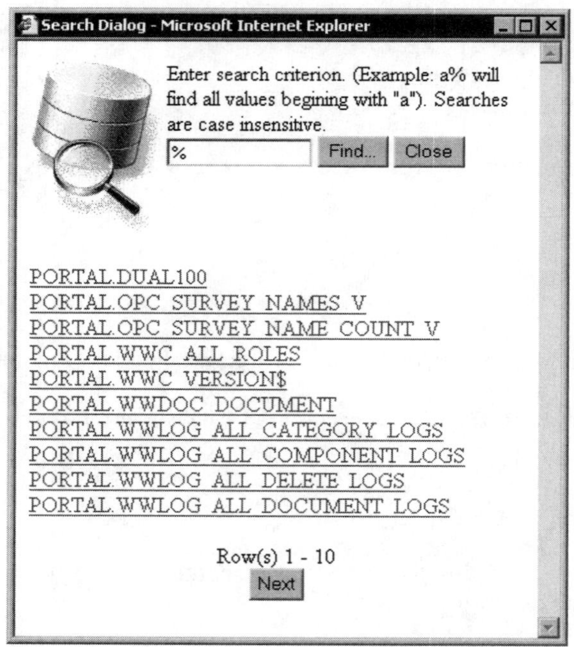

FIGURE 9-11. *The Search dialog*

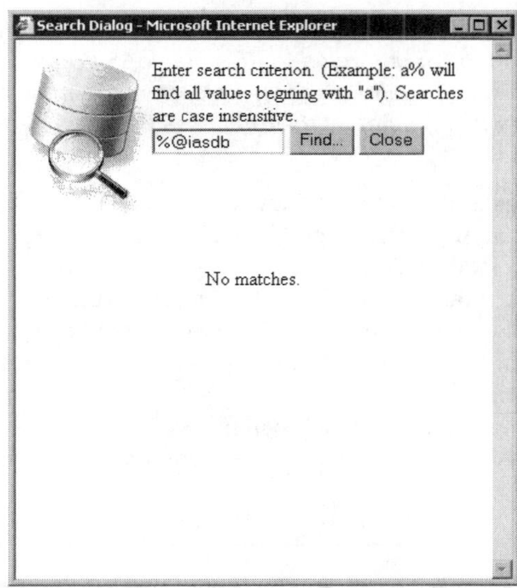

FIGURE 9-12. *The Search dialog attempting to search on the link name*

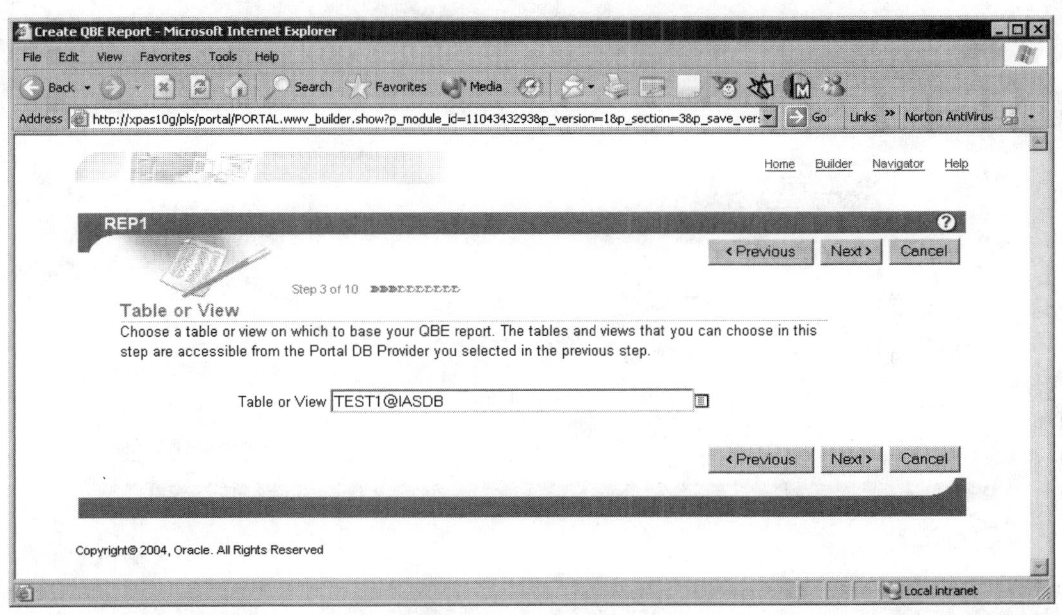

FIGURE 9-13. *The TEST1@IASDB table specified in the Table or View page of the Reports Wizard*

NOTE
Although this example shows database link functionality when building an OracleAS Portal Report, it is not limited to just OracleAS Portal Reports. Developers can specify valid database links any time they are prompted for a database object in any of the OracleAS Portal wizards.

Clicking Next > brings us to the Table or View Columns page, mistakenly labeled as "Step 5 of 10" (we're really only on Step 4). This page allows developers to specify what columns will be displayed on the report (Figure 9-14).

Clicking Next > brings us to the Column Formatting page (Figure 9-15). On this page, developers can specify the column heading of the report, whether we want the column to be a summary column, alignment, the format mask for the column, etc. Here are two of the interesting fields to note:

- **LOV** List of values; creation of LOVs will be discussed later in this chapter, but for now, understand that LOVs are one of two objects you can create in OracleAS Portal that are

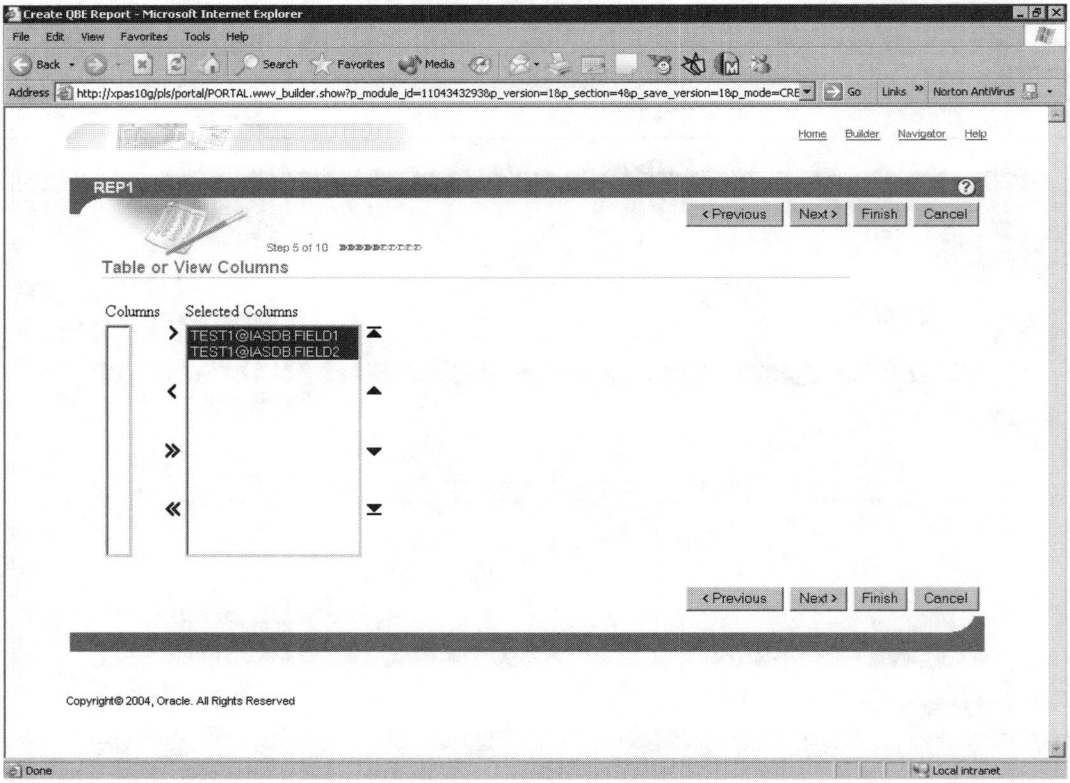

FIGURE 9-14. *The Table or View Columns page of the Reports Wizard*

not intended to be placed on an OracleAS Portal page (links, discussed in the next item, are the other). An LOV is designed to be used as an attribute for a field on an OracleAS Portal Report, as well as a few other OracleAS Portal components (discussed later).

- **Link** A link in OracleAS Portal is different from a database link but is similar to an HTML link. An OracleAS Portal link allows you to link one OracleAS component (such as a column in an OracleAS Portal Report) to another OracleAS component (such as an OracleAS Portal Form). Creation of links is discussed in the next chapter.

Clicking Next > brings us to the Formatting Conditions page (Figure 9-16). Unless you are using OracleAS Portal at an extremely high resolution (e.g., 1280 × 1024), part of this page will be off the right side of the screen. This page allows developers to graphically change the output of the report according to developer-defined criteria. Click the Condition drop-down box to see a list of conditions that can be checked for. The following graphical characteristics of the report can be modified at either the row or column level: color, background color, font (including bold, italic, and underline), blinking, and sequence displayed. Later in the wizard, we will define what

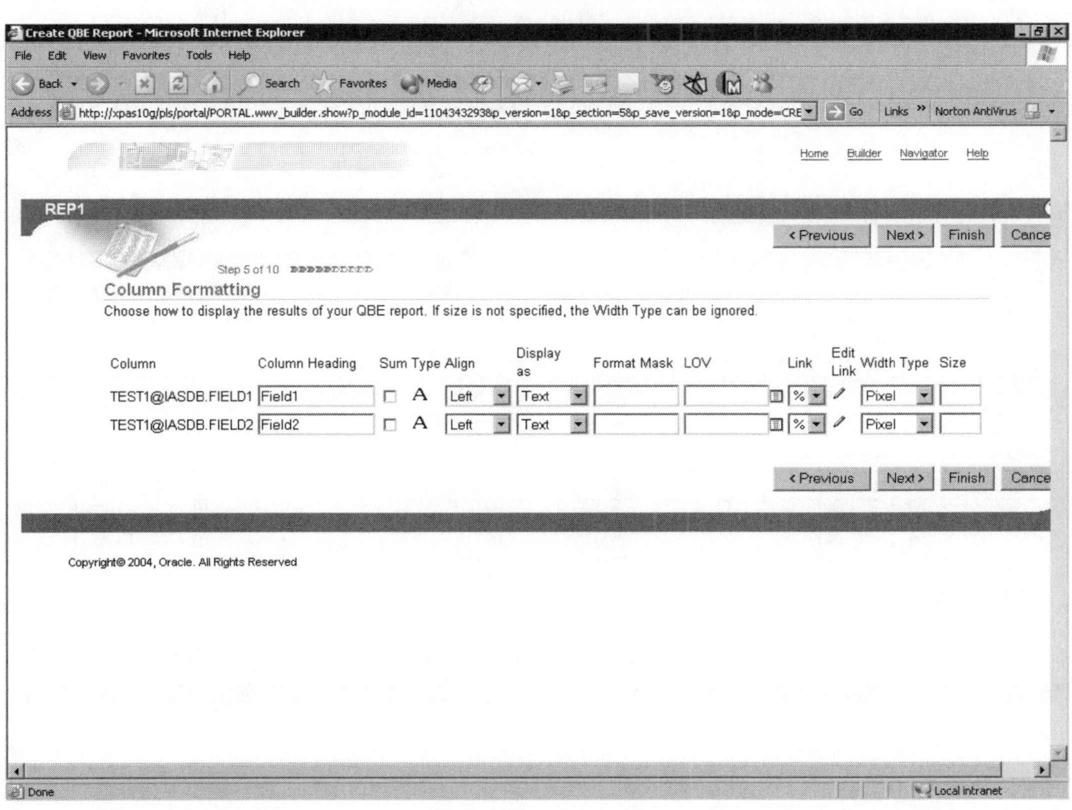

FIGURE 9-15. *The Column Formatting page*

characteristics the end user can customize for their report (if any), but remember that anything specified here will become permanently part of the report.

Clicking Next > displays the Display Options page (Figure 9-17). This page is divided into six sections from top to bottom:

- **Common Options** These options affect the entire report, regardless of whether it is displayed stand-alone or as a portlet. Of important note is the Expire After option. If the number specified is greater than 0, the OracleAS Portal engine will automatically cache the OracleAS Portal Report for each successive request to display it. While this greatly speeds the construction of an OracleAS Portal page (which may include a number of other OracleAS Portal objects), the developer must take into account the needs of the end users running the report. If end users need up-to-the-second information (as in a stock quote or ticketing application), caching the report would not be appropriate.
- **Full Page Options** These options affect how the report is displayed in stand-alone, or full-page, mode. All of the fields are self-explanatory. The Table Row Color(s) field takes a little explaining, however. Multiple colors can be selected by holding down the

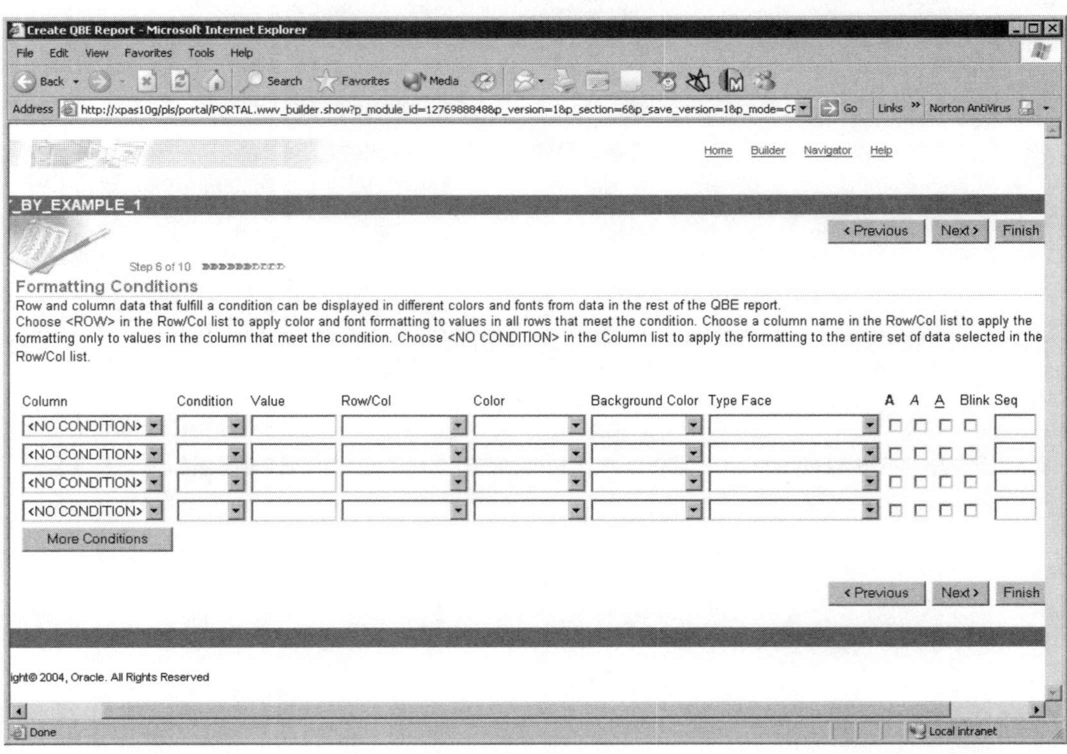

FIGURE 9-16. *The Formatting Conditions page*

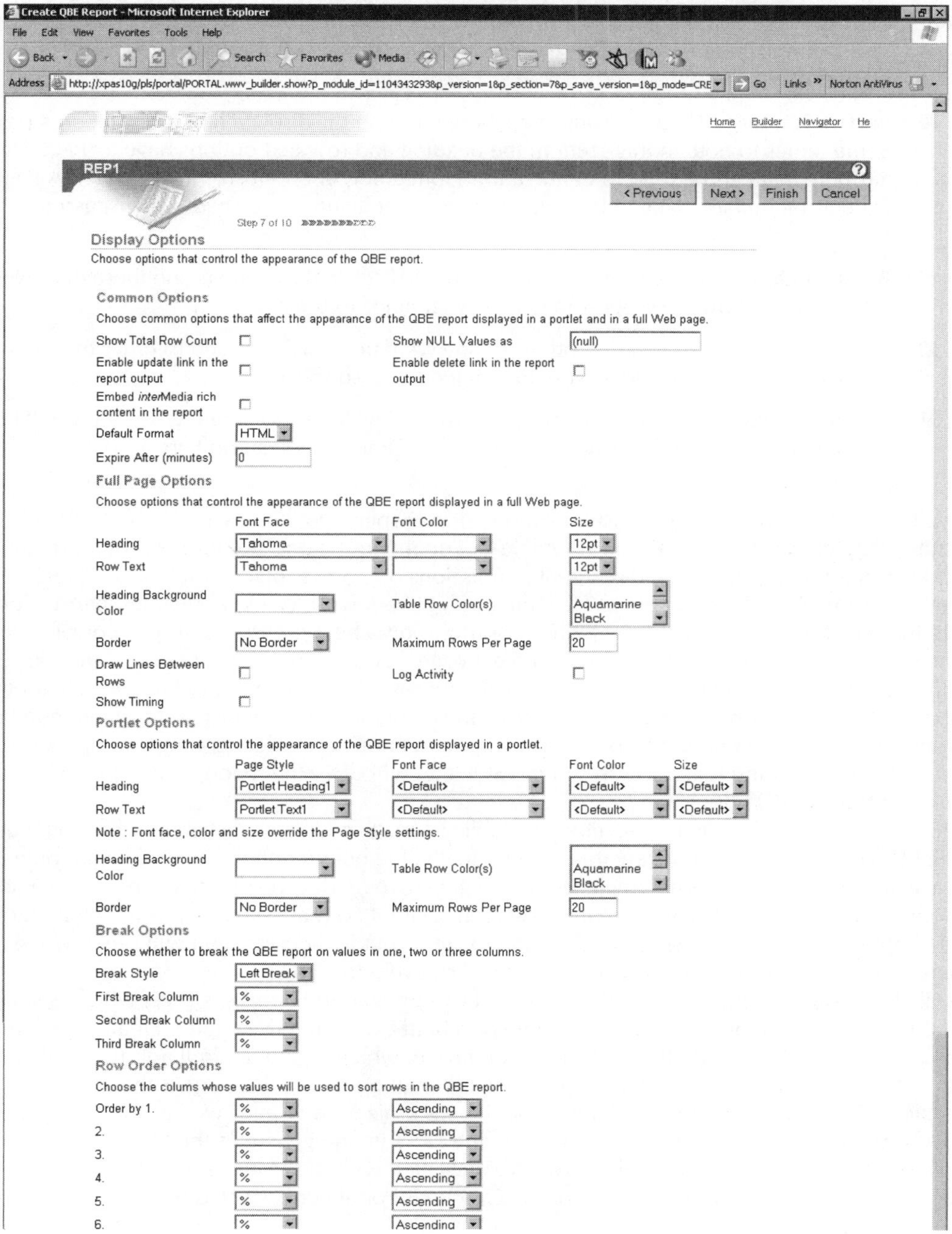

FIGURE 9-17. *The Display Options page*

SHIFT key and single-clicking the selected color(s). If more than one color is chosen, the OracleAS Portal engine will cycle through the colors when displaying the report. This can make the report much easier to read on the screen (provided you don't pick clashing colors).

- **Portlet Settings** These options affect how the report is displayed as a portlet on a page. Some things to note in this section: the heading and row text options have a "Page Style" attribute that can be used to define a font, font color, and font size for a portlet. A Page Style is a template that can be used over and over again; Page Styles are discussed in the next chapter.
- **Break Options** These options (for both reports displayed as portlets and those displayed stand-alone) allow developers to define what fields to break on.
- **Row Order Options** These options define what fields will be used to order the rows returned by a report's query. You are limited to six sort fields.
- **Mobile Display Options** These options allow developers to define what fields will be displayed for the Wireless options included in Oracle Application Server 10*g*.

Clicking Next > displays the Customization Form Display Options page (Figure 9-18). In the next chapter, we will take a look at OracleAS Portal permissions, but for now, understand that different users can be granted different permissions on portlets placed on a page. These permissions range from being able to view the portlet (the lowest, or least powerful, permission) up to modification of the portlet (the highest, or most powerful, permission). Those power users granted permission to modify the portlet will see a page that depends on what options are selected for the portlet by the developer on this page of the wizard. As you can see in Figure 9-18, for this report power users will have the ability to modify the output format, specify the maximum number of rows returned, select columns to perform summarizations on, select columns to break on, modify the order by and where clauses of the SQL that will drive the report, and define what to display as the report's title.

Below the Formatting Options section, the Public Formatting Options section lists those attributes available to all end users who view this report. Finally, the button options control which buttons are available to those users with privileges allowing them to modify the report. For now, remember the options that have been specified on this screen (Output Format, Maximum rows, etc.). In the next chapter, when we discuss OracleAS Portal page layout and design, you will see how the different privilege levels affect how the portlet is displayed on a page.

Clicking Next > displays the QBE Report and Customization Form Text page, which is similar to the Form Text page of the OracleAS Portal Form built earlier in this chapter. Finally, clicking Next > brings you to the Additional PL/SQL Code page, which, again, is similar to the final page of the OracleAS Portal Form Wizard. The only additional option on this page is the ability to execute PL/SQL code when events happen on the customization form as well as the report itself. When you click Finish, the OracleAS Portal engine kicks in and generates the PL/SQL code to display this report. After it is complete, you are presented with the Manage page for the report, which is identical to the Manage page for the OracleAS Portal Form created earlier.

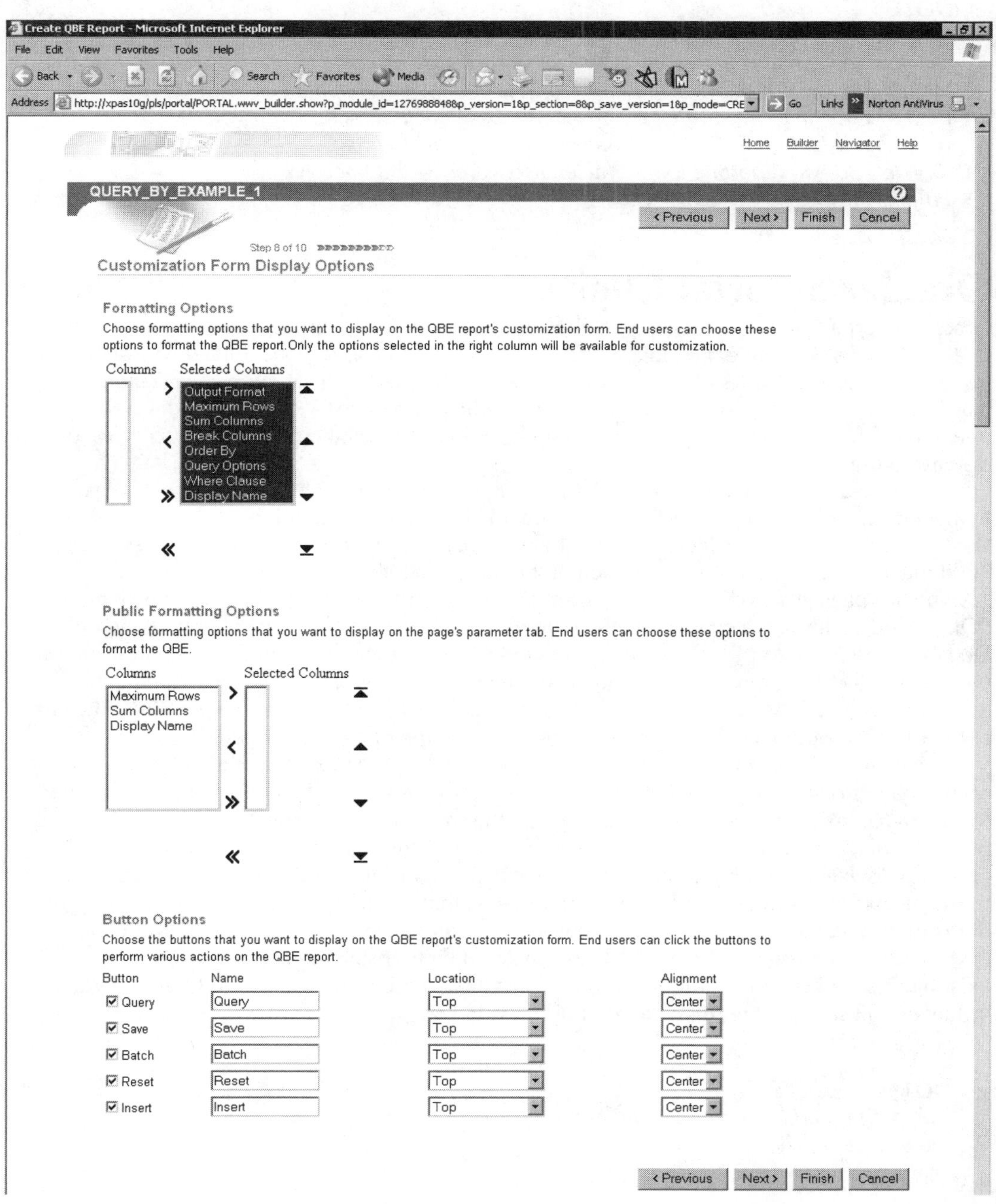

FIGURE 9-18. *The Customizations Form Display Options page*

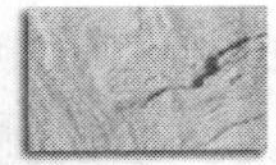

NOTE
Like the Forms component discussed earlier, the Reports component of OracleAS Portal is extremely powerful yet does not contain all of the functionality of the Oracle Reports 10g product. See Chapter 11 for a discussion of integrating reports created in Oracle Reports 10g with OracleAS Portal. Chapter 11 also discusses how to integrate Oracle's ad hoc reporting tool, Oracle Discoverer, with OracleAS Portal.

OracleAS Portal Charts

OracleAS Portal Charts give developers the ability to graphically display information as a portlet on their OracleAS Portal pages. Like OracleAS Portal Forms and Reports, OracleAS Portal Charts are developed using a series of wizard pages and can be created with various customization options that can then be granted to certain users. As you will see, OracleAS Portal gives developers great freedom in choosing the type of chart to display and what formatting options are to be used when displaying the chart.

To create a new OracleAS Portal Chart, bring up the Navigator by clicking the Navigator link in the top right of any OracleAS Portal page. Click the Providers tab if it is not already selected. Click the Locally Built Providers link, and then the name of the provider you have been using to build the examples so far. On the top left of the page, click the Create New... Chart link.

The first page gives you the option of creating a chart from the Query Wizard or a chart from a SQL Query. Building the chart using the Query Wizard allows you to quickly build and deploy a chart, but developers are restricted to a limited number of features. Building a chart from a SQL Query gives the developer greater flexibility but requires more work (particularly when constructing the driving SQL query). With either selection, you are presented with the now-familiar first page of the Chart Wizard (Figure 9-19) after choosing what type of chart to build.

If you are building a Chart from Query Wizard (CQW), the next step of the wizard, Step 3 of 10 (again, no Step 2), asks you to specify which table or view will be used to drive the chart (Figure 9-20). As in the wizards before, clicking the small notepad icon to the right of the text box will not display tables or views that can be resolved through database links; it will display only those database tables and views that the schema associated with the database provider of this chart has access to. Since Oracle recommends that production data not be stored in the infrastructure database, we have seen that this is of limited practical use. Most production environments will use the Repository Creation Assistant to install the Portal Repository into their existing Oracle Database, but portals accessing information from multiple Oracle database instances will still need to use database links.

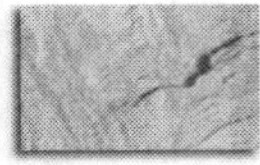

NOTE
You are limited to returning data from one, and only one, table or view when building a CQW.

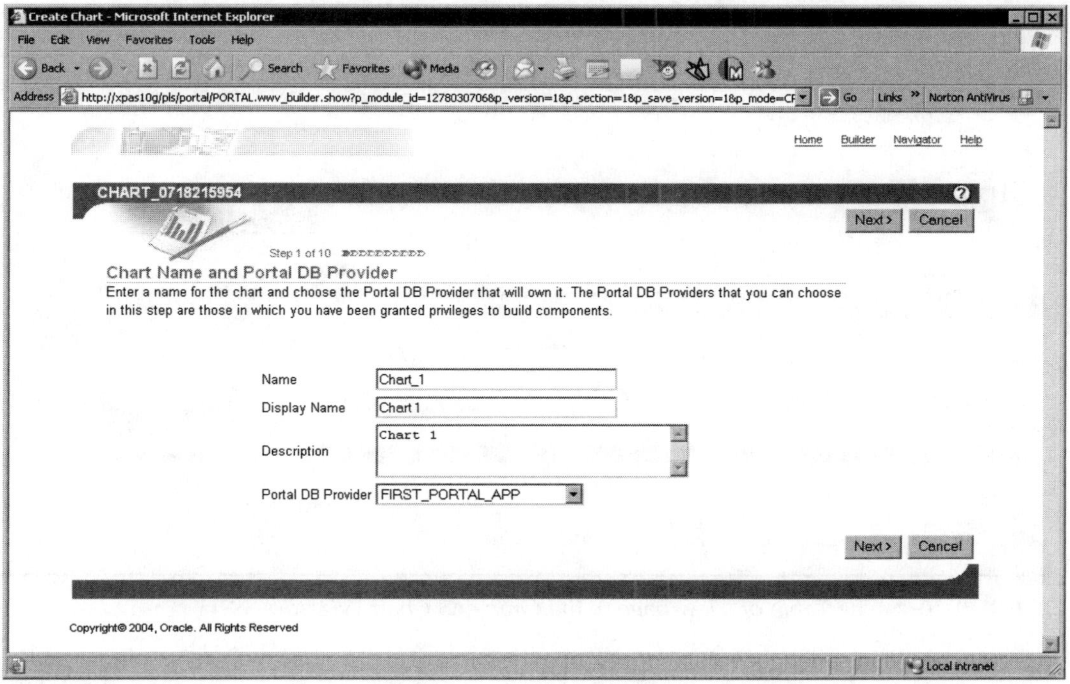

FIGURE 9-19. *The first page of the Chart Wizard*

If you are building a Chart from SQL Query (CSQ), the next step of the wizard, Step 3 of 10, asks you to specify an odd-looking query to retrieve the data that will drive your chart:

```
select
    null      the_link,
    ENAME     the_name,
    SAL       the_data
from SCOTT.EMP
order by SAL desc
```

In order to build a chart from a SQL query, you must construct the query in the format shown here: a select with three columns, all aliased:

- A link name, aliased as "the_link" (which can be NULL)
- A column that will supply the values for the y-axis (for a horizontal chart) or the x-axis (for a vertical chart), aliased as "the_name"
- A column that will provide data for the chart, aliased as "the_data"

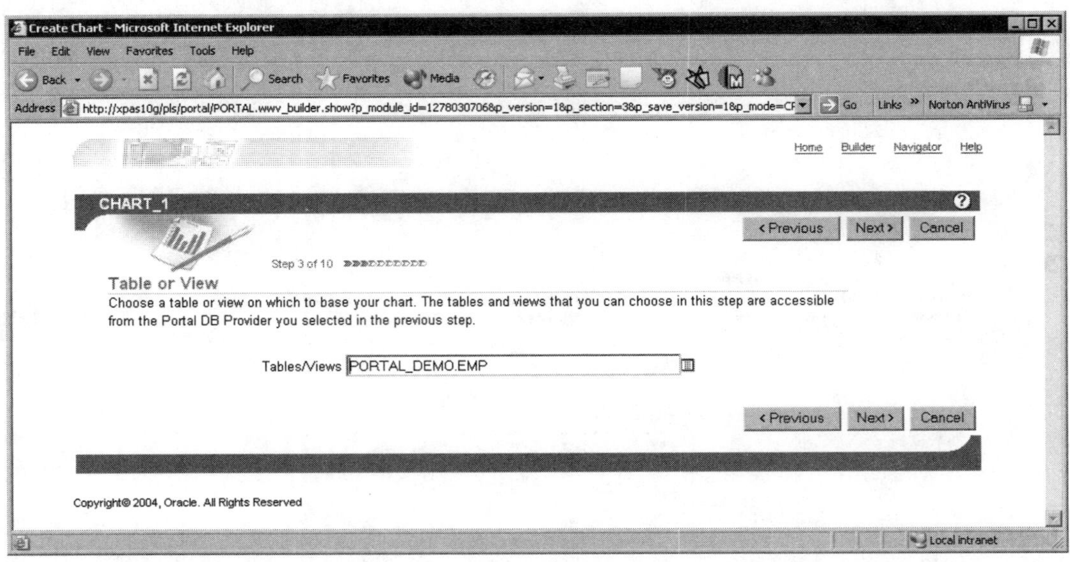

FIGURE 9-20. *The Table or View page of the OracleAS Chart Wizard*

The first time you try to construct a query in this manner, it may seem a little awkward, but after a few attempts, it will become second nature. The biggest difference between a CQW and a CSQ is the flexibility that can be incorporated into the query that drives a CSQ.

As mentioned earlier, a CQW is limited to only one table. It is only possible to apply the standard SQL functions provided for you in Step 4 (discussed shortly) of the chart wizard for a CQW: SUM, COUNT, AVERAGE, MAX, MIN, STDDEV, and VARIANCE. A CSQ can use multiple tables to return data and embed any SQL or user-defined function in the query. As an example, consider the following parent-child relationship between the ORDERS and LINE_ ITEMS tables:

```
SQL> desc orders
 Name                                      Null?    Type
 --------------------- ---- ------
 ORDER_ID                                           NUMBER
 CUSTOMER_NAME                                      VARCHAR2(20)

SQL> desc line_items
 Name                                      Null?    Type
 --------------------- ---- ------
 ORDER_ID                                           NUMBER
```

```
 LINE_ITEM                                                 NUMBER
 PRODUCT_DESC                                              VARCHAR2(20)
 AMOUNT                                                    NUMBER
```

If our requirements were to create an OracleAS Portal Chart that had the customer_name field as the y-axis (for a horizontal chart) and the amount of money each customer spent in our store, we could not use a CQW, as it allows only one table or view to be specified (we could create a view that joins the two tables together and then build a CQW off of that, but I digress). We can construct a query using a CSQ like this:

```
select
    null                    the_link,
    o.customer_name         the_name,
    sum(li.amount)          the_data
from orders@iasdb o, line_items@iasdb li
where o.order_id=li.order_id
group by o.customer_name
order by sum(li.amount) desc
```

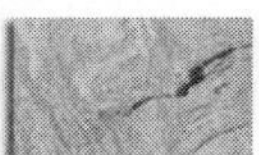

NOTE
To see the creation of the iasdb database link used in this example, see the section "OracleAS Portal Reports" earlier in this chapter.

If the data in the ORDERS and LINE_ITEMS tables looked like this:

```
SQL> select * from orders;
  ORDER_ID CUSTOMER_NAME
----- ----------
         1 Smith
         2 Jones
         3 Brown

SQL> select * from line_items;
  ORDER_ID  LINE_ITEM PRODUCT_DESC                AMOUNT
----- ----- ---------- -----
         1          1 Batteries                     4.99
         1          2 Cookies                       3.99
         2          1 Magazine                      5.99
         2          2 Fountain Drink                1.99
         2          3 Hot Dog                       2.99
         3          1 Big Gulp                      2.99
         3          2 Car Freshener                 6.99
```

the preceding query would produce a chart like Figure 9-21 (after we've completed the succeeding steps, of course).

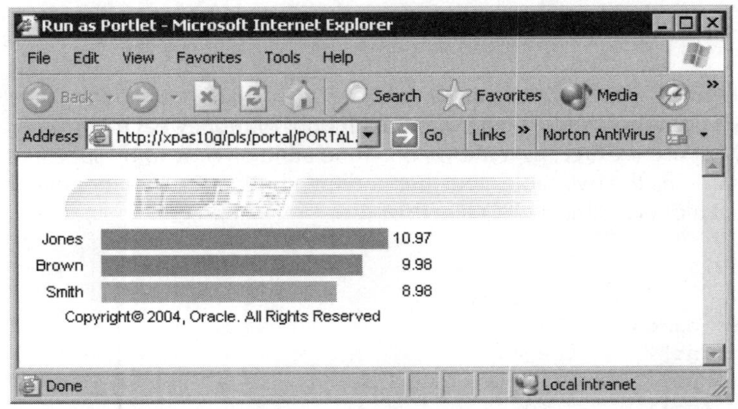

FIGURE 9-21. *A chart based on a multi-table query*

If you are creating a CQW, Step 4 of the chart wizard (Figure 9-22) asks you to specify what column from our table selected on the previous page will be used to drive the chart. The link field specified here is similar to the link field available to us in the Column Formatting page of the Reports Wizard. The purpose of a link, if you remember, is to create a pathway between OracleAS Portal objects. Since we have not created any links yet (we will do so in the next chapter), there is nothing to select here.

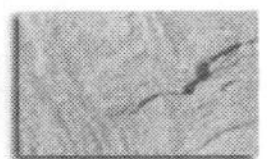

NOTE
After we create the links in the next chapter, we will revisit the reports and charts created in this chapter and update them with link capability.

The group function allows developers to specify what type of grouping function will be applied to the data. The following group functions can be applied: SUM, COUNT, AVERAGE, MAX, MIN, STDDEV, and VARIANCE.

Step 5 of the CQW Chart Wizard allows you to specify conditions for displaying the report. This is the equivalent of adding where clauses to the end of a SQL statement. Step 6 of the CQW Chart Wizard is similar to the Formatting Conditions page of the Report Wizard (if you are building a CSQ, the Formatting Conditions page is Step 4 in the wizard). Depending on the values returned by the query when the portlet is displayed, the bars or column headings that make up the chart can be altered to display specific colors, and the column headings can be changed (bold, italics, etc.) and have their sequence altered, changing the order that the columns of the chart are displayed.

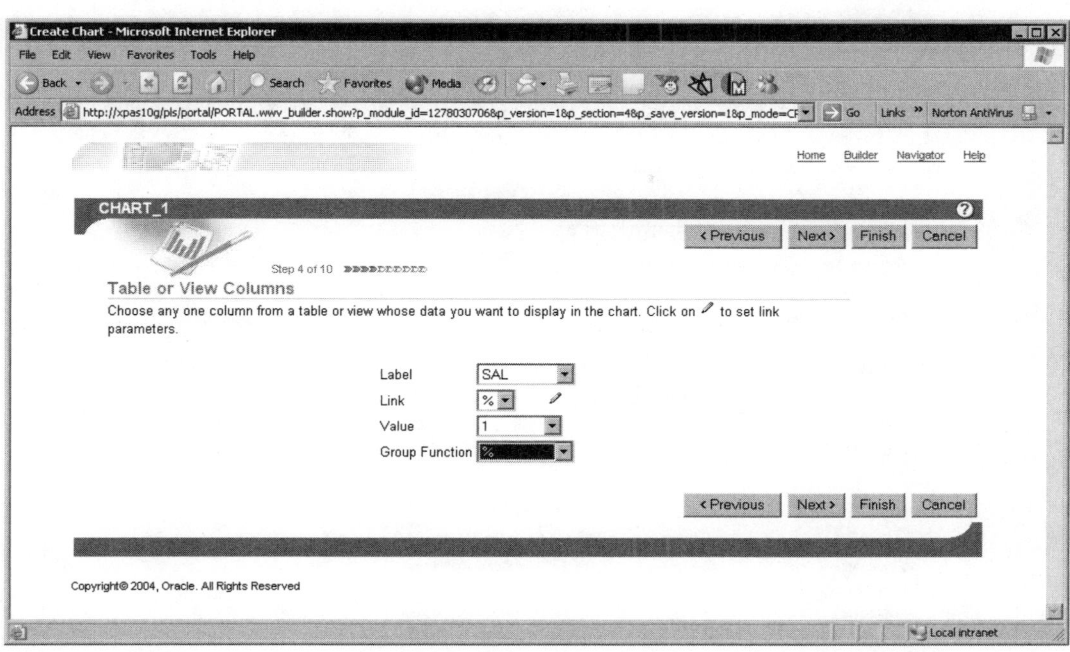

FIGURE 9-22. *The Table or View Columns page of the OracleAS Chart Wizard*

In Step 7 of the CQW Chart Wizard, the Display Options page (Figure 9-23) is displayed (if you are building a CSQ, this is Step 5). It is similar in functionality to the Display Options page of the OracleAS Portal Reports Wizard. It is broken into four sections:

- **Common Options** Affects the entire chart, regardless of whether it is displayed in stand-alone (full page) mode or as a portlet. The Expire After field serves the same purpose as the Expire After field on the Display Options page of the reports wizard: if the number specified here is greater than 0, the OracleAS Portal engine will cache the chart; if the number specified here is 0, a new chart will be generated every time it is accessed.
- **Full Page Options** Affects the chart when it is displayed in stand-alone mode. Multiple Summary Options can be selected by holding down the SHIFT key and single-clicking the desired option. The full page options also feature a "Chart Type," where the basic method that a chart uses to display data can be altered; this is not available for charts to be displayed as portlets.
- **Portlet Options** Affects the chart when it is displayed as a portlet on an OracleAS Portal page. Page Styles (discussed in the next chapter) can be used as templates for the portlet.

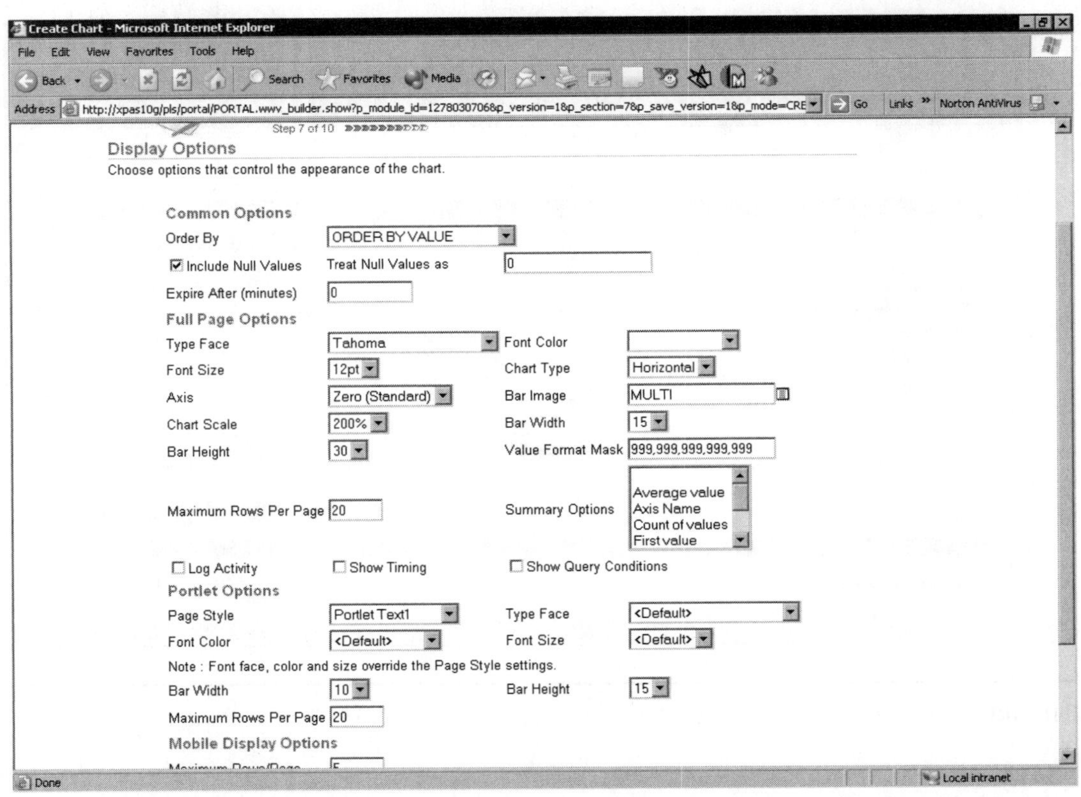

FIGURE 9-23. *The Display Options page of the OracleAS Portal Chart Wizard*

- **Mobile Display Options** Specifies what fields will be displayed for the Wireless component of Oracle Application Server 10*g* when a user requests a web page over a mobile device such as a web-enabled phone or personal digital assistant.

Step 8 of the CQW Chart Wizard (step 6 if you are building a CSQ), the Customization Form Display Options page (Figure 9-24), is similar to the corresponding page in the OracleAS Reports Wizard except for the introduction of a new concept: parameters. This page allows us to specify parameters that end users (who have been granted the necessary privileges) can use to alter the data that will drive the chart. If you click the Value Required check box, the end user will be forced to enter a value before the chart will be displayed.

The final two steps of the CQW and CSQ chart wizards, the Chart and Customization Form Text and Additional PL/SQL Code pages, are identical to their corresponding OracleAS Report Wizards pages. Figure 9-25 shows an example of an OracleAS Portal Chart run as a portlet.

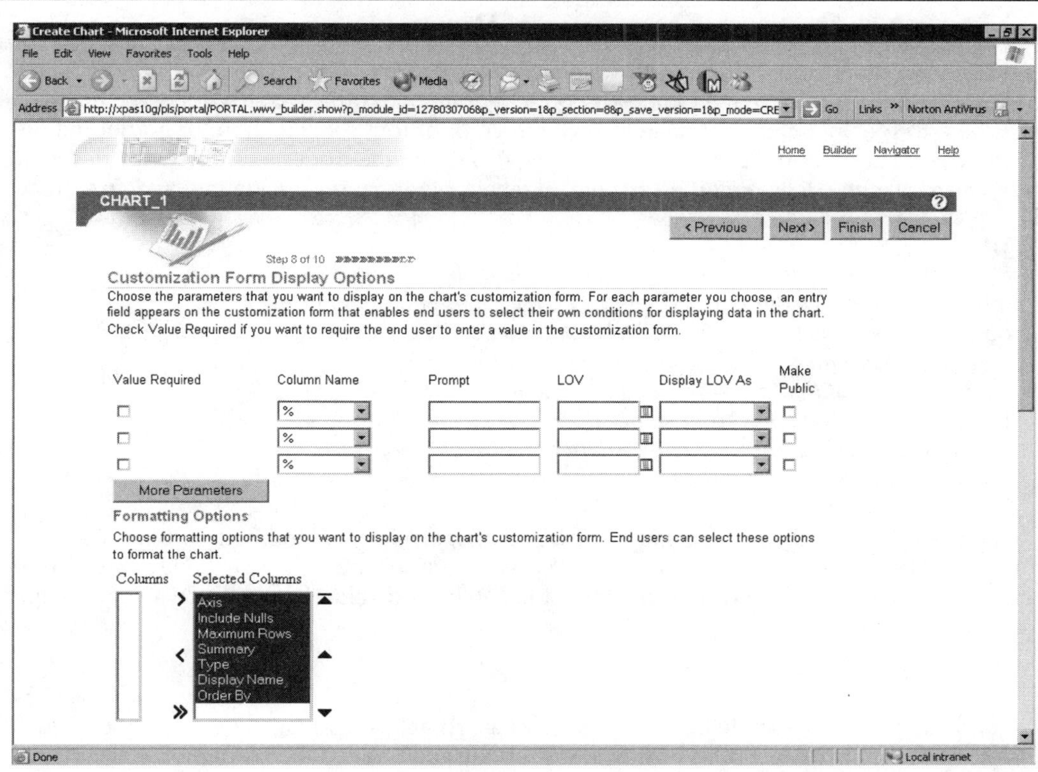

FIGURE 9-24. *The Customization Form Display Options page of the OracleAS Portal Chart Wizard*

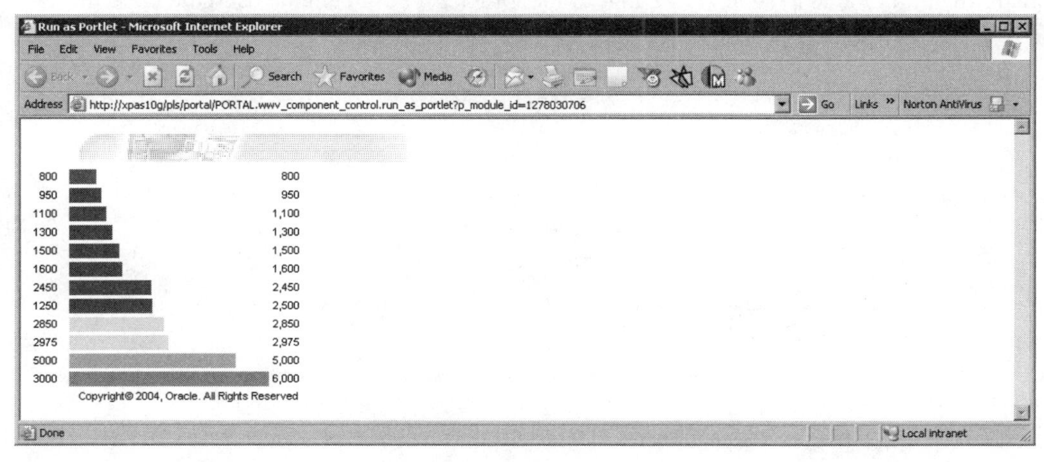

FIGURE 9-25. *An OracleAS Portal Chart run with default values*

OracleAS Portal Dynamic Pages

An OracleAS Portal Dynamic Page allows developers to control every aspect of their OracleAS Portal component. Unlike in the OracleAS Portal Reports and Forms wizards, there are no wizard pages here to specify column or page formatting, color or font specification, or portlet settings. While this OracleAS Portal component gives the developer the most flexibility when designing his or her portlet, the developer must handle all details of formatting, validation, and appearance.

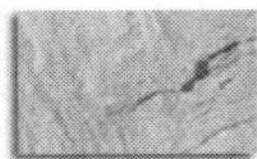

TIP

It is important to note that the name "Dynamic Page" can be a little misleading. Most of the time, developers create these components to be used as portlets that are then placed on OracleAS Portal pages. Placing a "Dynamic Page" portlet on a page does not affect the characteristics of that page—it's still an OracleAS Portal page. If the Dynamic Page is displayed in stand-alone mode, then it truly is a dynamic page; otherwise, it is just a dynamic portlet that is placed on an OracleAS Portal page.

Figure 9-26 shows the first page of the Dynamic Page Wizard. Figure 9-27 lists Step 3 of 8 (what does Oracle have against Step 2?). On this page, we specify the HTML code that will be used to drive our dynamic HTML page. If you look at the code closely, you'll see a code snippet that looks like this:

```
<oracle>select * from portal_demo.emp</oracle>
```

For dynamic pages, Oracle introduces a new tag: <oracle>. This tag allows you to embed SQL or PL/SQL code directly into your dynamic HTML page. When the portlet is displayed, the code between the <oracle> and </oracle> tags is automatically replaced with HTML code to display the results of the query. Multiple <oracle> and </oracle> tags can be specified, but you cannot embed <oracle> tags inside of other <oracle> tags.

One of the most overlooked capabilities of this feature is the ability to use the htp.print function within Oracle to send HTML tags to the OracleAS Portal engine as in the code that follows (line numbers have been added for readability):

```
<HTML>
<HEAD>
<TITLE>Employees</TITLE>
</HEAD>

<BODY  bgColor="#D3D3D3">

<H2>Employees</H2>
<ORACLE>
declare
  link_string        varchar2(500);
  link_string2       varchar2(500);
begin
  htp.print('<table border=5 bgColor="#D3D3D3"><th>Employee</th><th>Performance Reviews</th><th>Self Reviews</th>');
for x in (select person_id, full_name
          from hr.employees@test
          where sysdate <= effective_end_date
```

```
18          and sysdate >= effective_start_date
19          and employee_number is not null
20          order by full_name)
21    loop
22       link_string := '<td>'||x.full_name||'</td><td><a href="PORTAL.wwa_app_module.link?p_
arg_names=_moduleid&p_arg_values=1152450134&p_arg_names=_show_header&p_arg_values=YES&p_arg_
names=EMP_COMMENTS&p_arg_values='||x.person_id||'&p_arg_names=REVIEW_TYPE&p_arg_values=1">View
Performance Reviews</a></td>';
25       link_string2 := '<td><a href="PORTAL.wwa_app_module.link?p_arg_names=_moduleid&p_arg_
values=1135901415&p_arg_names=_show_header&p_arg_values=YES&p_arg_names=EMP_COMMENTS&p_arg_
values='||x.person_id||'">View Self Reviews</a></td>';
26       htp.print('<tr>'||link_string||link_string2||'</tr>');
27    end loop;
28 end;
29 </ORACLE>
30 </BODY>
31 </HTML>
```

Lines 9–29 provide the PL/SQL code that will make up this dynamic page. Line 14 makes use of the htp.print function to begin building an HTML table. Lines 15–21 begin a cursor loop for all

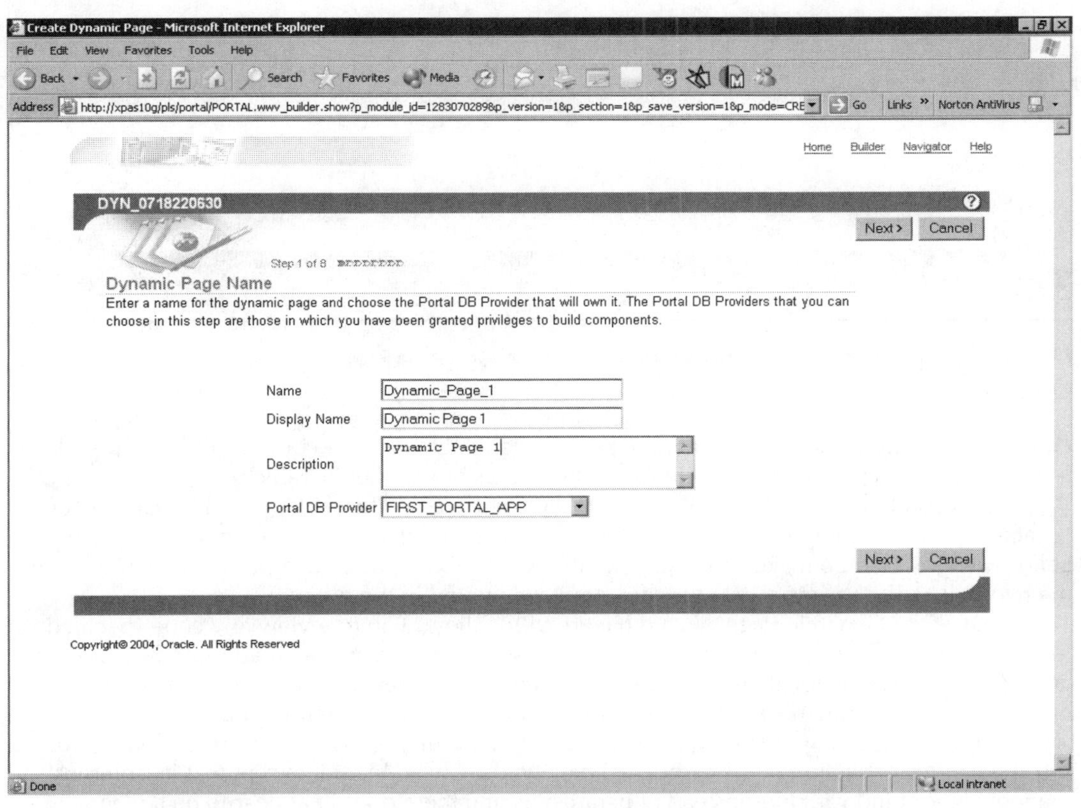

FIGURE 9-26. *The first page of the Dynamic Page Wizard*

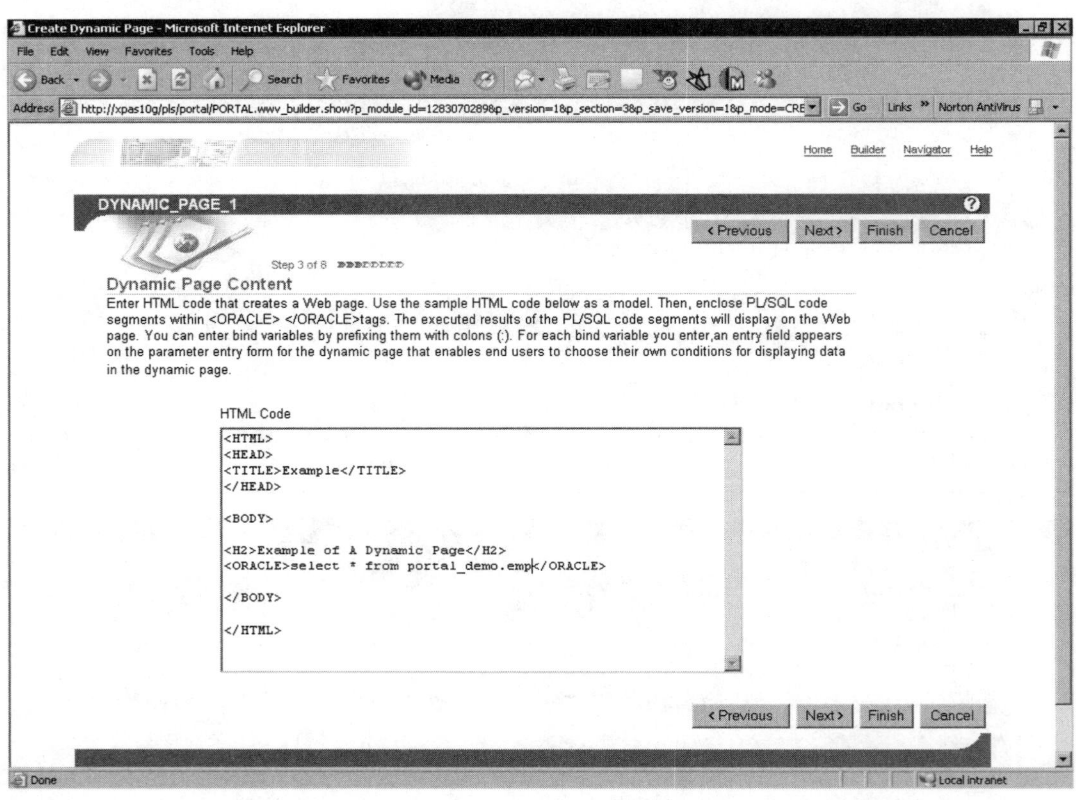

FIGURE 9-27. *The second page of the Dynamic Page Wizard*

current employees listed in the hr.employees@test table. Line 22 is a complex line that populates a string called link_string with a table row definition as broken out in Table 9-3.

Line 25 constructs a similar string, except that it references a different OracleAS Portal component (OracleAS Portal component ID: 1135901415) and uses a different link on the screen ("View Self-Reviews"). Line 26 makes use, again, of the htp database package to print a table row, with the two link_string's as table data for each employee found in the query.

Step 4 of the Dynamic Page Wizard (Figure 9-28) allows you to review any code specified in Step 3 between the <oracle> and </oracle> custom tags. If you specified multiple <oracle> and </oracle> tags, they will all be displayed on this page in separate text boxes. Step 5 displays options for the dynamic page (only available in stand-alone [full page] mode).

The top of Step 6 (Figure 9-29), the Customization Form Display Options page, looks a lot like the parameter section of the associated page in the Chart Wizard, except that its columns are looking for bind variables instead of parameters and there doesn't appear to be a place to specify any.

Code	Explanation
<td>	Tag to specify a table data element
x.full_name	The name of the employee
</td><td>	Combination to denote a new column for the row
<a href="PORTAL.wwa_app_module.link?p_arg_names=_moduleid&p_arg_values=1152450134	An HTML link to another OracleAS Portal component; in this case, we are referencing Portal component number 1152450134. Where does this number come from? It is generated automatically by Oracle and can be viewed in the manage page for the component
&p_arg_names=_show_header&p_arg_values=YES&p_arg_names=EMP_COMMENTS&p_arg_values='||x.person_id||'&p_arg_names=REVIEW_TYPE&p_arg_values=1">)	This link passes parameters (_show_header, EMP_COMMENTS, and REVIEW_TYPE) and values for those parameters (YES, x.person_id and 1, respectively)
View Performance Reviews</a>	The link to be displayed on the dynamic page
</td>	The end of the table data tag

TABLE 9-3. *Code Explanation of Line 22 of the Accompanying Listing*

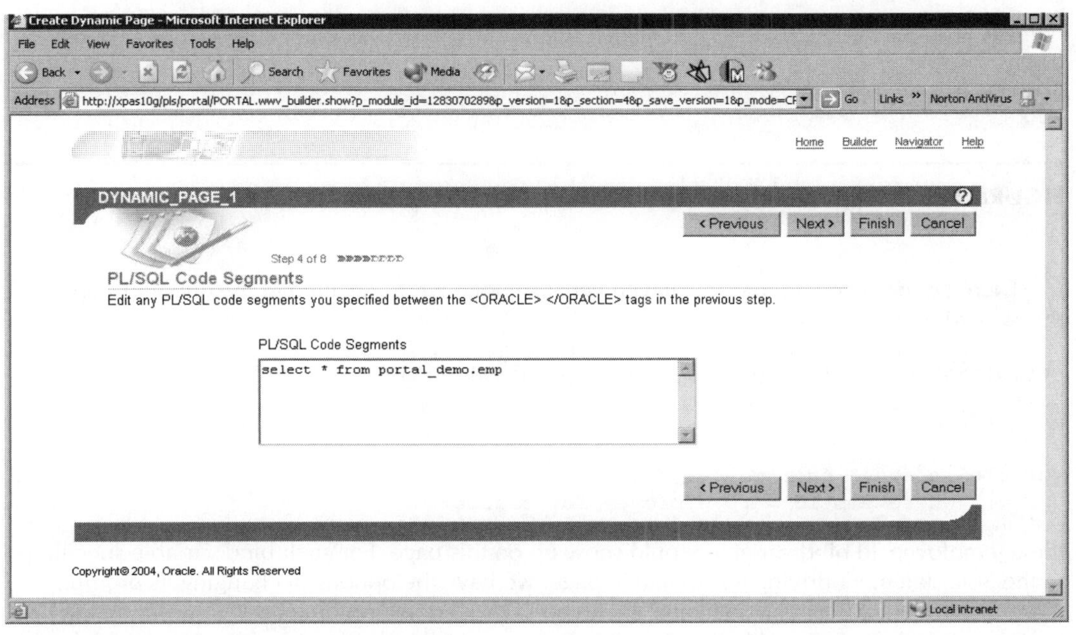

FIGURE 9-28. *The PL/SQL Code Segments page*

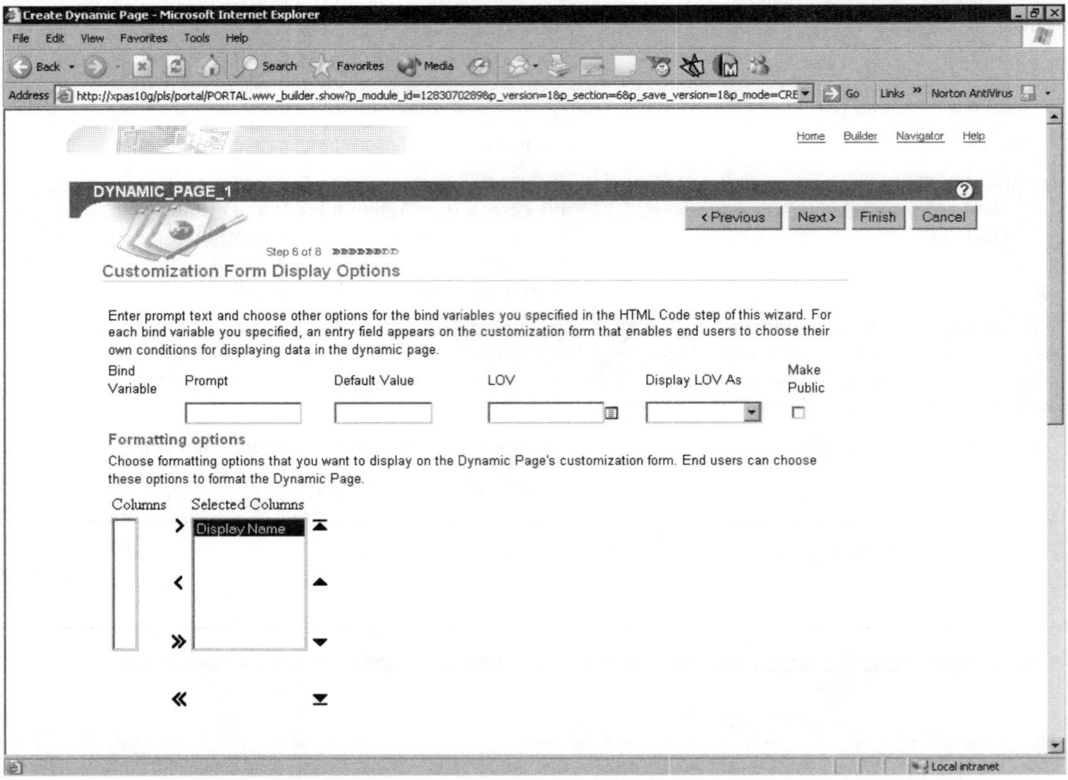

FIGURE 9-29. *The Customization Form Display Options page*

There are no bind variables displayed because none were specified in the query in step 3 of this wizard. If, instead of

```
<oracle>select * from portal_demo.emp</oracle>
```

we specified

```
<oracle>select * from portal_demo.emp
        where emp_id = :p_employee_id</oracle>
```

the p_employee_id bind variable would show up on this page. For each bind variable specified in the SQL statement driving this dynamic page, we have the options of changing its prompt, changing its default value, associating it with an LOV, and determining how we want that LOV to be displayed. Steps 7 and 8, the Dynamic Page and Customization Form Text and Additional PL/SQL Code pages, have the same functionality as the corresponding pages we've seen in the OracleAS Portal Forms, Reports, and Charts Wizards. Figure 9-30 shows an example of a Dynamic Page displayed after being generated with default values.

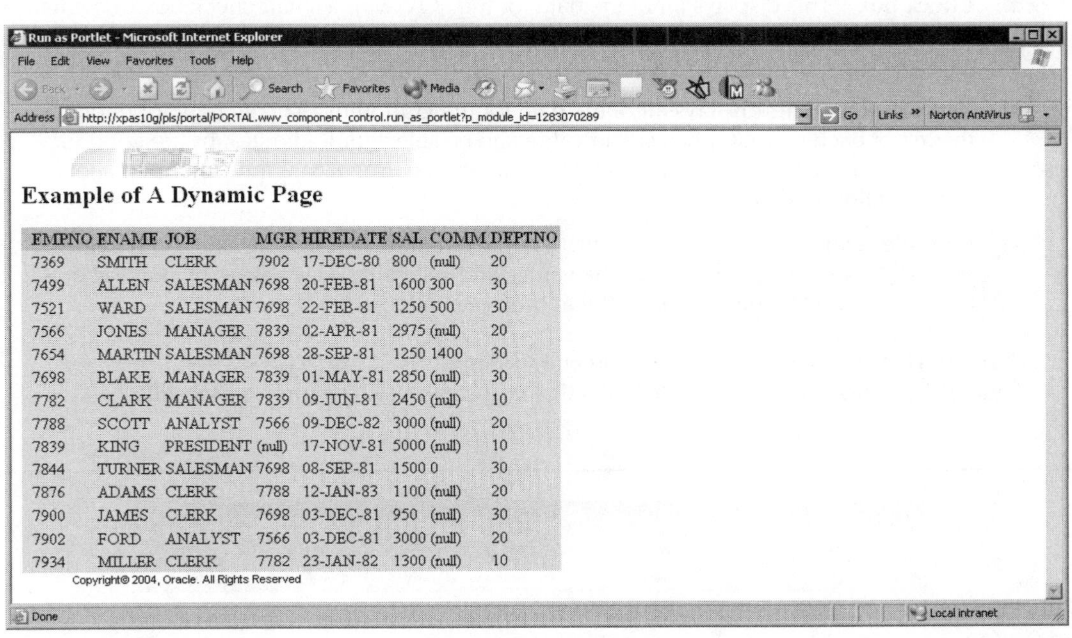

FIGURE 9-30. *A Dynamic Page displayed as a portlet*

OracleAS Portal List Of Values

An OracleAS Portal List of Values is a unique component in the sense that, along with OracleAS Portal Links, it is not designed to be placed on a page; rather, the purpose of an LOV is to be used as an attribute to provide data to other OracleAS Portal components. An LOV is invaluable when used in data entry–type applications for two reasons: 1) it eliminates incorrect data from being entered, and 2) it eliminates the need to memorize various codes needed to drive applications.

An LOV, after it is created, exists in OracleAS Portal but is not available to be placed on an OracleAS Portal page. Any new OracleAS component can use the LOV, and any existing OracleAS component can be modified to include the new LOV. LOVs can display values in different formats:

- **Combo box** This displays the data in a text box with a drop-down arrow on the text box's right side. When a user clicks the arrow, the box drops down to display all of the values of the LOV. Only a single value can be selected. Combo boxes are good for application screens that do not have a lot of free space on them.
- **Pop-up** This displays the data in a text box with a small notepad icon to its right. Clicking the icon opens another window, where the appropriate value can be selected. As in combo boxes, only a single value can be selected. We've seen pop-ups for selecting tables or views when we created our example OracleAS Portal Forms and Reports earlier in this chapter.

- **Check box** This displays all of the data for the LOV with a small check box to the left of each entry. Check boxes are good when you want to display all values in the LOV and give the end user the ability to select multiple values.
- **Radio group** This displays all of the data for the LOV with a small circular button to the left of each entry. Only a single value can be selected. Radio groups are good for applications that need to display all LOV data to the user at one time and then allow one selection to be made.
- **Multiple select** This displays the first couple of data elements for the LOV in a text box. The user can scroll through the values and select multiple values by holding down the SHIFT key and single-clicking the appropriate values.

Figure 9-31 displays a simple LOV in different formats.
Figure 9-32 shows the two types of LOVs that you can build (Dynamic and Static).

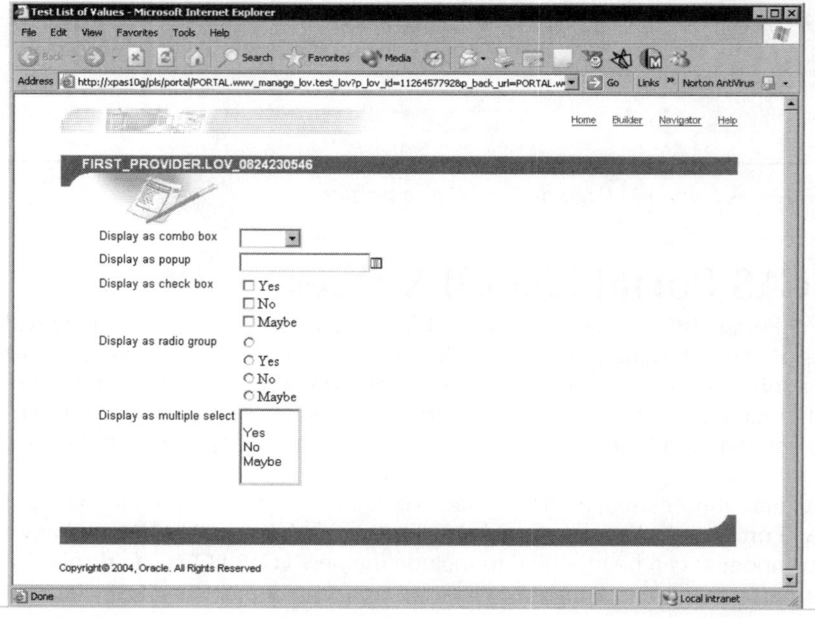

FIGURE 9-31. *The different formats in which an LOV can be displayed*

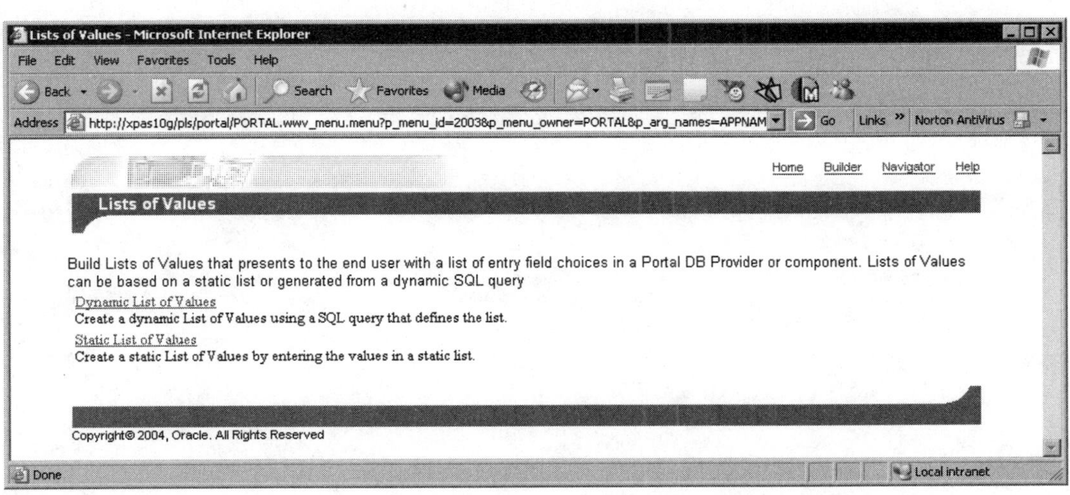

FIGURE 9-32. *The first page of the LOV wizard*

A static LOV is one where the developer hard-codes the values to be referenced in the database table, the display values, and the order in which they are displayed. Static LOVs are good for data elements on your OracleAS Portal components that have values that never change, such as a GENDER or STATE field. Figure 9-33 shows an example of the creation of a static LOV. Note that the fields do not have to be entered in order, as the Display Order field can be used to reorder the entries. If more than five entries are needed, clicking the More button on the bottom left of the screen will redraw the wizard page with more rows.

Dynamic LOVs query data out of the database and are populated on-the-fly (dynamically). Creation of a dynamic LOV (Figure 9-34) consists of specifying a query that is similar to the one we created for the OracleAS Portal Chart earlier in this chapter in the sense that it must be structured in a specific way. The syntax at the bottom of the page provides a template for how the SQL query needs to be constructed. Unlike in the SQL query needed to drive an OracleAS Portal Chart, the columns do not need to be aliased:

```
select [display_column], [return_column] from table
```

The query can be any valid SQL statement, so it can contain multiple tables, join conditions, where clauses, database links (as in Figure 9-34), references to stored procedures, etc. If bind variables are used, the end user will be prompted for a value before the LOV is rendered.

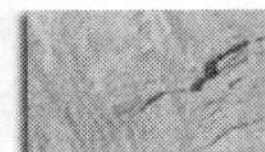

CAUTION
LOVs are intended to make the user's interaction with the application easier. Requiring the end user to enter a value before an LOV is rendered makes the interaction more complex and, in general, is not desirable.

Create a List of Values - Microsoft Internet Explorer

FIRST_PROVIDER.LOV_0824230546

Create a list of values based on a static hardcoded list. Choose the name of the Portal DB Provider that will own the list and enter a name to identify the list of values. Choose a format, whether or not to show null values, then enter a display value, return value, and display order for each item in the list of values.

Owner: FIRST_PROVIDER
Name: LOV_0824230546
Default Format: Check box
Show Null Value: Yes

Display Value	Return Value	Display Order
Yes	Y	1
Maybe	M	3
No	N	2

Copyright© 2004, Oracle. All Rights Reserved

FIGURE 9-33. *Example creation of a static LOV*

Figure 9-34 also shows a drop-down box named Default Format. On virtually every page where an LOV can be specified in OracleAS Portal, there is also an option to specify what type of LOV is to be displayed. If the type of LOV is left blank, the default format value specified here will be used. After the LOV is created, the values generated can be checked by clicking the Run link on the Manage page for the LOV.

Now that we have a valid LOV, the next example will show how to assign it as an attribute to an existing OracleAS Portal component. In the Navigator, click the Edit link next to the chart we created earlier in this chapter. You will see a screen similar to Figure 9-35.

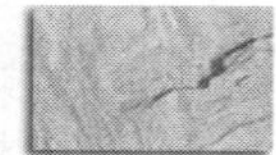

TIP

When editing an existing OracleAS Portal component, the tabs along the top right of the screen correspond to pages in the wizard used to create the OracleAS Portal component. Not every page has a corresponding tab, as some options (like the type of chart, form, or report and the provider it is associated with) cannot be modified.

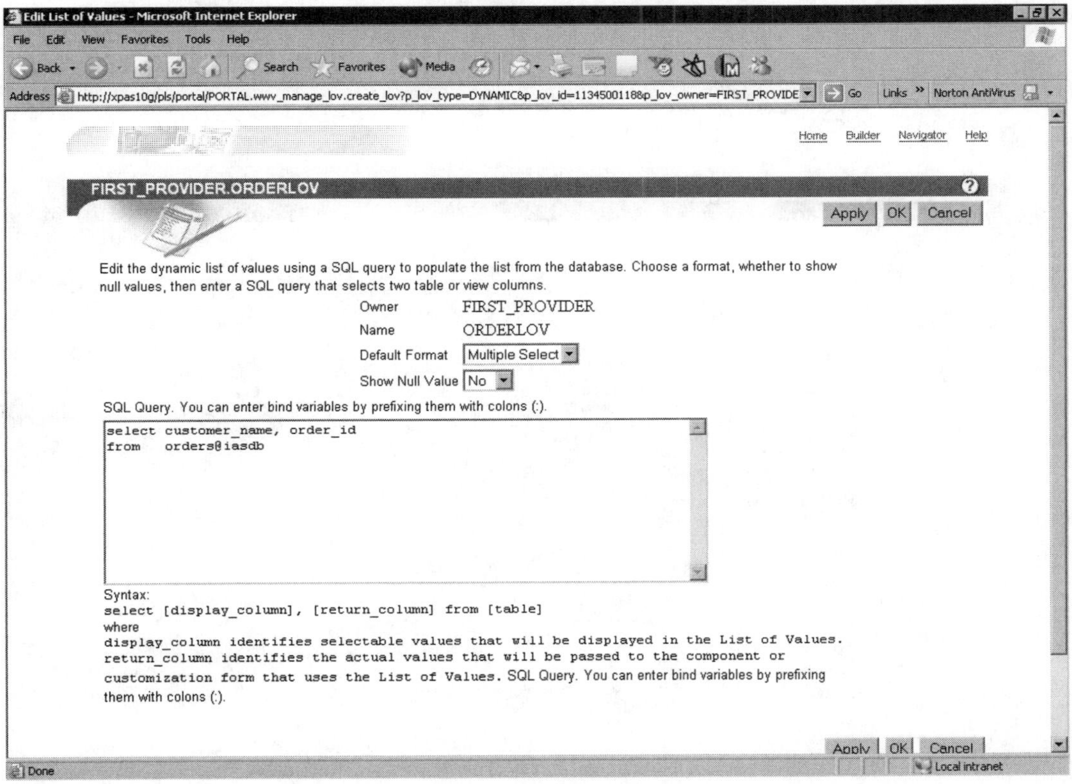

Edit List of Values - Microsoft Internet Explorer

File Edit View Favorites Tools Help

Address http://xpas10g/pls/portal/PORTAL.wwv_manage_lov.create_lov?p_lov_type=DYNAMIC&p_lov_id=1134500118&p_lov_owner=FIRST_PROVIDE

Home Builder Navigator Help

FIRST_PROVIDER.ORDERLOV

Apply OK Cancel

Edit the dynamic list of values using a SQL query to populate the list from the database. Choose a format, whether to show null values, then enter a SQL query that selects two table or view columns.

Owner FIRST_PROVIDER
Name ORDERLOV
Default Format Multiple Select
Show Null Value No

SQL Query. You can enter bind variables by prefixing them with colons (:).

```
select customer_name, order_id
from   orders@iasdb
```

Syntax:
select [display_column], [return_column] from [table]
where
display_column identifies selectable values that will be displayed in the List of Values.
return_column identifies the actual values that will be passed to the component or customization form that uses the List of Values. SQL Query. You can enter bind variables by prefixing them with colons (:).

Apply OK Cancel

Done Local intranet

FIGURE 9-34. *Example creation of a dynamic LOV*

CAUTION

It is also important to remember that clicking the Edit link on the Navigator page will edit the production copy of the OracleAS component. If you want to preserve the production version and edit a new copy, you would have to click the Manage link on the Navigator page and then click Edit As New on the Manage page for the component.

In order to demonstrate LOVs, we will need to add a bind variable to this chart. In the SQL query window of Figure 9-35, the line

```
and o.order_id = :p_order_id
```

was added. This creates a bind variable for the chart, which can then have an LOV associated with it. Click the fourth tab to display the Customization Display Form Options page (Figure 9-36).

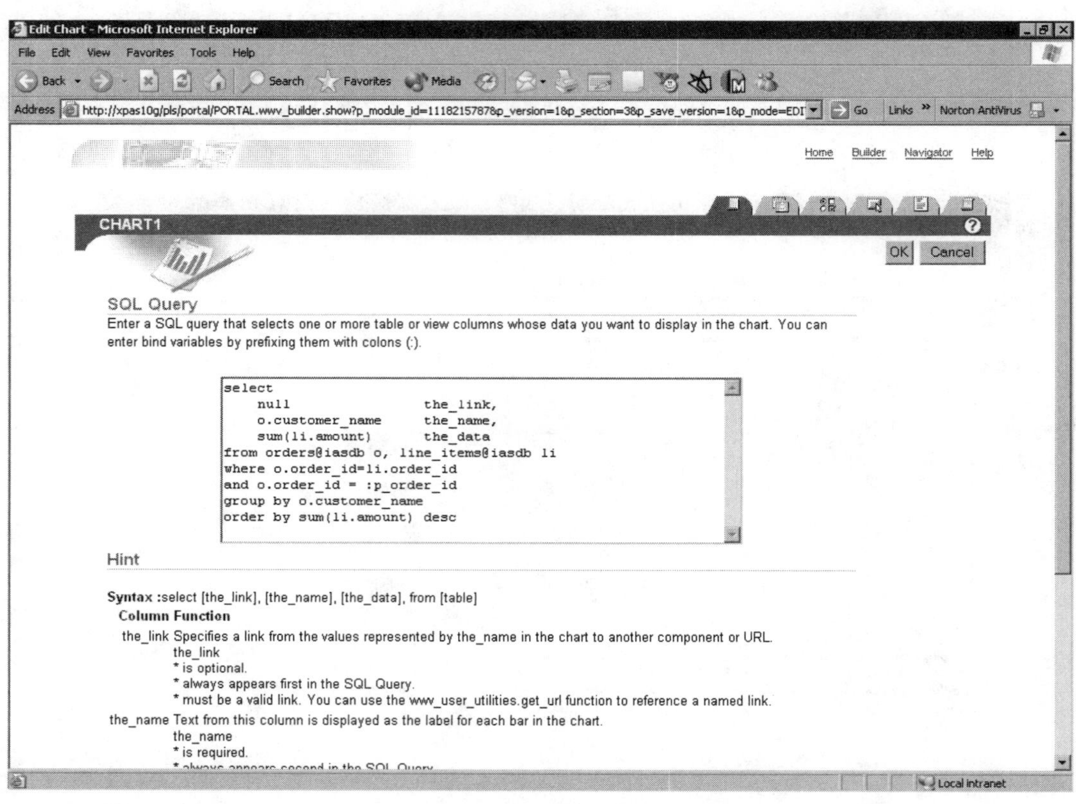

Edit Chart - Microsoft Internet Explorer
File Edit View Favorites Tools Help
Back Search Favorites Media
Address http://xpas10g/pls/portal/PORTAL.wwv_builder.show?p_module_id=1118215787&p_version=1&p_section=3&p_save_version=1&p_mode=EDI
Go Links Norton AntiVirus
Home Builder Navigator Help
CHART1
OK Cancel
SQL Query
Enter a SQL query that selects one or more table or view columns whose data you want to display in the chart. You can enter bind variables by prefixing them with colons (:).
select
null the_link,
o.customer_name the_name,
sum(li.amount) the_data
from orders@iasdb o, line_items@iasdb li
where o.order_id=li.order_id
and o.order_id = :p_order_id
group by o.customer_name
order by sum(li.amount) desc
Hint
Syntax :select [the_link], [the_name], [the_data], from [table]
Column Function
the_link Specifies a link from the values represented by the_name in the chart to another component or URL.
the_link
* is optional.
* always appears first in the SQL Query.
* must be a valid link. You can use the wwv_user_utilities.get_url function to reference a named link.
the_name Text from this column is displayed as the label for each bar in the chart.
the_name
* is required.
Local intranet

FIGURE 9-35. *Editing the OracleAS Portal chart from earlier in this chapter*

You will notice that our new bind variable, p_order_id, is automatically displayed in Bind Variable list at the top of the page. Clicking the small notepad icon to the right of the LOV text box will bring up a list of available LOVs. Select the LOV created in Figure 9-34 and select one of the LOV formats from the Display LOV As drop-down box.

Click OK to generate a new OracleAS Portal Chart, and then click Run on the Manage page. A page appears indicating that no data is returned—why? When we modified the query to include the line

```
and o.order_id = :p_order_id
```

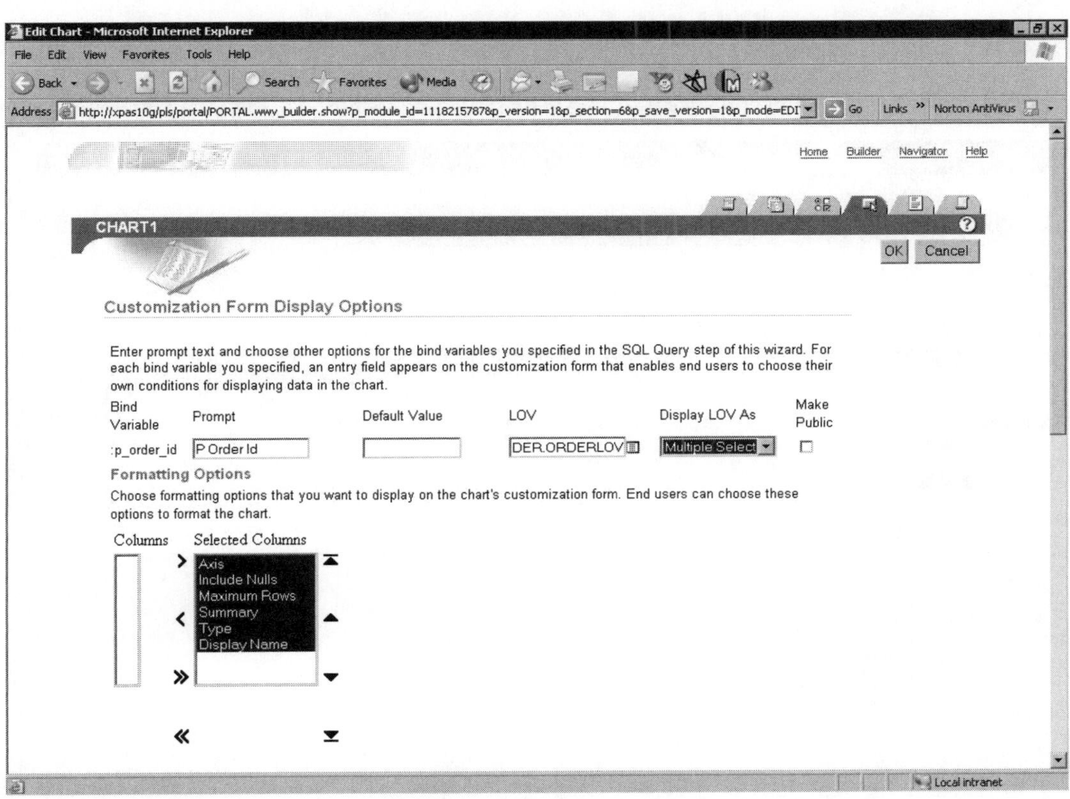

FIGURE 9-36. *Adding the LOV to the chart*

we added a clause that will exclude all rows if p_order_id is null, which it is, since we have not provided any value for it. Return to the Manage page for the chart and click the Customize link. This link will display a page similar to Figure 9-37. This page allows end users to enter specific information that will determine the dataset used to populate the OracleAS Portal component in question. Under Query Options, the bind variable specified in the query (P_ORDER_ID) along with the LOV we created are displayed, allowing the user to specify what data should be included on the chart. Selecting Brown and clicking Run Chart will display Figure 9-38.

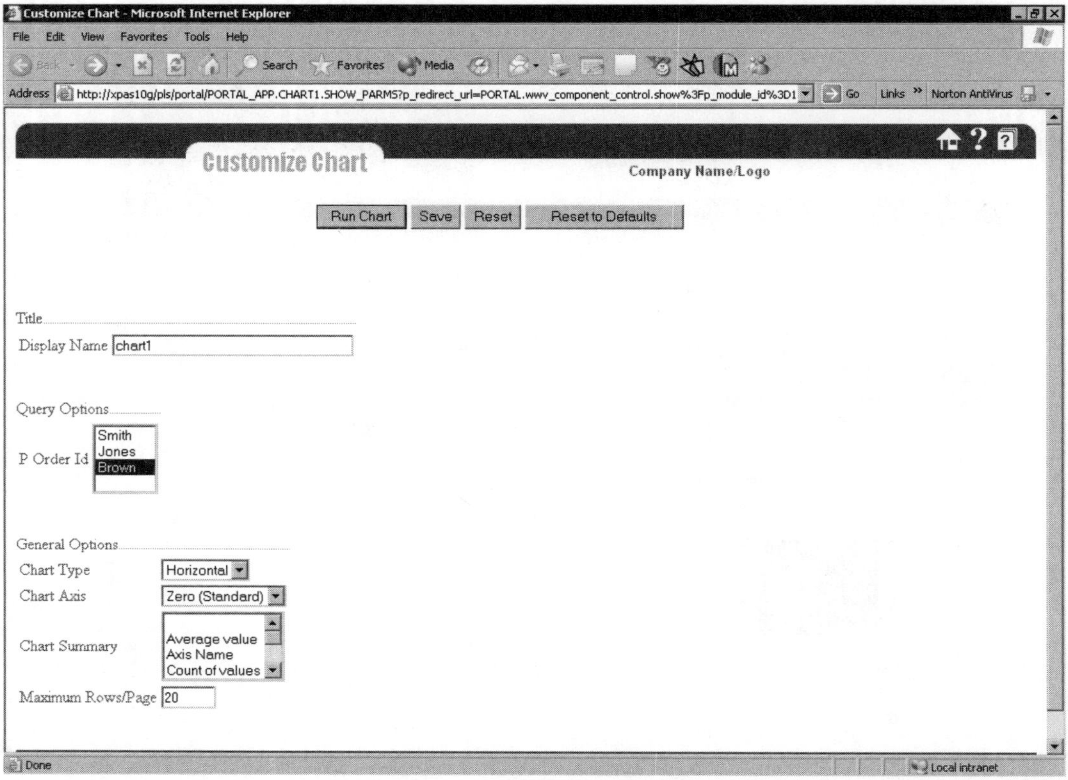

FIGURE 9-37. *The customize screen for the chart*

TIP

One of the really nice features of the Customize screen (Figure 9-37) is the Save button located at the top of the screen. If a user changes parameters for an OracleAS Portal component, that user can save their preferences by clicking the Save button. The next time the component is displayed, the OracleAS Portal engine will determine if that user has saved any preferences for that component and apply those preferences when displaying the component. This allows end users to customize their OracleAS Portal experience with a minimal amount of programming. In the next chapter, we will look at how OracleAS Portal administrators can grant "Customize" privileges on OracleAS Portal portlets.

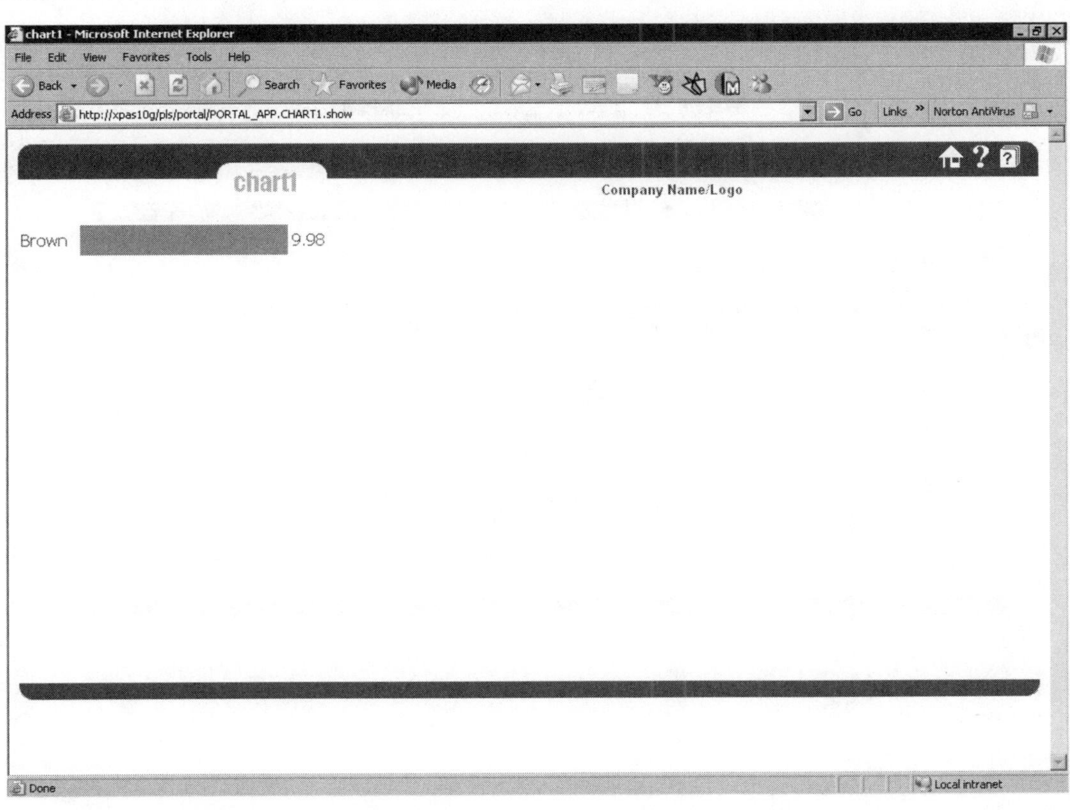

FIGURE 9-38. *The OracleAS Portal Chart displaying only "Brown's" data*

OracleAS Portal XML Components

The first step of the XML Component Wizard (Figure 9-39) shows the ubiquitous naming page of the wizard. Step 2 of the wizard (Figure 9-40) gives developers the opportunity to either enter a URL that points to an existing XML file or place the XML code on the page. Like the dynamic pages created earlier, OracleAS Portal allows developers to embed SQL or PL/SQL code within the XML text box by surrounding it with the <oracle> and </oracle> custom tags. You can also make use of bind variables to give your end users another layer of interaction with the portlet. Step 3 lists all of the code between <oracle> and </oracle> tags so that you can check it and make any modifications to it.

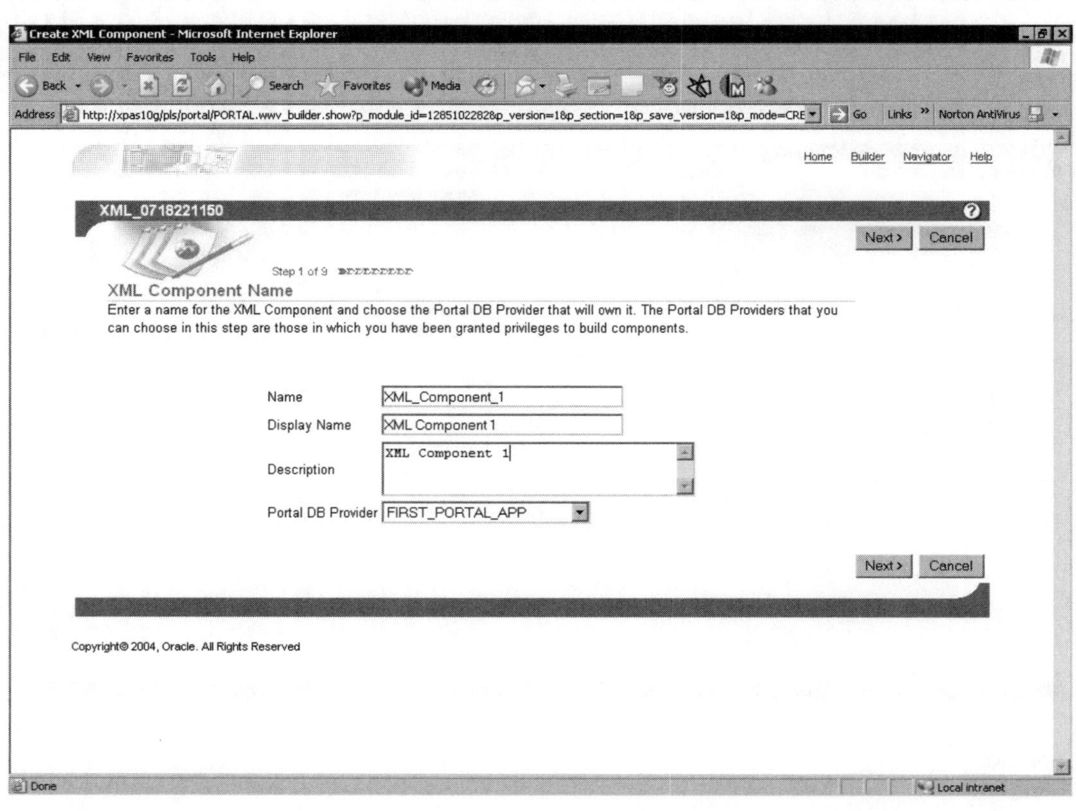

FIGURE 9-39. *The first page of the XML Component Wizard*

XSL (Extensible Stylesheet Language) is a language for creating a style sheet that describes how data sent over the Web using the Extensible Markup Language (XML) is to be presented to the user. Step 4 of the wizard (Figure 9-41) gives the developer the ability either to enter an URL to an XSL entry or to write the XSL code directly in the wizard.

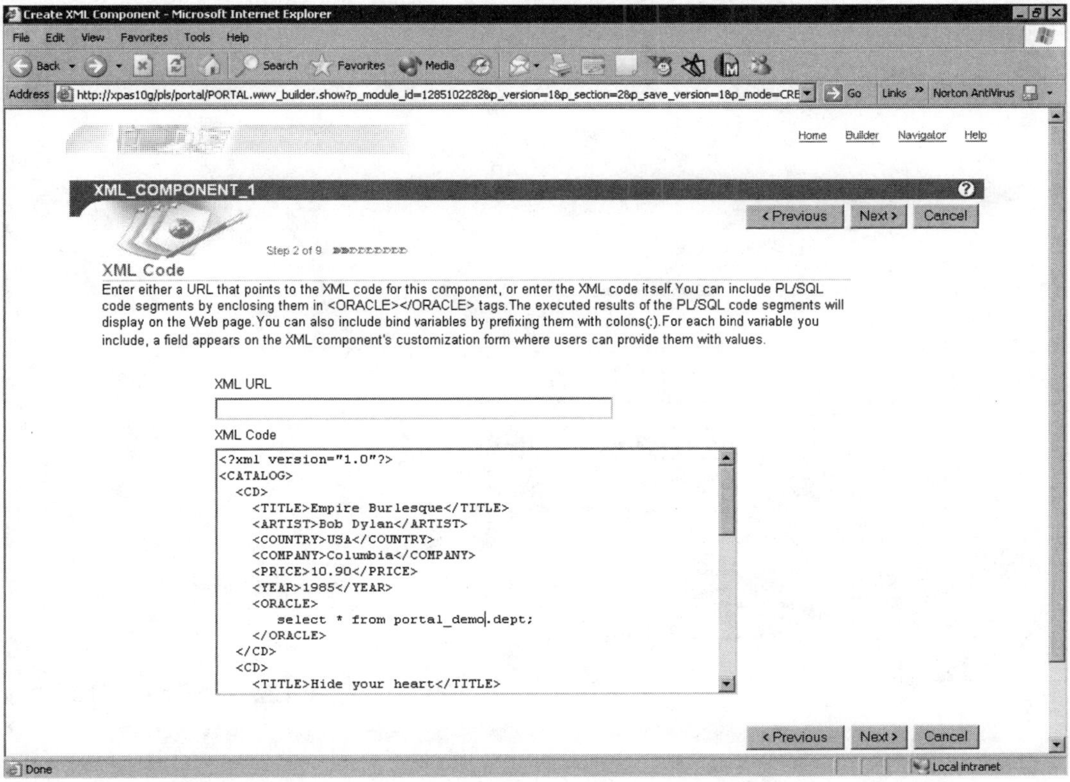

Create XML Component - Microsoft Internet Explorer

XML_COMPONENT_1

Step 2 of 9

XML Code

Enter either a URL that points to the XML code for this component, or enter the XML code itself. You can include PL/SQL code segments by enclosing them in <ORACLE></ORACLE> tags. The executed results of the PL/SQL code segments will display on the Web page. You can also include bind variables by prefixing them with colons(:). For each bind variable you include, a field appears on the XML component's customization form where users can provide them with values.

XML URL

XML Code

```
<?xml version="1.0"?>
<CATALOG>
  <CD>
    <TITLE>Empire Burlesque</TITLE>
    <ARTIST>Bob Dylan</ARTIST>
    <COUNTRY>USA</COUNTRY>
    <COMPANY>Columbia</COMPANY>
    <PRICE>10.90</PRICE>
    <YEAR>1985</YEAR>
    <ORACLE>
       select * from portal_demo.dept;
    </ORACLE>
  </CD>
  <CD>
    <TITLE>Hide your heart</TITLE>
```

FIGURE 9-40. *The second page of the XML Component Wizard*

NOTE
For more information on XSL, see Chapter 16 and Appendix A.

A DTD (Document Type Definition) is a collection of XML declarations that, as a collection, define the legal structure, elements, and attributes that are available for use in a document that

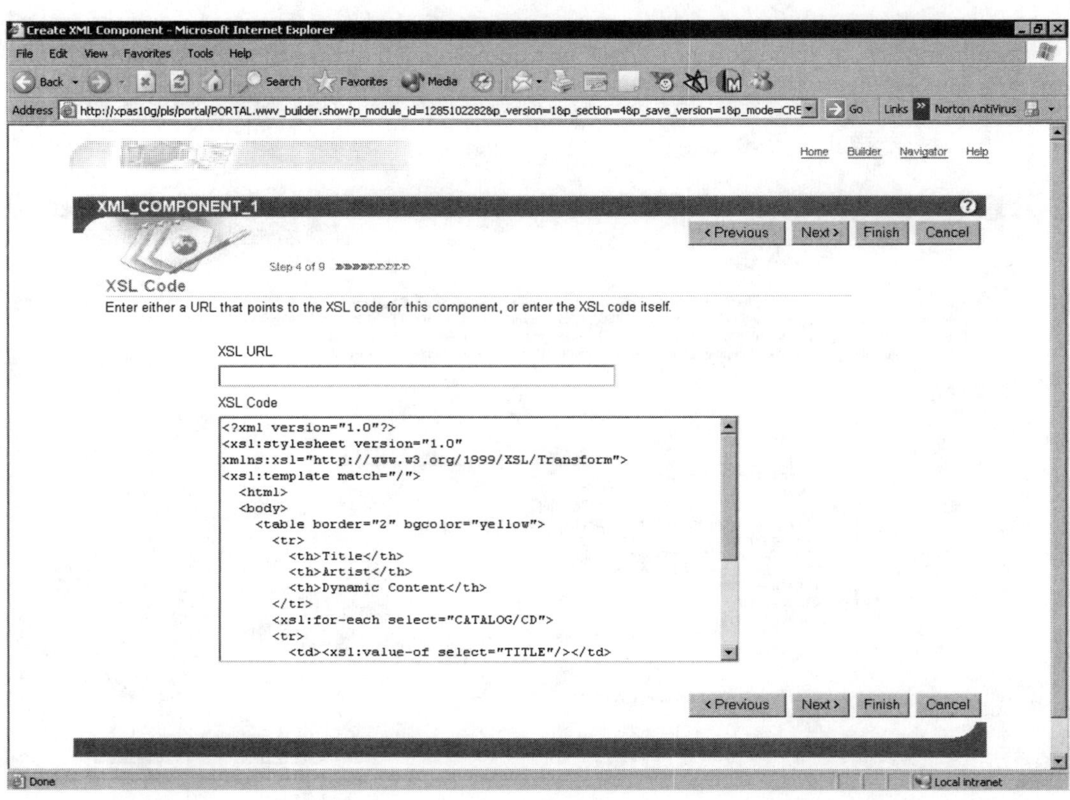

FIGURE 9-41. *The XSL Code page of the XML Component Wizard*

complies to the DTD. Step 5 of the XML Component Wizard (Figure 9-42) gives developers the opportunity to either enter a URL that contains the DTD or enter the DTD code on the page.

Step 6 has options for when the XML component is displayed in stand-alone (full page) mode. The Expire After (Minutes) text box allows the developer to specify how long a report generated by this XML component will be cached by the OracleAS Portal engine. For reports that need

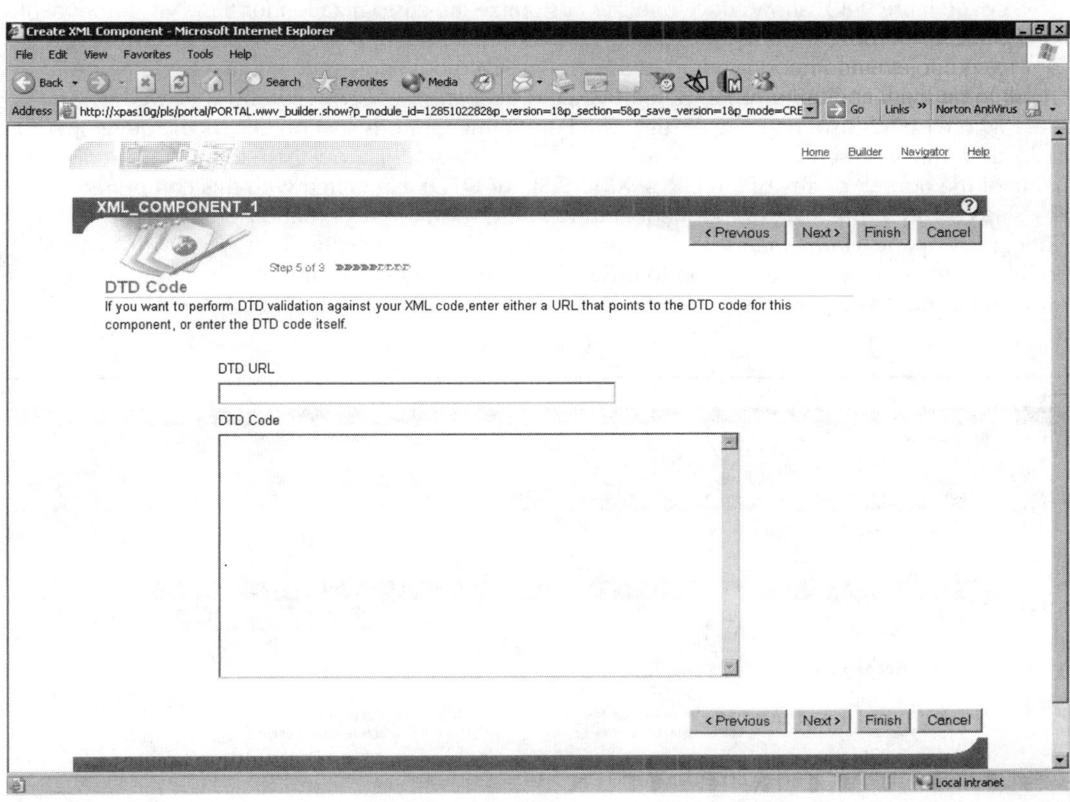

FIGURE 9-42. *The DTD code page of the XML Component Wizard*

up-to-the-second accuracy, leave this value at 0. This will force the OracleAS Portal engine to regenerate the report each time a user requests it. For XML-based reports that do not need up-to-the-second data, you can use the caching feature of OracleAS Portal to ease the workload placed upon the OracleAS Portal engine when rendering pages.

Step 7 (Figure 9-43) allows developers to customize the customization for the XML component. As with the Dynamic Page component built in the last chapter, this wizard page can take advantage of bind variables specified in any of the SQL or PL/SQL statements specified in Step 2 of the XML Component Wizard. The prompt, default value, LOV, and LOV type can be specified by end users who wish to customize the portlet. The Formatting Options section allows the developer to make customization screens available to the end user that would allow them to modify the display name of the portlet, or any of the URLs (XML, XSL, or DTD) associated with this component.

Steps 8 and 9, the XML Component and Customization Form Text and Additional PL/SQL Code, provide the same functionality as the corresponding screens for all of the other OracleAS Portal components we have seen up to this point. Figure 9-44 shows the results of running our XML component as a portlet.

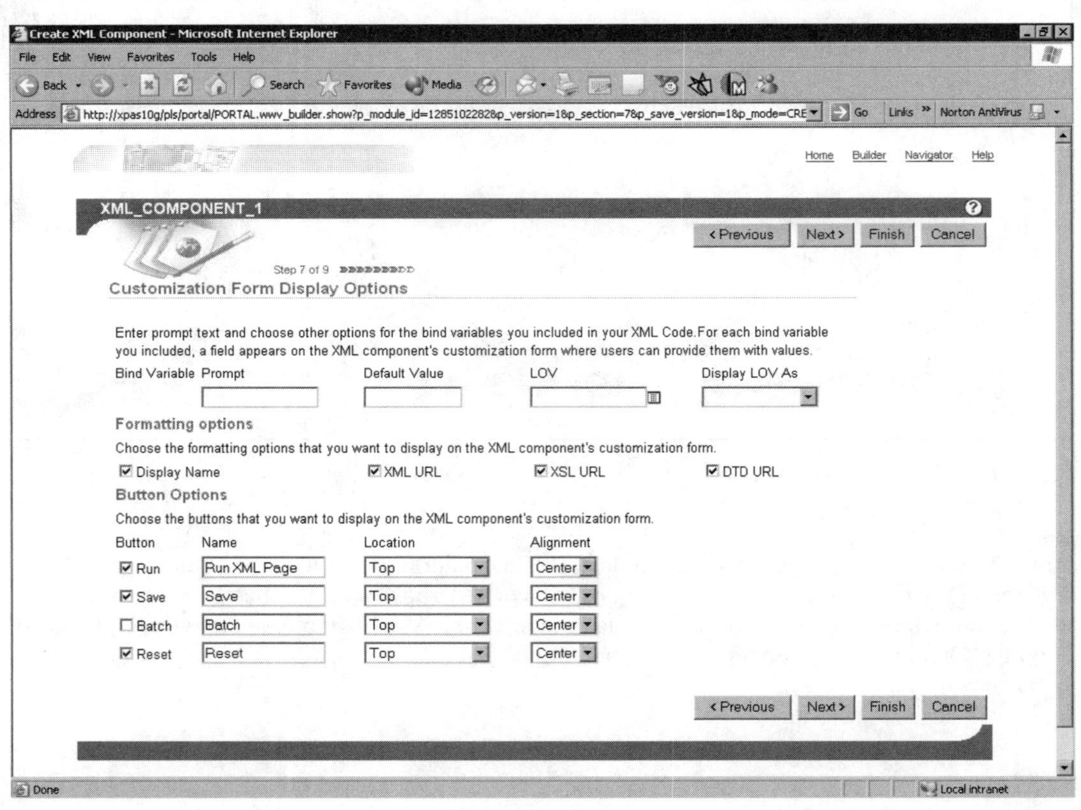

FIGURE 9-43. *The Customization Form Display Options page*

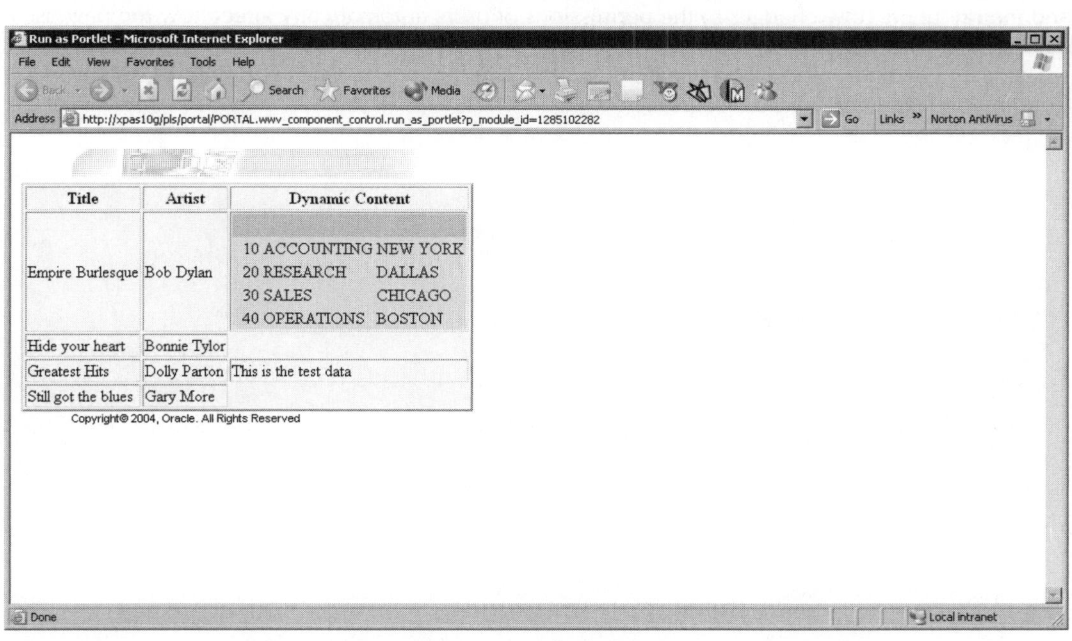

FIGURE 9-44. *The XML component run as a portlet*

Summary

OracleAS Portal is a feature-rich development environment that gives developers a multitude of tools and constructs to create and deploy web-based applications quickly and easily. This chapter has introduced the basic OracleAS Portal components that can be built using the wizards provided by Oracle: Forms, Reports, Charts, Dynamic Pages, Lists of Values, and XML Components. You have seen that each of these components (with the exception of LOVs) can be run either in portlet mode (where the intent is to place the component on an Oracle page) or in full-page, or stand-alone, mode. You have also seen that some of the components (like OracleAS Portal Forms and OracleAS Portal Reports) have subtypes (like a simple form based on a table, a master-detail form, or a form based on a procedure) that allow us to create different components based on complex structures within our Oracle database.

In the next chapter, we will explore the advanced OracleAS Portal components, such as calendars, hierarchies, menus, URLs, links, and Data Components. We will also spend some time bringing all of these components together by constructing our first OracleAS Portal page and then noticing how changes to the permissions of users automatically affect how the page is displayed, all without any administrator intervention or additional programming by the developer whatsoever. Another important advanced OracleAS Portal feature, OracleAS Portal Content and Content Management, is also discussed.

CHAPTER 10

Advanced Oracle Application Server Portal Components

In the previous chapter, we looked as some of the basic Oracle Application Server Portal components. These components provide a solid foundation for developers to create Oracle Application Server Portal pages that end users can use to interact with data stored within your organization. Those components, however, only make up a small percentage of what is available to you as an Oracle Application Server Portal administrator, developer, or content owner. There are more components that you can use to provide greater functionality to your end users, and content management features that allow you to place items that don't fit into traditional programming constructs such as forms or reports onto your portal. An example of content might be a Microsoft Word document or an Adobe Portable Document Format (PDF) file and, as we will see later in his chapter, content administrators have great flexibility as to how these content items are "published" (made available) on your web pages. The first half of this chapter will deal with the advanced Oracle Application Server Portal components, and the second half is devoted to other advanced topics such as Oracle Application Server Portal page design and Oracle Application Server Portal content.

Oracle Application Server Portal Advanced Components

In the previous chapter, we looked at the basic Oracle Application Server Portal components that can be built out of the box using the wizards provided for developers, including Oracle Application Server Portal Forms, Reports, Charts, Dynamic Pages, and list-of-values (LOVs). This chapter section will focus on the Oracle Application Server Portal advanced components:

- Oracle Application Server Portal Calendars
- Oracle Application Server Portal Hierarchies
- Oracle Application Server Portal Menus
- Oracle Application Server Portal URLs
- Oracle Application Server Portal Links
- Oracle Application Server Portal Data Components

Oracle Application Server Portal Calendars

A calendar is a graphical object that can be used to display links that reference specific records in your database. By default, the record must have a date field, or a field that can be converted into a date field by way of the TO_DATE SQL function if you intend to use it with an Oracle Application Server Portal Calendar. The calendar then displays with corresponding links in the calendar, which end users can drill down to get more information. As we will see, the trickiest part of building a calendar for use in our portal will be constructing the appropriate query to return data that will drive the calendar. This query is similar to the query we constructed when building the Oracle Application Server Portal Chart component in the previous chapter.

Figure 10-1 shows the first step of the Oracle Application Server Portal Calendar Wizard. Like the first pages of the other wizards we have seen up to this point, the developer is prompted for the name of the Oracle Application Server Portal Calendar object (which is stored internally, and has no spaces or special characters), the display name (what is displayed in the Oracle Application

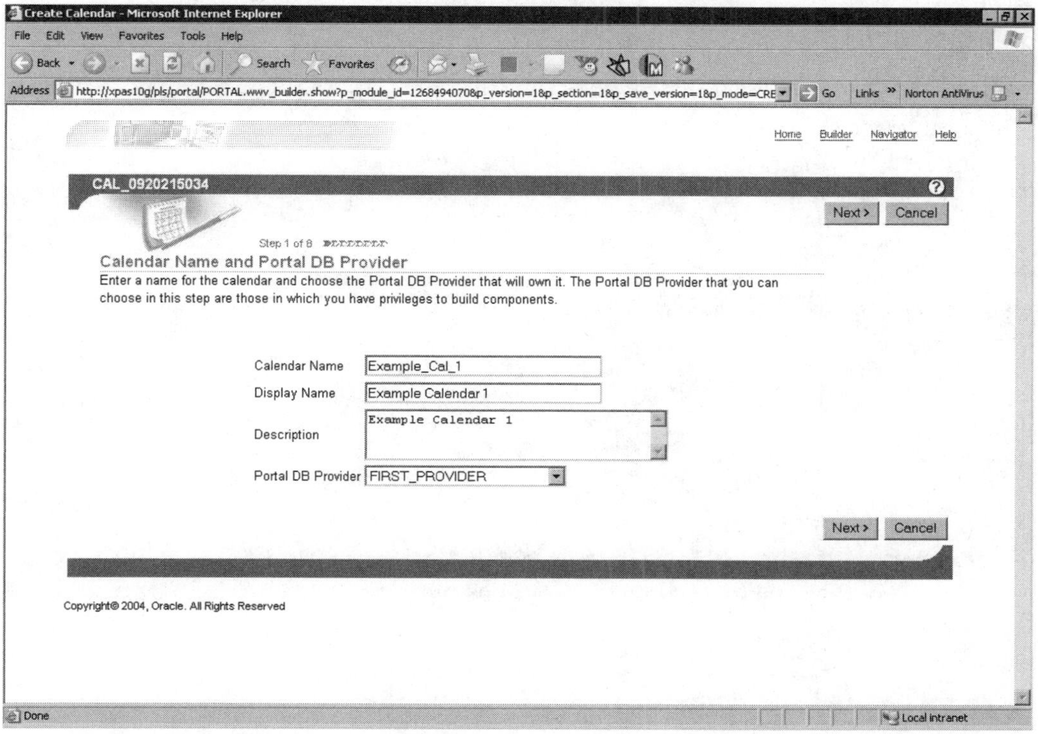

FIGURE 10-1. *The first step of the Calendar Wizard*

Server Portal Navigator, and can contain spaces and special characters), a free-form comment field, and which Oracle Application Server Portal provider this component is associated with. The next screen (Figure 10-2) is Step 3 in the wizard (as was the case with some of the wizards we explored in the previous chapter, there is no Step 2).

If you worked through the examples in the previous chapter, and the Oracle Application Server Portal Chart example in particular, this page should look familiar to you. On this page, we will need to construct a query in a specific format that the Oracle Application Server Portal engine will use to display the calendar when it is called. By default, the following query appears:

```
select
    EMP.HIREDATE the_date,
    EMP.ENAME    the_name,
    null         the_name_link,
    null         the_date_link,
    null         the_target,
    null         the_intermedia
from SCOTT.EMP
order by EMP.HIREDATE
```

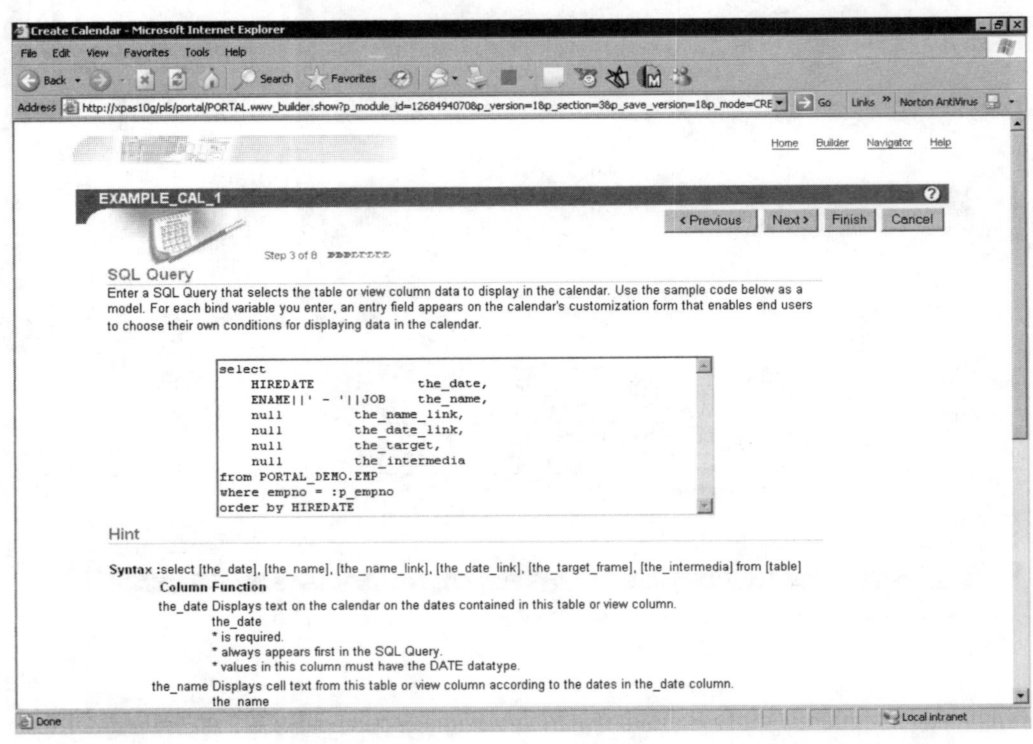

FIGURE 10-2. *The third step of the Oracle Application Server Portal Calendar Wizard*

This serves as a template for how the query is expected to look for this component. There are six aliases in the query. Only the first two fields (the_date and the_name) are required; the others can be ignored ("null" in the above query), but must still be aliased in the query:

- **the_date** This field is what the calendar uses to determine where to display the data. Normally, it's queried directly from a DATE column in the database, but this field can be modified with the TO_DATE SQL function to convert the field into a DATE.

Using the TO_DATE function can be very handy when dealing with Oracle 9i and 10g's external table function. External tables are defined as tables that do not reside in the database, and can be in any format for which an access driver is provided. This feature gives developers the ability to treat any data source (including text files) as if it were part of an Oracle database. If, for example, you wanted to reference a text file that looked like this:

```
101,Gregg Petri,Senior Consultant,31-AUG-2001
102,Robin Fingerson,Technical Management Consultant,01-FEB-2001
103,Gillian Kofal,Senior Consultant,30-NOV-2000
104,Shaun O'Brien,Technical Management Consultant,15-JUL-2000
105,Brad Gibson,Technical Management Consultant,01-JAN-2000
```

you could write a query like this to reference the data in an Oracle Application Server Portal Calendar:

```
select
to_date(REVIEW_DATE,'DD-MON-YYYY') the_date,
EMP_NAME        the_name,
null            the_name_link,
null            the_date_link,
null            the_target,
null            the_intermedia
from external_tab
```

- **the_name** This field displays cell text from this table or view column according to the dates in the_date column.
- **the_name_link** This field specifies a link from the values in the_name column to another component or URL.

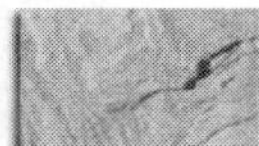

NOTE
We have not discussed links yet (they are covered later in this chapter in the section "Oracle Application Server Portal Links") but for now, understand that links are a way of "linking" two different Oracle Application Server Portal components together. When an Oracle Application Server Portal component is displayed that has a link on it, data on the component is displayed as an HTML link. The user can click on the link to be taken from the current component to another Oracle Application Server Portal component (form, report, etc.).

- **the_date_link** This field specifies a link from the values in the_date column to another component or URL.
- **the_target** This field specifies the URL of a frame in a web page. Enter this column if you want to link to a specific frame in a URL.

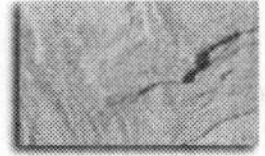

TIP
While it is possible to use frames in Oracle Application Server Portal by way of Frame Drivers, they are difficult to use and tedious to program. In general, it is much easier to use the various Page Layout features of Oracle Application Server Portal (discussed later in this chapter in the section "Oracle Application Server Portal Page Design") to format your page than it is to use Frame Drivers. As such, Frame Drivers are not discussed in this chapter.

- **the_intermedia** This field displays intermedia from this table or view column according to the dates in the_date column.

TIP

For more information on Oracle interMedia, see the Oracle interMedia User's Guide (Oracle Part number A88786-01, http://download-west.oracle.com/docs/cd/A91202_01/901_doc/appdev.901/a88786.pdf).

Some of the fields in the above query are database columns and some are Oracle Application Server Portal objects, which often confuses beginning Oracle Application Server Portal developers. The following fields must be columns in the database objects specified in the FROM clause:

- **the_date**
- **the_name**
- **the_intermedia**

The following fields must be Oracle Application Server Portal objects and are not found in any of the database objects referenced in the FROM clause of the query:

- **the_name_link**
- **the_date_link**
- **the_target**

```
select
    HIREDATE                the_date,
    ENAME||' - '||JOB       the_name,
    null          the_name_link,
    null          the_date_link,
    null          the_target,
    null          the_intermedia
from PORTAL_DEMO.EMP
order by HIREDATE
```

Figure 10-3 shows the next page of the Oracle Application Server Portal Calendar Wizard: the Formatting Conditions page. The page allows developers to change the way information is displayed in the calendars based on the values returned on the page. The color, font, and background and whether the data is underlined, italicized, or bolded can all be controlled from this page of the wizard.

Step 5, Display Options (Figure 10-4), allows developers to specify how the calendar is displayed and is broken into three sections:

- **Common Options** Any option specified in this section applies to the calendar display attributes whether it is displayed in stand-alone (full-page) mode or portlet mode. These options can control things such as starting and ending months, whether to display a Monday through Friday calendar only, and whether or not to show empty months.

- **Full-Page Options** Any option specified here applies only to calendars displayed in standalone mode.
- **Portlet Options** Any option specified here applies only to calendars displayed as portlets on Oracle Application Server Portal pages.

Step 6, the Customization Form Display Options page (Figure 10-5), is where developers can specify what options will be available to power users who have been granted the privilege of customizing their portlets. At the top of this page is the bind variable section. If any bind variables were specified in the query for this component, they show up here and we have the ability to specify the default value and LOV for this variable. Note the existence of the P_EMPNO variable we defined in the query in Step 3 of the wizard. Any options specified on the bottom half of the page under the heading "Public Formatting Options" will be available to all users.

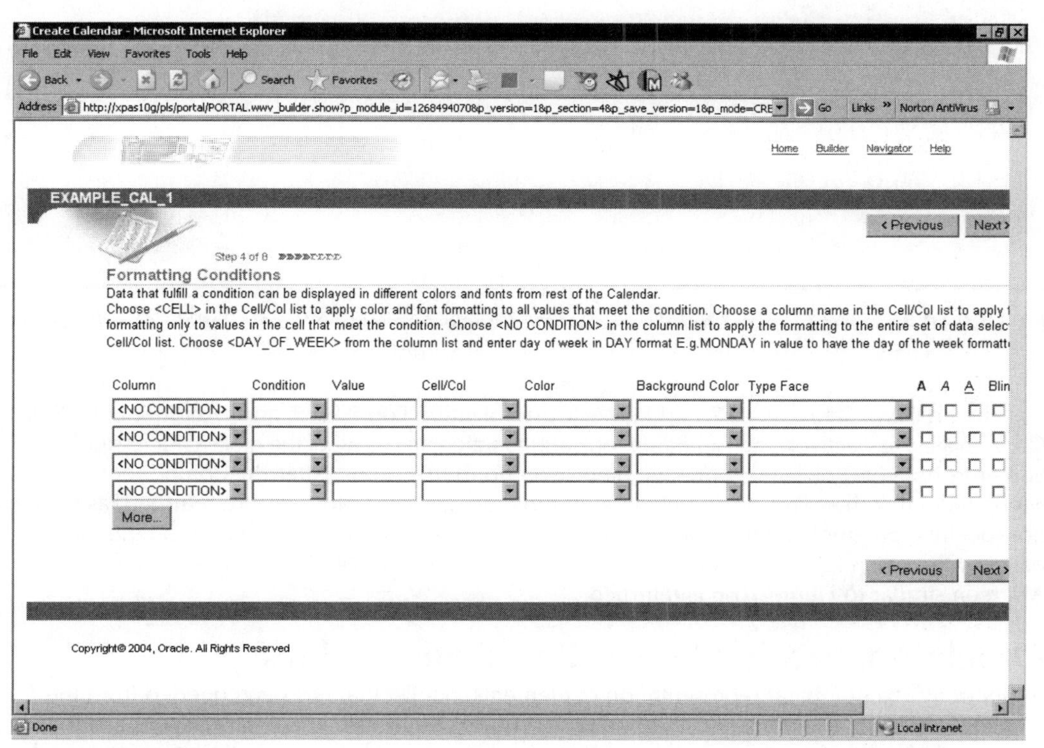

FIGURE 10-3. *The Formatting Conditions page of the Oracle Application Server Portal Calendar Wizard*

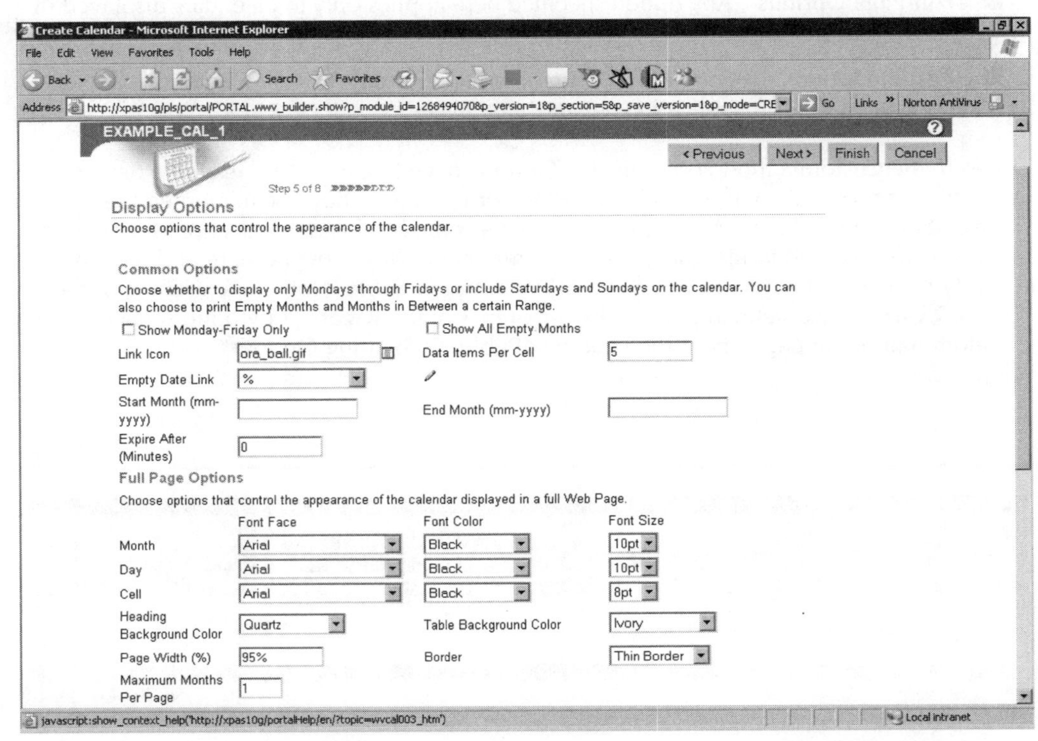

FIGURE 10-4. *The Display Options page of the Oracle Application Server Portal Calendar Wizard*

The final two steps, Steps 7 and 8, the "Customization Form Text" and "Additional PL/SQL Code" pages, respectively, are similar in look and functionality as all of the other Oracle Application Server Portal component wizards we have seen up to this point. After the component is generated, click the "Run As Portlet" link on the Manage page. No rows are returned, as we have not specified an employee number for our query. Click the "Customize" button on the manage page for the calendar component. In the P_EMPNO field, type **7499** and click "Run Calendar." A screen similar to Figure 10-6 is returned.

Oracle Application Server Portal Hierarchies

A hierarchy is a graphical representation of elements in a list that has been queried from the database. Hierarchies are very useful for things such as employee charts or a list of parts that makes up a large component such as an automobile or a computer server. Hierarchies can also be created with links so that they become a way of allowing end users to interact and drill down for more information based on what is displayed in the hierarchy.

The part of creating an Oracle Application Server Portal Hierarchy than can be complex is understanding the fact that the table you wish to base your hierarchy on must have what is called

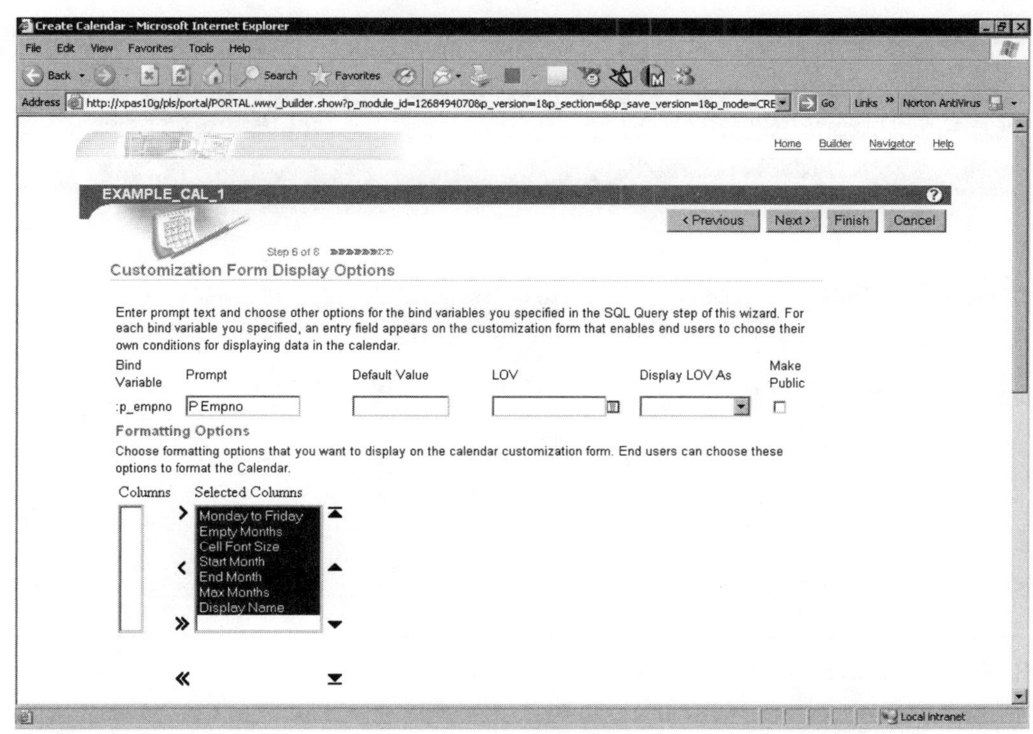

FIGURE 10-5. *The Customization Form Display Options page of the Oracle Application Server Portal Calendar Wizard*

a "recursive" relationship. Oracle defines a recursive relationship as one where values in a table column can be related to those in another column in the same table or another table; for example, relating the values between a primary key and foreign key. Consider, for a moment, the EMP table in the PORTAL_DEMO schema that is created in the infrastructure database during the installation of Oracle Application Server 10*g*:

```
SQL> desc portal_demo.emp;
 Name                                      Null?    Type
 ----------------------------------------- -------- ------------
 EMPNO                                     NOT NULL NUMBER(4)
 ENAME                                              VARCHAR2(10)
 JOB                                                VARCHAR2(9)
 MGR                                                NUMBER(4)
 HIREDATE                                           DATE
 SAL                                                NUMBER(7,2)
 COMM                                               NUMBER(7,2)
 DEPTNO                                             NUMBER(2)
```

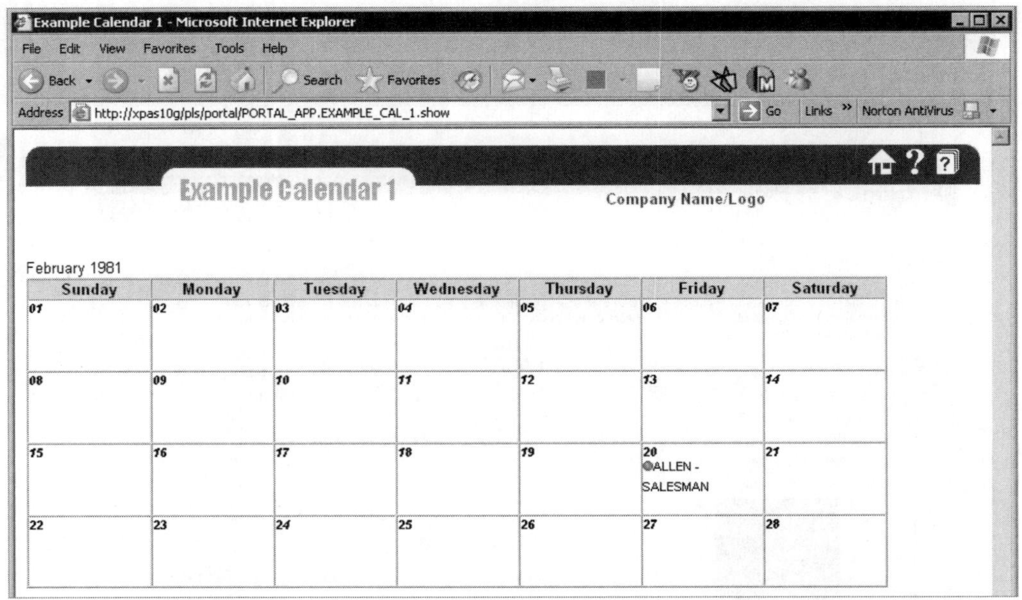

FIGURE 10-6. *The calendar object with employee 7499 displayed*

This table contains a recursive relationship between the MGR and EMPNO fields—that makes it a good candidate for a hierarchy. Step 1 of the hierarchy wizard asks us to specify the name of the hierarchy. Step 3 (again, no Step 2 exists) asks us to specify what table or view the hierarchy will be based off of. Figure 10-7 shows the fourth step of the wizard.

On this page, we are asked to specify the following fields:

- **Primary Key Column** This column must contain values that uniquely identify each row in the table.
- **Parent Key Column** This column must contain values that refer to the primary key. All parent key values must match an existing primary key value or be null.
- **Start With Column** This column contains a value that will be used to determine the topmost level in the hierarchy. After you choose a Start With Column, you can choose a Default Start With Value in this column to determine which value in the Start With Column displays in the topmost level of the hierarchy.
- **Default Start With Value** This column allows you to choose a value in the Start With Column that determines which table row data displays in the topmost level of the hierarchy. Default Start With Value is case-sensitive.
- **Start With LOVs** This column prompts you to choose a List of Values that allows end users of the hierarchy to choose a Default Start With Value on the hierarchy's customization form.

- **Display Column Expression** This column contains the actual values that will display in the hierarchy. In addition to the column name, you can specify text or an expression (such as concatenation).
- **Link** The column allows you to choose a link from the text you specified in the Display Column Expression to another Oracle Application Server Portal portlet or URL.

By default, the Oracle Application Server Portal engine will try to establish a relationship for you automatically. As you can see in Figure 10-7, the wizard was "smart" enough to determine the existence of the relationship between the EMPNO and MGR columns in the EMP table. By accepting the defaults, we will build a hierarchy with the parent (EMP.MGR) at the top, and all employees (EMP.EMPNO) associated with the parent underneath that. Next, we need to specify what is to be displayed in the hierarchy. For that, we need to fill in the "Display Column Expression" field. You can either enter the column name to be displayed (to display the employee name, enter EMP.ENAME) or click the small notepad icon next to the text box to display a list of acceptable columns.

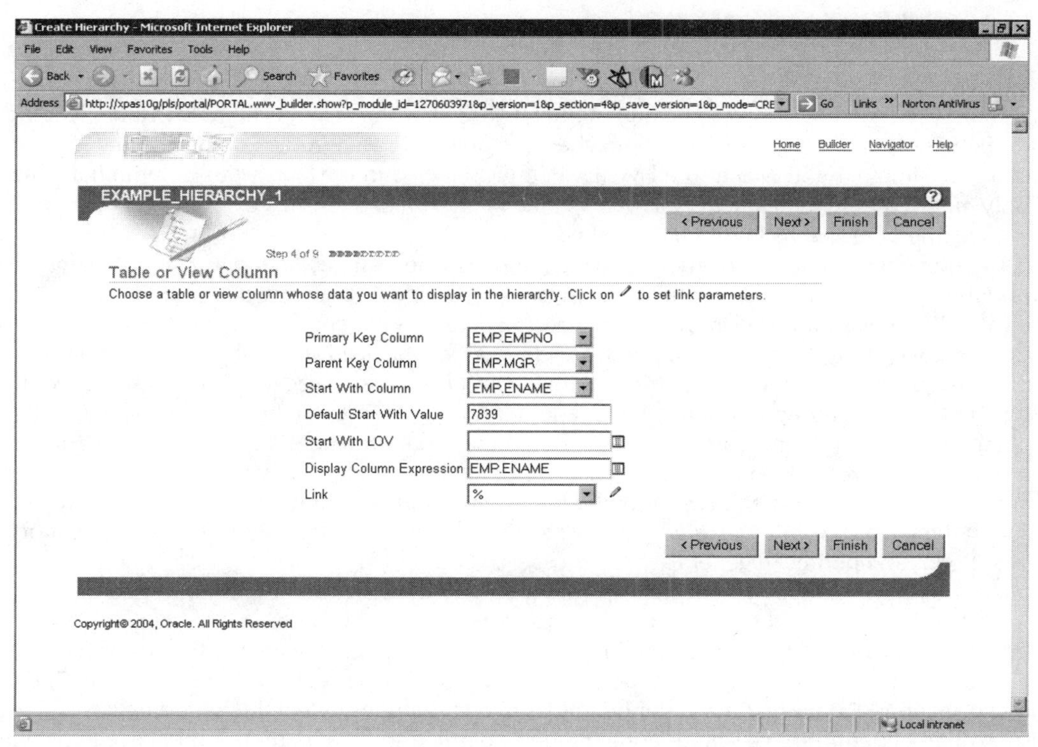

FIGURE 10-7. *The fourth step of the Oracle Application Server Portal Hierarchy Wizard*

Clicking Next> at this point will demonstrate what is perhaps the greatest limitation of using Oracle Application Server Portal Hierarchies. An error message will display:

```
Error: Default Start with Value cannot be null. Enter a valid value depending
on the Start with Column selected. (WWV-13026)
```

This error message is informing us that we need to specify the starting value (the topmost point) for our hierarchy. Looking at the data in the PORTAL_DEMO.EMP table, there is a record that looks like it would be a good candidate for our starting point:

```
     EMPNO ENAME      JOB              MGR HIREDATE         SAL       COMM
---------- ---------- --------- ---------- --------- ---------- ----------
    DEPTNO
----------
      7782 CLARK      MANAGER         7839 09-JUN-81       2450
        10

      7788 SCOTT      ANALYST         7566 09-DEC-82       3000
        20

      7839 KING       PRESIDENT            17-NOV-81       5000
        10
```

Employee King not only has the title of PRESIDENT, but she also has no MGR value, leading us to believe that employee 7839 is the highest-ranking employee in the company. That makes our choice simple, right? Make sure EMP.EMPNO is selected in the Start With Column field and simply enter **7839** in the Default Start With Value field. You can test this by clicking Finish on this page, then the Run as Portlet link on the Manage screen.

The hierarchy displays properly, but what happens when King is no longer the company president? Therein lies the limitation of hierarchies in Oracle Application Server Portal. Since the value 7839 was hard-coded into the portlet, it will always attempt to display the hierarchy using employee King as the starting point. For a hierarchy that's a list of parts contained within a complex product (such as a car), this probably won't be an issue because it is unlikely that all of the parts will need to be associated with another product immediately (most likely, you will build a new hierarchy for the new product). But in the situation where a company president retires (or is indicted), all employees will have to be re-assigned to a new president. You can make the argument that in this scenario, the hierarchy could be rebuilt by changing a single value in the wizard. While this is true, it goes against the dynamic nature of Oracle Application Server Portal and portals in general.

Developers also have the ability to assign an LOV to the start value. This allows end users to specify the starting value for the hierarchy. Click Edit on the Manage screen, then click the third tab on the top-right of the screen. The Display Options page (Figure 10-8) is displayed.

This page of wizard allows developers to specify how the hierarchy will be displayed. The top two sections, Common Options and Drill Up/Down Options, affect the hierarchy if it is displayed in either full-page (stand-alone) mode or portlet mode. Maximum Child Levels specifies how many levels are displayed on the page simultaneously. You can only set this value to 1 or 2.

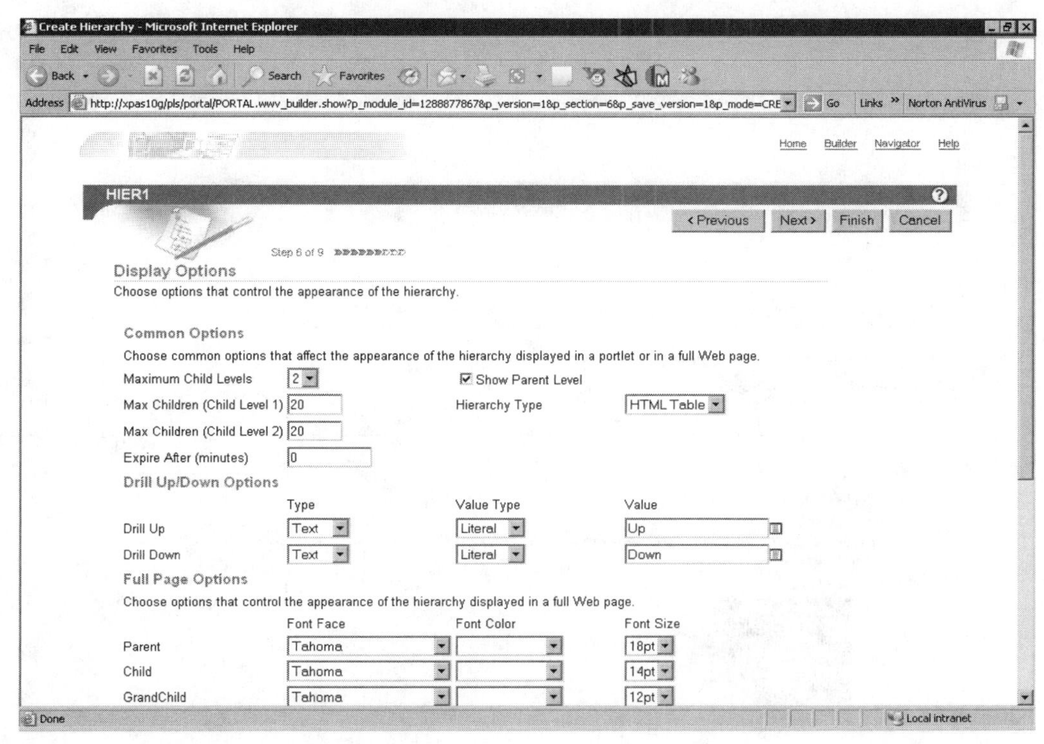

FIGURE 10-8. *The Display Options Page of the Hierarchy Wizard*

Setting this value will affect how many levels are displayed when the hierarchy is first rendered. The Drill Up/Down Options allow developers to control what the end user will see in order to drill up or down through the hierarchy. By default, the literal values Up and Down are displayed as links on the hierarchy allowing navigation. You can change the literal values by leaving the Value Type as Literal and entering new hard-coded values in the Value columns. You can also use values queried from the database as your links by changing the Value Type to Column and specifying a column in the value field. Oddly, clicking the small notepad icon to the right of the Value field does not bring up a list of database columns you can use; rather, it displays a list of images and buttons. These are used if you wish to use a button or image (by selecting Button or Image in the Type drop-down list) as your navigation tools. The third and fourth sections of the page (Full-Page Options and Portlet Options) affect how the portlet is displayed in stand-alone and when placed on an Oracle Application Server Portal page, respectively.

The next page of the wizard, the Customization Form Display Options page (Figure 10-9) allows developers to specify what options are to be displayed to power users who have been granted the ability to customize their portlets. At the top of the page is a section that allows you

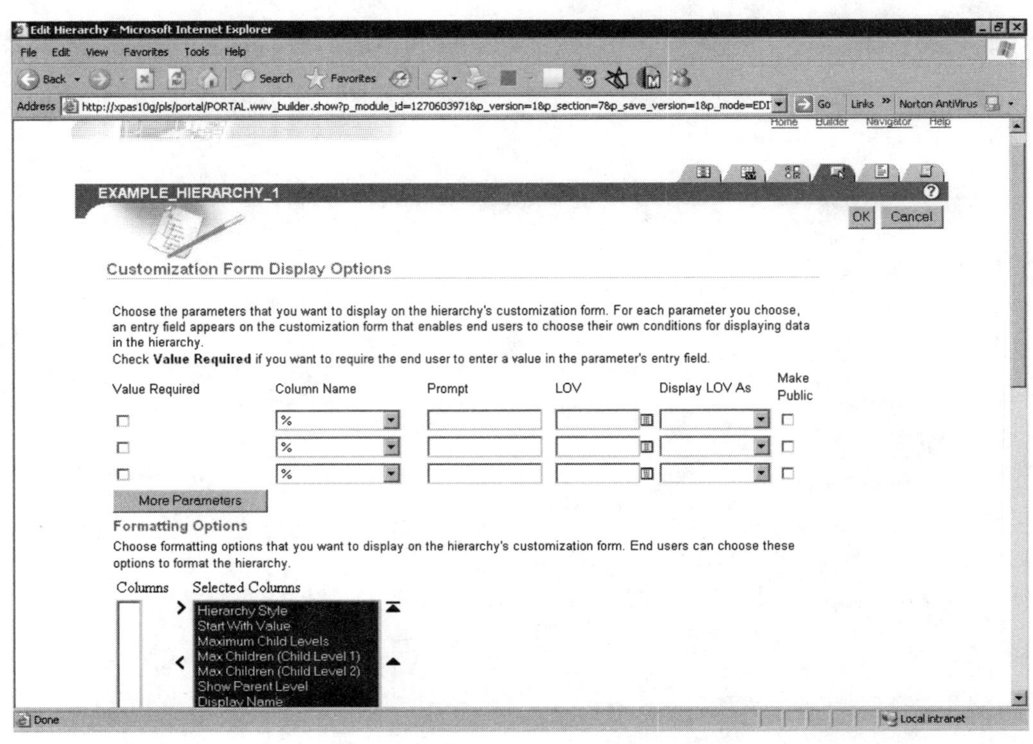

FIGURE 10-9. *The Customization form Display Options page of the hierarchy wizard*

to affect how any bind variables will be used on the customization page. The Formatting Options section allows you to specify what attributes of the hierarchy can be customized by those users who have been granted customization privileges. Any options specified in the Public Formatting Options section will be available to all users who view the hierarchy. The final section, Button Options, allows you to display or hide and change the values for buttons to be displayed on the customization form. The final two steps of the wizard, the Hierarchy and Customization Form Text and Additional PL/SQL code, have the same look and functionality as the wizards we have explored up to this point.

Figure 10-10 shows an example of a completed hierarchy. You can display this by clicking the "Run As Portlet" link on the Manage page for the hierarchy. As you can see, the initial page of the hierarchy displays two levels of depth, with employees Blake, Clark, and Jones under King at level one of the hierarchy and the next set of employees (Allen, James, Martin, etc.) at level two. The portlet displays these two levels based on the setting of Maximum Child Levels we specified on the Display Options page of the wizard. You can also see the Up and Down HTML link displayed on this page; if we had specified an image or button on the Display Options page, it would appear in place of these links.

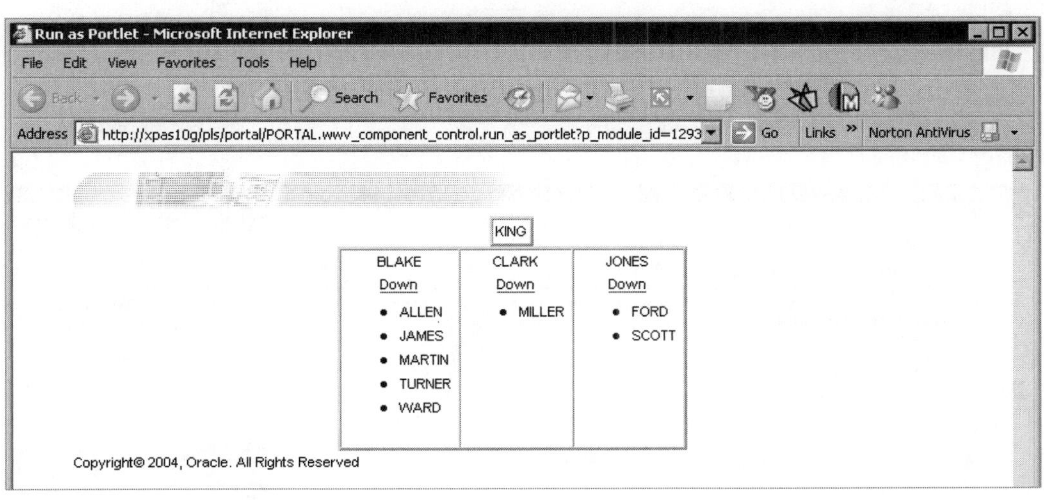

FIGURE 10-10. *The completed hierarchy*

Oracle Application Server Portal Menus

An Oracle Application Server Portal Menu is an HTML page that displays links to submenus, Oracle Application Server Portal database portlets, or external URLs. The menu, its submenus, and any links to Oracle Application Server Portal database portlets or URLs can be secured at the Oracle Application Server Portal role level to prevent access by unauthorized users. Oracle Application Server Portal Menus can display as many as five levels of a menu hierarchy, with each level indented on the menu to the right. Descriptive text can be added to links, and hyperlinks can be added to submenus that appear on menus. You can set an overall different look and feel for the menu and its submenus based on a template or you can set a different look and feel on a submenu by submenu basis.

To create a new menu, click the Navigator icon on the top right of any Oracle Application Server Portal page. Click the Providers tab if it isn't already selected. Click the Locally-Built Providers link and then click the provider you have been using to work through the examples. Click the Create New... Menu link on the top left of the page.

Menu creation via the wizard only has four steps (don't be fooled by the "Step 1 of 5" heading on the first page of the Oracle Application Server Portal Menu Wizard; as is the case with almost every other wizard we've seen up to this point, there is no Step 2), so it is one of the least complicated Oracle Application Server Portal components we can create. After we specify the name, display name, and provider of the menu on the first page of the wizard, we are taken to Step 3 of 5 (Figure 10-11).

This page of the wizard is where most of the characteristics of our menu will be set. On the left-hand side of the screen, there is a hierarchical display of the elements in our menu. When we first display this page of the wizard, the only element listed is named the same as the menu name specified in Step 1 of the wizard (in this case, "example_menu_1"). The right-hand side of the

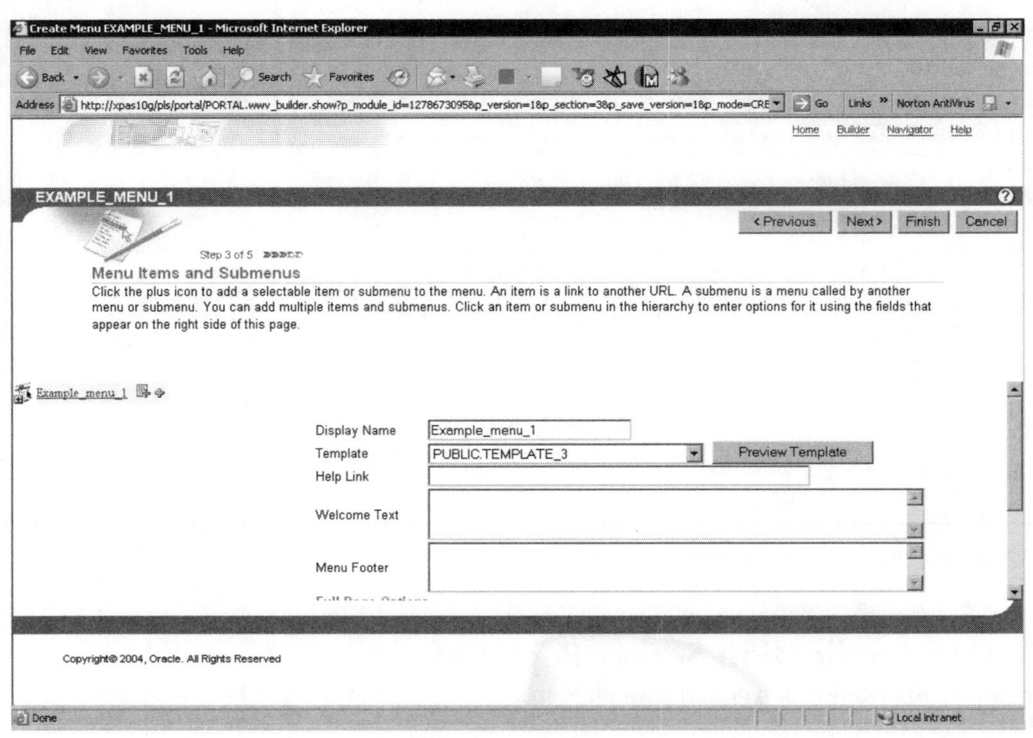

FIGURE 10-11. *The Menu Items and Submenus page of the Oracle Application Server Portal Menu Wizard*

screen will change to reflect the options associated with whatever is selected on the left-hand side of the screen. Since the only option that can be selected is the menu heading (example_menu_1), we see options like Display Name and Template displayed in the right-hand part of the screen. These options affect all menu items and submenus we create under the menu header. The template, help text, welcome text, and menu footer fields are only applicable when displaying the menu in stand-alone (full-screen) mode. The drop-down boxes labeled Full Page Options and Portlet Option determine how many levels of menu items will be displayed when the menu is initially loaded. If you remember, we mentioned earlier that up to five levels can be displayed; these drop-down boxes ask for the number of sublevels to be displayed, so the limit here is four.

On the left-hand side of the page, there are two "plus" signs next to the example_menu_1 menu element. One has a graphic of a page behind it, the other does not. These icons allow you to add elements to your menu. The graphic with the page will add a submenu when clicked; the other icon will add a menu item. Click the submenu icon to add a submenu below menu1. The right-hand side of the screen changes to reflect the newly-created submenu's properties. For the most part, these attributes are the same as the main menu's properties, with a few extra font properties for the submenu thrown in.

Up to this point, we have seen properties for the main menu item and submenu items. The third type of menu element, menu items, is where we specify where the portlet will "jump" to when it is selected. Click the Add Menu Item icon (the plus sign with no page graphic behind it) to add a new menu item to our menu (Figure 10-12). The right-hand side of the screen changes to reflect the attributes that can be set for this link. The most important ones are

- **Name** This will determine what is displayed when the menu is rendered.
- **Link Type** There are three types of links:
  - **Link** This refers to an Oracle Application Server Portal link (discussed later in this chapter in the section "Oracle Application Server Portal Links").
  - **Component** This refers to an Oracle Application Server Portal component; for those components with parameter (customization) pages, you can either specify running the component itself or running the customization page for that component.
  - **URL** This refers to a URL, which can be used to create a link to an external page or web site.
- **Link** Depending on what is selected as the link type, this field can either be populated with a predefined Oracle Application Server Portal link, an Oracle Application Server Portal component, or a URL. Clicking the small notepad icon to the right of the text box will only display a list of Oracle Application Server Portal components, even if "Link" or "URL" is selected.

The final two steps of the wizard, the Customization Form Display Options and the Menu Customization Form Text pages, have the same look and function as those pages we have already reviewed when looking at other wizards. Remember that the attributes specified on the Menu Customization Form Text screen are only applied to menus displayed in stand-alone (full-screen) mode. Click Finish, then Run on the Manage page for the menu. You will see the menu displayed with the Submenu link displayed on the page. Clicking the Submenu link will display the element in the submenu, namely the link to the calendar object.

Oracle Application Server Portal URLs

An Oracle Application Server Portal URL is, perhaps, the simplest component you can create in Oracle Application Server Portal. A URL portlet that is placed on a page does not display the HTTP hyperlink; rather, it resolves whatever is in the URL and displays that page in the portlet. To create an Oracle Portal URL, navigate to your provider page (if you don't remember how to do that, see the instructions at the beginning of the previous section, Oracle Application Server Portal Menus). Click the Create New… URL on the top left of the page.

The first step of the wizard is like all of the other Oracle Application Server Portal components we have seen up to this point. Clicking Next> brings us to Step 2 of the wizard (yes, there's actually a Step 2 in this wizard). Here, we specify the URL that we want to display. Remember, we will not display a link in the portlet; the Oracle Application Server Portal engine will resolve the URL and display that page as a portlet on the Oracle Application Server Portal page we will eventually place this portlet on. Later in this chapter, we will discuss placing portlets on pages. It is not necessary to specify HTTP:// at the beginning of the URL, but it certainly does not do any harm to do so. For this example, enter tusc.com and click Next>

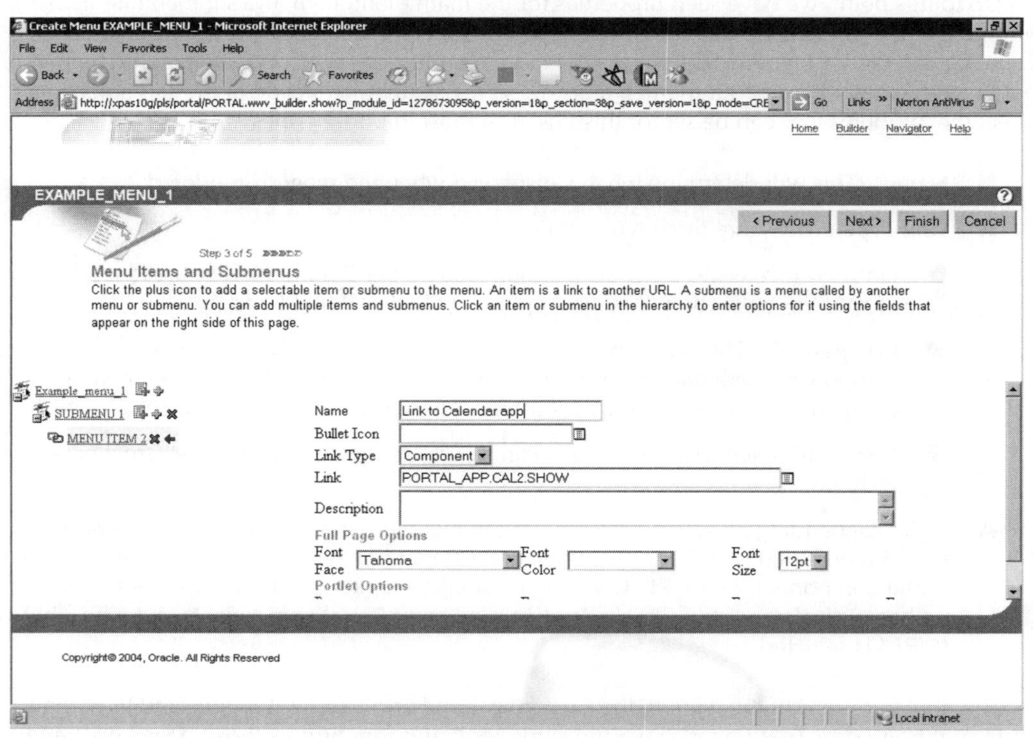

FIGURE 10-12. *The third step of the Oracle Application Server Portal Menu wizard*

Step 3 of 5 provides information about the URL component when displayed in full-page mode. If the Expire After (minutes) attribute is set to 0, the page will be requeried each time the URL is displayed in full-page mode. Any value greater than 0 will cause the Oracle Application Server Portal engine to cache (store) the web page for the allotted period of time. Anyone requesting the page within that time period will see the cached version. This shortens the time needed to display a page referenced by the URL, but can result in information being stale (i.e., cached by the Oracle Application Server Portal engine, while newer information was updated on the reference web page). The final two pages of the wizard, the Customization Form Display Options and URL and Customization Form Text pages, have similar functionality (this wizard has very few options for these pages) to pages for other Oracle Application Server Portal components we have reviewed.

Oracle Application Server Portal Links

Oracle Application Server Portal Links are a way of tying together your Oracle Application Server Portal components. With links, for example, you can produce a report that has one of its columns turned into a set of links. When an end user clicks on one of those links, he is taken to another component (such as an Oracle Application Server Portal Form) that provides more information about the selected record. There are two aspects of links that make them extremely powerful:

- **They can be used in multiple places.** Once a link is defined to a particular component, a component's customization form, or an HTML link, it can be placed on as many components as you like. This is very powerful as it easily gives you a way to allow a high level of interaction among portlets on your Oracle Application Server Portal portlets and provides a standardized, consistent way of handling this interaction.
- **They allow parameters to be passed.** Links are smart enough to pass the appropriate value(s) to the target (destination) Oracle Application Server Portal component. By doing so, the overhead of complex programming involving parameters is eliminated.

To create a new link, select the Create New… Link link on the Providers page in the Oracle Application Server Portal Navigator. If you don't remember how to get to the providers page, see the instructions at the beginning of the "Oracle Application Server Portal Menu" section earlier in this chapter. After entering the name information of your link on the first page of the wizard, you are presented with Step 2 of 3, the Link Target Type and Name screen (Figure 10-13).

On this page of the wizard, you will specify what type of link you wish to create and the target component. The target component is where the end user will be taken to when she clicks on the link. For this example, let's create a link to the calendar component we created earlier in this chapter. On page two of the wizard, select the Oracle Portal Component radio button, and when you click the small notepad to the right of the Target Component or URL text box, a list of

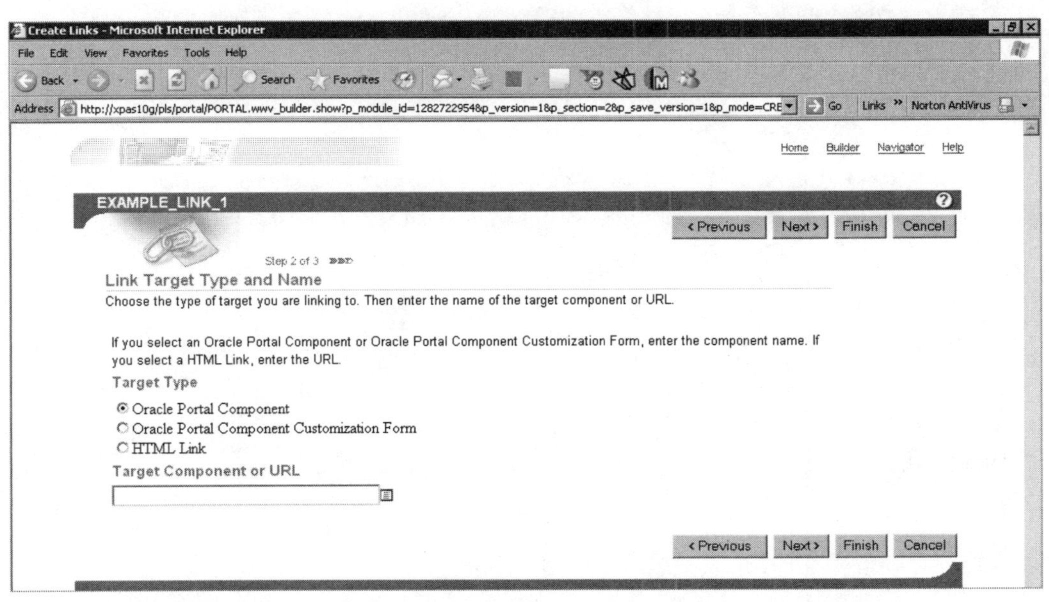

FIGURE 10-13. *The second page of the Oracle Application Server Portal Link Wizard*

Oracle Application Server Portal components will be displayed (Figure 10-14). Note that the internal name of the component, not the display name, is displayed in the dialog box. Select the name of the calendar component you created earlier and the Target Component or URL text box will be populated with your selection.

The final step of the wizard (Figure 10-15) allows us to specify default values for parameters that will be passed to our target component. There are two categories of parameters defined: user parameters and system parameters. User parameters are any parameter defined in the creation of the target component. Most often, this will be bind variables that have been defined for the target component. In this case, our calendar did not contain any bind variables, so nothing shows up under the "User Parameters" section. Under the "System Parameters" section, there are a number of system parameters defined, all starting with an underscore (_).

To understand system parameters, we need to go off on a tangent for a little bit. After we created our first Oracle Application Server Portal component in the previous chapter, you were encouraged to look at the source code that was generated by the Oracle Application Server Portal engine upon completion (you can view the source code that makes up any Oracle Application Server Portal component by going to the Manage page for that component and clicking on either the Package Spec or Package Body links). For even a simple component, the Oracle Application Server Portal engine generates a large amount of code. For many portals, this is an acceptable situation, but for most, developers will want greater control of how they can develop and enhance the components that make up their portal.

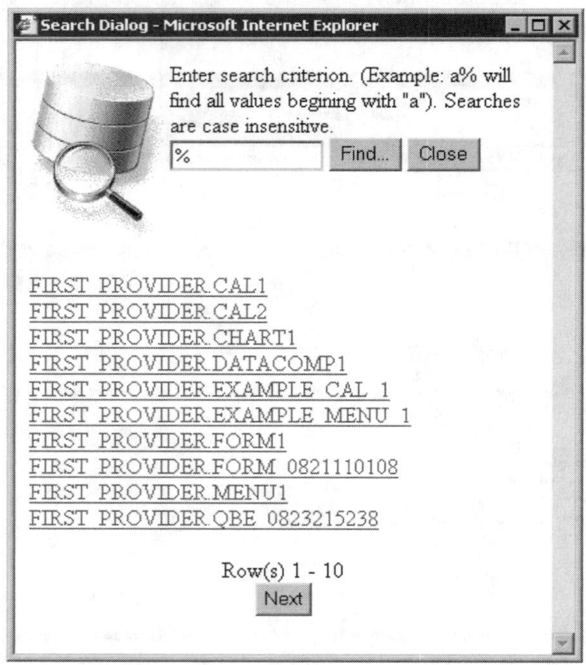

FIGURE 10-14. *The Search Dialog for the Link Wizard*

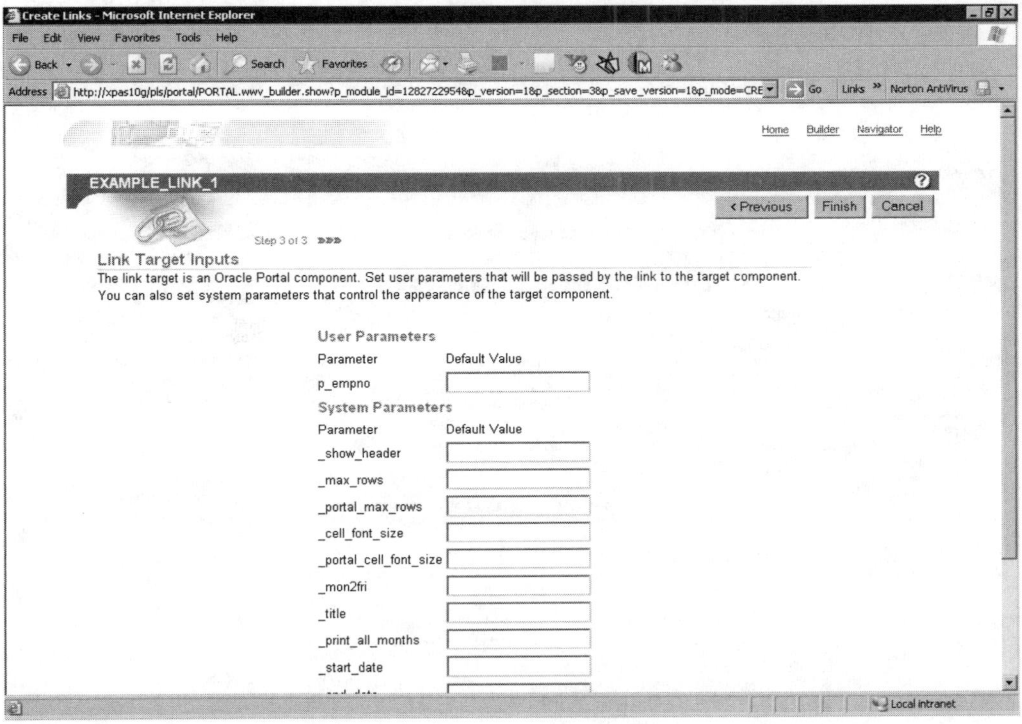

FIGURE 10-15. *Step 3 of the Oracle Application Server Portal Link Wizard*

The Portal Center web pages on Oracle's web site (http://www.oracle.com/technology/products/ias/portal/index.html) are an invaluable resource for Oracle Application Server Portal developers. On these pages, you will find numerous links to various pieces of documentation, including how-to guides and articles that provide step-by-step instructions on how to complete a specific task. While most of the documentation provided with Oracle Application Server 10*g* relates to configuring Oracle Application Server Portal and is, therefore, geared towards administrators, the documentation on this page is geared toward developers.

Behind the scenes, the Oracle Application Server Portal engine is doing a lot of work, most of which is hidden away from you, the developer. There is a way, however, for developers to interact and enhance their portal components outside of the Oracle Application Server Portal wizards: the Portal Developer Kit (PDK) (Figure 10-16). One of the things you can do from the Portal Center page is download the PDK.

The PDK, which is updated quarterly, provides a set of articles and documentation for the application programming interfaces (APIs) that developers can use to enhance their Oracle Application Server Portal components outside of the choices they can make in the various Oracle Application Server portal wizards. Part of this documentation deals with the various system parameters displayed in the "Link Target Inputs" screen of the Link wizard (Figure 10-15).

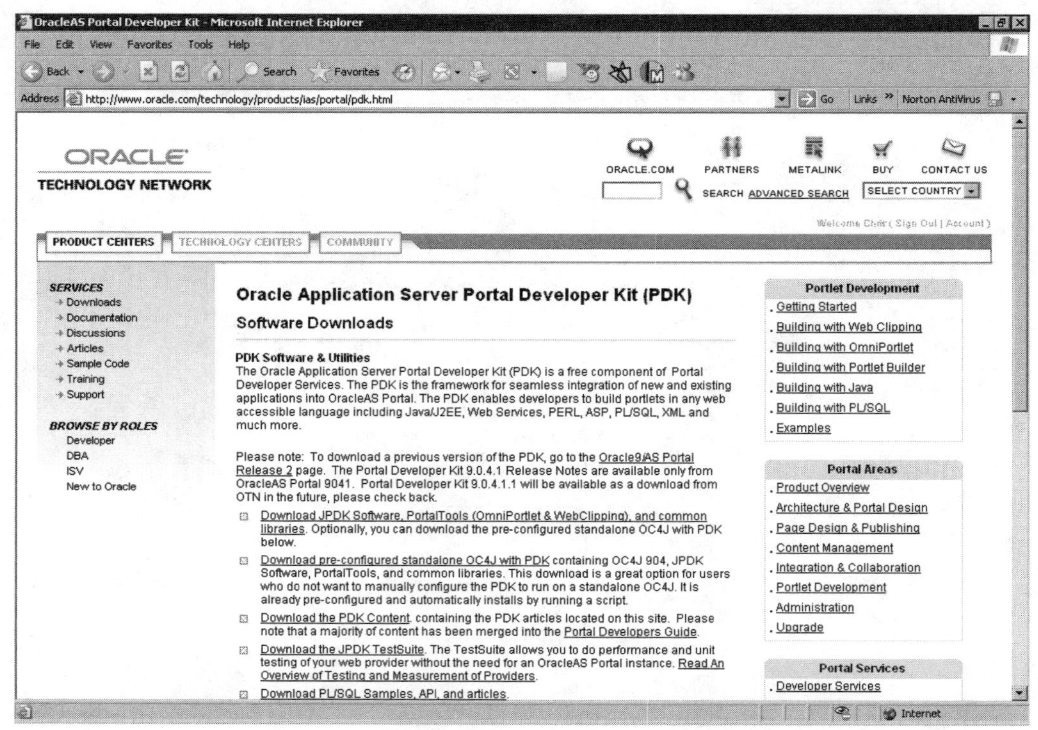

FIGURE 10-16. *The Portal Developer Kit download page*

A discussion of system parameters is beyond the scope of this book, but understand that Oracle provides additional functionality to developers beyond the normal attributes that can be set in the wizards by way of the APIs contained in the PDK.

Returning to our example, leave the fields blank and click Finish to generate the link. On the Manage screen for the component, there's a link called Run, but it's of little use, serving only to display what the link is pointing to (the Oracle Application Server Portal component destination). To see the usefulness of links, we'll need to associate them with another component. Let's start by building a simple Oracle Application Server Portal Report and then creating a link between this report and the calendar we built earlier in this chapter. Go to the Oracle Application Server Portal Navigator by clicking the link on the top-right of any Oracle Application Server Portal screen. Click the Providers tab, then the Locally-Built Providers link, then the name of the provider you have been using to create the components. Click the Create New… Report link and create a new Report From Query Wizard. Give the report a meaningful name in Step 1 of the wizard. On Step 3, base the report off of the PORTAL_DEMO.EMP table. Click Add and then Next >. Click the double greater-than signs (>>) to move all of the columns to the Selected Columns field on the page. Click Next > three times to get to the Column Formatting page.

Click the Link drop-down box for the EMP.EMPNO row. You will see a list of links that are available for us to use. Select the link you created earlier in this section, then click the pencil icon in the Edit Link column. Our link can use any of the fields to link to the calendar component, but only system parameters show up (Figure 10-17). Remember this fact, as we're going to revisit this page.

Click OK to close the Set Link Parameters dialog box, then click Finish to generate the report. On the Manage page, click the Run as Portlet link. You will see a report similar to Figure 10-18.

Note how the EMPNO column is a set of HTML links. Click on the first link (7369) and you will be taken to the calendar (Figure 10-19).

Looks pretty good, right? We clicked on the employee number for employee "Smith" and were taken to the calendar for the date he was hired; namely, December of 1980. Click the Back button in your browser, then click on the second link (7499). Based on Allen's starting date, we should be taken to February of 1981, but we're taken back to December of 1980. What happened?

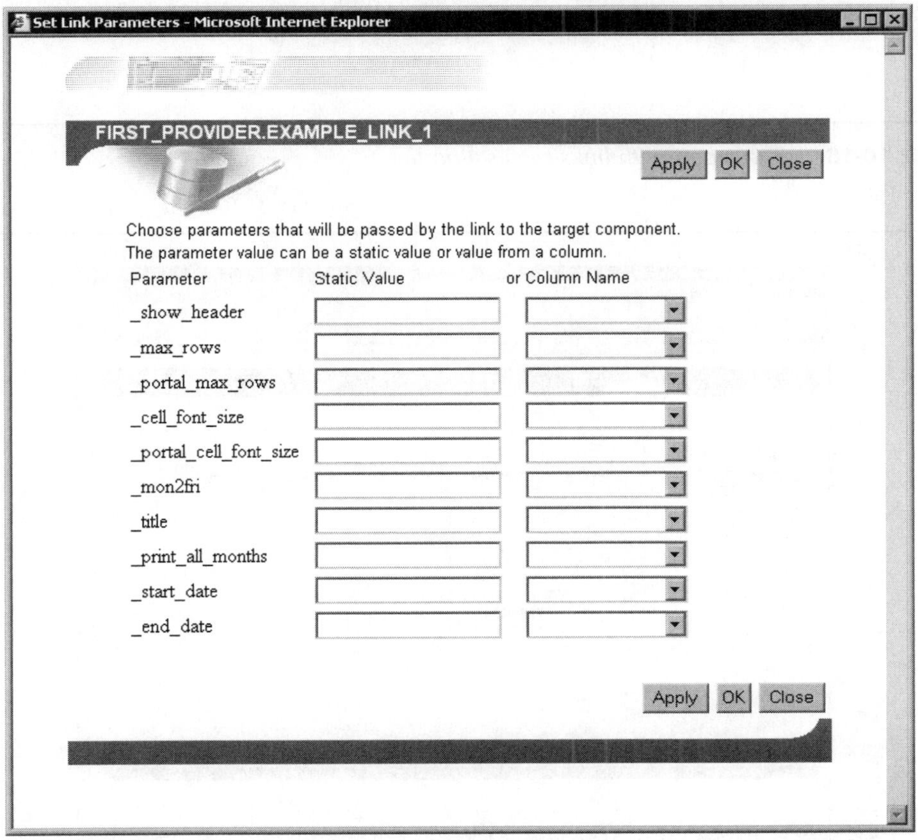

FIGURE 10-17. *Parameters for the link*

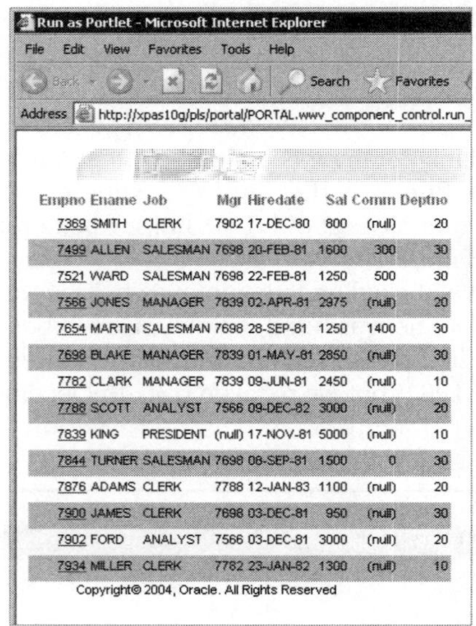

Empno	Ename	Job	Mgr	Hiredate	Sal	Comm	Deptno
7369	SMITH	CLERK	7902	17-DEC-80	800	(null)	20
7499	ALLEN	SALESMAN	7698	20-FEB-81	1600	300	30
7521	WARD	SALESMAN	7698	22-FEB-81	1250	500	30
7566	JONES	MANAGER	7839	02-APR-81	2975	(null)	20
7654	MARTIN	SALESMAN	7698	28-SEP-81	1250	1400	30
7698	BLAKE	MANAGER	7839	01-MAY-81	2850	(null)	30
7782	CLARK	MANAGER	7839	09-JUN-81	2450	(null)	10
7788	SCOTT	ANALYST	7566	09-DEC-82	3000	(null)	20
7839	KING	PRESIDENT	(null)	17-NOV-81	5000	(null)	10
7844	TURNER	SALESMAN	7698	08-SEP-81	1500	0	30
7876	ADAMS	CLERK	7788	12-JAN-83	1100	(null)	20
7900	JAMES	CLERK	7698	03-DEC-81	950	(null)	30
7902	FORD	ANALYST	7566	03-DEC-81	3000	(null)	20
7934	MILLER	CLERK	7782	23-JAN-82	1300	(null)	10

Copyright© 2004, Oracle. All Rights Reserved

FIGURE 10-18. *The report with links run as a portlet*

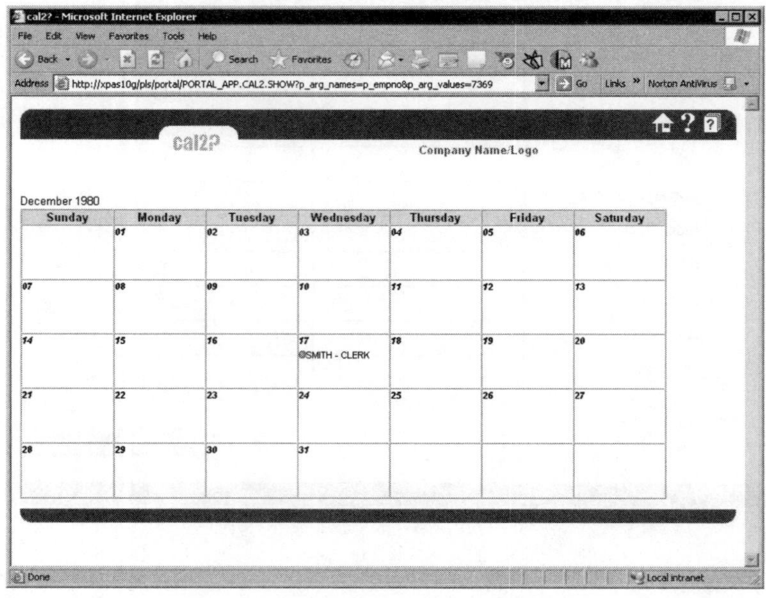

FIGURE 10-19. *The calendar displaying Smith's record*

In the Column Formatting page of the report wizard, we specified the link, but when we edited the link, there were no user parameters available for us to pass the employee number. Since we didn't pass the employee number to the calendar, it displayed the earliest month with an employee start date in it (December, 1980). It was just a coincidence that the link we chose (7369 - Smith) happened to be the earliest month with an employee start date in it. How can we fix this link?

The link is only useful if it passes the information about the row we clicked on, so we'll have to find a way to pass the row information from the report component to the calendar component. The calendar component will have to accept a passed parameter and, if you remember earlier, we said that the easiest way to have a component receive a user parameter is by way of a bind variable. We can add a bind variable to our calendar component by performing the following steps:

1. Edit the calendar component by clicking the Edit link next to the component in the navigator screen.
2. Modify the query to include a bind variable for the employee number (in the listing below, the line "where empno = :p_empno" was added):

```
select
HIREDATE                    the_date,
ENAME||' - '||JOB           the_name,
null            the_name_link,
null            the_date_link,
null            the_target,
null            the_intermedia
from PORTAL_DEMO.EMP
where empno = :p_empno
order by HIREDATE
```

3. Click OK to generate a new calendar component.
4. Edit the report by clicking the Edit link next to the report component in the navigator screen.
5. Click the third tab to display the Column Formatting page of the wizard.
6. Click the Edit Link pencil icon for the EMP.EMPNO row.
7. For the p_empno row, select the EMP.EMPNO column in the Column Name drop-down box.
8. Click OK to close the Set Link Parameters dialog box.
9. Click OK to generate a new report.

Click the Run as Portlet link and click a link other than 7369. Were you taken to the correct calendar page? Click the Back button on your browser and click different links to test it out.

Oracle Application Server Portal Data Components

An Oracle Application Server Portal data component is the equivalent of embedding a spreadsheet into your Oracle Application Server Portal pages. The wizard does not prompt you for any "source" information (such as a database table) since the spreadsheet is not populated upon being displayed on an Oracle Application Server Portal page. Based on whether you select a report or a chart in Step 3 of the wizard, you will see an entirely different set of wizard pages for this component (Table 10-1):

The steps in this wizard are identical to wizard pages we have visited in the past except for the Data Component Columns page, which will be either Step 4 or 5 depending on what type of object was selected in Step 3 of the wizard. On this page of the wizard, the developer is prompted for information that can be used to define links and group functions for specified columns. By default, there are four columns created in your data component, which are named "A" through "D."

When you first attempt to run this portlet, no data will be returned. Data has to be entered in a spreadsheet-like applet that is displayed when the developer clicks on the customize link on the Manage page for the component or the end user clicks on the Customize link when the portlet is displayed (assuming that the end user has customize privileges on the portlet). After the data is entered (Figure 10-20), the portlet can be redisplayed with the corresponding data.

Oracle Application Server Portal Page Design

Devoting one section of one chapter to Oracle Application Server Portal page design does not do it justice. The Oracle Application Server Portal page design mechanism is an extremely sophisticated environment giving page designers incredible flexibility to control every aspect of how their portal pages are presented to end users. This section will cover the basics of Oracle Application Server Portal page design. We encourage you to experiment with the various features contained in the product.

Up until this point, we have looked at creating various Oracle Application Server Portal components. How do we take them and place them on a page our end users can view? The answer lies in the Oracle Application Server Portal Design Page. To create a new page, enter the Navigator by clicking the Navigator link on the top right of any Oracle Application Server Portal page. Up to this point, all of our Oracle Application Server Portal examples have utilized the Providers tab on this page. To create a new page that can hold content, however, we will select the Page Groups tab (Figure 10-21).

Step 3 = Report	**Step 3 = Chart**
Step 4 - Data Component Columns	Step 5 - Data Component Columns
Step 6 - Column Formatting	Step 8 - Column Conditions
Step 7 - Formatting Conditions	Step 9 - Formatting Conditions
Step 10 - Display Options	Step 11 - Display Options
Step 12 - Customization Form Display Options	Step 13 - Customization Form Display Options
Step 14 - Data Component and Customization Form Text	Step 14 - Data Component and Customization Form Text

TABLE 10-1. *Steps in the Oracle Application Server Portal Data Component Wizard*

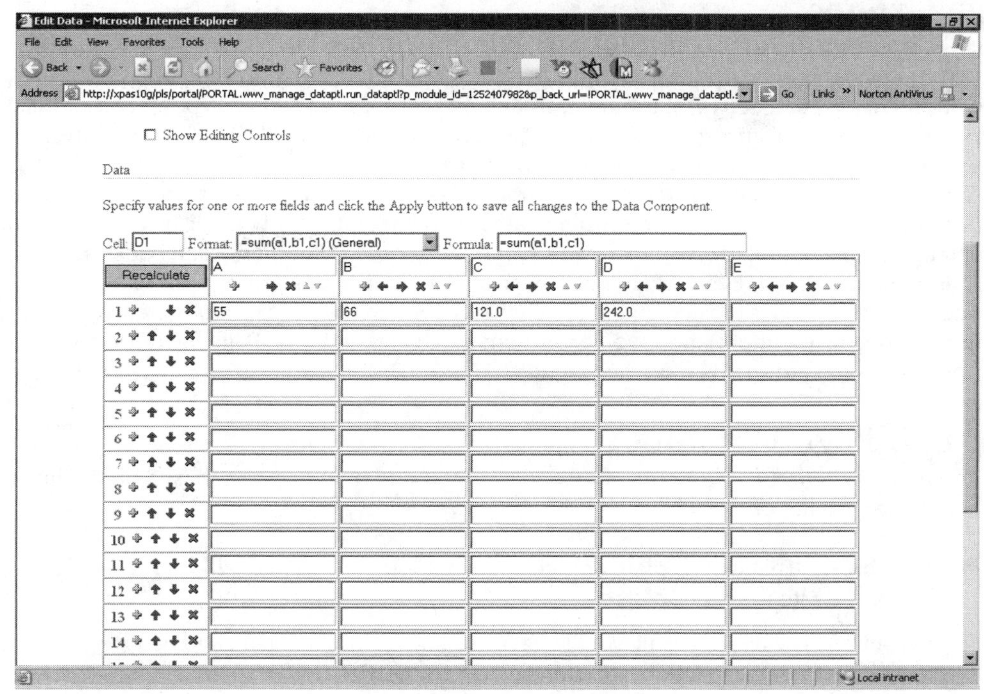

FIGURE 10-20. *The edit data/customize page of the Oracle Application Server Portal Data Component Wizard*

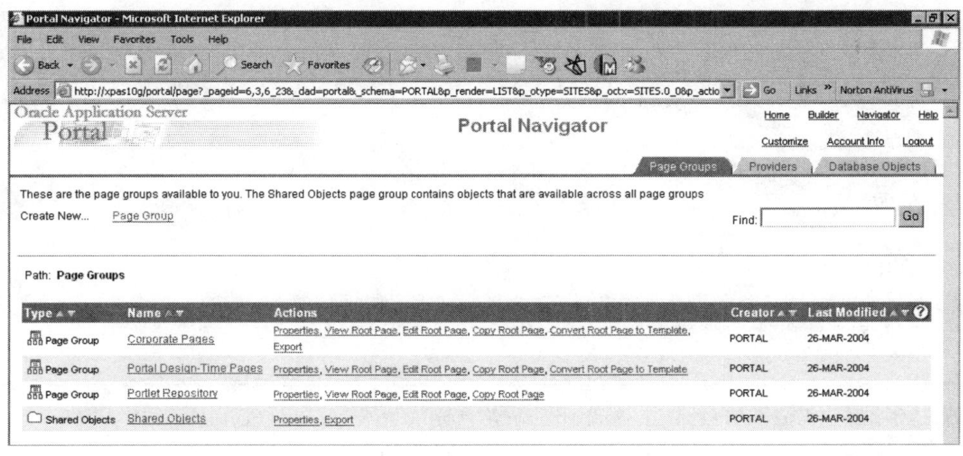

FIGURE 10-21. *The Page Groups tab displayed in the Navigator*

Page Groups

All pages must be associated with a Page Group.The Page Group tab on the Navigator allows us to create new page groups, where we can then create Subpages, Templates, Categories, Navigation Pages, Perspectives, Styles, Attributes, Page Types, and Item Types. Each of these components will be discussed later in this chapter in the sections "Styles," "Templates," "Navigation Pages," and "Categories and Perspectives." For now, click the Create New…Page Group link on the top left of the screen. The Create Page Group wizard is simple: It consists of one page that prompting for a name, display name, and language. Only English will appear in the Default Language drop-down box unless you have installed other language packs for Oracle Application Server Portal. Every page group has at least one page associated with it called the root page, and this page is created automatically for you when the page group is created. After entering the necessary information, you are automatically taken to the Page Layout screen for the root page of the group you have just created (Figure 10-22).

The Edit Page Window

You can edit a page in Oracle Application Server Portal one of three ways, based on the link selected on the top left of the screen:

- **Graphical** This will display a rough estimate of how the page will look as you add regions, content, and portlets to it.
- **Layout** This will display a layout page for adding regions, content, and portlets to a page (developers who have used earlier versions of Oracle Portal will be familiar with this page).
- **List** This provides a convenient way for developers to manage content on a page. It is not much use for managing portlets.

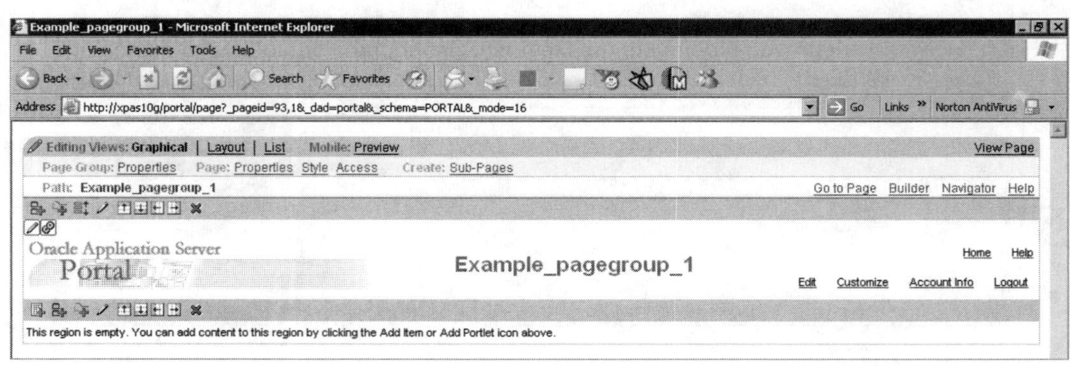

FIGURE 10-22. *The Edit Page screen of Oracle Application Server Portal*

Click the Graphical link on the top left of the page. By default, there are two regions created for you on the page: a banner region along the top of the page and an empty region below that. The banner region is considered a navigation page, which is one of the subcomponents of a page group listed above. After adding some portlets to our page, we will look at editing that part of the page. In the region below the banner, there is a set of nine icons along the top of the empty region. Moving your pointer over each one without clicking on it will bring up a tool tip telling you what action clicking each icon will perform. The first (left most) icon is the Add Item icon. Next to that is the Add Portlet icon.

Adding Portlets

A region, as we will soon discover, can contain items (content) or portlets but not both. If that's the case, why are both the Add Item and Add Portlet icons available for this region? The answer lies in the fact that, by default, the region is created as undefined, meaning we can place either items or portlets in the region now. As soon as we place either an item or portlet in the region, the region type becomes defined as that type. Place a portlet on the region by clicking the Add Portlet icon in the region below the banner.

The Add Portlets page (Figure 10-23) is displayed. From this page, we can select portlets that will be placed in the region we have selected. There are two ways to search for portlets that you would like to place in the region: If you know the name of your portlet (or a part of the name), type that in the search text box at the top of the screen and click Go. You can also search for portlets by looking through the categories provided to you by Oracle (portlets provided by Oracle are called "seeded" portlets):

- Portlet Builders
- Portal Community News
- Portal Content Tools
- Administration Portlets
- Published Portal Content
- Shared Portlets

Or, as another option, you can search for portlets you have created by looking in the Portlet Staging Area category.

Clicking on the portlet will move it to the right-hand side of the screen. Go to the Portlet Staging Area and click the name of the provider you have been creating your portlets under. You will see a list of the portlets you have created up to this point. Single-click on one of them and it will display on the right side of the page. Click OK to return to the Page Edit mode of your page with the portlet displayed graphically (Figure 10-24).

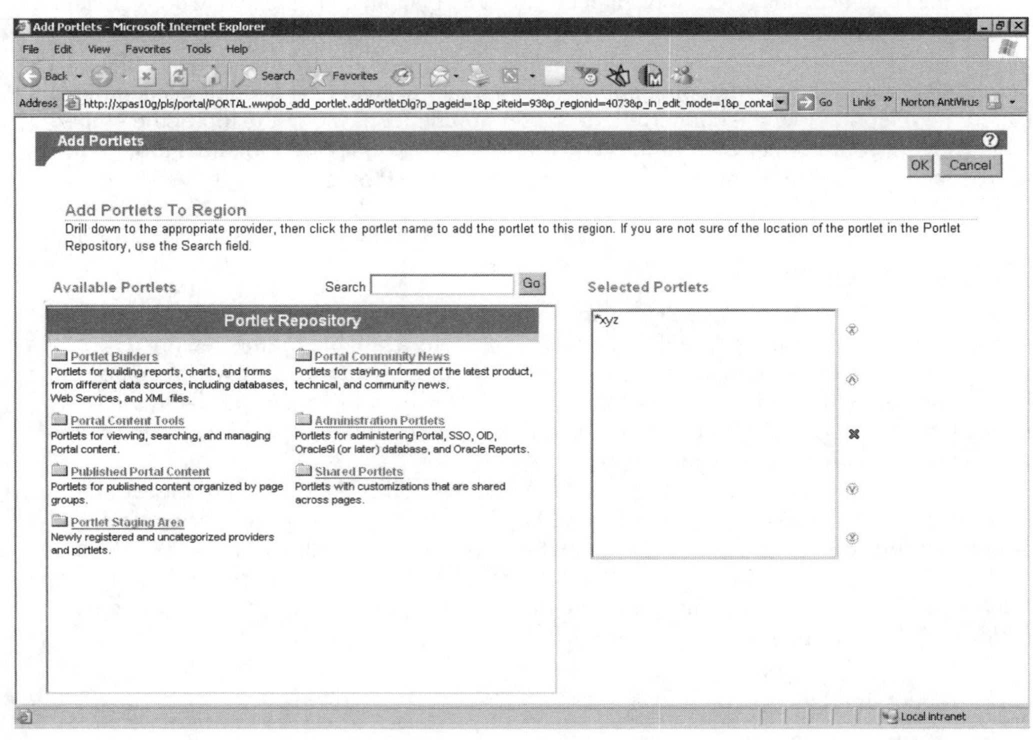

FIGURE 10-23. *The Add Portlets page*

Click the View Page link on the top right of the screen to see how the page will be displayed when end users request it. Click the Back button of your browser to return to the Edit Page window. Click the pencil icon (fourth from the left) in the region where you have just added your portlet. This displays the Edit Region page (Figure 10-25).

Regions

Regions are sections of a page. They can contain either items or portlets, but not both. They can be sized so that they take up a certain number of pixels on a page or a certain percentage of the page. Each region has its own set of attributes that affect how it displays items or portlets contained within it. The Edit Region page allows you to set attributes for a region on the page. The "Main" tab allows you to define whether the region is titled and how much space on the page it will take up. When we add regions to our pages in the next step, the Oracle Application Server Portal engine will automatically resize existing portlets so that they can fit on the page. The Oracle Application Server Portal engine will evenly divide the page depending on where we add regions, so we can

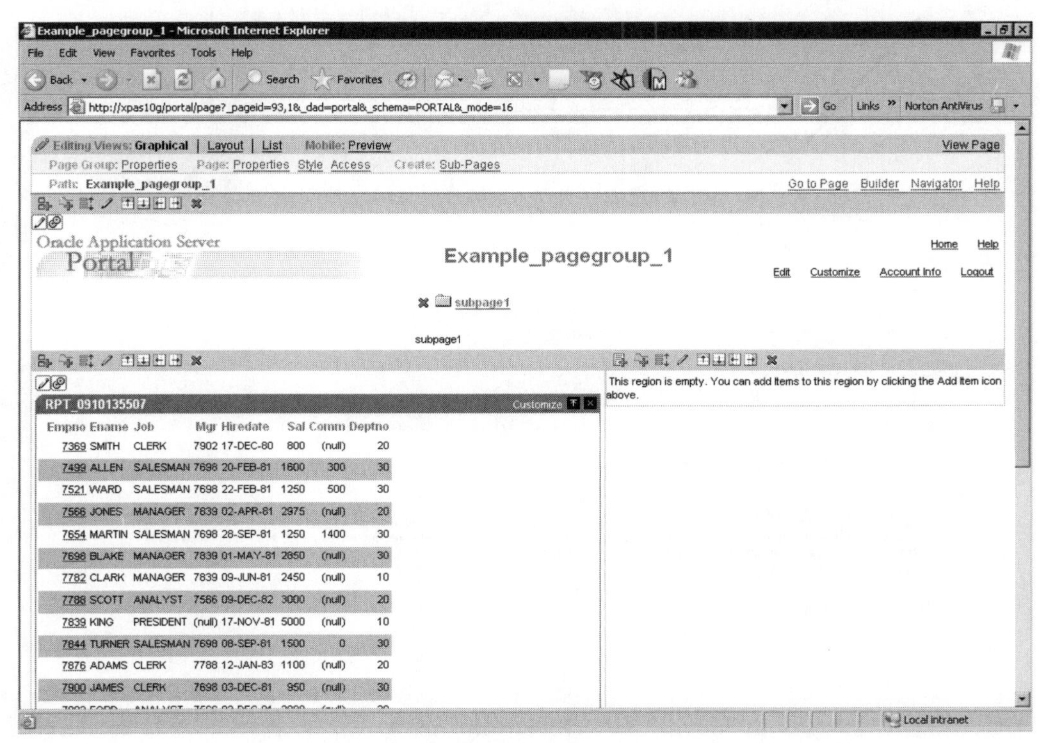

FIGURE 10-24. *The Edit Page screen with a portlet rendered*

return to this page to change the region size if we do not want evenly sized regions. The Attributes tab allows you to define what will be displayed along with which portlets or content are in the region. When we look at adding items (content) in the next section, we will revisit this page. Click Close to return to the Page Edit page.

Next to the pencil icon for the region there are four icons. These icons are used to add regions to the page. A region will be added in the direction that the arrow is pointing in the four icons. For this example, click the icon with the arrow pointing to the right (the eighth icon from the left). As we mentioned before, the Oracle Application Server Portal engine will automatically size the new and existing regions equally (Figure 10-26).

Changing the attributes for one of the regions will resize the others it affects automatically. To see an example of this, click the pencil icon for the left most region. Change the Width field on the Main tab to 66 percent. Click OK to redisplay the page (Figure 10-27). As you can see, the leftmost region now takes up 66 percent of the screen and the right-most region takes up 33 percent of the screen. To verify this, click the pencil icon on the right-most region and note how it has automatically been resized to have a width of 33 percent.

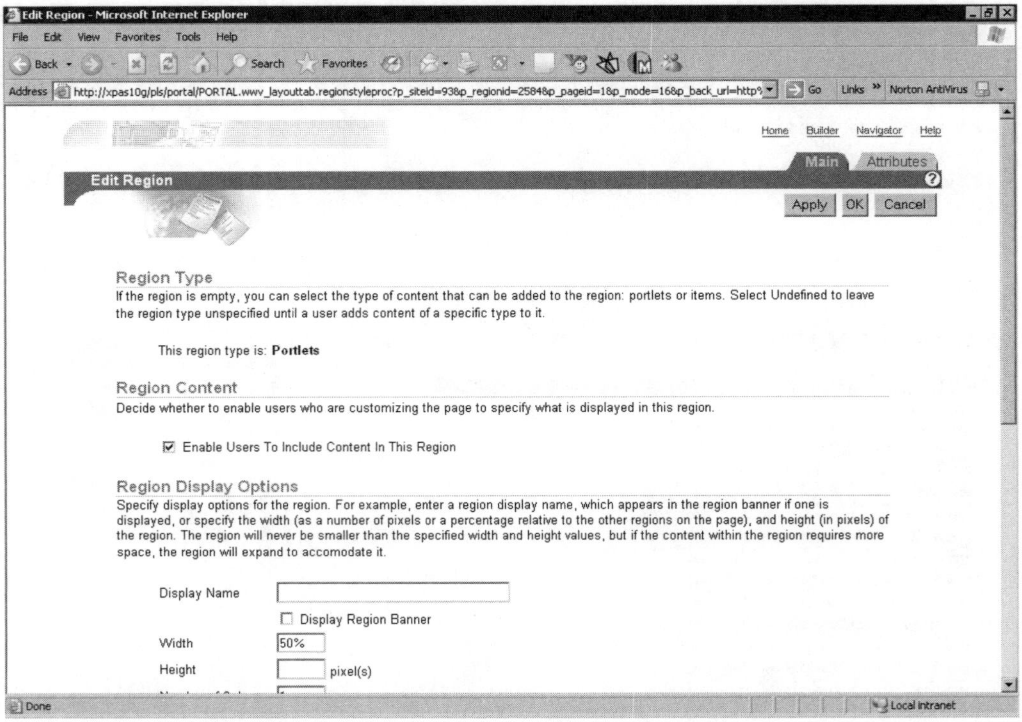

FIGURE 10-25. *The Edit Region page*

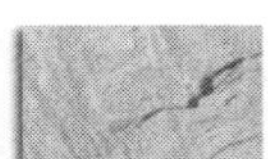

TIP

Because the rightmost region is an undefined region, the page properties will not display. Click the radio button next to "Items" and click the Apply button. The other attributes for the page will then display.

We now have a page with two regions on it: a portlet region on the left-hand side that takes up two-thirds of our page and an item region on the right-hand side that takes up one-third of our page. The colors and fonts that are displayed by default are pleasant enough, but we want to make our Portal distinctive. To change the colors and fonts that are displayed, we need to apply a Style to the page.

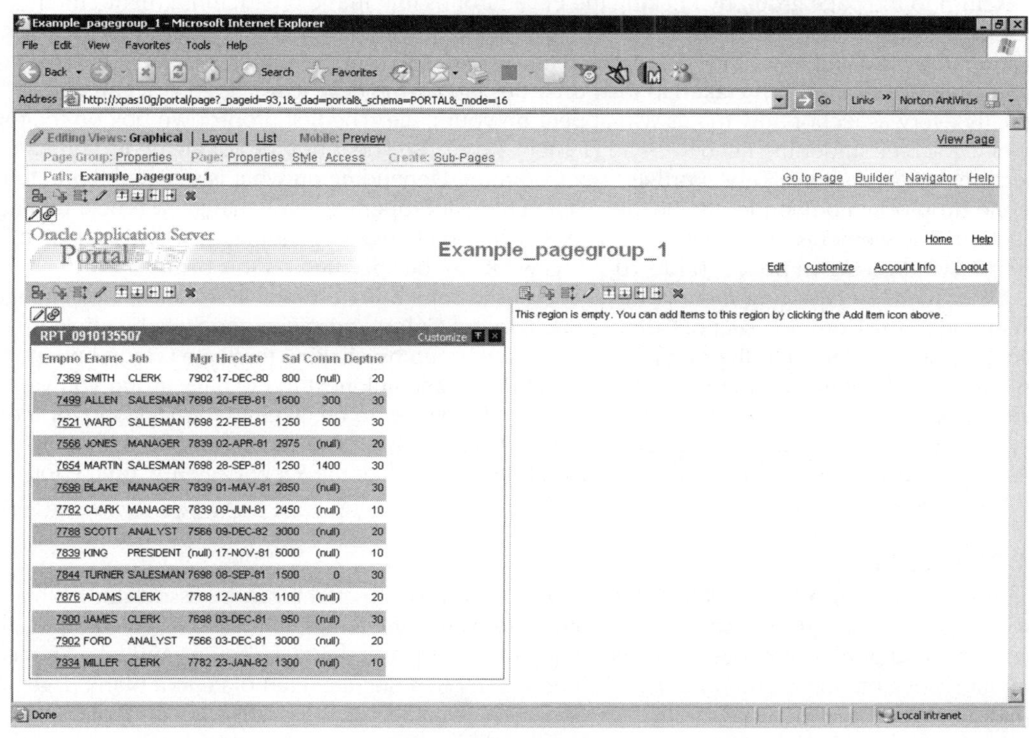

FIGURE 10-26. *The page with two equally-sized regions on it*

Styles

A Style is a set of colors and fonts that are used to define the look of a web page. By default, there are numerous styles provided for you when Oracle Application Server Portal is installed. You are not limited to the seeded styles: you can create your own styles and then apply them to pages if you'd like. To create a new Style, click on the Navigator link on the top right of any Oracle Application Server Portal screen. Click the Page Groups tab and then the link of the page group you have created in this chapter. Click the Style link. You'll notice that there are no styles there. What about the seeded styles? To see those, you'll have to navigate up to the root of the Page Groups section by clicking the Page Groups link in the breadcrumb menu. From there, click the Shared Objects link, then the Styles link. This will display all of the seeded styles available for you. If you choose to create a Style here, it will be available to all pages across all page groups. If you choose to create a Style under a specific page group, it will only be available for that page group.

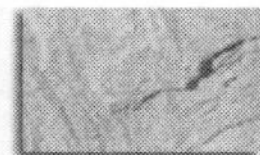

NOTE

The preceding sentence is true for all objects in the Shared Objects section of the Page Groups tab: Templates, Categories, Navigation Pages, Perspectives, Styles, Attributes, Page Types, and Item Types.

Return to the page group by clicking the Page Groups link in the breadcrumb menu, then clicking the link of the page group we have been working with. From here, click the Styles link and then the "Create New… Style" link to create a new style. After defining the name and display name, you are automatically taken to the Properties tab for the new style. Here, you can define virtually every aspect of how things will appear on your page. The first drop-down box on the top left of the screen under the header "Style Element Type" lists the four types of elements you can affect on the page: Items, Tabs, Portlets, and Common. Depending on what is selected there, the second drop-down box under the header "Style Element Properties" will change to reflect the first selection. The elements under the color palette will also change depending on what is selected in the first two drop-down boxes. Table 10-2 lists what can be specified on this page.

Experiment by changing some of the properties to something distinctive (it's easiest to change something in the Common section such as Background Color) and saving the Style by clicking the Close button. Return to the root page of the page group by clicking the Page Group link in the breadcrumb menu and then clicking the Edit Root Page link next to the page group you've been working with. Click the Style link on the top of the page to be taken to the Style tab for the page. Select the style you've just created from the Choose Style drop-down box. Click the OK button to return to the graphical editing view for the page. Click the View Page link on the top right of the screen (Figure 10-27).

Templates

A template can be used to predefine the tabs and regions on a page. It can be associated with a page when it is created, or it can be associated afterwards. If a template is associated with a page after items and portlets have been placed on it, you will be asked which regions and tabs on the template move the items and portlets. It is much easier to associate a template to a blank page right after it has been created.

Style Element Type	Style Element Properties
Items	Group By Banner, Group By Text, Group By Link, Default Attribute, Sub Page Title Associated Functions, Author, Base Item Type, Category, Create Date, Creator, Date Updated, Description, Display Name, Display Name and Image Link, Display Name Link, Document Size, Expiration Period, Expire Date, Help URL, Image or Display Name Link, Item Content, Keywords, Last Updated By, Page, Page Group, Perspectives, Portlet ID, Portlet Name, Provider ID, Provider Name, Publish ID, Score
Tabs	Active Tab Color, Active Tab Text, Inactive Tab Color, Inactive Tab Text
Portlet	Portlet Header Color, Portlet Header Text, Portlet Header Link, Portlet Header Style, Portlet Subheader Color, Portlet Subheader Text, Portlet Subheader Link, Portlet Body Color, Portlet Heading1, Portlet Text1, Portlet Heading2, Portlet Text2, Portlet Heading3, Portlet Text3, Portlet Heading4, Portlet Text4
Common	Background, Region Banner, Region Banner Text

TABLE 10-2. *Element Properties that Can Be Set on the Edit Style Page*

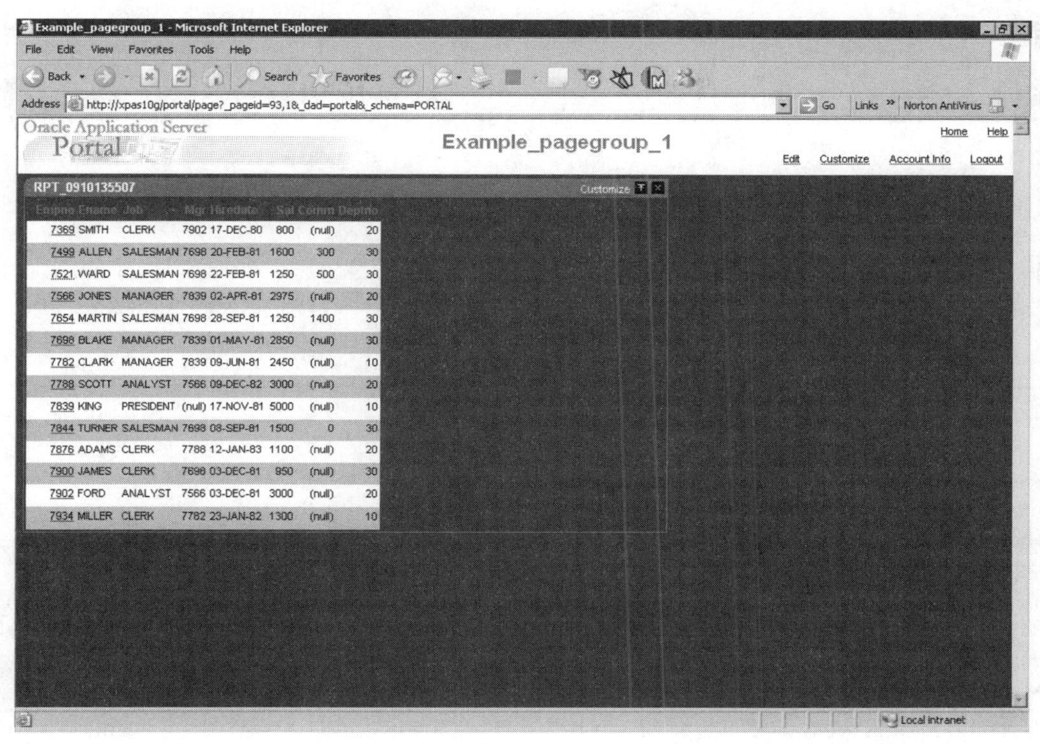

FIGURE 10-27. *A page with a style applied to it*

NOTE
Pages can also be detached from templates.

Create a new template by clicking on the name of the page group we have been working with in this chapter, then clicking on the Templates link. Click on the Create New… Template link on the top left of the page. Give the template a meaningful name, display name, and description, then click the "Make available for use in this page group" check box and click Next >. If you would like to restrict the Style to maintain a consistent look and feel, deselect the Enable Pages to Use a Different Style checkbox. When you click Finish, you will be taken to a page that looks very similar to the Edit Page screen (Figure 10-28).

On this screen, you can define regions and tabs, as well as place items and portlets, although the last two actions are rare. Experiment by adding some tabs and regions to this template. Changes are saved automatically as you add regions or tabs to the template. When you're finished, click the Navigator link in the top right of the screen. Click the name of the page group in the breadcrumb menu and then click the Pages link. Click the Create New… Page link on the top left of the screen. Leave Page Type as standard and enter meaningful information for the name, display name, and description fields. Click Next >. On the second page of the wizard,

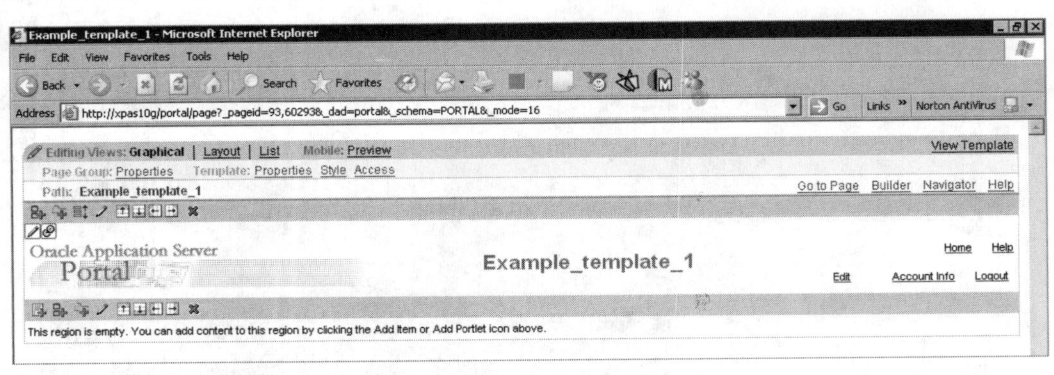

FIGURE 10-28. *The Edit Template Page screen*

select the template you created in the previous step. Automatically, the screen repaints to display what the new subpage will look like (Figure 10-29). Clicking Finish after this step will display the page in graphical edit mode. Note that the developer has no way to delete or add regions (they are locked by the template). It is also impossible to add portlets or items to the existing tabs as they have not been defined as portlet or item regions in the template.

Navigation Pages

Navigation pages are a special type of subpage that are intended to be used as a navigation area for your portal pages. When you create a navigation page, the steps and attributes of the navigation page are exactly the same as a subpage except for the following:

- Navigation pages can only be standard pages; subpages can be either standard or URL-type pages and can have their attributes modified.
- Navigation pages can be created from other navigation pages by selecting another page in the Copy From drop-down box.
- By default, navigation pages are published as portlets with the intent of placing them on a page.
- No banner region is created automatically.

Let's add a navigation window on the left-hand side of the page. Click the Navigator link on the top right of the page, then click the name of the page group you have created in this chapter. The page of the Navigator that is displayed lists all of the components that can be created that are associated with a page group. For now, click the Navigation Pages link. By default, there are two navigation pages created for each page group: a banner (which is displayed by default on the root page) and a navbar (which is not displayed by default on the root page). Create a new navigation page by clicking the Create New… Navigation Page link. Enter the name and display name and click Create. Click Close to return to the Navigator, then click the Edit link next to the navigation page you just created (Figure 10-30).

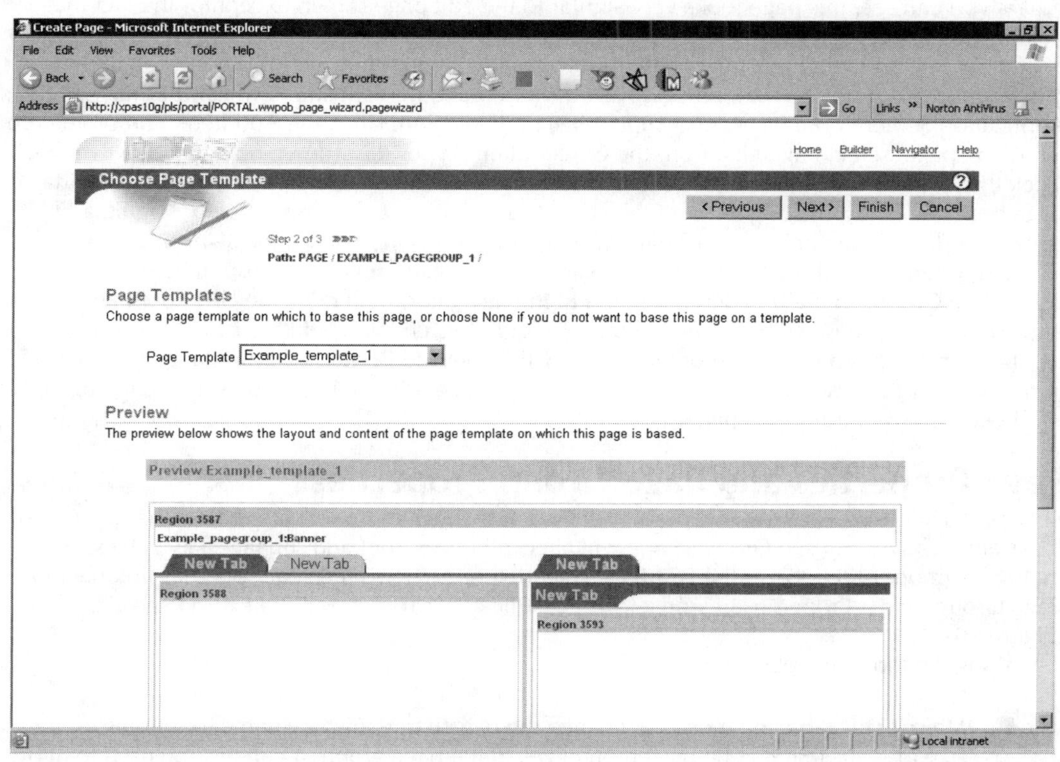

FIGURE 10-29. *The Create Page Wizard after a template has been selected*

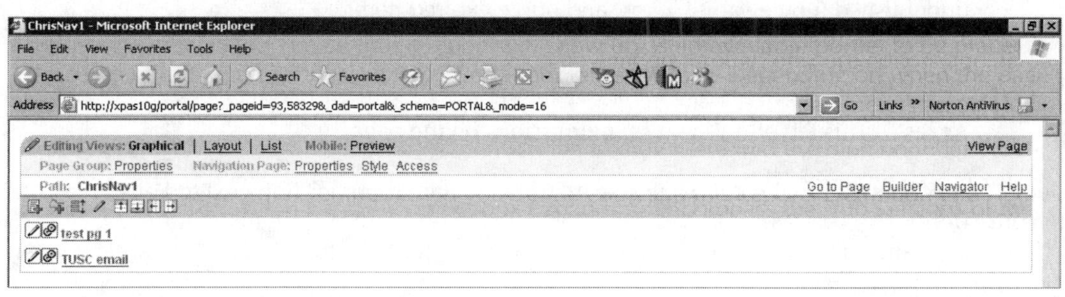

FIGURE 10-30. *The edit screen for the navigation page*

As you can see, this page looks very similar to the edit page screen except for the fact that there is no banner region created automatically. You can place either items or portlets on the default region, and you have full capabilities to create other regions and place tabs on them, but it is far more common to maintain one region and place items (usually links to other Oracle Application Server Portal pages or components) in this region. Click the Add Item icon on the top left of the page, select Page Link from the Content Item Types drop-down box and click Next >. Click the notepad icon next to the Path text box and select an Oracle Application Server Portal page from the list by clicking Return Object next to our selection. Return to Step 2 of the add item wizard, fill in the fields on this page with meaningful values, and click "Finish."

After returning to the edit page screen, click the Navigator link on the top right of the screen. Click Page Groups in the breadcrumb menu of the navigator, then click the Edit Root Page link next to the page group we have been working with in this chapter. Add the navigation page by creating a new region on the left of the screen. Click the Add Portlet icon for that new region and search for the navigation page you just created. Place it in the region by single-clicking on it. Click "OK" to return to the page.

Page Properties and Page Group Properties

Both pages and page groups have properties associated with them that affect how the page looks and behaves. A Page Group setting will affect all pages (root and subpages) associated with that page group. At the top of the Edit Page screen, there are two links: a Properties link next to Page Group: and a Properties link next to Page:. Click the Properties link next to Page Group: (Figure 10-31).

Along the top of the page, there are five tabs:

- **Main** This tab can be used to change the page name, display name, or quotas for the size of items that can be placed on pages in the page group. It can also be used to allow or deny end users from using or modifying page styles.
- **Configure** The tab can be used to allow or deny different page types and different types of content on the page.
- **Items** The tab allows you to enable/disable item versioning, set characteristics for unpublished (unviewable) items, and purge expired items.
- **Translations** This tab allows you to manage different language packs that may have been installed.
- **Access** This tab allows you set permissions on the pages.

Click OK to return to the edit page screen. Click on the Properties link next to Page (Figure 10-32).

This page shows a slightly different set of properties. Along the top, there are now eight tabs:

- **Main** This tab allows you to change the name/display name of the page and control its caching behavior.
- **Template** This tab allows you to attach the page to or detach the page from a template.
- **Style** This tab allows you to select a style for the page.

- **Access** This tab allows you to set access privileges for the page. You can use this tab to override settings made in the Access tab of the Page Group properties described above.
- **Optional** This tab allows you to publish your page as a portlet (which can then be placed on other pages), set default WebDAV properties, enable/disable item versioning, specify page images, and enable/disable links to subpages.

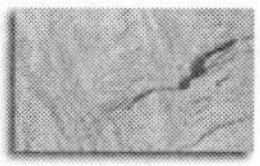

NOTE
WebDAV stands for WWW Distributed Authoring and Versioning and is a standard used to save data to web site (as opposed to just reading it). WebDAV is very useful when you have a large amount of content you wish to publish on your site.

- **Parameters** This tab allows you to define parameters for your page. You can then pass those parameters in calls to the page from the various packages in the Portal API.

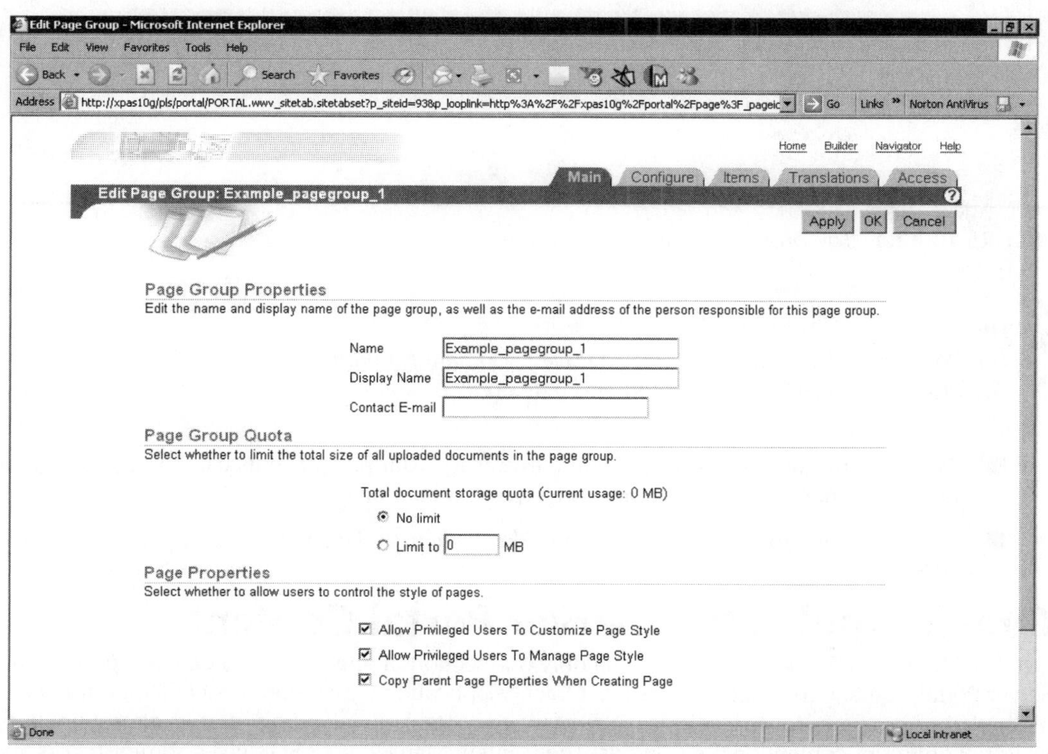

FIGURE 10-31. *The properties page for the page group*

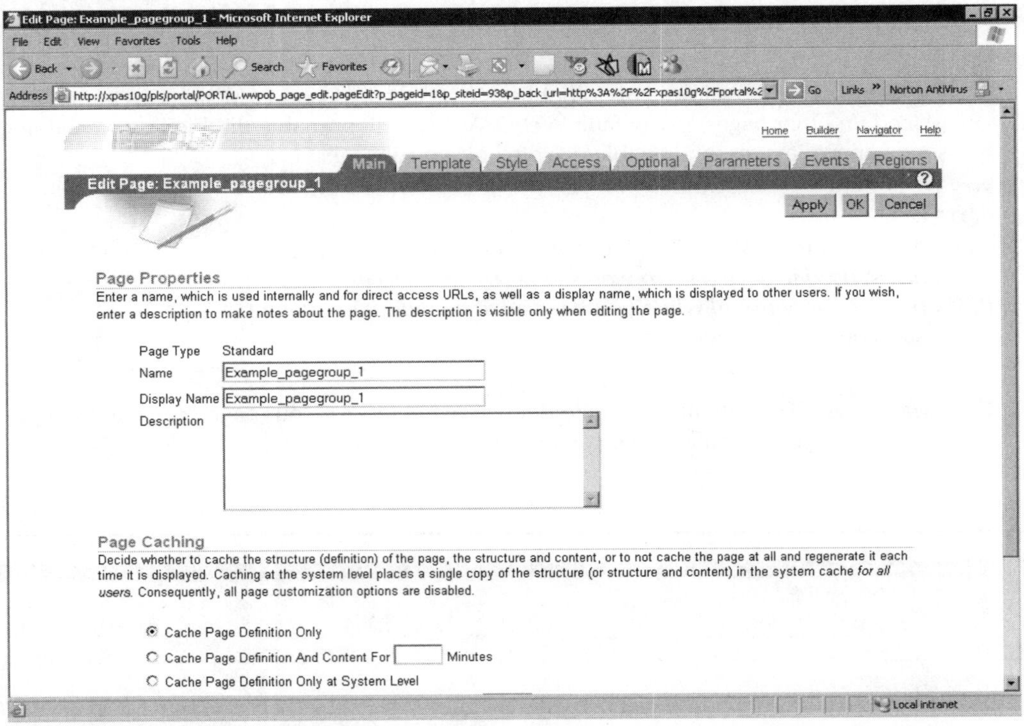

FIGURE 10-32. *The properties page for the page*

TIP
The Portal API is described in the Portal Development Kit (PDK), downloadable from http://portalcenter.oracle.com.

- **Events** This tab allows you to define events for your page. Events can be used to trigger certain actions when various events happen on the page.
- **Regions** This tab allows you to define a default item and default portlet region for the page.

Oracle Application Server Portal Content

Just as with the preceding section, devoting only one section of one chapter to Oracle Application Server Portal Content does not do it justice. Oracle Application Server Portal contains sophisticated methods and programs to store, display, and manage content, giving administrators almost limitless ways to administer content on their portals. The Content Management SDK gives administrators and developers the ability to automate many of the tasks of content management.

TIP
For more information on the Content Management SDK, go to http://www.oracle.com/technology/products/ifs/index.html.

A good place to start our discussion of Oracle Application Server Portal Content would be the definition of content. As we have seen, Oracle Application Server Portal allows developers to build components such as forms, reports, charts, calendars, etc. But what if you have information that you wish to display on your portal that does not fit into one of these component types; for example, you have a Microsoft Word document or an Adobe PDF file? The developers of Oracle Application Server Portal were smart enough to design it so that both types of objects can be displayed on your portal. Portlets query Oracle databases and display that data in a form, report, calendar, etc.; and items display content such as word processor files, spreadsheets, or images. Within the context of Oracle Application Server Portal, content can be defined as any piece of information displayed on a portal that does not fit into the traditional interface of an Oracle Application Server Portal component such as a form or report. There are two basic types of items that can be placed on a page: Content Item Types and Built-In Navigation Types. The following is a list of Content Item Types you can place on your Oracle Application Server Portal pages:

- **File** This option allows you to place a file on your portal and is the most common option selected when placing content on your portal. When a file is selected, it is converted to a binary large object and stored in the infrastructure database automatically. You also have the option of displaying a Simple File, which does not prompt you for advanced content attributes such as publish date or expiration (advanced content attributes are discussed shortly).
- **Text** This option displays a WYSIWYG (for What You See Is What You Get) editor that allows you to enter text for your content area. Just as with the File option, there is a Simple Text option.
- **URL** This option allows you to place a URL in your content area. Alternatively, the editor displayed in the text option allows you to create links in your text area. As with the File and Text options, there is also a Simple URL option.
- **Page Links** This option allows you to place links in your content area to other Oracle application Server Portal pages. There is also a Simple Link option.
- **Images** This option allows you to place an image in your content area. There is also a Simple Image option.
- **Zip Files** This option allows you to upload a zip (compressed) file to your content area. The only difference between this and a File is the existence of a link titled "Unzip" next to the item when displayed. Clicking the "Unzip" link gives end users the ability to unzip and store whatever is in the zip file on a page in the portal.
- **PL/SQL** This option allows you to store a PL/SQL code fragment as a content item in the content area. Clicking this link will execute the PL/SQL code.
- **Oracle Reports** This option allows developers to embed an Oracle Report on a content area. Clicking the link will display the Oracle Report on the Web.

The following is a list of Built-In Navigation Types you can place on your Oracle Application Server Portal pages:

- **Portal Smart Links** This option allows you to place various links in the content area to perform actions such as edit user account information, edit the page, display a help menu, take the user to her personal page, refresh the page, etc.
- **Login/Logout Links** This option places a "Logout" link on the content area page.
- **Basic Search Box** Two types of searches are available to end users in Oracle Application Server Portal: a basic search that allows users to search through their portals without reducing the information returned by category or perspective; and an advanced search that gives end users the ability to use various methods of reducing information returned by their search as well as advanced features such as Boolean operators. The Basic Search Box places a Search field on the content area allowing the end users to perform basic searches through content on the portal.

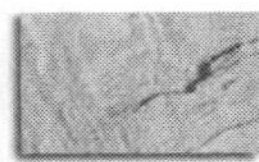

TIP
For now, understand that categories and perspectives are ways of organizing content in your portal. Categories organize the content based on what the content is. Perspectives organize the content based on who might be interested in it.

- **List Of Objects** This option allows you to return a set of Oracle Application Server Portal content that fits a certain criteria. You can return a drop-down list or a set of links that points to a page group, a perspective, or a category.
- **Portal Smart Text** This option can be used to display the current date, user, or page.
- **Object Map Link** This option can be used to create a link that will display a hierarchical map of pages and subpages when clicked by an end user.
- **Page Path** This option creates a breadcrumb menu on the page that allows end users to see where they are in the portal site and gives them the ability to navigate through levels quickly. Placing a Page Path navigation link on a root page has no effect; it is only useful on subpages.

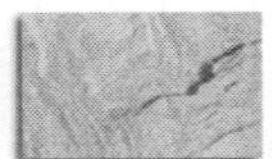

TIP
Not all of these types are available for pages by default. Some of the items will have to be enabled for a page group. To add these types, select the Properties link next to Page Group on the top left of the page editor. Select the Configure tab, then click the Edit link in the Content Type and Classification section of the page. Add the Item Types in the Item Types section of the page and click OK.

For this example, let's create a page and place content on it. You will need some basic content that is on the hard drive of the computer you are doing the exercise on. The content for these examples is not important—a simple text file will do. To begin, click the Navigator link on the top-right of any Oracle Application Server Portal page. Click the Page Groups tab (Figure 10-33).

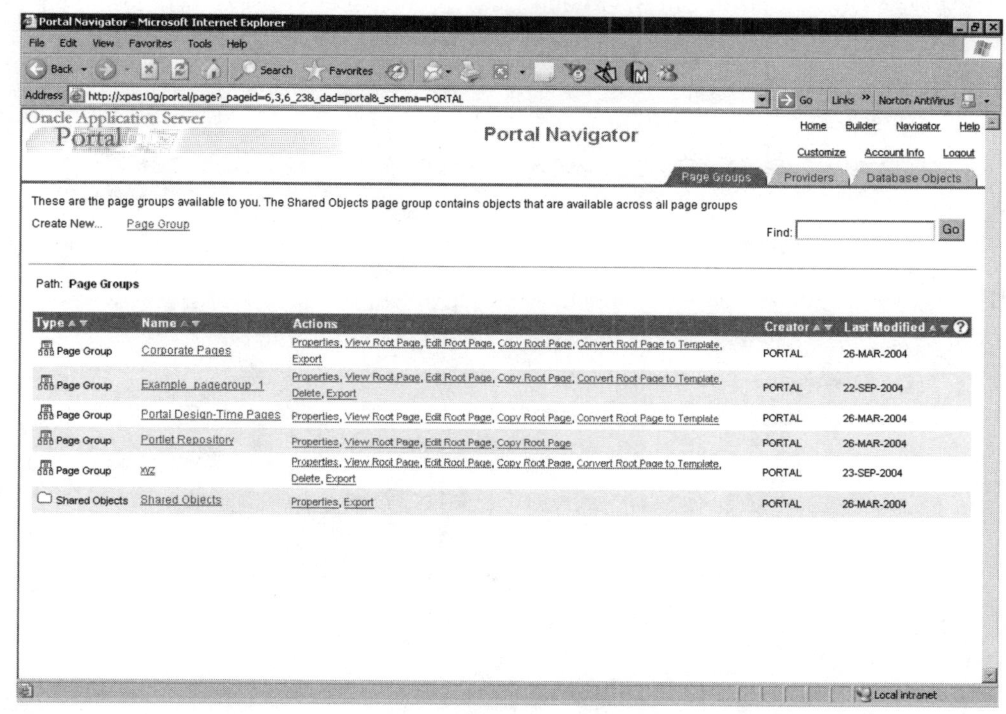

FIGURE 10-33. *The Page Groups tab of the Oracle Application Server Portal Navigator*

Click the Create New… Page Group link on the top-left of the screen. Give the page group a meaningful name and display name and click Create. The root page for the page group is created for you automatically and you are placed in the Edit Page for the root page (Figure 10-34).

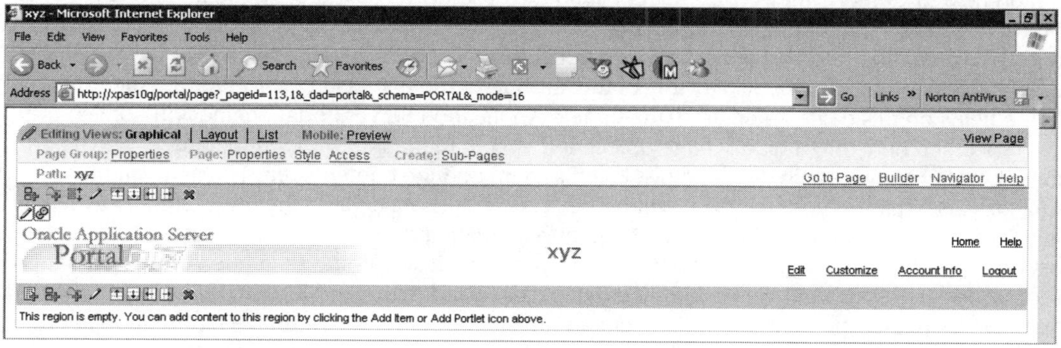

FIGURE 10-34. *The Edit Page screen for the default page of the new page group*

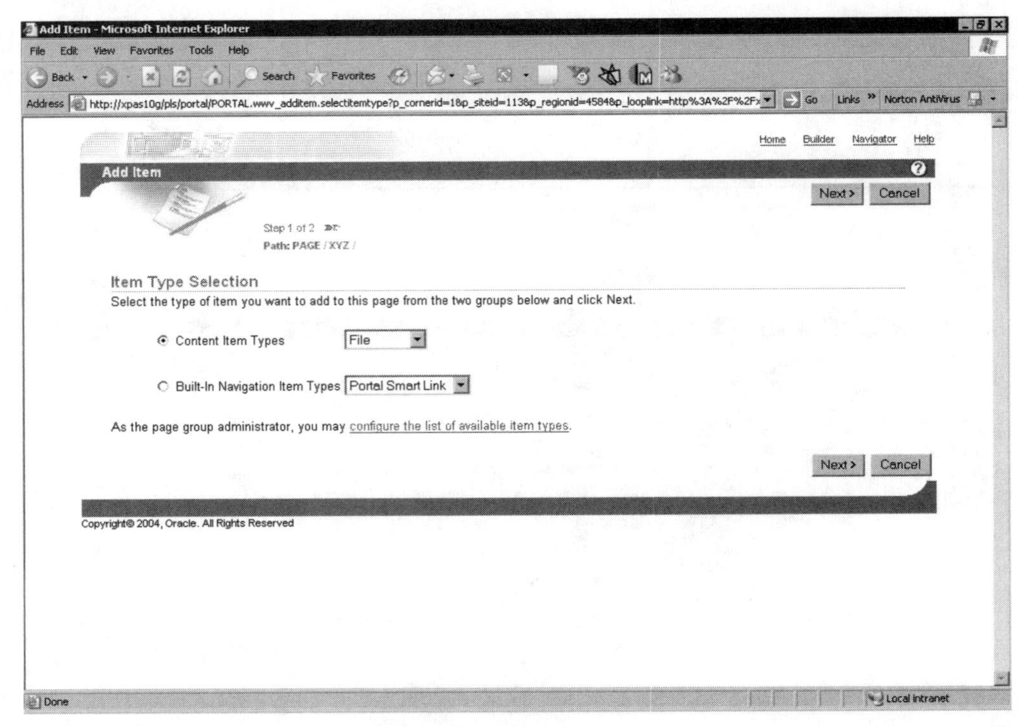

FIGURE 10-35. *The Add item Wizard*

Click on the Add Item icon for the lower region. You are presented with the Add Item Wizard (Figure 10-35).

This wizard will allow you to add content to your portal. As we mentioned earlier, there are two basic types of content: Content Item Types and Built-In Navigation Item Types. Select the radio button next to Content Item Types, select File in the drop-down box to the right, and click Next>. The following screen, the Item Attributes page, (Figure 10-36) allows us to set attributes for the content we are about to add. Again, as we mentioned earlier, if we had selected Simple File instead of File, this page would not display any of the attributes. The first field prompts for the file. After all of the fields on this page are entered, the Oracle Application Server Portal engine will convert the item specified here into a binary large object and store it in the infrastructure database. The next field, Display Name, is what will be displayed as a link on the content area. The field after that, Category, is what category this item will be associated with. By default, the only category available is "General." Later on, we will see how to go about creating new categories. Categories will become relevant when looking at the Oracle Application Server Portal search features later in this section and in the sections Categories and Perspectives and Advanced Search. Description, the next field, serves two purposes. It allows content administrators to enter descriptive information about the content item and provides information that the search capabilities of Oracle Application Server Portal can use when building indexes end users can use to search content.

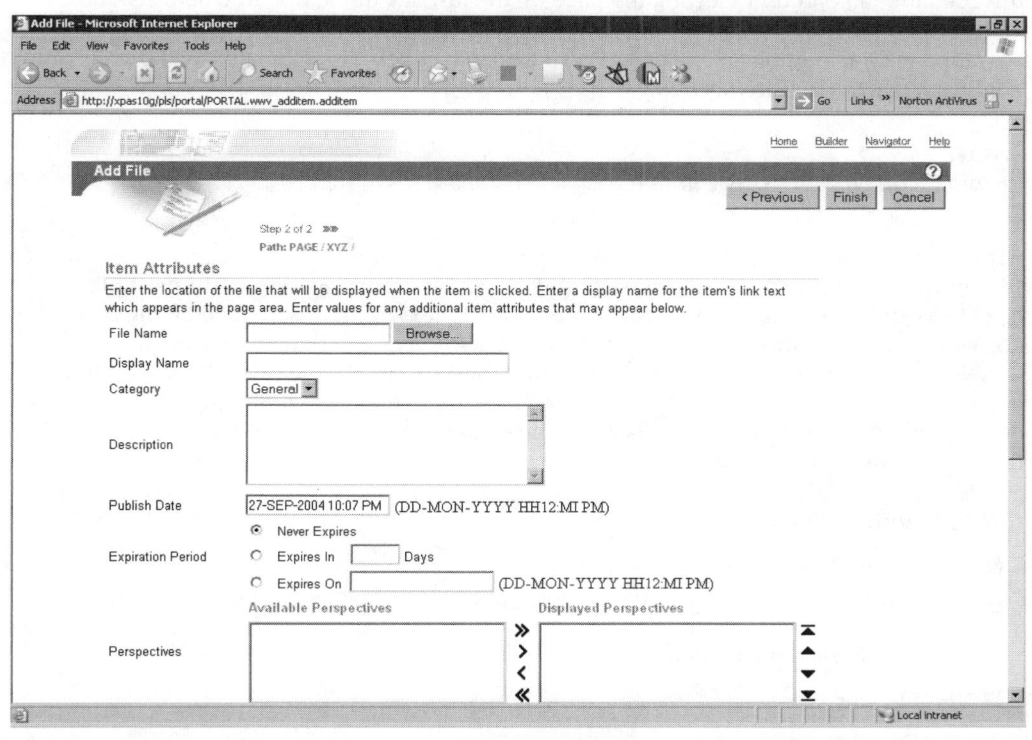

FIGURE 10-36. *The Item Attributes page for the item we wish to add*

The next field is called Publish Date. This date, which defaults to the current time, gives content managers that ability to control when a piece of content will become available to end users. If the default is taken, the content will be available immediately. If the time is set to the future, the content will not become available until that time threshold is reached. As a content coordinator, you will see the content on the edit page screen. End users, however, will not see it until the system time is greater than the time specified here.

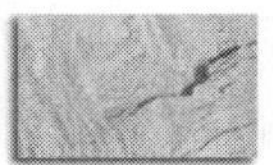

NOTE
The clock that determines when content is available is the system clock of the server running your Oracle Application Server Portal instance.

The next field, Expiration Date, gives content administrators the ability to expire an item; that is, make it unviewable after a certain date. This is particularly useful for something like a monthly report, which can be made available on a site and would expire on the final day of the month.

In this scenario, an end user viewing the page on the last day of the month would see the content item, but when he views the same page after the start of the next month, the item would not be displayed. The Oracle Application Server Portal engine handles this automatically; no programming or administrative actions are needed.

NOTE
Expired content still exists within the Oracle database.

The next field lists the perspectives available for this item. Perspectives organize content based on who might be interested in seeing it. A content item can belong to multiple perspectives simultaneously. An image can be placed next to the link by specifying an image file or web location in the Image field. The drop-down box next to the Image Alignment field allows you to align the image in the content area. Basic Search Keywords allows you to add keywords that will be indexed by the search engine. By default, the following attributes of a content item are indexed: its name, its description, and what is in the content, provided it is part of the following list:

- Microsoft Word documents
- Microsoft Powerpoint presentations
- Text files
- Microsoft Visio documents
- HTML files
- Microsoft Excel spreadsheets

The author allows you to enter an author for this content piece. Enable Item Check-Out allows you to lock the content item. In most organizations, there are numerous people who can add content. This can potentially be an issue if more than one person is updating a piece of content simultaneously. This issue can be overcome by clicking the check box next to this field. The content will not be able to be updated if someone has checked the item out. That will, in effect, lock the content, preventing anyone else from modifying it. Other users can still see the content; however, no one else is able to modify it until it is checked back in. The final set of radio buttons on the page, Display Options, control whether the item is displayed in the same page of the browser (if it is a supported Multipurpose Internet Mail Extensions (MIME) type for your browser) or if a new browser window opens up automatically.

For this example, create a text file on your local machine called sports.txt. In that, file type the line:

```
football hockey basketball baseball
```

Then save the file. Go back to your browser and add an Item by clicking the Add Item icon in the bar above the empty region. Select the radio button next to Content Item Types and select File in the drop-down box. Click Next >. Click the Browse button and select the sports.txt file you just created. Give it a display name and in the description field, type soccer lacrosse (without the quotes). Leave the rest of the fields the way they are and click Finish. The sports.txt file will be uploaded to your portal, and you will be taken back to the Edit Page window in your browser (Figure 10-37).

On the top right of the page, there is a link called "View Page." Click that link to show how the page will be displayed. Clicking the link will display the contents of the file in the browser. If the link pointed to a file with an extension that was associated with a MIME plug-in for your browser, the appropriate program would have executed and displayed in your browser. Click the back button in your browser to return to the Edit Page screen. In the banner region, click the "Add Portlet" icon on the top left of the screen. In the search text box, type "search" (without the quotes) and click the Go button. Single-click on "Basic Search" to move that portlet to the Selected Portlets window (Figure 10-38). Click "OK."

Click the "View Page" link to view the page. Note the search portlet on the top of the page. Type any of the keywords in the file we just uploaded. Remember, the following things are searchable: the title, the description, and the content, so any of the four sports in the sports.txt file (football, hockey, basketball, baseball) should be searchable along with the description (soccer, lacrosse) and the title (sports.txt). Type any combination of those keywords into the search dialog and click the Search button (Figure 10-39).

How come no results were returned? The answer lies in the fact that the indexes that maintain information about the content in our portal are not built dynamically. That is, they are not updated automatically when new content is added. The indexes must be rebuilt manually whenever new content is added. Luckily, this is an easy procedure and can be automated.

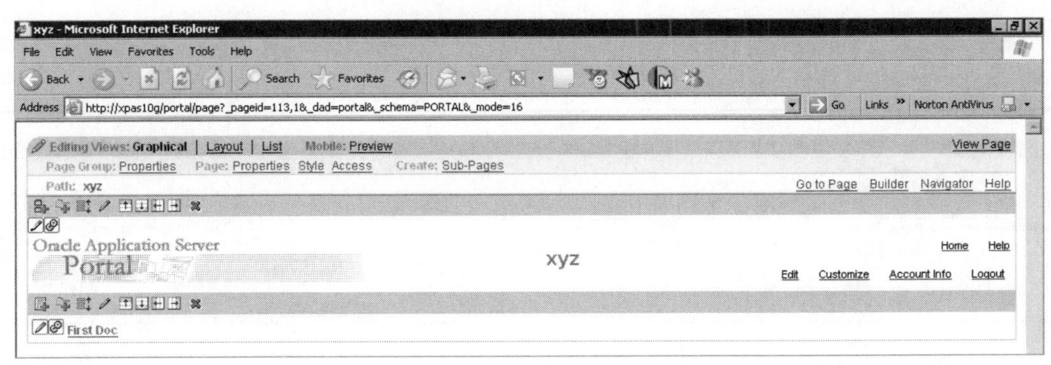

FIGURE 10-37. *The Edit Page screen displaying the newly added content*

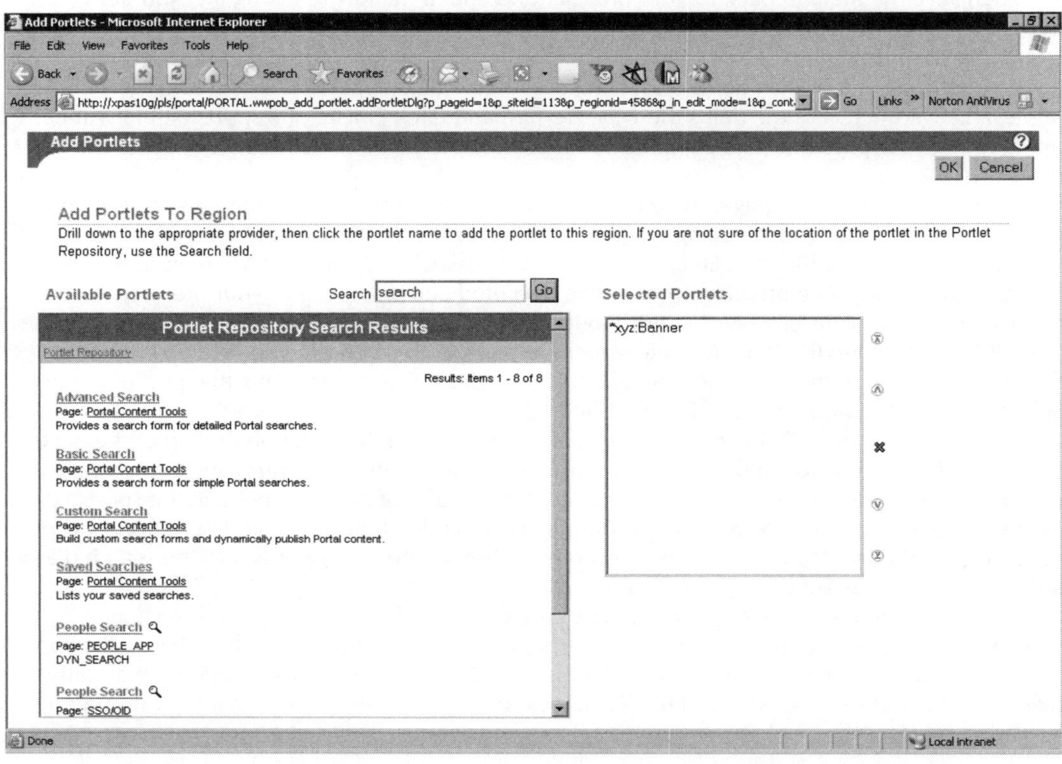

FIGURE 10-38. *The Selected Portlets window*

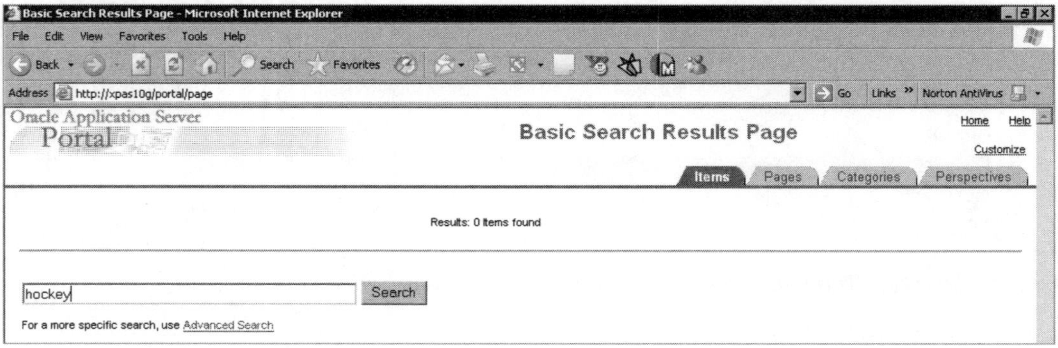

Basic Search Results Page - Microsoft Internet Explorer

Oracle Application Server Portal

Basic Search Results Page

Home Help Customize

Items Pages Categories Perspectives

Results: 0 Items found

hockey

Search

For a more specific search, use Advanced Search

FIGURE 10-39. *The Search results window*

The procedure to run is the SYNC procedure in the WWV_CONTEXT package owned by the PORTAL user in the infrastructure database. You can run it from a SQL*Plus session:

```
SQL*Plus: Release 10.1.0.2.0 - Production on Mon Sep 20 21:40:17 2004

Copyright (c) 1982, 2004, Oracle.  All rights reserved.


Connected to:
Oracle9i Enterprise Edition Release 9.0.1.5.1 - Production
With the Partitioning option
JServer Release 9.0.1.4.0 - Production

SQL> exec portal.wwv_context.sync;

PL/SQL procedure successfully completed.

SQL>
```

You can also run it from within Oracle Application Server Portal by performing the following steps:

1. Go back to the Navigator by clicking the Navigator link on the top right of the screen.
2. Click the Database Objects tab.
3. In the Find text box on the top right of the screen, type **wwv_context**.
4. Click the Show Properties link.
5. Scroll down until you see the procedures and packages in the wwv_context package (Figure 10-40).
6. Click the small icon next to the SYNC procedure.

After the procedure successfully executes (signified by a check mark displayed on the screen), return to the Navigator by clicking the Navigator link on the top right of the screen. Click the Page Groups tab, then the View Root Page link next to the Page Group you created. In the search text box on the top of the screen, enter one of the search items again. The Search page will now correctly display the results of the search (Figure 10-41).

Categories and Perspectives

Categories and perspectives are ways of organizing the content that is on your site. In general, categories are used to group items based on their content; that is, what purpose they serve for your company or organization. Perspectives are used to organize the content based on who would be interested in seeing it. Right now, these concepts may be hard to visualize, but when we look at the advanced search capabilities of Oracle Application Server Portal in the next section, having the ability to group information using these concepts will be invaluable, particularly when the content on your portal site grows to a large number.

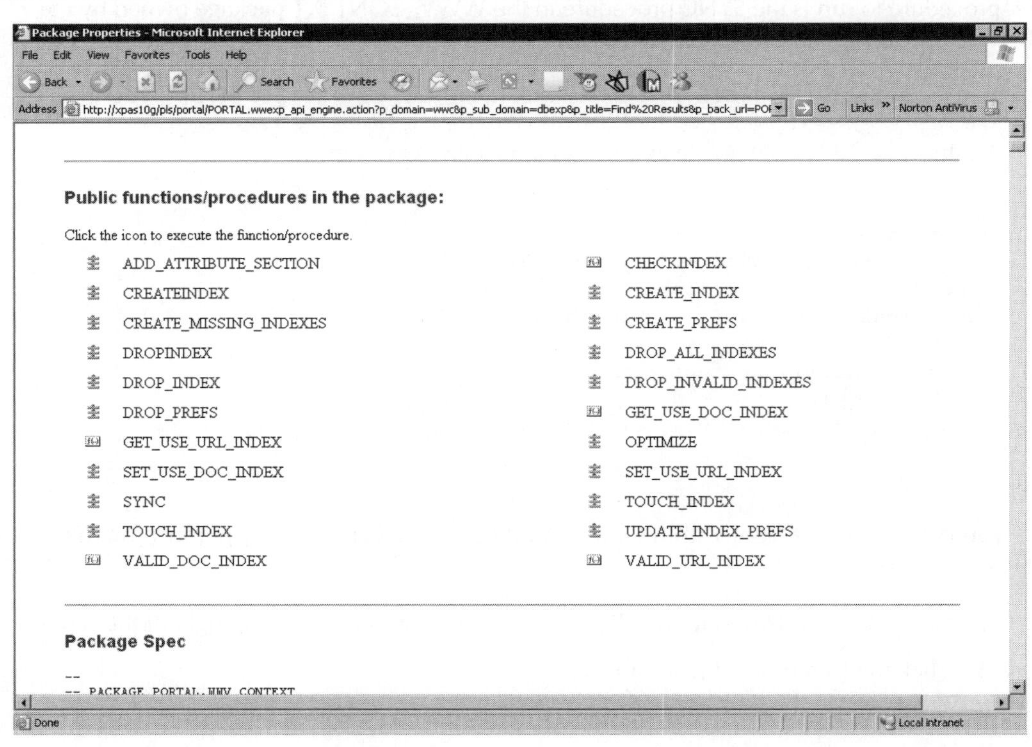

FIGURE 10-40. *The list of procedures/functions in the wwv_context package*

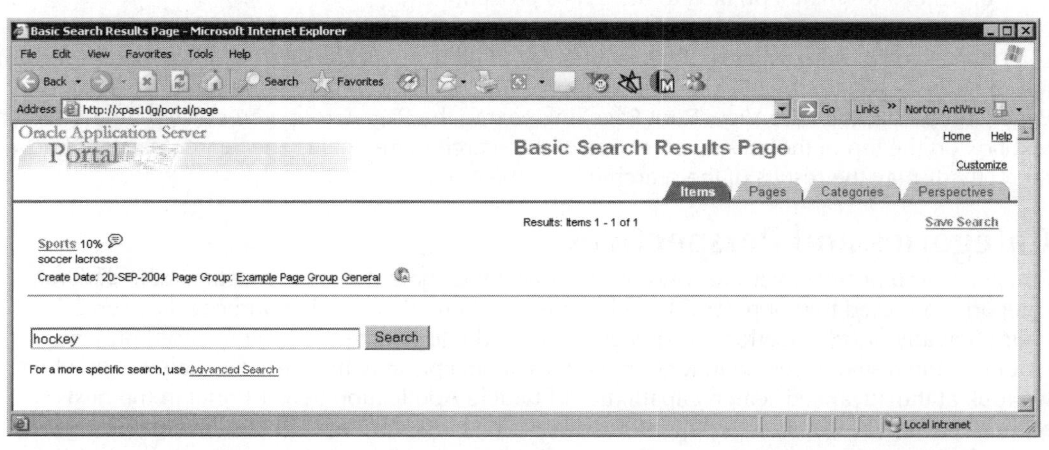

FIGURE 10-41. *The Search page returning expected results*

By default, there is only one category created for you: general. Categories can be created at either the page group level or at the shared objects level. A category created at the page group level will only be available to the root and subpages of the page group; a category created at the shared objects level will be available across all pages, subpages, and page groups. A category does not have many attributes—you can associate images with it—so the creation of a category is a relatively simple process. When adding content, you can specify your new category in the Category drop-down box. A content item can only be in one category.

Perspectives allow you to organize your content based on who might be interested in seeing it. The process of creating a perspective and the attributes that can be defined for a perspective is virtually identical to those of a category. The main difference is that an item can belong to multiple perspectives, whereas an item can belong to only one category. Also, there are no perspectives created by default.

Advanced Search

Go to the Edit Page screen for your page and click on the Add Portlets icon for a region that has been defined as a portlet region. In the Add Portlets to Region page, type search in the Search text box and click Go. This will list the eight seeded portlets that Oracle gives you to add searching capabilities to your portal. Earlier, we added the Basic Search portlet to our page. This time, add the Advanced Search portlet by single-clicking on it. Click on OK to return to the Edit Page screen (Figure 10-42).

The Advanced Search portlet gives the end user greater flexibility when she searches for content. End users can search by perspective, category, page group, page, or any combination of these. Users can also search for all items in a particular category or perspective by leaving the search text box blank and selecting the appropriate category or perspective.

Page Group Attributes

Content attributes are associated with item types and page types, and store information about an item or page, such as the associated category, description, or perspectives. These attributes are included in the add and edit screens where users can provide information about the item or page they are adding or editing. Content administrators can create their own item types and page types and specify exactly what information they want users to supply by choosing which attributes to include. In addition, page group administrators can create their own attributes for containing extra information. You can add attributes at either the Page Group level or the Shared Objects level. To add an attribute at the Page Group level, click on the page group link on the Navigator, click the Attributes link, then click Create New... Attribute on the top left of the page. To add an attribute at the Shared Objects level, click on the Shared Objects link on the Navigator, click the Attributes link, then click Create New... Attribute on the top left of the page. Table 10-3 lists the built-in content attributes that are provided with Oracle Application Server Portal:

Summary

This chapter has explored the advanced Oracle Application Server Portal components including calendars, hierarchies, menus, URLs, links, and data components. Coupled with the components explored in the previous chapter, Oracle Application Server Portal provides developers with a rich set of portlets that can be developed quickly and securely and deployed easily. The second half of this chapter detailed the basics of Oracle Application Server Portal page design. We saw

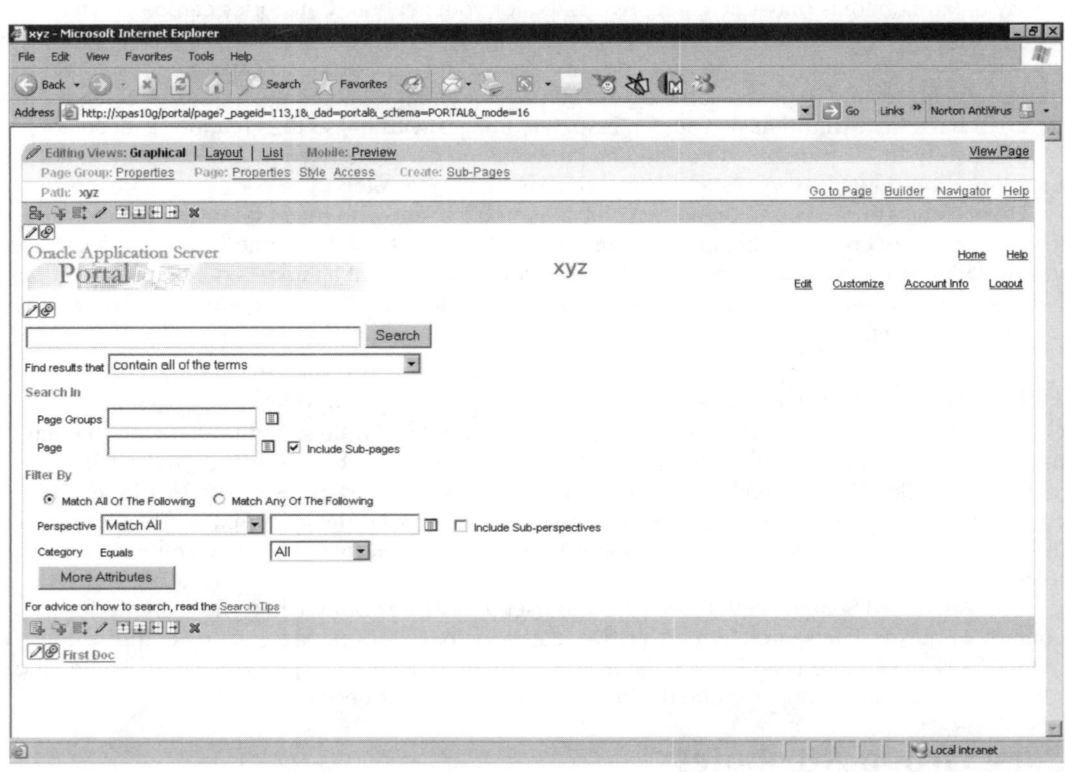

FIGURE 10-42. *The Edit Page screen with an Advanced Search portlet placed on it*

how the various user interface items (templates, styles, etc.) could be utilized to create Oracle Application Server Portal pages quickly while maintaining visual consistency with a minimum of effort. Finally, we explored Oracle Application Server Portal's content features and saw how easy it was to customize our content and its attributes with a minimum of programming effort. By utilizing the two main components of Oracle Application Server Portal (portlets and content items), developers can build a robust portal to serve all of an organization's information needs quickly and securely, with a minimum of programming effort that can grow as an organization's needs change.

Attribute	**Description**
Author	The name of the author of the item.
Category	The name of the category to which the item or page belongs.
Description	A short text description of the item or page.
Display Name	The display name of the item or page.
Display Option	Information about how the item or portlet should be displayed: Item Displayed Directly In Page Area Link That Displays Item In Full Browser Window Link That Displays Item In New Browser Window
Enable Item Check-Out	Information about whether or not the item can be checked out and checked in. This provides document control, allowing groups of users to edit items and not overwrite each other's work. Users cannot edit items that are checked out by another user.
Expiration Period	Information about how long an item should be displayed on a page.
Image	The image associated with the item or page.
Image Alignment	Information about where the item image should appear in the page.
Keywords	Keywords that describe the content or purpose of the item or page. When a user performs a search, the user's search criteria is compared to the keywords to find a match.
Perspectives	The names of the perspectives associated with the item or page.
Publish Date	The date (in the format DD-MON-YYYY HH12:MI PM) when the item should start being displayed to users.
Rollover Image	The second image associated with the item or page. This image is displayed whenever a user moves the mouse cursor over the original image on a navigation bar or tab.

TABLE 10-3. *A List of the Built-In Page Attributes*

CHAPTER 11

Integrating Forms, Reports, and Discoverer into Portal

Back in Chapters 3, 4, and 5, we looked at Oracle's suite of development tools, namely, Oracle Forms 10*g*, Oracle Reports 10*g*, and OracleAS Discoverer. We saw that each of those tools had its own strengths and weaknesses—no one tool is perfect for every situation—and that these legacy tools provide Oracle developers with a robust feature set, seamless integration with Oracle databases, and a wealth of existing knowledge available via various web resources (OTN, MetaLink, etc.). In Chapters 8, 9, and 10, we explored the OracleAS Portal environment and saw how its wizards make the development of OracleAS Portal Forms, Reports, and other various OracleAS Portal components a relatively simple task. Combined with OracleAS Portal's robust security, seamless integration with Single Sign-on and the LDAP-based Oracle Internet Directory, and ease with which OracleAS Portal applications can be deployed, OracleAS Portal is an extremely appealing environment for developers.

While OracleAS Portal is an exciting development environment, chances are your organization has existing Oracle Forms, Oracle Reports, and Oracle Discoverer Workbooks and Worksheets being used in production. For most organizations, it is not practical to discard all of their existing applications and begin coding OracleAS Portal Forms and Reports from scratch. Thankfully, Oracle provides a mechanism to ease your transition into OracleAS Portal development by facilitating the integration of existing Oracle Forms, Oracle Reports, and Oracle Discoverer Workbooks and Worksheets into OracleAS Portal. Developers can achieve the benefits inherent to OracleAS Portal, namely, its robust security and its ease of visual consistency, while moving existing applications to the Web with relative ease.

NOTE
It is also important to note that the forms and reports components of OracleAS Portal have a much smaller feature set and do not have all of the functionality of the Oracle Forms, Reports, and Discoverer products. Therefore, OracleAS Portal may not be the best choice as an exclusive tool to rewrite existing production applications in.

Is OracleAS Portal required to move existing Oracle Forms, Oracle Reports, and Oracle Discoverer Workbooks and Worksheets to the Web? No; it is entirely possible to move those components to the Web outside of OracleAS Portal—Chapter 6 discusses those methods in detail. This chapter discusses the integration of existing Oracle Forms, Oracle Reports, and Oracle Discoverer Workbooks and Worksheets into web pages that are served up by the OracleAS Portal engine in Oracle Application Server 10*g*. We will discuss the various methods for incorporating these components into OracleAS Portal, the pieces that need to be in place before attempting to integrate these components (like creation and administration of Discoverer connections), and the various methods of security we can apply to these components.

This chapter discusses the following topics:

- Benefits of integration
- "Native" support
- Integration of Oracle Reports
- Integration of Oracle Forms
- Integration of Oracle Discoverer Workbooks and Worksheets

Benefits of Integration

The benefits of developing in OracleAS Portal are numerous: the elimination of fat-client—based applications and maintenance, the simple implementation of security, the implementation of a consistent visual interface via the use of user interface templates, and the declarative, wizard-based development approach, allowing a minimum of code to be written, just to name a few. There are, however, several considerations that must be taken into account before moving development to OracleAS Portal.

First, and foremost, a great deal of time and effort may have been spent using Oracle's other development tools (Forms, Reports, Discoverer) to build existing applications—re-coding these applications may take resources that are impractical for many organizations to undertake. Second, Portal requires a new skill set and a new way of thinking—it may not be feasible to retrain all of your development staff. Finally, the forms and reports components in OracleAS Portal do not have the full feature set of the Oracle Forms and Oracle Reports products, which may further make it impractical to move production applications to OracleAS Portal. While these potential limitations may influence the types of applications to be developed in OracleAS Portal for your organization, it is important to note that Oracle has made a great effort to give developers and administrators the ability to incorporate existing applications into OracleAS Portal. This chapter is devoted to exploring these options.

Having mentioned those reasons, there are significant reasons *for* moving existing applications into OracleAS Portal. The most significant of these are security and the exploitation of Oracle Application Server 10*g*'s advanced security features, grouped together under the title "Identity Management." It is not uncommon for developers and administrators to spend as much time and effort devising and implementing security rules for web-based applications as coding and testing the application itself. OracleAS Portal provides an integrated security structure that allows administrators to quickly and easily maintain users within OracleAS Portal. OracleAS Portal pages can be designed to show or hide different portlets (in this case, the portlets would be your Oracle Forms, Reports, and Discoverer components), depending on the security privileges for your users defined in OracleAS Portal. Further security privileges can be granted to users allowing them to modify (or, in OracleAS Portal's terminology, "customize") individual portlets for their own purposes. The mechanism for these security features is handled automatically by the OracleAS Portal engine and, in most cases, does not require any additional programming by the OracleAS Portal developer.

Another significant challenge for developers and administrators deploying web-based applications involves the effort needed to maintain a consistent look and feel across the various pages that make up the web-based application. There is nothing less professional than constructing a web site where end users are forced to visit pages that differ in font, colors, and basic page design. Because of the maturity of most web sites, we take this consistency for granted, but in most cases, a great deal of work needs to go into maintaining this consistency. OracleAS Portal provides numerous features like templates that allow developers and administrators to greatly reduce the amount of effort needed to deploy an application with consistent visual attributes.

Native Support

OracleAS Portal has "native" support for two of the three components mentioned in this chapter: Oracle Reports and OracleAS Discoverer Worksheets and Workbooks. Oracle Forms does not have "native" support in OracleAS Portal, but we can still integrate Oracle Forms by way of a URL.

NOTE
You won't see the term "native support" in any of the OracleAS Portal documentation. In this chapter, the term "native support" is used to describe those features of OracleAS Portal that have been designed specifically to work with the three Oracle development tools mentioned in this chapter: Oracle Forms, Oracle Reports, and Oracle Discoverer. There are OracleAS Portal–specific features explicitly designed for Oracle Reports and Oracle Discoverer, but none for Oracle Forms. Hence, OracleAS Portal is said to have "native support" for Oracle Reports and Oracle Discoverer, but no "native support" for Oracle Forms.

The Oracle Reports and Oracle Discoverer Worksheets become portlets, once we "tell" OracleAS Portal about them. These portlets can then be manipulated like any other portlet in the OracleAS Portal Portlet Repository and be placed on a page, be placed on a tabbed page, and/or have customization options defined for them that can be made available to power users. Since Oracle Reports and OracleAS Discoverer are supported natively in OracleAS Portal, there are certain OracleAS Portal–specific features associated with them that enhance the OracleAS Portal developer's ability to work with them. For example, developers have the ability to set up a calendar in OracleAS Portal that determines when a particular Oracle Report can be run via OracleAS Portal or when a particular printer can be accessed by that Oracle Report running via OracleAS Portal.

Just because OracleAS Portal has native support for Oracle Reports, that doesn't mean developers have to use those features. If we choose not to, however, we lose out on using any OracleAS Portal–specific functionality (like the calendars just mentioned). To integrate OracleAS Discoverer Worksheets and Workbooks, however, we will have to use OracleAS Portal–specific methods. We can also integrate Oracle Forms into OracleAS Portal, but since there is no native support, no OracleAS Portal–specific features are associated with the integration of Oracle Forms.

Component #1: Oracle Reports

During the installation of Oracle Application Server 10*g*, a component called a Reports Server was automatically created, if the Business Intelligence and Forms option was chosen. The Reports Server component of Oracle Application Server 10*g* allows administrators to take an existing Oracle Report (either an .rep or .rdf file) and view it over the Web via a web browser. To view the report in OracleAS Portal, at least one Reports Server must be up and running, as we will associate the Oracle Report with an Oracle Applications Server 10*g* Reports Server when we turn the Oracle Report into an OracleAS Portal portlet. As you will see, we are not limited to just one Reports Server. We can have numerous servers running to handle the load of reports being generated, or Reports Servers with specific functions, security, and priorities.

Upon installation of Oracle Application Server 10*g*, a Reports Server called rep_<hostname> was created. Most of the administrative duties of Oracle Application Server 10*g* can be handled graphically through the Enterprise Manager Application Server Control web site. To view the status of this Reports Server, enter the Enterprise Manager Application Server Control web site for your installation. Point your browser to

```
http://<hostname>:1810
```

where the hostname is the name of the machine where the middle tier (also referred to as the Application Server) is installed. For the examples in this chapter, a server named xpas10g is used, so the URL to reference this server would look like

```
http://xpas10g:1810
```

The login user for the Enterprise Manager web site is ias_admin. The password is set during installation of the Oracle Application Server 10*g* mid-tier instance. If the infrastructure and middle tier are installed on the same machine, you will see a "Farm" page similar to Figure 11-1. If the infrastructure and the middle tier are on different servers, you will see a screen similar to the one in Figure 11-2.

In this example, I have two instances of Oracle Application Server 10*g* installed on my server. One is called IS_HOME (for InfraStructure home) and one called AS_HOME (for Application Server home). The names of these Oracle Application Server 10*g* instances are arbitrary and are set during installation of Oracle Application Server 10*g*. The Forms, Reports, and Discoverer Servers are deployed in the middle tier, so click the Application Server link (AS_Home.xpas10g in the preceding example). You will be taken to a screen similar to the one in Figure 11-2.

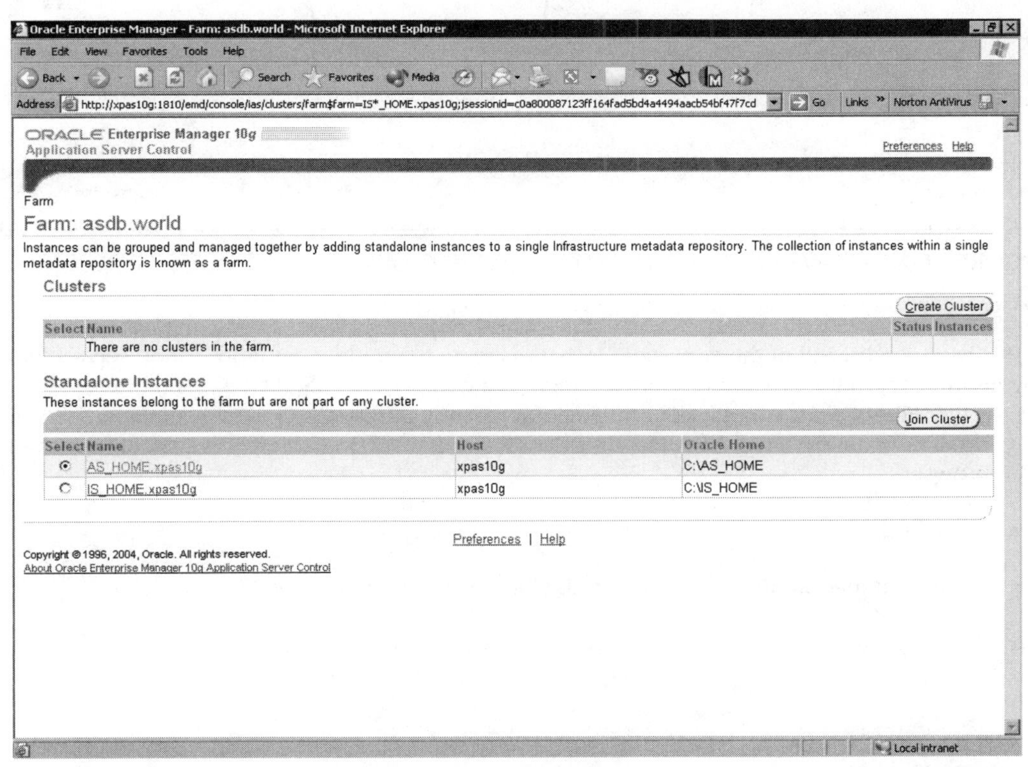

FIGURE 11-1. *The Enterprise Manager Application Control Farm page*

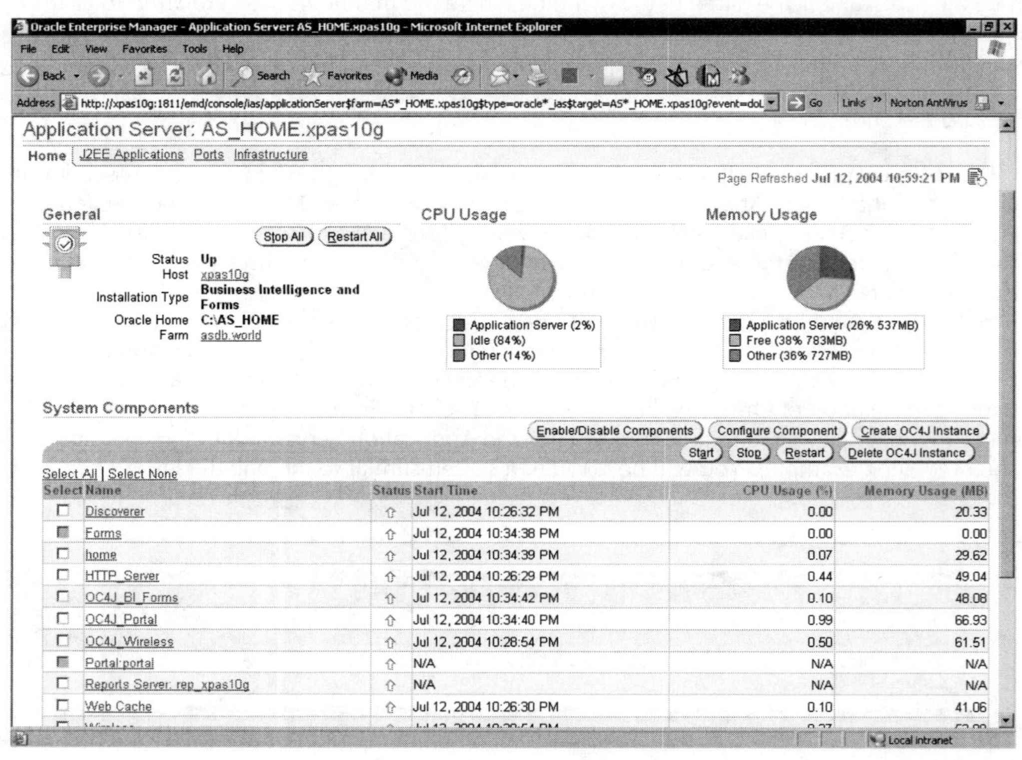

FIGURE 11-2. *The Enterprise Manager Web Page for the middle tier*

This screen lists all of the components that make up the middle tier (application server) for my installation. In the preceding example, there is a component called "Reports:rep_xpas10g." This is the Reports Server that was installed automatically during the Oracle Application Server 10*g* installation on my server. If you want to test to see if the Reports Server is, in fact, up, point your browser to

```
http://<Middle-tier server>:<port>/reports/rwservlet/showjobs?server=<server_name>
```

For the example server in this chapter, the URL would look like this:

```
http://xpas10g:7778/reports/rwservlet/showjobs?server=rep_xpas10g
```

If the infrastructure and middle tier are on the same machine, the port number is probably 7778. If they are on separate machines, the port number is probably 7777. You should see a page similar to Figure 11-3.

To test that all of the pieces are in place to actually serve up Oracle Reports in your browser, point your browser to the "Welcome" page for the Application Server (Figure 11-4).

```
http://<Middle-tier server>:<port>
```

For the example server in this chapter, the URL would look like this:

```
http://xpas10g:7778
```

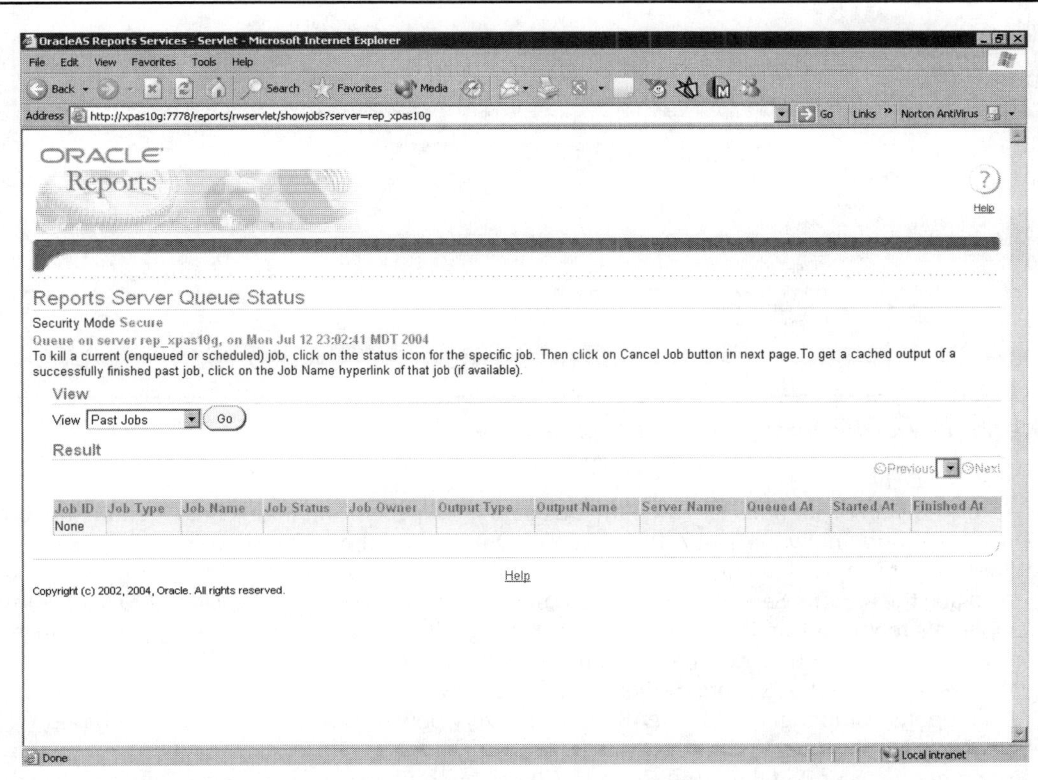

FIGURE 11-3. *The showjobs page for the Reports Server*

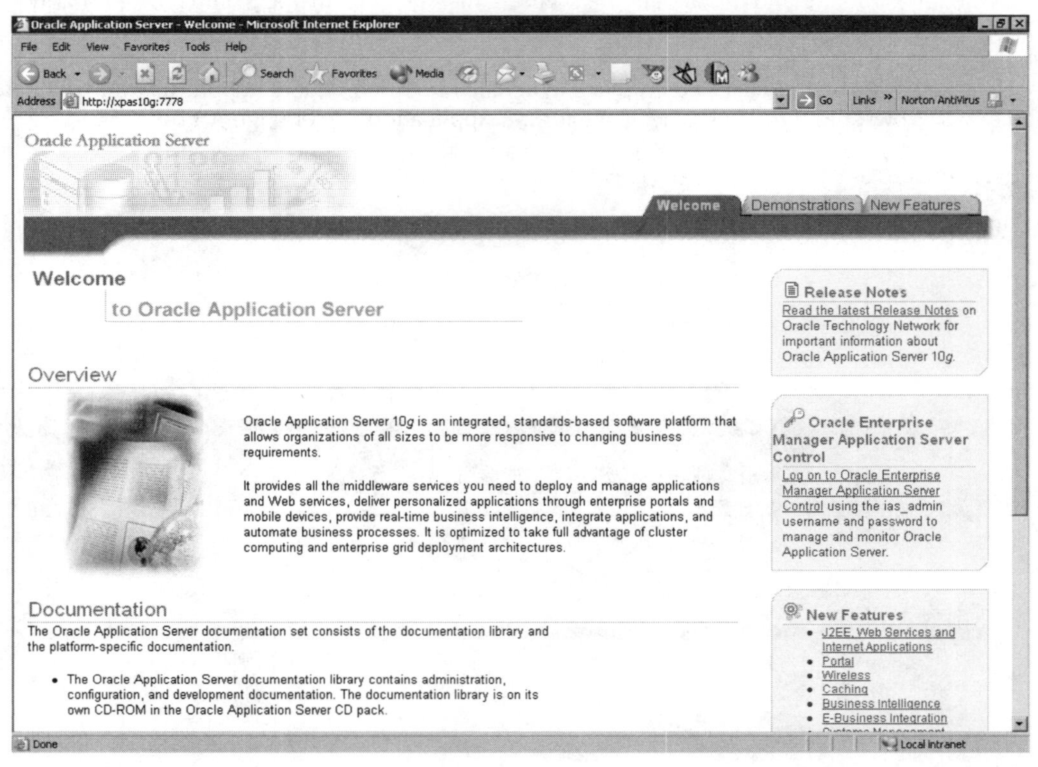

FIGURE 11-4. *The main page of the Application Server*

Click the Demonstrations tab, then the Business Intelligence And Forms link, then the Reports Services link, and finally the Test A Paper Report On The Web link. You should see a screen similar to Figure 11-5.

Replace the Reports Server name with the name of the Reports Server you want to test. In my example, it's rep_xpas10g. Replace the connect string with any valid connect string and change DesFormat to HTML 4.0. Leave the report name as test.rdf. Click Run Report. If you see a report in your web browser, the Reports Server is working.

The reports component in OracleAS Portal is a very powerful way to develop web-based reports in a very short period of time. It does, however, have some serious limitations. Since the major components of Portal (Forms, Reports, Charts) are built using wizards, a significant amount of control is handled by the code generator. Any development environment that uses code generators as its primary way of developing application components will hide many of the component details away from the developer. In many cases, this is not a prohibitive factor for your development needs. In other cases, developers will need total control of their components and this development environment will fall short of their development needs. If, for whatever reason, this limitation prohibits the development of OracleAS Portal reports, developers can integrate existing reports developed in Oracle Reports into OracleAS Portal.

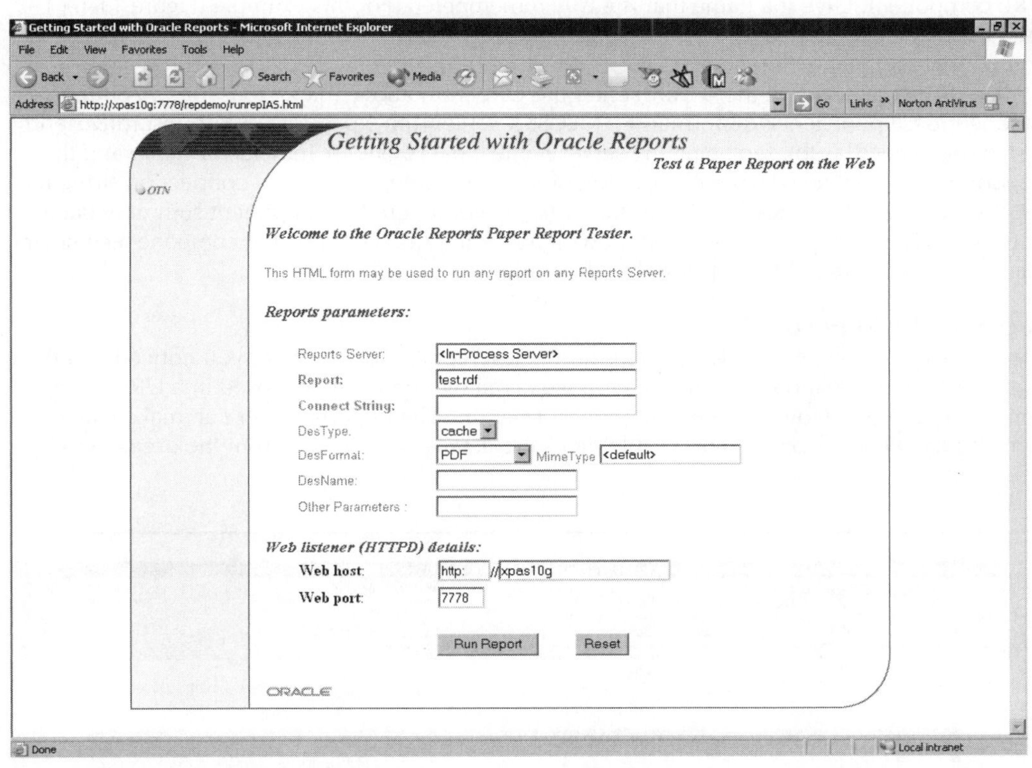

FIGURE 11-5. *Testing the Reports Server*

Reports Integration Method #1: Using the Portal URL Component

The simplest way to incorporate an Oracle Report into Portal is by way of a URL. This is not the "native" way of supporting Oracle Reports in OracleAS Portal, and while it is the quickest way to get an Oracle Report onto an OracleAS Portal page, it does not have the ability to use any of the Oracle Reports–specific functionality built into OracleAS Portal.

If you successfully ran the report from the "Getting Started with Oracle9*i* Reports" screen in Figure 11-5, you noticed that a new window popped up with a URL similar to

```
http://xpas10g:7778/reports/rwservlet?destype=cache&desformat=HTMLCSS&
server=rep_xpas10g&report=test.rdf&userid=system/manager@iasdb
```

This URL can be used to create an OracleAS Portal component (a URL component) that can then be placed on an OracleAS Portal page. Assuming you've already created a Database Provider in OracleAS Portal (if not, review Chapters 8 and 9), go into that provider and create a new

URL component. Give it a name that is easily remembered. For this example (Figure 11-6), I used the name test_reports_url. When we get to the next step in this process, we'll use this URL component and place it on a page.

On the second step of the wizard, enter the URL from above (http://xpas10g:7778/reports/rwservlet?destype=cache&desformat=HTMLCSS& server=rep_xpas10g&report=test.rdf&userid=system/manager@iasdb), replacing the server name (xpas10g) with your server name and the Reports Server (rep_xpas10g) with your Reports Server name, and a valid connection string for the userid parameter. Click Finish and then Run As Portlet on the component summary page. You should see the report in your web browser. Click the Access tab on the component summary page and make sure Publish To Portal is checked.

Securing the Reports URL

If you looked closely at the URL used to run the test report over the Web, you noticed that there was sensitive information in it; information we certainly don't want exposed in a URL for the entire world to see. How can we hide this information? The Reports Server can make use of something called a keymap file. This file hides the details of the report from the user's eyes by

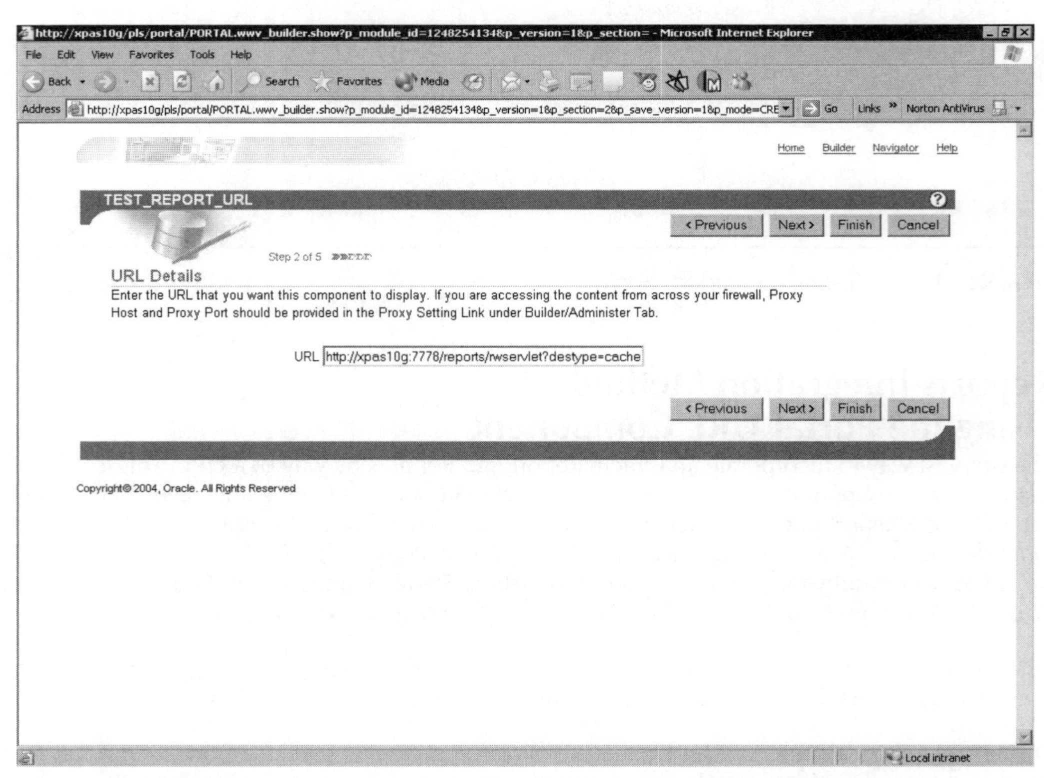

FIGURE 11-6. *Specifying the reports URL*

referencing a key in a file on the server. The keymap file for the Reports Server is called cgicmd.dat and is located in <Middle_Tier_Home>/reports/conf. Here's an example of some of the entries in that file:

```
orqa: report=breakb.rdf destype=cache desformat=html server=repserver
breakbparam: report=breakb.rdf destype=cache desformat=html server=repserver
userid=scott/tiger@mydb
```

The key name is to the left of the colon. The parameters associated with that key are to the right of the colon. The example contains two keys: orqa and breakparam. The orqa key uses the following parameters:

- report=breakb.rdf
- destype=cache
- desformat=html
- server=repserver
- userid=scott/tiger@mydb

Note that in the keymap file, the parameters are separated by spaces (in the URL they were separated by ampersands). Our URL in this example looks like this:

```
http://xpas10g:7778/reports/rwservlet?destype=cache&desformat=HTMLCSS&
server=rep_xpas10g&report=test.rdf&userid=system/manager@iasdb
```

We want to hide everything after the question mark, so we could create an entry in the cgicmd.dat file that looks like this:

```
test_report: destype=cache desformat=HTMLCSS server=rep_xpas10g
report=test.rdf userid=system/manager@iasdb
```

We could then reference the keymap file with the following URL:

```
http://xpas10g:7778/reports/rwservlet?cmdkey=test_report
```

To see all of the parameters that can be specified in the keymap file, look at the syntax for rwclient and rwservlet in Appendix A of "Oracle Application Server Reports Services Publishing Reports to the Web 10*g* (9.0.4)," Oracle Part Number B10314-01, or review Chapter 6 of this book. The most common parameters used are listed in Table 11-1.

If you want users to log on to the database, then omit the password portion of the USERID keyword from the report request. If you want users to log on every time they run report requests, then use the Reports key mapping file, cgicmd.dat, to specify the run-time command, and include the %D argument in the relevant key mapping entry. You can also use the SSOCONN parameter to reference a database resource for your OracleAS Portal user.

Things get a little confusing here: OracleAS Portal uses users created in Oracle's implementation of LDAP (Lightweight Directory Access Protocol) called Oracle Internet Directory. These LDAP users are not users in the database, even though the security

Parameter	Description
ARRAYSIZE	Use ARRAYSIZE to specify the size (in kilobytes) for use with ORACLE array processing. Generally, the larger the array size, the faster the report will run.
AUTHID	Use AUTHID to specify the user name and, optionally, the password to be used to authenticate users to the restricted Oracle9*i*AS Reports Server. User authentication ensures that the users making report requests have access privileges to run the requested report.
BUFFERS	Use BUFFERS to specify the size of the virtual memory cache in kilobytes. You should tune this setting to ensure that you have enough space to run your reports, but not so much that you are using too much of your system's resources.
DESFORMAT	Specifies the format for the job output. In bit-mapped environments, use DESFORMAT to specify the printer driver to be used when DESTYPE is FILE. In character-mode environments, use it to specify the characteristics of the printer named in DESNAME.
DESNAME	Use DESNAME to specify the name of the cache, file, printer, Oracle9*i*AS Portal, or e-mail ID (or distribution list) to which the report output will be sent. To send the report output by e-mail, specify the e-mail ID as you do in your e-mail application (any SMTP-compliant application). You can specify multiple user names by separating them with commas, and without spaces.
DESTYPE	Use DESTYPE to specify the type of device that will receive the report output. If you have created your own pluggable destination via the Reports Destination API, this is how the destination you created gets called.
REPORT	Use MODULE or REPORT to specify the name of the report to run.
RUNDEBUG	Use RUNDEBUG to turn on error messages/warnings that would otherwise not be displayed. For example, with RUNDEBUG=YES, you might get the error message "Frame 1 overlaps but does not contain Frame 2." This situation may or may not be acceptable, depending on the job being run.
SCHEDULE	Use SCHEDULE to set the day, time, and frequency a report should be run. The default is to run the report once, now. Time values are expressed according to a 24-hour day (i.e., one o'clock is expressed as 13:00).
SERVER	Use SERVER to specify the name of the Reports Server you want to use to run this report.
SSOCONN	Use SSOCONN to specify one or more connect strings to use to connect to one or more data sources in a single sign-on environment.
TRACEOPTS	TRACEOPTS indicates the tracing information that you want to be logged in the trace file when you run the report.
USERID	Use USERID only if you're not using single sign-on. Use USERID to specify your Oracle user name and password, with an optional database name for accessing a remote database. If the password is omitted, then a database logon form opens automatically before the user is allowed to run the report.

TABLE 11-1. *Common rwclient and rwservlet Parameters*

information about these users is stored in the infrastructure database (confusing enough?). In order for these nondatabase, LDAP users to have privileges to see (query) and potentially enter (insert), modify (update), and remove (delete) data in an Oracle database, a database resource must be set up for each of these LDAP users. The database resource is named, and then referenced with the SSOCONN parameter described in Table 11-1. LDAP users are commonly set up either in OracleAS Portal or by accessing the Oracle Internet Directory Delegated Authentication Server directly at: http://<infrastructure server>:<port>/oiddas.

This serves to hide the implementation details from the end user. The cgicmd.dat file is not read dynamically, however, so every change to it requires administrators to stop and start the OC4J_BI_FORMS component in the middle tier.

To put this component on a page, go back to the OracleAS Portal Navigator and click the Page Groups tab. If you don't have a page group defined, create one now. Edit the root page for your page group. You can edit the page in one of three ways: Graphical Mode, Layout Mode, or List Mode. Select Layout Mode and then click Add Portlets in the main region of the page (Figure 11-7).

Click New and then the name of your database provider. You should see Test_Report_URL (or whatever you named your URL) as one of the portlets that can be placed on this region. If it is not displayed, type **test_report_url** in the search field and click Go. Once it is displayed, single-click it to move it to the right-hand side ("Selected Portlets") of the page. Your Portal page now has an Oracle Report integrated into it. Back on the Edit Page screen, click the Graphical link on the top left of the page. You should see the report (albeit clumsily placed) on the page.

Reports Integration Method #2: Using the Native Portal Method

Using the URL component is a quick way to get an Oracle Report on an OracleAS Portal page, but we can't use any of OracleAS Portal's native support for Oracle Reports to enhance our functionality with this method. If you're logged into OracleAS Portal as a user with administration privileges, you'll see an Administer tab on the builder page (Figure 11-8).

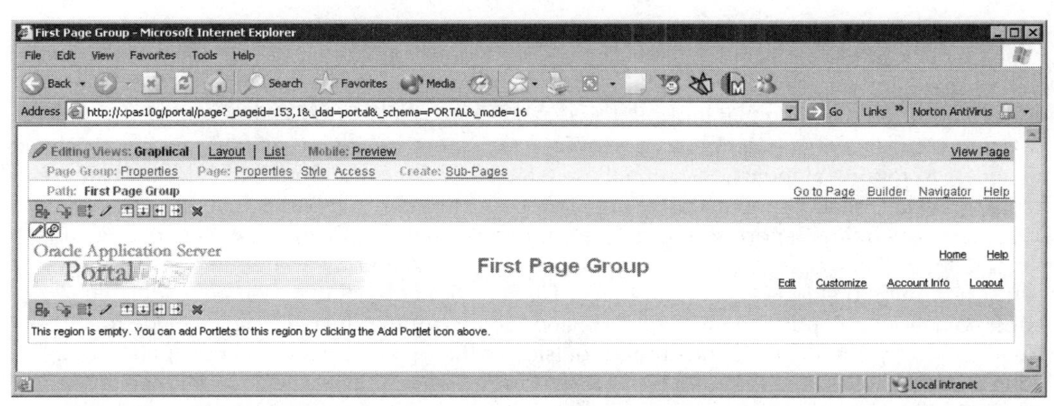

FIGURE 11-7. *Adding a portlet to a region*

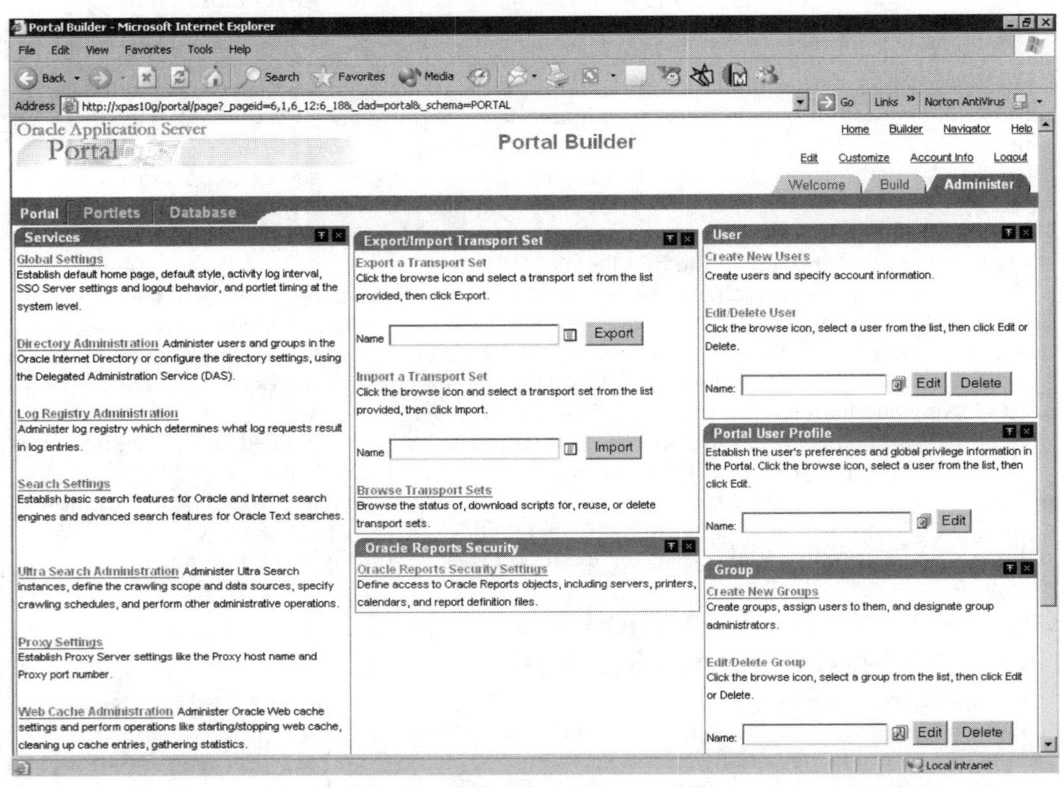

FIGURE 11-8. *The Portal subtab of the Administer tab*

If you click the Administer tab, and then on the "Portal" subtab on the top left of the screen, you will see a link on the bottom right that says Oracle Reports Security Settings. Clicking that link will take you to a page that looks like Figure 11-9.

On this screen, we can define access to Reports Servers, access to .rdf files, access to printers, and access to report calendars. By using these features of OracleAS Portal, developers can use OracleAS Portal's security mechanisms and added functionality to restrict access to the various components of Oracle Reports. For example, an OracleAS Portal Calendar Access object can be created that limits access to nonbusiness hours so that no report can be run during business hours, consuming precious system resources. That calendar object can then be associated to any combination of Reports Servers, .rdf files, and reports printers. If an attempt is made to access a Reports Server, .rdf file, or reports printer outside of the reports calendar access period (i.e., during working hours), the request fails and an error message is generated. Developers also have the ability to restrict access to any of these components according to the user and group privileges for the OracleAS Portal user.

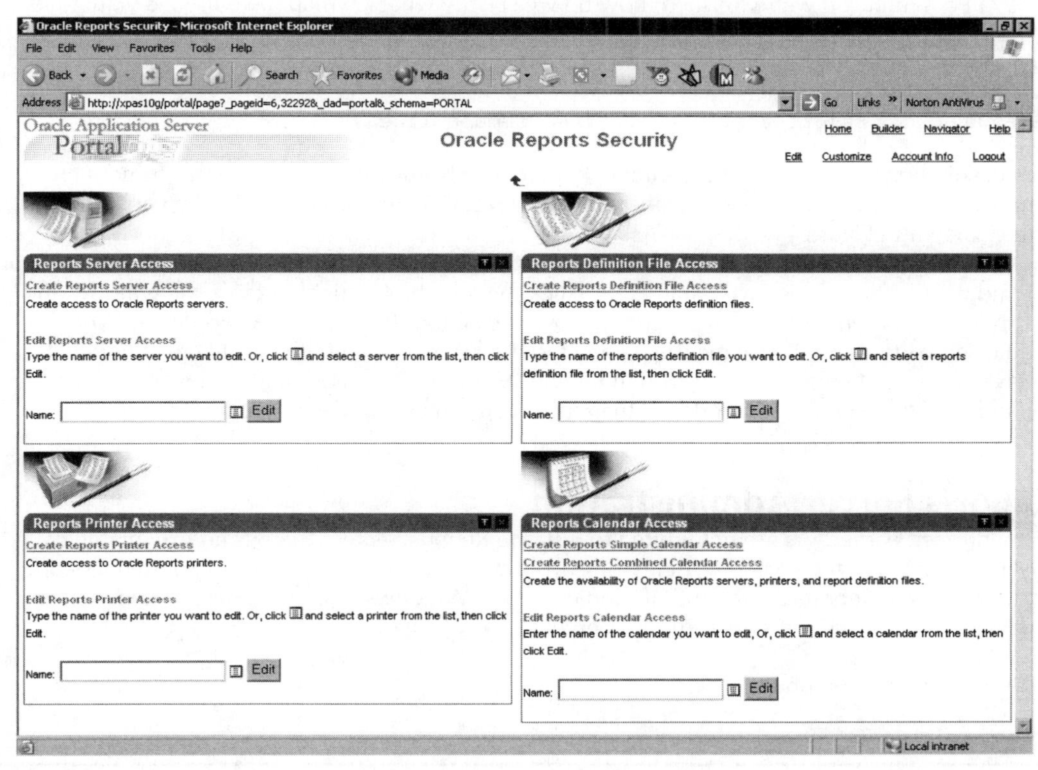

FIGURE 11-9. *The Oracle Reports Security Page*

When an .rdf file is defined in the Reports Definition File Access portlet, it must be associated with a Portal DB Provider. If that report has Publish To Portal checked in the Access tab of the component summary screen, then that report will show up as an available portlet to be placed on an OracleAS Portal page in the OracleAS Portal portlet repository. Depending on when the page is viewed, the report will then be displayed (if it falls within the calendar parameters associated with the Reports Server and .rdf file) or will display an error with absolutely no developer or system administration intervention whatsoever.

You can use keymap file entries when you define entries in the Reports Definition File Access portlet, but it's tricky to find and a little confusing to use. Click Create Reports Definition File Access. In step 1 of the wizard, give the report a meaningful name. On the second step of the wizard, you'll start entering characteristics of the report: its name on disk, the Reports Server you want to use, etc. Here's the tricky part: when we get to the final step, we can specify a keymap entry to use; any parameters specified in that keymap entry will override anything you enter in these screens. To prove this, leave the Oracle Reports File Name field blank. Click Finish to generate the report definition file access for Portal.

Wait a minute—if we're finished, how do we specify what keymap file entry we want to use? If you click either the Run or Run As Portlet link on the component summary screen, you'll get the following error message:

```
REP-50004: No report specified on the command line
```

This makes sense, since we left the Oracle Reports File Name field blank. On the component summary screen, you'll see a link that says Customize. Clicking this link will take you to the screen shown in Figure 11-10.

In the CGI/Servlet Command Key field, enter **test_report** (or a suitable name for a key in your cgicmd.dat file) and click Save Parameters. Click the *x* in the top right to close the window and return to the Component Summary screen. Now click either Run or Run As Portlet and you should see your report. By saving the parameter, the key specified in the CGI/Servlet field will always be used when this report is run in OracleAS Portal. The values have been taken from the cgicmd.dat file and have "overridden" the report's attributes that were specified in step 2 of the wizard.

Reports Server Administration

As mentioned earlier, we are not limited to just one Reports Server. There is an executable called rwserver located in the <Middle_Tier_Home>/bin directory. This program can be used to stop, start, or create a Reports Server and, if running on the Windows platform, create a Reports Server as a Windows service. To start a Reports Server,

```
rwserver server=<Reports Server>
```

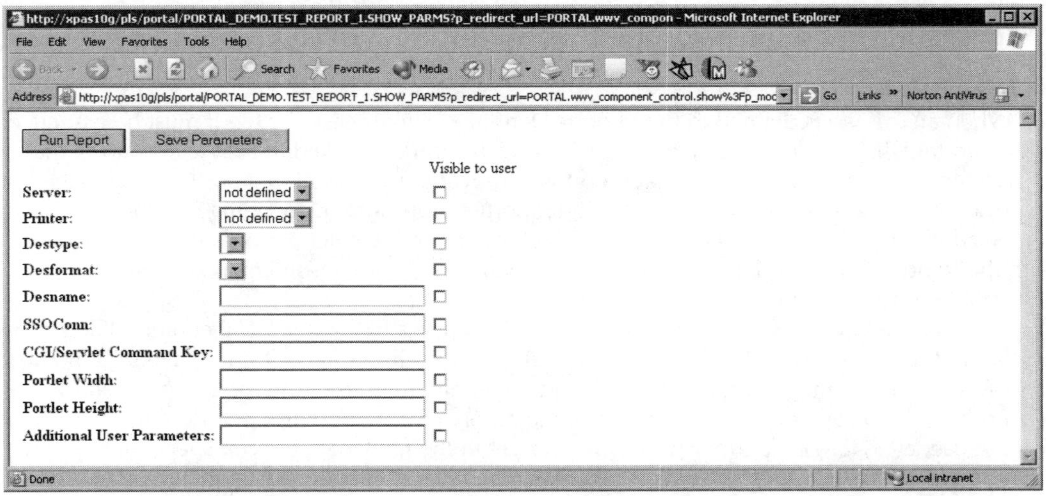

FIGURE 11-10. *The Configure page for OracleAS Portal Reports access*

TIP
If the Reports Server you specify does not exist, a new one will be created.

To stop a Reports Server,

```
rwserver server=<Reports Server> shutdown=immediate
```

To create a Reports Server as a Windows service, use the install keyword:

```
rwserver server=<Reports Server> install autostart=yes
```

Oracle provides the rwservlet executable to display information about your Reports Server. These are the most common parameters passed to rwservlet:

- **showjobs** Displays a web view of Reports Server queue status.

  Example syntax:

  http://xpas10g:7778/reports/rwservlet/showjobs?server=rep_xpas10g
- **showenv** Displays the `rwservlet` configuration file (`rwservlet.properties`).

  Example syntax:

  http://xpas10g:7778/reports/rwservlet/showenv
- **showmap** Displays `rwservlet` key mappings.

  Example syntax:

  http://xpas10g:7778/reports/rwservlet/showmap
- **showmyjobs** Displays the Reports Server queue status for a particular user.

  Example syntax:

  http://xpas10g:7778/reports/rwservlet/showmyjobs

Component #2: Oracle Forms

There is no "native" way to integrate Oracle Forms into OracleAS Portal, meaning that there are no OracleAS Portal–specific features for integrating and administering Oracle Forms within OracleAS Portal. In order to accomplish Forms–to–OracleAS Portal integration, we have to use a technique similar to method #1 for integrating Reports (i.e., using the URL component in Portal). First, we need to make sure the Forms Server is up and running. If you look back at Figure 11-2, you'll see a component called "Forms." If the status arrow is a check mark, we're up and running.

NOTE
One thing to notice about the Forms component: the check box next to the Forms component is grayed out. Normally, to stop, start, or restart a component, we select its check box and then click Start, Stop, or Restart in the right middle of the page. Why can't we do that with the Forms component? The Forms component is dependent on the OC4J_BI_FORMS component. When it's up, the Forms component is up; when it's down, the Forms component is down. So the next question becomes, if they're dependent on each other, why are there two of them? There are many reasons, but the most important one is that there are performance metrics associated with the Forms Server that allow administrators to see how efficiently the Forms Server is working. These metrics are viewable by clicking the Forms link. There is also a screen after you click the Forms link to view and modify the Forms Server configuration files. By separating these two components, administrators can get detailed information about both the OC4J_BI_FORMS and FORMS components of the Oracle Application Server 10g middle tier.

To test your Forms Server, we're going to follow steps similar to when we tested the Reports Server. Point your browser to the Welcome page for the Application Server. If the infrastructure and middle tier are on the same machine, the port number is probably 7778. If they are on separate machines, the port number is probably 7777:

```
http://<Middle-tier server>:<port>
```

You should see a page similar to Figure 11-4. Click the Demonstrations tab, then the Business Intelligence And Forms link, then the Forms Services link next to the text that starts "Demonstrates a test form...." If this is the first time you're attempting to run an Oracle Form, you will be prompted to install a browser plug-in called Jinitiator.

NOTE
Oracle JInitiator enables users to run Oracle9i Forms applications using Netscape Navigator or Internet Explorer. It provides the ability to specify the use of a specific Java Virtual Machine (JVM) on the client, rather than using the browser's default JVM. Oracle JInitiator runs as a plug-in for Netscape Navigator and as an ActiveX component for Internet Explorer. Oracle JInitiator does not replace or modify the default JVM provided by the browser. Rather, it provides an alternative JVM in the form of a plug-in. To get more information about JInitiator, refer to " Oracle Application Server Forms Services Deployment Guide 10g (9.0.4)," Oracle Part Number B10470-01, Appendix A.

After JInitiator installs, you should see a new browser window similar to Figure 11-11.

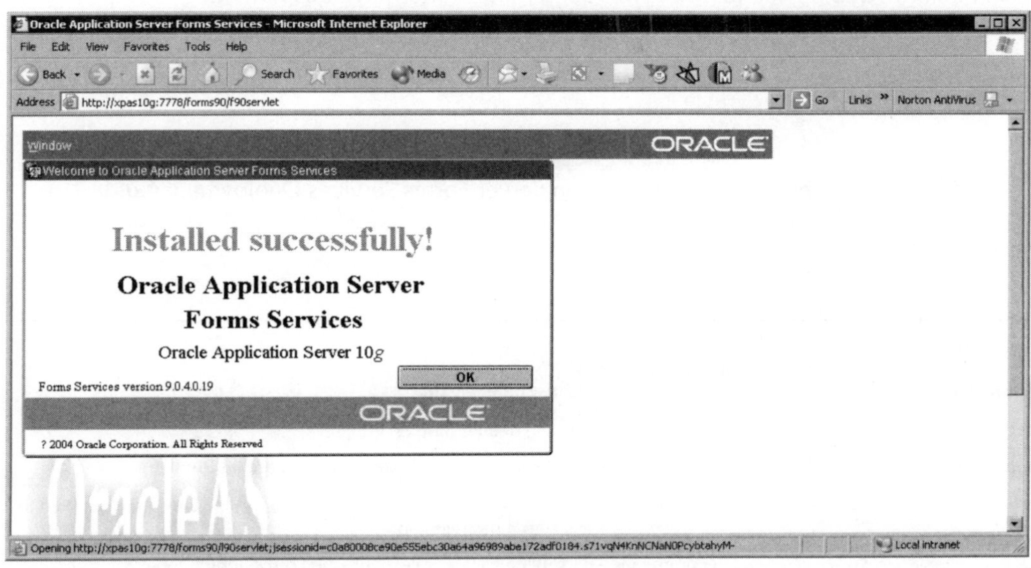

FIGURE 11-11. *The test page for the Oracle Forms Server*

Securing the Forms URL

Unlike the URL we used to run our first report, the URL to run our form seems pretty innocuous:

```
http://xpas10g:7778/forms90/f90servlet
```

Not much sensitive information you can get from the address in Figure 11-11, is there? But how do we specify what form we want to run and what characteristics we want to specify? Here's where Oracle is throwing you a bit of a curve ball. The demo to run a test report does not use a keymap entry (we saw all of the report's details in the URL), but the demo to run a form does use a keymap entry, even though there doesn't appear to be one specified.

Oracle Forms, like Oracle Reports, uses a keymap file, only for Oracle Forms, it's called the Forms Servlet Configuration File. It serves the exact same purpose as the Oracle Reports keymap file: namely, it hides sensitive details about the Oracle Form from the user's eyes in the URL of the browser. The Forms Servlet Configuration File is called formsweb.cfg and is located in <middle_tier_home>/forms90/server. The formats of the files are different, but the concept is the same: a key that will be referenced in the URL of the browser, followed by attributes that will determine what form is run and how the Forms Server is run for that particular Oracle Form. In Oracle's documentation, the "keys" in the formsweb.cfg file are called "named configurations."

In the cgicmd.dat file for the Reports Server, the entries had this format:

```
key: attribute1 attribute2 etc.
```

In the formsweb.cfg file for the Forms Server, the entries have this format:

```
[named configuration]
attribute1
attribute2
etc.
```

See Chapter 4 of the " Oracle Application Server Forms Services Deployment Guide 10*g* (9.0.4)" for a complete list of the parameters that can be specified. The most common parameters are specified in Table 11-2.

Parameter	**Required / Optional**	**Parameter Value**
`baseHTML`	Required	The default base HTML file.
`baseHTMLJInitiator`	Required	Physical path to HTML file that contains JInitiator tags.
`connectionDisallowedURL`	Required	This is the URL shown in the HTML page that is not allowed to start a new session.
`IE`	Recommended if there are users with Internet Explorer 5.0 or above browsers	Specifies how to execute the Forms applet under Microsoft Internet Explorer 5.0 or above. If the client is using an Internet Explorer 5.0 or above browser, either the native JVM or JInitiator can be used. A setting of "JInitiator" uses the basejini.htm file and JInitiator. A setting of "Native" uses the browser's native JVM.
`log`	Optional	Supports running and debugging a form from the Builder. Default value is `Null`.
`form`	Required	Specifies the name of the top-level Forms module (fmx file) to run.
`userid`	Optional	Login string. For example: `scott/tiger@ORADB`.
`otherparams`	Optional	This setting specifies command-line parameters to pass to the Forms run-time process in addition to `form` and `userid`. Default is `otherparams=buffer_records=%buffer% debug_messages=%debug_messages% array=%array% obr=%obr% query_only=%query_only% quiet=%quiet% render=%render% record=%record% tracegroup=%tracegroup% log=%log% term=%term%` Note: Special syntax rules apply to this parameter when it is specified in a URL: a + may be used to separate multiple name=value pairs (see Section 3.3.4, "Specifying Special Characters in Values of Runform Parameters" in the "Oracle Application Server - Forms Services Deployment Guide" (http://download-west.oracle.com/docs/cd/B10464_01/web.904/b10470/basics.htm) for more information). For production environments, in order to provide better control over which runform parameters end users can specify in a URL, use the `restrictedURLparams` parameter.

TABLE 11-2. *The Most Common Parameters Specified*

Parameter	Required / Optional	Parameter Value
debug	Optional	Allows running in debug mode. Default value is No.
buffer	Optional	Supports running and debugging a form from the Builder. Subargument for otherparams Default value is No.
log	Optional	Supports running and debugging a form from the Builder. Default value is Null.
pageTitle	Optional	HTML page title, attributes for the BODY tag, and HTML to add before and after the form.
serverURL	Required	/forms90/l90servlet (see Chapter 1, "Oracle Application Server—Forms Services Deployment Guide" (http://download-west.oracle.com/docs/cd/B10464_01/web.904/b10470/intro.htm) for more information).
codebase	Required	Virtual directory you defined to point to the physical directory <ORACLE_HOME>/forms90/java, where, by default, the applet JAR files are downloaded from. The default value is /forms90/java.
imageBase	Optional	Indicates where icon files are stored. Choose between • codeBase, which indicates that the icon search path is relative to the directory that contains the Java classes. Use this value if you store your icons in a JAR file (recommended). • documentBase, which is the default. In deployments that make use of the Forms Server CGI, you must specify the icon path in a custom application file.
logo	Optional	Specifies the .GIF file that should appear at the Forms menu bar. Set to NO for no logo. Leave empty to use the default Oracle logo.
width	Required	Specifies the width of the form applet, in pixels. Default is 650.
height	Required	Specifies the height of the form applet, in pixels. Default is 500.
separateFrame	Optional	Determines whether the applet appears within a separate window. Legal values: True or False.
splashScreen	Optional	Specifies the .GIF file that should appear before the applet appears. Set to NO for no splash. Leave empty to use the default splash image. To set the parameter, include the filename (for example, myfile.gif) or the virtual path and filename (for example, images/myfile.gif).
background	Optional	Specifies the .GIF file that should appear in the background. Set to NO for no background. Leave empty to use the default background.
lookAndFeel	Optional	Determines the application's look and feel. Legal values: Oracle or Generic (Windows look and feel).
jinit_download_page	Required (Netscape only)	If you create your own version of the Jinitiator download page, set this parameter to point to it. Default is /forms90/jinitiator/us/JInitiator/jinit.download.htm.

TABLE 11-2. *The Most Common Parameters Specified* (continued)

Parameter	Required / Optional	Parameter Value
jinit_classid	Required (IE only)	Default is clsid:CAFECAFE-0013-0001-0009-ABCDEFABCDEF
jinit_exename	Required	Default is jinit.exe#Version=1.3.1.9
jinit_mimetype	Required (Netscape only)	Default is application/x-jinit-applet;version=1.3.1.9
baseHTMLJInitiator	Required	Physical path to HTML file that contains JInitiator tags.
jpi_codebase	Required	Sun's Java Plug-in codebase setting.
jpi_classid	Required	Sun's Java Plug-in class ID.
jpi_download_page	Required	Sun's Java Plug-in download page.
em_mode	Required	1 is to enable. 0 is to disable. 1 indicates that all Enterprise Manager information is available, including metrics and servlet status. 0 indicates that only configuration information is available.
oid_formsid	Required	Configured during the OracleAS installation, so you do not need to change this.
ORACLE_HOME	Required	Configured during the OracleAS installation, so you do not need to change this.

TABLE 11-2. *The Most Common Parameters Specified* (continued)

The URL for the Reports Server to read the cgicmd.dat file looks like this:

```
http://<server name>:<port>/reports/rwservlet?key
```

The URL for the Forms Server to read the formsweb.cfg file looks like this:

```
http://<server name>:<port>/servlet/f90servlet?config=named configuration
```

Wait a minute—the demo form that is displayed in Figure 11-11 did not have a "config=" at the end of the URL. How did the Forms Server know what Oracle Form to display? At the beginning of the formsweb.cfg file, there is a "default configuration" section. Parameters specified in this section are used unless they are overridden by any named configurations referenced in the file. Since we didn't reference any, the default parameters were used. One of the default parameters is

```
Form=test.fmx
```

We could have specified a named configuration like this:

```
[test_form]

form=test.fmx
```

and then specified the URL like this:

```
http://xpas10g:7778/servlet/f90servlet?config=test_form
```

Here's a strange quirk. Try this:

```
http://xpas10g:7778/servlet/f90servlet?config=bogusbogusbogus
```

Now, bogusbogusbogus does not exist in the formsweb.cfg file, yet the form gets displayed with no error message. Why? Remember that the named configurations override any parameters specified in the default configuration section. Since bogusbogusbogus isn't in the formsweb.cfg file, the values from the default configuration are used (including the one that says "form=test.fmx"). This is why it's a good idea to comment out the form= parameter in the default configuration section or redirect users and developers to a help page. As in the case of the cgicmd.dat file, if you make any changes to the formsweb.cfg file, you must bounce the OC4J_BI_FORMS component before any changes will take effect.

Integrating the Oracle Form into OracleAS Portal is as simple as creating a URL object and performing the steps we did in the section "Reports Integration Method #1: Using the Portal URL Component" earlier in this chapter. The URL

```
http://xpas10g:7778/servlet/f90servlet?config=<named configuration>
```

can be used to construct the OracleAS Portal component (a URL component) that can then be placed on an OracleAS Portal page. Assuming you've already created a Database Provider in OracleAS Portal (if not, review Chapters 8 and 9), go into that provider and create a new URL component. Give it a name that is easily remembered. For this example (Figure 11-12), I used the name test_form_url. On the second step of the wizard, enter the URL from above (http://xpas10g:7778/servlet/f90servlet?config=<named configuration>). When we get to the next step in this process, we'll use this URL component and place it on a page.

Click Finish and then Run As Portlet on the component summary page. You should see the form in your web browser. Click the Access tab on the component summary page and make sure Publish To Portal is checked. You can now place this portlet on an OracleAS Portal page.

Component #3: Oracle Discoverer

Using either the URL or "native" methods to integrate Oracle Forms and Oracle Reports is a tricky, though relatively simple, process. Incorporating OracleAS Discoverer Workbooks into Portal requires a significantly greater number of steps. To start with, there is "native support" for OracleAS Discoverer in Portal, but we have to "tell" OracleAS Portal about OracleAS Discoverer first. In Oracle's documentation, this is called "Registering the Discoverer Portlet Provider."

Registering the Discoverer Portlet Provider

The Discoverer Portlet Provider is a program that runs on the server and facilitates communication between the Discoverer Server and OracleAS Portal. Thankfully, the first part of this process has to be performed only once, because once the Discoverer Portlet Provider is registered with OracleAS Portal, it remains there. The other steps in the process, however, must be repeated for each Discoverer Worksheet we wish to incorporate into OracleAS Portal.

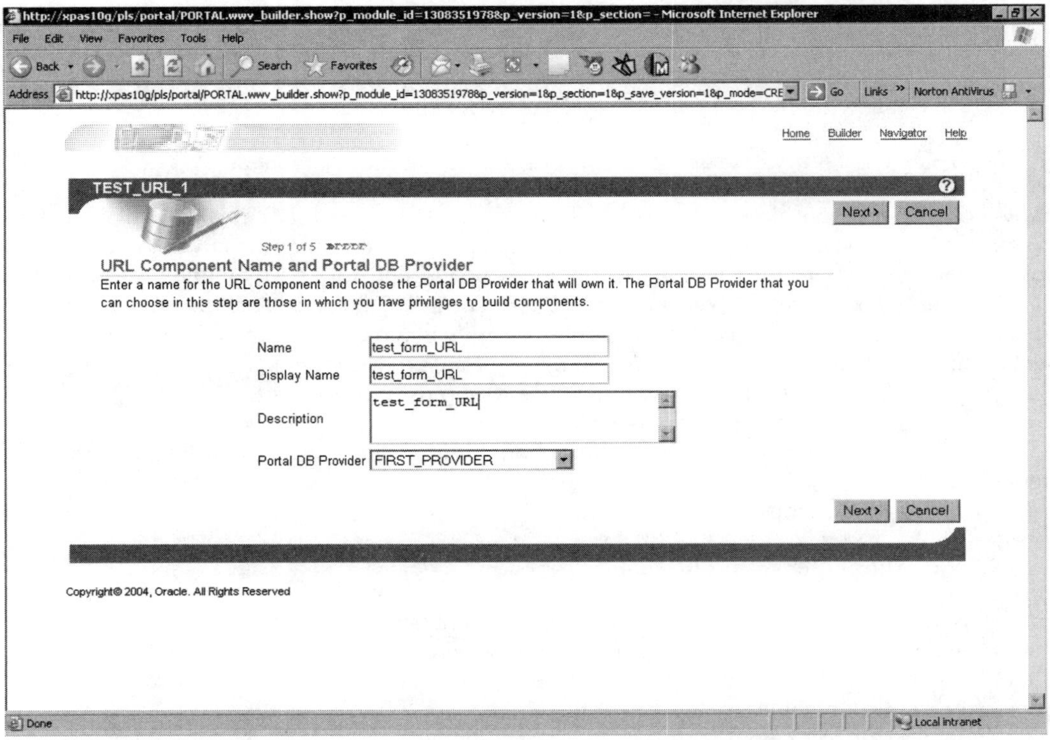

FIGURE 11-12. *Specifying the Oracle Forms URL for the OracleAS Portal component*

Before attempting to register the Discoverer Portlet Provider, we need to make sure all the pieces for OracleAS Portal and OracleAS Discoverer are in place and can "speak" to each other. Type the following in your browser:

```
http://<server>:<port>/discoverer/portletprovider
```

where <server> is the middle-tier server and <port> is the default port number of the middle-tier instance. In the examples in this chapter, I have been using a server named xpas10g with its middle tier installed on port 7778, so the URL on that server would look like this:

```
http://xpas10g:7778/discoverer/portletprovider
```

You should see a screen similar to Figure 11-13.

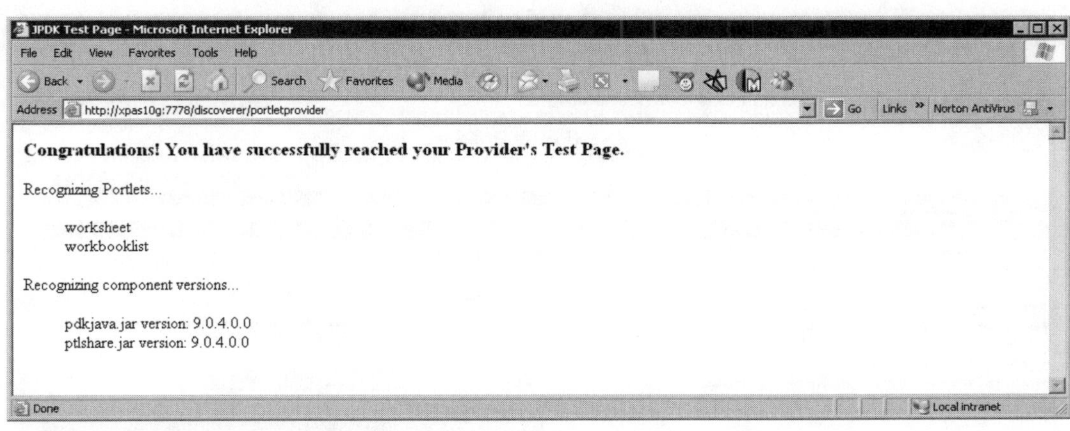

FIGURE 11-13. *Testing the Discoverer Portlet Provider*

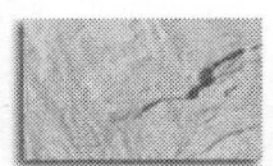

TIP
If you don't see a screen like Figure 11-13, make sure the OracleAS Discoverer background process is running on your server. You can start all services by typing ***opmnctl startall****. If this does not fix your problem, check Metalink docs 217185.1, 202268.1, and 236088.1 for suggestions on solutions.*

Next, we need to register the OracleAS Discoverer Portlet Provider in OracleAS Portal. Log into OracleAS Portal as a user with Portal administration privileges. On the main OracleAS Portal page, click the Administer tab on the top right of the page and select the Portlets subtab from the top left of the page. Click Register a Provider in the middle of the page (Figure 11-14).

The Name and Display Name fields in step 1 of the Register a Portlet Provider Wizard can contain anything, but the Display Name is what will be displayed to developers when they attempt to add an OracleAS Discoverer Portlet to a page, so make it meaningful. Make sure "Web" is chosen for implementation style. Click Next to display the General Properties page.

In the URL field, enter the URL we used to test the Discoverer Portlet Provider :

```
http://<server>:<port>/discoverer/portletprovider
```

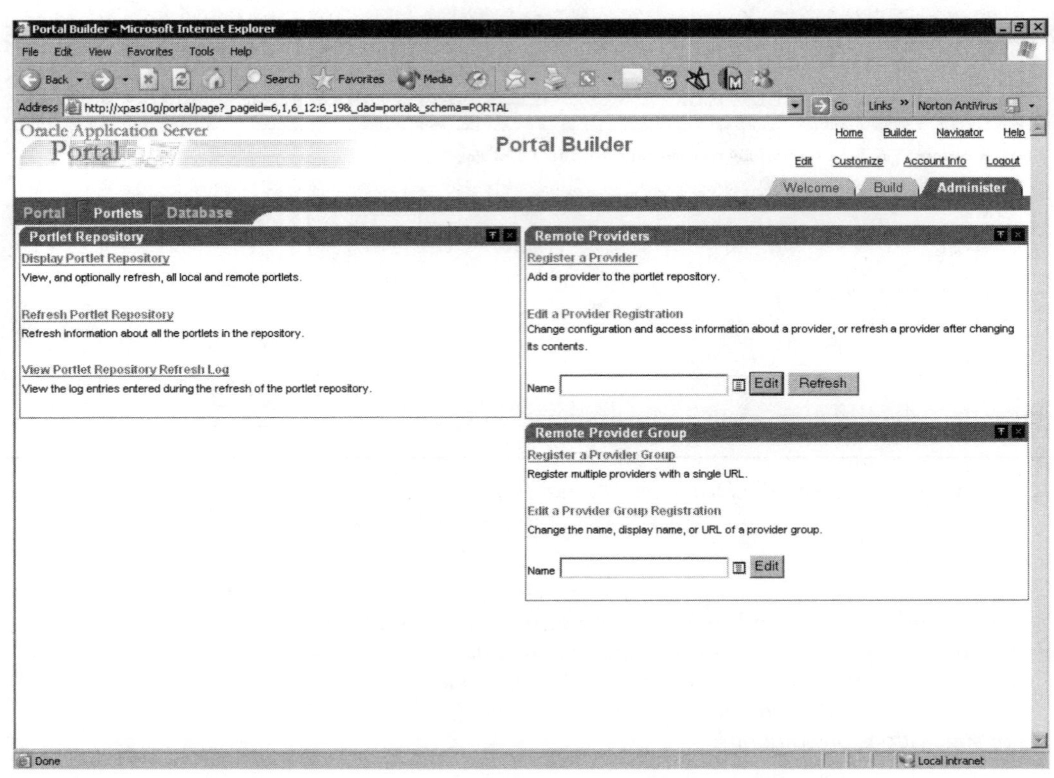

FIGURE 11-14. *The Portlets subtab of the Administer tab*

Make sure the radio button starting with "The user has the same identity…" is selected (Figure 11-15).

Click Next. Unless you want to change the default grant access settings, you do not need to enter details in the control access page. Click Finish. The Discoverer Portlet Provider is now registered with Portal.

Creating a Discoverer Connection in Oracle Application Server 10*g*

Before we can add OracleAS Discoverer portlets to a page, we have to establish an OracleAS Discoverer connection for Oracle Application Server 10*g*. Back in Figure 11-2, the first system component listed for the middle tier was one called "Discoverer." Clicking that link will take us to the screen where we can configure OracleAS Discoverer connections for Oracle Application Server 10*g*.

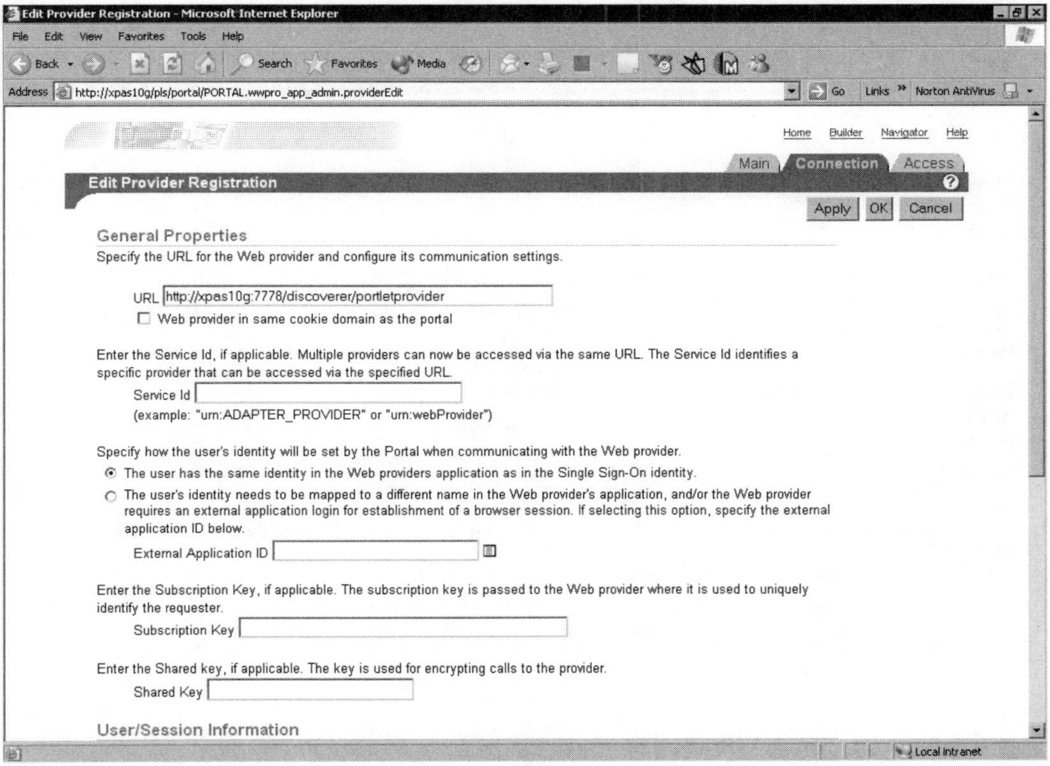

FIGURE 11-15. *Registering the OracleAS Discoverer Portlet*

Click the link that says Discoverer Public Connections. You will see a screen that looks like Figure 11-16.

Click Create Connection and enter connection information for a user that has a Discoverer EUL (End-User Layer) built. The connect string entered here must match an entry in the tnsnames.ora file in the <Middle-Tier-Home>/network/admin directory on the server. When it comes time to configure a OracleAS Discoverer portlet after it has been placed onto an OracleAS Portal page, we will be asked to enter the name of the OracleAS Discoverer connection defined on this page. Different Workbooks and different OracleAS Portal pages can use the same OracleAS Discoverer connection.

To place an OracleAS Discoverer portlet on a page, go to the Page Groups tab and select a page group. Click the Layout link on the top of the page. In a region on the page, click the Add Portlets icon, as we did in Figure 11-7. Click on the New link. You should see a new folder with the name you gave the OracleAS Discoverer Portlet Provider when you registered

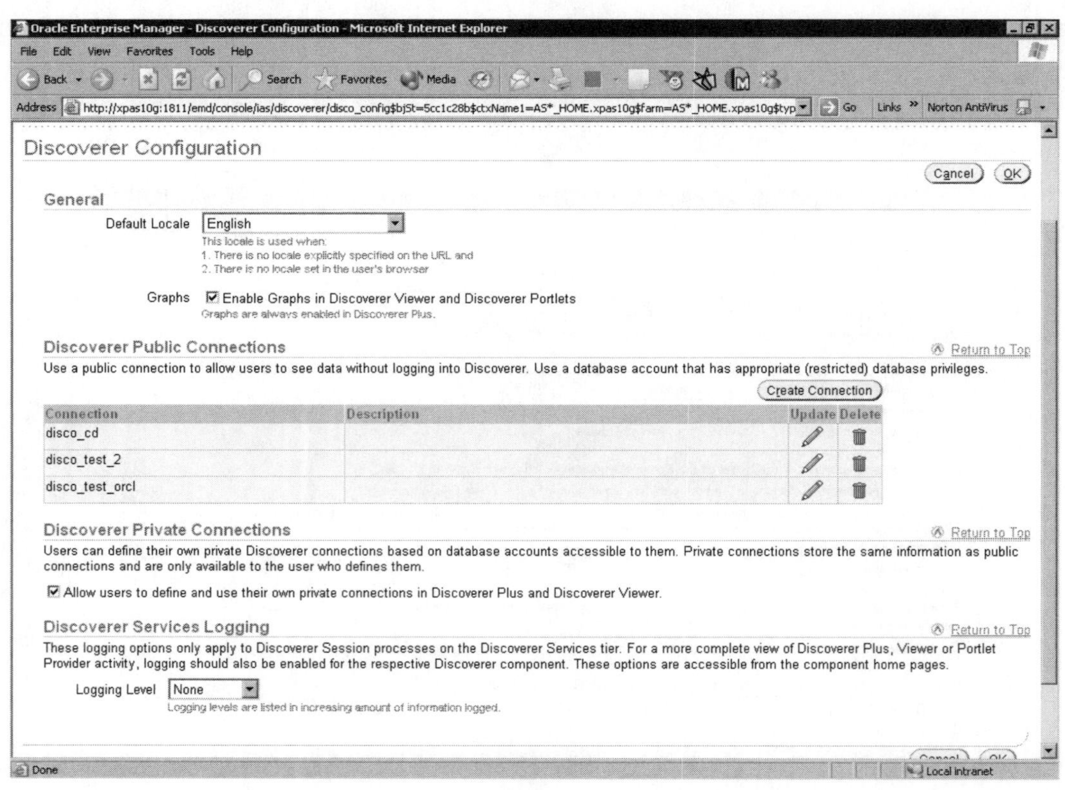

FIGURE 11-16. *Specifying an OracleAS Discoverer connection*

it in the steps right after Figure 11-13. In this example, it's called "discoverer_provider" (Figure 11-17).

If we click the Discoverer Portlet link, we have only two choices: adding a Worksheet portlet or a "List of Database Workbooks" portlet. Clicking the List Of Database Workbooks link will place a portlet on the screen that allows end users to specify which OracleAS Discoverer Workbook they would like to view. If we click the Worksheet portlet, we will have to perform another step—configuring the portlet to specify which OracleAS Discoverer Worksheet we would like to view.

Click Worksheet so that it appears on the right-hand side of the page under "Selected Portlets." We will specify which Worksheet we want to display in the next step. Clicking OK

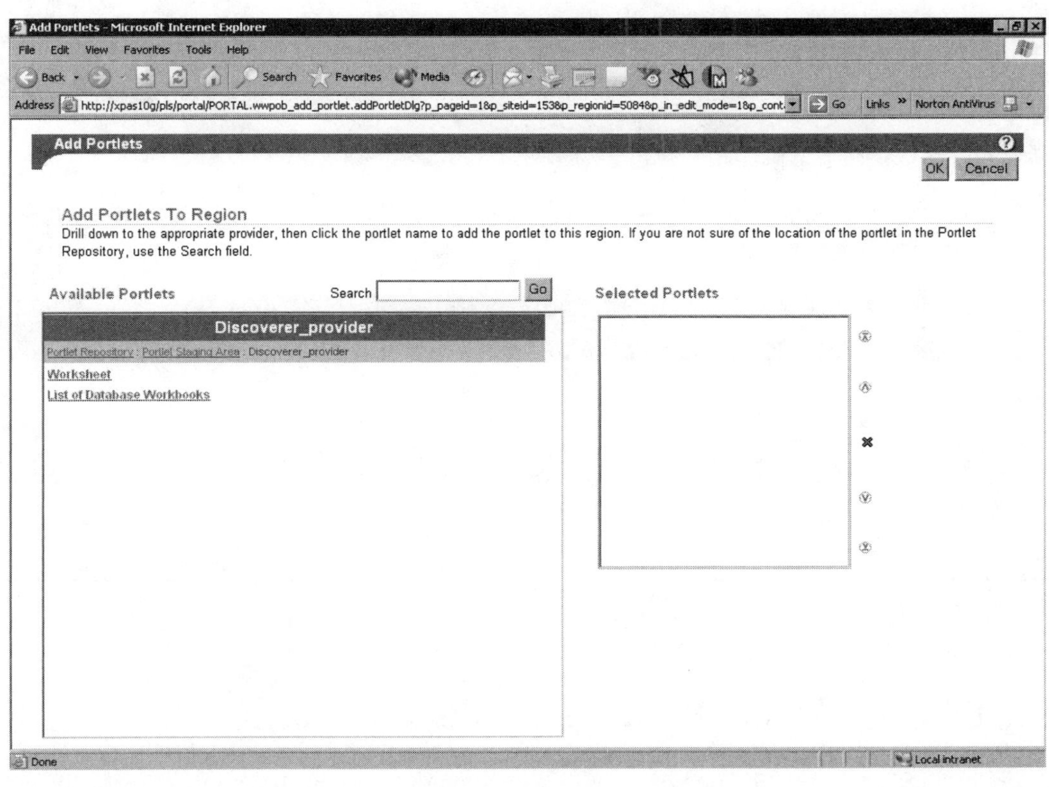

FIGURE 11-17. *The available portlets of the discoverer_provider*

on the top-right part of the screen will take us back to the Page Layout screen. Click Graphical in the top-left part of the screen to display the page graphically. You should see something like Figure 11-18.

The error makes sense because we haven't defined which OracleAS Discoverer Worksheet we want to display yet. We can't do that by editing the page in Graphical mode; we can do it only by editing the page in "Layout" mode, so click the Layout link on the top-left side of the page. In the middle of the page, in the region where you added the Discoverer portlet, you should see a link that says Edit Defaults next to the Discoverer portlet. Clicking that link will take you to the Edit Worksheet Portlet Defaults Wizard. This wizard will step you through the definition of the Discoverer portlet.

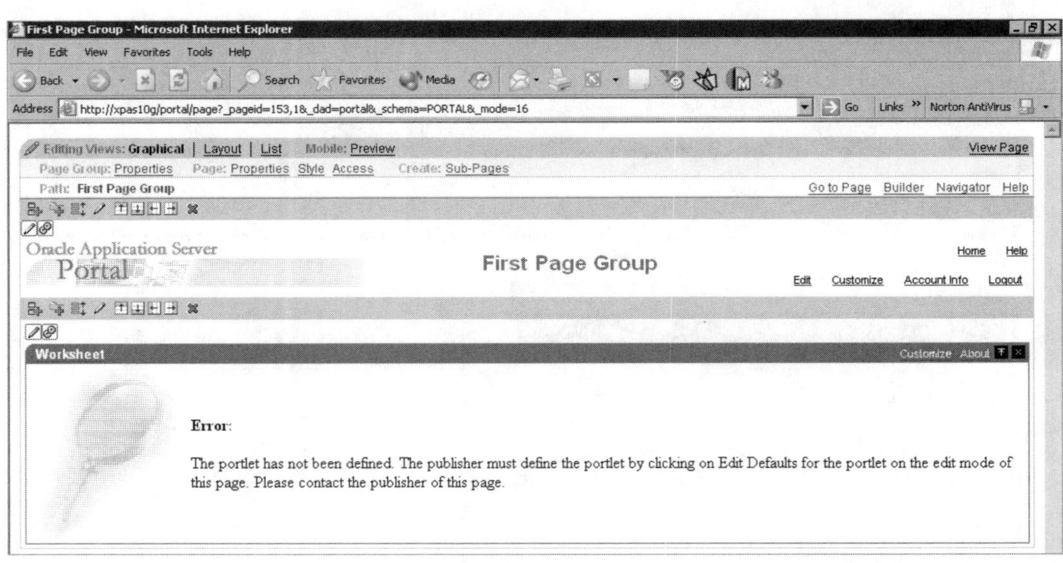

FIGURE 11-18. *Attempting to display the Oracle Discoverer Worksheet*

The Edit Worksheet Portlet Defaults Wizard

The first page of the Edit Worksheet Portlet Defaults Wizard asks us to enter the connection we created in Figure 11-15. The wizard will then attempt to establish a connection to the instance that has a Discoverer End-User Layer (EUL) already built in. On Step 1 of the wizard, the OracleAS Discoverer Workbooks available to us will be displayed. Leave the other selections with their default values for this example and click Next on the bottom right of the page (Figure 11-19).

On Step 2 of the wizard, we specify the Workbook to be displayed (Figure 11-20). An OracleAS Discoverer Workbook can be composed of numerous Worksheets, so on Step 3 of the wizard, we specify the Worksheet in the OracleAS Discoverer Workbook to be displayed (Figure 11-21).

If there are any parameters associated with the Worksheet, we are taken to Step 4 of the Edit Worksheet Portlet Defaults Wizard, where we can specify parameter values. If there are no parameters associated with the Worksheet, we are taken directly to Step 5, the Portlet Settings page, where we can specify the title of the portlet (Figure 11-22).

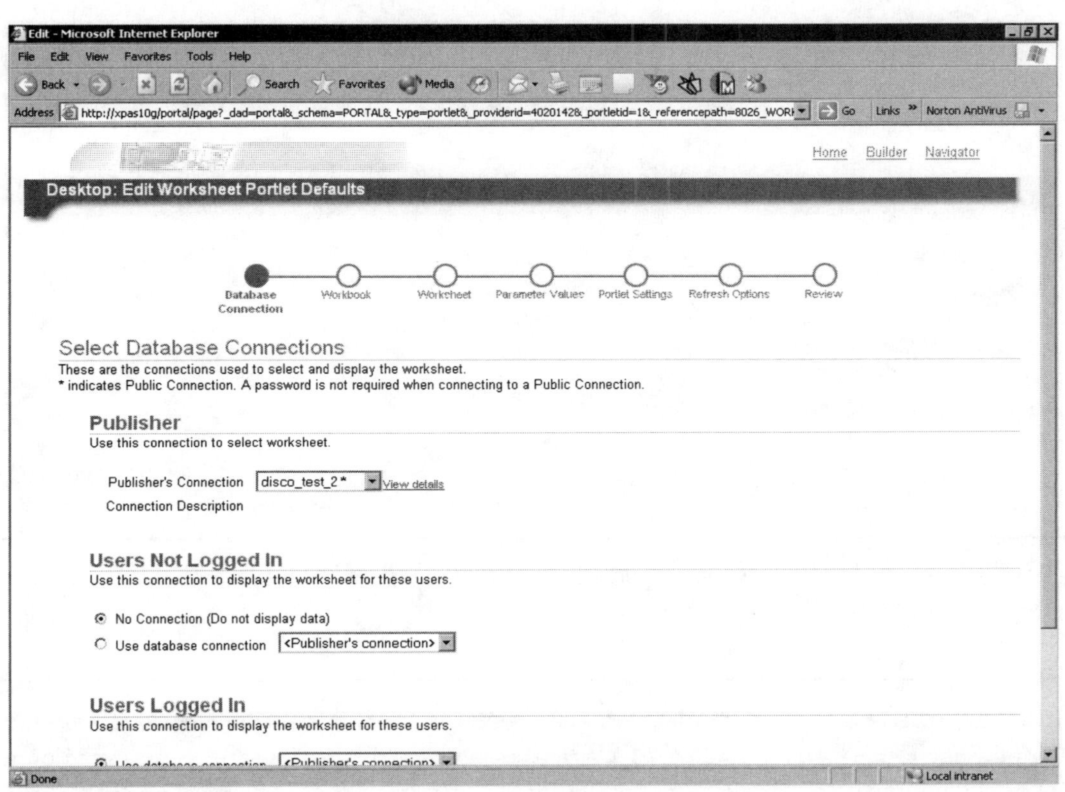

FIGURE 11-19. *The first page of the Edit Worksheet Portlet Defaults Wizard*

The sixth step, the Refresh Options page (Figure 11-23), takes a little explaining. When the page is constructed and the OracleAS Discoverer portlet is rendered, it is cached so that subsequent calls to display the page occur quickly. This may be a problem if the information on the OracleAS Discoverer portlet is dynamic and needs to be refreshed on a regular basis. You can specify a specific time or an interval to refresh the data in the OracleAS Discoverer portlet. The shortest refresh time that can be specified is one hour.

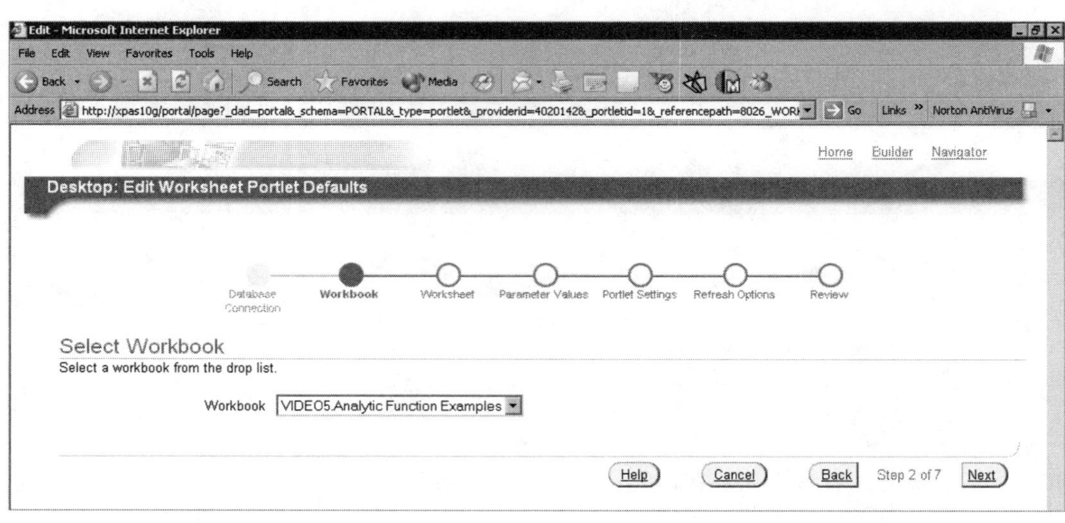

FIGURE 11-20. *The second page of the Edit Worksheet Portlet Defaults Wizard*

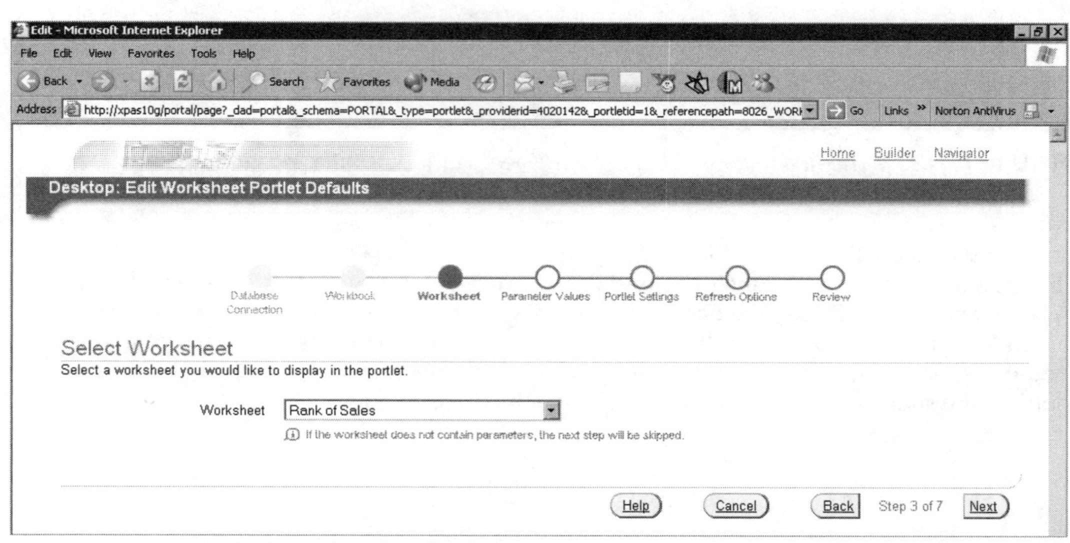

FIGURE 11-21. *The third page of the Edit Worksheet Portlet Defaults Wizard*

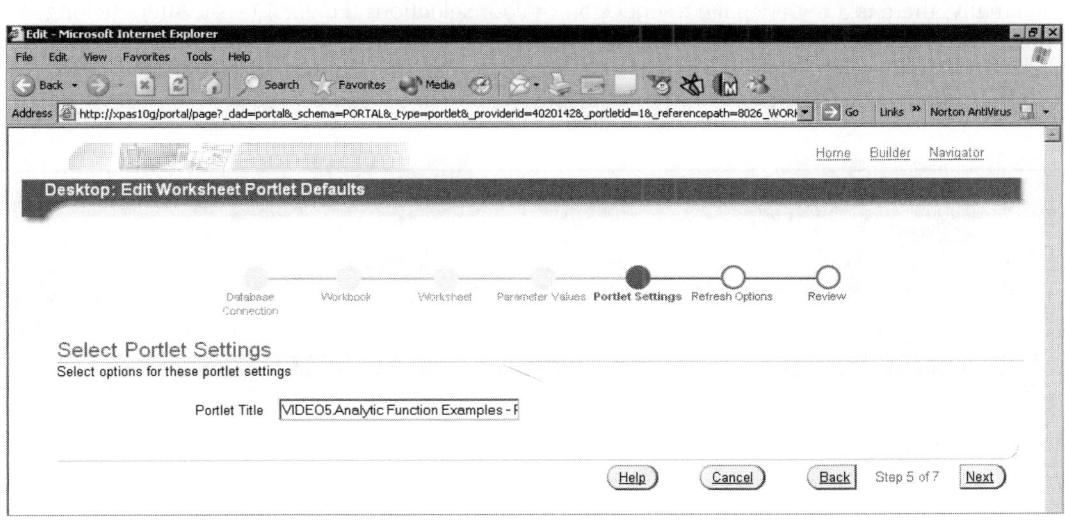

FIGURE 11-22. *The fifth page of the Edit Worksheet Portlet Defaults Wizard*

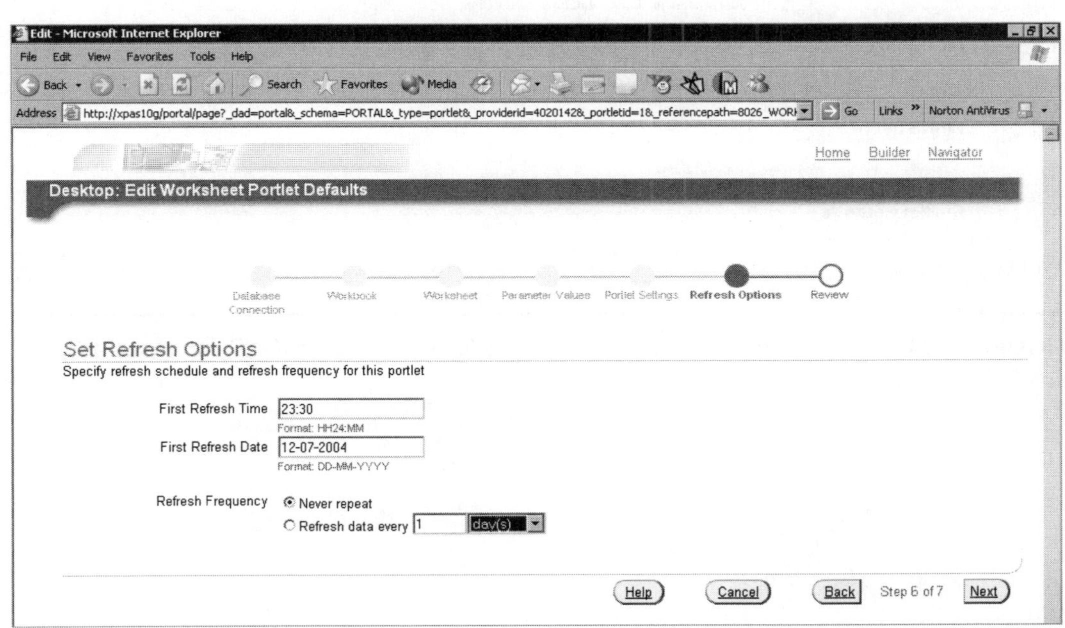

FIGURE 11-23. *The sixth page of the Edit Worksheet Portlet Defaults Wizard*

Finally, there is a review page to check all of your selections (Figure 11-24). After clicking Finish on the review screen, you can see the results of your work. You will automatically be taken back to the page layout screen. Click Graphical in the top right-hand part of the screen. You should now see the Discoverer report displayed similar to Figure 11-25.

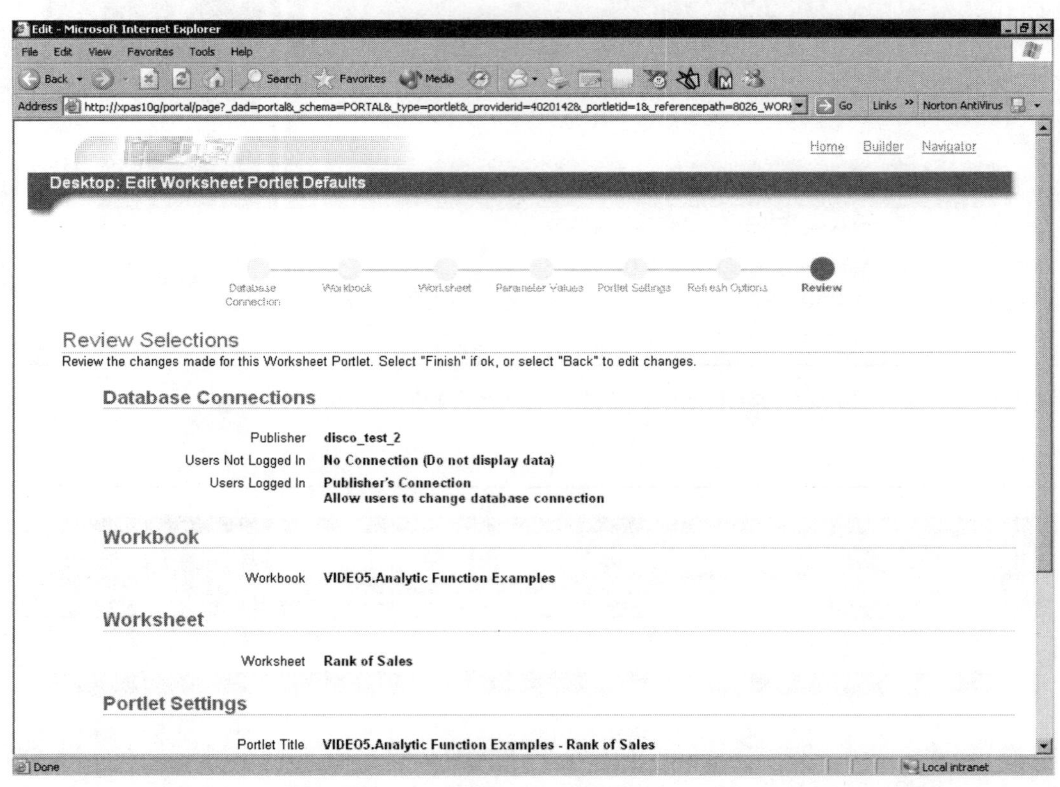

FIGURE 11-24. *The seventh and final page of the Edit Worksheet Portlet Defaults Wizard*

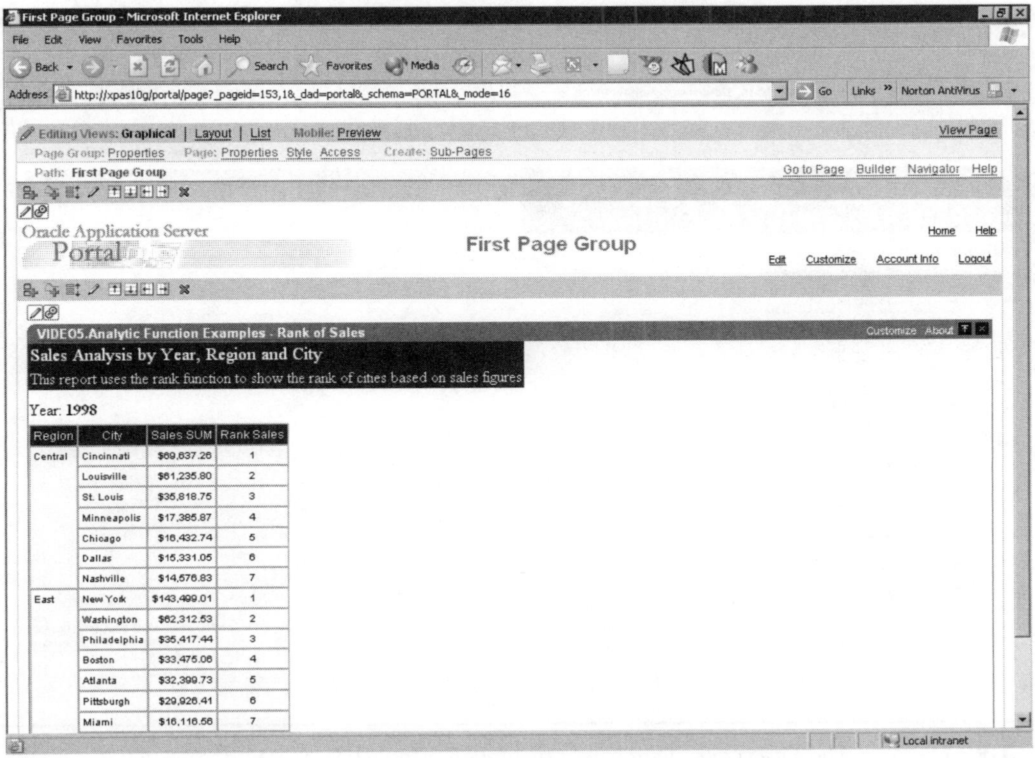

Year: 1998

Region	City	Sales SUM	Rank Sales
Central	Cincinnati	$69,637.26	1
	Louisville	$61,235.80	2
	St. Louis	$35,818.75	3
	Minneapolis	$17,385.87	4
	Chicago	$16,432.74	5
	Dallas	$15,331.05	6
	Nashville	$14,576.83	7
East	New York	$143,499.01	1
	Washington	$62,312.53	2
	Philadelphia	$35,417.44	3
	Boston	$33,475.06	4
	Atlanta	$32,399.73	5
	Pittsburgh	$29,926.41	6
	Miami	$16,116.56	7

FIGURE 11-25. *The Discoverer Worksheet displayed in graphical mode*

Click the View Page link in the top right of the screen to see how the page will look when deployed (Figure 11-26).

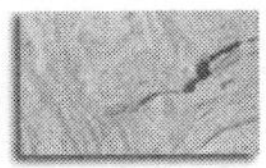

NOTE
Certain advanced OracleAS Discoverer features such as drill-downs are not available when you display your OracleAS Discoverer Worksheets in OracleAS Portal.

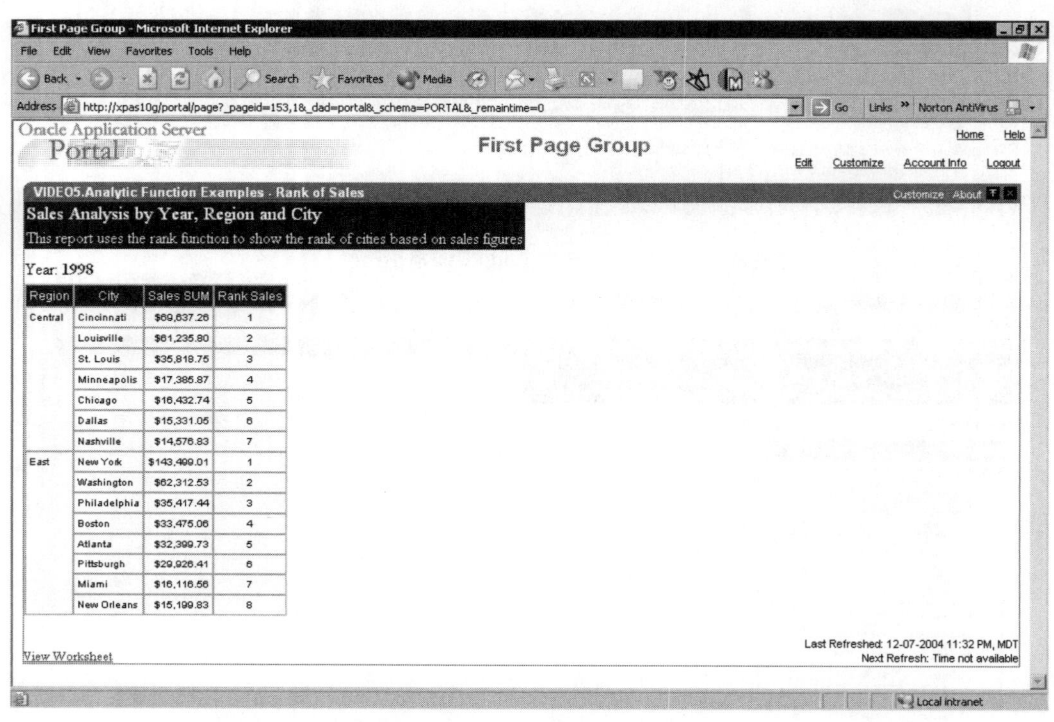

FIGURE 11-26. *The Discoverer Worksheet displayed as an OracleAS Portal portlet*

Summary

The designers of OracleAS Portal have given developers and administrators enough flexibility to incorporate non-Portal items into OracleAS Portal sites relatively easily. There is "native support" for Oracle Reports and Oracle Discoverer Worksheets, and even without "native support" for Oracle Forms, there are still methods for incorporating these Oracle Forms into OracleAS Portal. Integrating these existing components gives developers and administrators the benefit of not having to duplicate any existing development work, while gaining all of the benefits that OracleAS Portal provides.

PART IV

Java

CHAPTER 12

Java in the Oracle Database

Java, both a programming language and a platform developed by Sun Microsystems Inc., is a powerful tool for creating applications and application components at every level of a distributed architecture. Sun designed Java to be simple to learn, architecture neutral, object oriented, robust, secure, and multithreaded. Because Java is well suited for distributed application development, and has gained wide acceptance by the developer community, Oracle has made a strategic commitment to Java in the database, application server, and integrated development environments.

With a typical programming language, developers either compile a source program into native machine code, or execute the source program using an interpreter. With native machine code, a compiled program runs as fast as possible on the target platform, but it will not run on other platforms. Conversely, an interpreted program requires the overhead of an interpreter to run the program upon each invocation, and consequently runs slower than a binary executable. However, the interpreted program is portable to other platforms that support the interpreter. Java provides "write once, run anywhere" platform independence coupled with high performance because it is both compiled and interpreted.

The Java compiler reads source program instructions and creates a platform-independent program of Java bytecodes called a class file. The Java Virtual Machine (JVM) on the target platform interprets the class files at run time. Because of the overhead of the JVM, the performance of executing Java class files is inherently slower than the speed of executing native machine code. Early JVM implementations were very slow, but fortunately, vendors today design their JVM implementations for high performance. The benefits of platform-independence and increased security gained with Java outweigh the additional run-time cost.

Java packages consist of a group of related Java classes, which is similar to a schema in the Oracle database. Classes in Java are similar to packages in the database. Methods are similar to program units—i.e., procedures and functions in PL/SQL. The JVM includes many packaged classes, including the core language classes (in the java.lang package), the input/output classes (in the java.io package), relational database access classes (in the java.sql package), and so forth. Java platforms are differentiated by which packages are included in the platform.

One of the earliest uses of Java was to run programs and animated graphics within static web pages using applets. Because the client browser downloads the applet from the web server, and early implementations of the JVM were less efficient resulting in long interpretation times, Java earned a reputation of being slow. Today, most Java development is on the application and database tiers. In addition, significant improvements in JVM performance have enabled Java to prove itself as a capable language and platform for mission-critical application development. Application-tier Java uses include Enterprise JavaBeans (EJBs), servlets, JavaServer Pages (JSPs), and the SQL for Java (SQLJ) precompiler. The database tier allows the use of Java to develop stored procedures as an alternative to Procedural Language extension to Structured Query Language (PL/SQL). Because this book focuses on server-side development, this chapter only describes the use of Java in the application and database tiers.

This chapter does not teach you how to program in Java, as there are a multitude of books and tutorials dedicated to the various ways developers can write Java applications and application components. Rather, this chapter describes how to employ Java to develop server-side applications using the Oracle database and application server.

Because this book teaches Oracle web development and is aimed primarily at developers, it is assumed that most readers are Oracle developers and are already knowledgeable in programming PL/SQL. For PL/SQL programmers who are new to Java, this chapter starts with a section describing the basics of Java, and includes a comparison of the syntax and features of PL/SQL to Java. Programmers already comfortable with programming in Java can skip the introduction, or review the section to reinforce their knowledge.

Specifically, this chapter covers the following topics:

- Getting started with Java
- Java for the PL/SQL Developer
- Oracle's Java Virtual Machine (JVM)
- Java Database Connectivity (JDBC)
- SQLJ
- Java Stored Procedures
- DBMS_JAVA package
- Oracle Business Components for Java (OC4J): servlets, JavaServer Pages (JSPs), and Enterprise JavaBeans (EJBs)

There are many aspects of the Java programming language and entire books (often 1,000+ pages in length) have been written about them. While it is impossible to devote space to all of these technologies, we have made every effort to discuss what we feel are the most prevalent topics related to Oracle-based Java application development. This chapter discusses the fundamentals of the Java language. Chapter 13, while discussing Oracle's Java development tool, JDeveloper 10g, also touches on advanced Java topics such as Oracle's Application Development Framework (ADF), UIX (an extensible, J2EE-based framework for building web applications), and Oracle's Business Components for Java (BC4J). At the end of Chapter 14, is a listing of resources you can use to enhance your Java knowledge.

Getting Started with Java

The Java compiler is part of the Java Software Development Kit (SDK), formerly known as the Java Development Kit (JDK). The Java interpreter and JVM are part of the Java Run-time Environment (JRE). Both the Java SDK and JRE for various hardware platforms are available as a free download from http://java.sun.com.

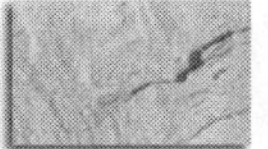

TIP

If you have access to a computer running an Oracle 8i Database or later, or an Oracle 9i Application Server or later, you may already have the software development kit available to you. To determine if the Java SDK was included in the Oracle installation, look for the jdk directory below the Oracle installation directory. If the jdk directory exists, ensure that <ORACLE_HOME>/ jdk/bin is in your executable search path.

Even if you have the Java compiler and run-time environment available, Sun's Java web site contains a wealth of information including the entire API specification for each release, tutorials and tools to assist in developing Java programs, and sample programs.

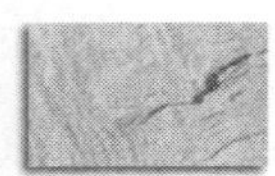

NOTE
Even though the software development kit is now the Java SDK, some developers and manuals, including the Oracle documentation, still refer to the software development kit as the JDK.

J2EE, J2SE, and J2ME Platforms

When selecting the version of the Java SDK to download, you need to choose between the J2EE, J2SE, and J2ME platforms. Each of these three editions contains a different set of packages, or APIs, to develop Java programs. The first two characters, "J2," stand for Java platform 2, which includes versions 1.2 and later of the Java SDK, and the fourth character, "E," simply stands for Edition. The third character, "E," "S," or "M," determines which libraries the download includes.

J2EE is the Enterprise Edition that contains the most libraries, and supports building enterprise-class server-side applications. J2SE is the Standard Edition that contains the tools to develop Java applets and applications. J2ME is the Micro Edition that contains a highly optimized run-time environment for deploying applications to consumer products such as cellular phones, Personal Digital Assistants (PDAs), and car navigation systems. If you are unsure which platform to choose, select the J2SE platform as it contains all of the tools you need to start learning Java.

Installing and Testing the Installation

Installing the Java SDK is as simple as running the downloaded executable file and following the installation prompts for both Windows and Unix platforms. For Unix platforms, first turn on the executable bit using the chmod +x command before running the downloaded executable file, and upon the completion of the installation, add the <INSTALL>/bin directory to your class path. The class path is an environment variable named CLASSPATH where Java programs search for dependent objects. For Unix installations, the class path is typically set in a run code script such as .profile or .cshrc, and for Windows installations the class path is set using the System Properties within the Control Panel.

To test the installation, create a small Java program named Hello.java using your favorite text editor. Do not worry if you do not understand all of the pieces of this program at this time; this step is only to verify the installation of the Java SDK.

```
public class Hello {
   public static void main(String[] args) {
      System.out.println("hello, world");
   }
}
```

At a command prompt, compile the program into Java bytecodes using the Java compiler javac.

```
prompt> javac Hello.java
```

If there are no errors, the compiler writes a class file named Hello.class in the same directory as your source code file. Test your JVM by running the Java interpreter java using the new class file. Note that you do not include the .class extension when running the interpreter.

```
prompt> java Hello
hello, world
```

Running the class file on any JVM produces the same results. For example, if the class file was created on a Windows platform, you can perform a binary transfer of the file to a Unix platform and run the same java command using the same class file, and the program will run perfectly.

Checking the Java Virtual Machine Version

You can verify the version of the JVM installed by passing the –version parameter to the interpreter:

```
prompt> java -version
java version "1.3.1_01"
Java(TM) 2 Runtime Environment, Standard Edition (build 1.3.1_01)
Java HotSpot(TM) Client VM (build 1.3.1_01, mixed mode)
```

There is no equivalent parameter for the Java compiler.

Integrated Development Environments

As shown in the installation test, all that you need to develop and compile a Java program is a text editor and the Java compiler. Once you become comfortable developing Java applications, you will most likely want to use an Integrated Development Environment (IDE) to simplify program development. IDEs provide useful features such as syntax highlighting, quick access to different source files, wizards to create template code for common program types, an interactive debugger, and source code control. IDEs will even point out errors in your program, such as not catching exceptions or mismatched braces, before you attempt to compile the program.

There is no shortage of capable IDEs to assist in your Java development, and Oracle's JDeveloper is a powerful IDE described in Chapter 13.

Java for the PL/SQL Developer

If you are a PL/SQL programmer and are new to Java, comparing the syntax and structure of a language you already know to a new language may help you get started with adding Java to your pool of programming skills. In many ways, matching PL/SQL up to Java is an "apples to oranges" comparison; however, as with all general purpose programming languages, there are also many things in common.

After reading this section, PL/SQL programmers will understand the basic differences between PL/SQL and Java. If you are already a knowledgeable Java programmer, you can either skip this section, or continue reading to refresh your Java knowledge.

Learning Java

As a PL/SQL developer, you may wonder if you need to learn how to program in Java. Because developers write entire applications in Java, as well as components at every tier of the application architecture, knowing how to program in Java is an important skill for all Oracle developers. Even though Oracle continues to improve PL/SQL, it is nonetheless a proprietary language. Java is not proprietary, and is useful in developing programs on a variety of platforms. As more business logic moves out of the database tier and into a middle tier, PL/SQL will play less of a role in new application development.

This is not to say that you should write all future programs in Java rather than PL/SQL. On the contrary, there are many tasks where PL/SQL is a more suitable programming language than Java, such as ones with heavy data manipulation. Rather, Java is another tool that a programmer can choose from when developing software.

Although PL/SQL now contains object-oriented features, the structure of a typical PL/SQL program is top-down programming. In contrast, Java is a pure object-oriented language, and as such is more difficult to learn. While the syntax of Java is relatively simple to learn, the difficult part is modeling objects in an efficient and clear manner. C and C++ programmers will instantly notice that the syntax and structure of Java programs closely resembles these languages, and all of the efficient constructs such as x++ (add 1 to x), y+=z (add z to y), and (a>b)?a:b (determine the greater of a and b) are available in Java as well. Java is especially similar to C++, the object-oriented version of C, but with important differences such as no pointers, no multiple inheritance, and automatic memory allocation and garbage collection.

Object-Oriented Program Features

Object-oriented programming languages, including Java, share several features that demonstrate the capabilities of developing in objects. Well-designed objects perform discrete functions and are often reusable, such that a specific function is only in one object. In many respects, designing an object-oriented application is analogous to normalizing a data model.

Features of all object-oriented languages include:

- **Classes** A program unit, consisting of attributes and methods.
- **Constructor methods** Code that is automatically executed when memory is allocated for an object.
- **Encapsulation** The capability to protect attributes and methods so that calling programs cannot access the attributes and methods directly.
- **Inheritance** Allows classes to be built in a hierarchical fashion.
- **Packages** A group of related classes.
- **Polymorphism** The capability of an object to respond to the same message in specific ways: Objects can have different implementations of the same message.

PL/SQL supports some, but not all of these features, as described below.

Classes

Java programs, as with all object-oriented languages, use templates called classes that define objects having common characteristics. The concept of a class is a difficult topic for programmers to learn who are new to object-oriented thinking, as there is no equivalent construct in top-down programming. On the plus side, once you understand the concept of a class, you are well on your way to being an object-oriented programmer.

In general, classes are object templates that contain either or both of the following:

- **Attributes** Attributes are similar to variables in PL/SQL. The data type for an attribute is either a native data type or a class.
- **Methods** Methods are similar to procedures and functions in PL/SQL. Methods either return a data type (as with PL/SQL functions), or use the keyword void specifying that no data type is returned (as with PL/SQL procedures).

Java programs allocate memory for objects defined by a class using a process called instantiation. An attribute or "object variable" stores the reference to the object, and the object holds the data for a single occurrence of the class. A program can create multiple instances of the same class. A small example is a purchase order class that defines all of the characteristics and business functions for a purchase order, and purchase order 1000 is a physical instance of the purchase order class.

In many ways, a class is like a PL/SQL package, as packages also contain variables, stored procedures, and functions. However, in other ways, a class is like a table, as each instance of the class contains data for one table row (a class can also be an entire table—i.e., a vector).

For example, attributes shapeSquare and shapeTriangle both store references to objects defined by the Shape class; in other words, the data type of both attributes is a Shape object. Attributes whose data type is an object are instantiated by using the `new` keyword. This following class example also contains an attribute named area whose data type is a native Java double-precision floating-point number. The Shape class contains a method named calcArea that does not take any parameters.

```
public class MyShapes {
   public static void main(String args[]) {
      Shape  shapeSquare   = new Shape("square",3.0);
      Shape  shapeTriangle = new Shape("triangle",2.0,4.0);
      double area;
      area = shapeSquare.calcArea();
      System.out.println("area of the square equals " + area);
   }
}
```

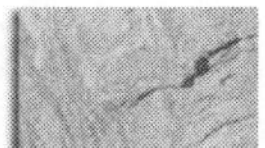

NOTE
Before the Java purists get upset with me, note that there is a better way to do this, as we'll see below. We will build off of this example.

It is important to notice the use of capitalization in the MyShapes class example. Unlike PL/SQL, Java is case-sensitive, and Java keywords such as public, class, new, and double must be lowercase. By convention, capitalize the first letter of every word within a class name; for example, MyShapes. Also by convention, capitalize the first letter of every word within an attribute and method name, except for the first letter. Attributes shapeSquare and shapeTriangle, and the Shape method getArea demonstrate this convention.

Another difference between PL/SQL and Java variables is the use of quotes around string values. Whereas PL/SQL requires single quotes around strings, Java requires double quotes. In Java, as in C, single quotes define a character.

Constructor Methods

All Java methods support parameter overloading, where the class contains multiple versions of the same method, and the parameters passed to the method determine which version of the method to execute. Consequently, each class may contain one or more constructor methods, often referred to as constructors. Recall that constructors are methods that the JVM executes automatically when an object is instantiated, and are useful for initializing variables and environment setup. Within a class, constructors have the same name as the class name, and do not specify a return data type. All other methods within the class must specify a return data type, where methods that do not return a value specify void for the return data type.

Upon instantiation of an object, the JVM automatically executes the constructor matching the parameter list passed using the new statement. Multiple constructors are a way to set default values for parameter values. A constructor with fewer parameters usually calls another constructor using the keyword "this," a system variable that contains a reference to the class itself, passing in default values for the missing parameters.

In the MyShapes class example, the Shape constructor for the shapeSquare attribute receives two parameters, a string, and a double precision floating-point number. For shapes such as squares, both the width and height dimensions require the same value, so the constructor only requires one dimension parameter. The Shape constructor for the shapeTriangle attribute requires three parameters, a string, and separate numbers for the width and height values.

The Shape class contains the two required constructors. This example demonstrates how the first constructor calls the second constructor with the same value for the second and third parameters.

```
public class Shape {
   private String shapeName;
   private double width, height;
   public Shape(String s,double x) {          // First constructor
     // Call the second constructor passing the same String parameter,
     // and the double parameter for the second and third parameters
     this(s,x,x);
   }
   public Shape(String s,double x,double y) { // Second constructor
      shapeName = new String(s);
      width     = x;
      height    = y;
   }
   public double calcArea() {
      if (shapeName.equals("square")) {
         return width * height;
      } else if (shapeName.equals("triangle")) {
         return (width / 2.0) * height;
      } else { // unknown shape
         return 0;
      }
   }
}
```

Similar to constructors, PL/SQL package bodies can contain an initialization part that the Relational Database Management System (RDBMS) automatically executes the first time a user session references the package. Because you cannot directly execute a PL/SQL package, only procedures and functions within the package, you cannot pass parameters to, or overload, the initialization part.

```
CREATE OR REPLACE PACKAGE my_shapes AS
   FUNCTION calc_area RETURN NUMBER;
END my_shapes;

CREATE OR REPLACE PACKAGE BODY my_shapes AS
   shape_name VARCHAR2(20);
   width      NUMBER(10,2);
   height     NUMBER(10,2);
   - Initialization part
   width  := 0;
   height := 0;
```

```
   FUNCTION calc_area RETURN NUMBER ...
END my_shapes;
```

Some object-oriented languages also have destructor methods, known as destructors, which execute automatically when destroying or freeing an object. Because Java automatically handles memory allocation, there is no built-in support for destructors within Java classes.

Encapsulation

Encapsulation provides the capability to control which attributes and methods within a class other methods can access. This capability allows the program to control the values set to the attributes, providing an added level of data integrity.

Java uses three keywords to encapsulate classes, attributes, and methods:

- **public** Allows access to attributes and methods by any calling program
- **protected** Allows access only by related methods
- **private** Attributes defined as private within a class are only accessible by methods within the class; methods defined as private within a class are not accessible by the calling program

If an attribute or method does not contain one of these three keywords, the attribute or method has the default package access. To state it another way, the attribute or method is accessible by all other classes within the same package, and not accessible by classes on other packages.

In addition to data integrity, this control also reduces the interdependence between classes. A developer can change the private and protected attributes and methods within a class without affecting other classes, given other classes cannot directly access these attributes and methods.

In the Shape class example, the shapeName, width, and height attributes are all private. The MyShape class example cannot reference these variable values directly. On the other hand, the calcArea method is public, so the MyShape class example can execute this method.

PL/SQL packages provide a similar scheme to encapsulate variables, functions, and procedures. The package specification exposes the public variables, and function and procedure prototypes, that calling programs can access. Variables, functions, and procedures defined only in the package body are private, and are not accessible by the calling programs.

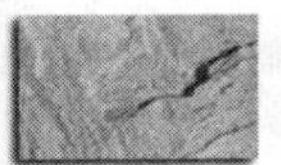

TIP
Oracle schemas and grants are similar to Java's "public" and "private." They indicate who can "get" to the objects.

Inheritance

The use of inheritance is a powerful object-oriented characteristic to implement a class hierarchy, and a properly designed class hierarchy is essential in creating modular, reusable objects. A derived, or child, class includes all of the attributes and methods of the parent, or base, class. A calling program that instantiates a derived class has access to the public attributes and methods of the derived class, plus the public attributes and methods of the ancestors of the derived class. If necessary, a derived class can redefine (known as overriding) a method in an ancestor class by defining the method in the derived class with the same name and parameter list.

Java uses the keyword `extends` to specify that the class will inherit the attributes and methods of the base class. The example below modifies the Shape class example to replace the constructors with a single default constructor that does not take any parameters, and removes all the variables and the calcArea method from the Shape class. Using inheritance, each derived shape class has its own of dimension attributes and area calculation method.

Also, add the keyword `abstract` to both the Shape class specification and the calcArea method specification. An abstract class restricts calling programs from directly instantiating an object of that class, forcing calling programs to instantiate one of the derived classes instead. Because the Shape class is an abstract class, you can also require that all derived classes code a calcArea method that returns a double precision floating-point number by placing the prototype of the calcArea method, without any code, in the Shape class template. Knowing that all nonabstract subclasses of this class will have the required calcArea() method has important implications for polymorphism, discussed in the next section.

```
public abstract class Shape {
   public Shape() {}                      // Default constructor
   public abstract double calcArea(); // Derived classes must implement
}
public class Square extends Shape {
   private double width;
   public Square(double x) {
      width = x;
   }
   public double calcArea() {
      return width * width;
   }
}
public class Triangle extends Shape {
   private double width, height;
   public Triangle(double x,double y) {
      width = x;
      height = y;
   }
   public double calcArea() {
      return (width / 2.0) * height;
   }
}
```

While there is no definitive "right" or "wrong" way to code in Java, most experienced Java developers would acknowledge that this code is closer to the "spirit" of the Java language.

It is easy to see how adding new shapes does not require any additional changes to the base Shape class, and how all attributes and methods specific to each shape are in their own objects. PL/SQL packages do not support inheritance, although Oracle object types, the equivalent of classes, provide this capability.

Polymorphism

Polymorphism builds on inheritance to allow the developer to create an attribute of a base class, but instantiate the attribute with a derived object. Building on the inheritance example where the Square and Triangle classes extend the Shape class, a single attribute can reference either a

Square or a Triangle object. This is a powerful object-oriented feature that significantly reduces the number of attributes and control statements required. Without polymorphism, the calling program would have to declare separate attributes to hold either a Square or a Triangle object. Although this example only has two possible objects, it is easy to imagine hundreds or thousands of possible objects, each requiring a separate attribute.

To demonstrate this feature, replace the MyShapes class with an example using a single attribute named shape whose data type is the base Shape class.

```
public class MyShapes {
   public static void main(String args[]) {
      Shape  shape;
      double area;
      // Instantiate a Square object into a Shape attribute
      shape = new Square(3);
      area = shapeSquare.calcArea();
      System.out.println("area of the square equals " + area);
   }
}
```

Because the Shape class is an abstract class that requires a calcArea method, the calling program is sure that regardless of what object derived from the Shape class the program instantiates into the shape attribute, the object will have a calcArea() method that returns a double precision floating-point number.

Polymorphism allows for easy processing of all Shape subclasses. For example, if you have an array of Shape subclass objects named shapeList, you could easily sum the areas of all shapes within the array. Without polymorphism, the same calculation would require an IF statement with a test for each type of shape, and would have to change whenever a developer created a new Shape subclass.

```
int totalArea = 0;
for (int i = 0;i < shapeList.size();i++)
   totalArea += ((Shape)shapeList.get(i)).calcArea();
```

In Java, you can raise specific exceptions that must be handled by the calling method; you can't do this in PL/SQL.

Oracle's Java Virtual Machine

Sun Microsystems furnishes the Java Compatibility Kit (JCK) to allow JVM vendors to ensure that their implementations meet the requirements for how the JVM compiles the bytecodes into native machine code. The Oracle Database and Application Server both contain the Oracle JVM, which Oracle has fully tested with the JCK.

The Oracle Database 10*g* Release 1 (10.1) includes version 1.4.1 of the Java Standard Edition platform, also known as the Enterprise Java Engine (EJE).

NOTE
Oracle 8i uses the 1.2 of the JVM; Oracle 9i uses 1.3 of the JVM.

The Oracle10*g* Application Server (9.0.4) includes version 1.3 of the Java Enterprise Edition platform. There is no way to change the version of the JVM other than upgrading to a new version of Oracle or applying an Oracle-supplied patch, if a patch is available. When developing Java programs that execute using the JVM in the database or the application server, you should use a version of the Java development platform that is the same or older than the version of the Oracle JVM.

Three major differences between the Oracle JVM and a typical client JVM are

- *main() method.* As shown in the previous examples, a standalone Java application, as with a C program, must contain a single method named main() that is the entry point to the application. Java programs within the database are not standalone applications; rather they are just methods that you can execute individually. Therefore, no main() method is required.
- *Graphical user interface (GUI).* The Oracle 10g Database supports the headless Abstract Windowing Toolkit (AWT). The Oracle JVM now includes the AWT classes, and your programs can manipulate graphical objects, such as using fonts and preparing printouts, as long as the programs do not attempt to display the GUI on the database server. For security reasons, the Oracle JVM cannot interact with the display and input hardware on the server where the Oracle Database is running.
- *The Java language allows applications to create multiple threads to increase scalability.* Developing multithreaded applications introduces another level of complexity, as the operating system is free to swap threads in and out of main memory as needed, which can lead to unexpected variable values if not properly controlled. One of the advantages of using the Oracle JVM is that the task scheduler built within the RDBMS efficiently handles thousands of simultaneous connections, and therefore provides for scalability without the use of multiple threads. Coding multiple-threaded applications in database programs does not increase scalability, and may hurt performance as the garbage collection process is less efficient.

JDBC

JDBC is an API included in the J2SE and J2EE platforms that provides access to a variety of data sources, typically relational database management systems such as Oracle, within Java programs. Sun Microsystems introduced JDBC in January 1997 as a standardized way to query and update data in the data sources. A common belief is that JDBC stands for "Java Database Connectivity" although Sun's JDBC specification does not list a definition of the abbreviation.

The JDBC API consists of two packages:

- **java.sql** Classes and interfaces to connect to data sources; process SQL statements that retrieve data into result sets; insert, update, and delete data; and execute stored procedures
- **javax.sql** Classes and interfaces for advanced server-side processing features, such as connection pooling and distributed transactions

The Oracle JDBC drivers also provide packages containing Oracle-specific extensions. The Oracle JDBC extension packages are

- oracle.sql

- oracle.jdbc
- oracle.jdbc.pool

To access the JDBC API in your program without having to specify the package name, use the import keyword to define the packages, classes, or interfaces you wish to reference before declaring the class. For example:

```
import java.sql.*;
public class MyClass {
}
```

JDBC Driver Types

Each underlying data source requires a Java Database Connectivity (JDBC) driver. The data source vendors as well as third parties develop JDBC drivers to allow Java programs to access data in the data source. Sun maintains a searchable database of available drivers, and a quick query shows 36 drivers are available to access Oracle databases. The search results show the driver type, and the version of the JDBC specification the driver supports. J2SE 1.4.1 and J2EE 1.3 both include JDBC 3.0.

There are four types of JDBC drivers. When selecting a driver, make sure the selected driver is of the driver type that best meets your individual needs.

- **Map to another data access API** The JDBC driver maps calls to another data access API, such as Open Database Connectivity (ODBC). One such Type 1 driver is the JDBC-ODBC Bridge that is included in the Java SDK. On Windows platforms, the Bridge can provide JDBC access to data sources using an existing ODBC connection. Due to its limited feature set, only use the JDBC-ODBC Bridge for experimenting with JDBC, or if no other JDBC driver is available.
- **Native-API partly Java** The JDBC driver converts the SQL statements to the equivalent calls for the native API on the client, such as the Oracle Call Interface (OCI).
- **Net-protocol fully Java** Net server middleware allows the same Java clients to access data in different data sources. The JDBC driver converts the SQL statements into a DBMS-independent protocol, which the middleware server converts to the specific DBMS protocol.
- **Native-protocol fully java** Allows for direct calls from a client to a server without requiring the data source native libraries, such as SQL*Net, to be installed on the client.

Oracle JDBC Drivers

Oracle Database 10*g* provides four JDBC drivers, three of which were available in prior Oracle releases. According to the Oracle documentation, Oracle has restructured all JDBC drivers from previous releases to improve performance. The four drivers are

- OCI driver
- Thin driver

- Server-Side Thin driver
- Server-Side Internal driver

Oracle JDBC drivers are available to download from the Oracle Technology Network at http://otn.oracle.com. If you have installed the Oracle Database Client software, the drivers are in <ORACLE_HOME>/jdbc/lib directory. The common Oracle JDBC drivers are

- **ojdbc14.jar** Java SDK 1.4
- **classes12.jar** Java SDK 1.2 and 1.3
- **classes111.jar** JDK 1.1 (Not supported with Oracle 10*g*)

In prior Oracle releases, the JDBC drivers were also available in ZIP archives. Starting with Oracle 10*g*, all JDBC drivers are only available in Java Archive (JAR) format.

OCI Driver

The Oracle OCI driver, also known as the fat (or thick) driver, is a Type 2 driver. Client/server Java programs using the OCI driver must have Net8 and the appropriate shared libraries installed; therefore, the OCI driver is best suited for server-side applications such as servlets. For client applications using the OCI driver, Oracle recommends installing the Oracle Database client software instead of the shared libraries separately. The following is an example of using the OCI driver:

```
Connection conn = DriverManager.getConnection
  ("jdbc:oracle:oci:@myhost:1521:inst1", "scott", "tiger);
```

Thin Driver

The Oracle Thin driver is a 100-percent Java Type 4 driver. The Thin driver is ideal for writing 100-percent pure Java applications, such as web-based and client-side applications where the client does not have Net8 installed. Instead, the Thin driver connects to the server using a protocol named TTC (Two-Task Common—a presentation layer type that is used in a typical Oracle Net connection to provide character set and data type conversion between different character sets or formats on the client and server) that Oracle developed to access an Oracle database. Data access using the Thin driver is slower than that using the OCI driver, but the applications are smaller and do not require the client-side Net8 installation.

If you are writing an application that must be portable, and does not require the OCI-specific features such as support for networks other than TCP/IP, use the Thin driver. In addition, applets can only use the Thin driver. The following is an example of using the Thin driver:

```
Connection conn = DriverManager.getConnection
  ("jdbc:oracle:thin:@//myhost:1521/orcl", "scott", "tiger");
```

Server-Side Thin Driver

The Server-Side Thin driver is new with Oracle Database 10*g*. It has the same functionality as the client Thin driver, but runs inside an Oracle database instead of a client machine. The benefit of this new driver is that it can access other Oracle databases, or different sessions within the same database.

NOTE
The Server-Side Thin driver is only available through Java Stored Procedures (JSProcs).

Using the Server-Side Thin driver opens a socket connection, and therefore requires granting access to the java.net.SocketPermission object to the users whose accounts open connections using the driver. You should create a role to group the user accounts that can create the socket connections. For example:

```
CREATE ROLE JDBCTHIN;
CALL dbms_java.grant_permission(
   'JDBCTHIN','java.net.SocketPermission','*','connect');
GRANT JDBCTHIN TO <user>;
```

Later in this chapter, the "DBMS_JAVA Package" section lists all of the procedures and functions within the DBMS_JAVA package.

Server-Side Internal Driver

The specially tuned Server-Side Internal driver is fully compatible with Sun's JDBC specification. Java stored procedures call the internal driver for quick access to the local database. It is used for code that runs inside the target server; that is, inside the Oracle server that it must access. The Server-Side Internal driver type is kprb and it actually runs within a default session. The connection should never be closed, as you are already "connected."

To access the default connection, use the Oracle-specific defaultConnection() method of the OracleDriver class:

```
OracleDriver ora = new OracleDriver();

Connection conn = ora.defaultConnection();
```

Using JDBC

Historically, accessing data sources in Java programs using JDBC involved registering the vendor-provided JDBC driver with the driver manager class. Once the JDBC driver is registered, you can establish connections to the data sources known to the driver manager, and use the connections to run queries and execute stored procedures.

More recently, the preferred method is to use standard, general-use objects for identifying databases and other sources of data called *datasources*. You can establish a database connection using datasources by specifying all connection information, similar to using the driver manager class. Alternatively, you create a connection to a datasource registered with the Java Naming and Directory Interface (JNDI).

JNDI allows for the use of logical names to locate resource such as databases, instead of requiring vendor-specific syntax in the application code. Instead, the vendor-specific syntax is only required when registering the datasource with JNDI. Typically, an administrator, instead of an application developer, creates the JNDI datasources. To connect to an Oracle datasource using JNDI, you must add jndi.jar to the class path.

Creating a Connection Using a Datasource

JDBC datasources are instances of a class that implements the DataSource interface in the javax.sql package. Each version of the getConnection() method returns a Connection object representing a connection to the database or other data resource. Several setter and getter methods are available to set and retrieve the properties required by the datasource. Table 12-1 lists the standard properties and the corresponding getter and setter methods.

You can also pass the values for user and password through the getConnection() call, which if set, overrides the corresponding properties.

Oracle provides an implementation of this interface using the OracleDataSource class in the oracle.jdbc.pool package. The implementation includes additional Oracle-specific properties. Table 12-2 lists the common Oracle-specific properties and the corresponding getter and setter methods. (Refer to the Oracle Database JDBC Developer's Guide and Reference (Oracle Part number: B10979-02) for a complete listing of all Oracle-specific datasource properties.)

The allowable driverType property values are thin for the Oracle Thin driver, oci for the Oracle OCI driver, or kprb for the Server-Side internal driver. If the driverType property equals kprb, the object ignores all other property settings.

To connect to an Oracle database using a datasource, import the oracle.jdbc.pool package into your program and instantiate an object of the OracleDataSource class. After instantiating the datasource object, set the appropriate property values and execute the Oracle datasource getConnection() method.

As an example, the following code uses the Oracle Thin JDBC driver to establish a database connection. The orcl database resides on the oski server and listens on port 1521.

```
try {
   OracleDataSource oracleDataSource = new OracleDataSource();
   oracleDataSource.setNetworkProtocol("tcp");
   oracleDataSource.setDriverType("thin");
   oracleDataSource.setServerName("oski");
   oracleDataSource.setPortNumber(1521);
   oracleDataSource.setDatabaseName("orcl");
   Connection conn = oracleDataSource.getConnection("scott","tiger");
} catch (SQLException e) {
   System.err.println("error:  cannot establish database connection");
   e.printStackTrace();
   System.exit(1);
}
```

This is not the recommended practice, however—using DataSources and JNDI is the preferred route for sure. Connections to the database using datasources registered with JNDI are much simpler and do not require vendor-specific coding. For example, if the JNDI administrator has created a datasource named oskidb within the jdbc naming subcontext of the JNDI namespace hierarchy, you can instantiate a Connection object using the datasource by:

```
Context ctx = new InitialContext();
OracleDataSource oracleDataSource =
   (OracleDataSource)ctx.lookup("jdbc/oskidb");
Connection conn = oracleDataSource.getConnection();
```

javax.sql.DataSource Property	Setter Method	Getter Method
DatabaseName	void setDatabaseName(String s)	String getDatabaseName()
DataSourceName	void setDataSourceName(String s)	String getDataSourceName()
Description	void setDescription(String s)	String getDescription()
NetworkProtocol	void setNetworkProtocol(String s)	String getNetworkProtocol()
Password	void setPassword(String s)	<none>
PortNumber	void setPortNumber(int i)	int getPortNumber()
ServerName	void setServerName(String s)	String getServerName()
User	void setUser(String s)	String getUser()

TABLE 12-1. *DataSource Properties and Methods*

To make this work, you will need to edit the data-sources.xml file, found in the $ORACLE_HOME/j2ee/<OC4J Container>/config directory. As an example, the following code listing is from the default data-sources.xml provided for the OC4J_BI_FORMS container:

```
<data-source
     class="com.evermind.sql.DriverManagerDataSource"
     name="OracleDS"
     location="jdbc/OracleCoreDS"
     xa-location="jdbc/xa/OracleXADS"
     ejb-location="jdbc/OracleDS"
     connection-driver="oracle.jdbc.driver.OracleDriver"
     username="scott"
     password="tiger"
     url="jdbc:oracle:thin:@localhost:5521:oracle"
     inactivity-timeout="30"
/>
```

oracle.jdbc.pool. OracleDataSource Property	Setter Method	Getter Method
connectionCacheProperties	void setConnectionCacheProperties (java.util.properties p)	java.util.properties getConnectionCacheProperties()
DriverType	void setDriverType(String s)	String getDriverType()
url	void setURL(String s)	String getURL()

TABLE 12-2. *OracleDataSource Common Properties and Methods*

The third line:

```
name="OracleDS"
```

defines the name of this data source.

Creating a Connection Using the Driver Manager

As we mentioned earlier, registering the driver with the driver manager is an older way of using JDBC. This technique requires specifying the Oracle JDBC driver name and connection information within a program, tying the program to a specific database vendor. However, because of its widespread use, the technique is included in this section.

The java.lang.Class class in Java provides information about the class itself, and enables the capability of dynamic class loading using a variable class name value. You can call the forName() method passing the class name to dynamically load an object of the specified class. If the program cannot locate the class file corresponding to the parameter, the forName() method throws a ClassNotFoundException exception.

All JDBC drivers are required to implement the Driver interface, and the implementation must contain a static constructor that registers a new instance of itself with the DriverManager interface. The DriverManager interface tracks all of the JDBC drivers available to your program.

The JDBC driver documentation provides the name of the driver class file, and should provide a code sample. The driver class name for both the Oracle OCI and the Oracle Thin driver classes is oracle.jdbc.driver.OracleDriver. For example, the following code dynamically loads the Oracle JDBC driver and registers the driver with the driver manager.

```
try {
   Class.forName("oracle.jdbc.driver.OracleDriver");
} catch (ClassNotFoundException e) {
   System.err.println("error:  cannot locate Oracle JDBC driver");
   e.printStackTrace();
   System.exit(1);
}
```

The DriverManager interface also provides a static registerDriver() method as an alternate approach for registering the JDBC driver. If this method is used, trap a SQLException instead of a ClassNotFoundException. For example:

```
try {
   DriverManager.registerDriver(new oracle.jdbc.driver.OracleDriver());
} catch (SQLException e) {
   System.err.println("error:  cannot locate Oracle JDBC driver");
   e.printStackTrace();
   System.exit(1);
}
```

Make sure the JDBC driver is located in the class path, and after you successfully register the driver with the driver manager, you are ready to connect your Java program to an Oracle database. The DriverManager class contains several versions of the getConnection() method to establish a database connection using a JDBC driver registered with the driver manager. The getConnection() methods accept a URL containing the details of how to connect to the database.

As with the driver class name, the driver documentation should include the format of the URL string. The getConnection() method returns a Connection interface representing an individual database connection.

The format of the URL for the JDBC driver is

```
jdbc:oracle:<driver_type>:<connect_string>
```

The driver type is set to one of the following values as shown in Table 12-3.

The connect string is set to one of the following:

- **<hostname>:<port>:<SID>** Only available for the Oracle Thin driver
- **net service name** Only available for the Oracle OCI driver; obtains the connect description from an entry in the TNSNAMES.ORA file or from Oracle Names
- **connection descriptor** Available for either driver, consisting of a complete entry in the TNSNAMES.ORA file

For example, the following code uses the Oracle Thin JDBC driver to establish a database connection. The orcl database resides on the oski server and listens on port 1521. If you do not know the hostname, port, or Oracle System ID (SID) of the target datasource, you can look up these values in the TNSNAMES.ORA file or ask the database administrator.

```
try {
   Connection conn = DriverManager.getConnection(
      "jdbc:oracle:thin:scott/tiger@oski:1521:orcl");
} catch (SQLException e) {
   System.err.println("error:  cannot establish database connection");
   e.printStackTrace();
   System.exit(1);
}
```

Connection Methods

After establishing the database connection using either a datasource or the driver manager, use the Connection object to control transactions and create SQL statements. The Connection class

Driver Type	Description
OCI	Oracle OCI driver
Thin	Oracle Thin driver
Kprb	Oracle Server-Side Internal driver
default	jdbc:default:connection

TABLE 12-3. *Valid driver types*

provides methods to create and prepare, or precompile, SQL statements. There are three types of available SQL statement classes:

- **Statement** A Dynamically Linked Library (DDL), select, insert, update, or delete query that does not contain bind variables
- **PreparedStatement** A precompiled select, insert, update, or delete query that can contain bind variables
- **CallableStatement** A stored procedure that can contain input and output bind variables

Transaction Control

Upon instantiation, Connection objects start out in auto-commit mode, except in the case of the Server-Side Internal driver, which does not support auto-commit mode. All inserts, updates, and deletes are automatically committed to the database for connections with auto-commit mode enabled. As an application developer, you will usually want to control when database changes are committed or rolled back; therefore, the first method usually called is to disable auto-commit mode.

```
Connection conn = oracleDataSource.getConnection();
conn.setAutoCommit(false);
```

Execute the commit() method to commit the changes to the database.

```
conn.commit();
```

Use either the Savepoint interface in the java.sql package, or the OracleSavepoint in the oracle.jdbc package (if the Java SDK 1.4 is not available) to set a savepoint. The Connection class provides setSavepoint() methods that return a Savepoint object.

```
Savepoint savepoint;
savepoint = conn.setSavepoint();
```

Execute the rollback() method to rollback all uncommitted changes, or the uncommitted changes to a savepoint.

```
conn.rollback();
conn.rollback(savepoint);
```

Statement

The createStatement() method of the Connection class creates a Statement object. Once it's created, run the SQL statement using the execute(), executeQuery(), or executeUpdate() method. All methods throw a SQLException in the event an error occurs. It is very important to call the close() method for each statement to ensure that database resources are released.

The simplest of the three methods, execute(), is typically used to run DDL statements or dynamic SQL statements, although you can run select, insert, update, or delete statements as well. However, for regular SQL statements, you should use executeQuery() or .executeUpdate() instead to save the extra calls to retrieve the result set or count of affected rows.

Call the executeQuery() method to process select statements that return a result set in a ResultSet object. The ResultSet class provides a next() method that attempts to retrieve the next row in the result set, and returns true if a row was fetched or false if the result set is exhausted. After successfully fetching a row, one of the getter methods can be used to retrieve the value for a specific column in the result set row. The appropriate getter method depends on the column datatype. For example, if the column datatype is CHAR or VARCHAR2, call the getString() method; if the column datatype is NUMBER, call the getLong() (integer) or getDouble() (float) method; and if the column datatype is DATE, call the getTimestamp() method. Specify which column to obtain by passing in either the column name or alias in the select clause, or specify the column's ordinal position starting with 1.

The executeUpdate() method is used to execute an insert, update, or delete statement. The method returns the number of rows that the query inserted, updated, or deleted.

The following example shows how you can use each of three execute methods for a Statement object created for a Connection object named conn.

```
try {
   String sqlDDL = new String(
      "CREATE TABLE shapes (shape VARCHAR2(10),size NUMBER(1)");
   String sqlIns = new String(
      "INSERT INTO shapes VALUES ('square',3)");
   String sqlSel = new String(
      "SELECT shape,size FROM shapes");
   boolean   rsAvailable;
   int       rows;
   Statement stmt = conn.createStatement();
   ResultSet rs;
   rsAvailable = stmt.execute(sqlDDL);
   rows = stmt.executeUpdate(sqlIns);
   rs = stmt.executeQuery(sqlSel);
   while (rs.next()) {
      System.out.println(
        "shape=" + rs.getString("shape") + " size=" + rs.getLong(2));
   }
   rs.close();
   stmt.close();
} catch (SQLException e) {
   e.printStackTrace();
}
```

PreparedStatement

The prepareStatement() method of the Connection class compiles a SQL statement into a PreparedStatement object. Question marks (?) within the SQL statement represent bind variables whose values must be set prior to executing the statement. Be careful not to enclose the question marks in single quotes for character and date values.

Similar to the getter methods of result sets, the appropriate setter method for the column datatype binds the appropriate value to the query. For example, for CHAR and VARCHAR2 columns use setString(); for NUMBER columns use setLong(); and for DATE columns use setTimestamp(). The first parameter for each setter method is the ordinal position of the bind variable starting with 1, and the second parameter is the value to bind to the query. You can use a version of the setNull() method to set a column to NULL.

Because PreparedStatement extends Statement, the same three execution methods are available to process the query. For example, you can use a PreparedStatement to create a dynamic select, insert, update, or delete statement.

```
try {
   String sql = new String("INSERT INTO shapes VALUES(?,?)");
   int     rows;
   PreparedStatement stmt = conn.prepareStatement(sql);
   stmt.setString(1,"circle"); - set bind variable 1 to 'circle'
   stmt.setLong(2,4);          - set bind variable 2 to 4
   rows = stmt.executeUpdate();
} catch (SQLException e) {
   e.printStackTrace();
}
```

CallableStatement

The prepareCall() method of the Connection class creates a CallableStatement object to execute a stored procedure or function. Oracle allows you to write store procedures and functions using either PL/SQL or Java. Similar to the PreparedStatement class, question marks represent input and output parameters that you must register (output) and set (input) prior to executing the statement. For functions, a CallableStatement object allows you to capture the return value using a question mark placeholder.

The format of the query that calls the stored procedure can conform to either the standard JDBC or Oracle-specific syntax. Table 12-4 shows the different syntax formats.

After instantiating the CallableStatement object, you must first register the OUT and IN OUT parameters using a version of the registerOutParameter() method. For CHAR, VARCHAR2, and DATE parameters, use the version that requires an index, starting at 1, and a SQL type. For NUMBER parameters, use the version that requires an index, SQL type, and scale. The appropriate SQL type is one of the constants defined in the Types class of the java.sql package, such as Types.CHAR for CHAR and VARCHAR2 values, Types.LONG or Types.DOUBLE for NUMBER values, and Types.TIMESTAMP for DATE values.

As with PreparedStatement objects, set the values of IN and IN OUT parameters using the setter method corresponding to the datatype. The first parameter for each setter method is the ordinal position of the question mark in the statement, starting at 1. If the statement is a function where a question mark captures the return value, the return value is at position 1 and the first parameter passed to the function is at position 2.

	Standard JDBC Syntax	**Oracle-specific Syntax**
Function	{ ? = call function_name[(?,...)] }	begin ? := function_name[(?,...)]; end;
Procedure	{ call procedure_name[(?,...)] }	begin procedure_name[(?,...)]; end;

TABLE 12-4. *CallableStatement Formats*

When you have completed registering the output parameters and setting the values of the input parameters, execute the stored procedure or function by calling the CallableStatement execute() method. The following example calls a function that takes an input string parameter and returns a number.

```
try {
   String sql = new String("{ ? = call callable_stmt_example(?) }");
   double returnValue;
   CallableStatement stmt = conn.prepareCall(sql);
   stmt.registerOutParameter(1,Types.DOUBLE,2); - scale is 2 digits
   stmt.setString(2,'square');
   stmt.execute();
   returnValue = stmt.getDouble(1);
   stmt.close();
} catch (SQLException e) {
   e.printStackTrace();
}
```

Closing JDBC Objects

After you are finished using the database connection, you must close the connection to release all of the resources assigned to the session. Typically, the call to the close() method is placed in a final section of a try/catch block to ensure the connection is always closed, regardless of whether an error occurred.

The following example determines if a connection is still open, and if it is, closes the connection. Connections and other JDBC objects that are still open will not be null. By this time, you should have also closed all ResultSet, Statement, PreparedStatement, and CallableStatement objects. If there is a possibility that any of these objects are not closed, execute their respective close() methods prior to closing the Connection object.

```
try {
   Java statements with JDBC calls
} catch (SQLException e) {
   e.printStackTrace();
} finally {
   if (conn != null) {
      conn.close();
   }
}
```

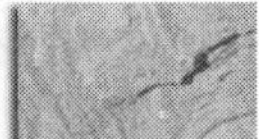

NOTE

As powerful as it is, JDBC alone is not suitable for enterprise-class applications, especially when you get into the areas of performance and transactions. A persistence framework for Java-based applications is required for any serious enterprise-class application development. Luckily, Oracle has created a robust tool for this very purpose. Oracle Application Server TopLink, an "out-of-the-box" solution, is discussed in the Oracle Application Server TopLink Getting Started Guide 10g (9.0.4), Part Number B10315-01.

SQLJ

SQLJ is an International Organization for Standardization (ISO) standard language specification for creating JDBC statements. For developers who do not wish to learn the native JDBC calls, SQLJ is a solution for embedding database directives within your Java program. Similar to Oracle's Pro*C, Pro*FORTRAN, and Pro*COBOL precompilers, the SQLJ translator reads a Java input file with a .sqlj extension, and converts the directives to the corresponding JDBC calls. Because JDBC is not dependent on any database vendor, all leading database vendors, including Oracle, support SQLJ.

There are some advantages to using SQLJ instead of coding calls to the JDBC API, including smaller program sizes, typed cursors and result sets, and compile-time checking of SQL statements. Because of these advantages, SQLJ is the default output of tools such as Oracle's JPublisher, a utility used to generate classes that represent data entities such as PL/SQL packages within a client application. Note that unless otherwise specified, JPublisher deletes the SQLJ source files after generating the output Java files with the corresponding JDBC calls.

When writing database calls for using a language such as C, it makes sense to use a precompiler to handle building the complex native Oracle Call Interface (OCI) API calls. Conversely, writing JDBC calls is straightforward; therefore, there is less of a need for this functionality with Java programs.

To use SQLJ, you must include the <ORACLE_HOME>/sqlj/lib/translator.jar and the <ORACLE_HOME>/sqlj/lib/runtime12.jar archives in your class path. Invoke the SQLJ translator using the sqlj command.

Java Stored Procedures (JSProcs)

With the introduction of the Oracle8*i* Database, Oracle allows developers to create stored procedures using Java in addition to the native PL/SQL procedural language. Because Java is not proprietary to Oracle, and enjoys a high level of acceptance within the development community, the support for Java stored procedure development allows developers to take advantage of the power of the Oracle stored procedures without having to learn PL/SQL. In addition, Java is a better choice than PL/SQL for many types of tasks, such as intensive computations. Java's object-oriented architecture, combined with all of the standard libraries included in the Java Run-time Environment (JRE), makes Java a powerful application development tool.

For Java Stored Procedures (JSProcs) that access data in the database, create a Connection object using the Server-Side Internal driver where the driver type is kprb. There are two key differences between standalone JDBC applications and Java Stored procedures. In JSProcs, you do not close the Connection object, and you do not provide a main() method.

NOTE
Do not confuse JSProcs with JSPs, which are JavaServer Pages, introduced later in this chapter and covered in detail in Chapter 14.

The following steps detail how to create and execute a JSProc within the database:

- Write the Java program

- Compile the Java program
- Load the class file into the Oracle database
- Create the PL/SQL call specification if client programs can execute the stored procedure or function
- Execute the JSProc

Write the Java Program

The first step is to create the Java program that will become a JSProc. For example, a JSProc accepts two parameters: a key value to the EMPLOYEES table, and a percentage to raise the employee's salary. The function updates the record and returns the new salary.

Prior to calling the function, the table contains the following data:

```
SQL> SELECT * FROM employees;
EMPLOYEE_ID      SALARY
------ -----
          1       50000
          2      100000
```

Create a new Employees class with the static raiseSalary() method. Note that you must declare methods that become Java Stored Procedures as static.

```
import java.sql.*;
import oracle.jdbc.pool.*;
public class Employees {
   public static double raiseSalary(long employeeID,double raisePct) {
      OracleDataSource  ods;
      Connection        conn = null;
      PreparedStatement stmt = null;
      ResultSet         rs = null;
      double            newSalary = 0.0;
      try {
         ods = new OracleDataSource();
         ods.setDriverType("kprb");
         conn = ods.getConnection();
         stmt = conn.prepareStatement(
            "UPDATE employees SET salary = " +
              "(salary + (salary * (?/100.0))) WHERE employee_id = ?");
         stmt.setDouble(1,raisePct);
         stmt.setLong(2,employeeID);
         stmt.executeUpdate();
         stmt.close();
         stmt = conn.prepareStatement(
             "SELECT salary FROM employees WHERE employee_id = ?");
         stmt.setLong(1,employeeID);
         rs = stmt.executeQuery();
```

```
            if (rs.next()) newSalary = rs.getDouble(1);
            conn.commit();
         } catch (SQLException e) {
            System.err.println(e.getMessage());
         } finally {
            try {
               if (rs != null) rs.close();
               if (stmt != null) stmt.close();
            } catch (SQLException e) {
               System.err.println(e.getMessage());
            }
         }
         return newSalary;
      }
   }
```

The try/catch/finally section of the code above is one of the "coolest" features of the Java language. For those programmers not familiar with it, it is a way to handle "exceptional situations" that happen at run time. This way, a programmer who knows an "exceptional situation" might happen during the execution of a piece of code can prepare for (and often recover from) it. It's important to note that the Java compiler doesn't care how the programmer handles the exception; it only cares that there is a way of handling it. In Java, the developer can raise specific exceptions that must be handled by the calling method; you can't do this in PL/SQL.

Compile the Java Program

JSProc are class files, just like other compiled Java applications. You can compile the JSProc source using the Java SDK with an IDE such as JDeveloper or at a command line prompt, or you can let the Oracle database compile the program. In general, it is easier to compile and test your Java program outside of the database, and then load the class file into the database.

Using CREATE JAVA SOURCE

You can execute the CREATE JAVA SOURCE SQL statement to compile and load the Java program within the database using SQL*Plus. Note the use of double quotation marks to maintain the case sensitivity of the class file.

```
CREATE OR REPLACE AND RESOLVE JAVA SOURCE NAMED "Employees" AS
import java.sql.*;
import oracle.jdbc.pool.*;
public class Employees {
   ...
}
/
```

Load the Class File into the Database

If you choose to compile and test your Java program outside of the database, load the source, class, and resource files into the database using either the loadjava utility or a CREATE JAVA SQL statement.

Using loadjava

The loadjava utility uploads Java source, class, and resource files into the database, storing the objects as Java schema objects in a system-generated database table. The utility then executes CREATE JAVA [SOURCE|RESOURCE|CLASS] SQL statements to load the files into the database. Note that you do not need to upload the source code, but the Oracle database can automatically recompile dependent objects if the source is available in a schema object.

The following example loads the Employees.class file into the SCOTT schema within the database:

```
prompt>loadjava -user scott/tiger@oski:1521:orcl -f -r -v Employees.class
arguments: '-user' 'scott/tiger@oski:1521:orcl' '-f' '-r' '-v'
           'Employees.class'
creating : class Employees
loading  : class Employees
resolving: class Employees
```

The -f option forces the utility to load the class even if an identical class already exists; the -r option resolves all of the classes after loading them, rather than at run-time; and the -v option specifies verbose output. There are several options available; execute loadjava –help to see all of the command line options.

You can also load ZIP and JAR files into the database using loadjava. The utility extracts all files from the archive and loads each file individually into the database. This capability is a very efficient way to load many Java classes into the database at once.

Using CREATE JAVA CLASS

To load a class file using SQL*Plus, create a directory object to reference where the class file is stored in the file system and execute the CREATE JAVA CLASS SQL statement.

```
CREATE OR REPLACE DIRECTORY BFILE_DIR AS 'C:\classes';
CREATE OR REPLACE JAVA CLASS USING BFILE(BFILE_DIR,'Employees.class');
```

Create the PL/SQL Call Specification

For each method that a trigger, or SQL or PL/SQL call, will execute within the Java class, you must create a PL/SQL call specification, similar to a package specification, for the method. In addition, the method must have public access. The call specification, also called a *wrapper*, maps the Java method names, parameter types, and return types to the matching SQL values.

At first glance, the PL/SQL call specification seems unnecessary, given you developed the stored procedure in Java and not PL/SQL. However, the call specification serves an important purpose in that it allows all stored procedures, regardless of their source language, to communicate easily. If Oracle supports another language for stored procedure development in the future, the new language will easily integrate into existing applications thanks to PL/SQL call specifications.

Because the raiseSalary() method within the Employee class returns a value, declare the PL/SQL call specification as a FUNCTION. You may be tempted to declare the employee_id input parameter as employees.employee_id%TYPE for maximum flexibility; however, Oracle does not allow you to constrain datatypes in PL/SQL call specifications.

```
CREATE OR REPLACE FUNCTION raise_salary (
   employee_id IN NUMBER,
   raise_pct   IN NUMBER)
RETURN NUMBER
AS LANGUAGE JAVA
NAME 'Employees.raiseSalary(long,double) return double';
/
```

Note the use of case within the PL/SQL call specification. Because PL/SQL is not case-sensitive, a common convention is to separate each word within method and parameter names by underscores; for example, the Java raiseSalary() method is referenced as the raise_salary function in PL/SQL. If the method was declared to return no value using the void keyword, you would declare the PL/SQL call specification as a PROCEDURE instead.

```
CREATE OR REPLACE PROCEDURE raise_salary (
   employee_id IN NUMBER,
   raise_pct   IN NUMBER)
AS LANGUAGE JAVA
NAME 'Employees.raiseSalary(long,double)';
```

Handling IN OUT and OUT Parameters

Because Java does not support pointers, you cannot pass nonarray parameters to Java methods by reference, only by value. To allow the JSProc to support IN OUT and OUT parameters, you must set up the parameters as one-dimensional arrays within the method signature. Within the method, access and set the parameter value as the first, and only, element of the array at index 0.

The following example shows a Java method and corresponding PL/SQL call specification that allows the calling program to change a parameter.

```
public class InOutExample {
   public static void incr(int[] i) {
      i[0]++;
   }
}
CREATE OR REPLACE PROCEDURE incr(i IN OUT NUMBER)
IS LANGUAGE JAVA
NAME 'InOutExample.incr(int[])';
```

Note that many developers consider using IN OUT and OUT parameters with functions as bad application design. Because of the side effects, Oracle does not allow you to call functions with IN OUT and OUT parameters within Data Manipulation Language (DML) statements, and returns an ORA-06572: Function <function> has out arguments error if such a call is attempted.

It is also important to note that as of Oracle 9*i* R2, the loadjava command will do this for you (for all public methods).

Execute the JSProc

Thanks to the PL/SQL call specification, you can execute the JSProc the same as a PL/SQL procedure or function. This includes calling the JSProc from PL/SQL procedures, functions, and triggers, as well as other Java classes. For example, to give employee 2 a 5 percent raise:

```
SQL> VARIABLE new_salary NUMBER
SQL> CALL raise_salary(2,5) INTO :new_salary;
Call completed.
SQL> PRINT new_salary
NEW_SALARY
-----
    105000
SQL> SELECT * FROM employees;
EMPLOYEE_ID     SALARY
------ -----
         1       50000
         2      105000
```

A second example shows running the incr stored procedure within an anonymous PL/SQL block. Make sure you turn on displaying output messages using SET SERVEROUTPUT ON in SQL*Plus.

```
SQL> DECLARE
  2     x NUMBER := 3;
  3  BEGIN
  4     incr(x);
  5     dbms_output.put_line('x=' || x);
  6  END;
  7  /
x=4
PL/SQL procedure successfully completed.
```

Capturing Output Messages

As shown in the second JSProc example, developers often use procedures within the Oracle-supplied DBMS_OUTPUT package to display debug messages. In Java programs, writing messages to standard output System.out or standard error System.err provides similar functionality.

By default, the Oracle JVM writes any output messages sent to System.out or System.err within JSProcs to a trace file in the user dump directory. You can choose to display these messages within a SQL*Plus session instead by turning on server output and calling the DBMS_JAVA.SET_OUTPUT method. For example:

```
SQL> SET SERVEROUTPUT ON SIZE(1000000)
SQL> CALL dbms_java.set_output(1000000);
Call completed.
```

Dropping Java Objects

To drop Java objects in the database, you must drop both the source, class, and resource files loaded with the loadjava utility or CREATE JAVA SQL statements.

The opposite of the loadjava utility is the dropjava utility that drops Java objects from the Oracle database. To drop the Employees class file, issue the dropjava command, as shown:

```
prompt>dropjava -user scott/tiger@oski:1521:orcl -v Employees.class
dropping: class Employees
```

Alternatively, you can drop the Java objects in SQL*Plus using DROP JAVA [SOURCE|CLASS|RESOURCE] SQL statements. As with the CREATE JAVA SQL statements, be sure to enclose the class name in double quotation marks to preserve case.

```
SQL> DROP JAVA CLASS "Employees";
Java dropped.
```

Dropping the Java class does not drop the corresponding PL/SQL call specification. After dropping the class, attempts to call the function will result in Oracle error ORA-29540: class <class> does not exist. Because the PL/SQL call specifications are simply PL/SQL procedures and functions, you can drop call specifications using DROP PROCEDURE and DROP FUNCTION SQL statements.

DBMS_JAVA Package

The Oracle Database 10*g* includes the DBMS_JAVA package containing procedures and functions to manage the Java objects in the database. A couple of the procedures in this package, grant_permission and set_output, were listed earlier in the chapter. The Oracle Database Java Developer's Guide 10*g* Release 1 describes all of the procedures and functions in detail, and Table 12-5 provides a summary of the same information.

Oracle Application Server Containers for J2EE

As described in Chapter 2, Oracle Application Server 10*g* provides a fully J2EE-compliant container called Oracle Application Server Containers for J2EE (OC4J). For development and small-scale installations, Oracle also provides for a separately downloadable standalone version of OC4J including full documentation. After successfully installing OC4J, either as the standalone version or the full version included with Oracle Application Server 10*g*, you can develop servlets, JavaServer Pages (JSPs), and Enterprise JavaBeans (EJBs) within the OC4J container.

NOTE
As of Oracle9i Database R2, you can no longer develop servlets, JSPs, and EJBs within the Oracle Database.

To verify that OC4J is properly running, open a web browser and set the address to http://localhost:8888. If OC4J is running, you will see a welcome page providing links to OC4J information, documentation, and sample applications. OC4J will be discussed further in Chapters 13-15.

Procedure or Function	Description
FUNCTION longname	Because Java object and method names may exceed the 30-character limit for Oracle object names, Oracle saves Java objects with both their original long name and a system generated short name. The longname function returns the long name for a Java object.
FUNCTION shortname	The shortname function returns the corresponding short name for a potentially truncated Java object long name.
FUNCTION get_compiler_option PROCEDURE set_compiler_option PROCEDURE reset_compiler_option	Set, retrieve, and reset are the options for the Java compiler included with the Oracle Database.
FUNCTION resolver	The resolver function returns the resolver specification for a Java object that contains the list of schemas to search for the dependent class objects.
FUNCTION derivedFrom	The derivedFrom function returns the source name for a Java object saved in the database.
FUNCTION fixed_in_instance	The fixed_in_instance function returns 1 if a Java object is permanently kept within the Database, and 0 if a Java object is not permanently kept. Objects included in the J2SE platform are permanently kept.
PROCEDURE set_output	The set_output procedure is used in conjunction with SET SERVEROUTPUT ON in SQL*Plus. It redirects output to System.out and System.err to the screen instead of a trace file in the user dump directory.
PROCEDURE start_debugging PROCEDURE stop_debugging PROCEDURE restart_debugging	The start_debugging, stop_debugging, and restart_debugging procedures start and stop the debug agent.
PROCEDURE export_source	The export_source procedure exports a Java source file stored in the database into an Oracle large object (LOB).
PROCEDURE export_class	The export_class procedure exports a Java class file stored in the database into an Oracle LOB (must be a BLOB, or binary large object).
PROCEDURE export_resource	The export_resource procedure exports a Java resource file stored in the database into an Oracle LOB.
PROCEDURE loadjava PROCEDURE dropjava	The loadjava and dropjava procedures load and drop classes using a database call rather than the command-line utilities.
PROCEDURE grant_permission PROCEDURE restrict_permission PROCEDURE grant_policy_permission PROCEDURE revoke_permission PROCEDURE disable_permission PROCEDURE delete_permission	The grant_permission, restrict_permission, grant_policy_permission, revoke_permission, disable_permission, and delete_permission procedures manage JVM permissions. Certain operations, such as opening sockets or writing to files, require extra permission.
PROCEDURE set_preference	The set_preference procedure sets system and user Java preferences.

TABLE 12-5. *DBMS_JAVA Procedures and Function*

Servlets

Servlets provide a way to create a dynamic HTML or XML response document—for example, a web page displaying data from an Oracle database—to an HTTP request. Specifically, servlets are server-side Java programs that run in a J2EE application server such as OC4J.

The first HTTP servers simply responded to HTTP requests by returning static HTML documents. Soon developers realized the enormous opportunity for web-based applications that such a worldwide network of HTTP servers could provide, if only the HTTP servers could execute programs to create dynamic response pages. The Common Gateway Interface (CGI) was one of the first practical solutions for creating dynamic pages, and soon web servers were running Perl programs, shell scripts, and almost any other language to create HTML pages. However, each HTTP request required the web server to spawn a new process in which to run the CGI program. The CGI program relied on environment variables, posted form values, and the request URL to create the response document, and could not interact with the web server once it began execution.

Because of the limited scalability of CGI programs, servlets soon replaced CGI programs as the tool of choice for creating dynamic web pages. Because servlets run as a continuous process within a single thread, they provide state maintenance and a high-performance solution to web-based application development. Because servlets are Java programs running within a JVM, they have access to all of the capabilities included within the J2EE platform, such as JDBC. As with all Java programs, the same servlets can execute in any J2EE-compliant container on any web server without having to recompile the program.

Similar to Java stored procedures, servlets are not standalone applications and do not have a static main() method. Rather, servlets extend one of the two standard servlets base classes, either javax.servlet.GenericServlet or javax.servlet.http.HttpServlet. Instead of having a main() method for the entrance point, the servlet overrides either or both base class methods doGet() to process an HTTP GET request, and doPost() to process an HTTP POST request. Both overridden methods accept two parameters with the following classes:

- **HttpServletRequest** The request from the client application, such as a web browser
- **HttpServletResponse** The response to return to the client application

The servlet container passes these parameters to the servlet, and once the servlet has completed processing, it passes the response back to the client application.

A servlet example uses an HTML document to send parameters to a servlet using an HTTP GET request. For this example, we will create both the HTML document containing the necessary form and input tags, and the servlet processed by the form action parameter. Using this example, the user enters the month, day, and year of his or her birthday, and the servlet displays the corresponding day of the week.

Create the HTML Document

Create an HTML document containing a form to capture and submit the parameters required by the servlet. Save the HTML tags and text listed below as a file named BirthdayServlet.html in the <j2ee_home>/default-web-app directory. The action tag specifies that the servlet is located in the default web application classes directory whose virtual path is set to /servlet.

```
<HTML>
<HEAD><TITLE>Birthday Servlet</TITLE></HEAD>
```

```
<BODY>
   <H1>When is your birthday?</H1>
   <FORM method="GET" action="/servlet/BirthdayServlet">
      Month <INPUT name="MONTH" size="2" type="TEXT"><BR>
      Day   <INPUT name="DAY"   size="2" type="TEXT"><BR>
      Year  <INPUT name="YEAR   size="4" type="TEXT"><BR>
      <INPUT type="SUBMIT">
   </FORM>
</BODY>
</HTML>
```

Note that the case of the action parameter of the FORM tag, and the values of the name parameters for the text input parameters, must match this example.

Create the Servlet

The servlet uses classes within the java.text.SimpleDateFormat and the java.util.Calendar J2SE packages to create a dynamic web page. Save the servlet code listed below as BirthdayServlet.java in the <j2ee_home>/default_web_app/WEB-INF/classes directory and compile the source file to BirthdayServlet.class.

NOTE
Before compiling the example servlet, make sure the <j2ee_home>/lib/servlet.jar archive is located in your class path.

```
// The following three imports are required for all servlets
import java.io.*;
import java.servlet.*;
import java.servlet.http.*;
import java.text.SimpleDateFormat;
import java.util.Calendar;
public class BirthdayServlet extends HttpServlet {
   public void doGet(HttpServletRequest  request,
                     HttpServletResponse response)
         throws ServletException, IOException {
      int year, month, day;
      Calendar cal = Calendar.getInstance();
      SimpleDateFormat sdf = new SimpleDateFormat("EEEE");
      // Set the response content MIME type
      response.setContentType("text/html");
      ServletOutputStream out = response.getOutputStream();
      out.println("<HTML">);
      out.println("<HEAD><TITLE>Birthday Servlet</TITLE></HEAD>");
      out.println("<BODY><H1>");
      try {
         // For calendars, subtract 1 from the month (0=Jan,11=Dec)
         cal.set(Integer.parseInt(request.getParameter("YEAR")),
                 Integer.parseInt(request.getParameter("MONTH"))-1,
                 Integer.parseInt(request.getParameter("DAY")));
         out.print("You were born on a ");
```

```
            out.println(sdf.format(cal.getTime()));
         } catch (NumberFormatException e) {
            out.println("Invalid date");
         }
         out.println("</H1></BODY></HTML>");
      }
   }
```

Test the Servlet

After creating the HTML document, and successfully compiling the servlet, you are ready to test creating a dynamic web page. Load the HTML document using the following URL:

```
http://localhost:8888/BirthdayServlet.html
```

Enter in the values for your birthday. For example, if you were born on January 26, 1967, enter "1" in the Month text box, "26" in the Day text box, and "1967" in the Year text box (without the quotes). Click the Submit button to pass these parameters within the URL to the servlet. You should receive a response HTML document showing:

```
You were born on a Thursday
```

JavaServer Pages

As shown by this example, servlets require the developer to code both the presentation logic by outputting the HTML tags, plus the business logic, all within the same program. This tight coupling

<table>
<tr><th>Element</th><th>Syntax</th></tr>
<tr><td>Include a file</td><td><%@ include file='relative url' %></td></tr>
<tr><td>Page attributes</td><td><%@ page import='package1,package2,...'
session="true|false"
errorPage='relative url'
isErrorPage="true|false"
contentType='content type'%></td></tr>
<tr><td>Forward to a new page</td><td><jsp:forward page='relative url'
<jsp:param name="name" value="value" />
</jsp:forward></td></tr>
<tr><td>Comment</td><td><%– comment –%></td></tr>
<tr><td>Declaration</td><td><%! declaration %></td></tr>
<tr><td>Scriptlet</td><td><% Java code %></td></tr>
<tr><td>Print a value</td><td><%= variable or expression %></td></tr>
</table>

TABLE 12-6. *Common JSP Elements*

of presentation and business logic is not flexible and is difficult to maintain. The responsibilities for developing the HTML framework might be a person or group using sophisticated web design tools, whereas the responsibilities for developing the business logic is usually a developer or group using an IDE such as JDeveloper. Changes to either the application presentation or the business logic require careful coordination between both parties.

JSPs (see Table 12-6) are a method to separate the HTML tags from the Java code containing the business logic so that the web designers and application developers can each focus on what they do best. A typical JSP file contains a mixture of HTML tags for the static content, and Java code snippets called scriptlets to create the dynamic content. J2EE-compliant web containers include a JSP translator for processing JavaServer Pages files.

The JSP translator is fundamentally a servlet precompiler. The JSP translator accepts requests for web pages containing a .jsp extension, and converts the JSP input files into servlets. Upon the first request for a JSP where the corresponding servlet does not yet exist or the JSP source is newer than the previously generated servlet, the container automatically creates and compiles a new servlet into a corresponding class file. You will usually notice slower performance during the translation and compilation time; however, all subsequent requests for the JSP are as fast as calling a servlet.

Within the Java code inside a JSP, there are several implicitly created objects to allow the JSP to access parameters available to servlets. Common implicit objects include request and response that correspond to the two parameters of the doGet() and doPost() servlet methods.

We will re-create the servlet example using a JSP to demonstrate how JSPs reduce coding complexity. You will need to modify the action parameter of the HTML form to call the JSP instead of a servlet, and then code the JSP. Note that this example only provides a brief introduction into the capabilities of JSPs; be sure to read Chapter 14 for a more complete explanation.

Create the HTML Document

Copy the BirthdayServlet.html document from the previous example, changing the title and the action parameter of the FORM tag to point to a JSP rather than a servlet. Save the new document as BirthdayJSP.html in the same <j2ee_home>/default-web-app directory.

```
<HTML>
<HEAD><TITLE>Birthday JSP</TITLE></HEAD>
<BODY>
   <H1>When is your birthday?</H1>
   <FORM method="GET" action="/Birthday.jsp">
      Month <INPUT name="MONTH" size="2" type="TEXT"><BR>
      Day   <INPUT name="DAY"   size="2" type="TEXT"><BR>
      Year  <INPUT name="YEAR   size="4" type="TEXT"><BR>
      <INPUT type="SUBMIT">
   </FORM>
</BODY>
</HTML>
```

Creating the JavaServer Page

Save the JSP as Birthday.jsp in the same <j2ee_home>/default-web-app directory as the HTML page. Unlike servlets, you do not manually compile the JSP or the servlet generated by the JSP translator.

```
<%@page import='java.text.SimpleDateFormat,java.util.Calendar'
        contentType='text/html' %>
<%! Calendar cal         = Calendar.getInstance(); %>
<%! SimpleDateFormat sdf = new SimpleDateFormat("EEEE"); %>
<HTML>
<HEAD><TITLE>Birthday JSP</TITLE></HEAD>
<BODY>
   <% try {
         cal.set(Integer.parseInt(request.getParameter("YEAR")),
                 Integer.parseInt(request.getParameter("MONTH"))-1,
                 Integer.parseInt(request.getParameter("DAY")));
   %>
         <H1>You were born on a <%= sdf.format(cal.getTime()) %> </H1>
   <% } catch (NumberFormatException e) { %>
         Invalid date
   <% } %>
</BODY>
</HTML>
```

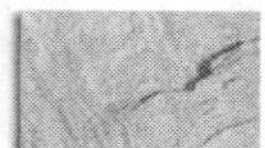

TIP
Do not place a semi-colon at the end of the Java scriptlet within the evaluation tags <%= ... %>.

Test the JSP

After creating the HTML document and saving the JSP source, you are ready to test creating a dynamic web page using the JSP. Load the HTML document using the following URL:

```
http://localhost:8888/BirthdayJSP.html
```

Enter in the values for your birthday, and click the Submit button to pass these parameters within the URL to the JSP. You should receive the same response HTML document as with the servlet example.

JavaBeans and Tag Libraries

Even with the separation of the static HTML tags from the JSP code, application logic still exists within the example JSP. JavaBeans, not to be confused with Enterprise JavaBeans, and tag libraries are two common methods to remove all of the business logic from the JSPs. Chapter 14 includes a thorough review of these topics, as well as other design improvements to JSPs.

Oracle Business Intelligence Beans

Oracle9*i* Business Intelligence Beans (BI Beans) is a set of standards-based JavaBeans that provides analysis-aware application building blocks. BI Beans functionality is fully integrated into JDeveloper 10*g*, allowing the developer to build Internet applications quickly and easily. These applications can expose the advanced analytic features of the Oracle database to both casual users and advanced users requiring ad-hoc query and analysis functionality. BI Beans fall into three categories:

- **Presentation** Presentations need to be easy to build so any level user within an organization can produce a high-quality report. BI Beans provide three flexible data-aware presentation components: graph, crosstab, and table.
- **OLAP** Online Analytical Processing (OLAP) beans make it easy to formulate complex questions and present answers in presentation beans. By using the graphical components provided with the BI Beans, a business user can specify complex queries in minutes, without knowing SQL. The OLAP beans also provide support to the APIs for advanced data manipulation including the capability to drill down on, change the layout of, or sort data.
- **Catalog services** The BI Beans Catalog is used to save, retrieve, and manage all developer- and user-defined analytical objects, such as reports, graphs, favorite queries, and custom measures. Object definitions are stored in the Catalog as XML. The BI Beans Catalog is designed to support large, distributed user communities who share analytical objects in collaborative environments.

Enterprise JavaBeans

Enterprise JavaBeans (EJBs) are distributed, server-side components that allow the developer to focus on implementing the business logic. The EJB container takes care of all of the common architecture requirements such as security, connection and resource pooling, persistence, and ensuring transactional integrity.

EJBs exist within an EJB container such as the container included with Oracle Application Server 10*g*. The EJB container is often a middle tier within an application, with a thin client at the presentation tier and a relational database such as Oracle at the database tier. There are fundamentally three types of EJBs:

- **Entity** Entity beans model business concepts that are expressible as nouns, and often model persistent records, such as those within a relational database table. Entity beans have persistent state using either container-managed persistence (CMP), where the container automatically synchronizes the data between the bean and the database, or bean-managed persistence (BMP), where the bean manages its own state.
- **Session** Session beans manage activities, and bring together various entity beans to process a transaction. Session beans do not have persistent state.
- **Message-driven** Message-driven beans subscribe to asynchronous messages and coordinate the interaction between entity and session beans. Message-driven beans also do not have persistent state.

Implementing EJBs is a complex process, and is beyond the scope of an introduction chapter. Improper use of EJBs without an understanding of how to best query and update data in Oracle databases can lead to a poorly performing, nonscalable enterprise-wide application. Therefore, it is important to learn the basics of how Java can interact with Oracle first. After building on your knowledge of Oracle with your new Java skills, you will be ready to learn more about building and deploying EJBs.

Business Components for Java

Business Components for Java (BC4J) is JDeveloper's programming framework for building multitier database applications from reusable business components. BC4J provides a standards-based, server-side framework for creating production-quality J2EE applications. It includes design-time facilities and run-time services to simplify the tasks of building, debugging, customizing, and reusing business components. Applications developed with BC4J can be deployed on any J2EE platform and can be accessed from a wide variety of clients. The framework handles common development cases with built-in behavior, and developers can take advantage of these benefits without compromising their ability to control the way an application works. Any behavior provided by the framework can be easily overridden with a few lines of code, so developers are never locked into a certain way of solving problems.

There are two key objects in the BC4J framework:

- **Entity objects** Entity objects store business logic and column information for a database table (or view, synonym, or snapshot).
- **View objects** View objects use a SQL query to specify sets of business data that can be related to attributes from entity objects. View objects provide clients with row sets they can scroll through and update without concern for or knowledge of the underlying entity objects. Clients manipulate data by navigating through the result set, getting and setting attribute values; changes are made to the data in the underlying database when the transaction is committed.

BC4J also has the concept of an application module. The application module is the object with which the client and the database will interact. It contains the view objects that represent your view of the data and manages the transactions on that data.

The business components framework is a class library (in oracle.jbo.*) with built-in application functionality. Using the framework involves specializing base classes to introduce application-specific behavior, allowing the framework to coordinate many of the basic interactions between objects. By using the BC4J design-time wizards and editors that are built into Oracle JDeveloper 10*g*, you can build business logic tiers by defining the characteristics of components. Wizards generate Java source code and XML metadata to implement the behavior you have specified. Because the generated code inherits from a framework, the Java source files are concise. You can use Oracle JDeveloper to edit the Java code to enhance or change the behavior, and test the application services, independent of the deployment platform.

Summary

The Java platform coupled with Oracle Database 10*g* and Oracle Application Server 10*g* is a powerful combination for robust and scalable application development. The platform independent, object-oriented Java architecture allows for the use of Java at all layers within an application, including presentation (applets, Swing applications), middle (servlets, EJBs), and database (stored procedures) layers. Combine this versatility with the highly robust and scalable Oracle Database and Application Server, and you now have an impressive set of tools to build applications to meet the needs of any size organization.

CHAPTER 13

Oracle JDeveloper 10*g*

In this chapter, we will cover the Oracle JDeveloper 10*g* Integrated Development Environment (IDE). We will cover the basics from acquisition and installation to basic structure and navigation through a simple Java development example. Next, some of the more advanced web development features of Oracle JDeveloper 10*g*, including the incredible Oracle ADF framework, will be discussed. Finally, we will wrap up with an advanced web development example utilizing this framework.

There are literally entire books devoted just to the topic of Oracle JDeveloper 10*g*, so we will by no means be able to cover every detail of the topic in this chapter. What we will hopefully be able to do is to provide information for newcomers to the tool as well as for those who have been working with Oracle JDeveloper 10*g* for a couple of versions. For those readers looking for a comprehensive manual on Oracle JDeveloper 10*g*, the authors recommend the *Oracle JDeveloper 10g Handbook.*

NOTE
The Oracle JDeveloper 10g Handbook is authored by Avrom Faderman, Peter Koletzke, and Paul Dorsey (ISBN: 0072255838). It is published by McGraw-Hill/Osborne and can be ordered from http://shop.osborne.com/cgi-bin/oraclepress/0072255838.html.

With that said, let's get started!

Acquisition and Installation

The installation of Oracle JDeveloper 10*g* is simpler than for most other Oracle products. There is no need to define an ORACLE_HOME environment variable prior to beginning the installation. Following a popular trend back toward simplicity in software management, Oracle JDeveloper 10*g* is provided as a Zip file (or appropriate compression type depending on your installation platform) that you simply extract to a directory you wish to work in. To begin execution of Oracle JDeveloper 10*g* on Windows, the developer simply executes the jdevw.exe file found in the <install location>\jdev\bin directory. To run on Linux/Unix, source the jdev script in the <install location>/jdev/bin directory:

```
. ./jdev
```

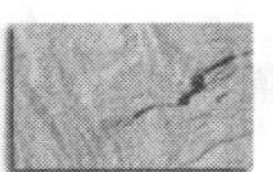

NOTE
Oracle JDeveloper 10g can be downloaded from OTN here: http://www.oracle.com/technology/products/jdev/index.html.

Oracle JDeveloper 10*g* Structure

One of the basic advantages that any IDE should provide to developers is increased levels of productivity. Oracle JDeveloper 10*g* excels in this area, particularly with the enhancement of its code generation tools as well as advanced integration of its visual modeling components. In this section, we will cover the basic structural segments of Oracle JDeveloper 10*g*, what each is utilized for, and how to navigate between them effectively.

After Oracle JDeveloper 10*g* is installed, click the jdevw.exe executable to load the application. You will be greeted with the Oracle JDeveloper 10*g* splash screen, and eventually the default Oracle JDeveloper 10*g* work environment is displayed.

The main display areas can be seen in Figure 13-1. Oracle JDeveloper 10*g* consists of the Applications Navigator, Structure pane, Editor pane, and message log. The function of each of these components will be discussed, as well as some additional panes and tabs included within.

Applications Navigator

The Applications Navigator is the main navigation point for visually identifying and managing the resources for your projects. It is the root position for all of the code that developers work with while developing applications in Oracle JDeveloper 10*g*. Applications are the highest level of organization for project code. In previous versions of Oracle JDeveloper 10*g*, these were called workspaces and had their configuration information maintained by a ".jws" (Oracle JDeveloper workspace) file on the file system. This file still exists in Oracle JDeveloper 10*g*, even though workspaces are now referred to as "applications." In reality, the term application is more suitable than workspace, particularly considering the role that this entity plays in the organization of project code.

Adding code to the Applications Navigator is easy. Click File | New to bring up the New Gallery. From here, select General in the drill-down on the left and Application Workspace on the right. This takes you into the New Application Workspace Wizard, as shown in Figure 13-2.

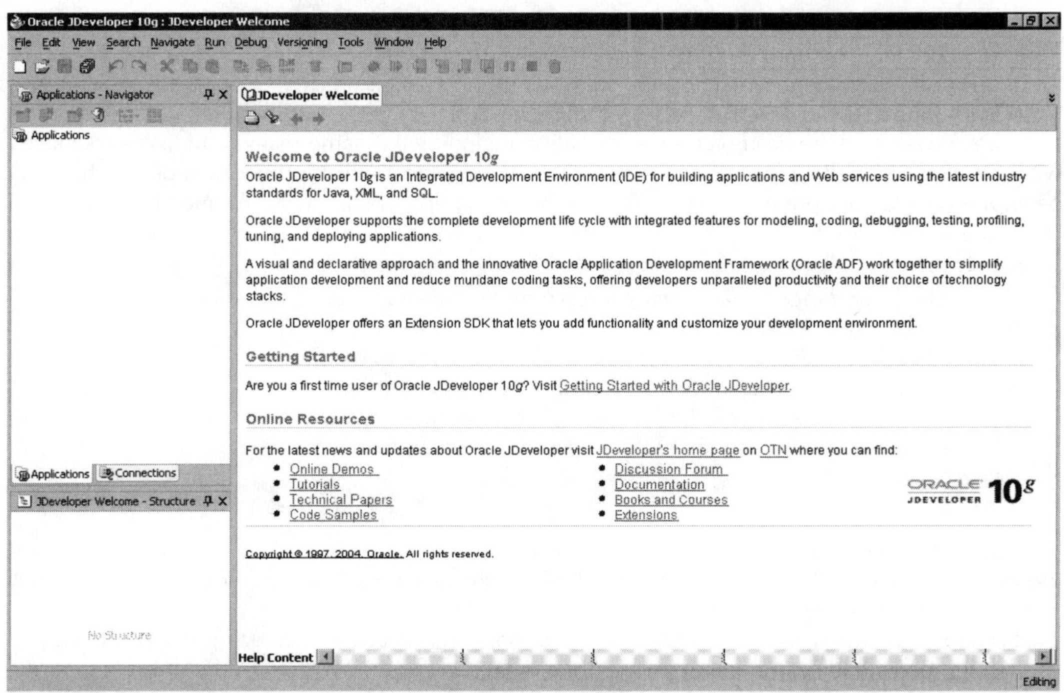

FIGURE 13-1. *The initial Oracle JDeveloper 10*g* screen*

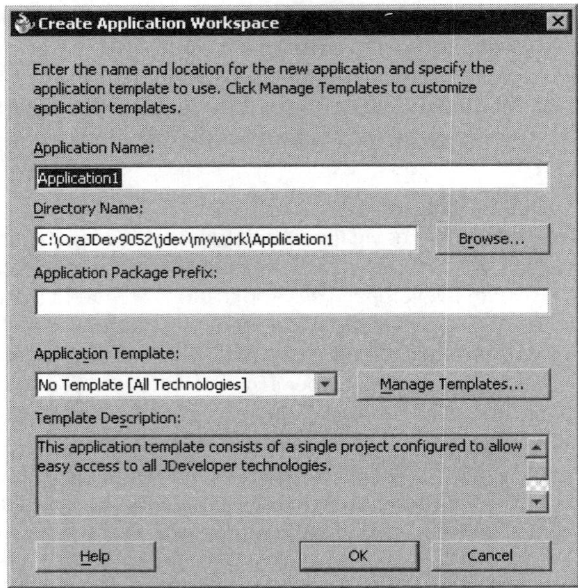

FIGURE 13-2. *The Create Application Workspace dialog box*

Here, developers are prompted for information including the name you would like associated with the application, the physical path to the source code, the application package prefix (this will be applied as the base prefix for any Java code included herein), and the application template.

NOTE

Of special importance is the application template. This is a new feature added with Oracle JDeveloper 10g that allows for an added measure of productivity. Templates essentially allow you to dictate a basic structure for the starting application. They also allow for management of the available technologies, structure, naming, and various other configuration details for the application and default projects.

You can also take a shortcut into the Application Workspace Wizard by simply right-clicking the word "applications" at the highest level of the Applications Navigator drill-down and selecting New Application Workspace.

Should you already have an existing application, you can add it to the Applications Navigator by clicking File | Add To Applications and then navigating to the location of the .jws file that contains the details of the application you wish to add. As a shortcut, you can also click the green + in the far upper left of the Applications Navigator pane.

After the application, the next highest level of organization is a "project." An application can consist of multiple projects. A project is utilized to segment subsystems or distinct units of work out into a set of logical groupings that provides for greater organization. As a developer, you view projects in the Applications Navigator by drilling down into the application that contains the project you are looking for. Like applications, projects have a file that resides on the file system that is utilized to maintain configuration information about that project. This file has the name of the project with a ".jpr" suffix.

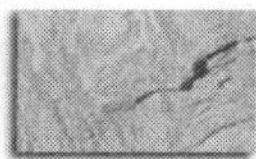

TIP
While on the topic of the file system, within the project folder on the file system you will find two additional subfolders, called classes and src. The src folder contains the folder tree that holds all of your source code for this project. The classes folder is a mirror of the src folder, with the exception that it contains the compiled code based on the code in the src folder.

There are several properties that can be managed from the project level that are of importance when doing development in Oracle JDeveloper 10*g*. To access the project properties as shown in Figure 13-3, you can right-click the project in question and select Project Properties. Alternatively, you can select the project you wish to manage and click Tools | Project Properties or just double-click the project. There is also a shortcut at the top of the Applications Navigator you can use by selecting the project in question and clicking the icon that is third from the left.

Most of the options are fairly self-explanatory; one option to pay particular attention to is the libraries option. This option allows you to configure what external libraries will be tied to your project.

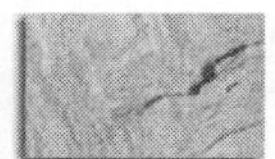

NOTE
Libraries are simply a way of binding a representative name to a set of code that is not directly a part of this project. In addition to all of the default libraries that come bundled with Oracle JDeveloper 10g, you can also create your own libraries when you wish to integrate custom-developed or third-party source trees. To do this, you simply select the New button in the dialog and follow the steps to bind a name to the source you wish to have comprise this library. Note that if you are utilizing source control, the type of library you select (user, project, or system) can have a bearing on how easily other people can pick up your code from source control and work with it. When creating a user library, it binds the library path to the absolute path on your machine, and this path may end up being different when a collaborator on your project pulls down and attempts to utilize your code during development. Project libraries, on the other hand, create the library as a relative path based on the project you're creating it from (which makes it more portable through a source control tool).

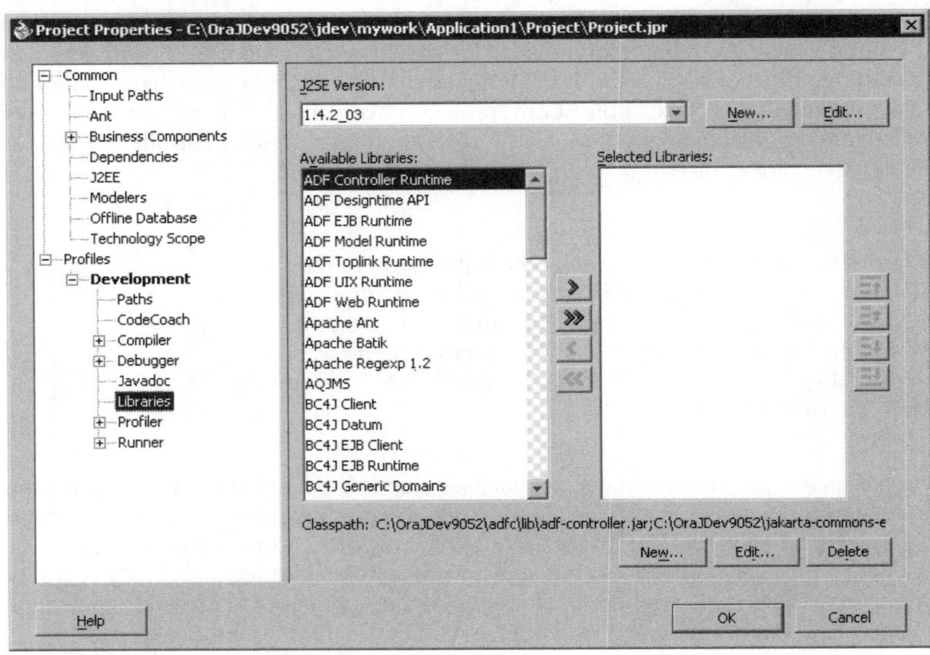

FIGURE 13-3. *The Project Properties dialog box*

There are two additional tabs in the Applications Navigator pane to be aware of. The first one is the Connections tab. This tab segregates out the external connection information that you have configured for Oracle JDeveloper 10*g*. This can include connections to an Application Server (like Oracle Application Server 10*g*), a database, a CVS server, a designer work area (for Oracle Designer repository), a SOAP server, a UDDI Registry (for web services), or a WebDAV server.

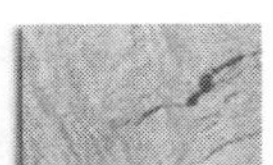

NOTE
WebDAV is a standard used to save data to a web site (as opposed to just reading it from a site). The IETF WWW Distributed Authoring and Versioning working group is responsible for a set of WebDAV standards (see http://www.ietf.org/html.charters/webdav-charter.html and http://www.ics.uci.edu/pub/ietf/webdav/).

Several excellent features are provided for each of the connection types. We will touch briefly on how to configure a connection to a database in the walk-through development of a simple web app later in the chapter.

The second additional tab of interest is the Run Manager tab. This tab allows you to keep track of the active processes that Oracle JDeveloper 10*g* has spawned. When you wish to do local testing or debugging, Oracle JDeveloper 10*g* loads your code into a local stand-alone version of the OC4J container that it spawns.

NOTE
See Chapters 1 and 2 for more information on OC4J.

When you reach a condition where you wish to bring down the local instance (for example, when you're done testing) you would navigate to the Run Manager tab and right-click the OC4J instance, selecting Shutdown.

Editor Pane

The Editor pane is exactly what it sounds like. It is the area where developers will be doing their actual coding. Whenever you wish to modify a file that is contained within your Applications Navigator, it is loaded into the Editor pane and edited as you choose. Loading something into the Editor pane also has a noticeable effect on your environment. First of all, the Structure pane in the lower left-hand corner becomes populated with the relevant information regarding the structure of the file you are editing. In addition, two other panes become visible on the right-hand side of the interface. These are the component palette and the property inspector. We will cover the functions of these panes in subsequent sections of this chapter.

The editor contains several productivity enhancements that would be expected of a fully realized IDE, including intelligent prompting for the completion of typed keywords, predictive dereferencing, and the ability to set bookmarks and breakpoints. If you have experience with other IDEs, none of these features should be new to you.

The absolute basics include compiling and running your code from the editor. To compile a source loaded into the editor, you right-click anywhere in the pane and select Make. The options to run and debug are also present in this pop-up menu. All of these options are also available from the Run and Debug menu options along the main toolbar at the top of the page. Setting a breakpoint is accomplished by clicking the line number of the line you wish to include a breakpoint at.

If you open multiple files within the editor, you can toggle between them by hitting CTRL-TAB or by selecting the tab at the top of the Editor pane with the name of the file you wish to work with. To close a file in the editor, hover over the tab for that file at the top of the editor and click the *x* that appears in the tab.

One of the nicer productivity enhancements made to the editor in 10*g* was the ability to split large documents into multiple panes and have them both available within the editor at the same time. To do this, select the Window | Split Document option. When you're finished, select Window | Unsplit Document to return to normal viewing. Also, if you have more than one document open, you can open up a new, separate Editor pane by selecting Window | New Tab Group.

Property Inspector

Those developers familiar with Microsoft Visual Studio should feel a familiarity with the property inspector added to Oracle JDeveloper 10*g*. With this dialog, the properties of elements selected within the editor can be manipulated irrespective of the explicit source. This is particularly important with the new emphasis being placed on visual building and model-driven development in Oracle JDeveloper 10*g*. To utilize the property inspector, you will need to have a file open in the Editor pane in design mode, as shown in Figure 13-4, and select a component with configurable properties. You can then edit the properties for that particular component and Oracle JDeveloper 10*g* will make modifications to the source, as needed. Design mode in the editor will be covered later in this chapter, when we walk through development of a simple web interface utilizing the ADF and Visual Builder capabilities.

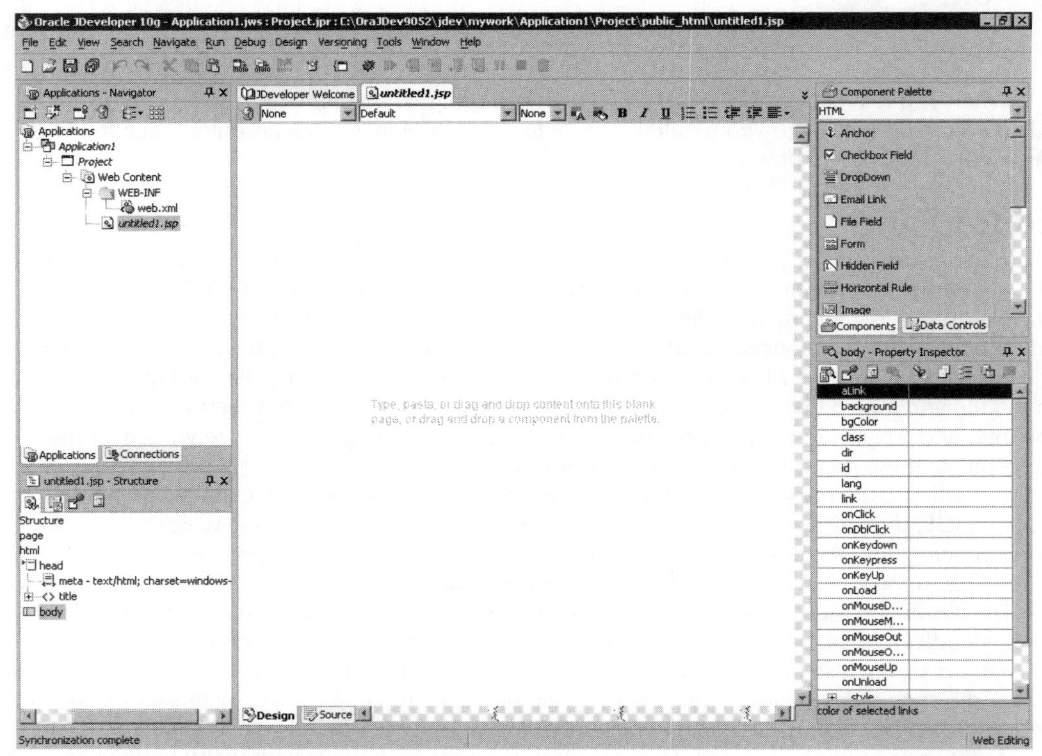

FIGURE 13-4. *Oracle JDeveloper10g in design mode*

Component Palette

The component palette is an essential part of the visual design process for client-facing elements in Oracle JDeveloper 10*g*. The component palette gives you a drop-down selection of technologies with canned functionality for the items listed on the palette for the selected technology (see Figure 13-5). When working on client-facing code, you can click an icon in the component palette and have Oracle JDeveloper 10*g* insert the appropriate code segment where your cursor is in your active source.

This can be done in design mode or source mode. When you're working in design mode, it is often a part of WYSIWYG (what you see is what you get) design and development. This, in conjunction with the property inspector and ADF framework (which we will cover later), makes Oracle JDeveloper 10*g* an excellent option for a RAD (Rapid Application Development) or rapid prototyping IDE.

One of the other included tabs in the component palette is the Data Controls tab. This contains items either that you have developed through the ADF framework as ADF BCs (ADF business components) or that you have explicitly requested Oracle JDeveloper 10*g* to construct

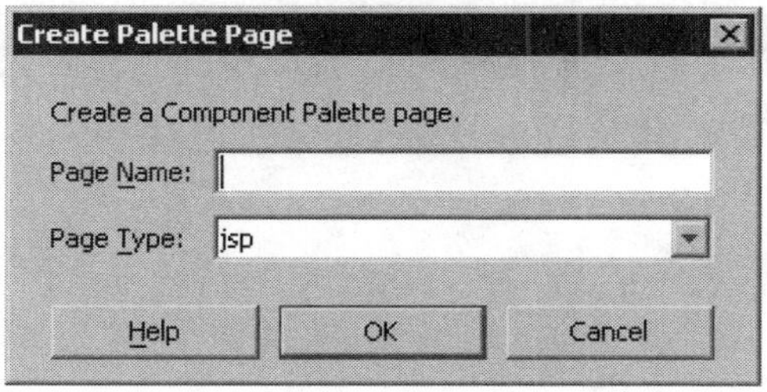

FIGURE 13-5. *The Create Palette Page dialog box*

data controls for based on code you have developed. We will be covering the Data Controls tab in greater detail in the walk-through creation of a simple web app.

Developers can also utilize the component palette to provide a way to disseminate reusable components to your project team. One of the major benefits of JSP development is that it provides for an architecture where presentation developers can be productive without necessarily having to understand Java. The idea is that JSP development can be done entirely with HTML and custom tags (which are, at heart, no more complex in usage than a standard HTML tag). Template JSP pages can be created that include the standard Java basics within them, and once a comprehensive custom tag library is developed that covers the needs of the project, the only skill required is to understand these concepts and the business requirements to develop.

How does the component palette help accomplish this? One of the capabilities of the component palette is to allow a project architect to disseminate the project's custom tag library to all of the presentation developers, while affording them access to it through a point-and-click interface. With the appropriate technology selected in the Technology drop-down, simply right-click the field of the palette. Suppose we want to create a page that contains all of the custom tags for our project. In this case, we will indicate that we want to Add Page from the pop-up menu. At this point, we will be prompted to input a name for our palette page and the technology it will contain (we will select JSP). Once this is completed, we are presented with a fresh component palette page that we can add the appropriate technology components to, in this case, JSP custom tags.

Now that we have our component palette page created, we can proceed to add custom tags to that page. The actual tags themselves will still need to be developed (third-party taglibs can be included easily as well). Once the taglib is developed, all developers have to do is to right-click the new page created in the preceding step and select Add Component from the pop-up menu. At this point, a list of registered taglibs appears in a drill-down menu. Select the New button on the right-hand side of the dialog to register your newly created taglib (or third-party taglib) in the dialog box shown in Figure 13-6.

You are then presented with another dialog box that prompts you for information about your taglib. This information is the same information that you would provide when registering your taglib in the web.xml file of a web application. This stands to reason, as the idea behind the component palette is to allow you to click your way to an application. The component palette needs this information so that it knows what to add to your web application when you request it to insert a particular tag into one of your pages.

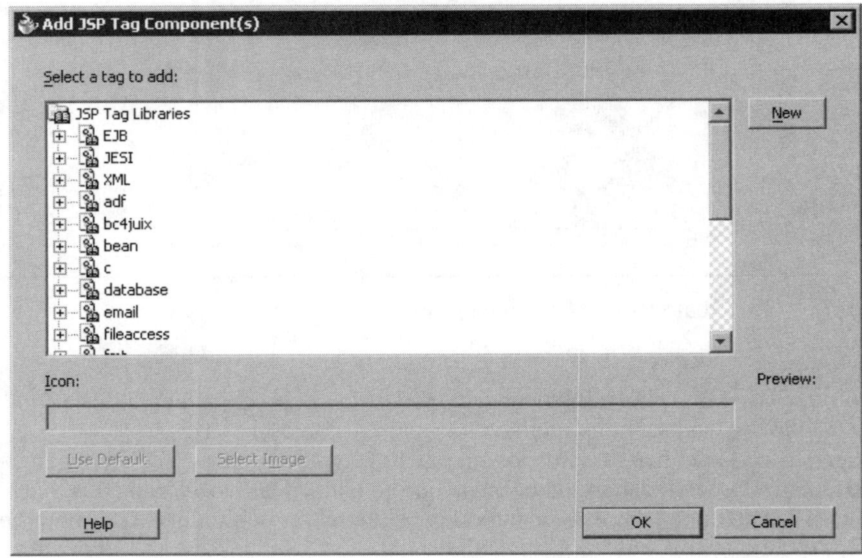

FIGURE 13-6. *The Add JSP Tag Components dialog box*

Once you have registered your taglib, the dialog containing the registered taglibs will now also contain your newly registered taglib. Locate your taglib and drill into it to list the available tags to be added to the project palette. Select the tag you would like to add (using SHIFT and CTRL as normal for multiselecting) and click OK. A confirmation dialog will come up asking you "Install jsp tag(s)?" Click Yes and your new tag should appear in the component palette.

Congratulations! You've just configured your project to take advantage of one of the biggest and most underused productivity tools provided for JSP development.

Structure Pane

The Structure pane is where you can see the structure of the selected item or active code in the Editor pane (if applicable). This can vary widely depending on what has been selected. For example, if you were using the Connections tab in the Applications Navigator to browse a connection to the database, one of the things you can do while exploring this connection is to view the tables that exist in the database (see Figure 13-7). If you were to drill down into the tables and actually select a table in the navigator, you would see a listing of the fields in the table within the Structure pane.

Example of Navigating Tables with the Structure Pane

As an example of how flexible the Structure pane is, if you shift your focus to an HTML source in the Editor pane, the Structure pane will reflect the structure of the HTML code displayed there. The Structure pane can be of assistance when doing web development in several ways. First of all, as HTML is an interpreted language, there is no compiler to do syntax checking. Most developers have had the experience of trying to put together HTML pages with the "type and

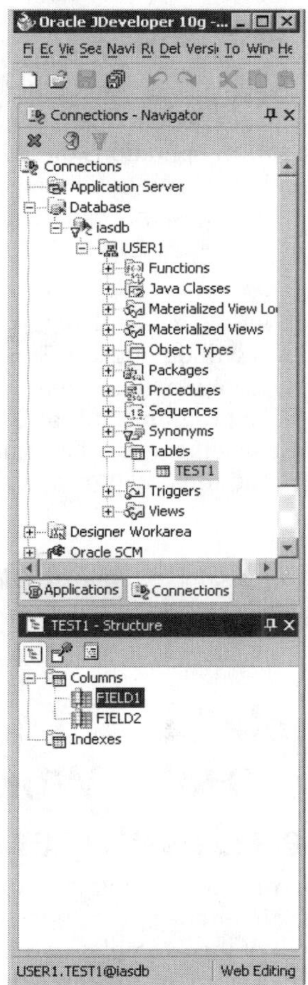

FIGURE 13-7. *The Connections view of the Oracle JDeveloper 10g Navigator*

test" method. This is where you are trying to get a page to look a certain way but for some reason it stubbornly refuses. Eventually, the development gets bogged down into changing a line or two, reloading the page and checking it, changing a few more lines, reloading again, ad nauseam.

The Structure pane can help developers avoid this fate by providing not only a visual cue of the structure of the page but also a substitute for a compiler over this interpreted language. This is provided in the drill-down called "HTML Errors" that appears at the top of the Structure pane when interrogating an HTML source. As you drill into this, it will list the warnings and errors that the pane has detected in the active source. From here, you can double-click the message and be taken to the location in the source that generated the message. This functionality isn't limited to HTML; when the focus is on a JSP page, the only difference is that the drill-down with the message is called "JSP Errors."

The Structure pane really isn't doing anything magical. HTML and JSPs are both tag-based code structures. All the Structure pane is doing is interpreting the tags it finds much as a browser would; instead of rendering the directives, it creates a structure navigator based on the tag hierarchy. However, it also aids developers by allowing selection of these elements to perform editing and customizations on the code without having to perform them directly on the source itself. For example, when working with a table, we can perform operations directly from the Structure pane such as merging or splitting cells, inserting or deleting rows or columns, modifying spans, or even inserting explicit HTML. When dealing with larger pages, this can be an extremely handy time saver.

Message Log

There really isn't a great deal to say about the message log. As is implied, the message log is an area where all of your message windows will be docked. This is where you will see compilation errors and compiler statistics when you compile. It is where you will see any output that would be generated to standard out by your Java programs. It is also where you will see the container messages from the embedded OC4J instance that is used for stand-alone testing. The rule of thumb is: if it would ordinarily go to standard out, there will be a tab in the message log to report on it.

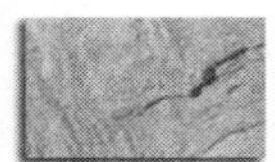

TIP
If the "Allow Program Input" option is selected in the project options, you can also enter in the parameters requested from an application (stdin.readLine();).

Development Example 1: Creating the Classic "Hello World" Java Class in Oracle JDeveloper 10*g*

In this section, we're going to put into practice the information you learned about the physical structure of the Oracle JDeveloper 10*g* interface to create the classic "Hello World" Java class in Oracle JDeveloper 10*g*. Throughout all of the examples in this chapter, we will be stressing the productivity benefits of the tool and, therefore, will be utilizing several of the code generating features of Oracle JDeveloper 10*g*.

Creating the Application Workspace

Recalling the unit of work structure in Oracle JDeveloper 10*g* from the preceding chapter, the first thing we will have to do is create an application workspace. As you may recall, there are several ways to do this. For this example, right-click the Applications node of the drill-down tree in the Applications Navigator and select New Application Workspace. The new application workspace dialog is displayed. Here, we enter our application workspace information. For this example, I have used the following settings, as shown in Figure 13-8:

- The application name is changed from the default to "JdevTutorial."
- The directory name should be automatically updated for you to correspond to your application name; if you wish, you can change it to anything you would like as long as Oracle JDeveloper 10*g* has visibility to the directory in question and there is enough space to hold the files needed.

FIGURE 13-8. *Application settings for our first Oracle JDeveloper 10g project*

- The application package prefix field allows you to specify a default package for all files that will be created in this application workspace. As you will see later when creating Java classes, it will auto-populate the package name with the value we have entered here. For this example, I used the package prefix of "com.tusc.tutorial." For our purposes, the default web application template will be sufficient, so it was left unchanged. Click OK to generate the application workspace.

Creating the Project

As mentioned earlier, the next level down in the application hierarchy in Oracle JDeveloper 10*g* is the project. This is used to organize pieces of code into units of work. Using the default web template, Oracle JDeveloper 10*g* created two projects for us, one named "Model" and the other called "ViewController." For this example, we will create a third project called "Example1." Our second example will be more in-depth and will take advantage of the default packages Oracle JDeveloper 10*g* created for us.

To create a new project, right-click the "JdevTutorial" application workspace and choose New Project. This brings up the New Project Wizard. Since we intend only to demonstrate the basic functions of Oracle Jdeveloper 10*g* in this example, let's keep things simple and leave the Empty Project option selected and click OK. In the next dialog, enter the project name; in this case, let's call it "Example1." The directory path will be automatically updated with the name of your project. Be cautious when changing the directory of your projects, as you can easily end up with an application structure that will cause problems when you try to deploy it, especially if you misplace folders, causing the application to become fragmented.

The last thing we need to do is to inspect the project properties. To do this, right-click the Example1 project and click Project Properties. Notice in the Input Paths tab under the common drill-down that our default package is listed as "mypackage1." At first glance, this might appear to be a bug—when we configured our application workspace, it was supposed to configure our projects to use the package prefix we specified, so why is "mypackage1" displayed? If you open up one of the projects that Oracle JDeveloper 10*g* created for us when we created our application workspace (Model or ViewController) and check the same properties we just checked for our Example1 project, you will see that the "com.tusc.tutorial" prefix is used with the project name appended on the end. The package prefix specified when we created the application workspace is automatically applied only to the projects it creates as part of the application template. Since it is configured in the projects, all classes created in those projects will also inherit these prefixes.

To bring our new project in line with the existing ones from the Application Workspace Wizard, let's re-open the Project Properties dialog box for Example1 and update the default package to read "com.tusc.tutorial.example1."

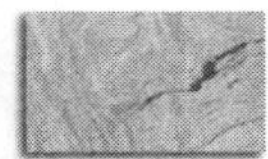

NOTE
We do not capitalize the "e" in example1 even though it is in our project name, since it is considered bad form to use capitals in package names.

Creating the Class

If you are unfamiliar with Java development, some of this section may be hard to follow. Unfortunately, covering the basics of Java development is outside the scope of this book, so in this case, you will simply have to follow along as best you can.

To create the class, right-click the Example1 project and select New. This brings up the now-familiar gallery for selecting what component we wish to create. In this case, drill into the General options, highlighting Simple Files and finally Java Class in the right-hand side, and click OK. In the Create Java Class dialog, change the name to **HelloWorld**. The package should now be properly prepopulated, since we reconfigured the default package for the project in the last section. Leave it as "extending Object," and the only thing we'll change in the Optional Attributes section is to request Oracle JDeveloper 10*g*'s code generator to generate a main method for us. Finally, click OK and you will taken back to the workbench with the new HelloWorld class active in the Editor pane. This is as good a time as any to save your work by selecting SAVE ALL from the menu bar.

Let's add the code to generate our "Hello World" message. For this example, we will stick with the simplest solution and have the class display the text to standard out, utilizing a System.out.println call. However, even something as simple as this provides the opportunity to detail another of Oracle JDeveloper 10*g*'s productivity-increasing features.

Code templates are, essentially, shorthand for creating code components in Oracle JDeveloper 10*g*. To invoke a code template, type the key for the template, press CTRL-ENTER, and Oracle JDeveloper 10*g* will expand the key into the code that is defined to be mapped to it. To view, edit, or create new code templates, you can go to Tools | Preferences and then drill into the code editor selection, choosing code templates from within the drill-down. Here, you will see a listing of the existing shortcuts and the code they will generate. These shortcuts create code ranging from things as simple as the System.out.println that's about to be demonstrated all the way up to things like fully generating a JDBC connection object. To create new code templates, click Add in this dialog and follow the instructions for specifying the shortcut and template code to be applied when it is invoked. Editing is even easier: just select the template you want to edit and edit it directly in the dialog.

Back to our hello world class: make sure the Editor window with your HelloWorld class is active and position your cursor at the end of the first line in the main method, which should read something like this:

```
HelloWorld helloWorld = new HelloWorld();
```

Hit ENTER to place the cursor on a new line, type **sop**, and then press CTRL-ENTER. Notice how Oracle JDeveloper 10*g* replaced the "sop" text with "System.out.println()" and automatically placed the cursor inside the parentheses that delineate the location of the parameter list for the println method. All we have to do now is place a string here saying "Hello World" (be sure to include the quotes to indicate it is a String) and we're done!

Compiling / Running the Class

Compiling is a simple process. There are three different ways to directly compile our HelloWorld class:

- The shortest is to use the shortcut CTRL-SHIFT-F9.
- If you are more visually driven or happen to have your hand on the mouse, you can do a quick right-click in the Editor pane and select Make from the pop-up menu.
- Finally, you can take the longest route and left-click the Run menu item, selecting Make HelloWorld.java from the drop-down menu.

Assuming you typed in everything correctly, you should see something like

```
Successful compilation: 0 errors, 0 warnings
```

displayed in your message log. If you missed something or typed something incorrectly, you will get compilation exceptions. You can double-click the exception message in your message log to jump to the line of code causing the error and repair it. Once you are able to successfully compile, let's move on to running.

If you tried the right-click option for compilation and you were paying attention, you probably noticed the Run option directly below the Make option. You will locate the menu item option under the same Run menu item drop-down as holds the make command.

Any of these options will work. Once you've run the class, you should notice a new Message Log window open with the project name as the name of the tab. Inside this window, you will see the Java command utilized to execute your class (good if you're ever trying to debug a stand-alone app), our text "Hello World!," and the exit condition (see Figure 13-9).

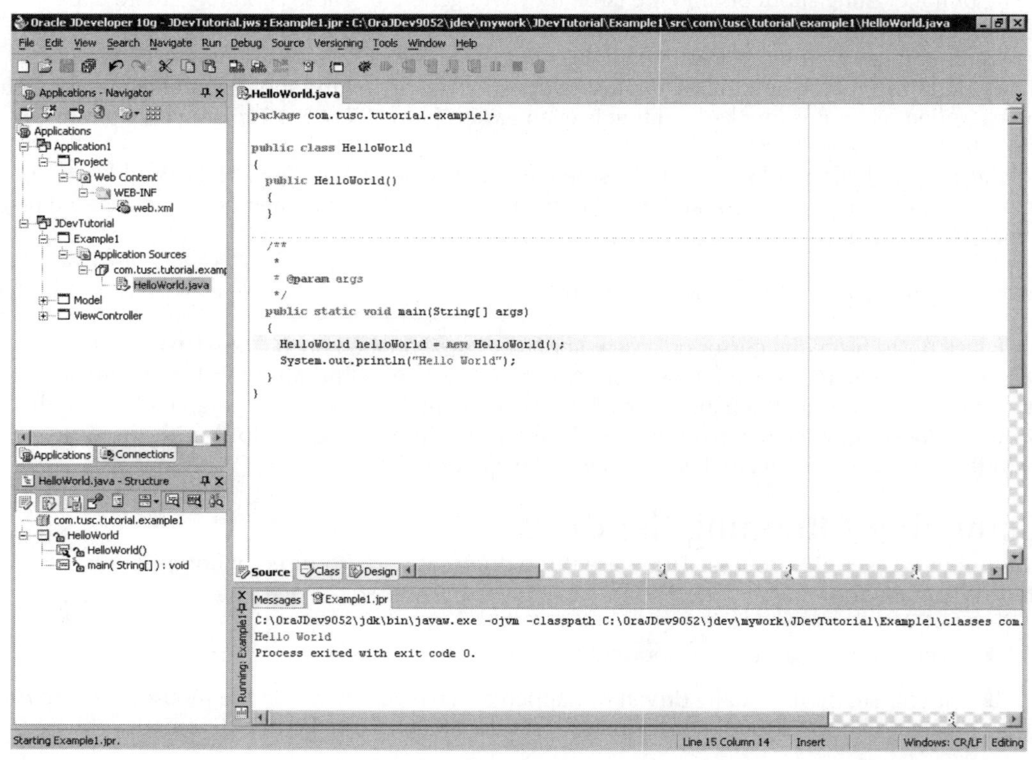

FIGURE 13-9. *Displaying the output of the HelloWorld.java program*

The Hello World Class in Oracle JDeveloper 10*g*

You can also run the class from the project level. The keyboard shortcut for this is F11. In a larger project, you will need to specify what should actually be run when you indicate that you wish to run a project. This is done by specifying it within the project properties for the project in question. The option to specify this can be found in the project properties dialog by drilling into Profiles | Development | Runner. In the Runner section, you can specify the default run target for the project, what VM you would like Oracle JDeveloper 10*g* to use, Java options, program arguments, and a default run directory. If you were building something that was command-line driven, the program arguments item would be of particular interest. This is where you would actually be able to specify what arguments were passed into your main method for testing and execution.

If you ever find you need to pass additional arguments to the Java executable for any reason (altering max heap size, configuring a system parameter using –D, etc.), you would use the Java Options section. This is where you would enter exactly what you would normally place directly between the Java executable and the run target, if you were typing it explicitly on the command line.

Debugging the Class

Debugging in Oracle JDeveloper 10*g* has enough features in and of itself that it could encompass an entire chapter. Few developers can write code perfectly on the first try, and as you add developers to a development project, the odds of needing to debug code grow exponentially as integration issues arise. Even syntactically correct code may not do what is expected, and even if your code compiles *and* does what it is expected, that does not mean that the code being developed by another team member is going to integrate with it successfully.

Having a rich debugging tool is a fundamental part of an efficient IDE. Having a developer who is skilled in its use is as essential as having a developer who knows the syntax of the language he or she is writing the application in. For a more in-depth look at the broad set of features included in the Oracle JDeveloper 10*g* debugging tool, you can refer to the Oracle JDeveloper 10*g* online help, or the Oracle JDeveloper 10*g* Handbook by Oracle Press referenced earlier in this chapter.

In this section, you will get a brief introduction to the debugger, including how to load it and the different command options to navigate your way through a debugging session. The class we've coded is extremely simple, so it doesn't provide very many debugging options. However, since the intent of this section is to illustrate how to get around in the debugger, it should suit our needs.

The first thing we're going to have to do is set a breakpoint. For this example, we will place a breakpoint on the line in the main method that is constructing a new instance of our class. It should look something like this:

```
HelloWorld helloWorld = new HelloWorld();
```

To place the breakpoint, click the line number to the left of the code. This should place a red dot on the line number, indicating that there is a breakpoint on this line and that while running the debugger, Oracle JDeveloper 10*g* will break on that line.

Next, start the debugger by one of these means:

- Click the small red bug in the toolbar.
- Right-click in the Editor pane and select Debug.
- Hit SHIFT-F9.
- Select Debug from the menu bar and then Debug from the drop-down menu.

You'll notice when you do this that Oracle JDeveloper 10*g* first compiles the class, then loads the debugger tool, and then loads your class into the debugger process. At this point, the debugger will stop at the breakpoint we designated in the editor; it tells you this by placing a check mark on the line it is currently at as well as by highlighting the line in light blue. You should also notice that a new window was brought up to the left of our Message Log window (the Message Log window will now be half its original size). This is the Data pane.

The primary use of the Data pane is to allow you to monitor the variables and values in memory for the code you are debugging. It has a couple of different tabs within it:

- The Smart Data tab shows you the variables, constants, arguments, and their values that are close to the execution point in your code (where the red arrow is).
- The Data tab will show all variables, constants, arguments, and their values for your code in general. If a particular element is out of scope, it will indicate this as well.

- The Watches tab allows you to specify particular elements that you want to watch. This is commonly used when you have an element that is key to the code you are working with and potentially nested into a complex relationship. Simply place a watch on it and you can monitor its progress through the Watches tab instead of having to drill through the relationships in one of the other tabs as you debug.

A couple of other tabs are available in the Data pane but are outside of the scope of this chapter. Now let's look at the navigation options once the debugger is loaded.

We'll traverse the buttons from left to right, as shown in Figure 13-10. The button furthest to the left is the Debugger button. This is the little red bug that we were referring to earlier when we were going to start the debugger.

The next button that looks like a green arrow is the Resume button (F9), which instructs the debugger to resume execution of your code until it either terminates (for whatever reason) or reaches the next debug point.

Next is the Step Over button (F8). This button instructs the debugger to step over the line of code that is the current execution point. This will still invoke the logic on that line and any

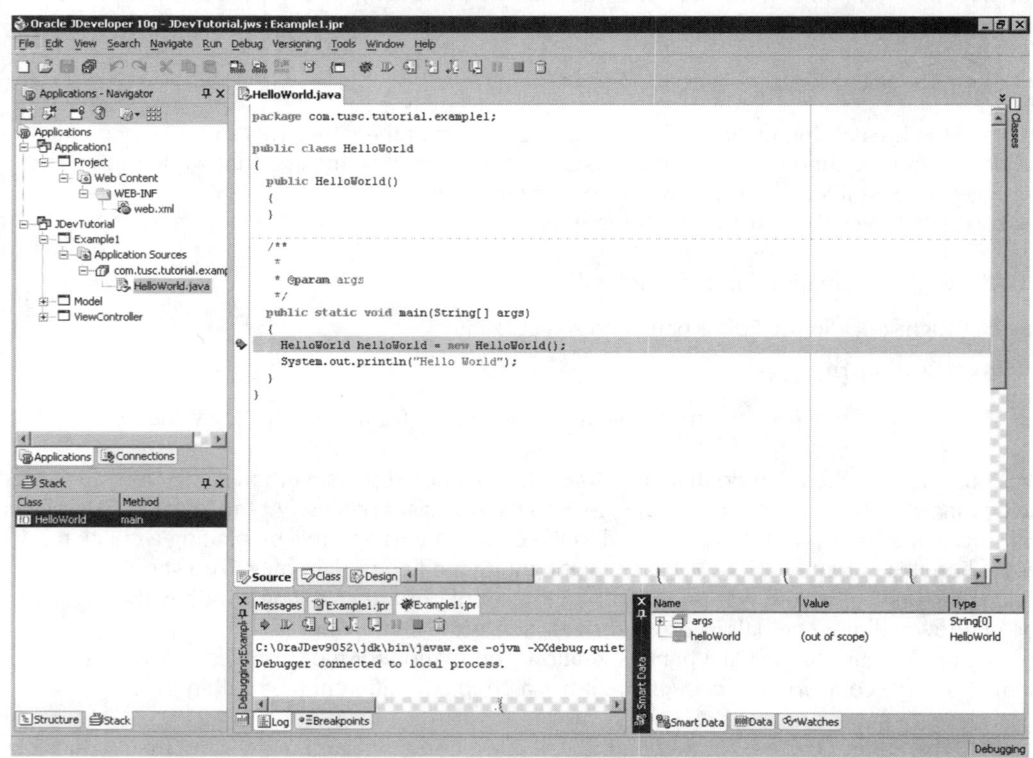

FIGURE 13-10. *Oracle JDeveloper 10g debugger navigation tool buttons*

nested calls therein and will return control to you on the next line in the current source. Keep in mind when debugging complex logic that if you have a breakpoint at some other point in your code that ends up being invoked by the call at the current execution point, the debugger will stop at that breakpoint even though you requested it to step over in the current source.

Next is the Step Into button (F7). This button will instruct the debugger to actually step into the call stack for the code at the current execution point. For example, if you are at the execution point in class A and the code at that execution point is calling a method in class B, hitting the Step Into button will bring up the code for class B in the editor and move the execution point to the first line of the method being called in class B. Should you ask the debugger to step into code that Oracle JDeveloper 10*g* does not have the source for but has a reference to, the class file for it will ask you if you wish to have Oracle JDeveloper 10*g* try to generate the code for you.

CAUTION
The results you will get from this vary, but in my experience you are better off to avoid trying to do this. In general, when you are debugging, you can be fairly certain that the code you are working with that is a "black box" is coded correctly and it is only a matter of getting your code to interoperate with it correctly.

The next button is the Step Out button (SHIFT-F7). This button once again relies on the call stack and instructs the debugger to try to step out of the current scope and back up the call stack one level. So in our example from the preceding button, if we are in class A and step into a method in class B, and then we realize that we're not really interested in what's happening in the method in class B, we can step out to return us to the next execution point in class A. This can also be a helpful remedy when we inadvertently step into something we really don't want to.

The next button is the Step To End Of Method button. This button will, as its name implies, step you to the end of the current method, placing the execution point at the line before the method would exit.

TIP
A very common use of this button is to assist you in locating where an element is being mutated into an incorrect value. Place a watch on the element in question, step into methods along the call stack, and step to the end of the method as you go until you notice the value change to the incorrect value. You now know what method is causing the problem. You can then reload the debugger with a breakpoint at the beginning of the offending method and step through it line-by-line to determine exactly where the problem is occurring.

Next, we have the Pause button. This button actually pauses execution of the program wherever it is. To resume execution, use the Resume button. To halt execution, use the Stop button (which we will discuss next).

As was stated in the description of the last button, the Stop button (CTRL-F2) halts execution of the program and terminates the debugger.

The final button is the Garbage Collection button. As we all know, there is no reliable way to directly invoke Java garbage collection. This button makes an attempt to manually trigger garbage collection, assuming the virtual machine supports such an action.

Back to our example: We currently have our HelloWorld class loaded into the debugger with the current execution point at the line that instantiates the class. If you look at the Smart Data tab in the Data pane, you notice that our helloWorld variable is currently out of scope. This means the debugger is aware of it but it has yet to have memory allocated for it. Essentially, it is just saying the debugger does not have a handle to this variable yet; in other cases, it could indicate the debugger once had a handle to it but does no longer. Step into this line using the Step Into toolbar button or the shortcut F7. Notice that it took us to the head of the constructor for this class, which is what was invoked by the "new" keyword that was at our previous execution point. We're not really interested in the constructor (particularly since it has no logic in it), so let's step out of the method using the Step Out toolbar button (or SHIFT-F7). This takes us back to our last execution point. Let's go ahead and step over this line now using the Step Over button (or F8). This takes us to the next line in our code, which is our call to System.out.println. Notice that the arrow marking our execution point and the highlight have now shifted to this line. If we once again look in the Smart Data tab of the Data pane, we notice that our helloWorld variable is no longer out of scope. If we had any variables declared within the HelloWorld class, we could now drill into that variable reference to look at them. For now, go ahead and step over this line as well (F8). You should now notice "Hello World!" show up in the output window for our Example1.jpr tab in the Message pane. That's all we were really interested in seeing, so go ahead and hit the Resume toolbar button (or F9). Our Example1.jpr tab in the Message pane should now show that the debugger has disconnected and that we have exited the process with an exit code of 0. This also terminates the debugger and closes our Data pane.

Something you may have noticed while running the debugger: an additional tab added to the bottom of the Message pane called Breakpoints. If you opened this, you would have seen the default breakpoints as well as the one we set in our HelloWorld class. This is also accessible while not running the debugger. To get it to appear, you can right-click the head of the Message pane (which actually appears on the left-hand side of the pane) and click breakpoints on the pop-up window.

Web Application Development Features of Oracle JDeveloper 10*g*

Up to this point, we have worked through some of the basic features of Oracle JDeveloper 10*g*. If all we are looking for is a basic IDE, it should be apparent that Oracle JDeveloper 10*g* covers all of the standard amenities one would expect from an IDE. But these days, developers aren't satisfied with "adequate"; companies and developers are looking for that "edge." Anything that can provide additional productivity is critical in an environment where time to develop takes ever-increasing precedence over the actual content being delivered. Make no mistake, however, projects are still expected to deliver rich content, robust frameworks, and ease of extension and maintainability. Following the traditional method of "roll your own" framework development is simply not possible for most modern projects and, with the advent of so many proven frameworks, is no longer nearly as necessary.

I recall one of the first frameworks I developed was a dynamic SQL generator that allowed me to collate data across differing databases (including differing database vendors). Later, I ended up taking over responsibility for our persistence layer. Simply maintaining this framework was nearly a full-time job. Several years later, I developed my first TCF (thin-client framework). The model was based on the J2EE BO-VO-DAO pattern and later had to incorporate EJBs. I spent over a year working with this.

I look back on these efforts now, and it amazes me how much time I spent working on things that could now be solved with off-the-shelf frameworks. My dynamic SQL generator could be replaced by Periscope (for more information about Periscope, go to http://www.tusc.com/periscope). The persistence framework could be replaced by any number of viable candidates, including Hibernate, JDO, TopLink, or ADF. And the idea of developing your own TCF these days is almost laughable with robust frameworks like Struts and Spring on the market. Open source development has really turned framework development on its ear; in many cases, it is now something that ambitious or passionate developers do as side projects rather than byproducts that get generalized out of finalized development efforts, but that is another discussion altogether.

So what is the relevance of this little aside? Well, as I was just saying, Oracle JDeveloper 10*g* is an adequate IDE if all we're looking for is just a standard development and debugging tool, but developers need more these days. What one needs to consider, beyond the basics when picking an IDE, is what that IDE offers above and beyond the standard amenities. What is critical is how easily it allows you to integrate with some of these frameworks. In the case of Oracle JDeveloper 10*g*, not only does it easily allow you to integrate with these frameworks, it actually comes bundled with some of the most popular major frameworks in the industry today. Oracle JDeveloper 10*g* comes integrated (out of the box) with Struts and ADF (which includes Oracle TopLink 10*g*). It also includes several other mission-critical components for successful project development such as native integration with Ant (automated build and deployment), a plug-in for JUnit (for unit testing and integration), and a rich suite of design and modeling tools.

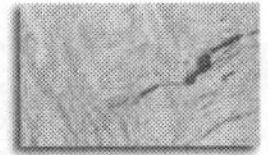

NOTE
OracleAS TopLink is a tool that provides mapping between relational databases (like Oracle) and object-oriented languages (like Java). OracleAS TopLink enables developers to: persist Java objects in virtually any relational database supported by a JDBC 2.0–compliant driver; map any object model to any relational schema, using the OracleAS TopLink Mapping Workbench graphical mapping tool; and use OracleAS TopLink successfully, even if they are unfamiliar with SQL or JDBC, because OracleAS TopLink provides a clean, object-oriented view of relational databases.

As we will see in our advanced examples later in the chapter, Oracle JDeveloper has taken major strides with version 10*g* to the point of providing rich functionality outside of the application-tier development realm. Oracle JDeveloper 10*g* has taken on additional capabilities to design and develop both the database structure as well as database-embedded functionality (triggers, packages, procedures, etc.). Instead of having your application development tool, your data modeling tool, your database management tool, and your PL/SQL development tool, you could just use Oracle JDeveloper 10*g*. Let's take a closer look at some of the features 10*g* offers.

Diagramming

Let's start with design. Oracle JDeveloper 10*g* has UML diagramming tools that allow you to design both the high-level and detail-oriented specifics of your system. Here are some of the diagrams that Oracle JDeveloper 10*g* provides:

- UML use case diagrams
- UML class diagrams

- UML class diagrams from XMI import
- Java class diagrams
- Activity diagrams
- Business components diagrams
- EJB diagrams
- Struts config diagrams
- Web service diagrams
- Database diagrams

Covering the specifics of each of these kinds of diagrams is outside of the scope of this chapter; however, we will touch on manipulating some of these later, in the advanced examples. The thing to gather from this list is that Oracle JDeveloper 10*g* offers a rich suite of UML diagramming capabilities and that many of these can be used to directly manipulate and/or generate code for you.

Struts Integration

Oracle JDeveloper 10*g* is integrated with the Jakarta Struts controller framework. Utilization of this framework is optional, but Oracle JDeveloper 10*g* has made major strides and taken great effort to ease the learning curve, the difficulty of implementation, and the maintenance involved with implementing this framework. As part of the Struts integration with the ADF framework (which we will discuss next), Oracle implemented extensions to the standard Struts framework, allowing it to seamlessly integrate with the ADF framework. This allows developers to do some of the amazingly easy prototyping that we will do in our advanced exercise later in the chapter.

The concept of a controller framework is to allow for a centralized configuration of the interactivity of your application while also allowing for modularity on a unit-of-work basis. Struts is also based around the BO-VO (Business Object–Value Object) or DTO (Data Transfer Object) pattern. The framework follows the MVC (Model-View-Controller) pattern by implementing the C (controller) portion of the framework completely and providing hooks to assist in the V (View) portion. The Struts framework consists of four key components:

- Struts request dispatcher
- Struts config.xml
- Struts action classes
- Struts form classes

The Struts request dispatcher and the Struts config file make up the brains of your application. You will likely never see the request dispatcher unless you end up stepping into it at one point during a debug session (if you're lucky, you'll never see your own brain either, but that doesn't make it any less important). The request dispatcher is what coordinates the transfer of control and handoff of requests within the Struts framework. Oracle created a custom extension to this class in 10*g* to integrate it with the data bindings layer of the framework as well as to provide the ability for it to handle event management of its custom extensions to the Struts action class.

The Struts config file is where you lay down the roadmap of your application. It is where all of the pages of your application are defined and linked together via actions, events, and paths to JSPs. This is also where you declare all of your action and form classes so that Struts knows which forms are associated with which actions and which JSP files.

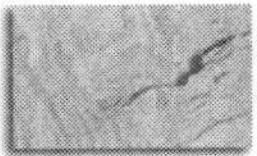

NOTE
We will cover the Struts config file in slightly more detail in the advanced example later in the chapter, but if you are really interested in Struts, my suggestion would be to check out the online documentation at http://Struts.apache.org.

Form classes implement the value object pattern in that their sole purpose is to contain data for the application. They can also provide some rudimentary validation logic. This can also be contained within the more advanced Struts validator system in the framework. The form classes are stand-alone Java classes that extend the org.apache.Struts.action.ActionForm class. As mentioned earlier, they are configured within the Struts config file. One of the major benefits of this class within the framework is that the Struts framework utilizes introspection to populate the form class that is associated with an action with the request parameters that map to the values defined within the class. This implies the standard reflection/introspection bean rules in that the values in the form class should be defined as private with appropriate accessors and mutators as needed.

The action class's primary responsibility is to operate between the HTTP request and the business logic defined for the application. It also has the job of determining what event condition applies to navigation and performing the lookup through the framework to locate the appropriate forward to be issued into the request dispatcher. The main entry point to the action class is the execute method, within which your custom decision logic can reside. With the introduction of the ADF framework and the custom Oracle extensions, a great deal of this work is abstracted away from developers so that you need not bother with it if you don't want to. You can now define methods on the DataAction extension for your unit of work (DataAction is an ADF extension of the Struts Action class) to handle specific events when the action is executed. You do this by defining a method in the DataAction that has a signature of

```
public void onEVENT(DataActionContext ctx)
```

where EVENT is equal to the name of the event you wish to handle. For more information on this, see the Oracle JDeveloper 10*g* online documentation.

Alternatively, you can actually view the specific source code by creating a unit of work that has a DataAction extension, opening that extension, highlighting the term DataAction anywhere in the stubbed-out class, right-clicking it, and selecting "go to declaration." This is an extremely nice feature of Oracle JDeveloper 10*g* in that you can highlight pretty much anything in your source code and select this option. Depending on the context of the item you have selected, either you will go to the line of code where the item was declared (if it is a variable), you will go to the header of the method (if it is a method), or it will open the source file for the class if it is a class type.

The ADF Framework

To cover the ADF framework in detail would require a minimum of a chapter unto itself. What we will try to do in this section is to at least give you some background on what the ADF framework is supposed to be and how it is relevant to the Oracle JDeveloper 10*g* environment.

NOTE
For a more detailed look at the high-level ADF features, refer to http://www.oracle.com/technology/products/jdev/collateral/papers/10g/ADF_overview.pdf.

ADF is really about "productivity with choice," and for once a corporate tag line delivers on its promise. ADF is a framework whose presence is felt as much or as little in your application as you desire. Its involvement can span all layers of the application development from presentation layer (with UIX or JClient) all the way to the persistence layer (ADF Business Components or TopLink). There are so many potential combinations of ways you could utilize some or all of the ADF framework that it is easier to introduce the framework in a visual manner. Figure 13-11 offers a diagram that is provided by Oracle to represent a high-level map of the ADF framework.

In Figure 13-11, the areas that show shading are those that are completely ADF. The other areas are technologies that ADF integrates with and that are available as integrated options when utilizing the ADF framework. Let's start closest to the client tier and work our way back toward the data tier.

ADF JClient

JClient is the ADF Swing extension. It allows a developer to develop a Swing GUI while still having the robust support of the ADF BC (business components) framework behind it. If you are familiar with BC4J, note that the ADF BC is just BC4J in the context of the ADF framework.

ADF UIX

ADF UIX is the newest incarnation of the UIX tag libraries. This gives an option to utilize the UIX structure as an alternative to the JSP page development.

ADF Data Bindings and Data Controls

The bindings and data controls are what allow the application components to integrate with the ADF BCs so easily. All of the presentation-layer technologies listed have been enhanced or extended to integrate with this new layer.

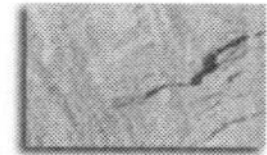

NOTE
The logic behind these technologies is rather complex and outside the scope of this chapter. If you're interested in the nuts and bolts of this layer, feel free to reference the Oracle white paper on the subject: http://www.oracle.com/technology/products/jdev/collateral/papers/10g/ADFBindingPrimer/index.html.

ADF Application Module

The next component is where we actually begin to encounter the components that were previously part of the BC4J framework. The concepts behind these components remain (relatively) the same, so if you're familiar with the BC4J framework, you may want to skip ahead a few sections. If you aren't, understand that the application module is the component that acts as the application interface into our persistence framework if we're utilizing the ADF BCs. The application module aggregates the view objects that we want to have available for this unit of work into a single container that we can access. We will cover working with application modules in more detail later, in the advanced example.

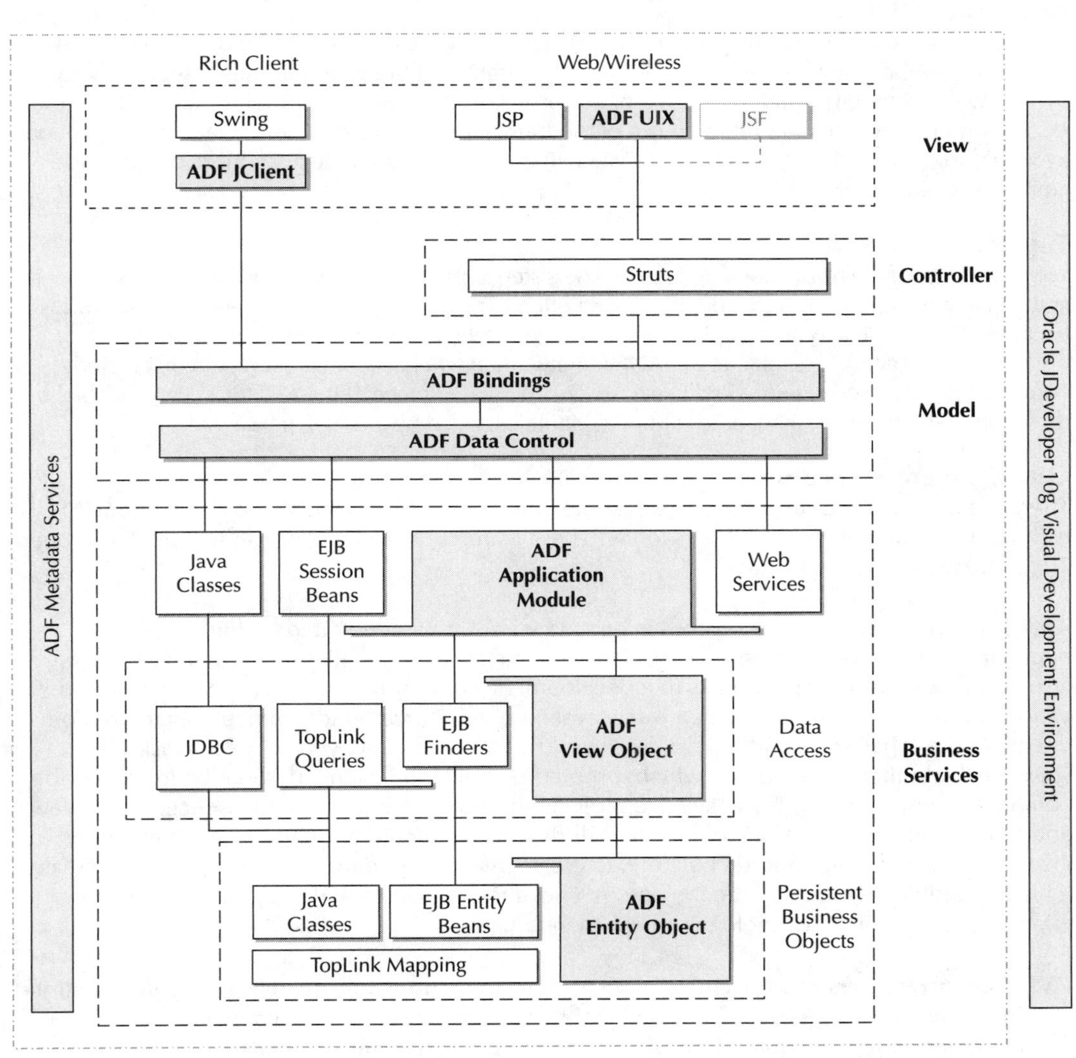

FIGURE 13-11. *The Oracle ADF framework*

ADF View Object

The view objects are what we utilize to create filtered views of data based on our persistent entity objects (which we will cover next). There are actually quite a few things we can do with the view objects to help us to define how this data is organized. We will cover working with view objects in more detail in the advanced example.

ADF Entity Object

The ADF entity objects are fairly simple to understand. These objects are the base data objects for our framework. Most often, they are a direct reflection of tables in our database, but there are several ways to specify what the source of our persistent data is. Entity objects manage both the storage and retrieval of data into and out of the framework. There are some configuration options available for how entity objects behave. We will cover the entity objects in more detail in the advanced example.

TopLink

TopLink is one of the most widely recognized persistence frameworks in the industry. While looking at the diagram we just covered, you may have noticed TopLink referenced in several places. This is because after Oracle acquired TopLink, it was immediately provided as an option in 9*i*. With 10*g*, Oracle has integrated TopLink into the ADF framework. If you have a migration path that includes TopLink, you're all set. If you would like to utilize TopLink in place of the ADF BCs, you are able to do so while still retaining other areas of functionality provided by the ADF framework.

Other Integrated Features

There are other features that make use of some of the latest development and deployment technologies available to developers today. These features are integrated into Oracle JDeveloper 10*g* and are summarized below.

Ant Oracle JDeveloper 10*g* comes integrated with Ant for automated building and deployment. Many of the most successful development methodologies recommend regular automated builds and deployments to a development environment to verify functionality and validity of the code base. Ant is the most prevalent open source build and deployment tool on the market. It is based around XML-defined build scripts that allow you to specify tasks, the source to be built, the method by which it should be built, and even a destination to deploy the completed application to. If you select a project within your application, right-click, select New, and look under the general section of the drill-down, you should find the Ant section, which gives you the option to import a buildfile, to create one based on the active project, or to create a blank buildfile. If you don't see the option, click the drop-down at the top of the gallery and change it from Project Technologies to All Technologies.

CVS (Concurrent Versions System) CVS is easily the most widely recognized source control tool in the industry. Besides having functional benefits, it is historically significant. Some of the familiar branded source control tools such as Microsoft Visual Source Safe were actually developed utilizing CVS as the source control tool for the project. Anyone who has been doing development for any period of time will attest to the need for a source control tool available for the project. Anyone who has worked with CVS will be able to speak to the capabilities of the tool, but many may also speak of the difficulty with surmounting its learning curve. Due to the history of the project, it was not developed with any sort of fancy graphical interface—it is essentially all command-line driven. Oracle JDeveloper 10*g* eases some of the integration tasks with this by providing menu-driven options that are translated into command-line executions against the CVS repository you configure. You configure your connection to the CVS repository through the Connections tab of the Applications Navigator and can access the CVS commands themselves through the versioning menu item or by right-clicking appropriate items in the Applications Navigator pane.

JUnit JUnit is one of the most popular unit testing tools on the market today. It was included as an optional plug-in for Oracle JDeveloper 9.0.3 and continues to be available in 10*g*. The concept behind JUnit is simple: Developers create classes that act as external testing units for the code you are developing. These units have individual test cases, which are then aggregated into test suites. By continued aggregation, you can have test suites that encompass a unit of work, aggregate several units of work into a subsystem, and aggregate several subsystems into your entire application. JUnit testing is also available to be executed as an Ant build task, such that when your Ant tasks execute for your nightly build, they execute all of the JUnit tests for the code being built. Thus, not only is the build being tested, but the compilation and functionality tests for the application are all being carried out simultaneously. In the next section, we are going to cover a more advanced application example that will demonstrate several of the features of the 10*g* ADF framework.

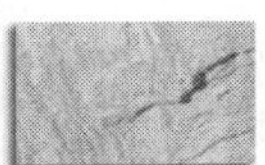

NOTE
The default install of Oracle JDeveloper 10g does not come with the Junit plug-in extension. You must go to OTN to download and install the plug-in. The current plug-in extension is Jdev9052_Junit.zip.

Development Example 2: Building a Completely Functional Web Application in Seven Steps with ADF

As discussed earlier, the productivity benefits of ADF are quite significant. This framework provides a greatly enhanced capability to develop in a RAD (Rapid Application Development) or agile development environment. It also allows for ease of rapid prototyping. It is this feature that we are going to focus on in this section. We're going to go from having only a database table defined to a fully functional web application integrated with the Struts open source controller framework in seven steps. This process is also capable of being almost entirely wizard and visually driven.

The image in Figure 13-12 should seem familiar, as it is a subset of the ADF architecture overview image from the last section. In this diagram, we see a segmented application architecture diagram outlining a typical MVC architecture and mapping it into ADF and Oracle JDeveloper 10*g* terms. It also diagrams what technologies from the ADF suite we will be utilizing in our example to implement our prototype site. Let's take a look at each tier, examine the standard mapping to the MVC pattern, discuss the ADF technology we will utilize at that level, and finally, relate the framework to the Oracle JDeveloper 10*g* project it is going to be mapped into.

Starting from the client-facing components and moving backward, we have the view layer. Classically, the view layer is composed of the components that actually make up the visual layer of the application; it is the view into the business domain data for the application. In the ADF framework, as we have discussed earlier, there are a great many choices of what technology to utilize at this level. Since we're interested in demonstrating how the ADF framework has been integrated into the Struts controller framework, our example will utilize JSP pages as our view layer. These components will be contained in the Oracle JDeveloper 10*g* ViewController project, which we will discuss in more detail later.

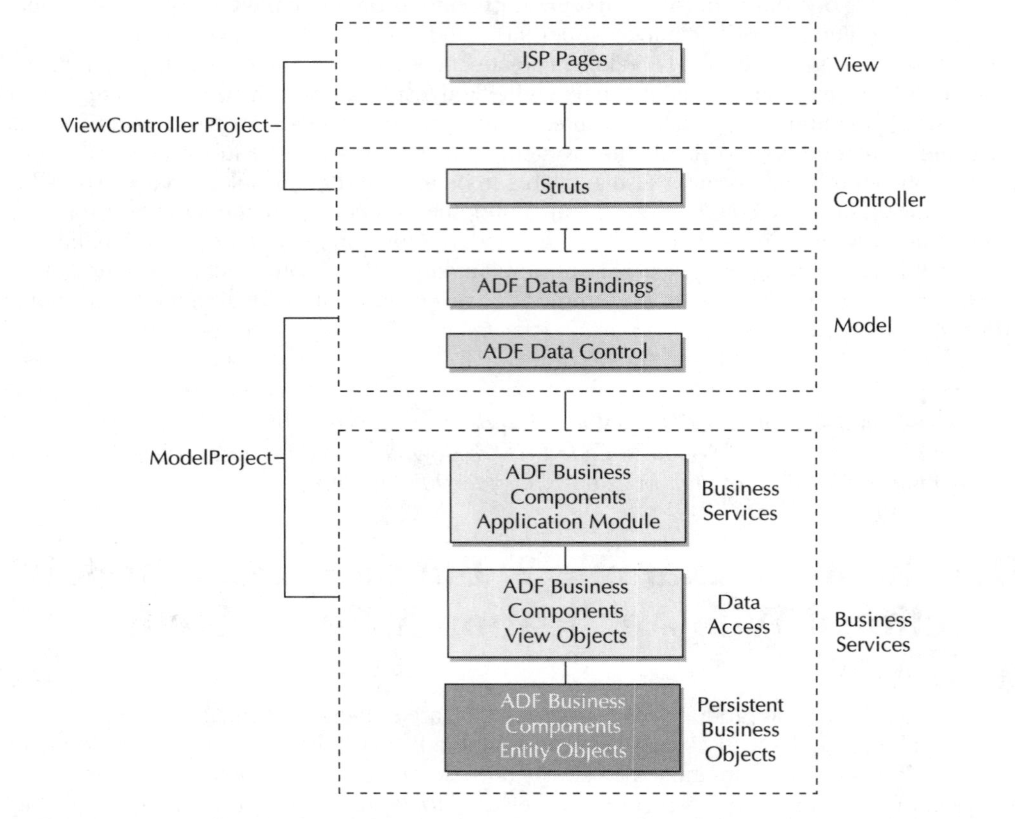

FIGURE 13-12. *The model-view-controller framework*

The next layer in our diagram is the controller layer. As discussed in the earlier section "Struts Integration," the controller is the architectural term for the component(s) in your application that manage the interaction and navigation of your site. They're also the components that manage interaction with your business components and data. In our diagram, we have the Struts framework classes represented as our controller layer, and indeed, that is what we will be using. Contrary to our discussion on Struts, however, in this example we will not code one line of an action or form class, nor will we actually enter the code that registers these classes in the Struts config.xml file (piqued your interest yet?). In our Oracle JDeveloper 10*g* environment, these classes will be contained within the ViewController project, the same as our JSPs.

Now is an appropriate time to discuss the first of our Oracle JDeveloper 10*g* projects associated with the example, the ViewController project. As you may recall from our basic Java example, when we selected the default web application template for our application workspace, Oracle JDeveloper 10*g* created two default projects for us, the ViewController and Model projects.

The naming convention here seems rather straightforward; the ViewController project contains anything that is related to the view (or controller) layers of an application (and so is visual and navigational), and the Model package contains our business services and model components. The ViewController project contains all of the web content for the application, and indeed there is a drop-down within the ViewController project that is labeled Web Content. Within this drop-down, you will find the structure of your eventually deployed doc root, including your Struts config.xml and web.xml files. Under the Application Sources drop-down, you will find the other configuration files for the presentation layer, including all of the UIModel files, the DataBindings files, and the ApplicationResources.properties file (as we have not created anything yet, only the ApplicationResources.properties file is present). Also, you will find any concrete Struts extensions made for your application in the application sources file.

Back to our diagram. Moving forward, we reach the Model portion of the MVC pattern. This is ordinarily the location of the application-tiered data container components. Coordinating some of the other J2EE patterns, this is where the BO-VO-DAO (or DTO) pattern would come into play. The model components would ordinarily be our BO/VO classes. ADF simplifies this pattern into the utilization of EL (expression language) to access the data by mapping the requested information through the data bindings, to the data control, and eventually through the application module, which serves as our persistence interface (or DAO).

NOTE
The application module was covered in our earlier section "The ADF Framework." For more information on EL, see Chapter 14.

Oddly enough, the Oracle JDeveloper 10*g* project that contains the components that make up the MVC Model concept reside in the Oracle JDeveloper 10*g* standard web application project called Model.

At this point, we have stepped back far enough that we have reached our true persistence layer. Labeled Business Services in our diagram, this would traditionally be developed utilizing a custom persistence framework, POJO (plain old Java object) or DAO (data access object) objects. In the ADF framework, this is made up of our ADF BCs. As you may recall, we have our application module, view objects, and persistent entity objects. These are bundled into the Oracle JDeveloper 10*g* Model class.

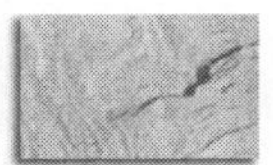

NOTE
In regard to the default projects, by no means are developers restricted to utilizing these default projects when developing an ADF application within Oracle JDeveloper 10g. You could name your projects whatever you would like, and even divide the classes up in a different manner, for example, placing all of your business components in separate folders according to their units of work. These folders are there only because we selected the default template and wish to utilize some of the default capabilities to accelerate our rapid prototype.

Now that we've discussed the basics, let's begin generating the prototype in Oracle JDeveloper 10*g*. The seven steps we are going to follow to generate our prototype from an existing table include:

1. Create the workspace.
2. Create the database connection (if necessary).
3. Model business components (entity).
4. Model business components (view).
5. Model business components (application module).
6. Create the page flow (controller).
7. Create the JSP page.

It should also be noted that to complete this example, it is assumed that you have access to the scott/tiger schema in an Oracle database, and that it is visible to the machine you are attempting to create this example on.

Create the Workspace

The first thing we need to do is to create our application workspace. You can refer to the sections earlier on the Application Workspace Navigator for the different methods. It is also perfectly acceptable to utilize the existing JDevTutorial workspace created for the previous exercise; this is the method used for this example. If you choose to create a new workspace, follow the directions for creating a workspace from the first example, remembering to make sure to select "Web Application [default]" as your application template.

Create the Database Connection

At this point, it is prudent to make sure we have a database connection created and configured properly. To create our business components, we will need access to a database instance to feed our tables to the ADF framework in Oracle JDeveloper 10*g*. As you may recall, we discussed the Connections tab within the Applications Navigator pane. This is where we will create and access our database connections from within Oracle JDeveloper 10*g*. Click the Connections tab at the bottom of the Applications Navigator pane to open this tab. Next, right-click the Database drill-down and select New Database Connection. This will take you to the new Database Connection Wizard. There are four basic steps to completing this wizard:

1. Provide a name for the connection.
2. Provide the username and password of the schema you are connecting to.
3. Provide the hostname and system identifier (SID) of the database box and instance you are connecting to.
4. Test the connection.

The wizard itself is fairly straightforward in this respect, and the test utility at the end of the wizard ensures that the connection is created correctly. If you get errors when creating your connection, make sure you have visibility to the box, the database is up, and the required information has been entered correctly. Once you have the database connection completed, we can continue on to investigating what information is provided in the Connections tab.

Once you have successfully completed the Connection Wizard, go ahead and connect to the database utilizing this new connection. To do this, you can either right-click the connection name and explicitly instruct it to connect, or you can simply drill down into the connection, causing Oracle JDeveloper 10*g* to automatically attempt to establish a connection. For this example, drill into the schema, and take note of the wide variety of options available and data provided. If you click the drill-down for the Tables option, you will see all of the tables located in the database for this schema. As was mentioned earlier in discussions of the Structure pane, if you left-click one of the tables, the relevant structure (columns, indexes, etc.) will be listed in the Structure pane below.

If you're looking for a little more information or would perhaps like to peruse the actual data in the table, you can double-click the table name in the Connections Navigator to open the table in the Editor pane. The Editor pane will display the table information with two tabs available (see Figure 13-13). The first and default one is the Structure tab. It includes much of the same information provided in the Structure pane with a bit more room to work with as well as an aggregation of all relevant data into a single view.

The other tab available in the Editor pane when viewing table information is the Data tab. As its name implies, it is for viewing the data contained within this table. It brings up a spreadsheet-like window that presents (by default) the first 100 rows of the table with all columns listed.

This is beneficial, but how often are developers working on production-level applications interested in the data from only a single table? Suppose you need to view data as a "real" application would, using a SQL query? Oracle JDeveloper 10*g* can accommodate you there as well. There are several options available: If you right-click the connection, you will notice in the drop-down menu where you have the option to run SQL*Plus from within Oracle JDeveloper 10*g*. In reality, this just automates the opening of a command window and execution of the default SQL*Plus executable (specified by the developer) the first time you choose this option. While somewhat limited in its practicality, it is still a nice convenience.

The second, and more impressive, option is to open the SQL Worksheet. This brings up a split window with the ability to enter SQL into the upper window and execute it against your connection to the database, producing a custom result in the lower pane (see Figure 13-14). This is extremely helpful when debugging an application. If you stumble across a query that isn't executing properly or is returning unexpected results, you can place a watch on the SQL statement and, once it is fully constructed, pull the value out, drop it in the SQL worksheet, and execute it.

Feel free to experiment with the other options available in the Connection drop-down. With this interface, you can perform a great deal of database development work, including management of table structures, definitions, and creation of database objects. You can also manage PL/SQL development, including packages, functions, and triggers, among other things. Oracle JDeveloper 10*g* has made major strides as a single IDE, capable of managing all development needs. For more information on the other capabilities of this section, see Avrom Faderman et al., *Oracle JDeveloper 10g Handbook* (McGraw-Hill/Osborne, 2004).

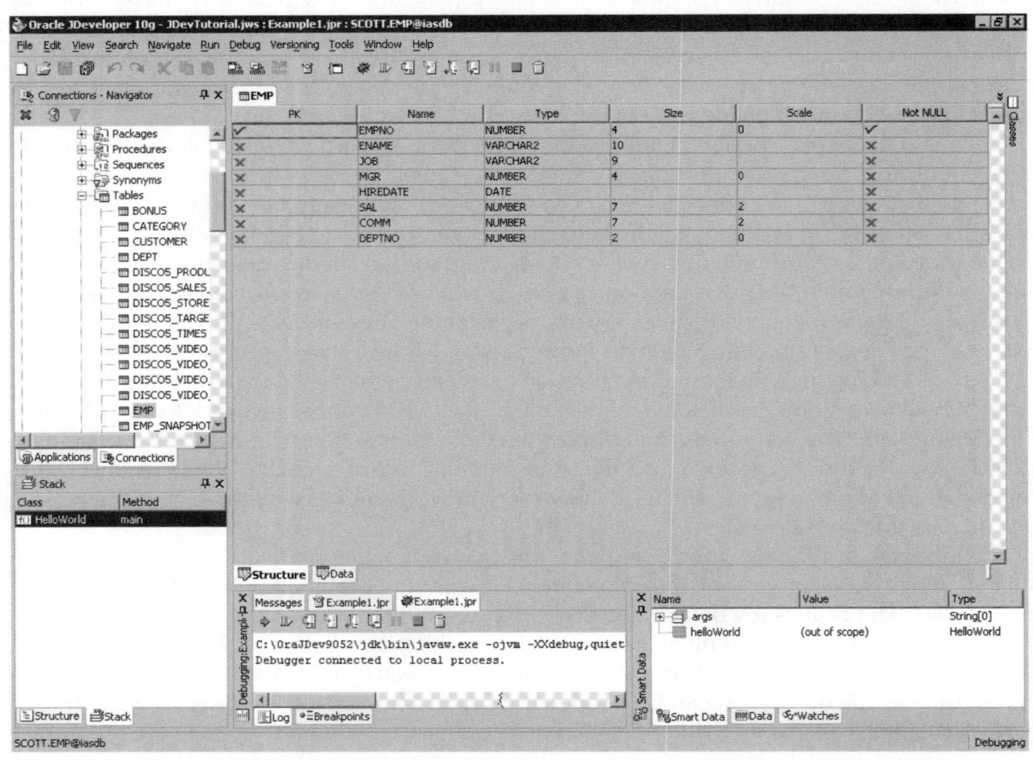

FIGURE 13-13. *The structure of the EMP table viewed in the Editor pane*

Model Business Components (Entity)

The next step in the creation of our web application is to model the business components (BCs). As you may recall from our discussion of ADF earlier, there are two distinct types of ADF BCs: entity and view. The base level of our business components is our persistent business components, or entity objects. Our entity objects are objects that implement the data access objects (DAO) or data access pattern and are responsible for the persistence, caching, and validation of data for our application. Oracle JDeveloper 10*g* gives us the ability to visually model these components, but first we have to create the business components diagram.

To create the diagram, make sure you have the Applications tab selected in the Applications Navigator and right-click our model project, selecting New from the drop-down menu that appears. From here, select the Business Components option under the Business Tier drop-down menu, in the right-hand pane select Business Components Diagram, and then click OK.

You will be prompted for the name you would like to give to your business components diagram; you can give it whatever name you would like. For our example, we're going to leave the default name of "Business Components Diagram1." The package name should be prepopulated with the package prefix (i.e., com.tusc.tutorial.model) we specified when creating the application workspace.

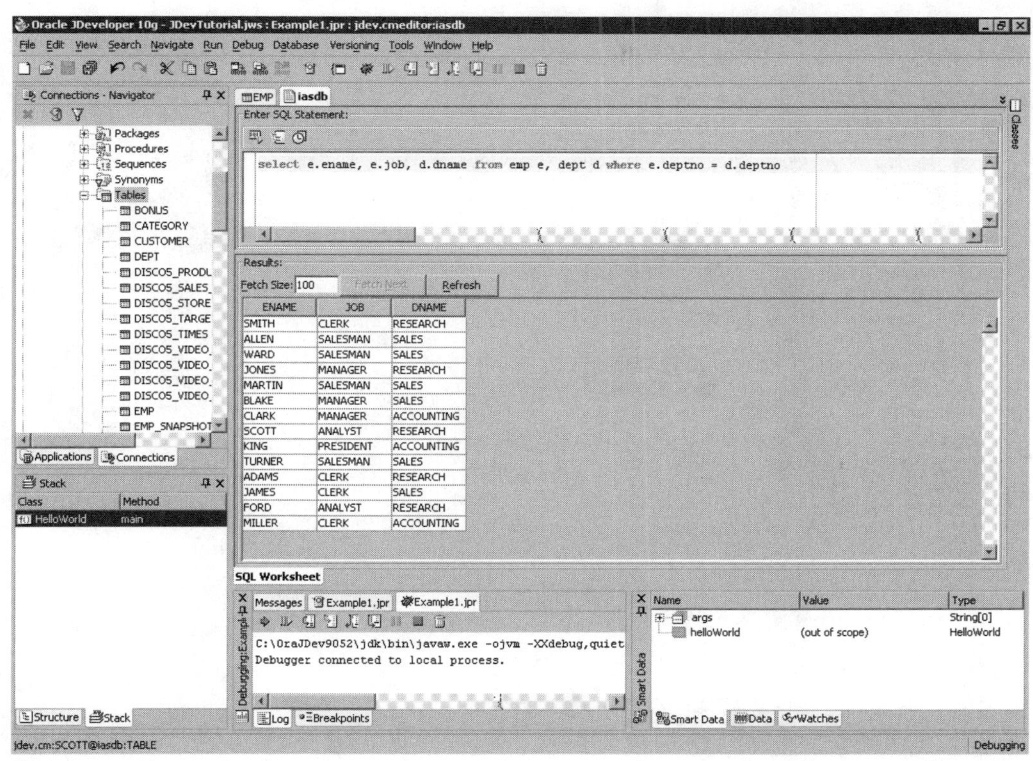

FIGURE 13-14. *Example of a custom query using the SQL worksheet*

To continue, click OK. This will create a blank page in the Editor pane. This is our business components diagram. Notice that the component palette now contains a new set of components for modeling business components.

To create our entity object, all we have to do is to go back to our Applications Navigator and select the Connections tab, drilling into our SCOTT schema until we find the tables in our schema. Creating an entity object with Oracle JDeveloper 10*g* is as simple as dragging and dropping one of the tables from our Connections tab into the business components diagram (see Figure 13-15). For this example, drag and drop the EMP table onto the blank page.

You can edit the entity object to customize several of its functions. To edit the entity object, double-click the object in the business components diagram. This will bring up the editor component, as seen in Figure 13-16.

Within this editor, you can alter the attributes that will be retrieved by this entity object. This allows you to exclude attributes such as audit fields that may not be relevant to your application, optimizing the functionality of the entity object by minimizing the amount of data it attempts to manage. You can also do things such as: enable batch updates, add control hints, establish validation and authentication rules, and publish and subscribe to events. Close this editor before proceeding.

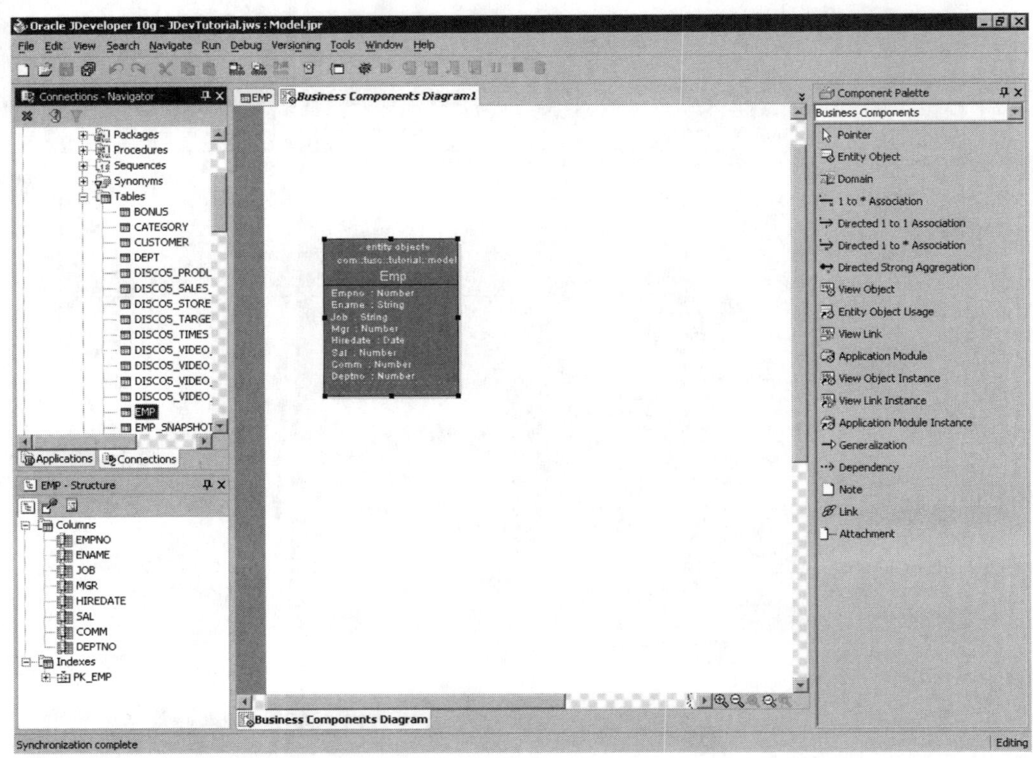

FIGURE 13-15. *Creation of the EMP entity object*

The business component modeling tool provides a great deal of power and flexibility as well as integrated intelligence when it comes to the structure of the database and how the application would most effectively integrate with the existing data structures. For example, when tables with referential integrity are brought into the business components diagram, Oracle JDeveloper 10*g* picks up on these dependencies and will model them appropriately, including referential integrity and multiplicity. Drag the DEPT table over from the Connections Navigator to the business component diagram (next to the EMP table) to see how this works.

Model Business Components (View)

Now that we have our base entity objects, we need to add view objects that preside over our entity objects to aggregate data. Our view objects each contain a SQL query that defines what data will be collected in that view object. To create a view object, go over to the component palette and click the View Object option. Then click the business components diagram where you want to place the view object container. The first thing you want to do with this new view object is to give it a name that will be relevant to our application. Click the name and edit its

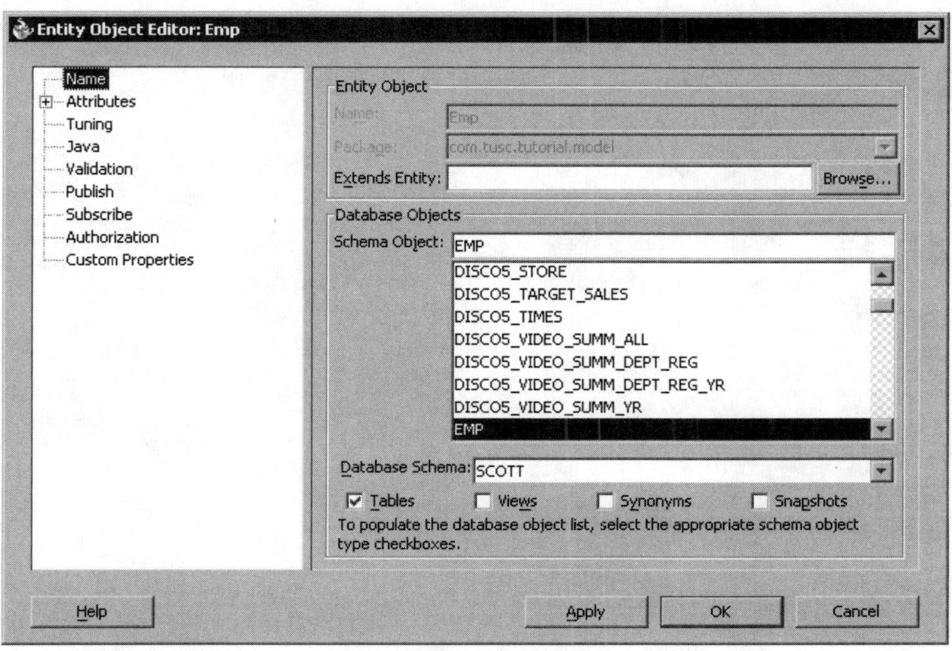

FIGURE 13-16. *Editing the entity object*

name to something more relevant, like **EmpView**. You should end up with a business component diagram that looks like Figure 13-17.

At this point, we have added a view object, but that view object doesn't have anything associated with it, so querying it will not produce meaningful results. We need to add components to the definition of the view object so that it knows what data it is pulling from the database. In the past, this would have involved making code changes to define what entity objects the defined view object was incorporating. This often involved navigation through obscure editors and actual physical code changes.

This is not the case with Oracle JDeveloper 10*g*. All we have to do now is choose which entity objects we want this view object to consist of and drag them into the blue boundary that defines the view object. Drag the EMP and DEPT entity objects into our new view object. As you do this, you will notice that the view object box expands to encompass the stub versions of the EMP and DEPT entity objects that are copied into the view object space. You will also notice that the view object definition box begins to list the attributes that are now being aggregated from the entity objects it is encapsulating. Adding the entity objects to the view object will, by default, create a one-to-one mapping of each entity object to the view object, creating entries for all values defined in the entity object. Also, when you add a dependent entity such as our DEPT entity, the view object automatically updates its SQL definition to reflect the need for a join statement.

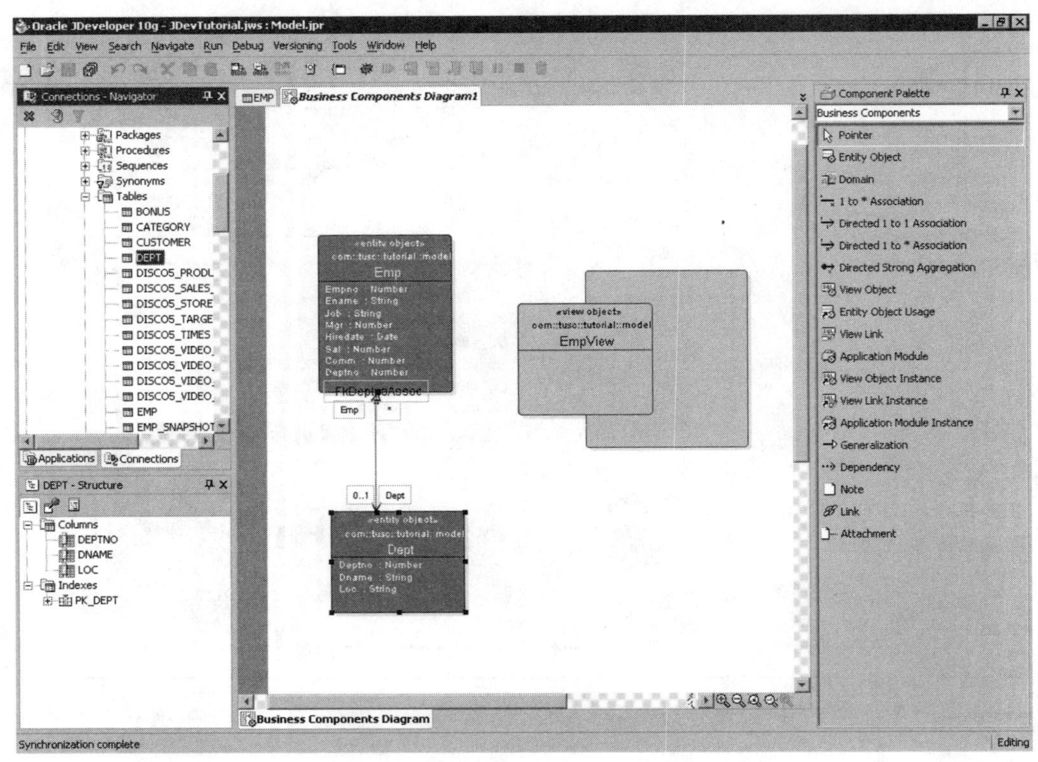

FIGURE 13-17. *Adding a view object to the business components diagram*

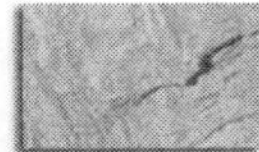

NOTE
Code generators can be fantastic productivity enhancers. However, they lack the creativity or flexibility of a human developer. As such, it is my personal experience that where they are utilized, it is often good to double-check high-profile operations they would perform, particularly in a persistence framework. As anyone who has done performance tuning on a web application knows, the items that an architect must be most keenly aware of are those that involve traffic over the wire. In the case of ADF, the business components designate how that traffic occurs and then how that data is aggregated in the application space.

One of the key places to perform checking for performance insurance is in the query definition of the view object. You enter the view object editor the same way you enter the entity object editor: by double-clicking the view object itself. Once inside the editor, click the query option in the left-hand pane to view the query that the ADF framework generated for you. If, upon examination of the view object query, you think you could do better (or, for example, you ran this through a query optimizer and determined a more efficient query), you can simply click the Expert Mode check box at the bottom of the dialog and replace the query at your discretion. You also have the option to utilize "?"-style bind parameters here or to directly manipulate the where clause.

CAUTION
Modifying the query itself is a bit of a radical step, and before doing so it might be prudent (particularly for the less DBA-inclined of us) to actually try the Tuning option in the left-hand pane first. Here, options to limit the query size, options covering how to iterate result sets, the option to add query hints, fetch mode options, and passivation options are presented. Covering the exact nature of each of these options is outside of the scope of this chapter.

Model Business Components (Application Module)

The final component of our data access (business services) tier for this example is the application module. This is the point of intersection for our application tier and the data access tier. The application module is utilized to aggregate the view objects we have defined into a "unit of work"–level component that can then be utilized by the application. The application module exposes a variety of API-level hooks to provide access and manipulation of the data contained further back in the data model.

As the intent of this example is to demonstrate how Oracle JDeveloper 10*g* provides developers with the ability to forego those API-level details in service of developing a rapid prototype, this chapter will not delve into the depths of those at this time. It is enough to know that they exist and that Oracle JDeveloper 10*g* utilizes a mechanism in the ADF framework to help developers interact with them at a higher level. We will cover the actual client interaction portion when we get to develop our JSPs.

Creation of an application module is done through the business components diagram, as with the view object. Our application module, at its simplest level, is a container to aggregate our view objects, much as a view object is a container object to aggregate our entity objects. By this logic, it stands to reason that the process of creating our application module should be extremely similar to that of our view object. (It is!)

To begin the application module creation process, we need to go back to the business component diagram and select the application module tool from the component palette. Just as with the view object, click the business components diagram and the application module will be created. Also, as with the view object, we should give this application module a name that is more relevant than "ApplicationModule." In this example, the name "EmpModule" is used.

We now need to indicate to the application module what view objects will be aggregated within it. To do this, we follow the same process we used with the view object: simply grab the view objects to be included in this application module and drag and drop them into the color-coded region of the application module control space. Since, in this example, we are currently working with only one view object, it should be fairly obvious which one we are going to utilize. Go ahead and drop the view object into the control space for the application module. As with all of our other business components, we can edit the attributes of our application module. To do so, follow the same approach as with the other business components; double-click the iconic representation on the business component diagram to enter the application module editor.

As our application module is our highest level of aggregation, most of the available editable features are centered on what data is being aggregated. You can manually select what view objects are included in the application module (although it is much easier to simply do it through the Visual Builder). You can also implement Java-like inheritance. You can specify through the Application Modules option which application modules this application module references. By doing this, you provide the application module you are editing with all of the functionality of the modules being referenced. This allows you to build application modules that are specific to a unit of work, while still maintaining the flexibility to build larger-grained objects that don't have to replicate the functionality of existing modules.

You can also interpose custom application module definitions if you choose to have base class extensions to the Oracle application module class. You do this by first creating an extension and then, in the application module, editing its options. Go to the Java option and push the Class Extends button, which provides Oracle JDeveloper 10*g* with the new base extension you created as the parent class to this application module.

The Remote option offers you choices in creating remote application modules. Oracle JDeveloper 10*g* gives developers the options to deploy application modules such as EJBs, CORBA, Web Service, etc. Creating a remote application module becomes particularly important if you're going to utilize the JClient interfaces provided in the ADF framework. The specifics of this framework are outside the scope of this chapter, however.

The Client Interface and Custom Properties Editor options are for enhancing the application module with extended functionality. For those developers familiar with writing business delegate–patterned J2EE applications, this is where that functionality comes into play. If you wish to have complex business service functionality at the application module level, you can provide the definitions for the exposed methods and attributes utilizing these options.

It is also possible to bypass the steps we have listed earlier with regard to the creation of the view and application modules for a given entity object by right-clicking the entity object and requesting it to generate default data model components. This is under the Generate option on the drop-down menu that pops up when you right-click an entity object. As you'll notice, there are also several other options in this drop-down, such as creating database objects, DDL, a web service, stubs/skeletons, and a simple Java client. Once again, the automation and productivity bonuses provided by Oracle JDeveloper 10*g* are extensive, and more details can be found in the *Oracle JDeveloper 10g Handbook.*

Create the Page Flow (Controller)

We now have a fully fleshed-out business service and data access layer for our application. Next, we will move on to utilizing Oracle JDeveloper 10*g*'s visual modeling and Struts integration via the ADF framework to generate our presentation layer. If you have done web development with Struts, you may be familiar with the effort required to generate a rapid prototype with the framework. Struts provides an integral piece of functionality to a well-designed and robust web application, but there is significant setup time and an increased development curve to create pages within this framework. Along with that is the issue of dealing with developers who may be new to the framework. Struts entails creation of at least two additional classes in addition to the actual physical page and integration with a Struts configuration file, requiring modification of an XML file that is by no means a simple task for a novice developer. These requirements hinder us from using Rapid Application Development techniques. Oracle JDeveloper 10*g* and the ADF framework come through for developers (yet again) in this area.

The Visual Builder functionality is not only limited to Oracle technologies such as the ADF BCs we just finished creating. With Oracle JDeveloper 10*g*, we now have a Visual Builder for the presentation components (in WYSIWYG form) and a visual representation of the Struts config file. For expert developers, there is still the ability to click a tab and have direct access to the explicit code definitions in the config file, but the Visual Builder is indispensable for novice developers as well as providing an at a glance view of how your web application is coming together. Particularly in the case of RAD, having a ready-made web flow diagram that mirrors the development of your prototype is an excellent feature.

Let's get into the code. The first thing we have to do is to create our Struts config diagram. There are a couple of options for doing this. The easiest is to right-click the ViewController default project in our application workspace and select Open Struts Page Flow Diagram. Alternatively, you can drill down into your ViewController project and double-click the Struts config file. You can find this by drilling ViewController | Web Content | WEB-INF | Struts-config.xml.

Once you have done this, you are presented with a blank canvas in the Editor pane similar to what you saw for the business components diagram. Notice again that the component palette has been updated to reflect our Struts-specific components. We will now create the Page Forward component for our first page. A Page Forward component defines a specific page in our action mappings for the Struts config file. If you not familiar with Struts, note that this is the configuration area in the config file that designates our individual pages and how the roadmap is laid out for the application. When an event occurs, the Struts request dispatcher checks the page that is being referenced along with the event or condition that is being reported and uses this information to determine what page the event is to be forwarded to.

First, take a look at the Struts config file source by clicking the Source tab at the bottom of the Editor pane. All we have in here at the moment are the opening and closing tags for the Struts config file and an entry for the message resources for the application. We can add an Action Forward component to the configuration by clicking the Page Flow Diagram tab again to return to visual design mode. Go to the component palette and click the Page Forward icon, and then click the page flow diagram to place the forward on the page.

We now need to provide a name for our forward; for this example, let's change the default name of "page1" to "EMP." Be sure that when you modify this, you do not remove the leading forward slash ("/"). Click the Source tab at the bottom of the editor again to look at the changes to the Struts config file. You will see that Oracle JDeveloper 10*g* has now added the action-mappings element to the file and has our /EMP path configured here. Notice also that the forward attribute of the element is listed as "unknown"; that is because we have yet to indicate to Oracle JDeveloper 10*g* what page is actually associated with this forward. All we have told Oracle JDeveloper 10*g* is that we plan to have an action mapping that is mapped to "/EMP." We now need to design and designate a physical page (a JSP, in this example) that this mapping is associated with.

Create the JSP Page

We now have a controller flow designation in place to map to our as-yet uncreated EMP page. We will now tell Oracle JDeveloper 10*g* that we wish to create an actual page to have mapped to our EMP action forward. In the Editor pane of the page flow diagram, double-click our EMP action forward. This brings up the option dialog for us either to choose a preexisting page to bind to this forward or to create a new one. In our example, we have yet to create any pages, so we will create a new one. Use the default name of "/EMP.jsp," leave the Edit This Page Now option checked, and click OK.

We now have a JSP file added to the web-inf folder in our application workspace structure, and the Page Builder will open up in the editor. As with our other builders, this looks more or less like a blank canvas with the appropriate components built up in our component palette. The Page Builder is a WYSIWYG (what you see is what you get) page builder similar to ones seen in Microsoft FrontPage or Dreamweaver. For our prototype, we are going to take advantage of yet another of Oracle JDeveloper 10*g*'s productivity-boosting features and have Oracle JDeveloper 10*g* create a page layout and supporting code to render one of our created ADF business components in a presentation format.

To do this, we are going to make use of the Data Controls tab in the component palette. If this view is not available, you need to enable it from the View | DataControl palette. After clicking the Data Controls tab, you will notice our empModule application module listed in a drop-down. This allows us to browse the existing data controls we have specified for this project and select data access components to have the page utilize.

Drill into the EmpModule module until you see the EmpView view object. We're going to create a page that will list the data from our employees table in a page. Click the view object in the Data Controls pane. Notice that there is a drop-down at the bottom of the Data Controls pane that has become active with the option of Read-Only Table selected. Click this drop-down and explore the available options. By selecting one of these options, you instruct Oracle JDeveloper 10*g* to insert code into your page to properly support the type of structure you designate and support it with the data from your selected data control.

For this example, we utilize an input form, so select the Input Form option from this drop-down. Much as when you were creating your business components, you will now drag the data control you have selected onto your page canvas. You are presented with two options in a pop-up dialog:

- You can convert the page to a data page, in which case your data interaction will be managed by the page.
- You can create a separate data action to manage the interaction with the data layer.

Although the former is the recommended option, select the option to create a separate data action and click OK. There are two reasons the second option is preferred for this example. The first arises from the concept of "separation of concerns." Separation of concerns refers to the idea that developers should have a clearly delineated set of functionality for every component in the application. By creating a data component, we have segregated the business service interaction into a class separate from the class that is responsible for displaying it (the JSP). The second reason is so that we can view how the builders interact.

Click the Struts-config.xml tab at the top of the Editor pane to examine the impact requesting Oracle JDeveloper 10*g* to create a separate data action has had on our Struts config. We now see that there is an /empDataAction with an arrow pointing to our original /EMP action and a label next to the arrow titled "success." If you have had some experience with Struts, take a look at the source view to see that Oracle JDeveloper 10*g* has now configured an action path for our data action with all of the requisite attributes configured. There is also our page action, which now maps to our EMP.jsp instead of to "unknown."

Also, when you clicked OK, our Page Builder canvas acquired a shell layout of a table with labels and controls configured to display our page. Notice that, for the labels, there are entries all beginning with "${bindings." This is code that has been placed there by Oracle JDeveloper 10*g* in EL (expression language) that takes advantage of the ADF data bindings and BC4J context to do automatic binding of the static values that define our business object to the physical layout of the page. If you look into the source for the page, you will notice that Oracle JDeveloper 10*g* and the ADF framework make use of the industry-standard JSTL tag libraries as well as integrating with the Struts tag libraries for optimization of the presentation. One of the most highly sought-after page design goals is to have the least possible actual scriptlet code in our JSPs, with as much logic as possible relegated to tag libraries and referenced beans. Oracle JDeveloper 10*g* strives to meet this goal (as much as is possible), and this is a very positive mark for a code generation tool.

But that's not all we get out of the box. Click back to the design view of our page. At the bottom, there is a Submit button. Suppose we are presented with the requirement for end users to have the ability to traverse the data from the table this page is bound to (the EMP table). Ordinarily, a developer would create a few more buttons on the page and then integrate them with the data container class (DTO or BO). We could then requery the result set to find the next value in the sequence and display its information. Not extremely difficult for an experienced programmer, but it would certainly be advantageous to exploit an existing feature that could provide this sort of canned functionality. Luckily for us, Oracle JDeveloper 10*g* does just that!

Examine the Data Controls pane in the component palette again. Listed there is the application module, which we drilled into to drag our view object over to our design view. If you then drill into the view object in the component palette, you are presented with a list of values that the view object contains (for reference, you can also drag these individual fields to the design view the same way you did the whole view object). Note that at the bottom of these values is yet another drop-down called Operations. Make sure you are looking at the one that is a child of our view object and drill into it. This presents you with a list of canned operations you can use in visually building your pages. All of them come fully integrated with the controller structure and the ADF framework so that all you have to do is click and drag to add that functionality to your pages.

Let's go ahead and add record traversal to our basic page. Drag the first, previous, next, and last operations over to your page, placing them in a line next to the Submit button. You may be wondering what the Submit button on the page is for. It does pretty much what one would expect, allowing us to submit changes from the form and save the data within it back to our persistence framework. We'll look at this more once we have the page running. When you're done, the design view of your page should look like Figure 13-18.

There you have it; we've just gone from a table to a fully functional JSP application in (almost) no time flat. We have even added record traversal to our page. Now let's go try it out!

Running the Page

At this point, we have done everything we need to have a fully functional web application. Granted, it is limited in the actual functionality it provides, but creating the same functionality with integration to a controller framework and the data integration capabilities we have by default by hand would have taken a great deal more time than it just took us to create this one using Oracle JDeveloper 10*g*'s wizards and ADF.

Let's run the application now to see what we have completed. Remember that we have created a data control action that serves our page. This means that if we try to run the JSP directly, we will get a cryptic error message telling us that the page encountered an error trying to find our data. This makes sense because if we bypass the data action, what data is the page going to display?

Navigate back to our Struts config diagram. From here, right-click the empDataAction and choose Run from the pop-up menu. After Oracle JDeveloper 10*g* is done compiling the code,

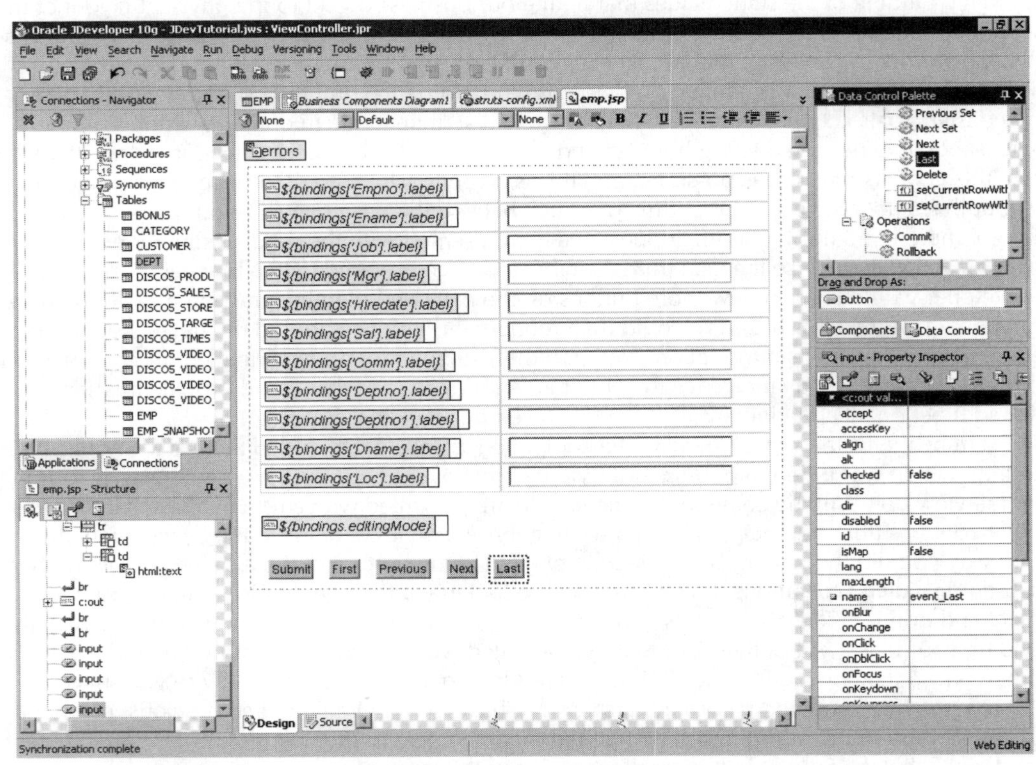

FIGURE 13-18. *A fully designed JSP page*

bringing up the embedded OC4J server, and loading our page into the container, we will see something like Figure 13-19 in our browser.

Navigate through the records a bit to get a feel for how our navigation controls work. Now, let's try to change some data. For example, update the salary for Smith, changing it from $800 to $1,000. Now hit Submit. Navigate around some more and come back to Smith. It should still reflect our changes, so obviously our update worked, right?

Let's check the data in the database. You can use your database tool of choice (SQL *Plus, PL/SQL Developer, etc.), or you can examine data from the connections manager in Oracle JDeveloper 10*g*. If you hit the Connections tab in the Applications Navigator, drill into the database connection, drill into the Scott schema, drill into tables, and then double-click the EMP table, the table is loaded into the Editor pane. Recall that you can then hit the Data tab at the bottom of the Editor pane to view the data in this table. Alternatively, you could use the SQL Worksheet option and issue a custom query against the table to pull back the data you're looking for. Either way, when we examine the data for Smith, we see that his salary has *not* been changed in the database!

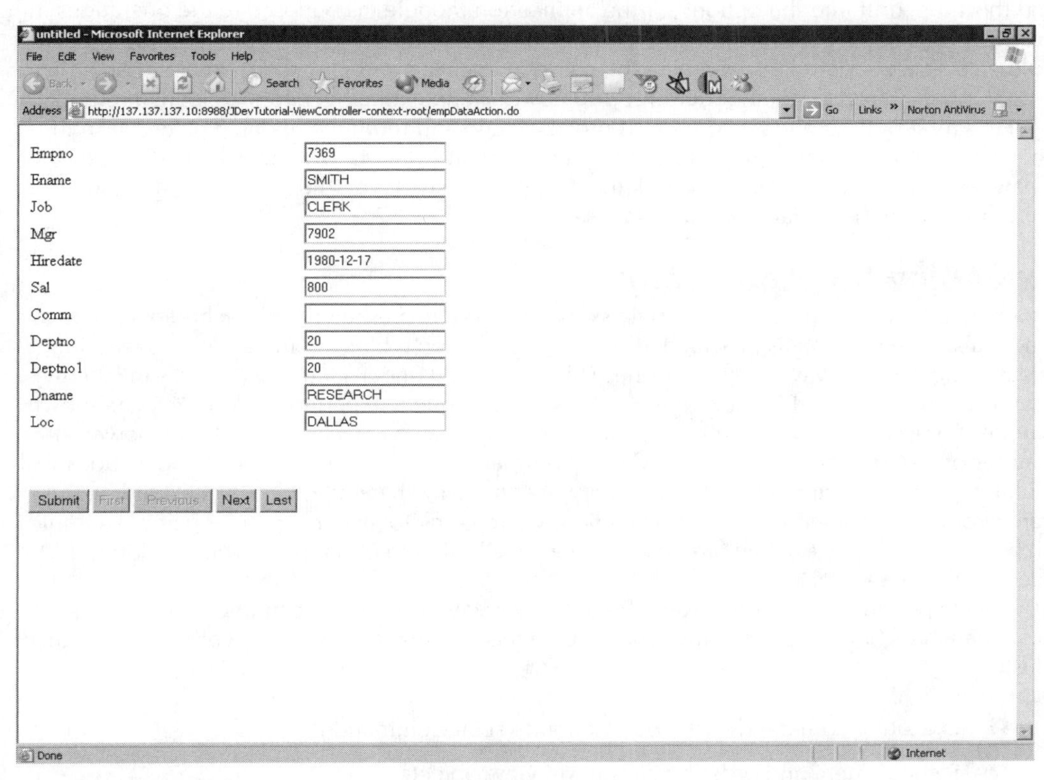

FIGURE 13-19. *The HelloWorld application running in a web browser*

We can confirm this by halting our running application and restarting it. To do this, select the Run Manager tab in the Applications Navigator. This will bring up a pane that displays all of the active processes you have running within Oracle JDeveloper 10*g*. To stop the current OC4J instance, drill into the processes and right-click Embedded OC4J Server. Select Terminate from the pop-up menu. This will stop the OC4J instance. You should then close the browser the application was in and run it again from the Struts config diagram.

Once you've done this, you will notice that Smith's salary was not altered. A seasoned developer might recognize this as a symptom of the data being updated in the application tier but not being propagated to the database. When we hit Submit, it submitted the change to the persistence tier (our ADF BCs), but we never instructed the business components to actually save and persist that data in the database. The change was accessible as long as we were accessing the cached data, but once we reloaded and the business components retrieved fresh data from the database, it was no longer there. All we need to do to get the data to save into the database, is to create something that instructs the business components to persist their data.

Fortunately for us, Oracle has thought of this as well and provided a canned component to do just that. If you go back to our EMP JSP, select the Data Controls tab in the component palette, and this time, drill into the options for the application module (as opposed to the operations for our view object that we utilized earlier), you will find two operations listed here: Commit and Rollback. These should be fairly self-explanatory. Go ahead and grab them both and drag them onto our page next to the other buttons. You now have integrated persistence logic in our page.

Let's try it out! Terminate your OC4J process again and rerun the updated page. Make the changes to Smith's salary again, hit Submit, and then hit Commit. Now check the data using whatever method you utilized to check the data previously. If you did everything right, Smith's data should now be updated in the database.

Extending the Application

Experienced programmers are extremely skeptical at being presented with technologies like this, where a simple example is provided as evidence of the technology being an earth-shattering advancement in the way things are done. This is perfectly understandable and was in fact my response when first working with the framework. Subsequent experience, however, has shown that this framework not only delivers on its promises but also goes far beyond. The powerful features of the ADF become evident when developers begin building complex applications with multiple pages and experience the simplicity of enhancing the application and extending the framework to meet their needs. In this section, we're going to give a very brief pair of examples on how to extend the existing functionality we have built into our app, as well as adding additional pages.

Oracle provides some great examples at http://www.oracle.com/technology/products/jdev/tips/muench/techniques/index.html. Some of the features that the example workspace provided illustrates:

- Executing commands with Transaction.executeCommand()
- Setting where and order by clauses on view objects
- Setting where clause parameter values
- Estimating the number of rows a view object's query will retrieve
- Setting query optimizer hints at run time on a view object
- Limiting the number of rows retrieved on a view object by setting max fetch size
- Executing view object queries and iterating through the results of their default rowset
- Resetting a view object's default iterator to reloop through the rows another time
- Setting up a view criteria collection of View Criteria Rows and applying the criteria
- Clearing the view criteria
- Finding a row in a view object with findByKey()
- Marshalling a single row of a view object into XML with a customized list of attributes to include
- Creating new rows in a view object
- Highlighting the built-in reference mechanism of join view objects to pull in foreign key–related information when the value of the foreign key attribute changes in a row

- Reading a row of information from an XML document
- Adding a dynamic attribute at run time to track "selected" rows
- Introspecting the run-time metadata of a view object
- Conditionally turning on SQL_TRACE to capture SQL statements into a TKPROF-analyzable trace file on the server
- Creating a view object at run time based on a SQL statement
- Illustrating the effect of calling postChanges() or not during a transaction
- Removing a row from a view object
- Registering warnings from entity object business logic
- Using a custom exception and warning handler (using different languages)
- Using custom exceptions
- Invoking custom application module methods from client code through the application module custom interface after exposing the methods as client-accessible
- Returning arrays of rows from a custom method

Enhancing an Existing Page

First, let's look at a simple enhancement to our existing page. If we look at our page, it is a nice representation of the data we're asking it to present. However, what if we were presented with the requirement that the Department ID were to be represented as a drop-down graphical object? To do this, developers only need to follow a few basic steps.

Open the EMP JSP in design mode and delete the row associated with the department numbers by right-clicking inside the deptno cell and selecting Delete Row. In addition, delete the input field associated with the department name (deptno, not deptno1). Next, find the deptno in the Data Controls pane. Select this and indicate in the Drag And Drop As drop-down that you wish to see it as a list of values and drop it on the page in the cell we just vacated. Since we're going to be creating a relationship here (associating our EMP record with a list of departments), we're going to need a department entity and view object.

Returning to our business components diagram, we find that we already have a DEPT entity object, so we don't need to replicate this. What we will need to do, however, is to create an independent view object that we can associate with our control. Create a department view object following the same steps you did to create our EMP view object, except this time you are only placing the department entity into the view object. Name this **DeptView**. Next, you need to add the DeptView object to the EmpModule application module. Do this the same way you added EmpView to the EmpModule. When you've completed these steps, your business components diagram should look something like Figure 13-20.

Now, we need to configure our list of values with a component for it to draw its values from and to indicate what information we would like displayed. We can configure this by going to our Structure pane and selecting the UI Model icon. The UI Model tab lists out the relevant components on our page that we can configure. If you are familiar with Java, you may recognize some of the terms listed here. The one we're most concerned with at this time is the Iterator components.

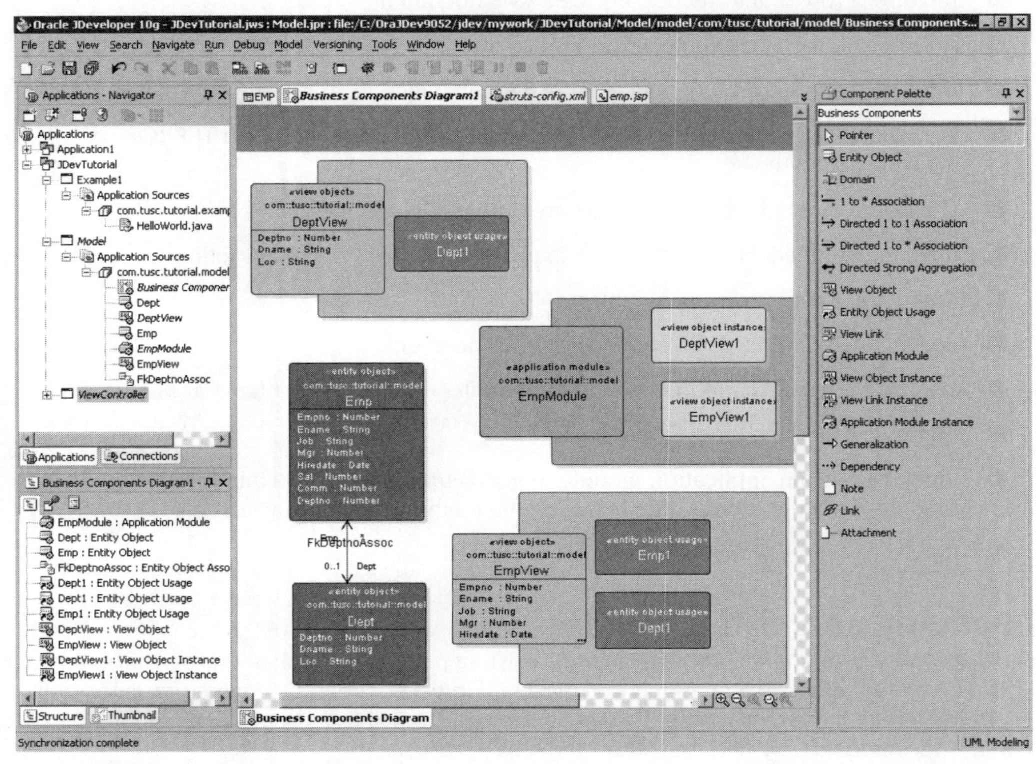

FIGURE 13-20. *The updated business components diagram*

The iterators indicate what elements we have to traverse our view objects with. In this case, we're going to need an iterator for our DeptView. Since none exists yet, we're going to have to create one.

Right-click the empUIModel element, go to Create Binding | Data | Iterator, and click. This will bring up the Iterator Binding editor. Here, we're going to create our DeptView iterator. Similar to our Data Controls tab, drill into the application module, select DeptView1, give the iterator the name **DeptView1Iterator**, and click OK. Now we're ready to configure our drop-down to use this iterator.

To figure out which control you're modifying, click the List of Values control you placed on the page and look in the property inspector for the name of the component, indicated by the "property *" field. In this case, the name of the component is Deptno2. Back to our UI Model pane, right-click the Deptno2 element and select Edit. This will take you into the list binding editor. Two tabs are listed, and we're going to work with both.

The LOV Update Attributes tab allows us to associate our source and target collections, our iterators, and what attributes we're using to bind these. The LOV Display Attributes tab is where we tell the control what values to display in its list of values. Starting with the LOV Update Attributes tab, drill down into the source data collection (which is actually our EmpModuleDataControl (application module)) and select DeptView as the source. In the target data collection, select EmpView if it is not already selected. You will bind the DeptViewIterator to the EmpViewIterator, so if these are not selected in the drop-downs below, do that as well. Finally, you need to tell the LOV how we are mapping the iterators to each other. Use the Deptno attribute for this; click Add and select deptno in both the LOV and Target attributes drop-downs that appear. Now click over to the LOV Display Attributes tab and select the Dname and Loc attributes as your display attributes and click OK.

To try it out, go to the Struts config diagram and run our data action again. You will now see the new page with a fully functional drop-down for the department (see Figure 13-21). All of the previous functionality still exists. In fact, if you added the Find button feature from the EmpViews operations drill-down in the data controls palette, you could also use this LOV to search by department. All with canned functionality!

Adding Additional Pages

We've seen that developers can make simple alterations to an existing page, so it is not all just canned functionality that will break as soon as we try to customize it. By no means is the change you made in the previous example indicative of the extent of what the framework will allow us to do. The Visual Builder gives developers the starting point from which they can customize to any depth they wish. Even with this level of functionality, the true test of a web development framework is not how it works in a single-instance example, but how it supports development of multiple units of work and how seamlessly it allows developers to tie those units of work together. In this section, we will enhance our little application to extend into a new page and tie our two pages together.

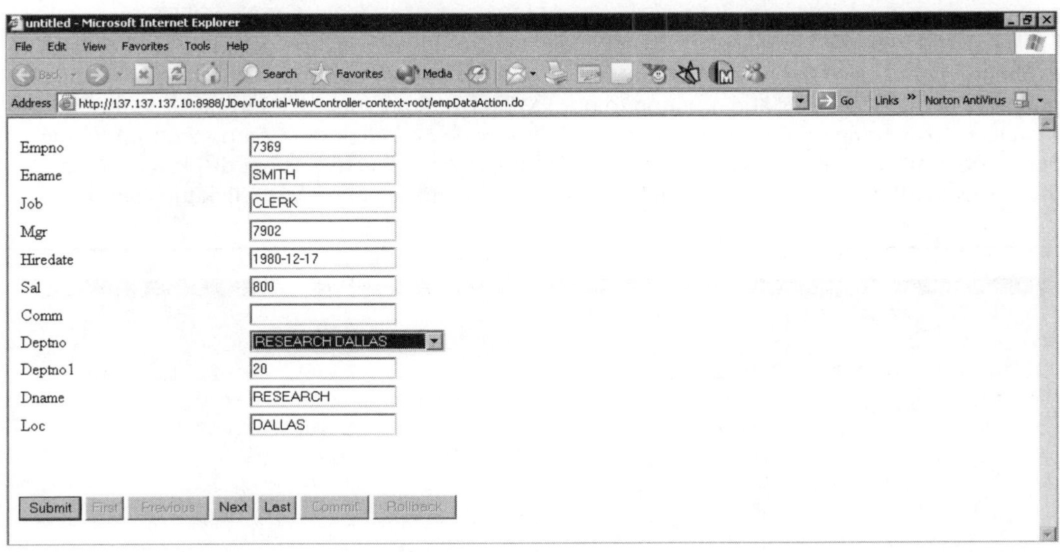

FIGURE 13-21. *The application reflecting the addition of the drop-down graphical object*

For the sake of brevity, we're going to create a page that lists out all of the available departments in the database and tie that to our EMP page. The reason for this choice is that the necessary business objects have already been constructed. We have already created the DEPT entity object in our first example; in the second, we created a view object and tied it into our application module. For this example, all we have to do is create the departments page and link it to our EMP page.

First, let's create the new page. To do this, we need to create a page forward in our Struts config diagram. Navigate back to our Struts config diagram and click the page forward icon, and then click the Struts config diagram to place it. Name this forward **DEPT** (remembering not to remove the "/"). Now, let's edit the page. Double-click the DEPT forward to bring up our page editor again, naming the JSP DEPT.jsp. The function of this page is to list all of the available departments and their relevant data. Remember that we do this by going to the application module in the Data Controls pane and drilling down until we find the DeptView view object. You may have to right-click and refresh the data control palette to show this object. Select this, and then in the Drag And Drop As drop-down, select Read-Only Table (if it is not already selected). Drag the DeptView over to our canvas and place it. For this example, we will create a separate data action, so click OK when prompted for this. If you followed these steps correctly, you now have a fully functional DEPT page.

Try it out by going back to our Struts config diagram, right-clicking the newly created deptDataAction, and selecting Run. Remember to terminate your currently running OC4J process if you didn't after we last ran the EMP page. Once Oracle JDeveloper 10*g* has loaded your page, you should see something like Figure 13-22 appear.

This isn't all that much more impressive than when we created our EMP page; all we have shown is that we can reuse our business objects on other pages. While that is a key feature of a good business objects framework, it is not the feature we are most interested about in this section. What we're going to do next is tie our two pages together without writing a single line of code. To do this, we're going to have to make modifications to our Struts config file to associate two pages together and create a control on the EMP page to direct us into the DEPT page.

Let's start with the changes to the EMP page. We could "cheat" and put in an anchor tag that explicitly directs us to the new page, but that would bypass our controller structure (which is the point of having one). Let's add a button to our EMP page. Stop your OC4J instance in the Run Manager. Now bring up the EMP page in the Editor pane and click the Components tab in the component palette pane to bring up the HTML components. If HTML is not displayed in the drop-down at the top of the pane, click the drop-down and select HTML. Click the "Submit

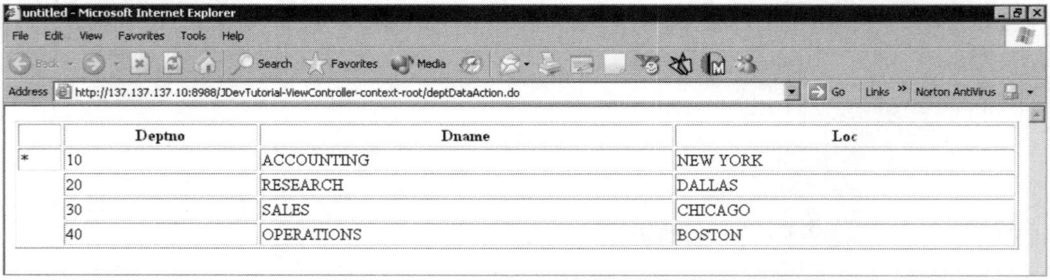

	Deptno	Dname	Loc
*	10	ACCOUNTING	NEW YORK
	20	RESEARCH	DALLAS
	30	SALES	CHICAGO
	40	OPERATIONS	BOSTON

FIGURE 13-22. *Running the new DEPT page*

Button" object in the component palette. Click the Editor pane to place the cursor where you would like the button (for this example, put it to the right of the Rollback button), and then click the Submit button control in the components palette. This will place a Submit button on our EMP page.

Click New in the Editor pane and scroll down the values in the property inspector until you see the "Value" element. Click this and edit it to say **Departments**. This should change the text in the button to say "Departments." Look for the name element and edit this to say **event_listdepts**. This is what the ADF extensions to the Struts request dispatcher will pick up as the event we are invoking on the page. It is crucial when defining your own events that if you wish them to be integrated with the ADF Struts framework, you prefix the event name with "event_."

Let's tie everything together in the Struts config diagram. Bring the diagram up in the Editor pane. Click the "forward" control in the component palette. The forward control allows developers to specify how pages link together. If you're familiar with Struts, you'll see that we're creating a forward entry in the action element for the page with the event equal to the event we configured on our EMP page and a path equal to our new DEPT pages action. Once you've clicked the forward control, click the empDataAction, and then click the deptDataAction to link them together. Oracle JDeveloper 10*g* should place an arrow between the two actions with a label next to it named something like "forward1." This indicates what the event is that Oracle JDeveloper 10*g* has associated with that path in your diagram. Run the application from the empDataAction element and click New. Nothing happens!

This didn't work because the framework doesn't recognize our event. If you click the Source tab for the Struts config diagram, you can take a look at what is actually in the file. Within the Struts config file, we have several sections:

- The form beans section defines what form classes are referenced within our app and gives us a name to reference them from within other sections of the config file.
- The next section defines the action mappings. This section is called action mappings because this is where we define our actions, which are the main controller classes for our pages. A subelement of each action consists of the mappings that it contains that define what events map to what paths. Thus, these are called forward elements.

This configuration should all seem familiar after our experience working with the Struts config diagram. A simple examination of the section of this document that defines the behavior of the empDataAction (which is the action we're attempting to invoke) shows us that it has two possible forwards defined for it. Examining the one that would direct us to our new departments page, we see that the event the Struts config file is set up for has an event name of "forward1." Obviously, this isn't going to work. If you like, you can change this here (that is how it was done in prior versions of Oracle JDeveloper), but with the visual editing capabilities of Oracle JDeveloper 10*g*, it is easy to do it in the diagram.

Click the Page Flow Diagram tab at the bottom of the Editor pane to return to the visual representation of the file. Here, we can now see, in a visual format, what we just saw in the source code. Look at the link between our empDataAction and our deptDataAction and notice that the name of that relationship is "forward1." To get our logic to work, it would seem that all we have to do is change this name to the name of the event that we defined on our button on our EMP page, and then when that event comes into our EMP action class, it will know where to send us.

Recall that our event was called "event_listdepts." You may think we should put "event_listdepts" in as the name of our association, but that would be incorrect. Oracle JDeveloper 10*g* imposes the rule that we must prefix our events with "event_," but that is something that gets stripped off by the Oracle extension to the request dispatcher before it reaches the Struts configuration file. The association name is actually only "listdepts." Go ahead and edit this by clicking the label next to the association and renaming it **listdepts**. Take a look back in the source file to see what has changed. When you're done, your Struts config diagram should look something like Figure 13-23.

Run the EMP page again and try out the new button. If you followed the preceding steps correctly, you will now have a fully functioning set of pages that allow you to traverse the records in the EMP table as well as navigate to a page that will list out all of the departments in the database.

If you want to continue to play with it, feel free to use the steps just outlined to put a button on the new Dept JSP to allow you to navigate back to the EMP page. You'll be surprised just how quickly playing around like this produces an extraordinarily large application. Remember the days that this used to be tedious work with little to show for it after hours of effort?

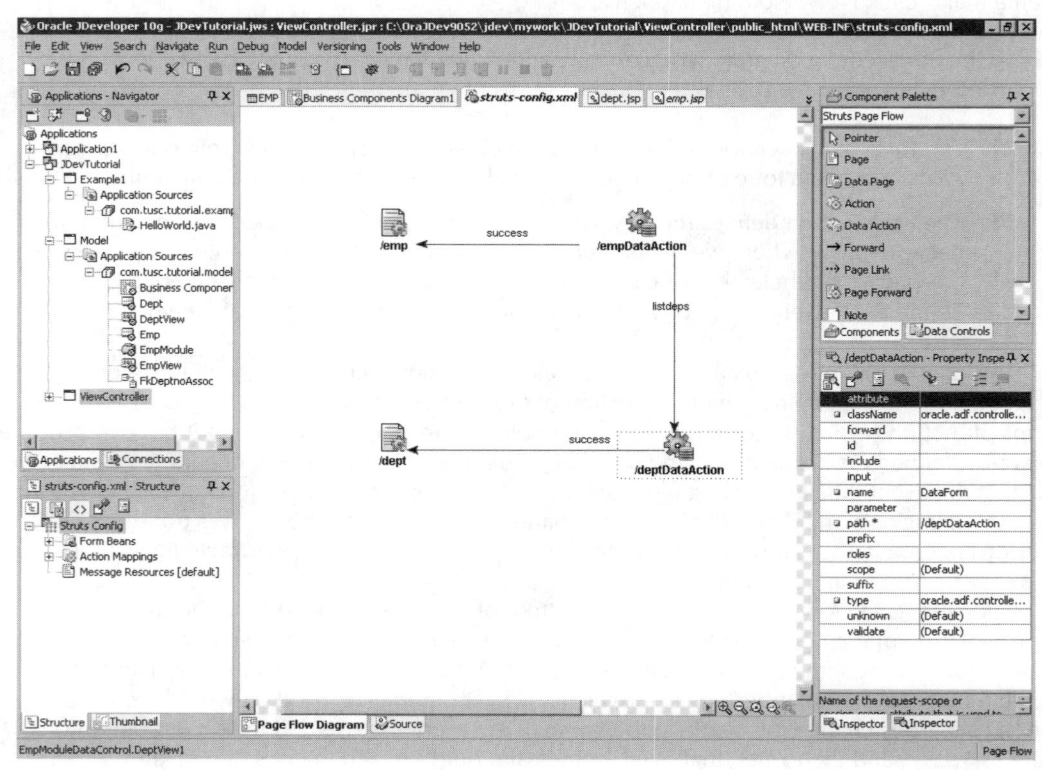

FIGURE 13-23. *The completed Struts config diagram*

Summary

We've spent a great deal of time in this chapter talking about the productivity benefits that Oracle JDeveloper 10*g* provides. As you have seen, Oracle JDeveloper 10*g* contains all of the expected capabilities of a top-of-the-line Java IDE. That alone would make it worthy of use, but add on the fact that Oracle JDeveloper 10*g* also contains the capabilities of a fairly robust database development and integration tool and we have a single development environment that combines the capabilities of three separate tools. Of course, we can't forget the integrated open source toolkits like JUnit for unit testing, Ant for nightly builds/deployments, log4j, and the ability to add in almost anything one could think of utilizing the Oracle JDeveloper 10*g* plug-in features, and so the tool continues to grow in capability and appeal.

We have yet to even come to the trump card, the ADF framework. With the ADF framework, Oracle took the robustness and enterprise capability of the BC4J framework and integrated it with multiple presentation delivery methods, among which is the leading controller framework in the industry today, Struts. It then removed the learning curve associated with BC4J and even eased the barrier to development with Struts by providing an amazing visual development environment based around UML diagramming and notation. In addition, the ADF framework augments the Oracle technology stack with the leading alternatives in the marketplace today.

CHAPTER 14

JavaServer Pages

JavaServer Pages (JSPs) are server-side components that allow developers to create applications that are accessible from the Internet. They combine Hypertext Markup Language (HTML) and Java to create a programming paradigm that does not require an extensive knowledge of Java. JSPs are specifically designed to handle the request and deliver a response in the form of HTML. The generated HTML page can also contain JavaScript to increase its functionality. Every action involves a request and the subsequent response in the form of an HTML document. It is possible to generate other types of documents such as Extensible Markup Language (XML) using JSPs. Behind the request/response cycle is the HTTP protocol. HTTP provides the mechanism that allows the client and server to communicate. The client is typically an Internet browser such as Microsoft's Internet Explorer or Netscape Navigator. If you have a good understanding of HTTP, it will make creating JSPs much easier.

NOTE
For a detailed description of the HTTP protocol, go to http://www.w3.org/Protocols/. Hundreds of other web resources are available as well.

Before a JSP can be served, it must be translated into a servlet, compiled, and deployed. Using the syntax elements available, JSPs are coded to deliver dynamic content in the form of an HTML page. The JSP compiler then does the work of translating it into a servlet. A JSP is what is requested, but a servlet is what delivers the response.

JSPs are accessed through a URL, just as HTML pages are. Typically, these URLs end in a .jsp extension. For example, the URL http://www.example.com/index.jsp requests that the index.jsp page handle the request. If the page has not yet been compiled or has been updated, the server will translate the JSP into the required Java code and then compile the servlet. The servlet then processes the request. Typically, the request involves interaction with an HTML form.

JSPs were designed with simplicity in mind so that JSP developers would not have to know Java. While in its purest implementation this is true, in practice this is normally not the case. A fair level of Java knowledge will go a long way in making you a better JSP developer.

JSPs give developers access to tag libraries that they can use that create dynamic content. Tag libraries are often created by developers with a good understanding of Java. Once the tag library is created, it can be used in any number of JSPs. Using the custom tag libraries allows JSP developers to code complex functionality into their pages without having to know how it is implemented.

You can place Java code directly in your JSP in the form of scriptlets, but this is not recommended as doing so increases the complexity and decreases the maintainability of your JSPs. More often than not, when you see Java code inside JSPs, you will find there is a lot of duplicated functionality across the application's pages.

Coding a JSP is similar to creating an HTML document. Oracle JDeveloper 10*g* provides a graphical user interface to develop JSPs. See Chapter 13, Oracle JDeveloper, for more information on using Oracle JDeveloper 10*g* to develop JSP applications. All of the examples created in this chapter were created with Oracle JDeveloper 10*g* 9.0.5.2.

NOTE
Oracle JDeveloper 10g can be downloaded from the Oracle Technology Network web site at: http://www.oracle.com/technology/software/products/jdev/index.html.

Model 1 vs. Model 2 Architecture

JSPs are usually coded using either a JSP Model 1 or Model 2 architecture. When designing an application using Model 1 architecture, the target of every request is a JSP. All business logic is coded inside the JSP or in JavaBeans. For very simple applications, this model is functional, but for even moderately complex applications, it is preferable to use the Model 2 architecture. In the Model 1 architecture, the JSP handles all of the work for authentication, creating and using JavaBeans to access data, and generating the HTML interface.

In the Model 2 architecture, also known as Model-View-Controller 2 (MVC2), all requests are first handled by servlets. The servlet processes the request, creating any required JavaBeans and then forwards the processing to the JSPs. The JSP can use the JavaBeans that were created by the servlet to generate the resulting HTML page. Using MVC2 increases the maintainability of your application by separating the presentation layer from the business logic. All but the simplest applications should use MVC2 architecture. When using MVC2, the only responsibility of the JSP is presentation to the client. Oracle has built-in support for the Jakarta Struts Framework that can be used to build MVC2 based applications.

Oracle Application Server 10*g* provides support for a Struts-based controller framework and is currently the standard controller mechanism for many web applications. When you combine Struts with your JSPs, your application's design is considerably more robust.

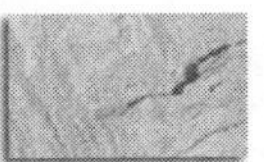

NOTE
This is what the Application Development Framework (ADF) in Oracle JDeveloper 10g is all about. We cover the ADF in Chapter 13.

Implicit Objects

JSPs provide you with a set of implicit objects that you can use to build your applications. These objects do not have to declared or initialized. Table 14-1 describes nine implicit objects/variables.

Implicit objects can be used in scriptlets to access or update values and access methods provided by the classes that they represent. The following example shows how to use the request and session implicit objects.

```
<%
session.setAttribute("username", request.getParameter("username"));
%>
```

JSP Scopes

JSPs provide a number of scopes for the sharing of data. Scopes equate to a predetermined lifetime for an object that is enforced by the container. There are four JSP scopes available: page, request, session, and application. All of the scopes contain various objects that can hold application data.

The shortest-lived of the scopes is the page scope, which is accessed through the pageContext implicit variable. The page scope is limited to a single JSP and a single request. Once the page has completed rendering the objects contained inside of it, the page scope is no longer available. From the pageContext object, you can also access all of the available scopes. Every object stored in the various scopes is always an object and not a primitive data type. The getAttribute method of the javax.servlet.jsp.PageContext can be used to retrieve data from the pageContext by name. The page

Object Name	Description
application	Provides access to the application's environment.
config	Provides access to the servlet configuration for JSPs.
exception	Only available if a JSP is marked as a JSP error page. This is covered in more detail in the "Error Pages" section of this chapter.
out	Provides access to the JSP's output stream.
page	Provides access to the JSP's implementation object that is created when the page is translated.
pageContext	Provides access to attributes stored in the page scope.
request	Provides access to attributes and parameters stored in the request scope.
response	Provides access to the response object.
session	Provides access to attributes stored in the session scope.

TABLE 14-1. *Implicit JSP Objects/Variables*

context provides a place to store key/value pairs that only need to be available during the rendering of the page. There is also a setAttribute method that allows you to set objects into the pageContext. Table 14-2 lists some of the commonly used pageContext methods.

The next shortest-lived scope is the request scope. This scope is available from the time the user submits the request until the page has completed rendering. The request scope is where the HTML form parameters are stored. Request parameters are always of type String and are populated from the submitted form. For example, if a user is completing a web form in their browser and clicks submit, all of the form fields are placed into the request scope. The parameters that are passed to the server are accessible from the request scope via the getParameter(String) method. The following

Methods	Description
Object getAttribute(String)	Retrieves an object from the page scope
void setAttribute(String, Object)	Sets an object into the page scope
HttpServletRequest getRequest()	Retrieves the request object
void removeAttribute(String)	Removes an attribute from the page scope

TABLE 14-2. *pageContext Methods*

code example checks to see if the username parameter is null or contains an empty string ("") and, if so, sets an ErrorMsg object into the request using the setAttribute(String, Object) method:

```
<%
      if(request.getParameter("username") == null
                   || "".equals(request.getParameter("username")) {
        request.setAttribute("errorMsg",
                               new ErrorMsg("Username is required.");
}
%>
```

The page can then print the message using the getAttribute(String) method. This method returns an object, so the retrieved object must be cast back to our Custom ErrorMsg object as follows:

```
<%= ((ErrorMsg) request.getAttribute("errorMsg") ).getErrorText()) %>
```

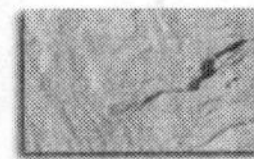

NOTE
As we cover JSP Standard Tag Library (JSTL) and the JSP Expression language in this chapter, you will learn how to access the object above without resorting to the expression tag or scriptlets.

The session scope is often one of the most misused scopes. Novice developers will often overuse the session scope by storing lots of objects that would be better stored in the request scope. The reason this is considered undesirable is that the session scope is fairly long lived. When a user creates a session, it has a specified timeout, which is set in the web.xml file. This timeout value is typically 30 minutes and sometimes longer. The session only times out when the client that owns the session has not made another request in 30 minutes. So while the user may be done, the objects that were created will not be garbage-collected for 30 minutes. The objects take up resources until the timeout is reached. Overusing the session will restrict your application's scalability. If you use the session to store transient objects, you must be sure to remove them when you're finished with them. A good general rule of thumb is to only store objects that are required throughout the life of the session. The session scope has the same set and get attribute methods as the request scope, though it does not have get and set parameter methods. All items stored in the session scope are also objects and must be typecast.

The application scope is the longest-lived scope and is available from the start of the application and exists until it is shut down. The objects in this scope are shared across all web components that make up the application. To access or set attributes in this context, you can use the getAttribute and setAttribute methods of the ServletContext interface.

Knowing what scope to put an object in is key to good web development. The rule of thumb is to place the objects you create in the shortest-lived scope possible. If you have a web form that spans multiple JSPs, use the HTML hidden fields to store and pass along the data until it is ready to be aggregated into an object. Do not create a temporary object and place it into the session.

Tag Type	Description	Syntax
Action	Used to provide request time instructions to the JSP container.	<jsp:actionName attributes />
Comment	Used to place comments in your JSPs. Comments are not sent to the client in the output.	<%-- This is a comment! --%>
Declaration	Used to declare and define methods and variables that are shared by all JSP requests.	<%! Any Java delcaration %>
Directive	Used to specify translation time instructions to the JSP compiler.	<%@ Any Java directive %>
Expression	Used as a shortcut for printing values.	<%= Any Java expression %>
Scriptlets	Used to include inline Java code in our JSPs.	<% Java code; %>

TABLE 14-3. *The Six JSP Tag Element Types*

JSP Syntax

There are six basic types of JSP tag elements. Table 14-3 defines each of the elements. Notice that all of the elements except the action type are enclosed in <% and %>.

JSP Directives

The first tag type we will discuss is the directive. All directives in a JSP are defined with the syntax:

```
<%@ directive-name   attribute-list %>
```

There are three types of JSP directives available: page, include, and taglib.

Page Directives

The page directive allows us to communicate properties at translation time. They let us specify which Java classes will be needed on the page and if a page must take part in a session. The following list describes the available page directive attributes:

- **autoFlush** Can be set to true or false. When it is set to true, the buffer should be flushed when it is full.
  - autoFlush="true" is the default.
- **buffer** The size of the page buffer.
- **contentType** The MIME type and character encoding of the output of the JSPs.
- **errorPage** A relative URL to a JSP that used to handle errors for this page.
  - errorPage="error.jsp"
  - This is not set by default.

- **extends** The class that this JSP will extend.
  - The class must implement the javax.servlet.jsp.JspPage interface.
- **import** A comma separated list of classes and packages that are to be imported. The following packages are imported by default:
  - java.lang.*
  - javax.servlet.*
  - javax.servlet.jsp.*
  - javax.servlet.http.*
- **info** Informational text about this JSP.
- **isErrorPage** Set to true if this page is a error handling page.
- **isThreadSafe** Set to true if the JSP is thread safe and set to false if the page is not thread safe.
- **language** The only valid value is java (JSP 1.2).
- **pageEncoding** The character encoding of the JSP.
- **session** Set to true if the page takes part in an HTTP session.

A typical page directive that sets the page's content type and imports the java.io and java.util packages might look like the following:

```
<%@ page contentType="text/html;charset=windows-1252"
                 import="java.io.*, java.util.*"
%>
```

Include Directive

The second type of directive is the include directive. This directive allows developers to include files in JSPs at translation time. This means that the contents of the included file are included when the JSP is translated into a servlet. The included file will be inserted at the point in the JSP where it is declared. The file attribute is used to specify the file that will be included. The value of the file attribute must be a valid relative URL. You cannot use run-time expressions for the file URL. The following example includes a JSP header and an HTML footer. The body of the page will be included between the include directives:

```
<%@ include file="header.jsp" %>
    … [BODY OF PAGE HERE]….
<%@ include file="footer.html" %>
```

When including files, you must remember that the included files may contain HTML tags that can cause a conflict. For example, suppose the header and the JSP that is including it both contain <html> tags. Since you can only have exactly one open and one close <html> tag in a valid HTML document, the page would not render correctly. For the preceding example to render correctly, you would have to have the open <html> tag in the header and the close </html> tag in the footer.

Taglib Directive

The third directive is the taglib directive. This directive tells the JSP engine that a tag library is going to be used. The syntax for the taglib directive is covered in the "Tag Libraries" section later in this chapter.

The Expression Tag Syntax

```
<%= %>
```

allows us to place Java expressions in our JSPs. For example, if we wanted to dynamically set the value of an HTML form field, we could do the following:

```
<input type="text" name="favoriteCar"
          value='<%= request.getAttribute("myFavoriteCar ") %>'>
```

This would draw a text field and populate it with the current value that the request parameter named myFavoriteCar is set to.

Declaration Elements

The declaration element:

```
<!% %>
```

allows us to declare variables and methods in our JSPs. The variables we declare are shared among all JSP requests, so you will not want to store elements that are tied to a request or session in a declaration. For example, if you stored your user information in a variable that was declared in a declaration, you will have issues with users suddenly seeing another users' information. User information is best stored in the session scope. The various JSP scopes are discussed earlier in this chapter, in the section "JSP Scopes." Any valid Java declaration is valid inside the declaration tags. The example below is a simple example:

```
<%!
     int requestCount = 0;
     public boolean isSet(String value) {
                         boolean valSet = false;
          if(value != null && !"".equals(value)) {
               valSet = true;
          }
                         return valSet;
     }
%>
```

Scriptlet Tags

The scriptlet JSP tag:

```
<% %>
```

is used to put Java code inline in our JSPs. While this is not desirable, as it increases page complexity, sometimes it is necessary. Most of the time, scriptlets can be eliminated by using tag libraries, JavaBeans, and the JSP Expression language. The following example is a loop that creates a simple select form element for a list of years ten years in the past and five years into the future.

```
<select name="years">

<%
      // build the option list for select
     int curYear = 2004;
     for(int cnt=curYear-10; cnt < curYear+5; cnt++) {
%>
          <option value="<%= cnt %>">
               <%= cnt %>
          </option>
<%
     }
%>
</select>
```

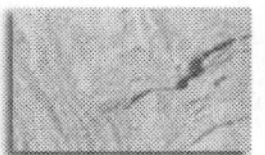

TIP
You can use // inside scriptlets for comments just as you can in Java.

Comment Tags

Comments in JSPs can be done two ways: comments that reach the client and hidden comments. The standard HTML comment can be used in JSPs but they will reach the client. Also, if any JSP tags are inside the comments, they will still be evaluated. To comment out JSP tags, you can use the comment tag:

```
<%-- your comment text --%>
```

The following example comments out a tag and places another descriptive comment in the JSP. The tag will be ignored by the JSP engine, and the comment will not reach the client:

```
...
<%-- BJG: removed functionality as per change request 1312934 --%>
<% -- <hr:displaySchedule startDate="${param.startDate}"/> --%>
...
```

Action Directives

We have saved JSP actions for last, as they are the most useful and complex. There are six standard JSP actions and an unlimited number of custom actions. The six standard JSP actions are: useBean, getProperty, setProperty, include, forward, and plugin. All actions use the jsp: prefix and have a tag-like syntax.

The useBean Action

The <jsp:useBean> allows for the creation and access of JavaBeans located in one of the JSP scopes. A JavaBean can be placed in the page, request, session, and application scopes. The following example retrieves a JavaBean from the session that represents a user:

```
<jsp:useBean id="userBean" class="mypackage.UserBean" scope="session" />
```

NOTE
A JavaBean is a reusable component that can be used in any Java application development environment. JavaBeans are "dropped" into an application container, such as a form, and can perform functions ranging from a simple animation to complex calculations.

The id property represents the handle that will be used to refer to the user JavaBean later in the JSPs. The class property tells the JSP engine what class to use and the scope property tells us which bean should be in the session scope.

Since the UserBean class has a no argument default constructor and public accessor methods, we can use the <jsp:setProperty> and <jsp:getProperty> actions to access and mutate the values contained in the bean. The following code sets the users' color preferences and displays their usernames:

```
<jsp:useBean id="userBean" class="mypackage.UserBean" scope="session" />
<jsp:setProperty name="userBean" property="colorPref" param="colorPref"/>
<font color='<jsp:getProperty name="userBean" property="colorPref"/>'>
<jsp:getProperty name="userBean" property="username"/>
</font>
```

The param property on the setProperty tag tells the JSP engine to load the beans property with the request parameter colorPref. This parameter would have been set most likely on a preceding form. Another great feature of the setProperty action is that you can populate the entire bean in one line. The following example sets the userBean from the request parameters:

```
<jsp:setProperty name="userBean" property="*"/>
```

If there is a parameter in the request that matches the name of any of the bean's properties, the JSP engine will update the userBean with the new values. If, for some reason, one of the bean's properties is not in the request, the value will be unchanged. Also, if a request parameter has more than one value, then only the first value is used. As you can see, the useBean action is very handy.

The include Action

The <jsp:include> action is similar to the include directive in that it forces the JSPs to include content from another JSPs. The include action is, however, evaluated at run time. This means you can dynamically include JSPs. Let's consider a user customization feature where the end user chooses from a list of pages to display as their page header. The JSPs can dynamically include one of many pages based on a user's preference. The following code will change the header and footer to match the user's preference:

```
<jsp:useBean name="userPrefs" scope="session" class="mypackage.UserPrefsBean"/>
<jsp:include page="<jsp:getProperty name="userPrefs" property="headerPage"/>
…. [PAGE_BODY]
<jsp:include page='<jsp:getProperty name="userPrefs"
property="footerPage"/>'/>
```

The page properties of the include actions are dynamically set using the values from the user's preferences object. The value that the page property is set to must be a relative URL to the included page and it must exist.

The forward Action

The <jsp:forward> tag forwards a request to a new JSP immediately when the action is encountered. The JSP forward tag requires that nothing has been sent back to the client's browser. The page forwarded to should handle this, as control is never returned to the forwarding page.

The plugin Action

Another JSP action is the <jsp:plugin>, which provides a mechanism to include client side JavaBeans or applets.

What Are the Benefits?

Many of the first web applications were developed using the Common Gateway Interface (CGI) and scripting languages to create dynamic pages. While this worked, it was very inefficient as every request spawned a process to handle the request. Using CGI scripts also often led to security risks. JSPs alleviate both of these issues. Since JSPs are translated into Java servlets, they are only loaded and initialized once. Once the generated servlet is loaded into memory, it can handle many simultaneous requests. Since servlets run inside a "protective sandbox" that is provided by the Java Virtual Machine, security is not an issue. Using JSPs and Servlets gives developers access to all Java APIs as well as the object-oriented features of Java. JSPs also facilitate the separation of the GUI design from coding; the ability to edit using a GUI WYSIWYG editor is an additional benefit of JSPs.

All JSPs must run inside an application server that adheres to the Servlet and JSP specifications. There are many J2EE application servers available on many different platforms, meaning your application can be built independent of both. A JSP application built on one vendor's implementation of the specification will run on another vendor's version.

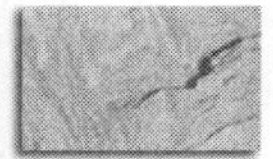

NOTE

The feature that differentiates an application server from a web server is its capability to provide a Java environment that supports the services outlined in the J2EE specification (servlets, JSPs, etc.). Microsoft's IIS product is a special case: it is considered an application server because it provides a .NET environment as opposed to a Java environment. Oracle Application Server 10g does this via the use of a technology called Oracle Application Server Containers for J2EE (OC4J), which supports all of the services in the J2EE 1.4 technology stack.

Most vendors also provide many value-added features with their implementation of the application server. Sometimes, these features cause a tight coupling between your application and a particular vendor. Oracle, however, has embraced the open source community and has incorporated many open source tools into Oracle Application Server 10*g*. As an example, the Oracle HTTP Server is based on the open source Apache HTTPD server. Oracle's Application Development Framework contains many value-added features that support the rapid development of applications that use JSPs as their presentation layer. Chapter 13, "JDeveloper," provides more information on Oracle ADF.

Developing any application usually involves a team of people that have varying levels of knowledge. Some team members may be very strong at presentations using HTML but are not well-versed in developing and designing Java classes. JSPs allow you to split development tasks among different team members according to their skill sets. Developers that are Java-focused can be tasked with the development of the servlets, tag libraries, and other required Java code. The JSP developers can then focus on the creation of the user interface and presentation logic using the JavaBeans and tag libraries.

JSP Implementation on OC4J

Since the JavaServer Pages and Servlet specifications are somewhat open in regards to how features are actually implemented by a container provider, there are certain items that are specific to Oracle's Java containers for Oracle Application Server 10*g*, called Oracle Application Server Containers for J2EE (OC4J). In this section, we will cover the specifics of how the specification is implemented in OC4J, as well as some value-added features to JSP development.

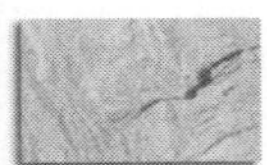

NOTE
For more information about OC4J, see Chapter 1, "Overview of Technologies".

The OC4J 9.0.4 J2EE container provided with Oracle Application Server 10*g* is fully JSP 1.2- and Servlet 2.3-compliant. Oracle does support the Servlet 2.0 model but recommends upgrading to the 2.3 model, if possible. OC4J provides all of the features that are in the specifications, as well as value-added features. These features are generally grouped into one of three categories:

- Extended Type JavaBeans
- Oracle-specific features
- Caching features

The Oracle HTTP Server (OHS)

Typically, the Apache-based Oracle HTTP Server (OHS) is the default entry point for all OC4J processes. When a user requests a JSP, it is first handled by OHS. OHS routes request for JSPs to the OC4J process by means of the Apache JServ Protocol (AJP), through the MOD_OC4J component. The MOD_OC4J Apache module is provided with Oracle Application Server 10*g* and is configured, by default, to service requests for JSPs. AJP was used instead of HTTP, as it has features that make it faster. MOD_OC4J also supports load balancing, stateless session routing of stateful servlets, and communicates with Oracle Process Monitoring and Notification (OPMN), which can then restart an OC4J instance in the event of a failure.

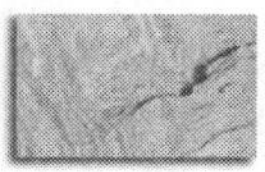

NOTE
In addition to MOD_OC4J, Oracle also supplies mod_jserv for the JServ servlet environment. This is mainly provided as a backward compatibility feature as older versions of the application server used this as the primary servlet container.

Configuration

Oracle Application Server 10*g* provides a highly configurable JSP container. While the application server comes preconfigured to run JSPs, there are a number of configuration parameters and features that are of particular interest to developers. This section will cover some of the features that are common to other J2EE containers as well as some that are specific to Oracle Application Server 10*g*.

Most of the configuration options for JSPs are available through the Oracle Enterprise Manager Application Server Control web site. This is good for applications that are ready for deployment to an Oracle Application Server 10*g* instance. However, Oracle JDeveloper 10*g* and OC4J stand-alone applications only provide access to the configuration via the configuration files. It is important that developers know how to access and change these parameters during development.

To set the Oracle JSP Container Properties, log into OEM and navigate to the OC4J instance you wish to modify by clicking on the OC4J instance name. To access the administration page for the selected instance, click on the Administration link located at either the top or bottom of the page. Once you are on the Administration page, select the JSP Container Properties link under the Instance Properties section to access the available JSP properties. From this page, you can modify any of the JSP properties for this instance. The global-web-application.xml file, located under the instance's config directory, is the file that is updated for all JSP configuration properties. The JSP servlet must be updated using the init-param element. The param-name and param-value elements should be added for each of the parameters that need to be modified. The excerpt below, from the global-web-applciation.xml file, shows how to set the emit_debug_info parameter to true:

```
<servlet>
     <servlet-name>jsp</servlet-name>
     <servlet-class>oracle.jsp.runtimev2.JspServlet</servlet-class>
<init-param>
<param-name>emit_debuginfo</param-name>
<param-value>true</param-value>
</init-param>
....
</servlet>
```

Table 14-4 describes the available properties, their purpose, valid values, and the property name that is updated:

JSP OEM Property	Valid Values [] = default	Property Name	Description
Debug Mode	[false] true	debug_mode	Causes a stack trace to be displayed when a run-time exception occurs. Valid values are true or false.
Emit Debug Info	[false]true	emit_debuginfo	Creates a line map from the JSPs for debugging.
External Resource for Static Content	[false]true	external_resource	When set to true, all static content for the JSPs will be placed in a separate Java resource file during page translation.
When a JSP Changes	[recompile]justrun	main_mode	This setting tells the JSP engine how to handle changed JSPs. By default, the server is set to recompile. To have the JSP save the resources expended checking for updated JSPs, set this value to justrun.
Generate Static Text as Bytes	[false]true	static_text_in_chars	By default, static text is generated as bytes. To have static text generated as characters, set this value to true.
Precompile Check	[false]true	precompile_check	Set this Boolean to true to check the HTTP request for a standard jsp_precompile setting. The default is false.
Tags Reuse Default	[runtime]compiletimecompiletime_with_release	tags_reuse_default	This specifies a default setting for JSP tag handler pooling (true to enable by default; false to disable by default). You can override this default setting for any particular JSP page. The default is true.
Reduce Code Size for Custom Tags	[false]true	reduce_tag_code	Set this Boolean to true for further reduction in the size of generated code for custom tag usage. The default is false.

TABLE 14-4. *JSP OEM Properties*

JSP Pre-translation

The default configuration for the OC4J Server is set to translate and compile each JSP the first time it is requested and every time the page changes. Oracle provides a utility for pre-translating JSPs for deployment. The ojspc utility can be used to pre-translate JSPs and eliminate the translation and compile time normally encountered during the initial request. This utility can also be used when deploying binary files only. If you elect to pre-translate your pages, you must configure the OC4J server accordingly.

Every J2EE application must have a web.xml file located in the application's WEB-INF directory. The web.xml file is used by the OC4J server to communicate configuration information for an application. This configuration file allows you to define servlets, servlet parameters, tag libraries, and other application-specific items. There are a number of JSP configuration parameters that are available for modifying the environment that JSPs run in.

Shared Resources in OC4J

OC4J allows for sharing tag libraries and their Tag Library Descriptor (TLD) files by providing a directory that is common to all deployed applications. It is recommended that all tag libraries that are shared be stored in the ORACLE_HOME/j2ee/OC4J_HOME/jsp/lib/taglib directory, by default.

Application Deployment

Deploying an application in Oracle Application Server 10*g* is a fairly simple process, thanks to the Oracle Enterprise Manager (OEM). By default, the OEM application is located on port 1810 but can be located on other ports. To deploy an application to Oracle Application Server 10*g*, you must first build a Web Archive (WAR) or Enterprise Application Archive (EAR) file. These files are specified by the J2EE specification and are of a standard format. The process of deploying applications to Oracle Application Server 10*g* is detailed in Chapter 15.

Oracle Specific Features

Oracle has provided developers with additional features that extend the functionality of JSPs and how they are processed by the Oracle Application Server 10g engine. These features are discussed in the next couple of sections.

Extended Type JavaBeans

The first feature we will discuss is the JavaBean-based extended types that are available. Storing primitive data types such as int, boolean, and float in the various JSP scopes is not allowed, and the standard Java wrapper classes do not comply with the JavaBeans API specification. Oracle's solution to this problem is a set of classes that act as JavaBean-compliant wrappers for the primitive data types. The oracle.jsp.jml package contains a set of classes that allow you to store representations of the primitive data types using the standard <jsp:useBean/> tag. Table 14-5 maps the available extended types to Java's primitive types.

The JSP Expression Language and the Java Standard Tag Libraries will be covered in detail later in this chapter in the section "Java Standard Tag Libraries."

In addition to the getValue method, there are several other methods that allow for comparison to other types. The getTypedValue(...) and setTypedValue(...) methods are overloaded to allow comparison and setting to or from a String, boolean, or JmlBoolean. These methods will generally be used in Java classes for comparison and initialization of the Java bean.

Oracle Extended Type JavaBean	Java Type
oracle.jsp.jml.JmlBoolean	boolean
oracle.jsp.jml.JmlFPNumber	double
oracle.jsp.jml.JmlNumber	int
oracle.jsp.jml.JmlString	String

TABLE 14-5. *Oracle-Java Primitive-Type Mapping*

The JmlFPNumber and JmlNumber classes are used to represent integer and floating-point values, respectively. These classes also use the value attribute setter method to initialize the value when used inside a JSP. Using these classes can cause your JSP to throw java.lang.NumberFomatException if the value cannot be converted to a number. The JmlString class is a wrapper for the java.lang.String class that is mutable and has a very handy isEmpty() method that returns false if the object contains an empty String (""). You can also compare JmlString objects to each other by using the overloaded .equals(JmlString) method.

Since most primitive data types are properties of objects and wrapped inside of JavaBeans, these classes are only useful if you do not have to model complex objects and simply need to store a single value. One advantage to using these classes is that the objects are mutable, unlike their java.lang counterparts.

JSP Markup Language (JML)

Oracle provides a set of custom tags that allows developers with little or no knowledge of Java to create JavaServer Pages. JSP Markup Language (JML) provides tags for conditional logic, database access, looping, and other useful elements. JML was introduced before the Java Standard Tag Libraries (JSTL) and contains many of the same features. If you are developing a new application, it is recommended that you use JSTL. There is, however, some functionality that JML has that JSTL does not. Table 14-6 lists the available tags, their purpose, and the equivalent JSTL or JSP tag.

In addition to JML basic tags, Oracle provides a set of Data-Access JavaBeans and SQL tags for data access. These provide a JSP developer with access to the database from within the JSPs. In simple applications, these components can be used to create dynamic data-driven pages. For medium to complex applications, you should use Oracle's Application Development Framework (ADF).

JML Tag Name	Purpose	JSTL/JSP Equivalent
useVariable	Declares simple variables in one of the JSP scopes.	jsp:useBean
useForm	Declares variables and uses the request parameters to set them.	jsp:useBean and jsp:setProperty
useCookie	Declares variables that are initialized from cookies.	
remove	Removes attributes from various scopes.	session.removeValue("Name")
if	Evaluates a single expression and executes the code in the body if the condition evaluates to true.	c:if
ChooseWhenotherwise	A multiple conditional statement similar to the standard if-else.	c:choose, c:when, c:if
for	Provides the ability to iterate through a loop.	c:for
foreach	Allows for iterating over Java arrays, Enumerations, and Vectors.	c:forEach
return	Stops page execution at the point it is encountered.	
flush	Flushes the page buffer if page buffering is enabled.	

TABLE 14-6. *JML/JSTL Comparison*

NOTE
See Chapter 13 for more on ADF.

Data-Access JavaBeans provide a set of reusable components that a developer can use to create database connections through a data source or a simple JDBC connection, run SQL queries, execute DML, and run stored procedures. The four JavaBeans available to the developer are contained in the oracle.jsp.dbutil package. To access this package, you must have the ojsputil.jar file in your classpath. This file is provided with the OC4J container.

Connecting to the database can be accomplished by the ConnBean, ConnCacheBean, or the DBBean. The ConnCacheBean provides connection pooling and uses datasources; the DBBean has its own connection mechanism. Using a data source is usually your best bet for scalability and maintainability. For more information on using these beans, see the Oracle Application Server 10*g* documentation. You will find descriptions of the tags and their interfaces in Chapter 4, "Data-Access JavaBeans and Tags," of the *Oracle Application Server Containers for J2EE JSP Tag Libraries and Utilities Reference 10g (9.0.4), Part Number B10319-01* (http://download-west.oracle.com/docs/cd/B10464_01/web.904/b10319/toc.htm).

Oracle Global Includes

Oracle Application Server 10*g* provides the ability to do global includes in your JSPs. This feature allows you statically include modules in your JSPs. You can use this feature to add headers or footers to your JSPs without having to code the include directives in every JSP. This feature is accomplished through an XML configuration file located in your applications WEB-INF directory. The ojsp-global-include.xml allows you to specify what, when, and how the include directives should be used. The root element <ojsp-global-include> has one subelement: include. The <include> element's attributes tell the JSP translator what to include and where in the page to include it. You can specify if the include should be at the top of the page (the default) or the bottom. The <include> element, in turn, has one subelement, <into>, that lets you specify what JSPs should process the global includes. You can specify a JSP by directory and, optionally, its subdirectories. For more information and examples on using global includes, see the Oracle Application Server 10*g* documentation, Chapter 7, "JSP Translation and Deployment," of the *Support for JavaServer Pages Developer's Guide* (http://download-west.oracle.com/docs/cd/B10464_01/web.904/b10320/toc.htm).

Edge Side Includes

Oracle Application Server 10*g* provides the ability to break a JSP up into cacheable components by using the Java Edge-Side Includes (JESI) tag library. JESI not only can cache static content but also dynamic content as well. Using JESI can reduce the load on your application server by caching static and dynamic content utilizing Oracle Application Server Web Cache. While learning the ESI framework that JESI is layered on is complex, it is well worth the effort. For a detailed description of Oracle's implementation of JESI, see *Oracle Application Server Containers for J2EE JSP Tag Libraries and Utilities Reference 10g (9.0.4) Part Number B10319-01* (http://download-west.oracle.com/docs/cd/B10464_01/web.904/b10319/toc.htm), Chapter 6, "JESI Tags for Edge Side Includes."

Tag Libraries

Without tag libraries, JSPs would be less useful. Tag libraries are reusable components that developers can use on multiple JSPs. A well-designed tag library encapsulates a set of reusable functionality. Using tag libraries keeps messy scriptlets out of our JSPs.

To use tag libraries, you must define them in the JSP using the taglib directive. You must specify either an absolute Uniform Resource Identifier (URI) or a logical URI. When using a logical URI, you must specify it in the web.xml file using the taglib element. The following entry in your web.xml file will allow you to use a logical URI to access the JSTL core library:

```
<taglib>
  <taglib-uri>http://java.sun.com/jstl/core</taglib-uri>
  <taglib-location>/WEB-INF/c.tld</taglib-location>
</taglib>
```

To use the tag library in your JSPs, you will also have to place the appropriate jar file in your classpath. In this case, it would be jstl.jar. The JSP taglib directive must be added to the JSPs to complete the configuration. The following example makes the JSTL core tags available to your JSPs:

```
<%@ taglib uri="http://java.sun.com/jstl/core" prefix="c" %>
```

NOTE
The c prefix used in the preceding example is the standard used by most developers, but the prefix can be any string that does not conflict with other tag libraries used on the page.

You can also add the taglib directive without adding the web.xml entry, as long as you set the URI to an absolute path. The following example allows you to access the core tag library without the web.xml entry:

```
<%@ taglib uri="/WEB-INF/c.tld" prefix="c" %>
```

Java Standard Tag Libraries

- **Core Tag Library** Provides functionality for variable support, flow control, URL management, and a couple of miscellaneous tags.
- **XML Tag Library** Provides functionality for working with XML documents.
- **Internationalization Tag Library** Provides functionality for internationalization of JavaServer Pages by providing mechanisms to set the locale, display internationalized messages, and format numbers and dates according to the locale.
- **SQL Tag Library** Provides functionality for accessing databases. You can perform queries and updates using this tag library.

The JSTL Core tag library provides many flow control tags and are categorized as either conditional or iterator tags. There are two flow control tags available in the core library. The simple if tag provides simple if functionality for use in our JSPs. If the test condition is true, then the body of the tag is evaluated. The following example checks to see if there is a nonempty request parameter named errorMsg:

```
<c:if test="${request.errorMsg != null && request.errorMsg != ''}">
     <font color="red">
Error: <c:out value="${request.errorMsg}"/>
     </font>
</c:if>
```

The first and last lines are the open and close if tags. The body of the tag is evaluated only when the result test condition is true. Here, the test condition is checking that the request-scoped object identified by the name errorMsg is not null and is not empty.

The <choose> and <when> tags work together to create an if-elseif-else type functionality where one of a number of actions is taken based on a test condition. The choose tag typically contains one or more when tags and one otherwise tag.

In addition to JSTL, there are many third-party and open-source tags available but many times the functionality required is specific to your application. Custom tag libraries fill this void. Custom tag libraries are developed by experienced Java developers and are used by JSP developers.

Oracle Tag Libraries

Oracle provides many tag libraries for use in JSPs. The following tag libraries are available to developers:

- Oracle Business Components for Java Tag Library
- Oracle JDeveloper 10*g* User Interface Extension (UIX) Tag Library
- Oracle JDeveloper 10*g* BC4J UIX JSP Tag Library
- Oracle Reports Tag Library
- Oracle Application Server Wireless Location Tag Library
- Oracle Application Server MapViewer Tag Library
- Oracle Ultra Search Tag Library
- Oracle Application Server Portal Tag Library
- Oracle Business Intelligence Beans Tag Library
- Oracle Application Server Multimedia Tag Library
- Oracle JESI Tag Library

These tags make developing JSPs much easier because they make use of the ADF. The ADF provides a large productivity advantage by using proven solutions to recurring problems. Problems such as, "How do I access persistent data?" are answered by the ADF, and in more than one way. All applications are written according to their own requirements and these requirements vary greatly. Many applications start out to solve a simple problem and do not require many advanced features to solve it. All applications will, however, benefit in the area of extensibility and maintainability if they make use of the features and services available in the ADF toolkit. For more information on developing applications with the ADF, see Chapter 13, Oracle JDeveloper 10*g*.

Custom Tag Libraries

Since tag libraries encapsulate common functionality and it is inevitable that you will find specific functionality that is common among your application's JSPs, they quickly become a very useful and productive tool. Creating custom tag libraries helps JSP developers keep a consistent look and feel across the various pages as well as reduce duplicated functionality. The following example is a simple custom tag that can access a list of employees from the database and create a select list. We will need to create a Tag Library Descriptor (TLD) file and the Java code to handle the tag. First, we will define our TLD file. This example uses the file name taglib.tld and is saved in the META-INF directory under the source directory. The source for the following TLD file defines one tag called selectEmployee. The selectEmployee tag has three attributes (name, selectedId, and size):

```
<?xml version = '1.0' encoding = 'windows-1252'?>
<!DOCTYPE taglib PUBLIC "-//Sun Microsystems, Inc.//DTD JSP Tag Library 1.2//EN" "http://
java.sun.com/dtd/web-jsptaglibrary_1_2.dtd">
<taglib>
  <tlib-version>1.1</tlib-version>
  <jsp-version>1.2</jsp-version>
  <short-name>taglib</short-name>
  <uri>/webapp/mytaglib</uri>
  <description>Human Resources Tag Library</description>
  <tag>
    <name>selectEmployee</name>
    <tag-class>com.tusc.examples.view.SelectEmployeeTag</tag-class>
    <body-content>empty</body-content>
    <display-name>selectEmployeeTag</display-name>
    <description>Custom tag for selecting an employee from a select list.</description>
    <attribute>
      <name>name</name>
      <required>true</required>
      <rtexprvalue>true</rtexprvalue>
    </attribute>
    <attribute>
      <name>selectedId</name>
      <required>false</required>
      <rtexprvalue>true</rtexprvalue>
    </attribute>
    <attribute>
      <name>size</name>
      <required>false</required>
      <rtexprvalue>true</rtexprvalue>
    </attribute>
    <example>
    &lt;hr:selectEmployee name="selectEmp" selectedId="&lt;%= empId %&gt;" size="7"/&gt;
    </example>
  </tag>
</taglib>
```

All of the lines above the first <tag> element apply to the entire tag library. The <tlib-version> element defines a version for the tag library. The <jsp-version> element refers to the version that is required by this tag library. The <short-name> element is a name that other tools and developers can use to refer to this tag library. The short-name must not contain white space and cannot start with a number or underscore. The <uri> element is the unique identifier for this tag library. This is commonly seen as a URL; for example, the uri for the JSTL core library is http://java.sun.com/jstl/core. The reason this is used is a domain name can only be owned by one entity. This makes creating a unique identifier simple and it can be used to attach a brand to the tag library. This example simply uses /myapp/mytaglib for its uri.

The child elements inside the <tag> element define the properties for the selectEmployee tag. The name element is how this tag will be referenced inside a JSP. The <tag-class> element points to the Java class that will provide the implementation for this tag. The <tag-class> must be fully qualified and the class file must be in your classpath. Since this is a simple tag and does not process the body of the tag, the <body-content> is set to empty.

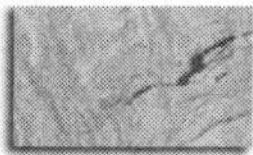

NOTE
For information on more complex tag examples, see http://java.sun.com/products/jsp/taglibraries.

The attribute elements describe the attributes that this tag will have. Each <attribute> element describes one element of the selectEmployee tag. It tells the element's name (if it is required), if it is calculated at run time, and the type of attribute it is. The <name> element is the only required field. The <required> element tells if the attribute is required when using the tag. Our name attribute must be specified and the selectedId is optional for the selectEmployee tag.

Now that we have a TLD defined, we can code the tag handler. This tag uses the SelectEmployeeTag class to implement the tag's functionality. This class extends the javax.servlet.jsp.tagext.TagSupport base class, which implements the required Tag interface. The doStartTag() method (which is the method we must override to implement our tag's functionality) is listed as follows (line numbers have been added for readability):

```
public int doStartTag() throws JspException {
System.out.println("Start SelectEmployeeTag-doStartTag(): " +
System.currentTimeMillis());
Connection conn = getConnection();
try {
selIdEval  = (String)ExpressionEvaluatorManager.evaluate(
"selectedId",             // attribute name
selectedId,               // expression
java.lang.String.class,   // expected type
this,                     // this tag handler
pageContext);              // the page context

JspWriter out = pageContext.getOut();
if(conn != null) {
SringBuffer optBuffer = new StringBuffer();
Statement st = conn.createStatement();
ResultSet rs = st.executeQuery("select * from employees order by last_name");
optBuffer.append("<select name='"+getName()+"' " + getSizeAttr() + " >\n");
while(rs.next()) {
BigDecimal empId = rs.getBigDecimal("employee_id");
optBuffer.append("<option value='"+empId+"' " + idIsSelected(empId)+">");
```

```
21 optBuffer.append(rs.getString("last_name")+", "+rs.getString("first_name")+"</option>\n");
22 }
23 optBuffer.append("</select>\n");
24 out.print(optBuffer.toString());
25 }else{
26 System.out.println("Unable to connect to Database");
27 }
28 }catch(SQLException sqlEx) {
29 sqlEx.printStackTrace();
30 }catch(Exception e) {
31 e.printStackTrace();
32 }finally{
33 try {
34 conn.close();
35 }catch(SQLException ex) {
36 //do nothing
37 }
38 }
39 System.out.println("End SelectEmployeeTag-doStartTag(): " + System.currentTimeMillis());
40 return SKIP_BODY;
41 }
```

The required method signature is defined on Line 1. On Line 3, we call the private getConnection() method to retrieve our datasource. The optBuffer variable that is declared and initialized on Line 14 is a StringBuffer that we will use to store our HTML that will be sent to the JSP's output stream. Once we have received a not null Connection object, we can create and execute our query to retrieve all of the employees on Lines 16 and 17. Line 17 sets up our HTML select tag by setting name to the value that was passed in with the name attribute. The optional size attribute, which defines the number of rows that will be visible by the select tag, is processed by the getSizeAttr(String) helper method. If the user does not specify a value for the size attribute, the select list is rendered as a simple drop-down list. If the size attribute is specified, it adds the text size="X" where X is the value passed in. Lines 18 thru 22 build the option list for the select. Lines 23 and 24 close the select and print the optBuffer to the output stream.

The following code is a test JSP for using the selectEmployee tag (again, line numbers have been added for readability):

```
<%@ page contentType="text/html;charset=windows-1252"%>
<%@ taglib prefix="hr" uri="/myapp/mytaglib"%>
<%@ taglib prefix="c" uri="http://java.sun.com/jstl/core"%>
<html>
  <head>
    <meta http-equiv="Content-Type" content="text/html; charset=windows-
1252">
    <title>Test selectEmployee Tag</title>
  </head>
  <body>
   <c:set var="empId" value="180" scope="page"/>
   <c:set var="empId" value="108" scope="request"/>
   <c:set var="firstName" value="Nicos" scope="request"/>
   <c:set var="lastName" value="Gibson" scope="request"/>
   <%-- Employee: hr:selectEmployee name="selectEmp" selectedId='<c:out
value="${lastName}, ${firstName}"/>'/ <br>
   <input type="text" name="fullName" value="<c:out value="${lastName}, ${firstName}"/>" >
   --%>
   <form name="negOrPos">
   Please enter a number.<br>
   <input type="text" name="numVal" value="<c:out value="${param.numVal}"/>" >
```

```
20   <input type="submit"><br>
21   <c:choose>
22     <c:when test="${param.numVal > 0}">
23       The number is positive.
24     </c:when>
25     <c:when test="${param.numVal < 0}">
26     The number is negative.
27     </c:when>
28     <c:otherwise>
29       <c:if test='${param.numVal != null}'>
30         <c:out value="The value \"${param.numVal}\""/> is zero!
31       </c:if>
32     </c:otherwise>
33   </c:choose>
34   </form>
35   </body>
36 </html>
```

Lines 2, 10, and 14 are the main lines needed to use the tag. Line 2 tells the JSP compiler that this page will be using hr prefix to refer to tag library identified by the /myapp/mytaglib uri as defined in the web.xml file. Line 10 sets a scripting variable to a constant value of 180 so we can test the selectedId functionality and the run-time evaluation of the attribute. Line 14 has the plain text Employee: and the selectEmployee tag call. The name attribute is set to the static value of selectEmp, for use in a web form, and the selectedId is set to the value of the empId specified on Line 10.

JSP Expression Language

You can also code this custom tag to make use of the JSP expression language. To do this, however, we must use a nonstandard class found in the org.apache.taglibs.standard.lang.support package. The ExpressionEvaluatorManager class gives us the ability to use the expression language in our custom tags. In the following code snippet, we see the code that would need to be added to make our tag process the expression:

```
selIdEval  = (String)ExpressionEvaluatorManager.evaluate(
           "map",                    // attribute name
           selectedId,               // expression
           java.lang.String.class, // expected type
           this,                      // this tag handler
           pageContext);              // the page context
```

The selIdEval is a new private String variable that will hold the results of the evaluated expression. We can now update the idIsSelected method to use this value instead of the selectedId. It is important to remember that variables that are defined in scriptlets are not placed into one of the JSP scopes. We can do this using the set core tag with the following call:

```
<c:set var="empId" value="180"/>
```

This will place the empId into the pageContext. You could also use the implicit variable pageContext and call the setAttribute method to place it into the page scope. Since avoiding scriptlets in our JSPs is good programming practice, using the tag is a better option.

NOTE
This is a very simple example and does not adequately show the power of the expression language. Ideally, JSPs are for presentation only and, generally, JavaBeans will be placed in one of the scopes by a servlet, so accessing them becomes the only concern for the JSP developer.

Accessing nested properties in the expression language (EL) is as simple as using the dot (.) operator. For example, if the employee data was stored in an EmployeeBean, then accessing the attributes could be done as follows:

```
${empBean.firstName}
```

The above expression causes the getFirstName() method to be called on the empBean object located in one of the JSP scopes. If there are two EmployeeBean objects referred to by the empBean name, and one in the page scope and one in the request scope, you will only be able to retrieve the object in the pageScope. The various JSP scopes are searched in the order of the shortest-lived to the longest: page, request, session, then application. It is a good idea to make the names unique across the scopes. You can, however, refer to a specific scope by name, such as in the following example:

```
${pageScope.empBean.firstName}
```

The pageScope element in the above expression is one of the implicit objects that the expression language provides. Table 14-7 describes each of the implicit objects that are available.

Variable	Description
pageScope	Provides access to the objects that are stored in the JSPs scope
requestScope	Provides access to the objects that are stored in the JSP request scope
sessionScope	Provides access to the objects that are stored in the JSP session scope
applicationScope	Provides access to the objects that are stored in the JSP application scope
cookie	Provides access to cookies and their values
header	Provides access to headers and their values
headerValues	Provides access to header values
initParam	Provides access to the initialization parameters as defined in your web.xml file
param	Provides access to requested parameters
paramValues	Provides access to the request parameters that have multiple values
pageContext	Provides access to the pageContext and the objects contained in the page context such as the request, response, session, servlet config, and servlet context

TABLE 14-7. *Available Implicit Objects*

Type	Operators
Arithmetic	* / div % mod
Grouping	
Identifier Access	. []
Logical	&& (and) || (or) ! (not) empty
Relational	== (eq) != (ne) < (lt) > (gt) <= (le) >= (ge)
Unary	-

TABLE 14-8. *Available Operators*

The EL also has set of operators that are used the same way you would use them in Java. As with Java, the operators have precedence. Table 14-8 is a summary of the available operators and the list that follows shows the operator precedence.

This list ranks the operator precedence from highest to lowest, left to right:

- []
- ()
- (unary) not ! empty
- / div % mod
- + - (binary)
- < > <= >= lt gt le ge
- == != eq ne
- && and
- || or

The following code example uses the JSTL choose, when, and otherwise tags and the expression language to create a web form that will determine if the supplied number is positive, negative, or zero. When the page is first displayed, the otherwise block is evaluated. Inside the otherwise tag's body, we have a JSTL if tag checking to make sure that the parameter is not null. If the numVal request parameter is not null, all of the “when” tags evaluate to false and “The value is zero!” message is displayed:

```
<form name="negOrPos">
Please enter a number.<br>
<input type="text" name="numVal"
        value="<c:out value="${param.numVal}"/>" >
<input type="submit"><br>
<c:choose>
```

```
    <c:when test="${param.numVal > 0}">
      The number is positive.
    </c:when>
    <c:when test="${param.numVal < 0}">
    The number is negative.
    </c:when>
    <c:otherwise>
      <c:if test='${param.numVal != null}'>
        The value is zero!
      </c:if>
    </c:otherwise>
  </c:choose>
  </form>
```

You can concatenate expressions together inside JSTL tags and custom tags that make use of the EL. To accomplish this, place the JSP expressions next to each other as in the following example. The resulting output would look like: Smith, Tom. Notice that the comma interpreted literally.

```
<c:out value="${firstName}, ${lastName}"/>
```

One of the confusing things about the syntax is its use of quotes. In JSP and HTML tags, you can use either a single quote or tick (') or double quotes ("). For example, the two following tags are equivalent:

```
<c:out value="${firstName}, ${lastName}"/>
<c:out value='${firstName}, ${lastName}'/>
```

Many times, you will find yourself placing JSTL tags inside HTML tag attributes or other custom tags. For example, a form field is being set using the JSTL <c:out> tag. Notice that the quotes of the HTML tag are single quotes and the quotes used for the value attribute of the out tag are double quotes:

```
<myTags:textInput name='fullName' value='<c:out value="${name}"/>'>
```

When working the HTML tags, it is not as important to alternate the quotes, but if you use the same quote type, testInput, and out value attributes, your page will not compile. You must also escape quotes that appear inside your attribute values. Escaping a quote is similar to escaping quotes in Java: to escape a single quote use \' and to escape a double quote use \".

Oracle ADF also uses the JSP EL in many of its tag libraries. Most experienced developers who first encounter the EL like it because it is simple to learn and makes JSP easier to read and maintain. The best resource for the details of the JSP expression language is the JavaServer Pages Standard Tag Library 1.0 specification. You can download it from the Sun Developer Network Site at http://java.sun.com.

Incorporating JSPs into Portal

One of the great features of Oracle Application Server Portal is that you can use JSPs to provide content to your user community. Oracle Application Server Portal is a great content management and information aggregation tool. It allows a business to create a streamlined process to publishing and approving content for your internal or external sites. Combining Oracle Application Server Portal with JSPs is a fairly simple process. This section will outline the process for incorporating your custom JSPs into Oracle Application Server Portal.

Everything in Oracle Application Server Portal is hierarchical in nature. At the top level of the tree is the Page Group. A Page Group is a grouping mechanism used to organize the content of your site. Inside each Page Group, there is a one-to-many relationship with Oracle Application Server Portal pages; inside each Oracle Application Server Portal page, there is a one-to-many relationship with regions; and inside each region is a one-to-many relationship to Oracle Application Server portlets. Developers can include many portlets that provide dynamic content in a single region. Using JSPs, developers can create portlets that generate dynamic content. You can even use the Struts Framework inside your portlets or convert existing Struts applications into Oracle Application Server Portal portlets. Oracle Application Server Portal also provides facilities to configure Partner applications (those built outside of Oracle Application Server Portal).

In order to create Java-based portlets, you must install the Oracle Application Server Portal Development Kit for Java. You can download the PDK for Java from http://portalstudio.oracle.com. The PDK allows you to create portlets that adhere to the Java Portlet Specification (JPS), which is based on Java Specification Request (JSR) 168.

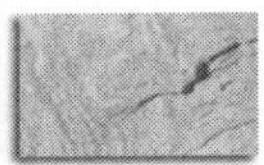

THE JSR 168
Portlet Specification was designed to enable interoperability between portlets and portals. This specification defines a set of APIs for portal computing, addressing the areas of aggregation, personalization, presentation, and security. To get more information about JSR 168, go to: http://www.jcp.org/en/jsr/detail?id=168.

The first step to understanding portlets is to understand the Show Modes available. Show Modes define the visualization and behavior of a portlet. There are eight basic show modes available, but you can also define custom Show Modes with JPS. The various modes are available as either JPS, Oracle Application Server Portal, or both. The eight basic types are

- **Shared Screen Mode** View mode for JPS
- **Edit Mode** JPS and Oracle Application Server Portal
- **Edit Defaults Mode** JPS and Oracle Application Server Portal
- **Preview Mode** JPS and Oracle Application Server Portal
- **Full Screen Mode** Oracle Application Server Portal
- **Help Mode** JPS and Oracle Application Server Portal
- **About Mode** JPS and Oracle Application Server Portal
- **Link Mode** Oracle Application Server Portal

When a portlet appears on a page with other portlets, it is in Shared Screen Mode. Anything that can be rendered inside a table cell can be rendered using Shared Screen Mode. When using this mode, you must remember that you do not have full control of the size and placement of the portlet. This is due to the varying browser width and user settings. For this section, we will focus on this mode. For additional information on various screen modes, see *Oracle® Application Server Portal Developer's Guide 10g (9.0.4) Part No. B13922-01* (http://download-west .oracle.com/docs/cd/B10464_05/portal.904/b13922/toc.htm).

To build and test our JPS compliant portlets, we will need the following items:

- Portal Development Kit
- Oracle Application Server 10*g* or Oracle Application Server Stand-alone Version 9.0.4
- Oracle Application Server Java Portlet Container Preview
- Oracle JDeveloper 10*g* Version 9.0.5.1 or 9.0.5.2
- Portal add-in for Oracle JDeveloper 10*g*

The first item that should be installed is Oracle Application Server 10*g* and Portal or the Oracle Application Server 10*g* Stand-alone server. To install Oracle Portal on Oracle Application Server 10*g*, you must have installed the infrastructure.

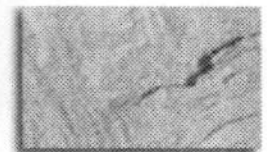

TIP

For detailed information on installing Oracle Application Server 10g, see the Oracle Application Server 10g Administration Handbook by John Garmany and Donald K. Burleson (Osborne Oracle Press Series, 2004).

To install the stand-alone version, first obtain it from http://portalstudio.oracle.com. Once you have downloaded the zip file, extract it to a suitable location. For this example, we will use c:\poc4j. This version of OC4J requires JDK version 1.4.1 to be installed on your computer before it will run. If you do not have the JDK installed, obtain it from http://java.sun.com and install it.

To start the stand-alone server, navigate to the directory where it was extracted and change to the bin directory. The startup and shutdown scripts are in this directory. If you are on Windows, run the startup.bat to start the server and shutdown.bat to stop the server.

By default, the server is configured on port 8888. To access the server, you can point your browser to http://localhost:8888. If you wish to change this port, you may do so by editing the $OC4J_HOME/j2ee/home/config/http-web-site.xml file. Update the <web-site port="8888" … > entry to the desired port. If the server has started correctly, you will see the default page. From this page, you will be able to access the Portal Tools Home Page.

The Oracle Application Server Portal Development Environment

Oracle Application Server Portal has a rich development environment. There are wizards that allow rapid development and deploying of reports, forms, charts, calendars, menus, etc. While the wizards for these components have evolved along with the Portal product to include greater and varied options, they are still not perfect for every situation. You may have the need for functionality that cannot be provided by the Oracle Portal wizards. It is also possible that you have already spent a significant amount of time and effort developing JSPs and do not wish to recode your applications from scratch. In either of these scenarios, the integration of JSPs into Portal gives your development staff the ability to leverage existing work while gaining the benefits of Oracle Portal, such as a robust, easy way to implement security features, page caching, as well the ability to easily pass parameters and visual templates that give your JSPs a common look and feel.

Integration with early versions of Portal (and Portal's predecessor, WebDB) were frustrating at best and arduous at worst. In Oracle 9*i* Application Server Release 2, the process of JSP integration with Portal became greatly simplified. Oracle Application Server 10*g* continues that trend by providing the developer with various methods for integrating JSP technology with Oracle Portal pages. In addition to the ability to integrate JSPs with Oracle Portal, Oracle also provides a set of tags that permit the JSP to communicate with Portal objects (discussed in the section "Portal-Specific JSP Tags").

Types of JSPs in Oracle Application Server Portal

There are two types of JSPs that can be used with Oracle Portal. Oracle refers to these pages as "external" and "internal" JSPs.

- **External pages** This refers to JSPs created and stored outside of the Oracle Portal environment. You can use any non-Portal tool or editor to create your JSPs. When it is time to integrate your JSP with Oracle Portal, a reference to the JSP file stored on disk is created. External pages offer the benefits of greater flexibility, and usually run faster than internal pages, but Oracle Portal does not provide them with any file management or security. The developer must manually configure file management and security for these external pages. The developer also must create a configuration file to reference the external JSP and modify configuration files on the server that will permit the external JSP to log into Portal.
- **Internal pages** This refers to JSPs created with Oracle Portal's page wizards. The resulting JSP is uploaded and stored within the Oracle Application Server 10*g* infrastructure database. Internal pages offer the benefits of easier creation and use Oracle Portal to manage and provide security for them.

Creating an Internal JSP

You will need to adjust few default Portal settings before you can create an internal JSP. In Portal, enter the Navigator by clicking on the "Navigator" link in the top right of the page. Click the "Page Groups" tab if it is not already selected. If you have an exiting page group you wish to work with, click the "Edit Properties" link next to that page group. If you wish to create a new page group, do so by clicking the "Page Group" link in the top left of the window. After creating the page group, click the link on the top of the page to edit the properties of the page group.

Click the "Configure" tab at the top of the Edit Page Group screen. At the top of that page, you'll see a section entitled Page Types and Template (Figure 14-1). By default, the only page types available for new page groups are "Standard" and "URL." To create a JSP, we will need to add the JSP type to the list of available page types. Do this by clicking the "Edit" link next to Current Selection in the Page Types and Template section. You will see a screen similar to Figure 14-2. Select JSP in the hidden page types and click the greater than symbol to move it to the Visible Page Types list. At the bottom of the "Configure" tab of the "Edit Page Group" page is a section entitled "JSP Access." Click the "Edit" link next to that section. On the following page, select the "Allow External Access" check box and type in a key (the key can be anything, but remember it for later). Click "OK" when complete. Click "OK" again to return to the Navigator.

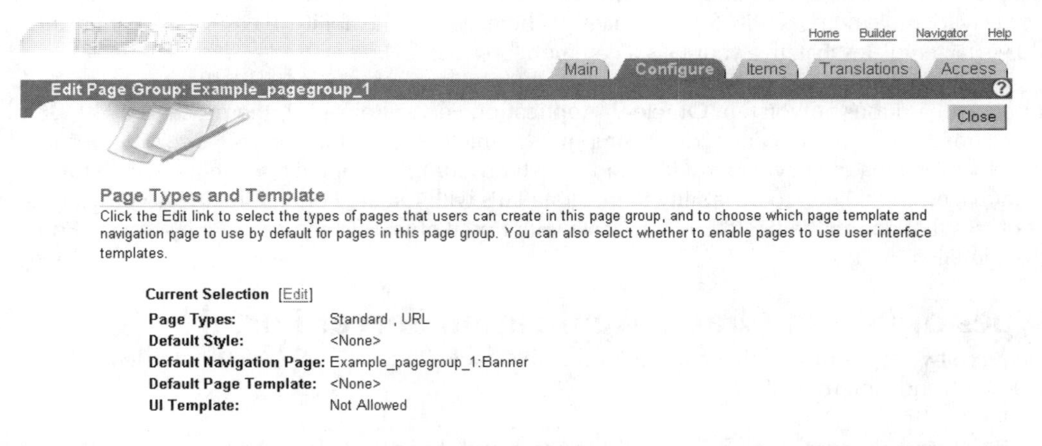

FIGURE 14-1. *The Page Types and Template screen in Oracle Application Server Portal*

Click the "Contents" link to enter the group objects page. Click the "Create" link next to Pages. JSP now shows up in the Page Type drop-down list for the page (Figure 14-3). Give your JSP a suitable name and click "Next >." On the following screen, the developer is prompted to enter the JSP file that will make up this page. When the JSP is specified here, the file will be uploaded and stored in the database. The developer can modify the JSP later on, but the step to upload the file to the database will need to be repeated. Click the "Browse" button and locate your JSP file.

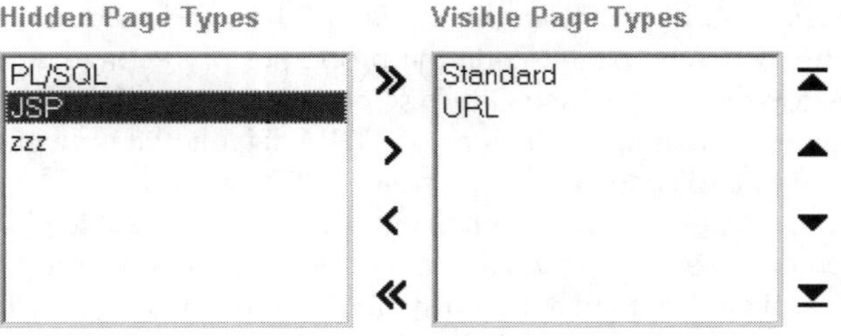

FIGURE 14-2. *The Page Types section*

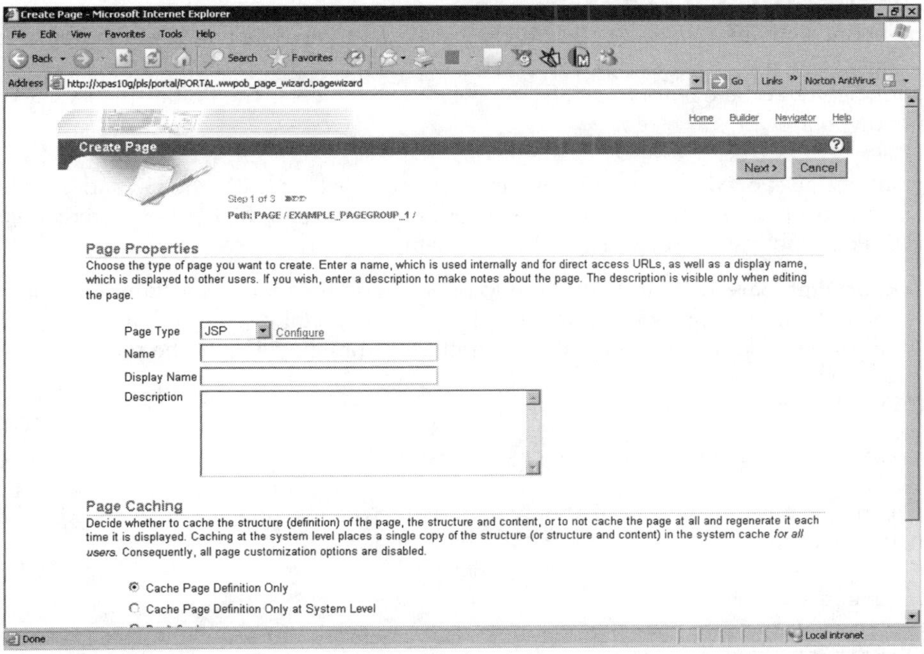

FIGURE 14-3. *The Create Page screen with "JSP" selected*

Note that on this page, you also have the option of specifying a Java Archive (JAR) or Web Archive (WAR) file. They are both files that have predefined directory structures and are made up of files that constitute an application. If you choose to specify a JAR or WAR file on this page, you must specify the initial JSP file within the archive, as an archive may contain multiple JSP files.

Click "Next >" to enter the Access page for your JSP. Leave the default values on that page and click "Finish." You can now view the JSP by clicking on its name in the Navigator (Figure 14-4).

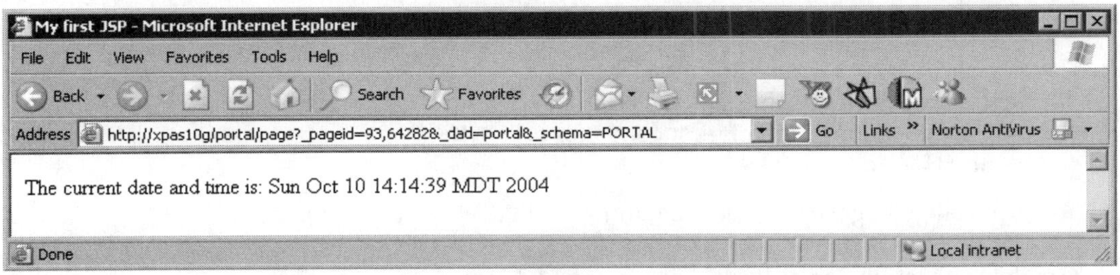

FIGURE 14-4. *The JSP displayed in Oracle Application Server Portal*

Portal-Specific JSP Tags

As we mentioned earlier, Oracle Application Server Portal provides a number of Portal-specific tags. These tags are used to extend your JSP's functionality so that it can run in the Oracle Application Server Portal environment and access Portal elements. The Portal-specific tags available to you are

- **<portal:usePortal>** This must be the first Portal-specific tag in the JSP and must be in the declaration section of the JSP. Its presence indicates the desire to interact with Oracle Application Server Portal portlets within the JSP.
- **<portal:prepare>** This tag is used to optimize portlet request by "bundling" portlet content requests for several portlets from the same portal instance. As an example, the following code would require three round-trips from the client to the server:

```
<showPortlet name = "StockQuotes"/>
<showPortlet name = "CompanyInfo"/>
<showPortlet name = "InvestmentPotfolio"/>
```

The prepare tag can be used so that only one trip between the client and server would be performed:

```
<portal:prepare>
<portal:Portlet name = "StockQuotes"/>
<portal:Portlet name = "CompanyInfo"/>
<portal:Portlet name = "InvestmentPotfolio"/>
</portal:prepare>
```

- **<portal:portlet>** This tag can only be used within a <portal:prepare> tag (see preceding example).
- **<portal:parameter>** This tag is used to set parameters for portlets.
- **<portal:showPortlet>** This tag puts the content of an existing portlet onto a JSP. Example syntax:

  For a default page group:

  ```
  <portal:showPortlet name="StockQuotes" />
  ```

  For a named page group:

  ```
  <portal:showPortlet name="/Page1/StockQuotes" />
  ```

- **<portal:useStyle>** This tag, placed in the <HEAD> section of your JSP file, specifies a style name defined in Portal. It generates a <LINK> that must be in the <HEAD> section of an HTML document.
- **<portal:getPageUrl>** The tag returns the URL of the current page.

Oracle Application Server Portal has expanded its capabilities, making integration with JSPs a much easier task than it was with earlier versions of Oracle Portal and WebDB. The page wizards save the developer from having to hand-modify any configuration files on the server, which often led to access issues (telnetting to the server) and human error when editing configuration files by hand. The developer also now has access to Oracle Application Server Portal-specific tags that allow the interaction of JSPs and existing Portlets. Through this functionality, the developer has the ability to exploit all of Portal's advanced functionality (security, visual templates, etc.) without sacrificing the power and time already invested in JSP development.

Example JSP Code

This section of the chapter shows how to create an HTML form with a JSP and process it. As discussed earlier in this chapter, there are two types of architecture we can follow: Model 1 or Model 2. This example uses Model 1 architecture. The target of our request will be another JSP. The code below provides a login mechanism for an application:

```
<%@ page contentType="text/html;charset=windows-1252"%>
<%@ taglib uri="http://java.sun.com/jstl/core" prefix="c" %>
<html>
  <head>
    <meta http-equiv="Content-Type" content="text/html; charset=windows-1252">
    <title>TUSC JSP Login Page</title>
  </head>
  <body>
    <%-- import the page header --%>
    <%@ include file="header.jsp" %>
    <h1>JSP Login Page Example</h1>
    <hr width="1024" align="left">
    <%-- if the user has submitted the form create a new UserBean object in the session scope --%>
    <c:if test="${param.submit == 'Login'}">
      <jsp:useBean id="userBean" scope="session" class="com.tusc.examples.jsp.UserBean"/>
      <jsp:setProperty name="userBean" property="firstName" param="firstName" />
      <jsp:setProperty name="userBean" property="lastName" param="lastName" />
    </c:if>

    <%-- if the userBean session object exists display the following information --%>
    <c:if test="${sessionScope.userBean != null}">
      <h3>Welcome <c:out value="${sessionScope.userBean.firstName}
${sessionScope.userBean.lastName}"/></h3>
      <br>
      <table width="1024" border="0">
        <tr>
          <td>
            A
            <a href="sessionScopeExamples.jsp">session</a> object (userBean) has been created
to hold your user information. This object is now available to every JSP page. This login page
does not authenticate the user; it simply creates an instance of the UserBean class and places
it in the session scope. This page does not contain any Java code. All of the logic is
accomplished using <a href="jstl.jsp">JSTL core tags</a>
            and <a href="jspDirectives.jsp">JSP tags</a>.
          </td>
        </tr>
      </table>
    </c:if>

    <%-- if the userBean session object does not exist, display the login form --%>
    <c:if test="${sessionScope.userBean == null}">
      <table width="1024" border="0">
        <tr>
```

```
          <td>
            This example makes use of Java Standard Tag Libraries, the session scope, an HTML
form, page directive and the include
            directive.  Once the user object is created in the session, the login form will no
longer be visible and a summary page
            of the example will be created.  Three things will cause the form to reappear: 1)
the user's session expires, 2) the user
            closes his browser windows, or 3) The userBean object is removed from the session
(logout).
          </td>
        </tr>
      </table>
      <form>
      <table width="1024" border="0">
        <tr>
          <td>
          <table cellspacing="2" cellpadding="3" border="0" width="100%">
            <tr>
              <td align="right">First Name:
              </td>
              <td align="left">
                <input type="text" name="firstName"/>
              </td>
            </tr>
            <tr>
              <td align="right">Last Name:</td>
              <td align="left">
                <input type="text" name="lastName"/>
              </td>
            </tr>
            <tr>
              <td> </td>
              <td>
                  <input type="submit" value="Login" name="submit"/>
              </td>
            </tr>
          </table>
          </td>
        </tr>
      </table>
      </form>
    </c:if>
    <%@ include file="footer.jsp" %>
  </body>
</html>
```

Invoking Servlets

Sometimes business logic requires functionality that is best implemented using servlets. A good example of this is an application that needs to use binary data. Given JSPs were designed for dynamic textual content, they do not contain the ability to convert raw bytes to text. For this type of development requirement, developers can use the jsp:include or jsp:forward actions to invoke servlets. The include action dispatches the request to a servlet and the servlets output is added to the resulting page. When the following tag is encountered, the page buffer is flushed and control is transferred to the servlet. Once the servlet completes execution, control is transferred back to the JSP.

```
<jsp:include page="/servlet/MyComplexOperation" flush="true"/>
```

The <jsp:forward> action can also be used with servlets. When the forward action is reached, the page buffer is cleared and the execution of the JSP is stopped. The servlet that is the target will then handle the request.

You can also use servlets in your HTML forms as the target of the action property. Using servlets as a central point of control for your application is a good practice. The following HTML form code snippet sets the form tag's action attribute to the processForm servlet:

```
<form name="myForm" action="/servlet/processform">
…. HTML FORM
</form>
```

You must make sure your web.xml file is configured correctly to process the servlet URL. The following entries added to your web.xml file will correctly configure the servlet:

```
  <servlet>
    <servlet-name>ProcessForm</servlet-name>
    <servlet-class>mypackage.ProcessForm</servlet-class>
  </servlet>
  <servlet-mapping>
    <servlet-name>ProcessForm</servlet-name>
    <url-pattern>/servlet/processform</url-pattern>
  </servlet-mapping>
```

Sometimes a servlet does not generate the HTML page that is the result of the request; it instead forwards the request to another JSP to render the HTML. This is accomplished using the getRequestDispatcher(String) method of the request object. The request dispatcher accepts a String argument that is the location of the JSP (or servlet) to forward the request.

Passing Data

There are many ways to pass data when using JSPs. Typically, objects are set into one of the JSP scopes and the request is forwarded to the target web component. You can also use the jsp:param tag to set parameters inside the body of forward and include. The following code snippet adds two request parameters to the request:

```
<jsp:include page="/servlet/MyComplexOperation" flush="true">
     <jsp:param name="userId" value="22322"/>
     <jsp:param name="managerId" value="34098"/>
</jsp:include>
```

Error Pages

When a run-time exception occurs in a JSP, the request is forwarded to the error page specified in the JSPs directive. Each JSP can have its own error page or they can share error pages. Error pages should always be user friendly. This means that displaying a Java stack trace to the user is not a good idea. Using scriptlets to catch exceptions inside your JSPs is also not a good idea; when errors happen, they should be forwarded (usually) to a page designed to handle the exception or error.

There are two ways to specify which page handles which error. You can specify the default location in your web.xml file using the <error-page> element, or you can specify the error page with the errorPage attribute of the page directive. Specifying default error pages is a feature that is new to the 2.3 version of the Java Servlet Specification; it is not available in older versions.

When specifying your default error pages in the web.xml file, you can map the pages to either an HTTP error code or to an exception type. The HTTP error code is the numeric error code returned when an error happens during a request. Examples of error codes are: 404 – File Not Found Error or 500 – Internal Server Error. You can specify a different error page for each of the HTTP error codes. The following snippet from the web.xml file defines an HTML page to handle the 404 – File Not Found Error and a JSP to handle the 500 – Internal Server Error. Typically, when you are developing web applications and you encounter a run-time exception, a 500 error code is returned. The following snippet, added to your web.xml file, will force all 500 errors to go to the unknownException.JSPs and "404 not found" errors to go to the notFound.html page.

```
<error-page>
<error-code>404</error-code>
<location>/errorPages/notFound.html</location>
</error-page>
<error-page>
<error-code>500</error-code>
<location>/errorPages/unknownException.jsp</location>
</error-page>
```

You can also specify different error pages for different exception types. For example, the following code forces all pages that throw a mypackage.ApplicationException exception to one page and all java.lang.NullPointer exceptions to another. The location must start with a "/" and is relative to the current application:

```
 <error-page>
    <exception-type>mypackage.ApplicationException</exception-type>
    <location>/errorPages/applicationException.jsp</location>
  </error-page>
  <error-page>
    <exception-type>java.lang.NullPointerException</exception-type>
    <location>/errorPages/nullPointer.jsp</location>
  </error-page>
```

As we discussed in the "JSP Expression Language" section of this chapter, the exception implicit object is available to all error pages. To make a JSP an error page, you must set the page directive's isErrorPage attribute to true, as in the following example:

```
<%@ page contentType="text/html" isErrorPage="true" %>
```

If you need a page to have its own error page, you can do this with the errorPage attribute of the page directive, as follows:

```
<%@ page contentType="text/html" errorPage="myErrorPage.jsp" %>
```

Using the implicit exception object, you can log and trace exceptions based on the type. Use the instanceof operator to compare instance types. The following JSP snippet will display a different message based on the instance type:

```
<% if(exception instanceof java.lang.NumberFormatException) { %>
    The specified text can not be converted to a number.
<% }else{ %>
    An unknown exception has occurred.
<% } %>
```

Exceptions that come from servlets can be wrapped in a javax.servlet.ServletException. This is an exception wrapper and contains the real or root exception. The ServletException class provides the getRootCause() method to retrieve the wrapped exception. The following JSP code retrieves the root cause of the exception and displays the message:

```
<%= ((ServletException)exception).getRootCause().getMessage() %>
```

As you can see, error handling in a servlet container is fairly simple and makes handling errors easy and consistent.

Summary

JavaServer Pages (JSPs) are an invaluable tool in modern web development. They provide developers with numerous benefits, including:

- ***Utilization of the Java programming language.*** Given JSPs use Java, they can be run on any application server that supports Java. Oracle Application Server 10*g* supports Java and Java Services such as JSP through the use of containers. Oracle Application Server Containers For J2EE (OC4J), which supports the JSP 1.2 specification, is included with Oracle Application Server 10*g*. An additional benefit is the fact that because Java has become ubiquitous, the learning curve for JSPs is often much smaller than those of competing technologies.
- ***Separation of roles.*** The Java 2 Enterprise Edition (J2EE) makes clear distinctions between the types of services that constitute a Java-based web application. The most commonly referred to categories include:
    - **Communication Services** Handles requests to and from the Web
    - **Business Logic Services** The development tools and languages for building applications
    - **Presentation Services** The development tools and languages for building dynamic web pages

    Technologies such as Business Components for Java (BC4J) and Oracle Forms are good for writing, testing, and maintaining your business logic but there are other technologies that are better suited for displaying your applications. Presentation Services deliver dynamic content to client browsers, supporting servlets, business intelligence, PL/SQL Server Pages, JSPs, Perl/CGI scripts, and PHP. You can use Presentation Services to build your presentation layer for your web applications. While Oracle puts these services into a separate group, you can think of them grouped with the Business Logic Services, in that your application logic can reside within these components. It is the authors' recommendation, however, that you break your business logic into executable components, which can then be called por invoked by these services.

- **Tag libraries** JSPs use tags to allow the insertion of dynamic content, which is invaluable for database-based applications. A tag library, which defines additional tags, can be used to replace sections of code.

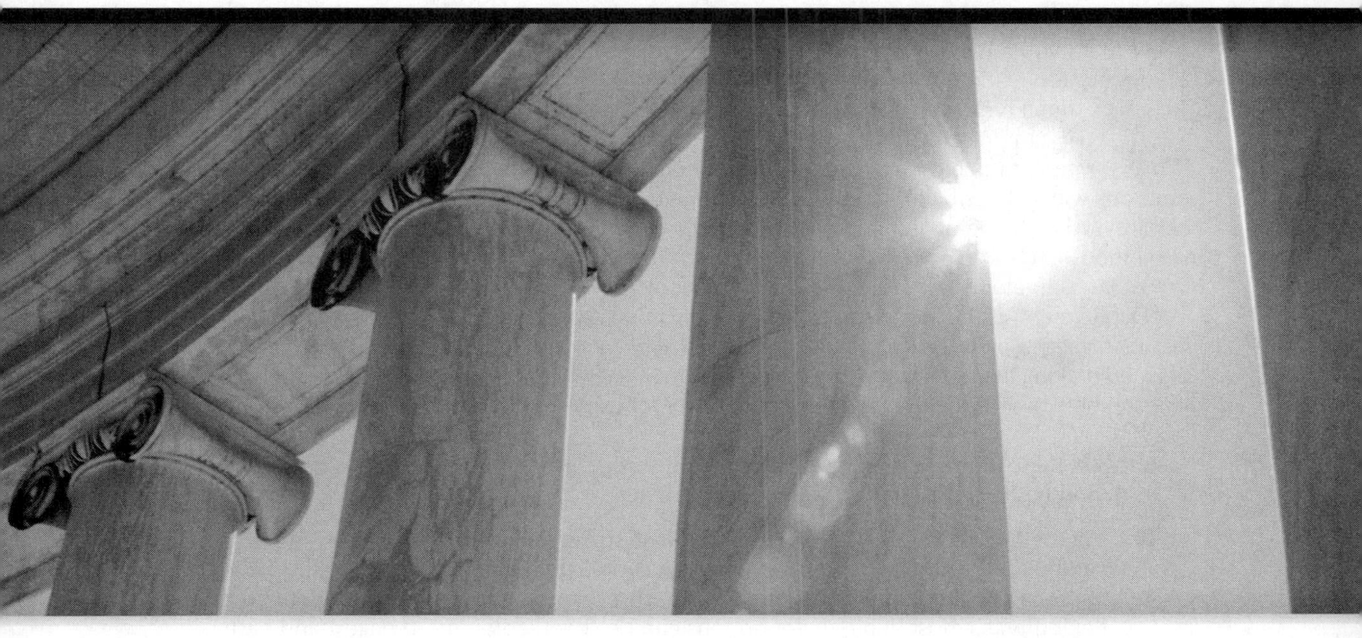

CHAPTER 15

Deploying EARs, WARs, JARs, and JSPs

If you have done Java development work, you know that except in the simplest of applications, the number of files that make up your application can grow very quickly. While this assists in the modularization of large-scale programming projects, it can present significant challenges to developers and administrators when it comes time to deploy those applications. Luckily, Oracle Application Server 10*g* supports numerous ways of deploying applications that give developers and administrators enormous flexibility. Also, by being fully compliant with the Java 2 Enterprise Edition (J2EE) specification, the methods and directory structures required for deployment are well documented and familiar to most Java developers.

"Deployment" is the process of taking an application and its associated files (which can be .java files, .class files, .jsp files, etc.), moving them to an application server (like Oracle Application Server 10*g*), and making the application available for end users to access. As we will see in this chapter, there are three basic ways of deploying applications for use with Oracle Application Server 10*g*:

- **Via the command line** We can manually copy files in the appropriate directories and modify the necessary OC4J configuration files.
- **Via the Oracle Enterprise Manager Application Server Control Web Site** Applications can be deployed via the Enterprise Application Server Control web pages provided for each OC4J container on your system. This option provides you with both great flexibility, as most deployment options can be specified on these pages, and ease of deployment, as most tasks can be handled via a graphical interface.
- **Via Oracle JDeveloper 10*g*** This method is the most flexible way of deploying applications to Oracle Application Server 10*g*. Its greatest limitation is that it requires, naturally, that you have developed your application in Oracle JDeveloper 10*g*.

This chapter will discuss the "packaging" of applications and then explore each of the deployment methods listed. As with most tasks associated with the development and deployment of web-based applications, there is no one "right" way to do it. Developers and administrators will need to evaluate the different options available to them and make decisions based on what is most appropriate for their development group, company, or organization.

Packaging Your Application

The J2EE specification outlines numerous Java-based technologies. Table 15-1 lists some of the Java technologies supported by Oracle Application Server 10*g* and the supported version of each of those technologies.

Since an application can be (and most likely will be) made up of a combination of these technologies, it would be helpful to have a standard way of organizing the various files that make up our applications so that when it came time to move these application components to an application server, the task could be handled in a standardized way. Luckily, the designers of the J2EE specification thought about this and have developed a standard that lists a set of directories for the components that make up your application. You can then group these files into an archive file using the jar (Java Archive) command. Depending on the complexity of your application, we may have JAR files that are made up of other JAR files. The different types of Java archive files are discussed in the next section. After the archive is created, it can be deployed to the application server container (OC4J) with ease.

Java Technology	Version of Specification Supported in Oracle Application Server 10*g*
Java Server Pages (JSPs)	1.2
Servlets	2.3
Entity Java Beans (EJBs)	2.0
Java Message Service (JMS)	1.0.2b
Java Database Connectivity (JDBC)	2.0
Simple Object Access Protocol (SOAP)	1.1
Web Services Description Language (WSDL)	1.1
Universal Description, Discovery, and Integration (UDDI)	2.0

TABLE 15-1. *Java Technologies Supported by Oracle Application Server 10g*

The Directory Structure

The key to building an archive file to be deployed is maintaining your application files in a standard directory structure. Figure 15-1 lists the directory structure outlined by the J2EE specification.

A description of each level of the directory follows. Any directory name in <> is arbitrary; others are exact matches of what has to be in the directory structure (including case-sensitivity):

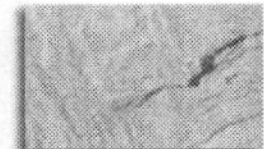

NOTE
The form <root> represents the root directory of your J2EE application; it is traditionally named after the application.

- **META-INF** Location of the application.xml file that describes the modules in your J2EE application (see Chapter 2 for a detailed look at the application.xml file)
- **<ejb_module>** Location of package(s) consisting of the EJB source code for the application; this directory is not mandatory and is omitted if your application does not make use of EJB technology
    - **bmp** Location of package(s) consisting of the source code of bean-managed persistent entity beans
    - **cmp** Location of package(s) consisting of the source code of container-managed persistent entity beans
- **META-INF** Location of the ejb-jar.xml deployment descriptor file
- **<web module>** Location of the web module, containing JSPs, JSP tag libraries, and HTML files
- **WEB-INF** Location of the web.xml file

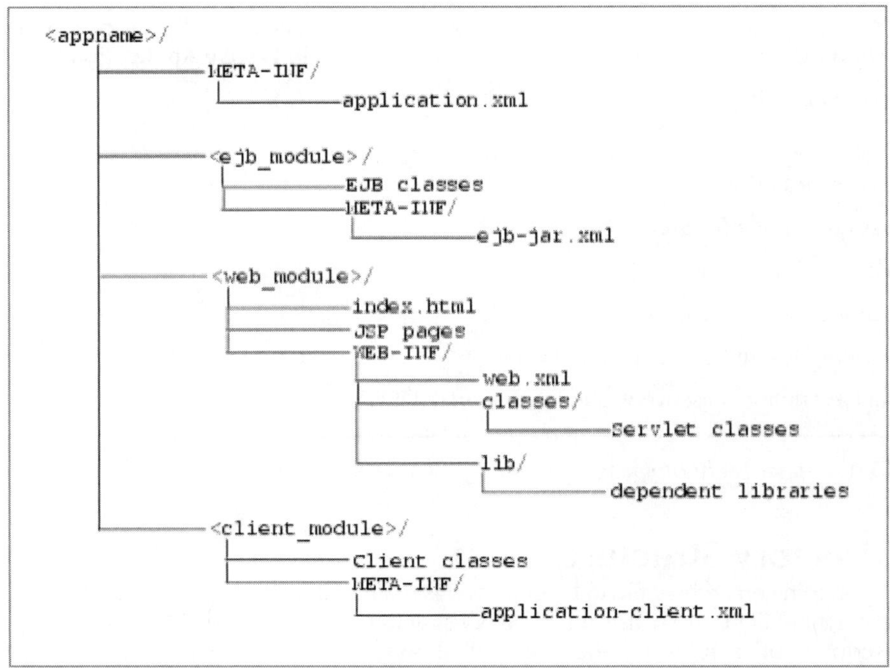

FIGURE 15-1. *The directory structure outlined by the J2EE specification*

- **classes** Starting location of the web module's/servlet classes
- **<package>** Location of package(s) classes
- **lib** dependent libraries
- **<client module>** Location of client classes
- **META-INF** Location of application-client.xml

Back in Chapter 2, we discussed the basic difference between EAR (Enterprise ARchive) and WAR (Web ARchive) files: an application that does not contain EJBs is considered a web application and is usually deployed as a WAR file. An application that contains EJBs is considered an EJB (or Enterprise) application and is deployed as an EAR file. Note that we said web applications are usually deployed as WAR files—you could deploy a web application as an EAR file by leaving the directories for EJB modules empty. This is commonly referred to as "wrapping" a WAR file into an EAR file. If the application contains EJBs, however, it must be deployed as an EAR file. EAR files are further complicated by the fact that they contain WAR files—the web-tier components of the application. The method of "wrapping" a WAR file into an EAR file is what

Oracle does automatically when you click the Deploy WAR file button on the Applications page for the OC4J container.

Let's start with the simpler of the two and create a WAR file. Assuming you have created a directory structure similar to Figure 15-1 for your application development, you can create a WAR file by going into the <web module> directory under the <root> directory for your application. If, for example, you had created an application called "hockeyapp," you might have a directory structure that looks like this:

```
C:\
hockeyapp\
        META-INF\                   application.xml
        hockeyweb\                  Various HTML, JSP and image files
                WEB-INF\            web.xml
                       classes\     Servlet classes
                       lib\         Tag libraries
```

Let's start with the first listing and build a WAR file from that. First cd to the <root>\<web module> directory—in this example, it would be C:\hockeyapp\hockeyweb. From that directory, you can create a WAR file by typing

```
jar cvf <name of war file> <directories to include in war file>
```

So for this example, it would be

```
jar cvf hockeyapp.war WEB-INF
```

If your application contained EJBs, there would also be an EJB directory (hockey_ejb\ as an example):

```
C:\
hockeyapp\
      META-INF\                     application.xml
      hockey_ejb\
            META-INF\               ejb-jar.xml
            hockey\                 Various EJB interface .java files
               impl\               Various Bean implementation files
      hockeyweb\                    Various HTML, JSP and image files
      WEB-INF\                      web.xml
            classes\                Servlet classes
            lib\                    Tag libraries
```

To create an EAR file from this directory, you need to perform a few more steps:

1. Create a WAR file by cd'ing to the <root>\<web module> directory (in this case, C:\hockeyapp\hockeyweb) and issuing the following command:

   ```
   jar cvf hockeyapp.war WEB-INF
   ```

2. Copy the newly created hockeyapp.war file up one level to the C:\hockeyapp directory.

3. Next cd to the <ejb> directory (in this example, C:\hockeyapp\hockey_ejb).
4. Create a jar file by issuing the following command:

   ```
   jar cvf <name of jar file> <directories to include in jar file>
   ```

   For this example, it would be:

   ```
   jar cvf hockeyapp-ejb.jar META-INF hockey
   ```

5. Copy the newly created hockeyapp-ejb.jar file up one level to the C:\hockeyapp directory.
6. Modify the application.xml file in the C:\hockeyapp\META-INF directory and add these two <module> sections:

   ```
   <?xml version="1.0"?>
   (!DOCTYPE application PUBLIC "-//Sun Microsystems,
       Inc.//DTD J2EE Application 1.2//EN"
     "http://java.sun.com/j2ee/dtds/application_1_2.dtd">
   <!-- The application element is the root element of a
       J2EE application deployment descriptor.    -->
   <application>
         <display-name>Hockey App</display-name>
         <module>
               <web>
                     <web-uri>hockeyapp.war</web-uri>
                     <context-root>/</context-root>
               </web>
         </module>
         <module>
               <ejb>hockeyapp-ejb.jar</ejb>
         </module>
   </application>
   ```

7. Now cd back to the root directory of the application (in this example, C:\hockeyapp).
8. Create the EAR file with the following command:

   ```
   jar cvf <name of ear file> <files/directories that will make up the ear file>
   ```

   For our example, it would be:

   ```
   jar cvf hockeyapp.ear hockeyapp.war hockeyapp-ejb.jar META-INF
   ```

Now that we have our EAR or WAR file, we can look at the next step we will need to perform before actually deploying our application to the application server.

The Data Sources File

If your application is going to access data in a database (and since you're reading a book with Oracle in its title, I'm assuming yours is), you need to set up a data source before your application can "speak" to your database. Most likely, you will be using a Java Database Connectivity (JDBC) driver to facilitate communications between your application and the

Oracle database. Depending on how you have coded your application, you will need to specify how your application will reference a data source in the data-sources.xml file (discussed shortly).

While there are an infinite number of ways to code connection routines for your application, the listing that follows demonstrates a simple way of attempting to establish a connection to an Oracle database:

```
private DataSource getDataSource() throws ConnectionException
{
DataSource ds = null;
try
{
       Context initContext = new InitialContext();
       ds = (DataSource) initContext.lookup ("jdbc/hockeyappDS");
} catch (NamingException e)
{
       e.printStackTrace();
       throw new ConnectionException("Cannot establish connection " + e.getMessage());
}
return ds;
}
```

The line

```
ds = (DataSource) initContext.lookup ("jdbc/hockeyappDS");
```

is searching for an entry in the data-sources.xml file with a name of "jdbc/hockeyappDS". Since this particular piece of code was implemented in a bean, Oracle will search the data-sources.xml file, attempting to match an entry with the ejb-location parameter.

During creation of an OC4J container, Oracle provides you with an example data source inside a default data-sources.xml file. You can use that as a template to create other data sources with the file. The location of the data-sources.xml file is <ORACLE_MID-TIER_HOME>/j2ee/<OC4J Container Name>/config. Here is a listing of the default data-sources.xml file that comes with Oracle Application Server 10*g*:

```
<?xml version="1.0" standalone='yes'?>
<!DOCTYPE data-sources PUBLIC "Orion data-sources" "http://xmlns.oracle.com/
ias/dtds/data-sources-9_04.dtd">
<data-sources>
       <!--
              An example/default DataSource that uses
              Oracle JDBC-driver to create the connections.
              This tag creates all the needed kinds
              of data-sources, transactional, pooled and EJB-aware sources.
              The source generally used in application code is the "EJB"
              one - it provides transactional safety and connection
              pooling. Oracle thin driver could be used as well,
              like below.
              url="jdbc:oracle:thin:@host:port:sid"
       -->
```

```
<data-source
      class="com.evermind.sql.DriverManagerDataSource"
      name="OracleDS"
      location="jdbc/OracleCoreDS"
      xa-location="jdbc/xa/OracleXADS"
      ejb-location="jdbc/OracleDS"
      connection-driver="oracle.jdbc.driver.OracleDriver"
      username="scott"
      password="->pwForScott"
      url="jdbc:oracle:thin:@localhost:1521:oracle"
      inactivity-timeout="30"
/>
```

Let's say we wanted to connect to an instance named "hockey" on a server named "avalanche" as user "sakic" with a password of "captain" using the data source specified in the preceding Java code segment ("jdbc/hockeyappDS"). We could copy the existing data-source section in the preceding file and create a new one that looks like this:

```
<data-source
      class="com.evermind.sql.DriverManagerDataSource"
      name="hockeyappDS"
      location="jdbc/hockeyappCoreDS"
      xa-location="jdbc/xa/hockeyappXADS"
      ejb-location="jdbc/hockeyappDS"
      connection-driver="oracle.jdbc.driver.OracleDriver"
      username="sakic"
      password="captain"
      url="jdbc:oracle:thin:@avalanche:1521:hockey"
      inactivity-timeout="30"
/>
```

As mentioned earlier, since the connection code listed here was part of a bean, Oracle will look at the ejb-location parameter attempting to find a match. If the code was implemented outside of a bean, it would attempt to find a match in the location parameter. Now that our data source is configured, it is time to deploy our application.

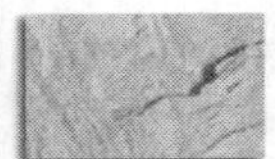

TIP
You can modify the container's data-sources.xml file, or you can include a new one in your EAR or WAR. That will create datasources specific to your application.

Creating a New OC4J Instance

Your Java-based applications must be associated with an OC4J instance when they are deployed to Oracle Application Server 10*g*. The OC4J instance has a set of properties that all applications that are deployed under them "inherit." In a moment, we will look at the properties that are associated with each OC4J instance. The easiest way of creating a new OC4J instance is to create one by way of the Oracle Enterprise Manager Application Server Control web site. Point your browser to

```
http://<mid-tier server>:1810
```

You will need the ias_admin password. If you do not have that password, contact your system administrator. If both the infrastructure and the middle tier are on the same server, you are presented with a "Farm" page. Select the mid-tier instance. You will see a page similar to Figure 15-2.

On this page, you can create a new OC4J instance. One OC4J instance can have multiple applications deployed to it, so we could use one of the existing OC4J containers to deploy our applications, but this is not a good idea. The parameters for the existing OC4J containers have been optimized for the applications that Oracle provides for you as part of the Oracle Application Server installation (things like the Forms server and the Portal environment). It's best to go ahead and create a new OC4J container for your application.

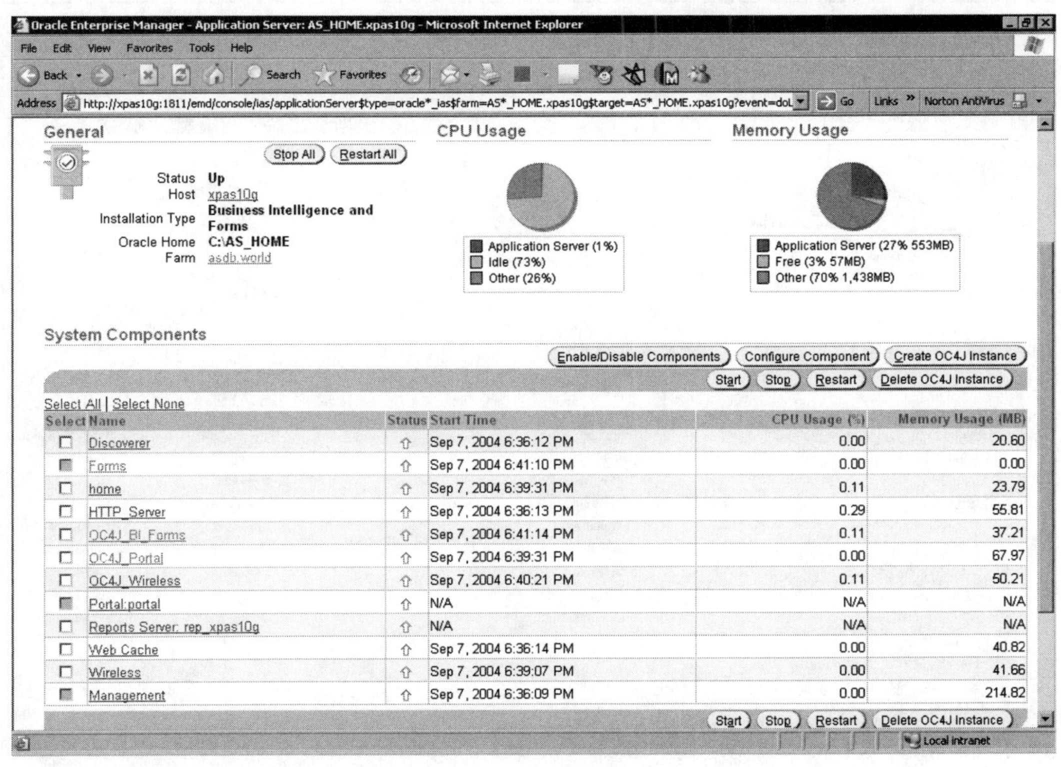

FIGURE 15-2. *The mid-tier components page*

To create a new OC4J instance, click the Create OC4J Instance button on the right of the page. Give the OC4J instance a meaningful name. Traditionally, developers give their instance an "OC4J_" prefix, but that is not required. Click the Create button. The Oracle Application Server will then create the instance and the directory structure on the server to support your new instance. After a few seconds, the Confirmation screen will display. After clicking OK, you will be returned to the main components screen for the middle tier with your new OC4J instance displayed (for this example, it is called "OC4J_HockeyApp" (Figure 15-3).

If you prefer command-line tools, you can create a new OC4J instance by way of the dcmctl command-line utility. You will find this executable (for Windows) or .sh script (for Unix/Linux) in the <ORACLE_MID-Tier_HOME>/dcm/bin directory. To create a new OC4J component named "OC4J_HockeyApp," use the following syntax:

```
C:\AS_HOME\dcm\bin>dcmctl createcomponent -ct OC4J -co OC4J_HockeyApp
```

The -ct switch is used to specify the component type (OC4J) you wish to create, and the -co switch specifies the component's name.

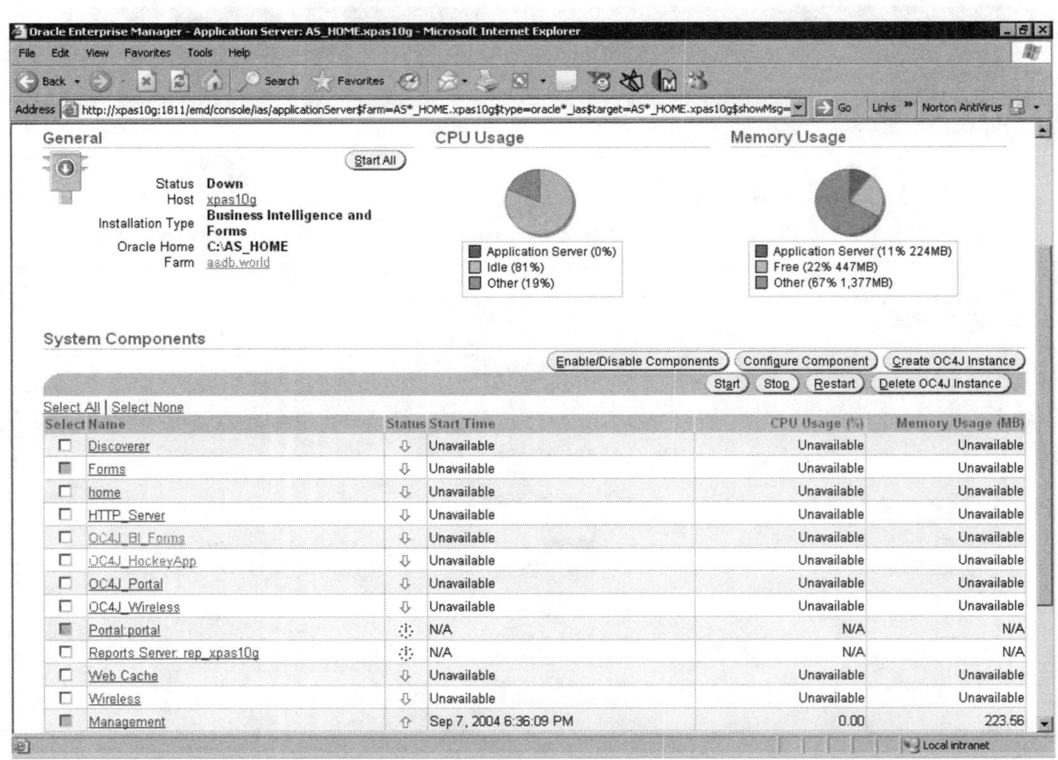

FIGURE 15-3. *The mid-tier components page with the new OC4J instance displayed*

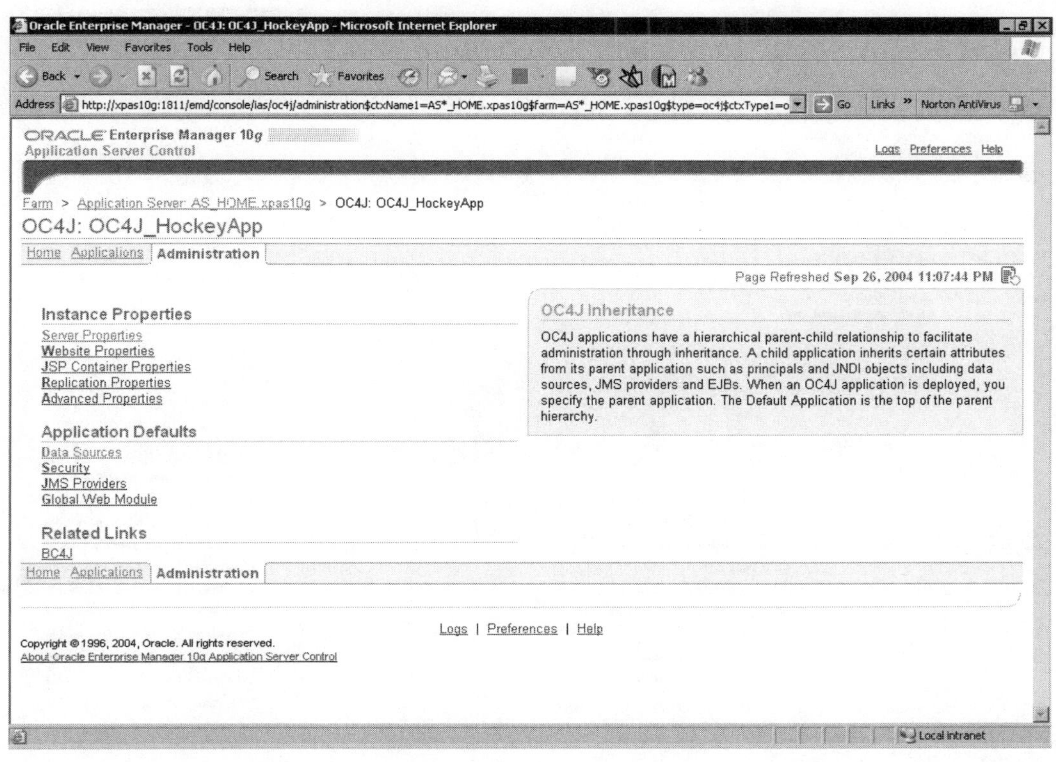

FIGURE 15-4. *The Administration tab of the new OC4J instance*

Returning to the Enterprise Manager Application Server Control web site, click the link for the new OC4J instance, then click the Administration tab along the top of the screen (Figure 15-4). Here, we can set values for all of the attributes for the instance. Of particular interest is the Data Sources link. This link allows us to create a new data source based on an existing data source in the data-sources.xml file. This page allows us to edit the file graphically through the web interface, making the need to grant telnet access to the server (if the server is Unix-based) or leaving the directory open as a shared directory (if the server is Windows-based) unnecessary for developers who need to make modifications to any of these files.

Click on the Applications tab (Figure 15-5) to see a list of the applications that have been deployed to this OC4J instance. Alternatively, you could use the listapplications switch of the dcmctl executable/shell script to see that information:

```
dcmctl listapplications -co OC4J_HockeyApp
```

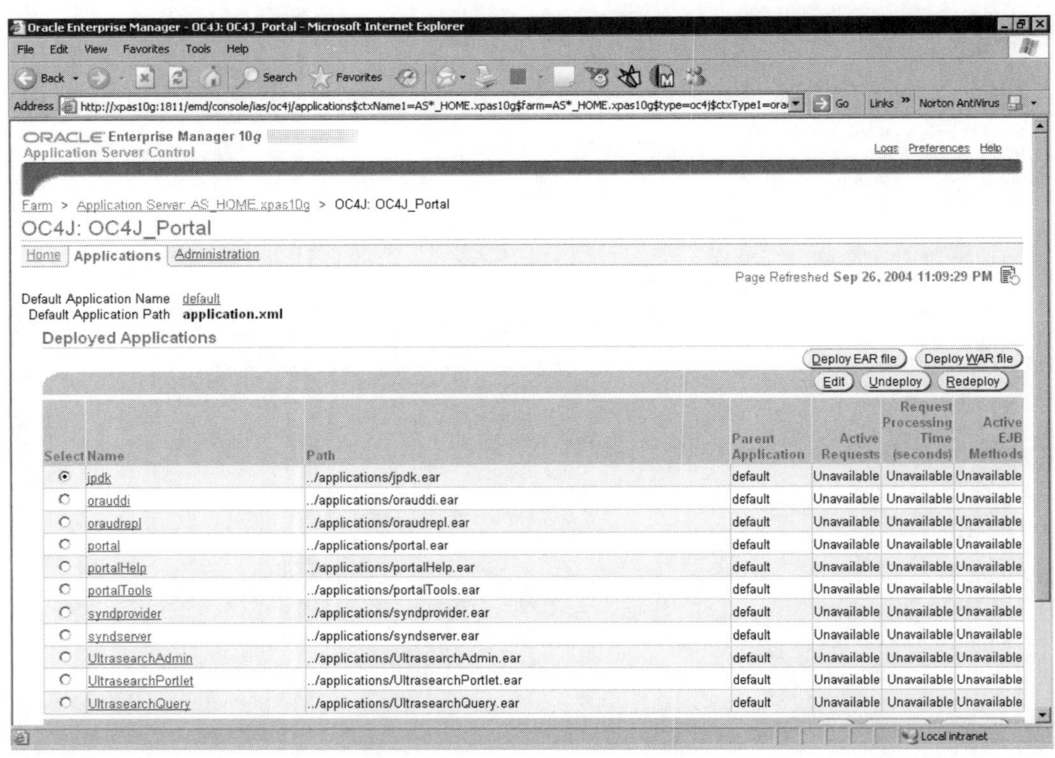

Select	Name	Path	Parent Application	Active Requests	Request Processing Time (seconds)	Active EJB Methods
⦿	jpdk	../applications/jpdk.ear	default	Unavailable	Unavailable	Unavailable
○	orauddi	../applications/orauddi.ear	default	Unavailable	Unavailable	Unavailable
○	oraudrepl	../applications/oraudrepl.ear	default	Unavailable	Unavailable	Unavailable
○	portal	../applications/portal.ear	default	Unavailable	Unavailable	Unavailable
○	portalHelp	../applications/portalHelp.ear	default	Unavailable	Unavailable	Unavailable
○	portalTools	../applications/portalTools.ear	default	Unavailable	Unavailable	Unavailable
○	syndprovider	../applications/syndprovider.ear	default	Unavailable	Unavailable	Unavailable
○	syndserver	../applications/syndserver.ear	default	Unavailable	Unavailable	Unavailable
○	UltrasearchAdmin	../applications/UltrasearchAdmin.ear	default	Unavailable	Unavailable	Unavailable
○	UltrasearchPortlet	../applications/UltrasearchPortlet.ear	default	Unavailable	Unavailable	Unavailable
○	UltrasearchQuery	../applications/UltrasearchQuery.ear	default	Unavailable	Unavailable	Unavailable

FIGURE 15-5. *The deployed applications tab of the OC4J instance named "OC4J_Portal"*

Deployment Method #1: Via the Command Line

Of the three ways we can deploy an application to Oracle Application Server 10*g*, the command line gives us the most flexibility. We can specify numerous parameters that affect how the application is deployed. While previous versions of the Oracle Application Server required you to copy files to the appropriate directories and manually edit the server.xml and http-web-site.xml files, the deployapplication switch of the dcmctl command in Oracle Application Server 10*g* will move the files that make up your application to appropriate directories automatically. From the command line, issue the following command:

```
dcmctl deployapplication -file hockeyapp.ear -a hockeyapp -co OC4J_HockeyApp
```

In this example, the -file switch lists the file we wish to deploy, the -a switch sets the name of the application, and the -co switch lists the OC4J container we are deploying to.

CAUTION
It is important to note that the application name specified after the -a switch must exactly match the name of the WAR file. The root will be the virtual path where OC4J can reach your application.

The dcmctl command is extremely powerful. There are too many options to explore in this chapter, but all options are listed in Table 15-2.

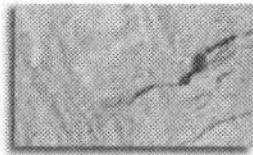

CAUTION
It is important to note that while the dcmctl command is extremely powerful, it also has the ability to misconfigure your application server if not used properly, making it unusable. The safest bet for interaction with Oracle Application Server 10g is by way of the Enterprise Manager Application Server Control web pages. The dcmctl command is a great, stable tool for deploying applications and modifying OC4J containers, but it should be used by experienced developers only. Accordingly, it is the authors' recommendation to use method 2 (Via the Oracle Enterprise Manager Application Server Control Web Site) or 3 (Via Oracle JDeveloper 10g) unless there is an explicit reason to do otherwise. Methods 2 and 3 are discussed later in this chapter.

addopmnlink	applyarchiveto	applyclusterto	applyinstanceto
configrepositoryssl	createarchive	createcluster	createcomponent
deployapplication	destroyinstance	echo	exit
exportarchive	exportrepository	getcomponenttype	geterror
getopmnport	getrepositoryid	getreturnstatus	getstate
help	importarchive	importrepository	isclusterable
iscompatible	joincluster	joinfarm	leavecluster
leavefarm	listapplications	listarchives	listclusters
listcomponents	listcomponenttypes	listinstances	quit
redeployapplication	removearchive	removecluster	removecomponent
removeopmnlink	repositoryrelocated	resetdcmcacheport	resetfiletransaction
resethostinformation	restart	restoreinstance	resyncinstance
saveinstance	set	setloglevel	shell
shutdown	start	stop	undeployapplication
updateconfig	validateearfile	whichcluster	whichfarm
whichinstance			

TABLE 15-2. *Options for the dcmctl Command*

Further information about any of the options can be printed out with this syntax:

```
dcmctl -help <command>
```

The following is an example of the dcmctl help system:

```
C:\AS_HOME\dcm\bin>dcmctl -help applyinstanceto
   applyInstanceTo
   Applies the configuration of the named instance to another instance or
   cluster.
   Type
   Configuration Management
   Syntax
   applyInstanceTo -src instanceName [-cl clusterName | -i instanceName]
   Description
   The configuration of the named instance is applied to the named
   instance or cluster. If no instance or cluster is specified, then the
   configuration of the named instance is applied to the current
   instance. The named source instance is not affected. The command will
   fail if the current instance and the named instance are the same (you
   cannot apply the configuration of an instance to itself).
   Example
   dcmctl applyinstanceto -src instance1
```

Deployment Method #2: Via the Oracle Enterprise Manager Application Server Control Web Site

This method allows developers and administrators to deploy their Java-based applications to an OC4J container within Oracle Application Server 10*g* graphically by way of a web browser. This approach has two main advantages:

- Developers who have been working with graphical tools will probably be more comfortable using graphical web pages to deploy their applications.
- By performing all of the deployment functions via a web interface, administrators do not have to develop security access methods for the various servers developers will be deploying their applications to. For Unix, this would involve granting telnet access and devising security policies for directories on the server. For Windows, this would entail sharing directories on the server(s) and devising security policies for each shared directory.

Deploying an application via the Oracle Enterprise Manager Web Server Control web site is a simple process after you have successfully built your EAR or WAR file and configured your data source. Go to the web site by pointing your browser to the following location:

```
http://<mid-tier server>:1810
```

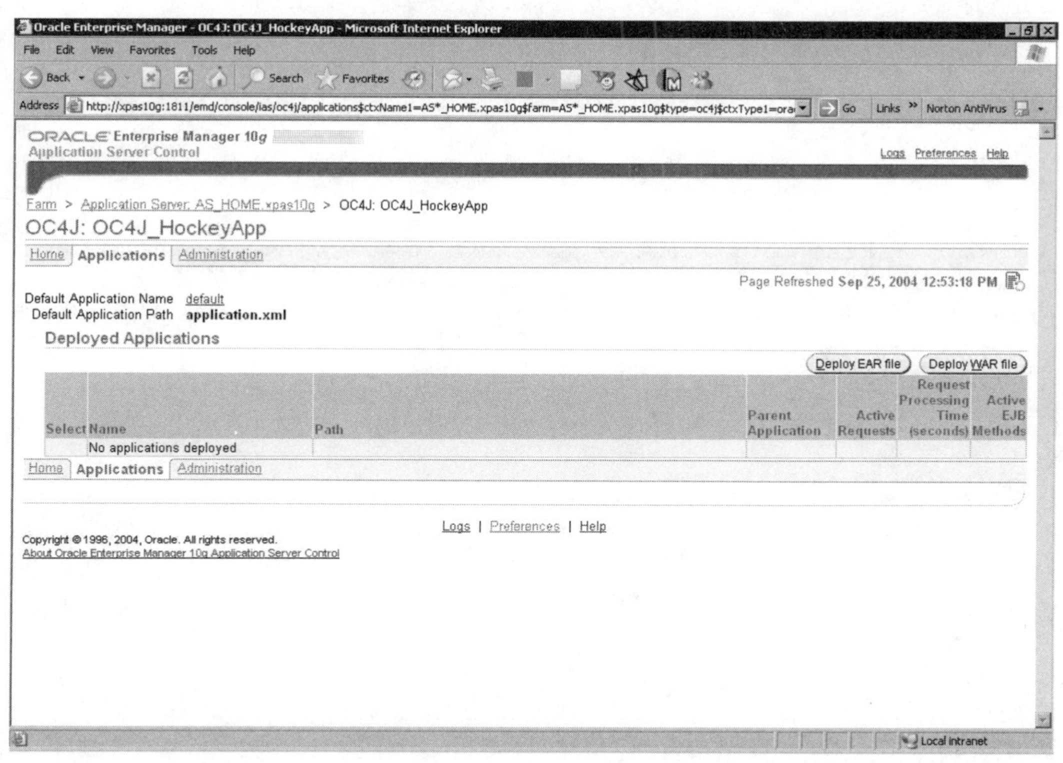

FIGURE 15-6. *The Applications tab of the OC4J component*

You will need to know the ias_admin password. If you do not have that information, check with your system administrator. Click the link of the OC4J container you wish to deploy your application to. Click the Applications tab on the top of the screen (Figure 15-6).

As you can see, no applications have been deployed to this OC4J container yet. There are two buttons on the right of the screen: Deploy EAR file and Deploy WAR file. As mentioned in Chapter 2, if you deploy a WAR file, it will be "wrapped" into an EAR file by creating empty EJB directories.

Clicking either the Deploy EAR file or Deploy WAR file button will begin a wizard that will prompt you with questions about the application you are about to deploy. On the first page (Figure 15-7), you are prompted for the name of the EAR file, the application name, and if this application is a subapplication of another, existing application. Remember that the application name must match the name of the web module in the EAR file.

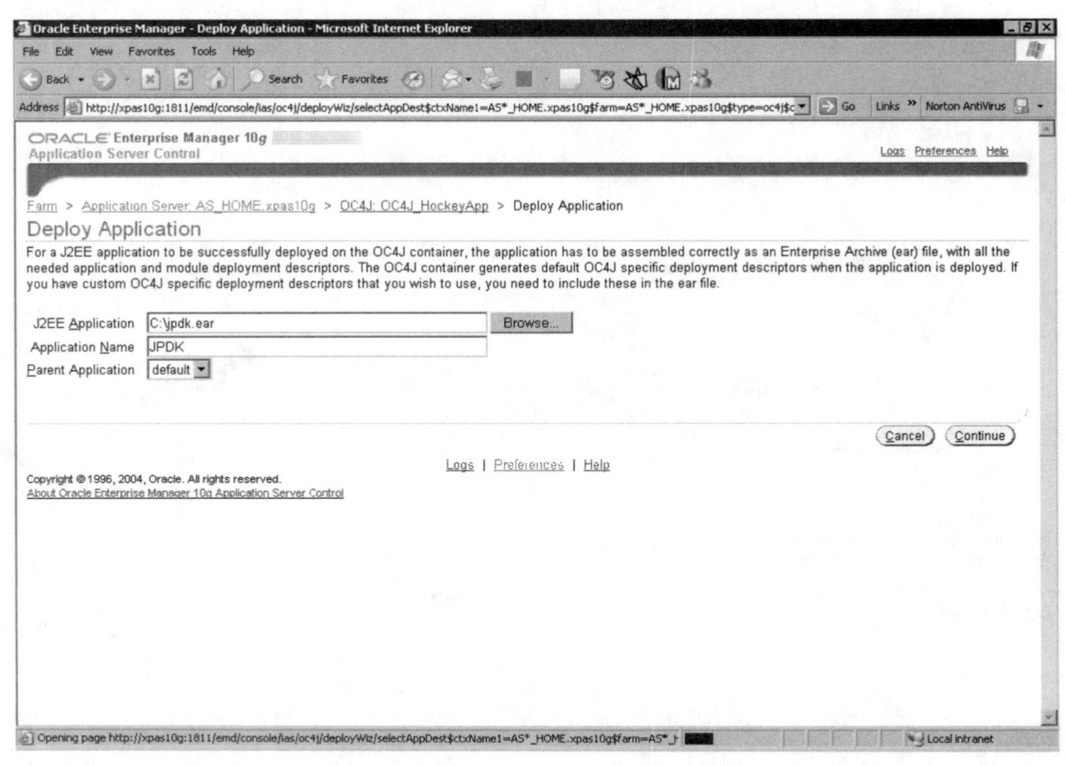

FIGURE 15-7. *The first page of the Deploy Application Wizard*

Next, we are taken to a screen where we can specify the URL mapping for our application. Under most circumstances, the default value generated (the name of the application) will be sufficient for your purposes (Figure 15-8).

What Is a User Manager and How Do You Specify the Information on This Page?

The next page of the wizard asks you to specify a User Manager (Figure 15-9). The Java Authentication and Authorization Service (JAAS) is a set of APIs that enable services to authenticate and enforce access controls upon users. It augments Java 2 security with support for user-based authentication and access control. It implements a Java technology version of the standard Pluggable Authentication Module (PAM) framework, and it supports user-based authorization, allowing applications to remain independent of the underlying authentication service. OC4J has two different security providers that offer user management services: one based on Oracle's JAAS implementation known as the JAAS Provider or JAZN, the other based on an XML file called principles.xml. The JAAS Provider implements the JAZNUserManager

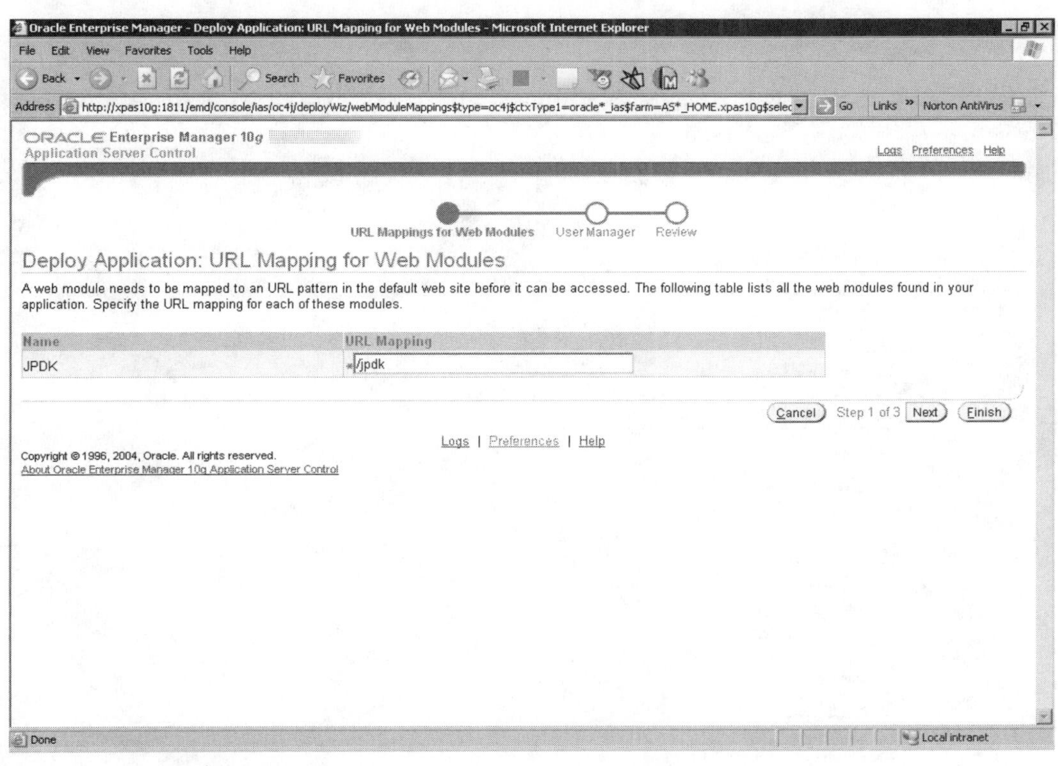

FIGURE 15-8. *The URL Mapping page of the Deploy Application Wizard*

class and can be configured with either an XML repository (JAZN-XML) or an Oracle Internet Directory (JAZN-LDAP). The user manager based on the principles.xml file implements the XMLUserManager class. Another option is to create a custom user manager by implementing the UserManager class.

When using the JAAS Provider, two configuration files are used: jazn.xml and jazn-data.xml. The jazn.xml file is the JAAS property file where the provider type is specified (XML or LDAP/OID). The jazn-data.xml file is used only when the XML provider type is specified; it contains JAAS data on users, roles, policy, and LoginModules. Unless you wish to implement a security method outside of what Oracle Application Server 10*g* provides for you by default, there is no need to change any of the values on this page.

The final step of the wizard asks you to review your selections. Clicking Deploy will restart the OC4J container, to pick up the new settings, and deploy the application. You can test your application by making sure your OC4J container is running (if not, click the check box to the left of it and click the Start button), opening up another browser window, and pointing your browser to the virtual path you specified in the URL mapping page when deploying the application.

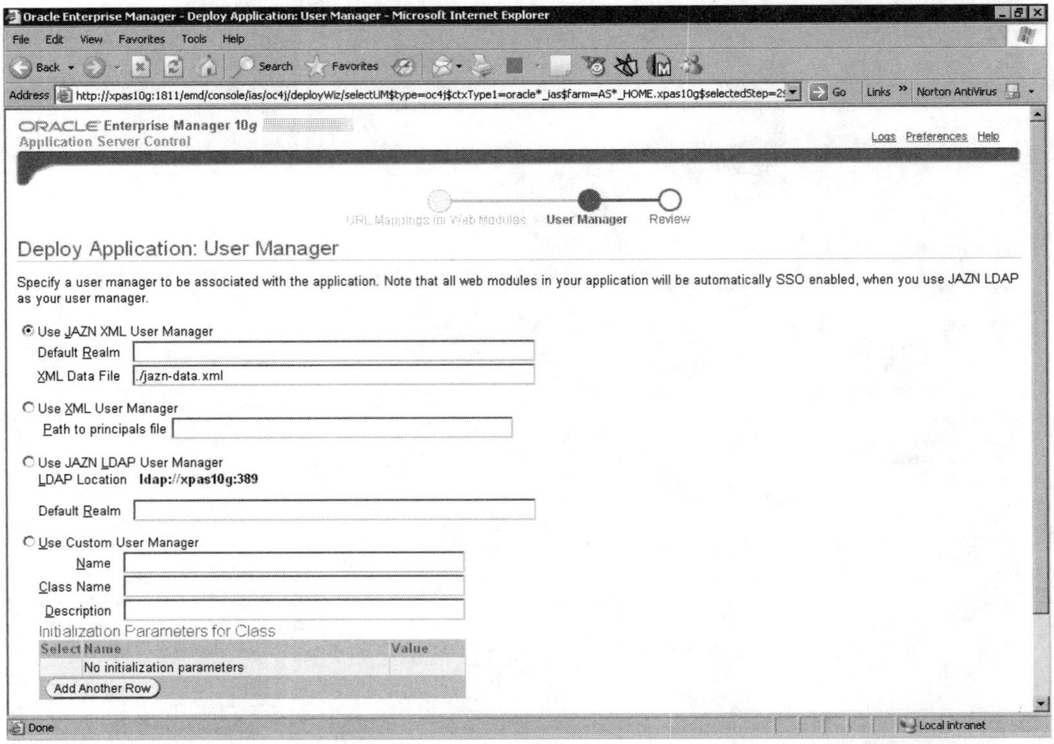

FIGURE 15-9. *The User Manager screen of the Deploy Application wizard*

Deployment Method #3: Via Oracle JDeveloper 10*g*

If you are using Oracle JDeveloper 10*g* to develop your Java-based applications, you can deploy them directly to Oracle Application Server 10*g* without ever leaving the JDeveloper 10*g* environment. As you will see, deploying an application is as simple as establishing a connection to the application server and specifying what OC4J container you want the application to be deployed to. Oracle has included a new framework in Oracle Application Server 10*g* called the Application Development Framework (ADF) that simplifies J2EE development by minimizing the need to write code that implements design patterns and an application's infrastructure. Oracle ADF provides these implementations as part of the framework. Recognizing that having a set of run-time services is not enough, Oracle ADF is also focused on the development experience, providing a visual and declarative approach to J2EE development. Oracle ADF is an extension of frameworks that were included with previous versions of JDeveloper. When it comes time to deploy applications developed with the ADF, there are some extra steps you will need to take. These are discussed at the end of this chapter.

Establishing a Connection in JDeveloper 10g

Before we can deploy applications to an OC4J instance from within Oracle JDeveloper 10*g*, there must be an EAR file, provided in the Oracle JDeveloper 10*g* installation, deployed to that OC4J container already. On the Oracle Enterprise Manager Application Server Control web site, go to the mid-tier components page. Select the OC4J container you will be deploying to. Click the Applications tab and then the Deploy EAR file button on the top right of the page. Click the Browse button and navigate to the directory where you have installed Oracle JDeveloper 10*g*. Now cd to the dcm\lib directory and select the oc4jdcmservlet.ear file. Continue through the other steps of the wizard to deploy this application.

Assuming you have deployed the oc4jdcmservlet.ear file successfully, have compiled and tested your application, and are ready to deploy it, select the Connections tab on the Oracle JDeveloper 10*g* Navigator. Right-click Application Server and select New Application Server Connection. The second page of the wizard asks you to name the connection and specify a target (Figure 15-10). Give the connection a meaningful name and select Oracle Application Server 10*g* in the connection type.

Step 2 asks you to specify the ias_admin password for the middle-tier instance. The third step of the wizard (Figure 15-11) asks you to specify the following information:

- **Enterprise Manager OC4J Host Name** This is the host where the Enterprise Manager Application Server Control web site is running.

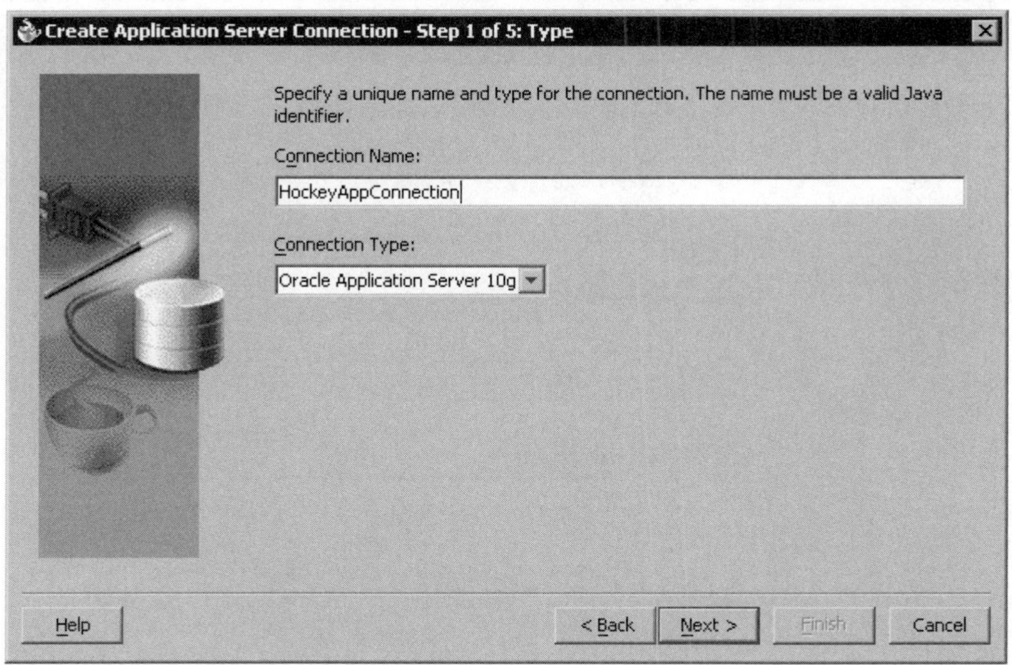

FIGURE 15-10. *Specifying the Application Server connection type*

- **Enterprise Manager OC4J HTTP Port** This is the port the Enterprise Manager is listening on; it is usually 1810 unless you have both the infrastructure and the middle tier on the same machine; in that case, it is usually 1811.
- **Remote Server's Oracle Home Directory** This is the home directory for the application server instance. If you have both the infrastructure and the middle tier on the same machine, make sure to specify the mid-tier Oracle home.
- **OC4J Instance Name (optional)** This is the OC4J instance where the application is to be deployed.

The fourth page of the wizard asks you to specify the EJB Client information for the connection. Enter the URL of the Remote Method Invocation server from which methods published to the EJBs will be accessible. Enter a username that has RMI login privileges on the OC4J instance within the Oracle Application Server. Enter the password for the RMI username. The final page of the wizard allows you to test your connection. If any errors appear, click the "Back" button and fix the incorrect information.

Constructing the EJB JAR File

After the connection has been successfully established, we can begin the process of deploying our application. Click the Applications tab in the Oracle JDeveloper 10*g* Navigator. Expand your

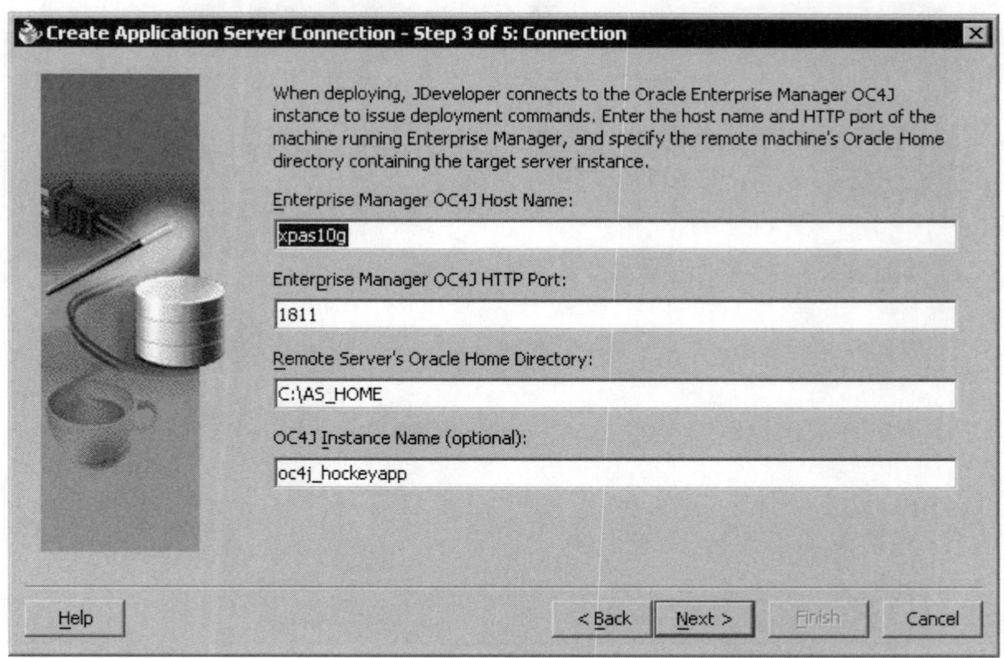

FIGURE 15-11. *The third step of the Application Server Connection Wizard*

application by clicking the plus sign to the left of the application name. Right-click the Model tree entry and select New. Select Deployment Profiles in the left-hand window and select EJB JAR file on the right-hand window. Click OK. Give the Deployment Profile Name a meaningful value and click OK. Under the General options on the next screen (Figure 15-12), give the Enterprise Application Name a meaningful value and click OK.

In the Oracle JDeveloper 10*g* Navigator, you will now see a new entry under <application name>/Model/Resources given the name you specified when prompted for the deployment profile name with a ".deploy" appended to it. Right-click that file and select Deploy To JAR File from the drop-down menu (Figure 15-13).

A file will be created with whatever name you specified when prompted for the deployment profile name plus a .jar extension. It is not important to know or remember where this file is—when it comes time to create your EAR file, the wizard will allow you to specify the resource files (the .JARs and .WARs) graphically.

Constructing the WAR File

Now, let's create the WAR file for our application. In the Navigator, right-click the View tree entry under your application. Select New and on the following page, make sure Deployment Profile is

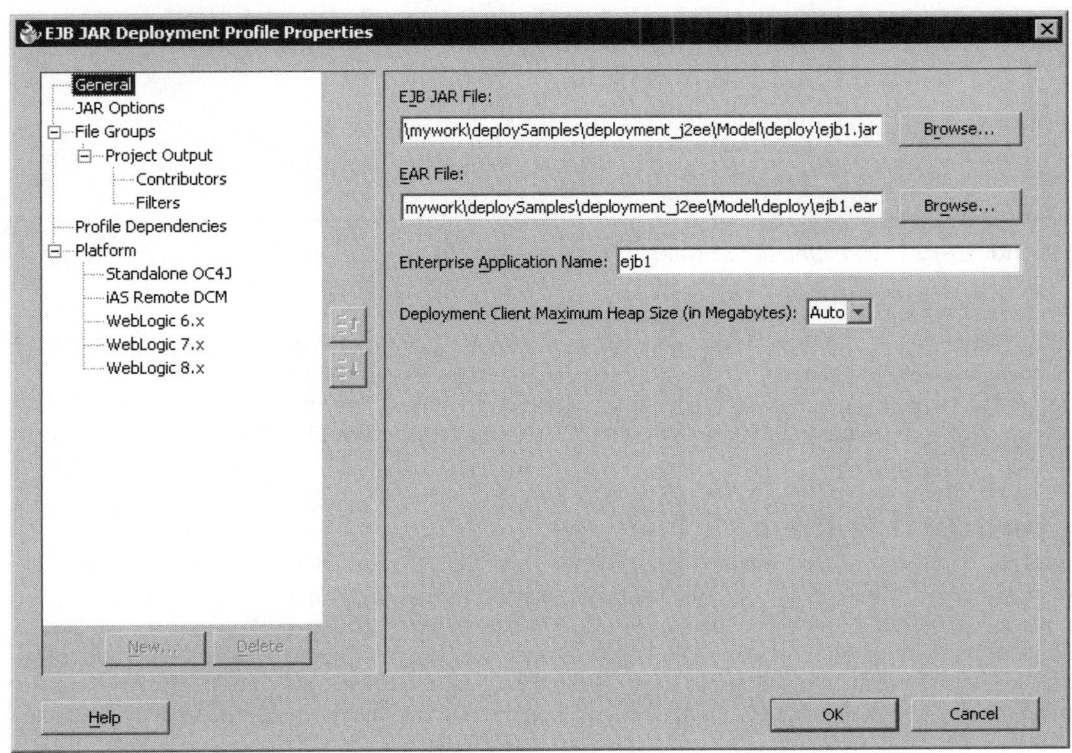

FIGURE 15-12. *The EJB JAR Deployment Profile Properties screen*

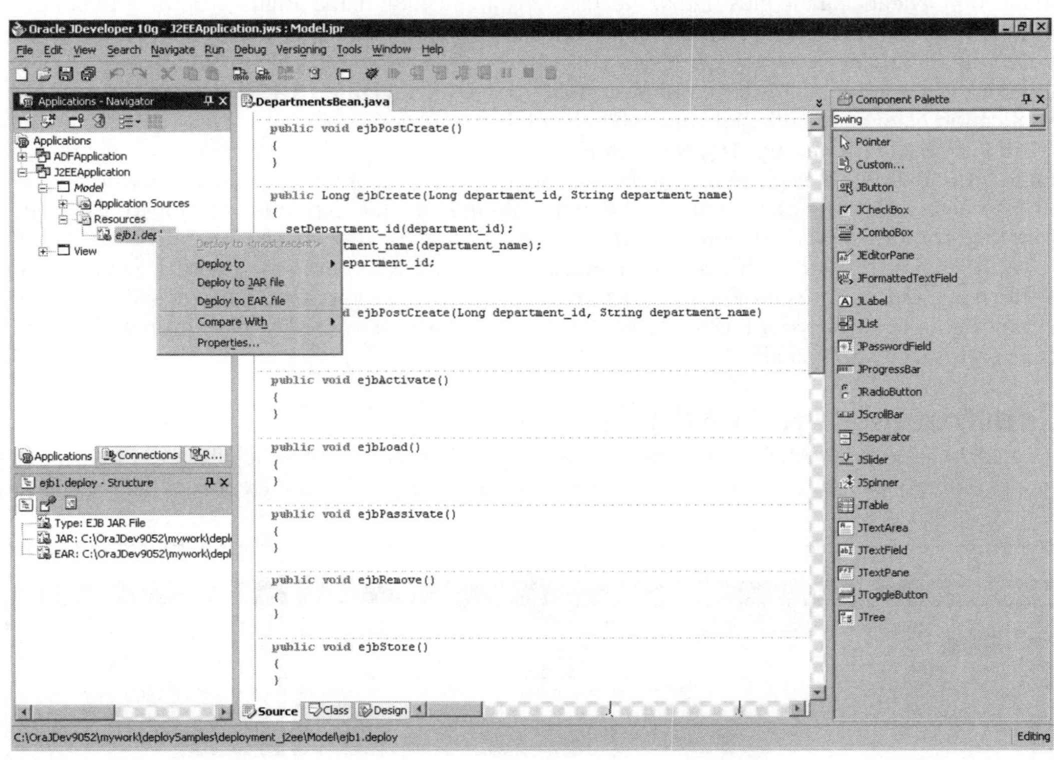

FIGURE 15-13. *Creating the JAR file*

selected on the left and WAR File is selected on the right. Click OK. Give the Deployment Profile Name a meaningful value and click OK. Give the Enterprise Application Name a meaningful value and click the Specify J2EE Web Context Root: radio button. Specify a name here and remember it—it is what will be used in your URL when it comes time to access the application. Click OK (Figure 15-14).

Constructing the EAR File

Now that we have created both the EJB jar and the WAR files, we can continue by creating and deploying the EAR file. With your application selected and expanded in the Navigator window, right-click View and select New from the drop-down box. Make sure Deployment Profiles is selected on the left-hand side of the screen and EAR File is selected on the right. Click OK. Give the Development Profile Name a meaningful value and click OK. In the General category, give the Application Name a meaningful name. Remember this name, as it will be the one that shows up on the Applications page of the OC4J container on the Oracle Enterprise Manage Application Server Control web page. Click

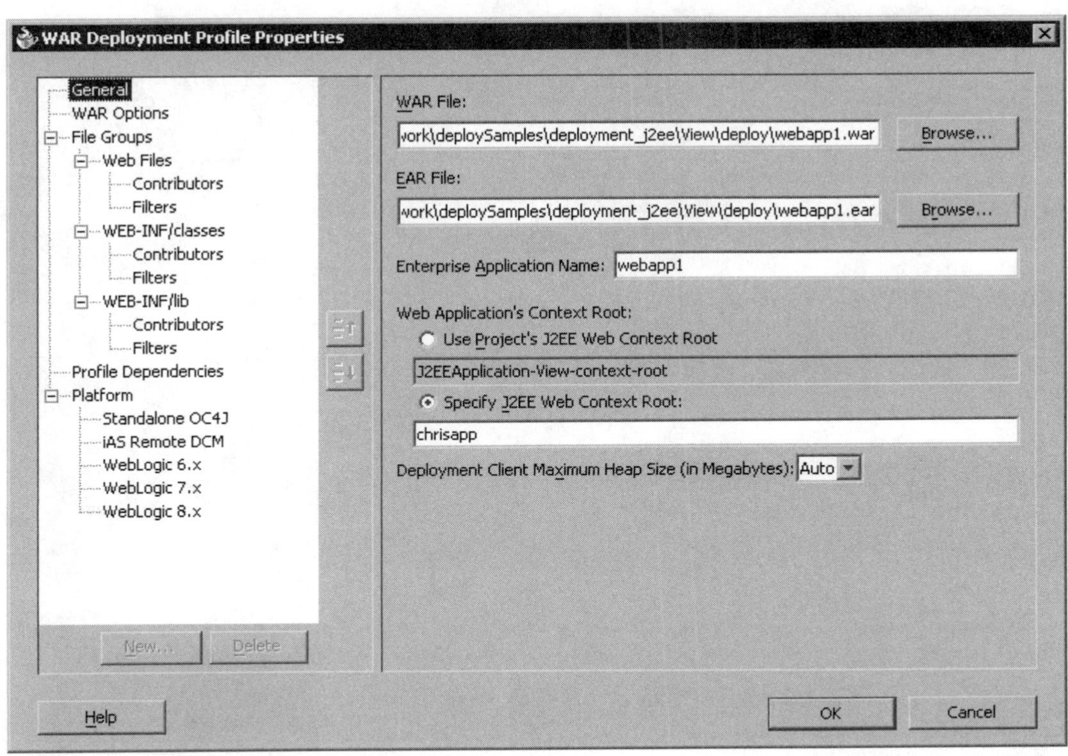

FIGURE 15-14. *The WAR Deployment Profile Properties screen*

Application Assembly on the left-hand side of the screen (Figure 15-15). Click the check boxes next to the .deploy files that you want to include. Click OK.

Final Step: Deploying the Application

The final step is to actually deploy our application. Right-click the <application name>.deploy file under Resources in the Navigator. Select the connection that you created earlier from the drop-down menu (Figure 15-16).

After a few minutes, you can test your deployment by opening up a new browser and going to the Oracle Enterprise Manager Application Server Control web page, clicking the middle tier, clicking the OC4J container, and clicking the Applications tab. You should see a new application deployed there with the name you specified as the application name when constructing the EAR file. You can then run your application by specifying the following URL in a new web browser:

```
http://<server>:<port>/<application>
```

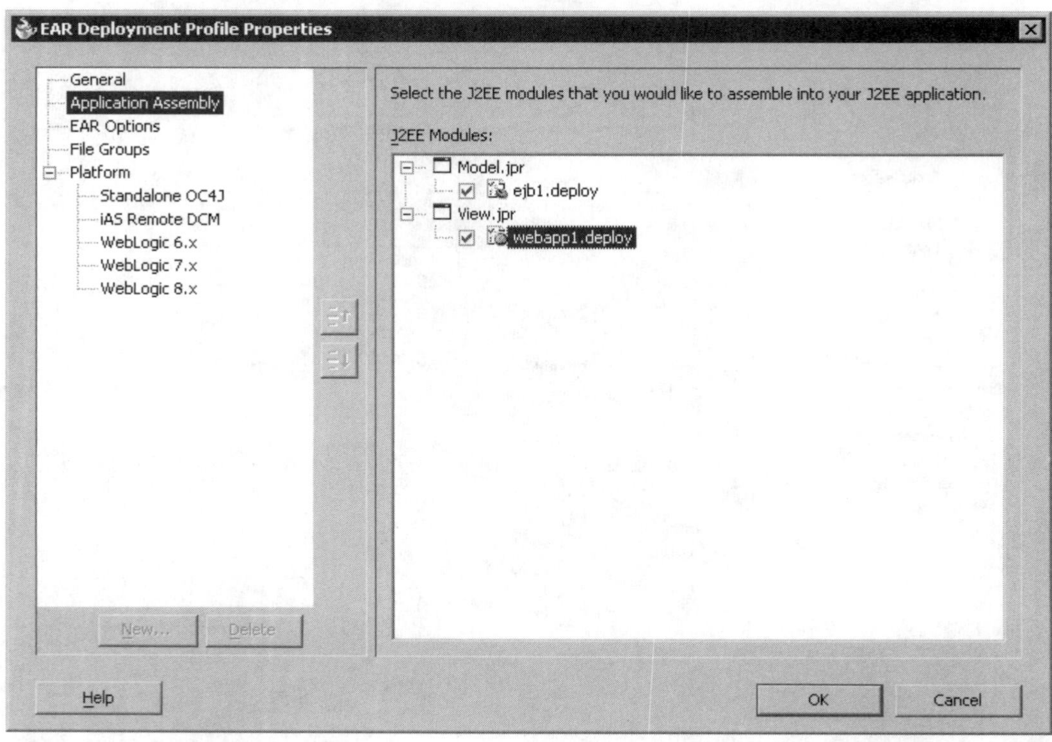

FIGURE 15-15. *Selecting the deployment location*

where <application> is the name of the J2EE Web Context Root you specified when setting the WAR deployment profile properties for your application.

Deploying Applications That Use ADF

Before we can deploy Oracle JDeveloper 10*g* applications that have been created using the ADF, we need to install the necessary run-time files by running the ADF Runtime Installer from within Oracle JDeveloper 10*g*. Luckily, this is a relatively simple process. One of the steps of the wizard will ask you to specify what directory on the server you wish to install the Application Runtime Files to. If you are running Oracle JDeveloper 10*g* on a Windows machine and your Oracle Application Server 10*g* mid-tier instance is on a Windows machine, you will need to map a network drive from your client to the server and specify that drive when you are prompted for the server directory. If you are running Oracle JDeveloper 10*g* on a Windows machine and your Oracle Application Server mid-tier instance is on a Unix or Linux machine, then things can get a little tricky. If this is your scenario, you basically have two options:

- Install Oracle JDeveloper 10*g* on your Unix/Linux box and perform the following steps that way.

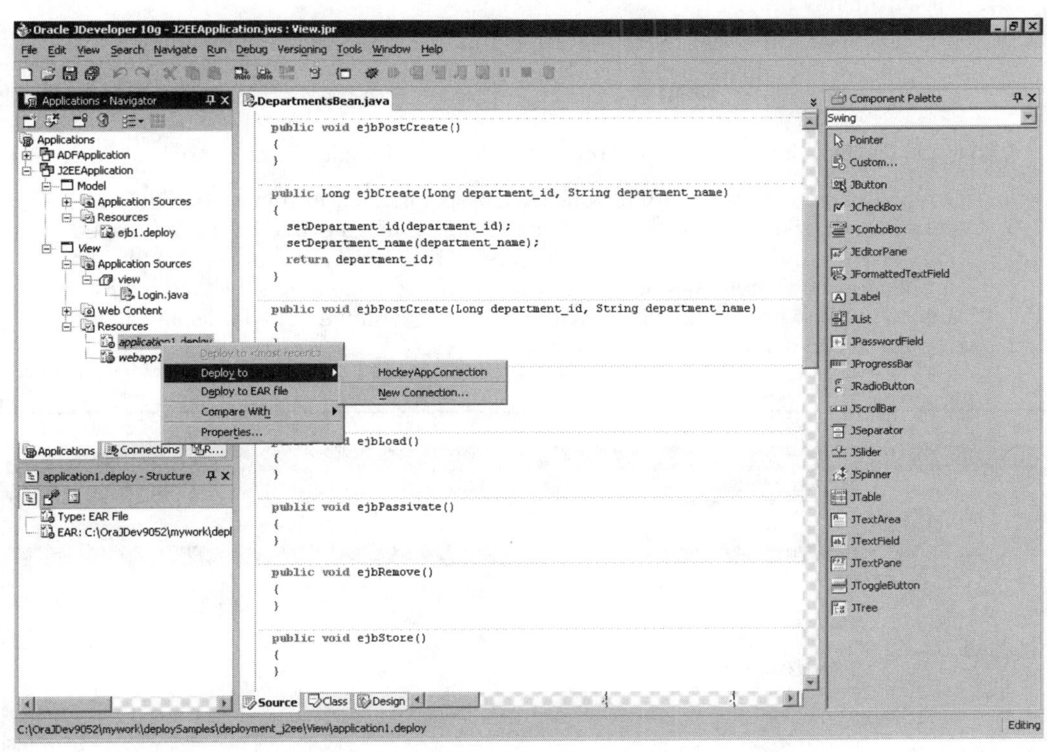

FIGURE 15-16. *The Application Assembly screen*

- Use a product like Hummingbird or Cygwin to map a drive from your Windows client to your Unix/Linux server.

Steps to Install the ADF Runtime Installer

The following steps need to be performed to install the ADF Runtime Installer.

1. Stop all of the mid-tier components by going to the Oracle Enterprise Manager Application Server Control web page at http://<servername>:1810 (1811 if both the middle tier and the infrastructure are on the same server).
2. Click the Stop All button on the top of the screen.
3. For Windows only:

   Stop the ASControl and ProcessManager services for the middle tier. In the Windows Services applet, these will be called Oracle<Oracle_Home>ASControl and Oracle<Oracle_Home>ProcessManager (where Oracle_Home is the name of the Oracle home for the mid-tier instance you specified when installing the software).

4. For Unix/Linux only:

   Stop all OPMN processes by cd'ing to the $ORACLE_HOME/opmn/bin directory for your middle tier and issue the following command:

   ```
   opmnctl stopall
   ```

5. In Oracle JDeveloper 10*g*, select Tools | ADF Runtime Installer | Oracle Application Server.

6. On the first step of the wizard (Figure 15-17), specify the location of the ORACLE_HOME for your mid-tier instance. In the example on Figure 15-17, I have mapped a drive on my laptop (Z:) to the server and AS_HOME is the directory where the Oracle Application 10*g* Server middle tier is installed (if you attempt to select a directory that is *not* a mid-tier home, the wizard will not let you continue but will display an error message when you click the Next button).

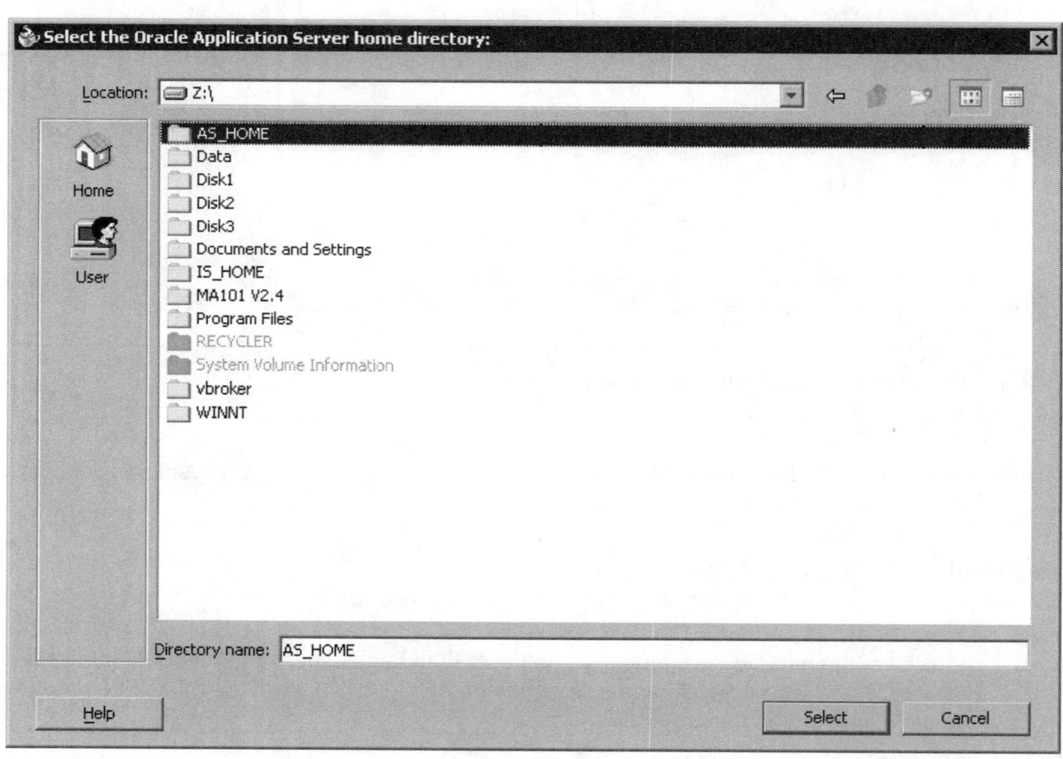

FIGURE 15-17. *Specifying the home directory of the application server middle tier*

6. If this is the first time you are installing the ADF run time, the only option available to you is "Install a new version of the ADF run time." If you have installed numerous versions of the ADF run time and need to return to an older version for whatever reason, the second radio button, "Restore an archived version of the ADF run time," will be available to you. Click Next>, and then Finish.

7. The run-time installer will archive any existing run-time files, display its progress both in a dialog box at the center of the screen and in the log section of the Oracle JDeveloper 10*g* desktop at the bottom of the screen (Figure 15-18). It will display the message "ADF Runtime Installer finished successfully" in the log window upon completion.

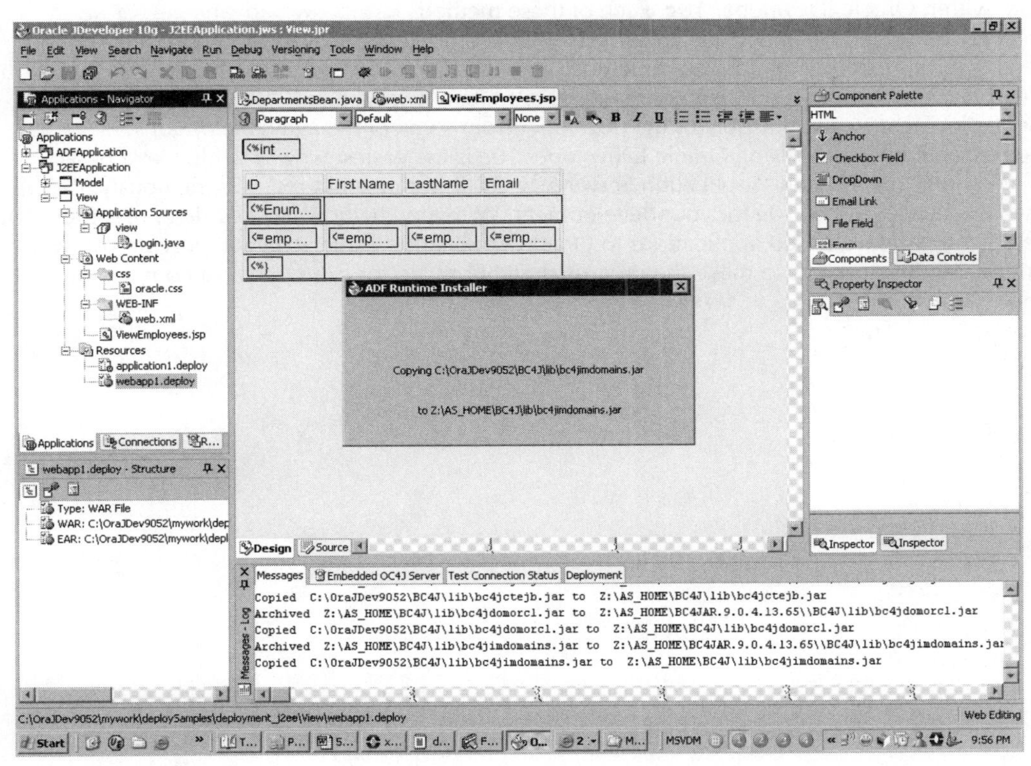

FIGURE 15-18. *The ADF Runtime installer status window*

Summary

The deployment of applications can be a challenge for developers and administrators, particularly when those applications incorporate things like JSPs or EJBs. The J2EE specification outlines how complex Java-based applications are expected to be organized ("packaged" in J2EE terms). This specification greatly simplifies the deployment of applications by forcing developers and administrators to adhere to a specific directory structure. Oracle Application Server 10*g*, being a fully compliant J2EE application server, is capable of taking these formatted directories and deploying the applications contained within them easily.

In this chapter, we explored the three basic ways of deploying J2EE applications to Oracle Application Server 10*g*: by way of the command line, by using the Oracle Enterprise Manager Application Server Control web site, and by deploying directly from within Oracle JDeveloper 10*g*. Each of these methods has its own advantages and drawbacks: the command line gives developers the most control over how applications are deployed, but it can be difficult to remember all of the necessary syntax. Deploying by way of the Enterprise Manager web site reduces the need to remember much of the deployment syntax but isolates the developer from some of the available options. Deployment by way of using Oracle JDeveloper 10*g* is the easiest way to deploy Java-based applications to an Oracle Application Server 10*g* OC4J instance but requires, obviously, that you use Oracle JDeveloper 10*g* for your development. With any method you decide to use, the deployment of Java-based applications to Oracle Application Server 10*g* will provide you with simple, intuitive options to make the process straightforward for even the most complex of applications.

CHAPTER 16

Extensible Markup Language (XML)

ML stands for Extensible Markup Language and like HTML, it is a subset of the Standard Generalized Markup Language (SGML). All three standards (XML, HTML, and SGML), are managed by the World Wide Web Consortium (W3C), and a page with details on XML can be found at (http://www.w3.org/XML/).

The XML standard was created to help tackle the challenges of electronic publishing because the limits of HTML were rapidly being reached. That original goal has gradually expanded so that XML now encompasses everything from electronic data interchange (EDI) applications to streaming news, stock quote feeds (such as Really Simple Syndication, or RSS), and Web Services.

How Does XML Differ from HTML?

While HTML and XML are derivations of the same SGML standard, they are used for entirely different purposes:

- HTML has a limited element set that is predefined by the HTML standard itself. In contrast, XML has an unlimited, user-definable element set.
- HTML is focused on the page presentation of data while XML focuses on the specification of data. In other words, the markup elements in HTML are concerned with describing how data to be displayed on a page will look. XML is concerned with describing what the data contained in an XML document is.
- HTML documents are inherently "flat" (non-hierarchical) and are largely unstructured. They are meant to be interpreted and rendered by a web browser in a top-to-bottom fashion. XML documents, however, have a tree structure to them. Different elements have a hierarchical relationship to each other. You can search an XML document along these hierarchical "paths," something you cannot do with an HTML document.
- An XML document can be easily transformed into other common document formats, including simple text, PDF, and HTML, to name only a few. While it is possible to convert HTML into other formats using third-party tools, the XML standard explicitly specifies a standardized methodology for converting XML documents.

While HTML is very good at displaying information, it is very difficult to do anything more with HTML than render it in a browser window. Information in standard HTML is not categorized or specified in any meaningful way. If you want to be able to manipulate and process data, then XML is the right tool.

```
<?xml version="1.0" encoding="UTF-8"?>
<ADDRESSBOOK>
     <ENTRY ID="1">
          <FIRSTNAME>John</FIRSTNAME>
          <LASTNAME>Doe</LASTNAME>
          <ADDRLINE1>100 Maple Lane</ADDRLINE1>
          <CITY>Dallas</CITY>
          <STATE>TX</STATE>
```

```
        <ZIP>75201</ZIP>
        <HOMEPHONE>555-555-1111</HOMEPHONE>
        <EMAIL>jdoe@someisp.com</EMAIL>
    </ENTRY>
    <ENTRY ID="2">
        <FIRSTNAME>Jane</FIRSTNAME>
        <LASTNAME>Doe</LASTNAME>
        <ADDRLINE1>1 Cherry Lane</ADDRLINE1>
        <ADDRLINE2>Apt 201</ADDRLINE2>
        <CITY>Buffalo</CITY>
        <STATE>NY</STATE>
        <ZIP>14201</ZIP>
        <HOMEPHONE>555-555-2222</HOMEPHONE>
        <EMAIL>doej@someisp.com</EMAIL>
    </ENTRY>
</ADDRESSBOOK>
```

This listing could be, for instance, an address book exported from an e-mail program into an XML file. We'll get into the mechanics of the file later in the chapter in the "XML Document Validation–Document Type Definition (DTD)" section, but for the moment we can make some initial observations about this XML document:

- XML uses the familiar <elementname> </elementname> markup syntax that HTML uses. Each piece of data is denoted by starting and ending elements. Note that unlike in HTML, element names are case-sensitive, so a <FIRSTNAME> element is not equivalent to a <firstname> element.
- The XML document has an XML declaration at the beginning of the file that designates that it is an XML document, what version of the XML specification it adheres to, and what character encoding is used to specify the data. You may encounter XML files in the real world that do not include this declaration (i.e., XML files used to hold configuration data for applications), but to follow the specification correctly, the declaration should be included.
- The XML document has only one "root" or outermost element; in this case, it is <ADDRESSBOOK>. The root element is allowed to contain data itself, but it often only contains other child elements.
- The elements are nested in a hierarchical fashion and no overlapping is allowed. In other words, the root element <ADDRESSBOOK> has <ENTRY> elements as its children. Each <ENTRY> element can have <FIRSTNAME>, <LASTNAME>, etc., elements as its children. Each element must remain in its proper scope. In other words, because a <FIRSTNAME> element starts under an <ENTRY> element, its closing tag (</FIRSTNAME>) must occur before the parent's closing tag (</ENTRY>) and before the opening tag of any other element at the same hierarchical level (<LASTNAME>, for instance).

  The actual data is presented between the opening and closing tags of an element (for this example, the last name is "Doe"):

```
<LASTNAME>Doe</LASTNAME>
```

NOTE
Unlike some HTML elements, XML elements are always required to be closed off.

- Elements may carry attributes. In the case of our example, there are multiple <ENTRY> elements. They can be distinguished from one another by the ID attribute included in the opening tag.

If we were to store this data in an Oracle table with a structure that matches the data, such as:

```
CREATE TABLE address_book
(id          number(5)
   CONSTRAINT address_book_pk PRIMARY KEY,
first_name     varchar2(50),
last_name     varchar2(50),
addr_line1     varchar2(60),
addr_line2     varchar2(60),
city          varchar2(60),
state_code     varchar2(2),
zip_code      number(9),
phone          number(12),
email_addr     varchar2(50));
```

we would need to insert a row into the address_book table for each <ENTRY> element in the XML document. We can use the ID attribute on each <ENTRY> element to populate the primary key.

The XML code in Listing 1 illustrates the fundamental and most significant difference between HTML and XML: XML clearly describes the data contained within the document, rather than how it should be displayed.

Fundamentals of XML

This chapter is not intended as a comprehensive guide to XML (for references on learning XML, see Appendix A). Addressing XML completely is beyond the scope of a single chapter in any book, and there are many fine texts available that cover the subject much more completely. Rather, in this section, we'll take a brief look at the fundamental aspects that make XML so useful to the task of communicating data to give you a basis for the subsequent sections on Oracle's implementation. We'll examine the basic structure of XML documents, parsing and validation, and converting XML data into other formats.

XML Document Declaration

Let's examine the first line of the XML document in Listing 1 again. Here is the first line:

```
<?xml version="1.0" encoding="UTF-8"?>
```

This is known as the XML declaration and it identifies the contents of the file as XML data that adheres to the XML standard. It is not uncommon to see XML data in a file without this declaration, but without it, there can be no expectation of adherence to the conventions. If it does appear in the document, it must appear before any data elements in the XML document.

The declaration specifies a couple pieces of information to both human readers and software parsers of the document.

The first piece of information is the version of the XML standard that the document follows. The XML standard is active and is being improved on an ongoing basis. The creators of the standard realized that there would be a need to indicate, especially to parsing software, what features of the various versions of the XML standard applied to a particular document. At the time of writing, the applicable version numbers are 1.0 and 1.1. The second piece of information specified is the document character encoding. The standard supports character sets listed by the Internet Assigned Numbers Authority (IANA) (http://www.iana.org/assignments/character-sets).

XML Document Structure

An XML document has one element called the root element. All other elements are children (or grandchildren of varying degrees) of the root element. Technically, the root element could have attributes and its own data, but more commonly, it has no attributes or data of its own as its primary purpose is to identify the document data at the highest conceptual level. An example of this case is the <ADDRESSBOOK> root element of the XML document in Listing 1. The XML standard also defines how elements are to be nested. More precisely, all XML elements must begin and end in the same element scope. For example, consider the following XML fragment:

```
<SITE>
     <NAME>Joe's Garage</NAME>
     <WEBURL>http://www.joesgarage.com/</WEBURL>
</SITE>
```

This XML fragment is correctly nested. The <SITE> element, because it is a parent of the <NAME> and <WEBURL> elements in the hierarchy, correctly nests the others within it. The <NAME> and <WEBURL> elements in Listing 2 do not overlap each other because they are at the same hierarchical level. However, the following copy of a similar fragment is incorrect (Listing 3):

```
<SITE>
     <NAME>Joe's Garage
     <WEBURL>http://www.joesgarage.com/
</NAME>
     </WEBURL>
</SITE>
```

Again, by the rules of proper XML element nesting, the </NAME> tag in Listing 3 must come before the <WEBURL> tag because the <NAME> and <WEBURL> elements are at the same hierarchical level. In short, once you are inside an XML element, another one cannot be specified at the same hierarchical level until the current one is closed.

```
<SITE>
     <NAME>Joe's Garage
          <WEBURL>http://www.joesgarage.com/</WEBURL>
     </NAME>
     </SITE>
```

This code fragment (Listing 6) is correct because the <NAME> element is closed off after the </WEBURL> tag, making the <WEBURL> element a hierarchical child of <NAME>. Note that the indentation used in the XML document examples in this chapter are there for readability only and to make them more understandable by pointing out the element hierarchy. An XML document does not require such formatting to be proper XML (i.e., the elements and text data can all be left aligned in the text file); however, it is good practice and makes it easier to track down problems when trying to troubleshoot a parsing error.

Document Type Definitions and Schemas

One of the benefits of XML is that it is easier to parse the data in XML documents, than, say, write custom code to parse a comma-separated value (CSV) file. In the former case, a prefabricated parser does all work. In the latter, you have to write the parsing code yourself. The XML standard defines a specific methodology for ensuring that the data in a given XML document will fit the expected model.

A Document Type Definition (DTD) is one way of accomplishing this. A DTD describes to a parser what type of data can be expected in an XML document, what values are allowed for elements and attributes, and how the hierarchy of elements will be arranged. In short, you, as the publisher of the XML document, can issue a DTD to declare (to any parser that might read the XML document) what parameters the data in the DTD must fit for the document to be considered valid. If the document is verified to be valid, the parser does its work. If the document is found to be invalid, the parser rejects the document and no work is done. The XML standard defines two structural verification concepts for its documents: well-formed and valid.

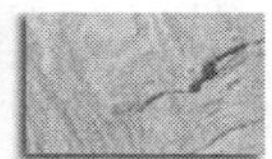

NOTE
A document must be well-formed to be valid, but the opposite is not necessarily true. In other words, a document can be well-formed without being valid. An XML document without an associated DTD is said to be well-formed, but, by definition, is not valid.

Well-Formed and Valid XML Documents

An XML document is said to be well-formed if it follows the basic structure rules of XML. For instance, a well-formed document contains one or more elements, only one of which can be the root element, and the subordinate elements all nest properly (i.e., adhere to proper element scope). No elements can be open-ended in XML. In other words, all XML elements must have a discernable beginning and end. For a complete description of well-formed XML, please see the XML specification (http://www.w3.org/XML/).

An XML document is valid if it has an associated DTD and the XML data in the document fits the constraints expressed in the DTD.

XML Document Validation–Document Type Definition (DTD)

In order for an XML document to be considered valid, we need something to validate its contents against. This is where the DTD comes in. The listing below (Listing 7) shows a possible DTD for the Address Book XML doc in Listing 1.

```
<?xml encoding="UTF-8"?>
<!ELEMENT ADDRESSBOOK (ENTRY)+>
<!ELEMENT ENTRY (FIRSTNAME,LASTNAME,ADDRLINE1,
ADDRLINE2?,CITY,STATE,ZIP,HOMEPHONE?,EMAIL?)>
```

```
<!ATTLIST ENTRY ID CDATA #REQUIRED>
<!ELEMENT FIRSTNAME (#PCDATA)>
<!ELEMENT LASTNAME  (#PCDATA)>
<!ELEMENT ADDRLINE1 (#PCDATA)>
<!ELEMENT CITY      (#PCDATA)>
<!ELEMENT STATE     (#PCDATA)>
<!ELEMENT ZIP          (#PCDATA)>
<!ELEMENT HOMEPHONE     (#PCDATA)>
<!ELEMENT EMAIL     (#PCDATA)>
```

You can think of a DTD as a set of instructions that identify what type of XML contents should be considered valid for a particular XML document. As we'll see later in this section, software called an XML parser uses DTDs in this way to determine whether an XML document is valid or not.

Let's look at the rules set forth by DTDs. In general, a DTD allows you to specify two major components of an XML document: the elements and their attributes (if any). The DTD also shows a clear relationship in the hierarchy of the elements represented in the XML documents it will be used to validate. Table 16-1 lists some of the more common DTD components:

<table>
<tr><th>DTD Element</th><th>Example Declaration</th><th>Definition</th></tr>
<tr><td><!ELEMENT ename EMPTY></td><td><!ELEMENT X EMPTY></td><td>The element declaration that specifies an empty element (i.e., an element containing no data or other elements) with a name specified by ename.</td></tr>
<tr><td><!ELEMENT ename ANY></td><td><!ELEMENT BOOK ANY></td><td>The element declaration of an element with name specified by ename. The element may contain any mixture of character data and elements. The exact content of the element is, therefore, undefined.</td></tr>
<tr><td><!ELEMENT ename (datatype)></td><td><!ELEMENT TITLE (#PCDATA)></td><td>The element declaration that specifies an element called ename that contains data of type datatype.</td></tr>
<tr><td><!ELEMENT ename (child,...)></td><td><!ELEMENT BOOK (TITLE, PUBLISHER, ISBN)></td><td>The element declaration that specifies an element called ename that contains a set of one or more child elements.</td></tr>
<tr><td><!ELEMENT ename (datatype|child1|child2)></td><td><!ELEMENT USERPROFILE (#PCDATA|CUSTOM|DEFAULT)></td><td>The element declaration that specifies an element called ename that contains either data of type datatype or child1 or child2 elements.</td></tr>
<tr><td>Attribute Declaration</td><td></td><td></td></tr>
<tr><td><!ATTLIST ename adef></td><td><!ATTLIST BOOK TITLE CDATA #REQUIRED></td><td>The attribute declaration for element ename. Attribute details are specified in adef, which consists of the attribute name, datatype, and default value handling.</td></tr>
<tr><td>Optionality</td><td></td><td></td></tr>
<tr><td>(child1,child2)</td><td><!ELEMENT PERSON (FIRSTNAME,LASTNAME)></td><td>The set of child elements consists of child1 AND child2.</td></tr>
</table>

TABLE 16-1. *Some of the More Common DTD Components*

<table>
<tr><td>Optionality</td><td></td><td></td></tr>
<tr><td>(child1|child2)</td><td><!ELEMENT PHONENUM (HOME|WORK|MOBILE)></td><td>The set of child elements consists of child1 AND/OR child2.</td></tr>
<tr><td>Datatypes</td><td></td><td></td></tr>
<tr><td>CDATA</td><td><!ELEMENT FIRSTNAME (#CDATA)></td><td>Specifies that data is a character string and that it does not contain markup that needs to be parsed. In other words, the data will be examined verbatim.</td></tr>
<tr><td>PCDATA</td><td><!ELEMENT SUBJECT (#PCDATA)></td><td>Specifies that the data is a character string but may contain markup information and needs to parsed.</td></tr>
<tr><td>Repeat Rules</td><td></td><td></td></tr>
<tr><td>?</td><td><!ELEMENT ADDRESS (ADDRL1, ADDRL2, CITY, STATE, ZIP)?></td><td>The element contains zero or one sets consisting of the elements ADDRL1, ADDRL2, CITY, STATE, ZIP.</td></tr>
<tr><td>?</td><td><!ELEMENT SINGLECOMMENT (CMTTEXT?)></td><td>The element contains a set consisting of zero or one instance of the CMTTEXT element.</td></tr>
<tr><td>*</td><td><!ELEMENT ADDRESS (ADDRL1, ADDRL2, CITY, STATE, ZIP)*></td><td>The element contains zero or more sets consisting of the elements ADDRL1, ADDRL2, CITY, STATE, ZIP.</td></tr>
<tr><td>*</td><td><!ELEMENT MULTICOMMENT (CMTTEXT*)></td><td>The element contains a set consisting of zero or more instances of the CMTTEXT element.</td></tr>
<tr><td>+</td><td><!ELEMENT ADDRESS (ADDRL1, ADDRL2, CITY, STATE, ZIP)+></td><td>The element contains one or more sets consisting of the elements ADDRL1, ADDRL2, CITY, STATE, ZIP.</td></tr>
<tr><td>+</td><td><!ELEMENT MULTICOMMENT (CMTTEXT+)></td><td>The element contains a set consisting of one or more instances of the CMTTEXT element.</td></tr>
</table>

TABLE 16-1. *Some of the More Common DTD Components* (continued)

Let's take a look at our DTD in Listing 2 and examine how it relates to our XML document from Listing 1 (Table 16-2).

Now that we have a DTD, we have to associate it with our XML document. There are two ways to do this. The internal DTD actually resides in the XML document itself:

```
<?xml version="1.0" encoding="ISO-8859-1"?>
<!DOCTYPE BOOKLIST [
     <!ELEMENT TITLE (#PCDATA)>
     <!ELEMENT ISBN (#PCDATA)>
     <!ELEMENT AUTHOR (#PCDATA)>
     <!ELEMENT PUBLISHER (#PCDATA)>
     <!ELEMENT PUBDATE (#PCDATA)>
]>
...
```

This method includes the DTD inside the XML document to be validated. The advantage to using an internal DTD is that everything a parser needs to validate the file is self-contained. The

DTD Declaration	XML Element Tags	Rule Description
<!ELEMENT ADDRESSBOOK (ENTRY)+>	<ADDRESSBOOK> ... </ADDRESSBOOK>	Specifies the root element for the Address. Book XML document; can contain one or more (+) ENTRY elements.
<!ELEMENT ENTRY (FIRSTNAME,LASTNAME,ADDRLINE1, ADDRLINE2?,CITY,STATE,ZIP, HOMEPHONE?,EMAIL?)>	<ENTRY ID="1">... </ENTRY>	Specifies the ENTRY element and that it contains one set of the following: one FIRSTNAME element, one LASTNAME element, one ADDRLINE1 element, zero or one ADDRLINE2 element, one CITY element, one STATE element, one ZIP element, zero or one HOMEPHONE element, and zero or one EMAIL element.
<!ATTLIST ENTRY ID CDATA #REQUIRED>	<ENTRY ID="1">	The ENTRY tag has an attribute called ID that contains unparsed character data. The attribute has no default value and is required on each ENTRY element.
<!ELEMENT FIRSTNAME (#PCDATA)> <!ELEMENT LASTNAME (#PCDATA)> <!ELEMENT ADDRLINE1 (#PCDATA)> <!ELEMENT CITY (#PCDATA)> <!ELEMENT STATE (#PCDATA)> <!ELEMENT ZIP (#PCDATA)> <!ELEMENT HOMEPHONE (#PCDATA)> <!ELEMENT EMAIL (#PCDATA)>	<FIRSTNAME>John </FIRSTNAME> <LASTNAME> Doe</LASTNAME> <ADDRLINE1> 100 Maple Lane </ADDRLINE1>	Each element contains parsed character data payload.

TABLE 16-2. *Analysis of the Address Book XML Document and DTD.*

disadvantage is that the inclusion of the DTD can bloat what might already be a rather large XML file to begin with. Also, if you are receiving this file to insert into your database and need to validate that it has followed the specifications you've provided to the publisher of the data, there is no guarantee of this; the publisher of the XML document has control over the DTD because the publisher has included it in the XML document.

An alternate methodology is to specify an external DTD. This method allows flexibility with regard to who controls the validation of the data.

```
<?xml version="1.0" encoding="ISO-8859-1"?>
<!DOCTYPE BOOKLIST SYSTEM "http://www.booksonline.com/booklist.dtd">
...
```

The SYSTEM keyword instructs the parser to look in the location of the specified Universal Resource Identifier (URI) (the http address in the preceding example) to find the document type definition information used to validate the XML document. The advantage to this method is added flexibility in regards to which party controls the DTD. In this case, it can be either the publisher or the consumer of the information. The disadvantage is that if a remote resource is specified but is unavailable due to network problems, parsing of the document cannot proceed.

XML Schemas

While the DTD serves as a necessary and useful component for validation of an XML document's contents, it has some shortcomings:

- DTDs do not provide a mechanism for strict data-type enforcement or support for complex data-types.
- Support for namespaces in DTDs is not inherent and what little support that can be simulated is complicated and involves difficult-to-implement techniques.
- DTDs use a specialized format that does not follow the XML standard.

These are just some of the disadvantages that have cropped up over time using DTDs. To solve these shortcomings and others, a W3C group (http://www.w3.org/XML/) was formed to draft a standard for XML Schemas (XSDs). Some of the benefits of XML Schemas are

- XML Schemas are capable of enforcing tighter data-type checking during validation as well as supporting complex data-types.
- XML Schemas support for namespaces is built in; no work-around is needed.
- XML Schema Definitions (XSDs) are XML files, so there is no new format to learn once you understand how to properly format an XML document.

The XML Schema Definition (XSD) language is much more powerful and complex than DTDs and does not lend itself easily to a short discussion of the subject.

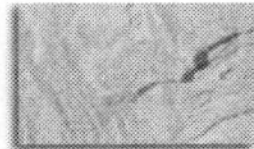

NOTE
XML Schemas are an advanced subject and there are entire texts written on the topic alone; therefore, this chapter will not go into detailed coverage of them. Keep in mind that the concepts applied to DTDs with respect to their usage with Oracle also apply to XSDs. If you wish to learn about XSDs, we urge you to consult a more comprehensive text on the subject.

XML Parsers—Manipulating and Searching an XML Document

While presenting data in an XML document format has strengths of its own, the real power behind XML is what you are able to do with it. An XML parser is a software component that allows developers to access and manipulate raw XML document data.

XML Parsers:

- Allow developers to write a minimal amount of code to extract the component data of the XML document for programmatic use. One application might be to populate Oracle tables with data from the XML document.
- Can manipulate XML data either as entire documents using the Document Object Model (DOM) or as individual "chunks" called events using the Simple API for XML (SAX).
- Are supported by multiple languages. Oracle supports SAX and DOM parsers for C/C++, Java, and PL/SQL (DOM only).

- Provide validation of the structure and content of XML documents, via the specification of a DTD or an XML Schema Definition (XSD).
- Allow developers (using the DOM parser) to search a parsed XML document using XPATH that resembles a URI path specification (somewhat) in style.

There are two major activities that XML parsers engage in: validation and parsing. A nonvalidating parser is an XML parser that only parses the XML given to it and does no active validation of the data. Most parsers, however, do both and the validation feature can usually be turned on or off with configuration parameters.

DOM Parsers

Document Object Model (DOM) is a platform-independent interface for accessing HTML and XML documents from within programming and scripting languages. The DOM presents documents in an object-oriented fashion. DOM exists in three levels. DOM Level 1 is a W3C Recommendation and is currently supported by lots of implementations. DOM Level 2 extends DOM Level 1 with regards to things like access to the DTD and namespaces. DOM Level 2 is yet another W3C Proposed Recommendation. DOM Level 2 is specified in a modularized document structure; i.e., Core Specification, HTML Specification, Views Specification, Style Specification, Events Specification, and Traversal-Range Specification. Core is the entry point to read the specification. The DOM group has recently published a first suggestion for DOM Level 3. A DOM interface is provided by Microsoft's XMLDOM ActiveXControl.

SAX Parsers

SAX is a simple, standardized API for XML parsers developed by the contributors to the xml-dev mailing list. The interface is mostly language-independent, as long as the language is object-oriented. The first implementation was written for Java, but a Python implementation is also available. SAX is supported by many XML parsers.

JAXP

JAXP stands for Java API for XML processing. It enables applications to parse and transform XML documents using an API that is independent of a particular XML processor implementation.

XSL Processors

Extensible Stylesheet Language (XSL) is a language for creating a style sheet that describes how data sent over the Web using XML is to be presented to the user. XSL specifies the styling of an XML document by using XSL Transformations (XSLT) to describe how the document is transformed into another XML document that uses the formatting vocabulary. XSLT is a language for transforming XML documents into other XML documents. It is designed to be used as part of XSL, which is a style sheet language for XML. In addition to XSLT, XSL includes an XML vocabulary for specifying formatting. XSLT is a W3C specification but also Part 2 of the XSL specification.

Oracle XDK–The XML Developer's Kit

The Oracle XML Developer's Kit (XDK) 10*g* is a set of components, tools, and utilities in Java, C, and C++ and is available in Oracle Database 10*g* and Oracle Application Server 10*g* that ease the task of building and deploying XML-enabled applications. Unlike many shareware and trial XML components, the Oracle XDK is fully supported. Oracle XDK consists of the following components:

- **XML parsers** Create and parse XML using DOM (including 3.0), SAX, and JAXP interfaces. Directly access XMLType in the Oracle Database 10*g* with unified C DOM interfaces.
- **XSLT processors** Transform or render XML. Supports XSLT 2.0 Java.
- **XSLT virtual machine (VM) and compiler** Provides high performance C XSLT transformation engine using compiled stylesheets.
- **XML Schema processors** Support XML schema validation. Include validation interfaces for stream-based processing.
- **XML Java Beans** Parse, transform, diff, retrieve, and compress XML documents via Java components.
- **XML Class Generator** Supports JAXP; automatically generates classes from DTDs and XML schemas to send XML from web forms or applications.
- **XML SQL Utility** Generates XML documents, DTDs, and XML schemas from SQL queries in Java and inserts XML documents into Oracle databases.
- **XSQL Servlet** Combines XML, SQL, and XSLT in the server to deliver dynamic web content and build sophisticated database-backed web sites and services.
- **XML Pipeline Processor** Invokes Java processes through XML control files.
- **TransX Utility** Makes it easier to load globalized seed data and messages into Oracle databases.

XML Technologies Supported by Oracle

This section will briefly discuss the XML technologies supported by Oracle. The XML technologies supported by Oracle can be separated into the following categories:

- Database XML Support
- XML Developer's Kit (XDK) for Java
- XDK for Java Beans
- XDK for C
- XDK for C++
- XDK for PL/SQL

Database XML Support

- **XMLType** A new datatype to store, query, and retrieve XML documents. XMLType is a system defined datatype with predefined member functions to access XML data. You can perform the following tasks with XMLType:
  - Create columns of XMLType and use XMLType member functions on instances of the type
  - Create PL/SQL functions and procedures, with XMLType as argument and return parameters

- Store, index, and manipulate XML data in XMLType columns

- **SYS_XMLGEN** A SQL function to create XML documents. SYS_XMLGEN is a SQL function, which generates XML within SQL queries. DBMS_XMLGEN and other packages operate at a query level, giving aggregated results for the entire query. SYS_XMLGEN operates on a single argument inside a SQL query and converts the result to XML. SYS_XMLGEN takes in a scalar value, an object type, or an XMLType instance to be converted to an XML document. It also takes an optional XMLGenFormatType object to specify formatting options for the result. SYS_XMLGEN returns a XMLType.
- **SYS_XMLAGG** A SQL function to aggregate multiple XML documents. SYS_XMLAGG is an aggregate function, which aggregates over a set of XMLTypes. SYS_XMLAGG aggregates all the input XML documents/fragments and produces a single XML document by concatenating XML fragments and adding a top-level tag.
- **DBMS_XMLGEN** A built-in package to create XML from SQL queries. DBMS_XMLGEN is a PL/SQL package that converts the results of SQL queries to canonical XML format, returning it as XMLType or CLOB. DBMS_XMLGEN is implemented in C, and compiled in the database kernel. DBMS_XMLGEN is similar in functionality to DBMS_XMLQuery package.
- **URI support** Store and retrieve global and intra-database references. The UriType family of types can store and query Uri-refs in the database. SYS.UriType is an abstract object type that provides functions to access the data pointed to by the URL. SYS.HttpUriType and SYS.DBUriType are subtypes of UriType. The HttpUriType can store HTTP URLs and the DBUriType can store intra-database references. You can also define your own subtypes of SYS.UriType to handle different URL protocols. The UriFactory package is
a factory package that can generate instances of these UriTypes automatically by scanning the prefix, such as http://, ftp://, etc. Users can also register their own subtypes with UriFactory, specifying the supported prefix. For example, a subtype to handle the gopher protocol can be registered with UriFactory, specifying that URLs with the prefix "gopher://" are to be handled by your subtype. UriFactory now generates the registered subtype instance for any URL starting with that prefix.
- **Text support** Supports XPath (the open standard syntax for addressing elements within a document used by XSL and XPointer) on XMLType and text columns.

XML Developer's *Kit (XDK) for Java*

- **XML Parser for Java** Library and command-line versions are provided that support the following standards and features:
- **XML** W3C XML 1.0 Recommendation
- **DOM** An integrated DOM (Document Object Model) API, compliant with: W3C DOM 1.0 Recommendation, W3C DOM 2.0 CORE Recommendation, W3C DOM 2.0 Traversal Recommendation, including Treewalker, Node Iterator, and Node Filter.
- **SAX** An integrated Simple API for XML (SAX) API, compliant with the SAX 2.0 recommendation. These APIs permit an application to process XML documents using an event-driven model.

- W3C Proposed Recommendation for XML Namespaces 1.0, thereby avoiding name collision, increasing reusability, and easing application integration. Supports Oracle XML Schema Processor. See also http://www.w3.org/TR/1999/REC-xml-names-19990114/.
- Validating and non-validating modes.
- Built-in error recovery until fatal error.
- DOM extension APIs for document creation.

- **XSLT Processor for Java** Includes the following features:
  - Integrated support for W3C XSLT 1.1 Working Draft
  - Provides new APIs to get XSL Transformation as SAX output
- **XML Schema Processor for Java** Supports XML Schema Processor that parses and validates XML files against an XML Schema Definition file (.xsd). It includes the following features:
  - Built on the XML Parser for Java v2
  - Supports the three parts of the XML Schema Working Draft :Part 0: Primer XML Schema, Part 1: Structures XML Schema, Part 2: Datatypes
  - Runs on Oracle and Oracle Application Server
- **XML Class Generator for Java** XML Class Generator for Java creates Java source files from an XML Document Type Definition (DTD) or XML Schema Definition. The generated classes can be used to programmatically construct XML documents. XML Class Generator for Java also optionally generates javadoc comments on the generated source files. XML Class Generator for Java requires the XML Parser for Java and the XML Schema Processor for Java. It works in conjunction with XML Parser for Java, which parses the DTD (or XML Schema) and sends the parsed XML document to the Class Generator. XML Class Generator for Java consists of the following two class generators (both of which can be invoked from the command line utility, oracg):
  - DTD Class Generator
  - XML Schema Class Generator
- **XSQL Servlet** XSQL Servlet is a tool that processes SQL queries and outputs the result set as XML. This processor is implemented as a Java servlet and takes an XML file containing embedded SQL queries as its input. It uses XML Parser for Java, XML-SQL Utility, and Oracle XSL Transformation (XSLT) Engine to perform many of its operations. You can use XSQL Servlet to perform the following tasks:
  - Build dynamic XML datapages from the results of one or more SQL queries and serve the results over the Web as XML datagrams or HTML pages using server-side XSLT transformations
  - Receive XML posted to your web server and insert it into your database
- **XML SQL Utility (XSU) for Java** Oracle XML SQL Utility (XSU) supports Java and PL/SQL. XML SQL Utility is comprised of core Java class libraries for automatically

and dynamically rendering the results of arbitrary SQL queries into canonical XML. It includes the following features:

- Supports queries over richly-structured user-defined object types and object views.
- Supports automatic XML Insert of canonically-structured XML into any existing table, view, object table, or object view. By combining with XSLT transformations, virtually any XML document can be automatically inserted into the database.
- XML SQL Utility Java classes can be used for the following tasks:
- Generate from an SQL query or Result set object a text or XML document, a DOM, DTD, or XML Schema.
- Load data from an XML document into an existing database schema or view.
- XML SQL Utility for Java consists of a set of Java classes that perform the following tasks:
- Pass a query to the database and generate an XML document (text or DOM) from the results or the DTD, which can be used for validation.
- Write XML data to a database table.

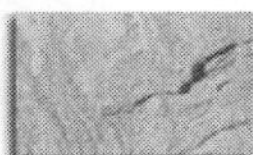

NOTE
Of all of the XML technologies supported by Oracle, XSU is one of the most frequently used. The final section of this chapter, "The XML SQL Utility (XSU) for Java and PL/SQL," explores the XSU.

XDK for Java Beans

- **XML Transviewer Beans** A set of XML components that constitute XML for Java Beans. These are used for Java applications or applets to view and transform XML documents. They are visual and nonvisual Java components that are integrated into Oracle JDeveloper 10*g* to enable the fast creation and deployment of XML-based database applications. The following beans are available:
  - **DOMBuilder Bean** This bean wraps the Java XML (DOM) parser with a bean interface, allowing multiple files to be parsed at once (asynchronous parsing). By registering a listener, Java applications can parse large or successive documents while having control return immediately to the caller.
  - **XML Source Viewer Bean** This bean extends JPanel by enabling the viewing of XML documents. It improves the viewing of XML and XSL files by color-highlighting XML and XSL syntax. This is useful when modifying an XML document with an editing application. Easily integrated with the DOM Builder Bean, it allows for preparsing, postparsing, and validation against a specified DTD.
  - **XML Tree Viewer Bean** This bean extends JPanel by enabling users' top view XML documents in tree form with the ability to expand and collapse XML parsers. It

displays a visual DOM view of an XML document, enabling users to easily manipulate the tree with a mouse to hide or view selected branches.

- **XSL Transformer Bean** This bean wraps the XSLT Processor with a bean interface and performs XSL transformations on an XML document based on an XSL stylesheet. It enables users to transform an XML document to almost any text-based format, including XML, HTML, and DDL, by applying an XSL style sheet. When integrated with other beans, this bean enables an application or user to view the results of transformations immediately. It can also be used as the basis of a server-side application or servlet to render an XML document, such as an XML representation of a query result, into HTML for display in a browser.
- **XML TransPanel Bean** This bean uses the other beans to create a sample application, which can process XML files. It includes a file interface to load XML documents and XSL style sheets. It uses these beans:

- Visual beans to view and edit files
- Transformer beans to apply the style sheet to the XML document and view the output

XDK for C

- **XML Parser for C** This parser will check if an XML document is well-formed, and optionally validate it against a DTD. It constructs an object tree, which can be accessed through a DOM interface or operated serially via a SAX interface. XML Parser for C is provided with Oracle and Oracle Application Server, located in $ORACLE_HOME/xdk/c/parser.
- **XML Schema Processor for C** See the preceding XML Schema Processor for Java entry.

XDK for C++

- **XML Parser for C++** See the preceding XML Parser for C entry
- **XML Schema Processor for C++** See the preceding XML Schema Processor for Java
- **XML Class Generator for C++** See the preceding XML Class Generator for Java

XDK for PL/SQL

- **XML Parser for PL/SQL** See the preceding XML Parser for C
- **XML SQL Utility (XSU) for PL/SQL** Comprised of a PL/SQL package that wraps the XML SQL Utility for Java (see preceding description)

The XML SQL Utility (XSU) for Java and PL/SQL

The XML SQL Utility allows developers to transform data retrieved from the Oracle database into XML, extract data from an XML document and insert the data into an Oracle database, and extract data from an XML document and apply the data to update or delete values of the appropriate columns or attributes. This is not the full list of capabilities within XSU, but it represents what will be discussed in this section.

Tasks To Complete Before Using XSU

Before you can use XSU, you will need to perform a few tasks. A valid JDBC driver must be available. XSU can work with any JDBC driver, but is only certified for use with Oracle JDBC drivers. Oracle XML Parser (included with Oracle8*i* of the database and every succeeding database version) must also be available. By default (in Oracle 8.1.7 and later), the installation of XSU is performed as part of the standard installation. If you chose not to install XSU when installing your database, refer to the *Oracle® Application Developer's Guide - XML 10g (9.0.4) Part Number B12099-01* (http://download-west.oracle.com/docs/cd/B10464_01/web.904/b12099/toc.htm), Chapter 7, "XML SQL Utility (XSU)."

Where Does XSU *"Live"*?

XSU can exist on any tier that supports Java:

- **In the database** The Java classes that make XSU can be loaded into Java-enabled Oracle8*i* or later. XSU contains a PL/SQL wrapper that publishes the XSU Java API to PL/SQL, creating a PL/SQL API. This way you can:
  - Write new Java applications that run inside the database and that can directly access the XSU Java API
  - Write PL/SQL applications that access XSU through its PL/SQL API
  - Access XSU functionality directly through SQL
- **In the middle tier** Your application architecture may need to use an application server in the middle tier, separate from the database. The application tier can be an Oracle database, an Oracle Application Server, or a third-party application server that supports Java programs. You may want to generate XML in the middle tier, from SQL queries or ResultSets, for various reasons. For example, if you want to integrate different JDBC data sources in the middle tier, you could install the XSU in your middle tier and your Java programs could make use of XSU through its Java API.
- **In a Web Server** XSU can live in the web server, as long as the web server supports Java servlets. This way, you can write Java servlets that use XSU to accomplish their task.

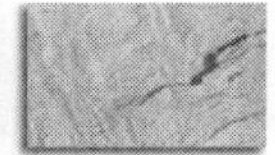

TIP
XSQL servlet is a standard servlet provided by Oracle. It is built on top of XSU and provides a template-like interface to XSU functionality. If XML processing in the web server is desired, use the XSQL servlet, as it will spare you from the intricacies of servlet programming.

- **In The Client Tier** XML SQL Utility can also be installed on a client system, where you can write Java programs that use XSU. You can also use XSU directly through its command line front end.

The OracleXML class

The XSU command line options are provided through the Java class, OracleXML, which can be invoked from a command line:

```
java OracleXML
```

By not passing any parameters, this command will print the options for using the class:

```
C:\oracle\product\10.1.0\db_1>java OracleXML
OracleXML-Error:wrong argument list
Call with

OracleXML getXML
 [-user "username/password"]     -- the username and password
 [-conn "JDBC_connect_string"]   -- JDBC connect string
 [-withDTD | -withSchema]        -- generate the DTD/Schema
 [-rowsetTag <rowsetTag>]        -- document tag name
 [-rowTag    <rowTag>]           -- row element tag name
 [-rowIdAttr <attrName>]         -- row-id attribute name
 [-rowIdColumn <column_name>]    -- db-column to use for the row id
 [-collectionIdAttr <attrName>] -- collection element-id attribute
 [-useTypeForCollElemTag]        -- use type name for coll-elem tag
 [-useNullAttrId]                -- use a null attribute
 [-styleSheet <URI>]             -- stylesheet processing instruction header
 [-styleSheetType <type>]        -- stylesheet header type (e.g.text/xsl)
 [-setXSLT <URI>]                -- XSLT to apply to XML doc
 [-setXSLTRef <URI>]             -- XSLT external entity reference
 [-useLowerCase| -useUpperCase] -- the case of the tag names
 [-withEscaping]                 -- if necessary do SQL-XML name escaping
 [-errorTag <errorTagName>]      -- error tag name
 [-raiseException]               -- raise exceptions for errors
 [-raiseNoRowsException]         -- raise exception if no returned
 [-maxRows   <maxRows>]          -- maximum rows in output
 [-skipRows  <skipRows>]         -- rows to skip in output
 [-encoding <encoding_name>]     -- encoding to be used
 [-dateFormat <date format>]     -- date format to be used
 (<query>| -fileName <sqlfile>) -- SQL query | file containing the query

 -- OR --

OracleXML putXML
 [-user "username/password"]     -- the username and password
 [-conn "JDBC_connect_string"]   -- JDBC connect string
 [-batchSize <size>]             -- number of inserts executed at a time
 [-commitBatch <size>]           -- number of inserts commited at a time
 [-rowTag <rowTagName>]          -- the name for row elements
 [-dateFormat <format>]          -- the format of date elements
 [-withEscaping]                 -- if necessary do SQL-XML name escaping
 [-ignoreCase]                   -- ignore the case of the tag names
```

```
 [-preserveWhitespace]          -- preserves any whitespaces
 [-setXSLT <URI>]               -- XSLT to apply to XML doc
 [-setXSLTRef <URI>]            -- external entity reference for XSLT doc
 [-fileName fileName |          -- the XML document file name or
  -URL url |                     - URL or
  -xmlDoc <XMLDocumentString>]   - XML string
 <tableName>                    -- the table name to put into
```

To generate XML, we will use the getXML parameter. To generate an XML document by querying the XYZ table in the user1 schema:

```
C:\oracle\product\10.1.0\db_1\BIN>sqlplus user1/user1@orcl
SQL*Plus: Release 10.1.0.2.0 - Production on Mon Aug 23 13:06:29 2004
Copyright (c) 1982, 2004, Oracle.  All rights reserved.
Connected to:
Oracle Database 10g Enterprise Edition Release 10.1.0.2.0 - Production
With the Partitioning, OLAP and Data Mining options

SQL> select * from xyz;
COL1                 COL2
-------------------- --------------------
abc                  def
ghi                  jkl
mno                  pqr
```

we can issue the following command:

```
C:\oracle\product\10.1.0\db_1\BIN>java OracleXML getXML -user "user1/user1" "select * from xyz"
<?xml version = '1.0'?>
<ROWSET>
   <ROW num="1">
      <COL1>abc</COL1>
      <COL2>def</COL2>
   </ROW>
   <ROW num="2">
      <COL1>ghi</COL1>
      <COL2>jkl</COL2>
   </ROW>
   <ROW num="3">
      <COL1>mno</COL1>
      <COL2>pqr</COL2>
   </ROW>
</ROWSET>
```

XSU's OracleXML getXML options are summarized in Table 16-3:

To insert an XML document into the XYZ table in the user1 schema, use the putXML keyword:

```
C:\oracle\product\10.1.0\db_1\BIN>java OracleXML putXML -user "user1/user1"
-filename "xyz_ins.xml" "xyz"
 successfully inserted 3 rows into xyz
```

XSU's OracleXML putXML options are summarized in Table 16-4:

getXML Option	Description
-user "<username>/<password>"	Specifies the username and password to connect to the database. If this is not specified, the user defaults to scott/tiger. Note that the connect string is also being specified; the username and password can be specified as part of the connect string.
-conn "<JDBC_connect_string>"	Specifies the JDBC database connect string. By default, the connect string is: "jdbc:oracle:oci8:@"):
-withDTD	Instructs the XSU to generate the DTD along with the XML document.
-rowsetTag "<tag_name>"	Specifies the rowset tag (the tag that encloses all the XML elements corresponding to the records returned by the query). The default rowset tag is ROWSET. Specifying an empty string for the rowset tells the XSU to completely omit the rowset element.
-rowTag "<tag_name>"	Specifies the row tag (the tag used to enclose the data corresponding to a database row). The default row tag is ROW. Specifying an empty string for the row tag tells the XSU to completely omit the row tag.
-rowIdAttr "<row_id-attribute-name>"	Names the attribute of the ROW element keeping track of the cardinality of the rows. By default, this attribute is called num. Specifying an empty string (i.e., "") as the rowID attribute will tell the XSU to omit the attribute.
-rowIdColumn "<row Id column name>"	Specifies that the value of one of the scalar columns from the query should be used as the value of the rowID attribute.
-collectionIdAttr "<collection id attribute name>"	Names the attribute of an XML list element keeping track of the cardinality of the elements of the list (Note: The generated XML lists correspond to either a cursor query or collection.) Specifying an empty string (i.e., "") as the rowID attribute will tell the XSU to omit the attribute.
-useNullAttrId	Tells the XSU to use the attribute NULL (TRUE/FALSE) to indicate if an element is null.
-styleSheet "<stylesheet URI>"	Specifies the style sheet in the XML PI (Processing Instruction).
-stylesheetType "<stylesheet type>"	Specifies the style-sheet type in the XML PI.
-errorTag "<error tag name>"	Specifies the error tag—the tag to enclose error messages that are formatted into XML.
-raiseNoRowsException	Tells the XSU to raise an exception if no rows are returned.
-maxRows "<maximum number of rows>"	Specifies the maximum number of rows to be retrieved and converted to XML.
-skipRows "<number of rows to skip>"	Specifies the number of rows to be skipped.
-encoding "<encoding name>"	Specifies the character set encoding of the generated XML.
-dateFormat "<date format>"	Specifies the date format for the date values in the XML document.
-fileName "<SQL query fileName>" | <sql query>	Specifies the file name that contains the query or specifies the query itself.

TABLE 16-3. *XSU's OracleXML getXML Options*

putXML Options	Description
-user "<username>/<password>"	Specifies the username and password to connect to the database. If this is not specified, the user defaults to scott/tiger. Note that the connect string is also being specified; the username and password can be specified as part of the connect string.
-conn "<JDBC_connect_string>"	Specifies the JDBC database connect string. By default, the connect string is: "jdbc:oracle:oci8:@"):
-batchSize "<batching size>"	Specifies the batch size, which controls the number of rows that are batched together and inserted in a single trip to the database. Batching improves performance.
-commitBatch "<commit size>"	Specifies the number of inserted records after which a commit is to be executed. Note that if the autocommit is true (default), then setting the commitBatch has no consequence.
-rowTag "<tag_name>"	Specifies the row tag (the tag used to enclose the data corresponding to a database row). The default row tag is ROW. Specifying an empty string for the row tag tells the XSU that no row enclosing tag is used in the XML document.
-dateFormat "<date format>"	Specifies the date format for the date values in the XML document.
-ignoreCase	Makes the matching of the column names with tag names case-insensitive (e.g., "EmpNo" will match with "EMPNO" if ignoreCase is on).
-fileName "<file name>" | -URL "<url>" | -xmlDoc "<xml document>"	Specifies the XML document to insert. The fileName option specifies a local file, the URL specifies a URL to fetch the document from, and the xmlDoc option inlines the XML document as a string on the command line.
<tableName>	The name of the table to put the values into.

TABLE 16-4. *XSU's OracleXML putXML Options*

The following two classes make up the XML SQL Utility Java API:

- XSU API for XML generation: oracle.xml.sql.query.OracleXMLQuery
- XSU API for XML save, insert, update, and delete: oracle.xml.sql.dml.OracleXMLSave

Here is a code example in Java to query the XYZ table owned by the USER1 user in the ORCL database:

```
import oracle.jdbc.driver.*;
import oracle.xml.sql.query.OracleXMLQuery;
import java.lang.*;
import java.sql.*;
// class to test the String generation.
class testXMLSQL {
```

```
    public static void main(String[] argv)
    {
      try{
       // Create the connection.
       Connection conn  = getConnection("USER1","USER1");
       // Create the query class.
       OracleXMLQuery qry = new OracleXMLQuery(conn, "select * from XYZ");
       // Get the XML string.
       String str = qry.getXMLString();
       // Print the XML output.
       System.out.println(" The XML output is:\n"+str);
       // Close the query to release resources.
      qry.close();
      }catch(SQLException e){
       System.out.println(e.toString());
      }
    }
    // Get the connection given the username and password.
    private static Connection getConnection(String username, String password)
      throws SQLException
    {
       // Register the JDBC driver.
        DriverManager.registerDriver(new oracle.jdbc.driver.OracleDriver());
       // Create the connection using the OCI8 driver.
        Connection conn =
         DriverManager.getConnection("jdbc:oracle:oci8:@",username,password);
       return conn;
    }
}
```

Summary

XML provides a general syntax for describing data that can be used in a wide variety of applications. It extends the feature set of HTML by providing human-readable, platform-independent code that is the perfect complement for modern databases that are required to exchange data over the Web. Oracle has shown its commitment to open standards by developing many technologies that allow organizations to integrate XML standards and technologies with their Oracle databases. There are general XML/database technologies such as the new XMLType database type, the SYS_XMLGEN and SYS_XMLAGG functions, and the DBMS_XMLGEN package available in the 10*g* version of the Oracle database; and XML/Database technologies specific to a particular programming language, such as the XML Developer's Kit (XDK) for Java, C, C++, and PL/SQL. Viewed as a whole, these robust technologies provide developers with the tools necessary to integrate XML with Oracle databases to satisfy virtually any application or organizational requirement.

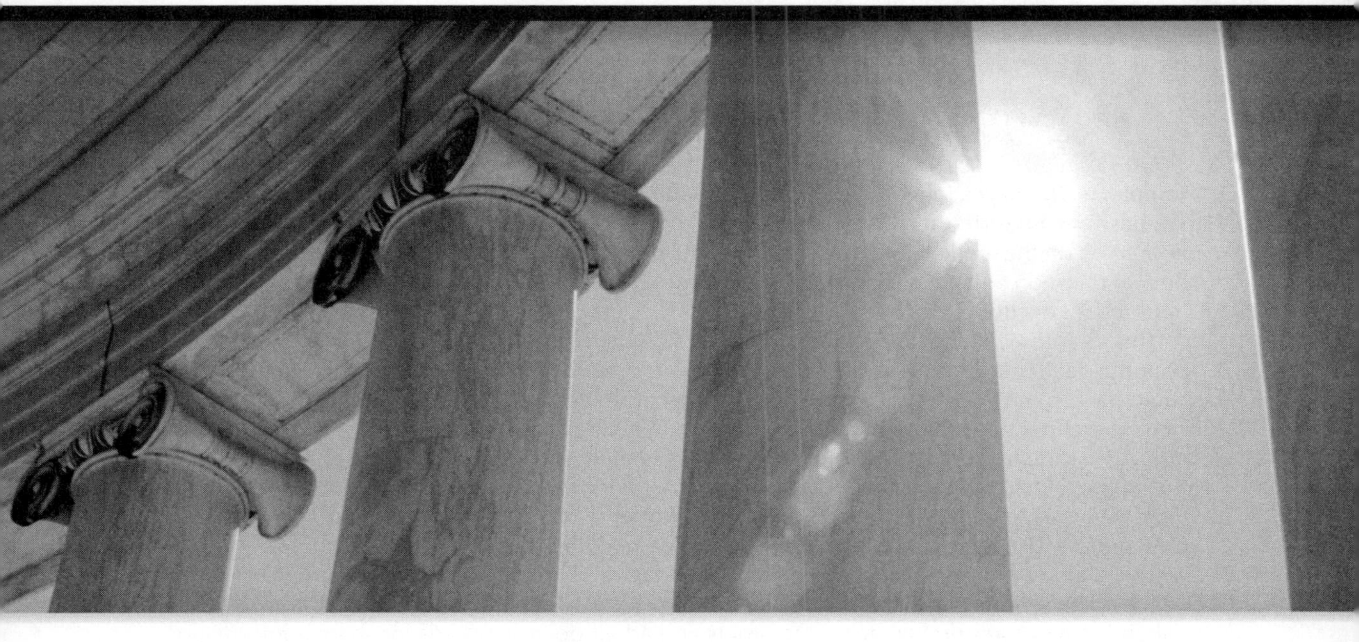

CHAPTER 17

Web Services

eb Services is a complex subject in and of itself. Entire books have been written on every facet of it, including books on Web Services architecture, security, managing Web Services, performance tuning, and more. As part of the Oracle documentation set for Oracle Application Server 10*g*, the "Oracle Application Server Web Services Developers Guide for 10*g*," as one example, is 382 pages long. A search on a popular online book site returned no less than 64,396 matches when queried for "Web Services." Programmers should have little trouble finding information on the architecture, implementation, and deployment of every aspect of Web Services. The real question at hand is how many pages does it really take to understand the technology? Thousands? Less than 50?

This chapter will provide all the typical Oracle developer will need to know to get excited about this technology, as well as properly demonstrate why everything you do going forward should have some Web Services component—because it should. All indications point to service-oriented architectures (i.e., an architecture with Web Services at the center) as the wave of the future. This chapter summarizes thousands of pages of information into the absolute essentials to begin developing Web Services applications. As Mark Twain once said, "If I had more time, I would have written a shorter letter." This is the shorter letter. You can read countless pages about SOAP and XML ... or you can take a few hours and read this part of the book.

This chapter represents one of the most important and least understood technologies: Web Services. The serious players in the software industry (Oracle, IBM, and Microsoft) have decided to abandon their proprietary technology roots and adopt open standards for sharing information. Sharing information across systems is a good thing for the IT industry.

It's important to know that Oracle Application Server 10*g* and the stand-alone Oracle Application Server Containers for J2EE (OC4J), which is available as a separate download from Oracle Technology Network (http://otn.oracle.com), both fully support Web Services. It's also important to understand that if you choose to use Oracle JDeveloper 10*g*, you'll be able to cut down your Web Services learning curve considerably. Oracle JDeveloper 10*g* allows the developer to easily create Web Services from existing Java classes or PL/SQL-packaged program units in a very short period of time. The wizards help you create, package, and deploy your Web Services. Oracle JDeveloper 10*g* automatically generates stubs and other files, such as Web Services Description Language (WSDLs). Oracle Application Server 10*g* also creates a home page automatically for each deployed Web Service. Simply put, if you are serious about Web Services and have the resources, make the effort to learn and use Oracle JDeveloper 10*g*. The examples in this chapter are built using it. Doing this work manually (i.e., not exploiting the various tools and wizards available in Oracle JDeveloper 10*g*) requires considerably more reading and more development work, and has a much higher potential for error.

Oracle has identified Web Services as a key technology. The Oracle Technology Network (OTN) at http://otn.oracle.com/tech/webservices/index.html offers a vast amount of good information. In particular, the site provides extensive information on such things as JDeveloper extensions, online documentation, step-by-step tutorials, code samples, discussion forums, technical documents, and much more.

What are Web Services? Stated in its simplest form, a service is a program. Web Services allow programs to be:

- Published
- Located

- Invoked from the network (i.e., the Web)

In other words, Web Services simply allow a program on another server to be run as if that program is running on your server. You could think of a Web Service as a remote subroutine which can be written in any language and could be running anyplace in the world. As you'll see in this chapter, this provides the ultimate scalability, reliability, and openness developers previously only dreamt about. Service-oriented architecture was mentioned above. It's made up of services (i.e., programs) that communicate via Web Services. Web Services are commonly described as:

- **Self-contained objects** "Black boxes" that live on their own. You'll see that this is true and they do stand on their own.
- **Self-describing** Meaning they can tell you all about their required inputs and expected outputs for each available method (i.e., program unit) within them. We'll talk about the WSDL (pronounced wiz-dil) in a minute.
- **Modular** We remember from our best practices that modular programming is good. A Web Service can be as granular as you want it to be.
- **Loosely coupled** If the Web Service is changed (i.e., new inputs and outputs are added), it won't break the programs calling it.
- **Platform and application independent** This one speaks for itself, but the fact that you can call a Web Service and it doesn't matter what platform it's running on, or what application it's part of, is very powerful.

You've probably heard that entire trade shows have been built around Web Services. Many vendors are making BIG bets on them (i.e., former Forte developers). While Web Services have revolutionary potential to transform technology, adoption of all new technologies is evolutionary (and MUCH slower than people had hoped). The adoption of Web Services should increase dramatically in the near future as Web Services have the additional benefit of making use of existing infrastructures. In other words, a Web Service can call existing programs that are in place today.

Can you think of something that has provided huge improvement in the business communications world? How about the fax machine? With fax machines, you can close a contract in 1/10th the time you could previously. It has been so successful that more than 150 billion faxes are now sent each year. What does that have to do with Web Services? One of the first business applications of Web Services is to enable better business communication, hence better business integration. Web Services are cheap business links that drive strategy. If you're interested in learning more on where to begin implementing Web Services into your organization, we recommend reading papers from Ted Schadler of Forrester Research (http://www.forrester.com/find).

Where to Start

Web Services can be used to crush the barriers to business integration. Business integration is a good idea at any time, but your recovery will accelerate if you use Web Services to work more closely with your suppliers and customers. Think of Web Services as XML links to customers, partners, and operating groups. Without them, you'll write one-to-one interfaces. You would write the interface for one vendor. Let's just say it takes you ten weeks to write the interface that would link your procurement system to your supplier's inventory system. Each additional vendor interface would take ten weeks, as well. Prior to Web Services, you had to have the same integration vendor on each side, too. A lot of resources (time, money, etc.) would need to be invested upfront on a proprietary technology and virtual area network (VAN) connection. Because Web Services use an open standard, you can use any vendor, can add a thin layer of technology over your existing systems, and, in many cases, send data encrypted over the public Internet. Instead of taking ten weeks to integrate the first vendor, it will take two to three weeks with Web Services. For subsequent vendors in the "old world," it took another ten weeks. With Web Services, it will take you about one week. That's ten times faster!

You can use Web Services to link to your suppliers, connect to customers, or simplify your internal interfaces—all using a fraction of the resources needed to develop, test, and implement using traditional (i.e., non-Web Services development) methods. The low-hanging fruit for Web Services is where the pain is greatest: linking to customers and suppliers. Maybe you want to open your production schedules to partners and suppliers or tie your order management system to your customer's purchasing software. There is also a great opportunity to simplify your internal systems. You could retool your pricing engine with Web Services interfaces to offer it as an internal service. Web Services also are the right technology for simplifying internal systems. Instead of building the same core functionality over and over again in each business unit or for each customer channel, build it once and reuse it everywhere. As an example, a very large bank has seven mortgage rate calculators—one for each channel and each kind of customer. That causes all kinds of problems: the rates can be different over the phone than from the web site, and the calculators are seven times the effort to build and maintain. What's the solution? One mortgage rate calculator with Web Services interfaces that is used in every channel and application. What does this mean? The Web Services solution provides a more consistent customer experience, more control over a business driver, and lower total cost of ownership.

Now that you know where to get started, the next question is how to get started. First, you must bring IT, business, and marketing together. Next, you'll need to prioritize the services you should build to the business.

Buzzwords of Web Services

All new technologies are inundated with buzzwords and acronyms that attempt to describe them, but these often produce the opposite effect of making the new technology harder to understand. The Web Services world has its share, as well. To explain the buzzwords, think of a Web Service as a package that will be shipped to a customer.

XML

XML, or eXtensible Markup Language, is used to build Web Service messages that go from one server to another. As you'll see in this chapter, by using JDeveloper, the developer will not need to know much about it to create a Web Service. When it comes to shipping our package to the customer, XML is the alphabet.

SOAP

SOAP, or Simple Object Access Protocol, is what enables the exchange of information over a network. SOAP is an XML-based (text) protocol specification. In other words, SOAP messages are built with XML. The messages are, therefore, platform, protocol, and language independent. The standard doesn't specify a transport mechanism. As a result, messages can travel on HyperText Transfer Protocol/Secure HyperText Transfer Protocol (HTTP/HTTPS); i.e., web site POSTs, Simple Mail Transfer Protocol, or SMTP; i.e., via e-mail, or File Transfer Protocol (FTP); i.e., file transfer. SOAP provides a standard so developers don't have to invent a custom XML message for every service they want to make available. The SOAP message specifies the service name, the method names implemented by the service, the method signature of each method, and address of the service implementation (expressed as a Uniform Resource Identifier, or URI). Oracle supports the HTTP and HTTPS transports only. The good news about HTTP and HTTPS is that this information is provided through firewall-friendly ports—messages are transported using existing communications protocols and methods. When it comes to the package that we're sending to our customer, SOAP addresses the envelope or package.

WSDL

WSDL, or Web Services Description Language, is actually a file containing XML that describes the Web Service interfaces and locations; it describes the methods or programs that you can call in the Web Service and input/output parameters for each method. When it comes to the package that we're sending to our customer, WSDL describes the message. Think of WSDL as the metadata about the Web Service. This is the mechanism that provides the "self-describing" qualities of a Web Service.

UDDI

UDDI, or Universal Description, Discovery, and Integration, specifies a standard business registry by which people can publish/discover information about Web Services. It also specifies a directory naming service (DNS) for business applications. UDDI registry components include:

- **White Pages** contact information for a given business
- **Yellow Pages** information that categorizes businesses (industry, product, etc.)
- **Green Pages** technical descriptions of provided Web Services

There are currently a number of UDDI providers, including Oracle (http://otn.oracle.com/tech/webservices/htdocs/uddi/otnuddi.html), Microsoft (http://uddi.microsoft.com), IBM (http://www-3.ibm.com/software/solutions/webservices/uddi/), and SAP (http://udditest.sap.com). When it comes to the package we're sending to our customer, UDDI is the directory of services that we can use.

Conceptual Technical Overview

It's important to understand how all of these acronyms come together to form a technical solution. Assuming a Web Service has been created (details of which will be discussed shortly), it is appropriate at this juncture to understand the mechanics of how a Web Service gets called. For a visualization of the following steps, refer to Figure 17-1:

- **Step 1** Once the service is created, a WSDL file is created that can be registered or published. The WSDL file can be published in a file, on the Internet, or in a service directory (i.e., using UDDI).
- **Step 2** A client that wishes to use the Web Service can learn about it via the self-describing WSDL file or through UDDI.
- **Step 3** Once a Web Service client understands the inputs, outputs, and methods available, it will execute the service remotely, but transparently, to the client. The request to execute the service is made via SOAP (which is composed of XML) through HTTP or HTTPS to the SOAP processor. The SOAP processor breaks down the SOAP message to understand which service is being called and to determine the input parameters to pass along to the service. The service is called, which returns its respective output parameters. The SOAP processor packages the results into a resulting SOAP message that is transmitted back to the Web Service client.
- **Step 4** The client extracts the output parameters from the SOAP message and returns this information to the calling program (in its native speak).

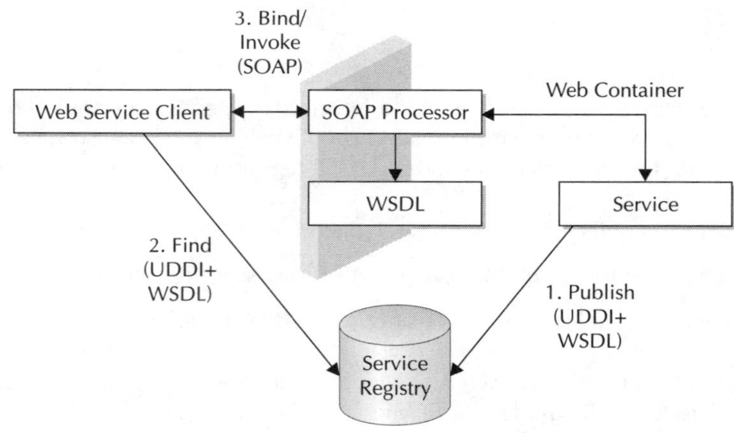

FIGURE 17-1. *Web Services conceptual overview*

The client program doesn't realize the "subroutine" that it just called exists on another server; rather, it just knows it received its results.

Creating/Developing Web Services

As we mentioned in the opening section of this chapter, the good news is that Oracle makes creating Web Services from existing code really easy for developers. In fact, by using Oracle JDeveloper 10*g*, any PL/SQL package or Java class can be turned into a Web Service by using the point-and-click options demonstrated in this chapter. All examples in this chapter were created using Oracle JDeveloper 10*g*.

Start a New Project

When working with a new set of codes, such as the following Web Services application, it is always a good idea to start a new project in Oracle JDeveloper 10*g*. Projects are also known as applications in Oracle JDeveloper 10*g*. In the Applications Navigator, which is shown in Figure 17-2, right-click on Applications and choose New Application Workspace.

The application needs to be named before working with it. For this example, as shown in Figure 17-3, the application is called Oracle10gWebServices. Files that constitute the application can be placed into a directory of your choice. Select No Application Template. Then click OK.

At this point, you will have a blank application with a single project in it. You're now ready to begin creating your Web Services.

It's best if you don't have any spaces in you application name. This can cause a problem when creating the Web Service. It has been known to return an internal error (No. 500) with a java compiler (javac) error. This is due to the space in the enterprise application name.

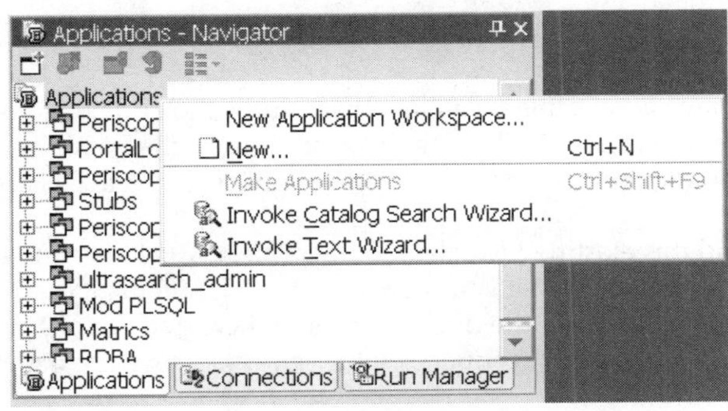

FIGURE 17-2. *The Applications Navigator*

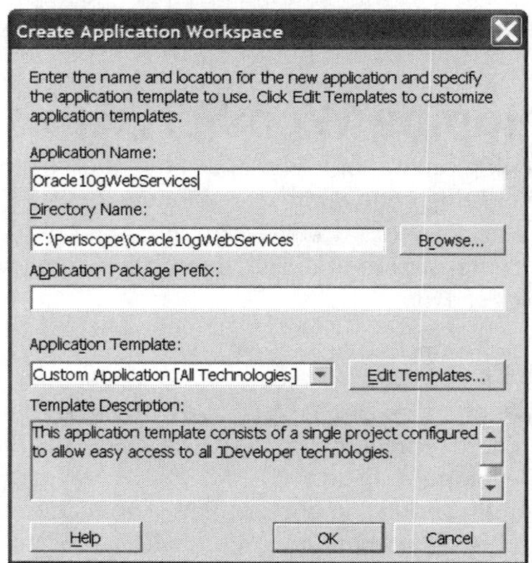

FIGURE 17-3. *Name your application*

Java Class-Based Web Services

In each of the examples below, we have existing Java classes we've written that we'd like to make available to the world via a Web Service. Java classes can be deployed as stateless or stateful Web Services—meaning that state is either preserved or not preserved between calls to the Web Service, respectively.

Stateless Java Web Services

For this example, we have an existing Java class that returns the current status of a database (i.e., up or down). Each time the class is called, the current status of the database will be displayed; it is not necessary to note if the class has been called previously, so this is an example of a stateless Java Web Service.

It's now time to add this existing Java class to my project. Click the Add to Project button, find the existing stateless Java class that you wish to add, as shown in Figure 17-4, and click Open.

If the file you're adding is not in the directory that you created your application in, you'll need to verify that you wish to add this directory to your project source path, as shown in Figure 17-5.

At this point, the Java class is now part of your project. In Oracle JDeveloper 10*g*, there are two ways to create a Web Service from this class. One method is to right-click on the class and then select Generate Web Service from Class (displayed in Figure 17-6):

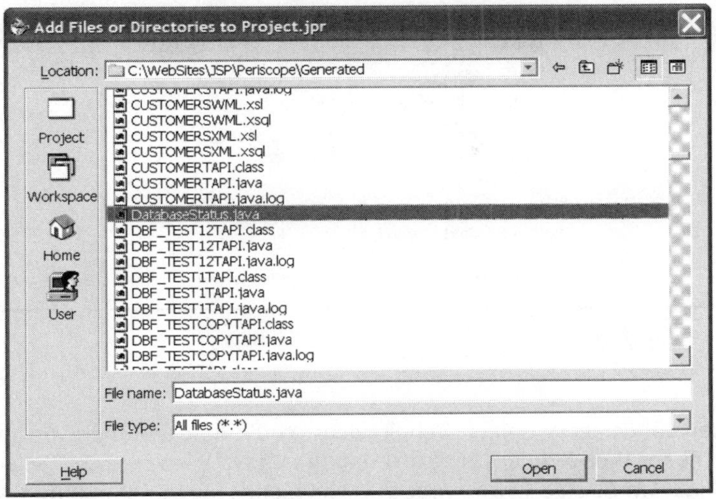

FIGURE 17-4. *Add a file to the project*

Using this method automatically generates all of the necessary components to turn this class into a Web Service without prompting you for any options. This option will name the Web Service "MyWebService1," expose all of the available methods in the class, and create a stateless class. Given this class only has one method (we wish to expose that method) and the desire is to create a stateless class, this method of automated Web Service creation works just fine. If you choose this method of Web Service creation, you can skip down to the section labeled Web Service Object Generated at this point.

The other method that can be used to create a Web Service is the wizard-based approach. Selecting File | New from the main Oracle JDeveloper 10*g* menu will bring up the New Gallery window, as shown in Figure 17-7.

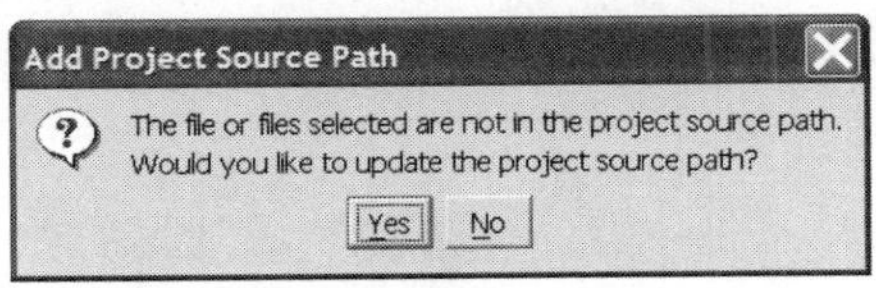

FIGURE 17-5. *Add the project source path*

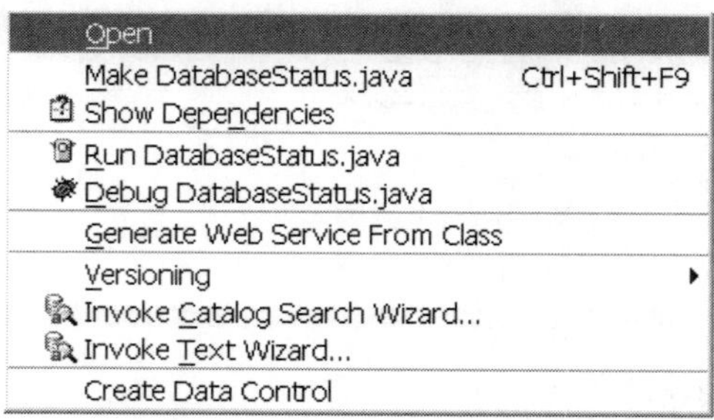

FIGURE 17-6. *Options for the Java class*

Under the General category, select Web Services. You'll note that there are a number of options available for Web Services. The first option is "Java Web Service." Select it, and then click OK. This starts a three-step wizard process, which ends up with the same results as the above right-click option. However, it does allow greater flexibility because the developer can specify choices relating to the generation and behavior of the Web Service as he goes through the wizard. Either option also allows modification of the Web Service with a three-tab Web Service modification window.

In Step 1, shown in Figure 17-8, a Java class needs to be selected that will be the basis of the Web Service you are attempting to create. In this figure, the DatabaseStatus Java class was selected—it was named DatabaseStatus.

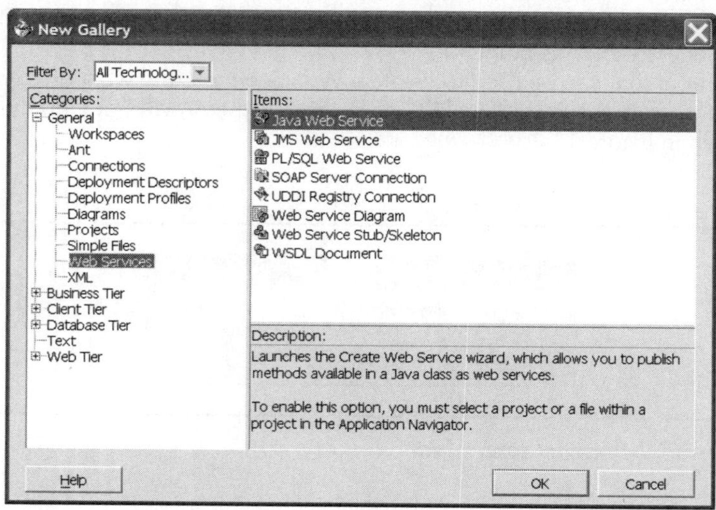

FIGURE 17-7. *The New Gallery window*

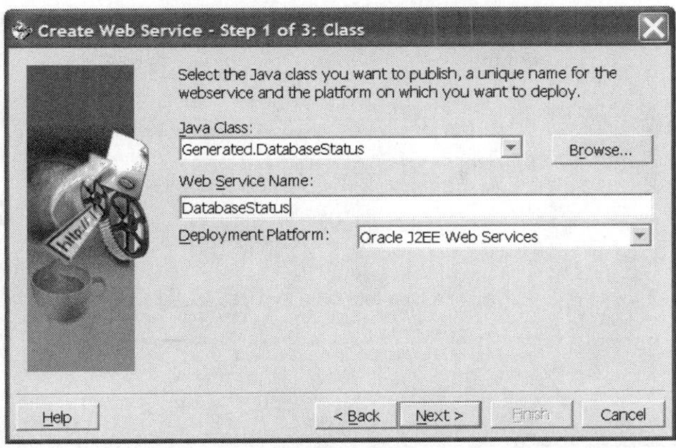

FIGURE 17-8. *Step 1 of 3 in the Web Service wizard*

Next, the methods to be exposed in the Web Service are selected (see Figure 17-9). Because this is going to be a stateless Web Service, the "Stateful" check box is left unselected. Clicking Next moves us to Step 3 in the wizard.

At this point, you can choose the port of your application server and the application server that this Web Service will be deployed to (commonly referred to as an endpoint), as well as the name space for the WSDL file that is generated (see Figure 17-10). The other fields on this page (Endpoint and Target Namespace) are automatically filled in (and not editable) based on the application server you choose to deploy the Web Service to.

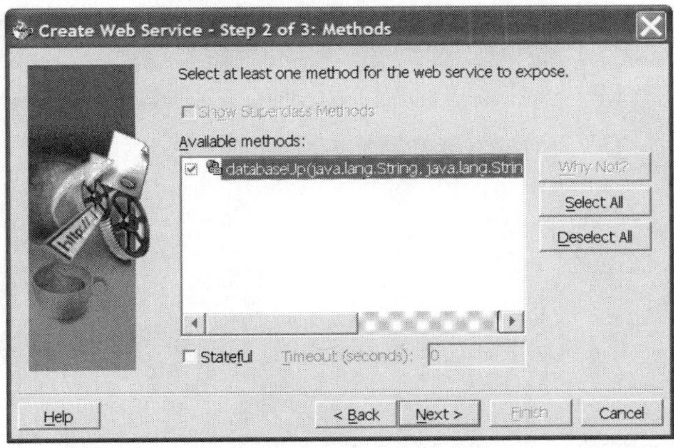

FIGURE 17-9. *Step 2 of 3 in the Web Services wizard*

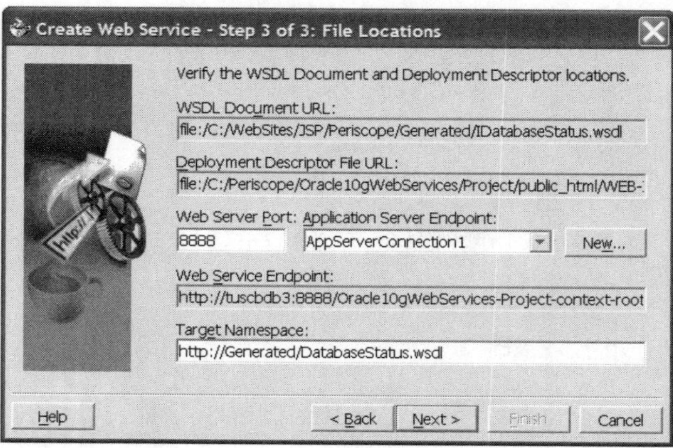

FIGURE 17-10. *Step 3 of 3 in the Web Service wizard*

If you haven't previously created an application server deployment profile, you can click on New at this time.

Once the appropriate fields on this page have been filled in, click Next.

The final page congratulates you on the completion of the creation of your Web Service, as shown in Figure 17-11. Simply click Finish at this point.

Web Service Object Generated The Applications Navigator will now include two new objects, as shown in Figure 17-12. The objects include the new Web Service (named DatabaseStatus) and the Web Service deployment resource (WebServices.deploy).

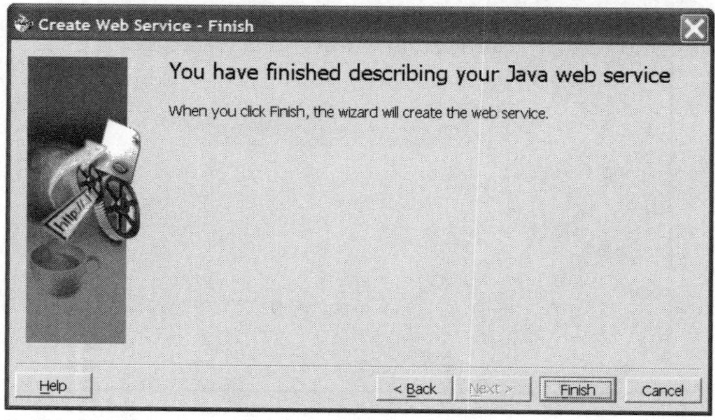

FIGURE 17-11. *Create Web Service finishing page*

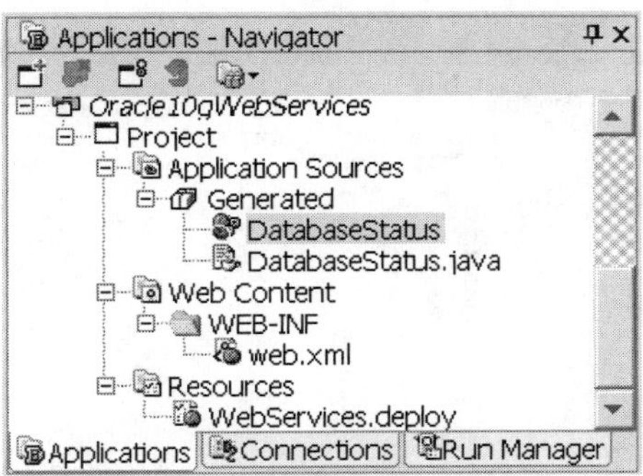

FIGURE 17-12. *Applications Navigator with new Web Service object*

Web Service Object Components Click on the new Web Service object (i.e., the first DatabaseStatus object in Figure 17-12). As shown in Figure 17-13, two objects appear in the structure window: a WSDL file and a Java file. You can select either object and view the contents of these automatically generated files. Oracle JDeveloper 10*g* automatically creates the WSDL file based on the inputs and outputs of the methods exposed. This is a prime example of the power of Oracle JDeveloper 10*g*'s Web Service wizard. If you read through the WSDL, you'll also understand why so many books require a considerable number of pages to discuss XML (the basis of the WSDL file) and WSDL structure. Using Oracle JDeveloper 10*g*, the developer is spared the details of learning the intricate syntax of XML and WSDL and only needs to focus on the purpose they fulfill in the Web Services architecture.

Editing the Web Service Object If you double-click the Web Service object, a three-tab form will pop up allowing you to edit the Web Service object. This should look very familiar, as the three tabs are the same as the three steps in the wizard (see Figure 17-14). If any of the fields are modified in the pop-up, the underlying Java and WSDL files are changed correspondingly.

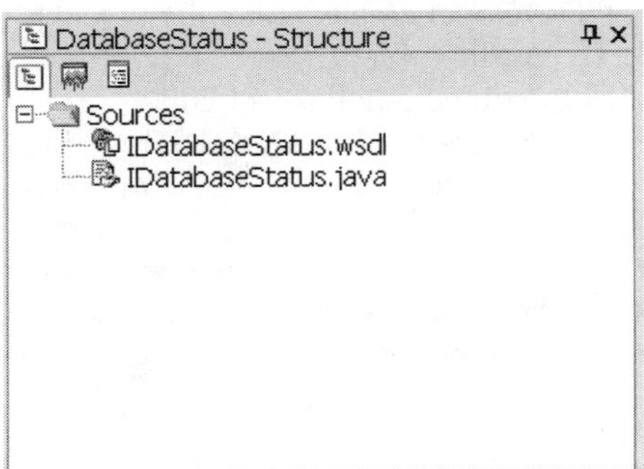

FIGURE 17-13. *Web Service structure*

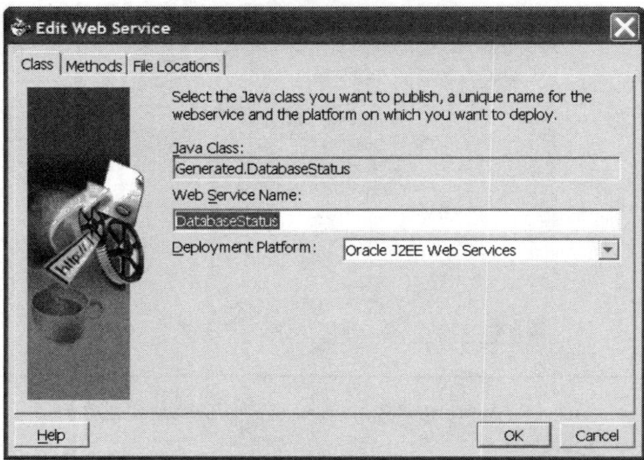

FIGURE 17-14. *Edit Web Service object*

We'll revisit deploying and executing this Web Service after covering stateful Java Web Services and PL/SQL-based Web Services. If you're interested in these topics, see the respective sections below.

Stateful Java Web Services

For this example, we had an existing Java class called DOMESTICTAPI that queries data from an Excel spreadsheet and returns batches of data as individual result sets. Because we plan on calling the service numerous times to get our complete result set, this Web Service needs to maintain state (i.e., know that it has been called before) between calls.

First, our Java class needs to be included in our project. Click the Add to Project icon to add the DOMESTICTAPI Java class as we did in Figure 17-4. Again, there are two ways to create a Web Service for this Java class. The object can be right-clicked, then edited, or the developer can go through the three-step Web Service wizard. For this example, we're going to right-click the object, then edit the object that JDeveloper creates. After the object is generated (see Figure 17-15), it is named MyWebService1. To edit the object, you can double-click it in the Applications Navigator window or right-click the object, then select Edit.

At this point, we renamed the Web Service to DOMESTICTAPI (the same name as the Java class). We then clicked on the Methods tab as you see in Figure 17-16. The Web Service is made stateful by clicking the Stateful check box. We changed the timeout (seconds) from 0 to 20.

Our thinking here is that you're going to retrieve the next record set within 20 seconds or you must be done fetching records. If the same user calls this stateful Web Service after the 20-second time-out, she will get the beginning of the record set once again — i.e., it will start over.

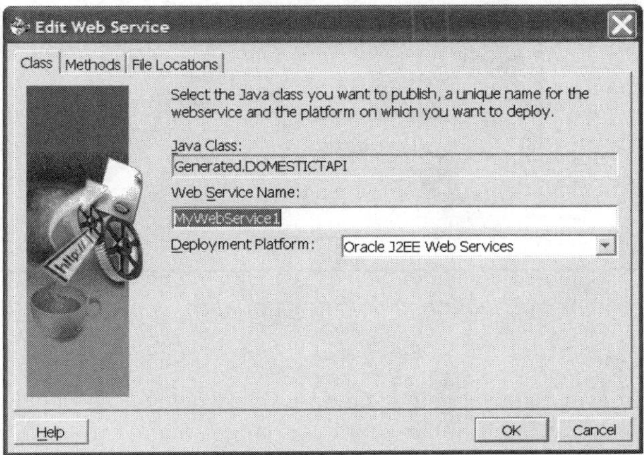

FIGURE 17-15. *Web Service for DOMESTICTAPI*

You can see in Figure 17-16 that the "fetchTable" method is grayed out. By clicking this method, then clicking the Why Not? button, as shown in Figure 17-17, you'll get a description as to why this method cannot be exposed as part of the Web Service.

In this case, it's because the oracle.sql.ARRAY object doesn't have an XML schema mapping. For this Web Service, we created another method called fetchTableSet and a record set called

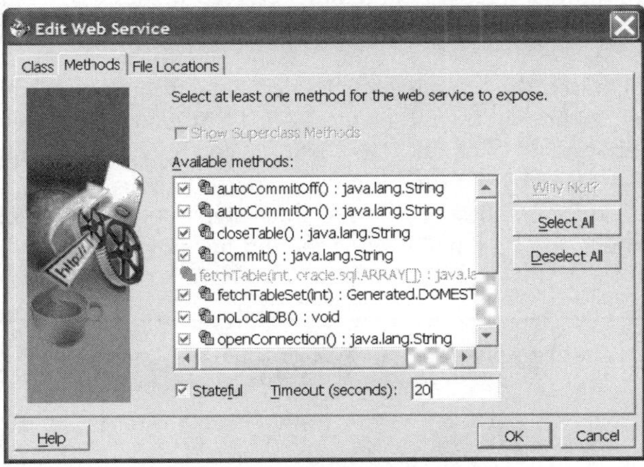

FIGURE 17-16. *Methods tab for DOMESTICTAPI*

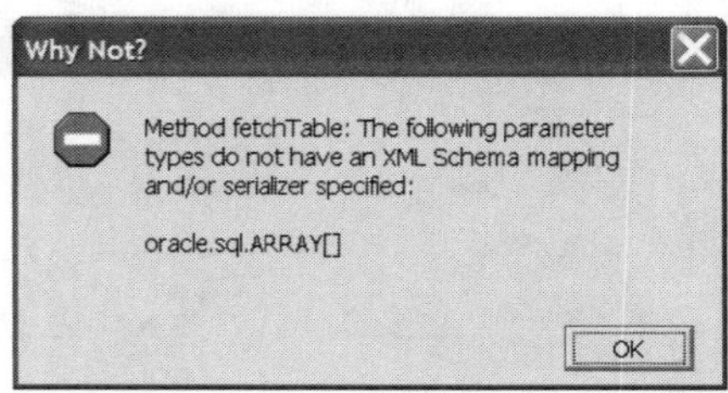

FIGURE 17-17. *The Why not? button and its functionality*

DOMESTICSet to return my data set using standard datatypes. Once the changes are made and you click OK" the wizard will notice that the changes made require regenerating the corresponding WSDL and Java files. Given these files already exist (and may have been hand-edited by you), Oracle JDeveloper 10*g* will prompt you, as shown in Figure 17-18, to confirm that you want to lose the changes.

Similar to the information shown in Figure 17-12, the new Web Service object will appear in the Navigation Window. We'll talk about the deployment and use of this stateful Java Class Web Service shortly.

PL/SQL-based Web Services

For this example, we will expose the "COMPANY" PL/SQL package that comes with the SCOTT example schema if you have created your test database by selecting the Load demo schemas option in the Database Configuration Assistant Wizard. This package contains procedures and functions to add new employees; retrieve an employee record, address, or status; set employee information; etc. This is a good example of a real-world package that can be exposed via a Web Service.

To create a PL/SQL-based Web Service, click File | New from the main JDeveloper menu. In the list of new gallery options shown in Figure 17-7, PL/SQL Web Service is one of the options available. Select this option and click OK. The PL/SQL Web Service publishing wizard begins, as shown in Figure 17-19. Click Next on this page.

The PL/SQL Web Service creation wizard has three steps (see Figure 17-20). You'll need to select a database connection. If a database connection has not previously been established,

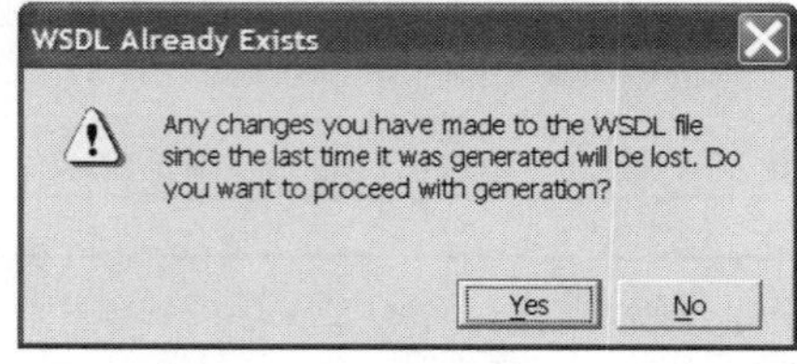

FIGURE 17-18. *Confirmation for generation*

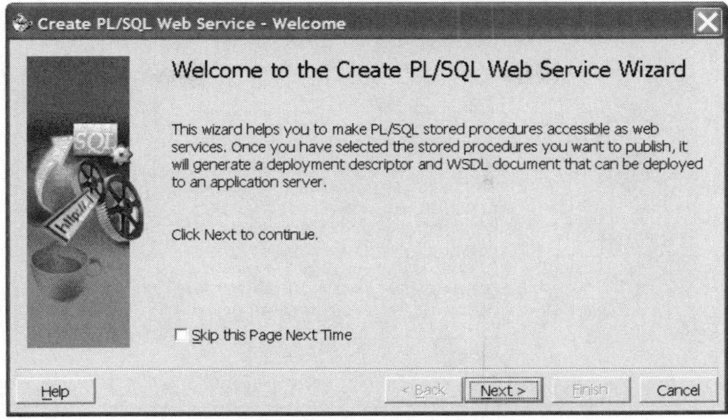

FIGURE 17-19. *The Create PL/SQL Web Service welcome page*

click New to create a new Java Database Connectivity (JDBC) connection to a specific username or schema (and password) in the database. In Figure 17-20, the SCOTT schema and specific package called COMPANY (from the drop-down list of packages in the SCOTT schema) was selected. A unique name is also provided for the service (COMPANY). The Web Service is packaged into a specific Java package (which is similar in concept to Oracle schemas). In this example, the Web Service is packaged into the same package as the other Web Services previously created, which is Generated.

It's now time to select which program units (procedures and functions) are to be exposed to the public in your Web Service (see Figure 17-21).

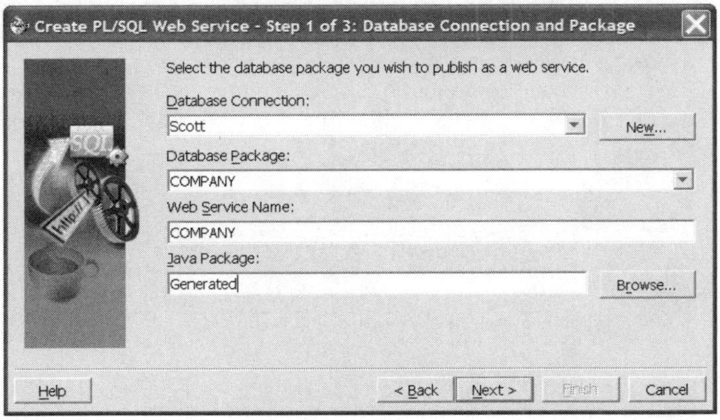

FIGURE 17-20. *Step 1 of 3 for create PL/SQL Web Service wizard*

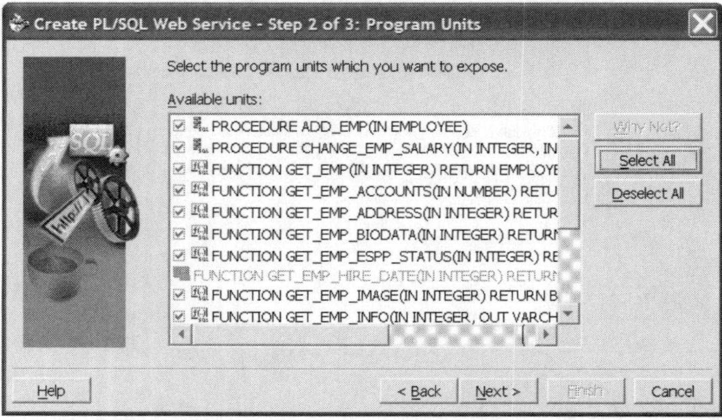

FIGURE 17-21. *Selecting program units to expose in Web Service*

We clicked on the Select All button. Again, you'll notice that some of the functions cannot be exposed. If you need to expose these functions, click the function, then click "Why Not?" You'll need to solve the problem before you create this Web Service. Once you're done, click "Next."

As you can see from Figure 17-22, the final step is the same as the final step when creating a Java class-based Web Service. The location of your target application server needs to be selected. The final page in the wizard is a success message.

Once you've completed the PL/SQL wizard, as shown in Figure 17-23, Oracle JDeveloper 10*g* will generate all of the necessary components for your PL/SQL-based Web Service.

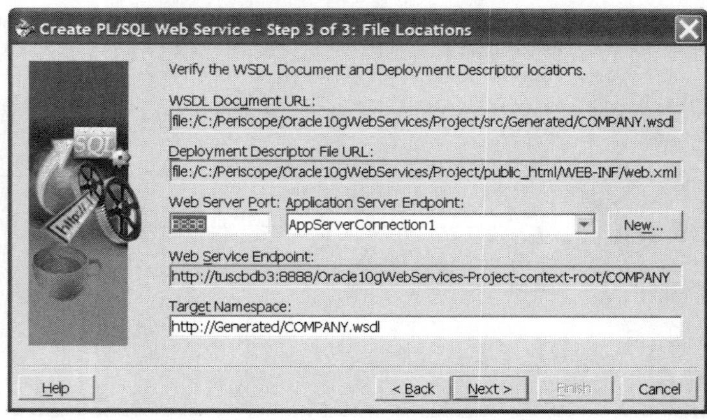

FIGURE 17-22. *Step 3 of 3 for the PL/SQL Web Service wizard*

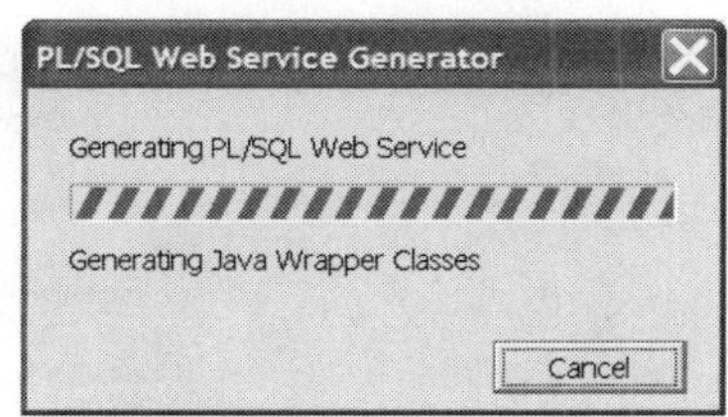

FIGURE 17-23. *PL/SQL Web Service generator*

Deploying Web Services

Now that we've created three different Web Services (i.e., stateless and stateful Java class-based Web Service and a PL/SQL-based Web Service), it's time to deploy our Web Services to an application server. As the Web Services were created, we were asked where we plan to deploy each one. A deployment profile (i.e., WebServices.deploy) was created based on your answer to this question.

At a minimum, you must include the Oracle SOAP library into your project. The Java classes that we deployed will require additional Java libraries. For our example Java classes, the specific JDBC libraries are required. If we're only going to connect to an Oracle Database via JDBC, this library is already included in the application server. In this example, we're going to include the Periscope libraries and a number of JDBC libraries.

First, we must include the libraries into our project. This is accomplished by editing the project properties. If you double-click the Project icon in the Application Navigator window, you'll be able to edit the project Libraries properties, as shown in Figure 17-24. We added the periscopeCom, JDBC Libraries, and Oracle SOAP to the Selected Libraries section.

Now it is time to edit the WebServices deployment profile to include the libraries for deployment. Double-click the WebServices.deploy icon and select the WEB-INF/lib section. As shown in Figure 17-25, you can include the libraries (probably the same libraries as above) needed to deploy this Web Service, and you can select the contributor libraries from the list of libraries set in the project properties.

When you're done selecting the libraries to include in the deployment, click OK. As shown in Figure 17-26, in the Applications Navigator right-click the WebServices.deploy icon and select Deploy to. Choose the application server profile (most likely previously created) to which you wish to deploy these Web Services.

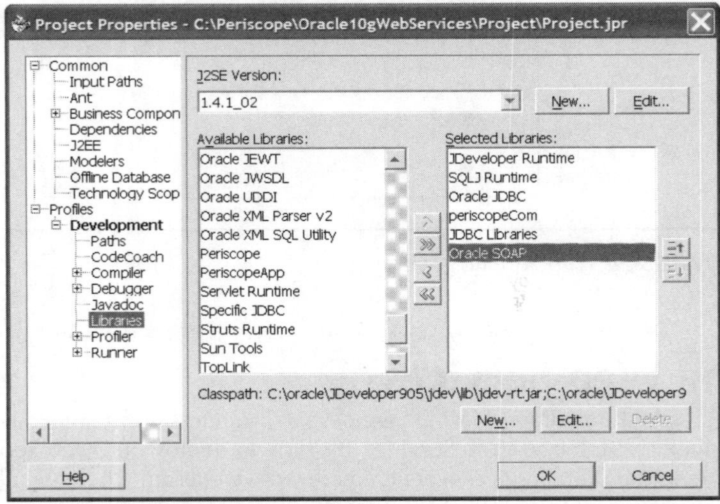

FIGURE 17-24. *Editing project libraries*

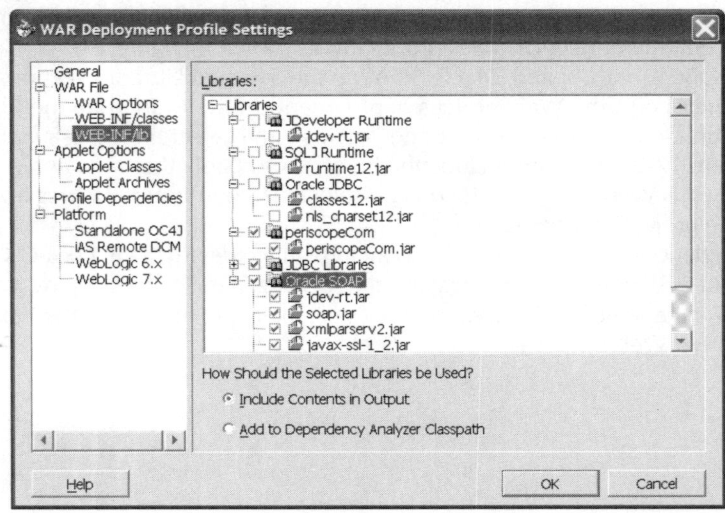

FIGURE 17-25. *Web Archive (WAR) deployment profile library settings*

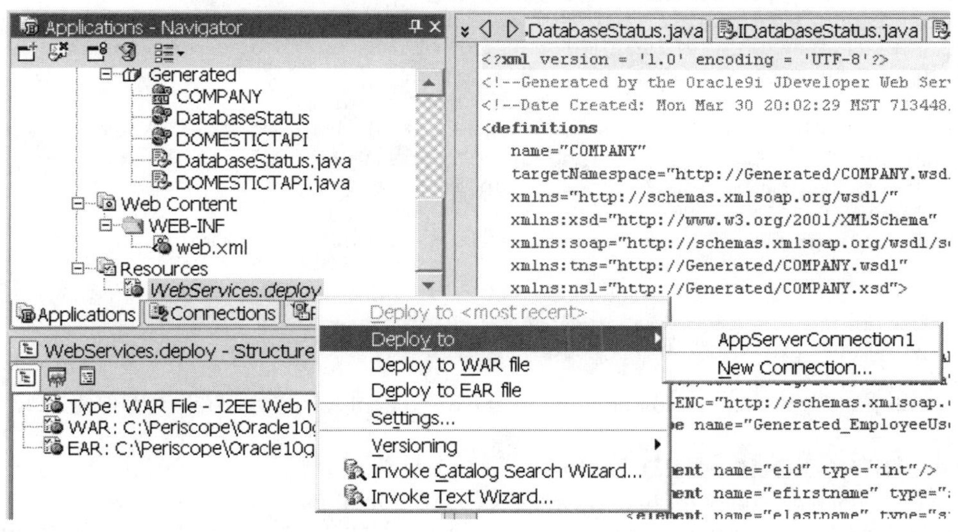

FIGURE 17-26. *Deploy the Web Service*

In the message window at the bottom of the JDeveloper window, a log of tasks to deploy the Web Services to the application server is displayed. That log might look something like this:

```
-- Deployment started. -- Jun 6, 69096798 2:45:52 AM
Target platform is Standalone OC4J (AppServerConnection1).
Wrote WAR file to C:\Periscope\Oracle10gWebServices\Project\WebServices.war
Wrote EAR file to
C:\Periscope\Oracle10gWebServices\Project\Oracle10gWebServices-Project-
WS.ear
Invoking OC4J admin tool...
C:\oracle\JDeveloper905\jdk\jre\bin\javaw.exe -jar C:\OC4J\j2ee\home\admin.jar
ormi://tuscbdb3/ admin **** -deploy -file C:\Periscope\Oracle10gWebServices\
Project\Oracle10gWebServices-Project-WS.ear -deploymentName
Oracle10gWebServices-Project-WS
Notification ==> Application Deployer for Oracle10gWebServices-Project-WS
STARTS [ 2004-02-08T00:15:01.167MST ]
Notification ==> Undeploy previous deployment
Notification ==> Copy the archive to C:\OC4J\j2ee\home\applications\
Oracle10gWebServices-Project-WS.ear
Notification ==> Unpacking Oracle10gWebServices-Project-WS.ear
Notification ==> Done unpacking Oracle10gWebServices-Project-WS.ear
Notification ==> Initialize Oracle10gWebServices-Project-WS.ear begins...
Notification ==> Unpacking WebServices.war
Notification ==> Done unpacking WebServices.war
Notification ==> Initialize Oracle10gWebServices-Project-WS.ear ends...
```

```
Notification ==> Initialize WebServices begins...
Notification ==> Initialize WebServices ends...
Notification ==> Application Deployer for Oracle10gWebServices-Project-WS
COMPLETES [ 2004-02-08T00:15:14.166MST ]
Exit status of OC4J admin tool (-deploy): 0
C:\oracle\JDeveloper905\jdk\jre\bin\javaw.exe -jar C:\OC4J\j2ee\home\admin.jar
ormi://tuscbdb3/ admin **** -bindWebApp Oracle10gWebServices-Project-WS
WebServices http-web-site /Oracle10gWebServices-Project-context-root
Exit status of OC4J admin tool (-bindWebApp): 0
Use the following context root(s) to test your web application(s):

http://tuscbdb3:8888/Oracle10gWebServices-Project-context-root
Elapsed time for deployment:  1 minute, 55 seconds
--  Deployment finished.  --    Jul 7, 68300421 5:27:17 AM
```

JDeveloper's one-click deployment makes it easy to deploy your Web Services.

Publishing Your Web Service to UDDI

Your Web Service can be published to Oracle's UDDI at http://otn.oracle.com/uddi/ui/publishingBase.jsp. You can get more information about UDDI at http://otn.oracle.com/tech/webservices/htdocs/uddi/index.html. The connections manager allows you to drill into each of the UDDI Registries.

Testing Web Services

Now that you have deployed your Web Service to an application server, it's time to test your Web Service. Ultimately you will want to write a client or at least a sample client to provide to your customers or vendors (i.e., users of the Web Service), but the quickest way to test the Web Service is via the Web Service home page.

Web Service Home Page

For each Web Service that you deploy, Oracle's Application Server automatically generates a supporting Web Service home page. The home page includes a link to the WSDL file, a link to each available method, and proxy links. If you forgot the URL to access each of your Web Services, simply double-click the Web Service and click the File Locations tab. As you can see in Figures 17-10 and 17-22, the Web Service endpoint field contains the URL.

For each of our three examples, the respective URLs are

- http://tuscbdb3.tusc.com:8888/Oracle10gWebServices-Project-context-root/DatabaseStatus
- http://tuscbdb3.tusc.com:8888/Oracle10gWebServices-Project-context-root/DOMESTICTAPI
- http://tuscbdb3.tusc.com:8888/Oracle10gWebServices-Project-context-root/COMPANY

Breaking down the above URLs:

- **http://** Hypertext transfer protocol that is used to access the application server from a browser (or client, too).
- **tuscbdb3.tusc.com** Name (including the domain name) of our application server.
- **8888** Port the application service is running on.
- **Oracle10*g*WebServices-Project-context-root** Root directory for our Web Services.
- **DatabaseStatus, DOMESTICTAPI, and COMPANY** Names of the specific Web Service.

We executed the DatabaseStatus URL, which resulted in a browser page showing the available methods (only one for this Web Service), as shown in Figure 17-27. Next, we clicked the databaseUp method, then entered a number of values, as shown in Figure 17-28. Finally, we executed the Web Service by clicking the Invoke button. You can see the results (in XML) of the invocation in Figure 17-29. As you can see from the result set, this procedure returns a Boolean (i.e., true or false) result.

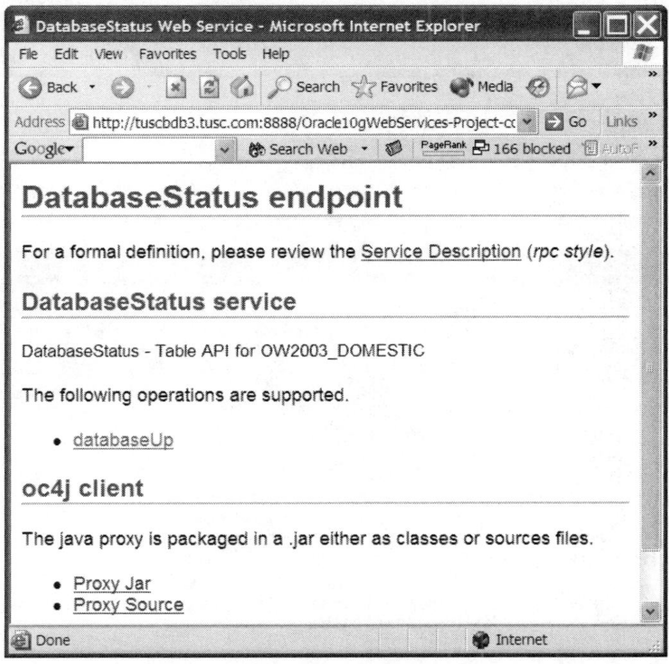

FIGURE 17-27. *DatabaseStatus browser home page filled in*

DatabaseStatus Web Service - Microsoft Internet Explorer

Address http://tuscbdb3.tusc.com:8888/Oracle10gWebServices-Project-context-root/

Click here for a complete list of operations.

databaseUp

Test

To test the operation using the HTTP GET protocol, click the 'Invoke' button.

Parameter	Type	Value
driver	string	easysoft.sql.jobDriver
connectionString	string	jdbc:easysoft://tuscbdb3/OW2003
username	string	username
password	string	password

Invoke

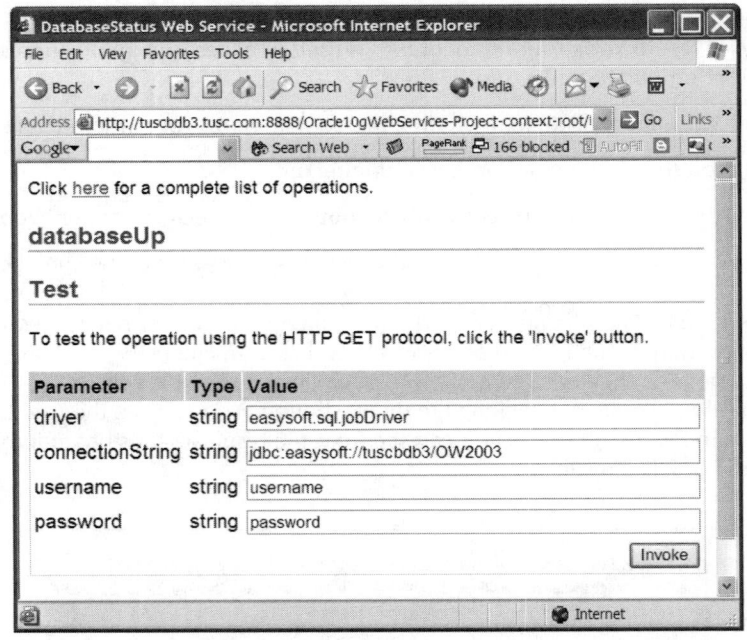

FIGURE 17-28. *databaseUp method's home page*

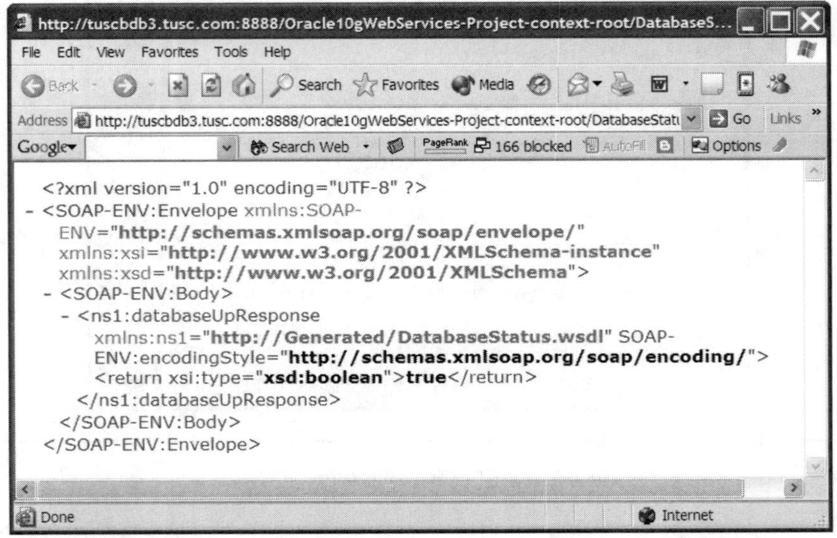

FIGURE 17-29. *Results of the databaseUp method Web Service execution*

We executed the DOMESTICTAPI URL, which resulted in the browser page showing the available methods, as depicted in Figure 17-30. This class required that we execute the openWebService, noLocalDB, and openTable methods before we could execute the fetchTableSet method. Finally, we executed the fetchTableSet method by clicking the Invoke button after entering the number of rows to return. You can see the results (in XML) of the invocation in Figure 17-31, which only shows a partial row from the DOMESTIC spreadsheet. If we execute the fetchTableSet method again within 20 seconds, we'll retrieve the next set of records from the DOMESTIC spreadsheet. Otherwise, the data set will again start at the beginning.

We executed the COMPANY URL, and then added an employee using the addEmp method. Next, we executed the getEmp method using an ID of 1, then clicked the Invoke button. You can see the results (in XML) of the invocation in Figure 17-32.

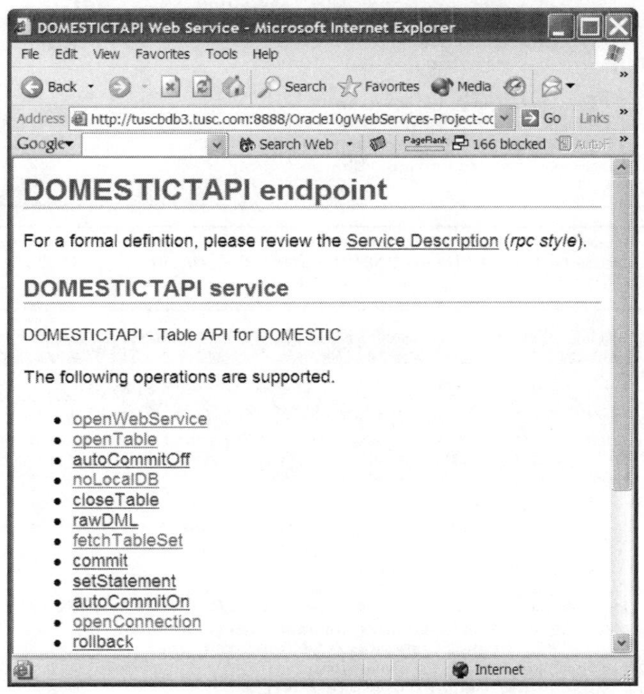

FIGURE 17-30. *DOMESTICTAPI browser home page filled in*

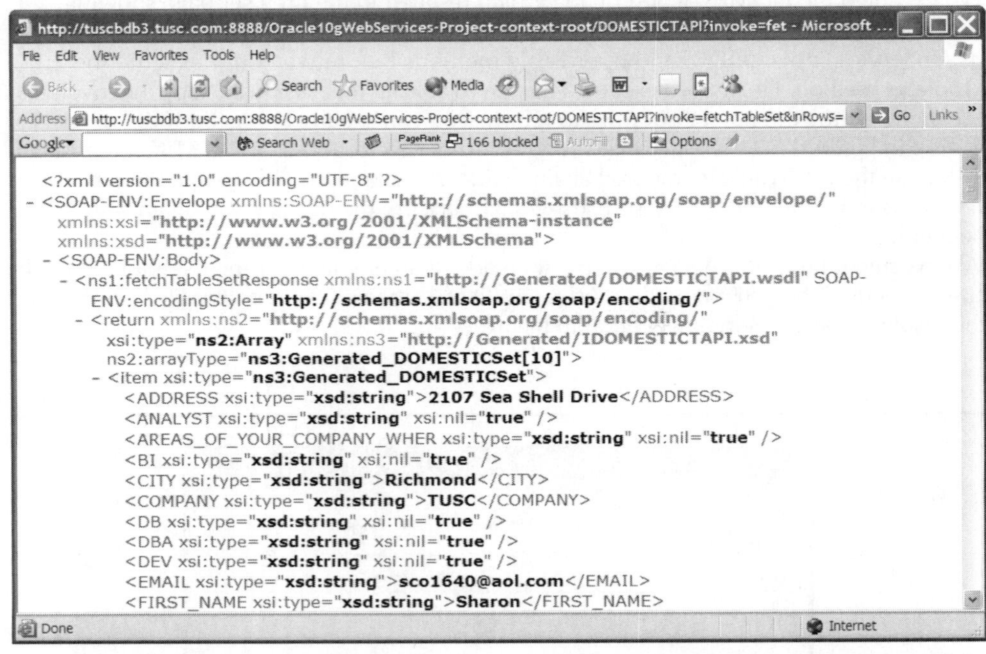

FIGURE 17-31. *Results of the fetchTableSet method execution*

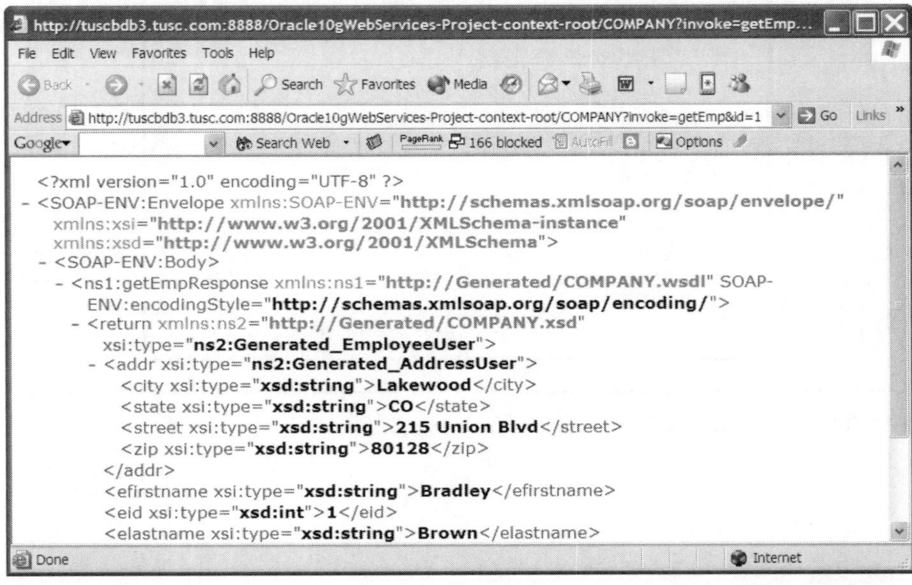

FIGURE 17-32. *Results of the getEmp method's execution*

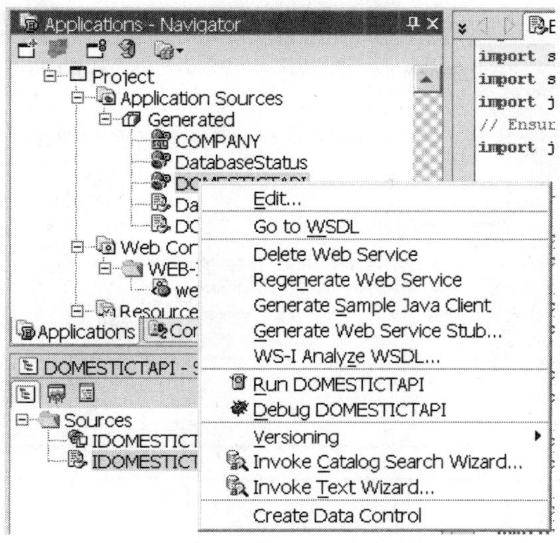

FIGURE 17-33. *Generate the Web Service stub wizard*

Building a Client that Uses a Web Service

This is where the process all comes together. Questions regarding the deployment of your Web Service will now need to be addressed:

- Is this Web Service going to be called internally?
- Are your partners, customers, or vendors going to call the Web Service?
- Have you been provided with a Web Service that you wish to call from your environment?

If you've created the Web Service and you want to write a stub so that it provides a client with a starting point to access the Web Service, Oracle JDeveloper 10*g* provides a wizard for this purpose. If you have been provided with the location of a WSDL file and you wish to create a stub based on a WSDL, Oracle JDeveloper 10*g* also provides a wizard for this purpose. We will discuss where Web Services that others have written can be located shortly.

Create Stub for Web Service Wizard

To create a stub for any of the Web Services created in this chapter, simply right-click on the Web Service's name and icon, then click the Generate Web Service Stub option, as shown in Figure 17-33.

There is also an option to generate a Web Service Client.

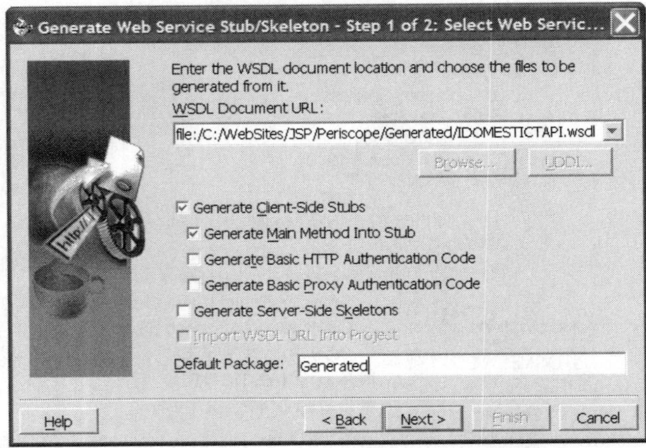

FIGURE 17-34. *Step 1 of 2*

This wizard will generate a stub that can be used as a starting point to call your Web Service. Figure 17-35 shows the generation of a stub for the DOMESTICTAPI Web Service.

In Figure 17-34, which is Step 1 of 2 in the Web Service Stub/Skeleton generation wizard, we chose to generate a main method in the stub. This allows us to easily test our Web Service by adding some code and running the Web Service stub class. Step 2 allows you to select the methods you wish to include/expose in the client. By default, all available methods are selected. The section labeled "Add your code here" is where the code in the main() method was added:

```
public static void main(String[] args)
  {
    try
    {
      DOMESTICTAPIStub stub = new DOMESTICTAPIStub();
      // Add your own code here.
      DOMESTICSet1 results[] = new DOMESTICSet1[5];
      stub.openWebService();
      stub.noLocalDB();
      System.out.println(stub.openTable("select distinct * from DOMESTIC where
COMPANY like '%TUSC%'"));
      results = stub.fetchTableSet(new Integer(10));
      for (int x=0; x<=10 && results[x] != null; x++)
      {
        System.out.println("Name of Person> " + results[x].getFIRST_NAME() + "
" + results[x].getLAST_NAME());
      }
    }
    catch(Exception ex)
    {
```

```
      ex.printStackTrace();
    }
  }
```

The output from the above stub class looks like:

```
OK
Name of Person> Anthony Catalano
Name of Person> Burk Sherva
Name of Person> Sharon Rogan
Process exited with exit code 0.
```

The stub class called the Web Service and returned the information as shown here. If you wish to monitor the Transmission Control Protocol/Internet Protocol (TCP/IP) packages and data that are transmitting from and to the Web Service, click the View menu, then select the TCP Packet Monitor on the menu as shown in Figure 17-35.

The TCP packet monitor (shown in Figure 17-36) allows you to browse through individual request and response TCP packets. This can be very helpful when debugging Web Service calls.

Create a Stub for Web Service Using a WSDL

If a URL to a WSDL file is provided, a stub can be created only knowing the URL. Oracle JDeveloper 10*g* knows how to read all of the information in the WSDL file. From the main menu, click File | New, then select the Web Services and Web Service Stub/Skeleton options. A window similar to the one shown in Figure 17-34 appears. The only difference is that Browse and UDDI are available for your selection. You can add a URL to the WSDL document URL

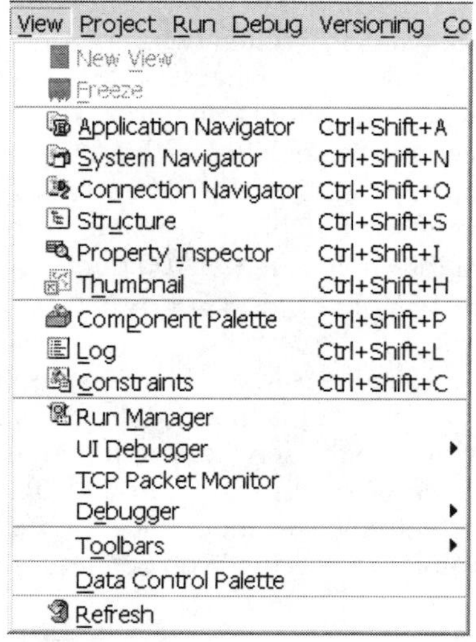

FIGURE 17-35. *A TCP packet monitor menu option*

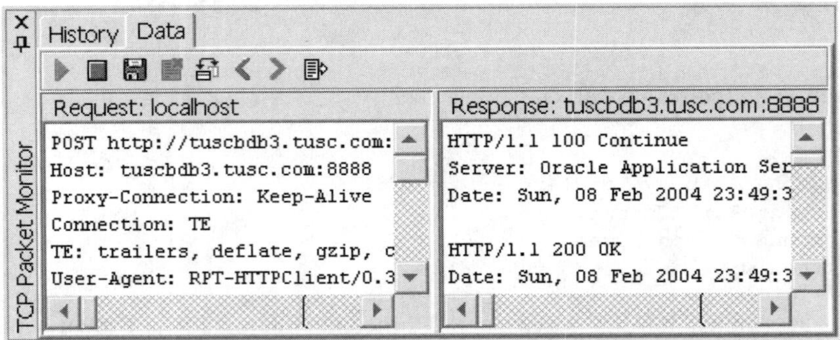

FIGURE 17-36. *A TCP packet monitor*

field. Once this information is filled in, Oracle JDeveloper 10*g* will read the WSDL file, figure out the available methods, show the list, and allow you to quickly develop a stub.

We'll discuss locations to find URLs shortly, but you can also click UDDI to find Web Services located in the Microsoft, IBM, Oracle, or, for that matter, any UDDI directory (UDDI will be discussed in more detail shortly). Oracle JDeveloper 10*g* makes this process very simple if you know the URL for the Web Service's WSDL file.

Locating a Web Service

If you're looking for a publicly available Web Service, there are two sites we like that provide this information: XMethods (http://www.xmethods.net/) and SalCentral (http://www.salcentral.com). When developers create a Web Service, they often register it on these sites. As time passes, more services will be listed in the UDDI directories because that's where they really belong. These web sites include complete descriptions, implementation information, etc., about each Web Service. Some of the services listed are "gamelike," such as "Letter Soup" and "Shakespeare," but most are business solutions such as "Stock Quotes," "View Area Codes For City," "Real Time Car Rental Quotes," and so forth. Many of the publicly available Web Services charge for the use of their service; some charge over a threshold, such as 100 quotes a day. When you use either site, you can search for a specific type of Web Service. For example, if you search for stock quotes on SalCentral, a list of available services is displayed.

This site tells whether the Web Service is free or if it charges per use; you can drill in for more information about each Web Service. Note that many of the services (on Salcentral) listed show that they are "FREE," but if you drill into the service, you'll find that the trial is free and that the use of the Web Service does cost money, typically per transaction. To determine whether a service is truly free, you must drill into the specific service for the details (i.e., read the fine print). On the XMethods site, once you select a specific Web Service, you'll see details for the delayed stock quotes Web Service.

Querying from UDDI

If you click UDDI in the Generate Web Service Stub/Skeleton or anyplace else, you will walk through a seven-step wizard for UDDI searches. Step 1 is simply a confirmation or informational step. In Step 2, you'll choose the UDDI directory that you wish to use (i.e., Oracle, Microsoft, or IBM) or you can click Create to add a new UDDI directory. In Step 3, you'll need to select whether you wish to search the directory by name (i.e., White Pages) or category (i.e., Yellow Pages). If you search by name, in Step 4 you'll type the text that you wish to search for and whether you wish to find an exact match and/or a case-sensitive match. Wildcards (i.e., %) can be used in your search. If you search by category, in Step 4 you'll be presented with a taxonomy of items to choose from based on the taxonomy classification you choose. Taxonomy classifications include UDDI types (i.e., based on the transport protocol, SOAP-based, or WSDL-based), NAICS (North American Industry Classification System, which includes breakdowns such as accommodations and food, agriculture, etc.), ISO 3166 (classifications are broken down by geographic area), or UNSPSC (United Nations Standard Products and Services Code, which uses the UNSPSC goods and services classifications). You can pick multiple categories. Once you select a category (or more than one), you can click Next. During Step 5, the UDDI directory is searched based on the search string or categories you selected in Step 4. During this step, you'll need to be connected to the Internet. If no matches are found, you'll need to go back to the prior page and change your criteria. For each match that is found, Oracle JDeveloper 10*g* will confirm whether a WSDL file exists for the Web Service and it will pull a description (if one exists) for each Model Name. You'll need to select a Web Service that is of interest to you. In step 6, you'll choose which services you wish to include in your stub. In the final step, you'll see a full description of the Web Service, the binds, and more information. This step is merely a confirmation step. From here, you simply continue creating the Stub as you did when you created a stub with the URL of a WSDL file.

If you have a favorite (or different than Oracle, Microsoft, or IBM) UDDI directory that you wish to use, you can add additional UDDI directories through the Oracle JDeveloper 10*g* interface, also.

Google's Free Web Service

Now you're ready to play with the power of Web Services. Google provides a truly free Web Service. You can get information about this Web Service at http://www.google.com/apis. From this site, download the Developers API archive and unzip it. It's packed with information about Google's free Web Services. You'll need to create an account with Google by providing an e-mail address (this information is provided in the instructions). The required license key is mailed to you. You're permitted to execute 1,000 queries per day per e-mail address (for free). We recommend that you create a new stub using the WSDL in the zip archive. It's fun to play with this Web Service. You'll need to edit the generated Java code to add the license key, query, and other information. All of the parameters are documented in an HTML file that is included in the documentation.

Periscope Virtualizes Google's Web Service

Using TUSC's Periscope, you can virtualize a Web Service to make it look like an Oracle table. In other words, you can make Google's HUGE database appear as if it's right in your own database, which allows us to execute a query such as the following:

```
SELECT *
FROM   google
WHERE  searchstring = 'RMOUG Brad Brown'
```

This query will read the results from Google's Web Service and return the data like it would any other Oracle table in your database.

To find out more about TUSC's Periscope, go to: http://www.tusc.com/oracle/technology/periscope_overview.html.

Summary

Today's Web Services are primarily behind the firewall. In fact, most Web Services are being deployed as low-cost integration alternatives. Vendors are integrating Web Services into their solutions and betting their future on this technology, but the overall adoption rate is slower than expected due to the IT slowdown.

The 10x factor makes Web Services a disruptive technology. You'll be betting on your application server vendor (i.e., Oracle). Web Services are not just for integration—they anchor a new software architecture. There are still plenty of opportunities in the Web Service space, such as service-level agreements (SLAs), for intracompany integration and service-oriented architectures, security, pricing models, monitors (for response times, load balancing, etc.), load balancing and failover, data integrity, and so much more.

One real strength of the Web Services model is that they can use your existing infrastructure and code base. This makes Web Services totally nondisruptive to implement within your environment.

We believe that every vendor (that has hopes of surviving in the future) will rewrite all of their APIs to make them Web Services. This will allow the likes of Oracle Applications, and software from PeopleSoft, Siebel, SAP, Baan, and others to integrate right out of the box.

Standards are a key part of the future if the service-oriented architecture is going to be successful. Fortunately NUMEROUS groups are working to come up with standards by industry. Without this, messages will be "proprietary"—making it more difficult to commoditize software products. These standards are similar to EDI X12 standards. If you're part of an industry, join a standards group. There are hundreds of groups out there (by industry) today. Our goal here is to give you a better feel for just how powerful Web Services (and Oracle JDeveloper 10*g*) are and why we believe they are the next big things for IT.

APPENDIX A

Further Reading

he following is a list of resources I found helpful when writing the book.

Chapter 1: Overview of Technologies

Documentation

"Oracle® Application Server 10*g* Administrator's Guide 10*g* (9.0.4)," Part Number B10376-02.

"Oracle® Application Server 10*g* Application Developer's Guide 10*g* (9.0.4)," Part Number B10378-01.

"Oracle® Application Server 10*g* Concepts 10*g* (9.0.4)," Part Number B10375-02.

"Oracle® Application Server 10*g* Installation Guide 10*g* (9.0.4) for AIX-Based Systems, hp HP-UX PA-RISC (64-bit), hp Tru64 UNIX, and Linux x86," Part Number B13658-02.

"Oracle® Application Server 10*g* Installation Guide 10*g* (9.0.4) for Microsoft Windows," Part Number B10433-01.

White Papers

Oracle Corporation. "Managing the Oracle Application Server with Oracle Enterprise Manager 10*g*."

Owen, Tracie A. "Oracle Application Server 10*g*: Basic Administration."

Web Sites

http://apache.org

http://jakarta.apache.org

http://java.sun.com/j2ee

http://modules.apache.org

http://portalcenter.oracle.com

http://www.oracle.com/technology/products/ias/as_sdk.html

http://www.oracle.com/technology/products/ias/index.html

http://www.oracle.com/technology/products/ias/toplink/index.html

http://www.oracle.com/technology/products/ias/web_cache/index.html

Chapter 2: Application Server Architecture

Documentation

"Oracle® Application Server 10*g* Security Guide 10*g* (9.0.4)," Part Number B10377-01.

"Oracle® Application Server Containers for J2EE User's Guide 10*g* (9.0.4)," Part Number B10322-01.

"Oracle® Application Server Single Sign-On Administrator's Guide 10*g* (9.0.4)," Part Number B13791-01.

"Oracle® Identity Management Concepts and Deployment Planning Guide 10*g* (9.0.4) for Windows or UNIX," Part Number B10660-01.

"Oracle® Internet Directory Administrator's Guide 10*g* (9.0.4)," Part Number B12118-01.

"Oracle® Process Manager and Notification Server Administrator's Guide 10*g* (9.0.4)," Part Number B12057-02.

White Papers

Oracle Corporation. "Oracle Application Server 10*g* (9.0.4): Overview of Oracle HTTP Server Components November 2003."

Web Sites

http://java.sun.com/j2ee

http://www.oracle.com/technology/products/id_mgmt/index.html

Chapter 3: Oracle Forms

Web Sites

http://www.oracle.com/technology/products/forms/index.html

Chapter 4: Oracle Reports

Documentation

"Oracle Reports Building Reports 10*g* (9.0.4)," Part Number B10602-01.

"Oracle Reports Tutorial 10*g* (9.0.4)," Part Number B10612-01.

White Papers

Weckerle, Philipp and Navneet Singh. "Oracle Reports – Tips and Techniques." Oracle Corporation.

Web Sites

http://www.oracle.com/technology/products/reports/index.html

Metalink note: Note:222332.1 – A Detailed Explanation of Oracle 9*i* Reports Security

Metalink note: Note:237301.1 – Logging and Tracing in Reports 9.0.2

Chapter 5: Oracle Discoverer

Documentation

"Oracle® Application Server Discoverer Plus Tutorial 10*g* (9.0.4)," Part Number B10269-01.

"Oracle® Application Server Discoverer Plus User's Guide 10*g* (9.0.4)," Part Number B10268-01.

"Oracle® Discoverer Administrator Tutorial 10*g* (9.0.4)," Part Number B10271-01.

"Oracle® Discoverer Desktop User's Guide 10*g* (9.0.4) for Windows," Part Number B10272-01.

White Papers

Sims, April. "Best Implementation Practices for Discoverer." Southern Utah University.

Slater, Phillip. "Putting Oracle9*i* Application Server Discoverer to Work on the Web: Best Practices." Oracle Corporation.

Web Sites

http://www.oracle.com/technology/products/discoverer/index.html

Chapter 6: Incorporating Forms, Reports, and Discoverer in AS

White Papers

Shmeltzer, Shay. "A Step by Step Guide to Upgrading Oracle Forms to the Web." Oracle Corporation.

Chapter 7: PL/SQL—The PL/SQL Web Toolkit and PSPs

Documentation

"Oracle® Database Application Developer's Guide—Fundamentals 10*g* Release 1 (10.1)," Part Number B10795-01.

Chapter 8: Portal Architecture

Documentation

"Oracle® Application Server Portal Configuration Guide 10*g* (9.0.4)," Part Number B13675-01.

"Oracle® Application Server Portal User's Guide 10*g* (9.0.4)," Part Number B10358-01.

White Papers

"Oracle® Application Server Portal 10*g* (9.0.4) Product Overview." Oracle Corporation.

"Oracle® Application Server Portal 10*g* (9.0.4) Technical Overview." Oracle Corporation.

Web Sites

http://portalcenter.oracle.com

http://www.oracle.com/technology/products/ias/portal/documentation.html

http://www.oracle.com/technology/products/ias/portal/index.html

Chapter 9: Portal Development, Part I

Documentation

"Oracle® Application Server Portal Developer's Guide 10*g* (9.0.4)," Part Number B13922-01.

"Oracle® Application Server Portal Error Messages Guide 10*g* (9.0.4)," Part Number B10608-01.

"Oracle® Application Server Portal User's Guide 10*g* (9.0.4)," Part Number B10358-01.

Web Sites

http://portalcenter.oracle.com

http://www.oracle.com/technology/products/ias/portal/documentation.html

http://www.oracle.com/technology/products/ias/portal/index.html

Chapter 10: Portal Development, Part II

Documentation

"Oracle® Application Server Portal Developer's Guide 10*g* (9.0.4)," Part Number B13922-01.

"Oracle® Application Server Portal Error Messages Guide 10*g* (9.0.4)," Part Number B10608-01.

"Oracle® Application Server Portal User's Guide 10*g* (9.0.4)," Part Number B10358-01.

"Oracle® Ultra Search User's Guide 10*g* (9.0.4)," Part Number B10896-01.

Web Sites

http://portalcenter.oracle.com

http://www.oracle.com/technology/products/ias/portal/documentation.html

http://www.oracle.com/technology/products/ias/portal/index.html

Chapter 11: Incorporating Forms, Reports, and Discoverer into Portal

Documentation

"Oracle® Application Server Portal Developer's Guide 10*g* (9.0.4)," Part Number B13922-01.

"Oracle® Application Server Portal User's Guide 10*g* (9.0.4)," Part Number B10358-01.

Web Sites

http://portalcenter.oracle.com

http://www.oracle.com/technology/products/ias/portal/documentation.html

Chapter 12: Java in the Oracle Database

Documentation

"Oracle® Database Java Developer's Guide 10*g* Release 1 (10.1)." Part Number B12021-02.

"Oracle® Database JDBC Developer's Guide and Reference 10*g* Release 1 (10.1)," Part Number B10979-02.

White Papers

Brown, Bradley D. "Introduction to Java for the PL/SQL Developer." TUSC.

Dorsey, Dr. Paul. "An Introduction to Java for PL/SQL Programmers." Dulcian, Inc.

Oracle Corporation, "Unleash the Power of Java Stored Procedures, An Oracle White Paper."

Web Sites

http://www.oracle.com/technology/tech/java/index.html

Java Technology Concept Map: http://java.sun.com/developer/onlineTraining/new2java/javamap/intro.html

Chapter 13: JDeveloper

White Papers

Brown, Bradley D. "Quick Web Development Using JDeveloper 10*g*." TUSC.

Dikmans, Lonneke. "Building Real-World Applications with JDeveloper: Best Practices." Transfer Solutions.

Web Sites

http://www.oracle.com/technology/products/jdev/index.html

Books

Faderman, Avrom, Peter Koletzke, and Paul Dorsey. *Oracle JDeveloper 10*g *Handbook."* Oracle Press, ISBN: 0072255838.

Oak, Harshad. *Oracle JDeveloper 10*g*: Empowering J2EE Development.* APress, ISBN: 1590591429.

Chapter 14: JSPs

Documentation

"Oracle® Application Server Containers for J2EE JSP Tag Libraries and Utilities Reference 10*g* (9.0.4)," Part Number B10319-01.

"Oracle® Application Server Containers for J2EE Support for JavaServer Pages Developer's Guide 10*g* (9.0.4)," Part Number B10320-01.

"Oracle® Application Server 10*g* Multimedia Tag Library for JSP User's Guide and Reference 10*g* (9.0.4)," Part Number B10445-01.

White Papers

Schalk, Chris. "Best Practices for Java Servlet and JSP Development." Oracle Corporation.

Web Sites

http://java.sun.com/products/jsp/

http://www.oracle.com/technology/tech/java/index.html

Metalink Note: Note:132992.1, "Developing and Deploying a BC4J JSP Application with 9*i*AS"

Chapter 15: Deploying EARs, WARs, JARs, and JSPs to AS

Documentation

"Oracle® Application Server 10*g* Administrator's Guide 10*g* (9.0.4)," Part Number B10376-01.

"Oracle® Application Server 10*g* Concepts 10*g* (9.0.4)," Part Number B10375-01.

"Oracle® Application Server Containers for J2EE User's Guide 10*g* (9.0.4)," Part Number B10322-01.

Chapter 16: XML

Documentation

"Oracle® Application Developer's Guide – XML 10*g* (9.0.4)," Part Number B12099-01.
"Oracle® XML Reference 10*g* (9.0.4)," Part Number B10926-01.

White Papers

Bernknopf, Jeff. "Developing XML Applications Using Oracle 9*i*'s XML DB Facility." MFG Systems Corporation.

King, John Jay. "Ready, Set, XML! Using Oracle XML Data." King Training Resources.

Kristjánsson, Magnús. "Doing XML with XML DB – Confessions of a Consultant." deCODE genetics & eMR software, Iceland.

Rosenow, Carol. "What a DBA Needs to know about XML." Qwest Communications.

Web Sites

http://www.oracle.com/technology/tech/xml/index.html

Books

Chang, Ben, Mark Scardina, and Stefan Kiritzov. "Oracle9*i* XML Handbook." Oracle Press, ISBN: 007213495X.

Chapter 17: Web Services

Documentation

"Oracle® Application Server Web Services Developer's Guide 10*g* (9.0.4)," Part Number B10447-01.

White Papers

Balusamy, Elangovan. "Web Services Development Made Easy."

Brown, Bradley D. "Oracle Web Services." TUSC.

Brown, Bradley. "Introduction to SOAP and Oracle Web Services." TUSC.

Louis, Regis. "Exploring Java and Web Services Development with Oracle JDeveloper 10*g*." Oracle Corporation.

Web Sites

http://www.oracle.com/technology/tech/webservices/index.html

Books

Deitel, Harvey M., Paul J. Deitel, and B. Duwaldt. *Web Services: A Technical Introduction.* Prentice Hall PTR, ISBN: 0613922808.

Symbols

A

B

C

P

Q

W

X

Y

INTERNATIONAL CONTACT INFORMATION

AUSTRALIA
McGraw-Hill Book Company
Australia Pty. Ltd.
TEL +61-2-9900-1800
FAX +61-2-9878-8881
http://www.mcgraw-hill.com.au
books-it_sydney@mcgraw-hill.com

CANADA
McGraw-Hill Ryerson Ltd.
TEL +905-430-5000
FAX +905-430-5020
http://www.mcgraw-hill.ca

GREECE, MIDDLE EAST, & AFRICA
(Excluding South Africa)
McGraw-Hill Hellas
TEL +30-210-6560-990
TEL +30-210-6560-993
TEL +30-210-6560-994
FAX +30-210-6545-525

MEXICO (Also serving Latin America)
McGraw-Hill Interamericana Editores
S.A. de C.V.
TEL +525-1500-5108
FAX +525-117-1589
http://www.mcgraw-hill.com.mx
carlos_ruiz@mcgraw-hill.com

SINGAPORE (Serving Asia)
McGraw-Hill Book Company
TEL +65-6863-1580
FAX +65-6862-3354
http://www.mcgraw-hill.com.sg
mghasia@mcgraw-hill.com

SOUTH AFRICA
McGraw-Hill South Africa
TEL +27-11-622-7512
FAX +27-11-622-9045
robyn_swanepoel@mcgraw-hill.com

SPAIN
McGraw-Hill/
Interamericana de España, S.A.U.
TEL +34-91-180-3000
FAX +34-91-372-8513
http://www.mcgraw-hill.es
professional@mcgraw-hill.es

UNITED KINGDOM, NORTHERN,
EASTERN, & CENTRAL EUROPE
McGraw-Hill Education Europe
TEL +44-1-628-502500
FAX +44-1-628-770224
http://www.mcgraw-hill.co.uk
emea_queries@mcgraw-hill.com

ALL OTHER INQUIRIES Contact:
McGraw-Hill/Osborne
TEL +1-510-420-7700
FAX +1-510-420-7703
http://www.osborne.com
omg_international@mcgraw-hill.com

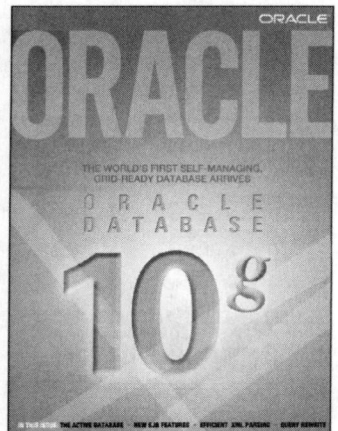

FREE SUBSCRIPTION

○ **Yes, please send me a FREE subscription to *Oracle Magazine*.** ○ **NO**

To receive a free subscription to *Oracle Magazine*, you must fill out the entire card, sign it, and date it (incomplete cards cannot be processed or acknowledged). You can also fax your application to +1.847.763.9638. **Or subscribe at our Web site at otn.oracle.com/oraclemagazine**

○ From time to time, Oracle Publishing allows our partners exclusive access to our e-mail addresses for special promotions and announcements. To be included in this program, please check this circle.

○ Oracle Publishing allows sharing of our mailing list with selected third parties. If you prefer your mailing address not to be included in this program, please check here. If at any time you would like to be removed from this mailing list, please contact Customer Service at +1.847.647.9630 or send an e-mail to oracle@halldata.com.

signature (required) X | date

name | title

company | e-mail address

street/p.o. box

city/state/zip or postal code | telephone

country | fax

YOU MUST ANSWER ALL TEN QUESTIONS BELOW.

① WHAT IS THE PRIMARY BUSINESS ACTIVITY OF YOUR FIRM AT THIS LOCATION? (check one only)

- □ 01 Aerospace and Defense Manufacturing
- □ 02 Application Service Provider
- □ 03 Automotive Manufacturing
- □ 04 Chemicals, Oil and Gas
- □ 05 Communications and Media
- □ 06 Construction/Engineering
- □ 07 Consumer Sector/Consumer Packaged Goods
- □ 08 Education
- □ 09 Financial Services/Insurance
- □ 10 Government (civil)
- □ 11 Government (military)
- □ 12 Healthcare
- □ 13 High Technology Manufacturing, OEM
- □ 14 Integrated Software Vendor
- □ 15 Life Sciences (Biotech, Pharmaceuticals)
- □ 16 Mining
- □ 17 Retail/Wholesale/Distribution
- □ 18 Systems Integrator, VAR/VAD
- □ 19 Telecommunications
- □ 20 Travel and Transportation
- □ 21 Utilities (electric, gas, sanitation, water)
- □ 98 Other Business and Services

② WHICH OF THE FOLLOWING BEST DESCRIBES YOUR PRIMARY JOB FUNCTION? (check one only)

Corporate Management/Staff

- □ 01 Executive Management (President, Chair, CEO, CFO, Owner, Partner, Principal)
- □ 02 Finance/Administrative Management (VP/Director/ Manager/Controller, Purchasing, Administration)
- □ 03 Sales/Marketing Management (VP/Director/Manager)
- □ 04 Computer Systems/Operations Management (CIO/VP/Director/ Manager MIS, Operations)

IS/IT Staff

- □ 05 Systems Development/ Programming Management
- □ 06 Systems Development/ Programming Staff
- □ 07 Consulting
- □ 08 DBA/Systems Administrator
- □ 09 Education/Training
- □ 10 Technical Support Director/Manager
- □ 11 Other Technical Management/Staff
- □ 98 Other

③ WHAT IS YOUR CURRENT PRIMARY OPERATING PLATFORM? (select all that apply)

- □ 01 Digital Equipment UNIX
- □ 02 Digital Equipment VAX VMS
- □ 03 HP UNIX
- □ 04 IBM AIX
- □ 05 IBM UNIX
- □ 06 Java
- □ 07 Linux
- □ 08 Macintosh
- □ 09 MS-DOS
- □ 10 MVS
- □ 11 NetWare
- □ 12 Network Computing
- □ 13 OpenVMS
- □ 14 SCO UNIX
- □ 15 Sequent DYNIX/ptx
- □ 16 Sun Solaris/SunOS
- □ 17 SVR4
- □ 18 UnixWare
- □ 19 Windows
- □ 20 Windows NT
- □ 21 Other UNIX
- □ 98 Other
- 99 □ None of the above

④ DO YOU EVALUATE, SPECIFY, RECOMMEND, OR AUTHORIZE THE PURCHASE OF ANY OF THE FOLLOWING? (check all that apply)

- □ 01 Hardware
- □ 02 Software
- □ 03 Application Development Tools
- □ 04 Database Products
- □ 05 Internet or Intranet Products
- 99 □ None of the above

⑤ IN YOUR JOB, DO YOU USE OR PLAN TO PURCHASE ANY OF THE FOLLOWING PRODUCTS? (check all that apply)

Software

- □ 01 Business Graphics
- □ 02 CAD/CAE/CAM
- □ 03 CASE
- □ 04 Communications
- □ 05 Database Management
- □ 06 File Management
- □ 07 Finance
- □ 08 Java
- □ 09 Materials Resource Planning
- □ 10 Multimedia Authoring
- □ 11 Networking
- □ 12 Office Automation
- □ 13 Order Entry/Inventory Control
- □ 14 Programming
- □ 15 Project Management
- □ 16 Scientific and Engineering
- □ 17 Spreadsheets
- □ 18 Systems Management
- □ 19 Workflow

Hardware

- □ 20 Macintosh
- □ 21 Mainframe
- □ 22 Massively Parallel Processing
- □ 23 Minicomputer
- □ 24 PC
- □ 25 Network Computer
- □ 26 Symmetric Multiprocessing
- □ 27 Workstation

Peripherals

- □ 28 Bridges/Routers/Hubs/Gateways
- □ 29 CD-ROM Drives
- □ 30 Disk Drives/Subsystems
- □ 31 Modems
- □ 32 Tape Drives/Subsystems
- □ 33 Video Boards/Multimedia

Services

- □ 34 Application Service Provider
- □ 35 Consulting
- □ 36 Education/Training
- □ 37 Maintenance
- □ 38 Online Database Services
- □ 39 Support
- □ 40 Technology-Based Training
- □ 98 Other
- 99 □ None of the above

⑥ WHAT ORACLE PRODUCTS ARE IN USE AT YOUR SITE? (check all that apply)

Oracle E-Business Suite

- □ 01 Oracle Marketing
- □ 02 Oracle Sales
- □ 03 Oracle Order Fulfillment
- □ 04 Oracle Supply Chain Management
- □ 05 Oracle Procurement
- □ 06 Oracle Manufacturing
- □ 07 Oracle Maintenance Management
- □ 08 Oracle Service
- □ 09 Oracle Contracts
- □ 10 Oracle Projects
- □ 11 Oracle Financials
- □ 12 Oracle Human Resources
- □ 13 Oracle Interaction Center
- □ 14 Oracle Communications/Utilities (modules)
- □ 15 Oracle Public Sector/University (modules)
- □ 16 Oracle Financial Services (modules)

Server/Software

- □ 17 Oracle9*i*
- □ 18 Oracle9*i* Lite
- □ 19 Oracle8*i*
- □ 20 Other Oracle database
- □ 21 Oracle9*i* Application Server
- □ 22 Oracle9*i* Application Server Wireless
- □ 23 Oracle Small Business Suite

Tools

- □ 24 Oracle Developer Suite
- □ 25 Oracle Discoverer
- □ 26 Oracle JDeveloper
- □ 27 Oracle Migration Workbench
- □ 28 Oracle9*i* AS Portal
- □ 29 Oracle Warehouse Builder

Oracle Services

- □ 30 Oracle Outsourcing
- □ 31 Oracle Consulting
- □ 32 Oracle Education
- □ 33 Oracle Support
- □ 98 Other
- 99 □ None of the above

⑦ WHAT OTHER DATABASE PRODUCTS ARE IN USE AT YOUR SITE? (check all that apply)

- □ 01 Access
- □ 02 Baan
- □ 03 dbase
- □ 04 Gupta
- □ 05 IBM DB2
- □ 06 Informix
- □ 07 Ingres
- □ 08 Microsoft Access
- □ 09 Microsoft SQL Server
- □ 10 PeopleSoft
- □ 11 Progress
- □ 12 SAP
- □ 13 Sybase
- □ 14 VSAM
- □ 98 Other
- 99 □ None of the above

⑧ WHAT OTHER APPLICATION SERVER PRODUCTS ARE IN USE AT YOUR SITE? (check all that apply)

- □ 01 BEA
- □ 02 IBM
- □ 03 Sybase
- □ 04 Sun
- □ 05 Other

⑨ DURING THE NEXT 12 MONTHS, HOW MUCH DO YOU ANTICIPATE YOUR ORGANIZATION WILL SPEND ON COMPUTER HARDWARE, SOFTWARE, PERIPHERALS, AND SERVICES FOR YOUR LOCATION? (check only one)

- □ 01 Less than $10,000
- □ 02 $10,000 to $49,999
- □ 03 $50,000 to $99,999
- □ 04 $100,000 to $499,999
- □ 05 $500,000 to $999,999
- □ 06 $1,000,000 and over

⑩ WHAT IS YOUR COMPANY'S YEARLY SALES REVENUE? (please choose one)

- □ 01 $500, 000, 000 and above
- □ 02 $100, 000, 000 to $500, 000, 000
- □ 03 $50, 000, 000 to $100, 000, 000
- □ 04 $5, 000, 000 to $50, 000, 000
- □ 05 $1, 000, 000 to $5, 000, 000

100103